To Jill and Ane

# CHILD SUPPORT:
# THE LEGISLATION

AUSTRALIA
Law Book Co.
Sydney

CANADA and USA
Carswell
Toronto

NEW ZEALAND
Brookers
Wellington

SINGAPORE and MALAYSIA
Sweet & Maxwell Asia
Singapore and Kuala Lumpur

# CHILD SUPPORT:
# THE LEGISLATION

Commentary by

## EDWARD JACOBS
*Barrister and Social Security and Child Support Commissioner*

and

## GILLIAN DOUGLAS
*Professor of Law at Cardiff Law School*

LONDON
SWEET & MAXWELL
2005

Published in 2005 by
Sweet & Maxwell Limited of
100 Avenue Road, Swiss Cottage
London NW3 3PF
*http://www.sweetmaxwell.co.uk*
Typeset by J&L Composition, Filey,
North Yorkshire.
Printed in Great Britain by
TJ International,
Padstow.

No natural forests were destroyed to make this product.
Only farmed timber was used and replanted.

A catalogue record for this book is
available from the British Library.

ISBN 0 421 91860 8

# FOREWORD

In keeping with the companion volumes in the Social Security Legislation series, this volume of Child Support legislation and accompanying commentary has rapidly become an indispensable source of information and guidance for those working in the difficult area of Child Support. I welcome this latest edition and commend it to all those who have an interest in this area of work, whether they are decision-makers, panel members or appellants.

His Honour Judge Michael Harris
President of Appeal Tribunals

# PREFACE

This edition is based on materials available to me at the end of May 2005.

The child support scheme as reformed by the Child Support, Pensions and Social Security Act 2000 has not been implemented as smoothly or as quickly as anticipated. This has led to a continuing demand for the material that was last provided in the 1999 edition of this book. The ideal solution would have been to include all the law that comprises both the reformed and the unreformed scheme. That, however, would have resulted in a large book that was cumbersome to use and expensive. I have instead opted for a compromise. What I have provided is the text of the four keys sets of provisions under the unreformed scheme: the original version of Schedule 1 to the Child Support Act 1991, the Child Support (Maintenance Assessment Procedure) Regulations 1992, the Child Support (Maintenance Assessments and Special Cases) Regulations 1992 and the Child Support Departure Direction and Consequential Amendments Regulations 1996. I have provided a commentary for the formula assessment provisions. Commentary for the other provisions is available, with suitable adjustment, under the equivalent provisions under the reformed scheme: the Social Security and Child Support (Decisions and Appeals) Regulations 1999 (for supersession and revision), the Child Support (Maintenance Calculation Procedure) Regulations 2000, the Child Support (Maintenance Calculations and Special Cases) Regulations 2000 and the Child Support (Variations) Regulations 2000.

As always I have to thank those who have drawn attention to my errors of omission and commission. Once again I owe a special debt to Professor Nick Wikeley whose attention to the details of my errors is fast making him indispensable and who has developed the valuable knack of anticipating my mistakes before they get into print.

Edward Jacobs
Social Security and Child Support Commissioner
Harp House
83 Farringdon Street
LONDON EC4A 4DH

# CONTENTS

# Contents

Contents

# Contents

## PART FOUR—MATERIAL AND COMMENTRY FOR THE ORIGINAL SCHEME

# TABLE OF ABBREVIATIONS

| | |
|---|---|
| Commencement No. 3 Order 2000 | Child Support, Pensions and Social Security Act 2000 (Commencement No. 3) Order 2000 |
| Commencement No. 5 Order 2000 | Child Support, Pensions and Social Security Act 2000 (Commencement No. 5) Order 2000 |
| Commencement No. 12 Order 2003 | Child Support, Pensions and Social Security Act 2000 (Commencement No. 12) Order 2003 |
| Commissioners Procedure Amendment Regulations 2005 | Social Security and Child Support Commissioners (Procedure) (Amendment) Regulations 2005 |
| Departure Regulations | Child Support Departure Direction and Consequential Amendments Regulations 1996 |
| Information, Evidence and Disclosure Regulations | Child Support (Information, Evidence and Disclosure) Regulations 1992 |
| Information, Evidence and Disclosure and Maintenance Arrangements and Jurisdiction Amendment Regulations 2000 2000 | Child Support (Information, Evidence and Disclosure and Maintenance Arrangements and Jurisdiction) (Amendment) Regulations 2000 |
| Jobseekers Amendment Regulations | Social Security and Child Support (Jobseeker's Allowance) (Consequential Amendments) Regulations 1996 |
| Jobseekers Miscellaneous Amendments Regulations | Social Security and Child Support (Jobseeker's Allowances) (Miscellaneous Amendments) Regulations 1996 |
| Maintenance Arrangements and Jurisdiction Regulations | Child Support (Maintenance Arrangements and Jurisdiction) Regulations 1992 |
| Maintenance Assessment Procedure Regulations | Child Support (Maintenance Assessment Procedure) Regulations 1992 |
| Maintenance Calculation Procedure Regulations | Child Support (Maintenance Calculation Procedure) Regulations 2000 |
| Maintenance Calculations and Special Cases Regulations | Child Support (Maintenance Calculations and Special Cases) Regulations 2000 |
| Maintenance Assessments and Special Cases Regulations | Child Support (Maintenance Assessments and Special Cases) Regulations 1992 |
| Miscellaneous Amendments Regulations 1994 | Child Support (Miscellaneous Amendments and Transitional Provisions) Regulations 1994 |
| Miscellaneous Amendments Regulations 1995 | Child Support (Miscellaneous Amendments) Regulations 1995 |

| | |
|---|---|
| Miscellaneous Amendments Regulations 1996 | Child Support (Miscellaneous Amendments) Regulations 1996 |
| Miscellaneous Amendments Regulations 1998 | Child Support (Miscellaneous Amendments) Regulations 1998 |
| Miscellaneous Amendments Regulations 1999 | Child Support (Miscellaneous Amendments) Regulations 1999 |
| Miscellaneous Amendments Regulations 2000 | Social Security and Child Support (Miscellaneous Amendments) Regulations 2000 |
| Miscellaneous Amendments Regulations 2002 | Child Support (Miscellaneous Amendments) Regulations 2002 |
| Miscellaneous Amendments Regulations 2003 | Child Support (Miscellaneous Amendments) Regulations 2003 |
| Miscellaneous Amendments Regulations 2004 | Child Support (Miscellaneous Amendments) Regulations 2004 |
| Miscellaneous Amendments Regulations 2005 | Child Support (Miscellaneous Amendments) Regulations 2005 |
| Miscellaneous Amendments (No.2) Regulations 1995 | Child Support (Miscellaneous Amendments) (No.2) Regulations 1995 |
| Miscellaneous Amendments (No.3) Regulations 1995 | Child Support (Miscellaneous Amendments) (No.3) Regulations 1995 |
| Miscellaneous Amendments (No.2) Regulations 1996 | Child Support (Miscellaneous Amendments) (No.2) Regulations 1996 |
| Miscellaneous Amendments (No.2) Regulations 1998 | Child Support (Miscellaneous Amendments) (No.2) Regulations 1998 |
| Miscellaneous Amendments (No.2) Regulations 1999 | Child Support (Miscellaneous Amendments) (No.2) Regulations 1999 |
| Miscellaneous Amendments (No. 2) Regulations 2003 | Child Support (Miscellaneous Amendments) (No.2) Regulations 2003 |
| State Pension Credit Regulations | State Pension Credit (Consequential, Transitional and Miscellaneous Provisions) (No.2) Regulations 2002 |
| Tax Credits Amendments Regulations 1999 | Social Security and Child Support (Tax Credits) Consequential Amendments Regulations 1999 |
| Transitional Amendments Regulations 2003 | Child Support (Transitional Provision) (Miscellaneous Amendments) Regulations 2003 |
| Transitional Provisions Order | Child Support Act 1991 (Commencement No.3 and Transitional Provisions) Order 1992 |
| Variation Regulations | Child Support (Variations) regulations 2000 |

# USING THIS BOOK

Those users who are unfamiliar with child support law or who are new to tribunal work may find it helpful to understand how the book is structured so that they can find their way around it. The structure may not always be apparent and may on occasions break down, but understanding it should stand users in good stead.

The book may need to be consulted in one of three ways: to find a known provision or decision; to find a definition of a word or phrase; or to find a provision or decision on a particular topic.

In order to find a known legislative provision or decision by a court or a Commissioner, consult the tables at the beginning of the book.

In order to find the meaning of a word or phrase in a particular provision, look at the "Definitions" list at the end of the provision in question. This will indicate which words and phrases are defined elsewhere and where the definitions may be found. In the case of regulations, also check the Act for any relevant definitions. If a definition is adopted from another statute, that definition will be reproduced in the General Note.

The most difficult task is to find a provision or decision on a particular topic. The key to doing this successfully is twofold. First think of the concept involved and the context in which it is likely to occur. Then use the statutes and the general notes to home in on the relevant provision or decision. The following example shows how this works in practice.

Suppose that the topic is the significance of the fact that the child is at a boarding school. Begin by identifying the concept involved in the topic or the context in which the topic is likely to occur. The "Overview" section may help with this. In the case of a child at a boarding school, the relevant concept is day to day care of the child. This may lead to the definition of person with care. Another possibility is that it may be identified as an exception, which in child support law is defined as a special case.

Once the concept and the likely context have been identified, use the "Arrangement of Sections" list at the beginning of the relevant statute in order to find the relevant statutory provision. The general note to that provision will refer to any relevant regulations. Relevant decisions will be referred to in the appropriate general note. The general note will contain cross references to any other significant related provisions. The index of the main work may also be helpful in finding the relevant pages.

Some concepts, such as waiver and estoppel, have no place in the legislative structure.

This process is easier to explain than to apply in practice and a number of possible avenues may have to be explored before the search is sucessful. Ultimately, however, it should lead to the relevant provision or decision.

# TABLE OF CASES

# Table of Cases

# Table of Cases

# Table of Cases

# Table of Cases

# Table of Cases

# Table of Cases

# Table of Cases

# Table of Cases

# Table of Cases

# Table of Cases

# Table of Cases

# TABLE OF STATUTES

References highlighted in bold indicate that the material shown is reproduced in full.

# TABLE OF STATUTORY INSTRUMENTS

References highlighted in bold indicate that the material shown is reproduced in full.

# TABLE OF COMMISSION DECISIONS

## Table of Commission Decisions

# PART I

# INTRODUCTION AND OVERVIEW

# AN OVERVIEW OF THE REFORMS TO THE CHILD SUPPORT SCHEME

The reforms made to the child support scheme by the Child Support, Pensions and Social Security Act 2000 can only be properly understood against the background of the original scheme and the amendments to it.

**1.1**

## History

The history and development of the child support scheme were covered in detail in the Introduction and Overview chapter in previous editions. The scheme was introduced in an attempt to remedy the deficiencies in the court child maintenance scheme. In summary, those deficiencies were: (i) the amounts of maintenance were usually unrealistically low; (ii) there was inconsistency in the amounts between courts; (iii) the amount was not automatically uprated and could not be easily varied; (iv) enforcement was costly and arrears were often remitted; (v) the courts and the parties were willing to place the burden on the social security scheme rather than on the parents.

**1.2**

The child support scheme tried to identify the cost of bringing up a child and then to allocate that cost between the parents according to their incomes. The amount of maintenance was based on a formula assessment that ensured consistency and was regularly uprated. Enforcement was be undertaken by the State. Responsibility for maintenance was placed on the parties rather than on the social security scheme.

As well as political opposition from interested parties, there were problems inherent in the scheme itself. The complexity of the scheme led to lengthy delays in making assessments both initially and when changes occured. The scheme contained so many elements that those changes were frequent. The rigidity of the scheme was capable of producing unfairness. Enforcement was sporadic and often ineffective, especially for the self-employed. The problems of enforcement were compounded by the complexity and delays in adjudication, which led to uncertainty in the amount of an absent parent's liability and to arrears for which the absent parent was not to blame.

The opposition to, and defects in, the scheme led to a regular procession of amendments. The most radical was the introduction of the departure direction scheme, which recognised that the formula was too rigid to take account of all matters that properly affected the amount of child support maintenance that should be payable.

## The new scheme

The new scheme is merely another, radical amendment of the scheme as it stood before the 2000 Act. Its essence is that the reforms are pragmatic.

**1.3**

They attempt to create a modified scheme that will be easier to operate, will command wider respect and will be more easily and effectively enforced.

## New terminology

1.4     There are some changes in terminology. The most important are:

| *was* | *becomes* |
|---|---|
| absent parent | non-resident parent |
| maintenance assessment | maintenance calculation |
| departure direction | variation |
| interim maintenance assessment | default maintenance decision |

(The expression "interim maintenance assessment" is still used but with a new meaning. It is now used in respect of variations only—s.12(2).)

## Retained concepts

1.5     Section 1 continues to make it the responsibilities of parents to support their children. Section 2 also continues to make the welfare of children affected a compulsory consideration in the exercise of the Secretary of State's discretionary powers.

The definitions in s.3 continue to apply, with the substitution of "non-resident parent" for "absent parent".

## The basic model

1.6     The basic model covers cases where the only children involved are those of the non-resident parent and for whom day to day care is provided exclusively by the parent or person with care; the non-resident parent provides no day to day care. For convenience, I refer to the non-resident parent as the father and the parent/person with care as the mother.

The father has to pay one of four rates: the basic rate, a reduced rate, a flat rate or the nil rate. It is fixed by reference to the circumstances of the father and his present family. There is no longer an attempt to take account of the circumstances of the mother or her present family.

The *nil rate* applies to a father of a prescribed description or whose net weekly income is below £5.

A *flat rate* of £5 a week applies to a father (a) whose net weekly income is £100 or less or (b) who (or whose partner) is receiving a prescribed benefit. A flat rate of a prescribed amount applies to a father (c) whose partner is also a non-resident parent for whom a maintenance calculation is in force and either of them is receiving a prescribed benefit.

The *reduced rate* applies if neither a flat rate nor the nil rate applies AND the father's net weekly income is more than £100 but less than £200.

Otherwise the *basic rate* applies. This is a percentage of net weekly income: 15 per cent for one child, 20 per cent for two children and 25 per cent for three children.

**More complicated models**

*Apportionment* applies where, for example, a father has four children, one                 1.7
by one mother and three by another. Each mother has exclusive day to day
care of her children. The basic, reduced or flat rate is apportioned between
the mothers in proportion to the number of children each cares for. So, in
the example, one mother has one quarter of the rate and the other mother
has three quarters.

*Shared care* applies where the mother is the parent with care, but the
father has overnight care of their children on some nights. The amount
payable as the basic or reduced rate is adjusted according to the number of
nights for which the father has day to day care of the children. The amount
payable is decreased by one seventh for one night a week, by two sevenths
for two nights a week, by three sevenths for three nights and by half for four
nights or more. There are more complications if more than one child is
involved. (Note that under the original scheme, provision for shared care
did not apply until the father had day to day care for at least two nights a
week; now it applies at one night a week.)

The amount payable as a flat rate is only adjusted if the father or his partner is receiving a prescribed benefit. If the father has day to day care for 52
nights a year, he pays nil.

*Other children.* If the father or his partner receives child benefit for children other than the qualifying children or there are children of a prescribed
description involved, the amount of income to which the basic rate percentage is applied is reduced. The reduction is 15 per cent for one other
child, 20 per cent for two other children and 25 per cent for three or more
others.

So, assume that a father has a child by the mother and is now married
with two stepchildren. He earns £500 a week net. If he did not have
stepchildren, he would pay 15 per cent of £500 = £75. With the stepchildren, his net weekly income is reduced by 20 per cent from £500 to
£400, and he pays 15 per cent of that = £60.

**Entry into the scheme**

Entry is still governed by ss.4, 6 and 7 of the 1991 Act. Sections 4 and 7                 1.8
are amended and there is a new version of s.6.

The new s.4(10)(aa) of the 1991 Act in effect allows an application for a
maintenance calculation after a maintenance order has been in force for
one year.

The new s.6 assumes that a parent with care is willing to comply with the
child support scheme. It is possible to opt out. There are no conditions to
be met, but there is the possibility of a reduced benefit decision under the
new s.46(1)(a). So, in effect, the use of the child support scheme is optional even for those parents who receive income support or income-based jobseeker's allowance, but subject to the penalty of a reduced benefit decision.

Jurisdiction still depends, under s.44, on habitual residence, but a new
s.44(2A) deems certain persons to be habitually resident here. This covers
civil servants, members of the armed forces, employees of prescribed
companies and employees of other prescribed bodies.

## Payment

### *Delay in adjudication*

1.9    The delays in making an assessment ensured that the absent parent would almost certainly begin by being in arrears. A delay in the effective date if a MAF was returned promptly gave some relief, but was not a complete solution to the problem of delay in adjudication. A new voluntary payment scheme is introduced under the new s.28J of the 1991 Act and by the Child Support (Voluntary Payments) Regulations 2000. A voluntary payment is a payment on account of child support maintenance in advance of the calculation being made and notified. It will be set off against arrears that arise as a result of the time taken to make a calculation by reducing payments due under the calculation. It may take the form of a cash payment to the person with care or the payment of a housing or utility liability for the child's home.

The voluntary payment scheme is additional to the repayment of overpaid child support maintenance under s.41B of the 1991 Act, which is amended to take account of it.

There is also a temporary compensation payment scheme introduced by s.27 of the 2000 Act. This puts onto a statutory basis the extra-statutory compensation scheme. It allows part of the arrears to be remitted in accordance with the terms of an agreement between the Secretary of State and the absent parent (note absent parent and not non-resident parent). In effect there is a cut off date of April 1, 2002; hence the reference to absent parent. The relevant regulations are the Child Support (Temporary Compensation Payment Scheme) Regulations 2000, which came into force on January 31, 2001.

### *Late payment or non-payment*

The original scheme envisaged that interest would be charged on arrears of child support maintenance. The 1995 Act introduced s.41A into the 1991 Act. This was intended to provide for penalties for late payment. It was never brought into force.

A new version of s.41A is introduced. It provides for the payment *to the Secretary of State* (not to the person with care) of a penalty that may not exceed 25 per cent of the weekly child support maintenance payable. This replaces the interest on arrears provisions in s.41, which are repealed.

Sections 39A and 40B bolster the already formidable array of penalties by authorising the court to disqualify a non-resident parent from holding or obtaining a driving licence.

## Compliance

### *Failure to provide the information needed to make a calculation, revision or supersession*

1.10    The previous law in s.14 continues to apply (subject to a technical amendment).

The new s.14A creates a new offence to make a statement or representation knowing it is false or to provide a document or other information that is known to be false in a material particular. It is also an offence to fail to comply with a request for information, subject to a defence of reasonable excuse. The penalty is a fine up to (currently) £1000.

Interim maintenance assessments are abolished, although the name is reused for a different purpose. Instead, there is provision for a default maintenance decision under the new s.12(1).

Parents with care receiving benefit who do not opt out under s.6(5) must provide information under s.6(7) or submit to a scientific test under s.27A, subject to the possibility of a reduced benefit decision under the new s.46(1)(b) or (c).

See also **Payment**—*Late Payment*

### Encouraging a person with care to take work

The child maintenance bonus was introduced by the 1995 Act to provide an incentive to parents with care to return to work. This is abolished. In its place, there will be a disregard (confusingly called a "premium") of a maximum of £10 in the income support or income-based jobseeker's allowance calculation under enabling provisions in the social security legislation. Payments in lieu of maintenance are treated as payments of maintenance for council tax and housing benefit purposes. The new arrangements are made in the Social Security (Child Maintenance Premium and Miscellaneous Amendments) Regulations 2000.

1.11

### Transitional arrangements

Some Regulations contain their own transitional provisions. General provision is made in the Child Support (Transitional Provisions) Regulations 2000. These provisions appear, and are, complex, but when the relevant dates and amounts are known, they should be relatively straightforward to apply in most cases.

There are transitional arrangements for the child maintenance bonus in reg.4 of the Social Security (Child Maintenance Premium and Miscellaneous Amendments) Regulations 2000.

1.12

# COMMISSIONERS' DECISIONS AND PRECEDENT

Apart from the legislation, the decisions of the Child Support    1.13
Commissioners and the decisions of the same Commissioners in the often
comparable social security jurisdiction will constitute the principal source
of law which tribunals will have to apply. Members and users of tribunals
will need to be familiar with how these decisions are cited and applied. This
not explains how Commissioners' decisions are cited and reported, together with the binding system of precedent which governs when they must be
followed.

## Reported decisions

Reported decisions of the Child Support Commissioners are cited in this    1.14
form: *R(CS) 1/98*. The R indicates that the decision is a reported one. The
letters in brackets stand for Child Support. The numbers show that this was
the first child support decision to be reported in 1998. The numbering is
separate from that used for the reported decisions of the Social Security
Commissioners.

This follows the format for the citation of the reported decisions of the
Social Security Commissioners which was introduced in 1951. Those deci-
sions are cited in this form: *R(IS) 4/91*. The R indicates that the decision is
a reported one. The letters in brackets indicate the benefit which was
involved in the appeal to the Commissioner. In this case IS stands for
Income Support. The numbers show that this was the fourth Income
Support decision reported in 1991. Each benefit is numbered separately.
There is, for example, an *R(SB) 4/91* as well as an *R(IS) 4/91*.

Where a decision is a decision of a tribunal of three Commissioners
rather than a decision of a single Commissioner, the citation is sometimes
followed by the words "Tribunal Decision" or (T). *R(IS) 4/91* was a
tribunal decision.

## Unreported decisions

Unreported decisions on appeals from tribunals in England and Wales    1.15
are cited in the following form: *CCS 7395/95*. The C indicates that the
decision is a Commissioner's decision and CS indicate that it was a decision on a Child Support appeal. In the case of Social Security appeals the
initial C is followed by letters which indicate the benefit involved. The
number indicates the year and the number of the appeal. In the numbering no distinction is drawn, as was once the case, between child support
and social security appeals or between appeals in relation to different
benefits.

There are no separate Scottish or Welsh Child Support Commissioners.
Child Support Commissioners are appointed for Great Britain as a whole,

although some sit as required in Wales and others sit permanently in Scotland. The Commissioners who are based in Scotland do not have an exclusive jurisdiction. Some cases from Scottish tribunals with be dealt with in England and equally some cases from English or Welsh tribunals will be dealt with in Scotland. Accordingly, no distinction is to be drawn between Commissioners' decisions from English and Welsh appeals on the one hand and Commissioners' decisions from Scottish appeals on the other *(R(U) 8/80)*, unless the decision is one which turns on principles which differ between the jurisdictions.

Unreported decisions on appeals from tribunals in Scotland are cited with an additional S after the C for Commissioner. They are numbered in the same way as appeals from tribunals in Wales and England, but separately from them. So, for example, *CSCS 1/94* was an appeal from a Scottish tribunal. There will also be a *CCS 1/94*, which will be an English or Welsh appeal. The additional S indicates the origins of the appeal and the possibility that the decision may turn on considerations which are unique to Scottish law. The Commissioners have reinstated the original practice of using W after the C for Commissioner to indicate that the case originates from Wales.

When a decision is reported it is given a new citation and number as explained above.

**Highlighted decisions**

1.16    All decisions of general interest or significance are on the Commissioners' website. Those that are considered of particular importance are highlighted by the Commissioners' editorial board, which advises the Chief Commissioner on reporting. This process draws them to the attention of those who visit the website. This system has replaced the starring system, described in the previous edition, which is no longer used by Commissioners.

The address of the Commissioners' website is: *www.osscsc.gov.uk*.

**Availability of decisions**

1.17    A copy of all reported decisions is available at every Child Support Appeal Tribunal venue. Members and chairmen who wish to consult an unreported decision will find all starred decisions in the Regional Offices. Unstarred decisions which are not held by the Regional Office can be obtained by that office for the member or chairman. Copies of unreported decisions, starred and unstarred, may be purchased from the Commissioners' office.

**Precedent**

1.18    Precedent is the name given to the principle which determines which decisions a court or tribunal must follow. They must follow all binding court decisions. Consent orders which are made without reasons being given and without the court hearing argument are only binding on the parties to them *(R(FC) 1/97*, para.28), although they may be of persuasive value. The reason is that, in English law, an appeal is against the decision rather than the reasons for the decision. The setting aside of the decision of a Commissioner on appeal does not of itself set aside the Commissioner's reasoning. This will only case to have authoritative value if reasons are given for allowing the appeal which are incompatible with the Commissioner's.

The Court of Appeal has held that judgments given by courts on applications for permission to appeal are not binding and, although they may be persuasive, reference to them is not encouraged (*Clark v University of Lincolnshire and Humbershire* [2000] 3 All E.R. 752 at 762 *per* Lord Woolf M.R.). This has been confirmed by a Practice Note that prohibits the citation as authority of judgments given on applications that were attended by one party only or were for permission to appeal, unless they purported to establish a new principle or to extend the present law ([2001] 2 All E.R. 510). For an example of the application of this principle, see *CCS 2567/98*, paras 14–22 in which the Commissioner considered both the accuracy of the remarks made by the Court of Appeal and their scope. The same principles apply to reasons given by Commissioners when granting or refusing leave to appeal.

The principles governing the relationship between tribunals themselves and between tribunals and the Commissioners are set out in *R(I) 12/75* and confirmed in *R(U) 4/88*, para.6:

1 An appeal tribunal is not bound by the decision of any other appeal tribunal.

2 An appeal tribunal is bound by all decisions of a single Commissioner or tribunal of Commissioners. This applies whether the decision is reported or unreported and whether or not it has been starred.

3 If there is a conflict between decisions of Commissioners an Appeal tribunal should give more weight to a reported decision than to an unreported decision. It should follow a decision of a tribunal of Commissioners in preference to that of a single Commissioner. A single Commissioners is entitled to disregard a decision of a tribunal of Commissioners. However, this is not a practice which should be followed by appeal tribunals.

4 Where it is not possible to choose between decisions on the bases indicated in 3 above, the tribunal is entitled to follow the decision which it considers the better. There is no obligation to prefer an earlier decision or a later decision. The only governing factor is the quality of the decision itself.

5 The child support jurisdiction is separate from the social security jurisdiction. However, the Commissioners are the same and the law is in many respects the same or similar. There will often be a "sufficient practical relationship" between child support and social security provisions such that they should be interpreted uniformly and differences between them may be assumed to have some significance (see the approach of the Tribunal of Commissioners in the Common Appendix to *R(IS) 3/91* and *R(IS) 4/91*, paragraph 9). In practice, therefore, tribunals will regard themselves as bound by relevant social security decisions just as they are by child support decisions in

accordance with the above rules of precedent. This is of course subject to the important proviso that neither the wording nor the context of a particular provision requires a different interpretation in child support law. Care will therefore always be needed to ensure that decisions are not applied without consideration first being given to whether they are relevant.

So far as Commissioners are concerned, single Commissioners will generally follow decisions of other single Commissioners, for reasons of comity and to avoid uncertainty and confusion, although they are not bound to do so and should not do so if it would lead to the perpetuation of error (*R(I) 12/75*, para.21). A single Commissioner will follow a decision of a Tribunal of Commissioners, unless there are compelling reasons to do otherwise (*R(I) 12/75*, para.21). This has been said to be as a matter of comity rather than law (*CSIS 118/90*, para.8), although *R(I) 12/75*, para.21, refers to comity only in the context of the practice of single Commissioners following decisions of other single Commissioners.

As between Tribunals of Commissioners, precedent applies on the principles followed by the House of Lords and not on the principles followed by the Court of Appeal. A Tribunal will normally follow the decision of an earlier Tribunal, but is free to depart from it if it is right to do so. There is no more specific principle. However, Tribunals bear in mind the danger of disturbing retrospectively the settled basis on which decisions have been made and which have passed the scrutiny of Parliament without adverse comment. See *R(U) 3/88*, paras 8 and 17.

The courts pay particular respect to decisions by Commissioners as being specialist, expert decisionmakers. Accordingly, both the Court of Appeal and the House of Lords have stated that courts should be slow to depart from a consistent, longstanding line of authority from the Commissioners (*R v National Insurance Commissioner Ex p. Strattton* [1979] 2 All E.R. 278 at 282, *per* Lord Denning M.R., *Presho v Insurance Officer* [1984] 1 All E.R. 97 at 102, *per* Lord Brandon and *Cockburn v Chief Adjudication Officer and Secretary of State for Social Security v Fairey (a.k.a. Holliday) R(A) 2/98*).

### Scotland

The jurisdiction of the Commissioners covers the whole of Great Britain. As a matter of practice, Commissioners follow decisions of both the Court of Appeal and the Court of Session regardless of where they are sitting and of where the tribunal heard the case under appeal. However, as a matter of strict precedent, decisions of the Court of Appeal are only binding in England and Wales and those of the Court of Session are only binding in Scotland (*Clarke v Frank Staddon Ltd* [2004] EWCA Civ 422).

### Scope of Commissioners' Decisions

1.19   Care needs to be taken in deciding the scope of a Commissioner's decision, as it will only be authority for those propositions of law which it decides. The need for care arises because a Commissioner only has power to set aside a decision on the ground that it is wrong in law. Accordingly, when dealing with the facts found by a tribunal, a Commissioner only has power to overturn the tribunal's decision if its findings were outside the scope of those which it was entitled to make. If the evidence was such that a tribunal, properly advised as to the law and acting judicially, might have come to more than one conclusion of fact, the appeal will not be allowed merely because the Commissioner would have reached a different conclusion on the evidence. In such a case it is essential that subsequent tribunals should not read into the acceptance of the tribunal's findings a decision by the Commissioner that the conclusion reached was the only permissible one so that, if the same facts should arise, the same conclusion must be drawn.

### Retrospective effect of decisions

In accordance with the general principle of the effect of judicial decisions, Commissioners are deemed to state the law as it has always been and their decisions have a retrospective effect (*CCS 8189/95*, para.6). This is subject to s.28ZC of the Act.

1.20

### Northern Ireland

Northern Ireland has its own structure of tribunals and its own Commissioners separate from those who hear appeals in England, Wales and Scotland. The proper approach of an appeal tribunal in Great Britain to a decision of a Child Support Commissioner in Northern Ireland or a court decision in Northern Ireland relating to child support law may be found in *R(SB) 1/90*. If there is no decision of a Commissioner in Great Britain a decision of a Child Support Commissioner in Northern Ireland should be followed, provided that two conditions are met. First, the relevant statutory provision must be identically worded to the provision to be applied in Great Britain. Second, if the decision is a court decision or that of a tribunal of Commissioners it must be unanimous. The precedent value of comments that are not necessary to the decision depends on the circumstances in which they are made (*R(IB) 4/04* at para.30). So express guidance given after hearing full argument on the interpretation of a controversial provision should generally be followed (*ibid.*)

1.21

Reported decisions of Commissioners for Northern Ireland are cited in the following form: *R 1/94 (CSC)*. The R indicates that the decision is a reported one. The numbers show that this was the first child support appeal decision reported in 1994. The letters in brackets indicate that this was a Child Support Commissioner's decision.

Unreported decisions are cited in the same form as British decisions, except that since 1999 they are reported by reference to the financial year rather than the calendar year: *CSC 2/01–02*. The CS indicates that the decision was on a Child Support appeal and the final C shows that it was a Commissioner's decision on the appeal. The numbers show that this was the second Child Support appeal received in the 2001–2002 financial year. Decisions are renumbered when they are reported. Thus *CSC 5/94* became *R 2/94 (CSC)* when reported.

# CHILD SUPPORT AND EUROPEAN LAW

European law in this context means the law of the European Community   1.22
and the European Convention on Human Rights. Each needs to be considered separately, but they are not wholly unconnected as the Court of
Justice of the European Community has recognised the European
Convention as part of the general principles of law to which it has regard.

## 1. European law—tribunals' powers and duties

The law of the European Community is part of UK law. The European   1.23
Communities Act 1972 provides that enforceable Community rights are to
be given legal effect in the UK and that in any clash between such a right
and national law the former shall prevail.

A tribunal has power to refer a question to the European Court of
Justice. A decision to make a reference is a final decision which is appealable to a Commissioner (*CIS 501/93*). However, tribunals should resist any
temptation to refer a question to the European Court. Such references are
better left to a Commissioner who will have the benefit of better researched
arguments and more time to consider the issues. In deciding whether to
make a reference, the normal doctrine of precedent does not apply (*Trent
Taverns Ltd v Sykes, The Times*, March 5, 1999). The Court of Appeal has
power to order the withdrawal of a reference (*Royscot Leasing Ltd v
Commissioners of Customs and Excise, The Times*, November 11, 1998).

The European Convention on Human Rights was not a part of domestic law. Accordingly, it could not be enforced directly by the domestic
courts in the UK or by the Commissioners (*CCS 11729/96*, para.9).
However, judges frequently had regard to its terms in interpreting
legislation and in analysing the proper exercise of discretions.

It is an error of law for a tribunal to fail to deal with an issue of European
Community law raised before it (*R(SB) 6/91*, para.5). It should use its
inquisitorial function to investigate any issue of European law raised on the
facts. The same principles are equally applicable to the European
Convention on Human Rights to the limited extent that it may be relevant
in domestic law.

## 2. The validity and interpretation of child support law under the European Convention on Human Rights

Under the Human Rights Act 1998 most but not all of the Convention   1.24
has become enforceable in accordance with, and within the limits set by,
the Act. However, the use of the terms of the Convention in interpreting
legislation and overseeing the exercise of discretions remains available as an
alternative to the procedures under the Act and in order to try to alleviate
any limitations in those procedures or in the extent of incorporation.

Little reference has been made by Child Support Commissioners to the Convention. In *R(CS) 3/96*, para.17, the Commissioner considered whether child support law might be inconsistent with Art.8 of the Convention which deals with the right to respect for private and family life. The issue had been raised formally on the appeal in order to ensure that all domestic remedies had been exhausted. The argument was not actively explored and was disposed of by the Commissioner on the basis of the opinion of Lord Bridge in *Brind v Secretary of State for the Home Department* [1991] 1 All E.R. 720 at 722–723, where his Lordship stated the power to take the Convention into account narrowly so as only to apply where the legislation was ambiguous.

The full extent of the possible use of the Convention in the interpretation of the legislation and in overseeing the operation of the discretions under that legislation remains to be explored, as does its use in relation to the new tribunal structure and procedures under the Social Security Act 1998. The coming into force of the Human Rights Act is likely to give impetus to such explorations.

### 3. The validity of child support law under European Community law

1.25    Challenges to all or part of the child support scheme by reference to European Community law have so far been unsuccessful.

In *R(CS) 3/96* it was argued that Directive 79/7 applied to child support law as that law had an indirect effect of providing a measure of protection to a parent with care against unemployment. The Commissioner held that the Directive had no application to child support law as it only applied to provisions which formed whole or part of a statutory scheme providing for protection against one of the risks specified in the Directive or a form of social assistance having the same objective. It was insufficient to point to some incidental connection (*R(CS) 3/96*, para.19).

In *R(CS) 2/95* it was argued that the obligation to pay child support maintenance and the duty to comply with a deducation from earnings order (wrongly called an Attachment of Earnings Order at para.6) issued by the Secretary of State were discriminatory on the grounds of sex under Art.119 EC Treaty and Directive 75/117 in that these obligations affected pay and, since the overwhelming majority of absent parents were male, therefore were contrary to the principle of equal pay for equal work. The argument was rejected by the Tribunal of Commissioners which held that child support was not directly or indirectly within the meaning of pay as defined by Art.119, as it did not arise as a consequence of the relationship of employer and employee.

Despite the lack of success of the arguments presented so far, there are other arguments which have not yet been tested and which may be more successful. It may be that the limitations on a child support officer's jurisdiction contained in s.44 of the Act render child support law discriminatory under European Community law.

The elimination of discrimination on the basis of nationality is of such central importance that it is the subject of special provision in Art.6 EC Treaty (formerly Art.7 EEC Treaty) which provides that:

"Within the scope of application of this Treaty, and without prejudice to any special provisions contained therein, any discrimination on grounds of nationality shall be prohibited."

In addition the removal of discrimination on the basis of nationality underlies specific provisions relating to freedom of movement within the Community. As the Union is an economic one, the concentration so far as freedom of movement is concerned is on the economic players, that is, workers and the self-employed. Art.3(c) EC Treaty defines one of the activities of the Community as being "an internal market characterised by the abolition, as between member States, of obstacles to the free movement of ... persons ..." Art.7a makes similar provision and has been held not to be of direct effect (*R. v Secretary of State for the Home Department Ex p. Flynn, The Times*, April 23, 1995). Art.48 EC Treaty lays down the objective of freedom of movement for workers while Art.52 makes equivalent provision for the self-employed. Both these articles have been held to have direct effect, although Art.48 only applies if there is some connecting factor with the European Community; it does not apply to purely internal matters (*R. v Saunders* [1979] E.C.R. 1129, para.11 and *Moser v Land Baden-Wurttemberg* [1984] E.C.R. 2539, para.15). Presumably the same applies to Art.52.

Regulation 1612/68 allows persons to take up and pursue employment in any Member State. Art.7(2) of the Regulation provides that migrant workers shall enjoy "the same tax and social advantages as national workers". Regulation 1251/70 complements Regulation 1612/68 by providing that workers (and their families) who have satisfied tests as to the periods of their residence and of their working in a State have a permanent right to remain and remain entitled to the equal treatment provided for by Regulation 1612/68. These rights arise when a worker reaches pensionable age, becomes incapable of work or wishes to continue to reside there while working in another Member State.

Persons who are merely seeking work are entitled to remain (*R. v Immigration Appeal Tribunal Ex p. Antonissen* [1991] I E.C.R. 745, para.22) and are entitled to equal treatment. However, European Community law only guarantees that work seekers will not be discriminated against so far as access to employment is concerned and does not grant them workers status (*Centre Public d'Aide Sociale de Courcelles v Lebon* [1987] E.C.R. 2811, para.26) with its associated benefits.

Consider the following example. Peter is British. Marie is French. They meet and marry. They live in France and have a child, Jean. They divorce. Peter returns to London to live with his parents. Marie comes to Cardiff with Jean and finds temporary part-time work. She is, therefore, a worker (*Levin v Staats-secretaris van Justitie* [1982] E.C.R. 1035, paras 11 and 16) and entitled to the protection of Regulation 1612/68. However, the likely duration of the work and the uncertainty of her position are such that Marie does not become habitually resident here. Accordingly, by virtue of the provisions of s.44 of the Act, she cannot obtain a child support maintenance assessment. However, if she were British she would find it easier to establish habitual residence here (see the general note to s.44 of the Act). Section 44 may, therefore, deprive her of equality of access to a social advantage (a child support maintenance assessment) and consequently represent a barrier to her free movement as a worker within the Community.

### 4. Relationship between European Community Law and the European Convention on Human Rights

1.26    The European Convention on Human Rights is part of the general principles of law whose observance the European Court of Justice ensures, but the Court will not give guidance to national courts on the interpretation of the Convention in an area which does not fall within the field of application of European law (*Kremzow v Republik Osterreich, The Times*, August 11, 1997).

### 5. References to the Court of Justice of the European Communities

1.27    If a tribunal considers it proper to refer a question or questions to the Court of Justice, it should have regard to President's Circular No.12 and to the following Guidance issued by the Court which is referred to in that Circular.

### Court of Justice of the European Communities

### Notes for Guidance on References by National Courts for Preliminary Rulings

1.28    The development of the Community legal order is largely the result of cooperation between the Court of Justice of the European Communities and national courts and tribunals through the preliminary ruling procedure under Art.177 of the EC Treaty and the corresponding provisions of the ECSC and Euratom Treaties.

In order to make this cooperation more effective, and so enable the Court of Justice better to meet the requirements of national courts by providing helpful answers to preliminary questions, this Note for Guidance is addressed to all interested parties, in particular all national courts and tribunals.

It must be emphasised that the Note is for guidance only and has no binding or interpretative effect in relation to the provisions governing the preliminary ruling procedure. It merely contains practical information which, in the light of experience in applying the preliminary ruling procedure, may help to prevent the kind of difficulties which the Court has sometimes encountered.

   1 Any court or tribunal of a Member State may ask the Court of Justice to interpret a rule of Community law, whether contained in the Treaties or in acts of secondary law, if it considers that this is necessary for it to give judgment in a case pending before it.

Courts or tribunals against whose decisions there is no judicial remedy under national law must refer questions of interpretation arising before them to the Court of Justice, unless the Court has already ruled on the point or unless the correct application of the rule of Community law is obvious.

2 The Court of Justice has jurisdiction to rule on the validity of acts of the Community institutions. National courts or tribunals may reject a plea challenging the validity of such an act. But where a national court (even one whose decision is still subject to appeal) intends to question the validity of a Community act, it must refer that question to the Court of Justice.

Where, however, a national court or tribunal has serious doubts about the validity of a Community act on which a national measure is based, it may, in exceptional cases, temporarily suspend application of the latter measure or grant other interim relief with respect to it. It must then refer the question of validity to the Court of Justice, stating the reasons for which it considers that the Community act is not valid.

3 Questions referred for a preliminary ruling must be limited to the interpretation or validity of a provision of Community law, since the Court of Justice does not have jurisdiction to interpret national law or assess its validity. It is for the referring court or tribunal to apply the relevant rule of Community law in the specific case pending before it.

4 The order of the national court or tribunal referring a question to the Court of Justice for a preliminary ruling may be in any form allowed by national procedural law. Reference of a question or questions to the Court of Justice generally involves stay of the national proceedings until the Court has given its ruling, but the decision to stay proceedings is one which is for the national court alone to take in accordance with its own national law.

5 The order for reference containing the question or questions referred to the Court will have to be translated by the Court's translators into the other official languages of the Community. Questions concerning the interpretation or validity of Community law are frequently of general interest and the Member States and Community institutions are entitled to submit observations. It is therefore desirable that the reference should be drafted as clearly and precisely as possible.

6 The order for reference should contain a statement of reasons which is succinct but sufficiently complete to give the Court, and those to whom it must be notified (the Member States, the Commission and in certain cases the Council and the European Parliament), a clear understanding of the factual and legal context of the main proceedings.

In particular, it should include:

— a statement of the facts which are essential to a full understanding of the legal significance of the main proceedings;

— an exposition of the national law which may be applicable;
— a statement of the reasons which have prompted the national court to refer the question or questions to the Court of Justice; and
— where appropriate, a summary of the arguments of the parties.

The aim should be to put the Court of Justice in a position to give the national court an answer which will be of assistance to it.

The order for reference should also be accompanied by copies of any documents needed for a proper understanding of the case, especially the text of the applicable national provisions. However, as the case-file or documents annexed to the order for reference are not always translated in full into the other official languages of the Community, the national court should ensure that the order for reference itself includes all the relevant information.

7 A national court or tribunal may refer a question to the Court of Justice as soon as it finds that a ruling on the point or points of interpretation or validity is necessary to enable it to give judgment. It must be stressed, however, that it is not for the Court of Justice to decide issues of fact or to resolve disputes as to the interpretation or application of the rules of national law. It is therefore desirable that a decision to refer should not be taken until the national proceedings have reached a stage where the national court is able to define, if only as a working hypothesis, the factual and legal context of the question; on any view, the administration of justice is likely to be best served if the reference is not made until sides have been heard.

8 The order for reference and the relevant documents should be sent by the national court directly to the Court of Justice, by registered post, addressed to:

The Registry
Court of Justice of the European Communities
L-2925 Luxembourg
Telephone: (352) 43031

The Court Registry will remain in contact with the national court until judgment is given, and will send copies of the various documents (written observations, Report for the Hearing, Opinion of the Advocate General). The Court will also send its judgment to the national court. The Court would appreciate being informed about the application of its judgment in the national proceedings and being sent a copy of the national court's final decision.

9 Proceedings for a preliminary ruling before the Court of Justice are free of charge. The Court does not rule on costs.

# PART II

# STATUTES

# Child Support Act 1991

## (1991 c.48)

### ARRANGEMENT OF SECTIONS

[This list is not part of the Regulations, but is added for the convenience of readers.]

*The basic principles*

2.1

*Information*

*Reviews and appeals*

An Act to make provision for the assessment, collection and enforcement of periodical maintenance payable by certain parents with respect to children of theirs who are not in their care; for the collection and enforcement of certain other kinds of maintenance; and for connected purposes. [25th July 1991.]

*The basic principles*

## The duty to maintain

**1.**—(1) For the purposes of this Act, each parent of a qualifying child is responsible for maintaining him.

   (2) For the purposes of this Act, [¹a non-resident parent] shall be taken to have met his responsibility to maintain any qualifying child of his by making periodical payments of maintenance with respect to the child of such amount, and at such intervals, as may be determined in accordance with the provisions of this Act.

   (3) Where a [²maintenance calculation] made under this Act requires the making of periodical payments, it shall be the duty of the [¹non-resident parent] with respect to whom the [²calculation] was made to make those payments.

2.2

AMENDMENTS

   1. Paragraph 11(2) of Sch.3 to the 2000 Act.
   2. Section 1(2) of the 2000 Act (March 3, 2003 under art.3 of, and the Schedule to, the Commencement No.12 Order 2003)

DEFINITIONS

   "maintenance calculation": see s.54.
   "non-resident parent": see s.3(2).
   "parent": see s.54.
   "qualifying child": see s.3(1).

GENERAL NOTE

   This section sets the framework of parental obligations around which the child support maintenance structure is built. Each parent of a qualifying child is responsible for maintaining that child. If a parent is a non-resident parent, a maintenance calculation may be made. It is the non-resident parent's duty to pay the amounts fixed by that calculation. If payment is made as required, the duty imposed by this section is discharged. The child support maintenance for which the non-resident parent is liable may be nil. If that is the case, the non-resident parent is effectively absolved from paying child support maintenance under this Act for so long as the calculation remains in force.

2.3

The obligations imposed by this section only apply for the purposes of this Act. They do not affect the rights and obligations which apply outside the scope of the Act (see Pt II of the Matrimonial Causes Act 1973, Pt I of the Domestic Proceedings and Magistrates' Courts Act 1978, Pt III of the Matrimonial and Family Proceedings Act 1984, Family Law (Scotland) Act 1985, Sch.1 to the Children Act 1989 and ss.78(6) and 105 of the Social Security Administration Act 1992). The principal limitations on the scope of the duty are therefore as follows: (i) it does not apply unless one of the parents (as defined by s.54) is a non-resident parent as defined by s.3(2); (ii) it does not apply unless the child has a home with someone who qualifies as a person with care under s.3(3); (iii) it ceases to apply when the child ceases to be a child for the purposes of the Act under s.55; (iv) the Act does not affect cases where the court has jurisdiction under s.8; (v) finally, the Act does not affect any consensual maintenance arrangements to which the parents may agree, except to the extent that the parties may not contract out of the Act (s.9).

For a survey of a non-resident parent's liability to maintain before and apart from this Act, see the judgment of Ward L.J. in *R. (Kehoe) v Secretary of State for Work and Pensions* [2004] 1 F.L.R. 1132.

## Welfare of children: the general principle

2.4    **2.** Where, in any case which falls to be dealt with under this Act, the Secretary of State [¹...] is considering the exercise of any discretionary power conferred by this Act, he shall have regard to the welfare of any child likely to be affected by his decision.

AMENDMENT

1. Paragraph 18 of Sch.7 to the Social Security Act 1998 (June 1, 1999).

DEFINITION

2.5    "child": see s.55.

GENERAL NOTE

This section attaches a general condition to all the discretionary powers given to the Secretary of State by this Act, that the welfare of any child likely to be affected by a decision must be taken into account.

The section contains the first of many references in the child support legislation to the Secretary of State. By virtue of s.5 of, and Sch.1 to, the Interpretation Act 1978, this means one of Her Majesty's Principal Secretaries of State. Nowhere in the legislation is the particular Secretary of State responsible for the legislation identified. Accordingly, the allocation falls with the Royal Prerogative exercised by the Prime Minister. Originally, the responsibility was allocated to the Secretary of State for Social Security, but in 2001 it became the responsibility of the Secretary of State for Work and Pensions.

Inevitably, the Secretary of State cannot and does not personally exercise the functions conferred under the legislation (*Carltona Ltd v Commissioners of Works* [1943] 2 All E.R. 560 at 563, *per* Lord Greene, M.R.). Instead the functions involved in the administration of the legislation are exercised in the name of the Secretary of State by officials who operate within the Child Support Agency. Even the power to make delegated legislation is in practice usually undertaken by a junior minister. The Secretary of State, however, remains personally answerable to Parliament, although in the case of Agencies there is a tendency for a distinction to be drawn between matters of policy, for which ministers are answerable, and matters of operation, for which the head of the Agency is answerable.

The section applies to appeal tribunals and to Commissioners when they are considering on appeal the decision which the Secretary of State should have made, but it does not apply when they are considering the exercise of powers of their own, such as the powers given to Commissioners by s.24(3). However, in cases to which this section does not apply, the welfare of any children likely to be affected will, on general principles, be a proper consideration in the exercise of any discretion.

The requirement imposed by this section is not a freestanding one authorising the welfare of children to be taken into account at any stage, but rather a qualification on the way in which powers conferred by this Act are to be exercised (*R(CS)* 2/98, para.17).

This section applies only to the exercise of discretionary powers in individual cases. It does not apply to the Secretary of State's general power to make delegated legislation (*R(CS)* 2/95, paras 11–12). As the section only applies to discretionary powers, it is irrelevant whether or not regard has been had to this section in the case where the exercise of a duty is involved, such as under s.11 (*R(CS)* 4/96, para.8 and *CCS 14/94*, para.10). Where, however, the exercise of discretionary power is involved, the tribunal should be satisfied that s.2 has been considered and, if in doubt, should require evidence or confirmation to be produced (*CCS 14/94*, para.9).

The Secretary of State must have regard to the welfare of any child likely to be affected by their decisions. It is only necessary that "regard" shall be had to the welfare of the child. This is less stringent than the requirement that the welfare of the child should be the "first" or "paramount" (*R(CS)* 4/96, para.8) consideration, which applies in s.25(1) of the Matrimonial Causes Act 1973 and s.1(1) of the Children Act 1989 respectively.

The children whose welfare must be considered are all those who are likely to be affected. Children other than the qualifying children may need to be considered. For example, if the non-resident parent has other children, their welfare must also be taken into account. One or both of the parents may also be a child within the meaning of the Act.

The welfare of children covers all the needs relating to their present condition and future development: physical, mental, emotional, educational and social (see especially the so-called "welfare checklist" in s.1(3) of the Children Act 1989, although it has no direct application to this Act). In an appropriate case the views of the child may be taken into account. A specific factor which should be taken into account is the possible prejudical effect of delay on the welfare of a child. So important is this consideration that it is expressly made a general principle for the purpose of the Children Act 1989 by s.1(2) of that Act.

In considering children's welfare, the emphasis will often be on the finances necessary and available to allow their needs to be met. These needs are not exclusively dependent upon money, but a minimum is necessary and among the most difficult decisions are likely to be those which involve assessing the impact of the distribution of limited resources on the welfare of the children affected. However, the requirement imposed by this section must be applied so as not to impede the basic objective of the child support legislation that non-resident parents should pay maintenance calculated in accordance with the child support scheme (*R(CS)* 4/96, para.8).

This section only applies to discretionary powers conferred *by* this Act. It does not, therefore, apply to such powers conferred by regulations made under the Act. This is to some extent underlined by the fact that elsewhere it has been felt necessary to make specific provision that the interests (rather than welfare) of a child are to be considered (reg.14(2) of the Maintenance Calculations and Special Cases Regulations). However, the welfare of any children likely to be affected will always be a factor which those exercising a power are entitled to take into consideration, regardless of whether or not there is specific provision to that effect.

In practice, this section is likely to have little impact on the decisions made. It is, however, important for the authorities to show that regard has been had to the welfare of children affected. A person who wishes to assert that welfare has not been considered may challenge the decision taken by means of judicial review (*R. v Secretary of State for Social Security Ex p. Biggin* [1995] 1 F.L.R. 851). However, Thorpe J. in that case considered that welfare appears to have no influence on the quantification of liability and very little on the discretion to enforce an assessment, so that the heading words of the section "seem hollow indeed". Indeed, the papers provided in some cases show that the officer involved has literally rubber stamped consideration of this section, as the officer has stamped the file with, and signed, a statement that the welfare of any child likely to be affected has been considered.

If a tribunal is faced with a question which involves the exercise of a discretion by the Secretary of State, it will need first to identify any children who might be affected by the decision. If the tribunal decides that the welfare of one of those children is not likely to be affected, it should decide why that is so. The tribunal's record of decision should record the children whose interests were considered, its decision and the reasons for it. If the welfare of any child is likely to be affected, the tribunal should decide how it might be affected. Then it will need to weigh the competing interests of all the children affected. Finally, it will have to decide the impact which its conclusions on these matters should have on the exercise of the discretion. These matters should be included in the record of decision.

In any case which directly affects the welfare of a child there is power in exceptional cases to bar disclosure to a party in the case of information which might be damaging to the child (*Re B (A minor) (Disclosure of Evidence)* [1993] 1 F.L.R. 191). Clearly, this can never be relied upon to prevent the disclosure of information to the Secretary of State.

Provisions like this section are inevitable in any legislation affecting children. However, the scope for the exercise of discretion is extremely limited in this Act. Where there is a discretion it may be supplemented by other specified criteria, as for example in s.46(3), although these do not displace the general duty created by this section. It may be that this section states one of the principles underlying the Act as a whole, but beyond that the recitation of the principle seems more to serve a ritual, political significance, than to provide a touch-stone for the practical implementation of the Act.

On the basis of the reasoning in *Jones v Department of Employment* [1988] 1 All E.R. 725 and *W v Home Office, The Times*, March 14, 1997, officers acting on behalf of the Secretary of State are not under a duty of care in negligence when exercising their powers under this section or any other provision of child support law.

## Meaning of certain terms used in this Act

2.6     **3.**—(1) A child is a "qualifying child" if—

(a) one of his parents is, in relation to him, [²a non-resident parent]; or

(b) both of his parents are, in relation to him, [²non-resident parents]

(2) The parent of any child is [²a non-resident parent], in relation to him, if—

(a) that parent is not living in the same household with the child; and

(b) the child has his home with a person who is, in relation to him, a person with care.

(3) A person is a "person with care", in relation to any child, if he is a person—

(a) with whom the child has his home

(b) who usually provides day to day care for the child (whether exclusively or in conjunction with any other person); and

(c) who does not fall within a prescribed category of person.

(4) The Secretary of State shall not, under subsection (3)(c), prescribe as a category—

(a) parents;

(b) guardians;

(c) persons in whose favour residence orders under section 8 of the Children Act 1989 are in force;

(d) in Scotland, persons [¹with whom a child is to live by virtue of a residence order under section 11 of the Children (Scotland) Act 1995].

(5) For the purposes of this Act there may be more than one person with care in relation to the same qualifying child.

(6) Periodical payments which are required to be paid in accordance with a [³maintenance calculation] are referred to in this Act as "child support maintenance".

(7) Expressions are defined in this section only for the purposes of this Act.

AMENDMENTS

1. Paragraph 52(2) of Sch.4 to the Children (Scotland) Act 1995 (November 1, 1996).

2. Paragraph 11(2) of Sch.3 to the 2000 Act (January 31, 2001 for the purposes of amendments to ss.15(4A) and 44(1) and (2A) under art.2(1)(b) of the Commencement No.3 Order 2000; March 3, 2003 under art.3 of, and the Schedule to, the Commencement No.12 Order 2003)

3. Section 1(2)(a) of the 2000 Act (March 3, 2003 under art.3 of, and the Schedule to, the Commencement No.12 Order 2003)

DEFINITIONS

"child": see s.55.                                                                                    2.7
"maintenance calculation": see s.54.
"parent": see s.54.
"prescribed": see s.54.

GENERAL NOTE

*Subsection (1)*

To be a qualifying child, a person must satisfy two conditions. First, the person      2.8
must be a child within the meaning of the Act. The basic definition in s.55 is elaborated on by Sch.1 to the Maintenance Calculation Procedure Regulations. Second, one or both of the child's parents must be non-resident as defined in subs.(2).

In this subsection "qualifying child" means a child who falls within the scheme at large regardless of whether or not there has been an application for a maintenance calculation in respect of the child (*CCS 806/95*, para.14).

*Subsection (2)*

If a person is to be a non-resident parent in relation to a child, three conditions must be satisfied. Two relate to the parent and one to the living arrangements of the child. First, the person must be a parent of the child as defined in s.54. Second, the person must not live in the same household with the child. Finally, the child's home must be with a person with care as defined in subs.(3). It is relevant only that these conditions are satisfied; it is irrelevant that the child is living apart from a parent against that parent's wishes (*CCS 3128/95*, paras 7–8).

*General approach*

The Act uses three different expressions: "household", "home" and "living [or residing] with". All three are used in this subsection. It is appropriate to make some general remarks on the proper use of the authorities and the application of the principles which they create to cases involving phrases such as these, *i.e.* cases where the application of the legal principles to the facts of a particular case turns on an individual analysis of the relevant factors of the case and their interrelation, and in which no single factor of itself is conclusive (*Simmons v Pizzey* [1977] 2 All E.R. 432 at 441–442 *per* Lord Hailsham, and *R(G) 1/79*) and no definitive list of relevant factors is possible (*Crake v Supplementary Benefits Commission* [1982] 1 All E.R. 498 at 502, *per* Woolf J.). It will often be possible for different members of a tribunal to attribute different significance to an individual factor and, even when all the factors are considered as a whole, the result will often depend upon the individual member's impression, with the result that different members may quite properly come to different conclusions on the same facts.

These, and similar phrases which have been given the same meaning, occur in a variety of contexts and there are a number of decisions by courts and Commissioners interpreting them. Since there is a broad level of consistency in these phrases across the various contexts, the decisions will be helpful in interpreting these phrases in the context of child support law. Indeed, in *Santos v Santos* [1972] 2 All E.R. 246 at 253, Sachs L.J. was able to identify a prima facie meaning of "living apart" (the antithesis, it was said, of "living together") before going on to consider whether it was displaced by the particular statutory context of the Divorce Reform Act 1969. However, it is clear from the nature of the analysis which the courts undertake and the comments which the judges make from time to time (for example, Ormrod L.J., in *Adeoso v Adeoso* [1981] 1 All E.R. 107 at 109) that the context in which they are used may affect the precise scope given to the words and the nature and weight of the factors relevant to their application. In using decisions from other contexts, therefore, it is necessary to take account of the statutory context in which they were made as well as to have due regard to the language and statutory context of child support law.

Usually it will be immediately obvious how the principles apply to the living arrangements of those concerned, because the circumstances will be such that the result will be the same whichever concept is being applied. In such cases failure to reach the correct conclusion will be an error of law (*R. v Birmingham Juvenile Court Ex p. N.* [1984] 2 All E.R. 688 at 690–691, *per* Arnold P.). However, the arrangements which can be entered into are subject to infinite variation, and tribunals will on occasion need to determine with precision both the scope of each concept and its application to the individual facts of the particular case. It is particularly likely in such cases that the facts of the case will be open to alternative analyses. If this is so, the decision will be one of fact and degree, and there will be no error of law, provided that (i) the decision is based on the correct legal principles and (ii) it is one that could reasonably be made on the facts of the case (*ibid.* and *Simmons v Pizzey*, above at 441–442, *per* Lord Hailsham L.C.).

Two particular types of case are likely to cause difficulties for tribunals: (i) those where the parties' financial and living arrangements are outside the usual range encountered in everyday experience and (ii) those where those arrangments are in a state of transition.

Applying the law in cases such as this requires the exercise of a number of skills by panel members who sit on tribunals. They must be aware of the manifold variations in living arrangements which exist and analyse them in a way which both reflects the individual circumstances of the case concerned and produces a sensible result within the structure of the legislation. Care will need to be taken in making and recording findings of fact on all relevant matters, as well as in making and explaining the reasons for the tribunal's decision, although it has been said (perhaps a little too broadly—see the general note to reg.53(4) of the Appeals Regulations) that in cases involving value judgments clear findings on the relevant issues are all that is required by way of reasons (*CIS 87/93*, para.9). Precedent must be used carefully: decisions must be followed in so far as they lay down general principles, but arguments based on the similarity of facts between two cases will always be misplaced, since minor differences can change the whole complexion of an arrangement. Reasons for decision which are framed by way of comparison with the facts in particular Commissioner's Decisions will lead to a successful appeal to a Commissioner, since it is not any single factor on its own which is decisive, but rather the combined effect of all relevant factors.

The conflicting decisions by Commissioners on consistency in decisions as between the same parties are of relevance in the context of decisions such as those being considered here, where different decisions may properly be reached on the same facts. The issue arises when a tribunal is dealing with an issue which has already been decided in the context of an earlier assessment. In *CM 140/92*, paras 19–22 and *CM 113/91*, the same Commissioner decided that, if there has been no change in the facts, the tribunal should as a matter of law follow the earlier decision unless to do so would be perverse. See the general note to reg.53(4) of the Appeals Regulations for a consideration of the recording of decisions in such cases. The principle in *CM 140/92* is concerned with the cases which turn on the interpretation of the same facts in successive decisions. It does not apply to cases where the facts in successive decisions are different, since each decision must be made on the facts and in the circumstances then prevailing (*CFC 5/93*, para.16). This approach to consistency has not found universal favour among the Commissioners, however, and in *R(M) 1/96*, para.14 a different Commissioner emphasised that each case must be decided on the evidence available without any bias in favour of following any earlier decision made between the same parties. In view of this conflict, tribunals may follow the approach which they prefer. Whatever the correct legal position, there is much to be said for ensuring that, where different decisions may properly be reached on the same facts, parties are treated consistently and are not subjected to differing decisions from time to time, and whatever decision is reached the reasons must be sufficient to explain the reason for it to the parties (see the general note to reg.53(4) of the Appeals Regulations).

*Household*

The criteria to be taken into account in deciding which households exist are discussed in the general note to reg.1 of the Maintenance Calculations and Special Cases Regulations. Although it will usually be obvious which households exist and who lives in which one, difficult cases will arise and attention will need to be paid to the relevant legal criteria. In the context of the definition of absent parent, the financial arrangements will be of central importance. The legal guidance on the factors to be taken into account in deciding whether a person is a member of a household is directed at the activities of adults. Where the circumstances do not provide an obvious answer, the approach to deciding the household in which a child lives should generally be as follows. First, consider the arrangements of the adults concerned and decide which households exist. Then, consider how the child fits into those arrangements by enquiring who bears the immediate financial responsibility for, and who fulfils the usual domestic responsibilities in respect of, that child. Findings of fact must be made on these matters. The relevant household will be the one with which the child has the closest connection. Deciding this will require the

2.9

exercise of judicial judgment. It will involve identifying the significance of each of the relevant factors and attributing the appropriate weight to each. The reasons for decision should record that this judgment has been exercised and indicate why it was exercised in the way it was. Where a child has a sufficient degree of maturity and financial independence, it may be possible to apply the legal criteria for the existence of a household directly to the child, rather than approach the question in the way suggested here. In all cases, the decision should be based on objective facts, rather than on the perceptions of the persons concerned as to whether they live in the same or separate households, although in marginal cases these perceptions, including (depending on the child's age and maturity) those of the child concerned, may be an important consideration.

The use of the words "lives with", in contrast to the "resides with", points to the emphasis being on the relationship between the parties rather than a connection with the property occupied by the parties (*South Northamptonshire District Council v Power* [1987] 3 All E.R. 831 at 833, *per* Kerr L.J.). The essential attribute of a household is the existence of a domestic establishment (paras 13–18 of the Appendix to *R(IS) 1/99*).

In the context of the Inheritance (Provision for Family and Dependants) Act 1975, the Court of Appeal has held that it is possible for persons to be living in the same household despite the fact that they are living separately at a particular time (*Gully v Dix* [2004] 1 F.L.R. 918). On the other hand, in the context of the Divorce Reform Act 1969, Wrangham J. thought that it was not possible for persons to live in the same household without also living with each other (*Mouncer v Mouncer* [1972] 1 All E.R. 289 at 291). However, as it is the purpose of child support law to require absent parents to contribute towards the cost of bringing up their children, it is possible that the position may be different and that there may be cases in which the arrangements within a family are such that one parent is a member of the same household as the child, but does not live in that household *with the child*. In such cases, attention will need to be given both to the question of which households exist and to the separate question of whether a particular member of a household may be described as living in it with the child. One type of case in which this distinction may need to be drawn is where one parent is working for substantial periods away from home, for example on an oil rig, or in another part of the country while the rest of the family stays in the family home until it is sold. Although the financial arrangements and emotional attachments may be such that the single household survives, the extent of the separation may result in it being inappropriate to regard the absent person as living in that household *with* the child. This analysis may also be appropriate where a relationship is coming to an end and the arrangements are moving in the direction of separate households. Those separate households may not yet have been completely established, but, in view of the steps being taken to separate the lives of the parties, it may nevertheless be appropriate to regard one of them as no longer living *with* the child in the surviving household, especially if responsibility for the child has for all practical purposes been abandoned by that parent. In practice, the evidence may not permit the distinctions suggested in this paragraph to be drawn and the making of the application for a maintenance assessment would be likely to lead to the household ceasing to exist.

It is possible that the child may be living with the non-resident parent, but not in the same household. If, for example, a father still lives in the family home, but has formed a separate household within it, the child may, depending on the circumstances, still be said to be living with both parents. Such circumstances will satisfy the definition in this subsection, since the child does not live in the same household as the father and the child's home is with the mother (albeit it is with the father as well) who can therefore qualify as a person with care. It is also possible for a child to be living under the same roof as a person but to have so little contact with that person that they are not living together. *(R(F) 1/71)*.

Each person in a household lives with every other member of that household (*Bate v Chief Adjudication Officer* [1996] 1 W.L.R. 814). Living in the same household involves more than a mere transitory presence and involves a settled course of daily living (*R(F) 2/81*, para.12; *R(CS) 8/99*, paras 14–15). A person will still "reside with" another despite a temporary absence, such as a holiday or a stay in hospital (*Camden London Borough Council v Goldenberg* [1997 1 F.L.R. 556 at 564, *per* Nourse L.J., quoting Denning L.J. in *Middleton v Bull* [1951] 2 T.L.R. 1010 at 1012). In *R(CS) 14/98*, para.16 the Commissioner declined to draw any distinction between *living* in the same household and *staying* in the same household on the ground that such fine distinctions would be highly contentious and not appropriate for legislation which was designed to produce fairly clear-cut answers by child support officers.

In *CCS 14625/96*, para.17 the Commissioner held that household had to be viewed in a realistic way and primarily with reference to the children themselves.

The meaning of "home" and some of the other problems associated with the concept of living or residing with someone are discussed in the general note to subs.(3).

*Subsection (3)*

A number of matters turn on whether or not a person is a person with care, for example it determines who is entitled to apply for a maintenance assessment under s.4, whether s.5(1) applies and whether the Secretary of State may treat an application for a maintenance calculation as having been made under s.6 below. It is not essential that the person with care should be a parent of the child. Some provisions, however, only apply to a person with care who is also a parent, for example s.6.

**2.10**

If a person is to be a person with care in respect of a child, three conditions must be satisfied. First, the child's home must be with the person. The tribunal's enquiry must concentrate on the nature and extent of the child's association with the person alleged to be the person with care, rather than on the child's association with particular premises. A child could still have a home with a person, although they have no fixed abode. (Compare the definition of "home" in reg.1(2) of the Maintenance Calculations and Special Cases Regulations, which is concerned with the accommodation.) The financial arrangements are much less important here than when considering the meaning of household. The living and caring arrangements for the child will be an important consideration and in this context an enquiry should always be made as to who has parental responsibility for, or parental rights over, the child, whether, and if so, in whose favour, a residence order under s.8 of the Children Act 1989 has been made in respect of the child, and in whose favour any existing order for custody or care and control of the child was made.

The meaning of "home" was considered in *CCS 1180/98*, para.10. The Commissioner laid down the following propositions. (i) A home is a domestic base. (ii) In some cases where the location of that base is unclear, an element of perception may be involved. (iii) No precise definition of "home" is possible. (iv) Where a person has a home is a question of fact. (v) The question must be answered by applying ordinary, common sense standards. (vi) A person may have a particular home despite lengthy absences from it. (vii) A home must be more than an occasional place of convenient resort.

In *CCS 5818/99*, the qualifying child was looked after by his grandmother, but they both stayed with and were kept by his mother during school holidays. The Commissioner held that in view of the lengths of the periods of time when all three were living together it was appropriate to take an overall view of whether the child had his home with his grandmother throughout the year.

In the case of a child, the perception of the adults who have legal responsibility for the child will be central considerations. However, as the emphasis here is on reality of parental responsibility (rather than lawfulness, as in the case when considering habitual residence; see the general note to s.44), it will be the wishes of those persons who have actual, as opposed to legal, responsibility for the child that will be the relevant ones. Moreover, the perceptions of the child may deserve consideration, depending on the degree of maturity.

In view of the importance of perception in identifying a child's home, it is possible for a home to be with a particular person despite considerable absences. This is emphasised by reg.12 of the Maintenance Calculations and Special Cases Regulations which makes clear that a child's home may be with a person, although the child lives elsewhere for a substantial part of the year. This regulation provides for the special case where a child is at boarding school or in hospital. It operates only in relation to para.(b) of the definition of "person with care" and does not affect para.(a). Clearly, therefore, reg.12 envisages that the fact that the child is separated from a person for lengthy periods does not of itself prevent that child's home being with that person. A child's home may be with a person despite the fact that they live in different households, for example, a child and a parent may maintain a separate household within a house which is shared with grandparents who share the care of the child. In such a case, the child does not live in the grandparents' household, but the arrangements may be such that the child's home is with them as well as with the mother.

The Court of Appeal has held that, although unusual, shared or split residence orders, whereby the child lives for part of the time with each parent, may be made under the Children Act 1989 (*A v A (Children) (Shared Residence Order)* [1994] 1 F.L.R. 669. This (which was in any case spelt out in s.11(4) of the Act) reverses the attitude of the courts under the old law, where, in *Riley v Riley* [1986] 2 F.L.R. 429, such orders had been disapproved. It may be expected, therefore, that there will be some increase in the making of orders of this type, with consequential implications for all three were living together it was the question of who is the parent with care. However, even where the more usual form of order is made, giving residence to one parent, and contact to the other, the total period spent by the child in "staying contact" with a parent may be relevant to the question whether there is a special case within the Maintenance Calculations and Special Cases Regulations.

In determining whether a qualifying child lives, resides or has a home with a parent or other person for the purposes of the definitions in this section, it is not necessary for the parent or other person to have a legal interest in the dwelling or for the child to be in a subordinate position in the dwelling (*Bate v Chief Adjudication Officer* [1996] 1 W.L.R. 814). It is possible, therefore, for the qualifying child to be the householder.

In *CCS 5818/99*, paras 9–10, the child lived with his grandmother, but they both lived with and were supported by his mother during school holidays. The Commissioner considered whether the child's home should be determined separately at different periods of the year or an overall view of the whole year should be taken. The Commissioner directed a rehearing, but suggested that, as the periods in that case varied from a few weeks to a few months, on the limited evidence available, it seemed appropriate to take an overall view.

The second limb of the definition of a person with care is that the person must provide day to day care for the child. This is not defined by the Act, but is defined by reg.1(2) of the Maintenance Calculations and Special Cases Regulations. It covers persons who on average over the previous 12 months (or such other period as is more representative of the current arrangements for the care of the child) provided care for not less than two nights per week. The need to provide day to day care is modified if (a) the qualifying child is a boarder at a boarding school or an in-patient at a hospital and (b) as a result, the person who would otherwise be providing day to day care is not doing so. These circumstances constitute a special case by virtue of reg.12 of the Maintenance Calculations and Special Cases Regulations. In this case, para.(b) of this sub-section is modified so as to apply to the person who would usually be providing day to day care were the child not a boarder or in-patient. If a child is allowed to live with a parent under s.23(5) of the Children Act 1989, there is a special case by virtue of reg.13 of the Maintenance Calculations and Special Cases Regulations and subs.3(b) is modified to apply to that parent rather than to the person who usually provides day to day care.

The definition of day to day care in terms of overnight care can create problems when arrangements for day and night care are separated. A parent who works night shifts, for example, may have overall care of a child, except that the child is looked after by a nanny or sleeps with a neighbour while the parent is at work. In cases like this, the child is still in the parent's care, although that care is exercised through the agency of someone else. The situation becomes more difficult, however, if the person with whom the child spends the night is someone who is not acting on the parent's behalf. The child might, for example, be looked after at night by grandparents, who might wish to set up a claim as persons with care in competition to the parent. In this case, the child's home might be with the parent, but day to day care with the grandparents, with the result that there would be no person with care. The only way to avoid this would be to rely on the fact that the definition of day to day care in terms of overnight care only applies unless the context otherwise requires. Freed from the definition, it would be possible to have regard to the overall pattern of care for a child. However, it is not the case that the context of the legislation requires a different meaning; rather it is that the meaning produces inappropriate results when applied to particular sets of circumstances and those circumstances could arise in relation to any of the provisions in which the words are used. In other words, in order to avoid the inappropriate results, it would be necessary to disregard the definition completely.

Paragraph (b) expressly caters for the possibility that there may be joint persons with care, that is, that the care for a child may be provided only in conjunction with someone else. It may be difficult to decide in a particular case who is the person with care of a child, for example both a mother and the maternal grandparents may live with and care for a child. The child's home may be said to be with both mother and grandparents. It will then be necessary to inquire closely into the care arrangements to see who has day to day care of the child. Findings of fact will need to be made on this matter and if there is any dispute, the record of decision of the tribunal must explain why the decision was made. Where the living and caring arrangements do not permit a sensible choice to be made between the persons involved, the appropriate decision will be that there are persons with joint care.

The third condition which must be satisfied if a person is to be a person with care in respect of a child is that the person must not fall within one of the prescribed categories of person who may not be persons with care. These are set out in reg.21 of the Maintenance Calculation Procedure Regulations and cover cases where the person with care is a local authority or a person with whom a child is placed or boarded by a local authority. In line with these exclusions, where a local authority has part-time care of a qualifying child, there is a special case by virtue of reg.9 of the Maintenance Calculations and Special Cases Regulations.

*Subsection (5)*

There may be more than one person with care in respect of a child. This subsection covers two possibilities. The first is the possibility expressly catered for by subs.(3)(b), that there may be persons who jointly have care of a child on a day to day basis. The second possibility is that care is shared between different persons (as opposed to being provided jointly by them) so that each is a person with part-time care. Where there is more than one person with care, only those who have parental responsibility for the child may apply for a maintenance assessment (s.5(1)). Where there are applications for maintenance assessments from more than one such person, the one to be proceeded with is determined under reg.4 of, and Sch.2 to, the Maintenance Calculation Procedure Regulations.

A court is entitled to consider the financial consequences of a child support assessment on the "non-resident parent" in determining which parent is to have a residence order in respect of the child, and may conclude that shared residence is appropriate (*Re R. (A Minor) (Residence Order: Finance)* [1995] 2 F.L.R. 612).

*Subsection (6)*

From the point of view of the non-resident parent, payment of child support maintenance is an obligation which must be met. Other debts, such as hire purchase or court fines, do not have priority and are not taken into account when making a maintenance calculation. The parent must renegotiate other financial obligations with the creditors in order to ensure that all obligations may be met, although those cases in which renegotiation is needed may well be those in which it will not be an attractive proposition to lenders. From the point of view of the person with care, child support maintenance is income and may result in this person receiving less benefit than before or ceasing to be entitled to benefit altogether.

In *R(CS) 8/98*, para.24 the Commissioner said that it was arguable that the payment of school fees by an absent parent in respect of a qualifying child at a time when the parent with care was treated as providing day to day care should be regarded as a payment of child support maintenance. However, in *CCS 37/97*, paras 25–26 the Deputy Commissioner, having said that matters for the Secretary of State were better identified as such as then left to the Secretary of State, gave his opinion that, as s.8(7) below preserved the power of the court to order payments "to meet some or all of the expenses incurred in the provision of the instruction" at an educational establishment, a payment of school fees under a court order would by definition be additional to a payment of child support maintenance and could not be regarded as if it were, in part at least, a payment of child support maintenance.

For the position of child support maintenance in insolvency, see the general note to s.33 below.

## Child support maintenance

2.11

**4.**—(1) A person who is, in relation to any qualifying child or any qualifying children, either the person with care or the [7non-resident parent] may apply to the Secretary of State for a [8maintenance calculation] to be made under this Act with respect to that child, or any of those children.

(2) Where a [8maintenance calculation] has been made in response to an application under this section the Secretary of State may, if the person with care or [7non-resident parent] with respect to whom the [9calculation] was made applies to him under this subsection, arrange for—

(a) the collection of the child support maintenance payable in accordance with the [9calculation]

(b) the enforcement of the obligation to pay child support maintenance in accordance with the [9calculation]

(3) Where an application under subsection (2) for the enforcement of the obligation mentioned in subsection (2)(b) authorises the Secretary of State to take steps to enforce that obligation whenever he considers it necessary to do so, the Secretary of State may act accordingly.

(4) A person who applies to the Secretary of State under this section shall, so far as that person reasonably can, comply with such regulations as may be made by the Secretary of State with a view to the Secretary of State [2. . . ] being provided with the information which is required to enable—

(a) the [ non-resident parent] to be [5identified or] traced (where that is necessary);

(b) the amount of child support maintenance payable by the [⁷non-resident parent] to be [⁹calculated]; and

(c) that amount to be recovered from the [⁷non-resident parent].

(5) Any person who has applied to the Secretary of State under this section may at any time request him to cease acting under this section.

(6) It shall be the duty of the Secretary of State to comply with any request made under subsection (5) (but subject to any regulations made under subsection (8)).

(7) The obligation to provide information which is imposed by subsection (4)—

(a) shall not apply in such circumstances as may be prescribed; and

(b) may, in such circumstances as may be prescribed, be waived by the Secretary of State.

(8) The Secretary of State may by regulations make such incidental, supplemental or transitional provision as he thinks appropriate with respect to cases in which he is requested to cease to act under this section.

(9) No application may be made under this section if there is in force with respect to the person with care and [⁷non-resident parent] in question a [⁸maintenance calculation] made in response to an application [⁶treated as made] under section 6.

[¹(10) No application may be made at any time under this section with respect to a qualifying child or any qualifying children if—

(a) there is in force a written maintenance agreement made before 5th April 1993, or a maintenance order [³made before a prescribed date] in respect of that child or those children and the person who is, at that time, the [⁷non-resident parent]; or

[⁴(aa) a maintenance order made on or after the date prescribed for the purposes of paragraph (a) is in force in respect of them, but has been so for less than the period of one year beginning with the date on which it was made; or],

(b) benefit is being paid to, or in respect of, a parent with care of that child or those children.

(11) In subsection (10) "benefit" means any benefit which is mentioned in, or prescribed by regulations under, section 6(1).]

AMENDMENTS

1. Section 18(1) of the 1995 Act (September 4, 1995).

2. Paragraph 19 of Sch.7 to the Social Security Act 1998 (June 1, 1999).

3. Section 2(2) of the 2000 Act (February 4, 2003 under art.2(a) of the Commencement No.12 Order 2003 for the purpose of making regulations; otherwise March 3, 2003 under art.3 of, and the Schedule to, the Commencement No.12 Order 2003).

4. Section 2(3) of the 2000 Act (March 3, 2003 under art.3 of, and the Schedule to, the Commencement No.12 Order 2003).

5. Paragraph 11(3)(a) of Sch.3 to the 2000 Act (March 3, 2003 under art.3 of, and the Schedule to, the Commencement No.12 Order 2003).

6. Paragraph 11(3)(b) of Sch.3 to the 2000 Act (March 3, 2003 under art.3 of, and the Schedule to, the Commencement No.12 Order 2003).

7. Paragraph 11(2) of Sch.3 to the 2000 Act (March 3, 2003 under art.3 of, and the Schedule to, the Commencement No.12 Order 2003).

8. Section 1(2)(a) of the 2000 Act (March 3, 2003 under art.3 of, and the Schedule to, the Commencement No.12 Order 2003).

9. Section 1(2)(b) of the 2000 Act (March 3, 2003 under art.3 of, and the Schedule to, the Commencement No.12 Order 2003).

DEFINITIONS

2.12     "child support maintenance": see s.3(6).
"maintenance agreement": see s.54.
"maintenance calculation": see s.54.
"non-resident parent": see s.3(2).
"person with care": see s.3(3).
"prescribed": see s.54.
"qualifying child": see s.3(1).

GENERAL NOTE

2.13     A child support maintenance calculation is initiated by an application that is actually made or treated as made. It may be initiated by a non-resident parent, a person with care or a child. An application may be made under this section by a non-resident parent or a person with care. In Scotland, an application may also be made under s.7 below by a child who has attained the age of 12. The Secretary of State may treat an application as having been made under s.6 (see s.6(3) below) or this section (see s.11(4) below).

*Subsection (1)*
Any non-resident parent and, subject to s.5(1), any person with care may apply for a maintenance assessment in respect of a child. This is subject to subs.(9). A non-resident parent may wish to apply in order to fix the extent of responsibility under this Act (see s.1(2)).

*Subsection (2)*
A person with care or a non-resident parent may authorise (see subss.(2) and (3)) the Secretary of State to arrange for the collection of child support maintenance and the enforcement of the obligation to pay it. The obligation to pay which is referred to in para.(b) is the duty created by s.1(3). Matters relating to the collection and enforcement of child support maintenance are for the Secretary of State and are dealt with in ss.29 to 41.

*Subsection (4)*
A person who authorises the Secretary of State to arrange for collection and enforcement under subss.(2) and (3) is required to co-operate by providing the information specified in this subsection. The regulations are to be found in Pt II of the Information, Evidence and Disclosure Regulations. The duty to co-operate is a qualified one. This subsection provides that it only applies in so far as it is reasonably possible for that person to comply and it is further limited by the conditions set out in regs 2(1) and 5. It may also be waived by the Secretary of State under subs.(7)(b), but only in prescribed circumstances. Wider duties concerning the provision of information are created under s.14(1) which are also contained in Pt II of the Regulations. This subsection applies only to the supply of information, whereas s.14(1) applies to both information and evidence. For a discussion of the meaning of "information" in this section and for enforcement see the general note to s.14(1). See also the offence under s.14A below.

*Subsection (5)*

This subsection only provides for the Secretary of State to *cease* acting. It does not authorise the cancellation of the maintenance assessment (*CCS 13/94*, para.6). Accordingly, the assessment remains valid for the period prior to the cessation of action by the Secretary of State. If a tribunal is in doubt whether an application under this section has been received by the Secretary of State, it is an error of law not to clarify this (by adjournment if necessary) if there is evidence to believe that such a request has been made (*ibid.*, para.8).

*Subsection (8)*

No regulations have been made under this subsection, although the circumstances in which the duty to disclose will arise are limited by reg.2(1) to cases where either the information or evidence is in the possession of the person concerned or it can reasonably be expected to be acquired by that person.

*Subsections (10) and (11)*

See the general note to s.18 of the 1995 Act. The non-resident parent referred to is the person who was the non-resident parent at the time when the order or agreement was made (*CCS 2567/98*, para.11, relying on the reasoning of the Court of Appeal in refusing leave to appeal against the decision in *R(CS) 4/96* in *Kirkley v Secretary of State for Social Security and the Child Support Officer*, unreported, December 15, 1995).

*Subsection (10)(a)*

March 3, 2003 is the date prescribed for the purposes of subs.(10)(a) by reg.2(a) of the Child Support (Applications: Prescribed Date) Regulations 2003.

*Subsection (10)(aa)*

A court order for child maintenance, whether or not made on consent, should use the child support maintenance figure as a starting point in order to discourage an application under this Act as soon as the year has expired (*GW v RW (Financial Provision: Departure from Equality)* [2003] 2 F.L.R. 108 at para.74).

## Child support maintenance; supplemental provisions

5.—(1) Where—

   (a) there is more than one person with care of a qualifying child; and

   (b) one or more, but not all, of them have parental responsibility for [1. . .] the child;

no application may be made for a [2maintenance calculation] with respect to the child by any of those persons who do not have parental responsibility for [1. . .] the child.

   (2) Where more than one application for a [2maintenance calculation] is made with respect to the child concerned, only one of them may be proceeded with.

   (3) The Secretary of State may by regulations make provision as to which of two or more applications for a [2maintenance calculation] with respect to the same child is to be proceeded with.

2.14

AMENDMENTS

1. Paragraph 52(3) of Sch.4, and Sch.5 to the Children (Scotland) Act 1995 (November 1, 1996).

2. Section 1(2)(a) of the 2000 Act (March 3, 2003 under art.3 of, and the Schedule to, the Commencement No.12 Order 2003).

DEFINITIONS

**2.15**     "maintenance calculation": see s.54.
"parental responsibility": see s.54.
"person with care": see s.3(3).
"prescribed": see s.54.
"qualifying child": see s.3(1).

GENERAL NOTE

*Subsection (1)*
**2.16**     If there is more than one person with care, only those with parental responsibility for the qualifying child may apply for a maintenance assessment. However, if there is only one person with care, that person may apply for an assessment regardless of who has parental responsibility.

*Subsections (2) and (3)*
Only one application for a maintenance assessment in respect of a child may be proceeded with. If more than one is made, the priority between any that cannot be eliminated under subs.(1) is determined under the provisions of reg.4 of, and Sch.2 to, the Maintenance Calculation Procedure Regulations. If an attempt is made to make an application for a maintenance assessment at a time when such an application may not be made (as to which see the general note to s.18 of the 1995 Act), that application is ignored and is irrelevant to the question of priority of applications.

## [¹Applications by those claiming or receiving benefit

**2.17**     **6.**—(1) This section applies where income support, an income-based jobseeker's allowance or any other benefit of a prescribed kind is claimed by or in respect of, or paid to or in respect of, the parent of a qualifying child who is also a person with care of the child.

(2) In this section, that person is referred to as "the parent".

(3) The Secretary of State may—

(a) treat the parent as having applied for a maintenance calculation with respect to the qualifying child and all other children of the non-resident parent in relation to whom the parent is also a person with care; and

(b) take action under this Act to recover from the non-resident parent, on the parent's behalf, the child support maintenance so determined.

(4) Before doing what is mentioned in subsection (3), the Secretary of State must notify the parent in writing of the effect of subsections (3) and (5) and section 46.

(5) The Secretary of State may not act under subsection (3) if the parent asks him not to (a request which need not be in writing).

(6) Subsection (1) has effect regardless of whether any of the benefits mentioned there is payable with respect to any qualifying child.

(7) Unless she has made a request under subsection (5), the parent shall, so far as she reasonably can, comply with such regulations as may be made

by the Secretary of State with a view to the Secretary of State's being provided with the information which is required to enable—

(a) the non-resident parent to be identified or traced;

(b) the amount of child support maintenance payable by him to be calculated; and

(c) that amount to be recovered from him.

(8) The obligation to provide information which is imposed by subsection (7)—

(a) does not apply in such circumstances as may be prescribed; and

(b) may, in such circumstances as may be prescribed, be waived by the Secretary of State.

(9) If the parent ceases to fall within subsection (1), she may ask the Secretary of State to cease acting under this section, but until then he may continue to do so.

(10) The Secretary of State must comply with any request under subsection (9) (but subject to any regulations made under subsection (11)).

(11) The Secretary of State may be regulations make such incidental or transitional provision as he thinks appropriate with respect to cases in which he is asked under subsection (9) to cease to act under this section.

(12) The fact that a maintenance calculation is in force with respect to a person with care does not prevent the making of a new maintenance calculation with respect to her as a result of the Secretary of State's acting under subsection (3).]

AMENDMENT

1. Section 3 of the 2000 Act (for the purpose of making regulations, November  2.18
10, 2000 under art.2(1) of, and Pt I of the Schedule to, the Commencement No.3
Order 2000; March 3, 2003 under art.4 of, and the Schedule to, the
Commencement No.12 Order 2003).

DEFINITIONS

"child": see s.55.
"child support maintenance": see s.54.
"income support": see s.54.
"income-based jobseeker's allowance": see s.54.
"non-resident parent": see s.54.
"parent": see s.54, but see also subs.(2).
"person with care": see s.54.
"prescribed": see s.54.
"qualifying child": see s.54.

GENERAL NOTE

This section applies to parents with care for whom a relevant benefit is claimed  2.19
or paid. It must be read together with s.46 below, which provides for reduced benefit decisions. Taken as a parcel, the two sections operate to limit the circumstances
in which a parent with care who is being supported by a social security benefit is
able to impose responsibility for the support of a child on the benefit systme rather
than on the non-resident parent.

The benefits covered are set out in or under subs.(1). The consequences of falling
within subs.(1) are that an application for a maintenance calculation is treated as

made and action to recover child support maintenance is taken: see subs.(3). The parent with care may opt out from the beginning (subs.(5)) or when subs.(1) is longer satisfied. In the former case, the parent with care may be subject to a reduced benefits decision. In the latter case, the parent with care may ask the Secretary of State to cease acting under subs.(9).

The Secretary of State is not required to consult the non-resident parent (if that parent's identify and whereabouts are known) before acting under this section (*R. v Secretary of State for Social Security Ex p. Lloyd* [1995] 1 F.L.R. 856).

The section refers to the parent with care as female and the non-resident parent as male. That reflects the reality of the majority of cases. However, the effect of s.6(a) of the Interpretation Act 1978 is that the gender of either parent is irrelevant.

### Subsection (1)

This section applies to parents with care, not to persons with care who are not parents. It applies to income support or an income-based jobseeker's allowance. No other benefit has been prescribed.

The benefit need not be claimed by or paid to the parent with care. It is sufficient if it is claimed or paid in respect of that parent. Paid means actually paid, not lawfully paid (*Secretary of State for Social Security v Harmon, Carter and Cocks* [1998] 2 F.L.R. 598). A Tribunal of Commissioners in Northern Ireland decided that this decision is no longer valid by virtue of s.3 of the Human Rights Act 1998 (*CSC7/03–04*), but this was reversed by the Court of Appeal in Northern Ireland in *Department for Social Development v MacGeagh* [2005] NICA 28(1).

It is irrelevant whether or not the benefit is payable with respect to the qualifying child: see subs.(6) below.

If the parent with care ceases to fall within this subsection before the application is determined, the section no longer applies, although the parent with care has one month within which to opt for the application to be treated as made under s.4 above (see s.11(3)–(4) below).

### Subsection (3)

If subs.(1) applies, the Secretary of State may treat an application for a maintenance calculation as having been made and take action to recover child support maintenance on the parent with care's behalf.

The Secretary of State is given a power, not a duty, to act (*CCS 12806/96*, para.8). The power is subject to s.2 above. The power is also subject to the parent with care's power to opt out under subss.(4) and (5) below.

This subsection ceases to apply if the parent with care ceases to fall within subs.(1) above, although the parent with care has the option of asking for the application to be treated as made under s.4 instead (see s.11(3)–(4) below).

### Subsection (5)

This is mandatory. It allows a parent with care who falls within subs.(1) to opt out of the child support scheme. However, the parent may then become subject to a reduced benefits decision under s.46 below.

### Subsection (7)

The regulations are to be found in Pt II of the Information, Evidence and Disclosure Regulations. The consequence of failure to comply with these regulations is that an officer may make a reduced benefit direction under s.46. The qualified nature of this duty to co-operate is discussed in the general note to s.4(4). It may also be waived by the Secretary of State under subs.(8)(b), but only in prescribed circumstances. Wider duties concerning the provision of information are created under s.14(1) which are also contained in Pt II of the Regulations. This subsection applies only to the supply of information, whereas s.14(1) applies to both information and evidence. For a discussion of the meaning of "information" in this section and for enforcement see the general note to s.14(1).

*Subsection (8)*

No regulations have been made under this subsection, although the circumstances in which the duty to disclose will arise are limited by reg.2(1) of the Information, Evidence and Disclosure Regulations to cases where either the information or evidence is in the possession of the person concerned or it can reasonably be expected to be acquired by that person.

*Subsection (9)*

This allows a parent with care who ceases to fall within subs.(1) above to opt out of the child support scheme. It is optional for the parent with care, not obligatory. If the option is exercised, the Secretary of State must comply. If it is not exercised, the Secretary of State *may* continue to act under this section. As action under this section is discretionary (see the general note to subs.(3) above), the Secretary of State's power in this subsection is also presumably discretionary. In practice, this issue is only likely to arise if a non-resident parent asks the Secretary of State to cease acting.

*Subsection (11)*

This subsection is narrower than similar provisions elsewhere in the Act in that it refers only to incidental and transitional provisions rather than to incidental, supplemental and transitional provisions: compare ss.4(8) and 7(9). However, any effect of this difference in wording is overriden by ss.51(1) and (3).

*Subsection (14)*

This allows a parent with care to be brought within the control of this section and s.46, despite the fact that a maintenance calculation is already in force as a result of another application.

## Right of child in Scotland to apply for assessment

7.—(1) A qualifying child who has attained the age of 12 years and who is habitually resident in Scotland may apply to the Secretary of State for a [8maintenance calculation] to be made with respect to him if— 2.20
 (a) no such application has been made by a person who is, with respect to that child, a person with care or [7a non-resident parent]; or
 [3(b) no parent has been treated under section 6(3) as having applied for a maintenance calculation with respect to the child.]
 (2) An application made under subsection (1) shall authorise the Secretary of State to make a [8maintenance calculation] with respect to any other children of the [7non-resident parent] who are qualifying children in the care of the same person as the child making the application.
 (3) Where a [8maintenance calculation] has been made in response to an application under this section the Secretary of State may, if the person with care, the [7non-resident parent] with respect to whom the [9calculation] was made or the child concerned applies to him under this subsection, arrange for—
 (a) the collection of the child support maintenance payable in accordance with the [9calculation];
 (b) the enforcement of the obligation to pay child support maintenance in accordance with the [9calculation].

(4) Where an application under subsection (3) for the enforcement of the obligation mentioned in subsection (3)(b) authorises the Secretary of State to take steps to enforce that obligation whenever he considers it necessary to do so, the Secretary of State may act accordingly.

(5) Where a child has asked the Secretary of State to proceed under this section, the person with care of the child, the [⁷non-resident parent] and the child concerned shall, so far as they reasonably can, comply with such regulations as may be made by the Secretary of State with a view to the Secretary of State [². . . ] being provided with the information which is required to enable—

(a) the [⁷non-resident parent] to be traced (where that is necessary);
(b) the amount of child support maintenance payable by the [⁷non-resident parent] to be [⁹calculated]; and
(c) that amount to be recovered from the [⁷non-resident parent].

(6) The child who has made the application (but not the person having care of him) may at any time request the Secretary of State to cease acting under this section.

(7) It shall be the duty of the Secretary of State to comply with any request made under subsection (6) (but subject to any regulations made under subsection (9)).

(8) The obligation to provide information which is imposed by subsection (5)—

(a) shall not apply in such circumstances as may be precribed by the Secretary of State; and
(b) may, in such circumstances as may be so prescribed, be waived by the Secretary of State.

(9) The Secretary of State may by regulations make such incidental, supplemental or transitional provision as he thinks appropriate with respect to cases in which he is requested to cease to act under this section.

[¹(10) No application may be made at any time under this section by a qualifying child if

[⁴(a)] there is in force a written maintenance agreement made before 5th April, 1993, or a maintenance order [⁵made before a prescribed date], in respect of that child and the person who is, at that time, the [⁷non-resident parent]; [⁶or
(b) a maintenance order made on or after the date prescribed for the purposes of paragraph (a) is in force in respect of them, but has been so for less than the period of one year beginning with the date on which it was made.]

AMENDMENTS

1. Section 18(2) of the 1995 Act (September 4, 1995).
2. Paragraph 21 of Sch.7 to the Social Security Act 1998 (June 1, 1999).
3. Paragraph 11(4)(a) of Sch.3 to the 2000 Act (March 3, 2003 under art.3 of, and the Schedule to, the Commencement No.12 Order 2003).
4. Paragraph 11(4)(b)(i) of Sch.3 to the 2000 Act (February 4, 2003 under art.2(b) of the Commencement No.12 Order 2003 the purpose of making regulations; otherwise March 3, 2003 under art.3 of, and the Schedule to, the Commencement No.12 Order 2003).

5. Paragraph 11(4)(b)(ii) of Sch.3 to the 2000 Act (February 4, 2003 under art.2(b) of the Commencement No.12 Order 2003 the purpose of making regulations; otherwise March 3, 2003 under art.3 of, and the Schedule to, the Commencement No. 12 Order 2003).

6. Paragraph 11(4)(b)(iii) of Sch.3 to the 2000 Act (March 3, 2003 under art.3 of, and the Schedule to, the Commencement No.12 Order 2003).

7. Paragraph 11(2) of Sch.3 to the 2000 Act (March 3, 2003 under art.3 of, and the Schedule to, the Commencement No.12 Order 2003).

8. Section 1(2)(a) of the 2000 Act (March 3, 2003 under art.3 of, and the Schedule to, the Commencement No.12 Order 2003).

9. Section 1(2)(b) of the 2000 Act (March 3, 2003 under art.3 of, and the Schedule to, the Commencement No.12 Order 2003).

DEFINITIONS

"child": see s.55.                                                          2.21
"child support maintenance": see s.3(6).
"maintenance agreement": see s.54.
"maintenance calculation": see s.54.
"non-resident parent": see s.3(2).
"person with care": see s.3(3).
"prescribed": see s.54.
"qualifying child": see s.3(1).

GENERAL NOTE

This section applies only to Scotland (s.58(10)) and is a consequence of the dif-      2.22
ferent age of legal capacity in Scotland from England and Wales as a result of the limited effect of the Age of Legal Capacity (Scotland) Act 1991. It allows a child who has attained the age of 12 to apply for a maintenance calculation. Two conditions must be satisfied. First, no application must have been made by a non-resident parent or a person with care. Second, the Secretary if State must not have treated an application as made under s.6 above. An application by a child authorises the Secretary of State to make a calculation in respect of all other qualifying children of the absent parent who are in the care of the person with care of the child who has applied under this section (subs.(2)).

After an application has been made the child may request the Secretary of State to cease acting under this section but the parent with care may not do so (subs.(6)). If requested by the child the Secretary of State must comply with the request, subject to any regulations made under subs.(9).

Except in these respects this section mirrors provisions in ss.4 and 6. Reference should be made to the general note to the equivalent provisions in those sections. The regulations referred to are to be found in the Information, Evidence and Disclosure Regulations. No regulations have been made under subss.(8) and (9), although the circumstances in which the duty to disclose will arise are limited by reg.2(1) to cases where either the information or evidence is in the possession of the person concerned or it can reasonably be expected to be acquired by that person. Wider duties concerning the provision of informations. be acquired by that person. Wider duties concerning the provision of information are created under s.14(1) which are also contained in Pt II of the Regulations. This subsection applies only to the supply of information, whereas s.14(1) applies to both information and evidence. For a discussion of the meaning of "information" in this section and for enforcement see the general note to s.14(1). See also the offence under s.14A below.

*Subsection (10)*

See the general note to s.18 of the 1995 Act.

March 3, 2003 is the date prescribed for the purposes of subs.(10)(a) by reg.2(b) of the Child Support (Applications: Prescribed Date) Regulations 2003.

## Role of the courts with respect to maintenance for children

2.23    **8.**—(1) This subsection applies in any case where [¹the Secretary of State] would have jurisdiction to make a [⁶maintenance calculation] with respect to a qualifying child and [⁸a non-resident parent] of his on an application duly made [²(or treated as made)] by a person entitled to apply for such [⁷a calculation] with respect to that child.

(2) Subsection (1) applies even though the circumstances of the case are such that [¹the Secretary of State] would not make [⁷a calculation] if it were applied for.

(3) [³Except as provided in subsection (3A),] in any case where subsection (1) applies, no court shall exercise any power which it would otherwise have to make, vary or revive any maintenance order in relation to the child and [⁸non-resident parent] concerned.

[⁴(3A) Unless a maintenance calculation has been made with respect to the child concerned, subsection (3) does not prevent a court from varying a maintenance order in relation to that child and the non-resident parent concerned—

  (a) if the maintenance order was made on or after the date prescribed for the purposes of section 4(10)(a) or 7(10)(a); or

  (b) Where the order was made before then, in any case in which section 4(10) or 7(10) prevents the making of an application for a maintenance calculation with respect to or by that child.]

(4) Subsection (3) does not prevent a court from revoking a maintenance order.

(5) The Lord Chancellor or in relation to Scotland the Lord Advocate may by order provide that, in such circumstances as may be specified by the order, this section shall not prevent a court from exercising any power which it has to make a maintenance order in relation to a child if—

  (a) a written agreement (whether or not enforceable) provides for the making, or securing, by [⁸a non-resident parent] of the child of periodical payments to or for the benefit of the child; and

  (b) the maintenance order which the court makes is, in all material respects, in the same terms as that agreement.

(6) This section shall not prevent a court from exercising any power which it has to make a maintenance order in relation to a child if—

  (a) a [⁶maintenance calculation] is in force with respect to the child;

  [⁵(b) the non-resident parent's net weekly income exceeds the figure referred to in paragraph 10(3) of Schedule 1 (as it has effect from time to time pursuant to regulations made under paragraph 10A(1)(b)); and]

  (c) the court is satisfied that the circumstances of the case make it appropriate for the [⁸non-resident parent] to make or secure the making of periodical payments under a maintenance order in addition to the child support maintenance payable by him in accordance with the [⁶maintenance calculation].

(7) This section shall not prevent a court from exercising any power which it has to make a maintenance order in relation to a child if—

(a) the child is, will be or (if the order were to be made) would be receiving instruction at an educational establishment or undergoing training for a trade, profession or vocation (whether or not while in gainful employment); and

(b) the order is made solely for the purposes of requiring the person making or securing the making of periodical payments fixed by the order to meet some or all of the expenses incurred in connection with the provision of the instruction or training.

(8) This section shall not prevent a court from exercising any power which it has to make a maintenance order in relation to a child if—

(a) a disability living allowance is paid to or in respect of him; or

(b) no such allowance is paid but he is disabled,

and the order is made solely for the purpose of requiring the person making or securing the making of periodical payments fixed by the order to meet some or all of any expenses attributable to the child's disability.

(9) For the purposes of subsection (8), a child is disabled if he is blind, deaf or dumb or is substantially and permanently handicapped by illness, injury, mental disorder or congenital deformity or such other disability as may be prescribed.

(10) This section shall not prevent a court from exercising any power which it has to make a maintenance order in relation to a child if the order is made against a person with care of the child.

(11) In this Act "maintenance order", in relation to any child, means an order which requires the making or securing of periodical payments to or for the benefit of the child and which is made under—

(a) Part II of the Matrimonial Causes Act 1973;

(b) The Domestic Proceedings and Magistrates' Courts Act 1978;

(c) Part III of the Matrimonial and Family Proceedings Act 1984;

(d) the Family Law (Scotland) Act 1985;

(e) Schedule 1 to the Children Act 1989; [⁹. . .]

[¹⁰(ea) Schedule 5, 6 or 7 of the Civil Partnership Act 2004; or]

(f) any other prescribed enactment,

and includes any order varying or reviving such an order.

AMENDMENTS

1. Paragraph 22 of Sch.7 to the Social Security Act 1998 (June 1, 1999).

2. Paragraph 11(5)(a) of Sch.3 to the 2000 Act (March 3, 2003 under art.3 of, and the Schedule to, the Commencement No.12 Order 2003).

3. Paragraph 11(5)(b) of Sch.3 to the 2000 Act (March 3, 2003 under art.3 of, and the Schedule to, the Commencement No.12 Order 2003).

4. Paragraph 11(5)(c) of Sch.3 to the 2000 Act (March 3, 2003 under art.3 of, and the Schedule to, the Commencement No.12 Order 2003).

5. Paragraph 11(5)(d) of Sch.3 to the 2000 Act (March 3, 2003 under art.3 of, and the Schedule to, the Commencement No.12 Order 2003).

6. Section 1(2)(a) of the 2000 Act (March 3, 2003 under art.3 of, and the Schedule to, the Commencement No.12 Order 2003).

7. Section 1(2)(b) of the 2000 Act (March 3, 2003 under art.3 of, and the Schedule to, the Commencement No.12 Order 2003).

8. Paragraph 11(2) of Sch. 3 to the 2000 Act (March 3, 2003 under art.3 of, and the Schedule to, the Commencement No.12 Order 2003).
9. Section 261(4) of, and Sch.30 to, The Civil Partnerhsip Act 2004.
10. Paragraph 1 of Sch.24 to the Civil Partnership Act 2004.

DEFINITIONS

2.24      "child": see s.55.
"child benefit": see s.54.
"child support maintenance": see s.3(6).
"disability living allowance": see s.54.
"maintenance calculation": see s.54
"non-resident parent": see s.3(2).
"person with care": see s.3(3).
"prescribed": see s.54.
"qualifying child": see s.3(1).

GENERAL NOTE

2.25      Section 8 to 10 provide for the relationship between maintenance calculation on the one hand and maintenance orders made by the courts and maintenance agreements on the other hand. Section 8 gives the child support scheme priority over the court system if the Secretary of State would have jurisdiction to make a maintenance calculation were an application to be made, regardless of whether or not an application has been made. In such a case the courts may not make, vary or revive a maintenance order, although they may revoke one.

A startling illustration of the effects of this section is given in *Phillips v Peace* [1996] 2 F.L.R. 230. The father lived in a house valued at £2.6 million and owned three motor cars together worth nearly £200,000. He carried on a share dealing business, and at the time of the child support maintenance assessment, was paid no salary by his (own) company. The child support officer accordingly assessed him as having as nil liability under the Act. The mother sought provision for the child under the remaining jurisdiction of the courts, to award lump sums and property adjustment orders (Sch.1 to the Children Act 1989). Johnson J. held that where jurisdiction to make an assessment lay with the Agency, the court should exercise its power to award a lump sum only in order to meet the need of a child in respect of a particular item of capital expenditure. Thus, he would order a sum of £90,000 to be paid so that a home could be purchased for the child and mother to live in, but he could not order a lump sum as a form of capitalised maintenance. If he had been able to do so, he would have ordered an amount based on £90 per week for the next year or so. His lordship commented that this appeared to be a suitable case for a departure direction (now called a variation), but it also seems strange that the child support officer apparently made no attempt to apply the regulations dealing with amounts treated as income (see Pt V of Sch.1 to the Maintenance Assessments and Special Cases, Regulations), still less to extract the minimum amount of support from the father. It is worth comparing the (apparent) powerlessness of the Child Support Agency in this case with the Court of Appeal decision in *Thomas v Thomas* [1995] 2 F.L.R. 668. There, a husband who ran a successful family business and was a Lloyds name, but had cash-flow problems, was ordered to pay a lump sum to his wife in a divorce settlement, even though in effect he would have to be helped to raise it by members of his family. The court considered that, where a husband has liquidity problems but possesses substantial means (a house and pension assets), the onus is on him to satisfy the court that all means of access to funds to make provision for the wife have been found to be impossible. The court was entitled to find that funds would be forthcoming to him. While the courts will be careful not to require a person to sell off a business which provides his livelihood, this case demonstrates that they are able, and willing, to look behind the ostensible picture and to ensure that fair liabilities to the family are met.

An award of child maintenance made under this section will be based on the assumption that a parent with care who has received a substantial share of the parents' assets on divorce will contribute to the support of the child (*GW v RW (Financial Provision: Departure from Equality)* [2003] 2 F.L.R. 108 at para.75). If the award is made in respect of a child who is living abroad, it should be expressed in the currency of the child's residence in order to avoid the risk of currency fluctuation (*ibid.*, at para.76).

*Subsection (3)*

Although the court loses it power to make, vary or revive a maintenance order, it retains the power to *enforce* such an order. This, however, will only apply to arrears which accured prior to the child support officer assuming jurisdiction.

The Family Proceedings (Amendment) Rules 1993 amend the Family Proceedings Rules 1991 as amended [FPR] to deal with the situation where there is a dispute as to whether the court or the Secretary of State has jurisdiction.

By r.10.24, where an application is made for an order which in the opinion of the District Judge, considering the matter in the first instance without holding a hearing, is one which the court would be precluded from making by virtue of s.8 or s.9 (below), the proper officer (the chief clerk of the family proceedings department of the principal registry or the chief clerk of any other court or registry—FPR r.1.2) may send a notice (Form M34) to the applicant. Where the applicant has been sent such a notice, and informs the proper officer in writing, within 14 days of the date of the notice, that he wishes to persist with his application, the proper officer shall refer the matter back to the district judge for action. The district judge shall give such directions as he considers appropriate for the matter to be heard and determined by the court, and may provide for the hearing to be *ex parte*. The proper officer shall inform the applicant of the directions, and, in relation to the other parties, send them a copy of the application. If the hearing is to be *ex parte*, he shall give them brief information of the matter and inform them that they will be told of the result of the hearing in due course. If the hearing is *inter partes*, he shall inform them of the circumstances which led to the directions being given, and the directions.

Where the applicant does not inform the officer that he wishes to persist with his application, the application shall be treated as having been withdrawn.

If, after the hearing, the court determines that it would be prevented by s.8 or 9 of the Act from making the order applied for, it shall dismiss the application, giving reasons in writing, copies of which will be sent to the parties by the proper officer. The applicant could then appeal to a circuit judge under FPR r.8, or go to the Secretary of State for a calculation.

Rule 10.25 deals with "non-free-standing applications" for child maintenance. Where an application for such maintenance is contained in a petition or other document and a notice is sent under r.10.24(1), the document shall be treated as if it did not include the maintenance application. (If the court decides, under r.10.24 that it *does* have jurisdiction to grant the application, it shall direct that the document be treated as if it contained the application.)

(Family proceedings forms and divorce petitions are amended by rr.7–16 and Schs1 and 2 to require an applicant for child or spousal maintenance to provide the court with details of any child support assessment or proceedings, to enable the court to decide whether it has jurisdiction, and if so, what payments should be ordered.)

The Family Proceedings Courts (Child Support Act 1991) Rules 1993, rr.6–12 make equivalent provision where applications are made to the family proceedings court.

Schedule 1 to the Child Maintenance Orders (Backdating) Order 1993 inserts s.31(11) into the Matrimonial Causes Act 1973, s.20(9A) into the Domestic Proceedings and Magistrates' Courts Act 1978, and Sch.1, para.6(9) into the Children Act 1989 to provide for backdating to the effective date or any later date where an application is made to vary or discharge an order which provided for periodical payments for children without apportioning the payments between them, and a maintenance calculation is made in respect of one or more, but not all of the children. This is to ensure that the non-resident parent is not obliged to continue paying the full amount under the order, in addition to the amount calculated under the maintenance calculation.

The Family Division of the High Court has held that the implementation of the Child Support Act is not an event which fundamentally undermines the assumption upon which a clean break settlement made some years previously between divorcing spouses was based, and thus does not justify the settlement being set aside. In *Crozier v Crozier* [1994] Fam. 114, the absent parent had made such a settlement, transferring his interest in the former matrimonial home to the wife at the time of the divorce in 1989. He had been paying £4 per week as a liable relative for his child's maintenance, and faced an increase to around £29 under the formula assessment. Booth J. regarded the increase as due to a procedural change and not because of any new power taken by the state. However, in *Mawson v Mawson* [1994] 2 F.L.R. 985, it was held that an appeal in respect of a divorce settlement made in 1993 would be allowed, *inter alia* because it had been predicated upon a maintenance assessment of some £600 per month, which had been reduced by £100 due to regulation changes in 1993. Thorpe J. stated that such changes, as distinct from changes in the absent parent's own circumstances, could not have been foreseen by the trial judge, and so should be taken into account in deciding on the appropriate settlement for the wife. It is not easy to discern how it is deemed possible to alter a settlement due to unforeseen changes to the child support formula, as in *Mawson*, but not possible to set aside a settlement due to unforeseen legislation, as in *Crozier*. The cases are distinguishable on the rather narrow point that the passage of time elapsing between the first court order and the attempt to appeal was much less in *Mawson*, and this is a factor which the courts are required to take into account under the leading authority concerning setting-aside, *Barder v Caluori* [1988] A.C. 20. However, this was not the basis of the courts' reasoning in the two decisions, and the cases would appear to be in conflict at the level of principle. In *Smith v McInerney* [1994] 2 F.L.R. 1077, another decision of Thorpe J., it was held that where a husband had parted with capital in part-commutation of his future obligation to maintain his children under a voluntary separation agreement, he should be provided with an indemnity, by means of a charge on the matrimonial home, in case the wife in future became a benefit recipient and hence probably required to seek a child support calculation under s.6 of the Act. Otherwise, the husband would end up being made to pay twice for his children. The case is distinguishable from *Crozier* in so far as it relates to a voluntary agreement rather than a consent order, but once more, it appears to highlight a difference of opinion among the Family Division judges on the principles which should apply to dealing with the relationship between child support and financial relief on divorce.

*Subsection (3A)*

**2.26**    See the general note to s.18 of the 1995 Act.

*Subsection (5)*

This subsection together with the Child Maintenance (Written Agreements) Order 1993 preserves the courts' power to make consent orders in respect of periodical payments to or for the benefit of a child, even though the Secretary of State has jurisdiction to carry out a calculation. Parents in receipt of benefit will not be able to seek a consent order as a means of avoiding the jurisdiction of the child support officer because of the mandatory nature of s.6.

*Subsection (7)*

A court may make a maintenance order the sole purpose of which is to cover some or all of the payments for a child's instruction or training. The child must be receiving or going to receive some instruction.

A court has made an order to cover school fees even where the maintenance assessment made by the child support officer is relatively modest. A district judge has ordered a husband who declared a gross income of £26,000 as a company director and who was required to pay £25 per week child maintenance to pay one-half of the child's school fees of £4,200 per year ([1994] N.L.J. 702).

*Subsection (8)*

A court may make a maintenance order the sole purpose of which is to meet some or all of the expenses attributable to a child's disability provided that either disability living allowance is payable to or in respect of the child or the child is disabled as defined in subs.(9).

*Subsections (6), (7) and (8)*

Maintenance orders covered by these subsections are prescribed for the purposes of s.30 by reg.2(a) of the Collection and Enforcement of Other Forms of Maintenance Regulations.

The Child Maintenance Orders (Backdating) Order 1993 adds s.29(7) and (8) to the Matrimonial Causes Act 1973, s.5(7) and (8) to the Domestic Proceedings and Magistrates' Courts Act 1978 and para.7(7) and (8) to Sch.1 to the Children Act 1989, to provide for where a maintenance calculation ceases to have effect or is cancelled under any provision of the Act, and an application for a periodical payments order in favour of the child is made. If the application for the order is made within six months of the date when the calculation ceased to have effect or, where the calculation was cancelled, the later of either the date it was cancelled or the date from which the cancellation first had effect, the order may begin from the date the calculation ceased to have effect, or the date with effect from which it was cancelled, or any later date. Again, the purpose is to remedy any shortfall in support which might otherwise occur between the ending of the assessment and the making of the order.

Schedule 1 to the Child Maintenance Orders (Backdating) Order 1993 allows maintenance orders to be backdated to the "earliest permitted date" which is the later of either (a) the date six months before the application was made, or (b) the effective date (see the general note to Sch.1, para.11 below) of a maintenance calculation made under the Child Support Act, (instead of to the date of the application to the court) provided that the application for the maintenance order is made within six months of the date of the calculation. The Order inserts s.29(5)(b) into the Matrimonial Causes Act 1973, s.5(5)(b) into the Domestic Proceedings and Magistrates' Courts Act 1978 and Sch.1, para.3(5)(b) into the Children Act 1989 to provide that where "top-up maintenance", etc. is awarded by a court, backdating can take place. This will protect the parent with care in the interim period between the making of the calculation (when an earlier order may have been superseded) and the application for the top-up.

*Subsection (9)*

This definition broadly follows that used in s.17(11) of the Children Act 1989 except that mental disorders must result in the child being substantially and permanently handicapped whereas under the 1989 Act any mental disorder is sufficient regardless of its effect. The extent to which the child must be blind or deaf is not specified. For the purpose of disability living allowance a person has to be 100 per cent blind and 80 per cent deaf: reg.12(2) of the Social Security (Disability Living Allowance) Regulations 1991. In the context of these provisions the test of blindness and deafness is assessed by reference to the criteria used for the purposes of assessing degrees of disablement for the purposes of Disablement Benefit *R(DLA) 3/95*). No regulations have been made under this subsection.

Although the definitions used in the Mental Health Act 1983 have not been adopted here, they give an indication of the breadth of the meaning of "mental disorder" in current legal usage. The relevant definitions from s.1(2) of that Act are as follows:

> " 'mental disorder' means mental illness, arrested or incomplete development of mind, psychopathic disorder and any other disorder or disability of mind . . .;
> 'psychopathic disorder' means a persistent disorder or disability of mind (whether or not including significant impairment of intelligence) which results in abnormal aggressive or seriously irresponsible conduct on the part of the person concerned."

Section 1(3) emphasises that a person does not fall within either of the above definitions "by reason only of promiscuity or other immoral conduct, sexual deviancy or dependence on alcohol or drugs".

*Subsection (10)*

A court may make a maintenance order against a person with care.

*Subsection (11)*

The other enactments are prescribed for the purposes of this subsection by reg.2 of the Maintenance Arrangements and Jurisdiction Regulations.

For a discussion of the meaning of "maintenance order", see the general note to s.18 of the 1995 Act.

## Agreement about maintenance

2.27
**9.**—(1) In this section "maintenance agreement" means any agreement for the making, or for securing the making, of periodical payments by way of maintenance, or in Scotland aliment, to or for the benefit of any child.

(2) Nothing in this Act shall be taken to prevent any person from entering into a maintenance agreement.

(3) [¹Subject to section 4(1)(a) and section 7(10),] the existence of a maintenance agreement shall not prevent any party to the agreement, or any other person, from applying for a [³maintenance calculation] with respect to any child to or for whose benefit periodical payments are to be made or secured under the agreement.

(4) Where any agreement contains a provision which purports to restrict the right of any person to apply for a [³maintenance calculation], that provision shall be void.

(5) Where section 8 would prevent any court from making a maintenance order in relation to a child and [⁴a non-resident parent] of his, no court shall exercise any power that it has to vary any agreement so as—

(a) to insert a provision requiring that [⁴non-resident parent] to make or secure the making of periodical payments by way of maintenance, or in Scotland aliment, to or for the benefit of that child; or

52

(b) to increase the amount payable under such a provision.

[[1](6) In any case in which section 4(10) or 7(10) prevents the making of an application for a [3maintenance calculation], and—

[[2](a) no parent has been treated under section 6(3) as having applied for a maintenance calculation with respect to the child; or

(b) a parent has been so treated but no maintenance calculation has been made,]

subsection (5) shall have effect with the omission of paragraph (b).]

AMENDMENTS

1. Section 18(4) of the 1995 Act (September 4, 1995).
2. Paragraph 11(6) of Sch.3 to the 2000 Act (March 3, 2003 under art.3 of, and the Schedule to, the Commencement No.12 Order 2003).
3. Section 1(2)(a) of the 2000 Act (March 3, 2003 under art.3 of, and the Schedule to, the Commencement No.12 Order 2003).
4. Paragraph 11(2) of Sch.3 to the 2000 Act (March 3, 2003 under art.3 of, and the Schedule to, the Commencement No.12 Order 2003).

DEFINITIONS

"child": see s.55.                                                                       2.28
"maintenance assessment": see s.54.
"non-resident parent": see s.3(2).

GENERAL NOTE

The Act does not prevent the making of a maintenance agreement, whether bind-   2.29
ing (contractually or otherwise) or not. However, a maintenance agreement cannot affect the operation of the Act. The provisions of such an agreement do not displace the child support scheme, nor can they provide that a person may not apply for a maintenance calculation. A maintenance agreement may still be useful, however. First, it may provide for the payment of a larger amount of maintenance than would be calculated under this Act. The Act does not affect the enforcement of such an arrangement. Second, even if the agreement does not provide for the payment of a larger sum than would be calculated under this Act, the parties may prefer to rely on the methods of enforcement available, in addition to or as a substitute for the mechanisms provided under the Act. Section 8(5) and the Child Maintenance (Written Agreements) Order 1993 allow for provision to be made to permit the incorporation of an agreement into a court order.

*Subsection (1)*

For a discussion of the meaning of "maintenance agreement", see the general note to s.18 of the 1995 Act.

In *CCS 12849/96*, para.5, the Commissioner left open the meaning of "securing the making" of periodical payments.

In *CCS 8328/95*, para.15, the Commissioner held that "for the benefit of any child" was not limited to cases where the child was expressly mentioned in the agreement. The words were not so wide as to cover any payment to a parent that might ultimately be to the advantage of a child, but there were cases where, without the child being expressly mentioned, the circumstances surrounding the making of the agreement made it abundantly clear that the payments were, at least in part, for the benefit of the child.

*Subsection (4)*

The effect of this subsection is, in line with the policy decision of Ministers (and with the approach of the private law on maintenance, see, *e.g.* s.23(4) of the Matrimonial Causes Act 1973 and s.3 of the Family Law (Scotland) Act 1985), to prevent clean breaks in respect of children. It refers to agreements in contrast to the other subsections which refer to *maintenance* agreements. It therefore catches all agreements which seek to restrict the right to apply for a maintenance calculation, regardless of whether they are maintenance agreements as defined by subs.(1) or not. This prevents the obvious avoidance measure of putting the restriction in a separate agreement, which would not be a maintenance agreement since it would provide for the avoidance of maintenance payments rather than for making or securing them. Agreements which, as part of an overall settlement on breakdown of a marriage or other relationship, make some provision conditional on no application for a maintenance calculation being made may, therefore, be caught by this provision. Whether or not these agreements expressly purport to restrict the right to apply for calculation, such is their clear effect and purpose. However, only the provision itself is void. Other terms in the agreement remain valid, so the other parts of the overall settlement will still be effective. It would appear, relying upon *Smith v McInerney* [1994] 2 F.L.R. 1077, that an agreement incorporating a charge-back arrangement, whereby, for example, the husband transfers his interest in the matrimonial home to the wife, subject to a charge back for the aggregate of any sums payable by him under the Child Support Act, would not be regarded as an attempt to restrict the wife's right to apply under the Act but would simply enable the husband to avoid effectively paying her twice over.

In *CCS 316/98*, para.23, the Commissioner held that an arrangement embodied in a consent order whereby payments of spousal maintenance were to reduce by the amount of any child support maintenance assessment were not void under this subsection, as it merely adjusted the absent parent's overall financial commitments in the light of his liability for child support maintenance. The decision in *Dorney-Kingdom v Dorney-Kingdom* [2000] 2 F.L.R. 855 shows that this is a standard form of order that is accepted as valid by the courts.

The Court of Appeal has held, in *N v N (Consent Order: Variation)* [1993] 2 F.L.R. 868, that a side letter to a maintenance and property settlement embodied in a consent order, whereby the wife agreed not to seek an extension of a fixed term spousal maintenance order, was void under the Matrimonial Causes Act 1973, s.34, as an attempt to oust the court's jurisdiction. Its suitability in a case where there was a child was also questionable, since it was impossible to anticipate what might have happened by the end of the fixed term. It was, however, highly relevant to a subsequent variation application, and should have been shown to the district judge who had to approve the original consent order. Query whether the court would regard a similar device, whereby the parent with care agrees in a side letter not to make a child support application, as "highly relevant" to subsequent proceedings between the parents.

*Subsections (3), (5) and (6)*

See the general note to s.18 of the 1995 Act.

## Relationship between maintenance assessments and certain court orders and related matters

2.30   **10.**—(1) Where an order of a kind prescribed for the purposes of this subsection is in force with respect to any qualifying child with respect to whom a [⁴maintenance calculation—] is made, the order—

   (a) shall, so far as it relates to the making or securing of periodical payments, cease to have effect to such extent as may be determined in accordance with regulations made by the Secretary of State; or

(b) Where the regulations so provide, shall, so far as it so relates, have effect subject to such modifications as may be so determined.

(2) Where an agreement of a kind prescribed for the purposes of this subsection is in force with respect to any qualifying child with respect to whom a [⁴maintenance calculation] is made, the agreement—

(a) shall, so far as it relates to the making or securing of periodical payments, be unenforceable to such extent as may be determined in accordance with regulations made by the Secretary of State; or

(b) where the regulations so provide, shall, so far as it so relates, have effect subject to such modifications as may be so determined.

(3) Any regulations under this section may, in particular, make such provision with respect to—

(a) any case where any person with respect to whom an order or agreement of a kind prescribed for the purposes of subsection (1) or (2) has effect applies to the prescribed court, before the end of the prescribed period, for the order or agreement to be varied in the light of the [⁴maintenance calculation] and of the provisions of this Act;

(b) the recovery of any arrears under the order or agreement which fell due before the coming into force of the [⁴ maintenance calculation], as the Secretary of State considers appropriate and may provide that, in prescribed circumstances, an application to any court which is made with respect to an order of a prescribed kind relating to the making or securing of periodical payments to or for the benefit of a child shall be treated by the court as an application for the order to be revoked.

(4) The Secretary of State may be regulations make provision for—

(a) notification to be given by [¹the Secretary of State] to the prescribed person in any case where [²he] considers that the making of a [⁴maintenance calculation] has affected, or is likely to affect, any order of a kind prescribed for the purposes of this sub-section;

(b) notification to be given by the prescribed person to the Secretary of State in any case where a court makes an order which it considers has affected, or is likely to affect, a [⁴maintenance calculation].

(5) Rules may be made under section 144 of the Magistrates' Courts Act 1980 (rules of procedure) requiring any person who, in prescribed circumstances, makes an application to a magistrates' court for a maintenance order to furnish the court with a statement in a prescribed form, and signed by [³an officer of the Secretary of State], as to whether or not, at the time when the statement is made, there is a [⁴maintenance calculation] in force with respect to that person or the child concerned.

In this subsection—

"maintenance order" means an order of a prescribed kind for the making or securing of periodical payments to or for the benefit of a child; and

"prescribed" means prescribed by the rules.

AMENDMENTS

1. Paragraph 23(1)(a) of Sch.7 to the Social Security Act 1998 (June 1, 1999).
2. Paragraph 23(1)(b) of Sch.7 to the Social Security Act 1998 (June 1, 1999).

3. Paragraph 23(2) of Sch.7 to the Social Security Act 1998 (June 1, 1999).

4. Section 1(2)(a) of the 2000 Act (March 3, 2003 under art.3 of, and the Schedule to, the Commencement No.12 Order 2003)

DEFINITIONS

2.31      "child": see s.55.
"maintenance calculation": see s.54.
"prescribed": see s.54.
"qualifying child": see s.3(1).

GENERAL NOTE

2.32      For the position in Scotland see the Child Support (Amendments to Primary Legislation) (Scotland) Order 1993 and Act of Sederunt (Child Support Act 1991) (Amendment of Ordinary Cause and Summary Cause) Rules 1993.

This section applies to all orders and agreements falling within its terms regardless of the date on which they were made and, in particular, the section is not limited to orders and agreements made after the Act received Royal Assent (*R(CS)* 2/95, para.16).

*Subsection (1)*

The maintenance orders to which this subsection applies are the same as those which fall within s.8(11) and regulations made thereunder (reg.3(1) of the Maintenance Arrangements and Jurisdiction Regulations). These orders cease to have effect in accordance with reg.3(2) to (4). In summary the orders cease to have effect in respect of any children with respect to whom a maintenance calculation has been made as from the effective date of the calculation. For this purpose the effective date is two days after the assessment is made. This is subject to some exceptions. These are: (i) where the order covers children in addition to those in respect of whom the maintenance calculation has been made without specifying separate amounts of maintenance for each child and (ii) where the order was made under s.8(7) or (8). In the case of Scotland when a maintenance order ceases to have effect and Secretary of State subsequently loses jurisdiction to make a maintenance calculation with respect to a particular child covered by the order, the order revives so far as that child is concerned.

If a maintenance calculation is made while a maintenance order is in force in respect of the same child but is subsequently cancelled as having been made in error, and the maintenance order has ceased to have effect by virtue of reg.3, the order is treated as having continued in force and any payments under the calculation are treated as if they were made under the order (reg.8(1) of the Maintenance Arrangements and Jurisdiction Regulations as amended).

Neither this subsection nor the Maintenance Arrangements and Jurisdiction Regulations expressly provide for the date on which the order must be in force. Normally the relevant date would be the effective date of the maintenance calculation. The wording of reg.3(2) provides that an order ceases to have effect when a maintenance calculation is made, which suggests that the relevant date on which the order must be in force is the date the calculation is made.

If a maintenance order is made while a maintenance calculation is in force in respect of the same child and subsequently revoked as having been made in error, the calculation is treated as not having been cancelled and any payments under the order are treated as if they were made under the calculation (reg.8(2) of the Maintenance Arrangements and Jurisdiction Regulations).

In England and Wales, an order that has ceased to have effect does not revive automatically and cannot be revived. The position is different in Scotland by virtue of reg.3(4) of the Maintenance Arrangements and Jurisdiction Regulations. See *CCS 2567/98*, paras 23–48.

*Subsection (2)*

The agreements to which this subsection applies are maintenance agreements as defined by s.9(1) (reg.4(1) of the Maintenance Arrangements and Jurisdiction Regulations). The extent of the enforceability of these agreements is covered by reg.4(2) and (3). In summary the agreements become unenforceable in respect of any children with respect to whom a maintenance calculation has been made as from the effective date of the calculation. For the effective date where a court order is or has been in force see reg.3 of those Regulations. This is subject to an exception where the agreement covers children in addition to those in respect of whom the maintenance calculation has been made without specfying separate amounts of maintenance for each child. When a maintenance agreement becomes unenforceable and the Secretary of State subsequently loses jurisdiction to make a maintenance calculation with respect to a particular child covered by the agreement, the agreement becomes enforceable again so far as that child is concerned.

*Subsection (3)(a)*

Schedule 1, para.3 to the Child Maintenance Orders (Backdating) Order 1993 inserts s.31(12) into the Matrimonial Causes Act 1973 and s.20(9B) into the Domestic Proceedings and Magistrates' Courts Act 1978 to permit an order varying or discharging/revoking periodical payments in favour of a spouse to be backdated to the effective date (see the general note to Sch.1, para.11 below) of a maintenance calculation provided that the application for the maintenance order is made within six months of the date of the calculation. This is intended, *inter alia*, to cater for the situation where a previous order which contained provision for spousal maintenance and child maintenance is partly superseded by a maintenance calculation. The order might have provided a relatively small element for spousal maintenance, and a relatively large portion for child maintenance. A spouse might seek an upward variation of *her* maintenance where the calculation has produced an amount for the child smaller than that contained in the maintenance order, in order to ensure no overall loss of income for the family.

*Subsection (4)*

Regulation 5 of the Maintenance Arrangements and Jurisdiction Regulations provides for the child support officer to give notice of any maintenance calculation which is likely to affect a court order to the persons in respect of whom the maintenance calculation is in force and to the court itself. Regulation 6 provides for the court to give notice to the Secretary of State of any maintenance order which it makes and which is likely to affect a maintenance calculation. The way in which an order or calculation might be "affected" would appear to be that it should cease to have effect, or be cancelled. Where a calculation is made, reg.3 will provide that the order, or part of it, will cease to have effect. A party to the order might seek a variation of the remaining part to take account of the calculation. Where an order is made, this will either be because the Secretary of State no longer has jurisdiction under s.44 or because it is an order which may continue to be made by virtue of s.8(6) to (8). Where the former is the case, the calculation should be cancelled under s.44. See s.8 for further discussion of the provision made to avoid clashes of jurisdiction between the courts and the secretary of state.

*Subsection (5)*

The Family Proceedings Courts (Child Support Act 1991) Rules 1993, rr.8–12 provide for the appropriate statement to be made on Forms CHA13, CHA14, CHA15 and Forms 1, 2, 3 and 4.

*[¹Maintenance calculations]*

## [²Maintenance calculations

2.33     **11.**—(1) An application for a maintenance calculation made to the Secretary of State shall be dealt with by him in accordance with the provision made by or under this Act.

    (2) The Secretary of State shall (unless he decides not to make a maintenance calculation in response to the application, or makes a decision under section 12) determine the application by making a decision under this section about whether any child support maintenance is payable and, if so, how much.

    (3) Where—

    (a) a parent is treated under section 6(3) as having applied for a maintenance calculation; but

    (b) the Secretary of State becomes aware before determining the application that the parent has ceased to fall within section 6(1),

he shall, subject to subsection (4), cease to treat that parent as having applied for a maintenance calculation.

    (4) If it appears to the Secretary of State that subsection (10) of section 4 would not have prevented the parent with care concerned from making an application for a maintenance calculation under that section he shall—

    (a) notify her of the effect of this subsection; and

    (b) if, before the end of the period of one month beginning with the day on which notice was sent to her, she asks him to do so, treat her as having applied not under section 6 but under section 4.

    (5) Where subsection (3) applies but subsection (4) does not, the Secretary of State shall notify—

    (a) the parent with care concerned; and

    (b) the non-resident parent (or alleged non-resident parent), where it appears to him that that person is aware that the parent with care has been treated as having applied for a maintenance calculation.

    (6) The amount of child support maintenance to be fixed by a maintenance calculation shall be determined in accordance with Part I of Schedule 1 unless an application for a variation has been made and agreed.

    (7) If the Secretary of State has agreed to a variation, the amount of child support maintenance to be fixed shall be determined on the basis he determines under section 28F(4).

    (8) Part II of Schedule 1 makes further provision with respect to maintenance calculation.]

AMENDMENTS

    1. Section 1(2)(a) of the 2000 Act (March 3, 2003 under art.3 of, and the Schedule to, the Commencement No.12 Order 2003).

    2. Section 1(1) of the 2000 Act (March 3, 2003 under art.3 of, and the Schedule to, the Commencement No.12 Order 2003).

DEFINITIONS

"application for a variation": see s.54.                    2.34
"child support maintenance": see s.54.
"maintenance calculation": see s.54.
"non-resident parent": see s.54.
"parent": see s.54.
"parent with care": see s.54.

GENERAL NOTE

*Decision making by the Secretary of State*

The duties and status of the Secretary of State when dealing with applications    2.35
under the child support legislation must largely be spelt out from the authorities on
the former social security adjudication officers.

The Secretary of State has a duty to act fairly and to obtain information necessary to deal with an application (*Duggan v Chief Adjudication Officer* reported as an
Appendix to *R(SB) 13/89; R(CS) 2/98,* para.20). Adjudication officers had administrative duties only and had no judicial or quasi-judicial function, because there
were no competing contentions on which the officer had to adjudicate (*R. v Deputy
Industrial Injuries Commissioner Ex p. Moore* [1965] 1 QB 456 at 486, *per* Diplock
Lord Justice; *R(SB) 11/89,* para.7). In child support cases, there is likely to be competing contentions and this may lead the Secretary of State to be held to have at
least a quasi-judicial function.

The officers acting for the Secretary of State have the same powers to decide on
the validity of delegated legislation as appeal tribunals and Commissioners. In *Chief
Adjudication Officer v Foster* [1993] 1 All E.R. 705 the House of Lords said in the
context of the social security legislation that an adjudication officer would be
expected to refer the question to a tribunal. This course is not available under the
child support legislation.

In dealing with application under the child support legislation, the officers acting
for the Secretary of State have an independent statutory function and are not bound
by an undertaking given by anyone else (*R(SB) 14/88,* paras 20–22), even when the
officer is exercising a discretion that could be exercised in accordance with the
undertaking (*R(SB) 14/89,* para.12). These principles apply in child support law, as
they applied to adjudication officers in social security law (*R(CS) 2/97*). See also
the discussion on *estoppel* in reg.49(1) of the Appeals Regulations.

Some decisions turn on the state of mind of the Secretary of State, such as opinion or suspicion. On appeal, the state of mind of the tribunal or Commissioner may
be substituted for that of the Secretary of State (*R(SB) 5/81,* para.8).

*Subsection (1)*

This imposes a duty on the Secretary of State to deal with an application that has
been made. It does not expressly refer to applications that are treated as made under
s.6 above, although it is clear from subs.(3) below that it does apply to them. It only
applies to effective applications. If the Secretary of State does not act under s.6(3),
no application is treated as made and this section does not apply.

For provisions governing applications for a maintenance calculation see Pt II of
the Maintenance Calculation Procedure Regulations.

For the position regarding proceedings for, or implementation and enforcement
of, a maintenance calculation pending resolution of a paternity issue, see the general note to Art.4 of the Child Support (Jurisdiction of Courts) Order Order 2002,
and the Child Support Appeals (Jurisdiction of Courts) (Scotland) Order 2003.

*Subsection (2)*

If an application is effective, the Secretary of State must (a) determine the application, (b) decide not to make a maintenance calculation or (c) make a decision under s.12 below. Unless the case falls within (b) or (c), the Secretary of State is under a duty to determine the application. There is no discretion and s.2 above does not apply (*R(CS) 4/96*, para.8; *R(CS) 2/98*, paras 17–21). For an example of (b), see the power given to the Secretary of State by s.6(3) above.

There is no limitation period on the Secretary of State making a maintenance calculation (*R(CS) 10/02*).

*Subsection (3)*

If the parent with care ceases to fall within s.6(1) above before the application is determined, s.6 ceases to apply and no application is treated as having been made under s.6. This applies if a parent with care's claim is refused or if an existing award is terminated. This reverses the effect of *R v Secretary of State for Social Security Ex p. Harris* unreported, July 1, 1998).

However, the parent with care has one month within which to opt under subs.(4) below for the application to be treated as if it had been made under s.4 above.

*Subsection (4)*

The Secretary of State may, at the parent with care's request, treat an application as having been made under s.4 above. However, this is not reflected elsewhere in the Act, which distinguishes between (a) applications made under s.4 and (b) applications treated as made under s.6. No reference is made to applications treated as made under s.4. See the wording of s.7(1)(b) above.

## [¹Default and interim maintenance decisions

2.36

**12.**—(1) Where the Secretary of State—

(a) is required to make a maintenance calculation; or

(b) is proposing to make a decision under section 16 or 17,

and it appears to him that he does not have sufficient information to enable him to do so, he may make a default maintenance decision.

(2) Where an application for a variation has been made under section 28A(1) in connection with an application for a maintenance calculation (or in connection with such an application which is treated as having been made), the Secretary of State may make an interim maintenance decision.

(3) The amount of child support maintenance fixed by an interim maintenance decision shall be determined in accordance with Part I of Schedule 1.

(4) The Secretary of State may by regulations make provision as to default and interim maintenance decisions.

(5) The regulations may, in particular, make provision as to—

(a) the procedure to be followed in making a default or an interim maintenance decision; and

(b) a default rate of child support maintenance to apply where a default maintenance decision is made.]

AMENDMENT

1. Section 4 of the 2000 Act (for the purpose of making regulations, November 10, 2000 under art.2(1) of, and Pt I of the Schedule to, the Commencement No.3

Order 2000; March 3, 2003 under art.3 of, and the Schedule to, the Commencement No.12 Order 2003).

DEFINITIONS

"application for a variation": see s.54.                                    2.37
"child support maintenance": see s.54.
"maintenance calculation": see s.54.

GENERAL NOTE

*Subsection (1)*

A default maintenance decision may be made if the Secretary of State has insuf-    2.38
ficient information to make a maintenance calculation or a revision or supersession
decision. The rate is set by reg.7 of the Maintenance Calculation Procedure
Regulations.

*Subsection (2)*

An interim maintenance decision may be made if an application for a variation is
made before a decision has been reached on an application for a maintenance calculation. The interim maintenance decision is made pending the determination of
the variation application. It may be subject to a regular payments condition under
s.28C below.

An interim maintenance decision is treated as replaced by the decision under s.11
below that is made when the application for a variation has been determined: see
s.28F(5) below.

Section 13 was repealed by the Social Security Act 1998 with effect from June 1,
1999.

*Information*

## Information required by Secretary of State

**14.**—(1) The Secretary of State may make regulations requiring any    2.39
information or evidence needed for the determination of any application
[6made or treated as made] under this Act, or any question arising in connection with such an application [5(or application treated as made), or
needed for the making of any decision or in connection with the imposition
of any condition or requirement under this Act], or needed in connection
with the collection or enforcement of child support or other maintenance
under this Act, to be furnished—
  (a) by such persons as may be determined in accordance with
      regulations made by the Secretary of State; and
  (b) in accordance with the regulations.
  [1(1A) Regulations under subsection (1) may make provision for notifying any person who is required to furnish any information or evidence
under the regulations of the possible consequences of failing to do so.]
  [2. . .]
  (3) The Secretary of State may be regulations make provision authorising the disclosure by him [3. . .], in such circumstances as may be prescribed, of such information held by [4him] for purposes of this Act as may
be prescribed.

(4) The provisions of Schedule 2 (which relate to information which is held for purposes other than those of this Act but which is required by the Secretary of State) shall have effect.

AMENDMENTS

1. Paragraph 3(1) of Sch.3 to the 1995 Act (October 1, 1995).
2. Paragraph 27(a) of Sch.7 to the Social Security Act 1998 (September 8, 1998).
3. Paragraph 27(b) of Sch.7 to the Social Security Act 1998 (June 1, 1999).
4. Paragraph 27(b) of Sch.7 to the Social Security Act 1998 (June 1, 1999).
5. Section 12 of the 2000 Act (March 3, 2003 under art.3 of, and the Schedule to, the Commencement No.12 Order 2003).
6. Paragraph 11(7) of Sch.3 to the 2000 Act (March 3, 2003 under art. 3 of, and the Schedule to, the Commencement No. 12 Order 2003).

DEFINITIONS

**2.40**    "benefit Acts": see s.54.
"prescribed": see s.54.

GENERAL NOTE

This section confers the general rule-making powers relating to the information or evidence needed by the Secretary of State. Subsections.(1) and (1A) deal with obtaining information. These are in addition to the more specific rule-making powers, such as that in ss.4(4), 6(7) and 7(5). They are supplemented by s.14A (offences) and s.15 (inspectors). Subsection (3) deals with disclosure of information held for the purposes of this Act.

The relevant regulations are the Information, Evidence and Disclosure Regulations. The Social Security (Claims and Information) Regulations 1999 are also relevant.

There is no definition of "information" or "evidence". The obvious difference is that information is what the Secretary of State needs to know and evidence is the documentary or other proof of it. So, if the Secretary of State needs to know a parent's wages, the amount of those wages is information and the wage slip that proves those wages is the evidence. In practice, the distinction is less clear cut, because the parent's statement of the amount of the wages is by itself evidence of that amount: see the general note to reg.49(1) of the Appeals Regulations. Moreover, this distinction causes problems if it is carried over into the disclosure provisions in s.50. They relate to information and not to evidence. If they do not include the evidence provided as proof, there is no provision authorising disclosure of that evidence to an appeal tribunal.

*Subsection (1)*

**2.41**    For the application of this subsection to the Crown see s.57(1).

This subsection contains the general enabling power under which the Secretary of State may obtain the information or evidence necessary for the implementation of the Act. It applies to both information and to evidence, and therefore covers cases where information has been supplied but the evidence is lacking to prove it. The regulations made under this subsection are contained in Pt II of the Information, Evidence and Disclosure Regulations. They create wider duties than those created under ss.4(4), 6(7) and 7(5). These subsections each limit the duty to cases where the person can reasonably comply. There is no equivalent to this limitation in this subsection. However, the duty created by reg.2(1) limits the duty to supply information or evidence to cases where the information or evidence is in a person's possession or it is reasonable to expect a person to acquire it. Thus the Act emphasises the reasonableness of compliance with the duty to *supply* whereas the regulation emphasises the reasonableness of *acquiring* the information or evidence. However, it is difficult to see any practical significance in this difference.

Information supplied to the Secretary of State is not subject to absolute privilege and so statements made therein may give rise to an action for libel (*Purdew v Seress-Smith* [1993] I.R.L.R. 77).

There is no single provision dealing with enforcement of the obligation to provide information or evidence. However, a variety of means exist by which pressure may be brought to bear to try to ensure that necessary information or evidence is obtained: (i) A default maintenance decision may be made under s.12 if the officer has insufficient information; (ii) A prosecution may be made for an offence under s.14A; (iii) An inspector may be appointed under s.15 and that may lead to an offence being committed under s.15(9). This may be directed against any person under a duty to supply information; (iv) A reduced benefit decision may be made under s.46. This will be directed against the parent with care; (v) Failure by one person to provide information or evidence may be remedied by obtaining it from another source under the wide powers given in the Information. Evidence and Disclosure Regulations; (vi) A person who fails to maintain a person whom he is liable to maintain may commit an offence under s.105 of the Social Security Administration Act 1992, but note that the duty to maintain created by s.1(1) of the Child Support Act cannot be used as a basis for that offence since it only applies for the purpose of this Act; (vii) It may also be possible to obtain an order under s.106 of the Social Security Administration Act 1992 for the recovery of benefit from a person liable to maintain another who receives income support. Once again the duty created by s.1(1) of this Act cannot be used for this purpose; (viii) The failure may provide the basis from which an inference may be drawn. This power is not used by the officers who act for the Secretary of State, but it may be used by an appeal tribunal.

*Subsection (3)*

The regulations made under this subsection are contained in Pt III of the Information, Evidence and Disclosure Regulations. The unauthorised disclosure of information may be an offence under s.50.

## [¹Information-offences

**14A.**—(1) This section applies to—                                         2.42
  (a) persons who are required to comply with regulations under section 4(4) or 7(5); and
  (b) persons specified in regulations under section 14(1)(a).

  (2) Such a person is guilty of an offence if, pursuant to a request for information under or by virtue of those regulations—
  (a) he makes a statement or representation which he knows to be false; or
  (b) he provides, or knowingly causes or knowingly allows to be provided, a document or other information which he knows to be false in a material particular.

  (3) Such a person is guilty of an offence if, following such a request, he fails to comply with it.

  (4) It is a defence for a person charged with an offence under subsection (3) to prove that he had a reasonable excuse for failing to comply.

(5    A person guilty of an offence under this section is liable on summary conviction to a fine not exceeding level 3 on the standard scale.]

AMENDMENT

1. Section 13 of the 2000 Act (January 31, 2001 under art.2(1) of the Commencement No.5 Order 2000).

GENERAL NOTE

**2.43**    This section provides for an offence, punishable by a fine, for failing to comply with some, but not all, of the duties to give information to the Secretary of State. This is outside the jurisdiction of the appeal tribunal, although the tribunal may invite the Secretary of State to consider a prosecution and make findings that show a basis for prosecution.

*Subsection (1)*
    This subsection identifies the persons who may be guilty of an offence under this section. Paragraph (a) applies to ss.4(4) and 7(5) above. It does not apply to the equivalent s.6(7) above.

*Subsection (2)*
    This makes it an offence knowingly to make false statements or representations and to provide or knowingly allow or cause to be provided false documents or information. It is not subject to the defence in subs.(4), but depending on the terms of the offence, the prosecution has to prove knowledge on the part of the defendant.

*Subsection (3)*
    This makes it an offence to fail to provide information required under s.4(4) or 7(5) above. This is subject to the defence under subs.(4) below.

*Subsection (4)*
    This provides a defence to subs.(3) above, but not to subs.(2). There is no definition or indication of what may constitute a reasonable excuse. The burden of proof is on the defendant.

*Subsection (5)*
    The maximum fine is £1000.

**Powers of inspectors**

**2.44**    **15.**—[[1](1) The Secretary of State may appoint, on such terms as he thinks fit, persons to act as inspectors under this section.

(2) The function of inspectors is to acquire information which the Secretary of State needs for any of the purposes of this Act.

(3) Every inspector is to be given a certificate of his appointment.

(4) An inspector has power, at any reasonable time and either alone or accompanied by such other persons as he thinks fit, to enter any premises which—

(a)  are liable to inspection under this section; and
(b)  are premises to which it is reasonable for him to require entry in order that he may exercise his functions under this section, and may there make such examination and inquiry as he considers appropriate.

(4A) Premises liable to inspection under this section are those which are not used wholly as a dwelling-house and which the inspector has reasonable grounds for suspecting are—

(a) premises at which a non-resident parent is or has been employed;

(b) premises at which a non-resident parent carries out, or has carried out, a trade, profession, vocation or business;

(c) premises at which there is information held by a person ("A") whom the inspector has reasonable grounds for suspecting has information about a non-resident parent acquired in the course of A's own trade, profession, vocation or business.]

(5) An inspector exercising his powers may question any person aged 18 or over whom he finds on the premises.

(6) If required to do so by an inspector exercising his powers, [²any such person] shall furnish to the inspector all such information and documents as the inspector may reasonably require.

(7) No person shall be required under this section to answer any question or to give any evidence tending to incriminate himself or, in the case of a person who is married [⁵or is a civil partner], his or her spouse [⁶or civil partner].

(8) On applying for admission to any premises in the exercise of his powers, an inspector shall, if so required, produce his certificate.

(9) If any person—

(a) intentionally delays or obstructs any inspector exercising his powers; or

(b) without reasonable excuse, refuses or neglects to answer any question or furnish any information or to produce any document when required to do so under this section,

he shall be guilty of an offence and liable on summary conviction to a fine not exceeding level 3 on the standard scale.

(10) In this section—

"certificate" means a certificate of appointment issued under this section;

"inspector" means an inspector appointed under this section;

"powers" means powers conferred by this section [⁴. . .]

[³(11) In this section, "premises" includes—

(a) moveable structures and vehicles, vessels, aircraft and hovercraft;

(b) installations that are offshore installations for the purposes of the Mineral Workings (Offshore Installations) Act 1971; and

(c) places of all other descriptions whether or not occupied as land or otherwise,

and references in this section to the occupier of premises are to be construed, in relation to premises that are not occupied as land, as references to any person for the time being present at the place in question.]

Amendments

1. Section 14(2) of the 2000 Act (January 31, 2001 under art.2(1) of the Commencement No.5 Order 2000).

2. Section 14(3) of the 2000 Act (January 31, 2001 under art.2(1) of the Commencement No.5 Order 2000).

3. Section 14(4) of the 2000 Act (January 31, 2001 under art.2(1) of the Commencement No.5 Order 2000).

4. Section 85 of, and Sch.9 to, the 2000 Act (March 3, 2003 under art.3 of, and the Schedule to, the Commencement No.12 Order 2003).

5. Paragraph 2(a) of Sch.24 to the Civil Partnership Act 2004.

6. Paragraph 2(b) of Sch.24 to the Civil Partnership Act 2004.

GENERAL NOTE

2.45
For the application of this section to the Crown see s.57(2) and (3). An inspector appointed under this section may enter Crown premises in order to exercise any powers conferred by this section provided that the Queen is not in residence (reg.7 of the Information, Evidence and Disclosure Regulations).

An inspector may only be appointed to acquire "information". However, the confusion noted in the general note to s.14 is apparent here also. Subsection (7) grants exemption from the giving of self-incriminating "evidence", while the offence created by subs.(9) applies to the failure to produce documents as well as to the failure to give information, so that the documents must be required as evidence rather than for the information they contain.

*Subsection (1)*

It is inconsistent with the terms of this subsection for a tribunal to direct the Secretary of State to appoint an inspector, although the tribunal could suggest this as a possible way of obtaining the information necessary in order to make a proper assessment (*CCS 13988/96*, paras 9 and 11).

*Subsection (4A)*

The limitation to this subsection only applies to premises which are used *solely* as a dwelling-house. Depending on the circumstances it may not apply in cases where the person is running a business from home. Where there is living accommodation which is separate from the work place, for example a flat over a shop, the inspector will be able to enter the shop but not the flat. However where a business is run from the study or a kitchen table, the inspector may enter the whole premises.

*Reviews and appeals*

[¹**Revision of decisions**

2.46
**16.**—(1) Any decision [²to which subsection 1A applies] may be revised by the Secretary of State—

(a) either within the prescribed period or in prescribed cases or circumstances; and

(b) either on an application made for the purpose or on his own initiative;

and regulations may prescribe the procedure by which a decision of the Secretary of State may be so revised.

[³(1A) This subsection applies to—

(a) a decision of the Secretary of State under section 11, 12 or 17;

(b) a reduced benefit decision under section 46;

(c) a decision of an appeal tribunal on a referral under section 28D(1)(b).

(1B) Where the Secretary of State revises a decision under section 12(1)—

(a) he may (if appropriate) do so as if he were revising a decision under section 11; and

(b) if he does that, his decision as revised is to be treated as one under section 11 instead of section 12(1) (and, in particular, is to be so treated for the purposes of an appeal against it under section 20).]

(2) In making a decision under subsection (1), the Secretary of State need not consider any issue that is not raised by the application or, as the case may be, did not cause him to act on his own initiative.

(3) Subject to subsections (4) and (5) and section 28ZC, a revision under this section shall take effect as from the date on which the original decision took (or was to take) effect.

(4) Regulations may provide that, in prescribed cases or circumstances, a revision under this section shall take effect as from such other date as may be prescribed.

(5) Where a decision is revised under this section, for the purpose of any rule as to the time allowed for bringing an appeal, the decision shall be regarded as made on the date on which it is so revised.

(6) Except in prescribed circumstances, an appeal against a decision of the Secretary of State shall lapse if the decision is revised under this section before the appeal is determined.]

AMENDMENTS

1. Section 40 of the Social Security Act 1998 (November 16, 1998 for the purposes of making Regulations: otherwise December 7, 1998).                              2.47
2. Section 8(2) of the 2000 Act (March 3, 2003 under art.3 of, and the Schedule to, the Commencement No.12 Order 2003).
3. Section 8(3) of the 2000 Act (March 3, 2003 under art 3 of, and the Schedule to, the Commencement No.12 Order 2003).

DEFINITION

"prescribed": see s.54.

GENERAL NOTE

This section deals with the revision of decisions. It is extended by reg.3A(6)      2.48
of the Appeals Regulations. It is subject to the saving and transitional provisions in art.3 of the Social Security Act 1998 (Commencement No.2) Order 1998 below.

*Subsection (1)*

Regulation 3A of the Appeals Regulations sets out the circumstances in which and the grounds on which a decision may be revised. They depend either on the time within which action is initiated or on the cause of the error. Regulation 4 of those Regulations deals with late applications for a revision. A change of circumstances cannot be dealt with by way of revision; it can only be dealt with under s.17: see reg.3A(2).

A decision that has been revised may be further revised (*CIS 3535/03*, paras 22–24).

*Subsection (1A)*

This subsection sets out decisions that may be revised. It is not exhaustive. Regulation 3A(6) of the Appeals Regulations extends it to include decisions under s.41A or s.47 below and to decisions on adjustment for overpayments or voluntary payments.

It is suggested that a decision is made by an appeal tribunal rather than by the Secretary of State even if the tribunal remits the case to the Secretary of State with directions under s.20(8) below: see the general note to that subsection.

*Subsection (2)*

The Secretary of State need not undertake a complete reconsideration of every issue covered by the original decision. This is in line with the general approach to determinations by both the Secretary of State and appeal tribunals.

*Subsections (3) and (4)*

These subsections deal with the effective date of a revision. Subsection (3) contains the basic rule governing the effective date of a revision. It is the date on which the original decision took effect or was to take effect. Subsection (4) allows for other cases to be dealt with by regulations. Regulation 5A of the Appeals Regulations is made under that authority.

*Subsections (5) and (6)*

These subsections deal with the impact of a revision on the appeal rights against the original decision and the revision. Time for appealing begins to run again from the date when the revision is made. Generally, an appeal against a decision lapses if it is revised before the appeal is determined. The exceptions are contained in reg.30 of the Appeals Regulations.

## [¹Decisions superseding earlier decisions

2.49    **17.**—(1)  Subject to subsection (2), the following, namely—

(a) any decision of the Secretary of State under section 11 or 12 or this section, whether as originally made or as revised under section 16;

(b) any decision of an appeal tribunal under section 20 [⁴. . .]

[²(c) any reduced benefit decision under section 46;

(d) any decision of an appeal tribunal on a referral under section 28D(1)(b);

(e) any decision of a Child Support Commissioner on an appeal from such a decision as is mentioned in paragraph (b) or (d)],

may be superseded by a decision made by the Secretary of State, either on an application made for the purpose or on his own initiative.

(2)  In making a decision under subsection (1), the Secretary of State need not consider any issue that is not raised by the application or, as the case may be, did not cause him to act on his own initiative.

(3)  Regulations may prescribe the cases and circumstances in which, and the procedure by which, a decision may be made under this section.

[³(4)  Subject to subsection (5) and section 28ZC, a decision under this section shall take effect as from the beginning of the maintenance period in which it is made or, where applicable, the beginning of the maintenance period in which the application was made.

(4A)  In subsection (4), a "maintenance period" is (except where a different meaning is prescribed for prescribed cases) a period of seven days, the first one beginning on the effective date of the first decision made by the Secretary of State under section 11 or (if earlier) his first default or interim maintenance decision (under section 12) in relation to the non-resident parent in question, and each subsequent one beginning on the day after the last day of the previous one.]

(5) Regulations may provide that, in prescribed cases or circumstances, a decision under this section shall take effect as from such other date as may be prescribed.]

AMENDMENTS

1. Section 41 of the Social Security Act 1998 (subss.(3) and (5) March 4, 1999; otherwise June 1, 1999).
2. Section 9(2) of the 2000 Act (for the purpose of making regulations, November 10, 2000 under art.2(1) of, and Pt I of the Schedule to, the Commencement No.3 Order 2000; March 3, 2003 under art.3 of, and the Schedule to, the Commencement No.12 Order 2003).
3. Section 9(3) of the 2000 Act (for the purpose of making regulations, November 10, 2000 under art.2(1) of, and Pt I of the Schedule to, the Commencement No.3 Order 2000; March 3, 2003 under art.3 of, and the Schedule to, the Commencement No.12 Order 2003).
4. Section 85 of, and Sch.9 to, the 2000 Act (March 3, 2003 under art.3 of, and the Schedule to, the Commencement No.12 Order 2003).

DEFINITION

"prescribed": see s.54.                                                                  **2.50**

GENERAL NOTE

This section deals with the supersession of decisions. It is extended by reg.6A(9)    **2.51**
of the Appeals Regulations. The nature of a supersession was analysed by the Court of Appeal in *Wood v Secretary of State for Work and Pensions* reported as *R(DLA) 1/03*. In the case of an application, it is permissible for the Secretary of State to give a decision refusing to supersede. That form of decision is appealable. It is the correct form of decision if no change is made either to the decision which is the subject of the application or to its basis. See further the general note to reg.6 of the Appeals Regulations.

*Subsection (1)*
The Secretary of State may act with or without an application. If a supersession is being considered on the Secretary of State's own initiative, the procedure set out in reg.7C of the Appeals Regulations must be followed.

It is suggested that a decision is made by an appeal tribunal rather than by the Secretary of State even if the tribunal remits the case to the Secretary of State with directions under s.20(8) below: see the general note to that subsection.

*Subsection (2)*
The Secretary of State need not undertake a complete reconsideration of every issue covered by the original decision. This is in line with the general approach to determinations by both the Secretary of State and appeal tribunals.

*Subsection (3)*
Regulations 6A and 6B of the Appeals Regulations are made under the authority of this provision.

*Subsections (4)–(5)*
These subsections deal with the effective date of a supersession. Subsection (4) contains the general rules. The general rule for a supersession made on the Secretary of State's own initiative is that it takes effect from the beginning of the maintenance period in which it was made. The general rule for a supersession made on an application is that it takes effect from the beginning of the maintenance period in which the application was made. Subsection (5) allows for other cases to be dealt with by regulations. Regulation 7C of the Appeals Regulations is made under that authority.

Sections 18 and 19 were repealed by s.41 of the Social Security Act 1998 with effect from June 1, 1999.

## [¹Appeals to appeal tribunals

2.52     **20.**—(1) A qualifying person has a right of appeal to an appeal tribunal against—
   (a) a decision of the Secretary of State under section 11, 12 or 17 (whether as originally made or as revised under section 16);
   (b) a decision of the Secretary of State not to make a maintenance calculation under section 11 or not to supersede a decision under section 17;
   (c) a reduced benefit decision under section 46;
   (d) the imposition (by virtue of section 41A) of a requirement to make penalty payments, or their amount;
   (e) the imposition (by virtue of section 47) of a requirement to pay fees.
   (2) In subsection (1), "qualifying person" means—
   (a) in relation to paragraphs (a) and (b)—
       (i) the person with care, or non-resident parent, with respect to whom the Secretary of State made the decision, or
       (ii) in a case relating to a maintenance calculation which was applied for under section 7, either of those persons or the child concerned;
   (b) in relation to paragraph (c), the person in respect of whom the benefits are payable;
   (c) in relation to paragraph (d), the parent who has been required to make penalty payments; and
   (d) in relation to paragraph (e), the person required to pay fees.
   (3) A person with a right of appeal under this section shall be given such notice as may be prescribed of—
   (a) that right; and
   (b) the relevant decision, or the imposition of the requirement.
   (4) Regulations may make—
   (a) provision as to the manner in which, and the time within which, appeals are to be brought; and
   (b) such provision with respect to proceedings before appeal tribunals as the Secretary of State considers appropriate.
   (5) The regulations may in particular make any provision of a kind mentioned in Schedule 5 to the Social Security Act 1998.
   (6) No appeal lies by virtue of subsection (1)(c) unless the amount of the person's benefit is reduced in accordance with the reduced benefit deci-

sion; and the time within which such an appeal may be brought runs from the date of notification of the reduction.

(7) In deciding an appeal under this section, an appeal tribunal—

(a) need not consider any issue that is not raised by the appeal; and

(b) shall not take into account any circumstances not obtaining at the time when the Secretary of State made the decision or imposed the requirement.

(8) If an appeal under this section is allowed, the appeal tribunal may—

(a) itself make such decision as it considers appropriate; or

(b) remit the case to the Secretary of State, together with such directions (if any) as it considers appropriate.]

AMENDMENT

1. Section 10 of the 2000, (for the purpose of making regulations, November 10, 2000 under art.2(1) of, and Pt I of the Schedule to, the Commencement No.3 Order 2000; March 3, 2003 under art.3 of, and the Schedule to, the Commencement No.12 Order 2003).

DEFINITIONS

"appeal tribunal": see s.54.　　　　　　　　　　　　　　　　　　　　　　　2.53
"child": see s.55.
"maintenance calculation": see s.54.
"non-resident parent": see s.54.
"parent": see s.54.
"person with care": see s.54.

GENERAL NOTE

This section is extended by reg.30A of the Appeals Regulations.　　　　　2.54

All heads of appeal presuppose a decision on a subsisting application or on the Secretary of State's own initiative. If an application is withdrawn before it is determined, no decision can be given, not even a refusal of the application (*CCS 2910/01*). It follows that an appeal tribunal has no jurisdiction to hear a dispute about whether an application was withdrawn.

*Jurisdiction*

The tribunal must not act outside its jurisdiction. In deciding whether a particular matter goes to the jurisdiction of the tribunal, the test to be applied is that set out in *Garthwaite v Garthwaite* [1964] 2 All E.R. 233 at 241 *per* Diplock L.J. as follows:

"In its narrow and strict sense, the 'jurisdiction' of a validly constituted court connotes the limits which are imposed on its power to hear and determine issues between persons seeking to avail themselves of its process by reference (i) to the subject-matter of the issue, or (ii) to the persons between whom the issue is joined, or (iii) to the kind of relief sought, or any combination of these factors."

This is in contrast to the wider use of "jurisdiction" to cover

"the settled practice of the court as to the way in which it will exercise its power to hear and determine issues . . ., or as to the circumstances in which it will grant a particular kind of relief . . ., including its settled practice to refuse to exercise such powers or to grant such relief in particular circumstances."

The significance of this distinction is that a tribunal created by statute cannot enlarge its jurisdiction in the strict sense, but has power to alter the way in which that jurisdiction is exercised in practice, subject of course to the limits set by legislation and precedent.

The tribunal's jurisdiction in the strict sense is limited to that given by statute. That jurisdiction cannot be extended by consent of the parties (*R(SB) 15/87*, paras 10–11; *R(SB) 1/95*, paras 13–16; *R. v Secretary of State for Social Services Ex p. CPAG* [1989] 1 All E.R. 1047 at 1056, *per* Woolf L.J.; *Rydqvist v Secretary of State for Work and Pensions* [2002] 1 W.L.R. 3343). It follows that a tribunal has no power simply to give effect to a maintenance agreement reached between the parents (*CCS 2083 and 2483/04*, paras 8–15). Likewise, it is not possible for a party to limit the tribunal's jurisdiction by seeking to restrict the appeal to certain issues only (*CCS 1992/97*, para.31). However, under subs.7(a) the appeal tribunal need not consider any issue that is not raised by the appeal.

It is in the strict sense of the word that Commissioners have held that tribunals have no inherent jurisdiction (*R 2/94 (CSC)*, para.10; *R(SB) 42/83*, paras 11–13).

There is no special rule of interpretation that allows tribunals or Commissioners to fill an apparent gap in the tribunal's statutory jurisdiction. Any apparent gap may only be filled if it is possible to do so by applying the normal principles of interpretation (*Pendragon plc v Jackson* [1998] I.C.R. 215).

A tribunal has power to determine whether a case falls within its jurisdiction (*R(SB) 29/83*, para.17; *CSB 105/89*, para.12; *R. v Fulham Rent Tribunal Ex p. Zerek* [1951] 1 All E.R. 482). The tribunal must determine whether it has jurisdiction by strict enquiry ("expiscate") (*CI 78/90*, para.12; *CI 79/90*, para.15). Once a question of jurisdiction has been raised, the tribunal must enquire and determine the question and cannot accept a concession that the argument was not valid (*CCS 499/95*, para.7).

The tribunal's enquiry into its jurisdiction may involve determining whether a decision on which its jurisdiction depends was valid. The tribunal has power to determine that a decision extending time to appeal was invalid (*R(SB) 1/95*, para.12). It also has power to determine that the setting aside of a decision was invalid (*CI 78/90*, para.12) and so ineffective, thereby depriving the present tribunal of jurisdiction to rehear the case (*CS 51/92*). The validity of the setting aside cannot be challenged on the basis that the tribunal set aside the decision on a ground that falls outside the scope of reg.57 of the Appeals Regulations (*R(I) 7/94*, paras 32 and 34). In this respect, the approach set by the Commissioners is narrower than the modern approach of the courts who veer towards permitting a collateral challenge whenever there has been an error of law in the approach taken.

It may be appropriate to hold a preliminary hearing into jurisdiction to deal with any issue of jurisdiction (*Potts v IRC* (1982) 56 T.C. 25 at 35, *per* Walton, J.). Generally, however, preliminary hearings of questions are not to be encouraged (*CA 126/89*, para.10; *Sutcliffe v Big C's Marine* [1998] I.C.R. 913). Guidance on when a preliminary issue is appropriate was given in *Steele v Steele, The Times*, June 5, 2001. This is subject to reg.48 of the Appeals Regulations.

*Nature of an appeal*

An appeal to an appeal tribunal lies on any ground. In other words, the decision under appeal may be challenged on fact or on law. The appeal tribunal undertakes a reconsideration of the issues arising for determination in substitution for the consideration of the Secretary of State. It is not revising or superseding the decision under s.16 or 17 below. The tribunal does not, therefore, have to identify a ground for revision or supersession in order to allow the decision under appeal to be changed (*CDLA 1392/01*).

*Delegated legislation*

Delegated legislation may only be made within the scope of the power conferred    2.55
by the Act. The scope of the enabling statutory power is relevant both to the interpretation and to the validity of delegated legislation which purports to be made
under it. If the language is susceptible to different meanings, one of which is within the scope of the enabling power and one of which is outside it, the provision will
(subject to the Human Rights Act 1998) be given the meaning which renders it
valid. There are, however, problems with this approach: (i) It may not be easy to
identify the relevant enabling power. Regulations may be made under stated sections and "all other powers enabling in that behalf" and the omission of a power to
make a particular type of provision from one enabling section does not prevent that
power falling within another (perhaps more generally worded) enabling section (*R.
v Secretary of State for Social Security Ex p. Rouse, The Times*, February 1, 1993); (ii)
The power may be worded very broadly (for example, s.51(1)).

If a provision in delegated legislation cannot be interpreted in a way which renders it valid, it is said to be *ultra vires* and is invalid and unenforceable. An appeal
tribunal and a Commissioner have power to interpret delegated legislation. They
have no power to carry out a judicial review and declare the delegated legislation to
be *ultra vires*, but they do have power to decide in the context of a particular appeal
that the legislation is of no effect because it is *ultra vires*. This power applies to cases
where the legislation is illegal, *i.e.* that it is outside the scope of the enabling power
(*Chief Adjudication Officer v Foster* [1993] 1 All E.R. 705). Commissioners (and,
therefore, appeal tribunals) also have power to determine whether delegated legislation is *ultra vires* on the ground of irrationality (*R(CS) 2/95*, paras 8–9), but
should only exercise that power if a serious issue arises and it it necessary to rule on
the question in order to determine the appeal (*R(IS) 26/95*, para.45). A decision on
whether a provision in Regulations is irrational must concentrate on the regulations
as laid before Parliament, without reference to any legislative drafting history (*CIS
14141/96*, para.21). A provision will only be held to be irrational if the argument for
this conclusion is compelling, and it will not be compelling merely because it points
to unfairness, absurdity or even perversity in the treatment of different parties (*ibid.*
para.21). There is no special test of irrationality where the legislation has been subject to Parliamentary scrutiny. The test to apply is the *Wednesbury* test (*O'Connor v
Chief Adjudication Officer*, [1999] 1 F.L.R. 1200 at 1210, *per* Auld L.J.). In an appropriate case a provision which has been held to be irrational can be severed so as to
preserve the remainder of the Regulations (*CIS 14141/96*, para.23). Presumably
Commissioners and appeal tribunals will also be held to have power to determine
the procedural regularity of delegated legislation. In addition to being within the
scope of its enabling provision the delegated legislation must not conflict with statutory rights already enacted by other primary legislation (*R. v Secretary of State for
Social Security Ex p. Joint Council for the Welfare of Immigrants* [1996] 4 All E.R. 385
and *C(IS) 7/99*, para.10). However, this will only be so in the most extreme cases,
and the effect of the delegated legislation must go beyond mere interference with
the statutory rights such that it renders them valueless in practice (*ibid.*, para.13).
For a fuller statement of the nature of and grounds for judicial review see the
introductory general note to the Appeals Regulations.

*Form of decision*

If an appeal is allowed, the appropriate form of decision is to give directions to
the officer acting on behalf of the Secretary of State, setting out the findings and
principles by reference to which the absent parent's liability for child support
maintenance is to be determined (*CCS 290/99*, para.1.3).

It is appropriate and valid to direct that the Secretary of State investigate and act
as required on the results of the enquiries, at least if these conditions are satisfied:
(i) the matter to be investigated is clear; (ii) the result of the investigation will be

uncontroversial; and (iii) once the results of the investigation are known, all that is required is the mechanical application of the legislation, without any element of judgment or discretion (*CCS 284/99*, paras 24–25).

*Duty of members*

It should be obvious, but history shows that it bears repeating, that it is the duty of members of to apply the law as it is and not as they would wish it to be (*R(U) 7/81*, para.8).

*Subsection (1)*

This subsection sets out decisions that are appealable to an appeal tribunal. Paragraph (c) is qualified by subs.(6).

The list in this subsection is not exhaustive of the decisions that are appealable. It is extended by reg.30A of the Appeals Regulations to cover (a) decisions on adjustments to take account of overpayments or voluntary payments and (b) super-session decisions made under s.17 above, including those that are later revised under s.16.

A refusal to revise is not an appealable decision. However, the original decision will be appealable, although the appeal may be late. Although time can be extend-ed under reg.32 of the Appeals Regulations, it may be safer to make an appeal at the same time as an application for a revision.

Variation decisions are made under s.11, 16 or 17. As there is no decision separate from the maintenance calculation, a separate right of appeal is not needed.

*Subsections (4)–(5)*

The relevant Regulations are the Appeals Regulations.

*Subsection (7)*

An appeal tribunal deals with a case on appeal by way of rehearing. The tribunal stands in the same position as the officer who made the decision under appeal. All aspects of the case that the officer could have considered may be considered by the tribunal. This does not mean that every aspect of the case is considered from scratch. The tribunal has power to reconsider any issue, but is only required to con-sider those that properly arise before it. See the general notes to paras (a) and (b) below. An issue is a point of fact or law that merits inquiry and decision on the information or evidence before the tribunal.

*Subsection (7)(a)*

Paragraph (a) provides that an appeal tribunal need not consider any issue that is not raised by the appeal.

An issue is raised by an appeal if it is raised by any of the parties before or at the hearing (*CH 1229/02*, paras 13–18).

The appeal tribunal retains power to deal with any issue that arose before the Secretary of State. Its decision will not automatically be wrong in law for consider-ing one of these questions. The appeal tribunal's decision may, though, be wrong in law for failing to exercise correctly its power to deal with other issues. The decision must be taken judicially. This means that it must be taken in accordance with the principles of natural justice and the Convention rights of the parties (*CCS 463/2000*, para.17). Commissioners will have to determine the extent to which an appeal tribunal is expected to exercise its inquisitorial approach to consider a ques-tion that was not raised by the appeal and how far that approach is limited by this provision.

In *CH 3513/03*, the Commissioner held that it was perverse in the circumstances of the case for the tribunal to take issues of fact that the claimant would surely have raised if they were relevant. He also held that, if the tribunal had been entitled to take the issue, it should have adjourned to allow the other party to produce evidence, as the pre-hearing directions had not been sufficient to alert that party to the need for further evidence.

This provision cannot be used as a device for extending the tribunal's jurisdiction: see the section on *Jurisdiction* at the beginning of this general note.

*Subsection (7)(b)*

Paragraph (b) provides that an appeal tribunal must not take into account any circumstances not obtaining at the time when the decision under appeal was made. In other words, it limits the tribunal's jurisdiction by excluding changes of circumstances after the date of the decision. It re-enacts the former s.20(5), which was introduced with effect from May 21, 1998 by para.9 of Sch.6 to the Social Security Act 1998.

In the case of appeals made before that date, the tribunal must apply the down to the date of hearing rule and the old review and revision procedures (*CIB 213/99*, paras 17 and 36–40; *CCS 2566/98*, paras 16–17).

The relevant date is that of the decision under appeal, not the effective date of the decision. The tribunal must consider any change of circumstances between the effective date and the time when the decision was made and take it into account by way of a series of calculations under Sch.1, para.15 below. See *CCS 2620/02*.

It is not possible or appropriate to give an abstract definition of what constitutes a circumstance (*GDLA 4734/99*, para.56).

The tribunal will usually be concerned not merely with the position on the date when a decision was made, but with the position over the period covered by the decision. Any circumstances that have existed during that period must be considered (*CDLA 4734/99*, para.55).

The provision deals with circumstances, not with evidence of circumstances. It does not prevent a tribunal from taking account of evidence of circumstances obtaining at or before the date of decision even if that evidence was only produced or obtained after that date. The tribunal may also consider evidence of what occurred after the date of the decision if it throws light on what occurred before that date. Evidence of earnings received after the date of the decision, for example, may throw light on whether before that date a relevant change of circumstances had occurred in the party's income to merit a fresh calculation. If a party wants to rely on evidence that was produced after the relevant date, the tribunal must determine whether it can be related to that date before taking it into account. See *R (DLA) 2/01* para.9 and *CDLA 4734/99*, para.58. If there is evidence of a change of circumstances after the date of the decision under appeal, it is good practice to identify the evidence on which the tribunal's decision was based in order to show that it complied with subs.(7)(b) (*CDLA 2822/99*, para.18). Depending on the circumstances, it may be a mistake of law not to make this clear.

Other provisions or principles may further limit the circumstances that the tribunal may take into account. In the case of an appeal against a decision that has been revised, the tribunal may not take account of circumstances that occurred after the date of the original decision but before the date of the revision. This is because a change of circumstances after the date of the original decision can only be considered on a supersession. See *R(CS) 1/03*.

Evidence relating to later than the time of the decision may be used to assess the credibility and reliability of evidence (*CSDLA 854/03*).

*Subsection (8)*

If an appeal tribunal allows an appeal, it may give its own decision or remit the case to the Secretary of State with directions. In the former case, the decision is clearly made by the appeal tribunal and not by the Secretary of State. In the latter case, it is suggested that the decision is also made by the appeal tribunal, albeit that the actual arithmetical calculations are carried out on behalf of the appeal tribunal by the Secretary of State in accordance with the tribunal's directions. This is relevant to the scope of the Secretary of State's power to revise and supersede decisions under ss.16 and 17. It also prevents an appeal against the decision implementing a tribunal's decision that was possible under the original scheme. An appeal to an appeal tribunal under subs.(1) above lies only against decisions and impositions of requirements by the Secretary of State. An appeal against a decision of an appeal tribunal now lies only to a Commissioner. See *CCS 2403/98*, paras 35.1 and 36.

Section 21 was repealed by s.42 of the Social Security Act 1998 with effect from June 1, 1999.

## Child Support Commissioners

2.56    **22.**—(1) Her Majesty may from time to time appoint a Chief Child Support Commissioner and such number of other Child Support Commissioners as she may think fit.

(2) The Chief Child Support Commissioner and the other Child Support Commissioners shall be appointed from among persons who—

(a)  have a 10 year general qualification; or

(b)  are advocates or solicitors in Scotland of 10 years' standing.

(3) The Lord Chancellor, after consulting the Lord Advocate, may make such regulations with respect to proceedings before Child Support Commissioners as he considers appropriate.

(4) The regulations—

(a)  may in particular, make any provision of a kind mentioned in [¹Schedule 5 to the Social Security Act 1998]; and

(b)  shall provide that any hearing before a Child Support Commissioner shall be in public except in so far as the Commissioner for special reasons directs otherwise.

(5) Schedule 4 shall have effect with respect to Child Support Commissioners.

AMENDMENT

1. Paragraph 29 of Sch.7 to the Social Security Act 1998 (June 1, 1999).

DEFINITION

"general qualification": see s.54.

GENERAL NOTE

*Subsection (3)*
The regulations are contained in the Child Support Commissioners (Procedure) Regulations 1999.

*Subsection (4) (b)*
This reflects the fact that when a case comes to a Commissioner the appeal may decide matters which are relevant to other cases.

## Child Support Commissioners for Northern Ireland

**23.**—(1) Her Majesty may from time to time appoint a Chief Child    2.57
Support Commissioner for Northern Ireland and such number of other
Child Support Commissioners for Northern Ireland as she may think fit.

(2) The Chief Child Support Commissioner for Northern Ireland and
the other Child Support Commissioners for Northern Ireland shall be
appointed from among persons who are barristers or solicitors of not less
than 10 years' standing.

(3) Schedule 4 shall have effect with respect to Child Support
Commissioners for Northern Ireland, subject to the modifications set out
in paragraph 8.

(4) Subject to any Order made after the passing of this Act by virtue of
subsection (1)(a) of section 3 of the Northern Ireland Constitution Act
1973, the matters to which this subsection applies shall not be transferred
matters for the purposes of that Act but shall for the purposes of subsection
(2) of that section be treated as specified in Schedule 3 to that Act.

(5) Subsection (4) applies to all matters relating to Child Support
Commissioners, including procedure and appeals, other than those specified
in paragraph 9 of Schedule 2 to the Northern Ireland Constitution Act 1973.

## [¹Redetermination of appeals

**23A.**—(1) This section applies where an application is made to a person    2.58
under section 24(6)(a) for leave to appeal from a decision of an appeal
tribunal.

(2) If the person who constituted, or was the chairman of, the appeal tribunal considers that the decision was erroneous in law, he may set aside the
decision and refer the case either for redetermination by the tribunal or for
determination by a differently constituted tribunal.

(3) If each of the principal parties to the case expresses the view that the
decision was erroneous in point of law, the person shall set aside the decision and refer the case for determination by a differently constituted
tribunal.

(4) The "principal parties" are—

(a) the Secretary of State; and

(b) those who are qualifying persons for the purposes of section 20(2) in
relation to the decision in question.]

AMENDMENT

1. Section 11 of the 2000 Act (February 15, 2001 under art.2(2) of the
Commencement No.5 Order 2000).

DEFINITION

"appeal tribunal": see s.54.    2.59

GENERAL NOTE

Subsection (4)(b) is subject to the transitional protection in reg.11 of the Child
Support (Consequential Amendments and Transitional Provisions) Regulations
2001 below.

**2.60**   Subsection (2) confers a power, but not a duty, to set aside a tribunal's decision for error of law. The power operates regardless of the views of the parties. Subsection (3) imposes a duty to set it aside if the parties agree that the tribunal went wrong in law. Given the antagonism that often exists between the non-resident parent and the person with care, it is unlikely that they will agree on the error that the tribunal is alleged to have made. However, it is only necessary that they agree that the tribunal has made an error.

The decision under either subsection can only be taken by the person who chaired or constituted the appeal tribunal in question: compare the wording of s.24(6)(a) below. The operation of this section is parasitic on an application for leave to appeal to the Commissioner. In other words, it only operates when a valid application has been made. There is no express provision to this effect, but it is the context in which it applies and explains why there is no time limit on its operation; it is subject to the time limits that apply to applications for leave (*CDLA 1685/04*, para.14). If there is no full statement of the tribunal's decision, the section cannot operate (*ibid.*, para.14). Nor can the section be operated once the person has granted or refused leave to appeal to the Commissioner (*CF 6923/99*).

In *CIB 4427/02*, the Social Security Commissioner was concerned with a case in which all the parties were agreed that the tribunal had gone wrong in law, but its decision was not set aside by a district chairman. The Commissioner said at para.17 that in those circumstances the parties' right to have the decision set aside had to be preserved, even if the Commissioner did not agree that the tribunal had gone wrong in law.

## Appeal to Child Support Commissioner

**2.61**   **24.**—(1) Any person who is aggrieved by a decision of [²an appeal tribunal, and the Secretary of State] may appeal to a Child Support Commissioner on a question of law.

[³ . . .]

(2) Where, on an appeal under this section, a Child Support Commissioner holds that the decision appealed against was wrong in law he shall set it aside.

(3) Where a decision is set aside under subsection (2), the Child Support Commissioner may—

(a) if he can do so without making fresh or further findings of fact, give the decision which he considers should have been given by [⁴the appeal tribunal];

(b) if he considers it expedient, make such findings and give such decision as he considers appropriate in the light of those findings; or

[¹(c) on an appeal by the Secretary of State, refer the case to [⁵an appeal tribunal] with directions for its determination; or

(d) on any other appeal, refer the case to [⁷the Secretary of State] or, if he considers it appropriate, to [⁶an appeal tribunal] with directions for its determination.]

[⁸(4) The reference under subsection (3) to the Secretary of State shall, subject to any direction of the Child Support Commissioner, be to an officer of his, or a person providing him with services, who has taken no part in the decision originally appealed against.]

(5) On a reference under subsection (3) to [⁹an appeal tribunal], the tribunal shall, subject to any direction of the Child Support Commissioner,

consist of persons who were not members of the tribunal which gave the decision which has been appealed against.

(6) No appeal lies under this section without the leave—

(a) of the person [[10] who constituted, or was the chairman of, the appeal tribunal] when the decision appealed against was given or of [[11]such other person] as may be determined in accordance with regulations made by the Lord Chancellor; or

(b) subject to and in accordance with regulations so made, of a Child Support Commissioner.

(7) The Lord Chancellor may by regulations make provision as to the manner in which, and the time within which, appeals under this section are to be brought and applications for leave under this section are to be made.

(8) Where a question which would otherwise fall to be determined by [[12]the Secretary of State] first arises in the course of an appeal to a Child Support Commissioner, he may, if he thinks fit, determine it even though it has not been considered by [[13]the Secretary of State].

(9) Before making any regulations under subsection (6) or (7), the Lord Chancellor shall consult the Lord Advocate.

AMENDMENTS

1. Paragraph 7(3) of Sch.3 to the 1995 Act (December 2, 1996).
2. Paragraph 30(1) of Sch.7 to the Social Security Act 1998 (June 1, 1999).
3. Paragraph 30(2) of Sch.7 to the Social Security Act 1998 (June 1, 1999).
4. Paragraph 30(3)(a) of Sch.7 to the Social Security Act 1998 (June 1, 1999).
5. Paragraph 30(3)(b) of Sch.7 to the Social Security Act 1998 (June 1, 1999).
6. Paragraph 30(3)(b) of Sch.7 to the Social Security Act 1998 (June 1, 1999).
7. Paragraph 30(3)(c) of Sch.7 to the Social Security Act 1998 (June 1, 1999).
8. Paragraph 30(4) of Sch.7 to the Social Security Act 1998 (June 1, 1999).
9. Paragraph 30(5) of Sch.7 to the Social Security Act 1998 (June 1, 1999).
10. Paragraph 30(6)(a) of Sch.7 to the Social Security Act 1998 (June 1, 1999).
11. Paragraph 30(6)(b) of Sch.7 to the Social Security Act 1998 (June 1, 1999).
12. Paragraph 30(7) of Sch.7 to the Social Security Act 1998 (June 1, 1999).
13. Paragraph 30(7) of Sch.7 to the Social Security Act 1998 (June 1, 1999).

DEFINITION

"appeal tribunal": see s.54.                                                    2.62

GENERAL NOTE

*Subsection (1)*

An appeal lies to a Commissioner from a decision of an appeal tribunal. It may    2.63
lie at the instance of either a person aggrieved by the tribunal's decision or the Secretary of State. The requirement of leave to appeal is compatible with Art.6 of the European Convention on Human Rights and Fundamental Freedoms (*CDLA 3432/01*).

The function of the Commissioners, like that of any other appellate body, is to correct wrong decisions in order to ensure justice between the parties and to ensure public confidence in the administration of justice by remedying wrong decisions and by clarifying and developing the law (*Taylor v Lawrence* [2002] 2 All E.R. 353 at para.66). An appeal to a Commissioner is a rehearing. Initially, the rehearing is confined to questions of law. However, if the tribunal's decision is wrong in law, the Commissioner may investigate the facts and make fresh or further findings in order to give a decision under subs.(3)(b) below. See *CIS 16701/96*.

The meaning of "person ... aggrieved" has been considered in a variety of statutory contexts, but so much depends on the context that it is difficult to distill from the authorities any general principles that are sufficiently precise to allow firm conclusions to be drawn about the meaning of the words in this section.

So far as is known, no one has attempted to appeal who was not an absent parent, a person with care or, in Scotland, a child. Others might wish to appeal. Grandparents have a recognised role to play in children cases in the courts. A partner of an absent parent might also object to the amount of the child support maintenance assessment. If persons like these tried to appeal, the question would arise whether they were sufficiently closely connected with and affected by the decision of the appeal tribunal to be "aggrieved" by it.

The requirement that the person be aggrieved prevents appeals by persons who have not been adversely affected by the decision of the appeal tribunal. In *R(CS) 15/98*, para.14 the Commissioner held that a person who was made subject to a reduced benefit direction would still be aggrieved by a decision despite that person's failure to take any part in the stages leading up to the making of the direction and that, even if the person's previous inaction did result in the loss of aggrieved status, the person could still be vicariously aggrieved on behalf of any qualifying child. The requirement that the person be aggrieved can be used to prevent appeals that are based solely on a point of principle with no practical effect on the decision.

The Secretary of State has no personal interest in a decision, but may appeal in the interests of one of the parties, or in order to obtain an authoritative decision on a particular point from a Commissioner. The decision appealed must be that of a tribunal. There can be no appeal against a decision or ruling of a chairman (*CSB 103/84*, paras 12–13 and *CSB 1182/89*, para.8 and the decisions cited therein). However, if a hearing follows a chairman's decision or ruling and the tribunal makes a decision, that decision may be subject to an appeal on the ground that the chairman's decision or ruling adversely affected the party's case or the presentation of it, or that it occasioned a breach of the rules of natural justice (*CSB 103/84*, para.14).

The precise scope of the word "decision" in this subsection is unclear. It certainly covers final decisions which dispose of all matters in dispute. This includes decisions which are subject to liberty to restore (*CIS 118/90*, para.17) and final decisions on any part of an appeal which has been decided separately (*CSIS 118/90*, para.10), if these are permissible in child support law (see the general note to reg.51(4) of the Appeals Regulations). It is also clear that determinations on applications for leave to appeal are not appealable (*Bland v Chief Supplementary Benefit Officer* [1983] 1 All E.R. 537; *White v Chief Adjudication Officer* [1986] 2 All E.R. 905; *R. v Secretary of State for Trade and Industry Ex p. Eastaway* [2001] 1 All E.R. 27 and see further in the general note to reg.30 of the Child Support Commissioners (Procedure) Regulations). A Tribunal of Commissioners in *CA 126/89*, para.9, has held, in the context of an adjournment following a decision on a preliminary point of law, that "decision" covers only final decisions rather than interlocutory ones and that an adjournment, being interlocutory, is not appealable. The same approach was taken by Commissioner Rice, who was a member of the Tribunal, in a case of an adjournment to allow an adjudication officer to carry out a calculation of overpayment (*CIS 64/91*, para.4). However, the Tribunal's decision has not been followed by two other Commissioners who have held that decisions to adjourn or to refuse to adjourn are appealable (*CSIS 118/90*, para.17 and *CSIS 110/91* para.14). The reasoning in these cases is equally applicable to cover directions given under reg.38(2) of the Appeals Regulations. The courts permit appeals against decisions to adjourn (*Kingcastle Ltd v Owen-Owen, The Times*, March 18, 1999).

It is suggested that the scope of this subsection is to be determined more by practical considerations of expedition and fairness than by analysis of the concept of "decision" in this context. The following approach is suggested: (i) Adjournments following a decision on a preliminary issue are not appealable (*CA 126/89*, paras 9–11). This is justified on the basis that decisions on preliminary points are not to be encouraged; (ii) Decisions to refuse to adjourn do not need to be appealable as such as the tribunal's final decision will be appealable. This will allow any adverse effect which the refusal may have had, or any breach of the rules of natural justice which may have occurred, to be taken into account by the Commissioner (on the principle of the reasoning in relation to decisions by chairmen in *CSB 103/84*, para.14); (iii) Appeals against adjournments will not normally be worth undertaking as they will merely delay matters even longer; (iv) However, if the adjournment is indefinite or for a particularly lengthy period, an appeal to a Commissioner may be quicker than waiting for the hearing and in such cases *CSIS 118/90*, para.17 and *CSIS 110/91*, para.14, provide authority for an appeal on the ground that the tribunal failed to exercise its discretion properly with the result that there was a miscarriage of justice or a breach of the rules of natural justice; (v) Appeals against decisions to issue directions under reg.38(2) of the Appeals Regulations, or to refuse to do so, will usually add delay to any other injustice occasioned and will not normally be worth appealing. (Point (iv) is very similar to the conclusion reached by the Commissioner in *CDLA 557/01* after an analysis of many of the court decisions considered later in this note. The Commissioner held that a decision to adjourn was only appealable if it (para.20) "makes some interim disposal of the case which either makes it more than likely that the case will be disposed of finally in a particular way or leaves one of the parties with no means of ensuring that there will be a final disposal of the case, or leaves one of the parties at the risk of an injustice.")

The above analysis is based on two assumptions: (i) that the Scottish decisions were correctly decided and (ii) that they establish principles which apply throughout Great Britain. Both these assumptions have been challenged by other Commissioners. In *CIS 628/92* the Commissioner preferred to follow the authorities which decide that the only decisions which are appealable are those which finally dispose of the matter in issue rather than the Scottish decisions. In *CIS 260/93* the Commissioner, after a detailed examination of the development of the different legal systems of the British Isles, decided that the decisions were only applicable to Scotland. Leaving aside this particular Commissioner's decision, it may be stated as a general proposition that, within the constraints imposed by the doctrine of precedent, it is a wise precaution to treat with care any statement by a London-based Commissioner on the principles of law which apply uniquely in Scotland.

The court decisions will be relevant to the extent that adjournment decisions are appealable to a Commissioner. The cases show that an appeal may be made against a decision to adjourn (*Re Yates' Settlement Trusts* [1954] 1 All E.R. 619) and against a decision not to do so (*Rose v Humbles* [1970] 2 All E.R. 519). A decision on adjournment is a discretionary one and the appellate body should be slow to interfere in the exercise of the discretion (*Maxwell v Keun* [1927] All E.R. Rep. 335 at 338, per Atkin L.J.). Nevertheless, it has power to do so (*Yates*, above at 621, *per* Evershed M.R.). A decision will only be overturned in an extreme case. The judges speak of such cases as being those where the result of the decision is to cause substantial injustice (*Rose*, above at 523, *per* Buckley J.), or to defeat the rights of the parties altogether (*Maxwell*, above at 339, *per Atkin* L.J.), or to defeat or deny justice altogether (*Hinckley and South Leicestershire Permanent Benefit Building Society v Freeman* [1940] 4 All E.R. 212 at 216, *per* Farwell J. and *Maxwell*, above at 341, *per* Lawrnece L.J.). Usually the decisions have related to the opportunity for a party or other person to attend to give evidence, but this is not exclusively so (*Hinckley*, above). It can be a proper exercise of the discretion if the adjournment is to await the outcome of a different case (*Yates*, above at 621, *per* Evershed, M.R.), but an indefinite adjournment, for whatever reason, is not an acceptable exercise of the discretion (*Hinckley*, above at 216, *per* Farwell J.). See also the general note to reg.51(4) of the Appeals Regulations.

In deciding whether a tribunal had jurisdiction to hear and decide an appeal Commissioners have taken to themselves powers to rule on the validity of decisions which are not appealable to them. Thus Commissioners have power to decide on the validity of a purported setting aside (*R(I) 7/94*, para.27), correction (*CM 264/93*, para.17) or a decision to extend the time for making an appeal (*R(SB) 1/95*, para.12). Clerks and chairmen should, therefore, resist the temptation to set aside or correct decisions on grounds other than those permitted under regs 56 and 57 of the Appeals Regulations. They may consider that in doing so they are avoiding the need for an appeal to a Commissioner with a view to achieving an earlier resolution of the points in issue. In fact the result may be to prolong the proceedings rather than to shorten them. The Commissioner may hold that the decision appealed is not valid, either because it represents an invalid correction or because it was a decision made following an invalid setting aside, and that the appellant must apply for leave to appeal out of time against the decision that was purportedly set aside or corrected in the invalid proceedings.

Before seeking leave to appeal it is worth considering whether an application to set aside the decision under reg.57 of the Appeals Regulations would be more appropriate. Such an application will be heard much more quickly than an appeal and does not affect the party's right to seek leave to appeal.

*Question of law*

**2.64**     An appeal lies to a Commissioner on a question of law. There can be no appeal, if a question of law cannot be identified (*R. v The Social Security Commissioner and the Social Security Appeal Tribunal Ex p. Pattni* [1993] Fam. Law 213). If the tribunal's decision is not wrong in law, a Commissioner has no power to direct a rehearing on the ground that it is justified by fresh evidence (*CCS 4687/00*, paras 6–9).

If the tribunal's decision is wrong in law, the decision will be set aside under s.24(2) below. The mistake of law may exist in the decision itself or in the proceedings that led to that decision (*R(I) 28/61*).

The cases in which a decision will be wrong in law are discussed below. It is impossible to give a comprehensive list of the ways in which a tribunal's decision may be wrong in law and any attempt to do so is likely to produce overlapping categories (*R(IS) 11/99*, para.4). It might be easier to identify those matters which are not questions of law. Perhaps the best attempt to distill the essence of what is involved in a mistake of law was that of Bridge J. in *Mountview Court Properties Ltd v Devlin* (1970) 21 P.&C.R. 689 at 695–696:

"... any ... language found in the statutes giving a right of appeal on a point of law, to my mind connotes that a successful appellant must demonstrate that the decision with which he is dissatisfied is itself vitiated by reason of the fact that it has been reached by an erroneous process of legal reasoning."

However, this does not cover all mistakes of law. It does not, for example, cover breaches of natural justice or inadequate reasons.

Reasonableness is a question of fact (*R(SB) 6/88*), although the process of determining it may contain a mistake of law.

A tribunal's decision will be wrong in law in at least the following cases:

(i) *No jurisdiction* If a tribunal purports to deal with a party or an issue over which it has no power or to grant relief that it has no power to grant, it acts without jurisdiction (*Garthwaite v Garthwaite* [1964] 2 All E.R. 233 at 241, *per* Diplock L.J.). If the whole of the tribunal's decision is outside its jurisdiction, it is of no force or effect *(R(S) 15/52*, para.10). If only part of the tribunal's decision is outside its jurisdiction, it may be possible to declare that part of the decision to be of no force or effect so that it may be disregarded as superfluous to the decision, leaving the remainder of the decision intact *(R(M) 1/98*, para.3; *CI 218/97*, para.13). On the reasoning in *R(I) 9/63*, paras 20–22 the decision or part of the decision that was made without jurisdiction nonetheless exists as a decision and must be set aside. This was what the Tribunal of Commissioners did in *R(SB) 42/83*, para.13, although it also left undisturbed part of the decision that was outside the tribunal's jurisdiction because it was not challenged on appeal to the Commissioners (*ibid.*, para.12). For the tribunal's power to consider the validity of determinations on which its jurisdiction depends, see the introductory general note to the new s.20 above.

(ii) *No power* If a tribunal purports to exercise a power which it does not possess, its decision will be wrong in law.

(iii) *Rejection of relevant evidence* If a tribunal rejects relevant evidence, whether by refusing to admit it or by refusing to consider it, its decision will be wrong in law (*Bailey v Stoke-on-Trent Assessment Committee* [1931] 1 K.B. 385 at 481–2, *per* Scrutton L.J.). There will also have been a breach of natural justice. A tribunal's decision will not be wrong in law merely because the tribunal took no account of evidence that was not before it *(R(S) 1/88*, para.3).

(iv) *Failure to adopt an inquisitorial approach* If the tribunal fails to take an inquisitorial approach to the case, the parties will not have had a fair hearing. This will be a breach of natural justice that makes the decision wrong in law. For a discussion of the inquisitorial approach, see the general note to reg.49(1) of the Appeals Regulations.

(v) *The decision or a finding of fact material to the decision is not supported by any evidence* If there is *no* evidence to support a finding of fact on which the tribunal's decision is based, the decision will be wrong in law *R(A) 1/72*, para.4; *R(SB) 11/83*, para.13(2)). It is a requirement of natural justice that each finding of fact by a tribunal must be based on some material logically tending to show the existence of that fact (*Mahon v Air New Zealand* [1984] 3 All E.R. 201 at 210, *per* Lord Diplock). The evidence relied on must have *some* probative value (*R. v National Industrial Injuries Commissioner Ex p. Moore* [1965] 1 All E.R. 81 at 94, *per* Diplock L.J.). On appeal a Commissioner is considering not whether the findings of fact made by the tribunal were the right ones to make on the evidence, but rather whether they were ones which the tribunal was entitled in law to make on the evidence before it. The evaluation of the evidence is for the fact finder, which in this case is the tribunal (*R. v Deputy Industrial Injuries Commissioner Ex p. Moore* [1965] 1 All E.R. 81 at 94, *per* Lord Diplock). The weight to be attached to any particular piece of evidence is determined by common sense (*Lord Advocate v Lord Blantyre* (1879) 4 App. Cas.770 at 792, *per* Lord Blackburn). If the evidence on a particular point is unchallenged and there are no facts or circumstances to displace or cast doubt on it, the tribunal would be wrong in law if it failed to accept it (*R. v Matheson* [1958] 2 All E.R. 87 at 90, *per* Lord Goddard C.J.). Likewise, a tribunal's finding will be wrong in law if it is out of tune with the evidence to such an extent that it can only have been the case that the tribunal misunderstood that evidence. (In *Hossack v General Dental Council, The Times*, April 22, 1997 the Privy Council reversed a finding of fact by the Council's professional conduct committee on this ground, although the appeal to the Council was not limited to mistakes of law.) These cases aside, there is no appeal on a question of fact (*CCS 7966/95*, para.9).

The generous margin of autonomy that the law allows to tribunals in the finding of facts reflects the fact that, unlike the tribunal, the Commissioner will not have seen the witnesses, and recognises that different persons may properly reach a different judgment on the same facts (*CDLA 5342/97*, para.13). A decision that a tribunal's decision was perverse should only be taken if an overwhelming case is made out (*Elmbridge Housing Trust v O'Donoghue, The Times*, June 24, 2004).

The mere fact that a party does not agree with a finding of fact or with a piece of evidence does not show that the tribunal's decision was wrong in law (*CSA 21/86*, para.5).

Findings of fact that are not reached on a rational or common sense basis are an example of this head. They merit special mention to show that there are limits to the autonomy allowed to tribunals in making findings of fact. If the tribunal's approach to the finding of facts is not a rational one that is in accordance with common sense, its decision will be erroneous in law. As the tribunal's approach will only be apparent from its reasoning, this head of error of law is closely connected with the adequacy of the tribunal's explanation for its findings. See *CDLA 5342/97*, paras 18–19.

(vi) *Errors of uncontroverted fact* A mere error of fact is not an error of law (*Inland Revenue Commissioners v George, The Times*, December 9, 2003). However, in some limited circumstances a mistake of uncontroverted fact may be an error of law in those jurisdictions where the parties share an interest in co-operating to achieve the correct outcome (*E and R v Secretary of State for the Home Department* [2004] EWCA Civ 49, para.66). The circumstances are: (i) there is a mistake of existing fact, including a mistake on the availability of evidence of a fact; (ii) the fact is uncontentious and objectively verifiable; (iii) the appellant and the appellant's advisers must not have been responsible for the mistake; (iv) the mistake must have played a material, but not necessarily decisive, part in the tribunal's reasoning (*ibid.*, at para. 66).

(vii) *Judgment exercised improperly or not at all* A tribunal must exercise judgment in a judicial manner. This means that it must be exercised in a selective and discriminating manner and not arbitrarily or idiosyncratically.

A tribunal may, and in almost every case will have to, exercise judgment at one or more stages as it reaches a decision. That judgment may be necessary because

(1) it is necessary to evaluate the evidence; or
(2) the rule with which the tribunal is concerned allows a degree of choice (*e.g.* where the tribunal is deciding whether to exercise its *discretion* to give a reduced benefit decision under s.46(5) below); or
(3) the tribunal is concerned with a broad concept under which it has to decide the significance to be attached to individual facts or has to weigh and balance the overall significance of the combinations of facts (*e.g.* whether a parent and child are living in the same *household* under s.3(2)(a) above, or whether it would be *just and equitable* under s.28F(1)(b) below to agree to a variation).

This classification should not be taken as establishing mutually exclusive categories. A case may come under more than one head.

It will be a mistake of law for a tribunal to fail to exercise a judgment when one is called or to introduce an element of judgment into a case which merely requires the tribunal to reach conclusions of fact. It will also be a mistake of law for a tribunal to exercise the wrong type of judgment. A tribunal is likely to have considerable leeway in fixing an appropriate deduction in a partner's housing costs when agreeing to a variation because the factors taken into account are unlikely to point to a precise figure, but there is no scope for the exercise of such deliberate choice in deciding whether a person is a member of a household because the tribunal must decide whether or not the facts show membership of a household. It is unfortunate that all cases involving the exercise of judgment are sometimes referred to as involving discretion, as by Lord Diplock in *Birkett v James* [1977] 2 All E.R. 801 at 804. The approach taken by the Commissioners differs according to the category of case concerned. They are particularly reluctant to find a mistake of law in the tribunal's analysis of the evidence.

The approach taken by Commissioners to cases where an element of judgment is **2.65** involved is based on the recognition that judgment might legitimately be exercised differently by different persons on the same facts (*Bellenden v Satterthwaite* [1948] 1 All E.R. 343 at 345, *per* Asquith L.J.). Decision will not be wrong in law merely because the Commissioners would have formed a different judgment (*Charles Osenton and Co v Johnson* [1941] 2 All E.R. 245 at 250, *per* Viscount Simon L.C.) and they should not and will not embark on the exercise of deciding what decision they would have reached on the facts (*Global Plant Ltd. v Secretary of State for Health and Social Security* [1971] 3 All E.R. 385 at 393, *per* Lord Widgery C.J.). See also *Birkett v James* [1977] 1 2 All E.R. 801 at 811, *per* Lord Salmon; *Cookson v Knowles* [1978] 2 All E.R. 604 at 607, *per* Lord Diplock; *Eagil Trust Co Ltd v Pigott-Brown* [1985] 3 All E.R. 119 at 121, *per* Griffiths L.J..

This approach is not affected by the Human Rights Act 1998 (*Biji v General Medical Council, The Times*, October 24, 2001).

The House of Lords has strongly reaffirmed the principles to be applied on an appeal against the exercise of a discretion, warning:

"An appellate court should resist any temptation to subvert the principle that they should not substitute their own discretion for that of the judge by a narrow textual analysis which enables them to claim that he misdirected himself."

(*Piglowska v Piglowski* [1999] 3 All E.R. 632 at 644, *per* Lord Hoffmann). The Court of Appeal has also emphasised that proper respect must be paid to the conclusions reached by tribunals within the area of expertise that legislation has left to them (*Bromley London Borough Council v Special Educational Needs Tribunal* [1999] 3 All E.R. 587 at 594, *per* Sedley L.J.).

On the assumption that there is no error in the findings of primary fact (see the *Evaluation of evidence* section of the general note to reg.49(1) of the Appeals Regulations), a decision will only be wrong in law in limited circumstances. These circumstances have been stated in slightly different terms in different cases. In *Ward v James* [1965] 1 All E.R. 563 at 570 Lord Denning M.R. said that a decision would only be set aside when the court was satisfied that it was wrong. In *R. v Birmingham Juvenile Court Ex p. N.* [1984] 2 All E.R. 688 at 690–691, *per* Arnold P. and *Simmons v Pizzey* [1977] 2 All E.R. 432 at 441–442, *per* Lord Hailsham L.C. it was said that a decision would be set aside if it was based on incorrect legal principles or if it was one that could not reasonably have been made on the facts of the case. In *Crake v Supplementary Benefits Commission* [1982] 1 All E.R. 498 at 501 Woolf J. said that a decision would be set aside if it was one that could not have been made on the facts by someone who was properly advised and acting reasonably. In *George Mitchell (Chesterhall) Ltd v Finney Lock Seeds Ltd* [1983] 2 All E.R. 737 at 743, *per* Lord Bridge it was said that a decision would only be set aside if proceeded upon some erroneous principle or was plainly and obviously wrong. Many variants of these different formulations can be found.

An exercise of judgment will be wrong in law in three circumstances: (a) if the tribunal took the wrong approach in law; (b) if the tribunal acted on the wrong material; and (c) if the tribunal went wrong in the balancing exercise.

A tribunal may take the wrong approach in law in two ways. (i) It may misdirect itself on the law. For example, it may misplace the burden of proof. (ii) It may also go wrong in principle. For example, it may disregard a principle that governs the exercise of a discretion.

A tribunal may act on the wrong material in two ways. (i) It may overlook a relevant consideration. (ii) It may take account of an irrelevant consideration.

A tribunal goes wrong in the balancing exercise if its conclusion "exceeded the generous ambit within which a reasonable disagreement is possible" (*G v G* [1985] 2 All E.R. 225 at 229 *per* Lord Fraser). This allows a wider margin for disagreement than the grounds on which a court will review the exercise of an administrative discretion (*Re F (a minor) (wardship: appeal)* [1976] 1 All E. R. 417, in which the majority rejected Stamp L.J.'s view at 429–430; (*G v G* at 232 *per* Lord Bridge). Judgment must always be exercised judicially, which limits the factors that may or must be taken into account. In some cases, the legislation sets out factors that must or must not be taken into account, as in reg.21 of the Variation Regulations.

The Commissioners should try to promote consistency where in closely comparable circumstances there are conflicting schools of opinion among tribunals as to the relative weight to be given to particular considerations (*Birkett v James* [1977] 2 All E.R. 801 at 804 and 811, *per* Lords Diplock and Salmon respectively).

This head may be seen as no more than a particular application of the rule that no tribunal acting judicially and properly instructed as to the relevant law could have come to the decision reached, with the Commissioner having to decide whether the tribunal's decision fell outside the range of permissible decisions that might be made.

Errors in the exercise of judgment may be established by being expressed in the tribunal's decision or they may be inferred from the decision which was reached (*Ward v James* [1965] 1 All E.R. 563 at 570, *per* Lord Denning M.R.). There is no special rule where the welfare of children is concerned (*G v G* [1985] 2 All E.R. 225 at 228, *per* Lord Fraser). There must be a particularly strong case that an exercise of judgment was wrong in law where it depended upon the tribunal having seen and heard witnesses (*Re F*, above at 439–440, *per* Bridge L.J.).

Where a tribunal is required to exercise its judgment, the mere fact that the decision fails to set out every one of the factors which led to the decision will not be sufficient to prove that the tribunal failed to consider those factors which are not mentioned (*Redman v Redman* [1948] 1 All E.R. 333 at 334–335, *per* Tucker L.J.). However, the reasons given for a decision must be adequate. It is not sufficient merely to recite the evidence taken into account. The reasons must go on to give an indication of how and why the tribunal reached its decision. See *B v B* (*Residence Order: Reasons for Decision*) [1997] 2 F.L.R. 602 at 606.

For the approach to cases involving case management decisions see the *Active case management* section of the introductory note to the Appeal Regulations.

(viii) *Inferences* Inferences are an example of the exercise of judgment. The courts have considered the proper approach that should be taken on appeal to inferences drawn below. Some of the cases involved the identification of an error of law on appeal on error of law grounds. Others involved the respect to be given to an inference on an appeal by way of rehearing on both fact and law.

The courts have drawn a distinction between inferences relating to perception and evaluation of facts.

Perception is concerned with what happened and who did it, proved not directly but by a process of reasoning from other facts. In these cases, there will be an error of law if there is no evidence to support the inference that has been drawn.

Evaluation is concerned with whether the facts as found satisfy a legal test or standard. If evaluation is involved, the issue may also be referred to as one of mixed law and fact or of fact and degree. The legal test or standard is a matter of law. Whether the facts are sufficient to satisfy that test or standard is a matter of fact. In these cases, there will be an error of law if the tribunal applied the wrong principle or came to a decision that was plainly wrong. The tribunal applied the wrong principle if it misdirected itself on the terms of the legal test or standard. That may be shown directly by the terms in which the tribunal explains its decision. The tribunal's decision will be plainly wrong if it has applied the test or standard to the facts in a way that the facts do not support. That is either seen as an error of law in itself or as evidence that the tribunal must have misdirected itself on the law. See also the previous section on the exercise of judgment.

Whichever the issue with which the case was concerned and whether the inference relates to perception or evaluation, the courts' reluctance to interfere with an inference varies with a variety of factors. The most important are: (a) whether it involved the assessment of oral evidence; (b) whether it involved the use of special experience or expertise, such as that of a financially qualified panel member; (c) how great is the range of variables that were taken into account in drawing the inference. The presence of these features increases the respect given to the inference and the reluctance to interfere with it on appeal.

The authorities and the distinctions were analysed by the Court of Appeal in *South Cone Inc v Bessant* [2002] EWCA Civ 763.

(ix) *The decision contains a false proposition on its face* If there is a false proposition on the face of the decision (*ex facie*), the decision is wrong in law (*R(A) 1/72*, para.4; *R(SB) 11/83*, para.13(1)). This applies where the tribunal has applied the wrong legal test in order to to determine an issue.

(x) *Ultra vires* The fact that a decision was based on a provision in delegated legislation which the minister had no power to make will make it wrong in law (*Chief Adjudication Officer v Foster* [1993] 1 All E.R. 705).

(xi) *Legislation or legal document wrongly interpreted* The proper interpretation of a piece of legislation or other legal document such as a contract is always a question of law. If the interpretation used by the tribunal is wrong, its decision will be wrong in law. It may also be wrong in law for a tribunal to rely on a concession on the interpretation of a document (*Bahamas International Trust Co Ltd v Threadgold* [1974] 3 All E.R. 881 at 884 *per* Lord Diplock) or on the interpretation of a statutory provision (*Cherwell District Council v Thames Water Authority* [1975] 1 All E.R. 763 at 767 *per* Lord Diplock). As these are questions of law for the tribunal to determine, it must satisfy itself that the concession is correctly made.

(xii) *No tribunal acting judicially and properly instructed as to the relevant law could have come to the decision* If the decision was one that no tribunal acting judicially and properly instructed on the law, the decision is said to be perverse and is wrong in law (*R(A) 1/72*, para.4; *R(SB) 11/83*, para.13(3)). This covers cases where the tribunal fails to make the only decision open to it on the facts as found (*R. v Birmingham Juvenile Court Ex p. N.* [1984] 2 All E.R. 688 at 690–691, *per* Arnold P.) and cases where the tribunal's decision falls outside the range of decisions that might properly be made (*Bellenden v Satterthwaite* [1948] 1 All E.R. 343 at 345, *per* Asquith L.J.). An argument based on this ground must be fully particularised, will only be accepted if an overwhelming case has been made out, and must not allow an appeal on a question of law to be turned into a rehearing of parts of the evidence (*Yeboah v Crofton* [2002] I.R.L.R. 634).

(xiii) *Failure to deal with all questions arising for decision* The tribunal must consider the case afresh. Although every aspect of the case is open for decision by the tribunal, it is only required to deal with those questions that put to it for decision by contention of one of the parties or that arise on the evidence. The appeal tribunal's decision will not be wrong in law for failing to deal with an obviously unsuccessful point that was not raised before the tribunal but which is raised on appeal in an attempt to obtain a rehearing (*Srimanoharan v Secretary of State for the Home Department, The Times,* June 29, 2000).

(xiv) *Decision incomplete or impossible to implement* If a tribunal's decision is incomplete or for some reason it cannot be implemented (*e.g.* if it is self-contradictory), the decision will be wrong in law.

(xv) *Inadequate reasons* The tribunal's decision will be wrong in law, if there has been a breach of reg.53 of the Appeals Regulations which requires a statement of the reasons for the tribunal's decision and of the findings on questions of fact material to that decision *(R(I) 18/61,* paras 10–11; *R(A) 1/72,* para.5; *R(SB) 11/82,* para.14; *R(SB) 11/83,* para.13(5)). A failure to give adequate reasons for a tribunal's decision may make its decision wrong in law in three ways:

(a) As the decision is the best indication of how the tribunal reached its decision, inadequate reasons may be evidence of a mistake of law.
(b) The lack of any, or of adequate, reasons may amount to a breach of natural justice.
(c) The failure to comply with reg.53 is itself a mistake of law.

In *Crake v Supplementary Benefits Commission* [1982] 1 All E.R. 498 at 506–508 Woolf J. held that the mere inadequacy of a Supplementary Benefit Appeal Tribunal's reasons was not as such an error of law. This was in line with *Mountview Court Properties Ltd v Devlin* (1970) 21 P.& C.R. 689 at 695–696, *per* Lord Parker C.J. and Bridge J. and the general principle has been restated in *R. v Legal Aid Area No.8 (Northern) Appeal Committee Ex p. Angell* [1990] C.O.D. 355 at 356. However, in the case of a Medical Appeal Tribunal the Court of Appeal had treated the inadequacy of reasons as sufficient to justify quashing the decision *(R. v Deputy National Injuries Commissioner Ex p. Howarth,* reported as an appendix to *R(I) 14/68).* In *R(SB) 11/82,* paras 13–14 *Crake* was distinguished as relating to a case in which there was a wide discretion whether or not to award benefit and no closely circumscribed legal framework designed to ensure uniformity of application of the rules. These characteristics certainly do not apply to the child support scheme and there is no doubt that the failure to give adequate reasons of itself makes the decision wrong in law.

The preponderance of authority favours the proposition that any failure to meet the standard required of a tribunal's reasons is a mistake of law. See *Norton Tool Co Ltd v Tewson* [1973] 1 All E.R. 183 at 187, *per* Donaldson P. and *Alexander Machinery (Dudley) Ltd v Crabtree* [1974] I.C.R. 120 at 122, *per* Donaldson P., although Lord Lane, C.J., speaking for himself in *R. v Immigration Appeal Tribunal Ex p. Khan* [1983] 2 All E.R. 420 at 423 doubted that every failure was of itself an mistake of law. The reason is that the giving of reasons is a function of due process and justice such that the failure to do so would deprive a party of the chance to identify a mistake of law on which to base an appeal *(Flannery v Halifax Estate Agencies Ltd* [2000] 1 All E.R. 373 at 377–8).

For a discussion of the standard of reasons required, see the general note to reg.53 of the Appeals Regulations.

There are a number of cases in which the courts have ordered that reasons be given or be supplemented. Some of these cases are based upon a variety of provisions and considerations that have no application to the child support jurisdiction. (a) The case may relate to the duty to give reasons under what is now s.10 of the Tribunals and Inquiries Act 1992 *(Crake v Supplementary Benefits Commission* [1982] 1 All E.R. 498 at 508, *per* Woolf J.). So in *Mountview Court Properties Ltd v Devlin* (1970) 21 P.&C.R. 689 the case was adjourned and remitted for further reasons to be supplied. The duty under the 1992 Act is displaced by the specific provision in the Appeals Regulations *(R(F) 1/70,* para.15). (b) The decision may turn on the power to issue (in the older terminology) an order of mandamus *(Mountview,* above 693, *per* Lord Parker C.J.) or in order to defeat an application for (in the older terminology) certiorari *(R. v Medical Appeal Tribunal Ex p. Gilmore* [1957] 1 QB 574 at 582–3, *per* Denning L.J.). (c) Some cases depend upon the interpretation of the particular legislation being considered *(ibid.* at 694, *per* Lord Parker C.J., discussing the *Givaudan* case). (d) Other cases turn on the fact that the remedy sought is discretionary (judicial review is discretionary) and the supplementary reasons show that no purpose would be served by granting it (*R. v Westminster City Council Ex p. Ermakov* [1996] 2 All E.R. 302 at 313).

There are, however, cases in which the reasoning can be applied to the child      **2.66** support jurisdiction. First, in *Yusuf v Aberplace Ltd* [1984] I.C.R. 850 at 853–854 the Employment Appeal Tribunal exercised the power, established by a line of authority, to remit a case to what is now called an employment tribunal for findings or reasons that were incomplete or obscure to be amplified. This power is based on the principle that a tribunal is not *functus officio* until adequate reasons have been given sufficient to tell the parties why they have won or lost. There is some support for this reasoning in *R(I) 18/61*, para.11 where the lack of adequate reasons was held to render the tribunal's decision a nullity. It is, however, usually said that a tribunal is *functus officio* as soon as its decision is promulgated (*Re Suffield and Watts Ex p. Brown* [1886–1890] All E.R. Rep.276 at 278, *per* Fry L.J.). This was the approach taken by the Employment Appeal Tribunal in *Reuben v Brent London Borough Council* [2000] I.C.R. 102. However, its reasoning is not consistent with the practice recommended and followed in other areas of law by the Divisional Court and the Court of Appeal. The Court of Appeal has confirmed that it is permissible to ask an employment tribunal to supplement reasons that it has already given (*Barke v SEETEC Business Technology Centre Ltd, The Times*, May 26, 2005). Second, in *Howarth*, above, Lord Denning suggested that, if the inadequacy of a Medical Appeal Tribunal's reasons had been the only error of law, it might have been possible to send the case back to the tribunal for the reasons to be better stated, but he did not cite any authority or explain any basis on which the court might have made the order. Third, the approach of the Court of Appeal in *English v Emery Reimbold and Strick Ltd* [2002] 3 All E.R. 385 at paras 22–25 favoured obtaining an amplification of reasons in preference to incurring the expense of an appeal.

It is possible to extract from the authorities some general principles which the Commissioners might apply were they to adopt this approach. It would mainly be used to confirm and elucidate a tribunal's reasons; only in exceptional circumstances would the tribunal be allowed to correct or add to the reasoning rather than merely elucidate the reasons (*R. v Westminster County Council Ex p. Ermakov* [1996] 2 All E.R. 302 at 315, *per* Hutchison L.J.). It would not be permissible to provide a subsequent rationalisation of the decision (*R. v Parole Board Ex p. Gittens, The Times*, February 3, 1994). The reasoning could not be supplemented if it were grossly flawed (*R. v Lambeth London Borough Council Housing Benefit Review Board Ex p. Harrington, The Times*, December 10, 1996). Nor can it be used to supplement the reasons substantially (*VK v Norfolk County Council, The Times*, January 6, 2005). This approach can only be applied if the case is identified sufficiently quickly for the chairman to have a realistic chance of recalling the case in sufficient detail to supply the additional information required (*Flannery v Halifax Estate Agencies Ltd* [2000] 1 All E.R. 373 at 379).

(xvi) *Breaches of natural justice* Although a breach of natural justice in a tribunal's decision may lead to a judicial review of a decision, it will also make the decision wrong in law and liable to be set aside on appeal (*R(I) 28/61; R(I) 29/61*, para.11; *R(A) 1/72*, para.5; *R(SB) 11/83*, para.13(5)). In theory "a tribunal which denies natural justice to one of the parties before it deprives itself of jurisdiction" (*Al-Mehdawi v Secretary of State for the Home Department* [1989] 3 All E.R. 843 at 849, *per* Lord Bridge). For a discussion of natural justice, see the introductory general note to the Appeals Regulations. Allegations of a breach of natural justice "should normally only be considered if 'full and sufficient particulars are set out in the grounds of appeal'" (*R(M) 1/89*, para.12). Usually there will only be an error of law if the breach of natural justice concerned the tribunal's proceedings rather than those of the officer who made the decision under appeal, although there may be exceptional cases in which appeal proceedings may not cure the breach by the officer (*CDLA 14884/96*, para.12).

Under s.11, Tribunals and Inquiries Act 1992, an appeal is allowed if information that was not put to a tribunal by a clerk might realistically have led to a different decision, even if that was not certain or even likely (*W. v Special Needs Appeal Tribunal, The Times*, December 12, 2000).

A procedural impropriety may be waived. This means that a party cannot rely on an incident as a breach of natural justice who has said or done anything inconsistent with treating the incident in this way. Usually a waiver arises from a failure to complain of what occurred. The sooner the complaint is made the less likely that the delay will give rise to a waiver. In most cases, there will be a waiver if a complaint is not made at the time the incident occurred or swiftly afterwards. However, there is no rule about the time when a complaint must be made if a waiver is to be avoided, it depends on the circumstances of the case. See the analysis in *CDLA 2559/97*, paras 28–31.

(xvii) *Cases analogous to breaches of natural justice* There are cases which are analogous to natural justice. They are cases where material information has not been provided to the tribunal by a party to the proceedings. See *R(SB) 18/83*, para.11 and *R(CS) 1/99*, para.18, both of which must be read in light of the reasoning and authorities in *CCS 16817/96*, para.10.

(xviii) *Record of proceedings* There will not automatically be a mistake of law if the chairman did not make a proper record of proceedings under reg.55 of the Appeals Regulations or the record is not available on the appeal to the Commissioner. There will be an error of law if in a particular case it is necessary to have regard to the evidence given at the hearing or to any contention put forward at the hearing in order to decide if the case falls within any of the recognised heads of error of law. The lack of any, or of an adequate, record of proceeding is not of itself and in all circumstances an error of law (*De Silva v Social Security Commissioner*, para.13, unreported, April 5, 2001). The absence of, or deficiency in, the notes of proceedings is not a separate head of error of law. However, it is subsidiary to, and protective and supportive of, the recognised heads of error of law in that it will be an error of law if it prevents a Commissioner from deciding whether a particular error of law has been shown. See *CDLA 1389/97*, para.18. This reasoning is in line with the protective approach taken by the courts to prevent their jurisdiction being defeated by a failure of a tribunal to provide a complete and correct record (*R. v Medical Appeal Tribunal Ex p. Gilmore* [1957] 1 QB 574 at 582–3, *per* Denning L.J.).

(xix) *Lengthy delay between hearing and decision* The tribunal's decision will usually be given on the day of the hearing. In exceptional cases, it may be given later, but the time between the hearing and the making of the decision should be short. Whether or not a delay or the effect of a delay raises a question of law was considered by the Court of Appeal in *Bangs v Connex South Eastern Ltd* [2005] 2 All ER 316. The basic position is that delay is a matter of fact that does not allow an appeal to a Commissioner, whose jurisdiction depends on there being a question of law (*ibid.* at para.43(2)). However, the delay will give rise to a question of law if it results in the decision being perverse (*ibid.* para.43(4)) or in a serious procedural error or material irregularity depriving a party to the proceedings of the substance of the right to a fair hearing such that it would be unfair or unjust to allow the decision to stand (*ibid.* para.43(7)). It is also possible that, outside the Commissioners' appeal structure, a delay may be a violation of the Convention right to a fair hearing that requires the party to be compensated in damages (*ibid.* para.43(2)).

(xx) *Delay in writing statement* A delay in providing a statement of the tribunal's reasons for decision is not of itself a mistake of law. However, the delay may make the tribunal's reasons unreliable, which will make them inadequate and therefore wrong in law. It may be possible to produce reliable reasons a long time after the hearing. Whether or not this is possible will depend on factors like (a) whether the hearing was oral or on the papers, (b) the detail in the record of proceedings, and (c) any personal notes the chairman may have retained. It is not appropriate to find that a tribunal's decision was wrong in law on this ground without giving the chairman the chance to explain how the tribunal's reasoning was reproduced. See *R (IS) 5/04* and *CJSA 322/01*, paras 8–9. In *CDLA 1761/02*, the Commissioner emphasised the relevance to this issue of reg.53(4) of the Appeals Regulations, which sets out the time limits for requesting a statement.

A chairman should approach an application for leave to appeal in two stages. The first question is to consider whether the application raises a question of law as discussed above. If it does raise a question of law, the chairman should then ask whether the question is an arguable one. There must be material in the case indicating that a sensible argument could be made that an error has occurred (*R(SB) 1/81*, para.4). If the case is an arguable one, leave to appeal should be given. The chairman is not required to decide whether or not the appeal will succeed. That is a matter for the Commissioner. Moreover, the granting of leave does not amount to an admission by the chairman that the decision is wrong. This is emphasised by the wording of the subsection which refers to a question, rather than to an error, of law. In order to obtain leave to appeal, the appellant must show that the case raises a question of law, and in order to succeed in the appeal, he or she must show that there has been an error of law.

If a question of law arises but there appears no realistic prospect of it being resolved in favour of the applicant for leave, it may still be appropriate to grant leave, for example if the issue is a controversial one or one that otherwise merits a decision by a Commissioner (*Smith v Cosworth Casting Processes Ltd* [1997] 4 All E.R. 840). Chairmen and Commissioners will, however, need to bear in mind that it may be unfair to raise false hopes or to impose on an individual the burden of resolving an issue for the benefit of others.

A chairman should as a general rule avoid commenting on an application for leave to appeal and merely grant or refuse the application. It is always inappropriate to attempt to justify the tribunal's decision, and it is quite wrong to try to supplement the reasoning of the tribunal (*CSDLA 336/00*, para.8). However, there are exceptional cases in which comment is appropriate and useful. There are at least two. The first case is where the chairman grants leave for a reason which is different from that advanced by the claimant in the application for leave to appeal. This will alert the Commissioner to the basis upon which leave has been given. The second case is where there is an allegation of impropriety in the conduct of the tribunal. A record of the chairman's recollection of events given relatively close to the events in question is useful, especially if the matters were not recorded in the notes of proceedings. See *CIS 4652/77*, para.13, Applications for leave to appeal which raise allegations of misconduct should be lodged as soon as possible after the hearing (*R(I) 11/63*, para.20).

*Subsection (3)*

This subsection gives Commissioners powers to make findings of fact, to give a final decision and to refer the case back to a tribunal or the Secretary of State. It is to be hoped that they will use these powers whenever possible to ensure that a final decision is made at as early a date as possible, especially in view of the possibility of a delay being prejudicial to the welfare of a child (see the general note to s.2). In particular, these powers allow Commissioners to give their own decisions in cases where the decision of the tribunal was clearly the correct one to reach, but it has to be set aside on appeal because of some technical defect. The Commissioners might

**2.67**

be able to avoid the need to allow an appeal by making use of the powers, discussed above, to require a tribunal to amplify its findings and reasoning.

However, Commissioners generally regard their fact-finding powers as subordinate to their principal duty of determining whether or not the tribunal's decision was wrong in law. There is a spectrum of cases and the Commissioners' willingness to substitute a decision for that of the tribunal without directing a rehearing depends on where the case falls on that spectrum. At one end of the spectrum is an appeal determined on a paper hearing that involves only the evaluation of the evidence by a legally qualified panel member. Commissioners readily substitute their own findings of fact in those circumstances. At the other end of the spectrum is the appeal determined following an oral hearing at which all the parties gave evidence and were questioned by panel members with particular expertise. In those circumstances, Commissioners are especially reluctant to reverse findings of fact and evaluations of evidence, including credibility. See *CCS 4473/00*, para.7.

A Commissioner has power under para.(b) without making any fresh or further findings of fact where the decision to be given is the same as that which the tribunal gave but for some technical reason had no power to give. In other words, this paragraph requires only that *any necessary* findings be made. See *CIS 16701/96*, para.25.

It is not expedient under para.(b) for a Commissioner to deal with a case simply because the appeal tribunal to which the case would otherwise be referred is not independent under the Convention right in Art.6(1) of the European Convention on Human Rights (*CI 4421/00*). If a case is referred to the Secretary of State or to a tribunal under para.(b) or (c), the officer or the tribunal has no power to deal with issues other than those referred by the Commissioner (*Aparau v Iceland Frozen Foods plc* [2000] 1 All E.R. 228). It is important to identify whether or not a Commissioner has referred the case generally, so that all issues arising may be considered, or has referred the case only on specific issues, so that others must not be considered. This limitation only applies to a tribunal rehearing a case after a successful appeal to a Commissioner. It does not affect the power of the Secretary of State to consider immediately issues outside the terms of the Commissioner's decision on a revision or supersession.

In view of the powers in paras (a) and (b), there is no scope or need for dismissing an appeal if the tribunal made a mistake in law that could not have affected the outcome (*CIS 869/99*, para.8, declining to follow *Bache v Essex County Council* [2000] 2 All E.R. 847).

By remitting a case to an appeal tribunal for rehearing, the Commissioner cures any procedural error that affected the decision set aside (*Pumahaven Ltd v Williams, The Times*, May 16, 2003).

*Subsection (4)*

The decision originally appealed against will be the decision made under s.18 or s.46. This subsection refers to the child support officer who made the decision, and not to the officer who made the decision which was reviewed.

*Subsections (6) and (7)*

The regulations are contained in Pt II of the Child Support Commissioners (Procedure) Regulations.

*Subsections (8)*

This procedural provision gives a Commissioner the discretion to deal with questions which might have been dealt with by an officer but have not been. It saves the need to refer the matter back to an officer for decision. It is, therefore, a convenient provision and is to be interpreted liberally (*R(I) 4/75*, para.12). It is unfortunate that no equivalent power has been conferred on tribunals.

The Commissioner should consider the application of this subsection in two stages. The first issue to decide is whether the question falls within the subsection. If the question does fall within the subsection, the next issue is whether, and if so in what manner, the discretion should be exercised.

*The scope of the subsection*

The subsection only applies to questions which would otherwise fall to be determined by a child support officer. It cannot be used for question which are for the Secretary of State or for the courts. It can be used to cure the Commissioner's lack of jurisdiction, for example, where there has been no decision on a s.18 review, the Commissioner can give a decision. It can also be used where there are questions which are relevant to the decision which the Commissioner will have to make, but which have not been dealt with by a child support officer. It is, therefore, an appropriate way to correct errors made by a child support officer *(R(F) 1/72)*. This is subject to the requirement, discussed below, that the question should first arise in the course of the appeal.

This subsection can, therefore, operate in two ways. It can operate to give a Commissioner power to make decisions which there would otherwise have been power to make, provided the matter had come to the Commissioner via a child support officer's decision. It can also operate to give a Commissioner power to make decisions which there would otherwise have been no power to take, for example, to review a child support officer's decision.

Only questions first arising in the course of the appeal are covered. This is ambiguous. It could mean that the question must first be identified in the course of the appeal, or it could mean that the question only arises because of the course taken by the appeal. The Commissioners have given it the first meaning. It has been held that a question does not arise until there is some doubt on the matter *(R. v Westminster (City) Borough Rent Officer Ex p. Rendall* [1973] 3 All E.R. 119 at 122, *per* Lord Denning M.R.).

The question must first arise in the course of *the appeal*. This is wider than "the course of *the hearing*" *(CS 101/86*, para.5). The question might, therefore, arise at an interlocutory stage or during an adjournment, as well as during the hearing itself.

The question must *first* arise in the course of the appeal and not before. So if the question has arisen and a decision has been given in respect of it whether by a child support officer or by a tribunal, it does not fall within this subsection *(CS 104/87*, para.2).

In the context of this power "consideration" means fully considered to the point where the officer is in a position to reach a decision *(CIS 807/92*, para.6). Consequently a case falls within the subsection if an officer has embarked upon consideration of a question, but has not fully considered it.

*The discretion*

The subsection gives a discretion to deal with a case. It must be exercised judicially. The Commissioner will consider (i) the wishes of the parties and (ii) whether a decision on the question is essential to the disposal of the case, but (iii) the paramount consideration will be the requirements of natural justice. It does not override the need for all parties to have a proper chance to prepare for, and to present evidence and argument on every matter in issue in, the appeal. The Commissioner will need to consider whether the parties have had an adequate chance to deal with the question. An important factor will be whether there has been notice of the question, either in the written submission of the child support officer or in the grounds stated in the notice of appeal or in some other document which has been sent to all the parties *(R(I) 4/75*, para.12). If the parties have not had a proper chance to deal with the question, the Commissioner may decide to adjourn to allow time for this. Alternatively, the Commissioner may decide to exercise the discretion against dealing with the question.

The Commissioner is under a duty to consider whether or not to exercise the discretion in respect of any question first arising (*R(IS) 15/93*, para.8). It will, though, seldom be an error of law for a Commissioner to decline to deal with a question first arising, although there may be cases in which the question is so clearly tied to the matter being considered that the Commissioner is effectively under a duty, given the technical nature of the jurisdiction and the inquistiorial approach, to deal with the question (*CIS 21/93*, para.13).

## Appeal from Child Support Commissioner on question of law

2.68  **25.**—(1) An appeal on a question of law shall lie to the appropriate court from any decision of a Child Support Commissioner.

(2) No such appeal may be brought except—

(a) with leave of the Child Support Commissioner who gave the decision or, where regulations made by the Lord Chancellor so provide, of a Child Support Commissioner selected in accordance with the regulations; or

(b) if the Child Support Commissioner refuses leave, with the leave of the appropriate court.

(3) An application for leave to appeal under this section against a decision of a Child Support Commissioner ("the appeal decision") may only be made by—

(a) a person who was a party to the proceedings in which the original decision, or appeal decision, was given;

(b) the Secretary of State; or

(c) any other person who is authorised to do so by regulations made by the Lord Chancellor.

[¹(3A) The Child Support Commissioner to whom an application for leave to appeal under this section is made shall specify as the appropriate court either the Court of Appeal or the Court of Session.

(3B) In determining the appropriate court, the Child Support Commissioner shall have regard to the circumstances of the case, and in particular the convenience of the persons who may be parties to the appeal.]

(4) In this section—

"appropriate court" [², except in subsections (3A) and (3B), means the court specified in accordance with those subsections], and

"original decision" means the decision to which the appeal decision in question relates.

(5) The Lord Chancellor may by regulations make provision with respect to—

(a) the manner in which and the time within which applications must be made to a Child Support Commissioner for leave under this section; and

(b) the procedure for dealing with such applications.

(6) Before making any regulations under subsection (2), (3) or (5), the Lord Chancellor shall consult the Lord Advocate.

AMENDMENTS

1. Paragraph 8(2) of Sch.3 to the 1995 Act (September 4, 1995).
2. Paragraph 8(3) of Sch.3 to the 1995 Act (September 4, 1995).

GENERAL NOTE

*Subsection (1)*

The meaning of "question of law" is discussed in the general note to s.24(1).     2.69

*Subsections (2), (3) and (5)*

The provisions are contained in reg.25 of the Child Support Commissioners (Procedure) Regulations.

For the test applied by the Court of Appeal on an application for permission to appeal, see the general note to reg.30 of the Social Security Commissioners (Procedure) Regulations 1999.

Permission may be given on limited grounds. The Court of Appeal's consideration is then confined to those grounds. See *Fieldman v Markovitch, The Times,* July 31, 2001. A grant of leave by the Court of Appeal may be reconsidered, but only for a compelling reason (*Hunt v Peasegood, The Times,* July 26, 2000).

Even if a Commissioner has granted leave, the Court of Appeal may refuse to hear the appeal if it is based on grounds that were not put to the Commissioner (*Secretary of State for Work and Pensions v Hughes (A Minor)*, reported as *R(DLA) 1/04*).

*Subsection (4)*

The Family Proceedings (Amendment) Rules 1993 amend the Family Proceedings Rules 1991 (as amended) to insert r.3.23 which applies to any appeal to the Court of Appeal.

**Disputes about parentage**

**26.**—(1) Where a person who is alleged to be a parent of the child     2.70
with respect to whom an application for a [⁹maintenance calculation] has been made [⁸(or treated as made)] ("the alleged parent") denies that he is one of the child's parents, [³the Secretary of State] shall not make a [⁹maintenance calculation] on the assumption that the alleged parent is one of the child's parents unless the case falls within one of those set out in subsection (2).

(2) The Cases are—

[⁶CASE A1

Where—
- (a) the child is habitually resident in England and Wales;
- (b) the Secretary of State is satisfied that the alleged parent was married to the child's mother at some time in the period beginning with the conception and ending with the birth of the child; and
- (c) the child has not been adopted.

CASE A2

Where—
- (a) the child is habitually resident in England and Wales;
- (b) the alleged parent has been registered as father of the child under section 10 or 10A of the Births and Deaths Registration Act 1953, or in any register kept under section 13 (register of births and

still-births) or section 44 (Register of Corrections Etc) of the Registration of Births, Deaths and Marriages (Scotland) Act 1965, or under Article 14 or 18(1)(b)(ii) of the Births and Deaths Registration (Northern Ireland) Order 1976; and

(c) the child has not subsequently been adopted.

## CASE A3

Where the result of a scientific test (within the meaning of section 27A) taken by the alleged parent would be relevant to determining the child's parentage, and the alleged parent—

(a) refuses to take such a test; or

(b) has submitted to such a test, and it shows that there is no reasonable doubt that the alleged parent is a parent of the child.]

## CASE A

Where the alleged parent is a parent of the child in question by virtue of having adopted him.

## CASE B

Where the alleged parent is a parent of the child in question by virtue of an order under section 30 of the Human Fertilisation and Embryology Act 1990 (parental orders in favour of gamete donors).

## [7CASE B1

Where the Secretary of State is satisfied that the alleged parent is a parent of the child in question by virtue of section 27 or 28 of that Act (meaning of "mother" and of "father" respectively).]

## CASE C

Where—

(a) either—

(i) a declaration that the alleged parent is a parent of the child in question (or a declaration which has that effect) is in force under section [555A or] 56 of the Family Law Act 1986 [1or Article 32 of the Matrimonial and Family Proceedings (Northern Ireland) Order 1989] (declarations of parentage); or

(ii) a declarator by a court in Scotland that the alleged parent is a parent of the child in question (or a declarator which has that effect) is in force; and

(b) the child has not subsequently been adopted.

[10. . .]

## CASE E

Where—

(a) the child is habitually resident in Scotland;

(b) [⁴the Secretary of State] is satisfied that one or other of the presumptions set out in section 5(1) of the Law Reform (Parent and Child) (Scotland) Act 1986 applies; and

(c) the child has not subsequently been adopted.

## CASE F

Where—

(a) the alleged parent has been found, or adjudged, to be the father of the child in question—

   (i) in proceedings before any court in England and Wales which are relevant proceedings for the purposes of section 12 of the Civil Evidence Act 1968 [²or in proceedings before any court in Northern Ireland which are relevant proceedings for the purposes of section 8 of the Civil Evidence Act (Northern Ireland) 1971]; or

   (ii) in affiliation proceedings before any court in the United Kingdom, (whether or not he offered any defence to the allegation of paternity) and that finding or adjudication still subsists; and

(b) the child has not subsequently been adopted.

(3) In this section—

"adopted" means adopted within the meaning of Part IV of the Adoption Act 1976 [¹¹or Chapter 4 of Part 1 of the Adoption and Children Act 2002] or, in relation to Scotland, Part IV of the Adoption (Scotland) Act 1978;

and

"affiliation proceedings", in relation to Scotland, means any action of affiliation and aliment.

AMENDMENTS

1. Article 13 of the Children (Northern Ireland Consequential Amendments) Order 1995 (November 4, 1996).

2. Article 13 of the Children (Northern Ireland Consequential Amendments) Order 1995 (November 4, 1996).

3. Paragraph 31(1) of Sch.7 to the Social Security Act 1998 (June 1, 1999).

4. Paragraph 31(2) of Sch.7 to the Social Security Act 1998 (June 1, 1999).

5. Paragraph 12 of Sch.8 to the 2000 Act.

6. Section 15(1) of the 2000 Act (January 31, 2001 under art.2(1) of the Commencement No.5 Order 2000).

7. Section 15(2) of the 2000 Act (January 31, 2001 under art.2(1) of the Commencement No.5 Order 2000).

8. Paragraph 11(8) of Sch.3 to the 2000 Act (March 3, 2003 under art.3 of, and the Schedule to, the Commencement No.12 Order 2003).

9. Section 1(2)(a) of the 2000 Act (March 3, 2003 under art.3 of, and the Schedule to, the Commencement No.12 Order 2003).

10. Section 85 of, and Sch.9 to, the 2000 Act.
11. Section 139(1) of, and Sch.3 para.81 to, the Adoption and Children Act 2002.

DEFINITIONS

2.71    "child": see s.55.
"maintenance calculation": see s.54.
"parent": see s.54.

GENERAL NOTE

2.72    This section allows the Secretary of State, appeal tribunals and Child Support Commissioners to make decisions on parentage in specified, clear-cut cases only. More contentious cases are within the jurisdiction of the court which has the appropriate powers to handle them. Section 27 gives the Secretary of State power to apply to a court for a declaration as to parentage. If the ground of appeal is that a person is or is not a parent of a child, the tribunal must decide that it has no jurisdiction as the appeal lies in such a case to the court: see s.45 below and the general note thereto.

In at least one case a small claims court has awarded compensation to a man who was wrongly approached by the Child Support Agency regarding maintenance for a child (*The Times*, April 8, 1994).

For the position where the issue of parentage is raised for the first time on appeal to a tribunal, see the Child Support Appeals (Jurisdiction of Courts) Order 2002 and the Child Support Appeals (Jurisdiction of Courts) (Scotland) Order 2003, and the general note to art.4 of the former Order.

If an application is made in respect of two children and parentage is disputed in respect of one of them, the application may proceed in respect of the other child without waiting for the dispute to be resolved (*CCS 2626/99*).

*Subsection (2)*

*Case F*

A person may have been found to be a parent of a child even if parentage was not in issue in the relevant proceedings, but such a finding is only relevant where it is open to the "parent" to make an application to the court for the finding to be set aside (*R(CS) 2/98*, para.24). If the finding is set aside, this will not always imply a finding that the person is not a parent of the child, and a reference under s.27 below may be necessary in order to determine the issue (*ibid.*, para.24). This question was before the Divisional Court on judicial review, leave having been granted by the Court of Appeal (*R. v Secretary of State for Social Security Ex p. West, The Times*, November 26, 1998). In granting leave, Henry L.J. said that it was arguable that the granting of a parental responsibility order in favour of a father on an application in which paternity was not contested was sufficient to bring the case within Case F. The parties were the same as in *R(CS) 2/98*, but the judicial review is not against the Commissioner's decision.

For the meaning of "relevant proceedings" for the purposes of s.12, Civil Evidence Act 1968 and the difficulties with the references to the various sections therein, see Halsbury, *Statutes* (4th ed.), Vol.17, pp.184–185. See also subs.(5) of this section.

## [¹Applications for declaration of parentage under Family Law Act 1986

**27.**—(1) This section applies where—       2.73

(a) an application for a maintenance calculation has been made (or is treated as having been made), or a maintenance calculation is in force, with respect to a person ("the alleged parent") who denies that he is a parent of a child with respect to whom the application or calculation was made or treated as made;

(b) the Secretary of State is not satisfied that the case falls within one of those set out in section 26(2); and

(c) the Secretary of State or the person with care makes an application for a declaration under section 55A of the Family Law Act 1986 as to whether or not the alleged parent is one of the child's parents.

(2) Where this section applies—

(a) if it is the person with care who makes the application, she shall be treated as having a sufficient personal interest for the purposes of subsection (3) of that section; and

(b) if it is the Secretary of State who makes the application, that subsection shall not apply.

(3) This section does not apply to Scotland.]

AMENDMENT

1. Paragraph 13 of Sch.8 to the 2000 Act.

DEFINITIONS

"child": see s.55.
"maintenance calculation": see s.54.
"parent": see s.54.
"person with care": see s.3(3).

GENERAL NOTE

Section 55A of the Family Law Act 1986 was inserted by s.83(2) of the 2000 Act.     2.74
It reads:

### "Declarations of parentage

**55A**—(1) Subject to the following provisions of this section, any person may apply to the High Court, a county court or a magistrates' court for a declaration as to whether or not a person named in the application is or was the parent of another person so named.

(2) A court shall have jurisdiction to entertain an application under subsection (1) above if, and only if, either of the persons named in it for the purposes of that subsection—

(a) is domiciled in England and Wales on the date of the application, or

(b) has been habitually resident in England and Wales throughout the period of one year ending with that date, or

(c) died before that date and either—

    (i)    was at death domiciled in England and Wales, or

>    (ii)   had been habitually resident in England and Wales through-
>            out the period of one year ending with the date of death.
>        (3) Except in a case falling within subsection (4) below, the court shall
>    refuse to hear an application under subsection (1) above unless it considers
>    that the applicant has a sufficient personal interest in the determination of
>    the application (but this is subject to section 27 of the Child Support Act
>    1991).
>        (4) The excepted cases are where the declaration sought is as to
>    whether or not—
>        (a) the applicant is the parent of a named person;
>        (b) a named person is the parent of the applicant; or
>        (c) a named person is the other parent of a named child of the applicant.
>        (5) Where an application under subsection (1) above is made and
>    one of the persons named in it for the purposes of that subsection is a
>    child, the court may refuse to hear the application if it considers that
>    the determination of the application would not be in the best interests
>    of the child.
>        (6) Where a court refuses to hear an application under subsection (1)
>    above it may order that the applicant may not apply again for the same
>    declaration without leave of the court
>        (7) Where a declaration is made by a court on an application under
>    subsection (1) above, the prescribed officer of the court shall notify the
>    Registrar General, in such a manner and within such period as may be
>    prescribed, of the making of that declaration."

The Court of Appeal sent a strong message to courts considering whether to
direct blood tests to establish paternity in *Re H (Paternity: Blood Test)* [1996] 2
F.L.R. 65. While it is clear that a party cannot be ordered to provide a sample, a
refusal to do so when certainty could be established justifies the inference that the
refusal is made to hide the truth. A child has a right, under Art.7 of the UN
Convention on the Rights of the Child, to know the truth about his or her identity
unless his welfare clearly justifies the cover-up. Thus, it is likely that a direction will
normally be given and, if there is a failure to comply, the court is entitled to draw
the appropriate inference, regardless of whether the refusal comes from the parent
with care or the absent parent. This was the approach taken in *F v Child Support
Agency, The Times*, April 9, 1999. A child was born to a wife, but she alleged that F
was the father and not her husband. The normal presumption that the child was her
husband's was rebutted by inferences drawn from F's refusal to provide a blood
sample and hearsay evidence that a DNA test had shown that the husband was not
the child's father. The same approach was taken in *Secretary of State for Work and
Pensions v Jones*, [2004] 1 F.L.R. 282.

## [¹Recovery of fees for scientific tests

2.75     **27A.**—(1) This section applies in any case where—
>        (a) an application for a [³maintenance calculation] has been made [⁴(or
>             treated as made)] or a [³maintenance calculation] is in force;
>        (b) scientific tests have been carried out (otherwise than under a direc-
>             tion or in response to a request) in relation to bodily samples
>             obtained from a person who is alleged to be a parent of a child with
>             respect to whom the application or [⁵calculation] is made [⁶or, as the
>             case may be, treated as made];

(c) the results of the tests do not exclude the alleged parent from being one of the child's parents; and

(d) one of the conditions set out in subsection (2) is satisfied.

(2) The conditions are that—

(a) the alleged parent does not deny that he is one of the child's parents;

(b) in proceedings under [²section 55A of the Family Law Act 1986], a court has made a declaration that the alleged parent is a parent of the child in question; or

(c) in an action under section 7 of the Law Reform (Parent and Child) (Scotland) Act 1986, brought by the Secretary of State by virtue of section 28, a court has granted a decree of declarator of parentage to the effect that the alleged parent is a parent of the child in question.

(3) In any case to which this section applies, any fee paid by the Secretary of State in connection with scientific tests may be recovered by him from the alleged parent as a debt due to the Crown.

(4) In this section—

"bodily sample" means a sample of bodily fluid or bodily tissue taken for the purpose of scientific tests;

"direction" means a direction given by a court under section 20 of the Family Law Reform Act 1969 (tests to determine paternity);

"request" means a request made by a court under section 70 of the Law Reform (Miscellaneous Provisions) (Scotland) Act 1990 (blood and other samples in civil proceedings); and

"scientific tests" means scientific tests made with the object of ascertaining the inheritable characteristics of bodily fluids or bodily tissue.

(5) Any sum recovered by the Secretary of State under this section shall be paid by him into the Consolidated Fund.]

AMENDMENTS

1. Section 21 of the 1995 Act (September 4, 1995).

2. Paragraph 14 of Sch.8 to the 2000 Act.

3. Section 1(2)(a) of the 2000 Act (March 3, 2003 under art.3 of, and the Schedule to, the Commencement No.12 Order 2003).

4. Paragraph 11(9)(a) of Sch.3 to the 2000 Act (March 3, 2003 under art.3 of, and the Schedule to, the Commencement No.12 Order 2003).

5. Section 1(2)(b) of the 2000 Act (March 3, 2003 under art.3 of, and the Schedule to, the Commencement No.12 Order 2003).

6. Paragraph 11(9)(b) of Sch.3 to the 2000 Act (March 3, 2003 under art.3 of, and the Schedule to, the Commencement No.12 Order 2003).

## Power of Secretary of State to initiate or defend actions of declarator: Scotland

**28.**—[¹(1) Subsection (1A) applies in any case where—

(a) an application for a [⁴maintenance calculation] has been made [⁵or treated as made], or a [⁴maintenance calculation] is in force, with respect to a person ("the alleged parent") who denies that he is a parent of a child with respect to whom the application [⁶was made or treated as made or the calculation was made]; and

2.76

(b) [³the Secretary of State] is not satisfied that the case falls within one of those set out in section 26(2).

(1A) In any case where this subsection applies, the Secretary of State may bring an action for declarator of parentage under section 7 of the Law Reform (Parent and Child) (Scotland) Act 1986.]

(2) The Secretary of State may defend an action for declarator of non-parentage or illegitimacy brought by a person named as the alleged parent in an application for a [⁴maintenance calculation] [²or in a [⁴maintenance calculation] which is in force].

(3) This section applies to Scotland only.

AMENDMENTS

1. Section 20(6) of the 1995 Act (September 4, 1995).
2. Section 20(7) of the 1995 Act (September 4, 1995).
3. Paragraph 33 of Sch.7 to the Social Security Act 1998 (June 1, 1999).
4. Section 1(2)(a) of the 2000 Act (March 3, 2003 under art.3 of, and the Schedule to, the Commencement No.12 Order 2003).
5. Paragraph 11(10)(a) of Sch.3 to the 2000 Act (March 3, 2003 under art.3 of, and the Schedule to, the Commencement No.12 Order 2003).
6. Paragraph 11(10)(b) of Sch.3 to the 2000 Act (March 3, 2003 under art.3 of, and the Schedule to, the Commencement No.12 Order 2003).

DEFINITIONS

2.77     "child": see s.55.
"maintenance calculation": see s.54.
"parent"; see s.54.

*[¹Decisions and appeals dependent on other cases*

## Decisions involving issues that arise on appeal in other cases

2.78     **28ZA.**—(1) This section applies where—
(a) a decision by the Secretary of State falls to be made under section 11, 12, 16 or 17 [²or with respect to a reduced benefit decision under section 46]; or
[³(b) an appeal is pending against a decision given in relation to a different matter by a Child Support Commissioner or a court.]

(2) If the Secretary of State considers it possible that the result of the appeal will be such that, if it were already determined, it would affect the decision in some way—
(a) he need not, except in such cases or circumstances as may be prescribed, make the decision while the appeal is pending;
(b) he may, in such cases or circumstances as may be prescribed, make the decision on such basis as may be prescribed.

(3) Where the Secretary of State acts in accordance with subsection (2)(b), following the determination of the appeal he shall if appropriate revise his decision (under section 16) in accordance with that determination.

(4) For the purposes of this section, an appeal against a decision is pending if—

(a) an appeal against the decision has been brought but not determined;

(b) an application for leave to appeal against the decision has been made but not determined; or

(c) in such circumstances as may be prescribed, an appeal against the decision has not been brought (or, as the case may be, an application for leave to appeal against the decision has not been made) but the time for doing so has not yet expired.

(5) In paragraphs (a), (b) and (c) of subsection (4), any reference to an appeal, or an application for leave to appeal, against a decision includes a reference to—

(a) an application for, or for leave to apply for, judicial review of the decision under section 31 of the Supreme Court Act 1981; or

(b) an application to the supervisory jurisdiction of the Court of Session in respect of the decision.]

AMENDMENTS

1. Section 43 of the Social Security Act 1998 (subss.(2)(b) and (4)(c) March 4, 1999; otherwise June 1, 1999).

2. Paragraph 11(11)(a) of Sched.3 to the 2000 Act (March 3, 2003 under art.3 of, and the Schedule to, the Commencement No.12 Order 2003).

3. Paragraph 11(11)(b) of Sched.3 to the 2000 Act (March 3, 2003 under art.3 of, and the Schedule to, the Commencement No.12 Order 2003).

## [¹Appeals involving issues that arise on appeal in other cases

**28ZB.**—(1) This section applies where—                                    2.79

[²(a) an appeal ("appeal A") in relation to a decision or the imposition of a requirement falling within section 20(1) is made to an appeal tribunal, or from an appeal tribunal to a Child Support Commissioner;]

(b) an appeal ("appeal B") is pending against a decision given in a different case by a Child Support Commissioner or a court.

(2) If the Secretary of State considers it possible that the result of appeal B will be such that, if it were already determined, it would affect the determination of appeal A, he may serve notice requiring the tribunal or Child Support Commissioner—

(a) not to determine appeal A but to refer it to him; or

(b) to deal with the appeal in accordance with subsection (4).

(3) Where appeal A is referred to the Secretary of State under subsection (2)(a), following the determination of appeal B and in accordance with that determination, he shall if appropriate—

(a) in a case where appeal A has not been determined by the tribunal, revise (under section 16) his decision which gave rise to that appeal; or

(b) in a case where appeal A has been determined by the tribunal, make a decision (under section 17) superseding the tribunal's decision.

(4) Where appeal A is to be dealt with in accordance with this subsection, the appeal tribunal or Child Support Commissioner shall either—

(a) stay appeal A until appeal B is determined; or

(b) if the tribunal or Child Support Commissioner considers it to be in the interests of the appellant to do so, determine appeal A as if—

    (i)

    (ii) the issues arising on appeal B had been decided in the way that was most unfavourable to the appellant.

In this subsection "the appellant" means the person who appealed or, as the case may be, first appealed against the decision [³or the imposition of the requirement] mentioned in subsection (1)(a).

(5) Where the appeal tribunal or Child Support Commissioner acts in accordance with subsection (4)(b), following the determination of appeal B the Secretary of State shall, if appropriate, make a decision (under section 17) superseding the decision of the tribunal or Child Support Commissioner in accordance with that determination.

(6) For the purposes of this section, an appeal against a decision is pending if—

(a) an appeal against the decision has been brought but not determined;

(b) an application for leave to appeal against the decision has been made but not determined; or

(c) in such circumstances as may be prescribed, an appeal against the decision has not been brought (or, as the case may be, an application for leave to appeal against the decision has not been made) but the time for doing so has not yet expired.

(7) In this section—

(a) the reference in subsection (1)(a) to an appeal to a Child Support Commissioner includes a reference to an application for leave to appeal to a Child Support Commissioner; and

(b) any reference in paragraph (a), (b) or (c) of subsection (6) to an appeal, or to an application for leave to appeal, against a decision includes a reference to—

    (i) an application for, or for leave to apply for, judicial review of the decision under section 31 of the Supreme Court Act 1981; or

    (ii) an application to the supervisory jurisdiction of the Court of Session in respect of the decision.

(8) Regulations may make provision supplementing that made by this section.]

AMENDMENTS

1. Section 43 of the Social Security Act 1998 (subs.(6)(c) March 4, 1999; otherwise June 1, 1999).

2. Paragraph 11(12)(a) of Sch.3 to the 2000 Act (March 3, 2003 under art.3 of, and the Schedule to, the Commencement No.12 Order 2003).

3. Paragraph 11(12)(b) of Sch.3 to the 2000 Act (March 3, 2003 under art.3 of, and the Schedule to, the Commencement No.12 Order 2003).

*[¹Cases of error*

## Restrictions on liability in certain cases of error

2.80    **28ZC.**—(1) Subject to subsection (2), this section applies where—

(a) the effect of the determination, whenever made, of an appeal to a Child Support Commissioner or the court ("the relevant determination") is that the adjudicating authority's decision out of which the appeal arose was erroneous in point of law; and

(b) after the date of the relevant determination a decision falls to be made by the Secretary of State in accordance with that determination (or would, apart from this section, fall to be so made)—

   (i) with respect to an application for a [7maintenance calculation] (made after the commencement date) [2or one treated as having been so made, or under section 46 as to the reduction of benefit];

   (ii) as to whether to revise, under section 16, [3any decision (made after the commencement date) referred to in section 16 (1A)]; or

   (iii) on an application under section 17 (made after the commencement date) [4any decision (made after the commencement date) referred to in section 17(1)].

(2) This section does not apply where the decision of the Secretary of State mentioned in subsection (1)(b)—

(a) is one which, but for section 28ZA(2)(a), would have been made before the date of the relevant determination; or

(b) is one made in pursuance of section 28ZB(3) or (5).

(3) In so far as the decision relates to a person's liability [5or the reduction of a person's benefit] in respect of a period before the date of the relevant determination, it shall be made as if the adjudicating authority's decision had been found by the Commissioner or court not to have been erroneous in point of law.

(4) Subsection (1)(a) shall be read as including a case where—

(a) the effect of the relevant determination is that part or all of a purported regulation or order is invalid; and

(b) the error of law made by the adjudicating authority was to act on the basis that the purported regulation or order (or the part held to be invalid) was valid.

(5) It is immaterial for the purposes of subsection (1)—

(a) where such a decision as is mentioned in paragraph (b)(i) falls to be made; or

(b) where such a decision as is mentioned in paragraph (b)(ii) or (iii) falls to be made on an application under section 16 or (as the case may be) section 17,

whether the application was made before or after the date of the relevant determination.

(6) In this section—

"adjudicating authority" means the Secretary of State, or a child support officer [6or, in the case of a decision made on a referral under s.28D(1)(b), an appeal tribunal];

"the commencement date" means the date of the coming into force of section 44 of the Social Security Act 1998; and

"the court" means the High Court, the Court of Appeal, the Court of Session, the High Court or Court of Appeal in Northern Ireland, the House of Lords or the Court of Justice of the European Community.

(7) The date of the relevant determination shall, in prescribed cases, be determined for the purposes of this section in accordance with any regulations made for that purpose.

(8) Regulations made under subsection (7) may include provision—

(a) for a determination of a higher court to be treated as if it had been made on the date of a determination of a lower court or a Child Support Commissioner; or

(b) for a determination of a lower court or a Child Support Commissioner to be treated as if it had been made on the date of a determination of a higher court.]

AMENDMENTS

1. Section 44 of the Social Security Act 1998 (to allow regulations to be made, March 4, 1999; otherwise June 1, 1999).

2. Paragraph 11(13)(a) of Sch.3 to the 2000 Act (March 3, 2003 under art.3 of, and the Schedule to, the Commencement No.12 Order 2003).

3. Paragraph 11(13)(b) of Sch.3 to the 2000 Act (March 3, 2003 under art.3 of, and the Schedule to, the Commencement No.12 Order 2003).

4. Paragraph 11(13)(c) of Sch.3 to the 2000 Act (March 3, 2003 under art.3 of, and the Schedule to, the Commencement No.12 Order 2003).

5. Paragraph 11(13)(d) of Sch.3 to the 2000 Act (March 3, 2003 under art.3 of, and the Schedule to, the Commencement No.12 Order 2003).

6. Paragraph 11(13)(e) of Sch.3 to the 2000 Act (March 3, 2003 under art.3 of, and the Schedule to, the Commencement No.12 Order 2003).

7. Section 1(2)(a) of the 2000 Act (March 3, 2003 under art.3 of, and the Schedule to, the Commencement No.12 Order 2003).

## [¹Correction of errors and setting aside of decisions

2.81    **28ZD.**—(1) Regulations may make provision with respect to—

(a) the correction of accidental errors in any decision or record of a decision given under this Act; and

(b) the setting aside of any such decision in a case where it appears just to set the decision aside on the ground that—

(i) a document relating to the proceedings in which the decision was given was not sent to, or was not received at an appropriate time by, a party to the proceedings or a party's representative or was not received at an appropriate time by the body or person who gave the decision; or

(ii) a party to the proceedings or a party's representative was not present at a hearing related to the proceedings.

(2) Nothing in subsection (1) shall be construed as derogating from any power to correct errors or set aside decisions which is exercisable apart from regulations made by virtue of that subsection.]

AMENDMENT

1. Section 44 of the Social Security Act 1998 (March 4, 1999 to allow regulations to be made; otherwise June 1, 1999).

GENERAL NOTE

*Subsection (2)*

2.82    The inherent powers of statutory tribunals was discussed by the Court of Appeal in *Akewushola v Secretary of State for the Home Department* [2000] 2 All E.R. 148 at

153–154. The court recognised that tribunals had an inherent power to correct accidental errors, but considered that they did not have an inherent power to rescind or review their own decisions. It seems, therefore, that there is no power apart from regulations made under subs.(1) for an appeal tribunal to set aside its decision.

*[¹ Variations*

## Application for variation of usual rules for calculating maintenance

**28A.**—(1) Where an application for a maintenance calculation is made under section 4 or 7, or treated as made under section 6, the person with care or the non-resident parent or (in the case of an application under section 7) either of them or the child concerned may apply to the Secretary of State for the rules by which the calculation is made to be varied in accordance with this Act.                                            2.83

(2) Such an application is referred to in this Act as an "application for a variation".

(3) An application for a variation may be made at any time before the Secretary of State has reached a decision (under section 11 or 12(1)) on the application for a maintenance calculation (or the application treated as having been made under section 6).

(4) A person who applies for a variation—

(a) need not make the application in writing unless the Secretary of State directs in any case that he must; and

(b) must say upon what grounds the application is made.

(5) In other respects an application for a variation is to be made in such manner as may be prescribed.

(6) Schedule 4A has effect in relation to applications for a variation.]

AMENDMENT

1. Section 5(2) of the 2000 Act (for the purpose of making regulations, November 10, 2000 under art.2(1) of, and Pt I of the Schedule to, the Commencement No.3 Order 2000; March 3, 2003 under art.3 of, and the Schedule to, the Commencement No.12 Order 2003).

DEFINITIONS

"application for a variation"; see s.54.
"child": see s.55.
"maintenance calculation": see s.54.
"non-resident parent": see s.54.
"person with care": see s.54.
"prescribed": see s.54.

GENERAL NOTE

The variation scheme reaches the parts that Sch.1 to the Act cannot reach (*CCS     2.84
8/00*, para.6). The statutory provisions are supplemented by the Variation Regulations.

By agreeing to a variation, the Secretary of State is permitted to alter the maintenance calculation. This can only be done on a small number of restrictively defined grounds. The scope of the scheme is not discretionary. There is a discretionary element in the scheme, but it only applies to qualify the application of the defined grounds. Some of the grounds for a variation relate to matters covered by Sch.1; others relate to matters outside that Schedule.

Uniquely in the child support scheme, the Secretary of State may either determine an application for a variation or refer it to an appeal tribunal (s.28D(1)).

### Subsection (1)

This is the main statutory authority under which a variation may be agreed by the Secretary of State. The application may be made before a decision is made on an application for a maintenance calculation (subs.(3)) or when a maintenance calculation is in force (s.28G(1)). If an application is made under s.28 G(1), this section applies as modified by reg.3 of the Child Support (Variations) (Modification of Statutory Provisions) Regulations 2000.

### Subsection (3)

This subsection allows an application for a variation to be made before the application for a maintenance calculation has been determined. Section 28G provides for an application for a variation when a maintenance calculation is in force.

If an application is made under this subsection, an interim maintenance decision may be made under s.12(2) above, which in turn may be subject to a regular payments condition under s.28C below.

### Subsection (4)(b)

The Secretary of State may treat an application made on one ground as if it were made on a different ground: see reg.9(8) of the Variation Regulations.

### Subsection (5)

Regulations 4 and 5 of the Variation Regulations have been made under this enabling power.

## [¹Preliminary consideration of applications

2.85     **28B.**—(1) Where an application for a variation has been duly made to the Secretary of State, he may give it a preliminary consideration.

(2) Where he does so he may, on completing the preliminary consideration, reject the application (and proceed to make his decision on the application for a maintenance calculation without any variation) if it appears to him—

(a) that there are no grounds on which he could agree to a variation;

(b) that he has insufficient information to make a decision on the application for the maintenance calculation under section 11 (apart from any information needed in relation to the application for a variation), and therefore that his decision would be made under section 12(1); or

(c) that other prescribed circumstances apply.]

AMENDMENT

1. Section 5(2) of the 2000 Act (for the purpose of making regulations, November 10, 2000 under art.2(1) of, and Pt I of the Schedule to, the Commencement No.3 Order 2000; March 3, 2003 under art.3 of, and the Schedule to, the Commencement No.12 Order 2003).

DEFINITIONS

"application for a variation"; see s.54.　　　　　　　　　　　　　　　　2.86
"maintenance calculation": see s.54.
"prescribed": see s.54.

GENERAL NOTE

This section allows the Secretary of State to dispose of an application without detailed consideration, if it becomes clear that it cannot succeed. None of the conditions set out in this section or in regulations made under it involve discretionary considerations.

If an application is made under s.28G(1), this section applies as modified by reg.4 of the Child Support (Variations) (Modification of Statutory Provisions) Regulations 2000.

*Subsection (2)(c)*
Regulation 6 of the Variation Regulations has been made under this enabling power.

## [¹Imposition of regular payments condition

**28C.**—(1) Where—　　　　　　　　　　　　　　　　　　　　　　　　2.87
  (a) an application for a variation is made by the non-resident parent; and
  (b) the Secretary of State makes an interim maintenance decision,
the Secretary of State may also, if he has completed his preliminary consideration (under section 28B) of the application for a variation and has not rejected it under that section, impose on the non-resident parent one of the conditions mentioned in subsection (2) (a "regular payments condition").
  (2) The conditions are that—
  (a) the non-resident parent must make the payments of child support maintenance specified in the interim maintenance decision;
  (b) the non-resident parent must make such lesser payments of child support maintenance as may be determined in accordance with regulations made by the Secretary of State.
  (3) Where the Secretary of State imposes a regular payments condition, he shall give written notice of the imposition of the condition and of the effect of failure to comply with it to—
  (a) the non-resident parent;
  (b) all the persons with care concerned; and
  (c) if the application for the maintenance calculation was made under section 7, the child who made the application.
  (4) A regular payments condition shall cease to have effect—
  (a) when the Secretary of State has made a decision on the application for a maintenance calculation under section 11 (whether he agrees to a variation or not);
  (b) on the withdrawal of the application for a variation.
  (5) Where a non-resident parent has failed to comply with a regular payments condition, the Secretary of State may in prescribed circumstances refuse to consider the application for a variation, and instead reach his decision under section 11 as if no such application had been made.

(6) The question whether a non-resident parent has failed to comply with a regular payments condition is to be determined by the Secretary of State.

(7) Where the Secretary of State determines that a non-resident parent has failed to comply with a regular payments condition he shall give written notice of his determination to—

(a) that parent;

(b) all the persons with care concerned; and

(c) if the application for the maintenance calculation was made under section 7, the child who made the application.]

AMENDMENT

1. Section 5(2) of the 2000 Act (for the purpose of making regulations, November 10, 2000 under art.2(1) of, and Pt I of the Schedule to, the Commencement No.3 Order 2000; March 3, 2003 under art.3 of, and the Schedule to, the Commencement No.12 Order 2003).

DEFINITIONS

2.88    "application for a variation": see s.54.
"child": see s.55.
"child support maintenance": see s.54.
"interim maintenance decision"; see s.54.
"maintenance calculation": see s.54.
"non-resident parent": see s.54.
"person with care": see s.54.
"prescribed": see s.54.

GENERAL NOTE

2.89    If an application is made under s.28G(1), this section applies as modified by reg.5 of the Child Support (Variations) (Modification of Statutory Provisions) Regulations 2000.

*Paragraph (1)*

This section is discretionary and subject to s.2 above. It only applies if the Secretary of State (a) has made an interim maintenance decision, (b) has given the application a preliminary consideration under s.28B above and (c) has not rejected the application under that consideration.

If the section applies, the Secretary of State is authorised to impose a condition on the non-resident parent to maintain regular payment of child support maintenance. This prevents a non-resident parent from using an outstanding application for a variation as an excuse for not making payments of child support maintenance. This is balanced by the power to fix a lower amount than that set by the interim maintenance decision (subs.(2)(b)). Notice of the imposition of a regular payments condition must be given under subs.(3) to the parties to the application.

*Subsection (2)*

Regulation 31(1) of the Variation Regulations has been made under the enabling power in para.(b).

*Subsection (4)*

A regular payments condition can last no longer than the application in respect of which it was made. So, this subsection provides that it ceases to have effect when the application is determined or withdrawn. Withdrawal is authorised by reg.5(1) of the Variation Regulations.

If the Secretary of State refuses to consider the application further under subss.(5)–(7), the regular payments condition does not cease to have effect. It only ceases to have effect once the Secretary of State has reached a decision under s.11 above.

*Subsection (5)*

The consequence of failing to comply with a regular payments condition is that the Secretary of State may refuse to consider the application and reach a decision under s.11 above as if the application had not been made. Notice of this determination must be given under subs.(7).

The application does not cease to have effect as soon as the Secretary of State refuses to consider it further: see the general note to subs.(4). That leaves open the possibility that the non-resident parent might try to remedy the breach by complying with the condition and paying any arrears that have built up. There is no provision for the Secretary of State to consider the application again if that happens, but neither is there anything to prohibit it. In practice, it is likely that there would not be the time for the non-resident parent to repent before the Secretary of State had made a decision under s.11. Although it is not expressly stated, the application must at that point be no longer capable of being considered.

Regulation 31(2) and (3) of the Variation Regulations have been made under the enabling power in this subsection. Regulation 31(3) contains the prescribed circumstances in which the Secretary of State may refuse to consider the application further.

*Subsection (7)*

Notice of the refusal to consider the application further must be given to the parties to the application. Reasons do not have to be given; they will be apparent from the circumstances.

## [¹Determination of applications

**28D.**—[²(1) Where an application for a variation has not failed, the Secretary of State shall, in accordance with the relevant provisions of, or made under, this Act—

    (a) either agree or not to a variation, and make a decision under section 11 or 12(1); or

    (b) refer the application to an appeal tribunal for the tribunal to determine what variation, if any, is to be made.]

(2) For the purposes of subsection (1), [³an application for a variation] has failed if—

    (a) it has [⁴. . . ] been withdrawn; or

    (b) the Secretary of State has rejected it on completing a preliminary consideration under section 28B [⁴or

    (c) the Secretary of State has refused to consider it under section 28C(5).]

(3) In dealing with [³an application for a variation] which has been referred to it under subsection (1)(b), [⁵an appeal tribunal] shall have the same powers, and be subject to the same duties, as would the Secretary of State if he were dealing with the application.]

2.90

AMENDMENTS

1. Section 4 of the 1995 Act (December 2, 1996).
2. Section 5(3)(a) of the 2000 Act (for the purpose of making regulations, November 10, 2000 under art. 2(1) of, and Pt I of the Schedule to, the Commencement No.3 Order 2000; March 3, 2003 under art.3 of, and the Schedule to, the Commencement No.12 Order 2003).
3. Section 5(3)(b) of the 2000 Act (for the purpose of making regulations, November 10, 2000 under art.2(1) of, and Pt I of the Schedule to, the Commencement No.3 Order 2000; March 3, 2003 under art.3 of, and the Schedule to, the Commencement No.12 Order 2003).
4. Section 5(3)(c) of the 2000 Act (for the purpose of making regulations, November 10, 2000 under art.2(1) of, and Pt I of the Schedule to, the Commencement No.3 Order 2000; March 3, 2003 under art.3 of, and the Schedule to, the Commencement No.12 Order 2003).
5. Paragraph 36 of Sch.7 to the Social Security Act 1998 (June 1, 1999).

DEFINITIONS

**2.91**     "application for a variation": see s.54.
"appeal tribunal": see s.54.

GENERAL NOTE

**2.92**     If an application is made under s.28G(1), this section applies as modified by reg.6 of the Child Support (Variations) (Modification of Statutory Provisions) Regulations 2000.

*Subsection (1)*
The Secretary of State must determine the application or refer it to an appeal tribunal. This is a unique power in the child support scheme, indeed it is the only instance of the power of referral to an appeal tribunal. It is used in the more complex and controversial disputes. The appeal tribunal may consider two or more applications for a variation together: see reg.45 of the Appeals Regulations.

A referral under para.(b) is a referral of the application. The application may be amended by notice in writing to the Secretary of State under reg.5 of the Variation Regulations, although see the general note to subs.(3) below. This allows the addition of a new head to the application before the case is decided by the appeal tribunal. Even if the additional head is contained in a letter addressed to the tribunal, that will be sufficient notice to the Secretary of State who is a party to the proceedings before the tribunal. So, the tribunal has jurisdiction to deal with the additional head, provided that the principles of natural justice and the Convention rights of the parties are observed. See *R(CS)3/01*, para.50.

An appeal tribunal may, if it considers it appropriate, consider a referral at the same time as an appeal under s.20 above against an interim maintenance decision: see Sch.4A, para.5(3) below.

*Subsection (3)*
On a referral the appeal tribunal has the same powers and duties as the Secretary of State. This *may* allow the appeal tribunal to receive notice of the amendment or withdrawal of an application under reg.5 of the Variation Regulations.

## [¹Matters to be taken into account

**28E.**—(1) In determining [²whether to agree to a variation], the Secretary of State shall have regard both to the general principles set out in subsection (2) and to such other considerations as may be prescribed.

**2.93**

(2) The general principles are that—

(a) parents should be responsible for maintaining their children whenever they can afford to do so;

(b) where a parent has more than one child, his obligation to maintain any one of them should be no less of an obligation than his obligation to maintain any other of them.

(3) In determining [²whether to agree to a variation], the Secretary of State shall take into account any representations made to him—

(a) by the person with care or [⁴non-resident parent] concerned; or

(b) where the application for the current [⁵calculation] was made under section 7, by either of them or the child concerned.

(4) In determining [²whether to agree to a variation], no account shall be taken of the fact that—

(a) any part of the income of the person with care concerned is, or would be if [³the Secretary of State agreed to a variation], derived from any benefit; or

(b) some or all of any child support maintenance might be taken into account in any manner in relation to any entitlement to benefit.

(5) In this section "benefit" has such meaning as may be prescribed.]

AMENDMENTS

1. Section 5 of the 1995 Act (to allow regulations to be made October 14, 1996; otherwise December 2, 1996).

2. Section 5(4)(a) of the 2000 Act (for the purpose of making regulations, November 10, 2000 under art.2(1) of, and Pt I of the Schedule to, the Commencement No.3 Order 2000; March 3, 2003 under art.3 of, and the Schedule to, the Commencement No.12 Order 2003).

3. Section 5(4)(b) of the 2000 Act (for the purpose of making regulations, November 10, 2000 under art.2(1) of, and Pt I of the Schedule to, the Commencement No.3 Order 2000; March 3, 2003 under art.3 of, and the Schedule to, the Commencement No.12 Order 2003).

4. Paragraph 11(2) of Sch.3 to the 2000 Act (March 3, 2003 under art.3 of, and the Schedule to, the Commencement No.12 Order 2003)

5. Section 1(2)(b) of the 2000 Act (March 3, 2003 under art.3 of, and the Schedule to, the Commencement No.12 Order 2003).

DEFINITIONS

"application for a variation": see s.54.

**2.94**

"benefit": see reg.32 of the Variation Regulations.

"child": see s.55.

"child support maintenance": see s.54.

"non-resident parent": see s.54.

"parent": see s.54.

"person with care": see s.54.

"prescribed": see s.54.

GENERAL NOTE

If an application is made under s.28G(1), this section applies as modified by reg.6 of the Child Support (Variations) (Modification of Statutory Provisions) Regulations 2000.

*Subsections (1)–(4)*

**2.95**     The principles set out in these subsections control the determining of an application for a variation. They, therefore, operate at the stage of applying the law to the facts of the case and are not relevant in interpreting the legislation, although the interpretation must be made in the context of the general scheme of the child support legislation of which these principles are part. They are not free-standing, but infuse all relevant stages of the determination. They are, therefore, relevant to the just and equitable test and to any judgment-based element of any of the heads under which a variation may be agreed.

The general principles in subs.(2) apply only to parents as defined by s.54 below and to children as defined by s.55 below. Expenses relating to other children may, however, constitute a special expense under reg.11 of the Variation Regulations. Also there is a wider requirement, in s.28F(2)(a) below, when considering the just and equitable condition, to have regard to the welfare of any child likely to be affected by a direction.

The requirement under subs.(3) to take into account representations is complemented by reg.21(2)(g) of the Variation which excludes representations other than by relevant persons from being taken into account in the application of the just and equitable test.

*Subsection (4)*

Tribunals will need to be careful to distinguish between para.(a) of this subsection and reg.21(1)(a)(i) of the Variation Regulations.

*Subsection (5)*

The prescribed benefits are contained in reg.32 of the Variation Regulations.

## [¹Agreement to a variation

**2.96**     **28F.**—(1)  The Secretary of State may agree to a variation if—

(a)  he is satisfied that the case is one which falls within one or more of the cases set out in Part I of Schedule 4B or in regulations made under that Part; and

(b)  it is his opinion that, in all the circumstances of the case, it would be just and equitable to agree to a variation.

(2)  In considering whether it would be just and equitable in any case to agree to a variation, the Secretary of State—

(a)  must have regard, in particular, to the welfare of any child likely to be affected if he did agree to a variation; and

(b)  must, or as the case may be must not, take any prescribed factors into account, or must take them into account (or not) in prescribed circumstances.

(3)  The Secretary of State shall not agree to a variation (and shall proceed to make his decision on the application for a maintenance calculation without any variation) if he is satisfied that—

(a)  he has insufficient information to make a decision on the application for the maintenance calculation under section 11, and therefore that his decision would be made under section 12(1); or

(b) other prescribed circumstances apply.

(4 Where the Secretary of State agrees to a variation, he shall—

(a) determine the basis on which the amount of child support maintenance is to be calculated in response to the application for a maintenance calculation (including an application treated as having been
made); and

(b) make a decision under section 11 on that basis.

(5) If the Secretary of State has made an interim maintenance decision,
it is to be treated as having been replaced by his decision under section 11,
and except in prescribed circumstances any appeal connected with it
(under section 20) shall lapse.

(6) In determining whether or not to agree to a variation, the Secretary
of State shall comply with regulations made under Part II of Schedule 4B.]

AMENDMENT

1. Section 5(5) of the 2000 Act (for the purpose of making regulations,
November 10, 2000 under art.2(1) of, and Pt I of the Schedule to, the
Commencement No.3 Order 2000; March 3, 2003 under art.3 of, and the Schedule
to, the Commencement No.12 Order 2003).

DEFINITIONS

"child": see s.55.                                                         **2.97**
"child support maintenance": see s.54.
"interim maintenance decision": see s.54
"maintenance calculation": see s.54
"prescribed": see s.54.

GENERAL NOTE

If an application is made under s.28G(1), this section applies as modified by reg.7     **2.98**
of the Child Support (Variations) (Modification of Statutory Provisions)
Regulations 2000.

*Subsection (1)(a)*
The cases are set out in regs.10–14 and 18–20 of the Variation Regulations.

*Subsection (1)(b)*
This paragraph imposes a general requirement that applies to all cases: it must be
just and equitable to agree to a variation. It is supplemented by subs.(2). There can
be no definitive list of considerations which must be taken into account (*Crake v
Supplementary Benefits Commission* [1982] 1 All E.R. 498 at 502, *per* Woolf J.). Still
less is it possible to give definitive guidance on the weight to be given to any
particular consideration.

Although the duty under this paragraph is expressed as a requirement that it be
just and equitable to agree to *a* variation, in practice this must refer to the effect that
the particular variation being considered would have under the Variation
Regulations.

The phrase "just and equitable" is used in a number of statutory contexts and
there are many authorities dealing with its interpretation in those contexts. It is,
however, the nature of the test that no general principles emerge from them beyond
the comments of Salmon L. J. in *Hanning v Maitland (No.2)* [1970] 1 All E.R. 812
at 819:

"I do not think that the words 'just and equitable' . . . are used in the Act as terms of art [i.e. as having a definite and fixed legal meaning]. Nor are they capable of precise defintion. The words should be interpreted broadly to mean just what they say."

The Secretary of State and an appeal tribunal must reach a positive conclusion that it would be just and equitable to agree to a variation. In *R(CS) 3/01*, the tribunal recorded that it did not have information on important and relevant matters, but that there was no reason to suspect that the giving of the direction would not be just and equitable. The Commissioner held that this was not sufficient (para.43). He also held that the tribunal had been wrong to apply a burden of proof, as the balance of probabilities had no application to the exercise of judgment involved (para.44). He left open whether the burden might apply to the finding of facts on which the judgment was based (*ibid.*).

The effect of satisfying a case for a variation is specified in the Variation Regulations in absolute terms. The Regulations make no allowance for a partial implementation of a variation, for example by allowing only part of the special expenses incurred by a non-resident parent. That appears to have the effect that a variation must be agreed to in full or not at all. A Commissioner has held that the just and equitable requirement is not as blunt an instrument as that and that it can be used to override the apparently absolute terms of the Regulations (*CCS 3151/99*, para.23). The case before the Commissioner concerned the amended departure direction scheme under which partial effect was expressly permitted. However, he was commenting on the effect of the original scheme, under which the effect of a departure direction was stated in absolute terms similar to the present Variation Regulations.

The application of the just and equitable requirement involves an exercise of judgment. This affects the approach of Commissioners to the adequacy of reasons given by tribunals. The reasons must be sufficient to show that the tribunal approached the exercise in the correct way and that its application was not perverse. It is not necessary for the reasons to include comment on every consideration on which there was evidence. It is sufficient for tribunals to deal with those considerations that were particularly significant in the circumstances of the case. See *CCS 3543/98*, paras 32 and 36.

*Subsection (2)(a)*

This duty to have regard to the welfare of any child likely to be affected by a variation is in similar terms to s.2 of the Act. There are two possible reasons why it has been included. The first reason is for emphasis. The second reason is that the tests like the just and equitable requirement may not be a disrectionary power for the purposes of s.2 (*George Mitchell (Chesterhall) Ltd v Finney Lock Seeds Ltd* [1983] 2 All E.R. 737 at 743 *per* Lord Bridge).

The one difference between this provision and s.2 is that this refers to a child likely to be affected if a *variation* is given whereas s.2 refers to a child likely to be affected by a *decision*. This may have the effect of excluding from this provision how a child would be affected if a variation were not given. In practice though, this is unlikely to be significant, because the provision does not exclude the broad power given by subs.(1)(b), under which that could be taken into account.

*Subsection (2)(b)*

Regulation 21 of the Variation Regulations has been made under this enabling power.

*Subsection (3)*

Regulation 30 of the Variations Regulations contains the prescribed circumstances.

*Subsection (5)*

This subsection deals with the possibility that an interim maintenance decision was made pending the determination of the application for a variation. If a variation is agreed to, a decision is made under s.11 of the Act. That decision replaces the interim maintenance decision. If an appeal was made against the interim maintenance decision, it lapses when the s.11 decision is made. However, a new right of appeal arises against the s.11 decision. No disadvantage arises, because the effective date of the s.11 decision will be the same as for the interim maintenance decision.

## [¹Variations: revision and supersession

**28G.**—(1) An application for a variation may also be made when a maintenance calculation is in force.    2.99

(2) The Secretary of State may by regulations provide for—

(a) section 16, 17 and 20; and

(b) section 28A to 28F and Schedules 4A and 4B, to apply with prescribed modifications in relation to such applications.

(3) The Secretary of State may by regulations provide that, in prescribed cases (or except in prescribed cases), a decision under section 17 made otherwise than pursuant to an application for a variation may be made on the basis of a variation agreed to for the purposes of an earlier decision without a new application for a variation having to be made.]

AMENDMENT

1. Section 7 of the 2000 Act (subs.(2)—for the purpose of making regulations, November 10, 2000 under art.2(1) of, and Pt I of the Schedule to, the Commencement No. 3 Order 2000 and for other purposes January 1, 2001 under art. 2(2) and Pt II of the Schedule to that Order. Other provisions: March 3, 2003 under art. 3 of, and the Schedule to, the Commencement No. 12 Order 2003).

DEFINITIONS

"appeal tribunal": see s.54.    2.100
"application for a variation": see s.54.
"maintenance calculation": see s.54.
"prescribed": see s.54.

GENERAL NOTE

*Subsection (1)*

Section 28A(3) allows an application for a variation to be made before the    2.101
Secretary of State has reached a decision on an application for a maintenance calculation. This subsection allows an application for a variation to be made when a maintenance calculation is in force. The application takes effect as an application for a revision of the maintenance calculation decision under s.16 above (see reg.3A(1)(a)(ii) of the Appeals Regulations) or for a supersession under s.17 (see reg.6A(6) of the Appeals Regulations).

*Subsection (2)(b)*

The provisions covered by this paragraph are drafted to apply to applications for a variation made under s.28A(3) above before a decision on an application for a maintenance calculation has been made. The Child Support (Variations)

(Modification of Statutory Provisions) Regulations 2000 have been made under the enabling power in this paragraph to modify those provisions so that they apply to applications under subs.(1) of this section.

*Subsection (3)*

Regulation 7 of the Variation Regulations has been made under this enabling power.

Sections 28H and 28I were repealed by para.11(14) of Sch.3 and by Sch.9 to the 2000 Act. Article 3 of, and the Schedule to, the Commencement No.12 Order 2003 provided that they ceased to have effect from March 3, 2003 for the purposes of the cases there specified.

## [¹Voluntary payments

**2.102**

**28J.** (1) This section applies where—
  (a) a person has applied for a maintenance calculation under section 4(1) or 7(1), or is treated as having applied for one by virtue of section 6;
  (b) the Secretary of State has neither made a decision under section 11 or 12 on the application, nor decided not to make a maintenance calculation; and
  (c) the non-resident parent makes a voluntary payment.
  (2) A "voluntary payment" is a payment—
  (a) on account of child support maintenance which the non-resident parent expects to become liable to pay following the determination of the application (whether or not the amount of the payment is based on any estimate of his potential liability which the Secretary of State has agreed to give); and
  (b) made before the maintenance calculation has been notified to the non-resident parent or (as the case may be) before the Secretary of State has notified the non-resident parent that he has decided not to make a maintenance calculation.
  (3) In such circumstances and to such extent as may be prescribed—
  (a) the voluntary payment may be set off against arrears of child support maintenance which accrued by virtue of the maintenance calculation taking effect on a date earlier than that on which it was notified to the non-resident parent;
  (b) the amount payable under a maintenance calculation may be adjusted to take account of the voluntary payment.
  (4) A voluntary payment shall be made to the Secretary of State unless he agrees, on such conditions as he may specify, that it may be made to the person with care, or to or through another person.
  (5) The Secretary of State may by regulations make provision as to voluntary payments, and the regulations may in particular—
  (a) prescribe what payments or descriptions of payment are, or are not, to count as "voluntary payments";
  (b) prescribe the extent to which and circumstances in which a payment, or a payment of a prescribed description, counts.]

AMENDMENT

1. Section 20(1) of the 2000 Act (for the purpose of making regulations, November 10, 2000 under art.2(1) of, and Pt I of the Schedule to, the

Commencement No.3 Order 2000; March 3, 2003 under art.5 of, and the Schedule to, the Commencement No.12 Order 2003).

DEFINITIONS

"child support maintenance": see s.54.  2.103
"maintenance calculation": see s.54.
"non-resident parent": see s.54.
"prescribed": see s.54.
"voluntary payment": see s.54.

GENERAL NOTE

This section makes provision to ameliorate the problems for non-resident parents that arise when arrears build up while their maintenance liability is being calculated. It provides a method that protects the non-resident parent without loss to the person with care. It avoids the need to meet the cost of delay to be met from public funds, as under s.27(7)(b) of the 2000 Act.

Only arrears that arise on the initial application for a maintenance calculation are covered. Arrears that arise from a delay in dealing with revisions and supersessions are not.

The impact of the arrears is lessened by the non-resident parent making voluntary payments pending the Secretary of State's decision on the application. Those payments are then offset against arrears of child support maintenance. If the amount of the voluntary payments exceed the arrears, they are dealt with under s.41B(1A) and (7) below as overpaid child support maintenance.

The Child Support (Voluntary Payments) Regulations 2000 supplement the provisions of this section. They prescribe the acceptable methods of payment (reg.3(a)), the matters to which the payments may be attributed (reg.3(b)) and the evidence that is acceptable as proof of payment (reg.4). The scheme is limited to payments made after the effective date of the maintenance calculation that was made or would have been made had the Secretary of State decided not to make one. The payments may be made to the person with care or to someone else, like an electricity supplier.

*Collection and enforcement*

**Collection of child support maintenance**

**29.**—(1) The Secretary of State may arrange for the collection of any  2.104
child support maintenance payable in accordance with a [¹maintenance calculation] where—
  (a) the [²calculation] is made by virtue of section 6; or
  (b) an application has been made to the Secretary of State under section 4(2) or 7(3) for him to arrange for its collection.

(2) Where a [¹maintenance calculation] is made under this Act, payments of child support maintenance under the [²calculation] shall be made in accordance with regulations made by the Secretary of State.

(3) The regulations may, in particular, make provision—
  (a) for payments of child support maintenance to be made—
    (i) to the person caring for the child or children in question;
    (ii) to, or through, the Secretary of State; or
    (iii) to, or through, such other person as the Secretary of State may, from time to time, specify;

(b) as to the method by which payments of child support maintenance are to be made;

(c) as to the intervals at which such payments are to be made;

(d) as to the method and timing of the transmission of payments which are made, to or through the Secretary of State or any other person, in accordance with the regulations;

(e) empowering the Secretary of State to direct any person liable to make payments in accordance with the [²calculation]

    (i) to make them by standing order or by any other method which requires one person to give his authority for payments to be made from an account of his to an account of another's on specific dates during the period for which the authority is in force and without the need for any further authority from him;

    (ii) to open an account from which payments under the [²calculation] may be made in accordance with the method of payment which that person is obliged to adopt;

(f) providing for the making of representations with respect to matters with which the regulations are concerned.

AMENDMENTS

1. Section 1(2)(a) of the the 2000 Act (March 3, 2003 under art.3 of, and the Schedule to, the Commencement No.12 Order 2003).

2. Section 1(2)(b) of the the 2000 Act (March 3, 2003 under art.3 of, and the Schedule to, the Commencement No.12 Order 2003).

DEFINITIONS

2.105    "child": see s.3(6).
"child support maintenance": see s.3(6).
"maintenance": calculation see s.54.

GENERAL NOTE

*Subsection (1)*

2.106    The Secretary of State may arrange for the collection of child support maintenance in two different cases. First, if the parent with care has been treated as applying for a maintenance calculation under s.6 above, recovery is automatic under s.6(3)(b) and no further application is necessary. Second, where an application for child support maintenance has been made under s.4(1) or 7(1), an application to the Secretary of State may be made under s.4(2) or 7(3). It is possible for parties to have sought a maintenance calculation under these sections, but to make their own private arrangements for collection of the child support maintenance so assessed. In such a case, either party may subsequently apply to use the collection service at a later date.

If collection of child support maintenance is arranged under this section in respect of a qualifying child whose parent with care is a spouse or former spouse to whom periodical payments under a maintenance order are payable, that order is prescribed for the purposes of s.30 by reg.2(b) of the Collection and Enforcement of Other Forms of Maintenance Regulations.

*Subsection (2)*

This subsection applies to payment of child support maintenance generally and not just to cases where collection is being arranged by the Secretary of State under subs.(1). The regulations are contained in Pt II of the Collection and Enforcement Regulations. They deal with the person to whom payment should be made (reg.2), the method, interval and method of transmission of payment and representations about these matters (regs 3 to 6), and notice to the liable person concerning payment (reg.7).

*Subsection (3)*
Payments may be required to be made by the "liable person" (see reg.2(2) and s.31 of the Act): (i) direct to the person caring for the child or children in question, or, where an application was made by a child under s.7, to that child; (ii) to or through the Secretary of State; or (iii) to or through such other person as is specified by the Secretary of State. The liable person and the person entitled to receive the payments will be provided with an opportunity to make representations as to the method of payment, and these will be taken into account when determining how the maintenance is to be paid. The aim is to arrange the most secure approach to payment.

The method of payment will vary according to the particular circumstances in the case. Payment direct by the liable person to the person caring for the child or children may be required to be made by standing order or equivalent, such as direct debit, cheque or postal order, or cash. Although para.(e)(ii) provides for the Regulations to give the Secretary of State the power to direct the liable person to open an account from which payments can be made, reg.3(2) more realistically empowers the Secretary of State to direct the liable person to take all reasonable steps to open an account. There may be situations where a bank or similar institution is not prepared to take a liable person on as a customer, in which case one of the other methods will have to be specified. These provisions may be compared with those under the Maintenance Enforcement Act 1991, where courts are given similar powers to collect maintenance. Under s.1(6) of that Act, the court must first give the debtor an opportunity to open an account, and may, if satisfied that the debtor has failed, without reasonable excuse, to do so, then order him or her to comply. Under s.29 and the regulations, the Secretary of State may require the liable person to take reasonable steps to comply without first offering an opportunity to him or her to do so voluntarily.

The date and intervals of payment will be specified by the Secretary of State, and timed to coincide with the liable person's receipt of salary or wages, with due allowance made for clearance of cheques, etc. Where the payments are made to or through the Secretary of State rather than to the person caring for the child or children, payments may be made to the recipient at different times or intervals from when they are received by the Secretary of State, but only where the Secretary of State is satisfied that it would otherwise cause undue hardship to either the person liable to make the payments or to the person entitled to receive them. For example, the liable person may make payments monthly, but the person caring for the child or children may be paid by the Secretary of State fortnightly.

A notice will be sent to the liable person under reg.7 as to the requirements about payment, as soon as is reasonably practicable after the making of the maintenance assessment and after any change in the requirements referred to in any previous such notice.

Ninety-seven per cent of payments received from absent parents in the financial year 1995–1996 were passed on within 10 working days, but the Secretary of State in any event now pays interest on payments of maintenance not passed on quickly to the person with care (reported in [1996] Fam. Law 344).

## Collection and enforcement of other forms of maintenance

**30.**—(1) Where the Secretary of State is arranging for the collection of any payments under section 29 or subsection (2), he may also arrange for    2.107

the collection of any periodical payments, or secured periodical payments, of a prescribed kind which are payable to or for the benefit of any person who falls within a prescribed category.

[²(2) The Secretary of State may, except in prescribed cases, arrange for the collection of any periodical payments, or secured periodical payments, of a prescribed kind which are payable for the benefit of a child even though he is not arranging for the collection of child support maintenance with respect to that child.]

(3) Where—

(a) the Secretary of State is arranging, under this Act, for the collection of different payments ("the payments") from the same [³non-resident parent];

(b) an amount is collected by the Secretary of State from the [³non-resident parent] which is less than the total amount due in respect of the payments; and

(c) the [³non-resident parent] has not stipulated how that amount is to be allocated by the Secretary of State as between the payments,

the Secretary of State may allocate that amount as he sees fit.

(4) In relation to England and Wales, the Secretary of State may by regulations make provision for sections 29 and 31 to 40 to apply, with such modifications (if any) as he considers necessary or expedient, for the purpose of enabling him to enforce any obligation to pay any amount which he is authorised to collect under this section.

(5) In relation to Scotland, the Secretary of State may by regulations make provision for the purpose of enabling him to enforce any obligation to pay any amount which he is authorised to collect under this section—

(a) empowering him to bring any proceedings or take any other steps (other than diligence against earnings) which could have been brought or taken by or on behalf of the person to whom the periodical payments are payable;

(b) applying sections 29, 31 and 32 with such modifications (if any) as he considers necessary or expedient.

[¹(5A) Regulations made under subsection (1) or (2) prescribing payments which may be collected by the Secretary of State may make provision for the payment to him by such person or persons as may be prescribed of such fees as may be prescribed.]

AMENDMENTS

1. Paragraph 9 of Sch.3 to the 1995 Act.
2. Paragraph 11(15) of Sch.3 to the 2000 Act (March 3, 2003 under art.7(b) of the Commencement No.12 Order 2003).
3. Paragraph 11(2) of Sch.3 to the 2000 Act (March 3, 2003 under art.3 of, and the Schedule to, the Commencement No.12 Order 2003).

DEFINITIONS

2.108 "child": see s.55.
"child support maintenance": see s.3(6).
"non-resident parent": see s.54.
"prescribed": see s.54.

GENERAL NOTE

The payments and categories of persons covered by this section are prescribed by    **2.109**
reg.2 of the Collection and Enforcement of Other Forms of Maintenance
Regulations. In the case of England and Wales, reg.3 applies the provisions of
subs.29(2) and (3) and 31 to 40 to payments covered by this section. In the case of
Scotland, reg.4 provides that the Secretary of State may bring any proceedings or
take any other steps other than diligence against earnings which could have been
taken by or on behalf of the person to whom the payments are payable, and applies
the provisions of subs.29(2) and (3), 31 and 32 to those payments.

This section empowers the Secretary of State to collect periodical payments
ordered by a court, when arranging for the collection of child support maintenance
under the Act. Periodical payments are not defined, but the Regulations (see below)
provide that secured periodical payments are included. The periodical payments
may be to or for the benefit of the person with care who is a spouse or former
spouse, and not just for children.

Magistrates may order that payments of other forms of maintenance be made
through the Agency's collection system where that is already being used in respect
of a maintenance assessment (Child Support Act 1991 (Consequential
Amendments) Order 1994).

*Subsection (1)*

Arrangements for the collection of other forms of maintenance are provided for
by the Collection and Enforcement of Other Forms of Maintenance Regulations.
These prescribe the following periodical payments and persons as covered by
s.30(1):

    (i) Payments under a maintenance order (note, not a maintenance agreement)
        made in relation to a child in accordance with s.8(6) (top-up maintenance);
        s.8(7) (maintenance to cover the costs of education or training); or s.8(8)
        (periodical payments to meet expenses attributable to disability);

   (ii) Periodical payments under a maintenance order (not a maintenance agree-
        ment in England and Wales, but, in Scotland, registered minutes of agree-
        ment are included) payable to or for the benefit of a spouse or former spouse,
        who is the person with care of a child who is a qualifying child in respect of
        whom a child maintenance assessment is in force for which collection has
        been arranged under s.29;

  (iii) Periodical payments under a maintenance order (not an agreement)
        payable to or for the benefit of a former child of the family of the person
        against whom the order is made, and who has his home with the person
        with care.

A child of the family is defined for England and Wales by s.52(1) of the
Matrimonial Causes Act 1973, as amended by Sch.12, para.33 to the Children Act
1989, as:

"in relation to the parties to a marriage . . .

    (a) a child of both of those parties; and

    (b) any other child, not being a child who is placed with those parties as foster
        parents by a local authority or voluntary organisation, who has been treated
        by both of those parties as a child of their family."

Whether a child has been treated as a child of the family is a question of fact judged
objectively (*Teeling v Teeling* [1984] F.L.R. 808). The fact that the husband mistak-
enly believes the child is his does not prevent the child being a child of the family,
if the husband treats the child as such (*W (RJ) v W (SJ)* [1972] Fam.152).

The aim of this third category is to provide a collection mechanism for all the
children having their home with the person with care, and to avoid the situation
where only one or some children are benefiting from the collection service because

they are the subjects of a maintenance assessment, while another or others are dependent upon the court machinery for enforcement.

*Subsection (2)*
This provides that periodical payments for the benefit of a child may be collected even though the Secretary of State is not collecting child support maintenance with respect to that child. This subsection has not been brought into force.

*Subsection (3)*
This provision gives the Secretary of State a discretion to apportion payments between different families to whom the absent parent is liable, as he sees fit. If the absent parent has stipulated how an amount is to be allocated, this would appear to be binding, but it is arguable that it would not be permitted where the absent parent chose to give priority to children whose carer is not a parent in receipt of benefit under s.6, or to a former spouse rather than the children.

*Subsection (4)*
The aim of the section is to enable the Secretary of State to use the same methods of collection and enforcement regardless of the origin of the payments. Hence, reg.3 of the Regulations provides that, in relation to England and Wales, subs.29(2) and (3) and 31 to 40 of the Act and any regulations made under those sections, apply for the purpose of enabling the Secretary of State to enforce any obligation to pay the prescribed forms of maintenance, as modified to provide that references to child support maintenance shall be read as references to periodical payments and references to maintenance assessments as maintenance orders.

*Subsection (5)*
Regulation 4 of the Regulations provides that, in relation to Scotland, the Secretary of State may bring any proceedings and take any other steps (other than diligence against earnings) which could have been brought or taken by or on behalf of the person to whom the periodical payments are payable. Sections 29(2) and (3), 31 and 32 of the Act and any regulations made under those sections, apply as modified to read as if referring to periodical payments and maintenance orders.

These Regulations do not apply to any periodical payments which fall due before the date specified by notice in writing to the absent parent that the Secretary of State is arranging for payments to be collected, and that date shall not be earlier than the date the notice is given (reg.5).

**Deduction from earnings orders**

2.110    **31.**—(1) This section applies where any person ("the liable person") is liable to make payments of child support maintenance.

(2) The Secretary of State may make an order ("a deduction from earnings order") against a liable person to secure the payment of any amount due under the [¹maintenance calculation] in question.

(3) A deduction from earnings order may be made so as to secure the payment of—
   (a) arrears of child support maintenance payable under the [²calculation];
   (b) amounts of child support maintenance which will become due under the [²calculation]; or
   (c) both such arrears and such future amounts.

(4) A deduction from earnings order—

(a) shall be expressed to be directed at a person ("the employer") who has the liable person in his employment; and

(b) shall have effect from such date as may be specified in the order.

(5) A deduction from earnings order shall operate as an instruction to the employer to—

(a) make deductions from the liable person's earnings; and

(b) pay the amounts deducted to the Secretary of State.

(6) The Secretary of State shall serve a copy of any deduction from earnings order which he makes under this section on—

(a) the person who appears to the Secretary of State to have the liable person in question in his employment; and

(b) the liable person.

(7) Where—

(a) a deduction from earnings order has been made; and

(b) a copy of the order has been served on the liable person's employer, it shall be the duty of that employer to comply with the order; but he shall not be under any liability for non-compliance before the end of the period of 7 days beginning with the date on which the copy was served on him.

(8) In this section and in section 32 "earnings" has such meaning as may be prescribed.

AMENDMENTS

1. Section 1(2)(a) of the 2000 Act (March 3, 2003 under art.3 of, and the Schedule to, the Commencement No.12 Order 2003).

2. Section 1(2)(b) of the 2000 Act (March 3, 2003 under art.3 of, and the Schedule to, the Commencement No.12 Order 2003).

DEFINITIONS

"child support maintenance": see s.3(6).  **2.111**
"maintenance calculation": see s.54.
"non-resident parent": see s.54.
"prescribed": see s.54.

GENERAL NOTE

The enforcement of a liability to pay child support maintenance is a matter for the   **2.112**
Secretary of State and not for the person with care. In securing the enforcement of a liability to pay, the Secretary of State must first consider whether or not a deduction from earnings order under this section is appropriate. If it is appropriate, one must be made and further action can only be taken if it proves ineffective (s.33(1)(b)(ii)). If it is inappropriate, any default in payment of child support maintenance allows the Secretary of State to proceed to the next step, which is to apply for a liability order from a magistrates' court or sheriff under s.33. This opens the way for steps to be taken to recover the maintenance. In England and Wales, these steps are distress and sale, garnishee proceedings and a charging order (ss.35 and 36). If these steps are unsuccessful, a warrant for commitment to prison may be issued under s.40. In Scotland, the relevant steps are arrestment and action of furthcoming or sale (s.38).

A deduction from earnings order operates as an instruction to the liable person's employer to deduct amounts from his or her earnings and pay these to the Secretary of State. It is similar to attachment of earnings in England and Wales (earnings arrestment in Scotland). As with attachment of earnings orders, as amended by the Maintenance Enforcement Act 1991 ss.1(4)(b) and 2(3)(d), an order can be made before the liable person has fallen into arrears. Nonetheless, such an order is intended to be used only when other methods have failed or appear likely to fail. The Secretary of State will first have tried to deal with arrears by means of agreement with the liable person or by trying a new method of payment (see s.41 below). A deduction from earnings order is also commonly made when an interim maintenance assessment is imposed. The limitations of the deduction from earnings order are that it can only be used where the liable person is employed and that it is not appropriate if the person changes jobs frequently. The fact that a person's earnings fluctuate is not a bar to the making of a deduction of earnings order (*R. v York Magistrates' Court Ex p. Grimes, The Times*, June 27, 1997). Regulations providing for the detailed arrangements are made under s.32.

Previous overpayments of child support maintenance are only relevant to the issue whether an absent parent is in arrears if they were expressly made to cover future liability (*R. v Secretary of State for Social Security Ex p. Newmarch Singh* [2000] 2 F.L.R. 664).

Where a deduction from earnings order is made in Great Britain and the liable person works for an employer in Northern Ireland, or vice versa, the deduction from earnings order will have effect in the territory in which the liable person is working, as if made under the provision for that territory. Any appeal in connection with the order shall be made under the provision for the territory in which the liable person is resident (Sch.1, paras 10 and 12 to the Child Support (Northern Ireland Reciprocal Arrangements) Regulations 1993).

For arrangements concerning deductions from the pay of servicemen and merchant seamen, see the Child Support Act 1991 (Consequential Amendments) Order 1993.

*Subsection (1)*
The "liable person" will be the non-resident parent.

*Subsection (2)*
A deduction from earnings order is made by the Secretary of State. This should make it possible for one to be made more quickly and easily than an attachment of earnings or earnings arrestment order, which has to be made by a court. Giving a public authority, rather than a court, the power to make such an order is not new. It also exists in relation to collection of council tax. A deduction from earnings order may be made against someone in the employment of the Crown, but in such a case the operation of s.32(8) is modified (s.57(4)).

*Subsection (8)*
"Earnings" is defined in reg.8 of the Collection and Enforcement Regulations.

## Regulations about deduction from earnings orders

2.113    **32.**—(1) The Secretary of State may by regulations make provision with respect to deduction from earnings orders.

(2) The regulations may, in particular, make provision—

(a) as to the circumstances in which one person is to be treated as employed by another;

(b) requiring any deduction from earnings under an order to be made in the prescribed manner;

[¹(bb) for the amount or amounts which are to be deducted from the liable person's earnings not to exceed a prescribed proportion of his earnings (as determined by the employer);]

(c) requiring an order to specify the amount or amounts to which the order relates and the amount or amounts which are to be deducted from the liable person's earnings in order to meet his liabilities under the maintenance assessment in question;

(d) requiring the intervals between deductions to be made under an order to be specified in the order;

(e) as to the payment of sums deducted under an order to the Secretary of State;

(f) allowing the person who deducts and pays any amount under an order to deduct from the liable person's earnings a prescribed sum towards his administrative costs;

(g) with respect to the notification to be given to the liable person of amounts deducted, and amounts paid, under the order;

(h) requiring any person on whom a copy of an order is served to notify the Secretary of State in the prescribed manner and within a prescribed period if he does not have the liable person in his employment or if the liable person ceases to be in his employment;

(i) as to the operation of an order where the liable person is in the employment of the Crown;

(j) for the variation of orders;

(k) similar to that made by section 31(7), in relation to any variation of an order;

(l) for an order to lapse when the employer concerned ceases to have the liable person in his employment;

(m) as to the revival of an order in such circumstances as may be prescribed;

(n) allowing or requiring an order to be discharged;

(o) as to the giving of notice by the Secretary of State to the employer concerned that an order has lapsed or has ceased to have effect.

(3) The regulations include provision that while a deduction from earnings order is in force—

(a) the liable person shall from time to time notify the Secretary of State, in the prescribed manner and within a prescribed period, of each occasion on which he leaves any employment or becomes employed, or reemployed, and shall include in such a notification a statement of his earnings and expected earnings from the employment concerned and of such other matters as may be prescribed;

(b) any person who becomes the liable person's employer and knows that the order is in force shall notify the Secretary of State, in the prescribed manner and within a prescribed period, that he is the liable person's employer, and shall include in such a notification a statement of the liable person's earnings and expected earnings from the employment concerned and of such other matters as may be prescribed.

(4) The regulations may include provision with respect to the priority as between a deduction from earnings order and—

(a) any other deduction from earnings order;

(b) any order under any other enactment relating to England and Wales which provides for deductions from the liable person's earnings;

(c) any diligence against earnings.

(5) The regulations may include a provision that a liable person may appeal to a magistrates' court (or in Scotland to the sheriff) if he is aggrieved by the making of a deduction from earnings order against him, or by the terms of any such order, or there is a dispute as to whether payments constitute earnings or as to any other prescribed matter relating to the order.

(6) On an appeal under subsection (5) the court or (as the case may be) the sheriff shall not question the [²maintenance calculation] by reference to which the deduction from earnings order was made.

(7) Regulations made by virtue of subsection (5) may include provision as to the powers of a magistrates' court, or in Scotland of the sheriff, in relation to an appeal (which may include provision as to the quashing of a deduction from earnings order or the variation of the terms of such an order).

(8) If any person fails to comply with the requirements of a deduction from earnings order, or with any regulation under this section which is designated for the purposes of this subsection, he shall be guilty of an offence.

(9) In subsection (8) "designated" means designated by the regulations.

(10) It shall be a defence for a person charged with an offence under subsection (8) to prove that he took all reasonable steps to comply with the requirements in question.

(11) Any person guilty of an offence under subsection (8) shall be liable on summary conviction to a fine not exceeding level two on the standard scale.

AMENDMENTS

1. Paragraph 11(16) of Sch.3 to the 2000 Act (March 3, 2003 under art.3 of, and the Schedule to, the Commencement No.12 Order 2003).
2. Section 1(2)(a) of the 2000 Act (March 3, 2003 under art.3 of, and the Schedule to, the Commencement No.12 Order 2003).

DEFINITIONS

2.114    "earnings": see s.31(8).
"liable person": see s.31(1).
"maintenance calculation": see s.54.
"prescribed": see s.54.

GENERAL NOTE

2.115    The regulations made under this section are contained in Pt III of the Collection and Enforcement Regulations.

They apply, as modified, to other forms of maintenance prescribed for the purposes of s.30 by the Collection and Enforcement of Other Forms of Maintenance Regulations (see above). The scheme set out is based closely on that which applies to the Attachment of Earnings Act 1971. However, the time limits for compliance by the liable person and the employer are more restrictive in relation to deduction from earnings orders (a seven-day requirement is used, compared with 10 days or a "specified period" in the Attachment of Earnings Act 1971). Whereas a court has power to order the debtor to attend to give employment details, the Secretary of State has no such power, although see below for powers to require these details to be supplied.

*Subsection (2)*

Regulation 8(2) provides that a relationship of employer and employee is treated as subsisting where one person, as principal and not as servant or agent, pays to the other any sum defined as earnings. Earnings are defined in paras (3) and (4) of this regulation. They are any sums payable by way of wages or salary (including fees, bonus, commission, overtime pay or other emoluments); sums payable by way of pension (including an annuity in respect of past service); and statutory sick pay. They do not include sums payable by any public department of the Government of Northern Ireland or a territory outside the UK; pay or allowances to members of Her Majesty's forces; pension, allowances or benefit payable under any enactment relating to social security; pension or allowances payable in respect of disablement or disability; guaranteed minimum pension within the meaning of the Social Security Pensions Act 1975. Regulation 9 provides that a deduction from earnings order shall specify certain items of information, including the name and address of the liable person, the normal deduction rate, protected earnings rate, and address to which the deducted amounts must be sent. Regulation 11 specifies various protected earnings rates where there is an interim maintenance assessment, dependent upon the amount of information which has been given by the absent parent.

As with the Attachment of Earnings Act 1971, a deduction from earnings order is made up of a normal deduction rate and a protected earnings rate. The former specifies the amount to be deducted from earnings by the employer at each pay-day (which amount could include payment of interest, when this becomes payable again, as well as arrears, as provided for by the Arrears, Interest and Adjustment of Maintenance Assessments Regulations, see s.41 below): the latter specifies that the liable person's earnings must not fall below his or her exempt income, as calculated for the current maintenance assessment. The employer may pay the amounts deducted to the Secretary of State by cheque, automated credit transfer, or other method specified by the Secretary of State.

In order to enable the Secretary of State to direct a deduction from earnings order to the employer, reg.15 requires the liable person, within seven days of being given written notice, to provide details of his or her employer's name and address, the amount of earnings, place and nature of work and any works or pay number. If the liable person leaves employment or becomes employed or reemployed, he or she must notify the Secretary of State in writing within seven days. Regulations 2(2) and 3 of the Information, Evidence and Disclosure Regulations also make provision for the liable person and/or a current or recent employer to provide information to enable the Secretary of State to discover the liable person's gross earnings and deductions from those earnings.

Regulation 23 provides for the case where the liable person is in the employment of the Crown.

In *Secretary of State for Social Security v Shotton and Others* [1996] 2 F.L.R. 241, the High Court ruled that magistrates hearing an appeal against a deduction from earnings order may not question the validity of the assessment in respect of which the order is made. The absent parent's remedy is to seek a review of the assessment.

*Subsection (7)*

Regulation 22 provides that a liable person may appeal against a deduction from earnings order to a magistrates' court in England and Wales, or the sheriff in Scotland, having jurisdiction in the area in which he or she resides. The grounds for such an appeal are: (a) that the order is defective; or (b) that the payments in question do not constitute earnings. A "defective" order is one, according to reg.8(1) (as amended by the Amendment Regulations 1995, codifying *R. v Secretary of State for*

*Social Security Ex p. Biggin* [1995] 1 F.L.R. 851), which does not comply with the requirements of regs 9 to 11, the failure having made it impracticable for the employer to comply with his obligations under the Act and Regulations. An appeal under reg.22 may not be used to argue that the Secretary of State has failed to consider the welfare of a child before making the deduction from earnings order. While considerable weight should be given to welfare before making the order, challenge on this ground must be by way of judicial review (*R. v Secretary of State Ex p. Biggin*, above). If justices declare a deduction from earnings order defective, they have no power to order the Child Support Agency to repay money paid under the order (*Secretary of State for Social Security v Shotton and Others* [1996] 2 F.L.R. 241).

*Subsection (8)*
The requirements for which failure to comply (in the absence of a defence under subs.(10)) will amount to an offence are: (i) the requirements on the liable person to supply details of his or her employment under reg.15; (ii) the requirements on the employer to notify the Secretary of State when the liable person is not, or has ceased to be in his or her employment, or when a person in relation to whom a deduction from earnings order is in force is one of his or her employees, under reg.16; (iii) the requirement on the employer to comply with any variation of a deduction from earnings order under reg.19.

If a deduction from an earnings order is made under s.31 against someone in the employment of the Crown, this section only applies to failures to comply with regulations made under this section (s.57(4)).

## Liability orders

2.116    **33.**—(1) This section applies where—
   (a) a person who is liable to make payments of child support maintenance ("the liable person") fails to make one or more of those payments; and
   (b) it appears to the Secretary of State that—
      (i) it is inappropriate to make a deduction from earnings order against him (because, for example, he is not employed); or
      (ii) although such an order has been made against him, it has proved ineffective as a means of securing that payments are made in accordance with the [³maintenance calculation] in question.

(2) The Secretary of State may apply to a magistrates' court or, in Scotland, to the sheriff for an order ("a liability order") against the liable person.

(3) Where the Secretary of State applies for a liability order, the magistrates' court or (as the case may be) sheriff shall make the order if satisfied that the payments in question have become payable by the liable person and have not been paid.

(4) On an application under subsection (2), the court or (as the case may be) the sheriff shall not question the [³maintenance calculation] under which the payments of child support maintenance fell to be made.

[¹(5) If the Secretary of State designates a liability order for the purposes of this subsection it shall be treated as a judgment entered in a county court for the purposes of section 73 of the County Courts Act 1984 (register of judgments and orders).]

[²(6) Where regulations have been made under section 29(3)(a)—
   (a) the liable person fails to make a payment (for the purposes of subsection (1)(a) of this section); and

(b) a payment is not paid (for the purposes of subsection (3)), unless the payment is made to, or through, the person specified in or by virtue of those regulations for the case of the liable person in question.]

AMENDMENTS

1. Paragraph 10 of Sch.3 to the 1995 Act (September 4, 1995).
2. Paragraph 11(17) of Sch.3 to the 2000 Act (January 1, 2001 under art.2(3) of, and the Schedule to, the Commencement No.3 Order 2000).
3. Section 1(2)(a) of the 2000 Act (March 3, 2003 under art.3 of, and the Schedule to, the Commencement No.12 Order 2003).

DEFINITIONS

"child support maintenance": see s.3(6).        **2.117**
"maintenance calculation": see s.54.

GENERAL NOTE

A liability order may be made if there has been any default in the payment of  **2.118** child support maintenance, but only if a deduction from an earnings order is inappropriate or has proved ineffective. Its effect is to permit other steps to be taken for enforcement. The Department of Social Security is not entitled to be granted a *Mareva* injunction to prevent a liable person from disposing of his assets before a liability order can be obtained: *Department of Social Security v Butler* [1996] 1 F.L.R. 65. The Child Support legislation, in the view of the Court of Appeal in that case, provides a complete code for the collection of payments due under maintenance assessments and the enforcement of liability orders made on the application of the Secretary of State. The duty to pay a maintenance assessment is not expressed as a civil debt and cannot be directly enforced by action in any civil court or by any means other than as provided in the Act. (If, however, a liability order has already been made under s.33, then the country court has jurisdiction to grant a *Mareva* injunction under the County Court Remedies Regulations 1991, r.3(3)(a), (c).)

Where payments have not been made or made regularly, the Secretary of State may decide to seek a liability order from the Magistrates' Court, in England and Wales, or the sheriff in Scotland. In determining whether to do so, the Secretary of State must have regard to the welfare of any child likely to be affected (s.2). Unlike a deduction from an earnings order, a liability order can only be made when payments have fallen into arrears, and it is therefore to be seen as a method of enforcement rather than collection. The liability order does not of itself operate to enforce the maintenance assessment, but enables the Secretary of State to use other enforcement measures to do so. It operates in the same way as liability orders used to enforce council tax. The enforcement measures which can be used are distress and sale of the liable person's goods, garnishee proceedings or charging order in England and Wales (ss.35 and 36); enforcement by diligence in Scotland (s.38); and commitment to prison in both jurisdictions (s.40). There is provision for enforcement of liability orders throughout the UK in s.39. Not all the mechanisms available to courts to enforce their orders have been included for the benefit of the Secretary of State. There is no provision for oral examination of the liable person as governed by r.7 of the Family Proceedings Rules 1991, which enables rigorous cross-examination of a respondent to take place as a means of discovering exactly what his income, assets and liabilities are, on pain of being in contempt of court. Nor can a judgment summons be sought, which enables the court to examine the respondent on oath as to his means, and to make such order as it considers appropriate as to the payment of arrears. The judgment summons has become popular as a means of enforcing financial orders made on divorce (see *Woodley v Woodley* [1992] 2 F.L.R. 417), but presumably it has been omitted from the Secretary of State's possible armoury because control vests with the court, not the applicant for the summons. The possibility of instituting bankruptcy proceedings has also been omitted, no doubt because this would not be appropriate to seeking to ensure that the liable person pays, and continues to pay his or her maintenance assessment. Access to the High Court for enforcement is also not available, perhaps because of the cost. Orders made in family proceedings (including lump sums—*Woodley v Woodley (No.2)* [1994] 1 W.L.R. 1167), and maintenance assessments made under the Child Support Act are not provable as debts against a bankrupt (reg.12.3 of the Insolvency Rules 1986 as amended by the Insolvency (Amendment) Rules 1993). It is not unknown for a maintenance debtor to petition for his own bankruptcy (as was indeed the case in *Woodley* above) to avoid liability to the creditor, and hence the availability of liability orders may be crucial to the enforcement of the child support obligation.

Where an application is to be made for a liability order against a liable person who is resident in Northern Ireland, it shall be made under the provision for that territory, even though the liability arose, or the maintenance assessment was made, under the provisions for Great Britain, and vice versa. Any appeal in connection with the liability order, or action as a consequence of the order, shall be made under the provision for the territory in which the liable person is resident (Sch.1, paras 11 and 12 to the Child Support (Northern Ireland Reciprocal Arrangements) Regulations 1993).

*Subsection (1)*

This subsection sets out the criteria which must be satisfied before the Secretary of State can seek a liability order. The liable person must have failed to make one or more payments of child support maintenance, and it must appear that a deduction from earnings order is inappropriate or has proved ineffective. A deduction from earnings order will be inappropriate where the liable person is unemployed, and unlikely to be appropriate where he or she is self-employed. It might also be inappropriate where it would prove embarrassing to the liable person for his or her employer to discover that child support maintenance had been assessed. Regulations 2(2) and 3 of the Information, Evidence and Disclosure Regulations, which make provision for the liable person and/or a current or recent employer to provide information to enable the Secretary of State or a child support officer to discover the liable person's gross earnings and deductions from those earnings, may be relevant to enable the Secretary of State to decide whether to seek the liability order.

*Subsection (2)*

The application for a liability order is made by way of complaint to the magistrates' court having jurisdiction in the area in which the liable person resides (reg.28(1) of the Collection and Enforcement Regulations). The application may not be instituted more than six years after the day on which the payment in question became due. For Scotland, see Act of Sederunt (Child Support Rules) 1993.

*Subsection (3)*

The position used to be as follows. The only questions for the Magistrates' Court or sheriff are whether the payments have become payable by the liable person and have not been paid. It may not question the amount of arrears (*Secretary of State for Social Security v Shotton and Others* [1996] 2 F.L.R. 241). The court may not, for example, question the desirability of the Secretary of State choosing to seek a liability order in the light of the welfare of any child likely to be affected, or the appropriateness of the enforcement mechanisms which result from obtaining the liability order. A liable person wishing to challenge the Secretary of State's decision to seek the order must go by way of judicial review.

However, the Court of Appeal has now held that Magistrates have jurisdiction to consider whether the parent had been liable to pay child support maintenance (*Farley v Secretary of State for Work and Pensions, The Times* January 27, 2005).

*Subsection (4)*

The magistrates' court or sheriff may not question the maintenance calculation. This is in line with the exclusive jurisdiction of the Secretary of State and appeal tribunals over calculations. If the maintenance calculation is to be challenged, the liable person would have to utilise the usual procedures for review in subs.17 or 18 (see above).

*Subsection (5)*

Entry on the register of judgments may affect a person's credit rating and may prove a useful incentive to the liable person to pay up. Liability orders have been designated by the Register of County Court Judgements (Amendment) Regulations 1996.

## Regulations about liability orders

**34.**—(1) The Secretary of State may make regulations in relation to England and Wales—    2.119

    (a) prescribing the procedure to be followed in dealing with an application by the Secretary of State for a liability order;

    (b) prescribing the form and contents of a liability order; and

    (c) providing that where a magistrates' court has made a liability order, the person against whom it is made shall, during such time as the amount in respect of which the order was made remains wholly or partly unpaid, be under a duty to supply relevant information to the Secretary of State.

(2) In subsection (1) "relevant information" means any information of a prescribed description which is in the possession of the liable person and which the Secretary of State has asked him to supply.

DEFINITIONS

"liability order"; see s.33(2).    2.120
"prescribed"; see s.54.

GENERAL NOTE

This section provides for regulations concerning England and Wales Section 37    2.121
below covers Scotland. The relevant regulations are contained in Pt IV of, and Sch.1 to, the Collection and Enforcement Regulations. They apply, as modified, to other forms of maintenance prescribed for the purposes of s.30 by the Collection and Enforcement of Other Forms of Maintenance Regulations (see above).

*Subsection (1)*

Part IV of the Regulations provides for the Secretary of State to give the liable    2.122
person at least seven days' notice of intention to apply for a liability order. The notice must set out the amount of child support maintenance which is claimed to be owing and not paid, and the amount of any interest on arrears payable (see s.41

below). The application may not be made more than six years after the day on which payment of the amount in question became due (see s.41 below for comparison with the courts' approach to payments in arrears). Schedule 1 to the Regulations sets out the form prescribed for the liability order. Regulation 29 provides for the enforcement of liability orders made in different parts of the UK.

*Subsection (2)*
    This subsection has not been brought into force.

### Enforcement of liability orders by distress

2.123      **35.**—(1) Where a liability order has been made against a person ("the liable person"), the Secretary of State may levy the appropriate amount by distress and sale of the liable person's goods.

(2) In subsection (1), "the appropriate amount" means the aggregate of—
   (a) the amount in respect of which the order was made, to the extent that it remains unpaid; and
   (b) an amount, determined in such manner as may be prescribed, in respect of the charges connected with the distress.

(3) The Secretary of State may, in exercising his powers under subsection (1) against the liable person's goods, seize—
   (a) any of the liable person's goods except—
      (i)  such tools, books, vehicles and other items of equipment as are necessary to him for use personally by him in his employment, business or vocation;
      (ii) such clothing, bedding, furniture, household equipment and provisions as are necessary for satisfying his basic domestic needs; and
   (b) any money, banknotes, bills of exchange, promissory notes, bonds, specialties or securities for money belonging to the liable person.

(4) For the purposes of subsection (3), the liable person's domestic needs shall be taken to include those of any member of his family with whom he resides.

(5) No person levying a distress under this section shall be taken to be a trespasser—
   (a) on that account; or
   (b) from the beginning, on account of any subsequent irregularity in levying the distress.

(6) A person sustaining special damage by reason of any irregularity in levying a distress under this section may recover full satisfaction for the damage (and no more) by proceedings in trespass or otherwise.

(7) The Secretary of State may make regulations supplementing the provisions of this section.

(8) The regulations may, in particular—
   (a) provide that a distress under this section may be levied anywhere in England and Wales;
   (b) provide that such a distress shall not be deemed unlawful on account of any defect or want of form in the liability order;
   (c) provide for an appeal to a magistrates' court by any person aggrieved by the levying of, or an attempt to levy, a distress under this section;

(d) make provision as to the powers of the court on an appeal (which may include provision as to the discharge of goods distrained or the payment of compensation in respect of goods distrained and sold).

DEFINITIONS

"liability order": see s.33(2).  2.124
"prescribed": see s.54.

GENERAL NOTE

This section does not extend to Scotland (s.58(9)).  2.125
Where the Secretary of State decides to levy distress as the appropriate means of enforcement, the liability order will operate to authorise the Secretary of State of levy distress within the terms of this section and of regs 30 to 32 of the Collection and Enforcement Regulations.

*Subsection (1)*

By reg.30, the person levying distress on behalf of the Secretary of State must carry written authorisation, which must be shown to the liable person if requested. Copies of regs 30 and 31 of, and Sch.2 to, the regulations, a memorandum setting out the appropriate amount (see below), a memorandum setting out details of any arrangement entered into regarding the taking into possession of goods distrained and a notice setting out the liable person's rights of appeal under reg.31 must be handed to the liable person or left at the premises where the distress is levied.

*Subsection (2)*

The amount to be raised by distress and sale is the amount of child support maintenance unpaid, which may include interest on the arrears (see s.41 below). The provisions dealing with charges in relation to distress are reg.32 of, and Sch.2 to, the Collection and Enforcement Regulations.

*Subsection (3)*

Under subs.(3)(b) cash belonging to the liable person may not be seized, contrary to the position under r.54(2) of the Magistrates' Courts Rules 1981.

*Subsection (7)*

The regulations are contained in Pt IV of the Collection and Enforcement Regulations.

*Subsection (8)*

Regulation 31(1) provides that a person aggrieved by the levy of, or attempt to levy, distress may appeal by way of complaint to the magistrates' court having jurisdiction in the area in which that person resides. The right is not limited to the liable person; it would appear that a member of that person's family, or a person disputing ownership of the goods seized, could appeal. However, the only ground for allowing the appeal is that the levy or attempted levy was irregular reg.31(3) and (4) of the Collection and Enforcement Regulations). The matrimonial courts have tended to use the threat of issuing a warrant for distress as an inducement to the debtor to pay up, and that approach is open to the Secretary of State as well. However, once the Secretary of State has decided to levy distress, the magistrates will not be able, as they could under their matrimonial powers, to postpone the process.

### Enforcement in county courts

2.126     **36.**—(1) Where a liability order has been made against a person, the amount in respect of which the order was made, to the extent that it remains unpaid, shall, if a county court so orders, be recoverable by means of garnishee proceedings or a charging order, as if it were payable under a county court order.

    (2) In subsection (1) "charging order" has the same meaning as in section 1 of the Charging Orders Act 1979.

DEFINITION

2.127     "liability order": see s.33(2).

GENERAL NOTE

2.128     The section gives jurisdiction only to the county courts, not the High Court.

    Garnishee proceedings are used to obtain arrears from the liable person, by diverting money owed to him or her by a third party or held by a third party on behalf of the liable person. The usual example will be where the liable person has a bank account with a credit balance, which is a debt owed to that person by the bank. The effect of a garnishee order is to require the third party to pay the money to the creditor. The procedures governing the making of garnishee orders are contained in the County Court Rules 1981, Ord.30.

    Charging orders secure payment of arrears from funds or property belonging to the liable person. They are governed by the Charging Orders Act 1979 and the County Court Rules 1981, Ord.31. Section 1(1) of that Act defines a charging order as one "imposing on any such property of the debtor as may be specified in the order a charge for securing the payment of any money due or to become due under the judgment or order." By s.2, a charge may be imposed only on a beneficial interest held by the debtor in land, securities consisting of government stock, stock of any body (other than a building society) incorporated within England and Wales, stock of any body incorporated outside England and Wales, but registered in England and Wales, or funds in court. The charge may be imposed, for example, upon a matrimonial home which is jointly owned by the debtor and a new spouse or partner, in respect of the debtor's beneficial interest in that home. The charging order may be enforced by an application for an order for sale. Difficulties may arise in deciding whether a charging order should take priority over the interest of the new spouse or partner. In *Harman v Glencross* [1986] 2 F.L.R. 241, the Court of Appeal held that the court must consider the position of the creditor and strike a balance between his normal expectation that an order enforcing a money judgment lawfully obtained would be made, and the hardship to the wife and children that such an order would entail, but the voice of the creditor will usually prevail unless there are exceptional circumstances (*Lloyds Bank plc v Byrne and Byrne* [1993] 1 F.L.R. 369). A *Mesher* order, whereby sale of the property is postponed until the children have grown up, may be appropriate (*Austin-Fell v Austin-Fell and Midland Bank* [1989] 2 F.L.R. 497). However, in *Harman v Glencross* the court noted that the creditor was an individual rather than a "faceless corporation" (*per* Balcombe L.J., at p.251). Section 1(5) of the Charging Orders Act requires the court to consider all the circumstances of the case in deciding whether to make the order; the Court considered that the competing interests of the spouse and the creditor should be weighed. Since the spouse is likely to suffer more hardship than the Secretary of State, it is arguable that a charging order might be refused where such hardship could be demonstrated.

## Regulations about liability orders: Scotland

**37.**—(1) Section 34(1) does not apply to Scotland.

2.129

(2) In Scotland, the Secretary of State may make regulations providing that where the sheriff has made a liability order, the person against whom it is made shall, during such time as the amount in respect of which the order was made remains wholly or partly unpaid, be under a duty to supply relevant information to the Secretary of State.

(3) In this section "relevant information" has the same meaning as in section 34(2).

DEFINITION

"liability order": see s.33(2).

2.130

GENERAL NOTE

*Subsection (2) and (3)*

2.131

These subsections have not been brought into force.

## Enforcement of liability orders by diligence: Scotland

**38.**—(1) In Scotland, where a liability order has been made against a person, the order shall be warrant anywhere in Scotland—

2.132

[¹. . .]

(b) for an arrestment (other than an arrestment of the person's earnings in the hands of his employers) and action of furthcoming or sale,

and shall be apt to found a Bill of Inhibition or an action of adjudication at the instance of the Secretary of State.

(2) In subsection (1) the "appropriate amount" means the amount in respect of which the order was made, to the extent that it remains unpaid.

AMENDMENT

1. Section 3(1) of, and the Schedule to, the Abolition of Poindings and Warrant Sales Act 2001 (December 31, 2002).

DEFINITION

"liability order": see s.33(2).

2.133

## Liability orders: enforcement throughout United Kingdom

**39.**—(1) The Secretary of State may be regulations provide for—

2.134

(a) any liability order made by a court in England and Wales; or

(b) any corresponding order made by a court in Northern Ireland, to be enforced in Scotland as if it had been made by the sheriff.

(2) The power conferred on the Court of Session by section 32 of the Sheriff Courts (Scotland) Act 1971 (power of Court of Session to regulate civil procedure in the sheriff court) shall extend to making provision for the registration in the sheriff court for enforcement of any such order as is referred to in subsection (1).

(3) The Secretary of State may by regulations make provision for, or in connection with, the enforcement in England and Wales of—

    (a) any liability order made by the sheriff in Scotland; or

    (b) any corresponding order made by a court in Northern Ireland, as if it had been made by a magistrates' court in England and Wales.

(4) Regulations under subsection (3) may, in particular, make provision for the registration of any such order as is referred to in that subsection in connection with its enforcement in England and Wales.

DEFINITION

2.135    "liability order": see s.33(2).

GENERAL NOTE

2.136    This section provides for the enforcement of liability orders throughout the UK. It obviates the need for the Secretary of State to seek fresh orders should the liable person move to another part of the UK. For the position concerning order made, or to be enforced, in Northern Ireland, see Sch.1, para.12 to the Child Support (Northern Ireland Reciprocal Arrangements) Regulations 1993 (provisions for the territory in which the liable person is resident to govern the action to be taken).

*Subsection (1)*

The provisions dealing with enforcement in Scotland are regs 26 and 29(2) of the Collection and Enforcement Regulations.

*Subsection (3)*

The provision dealing with enforcement in England and Wales is reg.29(3) and (4) of the Collection and Enforcement Regulations.

*Subsections (3) and (4)*

Before a liability order made in Scotland or Northern Ireland can be enforced in England and Wales it must be registered in accordance with the provisions of Pt II of the Maintenance Orders Act 1950. Regulation 29(4) provides that a Scottish liability order shall be treated as if it were a decree for payment of aliment within s.26(2)(b) of that Act, and that a liability order made in Northern Ireland shall be treated as if it were an order for alimony, maintenance or other payments within s.16(2)(c). Section 17 of the 1950 Act sets out the procedure for registration. It requires the application for registration to be made to the court which made the original order, which then sends a certified copy of the order to the appropriate court in England and Wales, which will be the magistrates' court for the area in which the liable person appears to be. The order will then be enforced as if it had been made by a magistrates' court in England and Wales.

## [¹Commitment to prison and disqualification from driving

2.137    **39A.**—(1) Where the Secretary of State has sought—

    (a) in England and Wales to levy an amount by distress under this Act; or

    (b) to recover an amount by virtue of section 36 or 38, and that amount, or any portion of it, remains unpaid he may apply to the court under this section.

(2) An application under this section is for whichever the court considers appropriate in all the circumstances of—

(a) the issue of a warrant committing the liable person to prison; or

(b) an order for him to be disqualified from holding or obtaining a driving licence.

(3) On any such application the court shall (in the presence of the liable person) inquire as to—

(a) whether he needs a driving licence to earn his living;

(b) his means; and

(c) whether there has been wilful refusal or culpable neglect on his part.

(4) The Secretary of State may make representations to the court as to whether he thinks it more appropriate to commit the liable person to prison or to disqualify him from holding or obtaining a driving licence; and the liable person may reply to those representations.

(5) In this section and section 40B, "driving licence" means a licence to drive a motor vehicle granted under Part III of the Road Traffic Act 1988.

(6) In this section "the court" means—

(a) in England and Wales, a magistrates' court;

(b) in Scotland, the sheriff.]

AMENDMENT

1. Section 16(1) of the 2000 Act (for the purpose of making regulations, November 10, 2000 under art.2(1) of, and Pt I of the Schedule to, the Commencement No.3 Order 2000; April 2, 2001 under art.2(3) of, and the Schedule to, the Commencement No.5 Order 2000).

GENERAL NOTE

Regulation 35 of the Collection and Enforcement Regulations is relevant to this section.  **2.138**

## Commitment to prison

**40.** [¹. . .]

(3) If, but only if, the court is of the opinion that there has been wilful refusal or culpable neglect on the part of the liable person it may—  **2.139**

(a) issue a warrant of commitment against him; or

(b) fix a term of imprisonment and postpone the issue of the warrant until such time and on such conditions (if any) as it thinks just.

(4) Any such warrant—

(a) shall be made in respect of an amount equal to the aggregate of—

　(i) the amount mentioned in section 35(1) or so much of it as remains outstanding; and

　(ii) an amount (determined in accordance with regulations made by the Secretary of State) in respect of the costs of commitment; and

(b) shall state that amount.

(5) No warrant may be issued under this section against a person who is under the age of 18.

(6) A warrant issued under this section shall order the liable person—

(a) to be imprisoned for a specified period; but

(b) to be released (unless he is in custody for some other reason) on payment of the amount stated in the warrant.

(7) The maximum period of imprisonment which may be imposed by virtue of subsection (6) shall be calculated in accordance with Schedule 4 to the Magistrates' Courts Act 1980 (maximum periods of imprisonment in default of payment) but shall not exceed six weeks.

(8) The Secretary of State may by regulations make provision for the period of imprisonment specified in any warrant issued under this section to be reduced where there is part payment of the amount in respect of which the warrant was issued.

(9) A warrant issued under this section may be directed to such person or persons as the court issuing it thinks fit.

(10) Section 80 of the Magistrates' Courts Act 1980 (application of money found on defaulter) shall apply in relation to a warrant issued under this section against a liable person as it applies in relation to the enforcement of a sum mentioned in subsection (1) of that section.

(11) The Secretary of State may be regulations make provision—

(a) as to the form of any warrant issued under this section;

(b) allowing an application under this section to be renewed where no warrant is issued or term of imprisonment is fixed;

(c) that a statement in writing to the effect that wages of any amount have been paid to the liable person during any period, purporting to be signed by or on behalf of his employer, shall be evidence of the facts stated;

(d) that, for the purposes of enabling an inquiry to be made as to the liable person's conduct and means, a justice of the peace may issue a summons to him to appear before a magistrates' court and (if he does not obey) may issue a warrant for his arrest;

(e) that for the purpose of enabling such an inquiry, a justice of the peace may issue a warrant for the liable person's arrest without issuing a summons;

(f) as to the execution of a warrant for arrest.

[²(12) This section does not apply to Scotland.]

AMENDMENTS

1. Section 16(2) of the 2000 Act and s.85 of, and Sch.9 to, that Act (for the purpose of making regulations, November 10, 2000 under art.2(1) of, and Pt I of the Schedule to, the Commencement No.3 Order 2000; April 2, 2001 under art.2(3) of, and the Schedule to, the Commencement No.5 Order 2000).

2. Section 17(1) of the 2000 Act (for the purpose of making regulations, November 10, 2000 under art.2(1) of, and Pt I of the Schedule to, the Commencement No.3 Order 2000; April 2, 2001 under art.2(3) of, and the Schedule to, the Commencement No.5 Order 2000).

DEFINITIONS

2.140    "liability order": see s.33(2).
"liable person": see s.33(1)(a).

GENERAL NOTE

2.141    The ultimate sanction for the Secretary of State will be to seek to have the liable person committed to prison for non-payment. Apart from council tax, the only civil debt for which imprisonment remains a sanction is maintenance. The sanction is intended for those who will not, rather than those who cannot, pay. It has been said that such a sanction is

> "a power of extreme severity. Indeed, it might be argued that the existence of such a power in a society which long ago closed the Marshalsea prison and abandoned imprisonment as a remedy for the enforcement of debts, is anomalous. Certainly, Parliament has made it plain that the power is to be exercised sparingly and only as a last resort."

(Waite J., in *R. v Luton Magistrates' Court Ex p. Sullivan* [1992] 2 F.L.R. 196 at 201.) Subsections (1) to (11) do not apply to Scotland (subs.(12)); subss.(13) and (14) provide that the Civil Imprisonment (Scotland) Act 1882 applies to commitment in Scotland for non-payment of child support maintenance.

The court has a discretion whether to commit, or suspend commitment of, the liable person to prison, and must take account of his or her means. It, therefore, has an opportunity to reassess the financial assumptions about the absent parent upon which the Secretary of State has worked in arriving at the maintenance assessment. No doubt, if the court considered that a warrant of commitment should not be made, the Secretary of State would consider reviewing his assessment.

*Subsection (1)*

The Secretary of State must have tried distress or enforcement through the county court first, emphasising that commitment is intended as a last resort. Regulations 33 and 34 of the Collection and Enforcement Regulations deal with the application and the warrant.

*Subsection (2)*

The liable person must be present at the hearing. To ensure his or her presence, reg.33(1) empowers a justice of the peace having jurisdiction for the area in which the liable person resides to issue a summons for him or her to appear before a magistrates' court and, if this is not obeyed, or as an alternative, to issue a warrant for the liable person's arrest.

The court must find wilful refusal or culpable neglect on the part of the liable person (*Bernstein v O'Neill* [1989] 2 F.L.R. 1). In *R. v Luton Magistrates' Court Ex p. Sullivan* [1992] 2 F.L.R. 196, the Divisional Court held, in relation to non-payment of maintenance under the private law, that the liable person's conduct must amount to deliberate defiance or reckless disregard; default by way of improvidence or dilatoriness was insufficient. Magistrates are entitled to disbelieve the debtor's evidence as to his past ability to pay, but they must go on to consider, in the light of that disbelief, whether he has the means to clear the stated arrears before imposing the prison sentence (*SN v ST (Maintenance Order: Enforcement)* [1994] 3 F.C.R. 229). Justices must be scrupulous in allowing the liable person the opportunity to make his or her case, and this will generally require that at least an opportunity be afforded for the liable person to obtain legal advice. Regrettably, the duty solicitor scheme operating at magistrates' courts does not extend to those facing commitment for non-payment; the result may be that where the liable person is brought to court and claims not to have been aware of the hearing, and hence not to have sought advice, the hearing should be adjourned to enable this to be done. The liable person should be allowed the assistance of a friend at any hearing if this is requested (*R. v Wolverhampton Stipendiary Magistrate Ex p. Mould* [1992] R.A. 309).

*Subsection (3)*

It is common to postpone issue of the warrant on condition that the liable person makes regular payments of maintenance as they fall due and pays towards clearing the arrears. A liable person who breaches the condition may be committed to prison in his or her absence, provided that notice of the hearing was given (*R. v Northampton Magistrates' Court Ex p. Newell* [1992] R.A. 283). The warrant must be in the form specified in Sch.3 to the Collection and Enforcement Regulations.

*Subsection (4)*

Regulation 34(2) provides that the amount in respect of costs shall be such amount as in the view of the court is equal to the costs reasonably incurred by the Secretary of State in respect of the costs of commitment.

*Subsection (7)*

Schedule 4 to the Magistrates' Courts Act 1980 provides a sliding scale relating the length of imprisonment to the amount of arrears.

*Subsection (8)*

The provision dealing with part-payment is reg.34(5) and (6) of the Collection and Enforcement Regulations.

*Subsection (11)*

The provisions dealing with these matters are regs 33 and 34 of, and Sch.3 to, the Collection and Enforcement Regulations.

## [¹Commitment to prison: Scotland

2.142

**40A.**—(1) If, but only if, the sheriff is satisfied that there has been wilful refusal or culpable neglect on the part of the liable person he may—

(a) issue a warrant for his committal to prison; or

(b) fix a term of imprisonment and postpone the issue of the warrant until such time and on such conditions (if any) as he thinks just.

(2) A warrant under this section—

(a) shall be made in respect of an amount equal to the aggregate of—

(i) the appropriate amount under section 38; and

(ii) an amount (determined in accordance with regulations made by the Secretary of State) in respect of the expenses of commitment; and

(b) shall state that amount.

(3) No warrant may be issued under this section against a person who is under the age of 18.

(4) A warrant issued under this section shall order the liable person—

(a) to be imprisoned for a specified period; but

(b) to be released (unless he is in custody for some other reason) on payment of the amount stated in the warrant.

(5) The maximum period of imprisonment which may be imposed by virtue of subsection (4) is six weeks.

(6) The Secretary of State may by regulations make provision for the period of imprisonment specified in any warrant issued under this section to be reduced where there is part payment of the amount in respect of which the warrant was issued.

(7) A warrant issued under this section may be directed to such person as the sheriff thinks fit.

(8) The power of the Court of Session by Act of Sederunt to regulate the procedure and practice in civil proceedings in the sheriff court shall include power to make provision—

(a) as to the form of any warrant issued under this section;
(b) allowing an application under this section to be renewed where no warrant is issued or term of imprisonment is fixed;
(c) that a statement in writing to the effect that wages of any amount have been paid to the liable person during any period, purporting to be signed by or on behalf of his employer, shall be sufficient evidence of the facts stated;
(d) that, for the purposes of enabling an inquiry to be made as to the liable person's conduct and means, the sheriff may issue a citation to him to appear before the sheriff and (if he does not obey) may issue a warrant for his arrest;
(e) that for the purpose of enabling such an inquiry, the sheriff may issue a warrant for the liable person's arrest without issuing a citation;
(f) as to the execution of a warrant of arrest.]

AMENDMENT

1. Section 17(2) of the 2000 Act (for the purpose of making regulations, November 10, 2000 under art.2(1) of, and Pt I of the Schedule to, the Commencement No.3 Order 2000; April 2, 2001 under art.2(3) of, and the Schedule to, the Commencement No.5 Order 2000).

GENERAL NOTE

The Child Support (Civil Imprisonment) Scotland) Regulations 2001 are made under the authority of this section.                              2.143

## [¹Disqualification from driving: further provision

**40B.**—(1) If, but only if, the court is of the opinion that there has been wilful refusal or culpable neglect on the part of the liable person, it may—   2.144
(a) order him to be disqualified, for such period specified in the order but not exceeding two years as it thinks fit, from holding or obtaining a driving licence (a "disqualification order"); or
(b) make a disqualification order but suspend its operation until such time and on such conditions (if any) as it thinks just.
(2) The court may not take action under both section 40 and this section.
(3) A disqualification order must state the amount in respect of which it is made, which is to be the aggregate of—
(a) the amount mentioned in section 35(1), or so much of it as remains outstanding; and
(b) an amount (determined in accordance with regulations made by the Secretary of State) in respect of the costs of the application under section 39A.
(4) A court which makes a disqualification order shall require the person to whom it relates to produce any driving licence held by him, and its counterpart (within the meaning of section 108(1) of the Road Traffic Act 1988).
(5) On an application by the Secretary of State or the liable person, the court—

(a) may make an order substituting a shorter period of disqualification, or make an order revoking the disqualification order, if part of the amount referred to in subsection (3) (the "amount due") is paid to any person authorised to receive it; and

(b) must make an order revoking the disqualification order if all of the amount due is so paid.

(6) The Secretary of State may make representations to the court as to the amount which should be paid before it would be appropriate to make an order revoking the disqualification order under subsection (5)(a), and the person liable may reply to those representations.

(7) The Secretary of State may make a further application under section 39A if the amount due has not been paid in full when the period of disqualification specified in the disqualification order expires.

(8) Where a court—

(a) makes a disqualification order;

(b) makes an order under subsection (5); or

(c) allows an appeal against a disqualification order,

it shall send notice of that fact to the Secretary of State; and the notice shall contain such particulars and be sent in such manner and to such address as the Secretary of State may determine.

(9) Where a court makes a disqualification order, it shall also send the driving licence and its counterpart, on their being produced to the court, to the Secretary of State at such address as he may determine.

(10) Section 80 of the Magistrates' Courts Act 1980 (application of money found on defaulter) shall apply in relation to a disqualification order under this section in relation to a liable person as it applies in relation to the enforcement of a sum mentioned in subsection (1) of that section.

(11) The Secretary of State may by regulations make provision in relation to disqualification orders corresponding to the provision he may make under section 40(11).

(12) In the application to Scotland of this section—

(a) in subsection (2) for "section 40" substitute "section 40A";

(b) in subsection (3) for paragraph (a) substitute—"(a) the appropriate amount under section 38;";

(c) subsection (10) is omitted; and

(d) for subsection (11) substitute—

"(11) The power of the Court of Session by Act of Sederunt to regulate the procedure and practice in civil proceedings in the sheriff court shall include power to make, in relation to disqualification orders, provision corresponding to that which may be made by virtue of section 40A(8)."]

AMENDMENT

1. Section 16(3) of the 2000 Act (for the purpose of making regulations, November 10, 2000 under art.2(1) of, and Pt I of the Schedule to, the Commencement No.3 Order 2000; April 2, 2001 under art.2(3) of, and the Schedule to, the Commencement No.5 Order 2000).

This is one of the provisions designed to ensure compliance with the child sup-   **2.145**
port scheme. It supplements s.39A, which allows the Secretary of State to apply for
the non-resident parent to be disqualified from holding or obtaining a driving
licence. It may be used as a punishment or as a threat. An order under this section
could be counter-productive, if it resulted in a non-resident parent being unable to
get to work or to pursue work as, for example, a taxi driver: see s.39A(3)(a) above.
The threat of disqualification may be more potent in those circumstances than actual disqualification. Even that will not be effective, if a recalcitrant non-resident parent calls the authorities' bluff and suffers a loss of livelihood rather than pay the
child support maintenance.

Regulation 35 of the Collection and Enforcement Regulations is relevant to this
section.

## Arrears of child support maintenance

**41.**—(1) This section applies where—   **2.146**
  (a) the Secretary of State is authorised under section 4, 6 or 7 to
    recover child support maintenance payable by [⁵a non-resident par-
    ent] in accordance with a maintenance [³maintenance calculation];
    and
  (b) the [⁵non-resident parent] has failed to make one or more payments
    of child support maintenance due from him in accordance with that
    [⁴calculation].

[¹(2) Where the Secretary of State recovers any such arrears he may, in
such circumstances as may be prescribed and to such extent as may be prescribed, retain them if he is satisfied that the amount of any benefit paid to
or in respect of the person with care of the child or children in question
would have been less had the [⁵non-resident parent] made the payment or
payments of child support maintenance in question.

(2A) In determining for the purposes of subsection (2) whether the
amount of any benefit paid would have been less at any time than the
amount which was paid at that time, in a case where the [³maintenance cal-
culation] had effect from a date earlier than that on which it was made, the
[⁴calculation] shall be taken to have been in force at that time.]

[². . .]

(6) Any sums retained by the Secretary of State by virtue of this section
shall be paid by him into the Consolidated Fund.]

1. Paragraph 11 of Sch.3 to the 1995 Act (October 1, 1995).
2. Section 18(1) of the 2000 Act and s.85 of, and Sch.9 to, that Act (March 3,
2003 under art.3 of, and the Schedule to, the Commencement No.12 Order 2003).
3. Section 1(2)(a) of the 2000 Act (March 3, 2003 under art.3 of, and the
Schedule to, the Commencement No.12 Order 2003).
4. Section 1(2)(b) of the 2000 Act (March 3, 2003 under art.3 of, and the
Schedule to, the Commencement No.12 Order 2003).
5. Paragraph 11(2) of Sch.3 to the 2000 Act (March 3, 2003 under art.3 of, and
the Schedule to, the Commencement No.12 Order 2003).

DEFINITIONS

2.147    "child": see s.55.
"child support maintenance": see s.3(6).
"maintenance calculation": see s.54.
"non-resident parent": see s.54.
"person with care": see s.3(3).
"prescribed": see s.54.

GENERAL NOTE

2.148    This section applies when the non-resident parent has failed to pay child support maintenance. It deals with recovery of arrears. In addition, the non-resident parent may be subject to a penalty payment under s.41A below, as well as to other enforcement and punitive provisions in ss.31 to 40B above. It relieves the person with care of the need to enforce payment of arrears by the non-resident parent and of the time and cost involved in doing so. Instead, the state accepts that responsibility.

If the Secretary of State is considering taking action to enforce a collection arrangement under s.29 of the Act, an arrears notice must be served under reg.2 of the Arrears, Interest and Adjustment of Maintenance Assessments Regulations.

If there are arrears, the Secretary of State has a discretion whether to attribute any payment that is made towards the satisfaction of those arrears or towards the discharge of the current liability for child support maintenance: reg.2 of the Arrears, Interest and Adjustment of Maintenance Assessments Regulations. An overpayment of child support maintenance may also be applied to reduce arrears owing under a previous maintenance calculation: reg.10(1)(a) of the Arrears, Interest and Adjustment of Maintenance Assessments Regulations.

*Subsection (2)*

Regulation 8 of the Arrears, Interest and Adjustment of Maintenance Assessments Regulations provides that where the person with care is paid income support or an income-based jobseeker's allowance, the Secretary of State may retain the amount of arrears equal to the difference between the amount of that benefit actually paid to that person, and the amount which would have been paid if the arrears had not accrued.

This prevents the person with care benefiting at the expense of the social security system from late payment by the non-resident parent.

## [¹Penalty payments

2.149    **41A.**—(1) The Secretary of State may by regulations make provision for the payment to him by non-resident parents who are in arrears with payments of child support maintenance of penalty payments determined in accordance with the regulations.

(2) The amount of a penalty payment in respect of any week may not exceed 25 per cent of the amount of child support maintenance payable for that week, but otherwise is to be determined by the Secretary of State.

(3) The liability of a non-resident parent to make a penalty payment does not affect his liability to pay the arrears of child support maintenance concerned.

(4) Regulations under subsection (1) may, in particular, make provision—

(a) as to the time at which a penalty payment is to be payable;
(b) for the Secretary of State to waive a penalty payment, or part of it.

(5) The provisions of this Act with respect to—

(a) the collection of child support maintenance;

(b) the enforcement of an obligation to pay child support maintenance,

apply equally (with any necessary modifications) to penalty payments payable by virtue of regulations under this section.

(6) The Secretary of State shall pay penalty payments received by him into the Consolidated Fund.]

AMENDMENT

1. Section 18(2) of the 2000 Act (for the purpose of making regulations, November 10, 2000 under art.2(1) of, and Pt I of the Schedule to, the Commencement No.3 Order 2000; March 3, 2003 under art.3 of, and the Schedule to, the Commencement No.12 Order 2003).

DEFINITIONS

"child support maintenance": see s.54.                                                              **2.150**
"non-resident parent": see s.54.

GENERAL NOTE

This is an enforcement measure. It allows the Secretary of State to impose a          **2.151**
penalty payment on the non-resident parent whose payments are in arrears. It may be up to 25 per cent of the weekly child support maintenance payable. It is in addition to liability for the arrears (subs.(2)). The penalty does not benefit the person with care, as it has to be paid into the Consolidated Fund (subs.(6)).

Regulation 7A of the Collection and Enforcement Regulations is made under the authority of this section.

## [¹Repayment of overpaid child support maintenance

**41B.**—(1) This section applies where it appears to the Secretary of State          **2.152**
that [⁴a non-resident parent] has made a payment by way of child support maintenance which amounts to an overpayment by him of that maintenance and that—

(a) it would not be possible for the [⁴a non-resident parent] to recover the amount of the overpayment by way of an adjustment of the amount payable under a [⁵maintenance calculation]; or

(b) it would be inappropriate to rely on an adjustment of the amount payable under a [⁵maintenance calculation] as the means of enabling the absent parent to recover the amount of the overpayment.

[²(1A) This section also applies where the non-resident parent has made a voluntary payment and it appears to the Secretary of State—

(a) that he is not liable to pay child support maintenance;

(b) that he is liable, but some or all of the payment amounts to an overpayment,

and, in a case falling within paragraph (b), it also appears to him that subsection (1)(a) or (b) applies.]

(2) The Secretary of State may make such payment to the [⁴non-resident parent] by way of reimbursement, or partial reimbursement, of the overpayment as the Secretary of State considers appropriate.

(3) Where the Secretary of State has made a payment under this section he may, in such circumstances as may be prescribed, require the relevant person to pay to him the whole, or a specified proportion, of the amount of that payment.

(4) Any such requirement shall be imposed by giving the relevant person a written demand for the amount which the Secretary of State wishes to recover from him.

(5) Any sum which a person is required to pay to the Secretary of State under this section shall be recoverable from him by the Secretary of State as a debt due to the Crown.

(6) The Secretary of State may by regulations make provision in relation to any case in which—

(a) one or more overpayments of child support maintenance are being reimbursed to the Secretary of State by the relevant person; and

(b) child support maintenance has continued to be payable by the [⁴non-resident parent] concerned to the person with care concerned, or again becomes so payable.

[³(7) For the purposes of this section—

(a) a payment made by a person under a maintenance calculation which was not validly made; and

(b) a voluntary payment made in the circumstances set out in subsection (1A)(a),

shall be treated as an overpayment of child support maintenance made by a non-resident parent.]

(8) Any sum recovered by the Secretary of State under this section shall be paid by him into the Consolidated Fund.]

AMENDMENTS

1. Section 23 of the Child Support Act 1995 (subss.(1), (2) and (7) September 4, 1995; remainder October 1, 1995).

2. Section 20(3) of the 2000 Act (for the purpose of making regulations, November 10, 2000 under art.2(1) of, and Pt I of the Schedule to, the Commencement No.3 Order 2000; March 3, 2003 under art.5 of, and the Schedule to, the Commencement No. 2 Order 2003).

3. Section 20(4) of the 2000 Act (for the purpose of making regulations, November 10, 2000 under art.2(1) of, and Pt I of the Schedule to, the Commencement No.3 Order 2000; March 3, 2003 under art.5 of, and the Schedule to, the Commencement No.12 Order 2003).

4. Paragraph 11(2) of Sch.3 to the 2000 Act (March 3, 2003 under art.3 of, and the Schedule to, the Commencement No.12 Order 2003).

5. Section 1(2)(a) of the 2000 Act (March 3, 2003 under art.3 of, and the Schedule to, the Commencement No.12 Order 2003).

DEFINITIONS

2.153     "child support maintenance": see s.54.
    "non-resident parent": see s.54.
    "person with care": see s.54.

GENERAL NOTE

This section deals with overpayments by the non-resident parent. If an adjust-    **2.154**
ment is not possible or appropriate, the overpayment may be reimbursed by the
Secretary of State: see reg.10 of the Arrears, Interest and Adjustment of
Maintenance Assessment Regulations. The Secretary of State may in turn recover
the amount reimbursed from the person who benefited from it: see regs 10A and
10B of those Regulations.

*Subsection (6)*

Where the circumstances set out in this subsection apply, the Secretary of State
may retain, out of the child support maintenance collected from the non-resident
parent in respect of a maintenance application made under ss.4 or 7, such sums as
are required from the person with care to offset his reimbursement of the non-resident parent for an overpayment (reg.10A(2) of the Arrears, Interest and
Adjustment of Maintenance Assessments Regulations).

*Special cases*

**Special cases**

**42.**—(1) The Secretary of State may be regulations provide that in    **2.155**
prescribed circumstances a case is to be treated as a special case for the
purposes of this Act.

(2) Those regulations may, for example, provide for the following to be
special cases—

(a) each parent of a child is [¹a non-resident parent] in relation to the
child;

(b) there is more than one person who is a person with care in relation
to the same child;

(c) there is more than one qualifying child in relation to the same [¹non-
resident parent] but the person who is the person with care in relation to one of those children is not the person who is the person with
care in relation to all of them;

(d) a person is [¹a non-resident parent] in relation to more than one
child and the other parent of each of those children is not the same
person;

(e) the person with care has care of more than one qualifying child and
there is more than one absent parent in relation to those children;

(f) a qualifying child has his home in two or more separate households.

(3) The Secretary of State may by regulations make provisions with
respect to special cases.

(4) Regulations made under subsection (3) may, in particular—

(a) modify any provision made by or under this Act, in its application to
any special case or any special case falling within a prescribed
category;

(b) make new provision for any such case; or

(c) provide for any prescribed provision made by or under this Act not
to apply to any such case.

AMENDMENT

1. Paragraph 11(2) of Sch.3 to the 2000 Act (March 3, 2003 under art.3 of, and the Schedule to, the Commencement No.12 Order 2003).

DEFINITIONS

2.156    "child": see s.55.
"non-resident parent" see s.54.
"parent": see s.54.
"person with care": see s.3(3).
"prescribed": see s.54.
"qualifying child": see s.3(1)

GENERAL NOTE

*Subsection (1)*

2.157    The basic structure of the Act presupposes the typical case of a child who has two parents, one of whom has left the household. However, there are a number of ways in which reality may vary from this model. These are represented by the special cases which adjust the provisions of the Act to cater for these variations. The regulations made under this section are contained in Pt III of the Maintenance Calculations and Special Cases Regulations.

*Subsection (3)*

The regulations made under this section are contained in Pt III of the Maintenance Calculations and Special Cases Regulations.

*Subsection (4)*

Where a statute permits regulations which modify its provisions, that modification must be expressed; it cannot be inferred or implied from the content of the regulation (*R(CS) 14/98*, para.10). However, the regulation will be validly made if the modification is on its proper interpretation expressly made, even if it is not clearly so (*ibid*, para.10).

This subsection is to be interpreted fairly widely, but it cannot be used to subvert the whole purpose of the Act or make provision beyond the scope of its long title. Moreover it must be read as a consistent whole such that other provisions may limit the scope of this subsection. See *R(CS) 14/98*, para.11.

## [¹Recovery of child support maintenance by deduction from benefit

2.158    **43.**—(1) This section applies where—
(a) a non-resident parent is liable to pay a flat rate of child support maintenance (or would be so liable but for a variation having been agreed to), and that rate applies (or would have applied) because he falls within paragraph 4(1)(b) or (c) or 4(2) of Schedule 1; and
(b) such conditions as may be prescribed for the purposes of this section are satisfied.

(2) The power of the Secretary of State to make regulations under section 5 of the Social Security Administration Act 1992 by virtue of subsection (1)(p) (deductions from benefits) may be exercised in relation to cases to which this section applies with a view to securing that payments in

respect of child support maintenance are made or that arrears of child support maintenance are recovered.

(3) For the purposes of this section, the benefits to which section 5 of the 1992 Act applies are to be taken as including was disablement pensions and war widows' pensions (within the meaning of section 150 of the Social Security Contributions and Benefits Act 1992 (interpretation)).]

AMENDMENT

1. Section 21 of the 2000 Act (for the purpose of making regulations, November 10, 2000 under art.2(1) of, and Pt I of the Schedule to, the Commencement No.3 Order 2000; March 3, 2003 under art.3 of, and the Schedule to, the Commencement No.12 Order 2003).

DEFINITIONS

"child support maintenance": see s.54.    2.159
"non-resident parent": see s.54.

GENERAL NOTE

*Subsection (2)*    2.160
This subsection is only worded as an enabling provision. The legal basis for liability to make payments in place of child support maintenance is provided by s.1 above which imposes an obligation on both parents to maintain their children which is to be met by an absent parent by making periodical payments of maintenance (*not* necessarily child support maintenance). See *CCS 16904/96*, para.21. The liability may be imposed directly and not only by deduction from benefits for a prospective period (*CCS 3488/04*).

Schedule 9, paras 2, 7A and 8 to the Social Security (Claims and Payments) Regulations 1987 (as amended) set out how deductions from benefit are to be made to third parties, including child support recipients, and the order of priorities in which various deductions are to be taken.

*Jurisdiction*

**Jurisdiction**

44.—(1) [¹The Secretary of State] shall have jurisdiction to make a    2.161
[⁶maintenance calculation] with respect to a person who is—
(a) a person with care;
(b) [⁵a non-resident parent]; or
(c) a qualifying child,
only if that person is habitually resident in the United Kingdom[², except in the case of a non-resident parent who falls within subsection (2A)].

(2) Where the person with care is not an individual, subsection (1) shall have effect as if paragraph (a) were omitted.

[³(2A) A non-resident parent falls within this subsection if he is not habitually resident in the United Kingdom, but is—
(a) employed in the civil service of the Crown, including Her Majesty's Diplomatic Service and Her Majesty's Overseas Civil Service;

(b) a member of the naval, military or air forces of the Crown, including any person employed by an association established for the purposes of Part XI of the Reserve Forces Act 1996;

(c) employed by a company of a prescribed description registered under the Companies Act 1985 in England and Wales or in Scotland, or under the Companies (Northern Ireland) Order 1986; or

(d) employed by a body of a prescribed description.]
[⁴. . .]

AMENDMENTS

2.162   1. Paragraph 41 of Sch.7 to the Social Security Act 1998 (June 1, 1999).
2. Section 22(2) of the the 2000 Act (January 31, 2001 under art.2(1) of the Commencement No. 5 Order 2000).
3. Section 22(3) of the 2000 Act (for the purpose of making regulations, November 10, 2000 under art.2(1) of, and Pt I of the Schedule to, the Commencement No.3 Order 2000; otherwise January 31, 2001 under art.2(1) of the Commencement No.5 Order 2000).
4. Section 22(4) of the 2000 Act (March 3, 2003 under art.3 of, and the Schedule to, the Commencement No.12 Order 2003).
5. Paragraph 11(2) of Sch 3 to the 2000 Act (March 3, 2003 under art.3 of, and the Schedule to, the Commencement No.12 Order 2003).
6. Section 1(2)(a) of the 2000 Act (March 3, 2003 under art.3 of, and the Schedule to, the Commencement No.12 Order 2003).

DEFINITIONS

2.163   "maintenance calculation": see s.54.
"non-resident parent": see s.54.
"person with care": see s.3(3).
"prescribed": see s.54.
"qualifying child": see s.3(1).

GENERAL NOTE

*Subsection (1)*
Jurisdiction depends on all the relevant parties being habitually resident in the UK. This is subject to subs.(2A) below.

The preponderance of authority is that there is no discernible difference between habitual residence and ordinary residence (*V v B* [1991] 1 F.L.R. 266; *Kapur v Kapur* [1984] F.L.R. 928; *I v I* [2001] 1 F.L.R. 913 confirmed in *Ikimi v Ikimi* [2001] 2 F.L.R. 1288). The authorities are used interchangeably in this note. Also, there is authority that a person may be habitually resident in more than one jurisdiction at the same time (*Ikimi v Ikimi* [2001] 2 F.L.R. 1288; *Armstrong v Armstrong* [2003] 2 F.L.R. 375). *C v FC (Brussels II: Free-standing application for parental responsibility)* [2004] 1 F.L.R. 317 is an extreme example in which the court decided that the parents had retained their habitual residence in England, despite being absent for more than two years and possibly having obtained habitual residence in Hong Kong.).

In order to apply the authorities, it is convenient to consider habitual residence in four categories. Regardless of category, the issue is one of fact (*Re M (Abduction: Habitual Residence)* [1996] 1 F.L.R. 887; *Cameron v Cameron* 1996 S.L.T. 306).

The first category is actual habitual residence. Most of the general note to this subsection is concerned with actual habitual residence. The leading authority is the decision of the House of Lords in *Shah v Barnet London Borough Council* [1983] 1 All E.R. 226, especially the speech of Lord Scarman at 234–236. In order to have actual habitual residence, two conditions must be satisfied. One is that the person must be resident in the UK. That requires the person to have established a home here. It is not sufficient to intend to do that. See *CCS 15927/96*, para.6–9. The other condition is that the person must have been resident for an appreciable period. In *CSCS 8/01*, para.16, the Commissioner relied on a Scottish authority for the proposition that a person could not be habitually resident in two jurisdictions at the same time. Outside of Scotland, dual habitual residence may be possible, albeit unlikely on the facts.

The second category is retained habitual residence. Habitual residence is retained if the person leaves the UK in circumstances that do not bring habitual residence to an end. In law, this is not a separate category. It is, however, convenient to label it in order to help identify the proper starting point if the issue of a person's habitual residence arises. It is often assumed that a person who has left the UK has thereby ceased to be habitually resident. The inquiry then centres on the circumstances of the person's return and when and whether habitual residence was again established. That is the wrong starting point. The person may never have ceased to be habitually resident. The proper starting point is not the person's return, but the person's departure.

The third category is resumed habitual residence. This was recognised by the House of Lords in *Nessa v Chief Adjudication Officer* [1999] 4 All E.R. 677. It arises when someone who was habitually resident in the UK returns after ceasing to be habitually resident here. This differs from actual habitual residence in that resumed habitual residence may be established more quickly, perhaps immediately. This category was analysed in detail in the joined cases of *CIS 1304/97* and *CJSA 5394/98*. These were his conclusions. The only difference between actual and resumed habitual residence is that the appreciable period of residence is reduced or removed in the latter. Habitual residence is not automatically resumed on return. The key consideration in establishing actual habitual residence is the character of a person's residence. That may be coloured by three factors: (a) the circumstances in which the person ceased to be habitually resident; (b) the links retained with the UK while absent; and (c) the circumstances of the return.

The fourth category is deemed habitual residence. This arises under subs.(2A) below. See the general note to that provision.

Decisions made on a person's residence (and on other matters) by officers acting in other capacities than under the child support legislation are persuasive but not conclusive *(R. (ota Nahar) v Social Security Commissioners* [2002] 1 F.L.R. 670).

From *Shah* and other authorities the following propositions emerge:  **2.164**
(i) The words are not a term of art and are to be given their ordinary and natural meaning unless it can be shown that the statutory framework or the legal context in which the words are used requires a different meaning (*Shah*). In *CCS 7207/95*, para.6 the Commissioner emphasised the importance of the context in which habitual residence has to be considered. The same Commissioner set out his view in *R(CS) 5/96* at para.9:

> "**the purpose underlying the child support legislation is the social need to require absent parents to maintain, or contribute to the maintenance of, their children**. In determining as question of fact whether in the above context a person has ceased to be habitually resident in this country, it appears to me that the emphasis should be put on factors directed to establishing the nature and degree of his past and continuing connection with this country and his intentions as to the future, albeit the original reason for his move abroad, and the nature of any work being undertaken there are also material. It is not enough merely to look at the length and continuity of the actual residence abroad."

(ii) The normal meaning of habitual residence is "a man's abode in a particular place or country which he has adopted voluntarily and for settled purposes as part of the regular order of his life for the time being, whether of short or long duration" (*Shah*). Residence is therefore something different from presence (*CA 35/92*, paras 5 and 14). Accordingly, a person may be habitually resident within the jurisdiction while working abroad. Residence must also be distinguished from the English concept of domicile (*R(U)8/88*, Appendix 1, para.6).

(iii) This basic definition of habitual residence is subject to the exception that the person's presence in a particular jurisdiction must be lawful (*Shah*). This is a rule of public policy, not of construction of legislation. So when, as in this section, the issue arises in the context of a jurisdictional rule, the court or tribunal has a margin of discretion whether or not the illegality is sufficient to oust jurisdiction. See *Marks v Marks (Divorce: Jurisdiction)* [2004] 1 F.L.R. 1069. In order to decide whether it does oust jurisdiction in a particular case, it may be relevant to know whether an immigrant is lawfully within the country or whether a child has been abducted. The habitual residence of children is discussed below.

(iv) For the most part the definition concentrates on observable facts, but there will seldom be direct evidence of a person's intention. The proper approach to dealing with conflicts of affidavit evidence on intention was explained by the Court of Appeal in *Re F (A Minor) (Child Abduction)* [1992] 1 F.L.R. 548. In the context of summary proceedings for the return of a child to a country in which it was alleged that he had been habitually resident before being abducted, the court held that where there is irreconcilable affidavit evidence and no oral testimony available, the judge should look to see if there is independent extraneous evidence in support of one side, although that evidence would have to be compelling before it could be preferred to the sworn testimony of a deponent. Usually, however, the person's intention will have to be inferred from all the circumstances of the case, in which case the primary facts will have to be included in the findings of fact and the drawing of the inference explained in the tribunal's reasons for decision.

(v) The person's intention will be relevant in two respects. First, the residence must be voluntary. Involuntary residence such as a result, for example, of kidnapping or imprisonment would negative the will to be there (*Shah*). However, this may not be a universal requirement. In *Re MacKenzie* [1940] 4 All E.R. 310 a lady came on a visit to this country which she intended to be temporary. She became insane while here and spent the next 54 years in an asylum. Morton J., discussed *I R C v Lysaght* [1928] A.C. 234, (one of the decisions relied on by the House of Lords in *Shah*), but distinguished it, holding that it did not decide that involuntary residence had to be wholly disregarded for ascertaining a person's habitual residence. In view of the very great degree of continuity in the case he held that the lady was habitually resident in this country despite her lack of choice. Where someone is looking after an adult who lacks the capacity to form an intention, the residence and wishes of the former will be relevant to the habitual residence of the latter: see the discussion of the habitual residence of children in (xi) below.

(vi) The second way in which intention is relevant is that there must be a settled purpose. There need be no intention to remain permanently or even indefinitely. A short and definite period will be sufficient. In *CA 35/92*, for example, a lady was held to be ordinarily resident in Malta when she went there for health reasons with the intention of returning within 18 months. All that is required is that there should be sufficient continuity that can properly be described as settled. Education can be a sufficient purpose (*Kapur v Kapur*), as would health (*CA 35/92*).

(vii) Lack of evidence of the actual places within a jurisdiction where a person has stayed is not fatal to a decision that a person has been habitually resident there, although it is a factor to be taken into account (*Re Brauch Ex p. Britannic Securities and Investments Ltd* [1978] 1 All E.R. 1004).

(viii) In order to acquire habitual residence it is necessary to show not only a settled purpose but also that the person has spent an appreciable period of time in the jurisdiction (*Re J (A Minor) (Abduction: Custody Rights)* [1990] 2 A.C. 562). What constitutes a sufficient period is a decision to be reached in the light of the circumstances of the individual case. Ultimately, however, it is the quality rather than the duration of the residence that is important (*Cruse v Chittum* [1974] 2 All E.R. 940). This suggests that in appropriate circumstances habitual residence could be acquired in a single day. However, it is unclear how quickly habitual residence can be acquired. The proposition attributed to *Re J* above appears inconsistent with *Lewis v Lewis* [1956] 1 All E.R. 375, in which it was held that the boarding of ship to resume a former home in this country would be sufficient to establish habitual residence here. This case is a clear authority for the proposition that habitual residence can be acquired in a single day if the person concerned has had an habitual residence in one place, moved to another, and then abandoned that other place to return to the former home. However, the authority on which this decision was based, *Macrae v Macrae* [1949] 2 All E.R. 34, is suspect in suggesting, contrary to the view of the House of Lords in *Re J*, that habitual residence may be acquired as easily as it is lost. The fact of resumption of a former home may be sufficient to distinguish *Re J*, although it must be admitted that the case of *R. v Lancashire County Council Ex p. Huddleston* [1986] 2 All E.R. 941, which is discussed below, is inconsistent with this argument. Moreover, in *Re M (Minors) (Residence Order: Jurisdiction)* [1993] 1 F.L.R. 495 a mother with parental responsibility for children allowed them to go to live in Scotland (a separate jurisdiction) and then decided on their returning to stay with her for a holiday that they should remain with her in England. Balcombe L.J., thought that the children did not thereby immediately become habitually resident in England, whereas Hoffmann L.J. thought they did. However, since the issue was not essential to the court's decision, these views are *obiter*. *Lewis* has been distinguished by the Court of Appeal on the ground that it applies where a period of ordinary (or habitual) residence has to be shown in order to establish jurisdiction (*Nessa v Chief Adjudication Officer* [1998] 1 F.L.R. 879 at 882–3, *per* Sir Christopher Staughton).

It appears to be accepted in the case law on the meaning of habitual residence for the purposes of the Child Abduction and Custody Act 1985 that habitual residence probably *cannot* be acquired in a single day. In *Re F (A Minor) (Child Abduction)* [1992] 1 F.L.R. 548 one month was accepted as sufficient. In *Re B (Minors) (Abduction) (No.2)* [1993] 1 F.L.R. 993 where parents went from England to live in the mother's home town in Germany "to provide a base for reconciliation and for planning a fresh start", it was held that after seven months' stay the habitual residence of the children was in Germany. Waite J., at p.995 said: "Although habitual residence can be lost in a single day, for example upon departure from the initial abode with no intention of returning, the assumption of habitual residence requires an appreciable period of time and a settled intention. ... Logic would suggest that provided the purpose was settled, the period of habitation need not be long." In *A v A (Child Abduction) (Habitual Residence)* [1993] 2 F.L.R. 225, habitual residence had been acquired after eight months.

(ix) Since habitual residence depends upon there being a settled purpose, a person will cease to be habitually resident once such a settled purpose ceases to exist. Habitual residence can therefore be lost in a single day (*Re J*). It is not necessary for the person to form a settled intention not to return (*Re R (Abduction: Habitual Residence)* [2004] 1 F.L.R. 216 at para.41). Since it may not be so easily acquired, it is possible that a person may have no place of habitual residence: see *CSCS 8/01*, para.16 and the discussion in (viii) above. A person who has been habitually resident in the UK has the evidential burden of proving that that habitual residence has ceased (*CSCS 8/01*, para.16).

(x) Absences from a place are not sufficient to lose habitual residence if they are purely temporary (*Shah* and *Lewis*). It will be necessary for the tribunal to establish the number and duration of any absences, as well as the reasons for them, in order to decide whether on balance they are sufficient to displace a person's habitual residence. However, lengthy absences will result in loss of habitual residence even if there is an intention ultimately to return. In *Huddleston* a family had left England for Hong Kong when their daughter was five-years-old, intending ultimately to return. However, they remained abroad for 13 years as a result of the father's employment which required him to be exclusively abroad. When the daughter returned, it was held that she was not ordinarily resident in the UK.

(xi) Usually the habitual residence of children will be determined by that of the persons with whom they live lawfully (*Re J*). If both parents have parental responsibility for a child, one of the parents cannot unilaterally change the child's habitual residence (*Re N (Abduction: Habitual Residence)* [2000] 2 F.L.R. 899). If parents want to sever a child's habitual residence from their own (for example, by sending the child to live with relatives abroad), they must have a settled intention that the child will not return, except for visits, and will live in a different jurisdiction from them for the long-term, although not necessarily permanently (*Re V (Jurisdiction: Habitual Residence* [2001 1 F.L.R. 253). If the child lives with only one parent by agreement, it will be that parent's residence which is significant. However, this will not be the case if the child has been abducted, unless the dispossessed parent has acquiesced. Acquiescence is the informed consent by a person to something which would otherwise amount to an infringement of that person's rights. Where the person has not expressly acquiesced, acquiescence may be inferred. The approach to be taken in deciding whether or not to infer that a person has acquiesced was explained by Balcombe L.J., in *Re A (Minors) (Abduction: Acquiescence)* [1992] 2 F.L.R. 14 at 22:

> "acquiescence can be inferred from inactivity and silence on the part of the parent from whose custody, joint or single, the child has been wrongfully removed. In such a case . . . the court would have to look at all the circumstances of the case, and in particular, the reasons for the inactivity on the part of the wronged parent and the length of the period over which the inactivity persisted, in order to decide whether it was legitimate to infer acquiescence on his or her part."

A parent does not need to have knowledge of his specific legal rights over a child to be held to have acquiesced in the child's wrongful retention abroad. The issue is whether the parent conducted himself in a way which would be inconsistent with him later seeking a summary order for the child's return. It is enough that the parent knows that the child has been retained in another jurisdiction against his wishes and he is capable of seeking legal advice as to what proceedings be might take, but does nothing to bring about the child's return (*Re AZ (A Minor) (Abduction: Acquiescence)* [1993] 1 F.L.R. 682).

An Australian father who, on being told by the mother that she was going to take their child to England for a holiday, said to her "Go for six months, 12 months, I do not care" had not acquiesced in the child's wrongful retention. On the other hand, his failure to take any effective steps to recover the child for the next 10 months did amount to such acquiescence: (*W v W (Child Abduction: Acquiescence)* [1993] 2 F.L.R. 211).

Acquiescence is primarily to be established by inference drawn from an objective survey of the acts and omissions of the parent, but it is permissible to inquire into the state of the parent's knowledge of his or her rights, and it may be necessary to examine private motives and other influences affecting the parent's conduct. Hence, where a parent does not take action to recover his child because of erroneous legal advice, he may be able to rebut the inference of acquiescence otherwise arising from his inactivity (*Re S (Minors) (Abduction: Custody Rights)* [1994] 1 F.L.R. 819).

It has been said that implied acquiescence will occur certainly after six months and in appropriate cases after as little as three months (*Re P (G E) (An Infant)* [1964] 3 All E.R. 977 at 982, *per* Lord Denning M.R.), although the authority is an old one and the proposition may be stated too starkly. In some cases children will be of sufficient age and maturity to form a settled purpose separate from that of the persons with whom they live. This of itself will not affect the children's habitual residence, unless the circumstances permit a separate habitual residence to exist. This might occur, for example, where a child is at a school or college abroad during term-time and returns home only for the vacations. In cases where children are of an age likely to be capable of forming their own settled purpose, an inquiry and findings of fact will be necessary as to their maturity to decide on such a purpose and on their freedom to act on it.

The important factor in the case of children is with whom they lawfully reside. In deciding this, any existing order for custody or care and control will be an important consideration as in *Re P (G.E) (An Infant)*. As cases in which the concept of custody is still relevant become fewer, as a result of the Children Act 1989, the emphasis will be on who has parental responsibility and on the effect of any residence order made under s.8 of that Act. In *Re M (Minors) (Residence Order: Jurisdiction)* [1993] 1 F.L.R. 495, for example, a decision by an unmarried mother, who lived in England and who had sole parental responsibility for children who were then living with their grandparents in Scotland, that they should henceforth live with her, was sufficient to end their habitual residence in Scotland.

The child's habitual residence remains unchanged until a court order which would have the effect of ending that habitual residence takes effect. In *Re O (A Minor) (Abduction: Habitual Residence)* [1993] 2 F.L.R. 594, an American court order had given custody of a child to the mother, whose habitual residence was the UK. A later American order that custody be transferred to the father, habitually resident in Nevada, the order to take effect at a later date, did not end the child's habitual residence being that of the mother *until* that later date. (Her removal of the child from Nevada in the interim was therefore not a wrongful removal within the terms of child abduction law, as the child was still habitually resident in the UK.)

*Re M* shows that it is not necessarily the place where the parent who has habitual residence (or custody) lives that matters, but the place where the parent allows the children to live; so the children's habitual residence was initially in Scotland until permission to live there was withdrawn by the mother. Where both parents have equal parental responsibility (*i.e.* they are married to each other, or the father has obtained parental responsibility under the Children Act 1989) and both are habitually resident in one country, there is a strong burden imposed upon anyone seeking to argue that the child's habitual residence is different. The parents may agree to change the child's habitual residence, but sending the child to a boarding-school abroad would not suffice. One parent cannot unilaterally change the child's habitual residence without the other's agreement (*Re A (A Minor) (Wardship: Jurisdiction)* [1995] 1 F.L.R. 767). In the context of the Child Abduction and Custody Act 1985 it has been held that whether consent to the removal of a child from one jurisdiction to another is valid depends upon the circumstances of the particular case, but that it is unlikely that consent which has been obtained by means of a calculated and deliberate fraud will be considered valid (*Re B (a Minor) (Child Abduction: Consent)* [1994] 2 F.L.R. 249).

It is impossible to lay down rigid rules as to the habitual residence of children. This is shown by *W and B v H (Child Abduction: Surrogacy)* [2002] 1 F.L.R. 1008 especially at para.25, in which Hedley J. decided that twin children were not habitually resident anywhere. The case concerned a surrogacy agreement between a husband and wife who lived in California and a surrogate mother. The twins were conceived of the husband's sperm and an anonymous donor's egg, and born to a surrogate mother. The surrogate mother gave birth in England and refused to honour the surrogacy agreement. Hedley J. found that although the husband had the right of custody under Californian law, the children were not habitually resident in California, where they had never been. He also found that although the children were physically present in this country and the surrogate mother was habitually resident here, they were not habitually resident here either, because the surrogate had no biological connection with them. There are comments in the judgment of Charles J. in *B v H (Habitual Residence:Wardship* [2002] 1 F.L.R. 388, which appear to suggest that children will always have the same habitual residence as their parents at birth, regardless of where in the world they happen to be born. Hedley J. disagreed with that proposition (para.23).

(xii) Whether or not habitual residence has been established is a question of fact to be decided in all the circumstances of the case (*Shah* and *Re J*). The tribunal will therefore need to make findings of fact on all of the factors considered above that are relevant to the appeal and to indicate in the reasons for decision that the correct test has been applied. It will be dangerous and an error of law to make decisions based on the similarity of the facts to those in other reported decisions, since each case depends on its own combination of facts. Commissioners' Decisions do, however, provide some indication of the range of factors which a CSAT might wish to investigate in deciding on habitual residence (see the factors taken into account in *R(U) 8/88* and the decisions cited therein).

(xiii) Although a person may retain habitual residence here despite being physically absent (as in *R(CS) 5/96*), there comes a time when absence outweighs all other considerations (as in *CCS 7207/95*, paras 9–10 where a tour of duty abroad for 20 years with only two and a half spent in this country was held to be incompatible with habitual residence here).

Where one of the parties is habitually resident abroad, the courts may still have powers to make maintenance and property orders for a child. Such powers are broad. In *A v A (A Minor) (Financial Provision)* [1994] 1 F.L.R. 657, for example, a wealthy father was required to pay as follows in respect of one particular child: a house was settled on trust for the child until she ceased education (including tertiary education); while the child remained under the control of the mother, the mother was to have the right to occupy the house rent-free in order to provide a home for the child; the father was to pay the child's school fees, extras, and secured periodical payments of £20,000 per annum for her maintenance (it being immaterial that some of this money would actually be spent on the mother's other children, of whom he was not the father). (Of course, even had the father been habitually resident in the UK, the circumstances suggest that the court would certainly have made a top-up order under s.8(6) and property adjustment orders under Sch.1 to the Children Act 1989.)

For a discussion of the possible conflict between this section and European Community law see the section on Child Support and European Law at the beginning of this book.

*Subsection (2A)*

This subsection operates effectively to deem a non-resident parent habitually resident in the UK if the person's employment relationship with the UK falls into one of the specified categories. Regulation 7A of the Maintenance Arrangements and Jurisdiction Regulations is made under the authority of this subsection. Regulation 7A(1) is made under para.(c) and reg.7A(2) is made under para.(d).

## Jurisdiction of courts in certain proceedings under this Act

**45.**—(1) The Lord Chancellor or, in relation to Scotland, the Lord    2.165
Advocate may by order make such provision as he considers necessary to
secure that appeals, or such class of appeals as may be specified in the
order—

  (a) shall be made to a court instead of being made to [¹an appeal
tribunal]; or

  (b) shall be so made in such circumstances as may be so specified.

  (2) In subsection (1), "court" means—

  (a) in relation to England and Wales and subject to any provision made
under Schedule 11 to the Children Act 1989 (jurisdiction of courts
with respect to certain proceedings relating to children) the High
Court, a county court or a magistrates' court; and

  (b) in relation to Scotland, the Court of Session or the sheriff.

  (3) Schedule 11 to the Act of 1989 shall be amended in accordance with
subsections (4) and (5).

  (4) [Adds Schedule 11, Part I, paragraph 1(2A) to the Children Act 1989.]

  (5) [Amends Schedule 11, Part I, paragraphs 1(3), 2(3) to the Children
Act 1989.]

  (6) Where the effect of any order under subsection (1) is that there are
no longer any appeals which fall to be dealt with by [²appeal tribunals], the
Lord Chancellor after consultation with the Lord Advocate may by order
provide for the abolition of those tribunals.

  (7) Any order under subsection (1) or (6) may make—

  (a) such modifications of any provision of this Act or of any other
enactment; and

  (b) such transitional provision,

as the Minister making the order considers appropriate in consequence of
any provision made by the order.

AMENDMENTS

1. Paragraph 42(1) of Sch.7 to the Social Security Act 1998 (June 1, 1999).
2. Paragraph 42(2) of Sch.7 to the Social Security Act 1998 (June 1, 1999).

DEFINITION

"appeal tribunal": see s.54.    2.166

GENERAL NOTE

*Subsection (1)*

  The Child Support Appeals (Jurisdiction of Courts) Order 2002 and the Child    2.167
Support Appeals (Jurisdiction of Courts) (Scotland) Order 2003 provides that
appeals under s.20 are to go to a court rather than to a tribunal where the question
involved is whether a particular person is a parent of the child. This will enable the
court to direct scientific tests to determine parentage by virtue of powers available
under ss.20–25 of the Family Law Reform Act 1969 as amended.

  Schedule 2 to the Child Maintenance Orders (Backdating) Order 1993 amends
s.65(1) of the Magistrates' Courts Act 1980 to provide that appeals under s.20, or
references for a declaration of parentage, brought to the magistrates by virtue of
s.27, are family proceedings.

*Subsections (3) to (5)*

The Children (Allocation of Proceedings) (Amendment) Order 1993 provides that child support cases heard by courts in accordance with ss.20, 27 and 45 are commenced in the magistrates' courts and may be transferred to another magistrates' court or up to the county court or High Court in line with the same criteria as apply in the Children (Allocation of Proceedings) Order 1991. The Family Proceedings Courts (Child Support Act 1991) Rules 1993 apply to parentage questions heard by the magistrates' court.

The High Court (Distribution of Business) Order 1993 provides that any proceedings under the Child Support Act which are heard in the High Court are to be assigned to the Family Division.

The Family Proceedings Rules 1991 (as amended) cater for where a child support case has been transferred up from the magistrates' court. Rules 3.21 and 3.22 provide that r.4.6 shall apply to an application under s.27 of the Child Support Act for a declaration of parentage, and to an appeal under s.20. The rules allow the court to give such directions as it thinks proper with regard to the conduct of the proceedings. In particular, the court may direct that the proceedings shall proceed as if they had been commenced by originating summons or originating application and that any document served or other thing done while the proceedings were pending in another court, including a magistrates' court, shall be treated for such purposes as may be specified in the direction as if provided for by the rules of court applicable in the court to which the proceedings have been transferred.

An application under s.27 (but not an appeal under s.20) may be heard and determined by a district judge (r.3.21(4)).

The Children (Admissibility of Hearsay Evidence) Order 1993 extends to civil proceedings under the Child Support Act in the magistrates' courts the power to admit evidence notwithstanding that it is hearsay.

*Miscellaneous and supplemental*

## [¹Reduced benefit decisions

2.168    **46.**—(1) This section applies where any person ("the parent")—

(a) has made a request under section 6(5);

(b) fails to comply with any regulation made under section 6(7); or

(c) having been treated as having applied for a maintenance calculation under section 6, refuses to take a scientific test (within the meaning of section 27A).

(2) The Secretary of State may serve written notice on the parent requiring her, before the end of a specified period—

(a) in a subsection (1)(a) case, to give him her reasons for making the request;

(b) in a subsection (1)(b) case, to give him her reasons for failing to do so; or

(c) in a subsection (1)(c) case, to give him her reasons for her refusal.

(3) When the specified period has expired, the Secretary of State shall consider whether, having regard to any reasons given by the parent, there are reasonable grounds for believing that—

(a) in a subsection (1)(a) case, if the Secretary of State were to do what is mentioned in section 6(3);

(b) in a subsection (1)(b) case, if she were to be required to comply; or

(c) in a subsection (1)(c) case, if she took the scientific test, there would be a risk of her, or of any children living with her, suffering harm or undue distress as a result of his taking such action, or her complying or taking the test.

(4) If the Secretary of State considers that there are such reasonable grounds, he shall—

    (a) take no further action under this section in relation to the request, the failure or the refusal in question; and

    (b) notify the parent, in writing, accordingly.

(5) If the Secretary of State considers that there are no such reasonable grounds, he may, except in prescribed circumstances, make a reduced benefit decision with respect to the parent.

(6) In a subsection (1)(a) case, the Secretary of State may from time to time serve written notice on the parent requiring her, before the end of a specified period—

    (a) to state whether her request under section 6(5) still stands; and

    (b) if so, to give him her reasons for maintaining her request,

and subsections (3) to (5) have effect in relation to such a notice and any response to it as they have effect in relation to a notice under subsection (2)(a) and any response to it.

(7) Where the Secretary of State makes a reduced benefit decision he must send a copy of it to the parent.

(8) A reduced benefit decision is to take effect on such date as may be specified in the decision.

(9) Reasons given in response to a notice under subsection (2) or (6) need not be given in writing unless the Secretary of State directs in any case that they must.

(10) In this section—

    (a) "comply" means to comply with the requirement or with the regulation in question; and "complied" and "complying" are to be construed accordingly;

    (b) "reduced benefit decision" means a decision that the amount payable by way of any relevant benefit to, or in respect of, the parent concerned be reduced by such amount, and for such period, as may be prescribed;

    (c) "relevant benefit" means income support or an income-based job-seeker's allowance or any other benefit of a kind prescribed for the purposes of section 6; and

    (d) "specified", in relation to a notice served under this section, means specified in the notice; and the period to be specified is to be determined in accordance with regulations made by the Secretary of State.]

AMENDMENT

1. Section 19 of the 2000 Act (for the purpose of making regulations, November 10, 2000 under art.2(1) of, and Pt I of the Schedule to, the Commencement No.3 Order 2000; March 3, 2003 under art.4 of, and the Schedule to, the Commencement No.12 Order 2003)

2.169    "maintenance calculation": see s.54.

GENERAL NOTE

2.170    This section, and the regulations made under it, provide for the consequences of a person with care's failure to co-operate under s.6 above. The relevant Regulations are contained in Pt IV of the Maintenance Calculation Procedure Regulations.

*Subsection (2)*
The period is prescribed by reg.9 of the Maintenance Calculation Procedure Regulations.

*Subsection (3)*
2.171    No reduced benefit decision may be made, if there are reasonable grounds to believe that there would be a risk of the parent or any child living with the parent suffering harm or undue distress. The risk need not be substantial and the tribunal must not concern itself with whether harm or undue distress would actually happen, but there must be a realistic possibility of it occurring (*CCS 1037/95*, para.9). The child who suffers harm or distress need not be the child of the absent parent. If more than one child might be affected, the possible impact on each must be considered separately (*ibid*, para.11). The emphasis is on the suffering of harm or distress. How it comes about is not relevant. Consequently, it will be sufficient if the person with care suffers undue distress as a result of believing, however unreasonably, that the giving of the authorisation might lead to violence on the part of the absent parent (*CCS 588/98*, paras 7 and 9). The harm which may be suffered may be physical or mental. It can come from any source; it need not be inflicted by the person who is or may be the non-resident parent (*R(CS) 8/02*, para.13). Any physical harm will suffice as will any mental effect which amounts to harm. However, if the mental effect does not amount to harm, it must be undue. Whether or not distress is undue is a matter of fact to be decided in the circumstances of each case, but if a child is likely to be distressed at never seeing a father again, it would be difficult to say that the distress would not be undue (*ibid*, para.10). This test is narrower than, but additional to (*ibid*, para.13), that which applies under s.2 where the "welfare" of a child has to be taken into account. In applying s.2 in the context of a reduced benefit decision, the issue is whether there is some exceptional or special factor, such as concerning the age or state of health of the child or parent with care, which would suggest that the welfare of a child would be adversely affected (*ibid*, para.13).

The bar to a reduced benefit decision only applies, if the risk of harm or distress would arise as a result of complying. If the risk would exist regardless of compliance and is not increased thereby, the bar does not apply and a direction may still be given, although these matters may not easily be susceptible to proof. Any consequence of non-compliance must be disregarded. Accordingly, it is not permissible to take into account the consequences of the reduction in benefit as a result of the making of the decision (*CSC 8/94*, para.6).

Statements made in the course of conciliation which indicate that the maker is likely to cause serious harm to the well-being of a child are admissible (*Re D (Minors) (Conciliation: Disclosure of Information)* [1993] 1 F.L.R. 932).

*Subsection (5)*
The officer has a discretion, even if reasonable grounds do not exist under subs.(3). The provisions of subss.(3), (4) and (5) do not displace the duty in s.2. The welfare of any children affected must still be considered, if the terms of subs.(3) are not satisfied.

The circumstances in which a child support officer may not make a reduced benefit direction are prescribed by reg.10 of the Maintenance Calculation Procedure Regulations.

*Subsection (6)*
The period is specified in reg.9A of the Maintenance Calculation Procedure Regulations.

## [¹Finality of decisions

**46A.**—(1) Subject to the provisions of this Act, any decision of the Secretary of State or an appeal tribunal made in accordance with the foregoing provisions of this Act shall be final.

2.172

(2) If and to the extent that regulations so provide, any finding of fact or other determination embodies in or necessary to such a decision, or on which such a decision is based, shall be conclusive for the purposes of—

(a) further such decisions;
(b) decisions made in accordance with sections 8 to 16 of the Social Security Act 1998, or with regulations under section 11 of that Act; and
(c) decisions made under the Vaccine Damage Payments Act 1979.]

AMENDMENT

1. Paragraph 44 of Sch.7 to the Social Security Act 1998 (subs.(2) March 4, 1999; otherwise June 1, 1999).

GENERAL NOTE

See also Sch.4, para.6(2) below and s.17 of the Social Security Act 1998.

2.173

The fact that a decision is final does not prevent it being subject to judicial review (*R. v Medical Appeal Tribunal Ex p. Gilmore* [1957] 1 QB 574).

A finding of fact in one decision is not conclusive for the purpose of later decisions, even if the decisions are related to each other. Subsection (2) does not provide for this. However, it follows from basic principle. Also, subs.(2) presupposes that findings of fact are not conclusive for later decisions. Otherwise, regulations to provide for that effect would be unnecessary. See *CIS 1330/02*, para.19.

## [¹Matters arising as respects decisions

**46B.**—(1) Regulations may make provision as respects matters arising pending—

2.174

(a) any decision of the Secretary of State under section 11, 12 or 17;
(b) any decision of an appeal tribunal under section 20; or
(c) any decision of a Child Support Commissioner under section 24.

(2) Regulations may also make provision as respects matters arising out of the revision under section 16, or on appeal, of any such decision as is mentioned in subsection (1).

[².. .]

AMENDMENTS

1. Paragraph 44 of Sch.7 to the Social Security Act 1998 (March 4, 1999 to allow regulations to be made; otherwise June 1, 1999).

2. Section 85 of, and Sch.9 to, the 2000 Act. (March 3, 2003 under art.3 of, and the Schedule to, the Commencement No.12 Order 2003).

## Fees

**2.175** **47.**—(1) The Secretary of State may be regulations provide for the payment, by the [⁵non-resident parent] or the person with care (or by both), of such fees as may be prescribed in cases where the Secretary of State takes [¹, or proposes to take,] any action under section 4 or 6.

(2) The Secretary of State may by regulations provide for the payment, by the [⁵non-resident parent], the person with care or the child concerned (or by any or all of them), of such fees as may be prescribed in cases where the Secretary of State takes [¹, or proposes to take,] any action under section 7.

(3) Regulations made under this section—

(a) may require any information which is needed for the purpose of determining the amount of any such fee to be furnished, in accordance with the regulations, by such person as may be prescribed;

(b) shall provide that no such fees shall be payable by any person to or in respect of whom income support [²an income-based jobseeker's allowance,] [⁶any element of child tax credit other than the family element, working tax credit] or any other benefit of a prescribed kind is paid; and

(c) may, in particular, make provision with respect to the recovery by the Secretary of State of any fees payable under the regulations.

[⁴(4) The provisions of this Act with respect to—

(a) the collection of child support maintenance;

(b) the enforcement of any obligation to pay child support maintenance, shall apply equally (with any necessary modifications) to fees payable by virtue of regulations made under this section.]

AMENDMENTS

1. Paragraph 13 of Sch.3 to the 1995 Act.
2. Paragraph 20(5) of Sch.2 to the Jobseekers Act 1995 (October 7, 1996).
4. Paragraph 11(18) of Sch.3 to the 2000 Act (for the purpose of making regulations, November 10, 2000 under art.2(1) of, and Pt I of the Schedule to, the Commencement No.3 Order 2000; March 3, 2003 under art.3 of, and the Schedule to, the Commencement No.12 Order 2003)
5. Paragraph 11(2) of Sch.3 to the 2000 Act (March 3, 2003 under art.3 of, and the Schedule to, the Commencement No.12 Order 2003).
6. Section 47 of and Sch.3, para.22 to the Tax Credits Act 2002 (April 6, 2003).

DEFINITIONS

**2.176** "absent parent": see s.3(2).
"child": see s.55.
"income support": see s.54.
"person with care": see s.3(3).
"prescribed": see s.54.
"working families' tax credit: see s.54.

The regulations made under this section (the Child Support Fees Regulations 1992) have been revoked by the Act.

2.177

## Right of audience

**48.**—(1) Any [¹officer of the Secretary of State who is authorised] by the Secretary of State for the purposes of this section shall have, in relation to any proceedings under this Act before a magistrates' court, a right of audience and the right to conduct litigation.

2.178

(2) In this section "right of audience" and "right to conduct litigation" have the same meaning as in section 119 of the Courts and Legal Services Act 1990.

AMENDMENT

1. Paragraph 14 of Sch.3 to the 1995 Act (September 4, 1995).

GENERAL NOTE

This section does not extend to Scotland (s.58(9)).

2.179

Section 119(1) of the Courts and Legal Services Act 1990 defines "right of audience" as meaning the right to exercise any of the functions of appearing before and addressing a court including the calling and examining of witnesses, and "right to conduct litigation" as meaning the right to exercise all or any of the functions of issuing a writ or otherwise commencing proceedings before any court and to perform any ancillary functions in relation to proceedings (such as entering appearances to actions).

## Right of audience: Scotland

**49.** In relation to any proceedings before the sheriff under any provision of this Act, the power conferred on the Court of Session by section 32 of the Sheriff Courts (Scotland) Act 1971 (power of Court of Session to regulate civil procedure in sheriff court) shall extend to the making of rules permitting a party to such proceedings, in such circumstances as may be specified in the rules, to be represented by a person who is neither an advocate nor a solicitor.

2.180

GENERAL NOTE

This section applies to Scotland only (s.58(10)).

2.181

## Unauthorised disclosure of information

**50.**—(1) Any person who is, or has been, employed in employment to which this section applies is guilty of an offence if, without lawful authority, he discloses any information which—

2.182

(a) was acquired by him in the course of that employment; and

(b) relates to a particular person.

(2) It is not an offence under this section—

   (a) to disclose information in the form of a summary or collection of information so framed as not to enable information relating to any particular person to be ascertained from it; or

   (b) to disclose information which has previously been disclosed to the public with lawful authority.

  (3) It is a defence for a person charged with an offence under this section to prove that at the time of the alleged offence—

   (a) he believed that he was making the disclosure in question with lawful authority and had no reasonable cause to believe otherwise; or

   (b) he believed that the information in question had previously been disclosed to the public with lawful authority and had no reasonable cause to believe otherwise.

  (4) A person guilty of an offence under this section shall be liable—

   (a) on conviction on indictment, to imprisonment for a term not exceeding two years or a fine or both; or

   (b) on summary conviction, to imprisonment for a term not exceeding six months or a fine not exceeding the statutory maximum or both.

  (5) This section applies to employment as—

   (a) the Chief Child Support Officer;

   (b) any other child support officer;

   (c) any clerk to, or other officer of, [¹an appeal tribunal or] a child support appeal tribunal;

   (d) any member of the staff of such a tribunal;

   (e) a civil servant in connection with the carrying out of any functions under this Act,

and to employment of any other kind which is prescribed for the purposes of this section.

  (6) For the purposes of this section a disclosure is to be regarded as made with lawful authority if, and only if, it is made—

   (a) by a civil servant in accordance with his official duty; or

   (b) by any other person either—

     (i) for the purposes of the function in the exercise of which he holds the information and without contravening any restriction duly imposed by the responsible person; or

     (ii) to, or in accordance with an authorisation duly given by, the responsible person;

   (c) in accordance with any enactment or order of a court

   (d) for the purpose of instituting, or otherwise for the purposes of, any proceedings before a court or before any tribunal or other body or person mentioned in this Act; or

   (e) with the consent of the appropriate person.

  (7) "The responsible person" means—

   (a) the Lord Chancellor;

   (b) the Secretary of State;

   (c) any person authorised by the Lord Chancellor, or Secretary of State, for the purposes of this subsection; or

   (d) any other prescribed person, or person falling within a prescribed category.

(8) "The appropriate person" means the person to whom the information in question relates, except that if the affairs of that person are being dealt with—

(a) under a power of attorney;

(b) by a receiver appointed under section 99 of the Mental Health Act 1983;

(c) by a Scottish mental health custodian, that is to say—

    (i) a curator bonis, tutor or judicial factor; or

    (ii) the managers of a hospital acting on behalf of that person under section 94 of the Mental Health (Scotland) Act 1984; or (b)

(d) by a mental health appointee, that is to say—

    (i) a person directed or authorised as mentioned in subparagraph (a) of rule 41(1) of the Court of Protection Rules 1984; or

    (ii) a receiver ad interim appointed under sub-paragraph (b) of that rule,

the appropriate person is the attorney, receiver, custodian or appointee (as the case may be) or, in a case falling within paragraph (a), the person to whom the information relates.

AMENDMENT

1. Paragraph 45 of Sch.7 to the Social Security Act 1998 (June 1, 1999).

DEFINITION

"prescribed": see s.54.

**2.183**

GENERAL NOTE

*Subsection (5)*

The other kinds of employment prescribed for the purposes of this subsection are contained in reg.11 of the Information. Evidence and Disclosure Regulations.

**2.184**

*Subsection (6)*

A court has no power under this section to give leave to, or direct the Secretary of State to disclose information to enable a child (or person with care) to trace the absent parent with a view to bringing proceedings for a s.8 order under the Children Act 1989 (*Re C (A Minor) (Child Support Agency: Disclosure)* [1995] 1 F.L.R. 201).

*Subsection (6)(a)*

The "official duty" of an officer may go beyond what is specified in the legislation. It includes the requirements of natural justice, so that matters may be notified to a party which are not expressly covered by the Maintenance Calculation Procedure Regulations (*Huxley v Child Support Officer and Huxley* [2000] 1 F.L.R. 898 at 906 *per* Hale L.J.).

*Subsection (6)(d)*

The rigid attitude taken by the Child Support Agency in disclosing information to tribunals reflects their stance on confidentiality which completely over-looks the significance of this paragraph.

See also the Data Protection Acts 1984 and 1998 below, which exempt from their provisions disclosure under an enactment or in relation to legal proceedings.

**Supplementary powers to make regulations**

2.185     **51.**—(1) The Secretary of State may be regulations make such incidental, supplemental and transitional provision as he considers appropriate in
connection with any provision made by or under the Act.

(2) The regulations may, in particular, make provision—

(a) as to the procedure to be followed with respect to—

(i) the making of applications for [³maintenance calculations];

[¹(ii) the making of decisions under section 11;

(iii) the making of decisions under section 16 or 17;]

[²(b) extending the categories of case to which section 16, 17 or 20
applies;]

(c) as to the date on which an application for a [³maintenance
calculation] is to be treated as having been made;

(d) for attributing payments made under [³maintenance calculations] to
the payment of arrears;

(e) for the adjustment, for the purpose of taking account of the retrospective effect of a [³maintenance calculation], of amounts payable
under the assessment;

(f) for the adjustment, for the purpose of taking account of overpayments or under-payments of child support maintenance, of amounts
payable under a [³maintenance calculation];

(g) as to the evidence which is to be required in connection with such
matters as may be prescribed;

(h) as to the circumstances in which any official record or certificate is
to be conclusive (or in Scotland, sufficient) evidence;

(i) with respect to the giving of notices or other documents;

(j) for the rounding up or down of any amounts calculated, estimated or
otherwise arrived at in applying any provision made by or under this
Act.

(3) No power to make regulations conferred by any other provision of
this Act shall be taken to limit the powers given to the Secretary of State by
this section.

AMENDMENTS

1. Paragraph 11(19)(a) of Sch.3 to the 2000 Act (March 3, 2003 under art.3 of,
and the Schedule to, the Commencement No. 12 Order 2003).

2. Paragraph 11(19)(b) of Sch.3 to the 2000 Act (March 3, 2003 under art.3 of,
and the Schedule to, the Commencement No.12 Order 2003).

3. Section 1(2)(a) of the 2000 Act (March 3, 2003 under art.3 of, and the
Schedule to, the Commencement No.12 Order 2003).

DEFINITIONS

2.186     "child support maintenance": see s.3(6).

"maintenance calculation": see s.54.

"prescribed": see s.54.

GENERAL NOTE

*Subsection (1)*

Words such as "incidental" and "supplemental" tend to be interpreted narrowly. **2.187**
Power to make "supplementary" provision has been held to mean power "to fill in
details or machinery for which the . . . Act itself does not provide—supplementary
in the sense that it is required to implement what was in the . . . Act" (*Daymond v
South West Water Authority* [1976] 1 All E.R. 39 at 53, *per* Viscount Dilhorne, followed in *R. v Customs and Excise Commissioners Ex p. Hedges and Bulter Ltd* [1986]
2 All E.R. 164 at 171, *per* Mustill L.J.). The terms of subs.(3) will not be sufficient
to displace this approach.

Subsection (2) below removes any doubt over the scope of this section in so far
as the matters there specified are concerned.

*Subsection (2) (a) (iii)*

The amendment to this provision is subject to the saving and transitional provisions in art.3(5) of the Social Security Act 1998 (Commencement No.2) Order 1998.

*Subsection (2) (f)*

The regulations dealing with the adjustment of the amount payable under a
maintenance assessment are contained in the Arrears, Interest and Adjustment of
Maintenance Assessments Regulations.

## Regulations and orders

**52.**—(1) Any power conferred on the Lord Chancellor, the Lord Advocate **2.188**
or the Secretary of State by this Act to make regulations or orders (other than
a deduction from earnings order) shall be exercisable by statutory instrument.

[¹(2) No statutory instrument containing (whether alone or with other
provisions) regulations made under—

(a) section 6(1), 12(4) (so far as the regulations make provision for the
default rate of child support maintenance mentioned in section
12(5)(b)), 28C(2)(b), 28F(2)(b), 30(5A), 41(2), 41A, 41B(6),
43(1), 44(2A)(d), 46 or 47;

(b) paragraph 3(2) or 10A(1) of Part I of Schedule 1; or

(c) Schedule 4B,

or an order made under section 45(1) or (6), shall be made unless a draft
of the instrument has been laid before Parliament and approved by a resolution of each House of Parliament.

(2A) No statutory instrument containing (whether alone or with other
provisions) the first set of regulations made under paragraph 10(1) of Part I
of Schedule 1 as substituted by section 1(3) of the Child Support, Pensions
and Social Security Act 2000 shall be made unless a draft of the instrument
has been laid before Parliament and approved by a resolution of each
House of Parliament.]

(3) Any other statutory instrument made under this Act (except an
order made under section 58(2)) shall be subject to annulment in
pursuance of a resolution of either House of Parliament.

(4) Any power of a kind mentioned in subsection (1) may be exercised—

(a) in relation to all cases to which it extends, in relation to those cases
but subject to specified exceptions or in relation to any specified
cases or classes of case;

(b) so as to make, as respects the cases in relation to which it is exercised—
  (i) the full provision to which it extends or any lesser provision (whether by way of exception or otherwise);
  (ii) the same provision for all cases, different provision for different cases or classes of case of different provision as respects the same case or class of case but for different purposes of this Act;
  (iii) provision which is either unconditional or is subject to any specified condition;
(c) so to provide for a person to exercise a discretion in dealing with any matter.

AMENDMENT

1. Section 25 of the 2000 Act (for the purpose of making regulations, November 10, 2000 under art.2(1) of, and Pt I of the Schedule to, the Commencement No.3 Order 2000; March 3, 2003 under art.3 of, and the Schedule to, the Commencement No.12 Order 2003).

## Financial provisions

2.189    **53.** Any expenses of the Lord Chancellor or the Secretary of State under this Act shall be payable out of money provided by Parliament.

## Interpretation

2.190    **54.** In this Act—
[9"appeal tribunal" means an appeal tribunal constituted under Chapter I of Part I of the Social Security Act 1998;]
[3"application for a [11variation]" means an application under section 28A [11or 28G];]
[14. . .]
"benefit Acts" means the [1Social Security Contributions and Benefits Act 1992 and the Social Security Administration Act 1992];
"child benefit" has the same meaning as in the Child Benefit Act 1975;
"child support maintenance" has the meaning given in section 3(6);
[15. . . ]
"deduction from earnings order" has the meaning given in section 31(2);
[12"default maintenance decision" has the meaning given in section 12]
[15. . . ]
"disability living allowance" has the same meaning as in the [2benefit Acts];
"general qualification" shall be construed in accordance with section 71 of the Courts and Legal Services Act 1990 (qualification for judicial appointments);
"income support" has the same meaning as in the benefit Acts;
[8"income-based jobseeker's allowance" has the same meaning as in the Job-seekers Act 1995;]
"interim maintenance [13decision]" has the meaning given in section 12;
"liability order" has the meaning given in section 33(2);
"maintenance agreement" has the meaning given in section 9(1);
[14"maintenance calculation" means a calculation of maintenance made under this Act and, except in prescribed circumstances,

includes a default maintenance decision and an interim maintenance decision;]

"maintenance order" has the meaning given in section 8(11);

[¹⁵ . . . ]

[¹⁷"non-resident parent"] has the meaning given in section 3(2);

"parent", in relation to any child, means any person who is in law the mother or father of the child;

[⁶"parent with care" means a person who is, in relation to a child, both a parent and a person with care;]

[⁷"parental responsibility", in the application of this Act—

(a) to England and Wales, has the same meaning as in the Children Act 1989; and

(b) to Scotland, shall be construed as a reference to "parental responsibilities" within the meaning given by section 1(3) of the Children (Scotland) Act 1995; "person with care" has the meaning given in section 3(3);

"prescribed" means prescribed by regulations made by the Secretary of State;

"qualifying child" has the meaning given in section 3(1);

[¹⁶"voluntary payment" has the meaning given in section 28J;] [¹⁷. . .].

AMENDMENTS

1. Schedule 2, para.114(a) to the Social Security (Consequential Provisions) Act 1992 (July 1, 1992).

2. Schedule 2, para.114(b) to the Social Security (Consequential Provisions) Act 1992 (July 1, 1992).

3. Paragraph 16 of Sch.3 to the 1995 Act (September 4, 1995).

6. Paragraph 16 of Sch.3 to the 1995 Act (September 4, 1995).

7. Paragraph 52(4) of Sch.4, and Sch.5 to the Children (Scotland) Act 1995 (November 1, 1996).

8. Paragraph 20(6) of Sch.2 to the Jobseekers Act 1995 (October 7, 1996).

9. Paragraph 47(a) of Sch.7 to the Social Security Act 1998 (June 1, 1999).

11. Paragraph 11(20)(a) of Sch.3 to the 2000 Act (March 3, 2003 under art.3 of, and the Schedule to, the Commencement No.12 Order 2003).

12. Paragraph 11(20)(b) of Sch.3 to the 2000 Act (March 3, 2003 under art.3 of, and the Schedule to, the Commencement No.12 Order 2003).

13. Paragraph 11(20)(c) of Sch.3 to the 2000 Act (March 3, 2003 under art.3 of, and the Schedule to, the Commencement No.12 Order 2003).

14. Paragraph 11(20)(d) of Sch.3 to the 2000 Act (March 3, 2003 under art.3 of, and the Schedule to, the Commencement No.12 Order 2003).

15. Paragraph 11(20)(e) of Sch.3 to the 2000 Act (March 3, 2003 under art.3 of, and the Schedule to, the Commencement No.12 Order 2003).

16. Paragraph 11(20)(f) of Sch.3 to the 2000 Act (March 3, 2003 under art.3 of, and the Schedule to, the Commencement No.12 Order 2003).

17. Paragraph 11(2) of Sch.3 to the 2000 Act (March 3, 2003 under art.3 of, and the Schedule to, the Commencement No.12 Order 2003)

18. Section 60 of and Sch.6 to the Tax Credits Act 2002 (April 6, 2003).

GENERAL NOTE

The definitions repealed by para.47(b) of Sch.7 to the Social Security Act 1998 are omitted without indication, although some of them still appear in s.50(5).    **2.191**

Although the definitions contained in this section are not prefaced by words such as "unless the contrary appears", they are subject to this qualification (*Meux v Jacobs* (1875) L.R. 7 H.L. 481 at 493, *per* Lord Selborne and *Robinson v Local Board of Barton-Eccles, Winton and Morton* (1883) 8 App. Cas. 798 at 801, *per* Lord Selborne L.C.).

By virtue of s.11 of the Interpretation Act 1978 expressions used in this Act bear, unless the contrary intention appears, the same meaning in delegated legislation made under this Act.

In interpreting the child support legislation it is permissible in order to resolve an ambiguity to have regard to reports of committees presented to Parliament in order to help to identify the mischief which the legislation was intended to remedy (*Black-Clawson International Ltd v Papierwerke Waldhof-Aschaffenburg A G* [1975] 1 All E.R. 810).

It is also permissible to have regard to parliamentary material as part of the objective circumstances to which the statutory language relates and in the context of which it must be interpreted (*R. (ota Westminster City Council) v National Asylum Support Service* [2002] 4 All E.R. 654 *per* Lord Steyn at para.5). The material may also be used as a direct indication of the meaning of a provision provided that three conditions are satisfied: (i) the legislation is ambiguous or obscure or its apparent interpretation would lead to absurdity: (ii) the material relied on consists of statements of a minister or promoter of the legislation, supplemented as necessary to understand the statements and their effect; and (iii) the statements are clear (*Pepper v Hart* [1993] 1 All E.R. 47 at 69, *per* Lord Browne-Wilkinson. The material that may be considered includes the explanatory notes to a statute (*R. (ota Westminster City Council) v National Asylum Support Service* [2002] 4 All E.R. 654 *per* Lord Steyn at para.5). However, where it is sought to interpret legislation consistently with provisions of European or international law, it is of particular importance that the true purpose of the legislation should be identified and reference to a wider range of material is permissible (*Three Rivers District Council v Govenor and Company of the Bank of England. (No.2)* [1996] 2 All E.R. 363). Citation of Hansard should take the form of reference to specific passages that satisfy the above conditions and it is not appropriate merely to produce a list of references to debates without referring specifically to particular passages *R(G) 1/98*, para.13). It is only in exceptional circumstances that a reference to Hansard will be relevant in identifying the scope of an enabling power (*R v Secretary of State for the Environment, Transport and the Regions Ex p. Spath Holme Ltd* [2001] 1 All E.R. 195).

If words have been left out of a statutory instrument by mistake, it can be rectified on interpretation by reference to the explanatory notes to the instrument and to the Secretary of State's letter authorising the making of the instrument (*Confederation of Passenger Transport UK v Humber Bridge Board* [2004] QB 310).

The general approach to interpretation of the child support legislation should be practical and purposive, rather than detached and literal, so as to produce a coherent structure devoid so far as possible of inconsistencies and arbitrary distinctions (*CCS 12/94*, paras 22–34). It is proper to bear in mind that the legislation "does seem designed to produce fairly clear-cut answers to most cases so that a relatively junior child support officer is able to apply the law" (*R(CS) 14/98*, para.16), although there are a number of decisions which cannot readily be reconciled with this approach.

In interpreting this Act, it is not proper to consider the contents of regulations made under it (*CCS 12806/96*, para.13). In interpreting the legislation, little of value is to be found in consulting any forms used by the Secretary of State (*ibid.*, para.17). The general scheme of the legislation should be initially determined as it originally existed, although it is legitimate to check that construction against subsequent amendments so that it may be reconsidered if those amendments are not consonant with it (*ibid*, para.25).

Regulations must be made under the authority of an enabling provision. Sometimes enabling provisions are compulsory, like s.22(4)(b) above. Usually, they are not. If an enabling provision is not compulsory, there is no duty to implement it and the regulations cannot be interpreted as if it were (*CCS 2348/00*, paras 8–10). In principle, the enabling provision under the authority of which a regulation is made sets the limit to what the regulation may provide. However, their value as guidance is reduced if there are a variety of enabling powers and no compelling reasons to maintain a strict separation between them (*Banks v Chief Adjudication Officer* [2001] 4 All E.R. 62 at 74 *per* Lord Hope).

*"child benefit."*

By virtue of s.17(2)(a). Interpretation Act 1978 reference to the Child Benefit Act 1975 is to be construed as a reference to the Social Security Contributions and Benefits Act 1992.

*"disability living allowance."*

By virtue of s.17(2)(a). Interpretation Act 1978 reference to the Social Security Act 1975 is to be construed as a reference to the Social Security Contributions and Benefits Act 1992.

*"maintenance agreement"*

See the general notes to s.9(1) above and s.18 of the 1995 Act.

*"parent."*

A parent is someone who is in law the mother or father of a child. The person may be a natural or adoptive parent. Step-parents, foster parents and persons who treat a child as their own are not within the definition, although they may become so if they adopt the child (*R(CS) 6/03*, paras 8–10). Likewise grandparents and other relatives are not within the definition unless they adopt the child (*CCS 3128/95*, para.8). Having parental responsibility or a residence order does not make a person a parent (*CCS 736/02*).

A person may not become a parent by virtue of estoppel (*Re M (Child Support Act: Parentage)* [1997] 2 F.L.R. 90 at 93–94, *per* Bracewell J.).

*"parental responsibility."*

This is defined by s.3 of the Children Act 1989 as all the rights, duties, powers, responsibility and authority which by law a parent of a child has in relation to the child and the child's property including those of a guardian of the child's estate.

## Meaning of "child"

55.—(1) For the purposes of this Act a person is a child if—          2.192

(a) he is under the age of 16;

(b) he is under the age of 19 and receiving full-time education (which is not advanced education)—

   (i)   by attendance at a recognised educational establishment; or

   (ii)  elsewhere, if the education is recognised by the Secretary of State; or

(c) he does not fall within paragraph (a) or (b) but—

   (i)   he is under the age of 18; and

   (ii)  prescribed conditions are satisfied with respect to him.

(2) A person is not a child for the purposes of this Act if he—

(a) is or has been married [¹or a civil partner];

   (b) has celebrated a marriage [²or been a party to a civil partnership] which
      is void; or

   (c) has celebrated a marriage in respect of which a decree of nullity has
      been granted [³or has been a party to a civil partnership in respect of which
      a nullity order has been made].

   (3) In this section—

"advanced education" means education of a prescribed description; and
"recognised educational establishment" means an establishment recog-
    nised by the Secretary of State for the purposes of this section as
    being, or as comparable to, a university, college or school.

   (4) Where a person has reached the age of 16, the Secretary of State may
recognise education provided for him otherwise than at a recognised educational establishment only if the Secretary of State is satisfied that education
was being so provided for him immediately before he reached the age of 16.

   (5) The Secretary of State may provide that in prescribed circumstances
education is or is not to be treated for the purposes of this section as being
full-time.

   (6) In determining whether a person falls within subsection (1)(b), no
account shall be taken of such interruptions in his education as may be
prescribed.

   (7) The Secretary of State may by regulations provide that a person who
ceases to fall within subsection (1) shall be treated as continuing to fall
within that subsection for a prescribed period.

   (8) No person shall be treated as continuing to fall within subsection (1)
by virtue of regulations made under subsection (7) after the end of the
week in which he reaches the age of 19.

AMENDMENTS

   1. Paragraph 3(a) of Sch.24 to the Civil Partnership Act 2004.
   2. Paragraph 3(b) of Sch.24 to the Civil Partnership Act 2004.
   3. Paragraph 3(c) of Sch.24 to the Civil Partnership Act 2004.

DEFINITION

2.193    "prescribed": see s.54.

GENERAL NOTE

2.194    This section must be read in conjunction with Sch.1 to the Maintenance
Calculation Procedure Regulations. References to paragraphs in this note are to
paragraphs in that Schedule.

   A child is a person who comes comes under one of the four heads established by
this section. The definition is modelled on the definition which is used for child benefit, although not without exception. There are many Commissioners' decisions on
provisions similar to those used here, but as the wording of those provisions has varied considerably from time to time great care is required in applying those decisions
to the present wording. The heads all require a decision on when a person attained
a particular age. A person attains an age on the beginning of the relevant anniversary of the date of his birth (s.9(1) of the Family Law Reform Act 1969 and s.6(1)
of the Age of Legal Capacity (Scotland) Act 1991).

   There is a general exception in subs.(2) for persons who are married or who have
been either married or through a ceremony of marriage. For the circumstances in

which a marriage will be void or voidable see ss.11 and 12 of the Matrimonial Causes Act 1973.

*1. Persons under the age of 16*

Every person under the age of 16 is a child (s.55(1)(a)). This applies whether or not the person is in education.

*2. Persons under the age of 19 who are in education*

For a person to be a child under this head, the following conditions must be satisfied (s.55(1)(b)).

(i) The person must be under the age of 19.

(ii) The person must be receiving full-time education.

This condition may be established in two ways. The first way is to bring the case within para.3. This paragraph does not provide an exhaustive definition of full-time education, but deems a person to be in full-time education if certain facts are established. These are that the person (a) attends (b) a course of education (c) at a recognised educational establishment and (d) that the hours spent on receiving instruction or tuition, undertaking supervised study, examination or practical work or taking part in any exercise, experiment or project for which provision is made in the curriculum of the course, exceed 12 per week. The time spent on meal breaks and unsupervised study is disregarded. Study is supervised if the person is in the presence or close proximity of a teacher or tutor who may preserve order, enhance diligence and give appropriate assistance *(R(F) 1/93*, para.13). Attendance requires physical presence, so following a correspondence course will not satisfy this definition *(R(F) 2/95*, para.5). In view of requirement (c), this way of proving full-time education is of no use to someone who is not in a recognised educational establishment. A tribunal will need to make findings of fact on all these matters. In the case of (c) the relevant facts will be the name of the establishment attended and whether or not the Secretary of State has recognised it as an educational establishment (s.55(3)). The relevant Secretary of State is the Secretary of State for Social Security, not the Secretary of State for Education *(R(F) 2/95*, para.6).

The second way is to prove as a matter of fact in all the circumstances of the case that the person is undergoing full-time education *(R(F) 2/85*, paras 13 and 17(2)). These words are to be given their natural and ordinary meaning *(R(F) 4/62*, para.5). In that case a course which involved attendance for 13 hours and 45 minutes a week did not constitute "full-time instruction". Attendance solely for the purpose of taking examinations was not sufficient in *R(F) 2/85*, since the person had left school and returned solely to sit for examinations. This must be distinguished from the normal case of someone who continues at school but whose time is free before and between examinations for revision. In such a case it is within the usual meaning of the words in this context to say that the person is receiving fulltime education.

(iii) The education must not be advanced education. This is defined by para.2. The precise terms of the definition are not repeated here. Put shortly, advanced education means education above A-level standard.

(iv) Finally, either the educational establishment attended or the education itself must be recognised by the Secretary of State. Where a person who has reached 16 is receiving education which is not provided at a recognised educational establishment, it can only be recognised by the Secretary of State if the person was receiving such education immediately before reaching 16 (s.55(4)). This provision differs from the similar provision in s.142(2) of the Social Security Contributions and Benefits Act 1992. As the legislation does not specify any particular Secretary of State, s.5 of, and Sch.1 to, the Interpretation Act 1978 apply so that it suffices if the education has been recognised by any of Her Majesty's Principal Secretaries of State *(CCS 2865/01*, para.9(e)).

Certain interruptions are ignored for the purpose of this head (s.55(6)) and these are set out in para.4. A period of up to six months of any interruption is ignored to the extent to which it is attributable to a reasonable cause. School holidays (provided the person intends to return to education afterwards), illness and delays associated with moving house or school are obvious examples of delays with reasonable causes. The six month period may be extended where the interruption or its continuance is attributable to the illness or disability of mind or body of the person concerned. The extension may be for such period as is reasonable in the circumstances. The illness or disability need not have been the original cause of the interruption; it is sufficient if it merely prolongs an interruption. The tribunal will need to find facts as to the duration of the interruption and the reasons for it. The reasons for decision will need to record that the tribunal gave its mind to the question of the reasonableness of the cause and, where appropriate, the extension of the six month period.

However, any interruption for whatever cause is not ignored in two cases (para.4(2)). The first case is where the interruption is, or is likely to be, immediately followed by a period during which youth training with an allowance is provided. The second case is where it is, or is likely to be, immediately followed by a period during which the person receives education by virtue of the person's employment or office.

*3. Persons under the age of 18 and available for work or training*

This head applies to persons under the age of 18 in respect of whom prescribed conditions are met (s.55(1)(c)). These conditions are set out in para.1 as follows: (i) The person must be registered for work, or for youth training with certain bodies. Youth training is defined in para.6; (ii) The person is not engaged in remunerative work. This means work of not less than 24 hours a week for which payment is made or which is done in the expectation of payment (para.6). Temporary work is disregarded if it is due to end before the so-called "extension period" expires; if there is evidence that the person is working, the tribunal in the exercise of its inquisitorial function will need to enquire whether that work is temporary, and if so when it is likely to end; (iii) The extension period has not expired; (iv) Immediately before the extension period began the person was a child under one of the other three heads. The definition of the extension period is in para.1(2). "Week" is defined in para.6 as a period of seven days beginning with a Monday. The period begins on the first day of the week in which a person ceased to be a child under any head other than this one (*i.e.* other than 3). When it ends depends on when the person ceased to come within head 1 or 4. This is called the cessation date in the table below.

| Cessation dates (inclusive) | Period ends |
| --- | --- |
| January 4, 1993 to April 18, 1993 | April 4, 1993 |
| April 19, 1993 to September 5, 1993 | July 18, 1993 |
| September 6, 1993 to January 2, 1994 | January 2, 1994 |
| January 3, 1994 to April 10, 1994 | April 3, 1994 |
| April 11, 1994 to September 4, 1994 | July 10, 1994 |
| September 5, 1994 to January 1, 1995 | January 1, 1995 |
| January 2, 1995 to April 23, 1995 | April 2, 1995 |
| April 24, 1995 to September 3, 1995 | July 23, 1995 |
| September 4, 1995 to December 31, 1995 | December 31, 1995 |
| January 1, 1996 to April 14, 1996 | March 31, 1996 |
| April 15, 1996 to September 1, 1996 | July 14, 1996 |
| September 2, 1996 to January 5, 1997 | January 5, 1997 |
| January 6, 1997 to April 6, 1997 | April 6, 1997 |
| April 7, 1997 to August 31, 1997 | July 6, 1997 |
| September 1, 1997 to January 4, 1998 | January 4, 1998 |

| | |
|---|---|
| January 5, 1998 to April 19, 1998 | April 5, 1998 |
| April 20, 1998 to September 6, 1998 | July 19, 1998 |
| September 7, 1998 to January 3, 1999 | January 3, 1999 |
| January 4, 1999 to April 11, 1999 | April 4, 1999 |
| April 12, 1999 to September 5, 1999 | July 11, 1999 |
| September 6, 1999 to January 2, 2000 | January 2, 2000 |
| January 3, 2000 to April 30, 2000 | April 2, 2000 |
| May 1 2000 to September 3, 2000 | July 30, 2000 |
| September 4, 2000 to December 31, 2000 | December 31, 2000 |
| January 1, 2001 to April 22, 2001 | April 1, 2001 |
| April 23, 2001 to September 2, 2001 | July 22, 2001 |
| September 3, 2001 to January 6, 2002 | January 6, 2002 |
| January 7, 2002 to April 7, 2002 | April 7, 2002 |
| April 8, 2002 to September 1, 2002 | July 7, 2002 |
| September 2, 2002 to January 5, 2003 | January 5, 2003 |
| January 6, 2003 to April 27, 2003 | April 6, 2003 |
| April 28, 2003 to August 31, 2003 | July 27, 2003 |
| September 1, 2003 to January 4, 2004 | January 4, 2004 |
| January 5, 2004 to April 18, 2004 | April 4, 2004 |
| April 19, 2004 to September 5, 2004 | July 18, 2004 |
| September 6, 2004 to January 2, 2005 | January 2, 2005 |
| January 3, 2005 to April 3, 2005 | April 3, 2005 |
| April 4, 2005 to September 4, 2005 | July 3, 2005 |
| September 5, 2005 to January 1, 2006 | January 1, 2006 |
| January 2, 2006 to April 23, 2006 | April 2, 2006 |
| April 24, 2006 to September 3, 2006 | July 23, 2006 |
| September 4, 2006 to December 31, 2006 | December 31, 2006 |
| January 1, 2007 to April 15, 2007 | April 1, 2007 |
| April 16, 2007 to September 2, 2007 | July 15, 2007 |
| September 3, 2007 to January 6, 2008 | January 6, 2008 |

The definition of the extension period and the terminal date which applies under head four below is based on the assumption that there are three school or college terms which end on more or less similar dates each year. As greater variation in practice arises, so the basis for these definitions will be undermined. Moreover, there is one instance where the extension period will end before it begins. The definition of the extension period makes sense for all persons who have at some time in their lives been in full-time non-advanced education. However, it does not make sense in those rare but real cases where a child has never been in such education. Take as an example a person who becomes 16 on September 1, 1994 and who has never been in such education. For this person the extension period began on September 1, 1994 but ended on July 10, 1994. In effect there was no extension period.

This head does not apply to a person who is engaged in training under youth training or who is entitled to income support (para.1(3)). A person is not entitled to income support unless a claim has been made or is treated as having been made (s.1(1) of the Social Security Administration Act 1992).

*4. Persons under the age of 19 who have left education*

A person who leaves full-time, non-advanced education may still be treated as a child for a period (s.55(7) and para.5). The period begins when the person leaves education or attains the age of 16, whichever is later. It ends at the end of the week which includes the terminal date. A week is a period of seven days beginning with a Monday (para.6). The terminal date is defined in para.5(3). It is the first of the following Mondays which occurs after the person's full-time education ceases: January 4, 1993; April 19, 1993; September 6, 1993; January 3, 1994; April 11,

1994; September 5, 1994; January 2, 1995; April 24, 1995; September 4, 1995; January 1, 1996; April 15, 1996; September 2, 1996; January 6, 1997; April 7, 1997; September 1, 1997, January 5, 1998, April 20, 1998, September 7, 1998, January 4, 1999, April 12, 1999, September 6, 1999, January 3, 2000; May 1, 2000; September 4, 2000; January 1, 2001; April 23, 2001; September 3, 2001; January 7, 2002; April 8, 2002; September 2; 2002, January 6, 2003; April 28, 2003; September 1, 2003; January 5, 2004; April 19, 2004; September 6, 2004; January 3, 2005; April 4, 2005 and September 5, 2005; January 2, 2006; April 24, 2006; September 4, 2006; January 1, 2007; April 16, 2007; September 3, 2007.

If the person attains the age of 19 on or before the day on which this period would expire, he or she ceases to be a child at the end of the week which includes the last Monday before the person attained the age of 19 (para.5(1)). If a person ceases full-time education before reaching the upper limit of compulsory school age, the terminal date is that which next follows the date on which the person would have attained that age (para.5(2)).

The provisions of para.5 do not apply to a person who is engaged in remunerative work as defined in para.6 unless the work is temporary and due to cease before the terminal date (para.5(5)). If there is evidence that the person is working, the tribunal in the exercise of its inquisitorial function will need to enquire whether that work is temporary and, if so, when it is likely to end.

Special provision is made for someone who takes examinations after leaving full-time education (para.5(6) to (8)). Such a person remains a child for a period after leaving education. The following matters must be established: (i) The person must have been in full-time education which is not advanced education. The meaning of these phrases has been discussed above; (ii) The person must have been entered as a candidate for an examination; (iii) The entry must have been made while the person was receiving the education; (iv) The examination must be an external one. Therefore, an internal college or school examination will not bring the case within this provision; (v) The entry to the examination must have been in connection with the education. If these conditions are satisfied, it is necessary to decide for what period the person is treated as a child after leaving full-time non-advanced education. The period begins with the date when the person ceases to receive such education or when the person attains the age of 16 if that is later. The period ends with the first terminal date after the examinations or with the expiry of the week (Monday to Sunday) which includes the last Monday before the person's nineteenth birthday, whichever is earlier.

## Corresponding provision for and co-ordination with Northern Ireland

2.195      56.—(1) An Order in Council made under paragraph 1(1)(b) of Schedule 1 to the Northern Ireland Act 1974 which contains a statement that it is made only for purposes corresponding to those of the provisions of this Act, other than provisions which relate to the appointment of Child Support Commissioners for Northern Ireland—

(a) shall not be subject to subparagraphs (4) and (5) of paragraph 1 of that Schedule (affirmative resolution of both Houses of Parliament); but

(b) shall be subject to annulment in pursuance of a resolution of either House of Parliament.

(2) The Secretary of State may make arrangements with the Department of Health and Social Services for Northern Ireland with a view to securing, to the extent allowed for in the arrangements, that—

(a) the provision made by or under this Act ("the provision made for Great Britain"); and

(b) the provision made by or under any corresponding enactment having effect with respect to Northern Ireland ("the provision made for Northern Ireland"),

provide for a single system within the United Kingdom.

(3) The Secretary of State may make regulations for giving effect to any such arrangements.

(4) The regulations may, in particular—

(a) adapt legislation (including subordinate legislation) for the time being in force in Great Britain so as to secure its reciprocal operation with the provision made for Northern Ireland; and

(b) make provision to secure that acts, omissions and events which have any effect for the purposes of the provision made for Northern Ireland have a corresponding effect for the purposes of the provision made for Great Britain.

## Application to Crown

57.—(1) The power of the Secretary of State to make regulations under section 14 requiring prescribed persons to furnish information may be exercised so as to require information to be furnished by persons employed in the service of the Crown or otherwise in the discharge of Crown functions.

2.196

(2) In such circumstances, and subject to such conditions, as may be prescribed, an inspector appointed under section 15 may enter any Crown premises for the purpose of exercising any powers conferred on him by that section.

(3) Where such an inspector duly enters any Crown premises for those purposes, section 15 shall apply in relation to persons employed in the service of the Crown or otherwise in the discharge of Crown functions as it applies in relation to other persons.

(4) Where a liable person is in the employment of the Crown, a deduction from earnings order may be made under section 31 in relation to that person; but in such a case subsection (8) of section 32 shall apply only in relation to the failure of that person to comply with any requirement imposed on him by regulations made under section 32.

DEFINITIONS

"deduction from earnings order": see s.31(2).
"liable person": see s.31(1)(a).
"prescribed": see s.54.

2.197

GENERAL NOTE

*Subsection (1)*
This subsection refers generally to s.14. However, since it relates to the Secretary of State's powers to "require" disclosure it only applies to s.14(1) and not to s.14(3) which allows him to "authorise" disclosure. For a discussion of the meaning of "information" in this section see the commentary to s.14(1).

2.198

### Short title, commencement and extent, etc.

**2.199**  **58.**—(1) This Act may be cited as the Child Support Act 1991.

(2) Section 56(1) and subsections (1) to (11) and (14) of this section shall come into force on the passing of this Act but otherwise this Act shall come into force on such date as may be appointed by order made by the Lord Chancellor, the Secretary of State or Lord Advocate, or by any of them acting jointly.

(3) Different dates may be appointed for different provisions of this Act and for different purposes (including, in particular, for different cases or categories of case).

(4) An order under subsection (2) may make such supplemental, incidental or transitional provision as appears to the person making the order to be necessary or expedient in connection with the provisions brought into force by the order, including such adaptations or modifications of—

(a) the provisions so brought into force;

(b) any provisions of this Act then in force; or

(c) any provision of any other enactment, as appear to him to be necessary or expedient.

(5) Different provision may be made by virtue of subsection (4) with respect to different periods.

(6) Any provision made by virtue of subsection (4) may, in particular, include provision for—

(a) the enforcement of a [¹maintenance calculation] (including the collection of sums payable under the assessment) as if the [²calculation] were a court order of a prescribed kind;

(b) the registration of [¹maintenance calculations] with the appropriate court in connection with any provision of a kind mentioned in paragraph (a);

(c) the variation, on application made to a court, of the provisions of a [¹maintenance calculation] relating to the method of making payments fixed by the [²calculation] or the intervals at which such payments are to be made;

(d) a [¹maintenance calculation], or an order of a prescribed kind relating to one or more children, to be deemed, in prescribed circumstances, to have been validly made for all purposes or for such purposes as may be prescribed.

In paragraph (c) "court" includes a single justice.

(7) The Lord Chancellor, the Secretary of State or the Lord Advocate may by order make such amendments or repeals in, or such modifications of, such enactments as may be specified in the order, as appear to him to be necessary or expedient in consequence of any provision made by or under this Act (including any provision made by virtue of subsection (4)).

(8) This Act shall, in its application to the Isles of Scilly, have effect subject to such exceptions, adaptations and modifications as the Secretary of State may by order prescribe.

(9) Sections 27, 35 [³40] and 48 and paragraph 7 of Schedule 5 do not extend to Scotland.

(10) Sections 7, 28 [⁴40A] and 49 extend only to Scotland.

(11)  With the exception of section 23 and 56(1), subsections (1) to (3) of this section and Schedules 2 and 4, and (in so far as it amends any enactment extending to Northern Ireland) Schedule 5, this Act does not extend to Northern Ireland.

(12)  Until Schedule 1 to the Disability Living Allowance and Disability Working Allowance Act 1991 comes into force, paragraph 1(1) of Schedule 3 shall have effect with the omission of the words "and disability appeal tribunals" and the insertion, after "social security appeal tribunals", of the word "and".

(13)  The consequential amendments set out in Schedule 5 shall have effect.

(14)  [Amends the Children Act 1989, Schedule 1, paragraph 2(6).]

AMENDMENTS

1. Section 1(2)(a) of the 2000 Act (March 3, 2003 under art.3 of, and the Schedule to, the Commencement No.12 Order 2003)
2. Section 1(2)(b) of the 2000 Act (March 3, 2003 under art.3 of, and the Schedule to, the Commencement No. 12 Order 2003)
3. Paragraph 11(21)(a) of Sch.3 to the 2000 Act (March 3, 2003 under art.3 of, and the Schedule to, the Commencement No.12 Order 2003)
4. Paragraph 11(21)(b) of Sch.3 to the 2000 Act (March 3, 2003 under art.3 of, and the Schedule to, the Commencement No.12 Order 2003)

DEFINITIONS

"child": see s.55.                                                                                  **2.200**
"maintenance calculation": see s.54.
"prescribed": see s.54.

GENERAL NOTE

*Subsection (12)*
It has not been necessary to bring this subsection into force.                **2.201**

SCHEDULE 1                                    **Section 11**

MAINTENANCE ASSESSMENTS

[¹²PART I

CALCULATION OF WEEKLY AMOUNT OF CHILD SUPPORT MAINTENANCE

*General rule*

1.—(1)  The weekly rate of child support maintenance is the basic rate unless a reduced     **2.202**
rate, a flat rate or the nil rate applies.
(2)  Unless the nil rate applies, the amount payable weekly to a person with care is—

(a)  the applicable rate, if paragraph 6 does not apply; or

(b)  if paragraph 6 does apply, that rate as apportioned between the persons with care in accordance with paragraph 6,

as adjusted, in either case, by applying the rules about shared care in paragraph 7 or 8.

*Basic rate*

**2.**—(1) The basic rate is the following percentage of the non-resident parent's net weekly income—

15% where he has one qualifying child;
20%; where he has two qualifying children;
25% where he has three or more qualifying children.

(2) If the non-resident parent also has one or more relevant other children, the appropriate percentage referred to in sub-paragraph (1) is to be applied instead to his net weekly income less—

15% where he has one relevant other child;
20% where he has two relevant other children;
25% where he has three or more relevant other children.

*Reduced rate*

**3.**—(1) A reduced rate is payable if—

(a)  neither a flat rate nor the nil rate applies; and

(b)  the non-resident parent's net weekly income is less than £200 but more than £100.

(2) The reduced rate payable shall be prescribed in, or determined in accordance with, regulations.

(3) The regulations may not prescribe, or result in, a rate of less than £5.

*Flat rate*

**4.**—(1) Except in a case falling within sub-paragraph (2), a flat rate of £5 is payable if the nil rate does not apply and—

(a)  the non-resident parent's net weekly income is £100 or less; or

(b)  he receives any benefit, pension or allowance prescribed for the purposes of this paragraph of this sub-paragraph; or

(c)  he or his partner (if any) receives any benefit prescribed for the purposes of this paragraph of this sub-paragraph.

(2) A flat rate of a prescribed amount is payable if the nil rate does not apply and—

(a)  the non-resident parent has a partner who is also a non-resident parent;

(b)  the partner is a person with respect to whom a maintenance calculation is in force; and

(c)  the non-resident parent or his partner receives any benefit prescribed under sub-paragraph (1)(c).

(3) The benefits, pensions and allowances which may be prescribed for the purposes of sub-paragraph (1)(b) include ones paid to the non-resident parent under the law of a place outside the United Kingdom.

*Nil rate*

**5.** The rate payable is nil if the non-resident parent—

(a)  is of a prescribed description; or

(b)  has a net weekly income of below £5.

*Apportionment*

**6.**—(1) If the non-resident parent has more than one qualifying child and in relation to them there is more than one person with care, the amount of child support maintenance payable is (subject to paragraph 7 or 8) to be determined by apportioning the rate between the persons with care.

(2) The rate of maintenance liability is to be divided by the number of qualifying children, and shared among the persons with care according to the number of qualifying children in relation to whom each is a person with care.

*Shared care—basic and reduced rate*

**7.**—(1) This paragraph applies only if the rate of child support maintenance payable is the basic rate or a reduced rate.

(2) If the care of a qualifying child is shared between the non-resident parent and the person with care, so that the non-resident parent from time to time has care of the child overnight, the amount of child support maintenance which he would otherwise have been liable to pay the person with care, as calculated in accordance with the preceding paragraphs of this Part of this Schedule, is to be decreased in accordance with this paragraph.

(3) First, there is to be a decrease according to the number of such nights which the Secretary of State determines there to have been, or expects there to be, or both during a prescribed twelve-month period.

(4) The amount of that decrease for one child is set out in the following Table—

| Number of nights | Fraction to subtract |
| :---: | :---: |
| 52 to 103 | One-seventh |
| 104 to 155 | Two-sevenths |
| 156 to 174 | Three-sevenths |
| 175 or more | One-half |

(5) If the person with care is caring for more than one qualifying child of the non-resident parent, the applicable decrease is the sum of the appropriate fraction in the Table divided by the number of such qualifying children.

(6) If the applicable fraction is one-half in relation to any qualifying child in the care of the person with care, the total amount payable to the person with care is then to be further decreased by £7 for each such child.

(7) If the application of the preceding provisions of this paragraph would decrease the weekly amount of child support maintenance (or the aggregate of all such amounts) payable by the non-resident parent to the person with care (or all of them) to less than £5, he is instead liable to pay child support maintenance at the rate of £5 a week, apportioned (if appropriate) in accordance with paragraph 6.

*Shared care- flat rate*

**8.**—(1) This paragraph applies only if—

(a) the rate of child support maintenance payable is a flat rate; and

(b) that rate applies because the non-resident parent falls within paragraph 4(1)(b) or (c) or 4(2).

(2) If the care of a qualifying child is shared as mentioned in paragraph 7(2) for at least 52 nights during a prescribed 12–month period, the amount of child support maintenance payable by the non-resident parent to the person with care of that child is nil.

*Regulations about shared care*

**9.** The Secretary of State may by regulations provide—

(a) for which nights are to count for the purposes of shared care under paragraphs 7 and 8, or for how it is to be determined whether a night counts;

(b) for what counts, or does not count, as "care" for those purposes; and

(c) for paragraph 7(3) or 8(2) to have effect, in prescribed circumstances, as if the period mentioned there were other than 12 months, and in such circumstances for the Table in paragraph 7(4) (or that Table as modified pursuant to regulations made under paragraph 10A(2)(a)), or the period mentioned in paragraph 8(2), to have effect with prescribed adjustments.

*Net weekly income*

**10.**—(1) For the purposes of this Schedule, net weekly income is to be determined in such manner as is provided for in regulations.

(2) The regulations may, in particular, provide for the Secretary of State to estimate any income or make an assumption as to any fact where, in his view, the information at his disposal is unreliable, insufficient, or relates to an atypical period in the life of the non-resident parent.

(3) Any amount of net weekly income (calculated as above) over £2,000 is to be ignored for the purposes of this Schedule.

*Regulations about rates, figures, etc.*

**10A.**—(1) The Secretary of State may by regulations provide that—

(a) paragraph 2 is to have effect as if different percentages were substituted for those set out there;

(b) paragraph 3(1) or (3), 4(1), 5, 7(7) or 10(3) is to have effect as if different amounts were substituted for those set out there.

(2) The Secretary of State may by regulations provide that—

(a) the Table in paragraph 7(4) is to have effect as if different numbers of nights were set out in the first column and different fractions were substituted for those set out in the second column;

(b) paragraph 7(6) is to have effect as if a different amount were substituted for that mentioned there, or as if the amount were an aggregate amount and not an amount for each qualifying child, or both.

*Regulations about income*

**10B.** The Secretary of State may by regulations provide that, in such circumstances and to such extent as may be prescribed—

(a) where the Secretary of State is satisfied that a person has intentionally deprived himself of a source of income with a view to reducing the amount of his net weekly income, his net weekly income shall be taken to include income from that source of an amount estimated by the Secretary of State;

(b) a person is to be treated as possessing income which he does not possess;

(c) income which a person does possess is to be disregarded.

*References to various terms*

**10C.**—(1) References in this Part of this Schedule to "qualifying children" are to those qualifying children with respect to whom the maintenance calculation falls to be made.

(2) References in this Part of this Schedule to "relevant other children" are to—

(a) children other than qualifying children in respect of whom the non-resident parent or his partner receives child benefit under Pt IX of the Social Security Contributions and Benefits Act 1992; and

(b) such other description of children as may be prescribed.

(3) In this Part of this Schedule, a person "receives" a benefit, pension, or allowance for any week if it is paid or due to be paid to him in respect of that week.

(4) In this Part of this Schedule, a person's "partner" is—

(a) if they are a couple, the other member of that couple;

(b) if the person is a husband or wife by virtue of a marriage entered into under a law which permits polygamy, another party to the marriage who is of the opposite sex and is a member of the same household.]

[$^{19}$(5) In sub-paragraph (4)(a), "couple" means—

(a) a man and a woman who are married to each other and are members of the same household,

(b) a man and a woman who are not married to each other but are living together as husband and wife,

(c) two people of the same sex who are civil partners of each other and are members of the same household,

(d) two members of the same sex who are not civil partners of each other but are living together as if they were civil partners.

(6) For the purposes of this paragraph, two people of the same sex are to be regarded as living together as if they were civil partners if, but only if, they would be regarded as living together as husband and wife were they instead two people of the opposite sex.]

PART II

GENERAL PROVISIONS ABOUT MAINTENANCE ASSESSMENTS

*Effective date of assessment*

**11.**—(1) A maintenance assessment shall take effect on such date as may be determined in accordance with regulations made by the Secretary of State.   **2.203**
(2) That date may be earlier than the date on which the assessment is made.

*Form of assessment*

**12.** Every maintenance assessment shall be made in such form and contain such information as the Secretary of State may direct.

[$^{13}$...]

*Consolidated applications and assessments*

**14.**[$^{14}$—(1)] The Secretary of State may by regulations provide—

(a) for two or more applications for maintenance assessments to be treated, in prescribed circumstances, as a single application; and

(b) for the replacement, in prescribed circumstances, of a maintenance assessment made on the application of one person by a later maintenance assessment made on the application of that or any other person.

[$^{14}$(2) In sub-paragraph (1), the references (however expressed) to applications for maintenance calculations include references to applications treated as made.]

*Separate assessments for different periods*

**15.** Where [$^7$the Secretary of State] is satisfied that the circumstances of a case require different amounts of child support maintenance to be assessed in respect of different periods, he may make separate maintenance assessments each expressed to have effect in relation to a different specified period.
**16.**—(1) A maintenance assessment shall cease to have effect—

(a) on the death of the [¹⁸non-resident parent], or of the person with care, with respect to whom it was made;

(b) on there no longer being any qualifying child with respect to whom it would have effect;

(c) on the [¹⁸non-resident parent] with respect to whom it was made ceasing to be a parent of—

  (i) the qualifying child with respect to whom it was made; or

  (ii) where it was made with respect to more than one qualifying child, all of the qualifying children with respect to whom it was made

[¹⁵and ¹⁶ . . .].

(10) A person with care with respect to whom a maintenance assessment is in force shall provide the Secretary of State with such information, in such circumstances, as may be prescribed, with a view to assisting the Secretary of State [¹¹. . . ] in determining whether the assessment has ceased to have effect [¹⁷. . .].

(11) The Secretary of State may by regulations make such supplemental, incidental or transitional provision as he thinks necessary or expedient in consequence of the provisions of this paragraph.

AMENDMENTS

11. Paragraph 48(5)(d) of Sch.7 to the Social Security Act 1998 (June 1, 1999).

12. Section 1(3) of, and Sch.1 to, the 2000 Act (for the purpose of making regulations, November 10, 2000 under art.2(1) of, and Pt I of the Schedule to, the Commencement No.3 Order 2000; March 3, 2003 under art.3 of, and the Schedule to, the Commencement No.12 Order 2003).

13. Paragraph 11(22)(a) of Sch.3 to the 2000 Act (March 3, 2003 under art.3 of, and the Schedule to, the Commencement No.12 Order 2003).

14. Paragraph 11(22)(b) of Sch.3 to the 2000 Act (March 3, 2003 under art.3 of, and the Schedule to, the Commencement No.12 Order 2003).

15. Paragraph 11(22)(c)(i) of Sch.3 to the 2000 Act (March 3, 2003 under art.3 of, and the Schedule to, the Commencement No.12 Order 2003).

16. Paragraph 11(22)(c)(ii) of Sch.3 to the 2000 Act (March 3, 2003 under art.3 of, and the Schedule to, the Commencement No.12 Order 2003).

17. Paragraph 11(22)(c)(iii) of Sch.3 to the 2000 Act (March 3, 2003 under art.3 of, and the Schedule to, the Commencement No.12 Order 2003).

18. Paragraph 11(2) of Sch.3 to the 2000 Act (March 3, 2003 under art.3 of, and the Schedule to, the Commencement No.12 Order 2003).

19. Paragraph 6 of Sch.24 to the Civil Partnership Act 2004.

DEFINITIONS

2.204

"child": see s.55.
"child benefit": see s.54.
"income support": see s.54.
"maintenance calculation": see s.54.
"non-resident parent": see s.3(2).
"parent": see s.54.
"person with care": see s.3(3).
"prescribed": see s.54.
"qualifying child": see s.3(1).

GENERAL NOTE

*Paragraph 1*

This paragraph makes three provisions.

First, it sets the basic rate as the relevant rate unless the conditions for one of the other rates is satisfied (subpara.(1)). All the rates are defined and fixed by reference to the circumstances of the non-resident parent's present family. The circumstances of the person with care's present family are irrelevant.

Second, it provides that, except if the nil rate applies, the weekly amount payable is the applicable amount (subpara.(2)).

Third, it determines the order in which that rate is reduced to take account of apportionment (between persons with care to which the non-resident parent is liable) and adjustment (for shared care). The rate is first apportioned and then adjusted (subpara.(2)).

Although the paragraph refers to the amount *payable*, it may not be the amount that the non-resident parent actually has to pay. That amount may be greater, to take account of arrears, or less, to take account of an overpayment.

*Paragraph 2*

It is not necessary to define the basic rate, because it is the one that applies if no other rate is applicable. So, this paragraph only needs to specify the percentage of the non-resident parent's net weekly income that is payable as the basic rate. The percentage varies according to the number of qualifying children (subpara.(1)) and the number of other relevant children, as defined by para.10C(2) below (subpara.(2)).

Net weekly income is determined under para.10 below. It is capped at £2000 by para.10(3). "Qualifying children" is defined in para.10C(1) below and "relevant other children" in para.10C(2).

*Paragraph 3*

This paragraph sets the conditions for, and determines the amount of, the reduced rate. It is defined by two criteria. The first is negative: neither a flat rate nor the nil rate must apply. The second is positive: the non-resident parent's weekly net income must be over £100 but under £200.

The amount of the reduced rate is fixed by regulations (subpara.(2)). Regulation 3 of the Maintenance Calculations and Special Cases Regulations is made under the authority of this provision.

The reduced rate payable must be at least £5 (subpara.(3)). This ensures that the reduced rate payable is never less than the flat rate of £5 (see para.4(1) below).

*Paragraph 4*

This paragraph sets the conditions for, and determines the amount of, the flat rate. There are two flat rates. They only apply if the nil rate does not.

Subparagraph (1) provides for a flat rate of £5. This is payable if one of three conditions is satisfied. The first is that the non-resident parent's net weekly income is £100 or less (subpara.(1)(a)). The second is that the non-resident parent is receiving a prescribed benefit, pension or allowance (subpara.(1)(b)), including non-UK ones (subpara.(3)). Regulation 4(1) of the Maintenance Calculations and Special Cases Regulations is made under the authority of this provision. The third is that the non-resident parent or that parent's partner receives a prescribed benefit (subpara.(1)(c)). Regulation 4(2) of the Maintenance Calculations and Special Cases Regulations is made under the authority of this provision.

Subparagraph (2) provides for a flat rate of a prescribed amount. The amount is prescribed by reg.4(3) of the Maintenance Calculations and Special Cases Regulations. This is payable if three conditions are satisfied. The first is that the non-resident parent has a partner who is also a non-resident parent (subpara.(2)(a)). The second is that a maintenance calculation is in force in respect of the partner (subpara.(2)(b)). The third is that the non-resident parent or the partner receives a benefit prescribed for subpara.(1)(c) (subpara.(2)(c)).

"Receives" is defined in para.10C(3) below and "partner" in para.10C(4) and (5).

*Paragraph 5*
This paragraph sets the conditions for the nil rate. It applies if one of two conditions is satisfied. The first is that the non-resident parent is of a prescribed description (subpara.(a)). Regulation 5 of the Maintenance Calculations and Special Cases Regulations is made under the authority of this provision. The second is that the non-resident parent's net weekly income is less than £5 (subpara(b)).

*Paragraph 6*
2.206    This paragraph deals with the possibility that a non-resident parent is liable to pay child support maintenance to different persons with care for different qualifying children. The child support maintenance payable by the non-resident parent is apportioned between the persons with care according to the number of children.

This paragraph is supplemented by reg.6 of the Maintenance Calculations and Special Cases Regulations.

"Qualifying children" is defined in para.10C(1) below.

*Paragraph 7*
This paragraph and para.8 deal with the possibility that the non-resident parent may sometimes have overnight care of the qualifying child. This is called shared care. Shared care is a concept that is separate from, but is linked to, day to day care under the Maintenance Calculations and Special Cases Regulations. Shared care is only relevant to the basic, reduced and flat rates. It is irrelevant to the nil rate, which obviously cannot be further reduced.

Care is shared if the non-resident parent from time to time has care of a qualifying child overnight. Two conditions must be satisfied: see reg.7(1)(a) and (b) of the Maintenance Calculations and Special Cases Regulations. First, the non-resident parent must have care of the child overnight. Care of a child means looking after that child: see reg.7(2) of those Regulations. Second, the child must stay at the same address as the non-resident parent. So, a non-resident parent whose child comes to stay and is looked after by a grandparent does not have care of the child.

The calculation of the number of nights is governed by reg.7(3)–(6) of the Maintenance Calculations and Special Cases Regulations.

The legislation refers to overnight care. This is in distinction to day to day care that is used elsewhere. In practice, there is likely to be no difference between the application of these two concepts. But there is a difference in the nuance of the language. Although day to day care is defined in terms of nights (see reg.1(2) of the Maintenance Calculations and Special Cases Regulations), it carries connotations of care from day to day, emphasising continuity over time appropriate to someone who is a principal carer and, therefore, a person with care under s.3(3)(b) of the Act. Overnight care, on the other hand, has connotations of occasional stays away from home. This may convey an accurate picture of some cases of shared care, like those where a child stays with a non-resident parent for one or two nights a week. But it can convey a misleading impression in cases in which the shared care is calculated by averaging over a period if, for example, a non-resident parent has a child for a period of time over a school holiday.

The effect of having shared care varies according to the rate of child support maintenance payable. This paragraph deals with shared care if the non-resident parent is paying the basic rate or a reduced rate. For these rates, the amount of child support maintenance payable by the non-resident parent is reduced. The reduction is determined by the number of nights for which the non-resident parent has the child overnight. Paragraph 8 below deals with the flat rate.

"Qualifying child" is defined in para.10C(1) below.

*Paragraph 8*

This paragraph and para.7 deal with shared care. See the general note to reg.7.

This paragraph deals with shared care if the non-resident parent is paying the flat rate. If that rate would otherwise apply, the amount payable is nil.

*Paragraph 10*

Net weekly income is calculated under the Schedule to the Maintenance Calculations and Special Cases Regulations. It is capped at £2000 under sub-para.(3).

*Paragraph 10C(2)(b)*

Regulations 1(3) and 10 of the Maintenance Calculations and Special Cases Regulations are made under the authority of this provision.

*Paragraph 10C(4) and (5)*

These definitions reflect those in reg.1(2) of the Maintenance Calculations and Special Cases Regulations.

*Paragraph 15*

This paragraph complements and extends reg.2(4) of the Maintenance Calculation and Special Cases Regulations. That provision applies to changes of circumstances that occur before the effective date. This paragraph is not so limited. It applies to changes of circumstances between the effective date and the date of decision and to future changes that can be anticipated. This bypasses the need to apply the revision and supersession rules. The result is a series of calculations that are separate but given as a parcel and part of a single process.

In contrast to reg.2(4) this paragraph is worded permissively, but it has been held that its operation is mandatory, not discretionary (*CCS 2657/98*, para.9).

The effective date of maintenance calculations made under this paragraph is governed by reg.25(5) of the Maintenance Calculation Procedure Regulations.

*Paragraph 16*

Where a person with care believes that an assessment has ceased to have effect or should be cancelled, that person is under a duty to notify the Secretary of State of this belief and the reasons for it, and to provide the Secretary of State with such information as he reasonably requires to allow a determination to be made as to whether the assessment has ceased to have effect or should be cancelled (reg.6 of the Information, Evidence and Disclosure Regulations).

If the non-resident parent returns to live with the person with care and the qualifying child, the child ceases to be a qualifying child under s.3(1) as there is no longer a non-resident parent. The case then falls within subpara.(1)(b). See *R(CS) 8/99*, para.16. The Commissioner considered the suggestion (set out in the 1997 edition) that in this subparagraph "qualifying child" concentrated on the person's status as a child, but rejected it on the ground that it was not appropriate in the context of the Act as a whole (paras 17–18). The Commissioner recognised that the effect of his decision was to leave little or no scope for the (now repealed) sub-para.(1)(d) (para.16). It was to avoid rendering this provision redundant that it was suggested that "qualifying child" must bear a different meaning in subpara.(1)(b).

PROVISION OF INFORMATION TO SECRETARY OF STATE

*Inland Revenue records*

2.207     **1.**—(1) This paragraph applies where the Secretary of State or the Department of Health and Social Services for Northern Ireland requires information for the purpose of tracing—

(a)   the current address of [²a non-resident parent]; or

(b)   the current employer of [²a non-resident parent].

(2) In such a case, no obligation as to secrecy imposed by statute or otherwise on a person employed in relation to the Inland Revenue shall prevent any information obtained or held in connection with the assessment or collection of income tax from being disclosed to—

(a)   the Secretary of State;

(b)   the Department of Health and Social Services for Northern Ireland; or

(c)   an officer of either of them authorised to receive such information in connection with the operation of this Act or of any corresponding Northern Ireland legislation.

(3) This paragraph extends only to disclosure by or under the authority of the Commissioners of Inland Revenue.

(4) Information which is the subject of disclosure to any person by virtue of this paragraph shall not be further disclosed to any person except where the further disclosure is made—

(a)   to a person to whom disclosure could be made by virtue of sub-paragraph (2); or

(b)   for the purposes of any proceedings (civil or criminal) in connection with the operation of this Act or of any corresponding Northern Ireland legislation.

[³**1A.**—(1) This paragraph applies to any information which—

(a)   relates to any earnings or other income of an absent parent in respect of a tax year in which he is or was a self-employed earner, and

(b)   is required by the Secretary of State or the Department of Health and Social Services for Northern Ireland for any purposes of this Act.

(2) No obligation as to secrecy imposed by statute or otherwise on a person employed in relation to the Inland Revenue shall prevent any such information obtained or held in connection with the assessment or collection of income tax from being disclosed to—

(a)   the Secretary of State;

(b)   the Department of Health and Social Services for Northern Ireland; or

(c)   an officer of either of them authorised to receive such information in connection with the operation of this Act.

(3) This paragraph extends only to disclosure by or under the authority of the Commissioners of Inland Revenue.

(4) Information which is the subject of disclosure to any person by virtue of this paragraph shall not be further disclosed to any person except where the further disclosure is made—

(a)   to a person to whom disclosure could be made by virtue of sub-paragraph (2); or

(b)   for the purposes of any proceedings (civil or criminal) in connection with the operation of this Act.

(5) For the purposes of this paragraph "self-employed earner" and "tax year" have the same meaning as in Parts I to VI of the Social Security Contributions and Benefits Act 1992.]
[¹. . .]

AMENDMENTS

1. Paragraph 49 of Sch.7 to the Social Security Act 1998 (September 8, 1998).
2. Paragraph 11(2) of Sch.3 to the 2000 Act (March 3, 2003 under art.3 of, and the Schedule to, the Commencement No.12 Order 2003).
3. Section 80 of the Welfare Reform and Pensions Act 1999 (November 11, 1999).

DEFINITION

"non-resident parent": see s.3(2).                                        2.208

[Schedule 3 was repealed by para.50 of Sch.7 to the Social Security Act 1998 with effect from June 1, 1999].

SCHEDULE 4                                        Section 22(5)

CHILD SUPPORT COMMISSIONERS

*Tenure of office*

**1.**—(1) Every Child Support Commissioner shall vacate his office [⁴on the date on which     2.209
he reaches the age of 70; but this subparagraph is subject to section 26(4) to (6) of the Judicial Pensions and Retirement Act 1993 (power to authorise continuance in office up to the age of 75)].
[⁵. . .]
(3) A Child Support Commissioner may be removed from office by the Lord Chancellor on the ground of misbehaviour or incapacity.

*Commissioners' remuneration and their pensions*

**2.**—(1) The Lord Chancellor may pay, or make such payments towards the provision of such remuneration, pensions, allowances or gratuities to or in respect of persons appointed as Child Support Commissioners as, with the consent of the Treasury, he may determine.
(2) The Lord Chancellor shall pay to a Child Support Commissioner such expenses incurred in connection with his work as such a Commissioner as may be determined by the Treasury.
[⁶(3) Subparagraph (1), so far as relating to pensions, allowances or gratuities, shall not have effect in relation to any person to whom Pt I of the Judicial Pensions and Retirement Act 1993 applies, except to the extent provided by or under that Act.]

*[⁹Expenses of other persons*

**2A.**—[¹²(1) The Lord Chancellor or, in Scotland, the Secretary of State may pay to any person who attends any proceedings before a Child Support Commissioner such travelling and other allowances as he may determine.].
(2) In sub-paragraph (1), references to travelling and other allowances include references to compensation for loss of remunerative time.
(3) No compensation for loss of remunerative time shall be paid to any person under this paragraph in respect of any time during which he is in receipt of other remuneration so paid.]

*Commissioners barred from legal practice*

**3.** Section 75 of the Courts and Legal Services Act 1990 (judges, etc. barred from legal practice) shall apply to any person appointed as a Child Support Commissioner as it applies to any person holding as a full-time appointment any of the offices listed in Schedule 11 to that Act.

*Deputy Child Support Commissioners*

**4.**—(1)  The Lord Chancellor may appoint persons to act as Child Support Commissioners (but to be known as deputy Child Support Commissioners) in order to facilitate the disposal of the business of Child Support Commissioners.

(2)  A deputy Child Support Commissioner shall be appointed—

(a)  from among persons who have a 10 year general qualification or are advocates or solictors in Scotland of 10 years' standing; and

(b)  [⁷subject to subparagraph (2A),] for such period or on such occasions as the Lord Chancellor thinks fit.

[⁷(2A)  No appointment of a person to be a deputy Child Support Commissioner shall be such as to extend beyond the date on which he reaches the age of 70; but this subparagraph is subject to section 26(4) to (6) of the Judicial Pensions and Retirement Act 1993 (power to authorise continuance in office up to the age of 75).]

(3)  Paragraph 2 applies to deputy Child Support Commissioners as if the reference to pensions were omitted and paragraph 3 does not apply to them.

*[¹Determination of questions by other officers*

**4A.**—(1)  The Lord Chancellor may by regulations provide—

(a)  for officers authorised—

(i)    by the Lord Chancellor; or
(ii)   in Scotland, by the Secretary of State,

to determine any question which is determinable by a Child Support Commissioner and which does not involve the determination of any appeal, application for leave to appeal or reference;

(b)  for the procedure to be followed by any such officer in determining any such question;

(c)  for the manner in which determinations of such questions by such officers may be called in question.

(2)  A determination which would have the effect of preventing an appeal, application for leave to appeal or reference being determined by a Child Support Commissioner is not a determination of the appeal, application or reference for the purposes of subparagraph (1).]

*Tribunals of Commissioners*

**5.**—(1)  If it appears to the Chief Child Support Commissioner (or, in the case of his inability to act, to such other of the Child Support Commissioners as he may have nominated to act for the purpose) [¹³that—

(a)  an application for leave under section 24(6)(b); or

(b)  an appeal,]

falling to be heard by one of the Child Support Commissioners involves a question of law of special difficulty, he may direct [¹⁴that the application or appeal] be dealt with by a tribunal consisting of any three [¹⁵or more] of the Child Support Commissioners.

(2)  If the decision of such a tribunal is not unanimous, the decision of the majority shall be the decision of the tribunal [¹⁶; and the presiding Child support Commissioner shall have a casting vote if the votes are equally divided].

[¹⁷(3)  Where a direction is given under subparagraph (1)(a), section 24(6)(b) shall have effect as if the reference to a Child Support Commissioner were a reference to such a tribunal as is mentioned in subparagraph(1).]

*Finality of decisions*

**6.**—(1) Subject to section 25, the decision of any Child Support Commissioner shall be final.

[¹¹(2) If and to the extent that regulations so provide, any finding of fact or other determination which is embodied in or necessary to a decision, or on which a decision is based, shall be conclusive for the purposes of any further decision.]

*Consultation with Lord Advocate*

**7.** Before exercising any of his powers under [²4(1) or (2)(b) or 4A(1)], the Lord Chancellor shall consult the Lord Advocate.

*Northern Ireland*

**8.** In its application to Northern Ireland this Schedule shall have effect as if—

(a) for any reference to a Child Support Commissioner (however expressed) there were substituted a corresponding reference to a Child Support Commissioner for Northern Ireland;

(b) in paragraph 2(1), the word "pensions" were omitted;

[¹⁰(bb) paragraph 2A were omitted;]

(c) for paragraph 3, there were substituted—

"**3.** A Child Support Commissioner for Northern Ireland, so long as he holds office as such, shall not practise as a barrister or act for any remuneration to himself as arbitrator or referee or be directly or indirectly concerned in any matter as a conveyancer, notary public or solicitor.";

(d) in paragraph 4—
    (i) for paragraph (a) of subparagraph (2) there were substituted—

"(a) from among persons who are barristers or solicitors of not less than 10 years' standing; and";

    (ii) for subparagraph (3) there were substituted—

"(3) Paragraph 2 applies to deputy Child Support Commissioners for Northern Ireland, but paragraph 3 does not apply to them."; and

(e) [³paragraphs 4A] to 7 were omitted.

AMENDMENTS

1. Section 17(1) of the 1995 Act (December 18, 1995).
2. Section 17(2) of the 1995 Act (December 18, 1995).
3. Section 17(3) of the 1995 Act (December 18, 1995).
4. Paragraph 23(2)(a) of Sch.6 to the Judicial Pensions and Retirement Act 1993 (March 31, 1995).
5. Paragraph 23(2)(b) of Sch.6 to the Judicial Pensions and Retirement Act 1993 (March 31, 1995).
6. Paragraph 21(2) of Sch.8 to the Judicial Pensions and Retirement Act 1993 (March 31, 1995).
7. Paragraph 23(3) of Sch.6 to the Judicial Pensions and Retirement Act 1993 (March 31, 1995).
8. Paragraph 23(4) of Sch.6 to the Judicial Pensions and Retirement Act 1993 (March 31, 1995).
9. Paragraph 18(1) of Sch.3 to the 1995 Act (December 18, 1995).

10. Paragraph 18(2) of Sch.3 to the 1995 Act (December 18, 1995).
11. Paragraph 52(4) of Sch.7 to the Social Security Act 1998 (March 4, 1999).
12. Paragraph 51 of Sch.7 to the Social Security Act 1998 (June 1, 1999).
13. Paragraph 52(1)(a) of Sch.7 to the Social Security Act 1998 (June 1, 1999).
14. Paragraph 52(1)(b) of Sch.7 to the Social Security Act 1998 (June 1, 1999).
15. Paragraph 52(1)(c) of Sch.7 to the Social Security Act 1998 (June 1, 1999).
16. Paragraph 52(2) of Sch.7 to the Social Security Act 1998 (June 1, 1999).
17. Paragraph 52(3) of Sch.7 to the Social Security Act 1998 (June 1, 1999).

DEFINITION

2.210    "general qualification": see s.54.

GENERAL NOTE

2.211    A person who is on the solicitors' roll but who does not hold a practising certificate is entitled to hold office as a Commissioner (see the reasons given by the Chief
Commissioner for refusing leave in *CIS 1344/04*).

[¹SCHEDULE 4A

APPLICATIONS FOR A VARIATION

*Interpretation*

2.212    1. In this Schedule, "regulations" means regulations made by the Secretary of State.

*Applications for a variation*

2. Regulations may make provision—

(a) as to the procedure to be followed in considering an application for a variation;

(b) as to the procedure to be followed when an application for a variation is referred to an
appeal tribunal under section 28D(1)(b).

*Completion of preliminary consideration*

3. Regulations may provide for determining when the preliminary consideration of an
application for a variation is to be taken to have been completed.

*Information*

4. If any information which is required (by regulations under this Act) to be furnished to
the Secretary of State in connection with an application for a variation has not been furnished
within such period as may be prescribed, the Secretary of State may nevertheless proceed to
consider the application.

*Joint consideration of applications for a variation and appeals*

5.—(1) Regulations may provide for two or more applications for a variation with respect
to the same application for a maintenance calculation to be considered together.

(2) In sub-paragraph (1), the reference to an application for a maintenance calculation
includes an application treated as having been made under section 6.

(3) An appeal tribunal considering an application for a variation under section 28D(1)(b)
may consider it at the same time as an appeal under section 20 in connection with an interim
maintenance decision, if it considers that to be appropriate.]

AMENDMENT

1. Section 6(1) of, and Pt I of Schedule 2 to, the 2000 Act (for the purpose of making regulations, November 10, 2000 under art.2(1) of, and Pt I of the Schedule to, the Commencement No.3 Order 2000; March 3, 2003 under art.3 of, and the Schedule to, the Commencement No.12 Order 2003).

DEFINITIONS

"appeal tribunal": see s.54.                                                      2.213
"application for a variation": see s.54
"maintenance calculation": see s.54.

GENERAL NOTE

If an application is made under s.28G(1), this Schedule applies as modified by     2.214
reg.8(1) of the Child Support (Variations) (Modification of Statutory Provisions)
Regulations 2000.

[¹SCHEDULE 4B

APPLICATION FOR A VARIATION: THE CASES AND CONTROLS

PART I

THE CASES

*General*

1.—(1) The cases in which a variation may be agreed are those set out in this Part of this    2.215
Schedule or in regulations made under this Part.
(2) In this Schedule "applicant" means the person whose application for a variation is being
considered.

*Special expenses*

2.—(1) A variation applied for by a non-resident parent may be agreed with respect to his
special expenses.
(2) In this paragraph "special expenses" means the whole, or any amount above a prescribed amount, or any prescribed part, of expenses which fall within a prescribed description
of expenses.
(3) In prescribing descriptions of expenses for the purposes of this paragraph, the Secretary
of State may, in particular, make provision with respect to—

(a)  costs incurred by a non-resident parent in maintaining contact with the child, or
     with any of the children, with respect to whom the application for a maintenance
     calculation has been made (or treated as made);

(b)  costs attributable to a long-term illness or disability of a relevant other child (within
     the meaning of paragraph 10C(2) of Schedule 1);

(c)  debts of a prescribed description incurred, before the non-resident parent became a
     non-resident parent in relation to a child with respect to whom the maintenance
     calculation has been applied for (or treated as having been applied for)—
     (i)    for the joint benefit of both parents;
     (ii)   for the benefit of any such child; or
     (iii)  for the benefit of any other child falling within a prescribed category;

(d)  boarding school fees for a child in relation to whom the application for a maintenance
     calculation has been made (or treated as made);

(e)   the cost to the non-resident parent of making payments in relation to a mortgage on the home he and the person with care shared, if he no longer has an interest in it, and she and a child in relation to whom the application for a maintenance calculation has been made (or treated as made) still live there.

(4)  For the purposes of sub-paragraph (3)(b)—

(a)   "disability" and "illness" have such meaning as may be prescribed; and

(b)   the question whether an illness or disability is long-term shall be determined in accordance with regulations made by the Secretary of State.

(5)  For the purposes of sub-paragraph (3)(d), the Secretary of State may prescribe—

(a)   the meaning of "boarding school fees"; and

(b)   components of such fees (whether or not itemised as such) which are, or are not, to be taken into account,

and may provide for estimating any such component.

*Property or capital transfers*

**3.**—(1)  A variation may be agreed in the circumstances set out in sub-paragraph (2) if before 5th April 1993—

(a)   a court order of a prescribed kind was in force with respect to the non-resident parent and either the person with care with respect to the application for the maintenance calculation or the child, or any of the children, with respect to whom that application was made; or

(b)   an agreement of a prescribed kind between the non-resident parent and any of those persons was in force.

(2)  The circumstances are that in consequence of one or more transfers of property of a prescribed kind and exceeding (singly or in aggregate) a prescribed minimum value—

(a)   the amount payable by the non-resident parent by way of maintenance was less than would have been the case had that transfer or those transfers not been made; or

(b)   no amount was payable by the non-resident parent by way of maintenance.

(3)  For the purposes of sub-paragraph (2), "maintenance" means periodical payments of maintenance made (otherwise than under this Act) with respect to the child, or any of the children, with respect to whom the application for a maintenance calculation has been made.

*Additional cases*

**4.**—(1)  The Secretary of State may by regulations prescribe other cases in which a variation may be agreed.

(2)  Regulations under this paragraph may, for example, make provision with respect to cases where—

(a)   the non-resident parent has assets which exceed a prescribed value;

(b)   a person's lifestyle is inconsistent with his income for the purposes of a calculation made under Part I of Schedule 1;

(c)   a person has income which is not taken into account in such a calculation;

(d)   a person has unreasonably reduced the income which is taken into account in such a calculation.

## PART II

### REGULATORY CONTROLS

**5.**—(1) The Secretary of State may by regulations make provision with respect to the variations from the usual rules for calculating maintenance which may be allowed when a variation is agreed.

(2) No variations may be made other than those which are permitted by the regulations.

(3) Regulations under this paragraph may, in particular, make provision for a variation to result in—

    (a) a person's being treated as having more, or less, income than would be taken into account without the variation in a calculation under Pt I of Schedule 1;

    (b) a person's being treated as liable to pay a higher, or a lower, amount of child support maintenance than would result without the variation from a calculation under that Part.

(4) Regulations may provide for the amount of any special expenses to be taken into account in a case falling within paragraph 2, for the purposes of a variation, not to exceed such amount as may be prescribed or as may be determined in accordance with the regulations.

(5) Any regulations under this paragraph may in particular make different provision with respect to different levels of income.

**6.** The Secretary of State may by regulations provide for the application, in connection with child support maintenance payable following a variation, of paragraph 7(2) to (7) of Schedule 1 (subject to any prescribed modifications).]

**2.216**

### AMENDMENT

1. Section 6(2) of, and Pt II of Sch.2 to, the 2000 Act (for the purpose of making regulations, November 10, 2000 under art.2(1) of, and Pt I of the Schedule to, the Commencement No.3 Order 2000; March 3, 2003 under art.3 of, and the Schedule to, the Commencement No. 12 Order 2003).

### DEFINITIONS

"child": see s.55.
"child support maintenance": see s.54.
"maintenance calculation": see s.54.
"non-resident parent": see s.54.
"parent": see s.54.
"person with care": See s.54.
"prescribed": see s.54.

**2.217**

### GENERAL NOTE

If an application is made under s.28G(1), this Schedule applies as modified by reg.8(2)–(5) of the Child Support (Variations) (Modification of Statutory Provisions) Regulations 2000.

**2.218**

*Paragraph 2*
These grounds are prescribed in regs 10–14 to of the Variation Regulations.

*Paragraph 3*
In essence, this paragraph allows for a variation to reflect the effect of property transfers made under a court order or written agreement that was made before the child support scheme came into force and had the consequence that the amount of maintenance payable for the qualifying child was less than it would otherwise have

been. The effect of satisfying the conditions in this paragraph is governed by reg.17 of the Variation Regulations.

*Subparagraph (1)*

The kinds of court orders and agreements are prescribed by reg.16(1) of the Variation Regulations.

*Subparagraph (2)*

The kind of transfer of property is prescribed by reg.16(2)–(3) of the Variation Regulations and the minimum value is prescribed by reg.16(4) of those Regulations.

On the strict wording of subpara.(2), the transfer need not have been made under the court order or agreement, although that will usually have been the case (*R(CS) 4/00*, para.18). In the rare case where it was not so made, there must still have been a link between the transfer and the amount of maintenance. Evidence will be needed to show the link, for example in the recitals.

It may be difficult to show that maintenance was reduced in consequence of the transfer, especially in view of the variation in practice between courts and the evidentiary problems of producing evidence often many years after the event. The issue is the effect of a transfer in the circumstances of a particular case. In practice, it will have to be determined on the probabilities having regard to the state of the law and common practice at the time.

In *R(CS) 4/00*, the Commissioner dealt with a case in which the transfer of property and the maintenance in respect of the children were dealt with by court orders.

(i) *Admissible evidence and considerations (paras 19–23)* The Commissioner held that the following were admissible. First, the terms of the court order must be considered, although it was unlikely that the effect of a transfer of property on maintenance payments would be spelt out. Second, any contemporaneous documents relevant to the making of the court order must be considered. (a) Correspondence between the parties or their legal advisers was relevant, although this had to be treated with caution, as it would be partisan and represent negotiating positions or posturing. (b) The documents filed in the court or created by a party's advisers for their own use were relevant and likely to be less partisan, but could not be treated as an entirely reliable basis for determining the effect of a transfer. (c) The best information would come from the terms of any judgment that was given to explain why the judge made the order. This is only likely to be available in the form of a note of the judgment taken by counsel or a solicitor. Third, the legal context in which the court order was made for (a) the transfer of the property and (b) the maintenance of the children must be considered. This includes (i) the range of orders that may be made, including an order for the capitalised payment of maintenance and (ii) the factors to which a judge must have regard when making particular orders. Specifically relevant to maintenance orders for children is ss.25(1), (2) and (3) of the Matrimonial Causes Act 1973. Fourth, oral evidence given to the tribunal or the Commissioner by the parties must be considered, although this evidence was likely to be of limited value, as it might be partisan and reflect a party's misunderstanding or later rationalisation of what happened and why.

(ii) *The causal link (paras 23, 26 and 27)* Except in the case of capitalised maintenance payment, there will not be a direct link between a transfer of capital or property and the amount of maintenance payable in respect of children. The causal link must be established in terms of the factors that a judge must take into account when making an order for maintenance. The link will be an indirect one. For example, a father who transfers his share in the family home to a mother will have a smaller deposit for a suitable home for himself than if some of the capital had been released to him. This will lead to higher mortgage payments, which will reduce the amount available for the payment of maintenance.

(iii) *The proximity of the link (paras 30 and 38)* The transfer and the maintenance order need not be contemporaneous in order to establish a causal link. A maintenance order may be affected by a transfer that has not taken place, provided that it was in contemplation of the court when the maintenance order was made. Likewise, a maintenance order may be affected by a transfer that occurred some time before; the passage of time is not alone sufficient to break the causal link.

*Subparagraph (3)*

This subparagraph contains does not define "maintenance". Instead, it limits its scope to maintenance that is provided by way of periodical payments and to a child with respect to whom an application for a maintenance calculation has been made.

A periodical payment is essential. The transfer of one parent's interest in the former family home to the other parent in order to provide a stable base for the upbringing and education of the couple's children does not constitute maintenance within this definition (*R(CS) 4/00*, para.16).

Maintenance is defined in reg.17(4) of the Variation Regulations as "the normal day-to-day living expenses of the qualifying child". This overcomes the apparent flaw in subpara.(3) which refers not to the qualifying child but to any child with respect to whom an application is made.

*Paragraph 4*

These grounds are prescribed in regs 18–20 to of the Variation Regulations.

*Paragraph 5*

*Subparagraph (1)*

The Variation Regulations contain the cases.

*Subparagraph (2)*

The cases listed in the Variation Regulations are exhaustive of the variations that the Secretary of State may agree to. There is no residual power to agree to others. This is surely obvious and, anyway, repeats para.1(1) above.

Schedule 4C was repealed by s.85 of, and Sch.9 to, the 2000 Act. Article 3 of, and the Schedule to, the Commencement No.12 Order 2003 provided that it ceased to have effect from March 3, 2003 for the purposes of the cases there specified.

# Child Support Act 1995

(1995 c.34)

## ARRANGEMENT OF SECTIONS

### *Miscellaneous*

2.219

*Supplemental*

26. Regulations and orders.
27. Interpretation.
28. Financial provisions.
29. Provision for Northern Ireland.
30. Short title, commencement, extent, etc.

An Act to make provision with respect to child support maintenance and other maintenance; and to provide for a child maintenance bonus. [19th July, 1995.]

2.220    Section 10 (child maintenance bonus) was repealed by s.23 of the 2000 Act. Article 6(1) of the Commencement No.12 Order 2003 provided that it ceased to have effect from March 3, 2003 for the purposes of the cases specified in art.6(2) of the Order. It is amended for those cases to which it continues to refer by para.126 of Sch.24 to the Civil Partnership Act 2004.

*Miscellaneous*

## Deferral of right to apply for maintenance assessment

2.221    **18.**—(1) to (4) omitted.
[¹ . . .]
(6) Neither section 4(10) nor section 7(10) of the 1991 Act shall apply in relation to a maintenance order made in the circumstances mentioned in subsection (7) or (8) of section 8 of the 1991 Act.
(7) The Secretary of State may by regulations make provision for section 4(10), or section 7(10), of the 1991 Act not to apply in relation to such other cases as may be prescribed.
(8) Pt I of the Schedule to the Child Support Act 1991 (Commencement No.3 and Transitional Provisions) Order 1992 (phased take-on of certain cases) is hereby revoked.
(9) At any time before 7th April 1997, neither section 8(3), nor section 9(5)(b), of the 1991 Act shall apply in relation to any case which fell within paragraph 5(2) of the Schedule to the 1992 order (pending cases during the transitional period set by that order).

AMENDMENT

1. Paragraph 13(2) of Sch.3 to the 2000 Act (March 3, 2003 under art.3 of, and the Schedule to, the Commencement No.12 Order 2003).

COMMENCEMENT

2.222    September 4, 1995

DEFINITION

2.223    "the 1991 Act": see s.27(1).

GENERAL NOTE

2.224

This section must be read in conjunction with ss.4(10) and (11), 7(10), 8(3A), 9(3) and (6) and 11(1A)—(1C) of the Act and reg.9 of the Maintenance Arrangements and Jurisdiction Regulations.

Subsection (8) of this section revokes Pt I of the Schedule to the Transitional Provisions Order which dealt with the phased take on of cases into the child support scheme, but re-enacts most of those provisions, although omitting the phasing element. The equivalent provisions are as follows:

| Transitional Provisions Order | Re-enactment |
|---|---|
| paras 1(1) and 2 | ss.4(10) and (11) of the Act |
| para.3 | s.7(10) of the Act |
| para.5(1)(i) | s.8(3A) of the Act |
| para.5(1)(ii) | s.9(3) of the Act |
| para.5(1)(iii) | s.9(6) of the Act |
| paras 1(2) and 5(2) | s.18(9) of the 1995 Act |

The effect of the parcel of provisions governing the take on of cases is set out below. The relevant time for applying the conditions is the time when a party seeks to make an application for a maintenance assessment. This may have an impact on what would otherwise be the priority of applications under s.5 of the Act and reg.4 of and Sch.2 to the Maintenance Assessment Procedure Regulations, since it may mean that one or more applications are not valid and have to be ignored.

*Applications under s.4 of the Act*

An absent parent or a person with care may apply for a maintenance assessment under s.4 of the Act except where either of the following two cases applies.

1. There is in force (see below for the meaning of "in force" in this context) in respect of every child covered by the application one of the following.
   (a) A written maintenance agreement made before April 5, 1993 (when the child support scheme came into force) (s.4(10)(a)—see below for a discussion of written maintenance agreement).
   (b) A maintenance order (s.4(10)(a) and (aa)), either made before a prescribed date or on or after that date but in force for less than one year, except
      (i) one dealing with educational needs or disability (subs.(6) of this section—the existence of such orders is not incompatible with a child support maintenance assessment as they have always been preserved for the courts' jurisdiction under s.8(7) and (8) of the Act); or
      (ii) one made after January 22, 1996, where the court has decided that it either has no power to vary the maintenance order or that it has no power to enforce it (reg.9 of the Maintenance Arrangements and Jurisdiction Regulations—this prevents parties being excluded from both the courts and the child support scheme).

Accordingly, when these limitations are taken into account alongside the limitations on the powers of the parties and the courts under ss.8 and 9, the overall effect is in essence that private client applications may not be made where there were in force at the inception of the child support maintenance scheme maintenance arrangements under a written agreement or court order.

2. The person with care is a parent of the child and a benefit which would trigger the operation of s.6 of the Act is in payment to or in respect of that parent (s.4(10)(b) and (11)). This ensures that the operation of s.4 and s.6 is mutually exclusive.

*Applications under s.7 of the Act*

In Scotland a qualifying child may apply for a maintenance assessment under s.7 of the Act unless there is in force (see below for the meaning of "in force" in this context) in respect of that child either

(a) a written maintenance agreement made before April 5, 1993 (when the child support scheme came into force) (s.7(10)—see below for a discussion of written maintenance agreement), or

(b) a maintenance order (ss.7(10)(a) and (b)), either made before a prescribed date or on or after that date but in force for less than one year, except

    (i) one dealing with educational needs or disability (subs.(6) of this section), or

    (ii) one made after January 22, 1996, where the court has decided that it either has no power to vary the maintenance order or that it has no power to enforce it (reg.9 of the Maintenance Arrangements and Jurisdiction Regulations).

See above under *Applications under s.4 of the Act* for the overall effect of these provisions and the reasons for the exceptions.

*Unsuccessful applications under s.6 of the Act*

If an application for a maintenance assessment under s.6 of the Act fails because, before the application is referred to a child support officer, the relevant benefit has been disallowed or withdrawn, the Secretary of State must invite the parent to apply for a maintenance assessment under s.4 if it appears that s.4(10) would not prevent the application (s.11(1A)–(1C) of the Act). The definition of "benefit" for the purposes of s.4(10) and s.6 is the same. Consequently, if a benefit claim is withdrawn or disallowed, it is only the existence of a maintenance agreement or order made before April 5, 1993 that can in the normal case prevent a parent with care having the option of switching from s.6 to s.4 (*CCS 12806/96*, para.21).

*Powers of the courts and the parties*

1. The courts retain jurisdiction to make maintenance orders in the following cases. Some are expressly reserved to the courts under the child support legislation. These are where the maintenance order:

(a) is the same as a written maintenance agreement (s.8(5) of the Act and the Child Maintenance (Written Agreements) Order 1993). In *V v V (child maintenance)* [2001] 2 F.L.R. 799, Wilson J. explained how the courts use this provision as a way of avoiding the child support scheme. The approach is certainly outside the spirit of the legislation and, as his Lordship admitted, sometimes even outside the letter as well;

(b) tops up a child support maintenance assessment (s.8(6));

(c) deals with educational needs (s.8(7));

(d) deals with needs arising from disability (s.8(8));

(e) is against a person with care of the child (s.8(10)).

Other cases arise because they fall outside the basic definitions which set the limits to the child support scheme. These are where

(f) the child falls outside the definition of child for the purposes of the legislation (s.55 and Sch.1 to the Maintenance Assessment Procedure Regulations);

(g) there is no one who is both the natural or adoptive parent of the child (s.54—definition of "parent") and an absent parent in relation to the child (ss.3(1) and (2));

(h) all the parties are not habitually resident in the UK (s.44).

2. In other cases, where the Secretary of State would have jurisdiction to make a maintenance assessment, even if one would not be made, the position is as follows in 3–7.

3. Courts have no power to make or revive a maintenance order (s.8(3)).

4. They have power to vary an existing order, if either:
   (a) a maintenance calculation has not been made and
      (i) the order was made on or after the prescribed date (s.8(3) and (3A)(a)), or
      (ii) the order was made before the prescribed date and s.4(10) or 7(10) prevents an application for a maintenance calculation being made (s.8(3) and (3A)(b)); or
   (b) there is at any time before April 7, 1997, pending before a court an application made before April 5, 1993, to make a maintenance order (subs.(9) of this section).

5. The child support legislation does not prevent parties making a maintenance agreement (s.9(3)).

6. If the agreement was a written maintenance agreement and was made before April 5, 1993, it prevents an application under s.4 and s.7 if it falls within s.4(10)(a) and s.7(10), respectively (s.9(3)).

7. Otherwise the existence of a maintenance agreement does not prevent an application being made for a maintenance assessment (s.9(3))

8. Where the courts have no power to make a maintenance order by virtue of s.8 of the Act (as to which see 1, 2 and 3 above), the position is as follows in 9–12.

9. The courts may not vary a maintenance agreement so as to insert a provision requiring the making or securing of periodical payments (s.9(5)(a)).

10. They have power to vary an agreement so as to increase the amount of periodical payments, if either
   (a) the following two conditions are satisfied
      (i) no application can be made under s.4 or s.7 because of subs.(10) of each of those sections; and
      (ii) no maintenance assessment has been made under s.6 even if there is an outstanding application under that section (s.9(5)(b) and (6)); or
   (b) there is at any time before April 7, 1997, pending before a court an application made before April 5, 1993, to vary a maintenance agreement (subs.(9) of this section).

11. When dealing with an application to vary the amount of maintenance payable, the court should take into account the amount which would be payable under a maintenance assessment, although this is not decisive (*E v C (Child Maintenance)* [1996] 1 F.L.R. 472).

12. The child support legislation makes no express provision in relation to the powers of the courts in any other area than periodical payments of maintenance for children. However, the courts have taken the child support scheme into account in making decisions in other areas. See *Phillips v Peace* [1996] 2 F.L.R. 230 (lump sum payments and property adjustment orders for children) and *Re R (Residence Order: Finance)* [1995] 2 F.L.R. 612 (residence).

*Maintenance*

There is no statutory definition of maintenance in the child support or any other legislation, except perhaps reg.17(4) of the Variation Regulations. It covers recurring payments of an income nature to meet the costs of daily living, but daily living is not to be interpreted literally and restrictively (*A v A (Maintenance Pending Suit: Provision for Legal Fees)* [2001] 1 F.L.R. 377). It includes payments to provide for education, including private education (*Secretary of State for Social Security v Foster*, reported as *R(CS) 1/01*).

*Written maintenance agreement*

For jurisdiction to decide whether a written maintenance agreement exists, see the discussion of *R(CS) 1/96*, paras 11–13, and *R(CS) 3/97* in the general note to reg.2 to the Maintenance Assessment Procedure Regulations.

2.225

It is essential that there should be an "agreement". It is not sufficient that there has been an offer, even an offer in writing, to make an agreement (*CCS 11052/95*, para.7). No agreement arises unless and until the offer is accepted. An agreement may be reached between the parties or through representatives. However, if solicitors are negotiating, it is necessary to distinguish between an agreement on terms that the clients might incorporate into an agreement and a final agreement on those terms (*CCS 1305/00*, para.13).

The agreement must be a "maintenance agreement". Section 54 of the Act defines this phrase as having the meaning given in s.9(1) of that Act. This will apply to regulations made under the statute unless the context otherwise requires (see the general note to s.54). There was no definition of this phrase in Pt I of the Schedule to the Transitional Provisions Order (see the 1995 edition of this book) most of which has been re-enacted as indicated above. Accordingly, on general principles, the phrase had the same meaning as in the Act, unless the context otherwise required (see again the general note to s.54). The whole of this reasoning, and in particular the definition in s.54, was unfortunately overlooked by the Commissioner in *CCS 12849/96*, para.5 when dealing with para.2 of the Schedule to the Order, which has been re-enacted as s.4(10) of the Act.

Payments by a parent under the social security liable relative provisions are not made under a maintenance agreement, even if the parent agrees to make them (*CCS 13475/95*, para.13).

The maintenance agreement must be a "written maintenance agreement". In *CCS 15849/96*, paras 9–13 the Commissioner drew attention to the difference between a written maintenance agreement and a maintenance agreement that was merely *evidenced* in writing. A maintenance agreement made in writing was a written maintenance agreement, but one merely evidenced in writing was not. The Commissioner's decision contains a helpful analysis of the types of evidence that are often produced to show that there was a written maintenance agreement. The Commissioner declined to follow *CCS 12767/96*, para.10 in which another Commissioner had treated an agreement that was evidenced in writing as a written maintenance agreement. That Commissioner had relied on wording in para.7(1)(a)(iii) of Pt II of the Schedule to the Transitional Provisions Order, but this was distinguishable on the ground that Pt II of the Schedule dealt with the phasing in of maintenance assessments and it was appropriate for a less strict test to be applied to that stage than to the question whether an application for a maintenance assessment could be made at all. The reasoning in *CCS 15849/96* is preferable as it is consistent with the interpretation that has been given to "written agreement" (in different contexts) by the courts (*Ahmed v Government of the Kingdom of Saudi Arabia* [1996] 2 All E.R. 248 at 254–55, *per* Peter Gibson L.J. and *CCS 5354/97*, para.6).

On general principles, an agreement may be formed in the course of discussions relating to a possible consent order and may be written by reason of being contained in the correspondence. However, in the case of consent orders which are dependent on the court accepting the proposed terms, there is no legally binding agreement unless and until the court incorporates the proposal into its order (*Xydhias v Xydhias* [1999] 1 F.L.R. 683). If in other proceedings a written agreement is reached, it is irrelevant that one party later seeks to resile from it, unless of course it is mutually rescinded. It is also irrelevant that it is not for some reason incorporated into a consent order, unless this step was a condition of the agreement coming into, or remaining, in force. An agreement may be concluded in correspondence even though the correspondence is labelled "without prejudice". See *CCS 12767/96*. The same principles apply if the maintenance agreed for the child is nominal (*CCS 12849/96*, para.6). Once the agreement has been incorporated into a consent order, the order thereafter subsumes and supersedes the agreement (*de Lasala v de Lasala* [1979] 2 All E.R. 1146 at 1155, *per* Lord

Diplock and *A M S v the Child Support Officer and L M* [1998] 1 F.L.R. 955 at 962, *per* Simon Brown L.J.).

An agreement may also be formed, and be written, by being given as an undertaking to a court *(CCS 8328/95*, para.18). The Commissioner did not discuss whether an agreement that is incorporated into an undertaking is superseded as it would be if it were incorporated into a consent order. For a discussion of when an undertaking may be part of a maintenance order, see the following section of this note.

The agreement must be one which is an enforceable legal agreement *(CCS 12797/96*, para.15). Accordingly an arrangement which is made and carried out without any legal obligation is not an agreement *(ibid.)*. This is another reason why negotiations leading to a possible consent order in divorce proceedings are not a contract; the negotiations are likely to be conditional on the court accepting the terms of the proposed order *(Xydhias v Xydhias* [1999] 1 F.L.R. 683).

In the context of child support law an agreement between the absent parent and the qualifying child does not fall within the meaning of "maintenance agreement" *(R(CS) 7/98*, paras 20–21).

*Maintenance order*

A consensual arrangement relating to financial payments following a divorce may consist in part of a court order by consent and in part of one or more undertakings by one of the parties to pay specified sums of money. Usually these undertakings will relate to matters which the court has no jurisdiction to order *(Jenkins v Livesey* [1985] 1 All E.R. 106 at 118–119, *per* Lord Brandon). The question arises of whether such undertakings are part of the order.

In the general law, an undertaking which is referred to in an order does not thereby become part of the order *(Re Hudson* [1966] 1 All E.R. 110). Support for this proposition is also to be found in *Thwaite v Thwaite* [1981] 2 All E.R. 789. That case involved an undertaking which was referred to in a court order and performance of which was a condition precedent to the operation of the order. Despite the close connection between the undertaking and the order, the Court of Appeal treated the undertaking as merely the basis of the bargain on which the consent order was based *(ibid.* at 795(iii)). For some purposes, an undertaking may be equivalent to an order *(e.g. Gandolfo v Gandolfo* [1980] 1 All E.R. 833 and *Symmons v Symmons* [1993] 1 F.L.R. 317), but this does not turn the undertaking into an order.

This approach has been followed in the child support legislation. "Order" bears its literal meaning and does not include an undertaking that is recited to order the performance of which is perhaps conditional upon compliance with the undertaking *(CCS 8328/95*, para.13 and *R(CS) 6/99*, para.22). It is, however, appropriate in the case of a consent order to interpret the undertakings and the orders of the court as a single whole, because the settlement was negotiated as a package *(CCS 316/98*, para.19).

Whether payments are for the benefit of the child is determined by the proper interpretation of the court order. Usually the language of the order will be decisive on the question. Exceptionally a payment may be for the benefit of the child, although the order is not so worded. When this is so, it is because this is the proper interpretation of the order. The effect of the payment or the use to which it is put or was intended to be put is irrelevant. See *CCS 316/98*, para.27, qualifying *CCS 8328/95*, para.15.

In Scotland, a Commissioner has held that an extract of a minute of agreement registered in the Books of Council and Session is an order *(R(CS) 3/99)*, but this has been doubted by Temporary Judge Coutts in *Woodhouse v Wright Johnston & Mackenzie*, 2004 S.L.T. 911.

*In force*

According to *R(CS) 4/96*, para.13, in this context a court order is "in force" only if it is of practical effect between the parties. It is not in force if, although not formally rescinded, it has ceased to have any bearing on the financial relationship between the parties, as for example where the order is predicated upon the assumption that one parent will have care of the children and the other parent now has care. In this case, the maintenance order had been made on the basis that the children would be looked after by their mother and maintenance would be paid by the father. Later the parents changed the arrangement and the father took over the children's care. Naturally the maintenance order ceased to be paid, but it was not formally rescinded. The mother (now the absent parent) argued that she should not have been assessed for child support maintenance on the father's application under s.4 of the Act, because the order continued in force and there was no jurisdiction to deal with the application under the Transitional Provisions Order. The Commissioner held that the order was wholly without effect since, if the absent parent had sought to enforce it against the parent with care, she would have stood no chance of success. Accordingly, in his view, the child support officer had jurisdiction to deal with the father's application. With respect it is open to question whether the Commissioner's view is correct. The duration of orders for financial provision for children, made under the Matrimonial Causes Act 1973 on divorce, is dealt with in s.29 of that Act, which provides that such orders continue (subject to certain exceptions) until the child's seventeenth or, if appropriate, eighteenth birthday. While provision is made for payments to cease on the payer's death (s.29(4)). no mention is made of an order ceasing to have effect due to a change of circumstances. It is contemplated, instead, that there would be an application to vary or discharge the order in such a situation (s.31). The only likelihood of it becoming inappropriate to enforce an order concerns a failure to enforce arrears timeously, which is catered for in s.32. This provides that arrears of maintenance may not be enforced if they became due more than 12 months before the proceedings to enforce them are begun. Other legislation dealing with child maintenance outside divorce makes similar provision and also deals with the situation where the parents commence, or resume, cohabitation. In such a case, orders for the benefit of the child (Domestic Proceedings and Magistrates' Courts Act 1978, s.25(1)) or made or secured to the child's parent (Children Act 1989, Sch.1, para.3(4)) cease to have effect if the parents live together for more than six months. Although the Commissioner made a strong pragmatic point that if the order had to be formally discharged, there would be a time-lag before any machinery could be put in hand to ensure that the mother contributed to the children's support, no legislation covers the point which arose in the present case and it is doubtful if the gap should have been filled in the way chosen by the Commissioner. In *CCS 2567/98*, para.18, the Commissioner decided that *R(CS) 4/96* was wrong on this point. The Commissioner relied on the reasoning of the Court of Appeal in refusing leave to appeal against the decision in *R(CS) 4.96*. (*Kirkley v Secretary of State for Social Security and the Child Support Officer*, unreported, December 15, 1995).

In *CCS 12849.96*, para.7 the Commissioner held, reluctantly, that an agreement to pay a nominal sum had a bearing on the financial relationship of the parties and so remained "in force". It is not clear from the decision whether the nominal sum of one pence per child per year was being paid.

2.226    Section 24 (compensation payments) was repealed by para.13(3) of Sch 3 to the 2000 Act. Article 3 of, and the Schedule to, the Commencement No.12 Order 2003 provided that it ceased to have effect from March 3, 2003 for the purposes of the cases there specified.

*Supplemental*

## Regulations and orders

**26.**—(1) Any power under this Act to make regulations or orders shall be exercisable by statutory instrument.

(2) Any such power may be exercised to make different provision for different cases, including different provision for different areas.

(3) Any such power includes power—

(a) to make such incidental, supplemental, consequential or transitional provision as appears to the Secretary of State to be expedient; and

(b) to provide for a person to exercise a discretion in dealing with any matter.

(4) Subsection (5) applies to—

(a) the first regulations made under section 10;

(b) any order made under section 18(5) [¹. . .].

(5) No regulations or order to which this subsection applies shall be made unless a draft of the statutory instrument containing the regulations or order has been laid before Parliament and approved by a resolution of each House.

(6) Any other statutory instrument made under this Act, other than one made under section 30(4), shall be subject to annulment in pursuance of a resolution of either House of Parliament.

2.227

Amendment

1. Section of, and Sch.9 to, the 2000 Act (March 3, 2003 under art.3 of, and the Schedule to, the Commencement No.12 Order 2003).

Commencement

Except subs.(4)(a) and (c) September 4, 1995
Subsection (4)(c) October 1, 1995
Otherwise October 14, 1996

2.228

## Interpretation

**27.**—(1) In this Act "the 1991 Act" means the Child Support Act 1991.

(2) Expressions in this Act which are used in the 1991 Act have the same meaning in this Act as they have in that Act.

2.229

Commencement

September 4, 1995

2.230

## Financial provisions

**28.**—There shall be paid out of money provided by Parliament—

(a) any expenditure incurred by the Secretary of State under or by virtue of this Act;

(b) any increase attributable to this Act in the sums payable out of money so provided under or by virtue of any other enactment.

2.231

COMMENCEMENT

2.232    September 4, 1995

**Provision for Northern Ireland**

2.233    **29.**—(1) An Order in Council under paragraph 1(1)(b) of Schedule 1 to the Northern Ireland Act 1974 (legislation for Northern Ireland in the interim period) which states that it is made only for purposes corresponding to those of this Act—
  (a) shall not be subject to paragraph 1(4) and (5) of that Schedule (affirmative resolution of both Houses of Parliament); but
  (b) shall be subject to annulment in pursuance of a resolution of either House of Parliament.
  (2) The Secretary of State may make arrangements with the Department of Health and Social Services for Northern Ireland with a view to securing, to the extent allowed for in the arrangements, that—
  (a) the provision made by or under sections 10 and 24 ("the provision made for Great Britain"); and
  (b) the provision made by or under any corresponding enactment having effect with respect to Northern Ireland ("the provision made for Northern Ireland"),
provide for a single system within the United Kingdom.
  (3) The Secretary of State may make regulations for giving effect to any such arrangements.
  (4) The regulations may, in particular—
  (a) adapt legislation (including subordinate legislation) for the time being in force in Great Britain so as to secure its reciprocal operation with the provision made for Northern Ireland; and
  (b) make provision to secure that acts, omissions and events which have any effect for the purposes of the provision made for Northern Ireland have a corresponding effect for the purposes of the provision made for Great Britain.

**Short title, commencement, extent etc.**

2.234    **30.**—(1) This Act may be cited as the Child Support Act 1995.
  (2) This Act and the 1991 Act may be cited together as the Child Support Acts 1991 and 1995.
  (3) Section 29 and this section (apart from subsection (5)) come into force on the passing of this Act.
  (4) The other provisions of this Act come into force on such day as the Secretary of State may by order appoint and different days may be appointed for different purposes.
  (5) Schedule 3 makes minor and consequential amendments.
  (6) This Act, except for—
  (a) sections 17, 27 and 29;
  (b) this section; and
  (c) paragraphs 1, 18, 19 and 20 of Schedule 3,
does not extend to Northern Ireland.

# Social Security Act 1998

(1998 c.14)

ARRANGEMENT OF SECTIONS

PART I

*Decisions and Appeals*

GENERAL

*Decisions*

2.235

*Appeals*

*Procedure etc.*

PART IV

MISCELLANEOUS AND SUPPLEMENTAL

SCHEDULES

An Act to make provision as to the making of decisions and the determination of appeals under enactments relating to social security, child support, vaccine damage payments and war pensions; to make further provision with respect to social security; and for connected purposes. [21st May 1998]

Part I

Decisions and Appeals

Chapter I

General

*Decisions*

**Transfer of functions to Secretary of State**

2.236      **1.** The following functions are hereby transferred to the Secretary of State, namely—
- (a) the functions of adjudication officers appointed under section 38 of the Social Security Administration Act 1992 ("the Administration Act");
- (b) the functions of social fund officers appointed under section 64 of that Act; and
- (c) the functions of child support officers appointed under section 13 of the Child Support Act 1991 ("the Child Support Act").

Commencement

2.237      June 1, 1999 for s.1(c).

**Use of computers**

2.238      **2.**—(1) Any decision, determination or assessment falling to be made or certificate falling to be issued by the Secretary of State under or by virtue of a relevant enactment, or in relation to a war pension, may be made or issued not only by an officer of his acting under his authority but also—
- (a) by a computer for whose operation such an officer is responsible; and
- (b) in the case of a decision, determination or assessment that may be made or a certificate that may be issued by a person providing services to the Secretary of State, by a computer for whose operation such a person is responsible.

(2) In this section "relevant enactment" means any enactment contained in—
- (d) the Child Support Act;
- (g) the Child Support Act 1995;

(3) In this section and section 3 below "war pension" has the same meaning as in section 25 of the Social Security Act 1989 (establishment and functions of war pensions committees).

Commencement

2.239      September 8, 1998, except for subs.(2)(a) which is not relevant to child support.

Definition

2.240      "the Child Support Act": see s.84.

**Use of information**

**3.**—(1) Subsection (2) below applies to information relating to social security, child support or war pensions which is held—
  (a) by the Secretary of State or the Northern Ireland Department; or
  (b) by a person providing services to the Secretary of State or the Northern Ireland Department in connection with the provision of those services.
  (2) Information to which this subsection applies—
  (a) may be used for the purposes of, or for any purposes connected with, the exercise of functions in relation to social security, child support or war pensions; and
  (b) may be supplied to, or to a person providing services to, the Secretary of State or the Northern Ireland Department for use for those purposes.
  (3) The following sections, namely—
  (a) section 122C of the Administration Act (supply of information to authorities administering benefit); and
  (b) section 122D of that Act (supply of information by authorities administering benefit),
shall each have effect as if the reference in subsection (1) to social security included references to child support and war pensions.
  (4) In this section "the Northern Ireland Department" means the Department of Health and Social Services for Northern Ireland.

2.241

COMMENCEMENT

September 8, 1998.

2.242

DEFINITION

"the Administration Act": see s.84.

2.243

*Appeals*

**Unified appeal tribunals**

**4.**—(1) Subject to the provisions of this Act—
  (a) the functions of social security appeal tribunals, disability appeal tribunals and medical appeal tribunals constituted under Part II of the Administration Act;
  (b) the functions of child support appeal tribunals established under section 21 of the Child Support Act; and
  (c) the functions of vaccine damage tribunals established by regulations made under section 4 of the Vaccine Damage Payments Act 1979 ("the Vaccine Damage Payments Act"),
are hereby transferred to appeal tribunals constituted under the following provisions of this Chapter.
  (2) Accordingly appeals under—
  . . .
  (b) section 20 of the Child Support Act, as substituted by section 42 below;

2.244

shall be determined by appeal tribunals so constituted (in the following provisions of this Chapter referred to as "appeal tribunals").

COMMENCEMENT

2.245 June 1, 1999 for subss.(1)(b) and (2)(b).

DEFINITIONS

2.246 "the Administration Act": see s.84.
"the Child Support Act": see s.84.

GENERAL NOTE

Subsection (1) transfers the functions of Child Support Appeal Tribunals to the appeal tribunal. Subsection 2(b) deals with appeals under s.20 of the Act. That section is applied, by para.3 of Sch.4C to the Act, to decisions with respect to departure directions, reduced benefit directions or liability under s.43 of the Act. In addition, the appeal tribunal has jurisdiction, under s.28D(1)(b) of the Act, on a reference of an application for a departure direction.

## President of appeal tribunals

2.247 **5.**—(1) The Lord Chancellor may, after consultation with the Lord Advocate, appoint a President of appeal tribunals.
(2) A person is qualified to be appointed President if—
(a) he has a 10 year general qualification (construed in accordance with section 71 of the Courts and Legal Services Act 1990); or
(b) he is an advocate or solicitor in Scotland of at least 10 years' standing.
(3) Schedule 1 to this Act shall have effect for supplementing this section.

COMMENCEMENT

2.248 June 1, 1999.

## Panel for appointment to appeal tribunals

2.249 **6.**—(1) The Lord Chancellor shall constitute a panel of persons to act as members of appeal tribunals.
(2) Subject to subsection (3) below, the panel shall be composed of such persons as the Lord Chancellor thinks fit to appoint after consultation, in the case of medical practitioners, with the Chief Medical Officer.
(3) The panel shall include persons possessing such qualifications as may be prescribed by regulations made with the concurrence of the Lord Chancellor.
(4) The numbers of persons appointed to the panel, and the terms and conditions of their appointments, shall be determined by the Lord Chancellor with the consent of the Secretary of State.
(5) A person may be removed from the panel by the Lord Chancellor on the ground of incapacity or misbehaviour.
(6) In this section "the Chief Medical Officer" means—

(a) in relation to England, the Chief Medical Officer of the Department of Health;

(b) in relation to Wales, the Chief Medical Officer of the Welsh Office; and

(c) in relation to Scotland, the Chief Medical Officer of the Scottish Office.

COMMENCEMENT

Subs.(3) on March 4, 1999 to allow regulations to be made. Otherwise June 1, 1999.    2.250

DEFINITION

"prescribe": see s.84.    2.251

GENERAL NOTE

The President is not made a member of the panel by virtue of his office.    2.252

## Constitution of appeal tribunals

7.—(1) Subject to subsection (2) below, an appeal tribunal shall consist    2.253
of one, two or three members drawn by the President from the panel
constituted under section 6 above.

(2) The member, or (as the case may be) at least one member, of an
appeal tribunal must—

(a) have a general qualification (construed in accordance with section 71 of the Courts and Legal Services Act 1990); or

(b) be an advocate or solicitor in Scotland.

(3) Where an appeal tribunal has more than one member—

(a) the President shall nominate one of the members as chairman;

(b) decisions shall be taken by a majority of votes; and

(c) unless regulations otherwise provide, the chairman shall have any casting vote.

(4) Where it appears to an appeal tribunal that a matter before it
involves a question of fact of special difficulty, then, unless regulations
otherwise provide, the tribunal may require one or more experts to provide
assistance to it in dealing with the question.

(5) In subsection (4) above "expert" means a member of the panel
constituted under section 6 above who appears to the appeal tribunal
concerned to have knowledge or experience which would be relevant in
determining the question of fact of special difficulty.

(6) Regulations shall make provision with respect to—

(a) the composition of appeal tribunals;

(b) the procedure to be followed in allocating cases among differently constituted tribunals; and

(c) the manner in which expert assistance is to be given under subsection (4) above.

(7) Schedule 1 to this Act shall have effect for supplementing this
section.

2.254    Subss.(6) and (7) on March 4, 1999 to allow regulations to be made. Otherwise June 1, 1999.

CHAPTER II

SOCIAL SECURITY DECISIONS AND APPEALS

*Procedure etc.*

## Finality of decisions

2.255    **17.**—(1) Subject to the provisions of this Chapter, any decision made in accordance with the foregoing provisions of this Chapter shall be final; and subject to the provisions of any regulations under section 11 above, any decision made in accordance with those regulations shall be final.

(2) If and to the extent that regulations so provide, any finding of fact or other determination embodied in or necessary to such a decision, or on which such a decision is based, shall be conclusive for the purposes of—

(a) further such decisions;

(b) decisions made under the Child Support Act; and

COMMENCEMENT

2.256    March 1999 to allow regulations to be made.

DEFINITION

2.257    "the Child Support Act": see s.84.

GENERAL NOTE

2.258    This section applies to the Child Support Act 1991, but not to the Child Support Act 1995. See also s.46A to the Act.

PART IV

MISCELLANEOUS AND SUPPLEMENTAL

## Regulations and orders

2.259    **79.**—(1) Subject to subsection (2) below and paragraph 6 of Schedule 4 to this Act, regulations under this Act shall be made by the Secretary of State.

(2) Regulations with respect to proceedings before the Commissioners (whether for the determination of any matter or for leave to appeal to or from the Commissioners) shall be made by the Lord Chancellor; and where the Lord Chancellor proposes to make regulations under this Act it shall be his duty to consult the Lord Advocate with respect to the proposal.

(3) Powers under this Act to make regulations or orders are exercisable by statutory instrument.

(4) Any power conferred by this Act to make regulations or orders may be exercised—

(a) either in relation to all cases to which the power extends, or in relation to those cases subject to specified exceptions, or in relation to any specified cases or classes of case;

(b) so as to make, as respects the cases in relation to which it is exercised—

(i) the full provision to which the power extends or any less provision (whether by way of exception or otherwise);

(ii) the same provision for all cases in relation to which the power is exercised, or different provision for different cases or different classes of case or different provision as respects the same case or class of case for different purposes of this Act;

(iii) any such provision either unconditionally or subject to any specified condition;

and where such a power is expressed to be exercisable for alternative purposes it may be exercised in relation to the same case for any or all of those purposes.

(5) Powers to make regulations for the purposes of any one provision of this Act are without prejudice to powers to make regulations for the purposes of any other provision.

(6) Without prejudice to any specific provision in this Act, a power conferred by this Act to make regulations includes power to make thereby such incidental, supplementary, consequential or transitional provision as appears to the authority making the regulations to be expedient for the purposes of those regulations.

(7) Without prejudice to any specific provisions in this Act, a power conferred by any provision of this Act to make regulations includes power to provide for a person to exercise a discretion in dealing with any matter.

(8) Any power conferred by this Act to make regulations relating to housing benefit or council tax benefit shall include power to make different provision for different areas or different authorities.

(9) In this section "Commissioner" has the same meaning as in Chapter II of Part I.

COMMENCEMENT

May 21, 1998.                                                                                     2.260

GENERAL NOTE

*Subsection (6)*

For a discussion of "incidental" and "supplementary" see the general note to     2.261
s.51(1) of the Act.

*Subsection (9)*

"Commissioner" is defined by s.39(1) for the purposes of Ch.II of Pt I as follows.

"'Commissioner' means the Chief Social Security Commissioner or any other Social Security Commissioner, and includes a tribunal of three of more Commissioners constituted under s.16(7) above"

## Parliamentary control of regulations

2.262     **80.**—(1) Subject to the provisions of this section, a statutory instrument containing (whether alone or with other provisions) regulations under—

     (a) section 7, 12(2) or 72 above; or

     (b) paragraph 12 of Schedule 1, paragraph 9 of Schedule 2 or paragraph 2 of Schedule 5 to this Act,

shall not be made unless a draft of the instrument has been laid before Parliament and been approved by a resolution of each House of Parliament.

    (2) A statutory instrument—

     (a) which contains (whether alone or with other provisions) regulations made under this Act by the Secretary of State; and

     (b) which is not subject to any requirement that a draft of the instrument be laid before and approved by a resolution of each House of Parliament,

shall be subject to annulment in pursuance of a resolution of either House of Parliament.

    (3) A statutory instrument—

     (a) which contains (whether alone or with other provisions) regulations made under this Act by the Lord Chancellor, and

     (b) which is not subject to any requirement that a draft of the instrument be laid before and approved by a resolution of each House of Parliament,

shall be subject to annulment in pursuance of a resolution of either House of Parliament.

COMMENCEMENT

2.263     May 21, 1998.

## Financial provisions

2.264     **82.**—(1) There shall be paid out of money provided by Parliament—

     (a) any expenditure incurred by the Secretary of State or the Lord Chancellor under or by virtue of this Act; and

     (b) any increase attributable to this Act in the sums which under any other Act are payable out of money so provided.

    (2) There shall be paid out of or into the Consolidated Fund any increase attributable to this Act in the sums which under any other Act are payable out of or into that Fund.

COMMENCEMENT

2.265     May 21, 1998.

## Interpretation—general

2.266     **84.** In this Act—

"the Administration Act" means the Social Security Administration Act 1992;

    . . .

"the Child Support Act" means the Child Support Act 1991;

. . .

"prescribe" means prescribe by regulations.

COMMENCEMENT

May 21 1998.

## Provision for Northern Ireland

**85.** An Order in Council under paragraph 1(1)(b) of Schedule 1 to the    **2.267**
Northern Ireland Act 1974 (legislation for Northern Ireland in the interim
period) which contains a statement that it is made only for purposes
corresponding to those of this Act—
  (a) shall not be subject to paragraph 1(4) and (5) of that Schedule
      (affirmative resolution of both Houses of Parliament); but
  (b) shall be subject to annulment in pursuance of a resolution of either
      House of Parliament.

COMMENCEMENT

May 21, 1998.    **2.268**

## Short title, commencement and extent

**87.**—(1) This Act may be cited as the Social Security Act 1998.    **2.269**
  (2) This Act, except—
  (a) sections 66, 69, 72 and 77 to 85, this section and Schedule 6 to this
      Act; and
  (b) subsection (1) of section 50 so far as relating to a sum which is
      chargeable to tax by virtue of section 313 of the Income and
      Corporation Taxes Act 1988, and subsections (2) to (4) of that
      section,
shall come into force on such day as may be appointed by order made by
the Secretary of State; and different days may be appointed for different
provisions and for different purposes.
  (3) An order under subsection (2) above may make such savings, or
such transitional or consequential provision, as the Secretary of State
considers necessary or expedient—
  (a) in preparation for or in connection with the coming into force of any
      provision of this Act; or
  (b) in connection with the operation of any enactment repealed or
      amended by a provision of this Act during any period when the
      repeal or amendment is not wholly in force.
  (4) This Act, except—
  (a) section 2 so far as relating to war pensions;
  (b) sections 3, 15, 45, to 47, 59, 78 and 85 and this section; and
  (c) section 86 and Schedules 7 and 8 so far as relating to enactments
      which extend to Northern Ireland,
does not extend to Northern Ireland.
  (5) The following provisions of this Act extend to the Isle of Man,
namely—

(a) in section 4, subsections (1)(c) and (2)(c);
(b) sections 6 and 7 and Schedule 1 so far as relating to appeals under the Vaccine Damage Payments Act;
(c) sections 45 to 47 and this section;
(d) paragraphs 5 to 10 of Schedule 7 and section 86(1) so far as relating to those paragraphs; and
(e) section 86(2) and Schedule 8 so far as relating to the Vaccine Damage Payments Act.

COMMENCEMENT

2.270    May 21, 1998.

## SCHEDULE I

### APPEAL TRIBUNALS SUPPLEMENTARY PROVISIONS

*Tenure of office*

2.271    1.—(1) Subject to the following provisions of this paragraph, the President of appeal tribunals shall hold and vacate office in accordance with the terms of his appointment.

(2) The President shall vacate his office on the day on which he attains the age of 70, but subject to section 26(4) to (6) of the Judicial Pensions and Retirement Act 1993 (power to authorise continuance in office up to the age of 75).

(3) The President may be removed from office by the Lord Chancellor on the ground of incapacity or misbehaviour.

(4) Where the Lord Chancellor proposes to exercise a power conferred on him by sub-paragraph (3) above, it shall be his duty to consult the Lord Advocate with respect to the proposal.

*Remuneration etc.*

2. The Secretary of State may pay, or make such payments towards the provision of, such remuneration, pensions or allowances to or in respect of the President as he may determine.

3. The Secretary of State may pay, or make such payments towards the provision of, such remuneration, pensions or allowances to or in respect of any person appointed under this Chapter to act as a member of an appeal tribunal, or as an expert to such a tribunal, as he may determine.

4.—(1) The Secretary of State may pay—

(a) to any person required to attend at any proceedings under section 12 of this Act or section 20 of the Child Support Act; or

(b) to any person required under this Part (whether for the purposes of this Part or otherwise) to attend for or to submit himself to medical or other examination or treatment.

such travelling and other allowances as he may determine.

(2) In this paragraph references to travelling and other allowances include references to compensation for loss of remunerative time but such compensation shall not be paid to any person in respect of any time during which he is in receipt of remuneration under paragraph 3 above.

5.—(1) Subject to sub-paragraph (2) below, the Secretary of State may pay such other expenses in connection with the work of any person or tribunal appointed or constituted under any provision of this Part as he may determine.

(2) Expenses are not payable under sub-paragraph (1) above in connection with the work of a tribunal presided over by a Social Security Commissioner.

*Officers and staff*

**6.** The Secretary of State may appoint such officers and staff as he thinks fit for the President and for appeal tribunals.

*Functions of President*

**7.** The President shall ensure that appropriate steps are taken by an appeal tribunal to secure the confidentiality, in such circumstances as may be prescribed, of any prescribed material or any prescribed classes or categories of material.

**8.**—(1) The President shall, after the requisite consultation, arrange such training for persons appointed to the panel constituted under section 6 above as he considers appropriate.

(2) In sub-paragraph (1) above "the requisite consultation" means—

(a)  except in the case of medical practitioners, consultation with the Secretary of State;

(b)  in the case of such practitioners, consultation with the Chief Medical Officers of the Department of Health, the Welsh Office and the Scottish Office.

**9.** The President shall supply the Secretary of State with such reports and other information with respect to the carrying out of the functions of appeal tribunals as the Secretary of State may require.

**10.** Each year the President shall make to the Secretary of State a written report, based on the cases coming before appeal tribunals, on the standards achieved by the Secretary of State in the making of decisions against which an appeal lies to an appeal tribunal; and the Secretary of State shall publish the report.

*Clerks to appeal tribunals*

**11.** The Secretary of State may by regulation provide—

(a)  for clerks to be assigned to service appeal tribunals; and

(b)  for clerks so assigned to be responsible for summoning members of the panel constituted under section 6 above to serve on such tribunals.

*Delegation of certain functions of appeal tribunals*

**12.**—(1) The Secretary of State may by regulations provide—

(a)  for officers authorised by the Secretary of State to make any determinations which fall to be made by an appeal tribunal and which do not involve the determination of any appeal, application for leave to appeal or reference;

(b)  for the procedure to be followed by such officers in making such determinations;

(c)  for the manner in which such determinations by such officers may be called in question.

(2) A determination which would have the effect of preventing an appeal, application for leave to appeal or reference being determined by an appeal tribunal is not a determination of the appeal, application or reference for the purposes of sub-paragraph (1) above.

*Certificates*

**13.** A document bearing a certificate which—

(a)  is signed by a person authorised in that behalf by the Secretary of State; and

(b)  states that the document, apart from the certificate, is a record of a decision of an appeal tribunal or of an officer of the Secretary of State,

shall be conclusive evidence of the decision; and a certificate purporting to be so signed shall be deemed to be so signed unless the contrary is proved.

COMMENCEMENT

Paragraphs 7, 11 and 12 on March 4, 1999 to allow regulation to be made.
Paragraphs 1–9 and 11–13 on June 1, 1999.

DEFINITIONS

"the Child Support Act": see s.84.
"prescribe": see s.84.

SCHEDULE 5

REGULATIONS AS TO PROCEDURE PROVISION WHICH MAY BE MADE

**2.272**     1. Provision prescribing the procedure to be followed in connection with—

(a)   the making of decisions or determinations by the Secretary of State, an appeal tribunal or a Commissioner; and

(b)   the withdrawal of claims, applications, appeals or references falling to be decided or determined by the Secretary of State, an appeal tribunal or a Commissioner.

2. Provision as to the striking out or reinstatement of proceedings.

3. Provision as to the form which is to be used for any document, the evidence which is required and the circumstances in which any official record or certificate is to be sufficient or conclusive evidence.

4. Provision as to the time within which, or the manner in which—

(a)   any evidence is to be produced; or

(b)   any application, reference or appeal is to be made.

5. Provision for summoning persons to attend and give evidence or produce documents and for authorising the administration of oaths to witnesses.

6. Provision with respect to the procedure to be followed on appeals to and in other proceedings before appeal tribunals.

7. Provision for authorising an appeal tribunal consisting of two or more members to proceed with any case, with the consent of the claimant, in the absence of any member.

8. Provision for empowering an appeal tribunal to give directions for the disposal of any purported appeal which the tribunal is satisfied that it does not have jurisdiction to entertain.

9. Provision for non-disclosure to a person of the particulars of any medical advice or medical evidence given or submitted for the purposes of a determination.

COMMENCEMENT

**2.273**     March 4, 1999 to allow regulations to be made.

DEFINITION

**2.274**     "prescribe": see s.84.

GENERAL NOTE

*Extension*

**2.275**     This Schedule is applied to child support cases before appeal tribunals by s.20(4) and (5) of the Act. Section 20(4)(a) deals only with the making of appeals and does not cover the making of references. Section 20(4)(b) deals with proceedings before an appeal tribunal. It is not limited to appeals and its wording is broad enough to cover references. The Schedule is also applied to child support cases before Commissioners by s.22(4)(a) of the Act.

*"Procedure"*

The purpose of a rule as to procedure is to enforce the right of appeal, and an enabling provision to make such rules does not permit a rule which has the effect of taking away that right (*The King v Tribunal of Appeal under the Housing Act 1919* [1920] 3 K.B. 334 at 342, 343 and 346, *per* Lord Reading C.J. and Shearman and Sankey JJ. respectively).

Rules as to procedure cannot extend the jurisdiction of the tribunal (*Garthwaite v Garthwaite* [1964] 2 All E.R. 233 at 246, *per* Diplock L.J.). It is for this reason that a provision may not be made for a tribunal to deal with questions first arising. For the meaning of jurisdiction see the general note to s.20.

*Paragraph 7*

Although this paragraph refers to "the claimant", s.20(5) of the Act has the effect of extending it to cover parties to the proceedings, presumably parties other than the Secretary of State.

# Human Rights Act 1998

## (1998 c.42)

### ARRANGEMENT OF SECTIONS

#### *Introduction*

2.276

#### *Legislation*

#### *Public authorities*

#### *Remedial action*

#### *Other rights and proceedings*

*Derogations and reservations*

14. Derogations.
15. Reservations.
16. Period for which designated derogations have effect.
17. Periodic review of designated reservations.

*Judges of the European Court of Human Rights*

18. Appointment to European Court of Human Rights.

*Parliamentary procedure*

19. Statements of compatibility.

*Supplemental*

20. Orders, etc. under this Act.
21. Interpretation, etc.
22. Short title, commencement, application and extent.

## SCHEDULES

Schedule 1—The Articles.
    Part I The Convention.
    Part II The First Protocol.
    [Part III Article 1 of the Thirteenth Protocol.]
Schedule 2—Remedial Orders.
Schedule 3—Derogation and Reservation.
    Part I Derogation.
    Part II Reservation.
Schedule 4—Judicial Pensions.

An Act to give further effect to rights and freedoms guaranteed under the European Convention on Human Rights; to make provision with respect to holders of certain judicial offices who become judges of the European Court of Human Rights; and for connected purposes. [9th November 1998]

GENERAL NOTE

2.277    This Act did not come into force until October 2, 2000. However, both the Lord Chief Justice and the Master of the Rolls said that, pending the coming into force, courts should be mindful of it and pay particular attention to it (*Reichhold Norway ASA v Goldman Sachs International (a Firm)* [2000] 2 All E.R. 679 and *R v North and East Devon Health Authority Ex p. Coughlan* [2000] 3 All E.R. 850). Even before the Act came into force, it was always appropriate to take account of Art.6(1) when exercising a judicial discretion (*CDLA 5413/99*, paras 38–48).

Inappropriate reference to a Convention right on appeal to a Commissioner is not encouraged (*CDLA 2259/00*, para.11)

All functions conferred by this Act on the Lord Chancellor are transferred to the Secretary of State (for Constitutional Affairs) by art.4 of, and Sch.1 to, the Secretary of State for Constitutional Affairs Order 2003. This does not apply to the provisions specified in Sch.1: ss.5, 10, 18 and 19 and Sch.4.

*Introduction*

## The Convention Rights

**1.**—(1) In this Act "the Convention rights" means the rights and
fundamental freedoms set out in—

    (a) Articles 2 to 12 and 14 of the Convention,

    (b) Articles 1 to 3 of the First Protocol, and

    (c) [²Article 1 of the Thirteenth Protocol], as read with Articles 16 to 18
of the Convention.

(2) Those Articles are to have effect for the purposes of this Act subject
to any designated derogation or reservation (as to which see sections 14
and 15).

(3) The Articles are set out in Schedule 1.

(4) The [¹Secretary of State] may by order make such amendments to
this Act as he considers appropriate to reflect the effect, in relation to the
United Kingdom, of a protocol.

(5) In subsection (4) "protocol" means a protocol to the Convention—

    (a) which the United Kingdom has ratified; or

    (b) which the United Kingdom has signed with a view to ratification.

(6) No amendment may be made by an order under subsection (4) so
as to come into force before the protocol concerned is in force in relation
to the United Kingdom.

2.278

AMENDMENTS

1. Article 9 of, and para.10(1) of Sch.2 to, the Secretary of State for
Constitutional Affairs Order 2003 (August 19, 2003).

2. Article 2(1) of the Human Rights Act 1998 (Amendment) Order 2004 (June
21, 2004).

DEFINITIONS

"amend": see s.21(1).

"the Convention": see s.21(1).

"the First Protocol": see s.21(1).

"the Thirteenth Protocol": see s.21(1).

2.279

GENERAL NOTE

This section incorporates parts of the Convention and its Protocols into domestic law, designating them "Convention rights". Those rights also retain their existence under the Convention itself and it may be that resort will be had directly to
them in the ways developed before this Act came into force, rather than to
Convention rights based on them, in order to avoid or alleviate problems with the
procedures under this Act.

The other parts of the Convention and its protocols are not incorporated as
Convention rights and cannot be relied on (*CCS 6373/99*, para.8). However, they
may still be relevant. (i) They may be relevant to the interpretation of Convention
rights. (ii) They may be taken into account in the variety of ways that the courts previously used, despite the apparently limiting effect of the decision of the House of
Lords in *Brind v Secretary of State for the Home Department* [1991] 1 All E.R 720, to
make use of the Convention. (iii) They be taken into account when applying

2.280

European law which recognises them as part of the general principles of law to which it has regard, although the European Court of Justice will not give interpretative guidance on whether national legislation complies with the convention unless the legislation falls within the field of application of European law (*Kremzow v Republik Österreich, The Times*, August 11, 1997).

## Interpretation of Convention rights

2.281  **2.**—(1) A court or tribunal determining a question which has arisen in connection with a Convention right must take into account any—

  (a) judgment, decision, declaration or advisory opinion of the European Court of Human Rights,

  (b) opinion of the Commission given in a report adopted under Article 31 of the Convention,

  (c) decision of the Commission in connection with Article 26 or 27(2) of the Convention, or

  (d) decision of the Committee of Ministers taken under Article 46 of the Convention,

whenever made or given, so far as, in the opinion of the court or tribunal, it is relevant to the proceedings in which that question has arisen.

  (2) Evidence of any judgment, decision, declaration or opinion of which account may have to be taken under this section is to be given in proceedings before any court or tribunal in such manner as may be provided by rules.

  (3) In this section "rules" means rules of court or, in the case of proceedings before a tribunal, rules made for the purposes of this section—

  (a) by [¹. . .] the Secretary of State, in relation to any proceedings outside Scotland;

  (b) by the Secretary of State, in relation to proceedings in Scotland; or

  (c) by a Northern Ireland department, in relation to proceedings before a tribunal in Northern Ireland—

   (i)  which deals with transferred matters; and

   (ii) for which no rules made under paragraph (a) are in force.

AMENDMENT

  1. Article 9 of, and para.10(2) of Sch.2 to, the Secretary of State for Constitutional Affairs Order 2003 (August 19, 2003).

DEFINITIONS

2.282  "the Commission": see s.21(1).
  "the Convention": see s.21(1).
  "the Convention rights": see s.1(1).
  "transferred matters": see s.21(1).
  "tribunal": see s.21(1).

GENERAL NOTE

*Subsection (1)*

2.283  The materials listed must be taken into account. They are not necessarily decisive (*Gough v Chief Constable of the Derbyshire Constabulary* [2001] 4 All E.R. 289

*per* Laws L.J. at para.32) and they do not have the status of Convention rights. This reflects the fact that the Court does not regard itself as bound by its previous decisions, which in turns reflects the fact that the Convention is interpreted in a dynamic way to keep up-to-date with changing conditions.

As the materials must be taken into account in determining a question which has arisen in connection with a Convention right, they are relevant both to the interpretation and to the application of those rights.

In *CH 4574/03*, the Commissioner considered how the duty under this section could be reconciled with the doctrine of precedent (paras 30–37). He decided that generally the doctrine of precedent applied. The duty under this section was relevant (a) as the starting point for consideration when an issue first arose in domestic law or (b) when changed conditions and developing Strasbourgh jurisprudence justified distinguishing domestic authority. In *Leeds City Council v Price, The Times*, March 17, 2005, the Court of Appeal decided that a conflict between a decision of the House of Lords and a subsequent decision of the European Court of Human Rights could only be resolved by the House of Lords itself.

*Legislation*

## Interpretation of legislation

**3.** (1) So far as it is possible to do so, primary legislation and subordinate legislation must be read and given effect in a way which is compatible with the Convention rights.    2.284

(2) This section—

(a) applies to primary legislation and subordinate legislation whenever enacted;

(b) does not affect the validity, continuing operation or enforcement of any incompatible primary legislation; and

(c) does not affect the validity, continuing operation or enforcement of any incompatible subordinate legislation if (disregarding any possibility of revocation) primary legislation prevents removal of the incompatibility.

DEFINITIONS

"the Convention rights": see s.1(1).    2.285
"primary legislation": see s.21(1).
"subordinate legislation": see s.21(1).

GENERAL NOTE

*Subsection (1)*

The Convention rights are not merely to be applied directly by courts and tribunals. They have to be taken into account both when interpreting ("read") and when applying ("given effect") domestic legislation in order to ensure as far as possible that the legislation operates compatibly with those rights.    2.286

The limits within which it will be "possible" to interpret and apply legislation which on its wording is incompatible with a Convention right will have to be set by the courts. In theory the present limit is set by the decision of the House of Lords in *Brind v Secretary of State for the Home Department* [1991] 1 All E.R. 720, which is authority that the Convention can only be taken into account if the domestic legislation is ambiguous. However, there are numerous examples of courts at all levels applying a less restrictive approach, showing that there are possibilities beyond ambiguity.

The courts have discussed the approach that must be taken under this section. The best guidance was given by the Court of Appeal in *Poplar Housing and Regeneration Community Association Ltd v Donoghue* [2001] 4 All E.R. 604. The court has no power to modify the meaning of a provision more than is necessary to ensure compatibility. Its function is one of interpretation. It is not given power to legislate. The more radical the modification of the meaning that is involved, the more likely it is that the court would be legislating rather than interpreting.

The proper approach was also considered by the Commissioner in *CI 4421/00*, paras 16–24. The Commissioner made the following points. First, in the absence of clear guidance from the courts, the only authoritative guide is the terms of this subsection. Second, the essential starting point was to identify the provision that had to be interpreted. The more closely that provision was connected with the violation of the Convention right, the greater the justification for stretching its meaning. Third, this subsection required a broad approach to be taken to the interpretation of the provision. However, fourth, that did not authorise the Commissioner to disregard completely the context in which the provision appeared.

It is permissible to refer to Hansard only as a source of background information on a statutory provision, such as the mischief it was intended to remedy and the impact it was likely to have (*Wilson v First County Trust Ltd* [2003] 4 All E.R. 97).

The proportionaltiy of a statutory provision as a response to a legitimate aim is determined at the time when the issue arises, not when the legislation was enacted or came into force (*Wilson v First County Trust Ltd* [2003] 4 All E.R. 97).

In *CCS 1153/03*, the Commissioner relied on the "unless the context otherwise requires" qualification in the definition section to disapply a definition, thereby removing its discriminatory effect. On appeal, the Court of Appeal disapproved of this approach (*M v Secretary of State for Work and Pensions* [2005] 1 F.L.R. 498). Sedley LJ said that this Act provided a filter not a context (para.84). The Court of Appeal's decision is now under appeal to the House of Lords.

*Subsection (2)*
This subsection makes three provisions.

*Paragraph (a)*
This paragraph provides that subs.(1) operates retrospectively on legislation enacted before this Act came into force.

*Paragraph (b)*
This paragraph provides that if primary legislation cannot be interpreted or applied compatibly with Convention rights, it nevertheless remains valid, continues to operate and must be applied. This may lead either to a case being taken to the European Court of Human Rights or to a declaration of incompatibility under s.4.

*Paragraph (c)*
This paragraph deals with incompatible subordinate legislation. It provides that subordinate legislation remains valid, continues to operate and must be applied if the enabling legislation prevents the removal of the incompatibility. It is not clear what is meant by primary legislation preventing removal. If subordinate legislation is declared *ultra vires*, it ceases to have effect. Any incompatibility with a Convention right is thereby removed by force of law and not under the primary legislation. If a tribunal or Commissioner has power to decide that subordinate legislation is not authorised by primary legislation, despite its clear wording, because it is incompatible with a Convention right, this paragraph would be redundant. Perhaps this paragraph prevents this approach being taken and *ultra vires* on this basis is confined to the nominated courts under s.4(4). Otherwise, this paragraph and s.4(4) would be redundant.

### Declaration of incompatibility

**4.**—(1) Subsection (2) applies in any proceedings in which a court 　　2.287
determines whether a provision of primary legislation is compatible with a
Convention right.

(2) If the court is satisfied that the provision is incompatible with a
Convention right, it may make a declaration of that incompatibility.

(3) Subsection (4) applies in any proceedings in which a court determines whether a provision of subordinate legislation, made in the exercise
of a power conferred by primary legislation, is compatible with a
Convention right.

(4) If the court is satisfied—

(a) that the provision is incompatible with a Convention right, and

(b) that (disregarding any possibility of revocation) the primary
legislation concerned prevents removal of the incompatibility,

it may make a declaration of that incompatibility.

(5) In this section "court" means—

(a) the House of Lords;

(b) the Judicial Committee of the Privy Council;

(c) the Courts-Martial Appeal Court;

(d) in Scotland, the High Court of Justiciary sitting otherwise than as a
trial court or the Court of Session;

(e) in England and Wales or Northern Ireland, the High Court or the
Court of Appeal.

(6) A declaration under this section ("a declaration of incompatibility")—

(a) does not affect the validity, continuing operation or enforcement of
the provision in respect of which it is given; and

(b) is not binding on the parties to the proceedings in which it is made.

DEFINITIONS

"the Convention rights": see s.1(1). 　　2.288
"primary legislation": see s.21(1).
"subordinate legislation": see s.21(1).

GENERAL NOTE

This section provides the procedure by which a court may deal with primary or 　　2.289
subordinate legislation that cannot be interpreted or applied compatibly with
Convention rights. If a court declares legislation to be incompatible with a
Convention right, remedial action may be taken under s.10 and Sch.2.

Neither tribunals nor Commissioners have power to make a declaration under
this section.

*Subsection (2)*
The court has a power, but not a duty, to make a declaration (*Poplar Housing and
Regeneration Community Association Ltd v Donoghue* [2001] 4 All E.R. 604).

*Subsection (4)*
See the general note to s.3(2)(c).

**Right of Crown to intervene**

2.290    **5.**—(1) Where a court is considering whether to make a declaration of incompatibility, the Crown is entitled to notice in accordance with rules of court.

(2) In any case to which subsection (1) applies—

(a) a Minister of the Crown (or a person nominated by him),

(b) a member of the Scottish Executive,

(c) a Northern Ireland Minister,

(d) a Northern Ireland department,

is entitled, on giving notice in accordance with rules of court, to be joined as a party to the proceedings.

(3) Notice under subsection (2) may be given at any time during the proceedings.

(4) A person who has been made a party to criminal proceedings (other than in Scotland) as the result of a notice under subsection (2) may, with leave, appeal to the House of Lords against any declaration of incompatibility made in the proceedings.

(5) In subsection (4)—

"criminal proceedings" includes all proceedings before the Courts-Martial Appeal Court; and

"leave" means leave granted by the court making the declaration of incompatibility or by the House of Lords.

DEFINITIONS

2.291    "declaration of incompatibility": see s.21(1).
"Minister of the Crown": see s.21(1).
"Northern Ireland Minister": see s.21(1).

*Public authorities*

**Acts of public authorities**

2.292    **6.**—(1) It is unlawful for a public authority to act in a way which is incompatible with a Convention right.

(2) Subsection (1) does not apply to an act if—

(a) as the result of one or more provisions of primary legislation, the authority could not have acted differently; or

(b) in the case of one or more provisions of, or made under, primary legislation which cannot be read or given effect in a way which is compatible with the Convention rights, the authority was acting so as to give effect to or enforce those provisions.

(3) In this section "public authority" includes—

(a) a court or tribunal, and

(b) any person certain of whose functions are functions of a public nature,

but does not include either House of Parliament or a person exercising functions in connection with proceedings in Parliament.

(4) In subsection (3) "Parliament" does not include the House of Lords in its judicial capacity.

(5) In relation to a particular act, a person is not a public authority by virtue only of subsection (3)(b) if the nature of the act is private.

(6) "An act" includes a failure to act but does not include a failure to—

(a) introduce in, or lay before, Parliament a proposal for legislation; or

(b) make any primary legislation or remedial order.

DEFINITIONS

"the Convention rights": see s.1(1).                                     2.293

"primary legislation": see s.21(1).

"remedial order": see s.21(1).

"tribunal": see s.21(1).

GENERAL NOTE

The tribunals and the Commissioners in both their administrative and judicial    2.294
capacities are public authorities under this section. An act by a public authority is
unlawful if it is avoidably incompatible with a Convention right. For what is
unavoidable, see subs.(2). Proceedings against the public authority in respect of the
unlawful act and compensation are governed by ss.7 and 9, subject in the case of
judicial acts to s.9.

## Proceedings

**7.**—(1) A person who claims that a public authority has acted (or    2.295
proposes to act) in a way which is made unlawful by section 6(1) may—

(a) bring proceedings against the authority under this Act in the
appropriate court or tribunal, or

(b) rely on the Convention right or rights concerned in any legal proceedings, but only if he is (or would be) a victim of the unlawful act.

(2) In subsection (1)(a) "appropriate court or tribunal" means such
court or tribunal as may be determined in accordance with rules; and
proceedings against an authority include a counterclaim or similar
proceedings.

(3) If the proceedings are brought on an application for judicial review,
the applicant is to be taken to have a sufficient interest in relation to the
unlawful act only if he is, or would be, a victim of that act.

(4) If the proceedings are made by way of a petition for judicial review
in Scotland, the applicant shall be taken to have title and interest to sue in
relation to the unlawful act only if he is, or would be, a victim of that act.

(5) Proceedings under subsection (1)(a) must be brought before the end
of—

(a) the period of one year beginning with the date on which the act
complained of took place; or

(b) such longer period as the court or tribunal considers equitable
having regard to all the circumstances,

but that is subject to any rule imposing a stricter time limit in relation to
the procedure in question.

(6) In subsection (1)(b) "legal proceedings" includes—

(a) proceedings brought by or at the instigation of a public authority;
and

(b) an appeal against the decision of a court or tribunal.

(7) For the purposes of this section, a person is a victim of an unlawful act only if he would be a victim for the purposes of Article 34 of the Convention if proceedings were brought in the European Court of Human Rights in respect of that act.

(8) Nothing in this Act creates a criminal offence.

(9) In this section "rules" means—

(a) in relation to proceedings before a court or tribunal outside Scotland, rules made by [1. . .] the Secretary of State for the purposes of this section or rules of court,

(b) in relation to proceedings before a court or tribunal in Scotland, rules made by the Secretary of State for those purposes,

(c) in relation to proceedings before a tribunal in Northern Ireland—

    (i) which deals with transferred matters; and
    (ii) for which no rules made under paragraph (a) are in force, rules made by a Northern Ireland department for those purposes,

and includes provision made by order under section 1 of the Courts and Legal Services Act 1990.

(10) In making rules, regard must be had to section 9.

(11) The Minister who has power to make rules in relation to a particular tribunal may, to the extent he considers it necessary to ensure that the tribunal can provide an appropriate remedy in relation to an act (or proposed act) of a public authority which is (or would be) unlawful as a result of section 6(1), by order add to—

(a) the relief or remedies which the tribunal may grant; or

(b) the grounds on which it may grant any of them.

(12) An order made under subsection (11) may contain such incidental, supplemental, consequential or transitional provision as the Minister making it considers appropriate.

(13) "The Minister" includes the Northern Ireland department concerned.

AMENDMENT

1. Article 9 of, and para.10(2) of Sch.2 to, the Secretary of State for Constitutional Affairs Order 2003 (August 19, 2003).

DEFINITIONS

2.296

"the Convention": see s.21(1).
"the Convention rights": see s.1(1).
"transferred matters": see s.21(1).
"tribunal": see s.21(1).

## Judicial remedies

2.297

**8.**—(1) In relation to any act (or proposed act) of a public authority which the court finds is (or would be) unlawful, it may grant such relief or remedy, or make such order, within its powers as it considers just and appropriate.

(2) But damages may be awarded only by a court which has power to award damages, or to order the payment of compensation, in civil proceedings.

(3) No award of damages is to be made unless, taking account of all the circumstances of the case, including—

(a) any other relief or remedy granted, or order made, in relation to the act in question (by that or any other court), and

(b) the consequences of any decision (of that or any other court) in respect of that act,

the court is satisfied that the award is necessary to afford just satisfaction to the person in whose favour it is made.

(4) In determining—

(a) whether to award damages, or

(b) the amount of an award,

the court must take into account the principles applied by the European Court of Human Rights in relation to the award of compensation under Article 41 of the Convention.

(5) A public authority against which damages are awarded is to be treated—

(a) in Scotland, for the purposes of section 3 of the Law Reform (Miscellaneous Provisions) (Scotland) Act 1940 as if the award were made in an action of damages in which the authority has been found liable in respect of loss or damage to the person to whom the award is made;

(b) for the purposes of the Civil Liability (Contribution) Act 1978 as liable in respect of damage suffered by the person to whom the award is made.

(6) In this section—

"court" includes a tribunal;

"damages" means damages for an unlawful act of a public authority; and

"unlawful" means unlawful under section 6(1).

DEFINITIONS

"the Convention": see s.21(1).           2.298
"tribunal": see s.21(1).

## Judicial acts

**9.**—(1) Proceedings under section 7(1)(a) in respect of a judicial act           2.299
may be brought only—

(a) by exercising a right of appeal;

(b) on an application (in Scotland a petition) for judicial review; or

(c) in such other forum as may be prescribed by rules.

(2) That does not affect any rule of law which prevents a court from being the subject of judicial review.

(3) In proceedings under this Act in respect of a judicial act done in good faith, damages may not be awarded otherwise than to compensate a person to the extent required by Article 5(5) of the Convention.

(4) An award of damages permitted by subsection (3) is to be made against the Crown; but no award may be made unless the appropriate person, if not a party to the proceedings, is joined.

(5) In this section—

"appropriate person" means the Minister responsible for the court concerned, or a person or government department nominated by him;

"court" includes a tribunal;

"judge" includes a member of a tribunal, a justice of the peace and a clerk or other officer entitled to exercise the jurisdiction of a court;

"judicial act" means a judicial act of a court and includes an act done on the instructions, or on behalf, of a judge; and

"rules" has the same meaning as in section 7(9).

DEFINITIONS

2.300  "the Convention": see s.21(1).
"tribunal": see s.21(1).

GENERAL NOTE

2.301  This section qualifies ss.7 and 8 in the case of judicial acts.

*Subsection (1)*
This subsection limits the way in which proceedings in respect of an unlawful judicial act may be brought to an appeal or an application for judicial review.

*Subsection (3)*
Compensation will be awarded in respect of an unlawful judicial act in two cases: (i) if the act was not done in good faith; (ii) under Art.5(5). As Art.5(5) cannot apply in child support cases, compensation can only be awarded if the judicial act was not done in good faith.

There will be no point in arguing before a Commissioner that a judicial act of a tribunal was done in bad faith, because the Commissioner has no power to award damages or order the payment of compensation and, therefore by virtue of s.8(2), has no power to award compensation for the unlawful judicial act.

*Remedial action*

**Power to take remedial action**

2.302  **10.**—(1) This section applies if—
(a) a provision of legislation has been declared under section 4 to be incompatible with a Convention right and, if an appeal lies—
(i) all persons who may appeal have stated in writing that they do not intend to do so;
(ii) the time for bringing an appeal has expired and no appeal has been brought within that time; or
(iii) an appeal brought within that time has been determined or abandoned; or
(b) it appears to a Minister of the Crown or Her Majesty in Council that, having regard to a finding of the European Court of Human Rights made after the coming into force of this section in proceedings against the United Kingdom, a provision of legislation is incompatible with an obligation of the United Kingdom arising from the Convention.

(2) If a Minister of the Crown considers that there are compelling reasons for proceeding under this section, he may by order make such amendments to the legislation as he considers necessary to remove the incompatibility.

(3) If, in the case of subordinate legislation, a Minister of the Crown considers—

(a) that it is necessary to amend the primary legislation under which the subordinate legislation in question was made, in order to enable the incompatibility to be removed, and

(b) that there are compelling reasons for proceeding under this section, he may by order make such amendments to the primary legislation as he considers necessary.

(4) This section also applies where the provision in question is in subordinate legislation and has been quashed, or declared invalid, by reason of incompatibility with a Convention right and the Minister proposes to proceed under paragraph 2(b) of Schedule 2.

(5) If the legislation is an Order in Council, the power conferred by subsection (2) or (3) is exercisable by Her Majesty in Council.

(6) In this section "legislation" does not include a Measure of the Church Assembly or of the General Synod of the Church of England.

(7) Schedule 2 makes further provision about remedial orders.

DEFINITIONS

"amend": see s.21(1).                    2.303
"the Convention": see s.21(1).
"the Convention rights": see s.1(1).
"Minister of the Crown": see s.21(1).
"primary legislation": see s.21(1).
"remedial order": see s.21(1).
"subordinate legislation": see s.21(1).

*Other rights and proceedings*

## Safeguard for existing human rights

**11.** A person's reliance on a Convention right does not restrict—    2.304

(a) any other right or freedom conferred on him by or under any law having effect in any part of the United Kingdom; or

(b) his right to make any claim or bring any proceedings which he could make or bring apart from sections 7 to 9.

DEFINITION

"the Convention rights": see s.1(1).                    2.305

GENERAL NOTE

This section ensures that Convention rights provide a minimum legal guarantee.    2.306
They do not affect any greater legal protection that may exist. Although the side note refers to safeguarding *human* rights, the section itself is not limited and applies to all rights and freedoms. It will not be necessary to determine whether other rights or freedoms are properly classifed as "human rights".

## Freedom of expression

2.307    **12.**—(1) This section applies if a court is considering whether to grant any relief which, if granted, might affect the exercise of the Convention right to freedom of expression.

(2) If the person against whom the application for relief is made ("the respondent") is neither present nor represented, no such relief is to be granted unless the court is satisfied—

(a) that the applicant has taken all practicable steps to notify the respondent; or

(b) that there are compelling reasons why the respondent should not be notified.

(3) No such relief is to be granted so as to restrain publication before trial unless the court is satisfied that the applicant is likely to establish that publication should not be allowed.

(4) The court must have particular regard to the importance of the Convention right to freedom of expression and, where the proceedings relate to material which the respondent claims, or which appears to the court, to be journalistic, literary or artistic material (or to conduct connected with such material), to—

(a) the extent to which—

(i)    the material has, or is about to, become available to the public; or

(ii)   it is, or would be, in the public interest for the material to be published;

(b) any relevant privacy code.

(5) In this section—

"court" includes a tribunal; and

"relief" includes any remedy or order (other than in criminal proceedings).

DEFINITIONS

2.308    "the Convention rights": see s.1(1).
"tribunal": see s.21(1).

## Freedom of thought, conscience and religion

2.309    **13.**—(1) If a court's determination of any question arising under this Act might affect the exercise by a religious organisation (itself or its members collectively) of the Convention right to freedom of thought, conscience and religion, it must have particular regard to the importance of that right.

(2) In this section "court" includes a tribunal.

DEFINITIONS

2.310    "the Convention rights": see s.1(1).
"tribunal": see s.21(1).

*Derogations and reservations*

## Derogations

**14.**—(1) In this Act "designated derogation" means—[¹. . . ]                    **2.311**
any derogation by the United Kingdom from an Article of the
Convention, or of any protocol to the Convention, which is
designated for the purposes of this Act in an order made by the [⁴. . .]
[². . .]

(3) If a designated derogation is amended or replaced it ceases to be a
designated derogation.

(4) But subsection (3) does not prevent the [⁵. . .] from exercising his
power under subsection (1) [³. . .] to make a fresh designation order in
respect of the Article concerned.

(5) The [⁶. . .] must by order make such amendments to Schedule 3 as
he considers appropriate to reflect—

(a) any designation order; or

(b) the effect of subsection (3).

(6) A designation order may be made in anticipation of the making by
the United Kingdom of a proposed derogation.

AMENDMENTS

1. Article 2(a) of the Human Rights Act (Amendment) Order 2001 (April 1,
2001).
2. Article 2(b) of the Human Rights Act (Amendment) Order 2001 (April 1,
2001).
3. Article 2(c) of the Human Rights Act (Amendment) Order 2001 (April 1,
2001).
4. Article 9 of, and para.10(1) of Sch.2 to, the Secretary of State for
Constitutional Affairs Order 2003 (August 19, 2003).
5. Article 9 of, and para.10(1) of Sch.2 to, the Secretary of State for
Constitutional Affairs Order 2003 (August 19, 2003).
6. Article 9 of, and para.10(1) of Sch.2 to, the Secretary of State for
Constitutional Affairs Order 2003 (August 19, 2003).

DEFINITIONS

"amend": see s.21(1).                                                         **2.312**
"the Convention": see s.21(1).

## Reservations

**15.**—(1) In this Act "designated reservation" means—                         **2.313**

(a) the United Kingdom's reservation to Article 2 of the First Protocol
to the Convention; and

(b) any other reservation by the United Kingdom to an Article of the
Convention, or of any protocol to the Convention, which is designated for the purposes of this Act in an order made by the Secretary
of State.

(2) The text of the reservation referred to in subsection (1)(a) is set out
in Part II of Schedule 3.

(3) If a designated reservation is withdrawn wholly or in part it ceases to be a designated reservation.

(4) But subsection (3) does not prevent the [¹. . .] from exercising his power under subsection (1)(b) to make a fresh designation order in respect of the Article concerned.

(5) The [². . .] must by order make such amendments to this Act as he considers appropriate to reflect—

(a) any designation order; or
(b) the effect to subsection (3).

AMENDMENTS

1. Article 9 of, and para.10(1) of Sch.2 to, the Secretary of State for Constitutional Affairs Order 2003 (August 19, 2003).
2. Article 9 of, and para.10(1) of Sch.2 to, the Secretary of State for Constitutional Affairs Order 2003 (August 19, 2003).

DEFINITIONS

**2.314**     "amend": see s.21(1).
"the Convention": see s.21(1).
"the First Protocol": see s.21(1).

## Period for which designated derogations have effect

**2.315**     **16.**—(1) If it has not already been withdrawn by the United Kingdom, a designated derogation ceases to have effect for the purposes of this Act—
[¹. . .]

at the end of the period of five years beginning with the date on which the order designating it was made.

(2) At any time before the period—

(a) fixed by subsection (1)[². . .], or
(b) extended by an order under this subsection, comes to an end, the [¹. . .] may by order extend it by a further period of five years.

(3) An order under section 14(1) [³...] ceases to have effect at the end of the period for consideration, unless a resolution has been passed by each House approving the order.

(4) Subsection (3) does not affect—

(a) anything done in reliance on the order; or
(b) the power to make a fresh order under section 14(1)[⁴. . .].

(5) In subsection (3) "period for consideration" means the period of forty days beginning with the day on which the order was made.

(6) In calculating the period for consideration, no account is to be taken of any time during which—

(a) Parliament is dissolved or prorogued; or
(b) both Houses are adjourned for more than four days.

(7) If a designated derogation is withdrawn by the United Kingdom, the [². . .] must by order make such amendments to this Act as he considers are required to reflect that withdrawal.

AMENDMENTS

1. Article 3(a) of the Human Rights Act (Amendment) Order 2001 (April 1, 2001).
2. Article 3(b) of the Human Rights Act (Amendment) Order 2001 (April 1, 2001).
3. Article 3(c) of the Human Rights Act (Amendment) Order 2001 (April 1, 2001).
4. Article 3(d) of the Human Rights Act (Amendment) Order 2001 (April 1, 2001).
5. Article 9 of, and para.10(1) of Sch.2 to, the Secretary of State for Constitutional Affairs Order 2003 (August 19, 2003).
6. Article 9 of, and para.10(1) of Sch.2 to, the Secretary of State for Constitutional Affairs Order 2003 (August 19, 2003).

DEFINITION

"amend": see s.21(1).                                                         2.316

## Periodic review of designated reservations

**17.**—(1) The appropriate Minister must review the designated     2.317
reservation referred to in section 15(1)(a)—

  (a) before the end of the period of five years beginning with the date on which section 1(2) came into force; and

  (b) if that designation is still in force, before the end of the period of five years beginning with the date on which the last report relating to it was laid under subsection (3).

(2) The appropriate Minister must review each of the other designated reservations (if any)—

  (a) before the end of the period of five years beginning with the date on which the order designating the reservation first came into force; and

  (b) if the designation is still in force, before the end of the period of five years beginning with the date on which the last report relating to it was laid under subsection (3).

(3) The Minister conducting a review under this section must prepare a report on the result of the review and lay a copy of it before each House of Parliament.

DEFINITION

"the appropriate Minister": see s.21(1).                                      2.318

*Judges of the European Court of Human Rights*

## Appointment to European Court of Human Rights

**18.**—(1) In this section "judicial office" means the office of—       2.319

  (a) Lord Justice of Appeal, Justice of the High Court or Circuit judge, in England and Wales;

  (b) judge of the Court of Session or sheriff, in Scotland;

  (c) Lord Justice of Appeal, judge of the High Court or county court judge, in Northern Ireland.

(2) The holder of a judicial office may become a judge of the European Court of Human Rights ("the Court") without being required to relinguish his office.

(3) But he is not required to perform the duties of his judicial office while he is a judge of the Court.

(4) In respect of any period during which he is a judge of the Court

(a) a Lord Justice of Appeal or Justice of the High Court is not to count as a judge of the relevant court for the purposes of section 2(1) or 4(1) of the Supreme Court Act 1981 (maximum number of judges) nor as a judge of the Supreme Court for the purposes of section 12(1) to (6) of that Act (salaries etc.);

(b) a judge of the Court of Session is not to count as a judge of that court for the purposes of section 1(1) of the Court of Session Act 1988 (maximum number of judges) or of section 9(1)(c) of the Administration of Justice Act 1973 ("the 1973 Act") (salaries etc.);

(c) a Lord Justice of Appeal or judge of the High Court in Northern Ireland is not to count as a judge of the relevant court for the purposes of section 2(1) or 3(1) of the Judicature (Northern Ireland) Act 1978 (maximum number of judges) nor as a judge of the Supreme Court of Northern Ireland for the purposes of section 9(1)(d) of the 1973 Act (salaries etc.);

(d) a Circuit judge is not to count as such for the purposes of section 18 of the Courts Act 1971 (salaries etc.);

(e) a sheriff is not to count as such for the purposes of section 14 of the Sheriff Courts (Scotland) Act 1907 (salaries etc.);

(f) a county court judge of Northern Ireland is not to count as such for the purposes of section 106 of the County Courts Act Northern Ireland) 1959 (salaries etc.).

(5) If a sheriff principal is appointed a judge of the Court, section 11(1) of the Sheriff Courts (Scotland) Act 1971 (temporary appointment of sheriff principal) applies, while he holds that appointment, as if his office is vacant.

(6) Schedule 4 makes provision about judicial pensions in relation to the holder of a judicial office who serves as a judge of the Court.

(7) The Lord Chancellor or the Secretary of State may by order make such transitional provision (including, in particular, provision for a temporary increase in the maximum number of judges) as he considers appropriate in relation to any holder of a judicial office who has completed his service as a judge of the Court.

*Parliamentary procedure*

### Statements of compatibility

2.320     **19.**—(1) A Minister of the Crown in charge of a Bill in either House of Parliament must, before Second Reading of the Bill—

(a) make a statement to the effect that in his view the provisions of the Bill are compatible with the Convention rights ("a statement of compatibility"); or

(b) make a statement to the effect that although he is unable to make a statement of compatibility the government nevertheless wishes the House to proceed with the Bill.

(2) The statement must be in writing and be published in such manner as the Minister making it considers appropriate.

DEFINITIONS

"the Convention rights": see s.1(1).                                          2.321
"Minister of the Crown": see s.21(1).

*Supplemental*

**Orders, etc. under this Act**

**20.**—(1) Any power of a Minister of the Crown to make an order under    2.322
this Act is exercisable by statutory instrument.

(2) The power of [¹. . .] the Secretary of State to make rules (other than rules of court) under section 2(3) or 7(9) is exercisable by statutory instrument.

(3) Any statutory instrument made under section 14, 15 or 16(7) must be laid before Parliament.

(4) No order may be made by [¹. . .] the Secretary of State under section 1(4), 7(11) or 16(2) unless a draft of the order has been laid before, and approved by, each House of Parliament.

(5) Any statutory instrument made under section 18(7) or Schedule 4, or to which subsection (2) applies, shall be subject to annulment in pursuance of a resolution of either House of Parliament.

(6) The power of a Northern Ireland department to make—

(a) rules under section 2(3)(c) or 7(9)(c), or

(b) an order under section 7(11),

is exercisable by statutory rule for the purposes of the Statutory Rules (Northern Ireland) Order 1979.

(7) Any rules made under section 2(3)(c) or 7(9)(c) shall be subject to negative resolution; and section 41(6) of the Interpretation Act (Northern Ireland) 1954 (meaning of "subject to negative resolution") shall apply as if the power to make the rules were conferred by an Act of the Northern Ireland Assembly.

(8) No order may be made by a Northern Ireland department under section 7(11) unless a draft of the order has been laid before, and approved by, the Northern Ireland Assembly.

AMENDMENT

1. Article 9 of, and para.10(2) of Sch.2 to, the Secretary of State for Constitutional Affairs Order 2003 (August 19,2003).

DEFINTION

"Minister of the Crown": see s.21(1).                                         2.323

**Interpretation, etc.**

2.324    **21.**—(1) In this Act—

"amend" includes repeal and apply (with or without modifications);

"the appropriate Minister" means the Minister of the Crown having charge of the appropriate authorised government department (within the meaning of the Crown Proceedings Act 1947);

"the Commission" means the European Commission of Human Rights;

"the Convention" means the Convention for the Protection of Human Rights and Fundamental Freedoms, agreed by the Council of Europe at Rome on 4th November 1950 as it has effect for the time being in relation to the United Kingdom;

"declaration of incompatibility" means a declaration under section 4;

"Minister of the Crown" has the same meaning as in the Ministers of the Crown Act 1975;

"Northern Ireland Minister" includes the First Minister and the deputy First Minister in Northern Ireland;

"primary legislation" means any—

(a) public general Act;

(b) local and personal Act;

(c) private Act;

(d) Measure of the Church Assembly;

(e) Measure of the General Synod of the Church of England;

(f) Order in Council—

    (i) made in exercise of Her Majesty's Royal Prerogative;

    (ii) made under section 38(1)(a) of the Northern Ireland Constitution Act 1973 or the corresponding provision of the Northern Ireland Act 1998; or

    (iii) amending an Act of a kind mentioned in paragraph (a), (b) or (c);

and includes an order or other instrument made under primary legislation (otherwise than by the National Assembly for Wales, a member of the Scottish Executive, a Northern Ireland Minister or a Northern Ireland department) to the extent to which it operates to bring one or more provisions of that legislation into force or amends any primary legislation;

"the First Protocol" means the protocol to the Convention agreed at Paris on 20th March 1952;

[1. . .]

"the Eleventh Protocol" means the protocol to the Convention (restructuring the control machinery established by the Convention) agreed at Strasbourg on 11th May 1994;

[2"the Thirteenth Protocol" means the protocol to the Convention (concerning the abolition of the death penalty in all circumstances) agreed at Vilnius on 3rd May 2002;]

"remedial order" means an order under section 10;

"subordinate legislation" means any—

(a) Order in Council other than one—

    (i) made in exercise of Her Majesty's Royal Prerogative;

    (ii) made under section 38(1)(a) of the Northern Ireland Constitution Act 1973 or the corresponding provision of the Northern Ireland Act 1998; or

(iii) amending an Act of a kind mentioned in the definition of primary legislation;

(b) Act of the Scottish Parliament;

(c) Act of the Parliament of Northern Ireland;

(d) Measure of the Assembly established under section 1 of the Northern Ireland Assembly Act 1973;

(e) Act of the Northern Ireland Assembly;

(f) order, rules, regulations, scheme, warrant, byelaw or other instrument made under primary legislation (except to the extent to which it operates to bring one or more provisions of that legislation into force or amends any primary legislation);

(g) order, rules, regulations, scheme, warrant, byelaw or other instrument made under legislation mentioned in paragraph (b), (c), (d) or (e) or made under an Order in Council applying only to Northern Ireland;

(h) order, rules, regulations, scheme, warrant, byelaw or other instrument made by a member of the Scottish Executive, a Northern Ireland Minister or a Northern Ireland department in exercise of prerogative or other executive functions of Her Majesty which are exercisable by such a person on behalf of Her Majesty;

"transferred matters" has the same meaning as in the Northern Ireland Act 1998; and

"tribunal" means any tribunal in which legal proceedings may be brought.

(2) The references in paragraphs (b) and (c) of section 2(1) to Articles are to Articles of the Convention as they had effect immediately before the coming into force of the Eleventh Protocol.

(3) The reference in paragraph (d) of section 2(1) to Article 46 includes a reference to Articles 32 and 54 of the Convention as they had effect immediately before the coming into force of the Eleventh Protocol.

(4) The references in section 2(1) to a report or decision of the Commission or a decision of the Committee of Ministers include references to a report or decision made as provided by paragraphs 3, 4 and 6 of Article 5 of the Eleventh Protocol (transitional provisions).

(5) Any liability under the Army Act 1955, the Air Force Act 1955 or the Naval Discipline Act 1957 to suffer death for an offence is replaced by a liability to imprisonment for life or any less punishment authorised by those Acts; and those Acts shall accordingly have effect with the necessary modifications.

AMENDMENTS

1. Article 2(2) of the Human Rights Act 1998 (Amendment) Order 2004 (June 21, 2004).

2. Article 2(2) of the Human Rights Act 1998 (Amendment) Order 2004 (June 21, 2004).

GENERAL NOTE

*Subsection (1)*

"*the appropriate Minister*" This expression is given a narrower definition for the purposes of Sch.4 by para.4 to that Schedule.

**2.325**

### Short title, commencement, application and extent

2.326    **22.**—(1)  This Act may be cited as the Human Rights Act 1998.

(2)  Sections 18, 20 and 21(5) and this section come into force on the passing of this Act.

(3)  The other provisions of this Act come into force on such day as the Secretary of State may by order appoint; and different days may be appointed for different purposes.

(4)  Paragraph (b) of subsection (1) of section 7 applies to proceedings brought by or at the instigation of a public authority whenever the act in question took place; but otherwise that subsection does not apply to an act taking place before the coming into force of that section.

(5)  This Act binds the Crown.

(6)  This Act extends to Northern Ireland.

(7)  Section 21(5), so far as it relates to any provision contained in the Army Act 1955, the Air Force Act 1955 or the Naval Discipline Act 1957, extends to any place to which that provision extends.

GENERAL NOTE

*Subsection (4)*

2.327    This subsection contains a comprehensive code for the application of the Act to decisions taken before it came into force. This limitation cannot be bypassed by relying on the duties in ss.3 and 6. See *R. v Lambert* [2001] 3 All E.R 577 and *Pearce v Governing Body of Mayfield School* [2001] EWCA Civ 1347. This reflects the views of the Commissioners in *CG/2356/00* and *CIS/1077/99*. It has been reaffirmed by the House of Lords in *R. v Kansal (No.2)* [2002] 1 All E.R. 257 and *Wilson v First County Trust Ltd* [2003] 4 All E.R. 97 especially at para.92.

## SCHEDULES

### SCHEDULE 1

#### THE ARTICLES

#### PART I

#### THE CONVENTION

GENERAL NOTE

2.328    There is probably no limit to the inventive ways in which a party in a child support case may try to identify a breach of the Convention. In *Logan v United Kingdom* (1996) 22 E.H.R.R CD 178, for example, one of the arguments used by the applicant absent parent was that the financial burden of the child support maintenance assessment interferred with his freedom of religion under Art.9. For this reason, the whole of the Convention as incorporated in British law is set out. However, most challenges are likely to be made under Arts 6 (fair hearing), 8 (family life) and 14 (discrimination). The commentary covers the general approach to the Convention and Arts 6(1) and 14. It is less easy to make useful general statements about the scope of Art.8 in the child support context.

*Interpretation and application*

The Convention is an international treaty. It must be interpreted as a treaty in accordance with the Vienna Convention on the Law of Treaties 1969, especially Arts 31–33 (*Golder v United Kingdom* (1975) 1 E.H.R.R 524).

There are two texts—English and French. As there is no provision for one or the other to take precedence, each is equally authoritative: Art.33 of the Vienna Convention. Only the English text is reproduced in the Act. Section 2 does not specify the French text as something to be taken into account. However, it must be taken into account when interpreting the English text in order to give a meaning that best reconciles the different language consistently with the object and purpose of the Convention: *Wemhoff v Federal Republic of Germany* (1968) 1 E.H.R.R 55.

Each provision must be interpreted in the context of the Convention and its Protocols as a whole. This means that account must be taken of those provisions that are not incorporated by this Act.

Sometimes the scope of a concept is determined by reference to domestic law of the State concerned. On these occasions, the classification by the State will determine whether a case falls within the scope of a Convention right. However, States do not always have this freedom. Sometimes the scope of a concept is determined autonomously under the Convention. On these occasions, the classification by the State will not automatically prevent a case from falling within the scope of a Convention right. A classification in domestic law that brings a case within the scope of a concept that has an autonomous meaning under the Convention is likely to be accepted, but a classification that takes a case outside the scope of a concept will not: *Engel v The Netherlands (No.1)* (1976) 1 E.H.R.R. 647.

Closely linked to the autonomous meaning of some concepts is the margin of appreciation that is allowed in the interpretation and application of some aspects of some Convention rights. The margin of appreciation applies in two ways. First, it applies to restrict the scope of a right when there is a divergence of views in the States who are parties to the Convention: *Handyside v United Kingdom* (1976) 1 E.H.R.R. 737. The greater the divergence of view, the wider the margin of appreciation: *X,Y and Z v United Kingdom* (1997) 24 E.H.R.R. 143. Second, the margin of appreciation applies when there are different ways in which a state may give effect to a right: *Airey v Ireland* (1979) 2 E.H.R.R. 305. Whichever way the margin of appreciation is used, it is only a margin and the courts police the boundary of the margin to ensure that it is not exceeded: *Stubbings v United Kingdom* (1996) 23 E.H.R.R. 213.

The courts and the Commissioners have referred in their decisions to a margin of appreciation. Sometimes they refer to a margin or degree of deference instead. This is not based on a recognition that different Member States have different laws on a point. Nevertheless, these expressions are useful in indicating the scope of freedom for action that is accorded under this Act to the legislature and executive. The extent of that freedom will vary according to the circumstances. It will be at its greatest in laws that deal with social and economic policy and at its least in laws which are of constitutional importance. See *R. (ota Carson) v Secretary of State for Work and Pensions* [2003] 3 All E.R. 577 *per* Laws L.J. at para.73. This freedom exists only for the purpose of justification that may be permitted within a Convention right; it does not apply to the scope of a Convention right (*ibid.* at para.62).

The margin of appreciation includes in appropriate cases an appropriate period of time in which to bring domestic law into compliance with the Convention rights (*R. (ota Hooper) v Secretary of State for Work and Pensions* [2003] 3 All E.R. 673 at para.78).

A purposive approach is taken to interpretation in order to ensure that the aim of the Convention is realised and its object is achieved (*Wemhoff*, above). This involves interpreting the Convention in a way that renders the rights practical and effective rather than theoretical or illusory: *Artico v Italy* (1980) 2 E.H.R.R. 7. It also means that the Convention is interpreted dynamically in order to reflect changing present day conditions: *Tyrer v United Kingdom* (1978) 2 E.H.R.R. 1.

As the Convention is interpreted dynamically, the European Court of Human Rights does not regard its case law as binding. However, it follows its previous decisions unless there are cogent reasons for doing otherwise: *Cossey v United Kingdom* (1990) 13 E.H.R.R. 622. It does not draw a distinction between those parts of its judgments that were essential to the decision in a particular case and those that were not. The highest British courts should take the same approach, although the doctrine or precedent will probably continue to apply.

Only live issues have to be considered. This prevents an issue being raised in the abstract. This is achieved in two ways. First, only someone who is a victim may rely on a Convention right. Second, the law is not concerned with theoretical or illusory violations of Convention rights where the victim had not in practice suffered as a consequence: *R (M) v Commissioner of Police for the Metropolis, The Times*, August 1, 2001.

RIGHTS AND FREEDOMS

*Article 2—Right to Life*

2.329    1.  Everyone's right to life shall be protected by law. No one shall be deprived of his life intentionally save in the execution of a sentence of a court following his conviction of a crime for which this penalty is provided by law.

2.  Deprivation of life shall not be regarded as inflicted in contravention of this Article when it results from the use of force which is no more than absolutely necessary:

(a)  in defence of any person from unlawful violence;

(b)  in order to effect a lawful arrest or to prevent the escape of a person lawfully detained;

(c)  in action lawfully taken for the purpose of quelling a riot or insurrection.

*Article 3—Prohibition of Torture*

2.330    No one shall be subjected to torture or to inhuman or degrading treatment or punishment.

*Article 4—Prohibition of Slavery and Forced Labour*

2.331    1.  No one shall be held in slavery or servitude.
2.  No one shall be required to perform forced or compulsory labour.
3.  For the purpose of this Article the term "forced or compulsory labour" shall not include:

(a)  any work required to be done in the ordinary course of detention imposed according to the provisions of Article 5 of this Convention or during conditional release from such detention;

(b)  any service of a military character or, in case of conscientious objectors in countries where they are recognised, service exacted instead of compulsory military service;

(c)  any service exacted in case of an emergency or calamity threatening the life or well-being of the community;

(d)  any work or service which forms part of normal civic obligations.

*Article 5—Right to Liberty and Security*

2.332    1.  Everyone has the right to liberty and security of person. No one shall be deprived of his liberty save in the following cases and in accordance with a procedure prescribed by law:

(a)  the lawful detention of a person after conviction by a competent court;

(b)  the lawful arrest or detention of a person for non-compliance with the lawful order of a court or in order to secure the fulfilment of any obligation prescribed by law;

(c)  the lawful arrest or detention of a person effected for the purpose of bringing him before the competent legal authority on reasonable suspicion of having committed an offence or when it is reasonably considered necessary to prevent his committing an offence or fleeing after having done so;

(d)  the detention of a minor by lawful order for the purpose of educational supervision or his lawful detention for the purpose of bringing him before the competent legal authority;

(e)  the lawful detention of persons for the prevention of the spreading of infectious diseases, of persons of unsound mind, alcoholics or drug addicts or vagrants;

(f)  the lawful arrest or detention of a person to prevent his effecting an unauthorised entry into the country or of a person against whom action is being taken with a view to deportation or extradition.

**2.** Everyone who is arrested shall be informed promptly, in a language which he understands, of the reasons for his arrest and of any charge against him.

**3.** Everyone arrested or detained in accordance with the provisions of paragraph 1(c) of this Article shall be brought promptly before a judge or other officer authorised by law to exercise judicial power and shall be entitled to trial within a reasonable time or to release pending trial. Release may be conditioned by guarantees to appear for trial.

**4.** Everyone who is deprived of his liberty by arrest or detention shall be entitled to take proceedings by which the lawfulness of his detention shall be decided speedily by a court and his release ordered if the detention is not lawful.

**5.** Everyone who has been the victim of arrest or detention in contravention of the provisions of this Article shall have an enforceable right to compensation.

### Article 6—Right to a Fair Trial

**1.** In the determination of his civil rights and obligations or of any criminal charge against him, everyone is entitled to a fair and public hearing within a reasonable time by an independent and impartial tribunal established by law. Judgment shall be pronounced publicly but the press and public may be excluded from all or part of the trial in the interest of morals, public order or national security in a democratic society, where the interests of juveniles or the protection of the private life of the parties so require, or to the extent strictly necessary in the opinion of the court in special circumstances where publicity would prejudice the interests of justice.

**2.** Everyone charged with a criminal offence shall be presumed innocent until proved guilty according to law.

**3.** Everyone charged with a criminal offence has the following minimum rights:

(a)  to be informed promptly, in a language which he understands and in detail, of the nature and cause of the accusation against him;

(b)  to have adequate time and facilities for the preparation of his defence;

(c)  to defend himself in person or through legal assistance of his own choosing or, if he has not sufficient means to pay for legal assistance, to be given it free when the interests of justice so require;

(d)  to examine or have examined witnesses against him and to obtain the attendance and examination of witnesses on his behalf under the same conditions as witnesses against him;

(e)  to have the free assistance of an interpreter if he cannot understand or speak the language used in court.

### GENERAL NOTE

This Article is not retrospective in its operation (*Law v Society of Lloyd's, The Times,* January 23, 2004).

The Article was considered by the Commission in *Logan v United Kingdom* (1996) 22 E.H.R.R. CD 178. The absent parent complained of a violation of Art.6

2.333

2.334

on the ground that the child support maintenance formula made no allowance for the costs of access to his children. He did not dispute that the formula had been correctly applied. The Commission decided that the complaint should be rejected as manifestly ill-founded because either there was no dispute as to the application of the domestic law (as opposed to a dispute about what that law should be) or there was dispute of a genuine or serious nature. This conclusion is not an authority that Art.6 has no application to the resolution of disputes about the application of the formula in an individual case. The Judicial Studies Board Seminar Paper on *Family Law and the Human Rights Act 1998* cites this case as authority that child support assessments are public rights rather than civil rights (para.9.1). The Commission's reasoning does not support that proposition.

The right given by this Article contains similar wording to s.11(1)(d) of the Canadian Charter of Rights and Freedoms, which guarantees as a Legal Right that:

"Any person charged with an offence has the right

    (d)  to be presumed innocent until proven guilty according to law in a fair and public hearing by an independent and impartial tribunal".

Decisions interpreting and applying the final words of this right are admissible in interpreting and applying Convention rights, subject to giving the appropriate weight to the Strasbourg jurisprudence under s.2(1) of the Act: *Starrs and Chambers v Procurator Fiscal, Linlithgow* [2000] H.R.L.R 191. No doubt the same approach will be taken with other comparable human rights provisions.

This right is a fundamental principle within a democratic society: *Sutter v Switzerland* (1984) 6 E.H.R.R. 272. As such it must be interpreted liberally. However, the right is not absolute and may be subject to limitation, provided that the limitations are not such that the very essence of the right is impaired: *Hall and Co v Simons* [2000] 2 F.L.R. 545 at 612.

Compliance with this right must be judged by reference to the adjudication system as a whole. If a decision of a body does not comply with this right, there will be no breach of the Convention if that body is under the control of a judicial body that does satisfy the right: *Albert and Le Compte v Belgium* (1983) 5 E.H.R.R. 533; *Bryan v United Kingdom* (1995) 21 E.H.R.R. 342. The higher body must undertake a rehearing or a careful review of the case on its merits: *In Re Medicaments and Related Classes of Goods (No.4), The Times,* August 7, 2001. It is not essential that the higher body rehears the evidence of witnesses: *Preiss v General Dental Council* [2001] 1 W.L.R. 1926. In particular, a violation by the appeal tribunal may be remedied by proceedings before a Commissioner. As a violation of Art.6(1) would be a mistake of law requiring a Commissioner to set aside a tribunal's decision, the Commissioner would be able to refer the case for rehearing before another tribunal that would comply with Art.6(1) or, if this is not possible, consider the case on its merits and give a decision without referring the case to another tribunal.

This Convention right does not give a right to any particular tribunal; only a right to *a* tribunal hearing: *OT Africa Line Ltd v Fayad Hijazy, The Times,* November 28, 2000.

*Determination*

A determination presupposes a dispute. This is emphasised by the word "contestation" in the French text. This underlines that the Article does not give a person a right to have an issue determined in the abstract. There must be an arguable case that a right exists under domestic law: *Lithgow v United Kingdom* (1986) 8 E.H.R.R. 329. There must a dispute about the right that is genuine and serious: *Benthem v Netherlands* (1985) 8 E.H.R.R. 1. The need for a genuine and serious dispute may mean that there is no violation of Art.6(1) in the striking out of misconceived appeals under reg.46 of the Appeals Regulations.

There will certainly be a dispute on an appeal to a tribunal. There may be some doubt about a referral to a tribunal of an application for a variation. The reason for the doubt lies in the reasoning of the European Court of Human Rights in *Feldbrugge v Netherlands* (1986) 8 E.H.R.R. 425, in which, at para.25, the Court referred to the dispute as arising only after the initial decision on entitlement to a sickness benefit. As the determination of a referral is a first determination, it may be that no dispute has arisen at that stage. However, the Court's reasoning may not apply. In the case of a social security benefit, the initial determination is by an officer whose concern is merely to ensure that the law is correctly applied. No dispute arises until a decision has been made. In the case of an application for a departure direction, in contrast, there will be disagreement between the absent parent and the person with care from the outset.

Article 6(1) is concerned with the determination of disputes. It is concerned with the way in which a dispute is handled. It is not concerned with the merits of the decision reached, provided that the procedure followed was fair. In other words, Art.6(1) must not be used as a further level of appeal. This is known as the *quatrième instance* doctrine. See *Locabail (United Kingdom) Ltd v Waldorf Investment Corporation (No.4)*, *The Times*, May 25, 2000.

Also, Art.6(1) is not concerned with the content of the rights which are in dispute. Any challenge to the content of rights must be made under other articles. So, it is not possible to use this Article to challenge either (i) the terms of the child support legislation: *Powell and Rayner v United Kingdom* (1990) 12 E.H.R.R. 355 or (ii) its interpretation by Commissioners and the courts: *X and Y v Netherlands* (1985) 8 E.H.R.R. 235.

If there is a dispute about civil rights, the party has a right to go before a tribunal. That right is not expressed in Art.6(1), but it is inherent: *Golder v United Kingdom* (1975) 1 E.H.R.R. 524. The right to access must, of course, be effective, but the means by which it is achieved is within the margin of appreciation: *Airey v Ireland* (1979) 2 E.H.R.R. 305. It may be achieved by legal aid or by other means, like simplified procedures (*ibid.*). The inquisitorial approach contributes to the access to the tribunal. However, in the most complex of cases, it may be arguable that financial assistance is essential: *Granger v United Kingdom* (1990) 12 E.H.R.R. 469, but it has been held that the restriction of legal aid is not a violation of this Convention right: *Procurator Fiscal, Fort William v McLean*, *The Times*, August 11, 2000.

The right of access may be subject to limitations provided that they pursue a legitimate objective, are proportionate to that objective and do not destroy the essence of the right: *Stubbings v United Kingdom* (1996) 23 E.H.R.R. 213 and *Ashingdane v United Kingdom* (1985) 7 E.H.R.R. 528. It has been held that an objective need has to be shown to justify a deemed notice provision like that in reg.2(b) of the Appeals Regulations: *R v Secretary of State for the Home Department, ex p. Saleem* [2000] 4 All E.R. 814, relying on *R. v Secretary of State for the Home Department Ex p. Leech* [1993] 4 All E.R 539. A Commissioner has held that reg.2(b) violates the equality of arms requirement of a fair hearing: *CDLA 5413/99*, paras 38–48.

The time limit for appealing to a tribunal is one month and it can only be extended on stringent conditions. It is possible for this type of restriction to be in violation of Art.6(1).

Some aspects of the child support legislation can only be challenged by judicial review. The European Court of Human Rights has left open whether judicial review satisfies Art.6(1): *Air Canada v United Kingdom* (1995) 20 E.H.R.R. 150. However, it has been held that judicial review would be sufficient to cure any lack of independence in the fact-finding tribunal: *R. (Hussain) v Asylum Support Adjudicator, The*

*Times*, November 15, 2001. It is very likely that judical review will be sufficient to do this if, regardless of appearances, there is no reason of substance to question the objective integrity of the decision-maker below (*R. (ota Beeson) v Dorset County Council, The Times*, December 18, 2002; *Begum v Tower Hamlets London Borough Council* [2003] 1 All E.R. 731).

The right of access is to a tribunal that complies with this Article. There is no right to a further appeal. However, the existence of a right of appeal to a body that complies with Art.6(1) may be sufficient to remedy a deficiency in the lower body. If there is a right of further appeal, it must not be discriminatory (*Belgian Linguistic Case (No.2)* (1968) 1 E.H.R.R. 252 at para.9).

### Civil rights and obligations

2.335   Article 6(1) is concerned with private rights and not with public rights. Private rights have an autonomous Convention meaning: *König v Federal Republic of Germany* (1978) 2 E.H.R.R. 170. The classification depends on the substantive content and effects of the right under domestic law and not on the legal classification of the right in domestic law (*ibid.*). The question to ask is: is the outcome of the determination decisive for private rights and obligations? (*Stran Greek Refineries and Stratis Andreadis v Greece* (1994) 19 E.H.R.R. 293).

It is suggested that child support rights and obligations, in so far as they come before appeal tribunals and Commissioners, are civil for the purposes of Art.6(1). There is an issue whether some other aspects of the scheme are criminal. This is determined by reference to (a) form of procedure involved, (b) whether an offence is created by the legislation and (c) whether the action taken by the court is in the form of a punishment: *R. (ota McCann) v Crown Court at Manchester* [2001] 4 All E.R. 264.

### Fair hearing

A margin of appreciation applies in the procedures adopted to ensure a fair hearing: *Dombo Beheer v Netherlands* (1993) 18 E.H.R.R. 213.

The margin of appreciation operates in respect of evidence, which is primarily a matter for the domestic court, provided that the proceedings as a whole are fair. This applies both to the admissibility of evidence (*Schenk v Switzerland* (1988) 13 E.H.R.R. 242) and to its evaluation (*Lüdi v Switzerland* (1992) 15 E.H.R.R. 173).

Equality of arms is an essential requirement for a fair hearing, although there is a margin of appreciation in how it is acheived: *Dombo Beheer v Netherlands* (1993) 18 E.H.R.R. 213. This means that a party must have a reasonable opportunity to present a case, including evidence, under conditions that do not put that party at a disadvantage as against the other parties (*ibid.*). It is the responsibility of the tribunal to ensure that the parties see, and have the chance to comment on, all evidence available to the tribunal (*H.A.L. v Finland* (Application No 38267/97) decided on January 27, 2004). Equality of arms is largely guaranteed by natural justice and the inquisitorial approach, if properly applied. There is, though, scope for a violation of this requirement. For example, the new style of submissions put to tribunals by the Secretary of State merely refer to, rather than quote, the relevant law, leaving the parties to find it for themselves (*CCS 3517/00*, para.10.2). Also, the difference of treatment between government departments and others in the deemed notice provisions of reg.2 of the Appeals Regulations was held to result in an inequality of arms (*CDLA/5413/99*, paras 38–48), although there is no objection in principle to the use of deemed service provisions (*Anderton v Clwyd County Council* [2002] 3 All E.R. 813).

Article 6 is concerned with the fairness of the hearing and not with extra-judicial activities: *R v Hertfordshire County Council Ex p. Green* [2000] 1 All E.R. 773. This means, for example, that it is not concerned with the way in which evidence is obtained, although it is concerned with the use of evidence at the hearing (*ibid.*).

The use of double translation from one language into another via a third language is not in principle a breach of Art.6: *R. v West London Youth Court Ex p. N* [2000] 1 All E.R. 823. However, a party is entitled to a professional service from an interpreter at a hearing and, if the service appears to be below that standard, the matter should be investigated by the tribunal (*CDLA 2748/02*, para.13).

Fairness also requires that reasons be given for a decision. The standard to be attained varies according to the circumstances of the case. Reasons are needed to show that an issue has been considered and how it was determined: *Ruiz Torija v Spain* (1994) Series A No. 303–A. The reasons must indicate with sufficient clarity the grounds on which the decision was based in order to allow a party usefully to exercise the rights of appeal: *Hadjianastassiou v Greece* (1992) 16 E.H.R.R. 219. Important issues must be covered: *Hiro Balani v Spain* (1994) 19 E.H.R.R. 565. However, it is not necessary to deal with every point. In particular, there is no need to deal with a point that is not raised timeously: *Van der Hurk v Netherlands* (1994) 18 E.H.R.R. 481. In considering reasons for detention under Art.5(3), the European Court of Human Rights has appeared unimpressed by reasons that are in identical or stereotyped form: *Mansur v Turkey* (1995) Series A No.319 B. These principles are broadly in line with the approach taken by the Commissioners.

Striking out a case for contempt is likely to be a breach of Art.6(1), unless the act which constituted the breach led to a real risk that a fair hearing could not happen: *Arrow Nominees Inc v Blackledge, The Times*, December 8, 1999. The reasoning does not appear from the short newspaper report, but it is unlikely to cover striking out for want of prosecution.

The Privy Council has held (but not in the context of a Convention right) that in an extreme case the incompetence of a representative can result in unfairness and deprive the representative's client of due process: *Boodram v Satet of Trinidad and Tobago, The Times*, May 15, 2001.

The Court of Appeal has held, albeit in a committal case, that the failure to give a party a reasonable opportunity to obtain legal funding may involve a breach of the party's right to a fair hearing (*Berry Trade Ltd v Moussavi* [2002] 1 W.L.R. 1910).

In *CCS 1018/02*, it was argued that there was an unfairness because the parent was an unrepresented and uninformed layman who was trying to negotiate the complex child support adjudication system. The parent was trying to challenge a decision of a child support appeal tribunal, which had given a departure direction against him. He tried to challenge it by way of appeal to a Commissioner and then to the Court of Appeal. He also applied for a revision of the tribunal's decision by the Secretary of State. The application for a revision was outside the maximum time allowed. His unfairness argument was presented in order to show that the relevant provision should be interpreted so that time would run not from the date of the decision of the tribunal, but from the date of the decision of the Court of Appeal. The Commissioner rejected the argument, making three points. First, the child support adjudication procedures are complex, but it is not necessary to understand them in order to operate them, because any attempt to challenge a decision is interpreted by reference to its substance and not its form. Second, the application for a revision was formally a separate proceeding from the proceedings before the tribunal, but in reality it was but another attempt by the parent to challenge the tribunal's decision. His argument had to be evaluated and applied in that context. Third, it was not appropriate to extend the time allowed for making an application, as this would not promote certainty or finality. The non-resident parent's application for leave to appeal was dismissed by the Court of Appeal (*Denson v Secretary of State for Work and Pensions*, reported as *R(CS) 4/04*). The court decided that the time limits on an appeal against a decision by the Secretary of State were compatible with the Convention right to a fair hearing. They did not impair his access to a tribunal. The non-resident parent had one month to appeal, subject to an extension for cause up to a maximum of 13 months. That was a legitimate and proportionate response to the need for certainty and finality in litigation.

The Secretary of State's power to enforce or not to enforce the non-resident parent's liability is not within the scope of this article (*R. (Kehoe) v Secretary of State for Work and Pensions* [2004] 1 F.L.R. 1132).

*Public hearing*

2.336   Oral hearings of child support appeals are held in public, unless a chairman directs otherwise on the ground that intimate personal or financial circumstances may have to be disclosed: see reg.49(6) of the Appeals Regulations. A private hearing is the normal practice in court cases involving children. This practice is consistent with the Convention (*Re PB (Hearings in open court)* [1996] 2 F.L.R 765 at 768, *per* Butler-Sloss L.J. and *B and P v United Kingdom* [2001] 2 F.L.R. 261). Article 6(1) expressly allows the public and the press to be excluded if the interests of juveniles or the private lives of the parties require it. A direction by a chairman in a child support case that the hearing be in private would not be a violation of this right. See further the general note to reg.49(6).

Also, the right may be waived: *Håkansson v Sweden* (1990) 13 E.H.R.R. 1. This is likely to be the wish of most parties in a child support case.

It has been held to be a contravention of this right to refuse an oral hearing if issues of fact may arise. A party has a right to require an oral hearing of an appeal before a tribunal under reg.39 of the Appeals Regulations. The Child Support Commissioners (Procedure) Regulations 1999 do not give a party a right to an oral hearing. However, if only an issue of law arises and no issue of fact is involved, an oral hearing is not required by this right. Also, if the whole of the system is considered, there is a right to an oral hearing below. There was a violation of this right in *Fischer v Austria* (1995) Series A No.312, but in that case there was no right to a hearing at all at any level.

There may be a conflict between the right to have evidence given at a public hearing and the Convention right under Art. 8 in respect of the content of that evidence. If this arises, the rights have to balanced. One solution is to hear the evidence that would breach Art. 8 in private (*XXX v YYY and ZZZ*, unreported decided by the Employment Appeal Tribunal on April 9, 2003).

*Within reasonable time*

There is no set time within which a case must be heard. The time that is reasonable depends on the individual circumstances of the case, including matters like the complexity of the legal and factual issues and the conduct of the parties. It has been held that particular diligence is required in social security cases: *Deumeland v Germany* (1986) 8 E.H.R.R. 448. No doubt the same approach applies to child support.

Only delays for which the State is responsible will be a violation of this right. So, it is necessary to show a causal link between the delay and something that is within the control of the State. It is not sufficient simply to prove that one of the parties has brought about a delay. However, the State must provide the tribunal and the Commissioners with the necessary powers and resources to prevent delays that can be anticipated and with the powers and resources to minimise unforeseeable delays when they occur: See *Zimmerman and Steiner v Switzerland* (1983) 6 E.H.R.R. 17 and *Buchholz v Federal Republic of Germany* (1981) 3 E.H.R.R. 597. The necessary powers exist, but resources are not always sufficient.

It is only appropriate to stay proceedings for delay if it has become impossible for there to be a fair hearing. Otherwise, the proceedings should continue and another, appropriate remedy be found for the delay. See *Attorney General's Reference (No.2 of 2001)* [2004] 1 All E.R. 1049.

The Commissioners have discussed when proceedings begin for the purposes of this provision *(R(IS)1/04 and 2/04)* . However, the value of this is debateable, because the Commissioners have no jurisdiction to give a remedy if there has been unreasonable delay. The House of Lords has decided that time begins at the earliest time when the likelihood of proceedings becomes known *(Attorney General's Reference (No. 2 of 2001)* [2004] 1 All E.R. 1049).

A person with care may be concerned about the delay in the enforcement of a child support maintenance assessment. However, that is not within the jurisdiction of appeal tribunals or Commissioners.

*Independent and impartial tribunal*

There is no doubt that both appeal tribunals and Commissioners have the necessary judicial function to be a tribunal under this right: *Benthem v Netherlands* (1985) 8 E.H.R.R. 1.

Although independence and impartiality are closely linked, each has a distinct role to play in ensuring a fair hearing.

*Independence* is concerned with the institutional relationship between the tribunal and (a) the executive and (b) the parties: *Campbell and Fell v United Kingdom* (1984) 7 E.H.R.R. 165.

The decision-maker who acts on behalf of the Secretary of State is not independent, even though in practice the officer may be impartial *(Begum v Tower Hamlets London Borough Council* [2003] 1 All E.R. 731). This can be remedied by an appeal to an appeal tribunal, which lies on both fact and law, if the appeal tribunal is itself independent *(R. (ota Beeson) v Dorset County Council, The Times*, December 21, 2001). It may even be remedied if the appeal tribunal does not have full fact-finding powers, provided that the decision-maker was impartial *(Begum*, above).

However, these authorities only apply if the appeal tribunal is itself independent. If it is not, the lack of independence of the decision-maker and the tribunal can only be remedied by the availability of an appeal to a Commissioner or by judicial review.

There are a number of features of the appeal tribunal that make it arguable whether it is independent. They cover matters of practice, some provisions in the Appeals Regulations and some provisions of statute *(CI/4421/00*, para.32). For example: an appeal is lodged with the Secretary of State who is a party to the proceedings and the Secretary of State makes the regulations that govern the tribunal's procedure and pays the panel members. The members are appointed by the Lord Chancellor, but part-time panel members are appointed for no more than five years at a time. See the decisions of the Employment Appeal Tribunal in *Smith v Secretary of State for Trade and Industry* [2000] I.C.R. 69 and of the High Court of Justiciary in Scotland in *Starrs and Chambers v Procurator Fiscal, Linlithgow* [2000] H.R.L.R. 191. However, it has been held that asylum support adjudicators are independent in view of their tenure of appointment: *R. (Hussain) v Asylum Support Adjudicator, The Times*, November 15, 2001.

*Impartiality* is concerned with the attitude, actual and perceived, of the judge to the parties and the issues.

Partiality may be subjective or objective. There is subjective partiality if the judge is actually prejudiced or biased. There is objective partiality if there is a legitimate doubt in this respect. See *Findlay v United Kingdom* (1997) 24 E.H.R.R. 221. Subjective partiality is covered by natural justice. So is objective partiality *(Porter v Magill* [2002] 1 All E.R. 465 *per* Lord Hope at paras 99–103, foreshadowed by Lord Browne-Wilkinson in *R. v Bow Street Metropolitan Stipendiary Magistrate Ex p. Pinochet Ugarte (No. 2)* [1999] 1 All E.R. 577 at 589).

Impartiality is presumed: *Le Compte, Van Leuven and D Meyere v Belgium* (1981) 6 E.H.R.R. 583.

It is permissible for judges to comment, critically or otherwise, on the law and its development, but the nature of a criticism or the language in which it is expressed may create a legitimate apprehension that they would not be able to apply the law impartially: *Hoekstra v H M Advocate, The Times*, April 14, 2000.

This Convention right may be waived. Waiver signifies a voluntary, informed and unequivocal election not to claim a right or raise an objection. It may be express or tacit. See *Millar v Dickson (Procurator Fiscal, Elgin)* [2002] 3 All E.R. 1041.

*Established by law*

The appeal tribunal and the Commissioner both satisfy this requirement.

*Judgment pronounced publicly*

The European Court of Human Rights has not required that every decision must be read in public. The degree of publicity depends on the circumstances of the case, especially the special features of the proceedings involved, judged by reference to the object and purpose of Art.6(1). It is sufficient in cases involving children and which do not establish an issue of general principle for the decision to be available to those who had a legitimate interest in the outcome of the case: *B and P v United Kingdom* [2001] 2 F.L.R. 261.

All decisions by Commissioners are publically available. Decisions by tribunals have been described as public documents (*CSDLA/5/95*, para.11). This is questionable. Certainly, they are not available to the public. See further the general note to reg.53(2) and (4) of the Appeals Regulations.

*Article 7—No Punishment Without Law*

**2.337**    **1.** No one shall be held guilty of any criminal offence on account of any act or omission which did not constitute a criminal offence under national or international law at the time when it was committed. Nor shall a heavier penalty be imposed than the one that was applicable at the time the criminal offence was committed.

**2.** This Article shall not prejudice the trial and punishment of any person for any act or omission which, at the time when it was committed, was criminal according to the general principles of law recognised by civilised nations.

*Article 8—Right to Respect for Private and Family Life*

**2.338**    **1.** Everyone has the right to respect for his private and family life, his home and his correspondence.

**2.** There shall be no interference by a public authority with the exercise of this right except such as is in accordance with the law and is necessary in a democratic society in the interests of national security, public safety or the economic well-being of the country, for the prevention of disorder or crime, for the protection of health or morals, or for the protection of the rights and freedoms of others.

GENERAL NOTE

*Paragraph (1)*

**2.339**    The right to a home is limited to issues of the right to privacy rather than a right to accommodation (*Harrow London Borough Council v Qazi* [2003] 4 All E.R. 461 at paras 70, 89 and 120; R. *(ota Erskine) v London Borough of Lambeth and the Office of the Deputy Prime Minster* [2003] EWHC 2479 (Admin)).

The Strasbourg authorities, the Commissioners and the courts have concluded that there is nothing in the general nature of the child support scheme or its application that renders it incompatible with this Article, although there is still scope for argument that there has been a violation on the facts of a particular case.

In *Logan v United Kingdom* (1996) 22 E.H.R.R. CD 178, the absent parent complained of a violation of Art.8 on the ground that the amount of child support maintenance for which he was liable left him insufficient money to enable him to maintain reasonable contact with his children. The Commission decided that the complaint should be rejected as manifestly ill-founded, because the child support legislation did not by its very nature affect family life and, looking at the absent parent's income and expenses including the costs of access, he had not shown that the effect of the operation of the legislation in his case was of such a nature or degree as to disclose a lack of respect for family life. This conclusion leaves open the possibility that a breach of this Article may be shown on the facts of another case.

The child support scheme, including the variation scheme, is not in violation of this Article, because it is necessary to the economic well-being of the country and for the protection of the rights and freedoms of qualifying children (*CCS 6373/99*, para.13). The courts have taken the same view, holding that neither the legislation nor the Child Support Agency's administration of the scheme is in violation *R. (ota Denson) v Child Support Agency* [2002] 1 F.L.R. 938 at para.22).

In *R. (ota Denson) v Child Support Agency* [2002] 1 F.L.R. 938, Munby J. held that the making of a liability order, as a lever for compliance or as a gateway to futher action, did not affect a person's private life under this paragraph (paras 38–45). The possibility was left open that this Article might be engaged if, for reasons known to the Agency, the person concerned was particulaly vulnerable (para. 44).

*Paragraph (2)*

The requirement that the interference must be in accordance with the law (the principle of legality) involves three elements: it must have a basis in domestic law; it must be sufficiently accessible to those affected by it and sufficiently precise for them to understand it and foresee the consequences of violating it; and it must not be applied in a way that is arbitrary, such as if its exercise was in bad faith or not proportionate (*R. v Shayler* [2002] 2 All E.R. 477 at paras 55–56).

Necessity also involves three elements: whether the objective justifies interfering with the right; whether the means chosen are rational, fair and not arbitrary; and whether the means impair the right as minimally as is reasonably possible (*R. v Shayler* [2002] 2 All E.R. 477 at paras 57 and 61).

So, proportionality is both an aspect of the third element of the principle of legality and an aspect of the third element of necessity. It requires, in both contexts, a consideration of the procedural safeguards to ensure that a decision is not made arbitrarily *R. (ota Denson) v Child Support Agency* [2002] 1 F.L.R. 938 at paras 55(iv) and 56).

In *R. (ota Denson) v Child Support Agency* [2002] 1 F.L.R. 938, Munby J. held that, even if this Article was engaged by the making of a liability order, the interference with the para.(1) right was justified and proportionate (para.46). The key issue was whether the order had been made arbitrarily (para.58). And in *R. (Qazi) v Secretary of State*, reported as *R(CS) 5/04*, Charles J held that any infringement with this article by the departure direction scheme (now replaced by the variation scheme) was a proportionate response to a pressing social need (para.45).

*Article 9—Freedom of Thought, Conscience and Religion*

**1.** Everyone has the right to freedom of thought, conscience and religion; this right includes freedom to change his religion or belief and freedom, either alone or in community with others and in public or private, to manifest his religion or belief, in worship, teaching, practice and observance.

**2.** Freedom to manifest one's religion or beliefs shall be subject only to such limitations as are prescribed by law and are necessary in a democratic society in the interests of public safety, for the protection of public order, health or morals, or for the protection of the rights and freedoms of others.

**2.340**

*Article 10—Freedom of Expression*

2.341     **1.** Everyone has the right to freedom of expression. This right shall include freedom to hold opinions and to receive and impart information and ideas without interference by public authority and regardless of frontiers. This Article shall not prevent States from requiring the licensing of broadcasting, television or cinema enterprises.
**2.** The exercise of these freedoms, since it carries with it duties and responsibilities, may be subject to such formalities, conditions, restrictions or penalties as are prescribed by law and are necessary in a democratic society, in the interests of national security, territorial integrity or public safety, for the prevention of disorder or crime, for the protection of health or morals, for the protection of the reputation or rights of others, for preventing the disclosure of information received in confidence, or for maintaining the authority and impartiality of the judiciary.

*Article 11—Freedom of Assembly and Association*

2.342     **1.** Everyone has the right to freedom of peaceful assembly and to freedom of association with others, including the right to form and to join trade unions for the protection of his interests.
**2.** No restrictions shall be placed on the exercise of these rights other than such as are prescribed by law and are necessary in a democratic society in the interests of national security or public safety, for the prevention of disorder or crime, for the protection of health or morals or for the protection of the rights and freedoms of others. This Article shall not prevent the imposition of lawful restrictions on the exercise of these rights by members of the armed forces, of the police or of the administration of the State.

*Article 12—Right to Marry*

2.343     Men and women of marriageable age have the right to marry and to found a family, according to the national laws governing the exercise of this right.

*Article 14—Prohibition of Discrimination*

2.344     The enjoyment of the rights and freedoms set forth in this Convention shall be secured without discrimination on any ground such as sex, race, colour, language, religion, political or other opinion, national or social origin, association with a national minority, property, birth or other status.

GENERAL NOTE

2.345     The right conferred by this Article has no independent existence. Its function is to safeguard the other rights. Those other rights may be violated alone or in conjunction with this Article. If there is a violation of another right, it is not necessary to consider this right, unless the clear inequality of treatment in the enjoyment of the other right is a fundamental aspect of the case. See *Airey v Ireland* (1979) 2 E.H.R.R. 305. Although the other right in respect of which there is discrimination need not have been violated alone, the facts must fall within the ambit of that right: *Rasmussen v Denmark* (1984) 7 E.H.R.R. 371.
Discrimination means treating differently, without an objective and reasonable justification, persons who are in relevantly similar situtations: *Fredin v Sweden* (1991) 13 E.H.R.R. 142. The difference of treatment may be on any ground. At one time, it was necessary for the difference in treatment to be based on a personal characteristic or status (*R. (ota Barber) v Secretary of State for Work and Pensions* [2002] 2 F.L.R. 1181 at paras 28–34). However, that line of Strasbourg authority is now out of date (*R. (ota Hooper) v Secretary of State for Work and Pensions* [2003] 3 All E.R. 673 at para.91).
Discrimination may take the form of treating persons in analogous circumstances differently or of failing to treat differently persons whose circumstances are significantly different (*Thlimmenos v Greece* (2001) 31 E.H.R.R. 411 at para.44).

The former approach of considering the application of this article in a series of questions was disapproved by the House of Lords in *R (Carson and Reynolds) v Secretary of State for Work and Pensions* [2005] UKHL 37 in favour of considering more simply whether the difference in treatment can stand scrutiny.

In *Barber* (at para.39), the judge doubted whether indirect discrimination was relevant under this article. However, in *CH 5125/02*, paras 36–55, the Commissioner expressed the view that any form of discrimination was relevant under this article, although this part of his reasoning was not essential to his decision. The Court of Appeal dismissed the appeal against the Commissioner's decision without dealing with this issue (*R(H) 8/04*).

A margin of appreciation applies, especially where there is a wide divergence of approaches between States: *Rasmussen v Denmark* (1984) 7 E.H.R.R. 371.

The reason for discrimination put forward by a State is not decisive. The reason must be examined to see if it is objective and reasonable. If there is a legitimate justification for discrimination, the means employed must be proportionate to the aim pursued: *Hoffmann v Austria* (1993) 17 E.H.R.R. 293.

As the Convention must be interpreted dynamically, the justification must be valid in current conditions.

In *CCS 1153/03*, the Commissioner decided that the distinction in the former protected income provisions between gay and straight couples discriminated against the former. The Commissioner removed the discrimination by holding that the context required that the definition giving rise to the discrimination did not apply. On appeal, the Court of Appeal approved of the Commissioner's decision, but justified it by simply deleting the offending definition (*M v Secretary of State for Work and Pensions* [2005] F.L.R. 498 at para.86). Sedley LJ said that discrimination on the ground of sexual orientation in respect of Art.8 was prohibited in the absence of a compelling and proportionate justification of the interests of the traditional family (para.48). The Court of Appeal's decision is now under appeal to the House of Lords.

There can be no discrimination on the basis of nationality on account of differences in English and Scottish law, because there is no such thing as Scottish nationality (*CG 1259/02*, para.7).

### Article 16—Restrictions on Political Activity of Aliens

Nothing in Articles 10, 11 and 14 shall be regarded as preventing the High Contracting Parties from imposing restrictions on the political activity of aliens.

**2.346**

### Article 17—Prohibition of Abuse of Rights

Nothing in this Convention may be interpreted as implying for any State, group or person any right to engage in any activity or perform any act aimed at the destruction of any of the rights and freedoms set forth herein or at their limitation to a greater extent than is provided for in the Convention.

**2.347**

### Article 18—Limitation on use of Restrictions on Rights

The restrictions permitted under this Convention to the said rights and freedoms shall not be applied for any purpose other than those for which they have been prescribed.

**2.348**

PART II

THE FIRST PROTOCOL

### Article 1—Protection of Property

Every natural or legal person is entitled to the peaceful enjoyment of his possessions. No one shall be deprived of his possessions except in the public interest and subject to the conditions provided for by law and by the general principles of international law. The preceding

**2.349**

provisions shall not, however, in any way impair the right of a State to enforce such laws as it deems necessary to control the use of property in accordance with the general interest or to secure the payment of taxes or other contributions or penalties.

GENERAL NOTE

Possession has an autonomous meaning in the Convention (*R. (ota Carson) v Secretary of State for Work and Pensions* [2003] 3 All E.R. 577 *per* Laws L.J. at para.45).

This Convention right is primarily concerned with the expropriation of property for a public purpose, not with the regulation of rights between persons in private law (*M v Secretary of State for Work and Pensions* [2005] F.L.R. 498 at para.52).

The making of a liability order, as a step towards possible enforcement measures, does not engage this Article (*R. (ota Denson) v Child Support Agency* [2002] 1 F.L.R. 938 at para.59). And in *R. (Qazi) v Secretary of State*, reported as *R(CS) 5/04*, Charles J. held that any infringement with this article by the departure direction scheme (now replaced by the variation scheme) was a proportionate response to a pressing social need (para.45).

*Article 2—Right to Education*

No person shall be denied the right to education. In the exercise of any functions which it assumes in relation to education and to teaching, the State shall respect the right of parents to ensure such education and teaching in conformity with their own religious and philosophical convictions.

*Article 3—Right to Free Elections*

2.350    The High Contracting Parties undertake to hold free elections at reasonable intervals by secret ballot, under conditions which will ensure the free expression of the opinion of the people in the choice of the legislature.

[¹PART III

ARTICLE OF THE THIRTEENTH PROTOCOL

*Abolition of the death penalty*

2.351    The death penalty shall be abolished. No one shall be condemned to such penalty or executed.]

AMENDMENT

2.352    1. Article 2(3) of the Human Rights Act 1998 (Amendment) Order 2004 (June 21, 2004).

SCHEDULE 2

REMEDIAL ORDERS

*Orders*

2.353    **1.**—(1) A remedial order may—

(a) contain such incidental, supplemental, consequential or transitional provision as the person making it considers appropriate;

(b) be made so as to have effect from a date earlier than that on which it is made;

(c) make provision for the delegation of specific functions;

(d) make different provision for different cases.

(2) The power conferred by sub-paragraph (1)(a) includes—

(a) power to amend primary legislation (including primary legislation other than that which contains the incompatible provision); and

(b) power to amend or revoke subordinate legislation (including subordinate legislation other than that which contains the incompatible provision).

(3) A remedial order may be made so as to have the same extent as the legislation which it affects.

(4) No person is to be guilty of an offence solely as a result of the retrospective effect of a remedial order.

*Procedure*

**2.** No remedial order may be made unless—

(a) a draft of the order has been approved by a resolution of each House of Parliament made after the end of the period of 60 days beginning with the day on which the draft was laid; or

(b) it is declared in the order that it appears to the person making it that, because of the urgency of the matter, it is necessary to make the order without a draft being so approved.

*Orders laid in draft*

**3.**—(1) No draft may be laid under paragraph 2(a) unless—

(a) the person proposing to make the order has laid before Parliament a document which contains a draft of the proposed order and the required information; and

(b) the period of 60 days, beginning with the day on which the document required by this sub-paragraph was laid, has ended.

(2) If representations have been made during that period, the draft laid under paragraph 2(a) must be accompanied by a statement containing—

(a) a summary of the representations; and

(b) if, as a result of the representations, the proposed order has been changed, details of the changes.

*Urgent cases*

**4.**—(1) If a remedial order ("the original order") is made without being approved in draft, the person making it must lay it before Parliament, accompanied by the required information, after it is made.

(2) If representations have been made during the period of 60 days beginning with the day on which the original order was made, the person making it must (after the end of that period) lay before Parliament a statement containing—

(a) a summary of the representations; and

(b) if, as a result of the representations, he considers it appropriate to make changes to the original order, details of the changes.

(3) If sub-paragraph (2)(b) applies, the person making the statement must—

(a) make a further remedial order replacing the original order; and

(b) lay the replacement order before Parliament.

(4) If, at the end of the period of 120 days beginning with the day on which the original order was made, a resolution has not been passed by each House approving the original or

replacement order, the order ceases to have effect (but without that affecting anything previously done under either order or the power to make a fresh remedial order).

*Definitions*

**5.** In this Schedule—

"representations" means representations about a remedial order (or proposed remedial order) made to the person making (or proposing to make) it and includes any relevant Parliamentary report or resolution; and

"required information" means—

 (a) an explanation of the incompatibility which the order (or proposed order) seeks to remove, including particulars of the relevant declaration, finding or order; and

 (b) a statement of the reasons for proceeding under section 10 and for making an order in those terms.

*Calculating periods*

**6.** In calculating any period for the purposes of this Schedule, no account is to be taken of any time during which—

 (a) Parliament is dissolved or prorogued; or

 (b) both Houses are adjourned for more than four days.

[¹**7.**—(1) This paragraph applies in relation to—

 (a) any remedial order made, and any draft of such an order proposed to be made,—
     (i) by the Scottish Ministers; or
     (ii) within devolved competence (within the meaning of the Scotland Act 1998) by Her Majesty in Council; and

 (b) any document or statement to be laid in connection with such an order (or proposed order).

(2) This Schedule has effect in relation to any such order (or proposed order), document or statement subject to the following modifications.

(3) Any reference to Parliament, each House of Parliament or both Houses of Parliament shall be construed as a reference to the Scottish Parliament.

(4) Paragraph 6 does not apply and instead, in calculating any period for the purposes of this Schedule, no account is to be taken of any time during which the Scottish Parliament is dissolved or is in recess for more than four days.]

AMENDMENT

1. Paragraph 21 of the Schedule to the Scotland Act 1998 (Consequential Modifications) Order 2000 (July 27, 2000).

DEFINITIONS

2.354  "amend": see s.21(1).
"primary legislation": see s.21(1).
"remedial order": see s.21(1).
"subordinate legislation": see s.21(1)

SCHEDULE 3

DEROGATION AND RESERVATION

[¹. . .]                                                                                              **2.355**

PART II

RESERVATION

At the time of signing the present (First) Protocol, I declare that, in view of certain provi-     **2.356**
sions of the Education Acts in the United Kingdom, the principle affirmed in the second sentence of Article 2 is accepted by the United Kingdom only so far as it is compatible with the
provision of efficient instruction and training, and the avoidance of unreasonable public
expenditure.
Dated 20 March 1952
Made by the United Kingdom Permanent Representative to the Council of Europe.

AMENDMENT

1. Article 2 of the Human Rights Act 1998 (Amendment) Order 2005 (April 8,
2005).

SCHEDULE 4

JUDICIAL PENSIONS

*Duty to make orders about pensions*

**1.**—(1) The appropriate Minister must by order make provision with respect to pensions     **2.357**
payable to or in respect of any holder of a judicial office who serves as an ECHR judge.
    (2) A pensions order must include such provision as the Minister making it considers is
necessary to secure that—

(a)  an ECHR judge who was, immediately before his appointment as an ECHR judge,
     a member of a judicial pension scheme is entitled to remain as a member of that
     scheme;

(b)  the terms on which he remains a member of the scheme are those which would have
     been applicable had he not been appointed as an ECHR judge; and

(c)  entitlement to benefits payable in accordance with the scheme continues to be deter-
     mined as if, while serving as an ECHR judge, his salary was that which would (but for
     section 18(4)) have been payable to him in respect of his continuing service as the
     holder of his judicial office.

*Contributions*

**2.** A pensions order may, in particular, make provision—

(a)  for any contributions which are payable by a person who remains a member of a
     scheme as a result of the order, and which would otherwise be payable by deduction
     from his salary, to be made otherwise than by deduction from his salary as an ECHR
     judge; and

(b)  for such contributions to be collected in such manner as may be determined by the
     administrators of the scheme.

*Amendments of other enactments*

**3.** A pensions order may amend any provision of, or made under, a pensions Act in such
manner and to such extent as the Minister making the order considers necessary or expedient
to ensure the proper administration of any scheme to which it relates.

*Definitions*

**4.** In this Schedule—

"appropriate Minister" means—

> (a) in relation to any judicial office whose jurisdiction is exercisable exclusively in relation to Scotland, the Secretary of State; and
> (b) otherwise, the Lord Chancellor;

"ECHR judge" means the holder of a judicial office who is serving as a judge of the Court;
"judicial pension scheme" means a scheme established by and in accordance with a pensions Act;
"Pensions Act" means—

> (a) the County Courts Act Northern Ireland) 1959;
> (b) the Sheriffs' Pensions (Scotland) Act 1961;
> (c) the Judicial Pensions Act 1981; or
> (d) the Judicial Pensions and Retirement Act 1993; and

"pensions order" means an order made under paragraph 1.

# Access to Justice Act 1999

## (1999 c.22)

### Legal Services Commission

2.358    **1.**—(1) There shall be a body known as the Legal Services Commission (in this Part referred to as "the Commission").
(2) The Commission shall have the functions relating to—
(a) the Community Legal Service, and
(b) the Criminal Defence Service,
which are conferred or imposed on it by the provisions of this Act or any other enactment.
. . .

### Services which may be funded

2.359    **6.** . . .
(6) The Commission may not fund as part of the Community Legal Service any of the services specified in Schedule 2.
. . .

(8) The Lord Chancellor—
2.360    (a) may by direction require the Commission to fund the provision of any of the services specified in Schedule 2 in circumstances specified in the direction, and
(b) may authorise the Commission to fund the provision of any of the services specified in Schedule 2 in specified circumstances or, if the Commission request him to do so, in an individual case.

SCHEDULE 2

COMMUNITY LEGAL SERVICE: EXCLUDED SERVICES

The services which may not be funded as part of the Community Legal Service are as follows.

2.361

. . .

**2.** Advocacy in any proceedings except—

. . .

(3) proceedings in a magistrates' court—

. . .

(g) under section 20 or 27 of the Child Support Act 1991

. . .

(4) proceedings before any person to whom a case is referred (in whole or in part) in any proceedings within paragraphs (1) to (3).

GENERAL NOTE

Section 6(6) and Sch.2 prevent the Commission from funding advocacy in proceedings in child support cases before appeal tribunals and Commissioners, unless the case is within a class covered by a direction under s.6(8)(a) or funding for the case is authorised under s.6(8)(b). The powers in s.6(8) might be used to provide funding of particular cases or classes of case in order to ensure compliance with the equality of arms requirement under the Convention right to a fair hearing under Art.6(1) of the European Convention on Human Rights and Fundamental Freedoms.

2.362

The reference to s.20 of the Child Support Act 1991 in Sch.2, para.2(3)(g) is difficult to understand, as that section deals only with appeals to appeal tribunals and does not cover appeals to a magistrates' court.

# Child Support, Pensions and Social Security Act 2000

## (2000 c.19)

An Act to amend the law relating to child support; to amend the law relating to occupational and personal pensions and war pensions; to amend the law relating to social security benefits and social security administration; to amend the law relating to national insurance contributions; to amend Part III of the Family Law Reform Act 1969 and Part III of the Family Law Act 1986; and for connected purposes. [28th July 2000]

2.363

PART I

CHILD SUPPORT

*Miscellaneous*

**Abolition of the child maintenance bonus**

**23.** Section 10 of the Child Support Act 1995 (which provides for the child maintenance bonus) shall cease to have effect.

2.364

**Periodical reviews**

2.365    **24.** Article 3(4) of the Social Security Act 1998 (Commencement No. 2) Order 1998 (which saved section 16 of the 1991 Act for certain purposes) is revoked; and accordingly that section shall cease to have effect for all purposes.

**Temporary compensation payment scheme**

2.366    **27.**—(1)  This section applies where—

(a) a maintenance assessment is made before a prescribed date following an application for one under section 4, 6 or 7 of the 1991 Act; or

(b) a fresh maintenance assessment has been made following either a periodic review under section 16 of the 1991 Act or a review under section 17 of that Act (as they had effect before their substitution by section 40 or 41 respectively of the Social Security Act 1998),

and the effective date of the assessment is earlier than the date on which the assessment was made, with the result that arrears of child support maintenance have become due under the assessment.

(2)  The Secretary of State may in regulations provide that this section has effect as if it were modified so as—

(a) to apply to cases of arrears of child support maintenance having become due additional to those referred to in subsection (1);

(b) not to apply to any such case as is referred to in subsection (1).

(3)  If this section applies, the Secretary of State may in prescribed circumstances agree with the absent parent, on terms specified in the agreement, that—

(a) the absent parent will not be required to pay the whole of the arrears, but only some lesser amount; and

(b) the Secretary of State will not, while the agreement is complied with, take action to recover any of the arrears.

(4)  The terms which may be specified are to be prescribed in or determined in accordance with regulations made by the Secretary of State.

(5)  An agreement may be entered into only if it is made before 1st April [¹2005] and expires before 1st April [²2006].

(6)  If the absent parent enters into such an agreement, the Secretary of State may, while the absent parent complies with it, refrain from taking action under the 1991 Act to recover the arrears.

(7)  Upon the expiry of the agreement, if the absent parent has complied with it—

(a) he ceases to be liable to pay the arrears; and

(b) the Secretary of State may make payments of such amounts and at such times as he may determine to the person with care.

(8)  If the absent parent fails to comply with the agreement he becomes liable to pay the full amount of any outstanding arrears (as well as any other amount payable in accordance with the assessment).

(9)  The Secretary of State may be regulations provide for this section to have effect as if there were substituted for the dates in subsection (5) such later dates as are prescribed.

(10)  In this section, "prescribed" means prescribed in regulations made by the Secretary of State.

(11) Regulations under this section shall be made by statutory instrument.

(12) No statutory instrument containing regulations under subsection (9) is to be made unless a draft of the instrument has been laid before Parliament and approved by a resolution of each House of Parliament; but otherwise a statutory instrument containing regulations under this section shall be subject to annulment in pursuance of a resolution of either House of Parliament.

COMMENCEMENT

November 10, 2000 for the purpose of making regulations; otherwise January 1, 2001 under art.2(2) of, and Pt II of the Sch. to, the Commencement No.3 Order 2000.

AMENDMENTS

1. Regulation 2(a) of the Child Support (Temporary Compensation Payment Scheme) (Modification and Amendment) Regulations 2002 (July 17, 2002).
2. Regulation 2(b) of the Child Support (Temporary Compensation Payment Scheme) (Modification and Amendment) Regulations 2002 (July 17, 2002).

DEFINITION

"the 1991 Act": see s.29(1).     **2.367**

GENERAL NOTE

This section deals with arrears that would otherwise be payable as a result of the   **2.368** delay in the making of a maintenance assessment under the child support scheme as it was applied before this Act came into force. It is a statutory replacement for the extra-statutory scheme that previously operated. The same problem is tackled differently under the new child support scheme by voluntary payments under s.28J of the 1991 Act.

Arrears may be remitted in accordance with an agreement reached with the absent parent: see subss.(3) and (7)(a). This only applies if the absent parent honours the agreement as to payment: see subs.(7). Otherwise, the whole of the arrears are payable, as well as any other sums payable under the assessment: see subss.(8). The person with care is protected by receiving payments from the Secretary of State: see subs.(7)(b). The agreement must have been made before April 1, 2005 and expire before April 1, 2006: see subs. (5). These dates may, though, be changed by regulations: see subs.(9).

The Child Support (Temporary Compensation Payment Scheme) Regulations 2000 are made under the authority of this section. References to regulations in the general notes to this section are to these Regulations. They came into force on January 31, 2002.

*Subsection (1)*
The date prescribed under para.(a) is April 1, 2002: see reg.3.

*Subsection (2)*
Regulation 2 is made under the authority of this subsection.

*Subsection (3)*
The circumstances are prescribed by reg.4.

*Subsection (4)*
The terms of the agreement are prescribed by reg.5.

## Pilot schemes

2.369    **28**—(1) Any regulations made under—
    (a) provisions inserted or substituted in the 1991 Act by this Part of this Act (or Schedule 1, 2 or 3); and
    (b) in so far as they are consequential on or supplementary to any such regulations, regulations made under any other provisions in the 1991 Act,
may be made so as to have effect for a specified period not exceeding 12 months.

(2) Any regulations which, by virtue of subsection (1), are to have effect for a limited period are referred to in this section as "a pilot scheme".

(3) A pilot scheme may provide that its provisions are to apply only in relation to—
    (a) one or more specified areas or localities;
    (b) one or more specified classes of person;
    (c) persons selected by reference to prescribed criteria, or on a sampling basis.

(4) A pilot scheme may make consequential or transitional provision with respect to the cessation of the scheme on the expiry of the specified period.

(5) A pilot scheme ("the previous scheme") may be replaced by a further pilot scheme making the same provision as that made by the previous scheme (apart from the specified period), or similar provision.

(6) A statutory instrument containing (whether alone or with other provisions) a pilot scheme shall not be made unless a draft of the instrument has been laid before Parliament and approved by resolution of each House of Parliament.

## Interpretation, transitional provisions, savings, etc.

2.370    **29**.—(1) In this Part, "the 1991 Act" means the Child Support Act 1991.

(2) The Secretary of State may in regulations make such transitional and transitory provisions, and such incidental, supplementary, savings and consequential provisions, as he considers necessary or expedient in connection with the coming into force of this Part or any provision in it.

(3) The regulations may, in particular—
    (a) provide for the amount of child support maintenance payable by or to any person to be at a transitional rate (or more than one such rate successively) resulting from the phasing-in by way of prescribed steps of any increase or decrease in the amount payable following the coming into force of this Part or any provision in it;
    (b) provide for a departure direction or any finding in relation to a previous determination of child support maintenance to be taken into

account in a decision as to the amount of child support maintenance payable by or to any person.

(4) Section 175(3) and (5) of the Social Security Contributions and Benefits Act 1992 (supplemental power in relation to regulations) applies to regulations made under this section as it applies to regulations made under that Act.

(5) The power to make regulations under this section is exercisable by statutory instrument.

(6) A statutory instrument containing regulations under this section shall be subject to annulment in pursuance of a resolution of either House of Parliament.

COMMENCEMENT

For the purpose of making regulations, November 10, 2000 under art.2(1) of, Pt I of the Schedule to, the Commencement No.3 Order 2000; March 3, 2003 under art.7(a) of, and the Schedule to, the Commencement No.12 Order 2003.

## Data Protection Act 1984

### Other exemptions

**34.** . . .                                                                                2.371

(5) Personal data are exempt from the non-disclosure provisions in any case in which the disclosure is—

(a) required by or under any enactment, by any rule of law or by the order of a court; or

(b) made for the purposes of obtaining legal advice or for the purposes of, or in the course of, legal proceedings in which the person making the disclosure is a party or a witness.

### General interpretation

**41.** In addition to the provisions of sections 1 and 2 above, the following    2.372
provisions shall have effect for the interpretation of this Act—

. . .

"enactment" includes an enactment passed after this Act;

. . .

## Data Protection Act 1998

### Disclosures required by law or made in connection with legal proceedings, etc.

**35.**—(1) Personal data are exempt from the non-disclosure provisions    2.373
where the disclosure is required by or under any enactment, by any rule of law or by order of a court.

(2) Personal data are exempt from the non-disclosure provisions where the disclosure is necessary—

(a) for the purposes of, or in connection with, any legal proceedings (including prospective legal proceedings), or

(b) for the purpose of obtaining legal advice,

or is otherwise necessary for the purpose of establishing, exercising or defending legal rights.

## Supplementary definitions

2.374     **70.** In this Act, unless the context otherwise requires,—

. . .

"enactment" includes an enactment passed after this Act;

. . .

## Gender Recognition Act 2004

## Parenthood

2.375     **12.** The fact that a person's gender has become the acquired gender under this Act does not affect the status of the person as the father or mother of a child.

# PART III

# REGULATIONS

# The Child Support (Information, Evidence and Disclosure) Regulations 1992

## (SI 1992/1812)

*Made by the Secretary of State for Social Security under sections 4(4), 6(9), 7(5), 14(1) and (3), 50(5), 51, 54 and 57 of, and paragraphs 16(10) of Schedule 1 to and 2(4) of Schedule 2 to, the Child Support Act 1991 and all other powers enabling him in that behalf.*

### ARRANGEMENT OF REGULATIONS

### PART I

*General*

### PART II

*Furnishing of information or evidence*

### PART III

*Disclosure of information*

### PART I

### GENERAL

## Citation, commencement and interpretation

**1.**—(1) These Regulations may be cited as the Child Support 3.2 (Information, Evidence and Disclosure) Regulations 1992 and shall come into force on 5th April 1993.

(2) In these Regulations, unless the context otherwise requires—

"the Act" means the Child Support Act 1991;

"appropriate authority" means—

    (a) in relation to housing benefit, the housing or local authority concerned; and

    (b) in relation to council tax benefit, the billing authority or, in Scotland, the levying authority,

[1"local authority" means, in relation to England, a county council, a district council, a London borough council, the Common Council of the City of London or the Council of the Isles of Scilly and, in relation to Wales, a county council or a county borough council and, in relation to Scotland, a council constituted under section 2 of the Local Government etc (Scotland) Act 1994;]

[2"Maintenance Calculations and Special Cases Regulations" means the Child Support (Maintenance Calculations and Special Cases) Regulations 2000;]

[3"Maintenace Calculation Procedure Regulations" means the Child Support (Maintenance Calculation Procedure) Regulations 2000;]

"parent with care" means a person who, in respect of the same child or children, is both a parent and a person with care;

"related proceedings" means proceedings in which a relevant court order was or is being sought;

"relevant court order" means—

    (a) an order as to periodical or capital provision or as to variation of property rights made under an enactment specified in paragraphs (a) to (e) of section 8(11) of the Act or prescribed under section 8(11)(f) of the Act in relation to a qualifying child or a relevant person; or

    (b) an order under Part II of the Children Act 1989 (Orders With Respect To Children In Family Proceedings) in relation to a qualifying child or, in Scotland, an order under section 3 of the Law Reform (Parent and Child) (Scotland) Act 1986 or a decree of declarator under section 7 of that Act in relation to a qualifying child;

"relevant person" means—

    (a) a person with care;

    (b) [4a non-resident parent];

    (c) a parent who is treated as [4a non-resident parent] under [5regulation 8 of the Maintenance Calculations and Special Cases Regulations];

    (d) where the application for [6a calculation] is made by a child under section 7 of the Act, that child,

in respect of whom [7a maintenance calculation has been applied for, or has been treated as applied for under section 6(3) of the Act, or is or has been in force.]

(3) In these Regulations, unless the context otherwise requires, a reference—

    (a) to a numbered regulation is to the regulation in these Regulations bearing that number.

(b) in a regulation to a numbered paragraph is to the paragraph in that regulation bearing that number;

(c) in a paragraph to a lettered or numbered subparagraph is to the subparagraph in that paragraph bearing that letter or number.

AMENDMENTS

1. Regulation 5(1)(a) of the Information, Evidence and Disclosure and Maintenance Arrangements and Jurisdiction Amendment Regulations 2000.
2. Regulation 3(1)(a) of the Information, Evidence and Disclosure and Maintenance Arrangements and Jurisdiction Amendment Regulations 2000.
3. Regulation 3(1)(b) of the Information, Evidence and Disclosure and Maintenance Arrangements and Jurisdiction Amendment Regulations 2000.
4. Regulation 2(1) of the Information, Evidence and Disclosure and Maintenance Arrangements and Jurisdiction Amendment Regulations 2000.
5. Regulation 3(2) of the Information, Evidence and Disclosure and Maintenance Arrangements and Jurisdiction Amendment Regulations 2000.
6. Regulation 2(2) of the Information, Evidence and Disclosure and Maintenance Arrangements and Jurisdiction Amendment Regulations 2000.
7. Regulation 5(1)(b) of the Information, Evidence and Disclosure and Maintenance Arrangements and Jurisdiction Amendment Regulations 2000.

## PART II

### FURNISHING OF INFORMATION OR EVIDENCE

**Persons under a duty to furnish information or evidence**

**2.**—[$^{10}$(1) A person falling within a category listed in paragraph (2) shall furnish such information or evidence—

    3.3

(a) with respect to the matter or matters specified in that paragraph in relation to that category; and

(b) which is in his possession or which he can reasonably be expected to acquire,

as is required by the Secretary of State to enable a decision to be made under section 11, 12, 16 or 17 of the Act.]

[$^{8}$(1A) A person falling within paragraph (2)(a) or (e) shall furnish such information or evidence as is required by the Secretary of State and is needed by him to enable a decision to be made in relation to the matters listed in regulation 3(1)(h) and (hh) where the person concerned has that information or evidence in his possession or can reasonably be expected to acquire it.]

(2) The persons who may be required to furnish information or evidence, and the matter or matters with respect to which such information or evidence may be required, are as follows—

(a) the relevant persons, with respect to the matters listed in regulation 3(1);

[$^{22}$(aa) where regulation 8(1) of the Maintenance Calculations and Special Cases Regulations applies (persons treated as non-resident parents), a parent of or a person who provides day to day care for the child in respect of whom a maintenance calculation has been applied for or has been treated as applied for or is or has been in force, with respect to the matter listed in sub-paragraph (1) of regulation 3(1);]

(b) a person who is alleged to be a parent of a child with respect to whom an application for a [[17]calculation has been made, or has been treated as made,] [[6]or in relation to whom a maintenance assessment has been made [[11]. . .] and that person] denies that he is one of that child's parents, with respect to the matters listed in subparagraphs (b) and (d) of regulation 3(1);

[[1](ba) the current or recent employer of a person falling within subparagraph (b), with respect to the matters listed in subparagraphs (d) and (e) of regulation 3(1);]

(c) the current or recent employer of the [[14]non-resident parent] [[15]. . .] in relation to whom an application for a maintenance [[17]calculation has been made, or has been treated as made,] [[7]or in relation to whom a maintenance assessment has been made [[12]. . .], with respect to the matters listed in subparagraphs (d), (e), (f), (h) [[16], (hh)] and (j) of regulation 3(1);

[[2](cc) persons employed in the service of the Crown or otherwise in the discharge of Crown functions, where they are the current or recent employer of the [[14]non-resident parent] [[15]. . .] in relation to whom an application for a maintenance [[17]calculation has been made, or has been treated as made,] [[7]or in relation to whom a maintenance assessment has been made [[13]. . .], with respect to the matters listed in subparagraph (d), (e), (f), (h) [[16], (hh)] and (j) of regulation 3(1);

(cd) persons employed in the service of the Crown or otherwise in the discharge of Crown functions, where they are the current or recent employer of a person falling within sub-paragraph (b), with respect to the matters listed in subparagraphs (d) and (e) of regulation 3(1);]

(d) the local authority in whose area a person falling within a category listed in subparagraphs (a) and (b) above resides or has resided, with respect to the [[18]matters] listed in subparagraph (a) [[19], (d), (e), (f), (h) and (hh)] of regulation 3(1);

(e) a person specified in paragraph (3) below, in any case where, in relation to the qualifying child or qualifying children or the [[14]non-resident parent]—

  (i)   there is or has been a relevant court order, or

  (ii)  there have been, or are pending, related proceedings before a court, with respect to the matters listed in subparagraphs [[9](aa), (ab),] (g), (h) and (k) of regulation 3(1);

[[20](f) a person who acts or has acted as an accountant for the [[14]non-resident parent] including where that person is self-employed, in relation to any business accounts of that parent with respect to the matters listed in sub-paragraphs (e), (f), (h) and (hh) of regulation 3(1);

(g) a company or partnership for whom the [[14]non-resident parent] is providing or has provided services under a contract for services with respect to the matters listed in sub-paragraphs (e) and (f) of regulation 3(1); and

(h) persons employed in the service of the Crown or otherwise in the discharge of Crown functions—

(i) under [[23]the Road Traffic (Northern Ireland) Order 1981,] sections 97 to 99A of the Road Traffic Act 1988 or Part II of the Vehicle Excise and Registration Act 1994 with respect to the matter listed in sub-paragraph (e) of regulation 3(1); or

(ii) under the Prison Act 1952 [[24], the Prison Act (Northern Ireland) 1953 or the Prisons (Scotland) Act 1989] with respect to the matter listed in sub-paragraph (e) of regulation 3(1).]

(3) The persons who may be required to furnish information or evidence in relation to a relevant court order or related proceedings under the provisions of paragraph (2)(e) are—

(a) in England and Wales—

(i) in relation to the High Court, the senior district judge of the principal registry of the Family Division or, where proceedings were instituted in a district registry, the district judge;

(ii) in relation to a county court, the proper officer of that court within the meaning of Order 1, Rule 3 of the County Court Rules 1981;

(iii) in relation to a magistrates' court, the [[21]justices' chief executive for] that court;

(b) in Scotland—

(i) in relation to the Court of Session, the Deputy Principal Clerk of Session;

(ii) relation to a sheriff court, the sheriff clerk.

AMENDMENTS

1. Regulation 2 of the Miscellaneous Amendments Regulations 1995 (February 16, 1995).

2. Regulation 22 of the Amendment Regulations 1995 (April 18, 1995).

6. Regulation 7(3) of the Miscellaneous Amendments (No.2) Regulations 1995 (January 22, 1996).

7. Regulation 7(4) of the Miscellaneous Amendments (No.2) Regulations 1995 (January 22, 1996).

8. Regulation 7(2) of the Miscellaneous Amendments Regulations 1996 (August 5, 1996).

9. Regulation 7(3) of the Miscellaneous Amendments Regulations 1996 (August 5, 1996).

10. Article 6(a) of the Commencement No.7 Order 1999 (June 1, 1999).

11. Article 6(b)(i) of the Commencement No.7 Order 1999 (June 1, 1999).

12. Article 6(b)(ii) of the Commencement No.7 Order 1999 (June 1, 1999).

13. Article 6(b)(ii) of the Commencement No.7 Order 1999 (June 1, 1999).

14. Regulation 2(1) of the Information, Evidence and Disclosure and Maintenance Arrangements and Jurisdiction Amendment Regulations 2000.

15. Regulation 5(2)(a) of the Information, Evidence and Disclosure and Maintenance Arrangements and Jurisdiction Amendment Regulations 2000.

16. Regulation 5(2)(b) of the Information, Evidence and Disclosure and Maintenance Arrangements and Jurisdiction Amendment Regulations 2000.

17. Regulation 5(2)(c) of the Information, Evidence and Disclosure and Maintenance Arrangements and Jurisdiction Amendment Regulations 2000.

18. Regulation 5(2)(d)(i) of the Information, Evidence and Disclosure and Maintenance Arrangements and Jurisdiction Amendment Regulations 2000.

19. Regulation 5(2)(d)(ii) of the Information, Evidence and Disclosure and Maintenance Arrangements and Jurisdiction Amendment Regulations 2000.

20. Regulation 5(2)(e) of the Information, Evidence and Disclosure and Maintenance Arrangements and Jurisdiction Amendment Regulations 2000.

21. Regulation 4 of the Information, Evidence and Disclosure and Maintenance Arrangements and Jurisdiction Amendment Regulations 2000.

22. Regulation 4(a) of the Miscellaneous Amendments Regulations 2002 (in force as ss.16, 17 and 20 of the Act).

23. Regulation 4(b)(i) of the Miscellaneous Amendments Regulations 2002 (April 30, 2002).

24. Regulation 4(b)(ii) of the Miscellaneous Amendments Regulations 2002 (April 30, 2002).

DEFINITIONS

3.4 "the Act": see reg.1(2).
"local authority": see reg.1(2).
"Maintenance Calculations and Special Cases Regulations": see reg.1(2).
"parent with care": see reg.1(2).
"related proceedings": see reg.1(2).
"relevant court order": see reg.1(2)
"relevant person": see reg.1(2).

GENERAL NOTE

*Paragraph (2)*
3.5 The Family Proceedings Rules 1991 (as amended) r.10.21A provides that nothing in rr.10.20 or 10.21 of those Rules (which limit the circumstances in which inspection, etc. of documents in court and disclosure of addresses can be required) shall prevent a person required to furnish information or evidence from doing so.

Paragraphs (1) and (1A) are amended for cases in respect of which s.12 of the 2000 Act is not yet in force. See reg.2(2) of the Child Support (Information, Evidence and Disclosure) Amendment Regulations 2003.

## Purposes for which information or evidence may be required

3.6 **3.**—(1) The Secretary of State [2. . .] may require information or evidence under the provisions of regulation 2 only if that information or evidence is needed to enable—

(a) a decision to be made as to whether, in relation to an application for a maintenance [19calculation], there exists a qualifying child, [12a non-resident parent] and a person with care;

[3(aa) a decision to be made as to whether there is in force a written maintenance agreement made before 5th April 1993, or a maintenance order [9made on or after the date prescribed for the purposes of section 4(10)(a) of the Act which has been in force for at least a year from the date it was made], in relation to a qualifying child and the person who is at that time the [12non-resident parent] of that child;

(ab) a decision to be made as to whether a person with care has parental responsibility for a qualifying child for the purposes of section 5(1) of the Act;]

(b) a decision to be made as to whether [7the Secretary of State] has jurisdiction to make a maintenance [19calculation] under section 44 of the Act;

(c) a decision to be made, where more than one application has been made, as to which application is to be proceeded with;

(d) [¹²a non-resident] parent to be identified;

(e) [¹²a non-resident] parent to be traced;

(f) the amount of child support maintenance payable by [¹²a non-resident] parent to be [²¹calculated];

(g) the amount payable under a relevant court order to be ascertained;

(h) the amounts specified in subparagraphs (f) and (g) to be recovered from [¹²a non-resident] parent;

[⁴(hh) a decision to be made as to whether to take action under section 35(1) or 38(1) of the Act or to apply under section 36(1) of the Act for an order for recovery by means of garnishee proceedings or a charging order;]

(i) the amount of interest payable with respect to arrears of child support maintenance to be determined;

(j) the amount specified in subparagraph (i) to be recovered from an absent parent;

(k) any related proceedings to be identified;

[¹⁰(l) a determination as to who is in receipt of child benefit, payable under Part IX of the Social Security Contributions and Benefits Act 1992, either for a child who may be a relevant other child for the purposes of Schedule 1 to the Act, or for the qualifying child where a parent may fall to be treated as a non-resident parent under the Maintenance Calculations and Special Cases Regulations.]

(2) The information or evidence to be furnished in accordance with regulation 2 may in particular include information and evidence as to—

(a) the habitual residence of the person with care, the [¹²non-resident parent] and any child in respect of whom [¹¹the maintenance calculation has been applied for, or has been treated as applied for];

(b) the name and address of the person with care and of the [¹²non-resident parent], their marital status, and the relationship of the person with care to any child in respect of whom [¹¹the maintenance calculation has been applied for, or has been treated as applied for];

(c) the name, address and date of birth of any such child, that child's marital status, and any education that child is undergoing;

(d) the persons who have parental responsibility for ([⁵and], in Scotland, parental rights over) any qualifying child where there is more than one person with care;

(e) the time spent by a qualifying child in respect of whom [¹¹the maintenance calculation has been applied for, or has been treated as applied for] with each person with care, where there is more than one such person;

(f) the matters relevant for determining, in a case falling within section 26 of the Act (disputes about parentage), whether that case falls within one of the Cases set out in subsection (2) of that section, and if it does not, the matters relevant for determining the parentage of a child whose parentage is in dispute;

(g) the name and address of any current or recent employer of [¹²a non-resident parent] [¹³. . .], and the gross earnings and the deductions from those earnings deriving from each employment;

(h) the address from which [¹²a non-resident parent] [¹⁴. . .] who is self-employed carries on his trade or business, the trading name, [⁸the total taxable profits derived from his employment as a selfemployed earner, as submitted to, or as issued to him by, the Inland Revenue,] and the gross receipts and expenses and other outgoings of the trade or business;

(i) any other income of [¹²a non-resident parent] [¹³. . .]; [²⁰. . .]

(k) amounts payable and paid under a relevant court order or a maintenance agreement;

(l) the persons living in the same household as the [¹²non-resident parent] [¹⁶. . .], their relationship to the [¹²non-resident parent] [¹⁶. . .], and to each other, and, in the case of the children of any such party, the dates of birth of those children; [²⁰. . .]

(q) the identifying details of any bank, building society or similar account held in the name of the [¹²non-resident parent] [¹⁷. . .], and statements relating to any such account;

(r) the matters relevant for determining whether—

   (i) a maintenance [¹⁹calculation] has ceased to have effect [¹⁸. . .] under the provisions of paragraph 16 of Schedule 1 to the Act;

   (ii) a person is a child within the meaning of section 55 of the Act. [²⁰. . .]

AMENDMENTS

2. Article 7(a) of the Commencement No.7 Order 1999 (June 1, 1999).

3. Regulation 8(2) of the Miscellaneous Amendments Regulations 1996 (August 5, 1996).

4. Regulation 8(3) of the Miscellaneous Amendments Regulations 1996 (August 5, 1996).

5. Regulation 32(a) of the Miscellaneous Amendments Regulations 1998 (January 9, 1998).

7. Article 7(b) of the Commencement No.7 Order 1999 (June 1, 1999).

8. Regulation 4(2) of the Miscellaneous Amendments Regulations 1999 (October 4, 1999).

9. Regulation 6(1)(a) of the Information, Evidence and Disclosure and Maintenance Arrangements and Jurisdiction Amendment Regulations 2000.

10. Regulation 6(1)(b) of the Information, Evidence and Disclosure and Maintenance Arrangements and Jurisdiction Amendment Regulations 2000.

11. Regulation 6(2)(a) of the Information, Evidence and Disclosure and Maintenance Arrangements and Jurisdiction Amendment Regulations 2000.

12. Regulation 2(1) of the Information, Evidence and Disclosure and Maintenance Arrangements and Jurisdiction Amendment Regulations 2000.

13. Regulation 6(2)(b)(i) of the Information, Evidence and Disclosure and Maintenance Arrangements and Jurisdiction Amendment Regulations 2000.

14. Regulation 6(2)(b)(ii) of the Information, Evidence and Disclosure and Maintenance Arrangements and Jurisdiction Amendment Regulations 2000.

15. Regulation 6(2)(b)(iii) of the Information, Evidence and Disclosure and Maintenance Arrangements and Jurisdiction Amendment Regulations 2000.

16. Regulation 6(2)(b)(iv) of the Information, Evidence and Disclosure and Maintenance Arrangements and Jurisdiction Amendment Regulations 2000.

17. Regulation 6(2)(b)(v) of the Information, Evidence and Disclosure and Maintenance Arrangements and Jurisdiction Amendment Regulations 2000.

18. Regulation 6(2)(b)(vi) of the Information, Evidence and Disclosure and Maintenance Arrangements and Jurisdiction Amendment Regulations 2000.

19. Regulation 2(2) of the Information, Evidence and Disclosure and Maintenance Arrangements and Jurisdiction Amendment Regulations 2000.

20. Regulation 6(2)(c) of the Information, Evidence and Disclosure and Maintenance Arrangements and Jurisdiction Amendment Regulations 2000.

21. Regulation 2(3) of the Information, Evidence and Disclosure and Maintenance Arrangements and Jurisdiction Amendment Regulations 2000.

DEFINITIONS

"the Act": see reg.1(2).                                                           **3.7**
"parent with care": see reg.1(2).
"related proceedings": see reg.1(2).

GENERAL NOTE

See the general note to reg.2.                                                     **3.8**
Paragraph (1A) is inserted for cases in respect of which s.12 of the 2000 Act is not yet in force. See reg.2(3) of the Child Support (Information, Evidence and Disclosure) Amendment Regulations 2003.

## [¹Contents of request for information or evidence]

[²3A. Any request by the Secretary of State in accordance with regula-    **3.9**
tions 2 and 3 for the provision of information or evidence shall set out the possible consequences of failure to provide such information or evidence] [³including details of the offences provided for in section 14A of the Act for failing to provide, or providing false, information.]

AMENDMENTS

1. Regulation 9 of the Miscellaneous Amendments (No. 2) Regulations 1995 (January 22, 1996).

2. Article 8 of the Commencement No.7 Order 1999 (June 1, 1999).

3. Regulation 6(3) of the Information, Evidence and Disclosure and Maintenance Arrangements and Jurisdiction Amendment Regulations 2000.

Regulation 4 is omitted by virtue of reg.7(1) of the Information, Evidence and Disclosure and Maintenance Arrangements and Jurisdiction Amendment Regulations 2000.

## [¹Time within which information or evidence is to be furnished

5.—(1) Subject to [². . .] the provisions of [⁵regulation 3(4) of the    **3.10**
Maintenance Calculation Procedure Regulations], information or evidence furnished in accordance with regulations 2 and 3 shall be furnished as soon as is reasonably practicable in the particular circumstances of the case.]
[⁴. . .]

AMENDMENTS

1. Regulation 10 of the Miscellaneous Amendments (No.2) Regulation 1995 (January 22, 1996).

2. Article 9(a)(i) of the Commencement No.7 Order 1999 (June 1, 1999).
4. Article 9(b) of the Commencement No.7 Order 1999 (June 1, 1999).
5. Regulation 3(3)(a) of the Information, Evidence and Disclosure and Maintenance Arrangements and Jurisdiction Amendment Regulations 2000.

DEFINITIONS

3.11    "the Act": see reg.1(2).
"Maintenance Calculation Procedure Regulations": see reg.1(2).

## Continuing duty of persons with care

3.12    **6.** Where a person with care with respect to whom a maintenance [²calculation] has been made believes that, by virtue of section 44 or 55 of, or paragraph 16 of Schedule 1 to, the Act, the [²calculation] has ceased to have effect [³. . .], she shall, as soon as is reasonably practicable, inform the Secretary of State of that belief, and of the reasons for it, and shall provide such other information as the Secretary of State may reasonably require, with a view to assisting the Secretary of State [¹. . .] in determining whether the [²calculation] has ceased to have effect [³. . .].

AMENDMENTS

1. Article 10 of the Commencement No.7 Order 1999 (June 1, 1999).
2. Regulation 2(2) of the Information, Evidence and Disclosure and Maintenance Arrangements and Jurisdiction Amendment Regulations 2000.
3. Regulation 7(2) of the Information, Evidence and Disclosure and Maintenance Arrangements and Jurisdiction Amendment Regulations 2000.

DEFINITION

3.13    "the Act": see reg.1(2)

## Powers of inspectors in relation to Crown residences

3.14    **7.** Subject to Her Majesty not being in residence, an inspector appointed under section 15 of the Act may enter any Crown premises for the purpose of exercising any powers conferred on him by that section.

DEFINITION

3.15    "the Act": see reg.1(2).

PART III

DISCLOSURE OF INFORMATION

## Disclosure of information to a court or tribunal

3.16    **8.**[¹—(1)] The Secretary of State [⁴. . .] may disclose any information held by [⁵him] for the purposes of the Act to—
(a) a court;

(b) any tribunal or other body or person mentioned in the Act;
[¹⁰(cc) a person with a right of appeal under the Act to an appeal tribunal,]
[⁶. . .]
where such disclosure is made for the purposes of any proceedings before any of those bodies relating to this Act[², to the benefit Acts or to the Jobseekers Act 1995].

[¹(2) For the purposes of this regulation "proceedings" includes the determination of an application referred to [⁷an] appeal tribunal under section 28D(1)(b) of the Act.]

[³(3) The Secretary of State [⁸. . .] may disclose information held by [⁹him] for the purposes of the Act to a court in any case where—

(a) that court has exercised any power it has to make, vary or revive a maintenance order or to vary a maintenance agreement; and

(b) such disclosure is made for the purposes of any proceedings before that court in relation to that maintenance order or that maintenance agreement or for the purposes of any matters arising out of those proceedings.]

AMENDMENTS

1. Regulation 63 of the Departure Regulations (December 2, 1996).
2. Regulation 33(2) of the Miscellaneous Amendments Regulations 1998 (January 19, 1998).
3. Regulation 33(3) of the Miscellaneous Amendments Regulations 1998 (January 19, 1998).
4. Article 11(a)(i) of the Commencement No.7 Order 1999 (June 1, 1999).
5. Article 11(a)(ii) of the Commencement No.7 Order 1999 (June 1, 1999).
6. Article 11(a)(iii) of the Commencement No.7 Order 1999 (November 29, 1999).
7. Article 11(b) of the Commencement No.7 Order 1999 (June 1, 1999).
8. Article 11(c)(i) of the Commencement No.7 Order 1999 (June 1, 1999).
9. Article 11(c)(ii) of the Commencement No.7 Order 1999 (June 1, 1999).
10. Regulation 3 of the Miscellaneous Amendments Regulations 2004 (September 16, 2004 or on the day on which the amended scheme comes into force for that type of case, whichever is later).

DEFINITION

"the Act": see reg. 1(2).                                                    **3.17**

GENERAL NOTE

*Paragraph 8(b)*
The reference to "person" here is qualified by the later reference to "proceedings     **3.18**
before any of those bodies". Thus, this paragraph permits disclosure to a person but only for the purpose of proceedings before one of the bodies covered.

There is no power to disclose information for the purposes of any other proceedings (*Re C (A Minor) (Child Support Agency: Disclosure)* [1995] 1 F.L.R. 201).

Regulation 9 was revoked by reg.4(3) of the Miscellaneous Amendments     **3.19**
Regulations 1999 with effect from April 6, 1999.

**[¹Disclosure of information to other persons**

3.20      **9A.**—(1) The Secretary of State [⁷. . .] may disclose information [⁶held by him for the purposes of the Act relating to] one party to a maintenance [¹²calculation] to another party to that assessment where, in the opinion of the Secretary of State [⁷. . .], such information is essential to inform the party to whom it would be given as to—

(a) [¹³why he has decided not to make a maintenance calculation in response to an application made under section 4 or 7 of the Act or treated as made under section 6 of the Act], or an application for a [⁸revision under section 16 of the Act or a decision under section 17 of the Act superseding an earlier decision] has been rejected;

(b) why, although an application for a maintenance [¹²calculation] referred to in subparagraph (a) has been accepted, that [¹²calculation] cannot, at the time in question, be proceeded with or why a maintenance [¹²calculation] will not be made following that application;

(c) why a maintenance [¹²calculation] has ceased to have effect [¹⁴. . .] [². . .];

(d) how a maintenance [¹²calculation] has been calculated, in so far as the matter has not been dealt with by the notification given under [¹⁵regulation 23 of the Maintenance Calculation Procedure Regulations];

[³(e) why a decision has been made not to arrange for, or to cease, collection of any child support maintenance under section 29 of the Act;

(f) why a particular method of enforcement, under section 31, 33, 35, 36, 38 or 40 of the Act of an amount due under a maintenance [¹²calculation] has been adopted in a particular case; or

(g) why a decision has been made not to enforce, or to cease to enforce, under section 31 or 33 of the Act an amount due under a maintenance [¹²calculation].]

(2) For the purposes of this regulation, "party to a maintenance [¹²calculation]" means—

(a) a relevant person;

(b) a person appointed by the Secretary of State under regulation [⁹34 of the Social Security and Child Support (Decisions and Appeals) Regulations 1999]:

[⁴(c) the personal representative of a relevant person where—

(i) a [¹⁰revision, supersession] or appeal was pending at the date of death of that person and the personal representative is dealing with that [¹⁰revision, supersession] or appeal on behalf of that person; or

(ii) an application for a departure direction had been made but not determined at the date of death of that person and the personal representative is dealing] [⁵on behalf of that person with any matters arising in connection with the determination of that application.]

(3) Any application for information under this regulation shall be made to the Secretary of State [⁷. . .] in writing setting out the reasons for the application.

(4) Except where a person gives written permission to the Secretary of State [7. . .] that the information in relation to him mentioned in subparagraphs (a) and (b) below may be conveyed to other persons, any information given under the provisions of paragraph (1) shall not contain—

(a) the address of any person other than the recipient of the information in question (other than the address of the office of the [11the officer concerned who is exercising functions of the Secretary of State under the Act]) or any other information the use of which could reasonably be expected to lead to any such person being located;

(b) any other information the use of which could reasonably be expected to lead to any person, other than a qualifying child or a relevant person, being identified.]

AMENDMENTS

1. Regulation 24 of the Amendment Regulations 1995 (April 18, 1995).
2. Regulation 11(2) of the Miscellaneous Amendments (No.2) Regulations 1995 (January 22, 1996).
3. Regulation 11(3) of the Miscellaneous Amendments (No.2) Regulations 1995 (January 22, 1996).
4. Regulation 64 of the Departure Regulations (December 2, 1996).
5. Regulation 34 of the Miscellaneous Amendments Regulations 1998 (January 19, 1998).
6. Regulation 4(4) of the Miscellaneous Amendments Regulations 1999 (April 6, 1999).
7. Article 12(a) of the Commencement No.7 Order 1999 (June 1, 1999).
8. Article 12(b) of the Commencement No.7 Order 1999 (June 1, 1999).
9. Article 12(c)(i) of the Commencement No.7 Order 1999 (June 1, 1999).
10. Article 12(c)(ii) of the Commencement No.7 Order 1999 (June 1, 1999).
11. Article 12(d) of the Commencement No.7 Order 1999 (June 1, 1999).
12. Regulation 2(2) of the Information, Evidence and Disclosure and Maintenance Arrangements and Jurisdiction Amendment Regulations 2000.
13. Regulation 7(3)(a) of the Information, Evidence and Disclosure and Maintenance Arrangements and Jurisdiction Amendment Regulations 2000.
14. Regulation 7(3)(b) of the Information, Evidence and Disclosure and Maintenance Arrangements and Jurisdiction Amendment Regulations 2000.
15. Regulation 3(3)(b) of the Information, Evidence and Disclosure and Maintenance Arrangements and Jurisdiction Amendment Regulations 2000.

DEFINITIONS

"the Act": see reg.1(2).                                                            3.21
"Maintenance Calculation Procedure Regulations": see reg.1(2).
"relevant person": see reg.1(2).

Regulations 10 and 10A are revoked by art.13 of the Commencement No.7        3.22
Order 1999 with effect from June 1, 1999.

## Employment to which section 50 of the Act applies

**11.** For the purposes of section 50 of the Act (unauthorised disclosure        3.23
of information) the following kinds of employment are prescribed in addition to those specified in paragraphs (a) to (e) of section 50(5)—

    (a)  the Comptroller and Auditor General;

    (b)  the Parliamentary Commissioner for Administration

    (c)  the Health Service Commissioner for England;

    (d)  the Health Service Commissioner for Wales;

    (e)  the Health Service Commissioner for Scotland;

    (f)  any member of the staff of the National Audit Office;

    (g)  any other person who carries out the administrative work of that Office, or who provides, or is employed in the provision of, services to it;

    (h)  any officer of any of the Commissioners referred to in paragraphs (b) to (e) above; and

    (i)  any person who provides, or is employed in the provision of, services to the Department of Social Security.

DEFINITION

3.24      "the Act": see reg.1(2).

GENERAL NOTE

The reference to the Department of Social Security in head (i) was not the subject of a specific amendment in the Secretaries of State for Education and Skills and for Work and Pensions Order 2002 and, as child support is not a social security function, it does not come within the general provision in art.9(5).

## The Child Support (Maintenance Assessment Procedure) Regulations 1992

### (SI 1992/1813)

3.25      The Child Support (Maintenance Assessment Procedure) Regulations 1992 were revoked by reg.30 of the Child Support (Maintenance Calculation Procedure) Regulations 2000 but are reproduced as one of the extracts from the original scheme below.

## The Child Support (Maintenance Assessment and Special Cases) Regulations 1992

### (SI 1992/1815)

3.26      The Child Support (Maintenance Assessments and Special Cases) Regulations 1992 were revoked by reg.15 of the Child Support (Maintenance Calculations and Special Cases) Regulations 2000 but are reproduced as one of the extracts from the original scheme below.

# The Child Support (Arrears, Interest and Adjustment of Maintenance Assessments) Regulations 1992

## (SI 1992/1816)

*Made by the Secretary of State for Social Security under sections 41, 51, 52(4) and 54 of the Child Support Act 1991 and all other powers enabling him in that behalf.*

ARRANGEMENT OF REGULATIONS

PART I

*General*

PART II

*Arrears of child support maintenance*

PART III

*Attribution of payments and adjustment of the amount payable under a maintenance calculation*

PART IV

*Miscellaneous*

PART I

GENERAL

## Citation, commencement and interpretation

3.28      **1.**—(1) These Regulations may be cited as the Child Support (Arrears, Interest and Adjustment of Maintenance Assessments) Regulations 1992 and shall come into force on 5th April 1993.

(2) In these Regulations, unless the context otherwise requires—

[1. . .]

"the Act" means the Child Support Act 1991;

"arrears" means arrears of child support maintenance;

"arrears of child support maintenance" is to be construed in accordance with section 41(1) and (2) of the Act;

"arrears notice" has the meaning prescribed in regulation 2;

[2"Maintenance Calculations Procedure Regulations" means the Child Support (Maintenance Calculations Procedure) Regulations 2000;

[1. . .]

[3"non-resident parent" includes a person treated as such under regulation 8 of the Child Support (Maintenance Calculation and Special Cases) Regulations 2000;]

"parent with care" means a person who, in respect of the same child or children, is both a parent and a person with care;

"relevant person" has the same meaning as in the [4Maintenance Calculations Procedure Regulations];

(3) In these Regulations, unless the context otherwise requires, a reference—

(a) to a numbered regulation is to the regulation in these Regulations bearing that number;

(b) in a regulation to a numbered paragraph is to the paragraph in that regulation bearing that number;

(c) in a paragraph to a lettered or numbered sub-paragraph is to the subparagraph in that paragraph bearing that letter or number.

AMENDMENTS

1. Regulation 5(2)(a) of the Collection and Enforcement and Miscellaneous Amendments Regulations 2000 (for in force date see regs 1 and 6 of SI 2001/162 below).

2. Regulation 5(2)(b) of the Collection and Enforcement and Miscellaneous Amendments Regulations 2000 (for in force date see regs 1 and 6 of SI 2001/162 below).

3. Regulation 5(2)(c) of the Collection and Enforcement and Miscellaneous Amendments Regulations 2000 (for in force date see regs 1 and 6 of SI 2001/162 below).

4. Regulation 5(2)(d) of the Collection and Enforcement and Miscellaneous Amendments Regulations 2000 (for in force date see regs 1 and 6 of SI 2001/162 below).

Part II

Arrears of Child Support Maintenance [[1]. . .]

## Applicability of provisions as to arrears [[2]. . .] and arrears notices

**2.**—(1) The provisions of paragraphs (2) to (4) and [[3]regulation 5 and 8] shall apply where—

(a) a case falls within section 41(1) of the Act; and

(b) the Secretary of State is arranging for the collection of child support maintenance under section 29 of the Act.

(2) Where the Secretary of State is considering taking action with regard to a case falling within paragraph (1), he shall serve a notice (an "arrears notice") on the [[5]non-resident parent].

(3) An arrears notice shall—

(a) itemize the payments of child support maintenance due and not paid;

(b) set out in general terms the provisions as to arrears [[4]. . .] contained in this regulation and [[3]regulations 5 and 8]; and

(c) request the [[5]non-resident parent] to make payment of all outstanding arrears.

(4) Where an arrears notice has been served under paragraph (2), no duty to serve a further notice under that paragraph shall arise in relation to further arrears unless those further arrears have arisen after an intervening continuous period of not less than 12 weeks during the course of which all payments of child support maintenance due from the [[5]non-resident parent] have been paid on time in accordance with regulations made under section 29 of the Act.

AMENDMENTS

1. Regulation 5(3)(a) of the Collection and Enforcement and Miscellaneous Amendments Regulations 2000 (for in force date see regs 1 and 6 of SI 2001/162 below).

2. Regulation 5(3)(b)(i) of the Collection and Enforcement and Miscellaneous Amendments Regulations 2000 (for in force date see regs1 and 6 of SI 2001/162 below).

3. Regulation 5(2)(b)(ii) of the Collection and Enforcement and Miscellaneous Amendments Regulations 2000 (for in force date see regs 1 and 6 of SI 2001/162 below).

4. Regulation 5(2)(b)(iii) of the Collection and Enforcement and Miscellaneous Amendments Regulations 2000 (for in force date see regs 1 and 6 of SI 2001/162 below).

5. Regulation 5(2)(b)(iv) of the Collection and Enforcement and Miscellaneous Amendments Regulations 2000 (for in force date see regs 1 and 6 of SI 2001/162 below).

DEFINITIONS

"the Act": see reg.1(2).
"arrears": see reg.1(2).

3.29

3.30

"arrears notice": see reg.1(2).
"non-resident parent": see reg.1(2).

Regulations 3 and 4 are omitted by virtue of regulation 5(3)(e) of the Collection and Enforcement and Miscellaneous Amendments Regulations 2000. For in force date see regs 1 and 6 of SI 2001/162 below.

## Payment of arrears by agreement

3.32    **5.**—[¹(1) The Secretary of State may at any time enter into an agreement with a [²non-resident parent] (an "arrears agreement") for the [²non-resident parent] to pay all outstanding arrears by making payments on agreed dates of agreed amounts.

(2) Where an arrears agreement has been entered into, the Secretary of State shall prepare a schedule of the dates on which payments of arrears shall be made and the amount to be paid on each such date, and shall send a copy of the schedule to such persons as he thinks fit.]

[³. . .]

(5) The Secretary of State may at any time enter into a further arrears agreement with the [²non-resident parent] in relation to all arrears then outstanding.

[³. . .]

(7) It shall be an implied term of any arrears agreement that any payment of child support maintenance that becomes due whilst that agreement is in force shall be made by the due date.

AMENDMENTS

1. Regulation 37 of the Amendment Regulations (April 5, 1993).
2. Regulation 5(3)(c)(i) of the Collection and Enforcement and Miscellaneous Amendments Regulations 2000 (for in force date see regs 1 and 6 of SI 2001/162 below).
3. Regulation 5(3)(c)(ii) of the Collection and Enforcement and Miscellaneous Amendments Regulations 2000 (for in force date see regs 1 and 6 of SI 2001/162 below).

DEFINITIONS

3.33    "arrears": see reg.1(2).
"non-resident parent": reg.1(2).

3.34    Regulations 6 and 7 are omitted by virtue of regulation 5(3)(e) of the Collection and Enforcement and Miscellaneous Amendments Regulations 2000. For in force date see regs 1 and 6 of SI 2001/162 below.

## [¹Retention of recovered arrears of child support maintenance by the Secretary of State

3.35    **8.**—(1) This regulation applies where—
(i) the Secretary of State recovers arrears from a [³non-resident parent] under section 41 of the Act; and

   (ii) income support [²or income-based jobseeker's allowance] is paid to or in respect of the person with care or was paid to or in respect of that person at the date or dates upon which the payment or payments of child support maintenance referred to in paragraph (2) should have been made.

(2) Where paragraph (1) applies, the Secretary of State may retain such amount of those arrears as is equal to the difference between the amount of income support [²or income-based jobseeker's allowance] that was paid to or in respect of the person with care and the amount of income support [²or income-based jobseeker's allowance] that he is satisfied would have been paid had the [³non-resident parent] paid, by the due dates, the amounts due under the child support [⁴maintenance calculation] in force or to be taken to have been in force by virtue of the provisions of section 41(2A) of the Act.]

AMENDMENTS

1. Regulation 2 of the Miscellaneous Amendments (No.2) Regulations 1995 (January 22, 1996).
2. Regulation 3(1) and (2)(b) of the Jobseekers Amendments Regulations (October 7, 1996).
3. Regulation 5(3)(d)(i) of the Collection and Enforcement and Miscellaneous Amendments Regulations 2000 (for in force date see regs 1 and 6 of SI 2001/162 below).
4. Regulation 5(3)(d)(ii) of the Collection and Enforcement and Miscellaneous Amendments Regulations 2000 (for in force date see regs 1 and 6 of SI 2001/162 below).

DEFINITIONS

"the Act".: see reg.1(2).                                   **3.36**
"arrears": see reg.1(2).
"non-resident parent": see reg.1(2).

PART III

ATTRIBUTION OF PAYMENTS AND ADJUSTMENT OF THE AMOUNT PAYABLE UNDER A MAINTENANCE [¹CALCULATION]

## Attribution of payments

**9.** Where a maintenance [²calculation] is or has been in force and there    **3.37** are arrears of child support maintenance, the Secretary of State may attribute any payment of child support maintenance made by a [³non-resident parent] to child support maintenance due as he thinks fit.

AMENDMENTS

1. Regulation 5(4)(a) of the Collection and Enforcement and Miscellaneous Amendments Regulations 2000 (for in force date see regs 1 and 6 of SI 2001/162 below).

2. Regulation 5(4)(b) of the Collection and Enforcement and Miscellaneous Amendments Regulations 2000 (for in force date see regs 1 and 6 of SI 2001/162 below).

3. Regulation 5(4)(c) of the Collection and Enforcement and Miscellaneous Amendments Regulations 2000 (for in force date see regs 1 and 6 of SI 2001/162 below).

DEFINITIONS

3.38  "arrears of child support maintenance": see reg.1(2).
"not-resident parent": see reg.1(2).

GENERAL NOTE

This regulation is part of the legislative mechanism for recovering arrears. It allows any payments made by the non-resident parent to be attributed as the Secretary of State thinks fit. A payment may be attributed wholly towards the non-resident parent's current liability for child support maintenance or towards discharge of arrears or part and part.

## [¹Adjustment of the amount payable under a maintenance [⁴calculation]

3.39  **10.**—(1) Where for any reason, including the retrospective effect of a [⁷. . .] maintenance [⁵calculation], there has been an overpayment of child support maintenance, [²the Secretary of State] may, for the purpose of taking account of that overpayment—

(a) apply the amount overpaid to reduce any arrears of child support maintenance due under any previous maintenance [⁵calculation] made in respect of the same relevant persons; or

(b) where there is no previous relevant maintenance [⁵calculation] or an overpayment remains after the application of subparagraph (a), and subject to paragraph (4), adjust the amount payable under a current maintenance [⁵calculation] by such amount as he considers appropriate in all the circumstances of the case having regard in particular to—

 (i) the circumstances of the [⁶non-resident parent] and the person with care;

 (ii) the amount of the overpayment in relation to the amount due under the current maintenance [⁵calculation]; and

 (iii) the period over which it would be reasonable for the overpayment to be rectified.

[¹¹. . .]

[⁸(3A) Where there has been a voluntary payment, the Secretary of State may—

(a) apply the amount of the voluntary payment to reduce any arrears of child support maintenance due under any previous maintenance calculation made in respect of the same relevant persons; or

(b) where there is no previous relevant maintenance calculation or an amount of the voluntary payment remains after the application of

sub-paragraph (a), and subject to paragraph (4), adjust the amount payable under a current maintenance calculation by such amount as he considers appropriate in all the circumstances of the case having regard in particular to—
  (i) the circumstances of the non-resident parent and the person with care;
  (ii) the amount of the voluntary payment in relation to the amount due under the current maintenance calculation; and
  (iii) the period over which it would be reasonable for the voluntary payment to be taken into account.]

(4) Any adjustment under the provisions of paragraph (1), [⁹(3A) or regulation 15D of the Social Security and Child Support (Decisions and Appeals) Regulations 1999] shall not reduce the amount payable under a maintenance [⁵calculation] to less than [¹⁰an amount equivalent to a flat rate fixed by paragraph 4(1)] of Schedule 1 to the Act.]

AMENDMENTS

1. Regulation 8 of the Amendment Regulations 1995 (April 18, 1995).
2. Article 26(a) of the Commencement No.7 Order 1999 (June 1, 1999).
4. Regulation 5(4)(a) of the Collection and Enforcement and Miscellaneous Amendments Regulations 2000 (for in force date see regs 1 and 6 of SI 2001/162 below).
5. Regulation 5(4)(b) of the Collection and Enforcement and Miscellaneous Amendments Regulations 2000 (for in force date see regs 1 and 6 of SI 2001/162 below).
6. Regulation 5(4)(c) of the Collection and Enforcement and Miscellaneous Amendments Regulations 2000 (for in force date see regs 1 and 6 of SI 2001/162 below).
7. Regulation 5(4)(d)(i) of the Collection and Enforcement and Miscellaneous Amendments Regulations 2000 (for in force date see regs 1 and 6 of SI 2001/162 below).
8. Regulation 5(4)(d)(ii) of the Collection and Enforcement and Miscellaneous Amendments Regulations 2000 (for in force date see regs 1 and 6 of SI 2001/162 below).
9. Regulation 5(4)(d)(iii)(aa) of the Collection and Enforcement and Miscellaneous Amendments Regulations 2000 (for in force date see regs 1 and 6 of SI 2001/162 below).
10. Regulation 5(4)(d)(iii)(bb) of the Collection and Enforcement and Miscellaneous Amendments Regulations 2000 (for in force date see regs 1 and 6 of SI 2001/162 below).
11. Regulation 14(1) of the Appeals Amendment Regulations 2000 (for in force date see regs 1 and 14 of SI 2000/3185 below).

DEFINITIONS

"absent parent": see reg.1(2).                                         **3.40**
"the Act": see reg.1(2).
"arrears of child support maintenance": see reg.1(2).

GENERAL NOTE

This regulation deals with overpayments of child support maintenance.         **3.41**

*Paragraph (1)*

Overpayments may be attributed to discharge of arrears under a previous maintenance calculation: see subpara.(1)(a). If that does not wipe out the overpayment, the Secretary of State may adjust the amount payable under the current maintenance calculation: see subpara.(b). The adjustment is to the amount payable under the calculation. It does not alter the calculation itself.

If a fresh maintenance calculation is made, the adjustment may (a) be continued into the fresh calculation, (b) cease to apply or (c) be itself adjusted: see reg.15D of the Appeals Regulations.

If an adjustment is not possible or appropriate, the Secretary of State may reimburse the non-resident parent under s.41B of the Act.

*Paragraph (2)*

This paragraph has not been amended to reflect the terminology of the amended scheme.

*Paragraph (3A)*

This makes equivalent provision to para.(1) for voluntary payments under s.28J of the Act. See the general note to that paragraph.

## [¹**Reimbursement of a repayment of overpaid child maintenance**

3.42    **10A.**—(1) The Secretary of State may require a relevant person to repay the whole or part of any payment by way of reimbursement made to a [⁴non-resident parent] under section 41B(2) of the Act where the overpayment referred to in section 41B(1) of the Act arose—

  (a) in respect of the amount payable under a maintenance [³calculation] calculated in accordance with Part I of Schedule 1 to the Act and where income support [²or income-based jobseeker's allowance] [⁵. . .] was not in payment to that person at any time during the period in which that overpayment occurred or at the date or dates on which the payment by way of reimbursement was made; or

[⁶. . .]

  (2) In a case falling within section 4 or 7 of the Act, where the circumstances set out in section 41B(6) apply, the Secretary of State may retain out of the child support maintenance collected by him in accordance with section 29 of the Act such sums as cover the amount of any payment by way of reimbursement required by him from the relevant person under section 41B(3) of the Act.]

AMENDMENTS

1. Regulation 3 of the Miscellaneous Amendments (No.2) Regulations (January 22, 1996).

2. Regulation 3(1) and (2)(c) of the Jobseekers Amendment Regulations (October 7, 1996).

3. Regulation 5(4)(b) of the Collection and Enforcement and Miscellaneous Amendments Regulations 2000 (for in force date see regs 1 and 6 of SI 2001/162 below).

4. Regulation 5(4)(c) of the Collection and Enforcement and Miscellaneous Amendments Regulations 2000 (for in force date see regs 1 and 6 of SI 2001/162 below).

5. Regulation 5(4)(e)(i) of the Collection and Enforcement and Miscellaneous Amendments Regulations 2000 (for in force date see regs 1 and 6 of SI 2001/162 below).

6. Regulation 5(4)(e)(ii) of the Collection and Enforcement and Miscellaneous Amendments Regulations 2000 (for in force date see regs 1 and 6 of SI 2001/162 below).

DEFINITIONS

"the Act": see reg.1(2).                                                                    3.43
"Maintenance Calculation Procedure Regulations": see reg.1(2).
"non-resident parent": see reg.1(2).
"relevant person": see reg.1(2).

GENERAL NOTE

The Secretary of State has power under s.41B of the Act to reimburse the non-          3.44
resident parent an overpayment of child support maintenance. This regulation provides for the Secretary of State to recover that amount from the person with care
who would otherwise benefit from the overpayment.

## [¹Repayment of a reimbursement of a voluntary payment

**10B.** The Secretary of State may require a relevant person to repay the             3.45
whole or any part of any payment by way of reimbursement made to a non-
resident parent under section 41B(2) of the Act where
    (a) a voluntary payment was made;
    (b) section 41B(1A) applies;
and income support or income-based jobseeker's allowance was not in payment to that person at any time during the period in which the voluntary
payment was made or at the date or dates on which the payment by way of
reimbursement was made.]

AMENDMENT

1. Regulation 5(4)(f) of the Collection and Enforcement and Miscellaneous
Amendments Regulations 2000 (for in force date see regs 1 and 6 of SI 2001/162
below).

DEFINITIONS

"the Act": see reg.1(2).                                                                    3.46
"non-resident parent": see reg.1(2).
"relevant person": see reg.1(2).

GENERAL NOTE

This regulation makes equivalent provision to reg.10A above. See the general          3.47
note to that regulation.

Regulations 11 to 17 were revoked by reg.14(1) of the Appeals Amendment             3.48–
Regulations 2000 (for in force date see regs 1 and 14 of SI 2000/3185 below).         3.55

# The Child Support (Collection and Enforcement) Regulations 1992

## (SI 1992/1989)

*Made by the Secretary of State for Social Security under sections 29(2) and (3), 31(8), 32(1) to (5) and (7) to (9), 34(1), 35(2), (7) and (8), 39(1), (3) and (4), 40(4), (8) and (11), 51, 52 and 54 of the Child Support Act 1991 and all other powers enabling him in that behalf.*

ARRANGEMENT OF REGULATIONS

### PART I

*General*

### PART II

*Collection of Child Support Maintenance*

### [PART IIA

*Collection of Penalty Payments]*

### PART III

*Deduction From Earnings Orders*

PART IV

*Liability Orders*

SCHEDULES

PART I

GENERAL

## Citation, commencement and interpretation

**1.**—(1) These Regulations may be cited as the Child Support 3.57 (Collection and Enforcement) Regulations 1992 and shall come into force on 5 April 1993.

[¹(2) In these Regulations—

"the Act" means the Child Support Act 1991;

"the 2000 Act" means the Child Support, Pensions and Social Security Act 2000;

"interest" means interest which has become payable under section 41 of the Act before its amendment by the 2000 Act; and

"voluntary payment" means a payment as defined in section 28J of the Act and Regulations made under that section.]

[²(2A) Except in relation to regulation 8(3)(a) and Schedule 2, in these Regulations "fee" means an assessment fee or a collection fee, which for these purposes have the same meaning as in the Child Support Fees Regulations 1992 prior to their revocation by the Child Support (Collection and Enforcement and Miscellaneous Amendments) Regulations 2000.]

(3) Where under any provision of the Act or of these Regulations—

(a) any document or notice is given or sent to the Secretary of State, it shall be treated as having been given or sent on the day it is received by the Secretary of State; and

(b) any document or notice is given or sent to any other person, it shall, if sent by post to that person's last known or notified address, be treated as having been given or sent on [³the day it was posted.]

(4) In these Regulations, unless the context otherwise requires, a reference—

(a) to a numbered Part is to the Part of these Regulations bearing that number;

(b) to a numbered regulation is to the regulation in these Regulations bearing that number;

(c) in a regulation to a numbered or lettered paragraph or subparagraph is to the paragraph or subparagraph in that regulation bearing that number or letter;

(d) in a paragraph to a lettered or numbered subparagraph is to the subparagraph in that paragraph bearing that letter or number;

(e) to a numbered Schedule is to the Schedule to these Regulations bearing that number.

AMENDMENTS

1. Regulation 2(2)(a) of the Collection and Enforcement and Miscellaneous Amendments Regulations 2000 (for in force date see regs 1 and 6 of SI 2001/162 below).

2. Regulation 2(2)(b) of the Collection and Enforcement and Miscellaneous Amendments Regulations 2000 (for in force date see regs 1 and 6 of SI 2001/162 below).

3. Regulation 2(2)(c) of the Collection and Enforcement and Miscellaneous Amendments Regulations 2000 (for in force date see regs 1 and 6 of SI 2001/162 below).

## PART II

### COLLECTION OF CHILD SUPPORT MAINTENANCE

**Payment of child support maintenance**

3.58     **2.**—(1) Where a maintenance [¹calculation] has been made under the Act and the case is one to which section 29 of the Act applies, the Secretary of State may specify that payments of child support maintenance shall be made by the liable person—

(a) to the person caring for the child or children in question or, where an application has been made under section 7 of the Act, to the child who made the application;

(b) to, or through, the Secretary of State; or

(c) to, or through, such other person as the Secretary of State may, from time to time, specify.

(2) In paragraph (1) and in the rest of this Part, "liable person" means a person liable to make payments of child support maintenance.

AMENDMENT

1. Regulation 2(3)(a) of the Collection and Enforcement and Miscellaneous Amendments Regulations 2000 (for in force date see regs 1 and 6 of SI 2001/162 below).

DEFINITION

"the Act": see reg.1(2).                                                        3.59

GENERAL NOTE

This regulation only applies if s.29 of the Act applies. It allows the Secretary of    3.60
State to specify in his notice (see reg.7) that payment shall be to the person caring for the child, the child (in the case of Scotland), or to or through the Secretary
or State or his nominee. The regulation does not refer to the person with care.
Instead it departs from the standard wording of the Act and the regulations made
under it by referring to the person caring for the child or children. In practice this
could be someone other than the person with care, as there could be persons with
part-time care or the care of the child could be temporarily entrusted to someone
other than the person with care. The use of different terminology may justify payments being made to someone who is not the person with care, such as a relative
looking after a child while the person with care is in hospital *(R(CS) 14/98*,
para.18).

## Method of payment

**3.**—(1) Payments of child support maintenance [[1], penalty payments,    3.61
interest and fees] shall be made by the liable person by whichever of the following methods the Secretary of State specifies as being appropriate in the
circumstances—

    (a) by standing order;

    (b) by any other method which requires one person to give his author-
        ity for payments to be made from an account of his to an account
        of another's on specific dates during the period for which the
        authority is in force and without the need for any further authority
        from him;

    (c) by an arrangement whereby one person gives his authority for pay-
        ments to be made from an account of his, or on his behalf, to another
        person or to an account of that other person;

    (d) by cheque or postal order;

    (e) in cash;

  [[2](f) by debit card.]

[[3](1A) In paragraph (1), "debit card" means a card, operating as a substitute for a cheque, that can be used to obtain cash or to make a payment
at a point of sale whereby the card holder's bank or building society
account is debited without deferment of payment.]

(2) The Secretary of State may direct a liable person to take all reasonable steps to open an account from which payments under the maintenance
[[4]calculation] may be made in accordance with the method of payment
specified under paragraph (1).

AMENDMENTS

1. Regulation 2(3)(b)(i) of the Collection and Enforcement and Miscellaneous
Amendments Regulations 2000 (for in force date see regs 1 and 6 of SI 2001/162
below).

2. Regulation 2(3)(b)(ii) of the Collection and Enforcement and Miscellaneous

Amendments Regulations 2000 (for in force date see regs 1 and 6 of SI 2001/162 below).

3. Regulation 2(3)(c) of the Collection and Enforcement and Miscellaneous Amendments Regulations 2000 (for in force date see regs 1 and 6 of SI 2001/162 below).

4. Regulation 2(3)(a) of the Collection and Enforcement and Miscellaneous Amendments Regulations 2000 (for in force date see regs 1 and 6 of SI 2001/162 below).

DEFINITIONS

3.62    "fee": see reg.1(2A).
       "interest": see reg.1(2).
       "liable person": reg.2(2).
       "penalty payment": see reg.7A(5).

GENERAL NOTE

*Paragraph (1)*
3.63    Methods (a) to (c) will be preferred to (d) and (e) since they will operate automatically provided there are sufficient funds in the account.

*Paragraph (2)*
This is a strange provision. It allows the Secretary of State to direct a person to take all reasonable steps to open a suitable account, but it does not operate until the Secretary of State has specified a method of payment under para.(1). However, if the liable person is unable to open a suitable account, the effect of specifying payment from an account will have been to delay the payment of child support maintenance. Perhaps this problem could be avoided by specifying an alternative method until (if at all) an account is opened. It would be better if the power in this paragraph could be employed before payment from an account was specified under para.(1), but this is not what the provision says.

## Interval of payment

3.64    **4.**—(1) The Secretary of State shall specify the day and interval by reference to which payments of child support maintenance are to be made by the liable person and may from time to time vary such day or interval.
       [¹(2) In specifying the day and interval of payment the Secretary of State shall have regard to the following factors—
       (a) the circumstances of the person liable to make the payments and in particular the day upon which and the interval at which any income is payable to that person;
       (b) any preference indicated by that person;
       (c) any period necessary to enable the clearance of cheques or otherwise necessary to enable the transmission of payments to the person entitled to receive them,
       and, subject to those factors, to any other matter which appears to him to be relevant in the particular circumstances of the case.]

AMENDMENT

1. Regulation 12 of the Amendment Regulations 1995 (April 18, 1995).

DEFINITION

"liable person": reg.2(2).    3.65

GENERAL NOTE

*Paragraph (1)*
The Secretary of State has power to vary the interval under reg.5(4).

*Paragraph (2)*
The Secretary of State must take account of all relevant circumstances in fixing    3.66
the day and interval of payments. The thrust of this regulation has been changed.
Whereas originally the Secretary of State was obliged to consider *inter alia* the needs
of the person entitled to receive the payment, the emphasis now is upon the needs
and preference of the payer.

## Transmission of payments

5.—(1) Payments of child support maintenance made through the    3.67
Secretary of State or other specified person shall be transmitted to the
person entitled to receive them in whichever of the following ways the
Secretary of State specifies as being appropriate in the circumstances—
  (a) by a transfer of credit to an account nominated by the person
      entitled to receive the payments;
  (b) by cheque, girocheque or other payable order;
  (c) in cash.
  (2) [¹Subject to paragraph (3), the Secretary of State] shall specify the
interval by reference to which the payments referred to in paragrapah (1)
are to be transmitted to the person entitled to receive them.
  [²(3) Except where the Secretary of State is satisfied in the circumstances of the case that it would cause undue hardship to either the person
liable to make the payments or the person entitled to receive them, the
interval referred to in paragraph (2) shall not differ from the interval
referred to in regulation 4.
  (4) Subject to paragraph (3) and regulation 4(2), the interval referred to
in paragraph (2) and that referred to in regulation 4 may be varied from
time to time by the Secretary of State.]

AMENDMENTS

1. Regulation 13(2) of the Amendment Regulations 1995 (April 18, 1995).
2. Regulation 13(3) of the Amendment Regulations 1995 (April 18, 1995).

GENERAL NOTE

*Paragraph (1)*
The Secretary of State has no power to require the person entitled to receive pay-    3.68
ment to take all reasonable steps to open a bank account. This is in contrast with
his power in relation to a liable person under reg.3(2).

*Paragraph (3)*

This regulation has been changed, presumably to simplify the administration of the collection machinery. The presumption is that the interval between payments will be the same both in respect of the liable person and the recipient. Only where undue hardship would be caused to either of these will the Secretary of State permit the interval to differ. Thus, for example, while it might be more convenient for the recipient to receive payments of child support maintenance weekly, if the liable person is paid monthly and prefers to have his payments collected monthly, the recipient will have to show that she would face undue hardship if she only received the payments monthly.

## [¹Voluntary Payments

3.69    **5A.**—(1) Regulation 5(1) shall apply in relation to voluntary payments as if—

(a) for the words "Payment of child support maintenance" there were substituted the words "Voluntary payments"; and

(b) the words "or other specified person" were omitted.

(2) In determining when the Secretary of State shall transmit a voluntary payment to the person entitled to it, the Secretary of State shall have regard to the factor in regulation 4(2)(c).]

AMENDMENT

1. Regulation 2(3)(d) of the Collection and Enforcement and Miscellaneous Amendments Regulations 2000 (for in force date see regs 1 and 6 of SI 2001/162 below).

DEFINITION

3.70    "voluntary payment": see reg.1(2).

## Representations about payment arrangements

3.71    **6.** The Secretary of State shall, insofar as is reasonably practicable, provide the liable person and the person entitled to receive the payments of child support maintenance with an opportunity to make representations with regard to the matters referred to in regulations 2 to 5 and the Secretary of State shall have regard to those representations in exercising his powers under those regulations.

DEFINITION

3.72    "liable person": reg.2(2).

GENERAL NOTE

3.73    The liable person and the person entitled to receive payment are entitled to an opportunity to make representations on the matters covered by regs 2 to 5, but only in so far as that is reasonably practicable. The person entitled to receive payment under this regulation means the person ultimately entitled to receive payment and not the Secretary of State or his nominee. That this is the meaning of these words is clear from the way in which the same words are used in reg.5(1).

## Notice to liable person as to requirements about payment

7.—(1) [¹In the case of child support maintenance,] the Secretary of     3.74
State shall send the liable person a notice stating—
  (a)  the amount of child support maintenance payable;
  (b)  to whom it is to be paid;
  (c)  the method of payment; and
  (d)  the day and interval by reference to which payments are to be
       made;
[²(e)  the amount of any payment of child support maintenance which is
       overdue and which remains outstanding.]
  [³(1A)  In the case of penalty payments, interest or fees, the Secretary of
State shall send the liable person a notice stating—
  (a)  the amount of child support maintenance payable;
  (b)  the amount of arrears;
  (c)  the amount of the penalty payment, interest or fees to be paid, as the
       case may be;
  (d)  the method of payment;
  (e)  the day by which payment is to be made; and
  (f)  information as to the provisions of sections 16 and 20 of the Act.]
  (2)  A notice under paragraph (1) shall be sent to the liable person as
soon as is reasonably practicable after—
  (a)  the making of a maintenance [⁴calculation] and
  (b)  after any change in the requirements referred to in any previous such
       notice.
  [⁵(3)  A notice under paragraph (1A) shall be sent to the liable person as
soon as reasonably practicable after the decision to require a payment of
the penalty payment, interest or fees has been made.]

AMENDMENTS

  1. Regulation 2(3)(e)(i)(aa) of the Collection and Enforcement and
Miscellaneous Amendments Regulations 2000 (for in force date see regs 1 and 6 of
SI 2001/162 below).
  2. Regulation 2(3)(e)(i)(bb) of the Collection and Enforcement and
Miscellaneous Amendments Regulations 2000 (for in force date see regs 1 and 6 of
SI 2001/162 below).
  3. Regulation 2(3)(e)(ii) of the Collection and Enforcement and Miscellaneous
Amendments Regulations 2000 (for in force date see regs 1 and 6 of SI 2001/162
below).
  4. Regulation 2(3)(a) of the Collection and Enforcement and Miscellaneous
Amendments Regulations 2000 (for in force date see regs 1 and 6 of SI 2001/162
below).
  5. Regulation 2(3)(e)(iii) of the Collection and Enforcement and Miscellaneous
Amendments Regulations 2000 (for in force date see regs 1 and 6 of SI 2001/162
below).

DEFINITIONS

  "fee": see reg.1(2A).     3.75
  "interest": see reg.1(2).
  "liable person": see reg.2(2).
  "penalty payment": see reg.7A(5).

[¹PART IIA

COLLECTION OF PENALTY PAYMENTS

**Payment of a financial penalty**

3.76    **7A.**—(1) This regulation applies where a maintenance calculation is, or has been, in force, the liable person is in arrears with payments of child support maintenance, and the Secretary of State requires the liable person to pay penalty payments to him.

(2) For the purposes of regulation 7(1)(e) a payment will be overdue if it is not received by the time that the next payment of child support maintenance is due.

(3) The Secretary of State may require a penalty payment to be made if the outstanding amount is not received within 7 days of the notification in regulation 7(1)(e) or if the liable person fails to pay all outstanding amounts due on dates and of amounts as agreed between the liable person and the Secretary of State.

(4) Payments of a penalty payment shall be made within 14 days of the notification referred to in regulation 7(1A).

(5) In this Part a "liable person" means a person liable to make a penalty payment and in Part II and in this Part "penalty payment" is to be construed in accordance with section 41A of the Act.]

AMENDMENT

1. Regulation 2(4) of the Collection and Enforcement and Miscellaneous Amendments Regulations 2000 (for in force date see regs 1 and 6 of SI 2001/162 below).

PART III

DEDUCTION FROM EARNINGS ORDERS

**Interpretation of this Part**

3.77    **8.**—(1) For the purposes of this Part—
[²"defective" means in relation to a deduction from earnings order that it does not comply with the requirements of regulations 9 to 11 and such failure to comply has made it impracticable for the employer to comply with his obligations under the Act and these Regulations;]
[⁸. . .]
"earnings" shall be construed in accordance with paragraphs (3) and (4);
[⁸. . .]
"net earnings" shall be construed in accordance with paragraph (5);
    "normal deduction rate" means the rate specified in a deduction from earnings order (expressed as a sum of money per week, month or other period) at which deductions are to be made from the liable person's net earnings;

"pay-day" in relation to a liable person means an occasion on which earnings are paid to him or the day on which such earnings would normally fall to be paid;

[⁸. . .]

[⁹"protected earnings proportion" means the proportion referred to in regulation 11(2).]

(2) For the purposes of this Part the relationship of employer and employee shall be treated as subsisting between two persons if one of them, as a principal and not as a servant or agent, pays to the other any sum defined as earnings under paragraph (1) and "employment", "employer" and "employee" shall be construed accordingly.

(3) Subject to paragraph (4), "earnings" are any sums payable to a person—

(a) by way of wages or salary (including any fees, bonus, commission, overtime pay or other emoluments payable in addition to wages or salary or payable under a contract of service);

(b) by way of pension (including an annuity in respect of past service, whether or not rendered to the person paying the annuity, and including periodical payments by way of compensation for the loss, abolition or relinquishment, or diminution in the emoluments, of any office or employment);

(c) by way of statutory sick pay.

(4) "Earnings" shall not include—

(a) sums payable by any public department of the Government of Northern Ireland or of a territory outside the United Kingdom;

(b) pay or allowances payable to the liable person as a member of Her Majesty's forces [⁷other than pay or allowances payable by his employer to him as a special member of a reserve force (within the meaning of the Reserve Forces Act 1996)];

(c) pension, allowances or benefit payable under any enactment relating to social security;

(d) pension or allowances payable in respect of disablement or disability;

(e) guaranteed minimum pension within the meaning of the Social Security Pensions Act 1975;

[¹⁰(f) working tax credit payable under section 10 of the Tax Credits Act 2002.]

(5) "Net earnings" means the residue of earnings after deduction of—

(a) income tax;

(b) primary class I contributions under Part I of the Contributions and Benefits Act 1992;

(c) amounts deductible by way of contributions to a superannuation scheme which provides for the payment of annuities or [¹lump] sums—

  (i) to the employee on his retirement at a specified age or on becoming incapacitated at some earlier age; or

  (ii) on his death or otherwise, to his personal representative, widow, relatives or dependants.

AMENDMENTS

1. Regulation 41 of the Amendment Regulations (April 5, 1993).

2. Regulation 14(2) of the Amendment Regulations 1995 (April 18, 1995).

7. Regulation 2(2) of the Miscellaneous Amendments Regulations 1999 (April 6, 1999).

8. Regulation 2(5)(a)(i) of the Collection and Enforcement and Miscellaneous Amendments Regulations 2000 (for in force date see regs 1 and 6 of SI 2001/162 below).

9. Regulation 2(5)(a)(ii) of the Collection and Enforcement and Miscellaneous Amendments Regulations 2000 (for in force date see regs 1 and 6 of SI 2001/162 below).

10. Regulation 2 of the Miscellaneous Amendments Regulations 2003 (April 6, 2003).

## Deduction from earnings order

3.78

**9.**—A deduction from earnings order shall specify—

(a) the name and address of the liable person;

(b) the name of the employer at whom it is directed;

(c) where known, the liable person's place of work, the nature of his work and any works or pay number;

[²(cc) where known, the liable person's national insurance number;]

[¹(d) the normal deduction rate or rates and the date upon which each is to take effect;

(e) the [³protected earnings proportion];]

(f) the address to which amounts deducted from earnings are to be sent.

AMENDMENTS

1. Regulation 15 of the Amendment Regulations 1995 (April 18, 1995).

2. Regulation 6 of the Miscellaneous Amendments (No.2) Regulations 1995 (January 22, 1996)

3. Regulation 2(5)(b) of the Collection and Enforcement and Miscellaneous Amendments Regulations 2000 (for in force date see regs 1 and 6 of SI 2001/162 below).

DEFINITIONS

3.79

"earnings": see reg.8(1), (3) and (4).

"employer": see reg.8(2).

"normal deduction rate": see reg.8(1).

"protected earnings proportion": see reg.8(1).

## Normal deduction rate

3.80

**10.**—(1) The period by reference to which [¹a normal deduction rate] is set shall be the period by reference to which the liable person's earnings are normally paid or, if none, such other period as the Secretary of State may specify.

[². . .]

AMENDMENTS

1. Regulation 16(2) of the Amendment Regulations 1995 (April 18, 1995).
2. Regulation 2(5)(c) of the Collection and Enforcement and Miscellaneous Amendments Regulations 2000 (for in force date see regs 1 and 6 of SI 2001/162 below).

DEFINITIONS

"the Act": see reg.1(2).  **3.81**
"normal deduction rate": see reg.8(1).

## [¹Protected earnings proportion]

**11.**—(1) The period by reference to which the [²protected earnings  **3.82** proportion] is set shall be the same as the period by reference to which the normal deduction rate is set under regulation 10(1).

(2) The amount to be specified as the [²protected earnings proportion] in respect of any period shall [³. . .] be an amount equal to [⁴60% of the liable person's net earnings] in respect of that period as calculated at the date of the current [⁵maintenance calculation].

[⁶. . .]

AMENDMENTS

1. Regulation 2(5)(d)(i) of the Collection and Enforcement and Miscellaneous Amendments Regulations 2000 (for in force date see regs 1 and 6 of SI 2001/162 below).
2. Regulation 2(5)(d)(ii) of the Collection and Enforcement and Miscellaneous Amendments Regulations 2000 (for in force date see regs 1 and 6 of SI 2001/162 below).
3. Regulation 2(5)(d)(iii)(aa) of the Collection and Enforcement and Miscellaneous Amendments Regulations 2000 (for in force date see regs 1 and 6 of SI 2001/162 below).
4. Regulation 2(5)(d)(iii)(bb) of the Collection and Enforcement and Miscellaneous Amendments Regulations 2000 (for in force date see regs 1 and 6 of SI 2001/162 below).
5. Regulation 2(5)(d)(iii)(cc) of the Collection and Enforcement and Miscellaneous Amendments Regulations 2000 (for in force date see regs 1 and 6 of SI 2001/162 below).
6. Regulation 2(5)(d)(iv) of the Collection and Enforcement and Miscellaneous Amendments Regulations 2000 (for in force date see regs 1 and 6 of SI 2001/162 below).

DEFINITIONS

"normal deduction rate": see reg.8(1).  **3.83**
"protected earnings proportion": see reg.8(1).

## Amount to be deducted by employer

**12.**—(1) Subject to the provisions of this regulation, an employer who  **3.84** has been served with a copy of a deduction from earnings order in respect of a liable person in his employment shall, each pay-day, make a deduction from the net earnings of that liable person of an amount equal to the normal deduction rate.

(2) Where the deduction of the normal deduction rate would reduce the liable person's net earnings below the [²protected earnings proportion] the employer shall deduct only such amount as will leave the liable person with net earnings equal to the protected earnings rate.

(3) Where the liable person receives a payment of earnings at an interval greater or lesser than the interval specified in relation to the normal deduction rate and the [²protected earnings proportion] ("the specified interval") the employer shall, for the purpose of such payments, take as the normal deduction rate and the [²protected earnings proportion] such amounts (to the nearest whole penny) as are in the same proportion to the interval since the last pay-day as the normal deduction rate and the [²protected earnings proportion] bear to the specified interval.

[¹(3A) Where on any pay-day the liable person receives a payment of earnings covering a period longer than the period by reference to which the normal deduction rate is set, the employer shall, subject to paragraph (2), make a deduction from the net earnings paid to that liable person on that pay-day of an amount which is in the same proportion to the normal deduction rate as that longer period is to the period by reference to which that normal deduction rate is set.]

(4) Where, on any pay-day, the employer fails to deduct an amount due under the deduction from earnings order or deducts an amount less than the amount of the normal deduction rate the shortfall shall, subject to the operation of paragraph (2), be deducted in addition to the normal deduction rate at the next available pay-day or days.

[³. . .]

(6) Where, on any pay-day, an employer makes a deduction from the earnings of a liable person in accordance with the deduction from earnings order he may also deduct an amount not exceeding £1 in respect of his administrative costs and such deduction for administrative costs may be made notwithstanding that it may reduce the liable person's net earnings below the [²protected earnings proportion].

AMENDMENTS

1. Regulation 6 of the Miscellaneous Amendments Regulations 1998 (January 19, 1998).
2. Regulation 2(5)(e)(i) of the Collection and Enforcement and Miscellaneous Amendments Regulations 2000 (for in force date see regs 1 and 6 of SI 2001/162 below).
3. Regulation 2(5)(e)(ii) of the Collection and Enforcement and Miscellaneous Amendments Regulations 2000 (for in force date see regs 1 and 6 of SI 2001/162 below).

DEFINITIONS

3.85    "earnings": see reg.8(1), (3) and (4).
"employer": see reg.8(2).
"employment": see reg.8(2).

"net earnings": see reg.8(1).
"normal deduction rate": see reg.8(1)
"pay-day": see reg.8(1).
"protected earnings proportion": see reg.8(1).

## Employer to notify liable person of deduction

**13.**—(1) An employer making a deduction from earnings for the pur-   3.86
pose of this Part shall notify the liable person in writing of the amount of
the deduction, including any amount deducted for administrative costs
under regulation 12(6).

(2) Such notification shall be given not later than the pay-day on which
the deduction is made or, where that is impracticable, not later than the
following pay-day.

DEFINITIONS

"employer": see reg.8(2).   3.87
"pay-day": see reg.8(1).

## Payment by employer to Secretary of State

**14.**—(1) Amounts deducted by an employer under a deduction from   3.88
earnings order (other than any administrative costs deducted under regulation 12(6)) shall be paid to the Secretary of State by the 19th day of the
month following the month in which the deduction is made.

(2) Such payment may be made—
(a) by cheque;
(b) by automated credit transfer; or
(c) by such other method as the Secretary of State may specify.

DEFINITION

"employer": see reg.8(2).   3.89

## Information to be provided by liable person

**15.**—(1) The Secretary of State may, in relation to the making or oper-   3.90
ation of a deduction earnings order, require the liable person to provide the
following details—
(a) the name and address of his employer;
(b) the amount of his earnings and anticipated earnings;
(c) his place of work, the nature of his work and any works or pay
    number;
and it shall be the duty of the liable person to comply with any such
requirement within 7 days of being given written notice to that effect.

(2) A liable person in respect of whom a deduction from earnings order
is in force shall notify the Secretary of State in writing within 7 days of
every occasion on which he leaves employment or becomes employed or
re-employed.

**3.91**   "employer": see reg.8(2).
"employment": see reg.8(2).

GENERAL NOTE

*Paragraph 1(a)*

**3.92**   The employer's address need not necessarily be the address of the office which is responsible for paying the liable person and therefore for administering the deduction from earnings order.

## Duty of employers and others to notify Secretary of State

**3.93**   **16.**—(1) Where a deduction from earnings order is served on a person on the assumption that he is the employer of a liable person but the liable person to whom the order relates is not in his employment, the person on whom the order was served shall notify the Secretary of State of that fact in writing, at the address specified in the order, within 10 days of the date of service on him of the order.

(2) Where an employer is required to operate a deduction from earnings order and the liable person to whom the order relates ceases to be in his employment the employer shall notify the Secretary of State of that fact in writing, at the address specified in the order, within 10 days of the liable person ceasing to be in his employment.

(3) Where an employer becomes aware that a deduction from earnings order is in force in relation to a person who is an employee of his he shall, within 7 days of the date on which he becomes aware, notify the Secretary of State of that fact in writing at the address specified in the order.

DEFINITIONS

**3.94**   "employer": see reg.8(2).
"employment": see reg.8(2)

## [¹Requirement to review deduction from earnings orders

**3.95**   **17.**—(1) Subject to paragraph (2), the Secretary of State shall review a deduction from earnings order in the following circumstances—
  (a) where there is a change in the amount of the maintenance [²calculation];
  (b) where any arrears [³, penalty payment, interest or fees] payable under the order are paid off.

(2) There shall be no obligation to review a deduction from earnings order under paragraph (1) where the normal deduction rates specified in the order take account of the changes which will arise as a result of the circumstances specified in subparagraph (a) or (b) of that paragraph.]

AMENDMENTS

  1. Regulation 18 of the Amendment Regulations 1995 (April 18, 1995).
  2. Regulation 2(5)(f)(i) of the Collection and Enforcement and Miscellaneous

Amendments Regulations 2000 (for in force date see regs 1 and 6 of SI 2001/162 below).

3. Regulation 2(5)(f)(ii) of the Collection and Enforcement and Miscellaneous Amendments Regulations 2000 (for in force date see regs 1 and 6 of SI 2001/162 below).

DEFINITION

"normal deduction rate": see reg.8(1).                                             **3.96**

## Power to vary deduction from earnings orders

**18.**—(1) The Secretary of State may (whether on a review under     **3.97**
regulation 17 or otherwise) vary a deduction from earnings order so as to—
  (a) include any amount which may be included in such an order or
      exclude or decrease any such amount;
  (b) substitute a subsequent employer for the employer at whom the
      order was previously directed.

(2) The Secretary of State shall serve a copy of any deduction from
earnings order, as varied, on the liable person's employer and on the liable
person.

DEFINITION

"employer": see reg.8(2).                                                          **3.98**

## Compliance with deduction from earnings order as varied

**19.**—(1) Where a deduction from earnings order has been varied and a    **3.99**
copy of the order as varied has been served on the liable person's employer it shall, subject to paragraph (2), be the duty of the employer to comply
with the order as varied.

(2) The employer shall not be under any liability for non-compliance
with the order, as varied, before the end of the period of 7 days beginning with the date on which a copy of the order, as varied, was served
on him.

DEFINITION

"employer": see reg.8(2).                                                          **3.100**

## Discharge of deduction from earnings orders

**20.**—[¹(1) The Secretary of State may discharge a deduction from
earnings order where it appears to him that—
  (a) no further payments are due under it;
  (b) the order is ineffective or some other way of securing that payments
      are made would be more effective;
  (c) the order is defective;
  (d) the order fails to comply in a material respect with any procedural
      provision of the Act or regulations made under it other than
      provision made in regulation 9, 10 or 11;

(e) at the time of the making of the order he did not have, or subsequently ceased to have, jurisdiction to make a deduction from earnings order; or

(f) in the case of an order made at a time when there is in force [²a default or interim maintenance decision], it is inappropriate to continue deductions under the order having regard to the compliance or the attempted compliance with the [³maintenance calculation] by the liable person.]

(2) The Secretary of State shall give written notice of the discharge of the deduction from earnings order to the liable person and to the liable person's employer.

AMENDMENTS

1. Regulation 19 of the Amendment Regulations 1995 (April 18, 1995).
2. Regulation 2(5)(g)(i) of the Collection and Enforcement and Miscellaneous Amendments Regulations 2000 (for in force date see regs 1 and 6 of SI 2001/162 below).
3. Regulation 2(5)(g)(ii) of the Collection and Enforcement and Miscellaneous Amendments Regulations 2000 (for in force date see regs 1 and 6 of SI 2001/162 below).

DEFINITIONS

**3.101**　　"the Act": see reg.1(2).
　　　　　　"defective": see reg.8(1).
　　　　　　"employer": see reg.8(2).

GENERAL NOTE

*Paragraphs (1)(c) and (d)*
**3.102**　　"Defective" is defined in reg.8(1) as meaning an order which does not comply with the requirements of regs 9 to 11 resulting in its being impracticable for the employer to comply with his obligations under the Act and regulations. This regulation enables the Secretary of State to discharge such an order. He may also discharge the order for any other failure of compliance with the Act or regulations. It is difficult to see why such failures are not deemed to make the order "defective" as such, especially since an appeal to the magistrates under reg.22 may only be made in respect of a "defective" order, *i.e.* one defective within reg.8(1).

## Lapse of deduction from earnings orders

**3.103**　　**21.**—(1) A deduction from earnings order shall lapse (except in relation to any deductions made or to be made in respect of the employment not yet paid to the Secretary of State) where the employer at whom it is directed ceases to have the liable person in his employment.

(2) The order shall lapse from the pay-day coinciding with, or, if none, the pay-day following, the termination of the employment.

(3) A deduction from earnings order which has lapsed under this regulation shall nonetheless be treated as remaining in force for the purposes of regulations 15 and 24.

(4) Where a deduction from earnings order has lapsed under paragraph (1) and the liable person recommences employment (whether with the same or another employer), the order may be revived from such date as may be specified by the Secretary of State.

(5) Where a deduction from earnings order is revived under paragraph (4), the Secretary of State shall give written notice of that fact to, and serve a copy of the notice on, the liable person and the liable person's employer.

(6) Where an order is revived under paragraph (4), no amount shall be carried forward under regulation 12(4) [2. . .] from a time prior to the revival of the order.

AMENDMENT

1. Regulation 2(5)(h) of the Collection and Enforcement and Miscellaneous Amendments Regulations 2000 (for in force date see regs 1 and 6 of SI 2001/162 below).

DEFINITIONS

"employer": see reg.8(2).                                                    3.104
"employment": see reg.8(2).
"pay-day": see reg.8(1).

## Appeals against deduction from earnings orders

**22.**—(1) A liable person in respect of whom a deduction from earnings       3.105
order has been made may appeal to the magistrates' court, or in Scotland
the sheriff, having jurisdiction in the area in which he resides.

(2) Any appeal shall—
(a) be by way of complaint for an order or, in Scotland, by way of applications;
(b) be made within 28 days of the date on which the matter appealed against arose.

(3) An appeal may be made only on one or both of the following grounds—
(a) that the deduction from earnings order is defective;
(b) that the payments in question do not constitute earnings.

(4) Where the court or, as the case may be, the sheriff is satisfied that the appeal should be allowed the court, or sheriff, may—
(a) quash the deduction from earnings order; or
(b) specify which, if any, of the payments in question do not constitute earnings.

DEFINITION

"defective": see reg.8(1).                                                    3.106
"earnings": see reg.8(1), (3) and (4).

GENERAL NOTE

*Paragraph (2)*
The appeal must be made within 28 days of the making of the deduction from    3.107
earnings order and not from a subsequent date at which point the liability to pay

the assessment might have ended, for example, when the qualifying child ceased to be such because he went to live with the liable person (*Secretary of State for Social Security v Shotton and Others* [1996] 2 F.L.R. 241).

*Paragraph (3)*
Magistrates, in deciding whether an order is defective, are limited to considering the matters referred to in regs 9 to 11 above and may not rule on the validity of the assessment itself (*Shotton*, above).

*Paragraph (4)*
An alleged failure to consider the welfare of any child affected, under s.2 of the Act, is not a ground for allowing an appeal against a deduction from earnings order (*R. v Secretary of State for Social Security Ex p. Biggin* [1995] 1 F.L.R. 851).

A magistrates' court made an order that a deduction of earnings order cease until a decision of a tribunal as to whether the child support officer had incorrectly taken into account monies of the absent parent which did not constitute earnings (*Bailey v Secretary of State*, (unreported, Lincoln District Magistrates' Court, October 6, 1993). It is open to question whether such an order is within the court's powers, given the terms of subs. (4), which seem to give the court only three options: to dismiss the complaint; to quash the deduction from earnings order; or itself to decide and specify which payments do not constitute earnings.

Magistrates have no power to order the repayment of monies paid under a defective deduction from earnings order (*Shotton*, above). However, overpayments may be reimbursed under s.41B of the Act (see above), or through an adjustment to the maintenance assessment (see reg.10 of the Arrears, Interest and Adjustment of Maintenance Regulations).

## Crown employment

3.108
**23.** Where a liable person is in the employment of the Crown and a deduction from earnings order is made in respect of him then for the purposes of this Part—
   (a) the chief officer for the time being of the Department, office or other body in which the liable person is employed shall be treated as having the liable person in his employment (any transfer of the liable person from one Department, office or body to another being treated as a change of employment); and
   (b) any earnings paid by the Crown or a minister of the Crown, or out of the public revenue of the United Kingdom, shall be treated as paid by that chief officer.

DEFINITIONS

3.109
"earnings": see reg.8(1), (3) and (4).
"employment": see reg.8(2).

## Priority as between orders

3.110
**24.**—(1) [². . .]
(2) Where an employer would, but for this paragraph, be obliged to comply with [⁴a deduction from earnings order] and one or more attachment of earnings orders he shall—
   (a) in the case of an attachment of earnings order which was made either wholly or in part in respect of the payment of a judgment debt or

payments under an administration order, deal first with the deduction from earnings order [³. . .] and thereafter with the attachment of earnings order as if the earnings to which it relates were the residue of the liable person's earnings after the making of deductions to comply with the deduction from earnings order [⁵. . .];

(b) in the case of any other attachment of earnings order, [³he shall—

    (i)  deal with the orders according to the respective dates on which they were made, disregarding any later order until an earlier one has been dealt with;

    (ii)  deal with any later order as if the earnings to which it relates were the residue of the liable person's earnings after the making of any deduction to comply with any earlier order.]

"Attachment of earnings order" in this paragraph means an order made under the Attachment of Earnings Act 1971 or under regulation 32 of the Community Charge (Administration and Enforcement) Regulations 1989 [1or under regulation 37 of the Council Tax (Administration and Enforcement) Regulations 1992].

(3) Paragraph (2) does not apply to Scotland.

(4) In Scotland, where an employer would, but for this paragraph, be obliged to comply with [⁴a deduction from earnings order] and one or more diligences against earnings he shall deal first with the deduction from earnings order [⁵. . .] and thereafter with the diligence against earnings as if the earnings to which the diligence relates were the residue of the liable person's earnings after the making of deductions to comply with the deduction from earnings order [⁵. . .].

AMENDMENTS

1. Regulation 42 of the Amendment Regulations (April 5, 1993).

2. Regulation 2(5)(i)(i) of the Collection and Enforcement and Miscellaneous Amendments Regulations 2000 (for in force date see regs 1 and 6 of SI 2001/162 below).

3. Regulation 2(5)(i)(ii) of the Collection and Enforcement and Miscellaneous Amendments Regulations 2000 (for in force date see regs 1 and 6 of SI 2001/162 below).

4. Regulation 2(5)(i)(iii)(aa) of the Collection and Enforcement and Miscellaneous Amendments Regulations 2000 (for in force date see regs 1 and 6 of SI 2001/162 below).

5. Regulation 2(5)(i)(iii)(bb) of the Collection and Enforcement and Miscellaneous Amendments Regulations 2000 (for in force date see regs 1 and 6 of SI 2001/162 below).

DEFINITIONS

"earnings": see reg.8(1), (3) and (4).     **3.111**
"employer": see reg.8(2).
"pay-day": see reg.8(1).

## Offences

**25.** The following regulations are designated for the purposes of section 32(8) of the Act (offences relating to deduction from earnings orders)—   **3.112**

[1(aa)  regulation 14(1);]
[2(ab)]  regulation 15(1) and (2);
  (b)  regulation 16(1), (2) and (3);
  (c)  regulation 19(1).

AMENDMENTS

1. Regulation 2(3)(a) of the Miscellaneous Amendments Regulations 1999 (April 6, 1999).
2. Regulation 2(3)(b) of the Miscellaneous Amendments Regulations 1999 (April 6, 1999).

## PART IV

### LIABILITY ORDERS

**Extent of this Part**

3.113    **26.** This Part, except regulation 29(2), does not apply to Scotland.

**Notice of intention to apply for a liability order**

3.114    **27.**—(1) The Secretary of State shall give the liable person at least 7 days notice of his intention to apply for a liability order under section 33(2) of the Act.

(2) Such notice shall set out the amount of child support maintenance which it is claimed has become payable by the liable person and has not been paid and the amount of any interest [1, penalty payments or fees which have become payable and have not been paid].

(3) Payment by the liable person of any part of the amounts referred to in paragraph (2) shall not require the giving of a further notice under paragraph (1) prior to the making of the application.

AMENDMENT

1. Regulation 2(6)(a) of the Collection and Enforcement and Miscellaneous Amendments Regulations 2000 (for in force date see regs 1 and 6 of SI 2001/162 below).

**Application for a liability order**

3.115    **28.**—(1) An application for a liability order shall be by way of complaint for an order to the magistrates' court having jurisdiction in the area in which the liable person resides.

(2) An application under paragraph (1) may not be instituted more than 6 years after the day on which payment of the amount in question became due.

(3) A warrant shall not be issued under section 55(2) of the Magistrates' Courts Act 1980 in any proceedings under this regulation.

GENERAL NOTE

*Paragraph (2)*

Payment of child support maintenance does not become due for the purposes of this paragraph until an assessment has been made (*R (ota Sutherland) v Secretary of State for Work and Pensions* [2004] EWHC 800 (Admin), paras 26–31). The 6 year period applies to the exclusion of the provisions under the Limitation Act 1980 (*ibid.*, para. 17).

## Liability orders

**29.**—(1) A liability order shall be made in the form prescribed in Schedule 1.

3.116

(2) A liability order made by a court in England or Wales or any corresponding order made by a court in Northern Ireland may be enforced in Scotland as if it had been made by the sheriff.

(3) A liability order made by the sheriff in Scotland or any corresponding order made by a court in Northern Ireland may, subject to paragraph (4), be enforced in England and Wales as if it had been made by a magistrates' court in England and Wales.

(4) A liability order made by the sheriff in Scotland or a corresponding order made by a court in Northern Ireland shall not be enforced in England or Wales unless registered in accordance with the provision of [¹Part II] of the Maintenance Orders Act 1950 and for this purpose—

  (a) a liability order made by the sheriff in Scotland shall be treated as if it were a decree to which section 16(2)(b) of that Act applies (decree for payment of aliment);

  (b) a corresponding order made by a court in Northern Ireland shall be treated as if it were an order to which section 16(2)(c) of that Act applies (order for alimony, maintenance or other payments).

AMENDMENT

1. Regulation 43 of the Amendment Regulations (April 5, 1993).

## Enforcement of liability orders by distress

**30.**—(1) A distress made pursuant to section 35(1) of the Act may be made anywhere in England and Wales.

3.117

(2) The person levying distress on behalf of the Secretary of State shall carry with him the written authorisation of the Secretary of State, which he shall show to the liable person if so requested, and he shall hand to the liable person or leave at the premises where the distress is levied—

  (a) copies of this regulation, regulation 31 and Schedule 2;

  (b) a memorandum setting out the amount which is the appropriate amount for the purposes of section 35(2) of the Act;

  (c) a memorandum setting out details of any arrangement entered into regarding the taking of possession of the goods distrained; and

(d) a notice setting out the liable person's rights of appeal under regulation 31 giving the Secretary of State's address for the purposes of any appeal.

(3) A distress shall not be deemed unlawful on account of any defect or want of form in the liability order.

(4) If, before any goods are seized, the appropriate amount (including charges arising up to the time of the payment or tender) is paid or tendered to the Secretary of State, the Secretary of State shall accept the amount and the levy shall not be proceeded with.

(5) Where the Secretary of State has seized goods of the liable person in pursuance of the distress, but before sale of those goods the appropriate amount (including charges arising up to the time of the payment or tender) is paid or tendered to the Secretary of State, the Secretary of State shall accept the amount, the sale shall not be proceeded with and the goods shall be made available for collection by the liable person.

GENERAL NOTE

*Paragraph (3)*

3.118     In *Evans v South Ribble Borough Council* [1992] 2 All E.R. 695, a case concerning unpaid community charge, a bailiff, finding no one at the debtor's home, put a notice of distress in a sealed envelope through the debtor's door. The Queen's Bench Divisional Court ruled that the bailiff had not effected a lawful distress. Regulation 30(3) provides that a distress shall not be deemed unlawful on account of any defect or want of form in the liability order, but query if it would be regarded as "irregular" and thus open to complaint under reg.31(3) below.

## Appeals in connection with distress

3.119     **31.**—(1) A person aggrieved by the levy of, or an attempt to levy, a distress may appeal to the magistrates' court having jurisdiction in the area in which he resides.

(2) The appeal shall be by way of complaint for an order.

(3) If the court is satisfied that the levy was irregular, it may—

(a) order the goods distrained to be discharged if they are in the possession of the Secretary of State;

(b) order an award of compensation in respect of any goods distrained and sold of an amount equal to the amount which, in the opinion of the court, would be awarded by way of special damages in respect of the goods if proceedings under section 35(6) of the Act were brought in trespass or otherwise in connection with the irregularity.

(4) If the court is satisfied that an attempted levy was irregular, it may by order require the Secretary of State to desist from levying in the manner giving rise to the irregularity.

GENERAL NOTE

*Paragraph (1)*

3.120     The County Court may also exercise its interlocutory jurisdiction to restrain the levying of excessive distress, provided that a powerful prima facie case for the distress being unlawful has been made out (*Steel Linings v Bibby and Co (a Firm)* [1993] R.A. 27).

*Paragraph (3)*

There appears to be no judicial guidance on the meaning of "irregular" and the term may be contrasted with that used in reg.30(3) above—"unlawful".

Where justices are faced with complicated factual or legal issues relating to the ownership of goods seized, they need not hear the complaint, but may leave the appellant to seek his remedy in the higher courts under the civil law (*R. v Basildon Justices Ex p. Holding and Barnes plc* [1994] R.A. 157).

## Charges connected with distress

**32.** Schedule 2 shall have effect for the purpose of determining the amounts in respect of charges in connection with the distress for the purposes of section 35(2)(b) of the Act.

3.121

## Application for warrant of commitment

**33.**—(1) For the purposes of enabling an inquiry to be made under section [¹39A] of the Act as to the liable person's conduct and means, a justice of the peace having jurisdiction for the area in which the liable person resides may—

3.122

 (a) issue a summons to him to appear before a magistrates' court and (if he does not obey the summons) issue a warrant for his arrest; or

 (b) issue a warrant for his arrest without issuing a summons.

(2) In any proceedings under [²sections 39A and 40] of the Act, a statement in writing to the effect that wages of any amount have been paid to the liable person during any period, purporting to be signed by or on behalf of his employer, shall be evidence of the facts there stated.

(3) Where an application under section [¹39A] of the Act has been made but no warrant of commitment is issued or term of imprisonment fixed, the application may be renewed on the ground that the circumstances of the liable person have changed.

AMENDMENTS

 1. Regulation 2(6)(b)(i) of the Collection and Enforcement and Miscellaneous Amendments Regulations 2000 and the Child Support (Miscellaneous Amendments) Regulations 2001 (May, 31, 2001).

 2. Regulation 2(6)(b)(ii) of the Collection and Enforcement and Miscellaneous Amendments Regulations 2000 and the Child Support (Miscellaneous Amendments) Regulations 2001 (May 31, 2001).

## Warrant of commitment

**34.**—(1) A warrant of commitment shall be in the form specified in Schedule 3, or in a form to the like effect.

3.123

(2) The amount to be included in the warrant under section 40(4)(a)(ii) of the Act in respect of costs shall be such amount as in the view of the court is equal to the costs reasonably incurred by the Secretary of State in respect of the costs of commitment.

(3) A warrant issued under section 40 of the Act may be executed any-where in England and Wales by any person to whom it is directed or by any constable acting within his police area.

(4) A warrant may be executed by a constable notwithstanding that it is not in his possession at the time but such warrant shall, on the demand of the person arrested, be shown to him as soon as possible.

(5) Where, after the issue of a warrant, part-payment of the amount stated in it is made, the period of imprisonment shall be reduced proportion-ately so that for the period of imprisonment specified in the warrant there shall be substituted a period of imprisonment of such number of days as bears the same proportion to the number of days specified in the warrant as the amount remaining unpaid under the warrant bears to the amount specified in the warrant.

(6) Where the part-payment is of such an amount as would, under para-graph (5), reduce the period of imprisonment to such number of days as have already been served (or would be so served in the course of the day of payment), the period of imprisonment shall be reduced to the period already served plus one day.

## [¹Disqualification from driving order

3.124

**35.**—(1) For the purposes of enabling an enquiry to be made under sec-tion 39A of the Act as to the liable person's livelihood, means and conduct, a justice of the peace having jurisdiction for the area in which the liable per-son resides may issue a summons to him to appear before a magistrates' court and to produce any driving licence held by him, and, where applica-ble, its counterpart, and, if he does not appear, may issue a warrant for his arrest.

(2) In any proceedings under sections 39A and 40B of the Act, a state-ment in writing to the effect that wages of any amount have been paid to the liable person during any period, purporting to be signed for or on behalf of his employer, shall be evidence of the facts there stated.

(3) Where an application under section 39A of the Act has been made but no disqualification order is made, the application may be renewed on the ground that the circumstances of the liable person have changed.

(4) A disqualification order shall be in the form prescribed in Schedule 4.

(5) The amount to be included in the disqualification order under sec-tion 40B(3)(b) of the Act in respect of the costs shall be such amount as in the view of the court is equal to the costs reasonably incurred by the Secretary of State in respect of the costs of the application for the disqual-ification order.

(6) An order made under section 40B(4) of the Act may be executed anywhere in England and Wales by any person to whom it is directed or by any constable acting within his police area, if the liable person fails to appear or produce or surrender his driving licence or its counterpart to the court.

(7) An order may be executed by a constable notwithstanding that it is not in his possession at the time but such order shall, if demanded, be shown to the liable person as soon as reasonably practicable.

(8) In this regulation "driving licence" means a licence to drive a motor vehicle granted under Part III of the Road Traffic Act 1988.]

AMENDMENT

1. Regulation 2(6)(c) of the Collection and Enforcement and Miscellaneous Amendments Regulations 2000 (for in force date see regs 1 and 6 of SI 2001/162 below).

DEFINITION

"the Act": see reg.1(2).                                                              **3.125**

SCHEDULE 1                                  **Regulation 29(1)**

LIABILITY ORDER PRESCRIBED FORM

Section 33 of the Child Support Act 1991 and regulation 29(1) of the Child Support     **3.126**
(Collection and Enforcement) Regulations 1992

... Magistrates' Court

Date:

Defendant:

Address:

On the complaint of the Secretary of State for Social Security that the sums specified below are due from the defendant under the Child Support Act 1991 and Part IV of the Child Support (Collection and Enforcement) Regulations 1992 and are outstanding, it is adjudged that the defendant is liable to pay the aggregate amount specified below.

Sum payable and outstanding
—child support maintenance
—interest
[¹—penalty payments
—fees]
—other periodical payments collected by virtue of section 30 of the Child Support Act 1991.
Aggregate amount in respect of which the liability order is made:

Justice of the Peace
[*or* by order of the Court
Clerk of the Court]

AMENDMENT

1. Regulation 2(7) of the Collection and Enforcement and Miscellaneous Amendments Regulations 2000 (for in force date see regs 1 and 6 of SI 2001/162 below).

SCHEDULE 2                                    **Regulation 32**

CHARGES CONNECTED WITH DISTRESS

**1.** The sum in respect of charges connected with the distress which may be aggregated     **3.127**
under section 35(2)(b) of the Act shall be set out in the following Table—

| (1) Matter connected with distress | (2) Charge |
|---|---|
| **A** For making a visit to premises with a view to levying distress (whether the levy is made or not): | Reasonable costs and fees incurred, but not exceeding an amount which, when aggregated with charges under this head for any previous visits made with a view to levying distress in relation to an amount in respect of which the liability order concerned was made, is not greater than the relevant amount calculated under paragraph 2(1) with respect to the visit. |
| **B** For levying distress: | An amount (if any) which, when aggregated with charges under head A for any visits made with a view to levying distress in relation to an amount in respect of which the liability order concerned was made, is equal to the relevant amount calculated under paragraph 2(1) with respect to the levy. |
| [¹BB For preparing and sending a letter advising the liable person that the written authorisation of the Secretary of State is with the person levying the distress and requesting the total sum due: | £10.00] |
| **C** For the removal and storage of goods for the purposes of sale: | Reasonable costs and fees incurred. |
| **D** For the possession of goods as described in paragraph 2(3)— | |
| (i) for close possession (the person in possession on behalf of the Secretary of State to provide his own board): | £4.50 per day |
| (ii) for walking possession: | [²10p per day.] |
| **E** For appraisement of an item distrained, at the request in writing of the liable person: | Reasonable fees and expenses of the broker appraising. |
| **F** For other expenses of, and commission on, a sale by auction— | |
| (i) where the sale is held on the auctioneer's premises: | The auctioneer's commission fee and out-of-pocket expenses (but not exceeding in aggregate 15 per cent of the sum realised), together with reasonable costs and fees incurred in respect of advertising. |
| (ii) where the sale is held on the liable person's premises: | The auctioneer's commission fee (but not exceeding 7\mh\ per cent of the sum realised), together with the auctioneer's out-of-pocket expenses and reasonable costs and fees incurred in respect of advertising. |
| **G** For other expenses incurred in connection with a proposed sale where there is no buyer in relation to it: | Reasonable costs and fees incurred. |

2.—(1) In heads A and B of the Table to paragraph 1, "the relevant amount" with respect to a visit or a levy means—

(a) where the sum due at the time of the visit or of the levy (as the case may be) does not exceed £100, £12.50;

(b) where the sum due at the time of the visit or of the levy (as the case may be) exceeds £100, 12½ per cent on the first £100 of the sum due, 4 per cent on the next £400, 2½ per cent on the next £1500, 1 per cent on the next £8000 and ¼ per cent on any additional sum, and the sum due at any time for these purposes means so much of the amount in respect of which the liability order concerned was made as is outstanding at the time.

(2) Where a charge has arisen under head B with respect to an amount, no further charge may be aggregated under heads A or B in respect of that amount.

(3) The Secretary of State takes close or walking possession of goods for the purpose of head D of the Table to paragraph 1 if he takes such possession in pursuance of an agreement which is made at the time that the distress is levied and which (without prejudice to such other terms as may be agreed) is expressed to the effect that, in consideration of the Secretary of State not immediately removing the goods distrained upon from the premises occupied by the liable person and delaying the sale of the goods, the Secretary of State may remove and sell the goods after a later specified date if the liable person has not by then paid the amount distrained for (including charges under this Schedule); and the Secretary of State is in close possession of goods on any day for these purposes if during the greater part of the day a person is left on the premises in physical possession of the goods on behalf of the Secretary of State under such an agreement.

**3.**—(1) Where the calculation under this Schedule of a percentage of a sum results in an amount containing a fraction of a pound, that fraction shall be reckoned as a whole pound.

(2) In the case of dispute as to any charge under this Schedule, the amount of the charge shall be taxed.

(3) Such a taxation shall be carried out by the district judge of the county court for the district in which the distress is or is intended to be levied, and he may give such directions as to the costs of the taxation as he thinks fit; and any such costs directed to be paid by the liable person to the Secretary of State shall be added to the sum which may be aggregated under section 35(2) of the Act.

(4) References in the Table in paragraph 1 to costs, fees and expenses include references to amounts payable by way of value added tax with respect to the supply of goods or services to which the costs, fees and expenses relate.

AMENDMENTS

1. Regulation 3(2)(a) of the Miscellaneous Amendments Regulations 1994 (February 7, 1994).

2. Regulation 3(2)(b) of the Miscellaneous Amendments Regulations 1994 (February 7, 1994)

GENERAL NOTE

The amendments to para.1 reflect the importance of correspondence with, as opposed to visits to, a debtor and reduce the fee as high charges are counter productive in achieving the aim of the distress, namely the collection of the debt.

SCHEDULE 3                                    **Regulation 34(1)**

FORM OF WARRANT OF COMMITMENT

Section 40 of the Child Support Act 1991 and regulation 34(1) of the Child Support    **3.128**
(Collection and Enforcement) Regulations 1992

. . . Magistrates' Court

Date:

Liable Person:

Address:

# Collection and Enforcement Regulations 1992

A liability order ("the order") was made against the liable person by the [ ] Magistrates' Court on [ ] under section 33 of the Child Support Act 1991 ("the Act") in respect of an amount of [ ].

The court is satisfied—

  (i) that the Secretary of State sought under section 35 of the Act to levy by distress the amount then outstanding in respect of which the order was made;

[and/or]

that the Secretary of State sought under section 36 of the Act to recover through the [ ] County Court, by means of [garnishee proceedings] [2. . .] [a charging order], the amount then outstanding in respect of which the order was made;

  (ii) that such amount, or any portion of it, remains unpaid; and

  (iii) having inquired in the liable person's presence as to his means and as to whether there has been [wilful refusal] [3. . .] [culpable neglect] on his part, the court is of the opinion that there has been [wilful refusal] [3. . .] [culpable neglect] on his part.

The decision of the court is that the liable person be [committed to prison] [detained] for [ ] unless the aggregate amount mentioned below in respect of which this warrant is made is sooner paid.

This warrant is made in respect of—
Amount outstanding (including any interest, [1penalty payments, fees,] costs and charges):
Costs of commitment of the Secretary of State:
Aggregate Amount:

And you [name of person or persons to whom warrant is directed] are hereby required to take the liable person and convey him to [name of prison or place of detention] and there deliver him to the [governor] [officer in charge] thereof; and you, the [governor] [officer in charge], to receive the liable person into your custody and keep him for [period of imprisonment] from the date of his arrest under this warrant or until he be sooner discharge course of law.

Justice of the Peace

[or by order of the Court

Clerk of the Court]

*Note: The period of imprisonment will be reduced as provided by regulation 34(5) and (6) of the Child Support (Collection and Enforcement) Regulations 1992 if part-payment is made of the aggregate amount.

## AMENDMENTS

1. Regulation 2(8)(a) of the Collection and Enforcement and Miscellaneous Amendments Regulations 2000 (for in force date see regs 1 and 6 of SI 2001/162 below).

2. Regulation 2(8)(b) of the Collection and Enforcement and Miscellaneous Amendments Regulations 2000 (for in force date see regs 1 and 6 of SI 2001/162 below).

3. Regulation 2(8)(c) of the Collection and Enforcement and Miscellaneous Amendments Regulations 2000 (for in force date see regs 1 and 6 of SI 2001/162 below).

[¹SCHEDULE 4

FORM OF ORDER OF DISQUALIFICATION FROM HOLDING OR OBTAINING A DRIVING
LICENCE

Section 39A and 40B of the Child Support Act 1991 and regulation 35 of the Child    **3.129**
Support (Collection and Enforcement) Regulations 1992.

... Magistrates' Court

Date:

Liable Person:

Address:
A liability order ("the order") was made against the liable person by the [ ] Magistrates' Court
on [ ] under section 33 of the Child Support Act 1991 ("the Act") in respect of an amount of [ ].
The court is satisfied—

(i) that the Secretary of State sought under section 35 of the Act to levy by distress
the amount then outstanding in respect of which the order was made;

[and/or]

that the Secretary of State sought under section 36 of the Act to recover through [ ] County
Court by means of [garnishee proceedings] [a charging order], the amount then outstanding
in respect of which the order was made;

(ii) that such amount, or any proportion of it, remains unpaid; and

(iii) having inquired in the liable person's presence as to his means and whether there
has been [wilful refusal] [culpable neglect] on his part.

The decision of the court is that the liable person be disqualified from [holding or obtain-
ing] a driving licence from [date] for [period] unless the aggregate amount in respect of which
this order is made is sooner paid*
This order is made in respect of—
Amount outstanding (including any interest, fees, penalty payments, costs and charges):
Aggregate amount:
And you [the liable person] shall surrender to the court any driving licence and counter-
part held.

Justice of the Peace

[or by order of the Court

Clerk of the Court]

*Note:* The period of disqualification may be reduced as provided by section 40B(5)(a)
of the Act if part payment is made of the aggregate amount. The order will be revoked by
section 40B(5)(b) of the Act if full payment is made of the aggregate amount.]

AMENDMENT

1. Regulation 2(9) of, and the Schedule to, the Collection and Enforcement and
Miscellaneous Amendments Regulations 2000 (for in force date see regs 1 and 6 of
SI 2001/162 below).

## The Child Support (Collection and Enforcement of Other Forms of Maintenance) Regulations 1992

### (SI 1992/2643)

*Made by the Secretary of State for Social Security under sections 30(1), (4) and (5), 51 and 54 of the Child Support Act 1991 and all other powers enabling him in that behalf.*

### Citation, commencement and interpretation

3.130     **1.**—(1) These Regulations may be cited as the Child Support (Collection and Enforcement of Other Forms of Maintenance) Regulations 1992 and shall come into force on 5th April 1993.
(2) In these Regulations—
"the Act" means the Child Support Act 1991;
"child of the family" has the same meaning as in the Matrimonial Causes Act 1973 or, in Scotland, the Family Law (Scotland) Act 1985; and
"periodical payments" includes secured periodical payments.

GENERAL NOTE

3.131     "child of the family" is defined by s.52(1) of the Matrimonial Causes Act 1973 as follows:
"child of the family", in relation to the parties to a marriage, means—

(a)  a child of both of those parties; and

(b)  any other child, not being a child who is placed with those persons as foster parents by a local authority or voluntary organisation, who has been treated by both of those parties as a child of their family.

### Periodical payments and categories of person prescribed for the purposes of section 30 of the Act

3.132     **2.** The following periodical payments and categories of persons are prescribed for the purposes of section 30(1) of the Act—
(a)  payments under a maintenance order made in relation to a child in accordance with the provisions of section 8(6) (periodical payments in addition to child support maintenance), 8(7) (periodical payments to meet expenses incurred in connection with the provision of instruction or training) or 8(8) of the Act (periodical payments to meet expenses at tributable to disability);
(b)  any periodical payments under a maintenance order [¹or, in Scotland, registered minutes of agreement] which are payable to or for the benefit of a spouse or former spouse who is the person with care of a child who is a qualifying child in respect of whom a child support [²maintenance calculation] is in force in accordance with which the Secretary of State has arranged for the collection of child support maintenance under section 29 of the Act; and

(c) any periodical payments under a maintenance order payable to or for the benefit of a former child of the family of the person against whom the order is made, that child having his home with the person with care.

AMENDMENTS

1. Regulation 44 of the Amendment Regulations (April 5, 1993).
2. Regulation 3(2) of the Collection and Enforcement and Miscellaneous Amendments Regulations 2000 (for in force date see regs 1 and 6 of SI 2001/162 below).

DEFINITIONS

"the Act": see reg.1(2).                                                           3.133
"child of the family": see reg.1(2).
"periodical payments": see reg.1(2).

GENERAL NOTE

From April 11, 1994 magistrates have had the power to order that payments       3.134
under qualifying maintenance orders be made in accordance with arrangements
made by the Secretary of State for their collection under s.30 of the Act (Child
Support Act 1991 (Consequential Amendments) Order 1994).

Thus, where a maintenance assessment is in force and payments are being collected through the Agency under it, but other types of periodical payments are still
in effect (these will be orders for "top up" maintenance, etc. and appear also to
include spousal maintenance) the magistrates may (see the Magistrates' Courts Act
1980, s.59(1) and (3)(cc)) order that all the monies due are paid through the collection machinery of the Child Support Act.

The power does not extend to the county or High Court, even though it is more
likely that those courts would have made top-up maintenance order, etc than the
magistrates. To take advantage of the magistrates' power, the creditor under the order
must have the order registered in the magistrates' court under the Maintenance
Orders Act 1958.

## Collection and enforcement—England and Wales

**3.** In relation to England and Wales, section 29(2) and (3) and 31 to        3.135
[²40B] of the Act, and any regulations made under those sections, shall
apply for the purpose of enabling the Secretary of State to enforce any obligation to pay any amount which he is authorised to collect under section
30 of the Act, with the modification that any reference in those sections or
regulations to child support maintenance shall be read as a reference to any
of the periodical payments mentioned in regulation 2 above, and any reference to a [¹maintenance calculation] shall be read as a reference to any of
the maintenance orders mentioned in that regulation.

AMENDMENTS

1. Regulation 3(2) of the Collection and Enforcement and Miscellaneous
Amendments Regulations 2000 (for in force date see regs 1 and 6 of SI 2001/162
below).

2. Regulation 3(3) of the Collection and Enforcement and Miscellaneous Amendments Regulations 2000 (for in force date see regs 1 and 6 of SI 2001/162 below).

DEFINITIONS

**3.136**      "the Act": see reg.1(2).
"periodical payments": see reg.1(2).

## Collection and enforcement—Scotland

**3.137**      **4.** In relation to Scotland, for the purpose of enforcing any obligation to pay any amount which the Secretary of State is authorised to collect under section 30 of the Act—

   (a) the Secretary of State may bring any proceedings and take any other steps (other than diligence against earnings) which could have been brought or taken by or on behalf of the person to whom the periodical payments are payable; and

   (b) sections 29(2) and (3), 31 and 32 of the Act, and any regulations made under those sections, shall apply, with the modification that any reference in those sections or regulations to child support maintenance shall be read as a reference to any of the periodical payments mentioned in regulation 2 above, and any reference to a [1maintenance calculation] shall be read as a reference to any of the maintenance orders mentioned in that regulation.

AMENDMENT

1. Regulation 3(2) of the Collection and Enforcement and Miscellaneous Amendments Regulations 2000 (for in force date see regs 1 and 6 of SI 2001/162 below).

DEFINITIONS

**3.138**      "the Act": see reg.1(2).
"periodical payments": see reg.1(2).

## Collection and enforcement—supplementary

**3.139**      **5.** Nothing in Regulations 3 or 4 applies to any periodical payment which falls due before the date specified by the Secretary of State by a notice in writing to the [1non-resident parent] that he is arranging for those payments to be collected, and that date shall be not earlier than the date the notice is given.

AMENDMENT

1. Regulation 3(2) of the Collection and Enforcement and Miscellaneous Amendments Regulations 2000 (for in force date see regs 1 and 6 of SI 2001/162 below).

Since the regulations made under s.29 of the Act apply to regs 3 and 4 above, the **3.140**
day when the notice is treated as given under reg.5 will be determined under
reg.1(2)(b) of the Collection and Enforcement Regulations.

## The Child Support Act 1991 (Commencement No.3 and Transitional Provisions) Order 1992

## (SI 1992/2644)

*Made by the Secretary of State for Social Security under section 58(2) to (6) of the Child Support Act 1991.*

## Citation

**1.** This Order may be cited as the Child Support Act 1991 **3.141**
(Commencement No.3 and Transitional Provisions) Order 1992.

## Date appointed for the coming into force of certain provisions of the Child Support Act 1991

**2.** Subject to the following provisions of this Order, the date appointed **3.142**
for the coming into force of all the provisions of the Child Support Act
1991, in so far as they are not already in force, except sections 19(3), 30(2),
34(2), 37(2) and (3) and 58(12), is 5th April 1993.

## Transitional provisions

**3.** The transitional provisions set out in the Schedule to this Order shall **3.143**
have effect.

SCHEDULE        Article 3

[. . .]

PART II

MODIFICATION OF MAINTENANCE ASSESSMENT IN CERTAIN CASES

**6.** In this Part of this Schedule— **3.144**

"the Act" means the Child Support Act 1991;
"formula amount" means the amount of child support maintenance that would, but for the
  provisions of this Part of this Schedule, be payable under an original assessment, or any
  fresh assessment made during the period specified in paragraph 8 [¹by virtue of a revision
  under section 16 of the Act or a decision under section 17 of the Act superseding an
  earlier decision];
"the Maintenance Assessment Procedure Regulations" means the Child Support
  (Maintenance Assessment Procedure) Regulations 1992;
"modified amount" means an amount which is £20 greater than the aggregate weekly
  amount which was payable under the orders, agreements or arrangements mentioned in
  paragraph 7(1)(a) below; and

"original assessment" means a maintenance assessment made in respect of a qualifying child where no previous such assessment has been made or, where the assessment is made in respect of more than one child, where no previous such assessment has been made in respect of any of those children.

AMENDMENT

1. Article 30(a) of the Commencement No.7 Order 1999 (June 1, 1999).

**3.145**   **7.**—(1) Subject to subparagraph (2), the provisions of this Part of this Schedule apply to cases where—

(a) on 4th April 1993[², and at all times thereafter until the date when a maintenance assessment is made under the Act] there is in force, in respect of all the qualifying children in respect of whom an application for a maintenance assessment is made under the Act and the absent parent concerned, one or more—

    (i) maintenance orders;
    (ii) orders under section 151 of the Army Act 1955 (deductions from pay for maintenance of wife or child) or section 151 of the Air Force Act 1955 (deductions from pay for maintenance of wife or child) or arrangements corresponding to such an order and made under Article 1(b) or 3 of the Naval and Marine Pay and Pensions (Deduction for Maintenance) Order 1959; or
    (iii) maintenance agreements (being agreements which are made or evidenced in writing); and

(b) the absent parent is responsible for maintaining a child or children residing with him other than the child or children in respect of whom the application is made; and

(c) the formula amount is not more than £60; and

(d) the formula amount exceeds the aggregate weekly amount which was payable under the orders, agreements or arrangements mentioned in sub-paragraph (a) above by more than £20 a week.

(2) Nothing in this Part of this Schedule applies to [³a Category A interim maintenance assessment within the meaning of regulation 8(1B) of the Child Support (Maintenance Assessment Procedure) Regulations 1992] made under section 12 of the Act.

AMENDMENTS

1. Article 2(2) of the Child Support Act 1991 (Commencement No.3 and Transitional Provisions) Amendment Order 1993 (March 31, 1993).
2. Article 2(3) of the Child Support Act 1991 (Commencement No.3 and Transitional Provisions) Amendment Order 1993 (March 31, 1993).

DEFINITIONS

**3.146**   "the Act": see para.6.
"formula amount": see para.6

**3.147**   **8.** In a case to which this Part of this Schedule applies, the amount payable under an original assessment, or any fresh assessment made [¹by virtue of a revision under section 16 of the Act or a decision under section 17 of the Act superseding an earlier decision], during the period of one year beginning with the date on which the original assessment takes effect or, if shorter, until any of the conditions specified in paragraph 7(1) is no longer satisfied, shall, instead of being the formula amount, be the modified amount.

1. Article 30(a) of the Commencement No.7 Order 1999 (June 1, 1999).

DEFINITIONS                                                                    **3.148**

"the Act": see para.6.
"formula amount": see para.6
"modified amount": see para.6
"original assessment": see para.6

**9.** For the purpose of determining the aggregate weekly amount payable under the orders,    **3.149**
agreements or arrangements mentioned in paragraph 7(1)(a) above any payments in kind and
any payments made to a third party on behalf of or for the benefit of the qualifying child or
qualifying children or the person with care shall be disregarded.

**10.** If, in making a maintenance assessment, [¹the Secretary of State] has applied the provisions of this part of this Schedule, regulation 10(2) of the Maintenance Assessment
Procedure Regulations shall have effect as if there was added at the end—

"(g) the aggregate weekly amount which was payable under the orders, agreements or
arrangements specified in paragraph 7(1)(a) of the Schedule to the Child Support Act
1991 (Commencement No.3 and Transitional Provisions) Order 1992 (modification of
maintenance assessment in certain cases)."

1. Article 30(b) of the Commencement No.7 Order 1999 (June 1, 1999).

DEFINITION

"the Maintenance Assessment Procedure Regulations": see para.6.                **3.150**

**11.** The first review of an original assessment under section 16 of the Act (periodical      **3.151**
reviews) shall be conducted on the basis that the amount payable under the assessment
immediately before the review takes place was the formula amount.

DEFINITIONS

"the Act": see para.6.                                                          **3.152**
"formula amount": see para.6.
"original assessment": see para.6.

**12.**—(1) The provision of the following sub-paragraphs shall apply where [¹a decision is      **3.153**
made under section 17 of the Act which supersedes an earlier decision on the ground that
there has been a material change of circumstances since the decision took effect] at any time
when the amount payable under that assessment is the modified amount.

(2) Where the [²Secretary of State determines that, were a fresh assessment to be made by
virtue of a decision under section 17 of the Act superseding an earlier decision], the amount
payable under it (disregarding the provisions of this Part of this Schedule) (in this paragraph
called "the reviewed formula amount") would be—

(a)  more than the formula amount, the amount of child support maintenance payable
     shall be the modified amount plus the difference between the formula amount and the
     reviewed formula amount;

(b)  less than the formula amount but more than the modified amount, the amount of child
     support maintenance payable shall be the modified amount;

(c) less than the modified amount, the amount of child support maintenance payable shall be the reviewed formula amount.

(3) [³The Secretary of State] shall, in determining the reviewed formula amount, apply the provisions of regulations [⁴21 and] 22 of the Maintenance Assessment Procedure Regulations.

AMENDMENTS

1. Article 30(c)(i) of the Commencement No.7 Order 1999 (June 1, 1999).
2. Article 30(c)(ii) of the Commencement No.7 Order 1999 (June 1, 1999).
3. Article 30(c)(iii) of the Commencement No.7 Order 1999 (June 1, 1999).
4. Article 30(c)(iii) of the Commencement No.7 Order 1999 (June 1, 1999).

DEFINITIONS

3.154    "the Act": see para.6.
"formula amount": see para.6
"the Maintenance Assessment Procedure Regulations": see para.6
"modified amount": see para.6.

GENERAL NOTE

3.155    This Order may still be of relevance to tribunals and is retained, but the general note has not been updated to reflect the new terminology.

*Phased Take-on of Cases*
Part I of the Schedule to this Order was revoked from September 4, 1995 by s.18(8) of the 1995 Act. Most of Pt I is re-enacted by s.18. For the re-enactment and a commentary see the general note to that section.

*Modified Maintenance Assessments*
Part II of the Schedule to this Order provides for a temporary reduction in the amount payable under a maintenance assessment in cases where low maintenance payments are being made at the time the child support scheme comes into operation so as to limit the increase in payments to be made to £20 a week for a maximum of one year.

This Part does not apply to Category A interim maintenance assessments (para.7(2)). It applies provided and only so long as the following conditions are met (paras 7(1) and 8).

(i) From April 4, 1993 until a maintenance assessment is made under the Act there is in force one or more maintenance orders or agreements in respect of all the qualifying children in respect of whom an application for a maintenance assessment has been made. Only maintenance agreements which are made or evidenced in writing are included. "Maintenance order", is not defined in this Order and will have the same meaning as in s.8(11) of the Act and regulations made the reunder. In calculating the amounts payable under the orders and agreements, payments in kind and payments to a third party on behalf of or for the benefit of a qualifying child are disregarded (para.9).

(ii) One or more children, other than children in respect of whom the maintenance assessment has been made, reside with the absent parent who is responsible for maintaining them. The Order uses the words "residing with" in contrast to "home" or "household" which are used elsewhere. It, therefore, covers cases where a child resides with someone but does not live in that person's household, although the need for the parent to be responsible for maintaining the child makes it likely that this will arise in very few cases. It is also more limited than "home" and would not cover cases where a child's home is with the absent parent but that child ceases to reside there, for example while away at boarding school. (For further discussion of these concepts, see the general note to s.3 of the Act.) The responsibility which the absent parent has to maintain the child may exist under a maintenance order or agreement or it may be one which the parent has assumed without any such order or agreement being made.

(iii) The amount of child support maintenance which would otherwise be payable is not more than £60.

(iv) This amount exceeds the sum of the amounts payable under (i) by more than £20 a week. If all four conditions are satisfied the child support maintenance payable is the total of the sums covered by (i) above plus £20. This applies to original assessments and to fresh assessments on review under s.17, 18 or 19 of the Act. This lasts for one year from the effective date of the *original* (not fresh) assessment, or until the time when one of the conditions above ceases to apply, whichever is the earlier (see para.8.) The one year maximum duration of the operation of these provisions is fixed independently of the date when a s.16 review is made or treated as made under reg.18 of the Maintenance Assessment Procedure Regulations.

When the original assessment is first reviewed under s.16 of the Act, the provisions of Pt II are disregarded and the assessment is treated as being for the amount of child support maintenance which would otherwise have been payable (para.11).

Where a review is conducted under s.17 of the Act while the provisions of Pt II apply, the result is determined in accordance with the provisions of para.12. Their effect is as follows. Assume that the absent parent pays £15 under a maintenance order and that the original assessment was for £50. The absent parent pays £15 plus £20, *i.e.* £35.

(a) If the effect of a s.17 review is that the assessment that would otherwise be payable is increased by £5 to £55, the absent parent must pay the £35 plus the additional £5, *i.e.* £40.

(b) If the effect of a s.17 review is that the assessment that would otherwise be payable is increased by £15 to £65 (*i.e.* above the £60 limit set by para.7(1)(c)), the case ceases to fall within Pt II: see the definition of "formula amount" in para.6. Accordingly, the absent parent must pay the full assessment of £65.

(c) If the effect of a s.17 review is that the assessment that would otherwise be payable is reduced from £50 to £30 (*i.e.* below the amount of the original assessment but more than the amount being paid by the absent parent), the amount paid by the absent parent remains unchanged at £35.

(d) If the effect of a s.17 review is that the assessment that would otherwise be payable is reduced from £50 to £30 (*i.e.* below the amount being paid by the absent parent), the absent parent must pay only the fresh assessment of £30.

In practice these provisions have been superseded by the new arrangements governing the phasing in of the full amount of child support maintenance contained tained in the Miscellaneous Amendments Regulations 1994 which are being used in all cases. If the phasing arrangements under this Order do not apply, the tribunal must consider whether the arrangements provided by Pt III of the 1994 Regulations apply (*CCS 14340/96*, para.6).

## The Child Support (Maintenance Arrangements and Jurisdiction) Regulations 1992

### (SI 1992/2645)

*Made by the Secretary of State for Social Security under sections 8(11), 10(1), (2) and (4), 44(3), 51, 52(4) and 54 of, and paragraph 11 of Schedule 1 to, the Child Support Act 1991 and all other powers enabling him in that behalf.*

### Citation, commencement and interpretation

3.156    **1.**—(1) These Regulations may be cited as the Child Support (Maintenance Arrangements and Jurisdiction) Regulations 1992 and shall come into force on 5th April 1993.

(2) In these Regulations—

"the Act" means the Child Support Act 1991;

[1"Maintenance Calculations and Special Cases Regulations" means the Child Support (Maintenance Calculations and Special Cases) Regulations 2000;]

[2"Maintenance Calculation Procedure Regulations" means the Child Support (Maintenance Calculation Procedure) Regulations 2000;]

"effective date" means the date on which a maintenance assessment takes effect for the purposes of the Act;

"maintenance order" has the meaning given in section 8(11) of the Act.

(3) In these Regulations, unless the context otherwise requires, a reference—

(a) to a numbered regulation is to the regulation in these Regulations bearing that number;

(b) in a regulation to a numbered paragraph is to the paragraph in that regulation bearing that number;

(c) in a paragraph to a lettered or numbered subparagraph is to the subparagraph in that paragraph bearing that letter or number.

AMENDMENTS

1. Regulation 3(1)(a) of the Information, Evidence and Disclosure and Maintenance Arrangements and Jurisdiction Amendment Regulations 2000.

2. Regulation 3(1)(b) of the Information, Evidence and Disclosure and Maintenance Arrangements and Jurisdiction Amendment Regulation 2000.

## [¹Prescription of enactments for the purposes of section 8(11) of the Act

**2.** The following enactments are prescribed for the purposes of section 8(11)(f) of the Act—     **3.157**
  (a)  the Conjugal Rights (Scotland) Amendment Act 1861;
  (b)  the Court of Session Act 1868;
  (c)  the Sheriff Courts (Scotland) Act 1907;
  (d)  the Guardianship of Infants Act 1925;
  (e)  the Illegitimate Children (Scotland) Act 1930;
  (f)  the Children and Young Persons (Scotland) Act 1932;
  (g)  the Children and Young Persons (Scotland) Act 1937;
  (h)  the Custody of Children (Scotland) Act 1939;
  (i)  the National Assistance Act 1948;
  (j)  the Affiliation Orders Act 1952;
  (k)  the Affiliation Proceedings Act 1957;
  (l)  the Matrimonial Proceedings (Children) Act 1958;
  (m) the Guardianship of Minors Act 1971;
  (n)  the Guardianship Act 1973;
  (o)  the Children Act 1975;
  (p)  the Supplementary Benefits Act 1976;
  (q)  the Social Security Act 1986;
  (r)  the Social Security Administration Act 1992.]

AMENDMENT

  1.  Regulation 26 of the Amendment Regulations 1995 (April 18, 1995).

DEFINITION

  "the Act": see reg.1(2).     **3.158**

## Relationship between maintenance assessments and certain court orders

**3.**—[¹(1) Orders made under the following enactments are of a kind     **3.159**
prescribed for the purposes of section 10(1) of the Act—
  (a)  the Conjugal Rights (Scotland) Amendment Act 1861;
  (b)  the Court of Session Act 1868;
  (c)  the Sheriff Courts (Scotland) Act 1907;
  (d)  the Guardianship of Infants Act 1925;
  (e)  the Illegitimate Children (Scotland) Act 1930;
  (f)  the Children and Young Persons (Scotland) Act 1932;
  (g)  the Children and Young Persons (Scotland) Act 1937;
  (h)  the Custody of Children (Scotland) Act 1939;
  (i)  the National Assistance Act 1948;
  (j)  the Affiliation Orders Act 1952;
  (k)  the Affiliation Proceedings Act 1957;
  (l)  the Matrimonial Proceedings (Children) Act 1958;
  (m) the Guardianship of Minors Act 1971;
  (n)  the Guardianship Act 1973;

(o) Part II of the Matrimonial Causes Act 1973;
(p) the Children Act 1975;
(q) the Supplementary Benefits Act 1976;
(r) the Domestic Proceedings and Magistrates Courts Act 1978;
(s) Part III of the Matrimonial and Family Proceedings Act 1984;
(t) the Family Law (Scotland) Act 1985;
(u) the Social Security Act 1986;
(v) Schedule 1 to the Children Act 1989;
(w) the Social Security Administration Act 1992.]

(2) Subject to paragraphs (3) and (4), where a maintenance [8calculation] is made with respect to—
(a) all of the children with respect to whom an order falling within paragraph (1) is in force; or
(b) one or more but not all of the children with respect to whom an order falling within paragraph (1) is in force and where the amount payable under the order to or for the benefit of each child is separately specified,

that order shall, so far as it relates to the making or securing of periodical payments to or for the benefit of the children with respect to whom the maintenance [8calculation] has been made, cease to have effect [6on the effective date of the maintenance calculation.]

(3) The provisions of paragraph (2) shall not apply where a maintenance order has been made in accordance with section 8(7) or (8) of the Act.

(4) In Scotland, where—
(a) an order has ceased to have effect by virtue of the provisions of paragraph (2) to the extent specified in that paragraph; and
(b) [5the Secretary of State] no longer has jurisdiction to make a maintenance [8calculation] with respect to a child with respect to whom the order ceased to have effect,

that order shall, so far as it relates to that child, again have effect from the date [5the Secretary of State] no longer has jurisdiction to make a maintenance [8calculation] with respect to that child.

[7. . .]

AMENDMENTS

1. Regulation 27(2) of the Amendment Regulations 1995 (April 18, 1995).
5. Article 31 of the Commencement No.7 Order 1999 (June 1, 1999).
6. Regulation 8(1)(a) of the Information, Evidence and Disclosure and Maintenance Arrangements and Jurisdiction Amendment Regulations 2000.
7. Regulation 8(1)(b) of the Information, Evidence and Disclosure and Maintenance Arrangements and Jurisdiction Amendment Regulations 2000.
8. Regulation 2(2) of the Information, Evidence and Disclosure and Maintenance Arrangements and Jurisdiction Amendment Regulations 2000.

DEFINITIONS

3.160     "the Act": see reg.1(2).
"effective date": see reg.1(2).
"maintenance order": see reg.1(2).

Non-resident parents become angry (and rightly so) when no steps are taken to terminate payments under a maintenance order once a maintenance assessment has been made. However, this failure does not invalidate the maintenance assessment as there is no obligation to notify the court of the making of a maintenance assessment under reg.10 of the Maintenance Assessment Procedure Regulations, since the court is not a "relevant person" within the definition in reg.1(2) of those Regulations.

**3.161**

## Relationship between maintenance assessments and certain agreements

**4.**—(1) Maintenance agreements within the meaning of section 9(1) of the Act are agreements of a kind prescribed for the purposes of section 10(2) of the Act.

**3.162**

(2) Where a maintenance [2calculation] is made with respect to—

(a) all of the children with respect to whom an agreement falling within paragraph (1) is in force; or

(b) one or more but not all of the children with respect to whom an agreement falling within paragraph (1) is in force and where the amount payable under the agreement to or for the benefit of each child is separately specified,

that agreement shall, so far as it relates to the making or securing of periodical payments to or for the benefit of the children with respect to whom the maintenance assessment has been made, become unenforceable from the effective date of the [2calculation].

(3) Where an agreement becomes unenforceable under the provisions of paragraph (2) to the extent specified in that paragraph, it shall remain unenforceable in relation to a particular child until such date as [1the Secretary of State] no longer has jurisdiction to make a maintenance [2calculation] with respect to that child.

1. Article 31(1) of the Commencement No.7 Order 1999 (June 1, 1999).

2. Regulation 2(2) of the Information, Evidence and Disclosure and Maintenance Arrangements and Jurisdiction Amendment Regulations 2000.

"the Act": see reg.1(2).

**3.163**

## Notifications by [1the Secretary of State]

**5.**—(1) Where [2the Secretary of State] is aware that an order of a kind prescribed in paragraph (2) is in force and considers that the making of a maintenance [3calculation] has affected, or is likely to affect, that order, he shall notify the persons prescribed in paragraph (3) in respect of whom that maintenance [3calculation] is in force, and the persons prescribed in paragraph (4) holding office in the court where the order in question was made or subsequently registered, of the [3calculation] and its effective date.

**3.164**

(2) The prescribed orders are those made under an enactment mentioned in regulation 3(1).

(3) The prescribed persons in respect of whom the maintenance [³calculation] is in force are—

(a) a person with care;

(b) [⁴a non-resident parent];

(c) a person who is treated as [⁴a non-resident parent] under [⁵regulation 8 of the Maintenance Calculations and Special Cases Regulations];

(d) a child who has made an application for a maintenance [³calculation] under section 7 of the Act.

(4) The prescribed person holding office in the court where the order in question was made or subsequently registered is—

(a) in England and Wales—

    (i) in relation to the High Court, the senior district judge of the principal registry of the Family Division or, where proceedings were instituted in a district registry, the district judge;

    (ii) in relation to a county court, the proper officer of that court within the meaning of Order 1, Rule 3 of the County Court Rules 1981;

    (iii) in relation to a magistrates' court, the [⁶justices' chief executive for] that court;

(b) in Scotland—

    (i) in relation to the Court of Session, the Deputy Principal Clerk of Session;

    (ii) in relation to a sheriff court, the sheriff clerk.

AMENDMENTS

1. Article 31(2) of the Commencement No.7 Order 1999 (June 1, 1999).
2. Article 31(1) of the Commencement No.7 Order 1999 (June 1, 1999).
3. Regulation 2(2) of the Information, Evidence and Disclosure and Maintenance Arrangements and Jurisdiction Amendment Regulations 2000.
4. Regulation 2(1) of the Information, Evidence and Disclosure and Maintenance Arrangements and Jurisdiction Amendment Regulations 2000.
5. Regulation 3(2) of the Information, Evidence and Disclosure and Maintenance Arrangements and Jurisdiction Amendment Regulations 2000.
6. Regulation 4 of the Information, Evidence and Disclosure and Maintenance Arrangements and Jurisdiction Amendment Regulations 2000.

DEFINITIONS

3.165    "effective date": see reg.1(2).

"Maintenance Calculations and Special Cases Regulations": see reg.1(2)

## Notification by the court

3.166    **6.**—(1) Where a court is aware that a maintenance [¹calculation] is in force and makes an order mentioned in regulation 3(1) which it considers has affected, or is likely to affect, that assessment, the person prescribed in paragraph (2) shall notify the Secretary of State to that effect.

(2) The prescribed person is the person holding the office specified below in the court where the order in question was made or subsequently registered—

(a) in England or Wales—
  (i) in relation to the High Court, the senior district judge of the principal registry of the Family Division or, where proceedings were instituted in a district registry, the district judge;
  (ii) in relation to a county court, the proper officer of that court within the meaning of Order 1, Rule 3 of the County Court Rules 1981;
  (iii) in relation to a magistrates' court, the [²justices' chief executive for] that court;
(b) in Scotland—
  (i) in relation to the Court of Session, the Deputy Principal Clerk of Session;
  (ii) in relation to a sheriff court, the sheriff clerk.

AMENDMENTS

1. Regulation 2(2) of the Information, Evidence and Disclosure and Maintenance Arrangements and Jurisdiction Amendment Regulations 2000.
2. Regulation 4 of the Information, Evidence and Disclosure and Maintenance Arrangements and Jurisdiction Amendment Regulations 2000.

Regulation 7 is omitted by virtue of reg.8(2) of the Information, Evidence and Disclosure and Maintenance Arrangements and Jurisdiction Amendment Regulations 2000.                                                              **3.167**

## [¹Prescription for the purposes of jurisdiction

**7A.**—(1) The companies prescribed for the purposes of section   **3.168**
44(2A)(c) of the Act (non-resident parents not habitually resident in the United Kingdom but employed by prescribed companies) are companies which employ employees to work outside the United Kingdom but make calculations and payment arrangements in relation to the earnings of those employees in the United Kingdom so that a deduction from earnings order may be made under section 31 of the Act in respect of the earnings of any such employee who is a liable person for the purposes of that section.

(2) The following bodies are prescribed for the purposes of section 44(2A)(d) of the Act (non-resident parents not habitually resident in the United Kingdom but employed by a prescribed body)—
  (a) a National Health Service Trust established by order made under section 5 of the National Health Service and Community Care Act 1990 ("the 1990 Act") or under section 12A of the National Health Service (Scotland) Act 1978 ("the 1978 Act");
  [²(aa) an NHS foundation trust within the meaning of section 1(1) of the Health and Social Care (Community Health and Standards) Act 2003;]
  (b) a Primary Care Trust established by order made under section 16A of the National Health Service Act 1977;
  (c) a Health Authority established under section 8 of the National Health Service Act 1977 ("the 1977 Act");
  (d) a Special Health Authority established under section 11 of the 1977 Act;

(e) a local authority, and for this purpose "local authority" means, in relation to England, a county council, a district council, a London borough council, the Common Council of the City of London or the Council of the Isles of Scilly and, in relation to Wales, a county council or a county borough council and, in relation to Scotland, a council constituted under section 2 of the Local Government etc (Scotland) Act 1994;

(f) a Health and Social Service Trust established by order made under Article 10 of the Health and Personal Social Services (Northern Ireland) Order 1991;

(g) a Health and Social Services Board established by order made under Article 16 of the Health and Personal Social Services (Northern Ireland) Order 1972 ("the 1972 Order");

(h) the Central Services Agency established by order made under Article 26 of the 1972 Order;

(i) a Special Agency established by order made under Article 3 of the Health and Personal Social Services (Special Agencies) (Northern Ireland) Order 1990;

(j) a Health Board constituted under section 2 of the 1978 Act; and

(k) a Special Health Board constituted under section 2 of the 1978 Act.]

AMENDMENTS

1. Regulation 8(3) of the Information, Evidence and Disclosure and Maintenance Arrangements and Jurisdiction Amendment Regulations 2000.

2. Article 3(1) of, and para.13 of Sch.1 to, the Health and Social Care (Community Health and Standards) Act 2003 (Supplementary and Consequential Provision) (NHS Foundation Trusts) Order 2004 (April 1, 2004).

DEFINITION

3.169     "the Act": see reg.1(2).

## Maintenance assessments and maintenance orders made in error

3.170     **8.**—(1) Where—

(a) at the time that a maintenance [¹calculation] with respect to a qualifying child was made a maintenance order was in force with respect to that child;

[¹(aa) the maintenance order has ceased to have effect by virtue of the provisions of regulation 3;]

(b) the [⁸non-resident parent] had made payments of child support maintenance due under that [⁷calculation]; and

(c) [⁴the Secretary of State revises the decision as to the maintenance calculation under section 16 of the Act and decides that no child support maintenance was payable on the ground that the previous decision was made in error,]

the payments of child support maintenance order shall be treated as payments under the maintenance order and that order shall be treated as having continued in force.

(2) Where—

(a) at the time that a maintenance order with respect to a qualifying child was made a maintenance [⁷calculation was in force with respect to that child;

[²(aa) the maintenance [⁷calculation] [⁵. . .] ceases to have effect;]

  (b) the [⁸non-resident parent] has made payments of maintenance due under that order, and

  (c) the maintenance order is revoked by the court on the grounds that it was made in error,

the payments under the maintenance order shall be treated as payments of child support maintenance and the maintenance [⁷calculation] shall be treated [⁶. . .] [³as not having ceased to have effect].

AMENDMENTS

1. Regulation 46(a) of the Amendment Regulations (April 5, 1993).
2. Regulation 46(b)(i) of the Amendment Regulations (April 5, 1993).
3. Regulation 46(b)(ii) of the Amendment Regulations (April 5, 1993).
4. Regulation 9(a) of the Information, Evidence and Disclosure and Maintenance Arrangements and Jurisdiction Amendment Regulations 2000.
5. Regulation 9(b) of the Information, Evidence and Disclosure and Maintenance Arrangements and Jurisdiction Amendment Regulations 2000.
6. Regulation 9(c) of the Information, Evidence and Disclosure and Maintenance Arrangements and Jurisdiction Amendment Regulations 2000.
7. Regulation 2(2) of the Information, Evidence and Disclosure and Maintenance Arrangements and Jurisdiction Amendment Regulations 2000.
8. Regulation 2(1) of the Information, Evidence and Disclosure and Arrangements and Jurisdiction Amendment Regulations 2000.

DEFINITION

"maintenance order": see reg.1(2).                                           **3.171**

GENERAL NOTE

*Paragraph (1)*
This paragraph provides for a court order that was cancelled in error to be treat-  **3.172**
ed as having continuing effect. However, where the order has been properly cancelled in accordance with the relevant provisions, there is no power to reinstate it
(*CSC 5/95*, para.7).

## [¹Maintenance calculations and maintenance orders—payments

  **8A.** Where—

  (a) a maintenance calculation has been made with respect to a qualify-ing child in response to an application made under section 4 or 7 of the Act;

  (b) at the time that maintenance calculation was made a maintenance order was in force with respect to that child;

  (c) the maintenance order has ceased to have effect by virtue of the pro-visions of regulation 3; and

  (d) the non-resident parent has made payments of maintenance due under that order after the date on which the maintenance calculation took effect in accordance with regulation 26 of the Maintenance Calculation Procedure Regulations, the payments made under the maintenance order shall be treated as payments of child support maintenance.]

AMENDMENT

1. Regulation 2 of the Miscellaneous Amendments Regulations (in force for the purposes of any type of case which is not one in relation to which 3rd March 2003 is the day appointed for the coming into force of section 1(2)(a) of the 2000 Act, on the day on which that provision comes into force in relation to that type of case).

DEFINITIONS

"Maintenance Calculation Procedure Regulations": see reg.1(2).
"maintenance order": see reg.1(2).

## [¹Cases in which application may be made under section 4 or 7 of the Act

3.173   **9.** The provisions of section 4(10) or 7(10) of the Act shall not apply to prevent an application being made under those sections after 22nd January 1996 where a decision has been made by the relevant court either that it has no power to vary or that it has no power to enforce a maintenance order in a particular case.]

AMENDMENT

1. Regulation 14 of the Miscellaneous Amendments (No.2) Regulations 1995 (January 22, 1996).

DEFINITIONS

3.174   "the Act": see reg.1(2).
"maintenance order": see reg.1(2)

GENERAL NOTE

3.175   See the general note to s.18 of the 1995 Act.

## The Child Support Fees Regulations 1992

### (SI 1992/3094)

3.176   The Child Support Fees Regulations 1992 were revoked by the Collection and Enforcement and Miscellaneous Amendments Regulations 2000 (for in force date see regs 1 and 6 of SI 2001/162 below).

## The Child Support (Northern Ireland Reciprocal Arrangements) Regulations 1993

### (SI 1993/584)

*Made by the Secretary of State for Social Security under section 56(3) and (4) of the Child Support Act 1991 and all other powers enabling him in that behalf.*

### Citation and commencement

**1.** These Regulations may be cited as the Child Support (Northern Ireland Reciprocal Arrangements) Regulations 1993 and shall come into force on 5th April 1993.

3.177

### Adaptation of the Child Support Act 1991 and regulations in respect of child support

**2.**—(1) The provisions contained in the Memorandum of Arrangements set out in Schedule 1 [¹as amended by the Exchange of Letters set out in Schedule 1A] to these Regulations shall have effect so far as the same relate to Great Britain.

3.178

(2) In particular and without prejudice to paragraph (1) above any act, omission and event which has effect for the purposes of the provision of the Northern Ireland legislation specified in column 2 of Schedule 2 to these Regulations shall also have effect as an act, omission and event for the purposes of the provision of the Child Support Act 1991 specified in the corresponding paragraph of column 1 of Schedule 2 to the said Regulations; and in the provisions specified in column 1 of Schedule 2 to these Regulations the references to—

    (a) "the Act" shall be construed as including references to the Child Support (Northern Ireland) Order 1991;

    (b) "the Secretary of State" shall be construed as including references to the Department of Health and Social Services for Northern Ireland;

    (c) any "child support officer" shall be construed as including references to such an officer appointed by the Department of Health and Social Services for Northern Ireland;

    (d) "child support maintenance" shall be construed as including references to child support maintenance within the meaning of the Child Support (Northern Ireland) Order 1991, and cognate expressions shall be construed accordingly.

AMENDMENT

1. Regulation 53 of the Miscellaneous Amendments No.2 Regulations 1995 (January 22, 1996).

## Northern Ireland Reciprocal Arrangements Regulations 1993

*Memorandum of Arrangements relating to the provision made for Child Support Maintenance in the United Kingdom between the Secretary of State for Social Security of the one part and the Department of Health and Social Services for Northern Ireland of the other part*

PART 1

INTERPRETATION AND GENERAL PROVISIONS

3.179      **1.** In this Memorandum, unless the context otherwise requires:

"the Act" means the Child Support Act 1991 and "the Order" means the Child Support (Northern Ireland) Order 1991;

"application", for the purposes of Article 5, includes an application by an absent parent and an application under section 7 of the Act;

"determining authority" means, in relation to Great Britain, a child support officer, a child support appeal tribunal, a Child Support Commissioner, or a tribunal consisting of any three of the Child Support Commissioners, and appointed or constituted under the Act, and, in relation to Northern Ireland, a child support officer or a child support appeal tribunal appointed or constituted under the Order, a Child Support Commissioner for Northern Ireland appointed under the Act or a tribunal consisting of any two or three of the Child Support Commissioners for Northern Ireland constituted under the Order;

"parent with care" means a person who, in respect of the same child or children, is both a parent and a person with care;

"territory" means Great Britain or Northern Ireland, as the case may be.

**2.**—(1) Unless the context otherwise requires, in the application of this Memorandum to a territory, expressions used in this Memorandum shall have the same respective meanings as in the Act, in relation to Great Britain, or in the Order, in relation to Northern Ireland.

(2) The rules for the construction of Acts of Parliament contained in the Interpretation Act 1978 shall apply for the purposes of the interpretation of this Memorandum as they apply for the purposes of the interpretation of an Act of Parliament or statutory instrument.

**3.**—(1) Subject to Articles 5 to 12 of this Memorandum, the provision made for Great Britain and the provision made for Northern Ireland shall operate as a single system within the United Kingdom.

(2) For the purposes of paragraph (1), all acts, omissions and events and in particular any application, declaration, direction, decision or order having effect for the provision made for Great Britain and having effect in that territory or for the provision made for Northern Ireland and having effect in that territory, shall have a corresponding effect for the purpose of the provision made for child support maintenance made in the other territory.

**4.** Nothing in this Memorandum shall require the payment of a fee under the provision made for one territory if such a fee is paid or liable to be paid in the same circumstances under the provision made for the other territory.

PART 2

CASE OWNERSHIP

3.180      **5.**—(1) Subject to paragraphs (2) and (4), where two or more applications for a maintenance assessment are made in relation to the same absent parent or a person treated as such, under the provision made for one territory and under the provision made for the other territory, all the said applications shall be dealt with in, and in accordance with the provision made for, the territory in which the person with care resides in respect of whom the first application was received.

(2) Subject to paragraph (4), where the applications specified in paragraph (1) include an application under section 7 of the Act by a qualifying child (right of child in Scotland to apply for assessment), all the applications shall be dealt with in, and in accordance with the provision made for, the territory in which the person with care of the said qualifying child resides.

(3) Subject to paragraph (4), where a person with care whose application is dealt with under the provisions of paragraph (1) makes an application in respect of another absent parent, that further application shall be dealt with in, and in accordance with the provision made for, the territory specified in that paragraph.

(4) Where paragraphs (1), (2) or (3) apply, the determining authority shall, in determining the amount of child support maintenance to be fixed by any maintenance assessment, take into account in calculating that amount, any provisions which would otherwise have been applicable to that calculation had the assessment been made in accordance with the provision made for the other territory.

### PART 3

#### MULTIPLE APPLICATIONS

**6.** Where—

(a) no maintenance assessment is in force and an application for such an assessment is made in one territory and another such application is made in the other territory in respect of the same qualifying child or children and the same person with care and absent parent or parents or person treated as such; and      **3.181**

(b) but for the fact that the person with care, and the absent parent or parents or person treated as such reside in different territories the provisions regarding multiple applications made under the provision for Great Britain or the provision made for Northern Ireland would apply,

those provisions shall have effect to determine which application shall be proceeded with.

### PART 4

#### DISCLOSURE OF INFORMATION AND INSPECTORS

**7.**—(1) Subject to paragraph (2) where the Secretary of State, the Department, or a child support officer appointed under the provision made for Great Britain or for Northern Ireland, has in his or its possession any information or evidence held for the purposes of the provision made for his or its territory, that information or evidence may be disclosed to the Secretary of State, the Department or the child support officer for the other territory for the purposes of the provision made for Great Britain or for Northern Ireland, as the case may be.      **3.182**

(2) Where information is disclosed under the provisions of paragraph (1), the provision made for Northern Ireland or, as the case may be, Great Britain, relating to unauthorised disclosure of information shall apply to that information.

**8.** Where in relation to a particular case, for the purposes of the provision made for one territory (the first provision) it is necessary for an inspector to be appointed, an inspector may be appointed under the provision for the other territory to exercise his powers of inspection for the purposes of the first provision.

### PART 5

#### APPEALS

**9.** Subject to Article 12, any appeal from any decision of a determining authority made under the provision for one territory shall be heard and determined—      **3.183**

(a) in a case which is being dealt with in accordance with the provisions of Article 5 above; or

(b) in a case where the relevant persons to the appeal are resident in different territories, in, and in accordance with the provision made for, the territory in which case is being dealt with.

PART 6

COLLECTION AND ENFORCEMENT

**3.184**    **10.** Where a deduction from earnings order is made under the provision made for one territory and the liable person works for an employer in the other territory, the deduction from earnings order shall have effect in the territory in which the liable person works as if it was made under provision for that territory.

**11.** Where an application for a liability order is to be made against a liable person under the provision made for one territory and the liable person is resident in the other territory, the application shall be made under the provision for the territory in which the liable person is resident, notwithstanding the fact that the liability arose or the maintenance assessment was made under the provision for the other territory.

**12.** Where a deduction from earnings order has been applied or a liability order has been obtained in accordance with Articles 10 or 11, any appeal in connection with that deduction from earnings order or liability order or action as a consequence of the deduction from earnings order or liability order shall be made under the provision for the territory in which the liable person is resident.

PART 7

ADMINISTRATIVE PROCEDURES

**3.185**    **13.** The Secretary of State and the Department may from time to time determine the administrative procedures appropriate for the purposes of giving effect to this Memorandum.

PART 8

OPERATIVE DATE

**3.186**    **14.** The arrangements in this Memorandum shall come into effect on 5th April 1993 but either Party may terminate them by giving not less than six months notice in writing to the other.

Signed on 8th day of March 1993.

*Peter Lilley*
*Secretary of State for Social Security*

Sealed with the Official Seal of the Department of Health and Social Services for Northern Ireland on 9th day of March 1993.

*F. A. Elliott*
*Permanent Secretary*

[¹SCHEDULE 1A    **Regulation 2(1)**

EXCHANGE OF LETTERS AMENDING THE MEMORANDUM OF ARRANGEMENTS RELATING TO THE PROVISION MADE FOR CHILD SUPPORT MAINTENANCE IN THE UNITED KINGDOM

No. 1

THE SECRETARY OF STATE FOR SOCIAL SECURITY AND THE DEPARTMENT OF HEALTH AND SOCIAL SERVICES FOR NORTHERN IRELAND

7th November 1995

Sir,

**3.187**    I now have the honour to refer to the Memorandum of Arrangements relating to the provision made for Child Support Maintenance between the Secretary of State for Social Security of the one part and the Department of Health and Social Services for Northern Ireland of the other part which came into effect on 5 April 1993 (which in this letter is referred to as "the Principal Memorandum") and to recent discussions between the Department of Social Security and the Department of Health and Social Services for Northern Ireland concerning the need to amend the Principal Memorandum so as to make further provision in relation to child support matters.

I now have the honour to propose the following amendments to the Principal Memorandum:

After paragraph (4) of Article 5 there shall be inserted:—

"(5) Subject to paragraph (7), where an application for a maintenance assessment is made under the provisions for one territory in relation to an absent parent, a person treated as such or an alleged absent parent who resides in the other territory, that application shall be dealt with in, and in accordance with the provision made for, the territory in which the person with care resides.

(6) Subject to paragraph (7), where an application for a maintenance assessment is made under section 7 of the Act by a qualifying child, the application shall be dealt with in, and in accordance with the provision made for, the territory in which the person with care of that child resides.

(7) Where paragraphs (5) and (6) apply, the determining authority shall, in determining the amount of child support maintenance to be fixed by a maintenance assessment, take into account in calculating that amount, any provisions which would otherwise have been applicable to that calculation had the assessment been made in accordance with the provision made for the other territory".

After Part 6 there shall be inserted the following Part:

"Part 6A

*Parentage*

12A Where a person with care resides in one territory and an alleged parent who denies    **3.188**
that he is one of the parents of a child in respect of whom an application for a maintenance assessment has been made resides in the other territory:—

(a) The person with care or the Secretary of State may apply for a declaration as to whether or not the alleged parent is one of the child's parents, under Article 28 of the Order;

(b) The person with care or the Department of Health and Social Services may apply for such a declaration under section 27 of the Act; and

(c) The Department of Health and Social Services may bring an action for declarator of parentage under the provisions of section 28 of the Act".

If the foregoing proposals are acceptable to you, I have the honour to propose that this letter and your reply to that effect shall constitute a Memorandum of Arrangements between us which shall come into effect on 21st January 1996.

*Andrew Mitchell*
*For the Secretary of State for Social Security*

No. 2

The Department of Health and Social Services for Northern Ireland
to the Secretary of State for Social Security

8th November 1995

Sir,

I refer to your letter of 7th November 1995 which reads as follows:

"I have the honour to refer to the Memorandum of Arrangements relating to the provision made for Child Support Maintenance between the Secretary of State for Social Security of the one part and the Department of Health and Social Services for Northern Ireland of the other part which came into effect on 5 April 1993 (which in this letter is referred to as "the Principal Memorandum") and to the recent discussions between the Department of Social Security and the Department of Health and Social Services for Northern Ireland concerning the need to amend the Principal Memorandum so as to make further provision in relation to child support matters.

I now have the honour to propose the following amendments to the Principal Memorandum:

After paragraph (4) of Article 5 there shall be inserted:—

"(5) Subject to paragraph (7), where an application for a maintenance assessment is made under the provisions for one territory in relation to an absent parent, a person treated as such, or an alleged absent parent, who resides in the other territory, that application shall be dealt with in, and in accordance with the provisions made for, the territory in which the person with care resides.

(6) Subject to paragraph (7), where an application for a maintenance assessment is made under section 7 of the Act by a qualifying child, the application shall be dealt with in, and in accordance with the provision made for, the territory in which the person with care of that child resides.

(7) Where paragraph (5) or (6) apply, the determining authority shall, in determining the amount of child support maintenance to be fixed by any maintenance assessment, take into account in calculating that amount, any provisions which would otherwise have been applicable to that calculation had the assessment been made in accordance with the provision made for the other territory".

After Part 6 there shall be inserted the following Part:—

## PART 6A

### *Parentage*

12A Where a person with care resides in one territory and an alleged parent whodenies that he is one of the parents of a child in respect of whom an application for a maintenance assessment has been made resides in the other territory:—

(a) The person with care or the Secretary of State may apply for a declaration as to whether or not the alleged parent is one of the child's parents, under Article 28 of the Order;

(b) The person with care or the Department of Health and Social Services may apply for such a declaration under section 27 of the Act; and

(c) The Department of Health and Social Services may bring an action for declarator of parentage under the provisions of section 28 of the Act".

I have the honour to confirm that the foregoing proposals are acceptable to the Department of Health and Social Services for Northern Ireland and agree that your letter and this reply shall constitute a Memorandum of Arrangements between us which shall come into effect on 21st January 1996.

Sealed with the Official seal of the Department of Health and Social Services for Northern Ireland on the 8th day of November 1995.

*F A Elliott*
*Permanent Secretary*

AMENDMENT

1. Regulation 54 of and the Sch. to the Miscellaneous Amendments (No.2) Regulations 1995 (January 22, 1996).


SCHEDULE 2                                    **Regulation 2(2)**

ADAPTATION OF CERTAIN PROVISIONS OF THE CHILD SUPPORT ACT 1991

| Column 1 | Column 2 | Column 3 | **3.189** |
|----------|----------|----------|------|
| Provisions of the Child Support Act 1991 | Provisions of the Child Support (Northern Ireland) Order 1991 | Subject Matter | |
| Section 1 | Article 5 | The duty to maintain | |
| Section 2 | Article 6 | Welfare of children: the general principle | |
| Section 8 | Article 10 | Role of the courts with respect to maintenance for children | |
| Section 9 | Article 11 | Agreements about maintenance | |
| Section 10 | Article 12 | Relationship between maintenance assessments and certain court orders and related matters | |
| Section 15 | Article 17 | Powers of inspectors | |
| [¹Sections 27 and 28 | Article 28 | Declaration of parentage] | |
| Section 29 | Article 29 | Collection of child support maintenance | |
| Section 30 | Article 30 | Collection and enforcement of other forms of maintenance | |

AMENDMENT

1. Regulation 55 of the Miscellaneous Amendments (No.2) Regulations 1995 (January 22, 1996).


## The Child Maintenance (Written Agreements) Order 1993

### (SI 1993/620 (L.4))

*Made by the Lord Chancellor under section 8(5) of the Child Support Act 1991*

**1.** This order may be cited as the Child Maintenance (Written      **3.190**
Agreements) Order 1993 and shall come into force on 5th April 1993.

**2.** Section 8 shall not prevent a court from exercising any power which it has to make a maintenance order in relation to a child in any circumstances in which paragraphs (a) and (b) of section 8(5) apply.

General Note

This Order was made only by the Lord Chancellor. It applies to England and Wales. Equivalent provision is made for Scotland by the Child Support (Written Agreements) (Scotland) Order 1997 below.

## The Child Support Appeals (Jurisdiction of Courts) Order 1993

### (SI 1993/961 (L.12))

*Made by the Lord Chancellor in relation to England and Wales and by the Lord Advocate in relation to Scotland under ss.45(1) and (7) and 58(7) of the Child Support Act 1991.*

This Order is revoked to the extent that it applies to England and Wales by art.2 of the Child Support Appeals (Jurisdiction of Courts) Order 2002 and to the extent that it applies to Scotland by art.6 of the Child Support Appeals (Jurisdiction of Courts) (Scotland) Order 2003. However, it is only revoked for those cases covered by the new s.20 of the Act, which was introduced by s.10 of the 2000 Act. For other cases, it remains in force.

### Title, commencement and interpretation

3.191
**1.** This order may be cited as the Child Support Appeals (Jurisdiction of Courts) Order 1993 and shall come into force on 5th April 1993.
**2.** In this Order, "the Act" means the Child Support Act 1991.

### Parentage appeals to be made in courts

3.192
**3.** An appeal under section 20 of the Act shall be made to a court instead of to a child support appeal tribunal in the circumstances mentioned in article 4.

General Note

3.193
This Article has not been amended to reflect the transfer of decision-making.

3.194
**4.** The circumstances are that—
(a) the decision against which the appeal is brought was made on the basis that particular person (whether the applicant or some other person) either was, or was not, a parent of a child in question, and
(b) the ground of the appeal will be that the decision should not have been made on that basis.

General Note

3.195
For a commentary to this article, see art.4 of the Child Support Appeals (Jurisdiction of Courts) Order 2002.

3.196
**5.**—(1) For the purposes of article 3 above, an appeal may be made to a court in Scotland if—

(a) the child in question was born in Scotland; or

(b) the child, the absent parent or the person with care of the child is domiciled in Scotland on the date when the appeal is made or is habitually resident in Scotland on that date.

(2) Where an appeal to a court in Scotland is to be made to the sheriff, it shall be to the sheriff of the sheriffdom where—

(a) the child in question was born; or

(b) the child, the absent parent or the person with care of the child is habitually resident on the date when the appeal is made.

### Modification of section 20(2) to (4) of the Act in relation to appeals to courts

**6.** In relation to an appeal which is to be made to a court in accordance with this Order, the reference to the chairman of a child support appeal tribunal in section 20(2) of the Act shall be construed as a reference to the court.          3.197

**7.** In relation to an appeal which has been made to a court in accordance with this Order, the references to the tribunal in section 20(3) and (4) of the Act shall be construed as a reference to the court.

### Amendment of the Law Reform (Parent and Child) (Scotland) Act 1986

**8.** In section 8 (Interpretation) of the Law Reform (Parent and Child) (Scotland) Act 1986 at the end of the definition of "action for declarator" there shall be inserted the words "but does not include an appeal under section 20 (Appeals) of the Child Support Act 1991 made to the court by virtue of an order made under section 45 (jurisdiction of courts in certain proceedings) of that Act;".          3.198

### The Child Support (Miscellaneous Amendments and Transitional Provisions) Regulations 1994

### (SI 1994/227)

*Made by the Secretary of State for Social Security under ss.16, 17(6)(b), 32(2)(c), 35(2)(b), 47, 51 and 52(4) of, and paras.1(3), 4(1), 6(6) and 8 of Sched. 1 to, the Child Support Act 1991 and all other powers enabling him in that behalf.*

PART I

GENERAL

### Citation and commencement

**1.** These Regulations may be cited as the Child Support (Miscellaneous Amendments and Transitional Provisions) Regulations 1994 and shall come into force on 7th February 1994.          3.199

PART II

AMENDMENT OF REGULATIONS

3.200    [The amendments made by this Part above are noted in relation to the relevant provisions.]

PART III

TRANSITIONAL PROVISIONS

3.201    **6.**—(1) In this Part and Part IV of these Regulations—
"the Act" means the Child Support Act 1991;
"excess" means the amount by which the formula amount exceeds the old amount;
"existing case" means a case in which before the date when these Regulations come into force, a maintenance assessment has been made which has an effective date which also falls before that date;
"formula amount" means the amount of child support maintenance that would, but for the provisions of this Part of these Regulations, be payable under the maintenance assessment in force on the date these Regulations come into force or, if these is no such assessment, under the first assessment to come into force on or after that date;
"new case" means a case in which the effective date of the maintenance assessment falls on or after the date when these Regulations come into force;
"old amount" means, subject to paragraph (2) below, the aggregate weekly amount which was payable under the orders, agreements or arrangements mentioned in regulation 7(1)(a) below;
"pending case" means a case in which an application for a maintenance assessment has been made before the date when these regulations come into force but no maintenance assessment has been made before that date;
"Procedure Regulations" means the Child Support (Maintenance Assessment Procedure) Regulations 1992;
"transitional amount" means an amount determined in accordance with regulation 8 below; and
"transitional period" means a period of, where the formula amount does not exceed £60, 52 weeks, and in any other case 78 weeks, beginning—
(a) in relation to an existing case, with the day that the maintenance assessment in that case [¹was reviewed or, as the case may be, a decision is made superseding an earlier decision,] following an application under regulation 10(1) to (3) below;
(b) in relation to a new case, the effective date of the maintenance assessment in that case;
(c) in relation to a pending case, the effective date of the maintenance assessment in that case or the date when these Regulations come into force, whichever is the later.

(2) In determining the old amount [²the Secretary of State] shall disregard any payments in kind and any payments made to a third party on behalf of or for the benefit of the qualifying child or qualifying children or the person with care.

AMENDMENTS

1. Article 32(a) of the Commencement No.7 Order 1999 (June 1, 1999).
2. Article 32(b) of the Commencement No.7 Order 1999 (June 1, 1999).

## Scope of this Part

7.—(1) Subject to paragraph (2) below, this Part of these Regulations applies to cases where—    **3.202**
  (a) on 4th April 1993, and at all times thereafter until the date when a maintenance assessment was or is made under the Act, there was in force, in respect of one or more of the qualifying children in respect of whom an application for a maintenance assessment was or is made under the Act and the absent parent concerned, one or more—
      (i) maintenance orders;
      (ii) orders under section 151 of the Army Act 1955 (deductions from pay for maintenance of wife or child) or section 151 of the Air Force Act 1955 (deduction from pay for maintenace of wife or child) or arrangements corresponding to such an order and made under Article 1(b) or 3 of the Naval and Marine Pay and Pensions (Deductions for Maintenance) Order 1959; or
      (iii) maintenance agreements (being agreements which are made or evidenced in writing); and
  (b) the absent parent was on the relevant date and continues to be a member of a family, as defined in regulation 1(2) of the Child Support (Maintenance Assessments and Special Cases) Regulations 1992, which includes one or more children;
  (c) the formula amount exceeds the old amount.
(2) Nothing in this Part of these Regulations applies to—
  (a) a Category A [¹or Category D] interim maintenance assessment within the meaning of [²regulation 8(3)]) of the Procedure Regulations and made under section 12 of the Act; [². . .]
  (b) a case falling within the provisions of Part II of the Schedule to the Child Support Act 1991 (Commencement No. 3 and Transitional Provisions) Order 1992 (modification of maintenance assessment in certain cases); [³or]
  [⁴(c) a maintenance assessment calculated in accordance with Part I of Schedule 1 to the Act which is made following a Category A or Category D interim maintenance assessment within the meaning of regulation 8 of the Procedure Regulations where that Category A or Category D interim maintenance assessment is made after 22nd January 1996.]
(3) In subparagraph (1)(b) above "the relevant date" means—
  (a) in an existing case, the date these Regulations come into force;
  (b) in a new case, the effective date of the maintenance assessment in that case; and

(c) in a pending case, the effective date of the maintenance assessment in that case or the date on which these Regulations come into force, whichever is the later.

AMENDMENTS

1. Regulation 60 of the Amendment Regulations 1995 (April 18, 1995).
2. Regulation 51(2) of the Miscellaneous Amendments (No.2) Regulations 1995 (January 22, 1996).
3. Regulation 51(3) of the Miscellaneous Amendments (No.2) Regulations 1995 (January 22, 1996).
4. Regulation 51(4) of the Miscellaneous Amendments (No.2) Regulations 1995 (January 22, 1996).

DEFINITIONS

3.203     "the Act": see reg.6(1)
"existing case": see reg.6(1)
"formula amount": see reg.6(1)
"new case": see reg.6(1)
"old amount": see reg.6(1)
"pending case": see reg.6(1)
"Procedure Regulations": see reg.6(1)
"transitional amount": see reg.6(1)

## Transitional amount of child support maintenance

3.204     **8.**—(1) In a case to which this Part of these Regulations applies the amount of child support maintenance payable under a maintenance assessment during the transitional period shall, instead of being the formula amount, be the transitional amount.

(2) The transitional amount is—

(a) where the formula amount is not more than £60, an amount which is £20 greater than the old amount;

(b) where the formula amount is more than £60—

    (i) during the first 26 weeks of the transitional period, the old amount plus either 25 per centum of the excess or £20.00, whichever is the greater;

    (ii) during the next 26 weeks of the transitional period, the old amount plus either 50 per centum of the excess or £40.00, whichever is the greater; and

    (iii) during the last 26 weeks of the transitional period, the old amount plus either 75 per centum of the excess or £60.00, whichever is the greater;

(3) If in any case the application of the provisions of this Part of these Regulations would result in an amount of child support maintenance becoming payable which is greater than the formula amount, then those provisions shall not apply or, as the case may be, shall cease to apply to that case and the amount of child support maintenance payable in that case shall be the formula amount.

DEFINITIONS

"excess": see reg.6(1)                                                      3.205
"formula amount": see reg.6(1)
"old amount": see reg.6(1)
"transitional amount": see reg.6(1)
"transitional period": see reg.6(1)

GENERAL NOTE

Part III of these Regulations extends the range of cases in which provision is made    3.206
for the phasing in of the full amount of the child support maintenance payable
under the formulae in the Act. Its effect is not cumulative with the provision for
phasing in contained in Pt II of the Transitional Provisions Order and so cannot be
used in cases which already benefit from the provisions of that Order (reg.7(2)(b)).
If a tribunal decides that the phasing arrangements under the Transitional
Provisions Order do not apply, it must consider whether the arrangements provided by this Part of these Regulations apply (*CCS 14340/96*, para.6). In in keeping
with the intended punitive effect of interim maintenance assessments, this Part has
no effect in the case of Category A or D interim maintenance assessments, that is,
those interim maintenance assessments which are made as a result of the default of
the absent parent (reg.7(2)(a)).

The phasing-in provisions of these Regulations apply where three conditions are
satisfied: (i) there must have been a maintenance order, arrangement or agreement
in force, in respect of the absent parent and one or more of the qualifying children,
continuously from April 4, 1993 (when child support maintenance came into
effect) until the date when the child support maintenance assessment is or was
made (reg.7(1)(a)); (ii) the absent parent lives with one or more children for whom
either that parent or that parent's partner has day to day care (reg.7(1)(b)); (iii) the
amount of child support maintenance that would be payable apart from this Part of
the Regulations exceeds the amount of the maintenance payable under the previous
order, arrangement or agreement (reg.7(1)(c)). In determining the amount previously payable, payments made in kind or to a third party are disregarded (reg.6(2)).

In those cases to which this Part applies provision is made for a reduced amount
of child support maintenance to be paid for the transitional period. In those cases
where the amount that would otherwise be payable is £60 or less, the transitional
period lasts for a year (reg.6(1)) and the reduced amount payable is the amount
previously payable plus £20 (reg.8(2)). In those cases where the amount that would
otherwise be payable is more than £60, the transitional period lasts for 18 months
(reg.6(1)) and the reduced amount payable is the previous amount plus £20 or 25
per cent (whichever is the greater) for the first 26 weeks, £40 or 50 per cent for the
next 26 weeks and £60 or 75 per cent for the final 26 weeks (reg.8(2)). These provisions do not apply, or case to apply, if they would result in the absent parent paying more than the amount of child support maintenance that would otherwise be
payable (reg.8(3)).

The provisions of this Part differ from those contained in the Transitional
Provisions Order in the following ways: (i) the previous maintenance order,
arrangement or agreement need not be in respect of all the children who are subject to the application for a child support maintenance assessment; (ii) there is no
restriction on the amount of child support maintenance that would otherwise be
payable; (iii) there is no provision for any minimum excess of the maintenance that
would otherwise be payable over the amount previously payable; (iv) the absent parent's family circumstances are now defined in terms of day to day care rather than
residence and maintenance and may include the qualifying child where the absent
parent has day to day care of that child (*CCS 14340/96*, para.8).

PART IV

PROCEDURE, ETC.

## Interpretation

3.207     **9.** In this part of these Regulations "the Procedure Regulations" means the Child Support (Maintenance Assessment Procedure) Regulations 1992.

GENERAL NOTE

3.208     This regulation is unnecessary as the same provision is made in relation to this Part of the Regulations by reg.6(1).

## Procedure

3.209     **10.**—(1) The Provisions of Part III of these Regulations shall not apply to a case in which there is a maintenance assessment in force on the date they come into force unless the absent parent in relation to whom that assessment was made makes an application for a review of that assessment under section 17 of the Act [¹before 1st June 1999 or an application on or after that date for a decision under section 17 of the Act superseding an earlier decision].

(2) Such an application must be made not later than 3 months after the date when these Regulations come into force, but if an application is made after that period it may be accepted if the Secretary of State is satisfied that there is good reason for its being made late.

[²(3) Regulation 10(2) of the Procedure Regulations shall not apply in respect of a decision made solely for the purpose of applying Part III of these Regulations but instead the Secretary of State shall notify the relevant persons (as defined in regulation 1(2) of the Procedure Regulations) of the detail of how the provisions of Part III of these Regulations have been applied in that case.]

AMENDMENTS

    1. Article 33(a) of the Commencement No.7 Order 1999 (June 1, 1999).
    2. Article 33(b) of the Commencement No.7 Order 1999 (June 1, 1999).

DEFINITIONS

3.210     "the Act": see reg.6(1).
    "Procedure Regulations": see regs 6(1) and 9.

GENERAL NOTE

3.211     The provisions of Pt III will only apply to cases in which there was a mainte-nance assessment in force on February 7, 1994 (the day the Regulations came into force) if the absent parent requests a review on the basis of a change of circum-stances (the change in the law being the relevant change) under s.17 of the Act within three months (subject to extension if there is a good reason for the late application). Unlike the provisions in the Transitional Provisional Order, the provisions of Pt III can, therefore, apply to cases where an assessment has already been made as well as to new assessments (see the definition of "formula amount" in reg.6(1) as above).

## [¹Revision and supersession

**11.**—(1) The provisions of the following paragraphs shall apply where the Secretary of State proposes to make a decision under section 16 (revision of decisions) or 17 (decisions superseding earlier decisions) of the Act with respect to a maintenance assessment under which the amount payable was the transitional amount.

(2) Where a fresh maintenance assessment would be made by virtue of a decision under section 16 or 17 of the Act and the amount payable under that assessment (disregarding the provisions of Part III of these Regulations) (in this regulation called "the new formula amount") would be—

(a) more than the formula amount, the amount of child support maintenance payable shall be the transitional amount plus the difference between the formula amount and the new formula amount;

(b) less than the formula amount but more than the transitional amount, the amount of the child support maintenance payable shall be the transitional amount;

(c) less than the transitional amount, the amount of child support maintenance payable shall be the new formula amount.

(3) Regulation 21 and 22 of the Procedure Regulations shall apply as if the new formula amount were the amount which would be fixed in accordance with a decision superseding an earlier decision.

(4) Where the effective date of a fresh maintenance assessment made by virtue of a revision under section 16 of the Act or of a decision under section 17 of the Act superseding an earlier decision would, apart from this regulation, be before 18th April 1995—

(a) the fresh maintenance assessment; and

(b) the decision under section 16 or, as the case may be, section 17, shall have effect as from 18th April 1995.]

3.212

AMENDMENT

1. Article 34 of the Commencement No.7 Order 1999 (June 1, 1999).

DEFINITIONS

"the Act": see reg.6(1).
"formula amount": see reg.6(1).
"Procedure Regulations": see regs 6(1) and 9.
"transitional amount": see regs 6(1) and 9.

3.213

## [¹Decisions] consequent on the amendments made by Part II

**12.**—(1) A fresh maintenance assessment shall not be made by virtue of a decision under section 17 of the Act superseding an earlier decision in consequence only of the amendments made by Part II of these Regulations

3.214

where the amount of child support maintenance fixed by the assessment currently in force and the amount that would be fixed if a fresh assessment were to be made under that section is less than £1.00 a week.

(2) Except in relation to the amendment made by regulation 4(8) above, where a fresh maintenance assessment is made by virtue of a decision under section 17 of the Act superseding an earlier decision in consequence only of the amendments made by Part II of these Regulations, the date as from which—

(a) the fresh maintenance assessment; and

(b) the decision under section 16 or, as the case may be, section 17, shall have effect shall be 7th February 1994.]

AMENDMENT

1. Article 35 of the Commencement No.7 Order 1999 (June 1, 1999).

DEFINITIONS

3.215    "the Act": see reg.6(1).
"Procedure Regulations": see regs 6(1) and 9.

GENERAL NOTE

*Paragraph (1)*
3.216    The £1 supplants the usual £10 threshold (*CCS 511/95*, para.30).

[Regulations 13 and 14 were revoked with effect from June 1, 1999 by art.36 of the Commencement No. 7 Order 1999.]

# Child Support and Income Support (Amendment) Regulations 1995

## (SI 1995/1045)

*Made by, the Secretary of State for Social Security under sections 8(11), 10(1), 12(2) and (3), 14(1) and (3), 16(1), 17(4), 18(11), 21(2), 29(2), 32, 41(3), 42, 43(1), 46(11), 47, 51, 52, 54 and 57 of, and paragraphs 4(3), 5(1) and (2), 6(2), (4) and (5), 7(1), 8, 9(a) and 11 of Schedule 1 to, the Child Support Act 1991 and sections 135(1), 137(1) and 175(1), (3) and (4) of the Social Security Contributions and Benefits Act 1992 and of all other powers enabling him in that behalf, after consultation with the Council on Tribunals in accordance with section 8 of the Tribunals and Inquiries Act 1992 and after agreement by the Social Security Advisory Committee that proposals in respect of regulation 62 should not be referred to it.*

## Citation, commencement and interpretation

3.217    **1.**—(1) These Regulations may be cited as the Child Support and Income Support (Amendment) Regulations 1995.

(2) This regulation and regulation 58 of these Regulations shall come into force on 13th April 1995 and all other regulations shall come into force on 18th April 1995.

(3) In these Regulations—

. . .

"the Arrears Regulations" means the Child Support (Arrears, Interest and Adjustment of Maintenance Assessments) Regulations 1992;

"the Maintenance Assessment Procedure Regulations" means the Child Support (Maintenance Assessment Procedure) Regulations 1992;

. . .

## Reviews consequent upon the amendments made by these regulations

**63.**—(1) [¹Subject to paragraph (3), a decision with respect to a maintenance assessment in force on 13th April 1995 or 18th April 1995 shall not be superseded by a decision under section 17 of the Act if the difference between the amount of child support maintenance currently in force and the amount that would be fixed if the fresh assessment were to be made as a result of a supersession is—]

   (a) less than £1.00 per week where the amount fixed by the assessment currently in force is more than the amount that would be fixed by the fresh assessment; or

   (b) less than £10.00 per week in all other cases.

(2) Paragraph (1) applies to the following provisions—

   (a) regulation 28(8);

   (b) regulation 43;

   (c) regulation 44(2);

   (d) regulation 45;

   (e) regulation 46(2)(d) and (e), (4) and (6);

   (f) regulation 47;

   (g) regulation 50;

   (h) regulation 51;

   (i) regulation 54(10) and (11).

(3) Paragraph (1) shall not apply to a [²decision under section 17 of the Child Support Act 1991 which fails to be made] in consequence only of the amendments made by regulations 44(2), 45, 46(2)(d) and (e) and 51 unless the person to whom the assessment relates [³notified] the Secretary of State before 18th July 1995 that he wishes a child support officer to consider whether the assessment in his case should be reviewed; but the Secretary of State may accept a later notification for the purposes of this paragraph if he is satisfied that there is good cause for the delay in giving it.

[⁴. . .]

(6) Where a maintenance assessment is in force on 18th April 1995 and—

   (a) the relevant person notifies the Secretary of State on or after 18th July 1995 that he wishes [⁵the question to be considered] of whether an amount should be allowed in the computation of the relevant person's exempt income or protected income in

3.218

respect of travelling costs or his exempt income in respect of a
qualifying transfer of property; and

(b) the Secretary of State is not satisfied that there was good cause
for the delay on the part of the relevant person in giving the
notification,

the effective date of any assessment made [⁶by virtue of a decision under
section 17 of the Act superseding an earlier decision] shall be the first day
of the maintenance period in which the Secretary of State is so notified.

AMENDMENTS

1. Article 37(a) of the Commencement No.7 Order 1999 (June 1, 1999).
2. Article 37(b)(i) of the Commencement No.7 Order 1999 (June 1, 1999).
3. Article 37(b)(ii) of the Commencement No.7 Order 1999 (June 1, 1999).
4. Article 37(c) of the Commencement No.7 Order 1999 (June 1, 1999).
5. Article 37(d)(i) of the Commencement No.7 Order 1999 (June 1, 1999).
6. Article 37(d)(ii) of the Commencement No.7 Order 1999 (June 1, 1999).

**Transitional provisions**

3.219    **64.**—(1) Where a maintenance assessment, other than an interim maintenance assessment, is in force on 18th April 1995 [¹and] the amount of
child support payable under that assessment would be affected by the provisions of these Regulations, only the provisions mentioned in paragraphs
(2) and (3) shall apply to that assessment until that assessment is reviewed
under section 16, 17 or 18 of the Act.

(2) The provisions of these Regulations to which paragraph (1) refers
are—

(a) regulation 34;
(b) regulation 43;
(c) regulation 46(6);
(d) regulation 47;
(e) regulation 50;
(f) regulation 54(10) and (11);
(g) [²...]

(3) The provisions of regulations 44(2), 45, 46(2)(d) and (e) and 51
and Schedules 1 and 2 to these Regulations shall not apply in a case
where there is a maintenance assessment in force on the 18th April 1995
until [³a relevant person applies for a decision under section 17 of the
Child Support Act 1991 superseding an earlier decision on the ground that
a qualifying transfer of property has been made or that he has travelling
costs.]

(4) Where on 18th April 1995 in any particular case there is in force a
maintenance assessment which is subject to an adjustment made under
the provisions of regulation 10 of the Arrears Regulations as in force prior
to that date that adjustment shall continue until whichever is the earlier
of—

(a) [⁴a decision under section 17 of the Child Support Act 1991 superseding a decision with respect to] that assessment on grounds other
than the coming into force of these Regulations; or

[[5](b) a decision under regulation 13 or 16 of the Arrears Regulations is made on an application made by a relevant person.]

(5) Regulations 12 and 13 shall not apply to a case in which there is an existing assessment until the Secretary of State first reviews the period by reference to which payments are to be made after these Regulations come into force.

AMENDMENTS

1. Regulation 50(2) of the Miscellaneous Amendments (No.2) Regulations 1995 (January 22, 1996).
2. Regulation 50(3) of the Miscellaneous Amendments (No.2) Regulations 1995 (January 22, 1996).
3. Article 38(a) of the Commencement No.7 Order 1999 (June 1, 1999).
4. Article 38(b)(i) of the Commencement No.7 Order 1999 (June 1, 1999).
5. Article 38(b)(ii) of the Commencement No.7 Order 1999 (June 1, 1999).

GENERAL NOTE

The provisions referred to in regs 63(2) and (3) and 64(2), (3) and (5) amend the Collection and Enforcement Regulations (CER), the Maintenance Assessment Procedure Regulations (MAP) and the Maintenance Assessments and Special Cases Regulations (MASC) as follows:

**3.220**

| Provision | Effect | Relevant to | | | | |
|---|---|---|---|---|---|---|
| | | reg. 63(2) | reg. 63(3) | reg. 64(2) | reg. 64(2) | reg. 64(5) |
| reg.12 | amends reg.4 of CER | | | | | ⋆ |
| reg.13 | amends reg.5 of CER | | | | | ⋆ |
| reg.28(8) | inserts paras (2D) to (21) into reg.8 of MAP | ⋆ | | | | |
| reg.34 | amends reg.17 of MAP | | | ⋆ | | |
| reg.43 | amends reg.6 of MASC | ⋆ | | ⋆ | | |
| reg.44(2) | amends para.(1) of reg.9 of MASC | ⋆ | ⋆ | | ⋆ | |

| Provision | Effect | Relevant to | | | | |
|---|---|---|---|---|---|---|
| | | reg. 63(2) | reg. 63(3) | reg. 64(2) | reg. 64(2) | reg. 64(5) |
| reg.45 | amends reg.10 of MASC | ⋆ | ⋆ | | ⋆ | |
| reg.46(2)(d) and (e) | inserts sub-para. (kk) into reg.11(1) of MASC and amends reg. 11(1)(I) of MASC | ⋆ | ⋆ | | ⋆ | |
| reg.46(4) | inserts head (ii) into reg.11(2)(a) of MASC | ⋆ | | | | |
| reg.46(6) | inserts paras (6) and (7) into reg.11 of MASC | ⋆ | | ⋆ | | |
| reg.47 | amends reg.12 of MASC | ⋆ | | ⋆ | | |
| reg.50 | revokes reg.17 of MASC | ⋆ | | ⋆ | | |
| reg.51 | amends reg.22 of MASC | ⋆ | ⋆ | | ⋆ | |
| reg.54(10) and (11) | amend paras 20 and 23 of Sch.1 to MASC | ⋆ | | ⋆ | | |
| reg.59 | amends Sch 5 to MASC | | | ⋆ | | |
| Sch 1 | inserts Sch 3A to MASC | | | | ⋆ | |
| Sch 2 | inserts Sch 3B to MASC | | | | ⋆ | |

Regulation 64(1) prevents certain provisions being applied to an assessment until it is reviewed under s.16, 17 or 18. They may not be applied under a s.19 review, even if the review was instigated for reasons other than the amendments made by these Regulations.

## The Child Support (Miscellaneous Amendments) (No.2) Regulation 1995

### (SI 1995/3261)

*Made by the Secretary of State for Social Security under sections 12(2) and (3), 14(1), (1A) and (3), 16, 17, 18, 32(1), 41(2), 41B(3) and (6), 42(1), 46(5) and (11), 51, 52, 54 and 56(3) of, and paragraphs 5(1) and (2), 6(2), 8 and 11 of Schedule 1 to, the Child Support Act 1991, section 18(7) of the Child Support Act 1995 and all other powers enabling him in that behalf.*

### Citation, commencement and interpretation

**1.**—(1) These Regulations may be cited as the Child Support (Miscellaneous Amendments) (No.2) Regulations 1995.

(2) This regulation . . . and regulation 56 of these Regulations shall come into force on 18th December 1995 and all other regulations shall come into force on 22nd January 1996.

(3) In these Regulations—

. . .

"the Maintenance Assessment Procedure Regulations" means the Child Support (Maintenance Assessment Procedure) Regulations 1992;

"the Maintenance Assessments and Special Cases Regulations" means the Child Support (Maintenance Assessments and Special Cases) Regulations 1992;

. . .

### [¹Supersessions consequent on amendments made by these Regulations

**56.** Where a fresh assessment is made by virtue of a decision under section 17 of the Child Support Act 1991 superseding an earlier decision in consequence of the coming into force of regulation 48—

(a) the decision under section 17; and

(b) that fresh maintenance assessment,

shall have effect as from the first day of the maintenance period following 18th December 1995.]

3.221

3.222

AMENDMENT

1. Article 39 of the Commencement No.7 Order 1999 (June 1, 1999).

## Transitional and consequential provisions

3.223    **57.**—[²(l)  A decision with respect to a maintenance assessment shall not be superseded by a decision under section 17 of the Child Support Act 1991 solely to give effect to the provisions set out in paragraph (2).]
(2)  The provisions referred to in paragraph (1) are—
(a)  regulation 40(3);
(b)  regulation 42;
(c)  regulation 43(3);
(d)  head (v) of subparagraph (a) of paragraph (2) of regulation 11 of the Maintenance Assessments and Special Cases Regulations as inserted by regulation 43(5) of these Regulations;
(e)  regulation 46; and
(f)  regulation 47.
(3)  [³Where a decision is made under section 17 of the Child Support Act 1991 superseding an earlier decision] is carried out wholly or partly in consequence of one or more of the provisions set out in [¹regulation 40, 42, 43(3) or (5), 46, 47 or 49], and the amount of any fresh assessment made following [⁴that decision] is different from the amount of any fresh assessment that would have been made had those provisions not been in force, the effective date of that fresh assessment shall not be earlier than 22nd January 1996.
[⁵. . .]

AMENDMENTS

1. Regulation 4 of the Miscellaneous Amendments (No.3) Regulations 1995 (January 22, 1996).
2. Article 40(a) of the Commencement No.7 Order 1999 (June 1, 1999).
3. Article 40(b)(i) of the Commencement No.7 Order 1999 (June 1, 1999).
4. Article 40(b)(ii) of the Commencement No.7 Order 1999 (June 1, 1999).
5. Article 40(c) of the Commencement No.7 Order 1999 (June 1, 1999).

DEFINITIONS

3.224    "Maintenance Assessment Procedure Regulations": see reg.1(3).
"Maintenance Assessments and Special Cases Regulations": see reg.(3)

GENERAL NOTE

*Paragraphs (2) and (3)*
3.225    The provisions specified in these paragraphs amend the Maintenance Assessments and Special Cases Regulations as set out in the following chart.

| Regulation | Amendment | Relevant to | |
|---|---|---|---|
| | | reg.57(1) | reg.57(3) |
| reg.40 | amends reg.1(2) and | | ⋆ |
| | amends reg.1(2A) | ⋆ | ⋆ |
| reg.42 | amends reg.9(1)(h) | ⋆ | ⋆ |
| reg.43(3) | amends reg.11(1)(i) | ⋆ | ⋆ |
| reg.43(5) | inserts reg.11(2)(a)(iv)and | | ⋆ |
| | inserts reg.11(2)(a)(v) | ⋆ | ⋆ |
| reg.46 | amends Sch.2, para.27(2) | ⋆ | ⋆ |
| reg.47 | inserts Sch.3, para.3(2)A, and amends Sch.3, para.6 | ⋆ | ⋆ |
| reg.48 | inserts Sch.3B, paras 17 and 17A | | ⋆ |

# The Child Support (Compensation for Recipients of Family Credit and Disability Working Allowance) Regulations 1995

## (SI 1995/3263)

*Made by the Secretary of State for Social Security under sections 24 and 27(2) of the Child Support Act 1995 and section 54 of the Child Support Act 1991 and all other powers enabling him in that behalf.*

GENERAL NOTE

The Child Support (Compensation for Recipients of Family Credit and Disability Working Allowance) Regulations 1995 were revoked by reg.6 of the Tax Credits Amendments Regulations 1999 with effect from October 5, 1999, but they continue to have effect in the case of an award of family credit or disability working allowance awarded with effect from a date falling before that date (the date when tax credits came into force).

3.226

These Regulations make detailed provision for the power to make compensation payments which was created by s.24 of the 1995 Act. The purpose of the payment is to provide some compensation for persons with care whose child support maintenance payments have been reduced as a result of certain changes to the child support scheme but whose benefit entitlement cannot immediately be adjusted to take account of that reduction. The key features of compensation payments are as follows:

1. A payment may be made when the amount of child support maintenance payable under an assessment is reduced on account of certain changes in child support legislation. The relevant changes are set out in the Schedule to these Regulations. They all came into force on April 18, 1995.

2. It may be made to a person with care, whether or not that person is a parent of the qualifying child (s.24(2) of the 1995 Act).

3. Compensation is only payable to those to, or in respect of, whom family

credit or disability living allowance was in payment (s.24(2) of the 1995 Act), as these benefits are awarded for 26 weeks and the amount of the award cannot be varied to take account of the reduction in the amount of child support maintenance payable.

4.  Compensation is payable for the remainder of the award in payment at the effective date of the assessment which implemented the change in legislation (reg.4) and, in essence, for any further award which began after that date but was calculated on the basis of the person with care's previous entitlement to child support maintenance (reg.5(5) and (6)).

5.  The compensation amounts to half of the reduction in child support maintenance (regs 4 and 5(5)). The calculation is linked by virtue of the terms of s.24(1) of the 1995 Act to the effects of the specified changes in the legislation on the child support maintenance payable. Where the assessment made on the review implementing the changes also relates to matters other than the changes consequent upon the specified changes in legislation, the effects of the specified changes will have to be isolated.

6.  Where there has been a fresh assessment on or after April 18, 1995, the reduction is to be calculated by reference to the child support maintenance payable under that assessment, provided that (a) it was made on a review under ss.16, 17, 18 or 19 of the Act; (b) both the review and the fresh assessment were made on or after April 18; (c) the review did not relate to the specified changes in legislation; (d) its effective date was before the effective date of the assessment implementing the changes (reg.5(1)).

7.  No compensation is payable unless it amounts to at least £5 (reg.6).

8.  Payment may be made as a lump sum or by instalments, and may be paid in such manner as the Secretary of State considers appropriate (reg.7).

9.  Provision is made for the recalculation of the payment in certain cases where there has been a revision of the amount of child support maintenance payable as a result of one of the following reviews:

(a)  a review on the grounds set out in s.18(6) or 19(2) which superseded the assessment which implemented the changes in the legislation from its effective date;

(b)  a review under s.16, 17, 18 or 19 of the Act which retrospectively altered the amount of child support maintenance payable immediately prior to the review which implemented the changes in the legislation.

The rules on recalculation are:

(i)  where a revision of type (a) has been made, a recalculation must be made to take account of changes resulting from that revision (reg.5(3));

(ii)  where revision of both type (a) and type (b) have been made, a recalculation must be made to take account of changes resulting from both those revisions (reg.5(4));

(iii)  but where only a revision of type (b) has been made, no recalculation is made (reg.5(2)).

## Citation, commencement and interpretation

3.227    1.—(1) These Regulations may be cited as the Child Support (Compensation for Recipients of Family Credit and Disability Working Allowance) Regulations 1995 and shall come into force on 23rd January 1996.

(2) In these Regulations—

"the 1995 Act" means the Child Support Act 1995 and "the 1991 Act" means the Child Support Act 1991;

"instrument for benefit payment" has the meaning prescribed in regulation 2(1) of the Social Security (Claims and Payments) Regulations 1987.

## Changes in child support legislation relevant for the purposes of compensation

**2.** A compensation payment under section 24 of the 1995 Act shall be made where a maintenance assessment in force is reduced as a result of the coming into force of any of the child support legislation set out in the Schedule to these Regulations.

**3.228**

DEFINITION

"the 1995 Act": see reg.1(2).

**3.229**

## Definition of relevant time

**3.** For the purposes of section 24 of the 1995 Act, the relevant time shall be the day immediately prior to the effective date of the revised assessment.

**3.230**

DEFINITION

"the 1995 Act": see reg.1(2).

## Calculation of compensation

**4.** Subject to regulation 5, the compensation payment referred to in section 24(2) of the 1995 Act shall be calculated by using the following formula—

**3.231**

$$C = \frac{A}{2} \times B$$

where—

C is the compensation payment payable.

A is the amount of the reduction referred to in section 24(2) of the 1995 Act;

B is the number of complete periods of 7 days within the period commencing on the effective date of the revised assessment and ending on the date of the expiry of the award of family credit or disability working allowance in force at that effective date.

DEFINITION

"the 1995 Act": see reg.1(2).

**3.232**

## Calculation of compensation in particular cases

**5.**—[1(1) Where a revised assessment is replaced by a fresh maintenance assessment of a different amount by virtue of a revision under section 16 of the 1991 Act, the compensation payment calculated under section 24 of the 1995 Act shall be recalculated using the amount due under the fresh maintenance assessment in place of the amount due under the revised assessment.

**3.233**

(2) Subject to paragraph (3), where the earlier assessment is replaced by a fresh assessment—

(a) which was made after the revised assessment; and

(b) the effective date of that fresh assessment is before the date on which the revised assessment was made,

the amount payable under the fresh assessment shall be ignored for the purposes of the calculation of a compensation payment under section 24 of the 1995 Act.

(3) In a case where the circumstances in paragraphs (1) and (2) apply the compensation payable under section 24 of the 1995 Act shall be recalculated using the amount due under the fresh assessments referred to in paragraphs (1) and (2).]

(5) Where the circumstances set out in paragraph (6) apply, the compensation payable under section 24 of the 1995 Act for the period of the further award shall be calculated in accordance with the following formula—

$$C = \frac{A}{2} \times 26$$

where C and A have the meaning given to them in regulation 4.

(6) The circumstances referred to in paragraph (5) are—

(a) the effective date of a revised assessment is not more than 4 weeks in the case of family credit or 6 weeks in the case of disability working allowance prior to the date upon which the existing award of that benefit ends;

(b) the person to whom that award was made has applied for a further award of that benefit to be paid from the date of expiry of the existing award;

(c) the amount payable under the further award has not taken account of the changes in child support legislation referred to in regulation 2 which are relevant to the further award.

(7) For the purposes of paragraph (6), the existing award means the award of family credit or disability working allowance in force at the effective data of the revised assessment and the further award means the award of family credit or disability working allowance made after the existing award has expired.

AMENDMENT

1. Article 41 of the Commencement No.7 Order 1999 (June 1, 1999).

DEFINITIONS

3.234  "the 1991 Act": see reg.1(2).
"the 1995 Act": see reg.1(2)

## Minimum payment

3.235  **6.**—(1) Subject to paragraph (2), compensation calculated under section 24 of the 1995 Act and these Regulations by reference to a revised assessment shall not be paid if the amount of that compensation is less than £5.00.

(2) Where paragraph (3) or (4) of regulation 5 applies, the prescribed minimum set out in paragraph (1) shall be applied to the recalculated compensation payment only.

(3) Where more than one revised assessment is made and a payment has been made in respect of compensation calculated by reference to one of those revised assessments, the amount of compensation to be paid in respect of any subsequent revised assessment shall be the difference between the payment that has already been made and the compensation calculated by reference to that subsequent revised assessment.

DEFINITION

"the 1995 Act": see reg. 1(2).                                    3.236

## Provisions for payment

7.—(1) The Secretary of State shall make any compensation payment    3.237
under section 24 of the 1995 Act in instalments or as a lump sum as he
considers appropriate in the circumstances.

(2) Any such compensation payment shall be paid on presentation of
an instrument for benefit payment or by means of an instrument of payment or by such other means as appears to the Secretary of State to be
appropriate in the circumstances of any particular case.

DEFINITIONS

"the 1995 Act": see reg. 1(2).                                    3.238
"instrument for benefit payment": see reg. 1(2)

SCHEDULE

CHANGES IN CHILD SUPPORT LEGISLATION RELEVANT FOR THE PURPOSES OF
COMPENSATION

| *Relevant legislation* | *Effect* | 2.239 |
|---|---|---|
| Regulation 43 of the Child Support Amendment Regulations | Amends regulation 6 of the Maintenance Assessments and Special Cases Regulations (additional element) | |
| Regulation 44(2)(a) and (b) of the Child *Relevant legislation* Support Amendment Regulations | Amend regulation 9 of the Maintenance *Effect* Assessments and Special Cases Regulations (exempt income) | |
| Regulation 46(2)(d) and (6) of the Child Support Amendment Regulations | Amend regulation 11 of the Maintenance Assessments and Special Cases Regulations (protected income) | |
| Regulation 48 of the Child Support Amendment Regulations | Amends regulation 15 of the Maintenance Assessments and Special Cases Regulations (housing costs) | |
| Regulation 50 of the Child Support Amendment Regulations | Revokes regulation 17 of the Maintenance Assessments and Special Cases Regulations (apportionment of housing costs) | |
| Regulation 54(11) of the Child Support Amendment Regulations | Amends paragraph 23 of Schedule 1 to the Maintenance Assessments and Special Cases Regulations (relevant income of child) | |

In this Schedule—

"The Child Support Amendment Regulations" means the Child Support and Income Support (Amendment) Regulations 1995.

"The Maintenance Assessments and Special Cases Regulations" means the Child Support (Maintenance Assessments and Special Cases) Regulations 1992.

## The Child Support (Maintenance Assessments and Special Cases) and Social Security (Claims and Payments) Regulations 1996

### (SI 1996/481)

*Made by the Secretary of State for Social Security under sections 51, 52 and 54 of, and paragraphs 5 and 7 of Schedule 1 to, the Child Support Act 1991 . . . and all other powers enabling him in that behalf . . .*

### Citation, commencement and interpretation

3.240    **1.**—(1) These Regulations may be cited as the Child Support (Maintenance Assessments and Special Cases) and Social Security (Claims and Payments) Amendment Regulations 1996 and shall come into force on 8th April 1996.

(2) In these Regulations—

"the Act" means the Child Support Act 1991;

. . .

### Transitional provisions

3.241    **4.** A maintenance assessment in force on 8th April 1996 shall not be reviewed solely to give effect to regulation 3 but, on review of that assessment under section 16, 17 or 18 of the Act, the provisions of that regulation shall have effect from the effective date of any fresh maintenance assessment made following that review.

GENERAL NOTE

3.242    This regulation applies only to amendments made by reg.3 which amends paras 19(1) and 20(1) of Sch.2 to the Maintenance Assessments and Special Cases Regulations (now revoked). It does not apply to amendments made by reg.2 which amends reg.13 of those regulations.

It applies only to reviews under ss.16, 17 and 18, but not to reviews under s.19.

# The Child Benefit, Child Support and Social Security (Miscellaneous Amendments) Regulations 1996

## (SI 1996/1803)

*Made by the Secretary of State for Social Security under sections 11(2),
43(1)(b), 51, 52(4) and 54 of, and paragraphs 1(3) and (5), 2(1), 4(3),
5(1) and (2), 6(2) and 9 of Schedule 1 to, the Child Support Act 1991
. . . and all other powers enabling him in that behalf . . .*

## Citation, commencement and interpretation

**1.**—(1) These Regulations may be cited as the Child Benefit, Child    3.243
Support and Social Security (Miscellaneous Amendments) Regulations
1996 and shall come into force—

. . .

(b) for the purposes of regulations 2 to 21 and 37 to 49, on 7th April
1997;

. . .

GENERAL NOTE

The relevant amendments were made to the Maintenance Assessments and
Special Cases Regulations by regs 7–17. Regulation 49 deals with decisions giving
effect to the changes and is set out below.

## Transitional provision relating to maintenance assessments

[¹**49.**—(1) A decision with respect to a maintenance assessment in force    3.244
on 7th April 1997 shall not be superseded by a decision under section 17
of the Child Support Act 1991 ("the Act") solely to give effect to these
Regulations.

(2) These Regulations shall apply to a fresh maintenance assessment
made by virtue of—

(a) a revision under section 16 of the Act of a decision with respect to a
maintenance assessment; or

(b) a decision under section 17 of the Act which supersedes a decision
with respect to a maintenance assessment, as from the effective date
of that revision under section 16 of the Act or, as the case may be,
decision under section 17 of the Act.]

AMENDMENT

1. Article 42 of the Commencement No.7 Order 1999 (June 1, 1999).

### The Child Support (Miscellaneous Amendments) Regulations 1996

### (SI 1996/1945)

*Made by the Secretary of State for Social Security under sections 14(1), 21(2), 32(1), 42(3), 46(11), 47(1) and (2), 51, 52(4) and 54 of, and paragraphs 5(1) and (2), 6, 8 and 11 of Schedule 1 to, the Child Support Act 1991 and all other powers enabling him in that behalf.*

### Citation, commencement and interpretation

3.245     **1.**—(1) These Regulations may be cited as the Child Support (Miscellaneous Amendments) Regulations 1996.

(2) . . .

(3) In these Regulations—

. . .

"the Maintenance Assessment Procedure Regulations" means the Child Support (Maintenance Assessment Procedure) Regulations 1992;
"the Maintenance Assessments and Special Cases Procedure Regulations" means the Child Support (Maintenance Assessments and Special Cases) Regulations 1992.

### Transitional provisions

3.246     **25.**—(1) The provisions of regulations 33 of the Maintenance Assessment Procedure Regulations in force prior to 5th August 1996 shall continue to apply to any application made prior to that date.

(2) The provisions of regulation 35 of the Maintenance Assessment Procedure Regulations in force prior to 7th October 1996 shall continue to apply to any case where the failure to comply referred to in paragraph (1) of that regulation arose prior to that date.

(3) The provisions of regulation 36 of the Maintenance Assessment Procedure Regulations in force prior to 7th October 1996 shall [¹apply with the amendments made by regulation 5(6) of the Social Security and Child Support (Jobseeker's Allowance) (Consequential Amendments). Regulations 1996] to a parent in respect of whom a reduced benefit direction was given prior to that date.

(4) The provisions of regulation 47 of the Maintenance Assessment Procedure Regulations in force prior to 7th October 1996 shall [²apply with the amendments made by regulation 5(11) of the Social Security and Child Support (Jobseeker's Allowance) (Consequential Amendments) Regulations 1996] to any reduced benefit direction made prior to that date, and in relation to an earlier direction referred to in paragraph (4) of that regulation, which was in force prior to that date, whether or not the further direction referred to in that paragraph was made after that date.

(5) The provisions of regulation 19 of the Maintenance Assessments and Special Cases Regulations in force prior to 7th October 1996 shall continue to apply to any application made prior to that date [³and a decision with respect to a maintenance assessment in force on that date shall not be superseded by a decision under section 17 of the Child Support Act 1991 solely to give effect to the provisions of regulation 19 as amended by regulation 23.]

AMENDMENTS

1. Regulation 3(2) of the Social Security and Child Support (Jobseeker's Allowance) (Transitional Provisions) (Amendment) Regulations 1996 (October 6, 1996).
2. Regulation 3(3) of the Social Security and Child Support (Jobseeker's Allowance) (Transitional Provisions) (Amendment) Regulations 1996 (October 6, 1996).
3. Article 43 of the Commencment No.7 Order 1999 (June 1, 1999).

DEFINITIONS

"the Maintenance Assessment Procedure Regulations": see reg.1(3).      **3.247**
"the Maintenance Assessments and Special Cases Procedure Regulations": see reg.1(3)


# Social Security (Adjudication) and Child Support Amendment (No. 2) Regulations 1996

## (SI 1996/2450)

*Made by the Secretary of State for Social Security under sections 21(2) and (3), 51 and 52 of the Child Support Act 1991 . . . and all other powers enabling him in that behalf, after consultation with the Council on Tribunals in accordance with section 8(1) of the Tribunals and Inquiries Act 1992.*

## Citation, commencement and interpretation

**1.**—(1) These Regulations may be cited as the Social Security    **3.248** (Adjudication) and Child Support Amendment (No. 2) Regulations 1996 and shall come into force on 21st October 1996.

(2) In these Regulations—
"the Appeal Regulations" means the Child Support Appeal Tribunals (Procedure) Regulations 1992.

## Saving Provision

**22.** In a case where an appeal, application or reference was made before    **3.249** the date on which these Regulations come into force, . . . regulations 3, 6(3) and 11(1) of the Appeal Regulations shall apply as if these Regulations had not been made.

DEFINITION

"the Appeal Regulations": see reg.1(2).      **3.250**

GENERAL NOTE

This regulation ensures that amendments to the specified regulations of the    **3.251** Tribunal Procedure Regulations (now revoked) do not have restrospective effect to appeals or applications made before October 21, 1996.

## The Child Support Departure Direction and Consequential Amendments Regulations 1996

### (SI 1996/2907)

3.252    The Child Support Departure Direction and Consequential Amendments Regulations 1996 were revoked by reg.33 of the Child Support (Variations) Regulations 2000 but are reproduced as one of the extracts from the original scheme below.

### The Social Security (Child Maintenance Bonus) Regulations 1996

### (SI 1996/3195)

*Made by the Secretary of State for Social Security under sections 10 and 26(1) to (3) of the Child Support Act 1995, sections 5(1)(p), 6(1)(q), 71(8), 78(2), 189(1), (3) and (4) and 191 of the Social Security Administration Act 1992, sections 136(5)(b), 137(1) and 175(1) and (3) of the Social Security Contributions and Benefits Act 1992 and of all other powers enabling in that behalf*

### Citation, commencement and interpretation

3.253    **1.**—(1) These Regulations may be cited as the Social Security (Child Maintenance Bonus) Regulations 1996 and shall come into force on 7th April 1997.

(2) In these Regulations—

"the Act" means the Child Support Act 1995;

"applicant", except where regulation 8 (retirement) applies, means the person claiming the bonus;

"appropriate office" means an Office of the [³Department for Work and Pensions];

"benefit week"—

(a) where the relevant benefit is income support, has the meaning it has in the Income Support (General) Regulations 1987(e) by virtue of regulation 2(1) of those Regulations; or

(b) where the relevant benefit is a jobseeker's allowance, has the meaning it has in the Jobseeker's Allowance Regulations 1996(a) by virtue of regulation 1(3) of those Regulations;

"bonus" means a child maintenance bonus;

"bonus period" comprises the days specified in regulation 4;

[¹"child maintenance" means maintenance in any of the following forms—

(a) child support maintenance paid or payable;

(b) maintenance paid or payable by an absent parent to a person with care of a qualifying child, under an agreement (whether enforceable or not) between them, or by virtue of an order of a court; or

(c) maintenance deducted from any benefit payable to an absent parent who is liable to maintain a qualifying child, which, as the case may be, is paid or payable or deducted on or after 1st April 1998, but does not include any maintenance paid or payable in respect of a former partner.]

"couple" means a married or an unmarried couple;

"income-based jobseeker's allowance" has the same meaning as in the Job-seekers Act by virtue of section 1(4) of that Act;

"the Jobseekers Act" means the Jobseekers Act (1995(b);

"jobseeker's allowance" means an income-based Jobseeker's allowance;

"partner" means where a person, whether an applicant or otherwise,—

(a) is a member of a married or unmarried couple, the other member of that couple;

(b) is married polygamously to two or more members of his house-hold, any such member; or

(c) is a member of a marriage to which section 133(1)(b) of the Social Security Contributions and Benefits Act 1992 (polygamous marriages) refers and the other party to the marriage has one or more additional spouses, the other party;

"work condition" means the conditions specified at regulation 3(1)(c).

(3) Expressions used in these Regulations and in the Child Support Act 1991 have the same meaning in these Regulations as they have in that Act.

(4) For the purposes of these Regulations, the qualifying benefits are a jobseeker's allowance and income support.

(5) In these Regulations, where—

(a) a payment is made in any benefit week by an absent parent to a person with care;

(b) the absent parent pays both child maintenance and maintenance for the person with care; and

(c) there is no evidence as to which form of maintenance that payment is intended to represent,

the first £5 of any such payment or, where the amount of payment is less than £5, that amount shall be treated as if it was a payment of child maintenance.

(6) For the purposes of these Regulations [³ other than regulation 4 (bonus period)], child maintenance is treated as payable where it is paid under an agreement which is not enforceable.

(7) Where a person is entitled to a qualifying benefit on any day but no qualifying benefit is payable to her in respect of that day, that person shall be treated for the purposes of these Regulations as not entitled to a qualifying benefit for that day.

(8) In these Regulations, unless the context otherwise requires, a reference—

(a) to a numbered section is to the section of the Act bearing that number;

(b) to a numbered regulation is to the regulation in these Regulations bearing that number;

(c) in a regulation to a numbered paragraph is to the paragraph in that regulation bearing that number;

(d) in a paragraph to a lettered or numbered sub-paragraph in that paragraph bearing that letter or number.

1. Regulation 2(2) of the Social Security (Miscellaneous Amendments) Regulations 1998 (April 1, 1998 as amended by reg.2 of the Social Security (Miscellaneous Amendment) (No.2) Regulations 1998).

2. Regulation 8(2)(b) of the Social Security (Miscellaneous Amendments) Regulations 1997 (April 6, 1997).

3. Article 29 of the Secretaries of State for Education and Skills and for Work and Pensions Order 2002 (June 27, 2002).

## Application of the Regulations

3.254    **2.**—(1) Subject to paragraph (2), these Regulations apply only in a case where on or after 7th April 1997 an absent parent has paid child maintenance in respect of a qualifying child and that maintenance has been—

    (a) taken into account in determining the amount of a qualifying benefit payable to the person with care or the partner of that person; or

    (b) retained by the Secretary of State in accordance with section 74A(3) of the Social Security Administration Act 1992 (payment of benefit where maintenance payments are collected by the Secretary of State)(a).

(2) Regulation 6 (Secretary of State to issue estimates) applies also where a child maintenance assessment has been made but no maintenance has been paid.

(3) No day falling before 7th April 1997 shall be taken into account in determining whether any condition specified in these Regulations is satisfied or whether any period specified in these Regulations commenced.

## Entitlement to a Bonus

3.255    **3.**—(1) An applicant is entitled to a bonus where—

    (a) she has claimed a bonus in accordance with regulation 10 (claiming a bonus);

    (b) the claim relates to days falling within a bonus period;

    (c) except where paragraph (2) applies; she satisfies the work condition, that is to say, she or her partner takes up or returns to work or increases the number of hours in which in any week she or her partner is engaged in employment or the earnings from an employment in which she or her partner are engaged is increased;

    (d) as a result of satisfying the work condition any entitlement to a qualifying benefit in respect of herself and, where she has a partner, her family ceases;

    (e) in a case where the qualifying benefit which ceased—

       (i) was income support, the person with care has not reached the day before her 60th birthday;

       (ii) was a jobseeker's allowance, the person with care has not reached the day before she attains pensionable age,

    at the time the work condition is satisfied; and

[¹(f)    the work condition is satisfied within the period of—

      (i)   in a case where an applicant with care cares for one child only and that child dies, 12 months immediately following the date of death;

    (ii)   in a case where the absent parent has—

       (aa)   died;

       (bb)   ceased to be habitually resident in the United Kingdom; or

       (cc)   has been found not to be the parent of the qualifying child or children,

             12 weeks immediately following the first date on which any of those events occurs;

   (iii)   in any other case, 14 days immediately following the day on which the bonus period applying to the applicant comes to an end.]

[²(1A) In the case of an applicant who satisfies the requirements of paragraph (1)(f) but whose entitlement, or whose partner's entitlement, to a qualifying benefit ceased otherwise than as a result of satisfying the work condition, for sub-paragraph (d) of paragraph (1) there shall be substituted the following sub-paragraph—

"(d) had the work condition been satisfied on the day she, or her partner, was last entitled to a qualifying benefit, that entitlement would as a consequence have ceased."]

(2) A person who is absent from work because of a trade dispute at her place of work and returns to work with the employer she worked for before the dispute began, does not thereby satisfy the requirements of paragraph (1)(c).

(3) In paragraph (2), "place of work", in relation to any person, means the premises at which she was employed.

(4) An applicant is also entitled to a bonus where she satisfies the requirements specified in regulation 8 (retirement).

Amendments

1. Regulation 2(3) of the Social Security (Miscellaneous Amendments) Regulations 1998 (April 1, 1998 as amended by reg.2 of the Social Security (Miscellaneous Amendment) (No.2) Regulations 1998).

2. Regulation 8(3) of the Social Security (Miscellaneous Amendments) Regulations 1997 (April 6, 1997).

**Bonus Period**

4.—(1) A bonus period comprises only days falling on or after 7th April 1997 [¹, other than days to which paragraph (9) applies,] on which—     3.256

  (a)  the applicant or, where the applicant has a partner, her partner is entitled to, or is treated as entitled to a qualifying benefit whether it is payable or not;

  (b)  the applicant has residing with her a qualifying child; and

  (c)  child maintenance is either—

     [²(i)   paid or payable to the applicant; or]

(ii) retained by the Secretary of State in accordance with section 74A(3) of the Social Security Administration Act 1992(a).

(2) Any two or more bonus periods separated by any one connected period shall be treated as one bonus period.

(3) For the purposes of these Regulations, "a connected period" is—

(a) any period of not more than 12 weeks falling between two bonus periods to which paragraph (1) refers;

(b) any period of not more than 12 weeks throughout which—

[³. . .]

    (ii) the applicant ceases to be entitled to a qualifying benefit on becoming one of a couple and the couple fail to satisfy the conditions of entitlement to a qualifying benefit; or

(c) any period throughout which maternity allowance is payable to the applicant; or

(d) any period of not more than 2 years through which incapacity benefit, severe disablement allowance or [⁷carer's allowance] is payable to the applicant.

(4) In calculating any period for the purposes of paragraph (3) no regard shall be had to any day which falls before 7th April 1997.

(5) Bonus periods separated by two or more connected periods shall not link to form a single bonus period but shall instead remain separate bonus periods.

(6) Where a qualifying child is temporarily absent for a period not exceeding 12 weeks from the home he shares with the applicant, the applicant shall be treated as satisfying the requirements of paragraph (1)(b) throughout that absence.

(7) A bonus period which would, but for this paragraph, have continued shall end—

(a) where the applicant or, where the applicant has a partner, her partner, satisfies the work condition and claims a bonus, on the last day of entitlement to a qualifying benefit to which any award made on that claim applies; or

[⁴(b) on the date of death of a person with care of a qualifying child to whom child maintenance is payable.]

[⁵(8) In paragraphs (1)(c)(i) and (9) "claimant"—

(a) where the qualifying benefit is income support, means a person who claims income support; and

(b) where the qualifying benefit is a jobseeker's allowance, means a person who claims a jobseeker's allowance.]

[⁶(9) This paragraph applies to days on which the claimant is a person to whom—

(a) regulation 70 of the Income Support (General) Regulations 1987 (urgent cases) applies other than by virtue of paragraph (2)(a) of that regulation (certain persons from abroad), or

(b) regulation 147 of the Jobseeker's Allowance Regulations 1996 other than by virtue of paragraph (2)(a) of that regulation.]

AMENDMENTS

1. Regulation 8(4)(a) of the Social Security (Miscellaneous Amendments) Regulations 1997 (April 6, 1997).

2. Regulation 2(4) of the Social Security (Miscellaneous Amendments) Regulations 1998 (April 1, 1998 as amended by reg.2 of the Social Security (Miscellaneous Amendment) (No.2) Regulations 1998).

3. Regulation 8(4)(b) of the Social Security (Miscellaneous Amendments) Regulations 1997 (April 6, 1997).

4. Regulation 8(4)(c) of the Social Security (Miscellaneous Amendments) Regulations 1997 (April 6, 1997).

5. Regulation 8(4)(d) of the Social Security (Miscellaneous Amendments) Regulations 1997 (April 6, 1997).

6. Regulation 8(4)(d) of the Social Security (Miscellaneous Amendments) Regulations 1997 (April 6, 1997).

7. Regulation 3 of, and Sched.2 to, the Social Security Amendment (Carer's Allowance) Regulations 2002 (April 1, 2003).

## Amount payable

**5.**—(1) The amount of the bonus shall be—  3.257

(a) subject to the following provisions of this regulation, a sum representing the aggregate of—

   (i) £5 for each benefit week in the bonus period in which the amount of child maintenance payable was not less than £5; and

   (ii) where in any benefit week in the bonus period the amount of child maintenance payable was less than £5, the amount that was payable;

(b) the amount of the child maintenance paid in the bonus period; or

(c) £1,000,

whichever amount is the least.

[¹. . .]

(3) So much of any child maintenance paid in excess of the amount either—

(a) declared for the purposes of determining the amount of qualifying benefit payable to the applicant or her partner; or

(b) retained by the Secretary of State in accordance with section 74A(3) of the Social Security Administration Act 1992,

shall be disregarded in determining the amount payable under paragraph (1).

[². . .]

(5) Where but for this paragraph the amount of bonus payable in accordance with paragraph (1) would be less than £5, the amount of the bonus shall be Nil.

1. Regulation 8(5) of the Social Security (Miscellaneous Amendments) Regulations 1997 (April 6, 1997).

2. Regulation 8(5) of the Social Security (Miscellaneous Amendments) Regulations 1997 (April 6, 1997).

## Secretary of State to issue estimates

**6.**—(1) Where it appears to the Secretary of State that a person [¹ with  3.258
care], or the partner of such a person, may satisfy the requirements of

regulation 3 (entitlement to a bonus) he may issue to [² that person] a written statement of the amount he estimates may be payable by way of a bonus in his particular case, and may provide such further statements as appear appropriate in the circumstances, stating the amount the estimates may be payable.

(2) The issue by the Secretary of State of a statement under paragraph (1) shall not be binding on the adjudication officer when he makes his determination on a claim for a bonus as to—

(a) whether the applicant satisfies the conditions of entitlement to the bonus; and

(b) the amount, if any, payable where the bonus is awarded.

AMENDMENTS

1. Regulation 8(6) of the Social Security (Miscellaneous Amendments) Regulations 1997 (April 6, 1997).

2. Regulation 8(6) of the Social Security (Miscellaneous Amendments) Regulations 1997 (April 6, 1997).

## Death of a person with care of a child

3.259

7.—(1) In a case where—

(a) the person (A) with care of a [¹ qualifying child to whom child maintenance is payable dies;]

(b) on the date of her death, the person (A) was entitled or, where she has a partner, her partner was entitled to a qualifying benefit or had been so entitled within the 12 weeks ending on the date of her death;

(c) after the death, another person (B), who is a close relative of the person (A) and who was not before the death a person with the care of the child, becomes the person with care; and

(d) that other person was entitled or, where the other person has a partner, the other person or her partner was entitled to a qualifying benefit on the day the person (A) died or becomes entitled to a qualifying benefit within 12 weeks of the day on which the person (A) was last entitled to a qualifying benefit,

then any weeks forming part of the bonus period of the person (A) which was current at the date of her death or within 12 weeks of the date on which she died shall be treated as part of the bonus period of the person (B) to the extent that those weeks are not otherwise a part of her bonus period.

(2) In this Regulation, "close relative" means a parent, parent-in-law, son, son-in-law, daughter, daughter-in-law, step-parent, step-son, step-daughter, brother, sister, or the spouse of any of the preceding persons or, if that person is one of an unmarried couple, the other member of that couple.

AMENDMENT

1. Regulation 8(7) of the Social Security (Miscellaneous Amendments) Regulations 1997 (April 6, 1997).

## Retirement

**8.**—(1) In a case where the person with care of the child in respect of     3.260
whom child maintenance is payable (the applicant) or the applicant's
partner, either—

   (a) is entitled to income support on the day before the applicant attains
       the age of 60; or

   (b) is entitled to a jobseeker's allowance on the day before the applicant
       attains pensionable age, the bonus period shall end on the day before
       the applicant attains 60 or, as the case may be, pensionable age and
       a bonus shall become payable to the applicant whether or not a claim
       is made for it.

(2) Where an applicant who ceases to be entitled to a jobseeker's
allowance after attaining the age of 60 without satisfying the condition in
paragraph (1)(b) above, becomes entitled to [¹state pension credit] within—

   (a) a period of 12 weeks of him ceasing to be entitled to a jobseeker's
       allowance; or

   (b) the duration of any connected period to which regulation 4(3)
       applies which immediately follows such an entitlement and which
       applies in his case,

he shall be entitled to the bonus as though paragraph (1) were satisfied in
his case and his bonus period shall be treated as though it ended on the day
he becomes entitled to [¹state pension credit].

[²(2A) In paragraph (2), "state pension credit" means the benefit of that
name payable under the State Pension Credit Act 2002.]

(3) No day which falls after the day the bonus period ends in accordance with paragraph (1) or (4) or is treated as ending in accordance with
paragraph (2), shall form part of that or any other bonus period.

(4) Paragraph (5) shall apply where—

   (a) the applicant or the applicant's partner—

      (i) ceased to be entitled to income support in the 12 weeks
          preceding the date of the applicant attaining the age of 60;

      (ii) ceased to be entitled to a jobseeker's allowance in the 12 weeks
          preceding the date of the applicant attaining pensionable age; and

   (b) the person who ceased to be so entitled failed to satisfy the
       requirements of regulation 3(1)(c) to (f).

(5) Where this paragraph applies—

   (a) the bonus periods shall end on the day entitlement to the qualifying
       benefit ceased; and

   (b) a bonus shall become payable to the applicant, but only where a
       claim is made for it in accordance with regulation 10 (claiming a
       bonus).

(6) In this regulation, "applicant" includes, where no claim is made, a
person who would have been an applicant had a claim for a bonus been
required.

AMENDMENTS

  1. Regulation 7(1)(a) of the State Pension Credit Regulations (October 6, 2003).
  2. Regulation 7(1)(b) of the State Pension Credit Regulations (October 6, 2003).

**Couples**

3.261     **9.**—(1) In the case of a couple, the person entitled to the bonus is the person who has the care of the child and to whom child maintenance is payable in respect of that child.

(2) Where each member of a couple has both the care of a child and child maintenance is payable in respect of the child for whom they have care, each of them may qualify for a bonus in accordance with these Regulations where a qualifying benefit ceases to be payable to either of them because one of them, whether or not the person to whom the benefit was payable, satisfies the work condition.

(3) A member of a couple to whom paragraph (2) applies shall not qualify for a bonus unless she claims it in accordance with regulation 10 (claiming a bonus).

(4) Subject to paragraph (5), these Regulations shall apply to both members of a couple who separate as if they had never been one of a couple.

(5) In the case of a couple who separate any entitlement to a qualifying benefit of one member of the couple during the time they were a couple shall be treated as the entitlement of both members of the couple for the purpose only of determining whether any day falls within a bonus period.

**Claiming a bonus**

3.262     **10.**—(1) A claim for a bonus shall be made in writing on a form approved for the purpose by the Secretary of State and shall be made—

    (a) not earlier than the beginning of the benefit week which precedes the benefit week in which an award of a qualifying benefit comes to an end; and

    (b) except in a case to which sub-paragraph [¹. . .] (d) applies, not later than 28 days after the day the qualifying benefit [². . .] ceases;

[³. . .]

    (d) in the case of a person to whom regulation 8(4) refers, not later than 28 days after the day the applicant attains the age of 60 or, as the case may be, pensionable age.

(2) A claim for a bonus shall be delivered or sent to an appropriate office.

(3) If a claim is defective at the time it is received, the Secretary of State may refer the claim to the person making it and if the form is received properly completed within one month, or such longer period, as the Secretary of State may consider reasonable, from the date on which it is so referred, the Secretary of State may treat the claim as if it had been duly made in the first instance.

(4) A claim which is made on the form approved for the time being is, for the purposes of paragraph (3), properly completed if it is completed in accordance with instructions on the form and defective if it is not.

(5) A person who claims a bonus shall furnish such certificates, documents, information and evidence in connection with the claim, or any questions arising out of it, as may be required by the Secretary of State and shall do so within one month of being required to do so or such longer period as the Secretary of State may consider reasonable.

(6) Where a person who has attained the age of 60 but has not attained pensionable age for the purposes of a jobseeker's allowance ceases to be entitled to a jobseeker's allowance and becomes instead entitled to income support, regulation 8 (retirement) and this regulation shall apply in his case as if he attained the age of 60 on the day he first became entitled to income support.

AMENDMENTS

1. Regulation 2(5)(a) of the Social Security (Miscellaneous Amendments) Regulations 1998 (April 1, 1998 as amended by reg.2 of the Social Security (Miscellaneous Amendment) (No.2) Regulations 1998).
2. Regulation 8(8)(a) of the Social Security (Miscellaneous Amendments) Regulations 1997 (April 6, 1997).
3. Regulation 2(5)(b) of the Social Security (Miscellaneous Amendments) Regulations 1998 (April 1, 1998 as amended by reg.2 of the Social Security (Miscellaneous Amendment) (No.2) Regulations 1998).

## Claims: further provisions

**11.**—(1) A person who has made a claim may amend it at any time by notice in writing received at an appropriate office before a determination has been made on the claim, and any claim so amended may be treated as if it had been so amended in the first instance.

(2) A person who has made a claim may withdraw it at any time before a determination has been made on it, by notice to an appropriate office and any such notice of withdrawal shall have effect when it is received.

(3) The date on which the claim is made shall be—

(a) in the case of a claim which meets the requirements of regulation 10(1), the date on which it is received at an appropriate office; or
(b) in the case of a claim treated under regulation 10(3) as having been duly made, the date on which the claim was received in an appropriate office in the first place.

(4) Where the applicant proves there was good cause throughout the period from the expiry of the 28 days specified in regulation 10(1), for failure to claim the bonus within the specified time, the time for claiming the bonus shall be extended to the date on which the claim is made or to a period of 6 months, whichever is the shorter period.

3.263

## Payment of bonus

**12.** A bonus calculated by reference to child maintenance paid during periods of entitlement to a jobseeker's allowance and to income support shall be treated as payable—

(a) wholly by way of a jobseeker's allowance, where the qualifying benefit last in payment in the bonus period was a jobseeker's allowance; or
(b) wholly by way of income support, where the qualifying benefit last in payment in the bonus period was income support.

3.264

**Payments on death**

3.265     **13.**—(1) Where a person satisfies the requirements for entitlement to a bonus other than the need to make a claim, but dies within 28 days of the last day of entitlement to a qualifying benefit, the Secretary of State may appoint such person as he may think fit to claim a bonus in place of the deceased person.

(2) Where the conditions specified in paragraph (3) are satisfied, a claim may be made by the person appointed for the purpose of claiming a bonus to which the deceased person would have been entitled if he had claimed it in accordance with regulation 10 (claiming a bonus).

(3) Subject to the following provisions of this regulation, the following conditions are specified for the purposes of paragraph (2)—

(a) the application to the Secretary of State to be appointed a fit person to make a claim shall be made within 6 months of the date of death; and

(b) the claim shall be made in writing within 6 months of the date the appointment was made.

(4) Subject to paragraphs (5) and (6), the Secretary of State may, in exceptional circumstances, extend the period for making an application or a claim to such longer period as he considers appropriate in the particular case.

(5) Where the period is extended in accordance with paragraph (4), the period specified in paragraph (3)(a) or (b) shall be shortened by a corresponding period.

(6) The Secretary of State shall not extend the period for making an application or a claim in accordance with paragraph (4) for more than 12 months from the date of death, but in calculating that period any period between the date when an application for a person to be appointed to make a claim is made and the date when the Secretary of State makes the appointment shall be disregarded.

(7) A claim made in accordance with paragraph (2) shall be treated, for the purposes of these Regulations, as if made on the date of the deceased's death.

**Bonus to be treated as capital for certain purposes**

3.266     **14.** Any bonus paid to an applicant shall be treated as capital of hers for the purposes of—

(a) housing benefit;

(b) council tax benefit;

(c) [¹working families' tax credit];

(d) [²disabled person's tax credit];

(e) income support;

(f) a jobseeker's allowance.

AMENDMENTS

1. Regulation 2(1) of the Tax Credits Amendments Regulations 1999 (October 5, 1999).

2. Regulation 2(2) of the Tax Credits Amendments Regulations 1999 (October 5, 1999).

### Capital to be disregarded

**15.** [As amended with effect from April 6, 1997 by regulation 8(9) of the Social Security (Miscellaneous Amendments) Regulations 1997, amends the Disability Working Allowance (General) Regulations 1991, the Family Credit (General) Regulations 1987, the Council Tax Benefit (General) Regulations 1992 and the Housing Benefit (General) Regulations 1987.]

**3.267**

### No deduction from bonus

**16.** [As amended with effect from April 6, 1997 by regulation 8(10) of the Social Security (Miscellaneous Amendments) Regulations 1997, amends the Social Security (Claims and Payments) Regulations 1987, the Social Security (Payments on account, Overpayments and Recovery) Regulations 1988 and the Social Fund (Recovery by Deductions from Benefits) Regulations 1988.]

**3.268**

## The Child Support (Miscellaneous Amendments) (No.2) Regulations 1996

### (SI 1996/3196)

*Made by the Secretary of State for Social Security under sections 12(2) and (3), 17(6) and (7), 21(2), 46(11), 47, 51, 52, and 54 of, and paragraphs 5(1), (2), and (4), 6(4), 8, and 11 of Schedule 1 to the Child Support Act 1991 and all other powers enabling in that behalf and after consultation with the Council on Tribunals in accordance with section 8 of the Tribunals and Inquiries Act 1992.*

### Citation, commencement and interpretation

**1.**—(1) These Regulations may be cited as the Child Support (Miscellaneous Amendments) (No. 2) Regulations 1996 and shall come into force on 13th January 1997.

**3.269**

(2) In these Regulations—

"the Act" means the Child Support Act 1991;

. . .

"the Maintenance Assessment Procedure Regulations" means the Child Support (Maintenance Assessment Procedure) Regulations 1992;

. . .

### Transitional provision

**16.**—[¹(1) A decision with respect to a maintenance assessment in force on 13th January 1997 shall not be superseded by a decision under section 17 of the Act solely to give effect to these Regulations.]

**3.270**

(2) Where the amount of child support maintenance fixed by any fresh assessment [². . .] is affected by the provisions of these Regulations, the effective date of that assessment shall not be earlier than the first day of the first maintenance period which commences on or after 13th January 1997.

(3) The provisions of regulations 40A and 49A of the Maintenance Assessment Procedure Regulations in force prior to 13th January 1997 shall continue to apply to a reduced benefit direction which at that date is suspended under the provisions of regulation 40A.

AMENDMENTS

1. Article 44(a) of the Commencement No. 7 Order 1999 (June 1, 1999).
2. Article 44(b) of the Commencement No. 7 Order 1999 (June 1, 1999).

DEFINITION

3.271     "the Act": see reg.1(2)
         "the Maintenance Assessment Procedure Regulations"; see reg.1(2)

## The Child Maintenance Bonus (Northern Ireland Reciprocal Arrangements) Regulations 1997

### (SI 1997/645)

*Made by the Secretary of State for Social Security under s. 29(3) and (4) of the Child Support Act 1991 and all other powers enabling in that behalf.*

### Citation, commencement and interpretation

3.272     **1.**—(1) These Regulations may be cited as the Child Maintenance Bonus (Northern Ireland Reciprocal Arrangements) Regulations 1997 and shall come into force on 7th April 1997.

(2) In these Regulations "the Child Support Act" means the Child Support Act 1995.

### Adaptation of section 10 of the Child Support Act and regulations made under it

3.273     **2.**—(1) The provisions contained in the Memorandum of Arrangements set out in the Schedule to these Regulations shall have effect so far as the same relate to Great Britain.

(2) In particular and without prejudice to paragraph (1) above, any act, omission, event or other matter which is relevant for the purposes of Article 4 of the Child Support (Northern Ireland) Order 1995 and regulations made under it is deemed to be an act, omission, event or other matter which is relevant for the purposes of section 10 of the Child Support Act (the child maintenance bonus) and regulations made under it.

(3) In section 10 of the Child Support Act and regulations made under it the references to—

"a child maintenance bonus" shall be construed as including references to a child maintenance bonus within the meaning of Article 4 of the Child Support (Northern Ireland) Order 1995;

"income support" shall be construed as including references to income support within the meaning of Part VII of the Social Security Contributions and Benefits (Northern Ireland) Act 1992;

"jobseeker's allowance" shall be construed as including references to job-seeker's allowance within the meaning of Article 3 of the Jobseekers (Northern Ireland) Order 1995;

"the Secretary of State" shall be construed as including references to the Department of Health and Social Services for Northern Ireland.

DEFINITION

"the Child Support Act": see reg.1(2).                                     3.274

SCHEDULE                                   **Regulation 2(1)**

*Memorandum of Arrangements Relating to the Provision made for child maintenance bonus in the United Kingdom between the Secretary of State for Social Security of the one part and the department of health and social services for Northern Ireland of the other part.*

1. In this Memorandum—                                                    3.275

"the provision made for Great Britain" means section 10 of the Child Support Act 1995 and regulations made under it;

"the provision made for Norther Ireland" means Article 4 of the Child Support (Northern Ireland) Order 1995 and regulations made under it.

**2.**—(1) The provision made for Great Britain and the provision made for Northern Ireland shall operate as a single system within the United Kingdom.

(2) For the purposes of paragraph (1), all acts, omissions, events and other matters and in particular any application, declaration, direction, decision or order having effect for the provision made for Great Britain and having effect in that territory or for the provision made for Northern Ireland and having effect in that territory, shall have a corresponding effect for the purposes of the provision made for child maintenance bonus in the other territory.

(3) The provisions of this Memorandum shall not confer a right to double benefit.

**3.** The Secretary of State and the Department of Health and Social Services for Northern Ireland may form time to time determine the administrative procedures appropriate for the purposes of giving effect to this Memorandum.

**4.** The arrangements in this Memorandum shall come into effect on 7th April 1997 but either Party may terminate them by giving not less than six months' notice in writing to the other.

Signed by the authority of the Secretary of State for Social Security on the 18th February 1997.

*Andrew Mitchell*
*Parliamentary Under-Secretary of State*
*Department of Social Security*

Sealed with the Official Seal of the Department of Health and Social Services for Northern Ireland on the 20th February 1997.

*A.F. Elliott*
*Permanent Secretary*

## The Child Support (Written Agreements) (Scotland) Order 1997

### (SI 1997/2943 (S.188))

*Made by the Lord Advocate under s.8(5) of the Child Support Act 1991
and all other powers enabling him in that behalf.*

3.276  **1.** This Order may be cited as the Child Support (Written Agreements) (Scotland) Order 1997 and shall come into force on 2nd January 1998.

**2.** Section 8 of the Child Support Act 1991 shall not prevent a court from exercising any power which it has to make a maintenance order in relation to a child in any circumstances in which paragraphs (a) and (b) of section 8(5) apply.

GENERAL NOTE

3.277  This Order makes provision for Scotland equivalent to that made for England and Wales by the Child Support (Written Maintenance) Order 1993 above. It applies to maintenance agreements, whether or not they have been registered for execution in the books of Council and Session.

## The Child Support (Miscellaneous Amendments) Regulations 1998

### (SI 1998/58)

*Made by the Secretary of State for Social Security under sections 12(2),
14(1) and (3), 16(1), 21, 28A(3), 28G(4), 29, 32(1), 42, 43(1), 51,
52(4) and 54 of, and paragraphs 1, 4, 5, 6, 8, 11 and 14 of Schedule 1,
paragraphs 2, 6 and 10 of Schedule 4A, and paragraphs 2, 3, 4, 5 and
6 of Schedule 4B to, the Child Support Act 1991 and of all other powers
enabling her in that behalf, after consultation with the Council on
Tribunals in accordance with section 8 of the Tribunals and Inquiries
Act 1992.*

### Citation, commencement and interpretation

3.278  **1.**—(1) These Regulations may be cited as the Child Support (Miscellaneous Amendments) Regulations 1997.

(2) Subject to paragraph (3), these regulations shall come into force on the first commencement day.

(3) Regulations 14, 39(3), 44, 45, 47, 49, 52, 54, 55 and paragraph (5) of regulation 56 shall come into force on the second commencement day.

(4) In these Regulations, unless the context otherwise requires—

. . .

"first commencement day" means 19th January 1998;

. . .

"second commencement day" means 6th April 1998.

**Transitional provisions**

[¹**59A.**—(1) A decision with respect to a maintenance assessment in 3.279
force on the first commencement day shall not be superseded by a decision
under section 17 of the Child Support Act 1991 ("the Act") solely to give
effect to regulation 42(2)(d), regulation 50 or regulation 56(2).

(2) The regulations specified in paragraph (1) shall apply to a fresh
maintenance assessment made by virtue of—

(a) a revision under section 16 of the Act of a decision with respect to a
    maintenance assessment; or
(b) a decision under section 17 of the Act which supersedes a decision
    with respect to a maintenance assessment, as from whichever is the
    later of—
    (i) the date as from which that revision or, as the case may be,
        supersession takes effect; or
    (ii) the first day of the first maintenance period which begins on or
        after the first commencement day, as the case may be.

(3) A decision with respect to a maintenance assessment in force on the
second commencement day shall not be superseded by a decision under
section 17 of the Act solely to give effect to regulations 44, 45, 47, 49, 52,
54, 55 and 56(5).

(4) The regulations specified in paragraph (3) shall apply to a fresh
maintenance assessment made by virtue of—

(a) a revision under section 16 of the Act of a decision with respect to a
    maintenance assessment; or
(b) a decision under section 17 of the Act which supersedes a decision
    with respect to a maintenance assessment, as from whichever is the
    later of—
    (i) the date as from which that revision or, as the case may be,
        supersession takes effect; or
    (ii) the first day of the first maintenance period which begins on or
        after the second commencement day, as the case may be.]

AMENDMENT

1. Article 45 of the Commencement No.7 Order 1999 (June 1, 1999).

**The Social Security Act 1998 (Commencement No.2) Order 1998**

**(SI 1998/2780 (C.66))**

*Made by the Secretary of State for Social Security under sections 79(3) and
87(2) and (3) of the Social Security Act 1998 and all other powers
enabling him in that behalf.*

**Citation and interpretation**

**1.**—(1) This Order may be cited as the Social Security Act 1998 3.280
(Commencement No. 2) Order 1998.

(2) In this Order, except where the context otherwise requires, references to sections and Schedules are references to sections and Schedules to the Social Security Act 1998.

## Savings and transitional provisions

3.281   **3.**—(1) From and including 16th November 1998 the references in section 16(1) and (6) of the Child Support Act 1991 to a decision of the Secretary of State shall be treated as including references to a decision of the child support officer made on or before the coming into force of section 1(c).

(2) From and including 16th November 1998 until the coming into force of section 41, section 16(1) of the Child Support Act 1991 shall have effect as if the reference to section 17 were omitted.

(3) From and including 16th November 1998 until the coming into force of section 44, section 16(3) of the Child Support Act 1991 shall have effect as if the reference to section 28ZC were omitted.

(4) Notwithstanding the commencement of section 40, section 16 of the Child Support Act 1991 shall continue to apply with respect to any maintenance assessment which takes effect of the purposes of that Act on or before 8th December 1996 as though section 40 had not been commenced.

(5) Notwithstanding the commencement of paragraph 46(a) of Schedule 7, section 51(2)(a)(iii) of the Child Support Act 1991 shall continue to apply with respect to—

(a) reviews under section 16 of that Act of maintenance assessments to which paragraph (4) of this article applies; and

(b) reviews under sections 17 to 19 of that Act as though paragraph 46(a) had not been commenced until such time as section 41 is commenced.

## The Social Security and Child Support (Tax Credits) Consequential Amendments Regulations 1999

### (SI 1999/2566)

*The Secretary of State for Social Security, in exercise of the powers set out in Schedule 1 to this Instrument and of all other powers enabling him in that behalf, by this Instrument, which contains only regulations consequential upon the Tax Credits Act 1999 and which is made before the end of the period of six months beginning with the coming into force of that Act and, in so far as they relate to housing benefit and council tax benefit, with the agreement of such organisations appearing to him to be representative of the authorities concerned that consultations should not be undertaken, hereby makes the following Regulations:*

### Citation, commencement and interpretation

**1.**—(1) These Regulations may be cited as the Social Security and Child Support (Tax Credits) Consequential Amendments Regulations 1999.

(2) These Regulations shall come into force on 5th October 1999.

. . .

## Revocation and Saving of the Child Support (Compensation for Recipients of Family Credit and Disability Working Allowance) Regulations 1995

**6.** The Child Support (Compensation for Recipients of Family Credit and Disability Working Allowance) Regulations 1995 are revoked except that they shall continue to have effect in the case of an award of family credit or disability working allowance awarded with effect from a date falling before 5th October 1999.

## The Child Support (Miscellaneous Amendments) Regulations 1999

### (SI 1999/977)

*Made by the Secretary of State for Social Security under sections 14(3), 32(1), (8) and (9), 42(1), 47(1) and (2), 52(4), 54 and 55(1) of, and paragraphs 5(1) and (2) of Schedule 1 to, the Child Support Act 1991, and of all other powers enabling him in that behalf.*

### Citation, commencement and interpretation

**1.**—(1) These Regulations may be cited as the Child Support (Miscellaneous Amendments) Regulations 1999.  **3.282**

(2) These Regulations shall come into force on 6th April 1999 with the exception of regulations 4(2), 6(2)(a) and (5)(a)(b)(c) and (d), which shall come into force on 4th October 1999.

(3) In these Regulations—

"the Act" means the Child Support Act 1991;

. . .

"the first commencement day" means 6th April 1999;

. . .

"the second commencement day" means 4th October 1999.

### [¹Transitional provisions

**7.**—(1) A decision with respect to a maintenance assessment in force on  **3.283** the first or second commencement day shall not be superseded by a decision under section 17 of the Act solely to give effect to these Regulations.

(2) These Regulations shall apply to a fresh maintenance assessment made by virtue of—

(a) a revision under section 16 of the Act of a decision with respect to a maintenance assessment; or

(b) a decision under section 17 of the Act which supersedes a decision with respect to a maintenance assessment, as from whichever is the later of—

    (i)  the date as from which that revision or, as the case may be, supersession takes effect; or

   (ii)  the first day of the first maintenance period which begins on or after the first or second commencement day, as the case may be.]

AMENDMENT

1. Article 47 of the Commencement No.7 Order 1999 (June 1, 1999).

## The Social Security and Child Support (Decisions and Appeals) Regulations 1999

(SI 1999/991)

ARRANGEMENT OF REGULATIONS

PART I

*General*

PART II

*Revisions, Supersessions and Other Matters*

*Social Security and Child Support*

CHAPTER I

*Revisions*

15D. Procedure in relation to the adjustment of the amount payable under a maintenance calculation.

## PART III

### SUSPENSION. TERMINATION AND OTHER MATTERS

### CHAPTER II

### OTHER MATTERS

## PART IV

### RIGHTS OF APPEAL AND PROCEDURES FOR BRINGING APPEALS

### CHAPTER I

#### *General*

#### *General Appeals Matters including*

#### *Child Support Appeals*

## PART V

#### *Appeal Tribunals for Child Support*

### CHAPTER I

#### *The Panel and Appeal Tribunals*

### CHAPTER II

#### *Procedure in Connection with Determination and Referrals of Appeals*

## CHAPTER III

### *Striking Out Appeals*

## CHAPTER IV

### *Oral Hearings*

## CHAPTER V

### *Decisions of Appeal Tribunals and Related Matters*

### *Appeal Tribunal Decisions*

## PART VI

### *Revocations*

## SCHEDULES

GENERAL NOTE

3.285    These Regulations deal with social security, child support and tax credits. Only the provisions relevant to child support are set out. The provisions that relate exclusively to social security have been omitted. Of those omissions those within regulations quoted are marked with three dots, while omissions of whole regulations are not marked. The amendments that have been made solely for the purposes of tax credits only are not included and the omissions are not marked.

*Determinations and decisions*

The Act, these Regulations and the Child Support Commissioners (Procedure) Regulations 1999 distinguish between determinations and decisions. The distinction is important for at least three reasons: (i) only decisions may be revised or superseded under ss.16 and 17 of the Act; (ii) only decisions are appealable to a Commissioner or a court under ss.24 and 25; (iii) only decisions are final under s.46A of the Act. The use of "decide" or "decision" signals that the conclusion must be a decision. So, for example, an appeal tribunal decides an appeal (see s.20(7)(a) and that decision is appealable to a Commissioner (see s.24(1)). The use of the word "determine" or "determination" is ambiguous. Sometimes it means a determination as opposed to a decision. So, a finding of fact is a determination and not a decision under s.46A(2). Sometimes it refers to the process by which a conclusion is reached, regardless of whether that conclusion is a decision or a determination. So, a Commissioner may refer a case to an appeal tribunal with directions for its determination under s.24(3)(d), although the outcome of the determination will be a decision by the tribunal.

Precise definition is difficult and not necessary. The following is tentatively suggested. A decision is the ultimate conclusion on a legal question. A determination is a conclusion on procedural matters or on the elements of that question (the building blocks of a decision). This suggestion is very similar to that used by the Court of Appeal in *Carpenter v Secretary of State for Department for Work and Pensions* reported as *R(IB) 6/03* at paras 14, 16 and 19.

*Who makes determinations and decisions?*

The persons authorised to exercise the powers conferred by these Regulations and the persons on whom the Regulations impose duties are identified in different ways. (i) *The clerk to the tribunal* So, reg.37 makes the clerk responsible for summoning members of the panel to sit on an appeal tribunal. (ii) *A legally qualified panel member* So, reg.38(1) gives the legally qualified panel member the power to determine the procedure in connection with the consideration and determination of the case. (iii) *The chairman, or sole member, of an appeal tribunal* The chairman will usually, but need not necessaily, be a legally qualified panel member. So, reg.53 imposes the duty to record the decision of the appeal tribunal on the chairman or sole member of the tribunal. (iv) *The appeal tribunal* So, reg.51(4) give the power to adjourn an oral hearing to the appeal tribunal. (v) *A panel member* Some provisions refer simply to a "panel member". The context usually makes it clear that only a particularly qualified panel member is covered. So, in reg.47(a) the reference to "the panel member" refers back to "legally qualified panel member". The only case of doubt is reg.51(3) which, if read in isolation, appears to give the power to postpone a hearing to any panel member. In the context of the regulation as a whole, this probably means the legally qualified panel member referred to in reg.51(1). (vi) Sometimes, the Regulations do not identify anyone as having responsibility. So, reg.49(2) does not impose the duty to give notice of the time and place on anyone in particular, although it will presumably be performed by the clerk as part of the clerk's service to the appeal tribunal under reg.37.

In the general notes to these Regulations, chairman is used to refer to (i) a panel member (usually a legally qualified panel member) who makes an interlocutory decision, (ii) the chairman of a tribunal that consists of more than one panel member and (iii) if an appeal tribunal consists of one member only, that member or the appeal tribunal itself.

*Natural justice and analogous cases*

The principles of natural justice are concerned with procedural fairness of the proceedings before the tribunal (or Commissioner), including the hearing of the appeal (*R(S) 4/82*, para.26). They are not concerned with the fairness of justice of the law applied by the appeal tribunal. They are only concerned with the merits of the application of the law in a particular case to the extent that this has been affected by procedural factors. The right to a fair hearing is separate from the outcome of the proceedings before the tribunal. Even if the outcome was unimpeachable, a failure to allow the parties a fair hearing is wrong as a fair hearing might have resulted in different findings of fact (*Stansby v Datapulse plc, The Times*, January 28, 2004).

The principles of natural justice ensure that the parties have a fair hearing (*McInnes v Onslow-Fane* [1978] 3 All E.R. 211 at 219, *per* Megarry V-C). They protect the parties to the proceedings against the failure by the appeal tribunal to give them a fair hearing. This covers the failings of the judicial members of the tribunal. It also covers the failings of a tribunal clerk in carrying out administrative duties ancillary to the tribunal's judicial function, as these are failings of "the appeal tribunal" for this purpose, provided that they affect the fairness of the hearing (*CIB 4812/97*, paras 12–21). Natural justice does not protect a party against the party's own failings or those of the party's advisers (*Al-Mehdawi v Secretary of State for the Home Department* [1989] 3 All E.R. 843 at 848, *per* Lord Bridge).

In *CJSA 5100/01*, the Commissioner argued that fair hearing issues would be better expressed in terms of striking a balance between the parties, language derived from the equality of arms aspect of the Convention right to a fair hearing under the Human Rights Act 1998, in order to emphasise this aspect to tribunals whose standards were, in his view, deteriorating.

On appeal, factual issues relating to the fairness of the hearing must be investigated and determined if that is necessary to deal with the issue on the appeal (*Stansby v Datapulse plc, The Times*, January 28, 2004). This may require a statement to be obtained from the members of the tribunal. In *CDLA 5574/02*, the Commissioner set out two circumstances in which a statement would be obtained (para.8). First, if the other evidence is insufficient but raised an issue worthy of investigation. Second, if personal misconduct by a panel member was alleged.

Principles have been developed by analogy with natural justice where the one party has failed to communicate material information to the other party (*Al-Mehdawi v Secretary of State for the Home Department* [1989] 3 All E.R. 843 at 848 *per* Lord Bridge). The failure by one of the parties to the proceedings before a tribunal to provide for the tribunal information material to the case has been treated as a breach of natural justice (*R(CS) 1/99*, para.8 following *R(SB) 18/83*, para.11), although the Commissioner did not refer to the reasoning in *Al-Mehdawi*. The reasoning has been extended to the failure by a tribunal clerk to pass material information to the tribunal (*CCS 16817/96*, para.10), but the reasoning was not followed by another Commissioner who treated the failure by the clerk as a failure by the appeal tribunal (*CIB 4812/97*, para.20). The Court of Appeal has allowed an appeal under s.11, Tribunals and Inquiries Act 1992 on the ground that information had been supplied to the clerk of a special needs appeal tribunal but not passed to the members (*W v Special Needs Appeal Tribunal, The Times*, December 12, 2000).

As the analogous principle is based on the suppression of information by one party to the proceedings to the detriment of another party, a party cannot rely on it if the reason for the information not being available lies in the party's own fault or in circumstances outside the control of any of the parties (*CIB 4951/97*, paras 5–6; *CIB 4853/98*, paras 18–20). This is especially so if the evidence that was not available was the subject of a direction under reg.38(2) below that was not complied with by the party (*CCS 4687/00*, para.12). The Convention right under Art.6(1) is no wider. It provides that a party is "entitled to a fair . . . hearing". If the absence of information is not attributable by cause or contribution to the appeal tribunal, the party's entitlement has not been affected. It has simply not been effective, because of the party's own fault or circumstances beyond anyone's control. See *CIB 2470/01*, paras.14–15. A party's recourse in a case that falls outside both the principles of natural justice and the analogous principle lies in the tribunal's wider discretionary power to set aside under reg.57 (*CIB 4853/98*, para.22).

Since the context in which the principles have to apply vary considerably, they are applied flexibly to ensure that standards are set that are appropriate to the circumstances. This point was made by Tucker L.J. in *Russell v Duke of Norfolk* [1949] 1 All E.R. 109 at 118:

> "There are, in my view, no words which are of universal application to every kind of inquiry and every kind of domestic tribunal. The requirements of natural justice must depend on the circumstances of the case, the nature of the inquiry, the rules under which the tribunal is acting, the subject matter that is being dealt with and so forth."

This point is of particular importance to a tribunal which takes an inquisitorial approach to its proceedings. The principles of natural justice in many ways reflect the features of the adversarial approach and have had to be adapted to other contexts.

In so far as these Regulations make no provision (*e.g.* for the procedure at a paper hearing), the tribunal must act "in accordance with natural justice and to promote the objective with which it was set up, and possibly by analogy with the rules of procedure prescribed for comparable tribunals or bodies" (*Qureshi v Qureshi* [1971] 1 All E.R. 325 at 342–3, *per* Simon P).

In so far as these Regulations make provision, their interpretation and operation **3.286** must be set in the context of the interplay between (i) the individual regulations, (ii) the wide powers given to a legally qualified panel member and the chairman to determine the appeal tribunal's procedure and (iii) the principles of natural justice (*CDLA 5509/97*, para.12). Legislation can never be in breach of natural justice (*R(CS) 4/99*, para.9). It may displace the requirements of natural justice, as in *R(SB) 55/83*, para.12. Before the effect of a regulation can be determined, it has to be interpreted and this must be done against the background of natural justice. Legislation will be interpreted, so far as the language allows, so as not to conflict with the requirement, in general terms, of natural justice (*John v Rees* [1969] 2 All E.R. 274 at 309, *per* Megarry J and *Fairmount Investments Ltd v Secretary of State for the Environment* [1976] 2 All E.R. 865 at 872, *per* Lord Russell). This applies to the enabling provisions under which secondary legislation is made as well as to the substantive terms of both primary and secondary legislation. Also, in deciding how to exercise discretions conferred by these Regulations, the chairman or tribunal must act judicially, which involves taking account of those requirements (*CDLA 5509/97*, para.12). So, for example, if the time available does not permit a hearing in accordance with natural justice, the tribunal must adjourn (*R. v Thames Magistrates' Court Ex p. Polemis* [1974] 2 All E.R. 1219).

The essence of natural justice is that the parties should be given a fair hearing. The test is an objective one. This is emphasised in the classic statement of Lord Hewart C.J. in *R. v Sussex Justices Ex p. McCarthy* [1924] 1 K.B. 256 at 259:

> "it is not merely of some importance but is of fundamental importance that justice should not only be done, but should manifestly and undoubtedly be seen to be done."

The extent to which this statement is given effect in the modern law varies from aspect to aspect of natural justice.

The appeal tribunal must not be biased. The standard required is the same for judges, arbitrators and jurors. The law is authoritatively laid down by the Court of Appeal in *Locabail (UK) Ltd v Bayfield Properties Ltd* [2000] 1 All E.R. 65. (References in this section of the general note are to paragraphs in the Court's judgment unless otherwise stated.) The British test was brought into line with the

European approach by the Court of Appeal in *In Re Medicaments and Related Classes of Goods (No. 2)* [2001] 1 W.L.R. 700 by modestly adjusting the reasoning of the House of Lords in *R. v Gough* [1993] A.C. 646. This was approved, subject to a slight alteration of the wording, by the House of Lords in *Porter v Magill* [2002] 1 All E.R. 465 *per* Lord Hope at paras 99–103.

There are three categories of bias. Bias involves a breach of the fundamental right of the parties to a fair hearing by reasons of partiality or prejudice (para.2).

*(i) Actual bias* This is regularly alleged on appeal, although usually on spurious grounds. It is rare in practice, because of the standards applied by members of the panel. It is difficult to prove in court, because the law does not allow judges to be questioned about extraneous matters that may have influenced a decision (para.3). In practice, it is unnecessary to show actual bias, because the lesser standard of real possibility of bias is always available as an alternative (paras 3 and 16).

*(ii) Presumed bias* Bias is presumed if a member of the tribunal has an interest in the outcome of the case (para.4). The interest is most likely to be financial, although there is an undefined category of cases where the member has a particularly close relationship with a party to the proceedings. This was exemplified in *R. v Bow Street Metropolitan Stipendiary Magistrate Ex p. Pinochet Ugarte (No.2)* [1999] 1 All E.R. 577. Cases of presumed bias should not be extended beyond existing authority, unless the extension is plainly required to give effect to the underlying principles on which the rule is based (para.14). An interest is disregarded if it is so small as to be incapable of affecting the decision (para.10). If the interest is that of a family member, the tribunal member must be so closely and directly affected that their interests are indistinguishable (para.10). Presumed bias can be waived by the parties to the proceedings against whom the bias is presumed (para.15), but the best practice is for the member to withdraw as soon as the interest becomes apparent, rather than present the parties to the proceedings with a last-minute choice between an adjournment or waiver (para.21).

*(iii) Real apprehension of bias* Bias will be shown if there is an objective apprehension of bias (para.16). The test is an objective one. It is decided by reference to the standard of a fair-minded and informed observer who is aware of legal traditions and culture (*Taylor v Lawrence* [2002] 2 All E.R. 353 at para.61). The issue is whether there is a reasonable apprehension of bias, not whether it was likely that the actual tribunal was in fact biased: *In Re Medicaments and Related Classes of Goods (No. 2)* [2001] 1 W.L.R. 700. The parties to the proceedings against whom the bias exists may waive it and allow the member to sit (paras 15 and 26). There is no comprehensive definition of what may or may not give rise to a real possibility of bias. Everything depends on the circumstances of the case, which may include the nature of the issue to be decided, although subject to this the Court of Appeal gave a detailed list of instances that might or might not show a real possibility of bias (para.25). It has been held in the Chancery Division that it is inconceivable that a real danger of bias could be shown on the basis of the religion, ethnic or national origin, gender, age, class, means or sexual orientation of a judge hearing a case (*Seer Technologies Ltd v Abbas, The Times*, March 16, 2000). Bias is particularly likely to arise from some connection between a member of the appeal tribunal and one of the parties. The connection might involve some relationship between the persons concerned or some dealing between or affecting them. Involvement in some earlier proceedings does not necessarily involve bias, although in the particular circumstances of the case this may be shown. Bias is not shown by professional or social contact between a member of the appeal tribunal and a representative of one of the parties (*CIB 5794/97*, para.9; *Taylor v Lawrence* [2002] 2 All E.R. 353 at para.63). Knowledge by the member of the factor alleged to create the bias is essential if the

allegation is to succeed and the member concerned may properly be asked whether the factor was known (paras 18 and 19). Disclosure should be made as soon as the member becomes aware of it and realises that it is relevant, regardless of the stage of the proceedings (para.26). It should only be made if there is objectively a real issue of the possibility of bias, but if it is made, it must be full (*Taylor v Lawrence* [2002] 2 All E.R. 353 at paras 64–65). Unfounded allegations of bias should not lead a tribunal to abort the hearing of a case (*Bennett v Southwark London Borough Council* [2002] I.C.R. 881).

The mere fact that a member of a tribunal has previously decided a case involving a party or made adverse comments about that party does not of itself entitle the party to claim bias and a differently constituted tribunal (*Lodwick v London Borough of Southwark* [2004] EWCA Civ 306, para.21).

If a panel member is called as a witness, care needs to be taken to avoid the appearance of bias in the constitution of the appeal tribunal by ensuring that it does not consist of members who regularly sit with the witness (*CIS 661/94*, para.14).

A lawyer who sits part-time as a chairman of an appeal tribunal should not appear before a tribunal if it contains a lay panel member before whom the lawyer has appeared (*Lawal v Northern Spirit Ltd* [2004] 1 All E.R. 187).

Bias is not the only aspect of natural justice. The principles cover everything that may deny a party to the proceedings a fair hearing. Many aspects of a fair hearing are covered by specific regulations. Each party to the proceedings must know that the hearing is to be held and, subject to the rules on opting for an oral hearing, be entitled to attend. The party must be entitled to know the issues involved and the evidence and arguments put forward by other parties. They should have a chance, in person or in writing, to contribute by presenting evidence and arguments and by challenging those presented by other parties. This involves having adequate notice of the hearing (in the case of a paper hearing, adequate notice of the earliest date on which it will be held) and adequate time to prepare a case. A record of the proceedings should be kept. The decision must be notified to the parties, along with reasons if they are requested in time. The decision must not be based on factors on which a party adversely affected by them has not had a chance to comment, although this chance may (depending on the factors and the circumstances of the case) have been forfeited if the party did not ask for and attend an oral hearing. The decision must be based on material that tends logically to show the existence of non-existence of relevant facts or the likelihood of the occurrence or non-occurrence of some future relevant event. See generally *R(IS)* 5/93, para.17.

A tribunal should usually hear both sides of a case and not dismiss the appeal having heard only the appellant. The only exception is if the case is hopeless. Otherwise, the tribunal should hear all parties, whether or not there is a burden of proof on the appellant. See *Logan v Commissioners for Customs and Excise* [2004] I.C.R. 1.

Reliance by a tribunal on an authority or provision that was not cited to it by the parties and not drawn to the parties' attention by the tribunal will only render the hearing unfair if it was central to the issue and resulted in substantial prejudice or material injustice to one of the parties (*Stanley Cole (Wainfleet) Ltd v Sheridan, The Times*, September 5, 2003).

If it appears that a member of the tribunal is not concentrating on a significant part of the proceedings, for example by appearing to be asleep, there will not have been a fair hearing. Compare *Stansby v Datapulse plc, The Times*, January 28, 2004 (no fair hearing when member appeared to be asleep after drinking alcohol) and *R. v Betson and Cockran, The Times*, January 28, 2004 (in which a judge fell asleep during counsel's speech to the jury—outcome not influenced by this).

If a remark (such as a racial remark) is made in an impersonal way which could not be taken as relating to any party to the proceedings, an immediate apology may remove the appearance of bias (*Reid v Chief Constable of Merseyside, The Times*, February 5, 1996). This authority is very limited in scope and it is, of course, better for the remark not to be made at all.

In *CU 270/86*, paras 11–12 the claimant had been too ill to attend the hearing of his appeal. He applied for the decision to be set aside. This application was rejected. The claimant was not invited to attend the hearing of his application in order to explain his illness. Although there was no duty on the tribunal to do so and the original tribunal had correctly exercised its power to proceed in the claimant's absence, the Commissioner held that the failure to allow the claimant to give evidence on the setting aside application coupled with his earlier illness retrospectively produced a breach of natural justice in the original hearing. With respect, this must be wrong. A breach is respect of later proceedings cannot relate back to an earlier hearing.

*Natural justice and the proper approach to a hearing*

The members of an appeal tribunal should have read the papers before an oral hearing. If there is more than one member of the appeal tribunal, it is good practice for the members to have previewed the case, in so far as that is possible from the papers, before the start of the hearing. This involves identifying the issues that will arise and the questions that the tribunal will have to investigate, and deciding how to conduct the hearing. No question of prejudgement is involved in this practice, which is in accordance with the principles of natural justice. The point was nicely made by Bill Tillyard, a former full-time chairman in the Wales and the South West Region of the Independent Tribunal Service, when he said that a hearing must be approached with an open mind, but not with an empty one.

It is consistent with the principles of natural justice, and indeed a contribution to a fair hearing, for an appeal tribunal to keep the parties informed during a hearing of its assessment of the evidence or arguments, provided that no impression is created that a conclusion has been reached. Decisions taken by the chairman on the conduct of the proceeding, such as to ensure that they are conducted as expeditiously as possible, are consistent with the principles of natural justice. See *Arab Monetary Fund v Hashim (No.8)* (1993) 6 Admin L.R. 348, *Mahomed v Morris, The Times*, March 1, 2000 and *R(IS) 5/78*, para.18.

An appeal tribunal has to take an inquisitorial approach to the proceedings before it. This is an aspect of natural justice that is necessary in order to ensure a fair hearing for every party to the proceedings. The proper exercise of this approach is not inconsistent with the principles of natural justice. The following will not, therefore, automatically be in breach of natural justice: interrupting the presentation of a party's case (*R(SB) 6/82*, para.6); asking probing questions that the party would prefer were not asked (*R(S) 4/82*, para.27; indicating scepticism, but not a closed mind (*Arab Monetary Fund v Hashim (No.8)* (1993) 6 Admin L.R. 348 *per* Sir Thomas Bingham M.R.).

In order to apply the just and equitable test to a possible variation of a maintenance calculation, the tribunal has to know the impact that it will have on the calculation. In some cases, it will be sufficiently obvious not to require more detailed consideration. In most cases, it can only be known by using the presenting officer's laptop computer. The parties may not be able to make a useful contribution to that exercise, but it is a breach of natural justice for the parties not to be present. However, if it did not affect the outcome of the appeal, the Commissioner may on an application for leave exercise the discretion to refuse leave to appeal or on an appeal may decline to direct a rehearing. See *CCS 7502/99*.

*Appeal and judicial review*

An appeal lies to a Child Support Commissioner only against the decision of an appeal tribunal and only on the ground that the decision was wrong in law. A determination by an appeal tribunal or a chairman can only be challenged in a court by judicial review. A decision of an appeal tribunal may also be subject to judicial review, but the scope for this is limited, because of the power to appeal to a Commissioner. In view of the wide grounds on which a Commissioner may hold a decision to be wrong in law, it is likely that an appeal to a Commissioner will be an adequate alternative remedy, rendering a judicial review inappropriate. This will not, however, necessarily prevent a judicial review, as the test applied by the courts is not whether or not a power of appeal exists, but whether the court or the Commissioner is the more appropriate venue for determining the question that arises (*R. v Leeds City Council Ex p. Hendry, The Times*, January 20, 1994). However, it will only be in the most exceptional circumstances that the court will entertain an application for judicial review if an appeal is available (*R. (Davies) v Financial Services Authority* [2003] 4 All E.R. 1196). A judicial review will be the only way to challenge a decision of an appeal tribunal outside the time limit on applications for appeal to a Commissioner under reg.11 of the Child Support Commissioners (Procedure) Regulations 1999.

A judicial review of a decision lies on the three grounds set out by Lord Diplock in *Council of Civil Service Unions v Minister for the Civil Service* [1984] 3 All E.R. 935 at 950–951: (i) illegality—a decisionmaker fails to give effect to the law that regulates his power to make decisions, such as an appeal tribunal acting outside its jurisdiction; (ii) irrationality—a decision is "so outrageous in its defiance of logic or of accepted moral standards that no sensible person who had applied his mind to the question to be decided could have arrived at it", such as a decision by an appeal tribunal that was not supported by any evidence; (iii) procedural impropriety—the decisionmaker fails to comply with the principles of natural justice or its own rules of procedure.

### Appeal and supersession

For a discussion of the relationship between appeals and applications for supersession, see the preliminary general note to reg.6A below.

### Reconsideration of determinations and decisions

Interlocutory determinations, whether or not made after giving notice to all the parties, are open to reconsideration and, if appropriate, they may be reversed or varied (*CIS 93/92*, para.15). This reflects the principle that a determination or decision made without notice being given to all the parties may be discharged (*Boyle v Sacker* (1888) 39 Ch. D. 249). There is, however, no duty to reconsider (*CIS 93/92*, para.16). There is no authority on whether an interlocutory decision may only be reconsidered on request, but in principle this should not be necessary.

A final decision by a tribunal may be reconsidered at any time until it is promulgated (*CSB 226/81*, para.11; *R(I) 14/74*, para.14(a)). This may be done on application of the one of the parties or on the tribunal's own initiative (*Re Harrison's Settlement* [1955] 1 All E.R. 185). Reconsideration is only permissible to further the interests of justice in exceptional circumstances or for strong reasons; it must not be allowed to subvert the appeal process (*Compagnie Noga D'Importation et D'Exportation SA v Abacha* [2001] 3 All E.R. 513 at paras 42–43 and 47). On principle, reconsideration should only be possible if undertaken by the same tribunal (*R. v Cripps Ex p. Muldoon* [1984] 2 All E.R. 705 at 710, *per* Sir John Donaldson M.R.). Natural justice may require that the parties be given notice that the decision is to be reconsidered and an opportunity to make submissions or produce further evidence, if appropriate (*ibid.*).

After a final decision has been promulgated, it may be corrected or set aside and may be the subject of an appeal. These possibilities apart, reconsideration is not possible (*CSI 559/98*, para.11; *R. v Immigration Appeal Tribunal Ex p. Wanyoike, The Times*, March 10, 2000). There are, however, two suggestions in the authorities that reconsideration of a final decision may be possible after promulgation. First, in *R.*

*v Cripps Ex p. Muldoon* [1984] 2 All E.R. 705 at 710. Sir John Donaldson M.R. said that a final decision that is irregular may be open to reconsideration after promulgation, but no examples of irregularities were given. Second, there was a possibility that an appeal tribunal might have had power to reconsider a decision given on a setting aside application (*R(I) 7/94*, paras 16 and 35; *CIS 30/93*, para.11), but only at the request of one of the parties and not on the tribunal's own initiative (*R(I) 7/94*, para.35). This was only a suggestion made in the course of argument. No ruling was made on the point, except to say that *if* the power existed it could only be exercised on an application by one of the parties. The determination of a setting aside application is now made by a legally qualified panel member and not by an appeal tribunal. So, the decision is no longer directly applicable. Anyway, it is not clear whether the reasoning underlying the suggestion applied only to determinations of setting aside applications or was wider and applied to other determinations, perhaps to all final decisions. Certainly the authorities cited in *CI 79/90*, para.16 are not limited to setting aside applications. The Commissioner in *CSI 559/98* did not refer to these authorities dealing with reconsideration of final decisions.

If there is power to reconsider a final decision after promulgation, it is difficult to understand why it should only be exercised on application by one of the parties. If, for example, the tribunal rejected an application to set aside a decision, but then discovered that relevant information had not been put to the tribunal by the clerk, there seems no point in requiring one of the parties to make an application for the refusal to be reconsidered and every reason for the tribunal to be able to act on its own initiative. As the tribunal that gave the decision which is to be reconsidered no longer has jurisdiction once the decision has been promulgated, any power to reconsider may be exercised by any tribunal and need not be exercised by the same tribunal (*R. v Cripps Ex p. Muldoon* [1984] 2 All E.R. 705 at 710, *per* Sir John Donaldson M.R.), although courtesy would normally suggest that, if possible, the original tribunal should exercise the power. As a reconsideration does not involve an appeal, there is no violation of Art.6(1) of the European Convention on Human Rights if it is undertaken by the same tribunal (*Khreino v Khreino* [2000] 1 F.L.R. 578).

There is no authority on what factors allow a decision to be reconsidered. Usually, a decision will be reconsidered because further evidence has been obtained or a new argument had been advanced. It is difficult to imagine a case in which a decision would, or should, be reconsidered without the presence of some new factor. This is particularly the case for final decisions. If reconsideration is permissible without a new factor being present, the circumstances in which it is appropriate must be exceptional and there is a strong argument that it should only be undertaken by the person or tribunal who made the decision. In the case of a final decision, the argument of courtesy is especially strong.

The courts regard it as undesirable for an application for reconsideration to be made unless there are strong reasons to support it (*In Re Blenheim Leisure (Restaurants) Ltd (No.3), The Times*, November 9, 1999). In view of the limited information on which interlocutory decisions often have to be made, this approach is not appropriate to tribunals. The power to reconsider is discretionary, so any applications that appear unmeritious may be refused without consideration.

The courts have accepted the possibility of a reconsideration without legislative authority in an administrative context (*R. (ota C) v Lewisham London Borough Council* [2003] 3 All E.R. 1277 at para.59).

*Active case management*

3.287    Regulation 38(1) and (2) and 49(1) provide the legislative basis for chairmen to take a proactive role at all stages of the proceedings. The days are past when the parties to the proceedings or their representatives are allowed to dictate the speed of the proceedings and the evidence that they wish to make available. The appeal tribunals are run from public funds and those who organise them and those who sit on them must ensure that those funds are expended efficiently. There is ample authority from the courts in the days before the Woolf reforms to support a proactive approach by chairmen in exercising control over the nature and quantity of the evidence that may be produced and over the speed at which and the manner in which the proceedings are to be conducted. See *CIB 5595/97*, para.17 and *CDLA 1834/98*, para.19.

The parties must co-operate with the tribunal in fixing a suitable date for hearing, showing flexibility and giving appropriate priority to a judicial proceeding (*CCS 5315/99*).

### Inherent or implied powers

It is sometimes said that a statutory tribunal has no inherent jurisdiction. The word "jurisdiction" is ambiguous. A statutory tribunal has no inherent jurisdiction in the sense that it has no power to deal with parties or issues, or to give a form of relief, that is not permitted by legislation. So, it has been held that a tribunal could not deal with a question first arising in the course of an appeal (*R 2/94 (CSG)*, para.10) or deal with entitlement in the absence of a claim (*R(SB) 42/83*, paras 8 and 12). Both of these were issues that were outside the tribunal's statutory jurisdiction. This is the narrower and stricter meaning of "jurisdiction". The word is also used more broadly to cover the powers that a tribunal may exercise within its jurisdiction in the stricter sense. In this broader sense, a statutory tribunal may have inherent powers. (There is some difference in the use of terminology. In *Akewushola v Secretary of State for the Home Department* [2000] 2 All E.R. 148 at 153, Sedley L.J. referred to "inherent" powers of statutory tribunals, while in *CCS 910/99*, paras 8 and 11, the Commissioner preferred to use "implied" rather than "inherent". In *Taylor v Lawrence* [2002] 2 All E.R. 353, the Court of Appeal used the terms interchangeably.)

The inherent powers are part of the tribunal's control over its procedure in order to allow it to do justice between the parties (*Lloyd v McMahon* [1987] 1 All E.R. 1118 at 1161, *per* Lord Bridge; *R(U) 3/89*, para.5). The starting point is that they cover all acts necessary to maintain the character of a court of justice (*Taylor v Lawrence* [2002] 2 All E.R. 353 at para.53), although this is subject to the legislative context (see below).

Section 28ZD(2) of the Act preserves any power that tribunals would otherwise have to correct or set aside their decisions. See the general note to that subsection.

The need to rely on a tribunal's inherent or implied procedural powers is reduced by the power to give directions under reg.38(2) and to control procedure under regs 38(1) and 49(1). The scope of the inherent powers of tribunals (and Commissioners) must now be considered in the light of the decision of the Court of Appeal in *Akewushola v Secretary of State for the Home Department*, above at 153–154, in which the court held that there was no inherent power to rescind or review a tribunal's own decision. Subject to that case, the position as laid down by Commissioners is set out in the following two paragraphs.

Some inherent powers of an appeal tribunal are well-established: (i) the tribunal's control over its decision until it is promulgated: see the general note to reg.56(1); (ii) the power to correct accidental errors; (iii) the power to set aside decisions made without jurisdiction. Powers (ii) and (iii) are inherent or implied in order to allow the tribunal to do justice between the parties (*R(U) 3/89*, para.5).

Others are less clear: (i) the power of a chairman to initiate the procedure for setting aside the decision of an appeal tribunal: see the general note to reg.57(1); (ii) a wider power to set aside decisions than permitted by reg.57—it has been suggested that the Commissioners' power to set aside decisions is wider than that given by their procedure regulations (*R(U) 3/89*, para.5(3); *CCS 910/99*, paras 11–14).

The question always arises whether the existence of the inherent power is consistent with or displaced by the provisions of these regulations.

Although clerks have power under reg.56 to correct a decision or record of decision, they have no inherent power to alter a decision (*Memminger-IRO GmbH v Trip-Lite Ltd (No.2), The Times*, July 9, 1992).

*Failure to comply with procedural requirements*

The question may arise of the effect of a failure to comply with procedural requirements. The same principles apply whether the failure was that of the Secretary of State, a clerk, a chairman, a tribunal or a party to the proceedings.

The argument may be expressed in terms of the decision being "void", "nullity" and "ineffective". As these words have many shades of meaning, it is preferable to refer to correctable and uncorrectable defects in a legal process (*CCS 1992/97*, paras 12–13). Correctable defects are defects in a process which can be corrected by some later action, leaving the rest of the process intact, subject of course to any other mistakes that need to be corrected. Uncorrectable defects are defects which can only be corrected, if at all, by beginning the whole process afresh.

In *CCS 16904/96*, para.25 the Commissioner gave the following as cases where the failure involved would render the officer's decision invalid and ineffective: (i) where the decision was given by an officer who had no authority to make it; (ii) where the decision had already beenmade by another officer; (iii) there was an absence of some application, leave, notice or other step necessary to give the officer authority. This is similar to the matters considered as going to a tribunal's jurisdiction in *R(I) 7/94* para.30.

In *CCS 16904/96* the absent parent had been assessed as liable to pay nil child support maintenance, but had been held liable to pay a contribution from his income support in lieu of child support maintenance. The officer had failed to consider whether the condition contained in reg.28(1)(c) of the Maintenance Assessments and Special Cases Regulations was satisfied. The Commissioner held that none of the above conditions was satisfied and that the decision, though flawed, was valid and effective until set aside on review. In contrast, in *CCS 12848/96*, para.9 the Commissioner held that failure to give notice under reg.25 of the Maintenance Assessment Procedure Regulations of an intended review rendered the decision on that review a nullity. This case involved a defective of type (iii) above.

The argument may also be expressed in terms of the procedural provision being "mandatory" or "directory". These terms have been rejected as unhelpful by the Court of Appeal in *R. v Immigration Appeal Tribunal Ex p. Jeyeanthan* [1999] 3 All E.R. 231. Lord Woolf M.R. set out (at pages 238–9) the three questions which were most likely to determine the effect of failure to comply with a procedural requirement.

"Is the statutory requirement fulfilled if there has been substantial compliance with the requirement and, if so, has there been substantial compliance in the case in issue even though there has not been strict compliance? (The substantial compliance question.) Is the non-compliance capable of being waived, and if so, has it, or can it be waived in this particular case? (The discretionary question.) I treat the grant of an extension of time for compliance as a waiver. If is is not capable of being waived or is not waived then what is the consequence of the non-compliance? (The consequences question.)

"Which questions arise will depend upon the facts of the case and the nature of the particular requirement. The advantage of focusing on these questions is that they should avoid the unjust and unintended consequences which can flow from an approach solely dependent on dividing requirements into mandatory ones, which oust jurisdiction, or directory, which do not. If the result of non-compliance goes to jurisdiction it will be said jurisdiction cannot be conferred where it does not otherwise exist by consent or waiver."

A breach of a tribunal's procedural rules does not usually render further proceedings of no force or effect, even if the rule is framed in mandatory terms (*R v Sekhon* [2003] 3 All E.R. 508).

*Representation*

The scope of the rights and powers of a representative under these Regulations is unclear. A representative may sign an appeal on behalf of an appellant under reg.33(1)(a)(ii) and may withdraw an appeal under reg.40(1). A party to the proceedings may be represented at an oral hearing under reg.49(8), which gives to the representative "for the purposes of the proceedings *at the hearing*" only the rights and powers of the party. There is no other provision giving rights or powers to representatives. Regulation 57(1)(a) envisages that the representative is entitled to be given documents relating to the proceedings, although there is no provision requiring this to be done and the duty to notify the time and place of an oral hearing under reg.49(2) applies only to the parties to the proceedings. The existence of the express powers under regs 33(1), 40(1) and 49(8) suggests that they are the only circumstances in which a representative may act for a party to the proceedings and that, for example, applications for a full statement of the tribunal's decision or to set aside a decision of an appeal tribunal must be made personally by the party to the proceedings.

PART I

GENERAL

## Citation, commencement and interpretation

**1.**—(1) These Regulations may be cited as the Social Security and Child Support (Decisions and Appeals) Regulations 1999.     3.288

(2) These Regulations shall come into force—

(a) in so far as they relate to child support and for the purposes of this regulation and regulation 2 on Ist June 1999;

. . .

(3) In these Regulations, unless the context otherwise requires—

"the Act" means the Social Security Act 1998;

. . .

[3"the Arrears, Interest and Adjustment of Maintenance Assessments Regulations" means the Child Support (Arrears, Interest and Adjustment of Maintenance Assessments) Regulations 1992;]

. . .

"appeal" means an appeal to an appeal tribunal;

. . .

"clerk to the appeal tribunal" means a clerk assigned to the appeal tribunal in accordance with regulation 37;

"the date of notification" means—

(a) the date that notification of a decision of the Secretary of State is treated as having been given or sent in accordance with regulation 2(b); or

(b) in the case of a social fund payment arising in accordance with regulations made under section 138(2) of the Contributions and Benefits Act—

(i) the date seven days after the date on which the Secretary of State makes his decision to make a payment to a person to meet expenses for heating;

(ii) where a person collects the instruments of payment at a post office, the date the instrument is collected;

(iii) where an instrument of payment is sent to a post office for collection but is not collected and a replacement instrument is issued, the date on which the replacement instrument is issued; or

(iv) where a person questions his failure to be awarded a payment for expenses for heating, the date on which the notification of the Secretary of State's decision given in response to that question is issued;

. . .

"financially qualified panel member" means a panel member who satisfies the requirements of paragraph 4 of Schedule 3;

. . .

"legally qualified panel member" means a panel member who satisfies the requirements of paragraph 1 of Schedule 3;

[⁴"the Maintenance Calculation Procedure Regulations" means the Child Support (Maintenance Calculation Procedure) Regulations 2000;]

[⁵"the Maintenance Calculations and Special Cases Regulations" means the Child Support (Maintenance Calculations and Special Cases) Regulations 2000;]

"medically qualified panel member" means a panel member who satisfies the requirements of paragraph 2 of Schedule 3;

[¹³. . .]

[¹⁰"official error" means an error made by—

(a) an officer of the Department for Work and Pensions or the Board acting as such which no person outside the Department or the Inland Revenue caused or to which no person outside the Department or the Inland Revenue materially contributed;

(b) a person employed by a designated authority acting on behalf of the authority, which no person outside that authority caused or to which no person outside that authority materially contributed,

but excludes any error of law which is shown to have been an error by virtue of a subsequent decision of a Commissioner or the court;]

[¹²"out of jurisdiction appeal" means an appeal brought against a decision which is specified in—

(a) Schedule 2 to the Act or a decision prescribed in regulation 27 (decision against which no appeal lies); or

(b) . . .;]

"panel" means the panel constituted under section 6;

"panel member" means a person appointed to the panel;

. . .

[¹¹"partner" means—

(a) where a person is a member of a married couple or an unmarried couple, the other member of that couple; or

(b) where a person is polygamously married to two or more members of his household, any such member;]

"party to the proceedings" means the Secretary of State and any other person—

(a) who is one of the principal parties for the purposes of sections 13 and 14;

(b) who has a right of appeal to an appeal tribunal under section 11(2) of the 1997 Act, section 20 of the Child Support Act [⁶. . .] or section 12(2);

"President" means the President of appeal tribunals appointed under section 5;

"referral" means a referral of an application for a [⁷variation] to an appeal tribunal under section 28D(1)(b) of the Child Support Act;

[⁸except where otherwise provided "relevant person" means—

(a) a person with care;

(b) a non-resident parent;

(c) a parent who is treated as a non-resident parent under regulation 8 of the Maintenance Calculations and Special Cases Regulations;

(d) a child, where the application for a maintenance calculation is made by that child under section 7 of the Child Support Act,

in respect of whom a maintenance calculation has been applied for, or has been treated as applied for under section 6(3) of that Act, or is or has been in force;]

. . .

[⁹"the Variations Regulations" means the Child Support (Variations) Regulations 2000];

. . .

(4) In these Regulations, unless the context otherwise requires, a reference—

(a) to numbered section is to the section of the Act bearing that number;

(b) to a numbered Part is to the Part of these Regulations bearing that number;

(c) to a numbered regulation or Schedule is to the regulation in, or Schedule to, these Regulations bearing that number;

(d) in a regulation or Schedule to a numbered paragraph is to the paragraph in that regulation or Schedule bearing that number;

(e) in a paragraph to a lettered or numbered sub-paragraph is to the sub-paragraph in that paragraph bearing that letter or number.

AMENDMENTS

3. Regulation 2(a) of the Appeals Amendment Regulations 2000 (for in force date see regs 1 and 14 of SI 2000/3185 below).

4. Regulation 2(b) of the Appeals Amendment Regulations 2000 (for in force date see regs 1 and 14 of SI 2000/3185 below).

5. Regulation 2(b) of the Appeals Amendment Regulations 2000 (for in force date see regs 1 and 14 of SI 2000/3185 below).

6. Regulation 2(c) of the Appeals Amendment Regulations 2000 (for in force date see regs 1 and 14 of SI 2000/3185 below).

7. Regulation 2(d) of the Appeals Amendment Regulations 2000 (for in force date see regs 1 and 14 of SI 2000/3185 below).

8. Regulation 2(e) of the Appeals Amendment Regulations 2000 (for in force date see regs 1 and 14 of SI 2000/3185 below).

9. Regulation 2(f) of the Appeals Amendment Regulations 2000 (for in force date see regs 1 and 14 of SI 2000/3185 below).

10. Regulation 2(a) of the Appeals Amendment Regulations 2002 (May 20, 2002).

11. Regulation 2(b) of the Appeals Amendment Regulations 2002 (May 20, 2002).

12. Regulation 3(1) of the Social Security and Child Support (Miscellaneous Amendments) Regulations 2003 (May 5, 2003).

13. Regulation 2(2) of the Social Security, Child Support and Tax Credits (Decisions and Appeals) Amendment Regulations 2004 (December 21, 2004).

GENERAL NOTE

*"official error"*

3.289 　In *CCS 2819/2000*, the tribunal had reached a decision on the basis of incorrect information provided by the presenting officer at the hearing. When this was discovered during the proceedings before the Commissioner, the Secretary of State revised the decision of the tribunal from its effective date. The Commissioner gave a direction that in those circumstances the appeal before him had lapsed. He accepted that the words "the decision arose from an official error" were sufficiently wide to cover the circumstances of the case.

In *CDLA 3440/03*, para.8 the Commissioner held that official error refers to mistakes in adjudication decisions or to mistakes that affect those decisions. On that basis, making a computer record of a decision was a purely administrative matter that required no legislative authority so that a mistake in doing so could not have had any impact on the decision that was made. In *R(CS) 3/04*, the Commissioner held that official error included mistakes made by officials acting in the former capacity of child support officers. In *CH 943/03*, the Commissioner held that a decision by a decision-maker that was reversed by an appeal tribunal was made in official error. In *R(H) 2/04*, the Commissioner held that it was not an error or mistake for decision-makers to rely on the best information currently available and to trust the parties concerned to inform them if it was not correct.

*"out of jurisdiction appeal"*

This definition refers to reg.27 and Sch.2, both of which deal exclusively with social security decisions. There will, of course, be attempts to appeal to an appeal tribunal against child support decisions over which the tribunal has no jurisdiction, but they will not be out of jurisdiction appeals for the purposes of reg.46(1)(a), where this definition is used. They will have to be considered by an appeal tribunal, which has power to determine whether a case falls within its jurisdiction.

*"panel member"*

The President is not automatically made a panel member and in order to sit must be appointed as a legally qualified panel member.

*"party to the proceedings"*

There is no power for anyone other than the persons specified to be identified as, or made, a party to the proceedings.

The Secretary of State is not personally a party to the proceedings and is not a party in a contentious sense. The duty of the officer who makes a decision on behalf of the Secretary of State is to apply the law. It follows that the duty of the officer who attends an oral hearing as a presenting officer is to assist the tribunal in identifying and analysing the evidence and issues relevant to the decision that the appeal tribunal has to make. This role is more like that of a friend of the court than a true party to litigation (*R. v Deputy Industrial Injuries Commissioner Ex p. Moore* [1965] 1 All E.R. 81 at 93, *per* Diplock L.J.). The officer should, though, be cautious of supporting an appeal so as not to raise false hopes, or cause, unfounded fears, in the other parties (*CM 361/92*, para.11). Also, inappropriate support may induce a party not to present all relevant evidence and argument in the belief that the decision of the appeal tribunal is a foregone conclusion.

## Service of notices or documents

**2.** Where, by any provision of the Act [¹, of the Child Support Act] or of these Regulations—    **3.290**

(a) any notice or other document is required to be given or sent to the clerk to the appeal tribunal or to an officer authorised by the Secretary of State, that notice or document shall be treated as having been so given or sent on the day that it is received by the clerk to the appeal tribunal or by an officer authorised by the Secretary of State, as the case may be, and

(b) any notice (including notification of a decision of the Secretary of State) or other document is required to be given or sent to any person other than the clerk to the appeal tribunal or to an officer authorised by the Secretary of State, as the case may be, that notice or document shall, if sent by post to that person's last known address, be treated as having been given or sent on the day that it was posted.

AMENDMENT

1. Regulation 3 of the Appeals Amendment Regulations 2000 (for in force date see regs 1 and 14 of SI 2000/3185 below).

DEFINITIONS

"the Act": see reg.1(3).    **3.291**
"clerk to the appeal tribunal": see reg.1(3).

GENERAL NOTE

*Head (a)*
When is a document received by the clerk? Usually the answer to this question    **3.292**
will be decided by the evidence available. In most cases the only evidence of the date of receipt will be the date stamped on the document, not infrequently in a position which obscures important contents. A party will seldom be in a position to challenge this date. Such a challenge is most likely to be made when the party alleges that the document was delivered by hand on a different day, perhaps late in the afternoon or at a weekend. The usual meaning of receipt involves something coming into someone's hands, here the clerk's. This suggests that mere delivery to the building is insufficient. There is authority for the proposition that delivery through a letter box is sufficient to constitute *notice* on the basis that the presence of the letter box impliedly invites communication by that means (*Holwell Securities Ltd v Hughes* [1974] 1 All E.R. 161 at 164). However, that decision turned on notice. "Receipt," in contrast, is a word which is to be given its natural meaning.

*Swainston v Hetton Victory Club Ltd* [1983] 1 All E.R. 1179 dealt with when a complaint could be "presented" to an industrial tribunal. In particular, the issue was whether a complaint could be presented on a day when the tribunal office was closed. The Court of Appeal held that, as the tribunal was not required to take any steps, the complaint could be presented by being put through the letter box of the tribunal office on a Sunday. Accordingly, it was not necessary to disregard that day as one when the tribunal office was closed. This analysis is in accordance with the Court of Appeal in *Van Aken v Camden London Borough Council* [2003] 1 All E.R. 552. The case was concerned with when a document was filed. The court distinguished between a unilateral act, in which the recipient does not need to take any action and has a purely passive role, and a transactional act, in which the recipient has to take action and has an active role. It decided that the filing of a document was a unilateral act, so that delivery to the court was all that was required. It is possible that these cases are distinguishable in the interpretation of this provision. Presenting a complaint or filing a document concentrates on the action of the person initiating the communication. This is in contrast to receipt which concentrates on the person to whom the communication is directed.

If the Post Office fails to deliver under-stamped mail in accordance with a bulk surcharging arrangement, it holds the mail as bailee for the addressee, and the mail is treated as being delivered on the day it would have arrived in the ordinary course of post (*CIS 4901/02*).

If a document is sent to a clerk by fax at a dedicated tribunal venue, it is received when it is successfully transmitted to the tribunal's number at that venue, even if it is not collected by the clerk until later, unless the tribunal specified that communication should be made only to a different number (*CDLA 2149/04*).

*Head (b)*

The rule applies regardless of whether or not the notice or document is actually received (*R(SB) 55/83*). There will be no automatic breach of the rules of natural justice by relying on this provision since it displaces any rule of natural justice which would otherwise have required a party to have received notices or documents (*ibid.* para.12). However, this potentially harsh rule must be considered in the context of two other powers available; the power to adjourn a hearing and the power to set aside a decision of a tribunal.

In *CCS 6302/99*, paras 13–16 the Commissioner raised the issue whether this provision was authorised by statute. The case concerned a non-resident parent who had notified a change of address to the Child Support Agency. The Agency had not passed the new address to the tribunal. The Commissioner referred to authorities in which it had been held that a deemed notice provision will only be valid if (a) it is authorised expressly by statute or (b) it is authorised by necessary implication, which must be shown by demonstrating an objective need for it: *R. v Immigration Appeal Tribunal Ex p. Saleem* [2000] 4 All E.R. 814, relying on *R. v Secretary of State for the Home Department Ex p. Leech* [1993] 4 All E.R. 539. (This issue was not considered by the Commissioner in *CCS 910/99*, where a parent did not receive notice of a tribunal hearing, because he had not notified the Child Support Agency that he had moved.) However, the Commissioner accepted the argument for the Secretary of State that those decisions were distinguishable. Unlike the immigration procedural rules considered in *Saleem*, there is provision in the tribunal's rules for a decision to be set aside if a party to the proceedings did not receive notice of the hearing as well as power to extend some time limits. However, although the deemed notice provision itself might be valid in law, the Commissioner gave a warning that the operation by the legally qualified panel members of the tribunal's procedural rules that could protect a party to the proceedings against an inappropriate application of the provision might result in a violation of Art.6(1) of the European Convention on Human Rights and Fundamental Freedoms.

The address to which the notice or document must have been sent is the person's last *known* address. Usually an address will be known because it will have been notified to the clerk to the tribunal by the person concerned. However, if someone else has suggested that a person who has moved may be living at another address, it will have to be decided whether that person's knowledge and the confidence with which the information was conveyed are such that that address is so certain that it may be said to be the person's last *known* address. The wording of this paragraph is in line with that of reg.15(5). However, it is in contrast to ordinary or last notified address, which is used in reg.24(1) of the Child Support Commissioners (Procedure) Regulations 1999, and to "last known or notified address," which is used in reg.8(1)(b) of the Child Support Fees Regulations, reg.1(3)(b) of the Collection and Enforcement Regulations, and regs 1(6)(b) and 55(6) of the Maintenance Assessment Procedure Regulations. There is a clear pattern with one formulation being used for tribunals, another for Commissioners and a third for the Secretary of State. However, there is no obvious reason for the differences in wording and one can only wonder at how and why they came to be used in each case.

A document is only sent by post if it is sent by the Royal Mail rather than by courier or through a document exchange system (*CIS 550/93*, para.6).

The power to adjourn under reg.51(4) will be relevant if the tribunal suspects or becomes aware that a document has not been received. If a party does not attend and has not contacted the tribunal to say that he will not be attending, the tribunal should investigate whether the appropriate notice has been sent to the proper address. The same procedure should be followed if a party alleges that a document has not been received. A Commissioner has held in the social security jurisdiction that it is the duty of the clerk to be in a position to advise the tribunal as to the fact of posting of notices and documents and the addresses to which they were sent (*R(SB) 19/83*, para.7).

If the issue becomes contentious, the chairman should bear in mind the position of the tribunal clerks. They are junior officials and should play a neutral administrative role at the hearing. It is appropriate that the tribunal should look to them for information about the handling of the case and advice on the procedures of the tribunal office. However, they should not be drawn into a contentious issue, still less should they become the target of antagonism for an aggrieved party. In order to prevent this, the chairman should ensure that the clerk's administrative role and the giving of evidence necessary for the tribunal to decide an issue are kept distinct, if need be by being fulfilled by different people.

The chairman should record both the fact that the investigation has been carried out and the results of the inquiry in the notes of proceeding. The tribunal should then consider whether it is appropriate to adjourn the hearing. The chairman should record that this consideration has taken place. If the hearing is adjourned, this will be the decision of the tribunal. In any event the statement of reasons, if issued, should say why the hearing was or was not adjourned.

The power to set aside under reg.57 will be relevant where a document has not been received with the result that a party to the proceedings is not present at the hearing or is in some other way prejudiced. Every decision is sent out with a covering letter drawing the party's attention to the setting aside power. This may prompt an express application, but if it becomes known to the tribunal, the clerk or the Secretary of State by any means that a document may not have been received, advice as to the possibility of a setting aside application should be given. If the awareness followed from a written communication from or on behalf of the party affected, that can itself be treated as an application (*R(SB) 19/83*, para.4).

PART II

REVISIONS, SUPERSESSIONS AND OTHER MATTERS

SOCIAL SECURITY [¹AND CHILD SUPPORT]

CHAPTER I

*Revisions*

AMENDMENT

1. Regulation 3 of the Appeals Amendment Regulations 2000 (for in force date see regs 1 and 14 of SI 2000/3185 below).

## [¹Revision of child support decisions

3.293      **3A.**—(1) Subject to paragraph (2), any decision as defined in paragraph (3) may be revised under section 16 of the Child Support Act by the Secretary of State—

    (a) if he receives an application for the revision of a decision either—

        (i) under section 16; or

        (ii) by way of an application under section 28G,

    of the Child Support Act, within one month of the date of notification of the decision or within such longer time as may be allowed under regulation 4;

    (b) if—

        (i) he notifies the person who applied for a decision to be revised within the period specified in sub-paragraph (a), that the application is unsuccessful because the Secretary of State is not in possession of all of the information or evidence needed to make a decision; and

        (ii) that person reapplies for the decision to be revised within one month of the notification described in head (i) above, or such longer period as the Secretary of State is satisfied is reasonable in the circumstances of the case, and provides in that application sufficient information or evidence to enable a decision to be made;

    (c) if he is satisfied that the decision was erroneous due to a misrepresentation of, or failure to disclose, a material fact and that the decision was more advantageous to the person who misrepresented or failed to disclose that fact than it would have been but for that error;

    [²(cc) if an appeal is made under section 20 of the Child Support Act against a decision within the time prescribed in regulation 31, or in a case to which regulation 32 applies within the time prescribed in that regulation, but the appeal has not been determined;]

    (d) if he commences action leading to the revision of the decision within one month of the date of notification of the decision; or

(e)  if the decision arose from an official error [³; or

(f)  if the grounds for revision are that a person with respect to whom a maintenance calculation was made was not, at the time the calculation was made, a parent of a child to whom the calculation relates.]

(2) Paragraph (1)(a) to (d) shall not apply in respect of a change of circumstances which—

(a)  occurred since the date on which the decision had effect; or

(b)  according to information or evidence which the Secretary of State has, is expected to occur.

[⁴(3) In paragraphs (1), (2) and (5A) and in regulation 4(3) "decision" means a decision of the Secretary of State under section 11, 12 or 46 of the Child Support Act, or a determination of an appeal tribunal on a referral under section 28D(1)(b) of that Act, or any supersession of a decision under section 17 of that Act, whether as originally made or as revised under section 16 of that Act.]

(4) A decision made under section 12(2) of the Child Support Act may be revised at any time before it is replaced by a decision under section 11 of that Act.

(5) Where the Secretary of State revises a decision made under section 12(1) of the Child Support Act in accordance with section 16(1B) of that Act, that decision may be revised under section 16 of that Act at any time.

[⁵(5A) Where—

(a)  the Secretary of State makes a decision ("decision A") and there is an appeal;

(b)  there is a further decision in relation to the appellant ("decision B") after the appeal but before the appeal results in a decision by an appeal tribunal ("decision C"); and

(c)  the Secretary of State would have made decision B differently if he had been aware of decision C at the time he made decision B,

decision B may be revised at any time.]

(6) Section 16 of the Child Support Act shall apply in relation to any decision of the Secretary of State—

(a)  under section 41A or 47 of the Child Support Act; or

(b)  that an adjustment shall cease or with respect to the adjustment of amounts payable under maintenance calculations for the purpose of taking account of overpayments of child support maintenance and voluntary payments,

as it applies in relation to any decision of the Secretary of State under sections 11, 12, 17 or 46 of that Act, or the determination of an appeal tribunal on a referral under section 28D(1)(b) of that Act.

(7) In paragraph (6)(b) and in regulations 6A(9), 6B(4)(d) and 30A "voluntary payments" means the same as in the definition in section 28J of the Child Support Act and Regulations made under that section.]

AMENDMENTS

1. Regulation 5 of the Appeals Amendment Regulations 2000 (for in force date see regs 1 and 14 of SI 2000/3185 below).

2. Regulation 2(2)(a)(i) of the Miscellaneous Amendments Regulations 2002 (in force as ss.16, 17 and 20 of the Act).

3. Regulation 2(2)(a)(ii) of the Miscellaneous Amendments Regulations 2002 (in force as ss.16, 17 and 20 of the Act).

4. Regulation 2(2)(b) of the Miscellaneous Amendments Regulations 2002 (in force as ss.16, 17 and 20 of the Act).

5. Regulation 2(2)(c) of the Miscellaneous Amendments Regulations 2002 (in force as ss.16, 17 and 20 of the Act).

DEFINITIONS

3.294    "date of notification": see reg.1(3).
"official error": see reg.1(3).
"referral": see reg.1(3).

GENERAL NOTE

*Paragraph (1)*

3.295    A decision may be revised if an application is made or action is initiated by the Secretary of State within the one month time limit. That limit may be extended under reg.4 below. The grounds on which a decision may be revised are not specified. An error of fact or law will justify a revision, but the revision jurisdiction is not so limited. A revision may be based on any ground, except a change of circumstances (see para.(2) below). This includes a different exercise on the same facts of a discretion relevant to the decision.

Outside the time limit, a revision may only be made if an error arose from one of the specified causes.

The powers to revise and to supersede are mutually exclusive. If revision is possible, the decision must be revised and not superseded: see reg.6A(7) below. In the case of a supersession on the Secretary of State's own initiative, the relevant date for determining whether a revision or a supersession is permissible is the date when the decision is taken. If it is taken within one month of the decision under consideration, only a revision is permissible. If it is taken outside that period, a supersession is permissible. Action on the Secretary of State's own initiative does not require an application. See *CDLA 3688/01*, paras 7–16.

The power to revise is additional to the provisions that provide for a maintenance calculation to cease to have effect under Sch.1, para.16 to the Act.

The subparagraphs specify circumstances in which a decision may be revised. Subparagraphs (a), (b) and (d) contain tight timetables. The circumstances covered by subparas (c) and (e) make it inappropriate for there to be time limits. Separate provision is made for interim maintenance decisions in para.(4) below and for subsequent revisions of default maintenance decisions in para.(5) below.

On appeal, a tribunal has jurisdiction to substitute a revision for a supersession and a supersession for a revision (*R(IB) 2/04*).

*Subparagraph (a)*

This is the companion to subpara.(d). It is the basic provision under which a decision may be challenged. The application must be made within one month, subject to the possibility of an extension under reg.4 below.

*Subparagraph (b)*

This allows a further chance to someone whose application for a revision was rejected because of lack of information or evidence. The person is allowed a period of grace in which to provide the information or evidence. The default period is one month, but this may be extended by the Secretary of State.

*Subparagraph (c)*
This applies without time limit.

*Subparagraph (cc)*
This allows a decision to be revised if it is under appeal, provided that the appeal has not been determined.

*Subparagraph (d)*
This is the companion to subpara.(a). It gives a correction power to the Secretary of State provided that action is initiated within one month. The time cannot be extended. If the Secretary of State wishes to alter a decision outside this time limit, it may be done by revision for official error under subpara.(e) or by supersession under reg.6A below.

*Subparagraph (e)*
This applies without time limit. It allows the Secretary of State to correct offical errors.

*Subparagraph (f)*
This allows a decision to be revised if it is was made on the incorrect basis that a person in respect of whom the maintenance calculation was made was a parent.

*Paragraph (2)*
A change of circumstances can only be dealt with by way of supersession under s.17 of the Act.

*Paragraph (5A)*
This allows a decision to be revised in order to give knock-on effect to a decision by an appeal tribunal on an earlier decision into another decision that was made while the appeal was pending. Assume that a calculation is made in which the non-resident parent's income is calculated in a particular way. The non-resident parent appeals against that decision. While the appeal is pending another calculation is made on the same basis. If the appeal tribunal changes the basis of calculation of the non-resident parent's income, that can be given effect in respect of the second calculation by revision under this paragraph.

## Late application for a revision

**4.**—(1) The time limit for making an application for a revision specified in regulation 3(1) or (3) [¹or 3A(1)(a)] may be extended where the conditions specified in the following provisions of this regulation are satisfied.

3.296

(2) An application for an extension of time shall be made by [²the relevant person,] the claimant or a person acting on his behalf.

(3) An application shall—
(a) contain particulars of the grounds on which the extension of time is sought and shall contain sufficient details of the decision which it is sought to have revised to enable that decision to be identified; and
(b) be made within 13 months of the date of notification of the decision which it is sought to have revised[⁶, but if the applicant has requested a statement of the reasons in accordance with regulation 28(1)(b) the 13 month period shall be extended by—
    (i) if the statement is provided within one month of the notification, an additional 14 days; or

      (ii)   if it is provided after the elapse of a period after the one month ends, the length of that period and an additional 14 days.]

(4) An application for an extension of time shall not be granted unless the applicant satisfies the Secretary of State that—

    (a)   it is reasonable to grant the application;

    (b)   the application for revision has merit; and

    (c)   special circumstances are relevant to the application and as a result of those special circumstances it was not practicable for the application to be made within the time limit specified in regulation 3 [³or 3A].

(5) In determining whether it is reasonable to grant an application, the Secretary of State shall have regard to the principle that the greater the amount of time that has elapsed between the expiration of the time specified in regulation 3(1) and (3) [⁴and regulation 3A(1)(a)] for applying for a revision and the making of the application for an extension of time, the more compelling should be the special circumstances on which the application is based.

(6) In determining whether it is reasonable to grant the application for an extension of time, no account shall be taken of the following—

    (a)   that the applicant or any person acting for him was unaware of or misunderstood the law applicable to his case (including ignorance or misunderstanding of the time limits imposed by these Regulations); or

    (b)   that a Commissioner [⁵, a Child Support Commissioner] or a court has taken a different view of the law from that previously understood and applied.

(7) An application under this regulation for an extension of time which has been refused may not be renewed.

## Amendments

1. Regulation 6(a) of the Appeals Amendment Regulations 2000 (for in force date see regs 1 and 14 of SI 2000/3185 below).

2. Regulation 6(b) of the Appeals Amendment Regulations 2000 (for in force date see regs 1 and 14 of SI 2000/3185 below).

3. Regulation 6(c) of the Appeals Amendment Regulations 2000 (for in force date see regs 1 and 14 of SI 2000/3185 below).

4. Regulation 6(d) of the Appeals Amendment Regulations 2000 (for in force date see regs 1 and 14 of SI 2000/3185 below).

5. Regulation 6(e) of the Appeals Amendment Regulations 2000 (for in force date see regs 1 and 14 of SI 2000/3185 below).

6. Regulation 2(3) of the Amendment Regulations 2005 (March 18, 2005).

## Definitions

**3.297**    "the date of notification": see reg.1(3).

"decision": see reg.3A(3).

"relevant person": see reg.1(3).

## General Note

**3.298**    This regulation allows the time for an application for a revision under reg.3A(1)(a) above to be extended. It does not apply to reg.3A(1)(b), which contains its own power to extend or to reg.3A(1)(d), under which action may be initiated by the Secretary of State.

If the Secretary of State refuses to extend time under this regulation, the party may seek to appeal to an appeal tribunal. The appeal is against the original decision and will be late. The issue arises whether a legally qualified panel member will extend the time for appealing under reg.32. If time is extended, the tribunal has power to consider the application for revision without considering this regulation. If time is not extended, the case does not come before an appeal tribunal. There is no power, and no need, for there to be an appeal against the refusal to extend time under this regulation. See *CTC 3433/03*.

## [¹Date from which a decision revised under section 16 of the Child Support Act takes effect

**5A.**—(1) Where the date from which a decision took effect is found to be erroneous on a revision under section 16 of the Child Support Act, the revision shall take effect from the date on which the decision revised would have taken effect had the error not been made.

3.299

(2) Where the Secretary of State considers it appropriate to revise a decision under section 12(1) of the Child Support Act as if he were revising a decision under section 11 of that Act, the revision shall take effect from the first day of the maintenance period in which the information required to make a maintenance calculation was provided, except where—
   (a) the non-resident parent satisfies the Secretary of State—
      (i) that he used his best endeavours to obtain the information required by the Secretary of State; and
      (ii) the failure to provide the information was not his fault; or
[²(b) the total amount of child support maintenance which would be fixed for the relevant period by the decision which is treated as a decision made under section 11 of the Child Support Act is greater than the total amount of child support maintenance which was fixed for that period by the decision made under section 12(1) of the Child Support Act (whether as originally made, or as revised or superseded under sections 16 or 17 of that Act respectively, or decided on appeal).]
[³(3) For the purposes of paragraph (2)(b), "the relevant period" means the period during which the decision under section 12(1) of the Child Support Act (whether as originally made, or as revised or superseded under sections 16 or 17 of that Act respectively, or decided on appeal) applied.]

AMENDMENTS

1. Regulation 7 of the Appeals Amendment Regulations 2000 (for in force date see regs 1 and 14 of SI 2000/3185 below).
2. Regulation 2(a) of the Child Support (Decisions and Appeals) (Amendment) Regulations 2003 (in force as s.16 of the Act).
3. Regulation 2(b) of the Child Support (Decisions and Appeals) (Amendment) Regulations 2003 (in force as s.16 of the Act).

GENERAL NOTE

The basic rule on the effective date of a revision is contained in s.16(3) of the Act. This regulation deals with two circumstances in which special provision is required, as authorised by s.16(4).

3.300

413

**[¹Supersession of child support decisions**

3.301 **6A.**—(1) Subject to paragraphs (7) and (8), the cases and circumstances in which a decision ("a superseding decision") may be made by the Secretary of State for the purposes of section 17 of the Child Support Act are set out in paragraphs (2) to (6).

(2) A decision may be superseded by a decision made by the Secretary of State acting on his own initiative where—

(a) there has been a relevant change of circumstances since the decision had effect; or

(b) the decision was made in ignorance of, or was based upon a mistake as to, some material fact.

(3) Subject to regulation 6B, a decision may be superseded by a decision made by the Secretary of State where—

(a) an application is made on the basis that—

(i) there has been a change of circumstances since the date from which the decision had effect; or

(ii) it is expected that a change of circumstances will occur; and

(b) the Secretary of State is satisfied that the change of circumstances is or would be relevant.

(4) A decision may be superseded by a decision made by the Secretary of State where—

(a) an application is made on the basis that the decision was made in ignorance of, or was based upon a mistake as to, a fact; and

(b) the Secretary of State is satisfied that the fact is or would be material.

[²(4A) A decision may be superseded by a decision made by the Secretary of State—

(a) where an application is made on the basis that; or

(b) acting on his own initiative where,

the decision to be superseded is a decision of an appeal tribunal or of a Commissioner that was made in accordance with section 28ZB(4)(b) of the Child Support Act, in a case where section 28ZB(5) of that Act applies.]

(5) A decision, other than a decision made on appeal, may be superseded by a decision made by the Secretary of State—

(a) acting on his own initiative, where he is satisfied that the decision was erroneous in point of law; or

(b) where an application is made on the basis that the decision was erroneous in point of law.

(6) A decision may be superseded by a decision made by the Secretary of State where he receives an application for the supersession of a decision by way of an application made under section 28G of the Child Support Act.

(7) The cases and circumstances in which a decision may be superseded shall not include any case or circumstance in which a decision may be revised.

(8) Paragraphs (2) to (6) shall not apply in respect of a decision to refuse an application for a maintenance calculation.

(9) For the purposes of section 17 of the Child Support Act, paragraphs (2) to (6) shall apply in relation to any decision of the Secretary of State that an adjustment shall cease or with respect to the adjustment of amounts

payable under a maintenance calculation for the purpose of taking account of overpayments of child support maintenance and voluntary payments, whether as originally made or as revised under section 16 of that Act.]

AMENDMENTS

1. Regulation 8 of the Appeals Amendment Regulations 2000 (for in force date see regs 1 and 14 of SI 2000/3185 below).
2. Regulation 3(4) of the Social Security and Child Support (Miscellaneous Amendments) Regulations 2003 (in force on whichever is the later of May 5, 2003 or as s.9 of the 2000 Act, which amends s.17 of the Act).

DEFINITION

"voluntary payments": see reg.3A(7). 3.302

GENERAL NOTE

*Appeal and supersession*

It may be sensible for a person who disagrees with a decision both to appeal against the decision and to apply for a supersession. One particular reason for doing this is the effect of s.20(7)(b) of the Act. This prevents a tribunal from considering change of circumstances that occur after the time of the decision under appeal. These changes may be taken into account on a supersession. The possibility of concurrent appeals and applications can give rise to problems about their interrelation.

One bundle of problems arose in *CDLA 2050/02*. The claimant both appealed against a decision and applied for it to be superseded. The application related to a change of circumstances that had occurred after the decision, but before tribunal heard the appeal. The tribunal dismissed the appeal before the application for supersession was decided. This raised two issues. Which decision was the subject of the supersession application when it was decided—the original decision or the decision of the tribunal dismissing the appeal? And if the latter, could the Secretary of State's decision-maker take account of the change of circumstances that had occurred before the tribunal made its decision? The Commissioner decided that the decision that was the proper subject of the supersession became the tribunal's decision, but that it was permissible to take account of changes of circumstances that has occurred before the tribunal made its decision (para.8). He achieved this result by interpreting "decision" in the equivalent of head (a) in paras (2) and (3) as referring to the last decision before the change of circumstances occurred. This result is more easily justified under the child support legislation than under the social security legislation that the Commissioner was interpreting. In that legislation, the provision referred to a change of circumstances "since the decision was made", whereas paras (2)(a) and (3)(a) here refer to a change "since the decision had effect".

Another bundle of problems arose in *R(DLA) 2/04*. The claimant appealed against a decision and the tribunal allowed the appeal in part only. The claimant appealed to the Commissioner against the tribunal's decision, who set aside the tribunal's decision and directed a rehearing. The claimant then applied to the Secretary of State for a supersession. This was refused. This raised the issue whether the tribunal's decision could extend beyond the date of the Secretary of State's decision refusing to supersede. The Commissioner held that it could. He set out three rules (para.12):

"1. An application for supersession that results in a refusal to supersede the original decision does not terminate the period under consideration on an appeal against the original decision.

2. Live proceedings arising out of an application for supersession based on ignorance of, or mistake as to, a material fact lapse when the decision to be superseded is set aside on appeal (provided that there is no further appeal in respect of the original decision).

3. Live proceedings arising out of an application for supersession based on a change of circumstances do not lapse when the decision to be superseded is set aside on appeal (but the application may have to be treated as an application for supersession of a different decision, or perhaps, as a new claim, depending of the circumstances)."

### General

**3.303**   This regulation specifies the circumstances in which a decision may be superseded. Action may be taken on the Secretary of State's own initiative or on application. A decision may be superseded to reflect an actual or anticipated change of circumstances, to correct an error of fact or law, or to give effect to a variation. Some decisions cannot be superseded: see para.(8) below. Other decisions may not be superseded in specified circumstances: see para.(7) and reg.6B below. If action is taken on the Secretary of State's initiative, the procedure in reg.7C must be followed.

The nature of a supersession was analysed by the Court of Appeal in *Wood v Secretary of State for Work and Pensions* reported as *R(DLA) 1/03*. The court decided that the cases and circumstances specified in these Regulations were outcome criteria, not threshold criteria. In other words, they are criteria that must be satisfied before a decision can be given on supersession. If after consideration of an application, no change is made to the decision or to the basis of the decision, the proper course is to refuse to supersede rather than to give a supersession in the same terms.

On appeal, a tribunal has jurisdiction to substitute a revision for a supersession and a supersession for a revision (*R(IB) 2/04*). If a supersession is instigated by an application, a tribunal on appeal is not limited to the issues raised by the application, but may also consider issues that were not raised and might be decided adversely to the applicant (*ibid.*).

### Paragraph (2)

This allows the Secretary of State to supersede without an application on two grounds: change of circumstances or error of fact. The change of circumstances must have occurred. An anticipated change of circumstances may only be considered on application under para.(3).

The change of circumstances must be a change from the circumstances taken into account in making the decision that is subject to the supersession procedure (*CDLA 2115/03*, para.8).

It is not necessary for a specific change to be identified and recorded; what is required is a decision that involves a process of continuous comparison (*Smith v Secretary of State for Work and Pensions* unreported [2003] EWCA Civ 437, para.23).

The tolerance, or minimum change, provisions do not apply to a supersession undertaken on the Secretary of State's own initiative (*CCS 509/02*).

### Paragraph (3)

This allows the Secretary of State to supersede on application to reflect an actual or anticipated change of circumstances. For further discussion, see the general note to para.(2) above.

### Paragraph (4)

This allows the Secretary of State to supersede on application to correct an error of fact.

*Paragraph (5)*

This allows the Secretary of State to supersede, with or without an application, to correct an error of law.

For a detailed discussion of error of law, see the general note to s.24(1) of the Act.

Difficulties arise in cases involving issues of fact and degree, such as whether two people are living together as husband and wife in the same household or whether a person is habitually resident in the UK. It is the nature of these issues that different decision-makers may be entitled to form different judgments on the same facts without being in error of law. The decision of one decision-maker will not necessarily be erroneous in law just because a later decision-maker would form a different judgment on the same facts. There will only be an error of law if the first decision-maker forms a judgment that no officer, properly advised and acting reasonably, was entitled to reach on the facts: *Crake v Supplementary Benefits Commission* [1982] 1 All E.R. 498 at 501, *per* Woolf J. If the case is one that merely involves a legitimate difference of judgment without any accompanying error of fact, the proper challenge is by an application for a revision.

*Paragraph (6)*

This allows a supersession to give effect to a variation.

*Paragraph (7)*

This paragraph gives the revision procedure priority over the supersession procedure in any case or circumstance in which they would otherwise overlap. It is stated in absolute terms and cannot be disregarded under the powers given to the Secretary of State and appeal tribunals to limit their consideration under ss.16(2), 17(2) and 20(8)(a) of the Act.

*Paragraph (8)*

A decision to refuse an application for a maintenance calculation cannot be superseded; it may only be revised under s.16 of the Act. This prevents a refusal being revised on the ground of error of material fact unless the application for a revision was made within the time limit or the mistake of fact arose from misrepresentation, failure to disclose or official error.

## [¹Circumstances in which a child support decision may not be superseded

**6B.**—(1) Except as provided in paragraph (4), and subject to paragraph (3), a decision of the Secretary of State, appeal tribunal or Child Support Commissioner, on an application made under regulation 6A(3), shall not be superseded where the difference between—

    (a) the non-resident parent's net income figure fixed for the purposes of the maintenance calculation in force in accordance with Part I of Schedule 1 to the Child Support Act; and

    (b) the non-resident parent's net income figure which would be fixed in accordance with a superseding decision, is less than 5% of the figure in sub-paragraph (a).

(2) In paragraph (1) "superseding decision" means a decision which would supersede the decision subject to the application made under regulation 6A(3) but for the application of this regulation.

[³(3) Where the application for a supersession is made on more than one ground, if those grounds which do not relate to the net income of the

3.304

non-resident parent lead to a superseding decision this regulation shall not apply to the ground relating to the net income of that parent.]

(4) This regulation shall not apply to a decision under regulation 6A(3) where—

(a) the superseding decision is made in consequence of the determination of an application made under section 28G of the Child Support Act;

(b) the superseding decision affects a variation ground in a decision made under section 11 or 17 of the Child Support Act, whether as originally made or as revised under section 16 of that Act;

(c) the decision being superseded was made under section 12(2) of the Child Support Act, or was a decision under section 17 of that Act superseding an interim maintenance decision, whether as originally made or as revised under section 16 of that Act;

(d) the decision being superseded was a decision that an adjustment shall cease or with respect to the adjustment of amounts payable under maintenance calculations for the purpose of taking account of overpayments of child support maintenance and voluntary payments or was a decision under section 17 of the Child Support Act superseding that decision, whether as originally made or as revised under section 16 of that Act; or

(e) the superseding decision takes effect from the dates prescribed in regulation 7B(1) to (3) [². . .] or (20).]

[⁴(5) Where an application has been made to which paragraph (1) applied ("application A") and a further application ("application B") is made for a supersession on a ground other than one relating to the net income of the non-resident parent, the Secretary of State may make a superseding decision on the basis that application A was made at the same time as application B.]

AMENDMENTS

1. Regulation 8 of the Appeals Amendment Regulations 2000 (for in force date see regs 1 and 14 of SI 2000/3185 below).

2. Regulation 2(3) of the Miscellaneous Amendments Regulations 2002 (in force as ss.16, 17 and 20 of the Act).

3. Regulation 2(2)(a)of the Miscellaneous Amendments Regulations 2004 (September 16, 2004 or on the day on which the amended scheme comes into force for that type of case, whichever is later).

4. Regulation 2(2)(b) of the Miscellaneous Amendments Regulations 2004 (September 16, 2004 or on the day on which the amended scheme comes into force for that type of case, whichever is later).

DEFINITION

3.305    "voluntary payments": see reg.3A(7).

GENERAL NOTE

3.306    This regulation sets out circumstances in which a child support decision may not be superseded.

*Paragraphs (1)–(3)*

These paragraphs impose a threshold to be satisfied before a decision may be superseded on a ground relating solely to the net income of the non-resident parent. The restriction only applies to supersession on an application under reg.6A(3) above. It does not apply to any other provision in reg.6A. It is subject to the exceptions in para.(4).

## [¹Date from which a decision superseded under section 17 of the Child Support Act takes effect

**7B.**—(1) Subject to paragraphs (17) to (22), where a decision is superseded by a decision made by the Secretary of State in a case to which regulation 6A(2)(a) applies on the basis of information or evidence which was
also the basis of a decision made under section 8, 9 or 10 of the Act, the
decision under section 17 of the Child Support Act shall take effect from
the first day of the maintenance period in which that information or evidence was first brought to the attention of an officer exercising the functions of the Secretary of State under the Child Support Act ("the officer").

3.307

[²(1A) Where a decision is superseded by a decision made by the
Secretary of State in a case to which regulation 6A(2)(a) or (3) applies and
the relevant circumstance is that—
  (a) paragraph 4(2) of Schedule 1 to the Child Support Act applies, the
      decision shall take effect from the first day of the maintenance period
      on or after—
      (i)  the date on which the non-resident parent becomes the partner
           of a non-resident parent; or
      (ii) where a maintenance calculation is first made in respect of the
           non-resident parent's partner, the date on which that calculation
           takes effect for the purposes of the Child Support Act; or
  (b) paragraph 4(2) of Schedule 1 to the Child Support Act ceases to
      apply, the decision shall take effect from the first day of the
      maintenance period on or after the date on which—
      (i)  the non-resident parent or his partner ceases to be a non-
           resident parent; or
      (ii) the non-resident parent ceases to be the partner of a non-
           resident parent.]

(2) Where a decision is superseded by a decision made by the Secretary
of State in a case to which regulation 6A(3)(a) applies and the relevant circumstance is that the non-resident parent or his partner has notified the
officer that he or his partner had made a claim for a relevant benefit and,
where the relevant benefit is payable, that the officer was notified within
one month of notification of the award, the decision shall take effect from
the first day of the maintenance period in which—
  (a) the non-resident parent or his partner notified the officer that he or
      his partner had made a claim for a relevant benefit, where entilement
      to that benefit commences on or before the date of notification; or
  (b) entitlement to the relevant benefit commences, where that entitlement
      commenced after the date of notification.

(3) Where a decision is superseded by a decision made by the Secretary
of State in a case to which regulation 6A(4) applies and the material fact is
that the non-resident parent or his partner has notified the officer that he

or his partner had made a claim for a relevant benefit before the Secretary of State notified him of an application for a maintenance calculation in accordance with regulation 5 of the Maintenance Calculation Procedure Regulations (notice of an application for a maintenance calculation) and, where the relevant benefit is payable, that the officer was notified within one month of notification of the award, the decision shall take effect from the first day of the maintenance period in which—

    (a) the non-resident parent or his partner notified the officer that he or his partner had made a claim for a relevant benefit, where entitlement to that benefit commences on or before the date of notification; or

    (b) entitlement to the relevant benefit commences, where that entitlement commenced after the date of notification.

(4) Subject to paragraphs (17) to (22), where the superseding decision is made in a case to which regulation 6A(3)(a)(i) applies and that decision supersedes one which has been made under section 12(2) of the Child Support Act, the decision shall take effect from the first day of the maintenance period in which the change of circumstances occurred.

(5) Where the superseding decision is made in a case to which regulation 6A(3)(a)(ii) applies, the decision shall take effect from the first day of the maintenance period in which the change of circumstances is expected to occur.

(6) Where the superseding decision is made in a case to which regulation 6A(6) applies and the relevant circumstance is that a ground for a variation is expected to occur, the decision shall take effect from the first day of the maintenance period in which the ground for the variation is expected to occur.

(7) Except in a case to which paragraph (1) applies, where the superseding decision is made in a case to which regulation 7C applies, that decision shall take effect from the first day of the maintenance period which includes the date which is 28 days after the date on which the Secretary of State gave notice to the relevant persons under that regulation.

(8) For the purposes of paragraph (7)—

    (a) where the relevant persons are notified on different dates, the period of 28 days shall be counted from the date of the latest notification;

    (b) notification includes oral and written notification;

    (c) where a person is notified in more than one way, the date on which he is notified is the date on which he was first given notification; and

    (d) the date of written notification is the date on which it was given or sent to the person.

(9) Where—

    (a) a decision made by an appeal tribunal or by a Child Support Commissioner is superseded on the ground that it was erroneous due to a misrepresentation of, or that there was a failure to disclose, a material fact; and

    (b) the Secretary of State is satisfied that the decision was more advantageous to the person who misrepresented or failed to disclose that fact than it would otherwise have been but for that error,

the superseding decision shall take effect from the date on which the decision of the appeal tribunal or, as the case may be, the Child Support Commissioner took, or was to take, effect.

(10) Any decision made under section 17 of the Child Support Act in consequence of a determination which is a relevant determination for the purposes of section 28ZC of that Act shall take effect from the date of the relevant determination.

(11) Where a decision with respect to a reduced benefit decision is superseded because the decision ceases to be in force in accordance with regulation 16(a) of the Maintenance Calculation Procedure Regulations (termination of a reduced benefit decision), the superseding decision shall have effect—

(a) where the decision is in operation immediately before it ceases to be in force, from the last day of the benefit week during the course of which the parent concerned falls within the provisions of section 46(1) of the Child Support Act; or

(b) where the decision is suspended immediately before it ceases to be in force, from the date on which the parent concerned falls within the provisions of section 46(1) of that Act.

(12) Where a decision with respect to a reduced benefit decision is superseded because the decision ceases to be in force in accordance with regulation 16(b) of the Maintenance Calculation Procedure Regulations, the superseding decision shall have effect—

(a) where the decision is in operation immediately before it ceases to be in force, from the last day of the benefit week during the course of which the parent concerned complied with the obligations imposed by section 46(6)(b) of the Child Support Act; or

(b) where the decision is suspended immediately before it ceases to be in force, from the date on which the parent concerned complied with the obligations imposed by section 46(6)(b) of the Child Support Act.

(13) Where a decision with respect to a reduced benefit decision is superseded because the decision ceases to be in force in accordance with regulation 16(c) of the Maintenance Calculation Procedure Regulations, the superseding decision shall have effect from the last day of the benefit week in which entitlement to benefit ceased.

(14) Where a decision with respect to a reduced benefit decision is superseded because the decision ceases to be in force in accordance with regulation 16(d) of the Maintenance Calculation Procedure Regulations, the superseding decision shall have effect—

(a) where the decision is in operation immediately before it ceases to be in force, from the last day of the benefit week during the course of which the Secretary of State is supplied with information that enables him to make the calculation; or

(b) where the decision is suspended immediately before it ceases to be in force, from the date on which the Secretary of State is supplied with information that enables him to make the calculation.

(15) Where a decision with respect to a reduced benefit decision is superseded because the decision ceases to be in force in accordance with regulation 17(1) of the Maintenance Calculation Procedure Regulations (reduced benefit decisions where there is an additional qualifying child), the superseding decision shall have effect from—

(a) the last day of the benefit week preceding the benefit week which includes, in accordance with the provisions of regulation 11(3) of the Maintenance Calculation Procedure Regulations (amount of and period of reduction of relevant benefit under a reduced benefit decision), the first day on which the further decision comes into operation; or

(b) the first day on which the further decision would come into operation but for the provisions of regulation 14 of the Maintenance Calculation Procedure Regulations (suspension of a reduced benefit decision when a modified applicable amount is payable (income support)) or 15 (suspension of a reduced benefit decision when a modified applicable amount is payable (income-based jobseeker's allowance)) of those Regulations.

(16) Where a decision with respect to a reduced benefit decision is superseded because the decision ceases to be in force in accordance with regulation 18(2) of the Maintenance Calculation Procedure Regulations (suspension and termination of a reduced benefit decision where the sole qualifying child ceases to be a child or where the parent concerned ceases to be a person with care), the superseding decision shall have effect from the last day of the benefit week which includes the day on which the child ceases to be a child within the meaning of section 55 of the Child Support Act as supplemented by Schedule 1 to those Regulations, or the parent ceases to be the person with care.

(17) Where a superseding decision is made in a case to which regulation 6A(2)(a) or (3) applies and the relevant circumstance is the death of a qualifying child or a qualifying child ceasing to be a qualifying child, the decision shall take effect from the first day of the maintenance period in which the change occurred.

[⁴(17A) Where a superseding decision is made in a case to which regulation 6A(2)(a) or (3) applies, and the relevant circumstance is that a person has ceased to be a person with care in relation to a qualifying child in respect of whom the maintenance calculation was made, the decision shall take effect from the first day of the maintenance period in which that person ceased to be a person with care in relation to that qualifying child.

(17B) Where a superseding decision is made in a case to which regulation 6A(3) applies, and the relevant circumstance is that there is a further qualifying child in respect of the non-resident parent and the person with care to whom the maintenance calculation being superseded relates, the superseding decision shall take effect from—

(a) subject to sub-paragraph (b), the first day of the maintenance period in respect of the maintenance calculation in force, following—

  (i) where an effective application is made under section 17(1) of the Child Support Act by the non-resident parent, the date on which that application is made; or

  (ii) where the application made under section 17(1) of that Act is made by the person with care, or, where a maintenance calculation has been made in response to an application by a child under section 7 of that Act, by the child, the date of notification to the non-resident parent of that application;

(b) the first day of the maintenance period in respect of the maintenance calculation in force where the date set out in head (i) or (ii) falls on the first day of that maintenance period.

(17C) For the purposes of paragraph (17B)—
(a) in head (i) of sub-paragraph (a), an application is effective if, were it an application for a maintenance calculation, it would comply with regulation 3(1) of the Maintenance Calculation Procedure Regulations;
(b) in head (ii) of sub-paragraph (a), notification to the non-resident parent shall take the same form in respect of an application for a supersession as it would in regulation 5 of the Maintenance Calculation Procedure Regulations, in respect of an application for a maintenance calculation.]

(18) Where a superseding decision is made in a case to which regulation 6A(2)(a) or (3) applies and the relevant circumstance is that the non-resident parent, person with care or the qualifying child has moved out of the jurisdiction, the decision shall take effect from the first day of the maintenance period in which the non-resident parent, person with care or qualifying child leaves the jurisdiction and jurisdiction is within the meaning of section 44 of the Child Support Act.

[³. . .]

(20) Where a superseding decision is made in a case to which regulation 6A(2)(a) or (3) applies and the relevant circumstance is that both the non-resident parent and the person with care with respect to whom a maintenance calculation was made request the Secretary of State to decide that the maintenance calculation shall cease and he is satisfied that they are living together, the decision shall take effect from the first day of the maintenance period in which the later of the two requests was made.

(21) Where a superseding decision is made in a case to which regulation 6A(2)(a) or (3) applies and the relevant circumstance is that—
(a) an application for a maintenance calculation is made under section 4 or 7 of the Child Support Act, or treated as made under section 6(3) of that Act, in respect of a non-resident parent; and
(b) before the decision as to a maintenance calculation is made at least one other maintenance calculation is in force with respect to the same non-resident parent but to a different person with care and a different child,
the effective date of the maintenance calculation made in respect of the application shall be a date which is not later than 7 days after the date of notification to the non-resident parent and which is the day on which a maintenance period in respect of the maintenance calculation in force begins.

(22) Where a superseding decision is made in a case to which regulation 6A(3) applies and in relation to that decision a maintenance calculation is made to which paragraph 15 of Schedule 1 to the Child Support Act applies, the effective date of the calculation or calculations shall be the beginning of the maintenance period in which the change of circumstance to which the calculation or calculations relates occurred or is expected to occur and where that change occurred before the date of the application for the supersession and was notified after that date, the date of that application.

[⁵(22A) Where a superseding decision is made in a case to which regulation 6A(4A) applies the decision shall take effect from the first day of the maintenance period following the date the appeal tribunal or the Commissioner's decision would have taken effect had it been decided in accordance with the determination of the Commissioner or the court in the appeal referred to in section 28ZB(1)(b) of the Child Support Act.]

(23) In this regulation—

"benefit week" in relation to income support has the same meaning as in regulation 2(1) of the Income Support Regulations, and in relation to jobseeker's allowance has the same meaning as in regulation 1(3) of the Jobseeker's Allowance Regulations;

"partner" has the same meaning as in regulation 2 of the Income Support Regulations; and

"relevant benefit" means a benefit which is prescribed in regulation 4 of the Maintenance Calculations and Special Cases Regulations for the purposes of paragraph 4(1)(b) of Part I of Schedule 1 to the Child Support Act, and child benefit as referred to in paragraph 10C(2)(a) of Part I of Schedule 1 to that Act.]

AMENDMENTS

1. Regulation 9 of the Appeals Amendment Regulations 2000 (for in force date see regs 1 and 14 of SI 2000/3185 below).
2. Regulation 2(4)(a) of the Miscellaneous Amendments Regulations 2002 (in force as ss.16, 17 and 20 of the Act).
3. Regulation 2(4)(b) of the Miscellaneous Amendments Regulations 2002 (in force as ss.16, 17 and 20 of the Act).
4. Regulation 3(2) of the Miscellaneous Amendments Regulations 2003 (in force as s.17 of the Act).
5. Regulation 3(6) of the Social Security and Child Support (Miscellaneous Amendments) Regulations 2003 (in force on whichever is the later of May 5, 2003 or as s.9 of the 2000 Act, which amends s.17 of the Act).

DEFINITIONS

3.308     "Maintenance Calculation Procedure Regulations": see reg.1(3).
"Maintenance Calculations and Special Cases Regulations": see reg.1(3)
"relevant person": see reg.1(3)

## [¹Procedure where the Secretary of State proposes to supersede a decision under section 17 of the Child Support Act on his own initiative

3.309     **7C.** Where the Secretary of State on his own initiative proposes to make a decision superseding a decision he shall notify the relevant persons who could be materially affected by the decision of that intention.]

AMENDMENT

1. Regulation 9 of the Appeals Amendment Regulations 2000 (for in force date see regs 1 and 14 of SI 2000/3185 below).

DEFINITION

"relevant person": see reg.1(3).                                                          3.310

GENERAL NOTE

This ensures that those affected by the Secretary of State's proposed action know          3.311
of it so that they may make representations.

## [¹Provision of information

**15A.**—(1) Where the Secretary of State has received an application          3.312
under section 16 or 17 of the Child Support Act in connection with a previously determined variation which has effect on the maintenance calculation in force, he may request further information or evidence from the
applicant to enable a decision on that application to be made and any such
information or evidence shall be provided within one month of the date of
notification of the request, or such longer period as the Secretary of State
is satisfied is reasonable in the circumstances of the case.

(2) Where any information or evidence requested in accordance with
paragraph (1) is not provided within the time limit specified in that paragraph, the Secretary of State may, where he is able to do so, proceed to
make the decision in the absence of that information or evidence.]

AMENDMENT

1. Regulation 10 of the Appeals Amendment Regulations 2000 (for in force date
see regs 1 and 14 of SI 2000/3185 below).

GENERAL NOTE

This regulation applies to applications for revision or supersession that relate to         3.313
a variation. It gives the Secretary of State power to require information or evidence
from the applicant. It must be provided within one month, subject to extension by
the Secretary of State. If the information or evidence is not provided, the Secretary
of State may (if possible) determine the application without it. The Secretary of
State may also accept the information or evidence late under reg.15B(7) below.

## [¹Procedure in relation to an application made under section 16 or 17 of the Child Support Act in connection with a previously determined variation

**15B.**—(1) Subject to paragraph (3), where the Secretary of State has          3.314
received an application under section 16 or 17 of the Child Support Act in
connection with a previously determined variation which has effect on the
maintenance calculation in force, he—
  (a) shall give notice of the application to the relevant persons, other than
      the applicant, informing them of the grounds on which the applica-
      tion has been made and any relevant information or evidence the
      applicant has given, except information or evidence falling within
      paragraph (2);
  (b) may invite representations, which need not be in writing but shall be
      in writing if in any case he so directs, from the relevant persons other

than the applicant on any matter relating to that application, to be submitted to the Secretary of State within 14 days of notification or such longer period as the Secretary of State is satisfied is reasonable in the circumstances of the case; and

(c) shall set out the provisions of paragraphs (2)(b) and (c), (4) and (5) in relation to such representations.

(2) The information or evidence referred to in paragraphs (1)(a), (4)(a) and (7), is—

(a) details of the nature of the long-term illness or disability of the relevant other child which forms the basis of a variation application on the ground in regulation 11 of the Variations Regulations (special expenses-illness or disability of relevant other child) where the applicant requests they should not be disclosed and the Secretary of State is satisfied that disclosure is not necessary in order to be able to determine the application;

(b) medical evidence or medical advice which has not been disclosed to the applicant or a relevant person and which the Secretary of State considers would be harmful to the health of the applicant or that relevant person if disclosed to him;

(c) the address of a relevant person or qualifying child, or any other information which could reasonably be expected to lead to that person or child being located, where the Secretary of State considers that there would be a risk of harm or undue distress to that person or that child or any other children living with that person if the address or information were disclosed.

(3) The Secretary of State need not act in accordance with paragraph (1) if—

(a) he is satisfied on the information or evidence available to him, that he will not agree to a variation of the maintenance calculation in force, but if, on further consideration he is minded to do so he shall, before doing so, comply with the provisions of this regulation; and

(b) were the application to succeed, the decision as revised or superseded would be less advantageous to the applicant than the decision before it was so revised or superseded.

(4) Where the Secretary of State receives representations from the relevant persons he—

(a) may, if he considers it reasonable to do so, send a copy of the representations concerned (excluding material falling within paragraph (2) above) to the applicant and invite any comments he may have within 14 days or such longer period as the Secretary of State is satisfied is reasonable in the circumstances of the case; and

(b) where the Secretary of State acts under sub-paragraph (a), shall not proceed to make a decision in response to the application until he has received such comments or the period referred to in sub-paragraph (a) has expired.

(5) Where the Secretary of State has not received representations from the relevant persons notified in accordance with paragraph (1) within the time limit specified in sub-paragraph (b) of that paragraph, he may proceed

to make a decision under section 16 or 17 of the Child Support Act in response to the application, in their absence.

(6) In considering an application for a revision or supersession the Secretary of State shall take into account any representations received at the date upon which he makes a decision under section 16 or 17 of the Child Support Act, from the relevant persons including any representations received in connection with the application in accordance with paragraphs (1)(b), (4)(a) and (7).

(7) Where any information or evidence requested by the Secretary of State under regulation 15A is received after notification has been given under paragraph (1), he may, if he considers it reasonable to do so and except where such information or evidence falls within paragraph (2), send a copy of such information or evidence to the relevant persons and may invite them to submit representations, which need not be in writing unless the Secretary of State so directs in any particular case, on that information or evidence.

(8) Where the Secretary of State is considering making a decision under section 16 or 17 of the Child Support Act in accordance with this regulation, he shall apply the factors to be taken into account for the purposes of section 28F of the Child Support Act set out in regulation 21 of the Variations Regulations (factors to be taken into account and not to be taken into account) as factors to be taken into account and not to be taken into account when considering making a decision under this regulation.

(9) In this regulation "relevant person" means—

(a) a non-resident parent, or a person treated as a non-resident parent under regulation 8 of the Maintenance Calculations and Special Cases Regulations (persons treated as non-resident parents), whose liability to pay child support maintenance may be affected by any variation agreed;

(b) a person with care, or a child to whom section 7 of the Child Support Act applies, where the amount of child support maintenance payable by virtue of a calculation relevant to that person with care or in respect of that child may be affected by any variation agreed.]

AMENDMENT

1. Regulation 10 of the Appeals Amendment Regulations 2000 (for in force date see regs 1 and 14 of SI 2000/3185 below).

DEFINTION

"Variations Regulations": see reg.1(3).                                        3.315

GENERAL NOTE

This regulation provides for the procedure to be followed on consideration of     3.316
revision or supersession of the effect of a variation. It reflects the procedure followed
on an application for a variation under reg.9 of the Variation Regulations.

*Paragraph (9)*
This definition overrides the one in reg.1(3) above.

**[¹Notification of a decision made under section 16 or 17 of the Child Support Act**

3.317

**15C.**—(1) Subject to paragraph (2) and (5) to (11), a notification of a decision made following the revision or supersession of a decision made under section 11, 12 or 17 of the Child Support Act, whether as originally made or as revised under section 16 of that Act, shall set out, in relation to the decision in question—

(a) the effective date of the maintenance calculation;

(b) where relevant, the non-resident parent's net weekly income;

(c) the number of qualifying children;

(d) the number of relevant other children;

(e) the weekly rate;

(f) the amounts calculated in accordance with Part I of Schedule 1 to the Child Support Act and, where there has been agreement to a variation or a variation has otherwise been taken into account, the Variations Regulations;

(g) where the weekly rate is adjusted by apportionment or shared care or both, the amount calculated in accordance with paragraph 6, 7 or 8, as the case may be, of Part I of Schedule 1 to the Child Support Act; and

(h) where the amount of child support maintenance which the non-resident parent is liable to pay is decreased in accordance with regulation 9 of the Maintenance Calculations and Special Cases Regulations (care provided in part by local authority) or 11 (non-resident parent liable to pay maintenance under a maintenance order) of those Regulations, the adjustment calculated in accordance with that regulation.

(2) A notification of a revision or supersession of a maintenance calculation made under section 12(1) of the Child Support Act shall set out the effective date of the maintenance calculation, the default rate, the number of qualifying children on which the rate is based and whether any apportionment has been applied under regulation 7 of the Maintenance Calculation Procedure Regulations (default rate) and shall state the nature of the information required to enable a decision under section 11 of that Act to be made by way of section 16 of that Act.

(3) Except where a person gives written permission to the Secretary of State that the information in relation to him, mentioned in sub-paragraphs (a) and (b), may be conveyed to other persons, any document given or sent under the provisions of paragraph (1) or (2) shall not contain—

(a) the address of any person other than the recipient of the document in question (other than the address of the office of the officer concerned who is excercising functions of the Secretary of State under the Child Support Act) or any other information the use of which could reasonably be expected to lead to any such person being located;

(b) any other information the use of which could reasonably be expected to lead to any person, other than a qualifying child or a relevant person, being identified.

(4) Where a decision as to the revision or supersession of a decision made under section 11, 12 or 17 of the Child Support Act, whether as originally

made or as revised under section 16 of that Act, is made under section 16 or 17 of that Act, a notification under paragraph (1) or (2) shall include information as to the provisions of sections 16, 17 and 20 of that Act.

(5) Where the Secretary of State makes a decision that a maintenance calculation shall cease to have effect—

(a) he shall immediately notify the non-resident parent and person with care, so far as that is reasonably practicable;

(b) where a decision has been superseded in a case where a child under section 7 of the Child Support Act ceases to be a child for the purposes of that Act, he shall immediately notify the persons in sub-paragraph (a) and the other qualifying children within the meaning of section 7 of that Act; and

(c) any notice under sub-paragraphs (a) and (b) shall specify the date with effect from which that decision took effect.

(6) Where the Secretary of State, under the provisions of section 16 or 17 of the Child Support Act, has made a decision that an adjustment shall cease, or adjusted the amount payable under a maintenance calculation, he shall immediately notify the relevant persons, so far as that is reasonably practicable, that the adjustment has ceased or of the amount and period of the adjustment, and the amount payable during the period of the adjustment.

(7) Where the Secretary of State has made a decision under section 16 of the Child Support Act, revising a decision under section 41A or 47 of that Act, he shall immediately notify the relevant persons so far as that is reasonably practicable, of the amount of child support maintenance payable, the amount of arrears, the amount of the penalty payment or fees to be paid, as the case may be, the method of payment and the day by which payment is to be made.

(8) Where the non-resident parent appeals against a decision made by the Secretary of State under section 41A or 47 of the Child Support Act and the Secretary of State makes a decision under section 16 of that Act, before the appeal is decided he shall notify the relevant persons, so far as that is reasonably practicable of either the new amount of the penalty payment or the fee to be paid or that the amount is no longer payable, the method of payment and the day by which payment is to be made.

(9) Paragraphs (1) to (3) shall not apply where the Secretary of State has decided not to supersede a decision under section 17 of the Child Support Act, and he shall, so far as that is reasonably practicable, notify the relevant persons of that decision.

(10) A notification under paragraphs (6) to (9) shall include information as to the provisions of sections 16, 17 and 20 of the Child Support Act.

(11) Where paragraph (9) applies, and the Secretary of State decides not to supersede under regulation 6B, he shall notify the relevant person, in relation to the decision in question of—

(a) the fact that regulation 6B applies to the decision;

(b) the non-resident parent's net income figure fixed for the purposes of the maintenance calculation in force in accordance with Part I of Schedule 1 to the Child Support Act;

(c) the non-resident parent's net income figure provided by that parent to the Secretary of State with the application for supersession under regulation 6A(3);

(d) the decision of the Secretary of State not to supersede; and

(e) the right to appeal against the decision under section 20 of the Child Support Act.

(12) Where an appeal lapses in accordance with section 16(6) or 28F(5) of the Child Support Act, the Secretary of State shall, so far as that is reasonably practicable, notify the relevant persons that the appeal has lapsed.]

AMENDMENT

1. Regulation 10 of the Appeals Amendment Regulations 2000 (for in force date see regs 1 and 14 of SI 2000/3185 below).

DEFINITIONS

3.318    "Maintenance Calculation Procedure Regulations": see reg.1(3).
"Maintenance Calculations and Special Cases Regulations": see reg.1(3).
"relevant person": see reg.1(3).

## [¹Procedure in relation to the adjustment of the amount payable under a maintenance calculation

3.319    **15D.**—(1) Where the Secretary of State has adjusted the amount payable under a maintenance calculation under the provisions of regulation 10(1) and (3A) of the Arrears, Interest and Adjustment of Maintenance Assessments Regulations and that maintenance claculation is subsequently replaced by a fresh maintenance calculation made by virtue of a revision under section 16 of the Child Support Act or of a decision under section 17 of that Act superseding an earlier decision, that adjustment shall, subject to paragraph (2), continue to apply to the amount payable under that fresh maintenance calculation unless the Secretary of State is satisfied that such adjustment would not be appropriate in all the circumstances of the case.

(2) Where the Secretary of State is satisfied that the adjustment referred to in paragraph (1) would not be appropriate, he may make a decision under section 17 of the Child Support Act, superseding an earlier decision making an adjustment, and—

(a) the adjustment shall cease; or

(b) he may adjust the amount payable under that fresh maintenance calculation,

as he sees fit, having regard to the matters specified in regulation 10(1)(b)(i) to (iii) of the Arrears, Interest and Adjustment of Maintenance Assessments Regulations.]

AMENDMENT

1. Regulation 10 of the Appeals Amendment Regulations 2000 (for in force date see regs 1 and 14 of SI 2000/3185 below).

DEFINITION

"Arrears, Interest and Adjustment of Maintenance Assessments Regulations":    **3.320**
see reg.1(3).

GENERAL NOTE

Despite the reference to procedure in the heading to this regulation, it is not con-    **3.321**
cerned with procedure but with substance. It allows for an adjustment to carry over
to a decision given on revision or supersession. However, this does not apply if the
Secretary of State is satisfied that it would not be appropriate. In that case, the
adjustment either ceases or is itself adjusted.

## PART III

### CHAPTER II

*Other Matters*

## Child support decisions involving issues that arise on appeal in other cases

**23.**—(1) For the purposes of section 28ZA(2)(b) of the Child Support    **3.322**
Act (prescribed cases and circumstances in which a decision may be made
on a prescribed basis), a case which satisfies either of the conditions in
paragraph (2) is a prescribed case.

(2) The conditions referred to in paragraph (1) are that—

(a) if a decision were not made on the basis prescribed in paragraph (3),
the parent with care would become entitled to income support if a
claim were made, or to an increased amount of that benefit;

(b) the [¹non-resident parent] is an employed earner or a self-employed
earner.

(3) For the purposes of section 28ZA(2)(b) of the Child Support Act,
the prescribed basis on which the Secretary of State may make the decision
is as if—

(a) the appeal in relation to the different maintenance [³calculation],
which is referred to in section 28ZA(1)(b) of that Act had already
been determined; and

(b) that appeal had been decided in a way that was the most
unfavourable to the applicant for the decision mentioned in section
28ZA(1)(a) of that Act.

(4) The circumstances prescribed under section 28ZA(4)(c) of the
Child Support Act (where an appeal is pending against a decision for the
purposes of that section, even though an appeal against the decision has not
been brought or, as the case may be, an application for leave to appeal
against the decision has not been made but the time for doing so has not
expired), are that the Secretary of State—

(a) certifies in writing that he is considering appealing against that
decision; and

(b) he considers that, if such an appeal were to be determined in a particular way—
  (i) there would be no liability for child support maintenance, or
  (ii) such liability would be less than would be the case were an appeal not made.

(5) In this regulation—

"[²non-resident parent]" and "parent with care" have the same meaning as in section 54 of the Child Support Act;

"employed earner" and "self-employed earner" have the same meaning as in section 2(1) of the Contributions and Benefits Act.

AMENDMENTS

1. Regulation 4(2) of the Child Support (Consequential Amendments and Transitional Provisions) Regulations 2001 (in force as s.11 of the Act).
2. Regulation 4(2) of the Child Support (Consequential Amendments and Transitional Provisions) Regulations 2001 (in force as s.11 of the Act).
3. Regulation 4(3) of the Child Support (Consequential Amendments and Transitional Provisions) Regulations 2001 (in force as s.11 of the Act).

DEFINITION

3.323    "appeal": see reg.1(3).

**Child support appeals involving issues that arise in other cases**

3.324    **24.** The circumstances prescribed under section 28ZB(6)(c) of the Child Support Act, where an appeal is pending against a decision in the case described in section 28ZB(1)(b) even though an appeal against the decision has not been brought (or, as the case may be, an application for leave to appeal against the decision has not been made), is where the Secretary of State—
  (a) certifies in writing that he is considering appealing against that decision, and
  (b) considers that, if such an appeal were already determined, it would affect the determination of the appeal described in section 28ZB(1)(a).

DEFINITION

"appeal": see reg.1(3).

## PART IV

RIGHTS OF APPEAL AND PROCEDURE FOR BRINGING APPEALS

### CHAPTER 1

### *General*

### *General Appeals Matters Including Child Support Appeals*

## Appeal against a decision which has been [¹replaced or] revised

**30.**—(1) An appeal against a decision of the Secretary of State shall not lapse where the decision [²is treated as replaced by a decision under section 11 of the Child Support Act by section 28F(5) of that Act, or is revised under section 16 of that Act] or section 9 before the appeal is determined and the decision as [¹replaced or] revised is not more advantageous to the appellant than the decision before it was [⁴replaced or] revised.

3.325

(2) Decisions which are more advantageous for the purposes of this regulation include decisions where—

. . .

    (f) a financial gain accrued or will accrue to the appellant in consequence of the decision.

(3) Where a decision as [⁵replaced under section 28F(5) of the Child Support Act or revised under section 16 of that Act] or under section 9 is not more advantageous to the appellant than the decision before it was [⁶replaced or] revised, the appeal shall be treated as though it had been brought against the decision as [⁷replaced or] revised.

(4) The appellant shall have a period of one month from the date of notification of the decision as [⁸replaced or] revised to make further representations as to the appeal.

(5) After the expiration of the period specified in paragraph (4), or within that period if the appellant consents in writing, the appeal to the appeal tribunal shall proceed except where, in the light of the further representations from the appellant, the Secretary of State further revises his decision and that decision is more advantageous to the appellant than the decision before it was [⁹replaced or] revised.

AMENDMENTS

1. Regulation 11(a) of the Appeals Amendment Regulations 2000 (for in force date see regs 1 and 14 of SI 2000/3185 below).

2. Regulation 11(b)(i) of the Appeals Amendment Regulations 2000 (for in force date see regs 1 and 14 of SI 2000/3185 below).

3. Regulation 11(b)(ii) of the Appeals Amendment Regulations 2000 (for in force date see regs 1 and 14 of SI 2000/3185 below).

4. Regulation 11(b)(iii) of the Appeals Amendment Regulations 2000 (for in force date see regs 1 and 14 of SI 2000/3185 below).

5. Regulation 11(c)(i) of the Appeals Amendment Regulations 2000 (for in force date see regs 1 and 14 of SI 2000/3185 below).
6. Regulation 11(c)(ii) of the Appeals Amendment Regulations 2000 (for in force date see regs 1 and 14 of SI 2000/3185 below).
7. Regulation 11(c)(iii) of the Appeals Amendment Regulations 2000 (for in force date see regs 1 and 14 of SI 2000/3185 below).
8. Regulation 11(d) of the Appeals Amendment Regulations 2000 (for in force date see regs 1 and 14 of SI 2000/3185 below).
9. Regulation 11(e) of the Appeals Amendment Regulations 2000 (for in force date see regs 1 and 14 of SI 2000/3185 below).

DEFINITIONS

3.326   "appeal": see reg.1(3).
"the date of notification": see reg.1(3).

GENERAL NOTE

If an appeal does not survive under this regulation, it lapses under s.16(6) of the Act.

## [¹Appeals to appeal tribunals in child support cases

3.327   **30A.** Section 20 of the Child Support Act shall apply to any decision of the Secretary of State that an adjustment shall cease or with respect to the adjustment of amounts payable under a maintenance calculation for the purpose of taking account of overpayments of child support maintenance and voluntary payments, or a decision under section 17 of that Act, whether as originally made or as revised under section 16 of that Act.]

AMENDMENT

1. Regulation 12 of the Appeals Amendment Regulations 2000 (for in force date see regs 1 and 14 of SI 2000/3185 below).

DEFINITION

3.328   "voluntary payments": see reg.3A(7).

GENERAL NOTE

This regulation extends the scope of s.20 of the Act, which deals with appeals to appeal tribunals, to include two types of decision: (a) decisions on adjustments to take account of overpayments and voluntary payments and (b) supersessions decisions made under s.17 of the Act, including those that are later revised under s.16 of the Act.

## Time within which an appeal is to be brought

3.329   **31.**—(1) Where an appeal lies from a decision of the Secretary of State to an appeal tribunal . . . the time within which that appeal must be brought is, subject to the following provisions of this Part—
[³(a) subject to regulation 9A(3), within one month of the date of notification of the decision against which the appeal is brought;

(b) where a written statement of the reasons for that decision is requested and provided within the period specified in sub-paragraph (a), within 14 days of the expiry of that period; or

(c) where a written statement of the reasons for that decision is requested but is not provided within the period specified in sub-paragraph (a), within 14 days of the date on which the statement is provided.]

(2) Where the Secretary of State—

(a) revises, or following an application for a revision under regulation . . . [¹, 3A(1) or regulation 17(1)(a) of the Child Support (Maintenance Assessment Procedure) Regulations 1992] does not revise, a decision under section 16 of the Child Support Act . . ., or

(b) supersedes a decision under section 17 of the Child Support Act . . ., the period of one month specified in paragraph (1) shall begin to run from the date of notification of the revision or supersession of the decision, or following an application for a revision under regulation 3(1) or (3) [², 3A(1) or reg.17(1)(a) of the Child Support (Maintenance Assessment Procedure) Regulations 1992], the date the Secretary of State issues a notice that he is not revising the decision.

. . .

(4) Where a dispute arises as to whether an appeal was brought within the time limit specified in this regulation, the dispute shall be referred to, and be determined by, a legally qualified panel member.

(5) The time limit specified in this regulation for bringing an appeal may be extended in accordance with regulation 32.

AMENDMENTS

1. Regulation 2(8) of the Amendment Regulations 2005 (March 18, 2005).
2. Regulation 2(8) of the Amendment Regulations 2005 (March 18, 2005).
3. Regulation 9 of the Appeals Amendment Regulations 2002 (May 20, 2002).

DEFINITIONS

"appeal": see reg.1(3).                                                                          3.330
"the date of notification": see reg.1(3)
"legally qualified panel member": see reg.1(3)

GENERAL NOTE

In the case of parentage appeals in England and Wales, this regulation applies as modified by art.5 of the Child Support Appeals (Jurisdiction of Courts) Order 2002 and for appeals in Scotland, as modified by art.5 of the Child Support Appeals (Jurisdiction of Courts) (Scotland) Order 2003.

The date from which time begins to run for the purposes of this paragraph is the date when the decision is correctly notified, because it is only then that the right to appeal can be exercised effectively (*CDLA 3440/03*, para.17).

If the period within which an appeal must be made ends on a day when the relevant office is closed, it may be that the end of the period will be extended to the next day on which the tribunal office is opened. The decision of the Court of Appeal in *Swainston v HettonVictory Club Ltd* [1983] 1 All E.R. 1179 may be distinguishable: see the general note to reg.2(a).

**3.331**    If the date of the decision against which the appellant seeks to appeal is not identified, there is no valid application. If the wrong date is given, any decision on it is a nullity. See *R(SB) 1/95*, para.12. In either case, the decision of the appeal tribunal on the appeal will be wrong in law (*ibid.*, para.12)

*Paragraph (2)*

Subparagraph (a) makes sense, as there is no power to appeal against a revision decision, only against the earlier decision as revised: see s.20(1)(a) of the Act. However, there is no need for subpara.(b). A decision on supersession is itself appealable: see s.20(1)(a) of the Act. That applies whether the supersession decision is to substitute a new decision for the earlier decision or to refer to supersede that decision. For some reason, this subpara.(b) is limited to decisions to supersede and does not cover refusals to supersede.

## Late appeals

**3.332**    **32.**—(1) The time within which an appeal must be brought may be extended where the conditions specified in paragraphs (2) to (8) are satisfied, but no appeal shall in any event be brought more than one year after the expiration of the last day for appealing under regulation 31.

(2) An application for an extension of time under this regulation shall be made in accordance with regulation 33 and shall be determined by a legally qualified panel member [[1], except that where the Secretary of State . . ., as the case may be, consider that the conditions in paragraphs (4)(b) to (8) are satisfied, the Secretary of State . . ., as the case may be, may grant the application.]

(3) An application under this regulation shall contain particulars of the grounds on which the extension of time is sought, including details of any relevant special circumstances for the purposes of paragraph (4).

[[2](4) An application for an extension of time shall not be granted unless—

(a) the panel member is satisfied that, if the application is granted, there are reasonable prospects that the appeal will be successful; or

(b) the panel member, the Secretary of State . . ., as the case may be, are satisfied that it is in the interests of justice for the application to be granted.]

(5) For the purposes of paragraph (4) it is not in the interests of justice to grant an application unless the panel member [[3], the Secretary of State . . ., as the case may be,] is satisfied that—

(a) the special circumstances specified in paragraph (6) are relevant to the application; or

(b) some other special circumstances exist which are wholly exceptional and relevant to the application,

and as a result of those special circumstances, it was not practicable for the [[4]appeal to be made] within the time limit specified in regulation 31.

(6) For the purposes of paragraph (5)(a), the special circumstances are that—

(a) the applicant or a [[5]partner] or dependant of the applicant has died or suffered serious illness;

(b) the applicant is not resident in the United Kingdom; or

(c) normal postal services were disrupted.

(7) In determining whether it is in the interests of justice to grant the application, [[6]regard shall be had] to the principle that the greater the

amount of time that has elapsed between the expiration of the time within which the appeal is to be brought under regulation 31 and the making of the application for an extension of time, the more compelling should be the special circumstances on which the application is based.

(8) In determining whether it is in the interests of justice to grant an application, no account shall be taken of the following—

    (a) that the applicant or any person acting for him was unaware of or misunderstood the law applicable to his case (including ignorance or misunderstanding of the time limits imposed by these Regulations); or

    (b) that a Commissioner or a court has taken a different view of the law from that previously understood and applied.

(9) An application under this regulation for an extension of time which has been refused may not be renewed.

(10) The panel member who determines an application under this regulation shall record a summary of his decision in such written form as has been approved by the President.

(11) As soon as practicable after the decision is made a copy of the decision shall be sent or given to every party to the proceedings.

AMENDMENTS

1. Regulation 10(a) of the Appeals Amendment Regulations 2002 (May 20, 2002).

2. Regulation 10(b) of the Appeals Amendment Regulations 2002 (May 20, 2002).

3. Regulation 10(c)(i) of the Appeals Amendment Regulations 2002 (May 20, 2002).

4. Regulation 10(c)(ii) of the Appeals Amendment Regulations 2002 (May 20, 2002).

5. Regulation 10(d) of the Appeals Amendment Regulations 2002 (May 20, 2002).

6. Regulation 10(e) of the Appeals Amendment Regulations 2002 (May 20, 2002).

DEFINITIONS

"appeal": see reg.1(3).                                     3.333
"legally qualified panel member": see reg.1(3).
"partner": see reg.1(3)
"President": see reg.1(3).

GENERAL NOTE

In the case of parentage appeals in England and Wales, this regulation applies as   3.334
modified by art.5 of the Child Support Appeals (Jurisdiction of Courts) Order 2002
and for appeals in Scotland, as modified by art.5 of the Child Support Appeals
(Jurisdiction of Courts) (Scotland) Order 2003.

## Making of appeals and applications

**33.**—(1) An appeal, or an application for an extension of time for   3.335
making an appeal to an appeal tribunal shall be in writing either on a form

approved for the purpose by the Secretary of State or in such other format
as the Secretary of State accepts as sufficient for the purpose and shall—
  (a) be signed by—
    (i) the person who, under section 20 of the Child Support Act
       [³. . .] . . . has a right of appeal; or
    (ii) where the person in head (i) has provided written authority to a
       representative to act on his behalf, by that representative;
  (b) be sent or delivered to an appropriate office;
  (c) contain particulars of the grounds on which it is made; and
  (d) contain sufficient particulars of the decision, the certificate of recov-
    erable benefits or the subject of the application, as the case may be,
    to enable that decision, certificate or subject of the application to be
    identified.
  (2) In this regulation, "an appropriate office" means—. . .
. . .
  (d) in the case of an appeal under section 20 of the Child Support Act
    [⁴. . .], an office of the Child Support Agency;
  (3) A form which is not completed in accordance with the instructions
on the form—
  (a) except where paragraph (4) applies, does not satisfy the requirements
    of paragraph (1), and
  (b) may be returned by the Secretary of State to the sender for
    completion in accordance with those instructions.
  (4) Where the Secretary of State is satisfied that the form, although not
completed in accordance with the instructions on it, includes sufficient
information to enable the appeal or application to proceed, he may treat the
form as satisfying the requirements of paragraph (1).
  (5) Where an appeal or application is made in writing otherwise than on
the approved form ("the letter"), and the letter includes sufficient information to enable the appeal or application to proceed, the Secretary of
State may treat the letter as satisfying the requirements of paragraph (1).
  (6) Where the letter does not include sufficient information to enable
the appeal or application to proceed, the Secretary of State may request
further information in writing ("further particulars") from the person who
wrote the letter.
  [¹(7) Where a person to whom a form is returned, or from whom further particulars are requested, duly completes and returns the form or
sends the further particulars, if the form or particulars, as the case may be,
are received by the Secretary of State . . . within—
  (a) 14 days of the date on which the form was returned to him by the
    Secretary of State . . ., the time for making the appeal shall be
    extended by 14 days from the date on which the form was returned;
  (b) 14 days of the date on which the Secretary of State's . . . request was
    made, the time for making the appeal shall be extended by 14 days
    from the date of the request; or
  (c) such longer period as the Secretary of State . . . may direct, the time
    for making the appeal shall be extended by a period equal to that
    longer period directed by the Secretary of State or the Board.]
  (8) Where a person to whom a form is returned or from whom further particulars are requested does not complete and return the form or

send further particulars within the period of time specified in paragraph (7)—

(a) the Secretary of State shall forward a copy of the form, or as the case may be, the letter, together with any other relevant documents or evidence to a legally qualified panel member, and

(b) the panel member shall determine whether the form or the letter satisfies the requirement of paragraph (1), and shall inform the appellant or applicant and the Secretary of State of his determination.

(9) Where—

(a) a form is duly completed and returned or further particulars are sent after the expiry of the period of time allowed in accordance with paragraph (7), and

(b) no decision has been made under paragraph (8) at the time the form or the further particulars are received by the Secretary of State,

that form or further particulars shall also be forwarded to the legally qualified panel member who shall take into account any further information or evidence set out in the form or further particulars.

[²(10) The Secretary of State or the Board may discontinue action on an appeal where the appeal has not been forwarded to the clerk to an appeal tribunal or to a legally qualified panel member and the appellant or an authorised representative of the appellant has given written notice that he does not wish the appeal to continue.]

AMENDMENTS

1. Regulation 11(b) of the Appeals Amendment Regulations 2002 (May 20, 2002).

2. Regulation 11(c) of the Appeals Amendment Regulations 2002 (May 20, 2002).

3. Regulation 4(4) of the Child Support (Consequential Amendments and Transitional Provisions) Regulations 2001 (in force as s.1 of the 2000 Act).

4. Regulation 4(4) of the Child Support (Consequential Amendments and Transitional Provisions) Regulations 2001 (in force as s.1 of the 2000 Act).

DEFINITION

"appeal": see reg.1(3).

3.336

## Death of a party to an appeal

**34.**—(1) In any proceedings, on the death of a party to those proceedings (other than the Secretary of State), the Secretary of State may appoint such person as he thinks fit to proceed with the appeal in the place of such deceased party.

3.337

(2) A grant of probate, confirmation or letters of administration to the estate of the deceased party, whenever taken out, shall have no effect on an appointment made under paragraph (1).

(3) Where a person appointed under paragraph (1) has, prior to the date of such appointment, taken any action in relation to the appeal on behalf of the deceased party, the effective date of appointment by the Secretary of State shall be the day immediately prior to the first day on which such action was taken.

DEFINITION

3.338    "party to the proceedings": see reg.1(3).

PART V

APPEAL TRIBUNALS FOR . . . CHILD SUPPORT

CHAPTER 1

*The Panel and Appeal Tribunals*

**Persons appointed to the panel**

3.339    **35.** For the purposes of section 6(3), the panel shall include persons with the qualifications specified in Schedule 3.

DEFINITION

3.340    "panel": see reg.1(3).

**Composition of appeal tribunals**

3.341    **36.**—(1) Subject to the following provisions of this regulation, an appeal tribunal [².. .] shall consist of a legally qualified panel member.

. . .

(3) An appeal tribunal shall consist of a financially qualified panel member and a legally qualified panel member where—

(a) the issue raised, or one of the issues raised on appeal or referral, relates to child support or a relevant benefit; and

(b) the appeal or referral may require consideration by members of the appeal tribunal of issues which are, in the opinion of the President, difficult and which relate to—

(i) profit and loss accounts, revenue accounts or balance sheets relating to any enterprise;

(ii) an income and expenditure account in the case of an enterprise not trading for profit; or

(iii) the accounts of any trust fund.

(4) Where the composition of an appeal tribunal would fall to be prescribed under both paragraphs (2) and (3), it shall consist of a medically qualified panel member, a financially qualified panel member and a legally qualified panel member.

(5) Where the composition of an appeal tribunal is prescribed under [¹paragraph (1), (2)(a)] [⁴or (3)] the President may determine that the appeal tribunal shall include such an additional member drawn from the panel constituted under section 6 as he considers appropriate for the purposes of providing further experience for that additional member or for assisting the President in the monitoring of standards of decision making by panel members.

(6) An appeal tribunal shall consist of a legally qualified panel member, a medically qualified panel member and a panel member with a disability qualification in any appeal which relates to an attendance allowance or a disability living allowance under Part III of the Contributions and Benefits Act or [³a disabled person's tax credit] under section 129 of that Act.
. . .
[⁵. . .]

AMENDMENTS

1. Regulation 2(b)(b) of the Social Security and Child Support (Decisions and Appeals) (Amendment) Regulations 1999 (June 1, 1999).
2. Regulation 24(a) of the Social Security and Child Support (Miscellaneous Amendments) Regulations 2000 (June 19, 2000).
3. Regulation 24(f) of the Social Security and Child Support (Miscellaneous Amendments) Regulations 2000 (June 19, 2000).
4. Regulation 2(4)(b) of the Social Security, Child Support and Tax Credits (Decisions and Appeals) Amendment Regulations 2004 (December 21, 2004).
5. Regulation 2(4)(c) of the Social Security, Child Support and Tax Credits (Decisions and Appeals) Amendment Regulations 2004 (December 21, 2004).

DEFINITIONS

"appeal": see reg.1(3).                                                3.342
"financially qualified panel member": see reg.1(3).
"legally qualified panel member": see reg.1(3)
"panel": see reg.1(3).
"panel member": see reg.1(3).
"President": see reg.1(3).
"referral": see reg.1(3).

GENERAL NOTE

*Paragraph (3)*
The presence on a tribunal of a financially qualified panel member is valuable in      3.343
order to avoid the need for expert evidence and to allow a tribunal to make an expert decision on a point that involves an understanding of accounting practice (*CIS 548/97*, paras 2–3). The tribunal is entitled to rely on the expertise of the financially qualified panel member and the adequacy of its reasons will be evaluated in that context (*CCS 1626/02*, para.13).

## Assignment of clerks to appeal tribunals: function of clerks

**37.** The Secretary of State shall assign a clerk to service each appeal      3.344
tribunal and the clerk so assigned shall be responsible for summoning members of the panel constituted under section 6 to serve on the tribunal.

DEFINITION

"panel": see reg.1(3).                                                3.345

CHAPTER II

*Procedure in Connection with Determination of Appeals and Referrals*

GENERAL NOTE ON PAPER HEARINGS

3.346      The procedure at a paper hearing is such as a legally qualified panel member determines: see reg.38(1) below. The panel member is not specified, but at a paper hearing it will obviously be the panel member who chairs the tribunal. As only the members of the tribunal will be present, there is no need for any formal procedural rules. In so far as procedural rules are needed, the tribunal must act "in accordance with natural justice and to promote the objective with which it was set up, and possibly by analogy with the rules of procedure prescribed for comparable tribunals or bodies" (*Qureshi v Qureshi* [1971] 1 All E.R. 325 at 342–3, *per* Simon P.). It must act judicially: see the general note to reg.49. Much of the commentary in the general notes to the following regulations will be as relevant to paper hearings as to oral hearings.

The tribunal must satisfy itself that one of the parties has not opted for an oral hearing (*CDLA 245/98*, para.13). The decision will be wrong in law if no oral hearing is held when a party has exercised the power to have one. In cases where there may be a doubt on the point, the tribunal's reasons should explain why the tribunal proceeded without an oral hearing (*ibid.*, para.13)

The "paper" hearing may be part of a session comprised entirely of such hearings or it may be part of a session which also involves oral hearings. In either case the presenting officer, even if present at the venue, must not be involved in the "paper" hearing, however helpful that officer's assistance might be (*CS 2810/98*). Whether the hearing is the whole or only a part of the session, there must be a proper hearing in the sense that the tribunal must consider, as a single adjudicating body, all the relevant evidence and contentions before reaching a conclusion. This means that the tribunal must meet; it is not sufficient for the members to read the documents and reach a conclusion in isolation. See *R. v Army Board Ex p. Anderson* [1991] 3 All E.R. 375 at 387, *per* Taylor L.J.

There is no express requirement in respect of paper hearing for the parties to be sent a copy of the appeal documents or to be given notice of the date of the hearing. However, the principles of natural justice apply. These require that a party should be aware of the basis of the officer's decision and the evidence available to the tribunal. Each party should also have an opportunity to place further evidence or representations before the tribunal once these have been seen. See *The King v Tribunal of Appeal under the Housing Act 1919* [1920] 3 K.B. 334. This requires that the parties should know either the date of the hearing, or at least the earliest date on which the case will be heard, and that there should be sufficient notice of this to allow additional material to be placed before the tribunal.

It is only in an exceptional case that it would be an error of law for a tribunal to proceed in the absence of the parties to the proceedings when no oral hearing has been requested (*CDLA 4683/97*, para.23). The absence of the parties will inevitably limit the inquiries that the tribunal can make (*CIB 17622/96*, para.8), unless it is appropriate for the chairman to direct an oral hearing under reg.39(5).

If a substantial new point arises in the course of a paper hearing, there will be a breach of natural justice if the tribunal does not adjourn to allow the parties to produce evidence or to make submissions on the point (*CIB 3899/97*, paras 18–19), if appropriate at an oral hearing directed by the chairman or appeal tribunal under reg.39(5).

The Social Security Commissioners held that a paper hearing of Attendance Allowance cases was not appropriate where integrity was in question (*R(A) 4/89* and *R(A) 7/89)*.These decisions were made in the context of the adjudication of the pre-1992 Attendance Allowance, which did not allow a party a chance to opt for an oral hearing. Under these Regulations, the parties have that power. So, these decisions are not authority that an oral hearing should be held whenever a party's integrity is in question. This is, though, a factor that the chairman should consider when deciding whether to exercise the power to direct that an oral hearing be held under reg.39(5).

There is no general requirement in human rights law that there must be an oral hearing, even if disputed issues of fact or opinion are involved (*R. (N) v Doctor M* [2003] 1 F.L.R. 667 at para.41).

The duty to make a record of proceedings under reg.55(1) does not apply to paper hearings. Under the principles applied by the Social Security Commissioners before there was a legislative duty to keep a record, the lack of a record may result in the tribunal's decision being wrong in law on the principles set out in the *Significance of the record* section in the general note to reg.55(1). In practice, however, it is unlikely that anything that might be recorded at a paper hearing would be sufficiently important to make the tribunal's decision wrong in law if it were not recorded, although there may be exceptional cases. The most useful function of a record of proceedings at a paper hearing is to note the receipt of additional documents from one of the parties to the proceedings. It is often difficult for a Commissioner to tell which documents were before the tribunal. If the chairman does not keep a record of this, there is the risk that the decision will be set aside because it cannot be shown that a document was considered. See *CCS 4742/97*, para.11.

## Consideration and determination of appeals and referrals

**38.**—(1) The procedure in connection with the consideration and determination of an appeal or a referral shall, subject to the following provisions of these Regulations, be such as a legally qualified panel member shall determine.

3.347

(2) A legally qualified panel member may give directions requiring a party to the proceedings to comply with any provision of these Regulations and may at any stage of the proceedings, either of his own motion or on a written application made to the clerk to the appeal tribunal by any party to the proceedings, give such directions as he may consider necessary or desirable for the just, effective and efficient conduct of the proceedings and may direct any party to the proceedings to provide such particulars or to produce such documents as may be reasonably required.

(3) Where a clerk to the appeal tribunal is authorised to take steps in relation to the procedure of the tribunal he may give directions requiring any party to the proceedings to comply with any provision of these Regulations.

DEFINITIONS

"appeal": see reg.1(3).

3.348

"clerk to the appeal tribunal": see reg.1(3).
"legally qualified panel member": see reg.1(3).
"party to the proceedings": see reg.1(3).
"referral": see reg.1(3).

GENERAL NOTE

*Paragraph (1)*

**3.349**     See also reg.49(1) under which the same power is given to the chairman or only member of the appeal tribunal. Unlike that provision, this paragraph is not limited to the procedure at an oral hearing. It covers paper hearings. This power may not extend to an application to set aside the decision of an appeal tribunal: see the general note to reg.57(1).

*Paragraph (2)*

The power to give directions that a party to the proceedings comply with any provision of these Regulations exists as a preliminary step to striking out proceedings under reg.46(1)(c) for failure to comply with the direction. A direction under this paragraph can only override a tribunal's directions given on an adjournment if the tribunal's directions are impossible or very difficult to implement or if they frustrate the determination of an appeal within a reasonable time (*CSDLA 866/02*).

The chairman acquires the power to give directions as soon as proceedings begin, which means as soon as the appeal or referral is lodged. A direction may be given on the chairman's own motion or at the request of any party. A written request in writing before the hearing causes little inconvenience. The requirement for a written request at the hearing appears cumbersome. However, if an oral request is made at the hearing, a direction may be given on the chairman's own motion. The same procedure may be followed in the case of requests telephoned to the chairman via the clerk.

The express wording of the regulation makes it clear that the power to give directions is one which is given to the chairman alone and which remains with him to the exclusion of the tribunal throughout the proceedings.

It is good practice for the chairman on receipt of the papers to read through them in order to identify any directions which could be given which would contribute to the just, effective and efficient conduct of the proceedings. The chairman will need to bear in mind, if directions are given to a party, that there will only be a limited time before the hearing within which the party can comply with the directions.

This regulation gives chairmen the power to make orders which would require the hearing of an appeal to be postponed or even the whole session to be aborted. This might arise, for example, if a chairman issued directions that fresh evidence should be disclosed to all parties or written submissions be presented to the tribunal in advance. Chairmen will wish to exercise their powers under this regulation sesibly and with caution in order to balance their desire to ensure that the proceedings are conducted in a just, effective and efficient manner with the undesirability of bringing disruption to the listing of appeals with resulting delay to the parties to other appeals, including the Secretary of State. They will also need to bear in mind that the administrative arrangements necessary to carry out their directions may not exist.

Despite the broad wording of the power, it is limited to procedural matters. It cannot be used to usurp the tribunal's powers over substantive issues. One direction which might be made in an appropriate case is for evidence to be given by video or through a television link. The administrative arrangements by which such a direction could be implemented are not in place. Another use of the power might be to restrict circulation of certain evidence. By analogy with the power of a court dealing with the welfare of a child, the chairman might in exceptional cases order that evidence which would be detrimental to the welfare of the child should not be disclosed to another party to the appeal (*Re B (A Minor) (Disclosure of Evidence)* [1993] 1 F.L.R. 191). A number of other occasions on which the exercise of this power to give directions should be considered are pointed out in the general notes to specific regulations.

In giving a direction, a chairman should be mindful of whether it will be possible to enforce the direction if it is not complied with. If the failure to comply is that of an appellant or applicant, the chairman has the ultimate sanction of striking out the appeal. However, this may be considered too draconian a penalty in all but the most serious cases A chairman could direct the party to attend to give evidence, or issue a summons or citation to the person to produce documents, but this latter power has its own problems of enforcement (see the general note to reg.43). Alternatively, a chairman or the tribunal could ask the Secretary of State to use an inspector under s.15 of the Act. An inspector can only be appointed to obtain information required by the Secretary of State, not by a tribunal, although it would be sufficient if the information was needed as evidence before a tribunal. The appointment of an inspector is a matter for the Secretary of State; the tribunal or its chairman can only request an appointment. Beyond these powers, the consequences of failure to comply will depend upon the nature of the direction and whether compliance will be for the benefit of the person to whom the direction is given. If compliance is against the person's interests, the tribunal may be able to apply the law to the advantage of the appellant and the disadvantage of the other party by relying on any evidence that the appellant can give or by drawing an adverse inference. Failing any device such as these, the tribunal will have to accept the facts that the burden of proof is on the appellant, that the tribunal has an inquisitorial function, which it must exercise impartially even if one party has disobeyed a direction, and that it can only act on evidence before it.

At the end of the day the key to compliance lies not in coercion or powers of enforcement, but in the willingness of the person concerned to comply with the directions given. The power under this regulation should be used in a constructive manner to guide the parties in the preparation and presentation of their cases, and to assist them to proceed in a spirit and atmosphere of co-operation which should be fostered by the whole appeal system in implementing the enabling role of the tribunal which extends beyond the hearing of the appeal itself to the entire proceedings. This will, no doubt, often be an unattainable ideal, but it, rather than confrontation and compulsion, will make this power effective. See the comments of the Commissioner in *CCS 2061/00*, paras 12–16 and *CIB 4252/04*, paras 11–15.

Despite this exhortation, a note of caution is required. Chairmen will need to be mindful that the resources available to provide the administrative and budgetary support that may be required by, or as a result of, their directions are limited, as are the means by which compliance with a direction can be encouraged or secured. They should not exercise this power in a manner that will undermine confidence in the tribunal system.

If a party fails to provide the evidence that a chairman has directed to be produced, the tribunal may be able to draw adverse inferences against the party in breach. However, it may only do this if the evidence before it does not provide an adequate basis for determining the issue. See the *Evaluation of evidence* section of the general note to reg.49(1). A failure to provide evidence in accordance with a direction does not automatically make a decision made without the evidence wrong in law. See *CCS 2061/00*, paras 17–19.

A Commissioner has said that it is doubtful whether a direction that further evidence or statements shall only be filed with the leave of a chairman is of any effect (*CCS 37/97*, para.7). However, the Employment Appeal Tribunal has said that Employment Tribunal could give directions about the production of witness statements and the calling of witnesses without leave (*Eurobell (Holdings) plc v Barker* [1998] I.C.R. 299).

One direction that might be made is an order to hold a hearing to deal with a preliminary issue. However, the holding of such hearings is not to be encouraged (*CA 126/89*, para.10 and *Sutchiffe v Big C's Marine* [1998] I.C.R. 913), although they may be useful if there is dispute as to the tribunal's jurisdiction. Another direction that might be given in exceptional cases is that there be a domiciliary hearing.

Chairmen are advised to read the papers as soon as they are received and, if need be, issue directions to ensure that all the relevant information is available on the day of the hearing, with a view to avoiding unnecessary adjournments. However, chairmen should not telephone the clerks and dictate directions to be issued to a party to the appeal, since this practice can lead to misunderstandings.

Usually a direction will be issued in writing. Sometimes, however, it may be appropriate at a hearing to give a direction orally. A chairman might, for example, direct a party to an appeal not to tape record the proceedings. When a direction is given orally, the chairman should record the fact that it has been given and its terms in the notes of proceedings as evidence of the direction having been issued.

Any response based on a party's failure to comply with a direction must be proportionate. In gauging what is proportionate, it is proper to consider among other matters: (a) the impact of the breach on the other party; (b) the purpose for which the direction was given; and (c) whether the response being considered would prolong proceedings in view of the Secretary of State's powers to correct errors of fact (*CDLA 4977/01*, para.35).

*Paragraph (3)*

This paragraph gives a limited power to the clerk to the tribunal to give directions. The power is not of the nature of that given to the chairman under para.(1). It is limited to the power to give directions requiring a party to comply with any provision of these Regulations. It applies whenever the clerk is authorised to take steps in relation to the tribunal's procedure, but is not expressly limited to requiring a party to comply with those aspects of tribunal procedure over which the clerk has power to act.

## [¹Choice of hearing

3.350    **39.**—(1) Where an appeal or a referral is made to an appeal tribunal the appellant and any other party to the proceedings shall notify the clerk to the appeal tribunal, on a form approved by the Secretary of State, whether he wishes to have an oral hearing of the appeal or whether he is content for the appeal or referral to proceed without an oral hearing.

(2) Except in the case of a referral, the form shall include a statement informing the appellant that, if he does not notify the clerk to the appeal tribunal as required by paragraph (1) within the period specified in paragraph (3), the appeal may be struck out in accordance with regulation 46(1).

(3) Notification in accordance with paragraph (1)—

(a) if given by the appellant or a party to the proceedings other than the Secretary of State, must be sent or given to the clerk to the appeal tribunal within 14 days of the date on which the form is issued to him; or

(b) if given by the Secretary of State, must be sent or given to the clerk-

(i)  in the case of an appeal, within 14 days of the date on which the form is issued to the appellant; or

(ii) in the case of a referral, on the date of referral,

or within such longer period as the clerk may direct.

(4) Where an oral hearing is requested in accordance with paragraphs (1) and (3) the appeal tribunal shall hold an oral hearing unless the appeal is struck out under regulation 46(1).]

(5) The chairman, or in the case of an appeal tribunal which has only one member, that member, may of his own motion direct that an oral hearing of the appeal or referral be held if he is satisfied that such a hearing is necessary to enable the appeal tribunal to reach a decision.

AMENDMENT

1. Regulation 2(5) of the Social Security, Child Support and Tax Credits (Decisions and Appeals) Amendment Regulations 2004 (December 21, 2004).

DEFINITIONS

"appeal": see reg.1(3).                                                                    **3.351**
"clerk to the appeal tribunal": see reg.1(3).
"party to the proceedings": see reg.1(3).
"referral": see reg.1(3).

GENERAL NOTE

For paper hearings, see the introductory general note to this Chapter of these Regulations.

*Paragraph (1)*
If a party does not return a notice issued under this paragraph, the only evidence     **3.352**
that will be available to show that it was sent will be a note on the tribunal's file or
a copy of a computer record. This is admissible as evidence that the notice was sent,
although the weight given to it will depend on the evidence as a whole. See *CIB
6180/97*, para.5.

In exceptional cases, an oral hearing may be held at a party's home.

There is no duty to allow a domiciliary hearing. Underlying the exercise of this discretion is the proper allocation of public funds. The judicial members of tribunals share with the administrators who organise the tribunals responsibility for the proper use of the public money which is provided to run them. The efficient allocation of resources is a legitimate consideration. The reasons given by a tribunal for refusing to allow a domiciliary hearing need not be elaborate; a sentence or two will usually suffice. See *CDLA 1834/98*.

When considering whether to allow a domiciliary hearing, alternative sources of evidence always have to be considered. However, it would not be proper to refuse a domiciliary hearing on the ground that evidence could be given by someone else and then reject that evidence because it did not come from the party personally. If a domiciliary hearing is refused on the ground that evidence may be obtained from an alternative source, that source must be an adequate substitute for the party's own evidence. It will not be adequate if it is less satisfactory than evidence from the party and if the evidence given is liable to be rejected as not coming from the party. See *CS 3326/99*, para.25.

A party who cannot attend a hearing will be at a disadvantage. In the social security context a Commissioner has said that in this eventuality a party is unlikely to have a fair hearing under Art.6(1) of the European Convention on Human Rights (*CS 3326/99*, para.26). However, in the child support context the practicalities must also be considered, as the parties may live a long way apart and their relationship may make a domiciliary hearing inappropriate.

*Paragraph (5)*

A chairman has power to direct that an oral hearing be held, but no power to override a notification under para.(1) that one is required.

The power to direct an oral hearing be held only arises if it is "necessary to enable the appeal tribunal to reach a decision". If this condition were interpreted literally, it would never be fulfilled, because a decision can always be reached by relying on the burden of proof. It means "reasonably" necessary (*CI 1533/98*, para.13). It is most likely to be used where a substantial new point is identified that was not known to all the parties to the proceedings when the clerk to the appeal tribunal gave the direction under para.(1) or where it appears that a party to the proceedings did not appreciate the importance of an oral hearing. An oral hearing is particularly useful if an issue turns on a party's integrity.

The fact that an oral hearing is held does not mean that the parties to the proceedings must, or will, attend. This is a factor to be kept in mind when deciding whether to exercise the power to direct that an oral hearing be held.

An alternative to directing that an oral hearing be held is the giving of a direction under reg.38(2) that evidence be produced. This may be a more appropriate way of obtaining evidence. It is relevant to consider this possibility when deciding whether to exercise the power under this paragraph. It also avoids the need to consider whether an oral hearing is reasonably necessary.

The failure by a chairman to order that an oral hearing be held is not an error of law by the appeal tribunal itself for the purposes of an appeal to a Commissioner (*CI 1533/98*, para.15). In the case of a single member appeal tribunal, the power is given to the appeal tribunal itself and a failure by the tribunal to order that an oral hearing be held may amount to, or involve, an error of law.

## Withdrawal of appeal or referral

3.353     **40.**—(1) An appeal may be withdrawn by the appellant or an authorised representative of the appellant and a referral may be withdrawn by the Secretary of State, as the case may be, either—

(a) at an oral hearing; or

(b) at any other time before the appeal or referral is determined, by giving notice in writing of withdrawal to the clerk to the appeal tribunal.

(2) If an appeal or a referral is withdrawn (as the case may be) in accordance with paragraph (1)(a), the clerk to the appeal tribunal shall send a notice in writing to any party to the proceedings who is not present when the appeal or referral is withdrawn, informing him that the appeal or referral (as the case may be) has been withdrawn.

(3) If an appeal or a referral is withdrawn (as the case may be) in accordance with paragraph (1)(b), the clerk to the appeal tribunal shall send a notice in writing to every party to the proceedings informing them that the appeal or referral (as the case may be) has been withdrawn.

DEFINITIONS

3.354     "appeal": see reg.1(3).
"clerk to the appeal tribunal": see reg.1(3).
"party to the proceedings": see reg.1(3).
"referral": see reg.1(3).

GENERAL NOTE

This regulation provides for the withdrawal of appeals and referrals. Withdrawal is solely a matter for the appellant in the case of an appeal and for the Secretary of State in the case of a referral. The consent of any other party to the proceedings, of a chairman, or of an appeal tribunal is not needed.

If it is unclear whether a party wishes to withdraw an appeal or a referral, it is an error of law for the appeal tribunal to fail to clarify the party's wishes (*CCS 13/94*, para.8).

If a withdrawal is made at an oral hearing, the chairman should record this in the record of proceedings.

There is no power to reinstate an appeal that has been withdrawn. Unlike the position in a court (see *Ogwr Borough Council v Knight. The Times*, January 13, 1994), a withdrawn appeal is not dismissed. A fresh appeal may be made (whether by the original appellant or by someone else) and a fresh referral may be made by the Secretary of State (*R(IS) 5/94*). The requirements of reg.32 must be satisfied in the case of a fresh but late appeal.

Withdrawal may be made by "an authorised representative". In contrast to reg.30(1)(a)(ii), there is no need for the authority to be given in writing. In practice, writing may be needed to ensure that the person has authority to act.

## Non-disclosure of medical advice or evidence

**42.**—(1) Where, in connection with [[1]. . .] an appeal or referral there is before an appeal tribunal medical advice or medical evidence relating to a person which has not been disclosed to him and in the opinion of [[2]a legally qualified panel member], the disclosure to that person of that advice or evidence would be harmful to his health, such advice or evidence shall not be required to be disclosed to that person.

(2) Advice or evidence such as is mentioned in paragraph (1) shall not be disclosed to any person acting for or representing the person to whom it relates or, in a case where a claim for benefit is made by reference to the disability of a person other than the claimant and the advice or evidence relates to that other person, shall not be disclosed to the claimant or any person acting for or representing him, unless [[3]a legally qualified panel member], is satisfied that it is in the interests of the person to whom the advice or evidence relates to do so.

(3) A tribunal shall not be precluded from taking into account for the purposes of the determination advice or evidence which has not been disclosed to a person under the provisions of paragraph (1) or (2).

AMENDMENTS

1. Regulation 25(a)(i) of the Social Security and Child Support (Miscellaneous Amendments) Regulations 2000 (June 19, 2000).
2. Regulation 25(a)(ii) of the Social Security and Child Support (Miscellaneous Amendments) Regulations 2000 (June 19, 2000).
3. Regulation 25(b) of the Social Security and Child Support (Miscellaneous Amendments) Regulations 2000 (June 19, 2000).

3.355

3.356

DEFINITIONS

3.357    "appeal": see reg.1(3).
       "referral": see reg.1(3).

## Summoning of witnesses and administration of oaths

3.358    **43.**—(1) A chairman, or in the case of an appeal tribunal which has only one member, that member, may by summons, or in Scotland, by citation, require any person in Great Britain to attend as a witness at a hearing of an appeal, application or referral at such time and place as shall be specified in the summons or citation and, subject to paragraph (2), at the hearing to answer any question or produce any documents in his custody or under his control which relate to any matter in question in the appeal, application or referral but—

    (a)  no person shall be required to attend in obedience to such summons or citation unless he has been given at least 14 days' notice of the hearing or, if less than 14 days' notice is given, he has informed the tribunal that the notice given is sufficient; and

    (b)  no person shall be required to attend and give evidence or to produce any document in obedience to such summons or citation unless the necessary expenses of attendance are paid or tendered to him.

(2) No person shall be compelled to give any evidence or produce any document or other material that he could not be compelled to give or produce on a trial of an action in a court of law in that part of Great Britain where the hearing takes place.

(3) In exercising the powers conferred by this regulation, the chairman, or in the case of an appeal tribunal which has only one member, that member, shall take into account the need to protect any matter that relates to intimate personal or financial circumstances, is commercially sensitive, consists of information communicated or obtained in confidence or concerns national security.

(4) Every summons or citation issued under this regulation shall contain a statement to the effect that the person in question may apply in writing to a chairman to vary or set aside the summons or citation.

(5) A chairman, or in the case of an appeal tribunal which has only one member, that member, may require any witness, including a witness summoned under the powers conferred by this regulation, to give evidence on oath or affirmation and for that purpose there may be administered an oath or affirmation in due form.

DEFINITIONS

3.359    "appeal": see reg.1(3).
       "referral": see reg.1(3).

GENERAL NOTE

3.360    This regulation gives power to a chairman to summon a witness to attend to answer questions or produce documents. The regulation provides for no penalty if the person fails to attend or to produce the documents, although the operation of this regulation is to be kept under review and penalty powers added if they are needed. However, the High Court has power to issue a *subpoena* in aid of an inferior jurisdiction. (There is no equivalent power in Scotland.) That procedure involves attendance in person or through a solicitor and the payment of a fee before the *subpoena* will be issued. The tribunal is not equipped with the appropriate administrative machinery or prepared to pay the expenses for obtaining a *subpoena*. Chairmen should therefore be wary of issuing a summons or citation of their own motion.

Obviously, this regulation only applies where there is to be an oral hearing.

*Paragraph (1)*

A chairman may require a person to attend at a hearing. That person may be a party to the proceedings or some other person (*R. v B. County Council Ex p. P* [1991] 2 All ER. 65 at 69, *per* Butler-Sloss L.J.). The power given to the chairman is discretionary and, in the case of a child, it should be exercised with caution (*ibid.* at 70–71 and 75, *per* Butler-Sloss L.J. and Lord Donaldson M.R. respectively). No summons will be issued, whether to a child or to an adult, if to do so would be oppressive (*ibid.*, 475, *per* Butler-Sloss L.J.). In the case of a child, the older the child the more likely it is that it will be appropriate to issue a summons (*Re P (Witness Summons)* [1997] 2 F.L.R. 447 at 454, *per* Wilson J.). If a child is aged 12 or younger the issue of a summons would in most cases be inappropriate (*ibid.*). However, in *R. v Highbury Corner Magistrates's Court Ex p. D.* [1997] 1 F.L.R. 683 the Divisional Court held that it was proper to issue a witness summons against a nine-year-old-boy whose evidence was potentially relevant and take the decision of whether it was appropriate for him to be called as a witness at the time when he was called upon to give evidence so that the decision could be taken in the light of the circumstances then prevailing. If the person is to give evidence through a television link, that would constitute attending at the hearing. However, if evidence is to be given by video recorded in advance, it is difficult to treat this as attending at a hearing. Thus, this regulation cannot be used to order a person to give evidence in this way. There is no express provision dealing with who must ultimately meet the cost and it appears that the tribunal may have to do so.

In relation to the equivalent powers as exercised by the courts a wide interpretation has been given to the word "documents" so that it includes any medium which can record evidence or information including tape recordings (*Grant v Southerwestern and County Properties Ltd* [1974] 2 All E.R. 465) and film (*Senior v Holdsworth* [1975] 2 All E.R. 1009).

A chairman has a discretion whether or not to compel an expert to attend to give evidence and in exercise of that discretion may take account of whether or not attendance would disrupt or impede other important work which the expert has to do (*Society of Lloyd's v Clementson (No.2)*, *The Times*, February 29, 1996).

*Paragraph (2)*

It is usual to distinguish between admissibility of evidence and compellability of witnesses. This paragraph by referring to compellability to give evidence fails to make that distinction. It may, therefore, appear to introduce all the rules of evidence which apply in a court on a trial of an action. After all, a person cannot be compelled to give evidence which is inadmissible. However, the location of this provision in a regulation dealing with summoning of witnesses and before the regulation dealing with the hearing itself shows that it is not intended to have that effect. Its only concern is with the compellability of the person as a witness.

For parties who are not compellable see Halsbury, *Laws of England* (4th ed.), Vol.17, para.234.

Production may be required on the date of hearing or before (*Khanna v Lovell White Durrant (a firm)* [1994] 4 All E.R. 267).

Normally tax documents are protected from disclosure by a public interest immunity, regardless of whether or not this immunity is claimed by the tax authorities. However, this immunity may be overridden by public interest in the administration of justice. The burden of justifying disclosure is on the person seeking disclosure. In making the decision, the chairman should have regard to the relevance of the documents and to the necessity of disposing fairly of the case. See *Lonrho plc v Fayed (No.4)* [1994] QB 775.

The test to apply in deciding whether to order a person who is not a party to produce a document is whether the production of the document is necessary for disposing of the case or for saving costs (*Macmillan Inc v Bishopsgate Investment Management plc (No.1)* [1993] 4 All E.R. 998.

In requiring production of information held by a bank it will be necessary to take account of the Bankers' Books Evidence Act 1879 as amended. A bank may be required to produce a customer's bank statement and is not in breach of its duty of confidentiality to its customer in doing so (*Robertson v Canadian Imperial Bank of Commerce* [1995] 1 All E.R. 824). However, it is an offence to disclose information which relates to the business or other affairs of any person and which has only been acquired for the purposes of the Banking Act 1987 (s.82 and *Bank of Credit and Commerce International (Overseas) Ltd (in liquidation) v Price Waterhouse*, [1997] 4 All E.R. 781). The only exceptions which may be relevant to a tribunal where (a) the person concerned consents to such disclosure, or (b) the information is already public.

*Paragraph (5)*

For a discussion of who has power to administer the oath, see the general note to reg.49(11).

There is no express mention of an interpreter's oath.

## Confidentiality in child support appeals or referrals

3.361     **44.**—(1)  In the circumstances specified in paragraph (2), for the purposes of paragraph 7 of Schedule 1 to the Act (President to secure confidentiality), in a child support appeal or referral, the prescribed material is—

(a) the address of the [1non-resident parent]; the parent with care; the child; a parent of the child or any other person with care of the child; or

(b) any information the use of which could reasonably be expected to lead to the location of any person specified in paragraph (a).

(2) Except where the appeal is brought against a reduced benefit [4decision] within the meaning of [5section 46(10)(b)] of the Child Support Act, paragraph (1) applies where in response to an enquiry from the Secretary of State, the [2non-resident parent] or, as the case may be, the parent with care, has within 14 days of issue of that enquiry notified the Secretary of State that he would like the information specified in paragraph (1) which relates to him to remain confidential.

(3) In this regulation, the expressions "[3non-resident parent]" and "parent with care" have the meanings those expressions bear in section 54 of the Child Support Act.

Amendments

1. Regulation 4(2) of the Child Support (Consequential Amendments and Transitional Provisions) Regulations 2001 (in force as s.11 of the Act).

2. Regulation 4(2) of the Child Support (Consequential Amendments and Transitional Provisions) Regulations 2001 (in force as s.11 of the Act).
3. Regulation 4(2) of the Child Support (Consequential Amendments and Transitional Provisions) Regulations 2001 (in force as s.11 of the Act).
4. Regulation 4(5) of the Child Support (Consequential Amendments and Transitional Provisions) Regulations 2001 (in force as s.11 of the Act).
5. Regulation 4(5) of the Child Support (Consequential Amendments and Transitional Provisions) Regulations 2001 (in force as s.11 of the Act).

DEFINITIONS

"appeal": see reg.1(3).　　　　3.362
"President": see reg.1(3).
"referral": see reg.1(3).

GENERAL NOTE

This regulation sets the terms of the duty of the President under Sch.1, para.7 to　3.363 the Social Security Act 1998. It is in addition to the duty of non-disclosure to a party to the proceedings in order to protect the welfare of a child, which is discussed in the general note to s.2 of the Act. For the duties of confidentiality imposed on the Office of the Child Support Commissioners and on the Commissioners themselves see regs 9 and 26(5) of the Child Support Commissioners (Procedure) Regulations 1999, and for the duties imposed on the Secretary of State see reg.23(3) of the Maintenance Calculation Procedure Regulations and reg.9(2)(c) of the Variation Regulations.

Subparagraph (2)(b) must be interpreted narrowly and applied sensibly, Persons might be located from information which relates directly to themselves or from information that relates to them only indirectly in that it relates to some other person, inquiry or observation of whom might lead to their being located (such as a grandparent, employer or solicitor). The key to the realistic application of this provision is the "reasonably".

All documents are covered regardless of who provides them, including the documents supplied by the Child Support Agency.

Natural justice requires a fair hearing and this usually requires that a person should know and have a chance to answer the case of the other party (*Doody v Secretary of State for the Home Department* [1993] 3 All E.R. 92 at 106; *R. (ota S) v Plymouth City Council* [2002] 1 F.L.R. 1177). However, the requirements of natural justice must give way to contrary statutory provision. Where a provision such as this regulation applies the question, therefore, becomes one of the extent to which as a matter of interpretation the provision replaces this aspect of natural justice and how it relates to the requirements of regs 53 and 55.

Some help can be found in the approach taken and principles laid down by the Commissioner in *CSDLA 5/95*, paras 16–23, in the context of a provision permitting non-disclosure of harmful medical evidence. Adapting that approach and those principles to the present context produces the following guidance on the operation of this regulation.

(i) The regulation should be given as narrow a scope as its wording permits.

(ii) It prevents disclosure without consent but does not exclude the fundamental right to a fair hearing.

(iii) All parties should be told that information exists which has not been disclosed. This will be obvious from the masking.

(iv) Sufficient details should be disclosed to allow other parties to respond.

(v) The disclosure to which reg.17(1) is directed must mean direct or indirect disclosure to another party. It may, therefore, be possible to disclose information to a representative subject to appropriate, credible undertakings as to the extent to which it may be disclosed to the party.

(vi) The concept of non-disclosure necessarily involves an assumption that the information or the party's location is not already known. However, the terms of para.(3) give an unqualified right to protect information even if this protection is unnecessary.

(vii) This regulation may be in breach of the European Convention on Human Rights (see the case of *McMichael v United Kingdom* (1995) 20 E.H.R.R. 205 referred to by the Commissioner at paras 16 and 17).

*McMichael* concerned the non-disclosure of documents in a children's hearing in Scotland. Before the Court the Government accepted that non-disclosure of the documents constituted a breach of Art.6(1) of the Convention in that the lack of knowledge of the contents of those documents prevented there being a fair hearing in that the power of the parents to influence the outcome of the proceedings and to assess the prospects of a successful appeal to a higher court were affected. See especially at para.80 of the judgment. Unless this regulation is protected by some other provision of the Convention, the same reasoning will apply to render it a breach of Art.6(1).

The principles set out above are in line with the general approach taken by the courts to non-disclosure of evidence (*Re K (Adoption: Disclosure of Information)* [1997] 2 F.L.R. 74).

In *CCS/2997/97*, the Deputy Commissioner held that

(i) the regulation only prevented disclosure of evidence and information to the parties to the proceedings and did not prevent disclosure to the members of the tribunal;

(ii) the regulation did not displace the requirements of natural justice and that, if the evidence and information contained in the masked passages could not be obtained from a reliable source at the hearing, there would be a breach of natural justice unless the tribunal adjourned for an unmasked set of documents to be made available;

(iii) the chairman had a duty, in order to avoid a breach of natural justice, to ensure that a procedure was adopted that was consistent with this regulation but allowed the parties to know the case that had to be answered and to have a reasonable opportunity to respond to it.

There are four cases in which information which might be covered by this regulation may be of significance in a tribunal hearing. The first is where it is necessary to decide whether papers and notice of the hearing have been properly served on a party who does not come to the hearing. The other cases are where a person's address is relevant to a question as to habitual residence or housing costs and where a person's employer is relevant to income. In all these cases it should be possible, if necessary, to discuss matters in sufficient generality to prevent inappropriate disclosure while allowing sufficient detail to be disclosed to allow a fair hearing on the issue.

So far as the record of proceedings and the findings and reasons are concerned, it should usually be relatively easy for the chairman to record sufficient relevant detail without referring to any matters which would conflict with this regulation.

Accordingly, in practice it is unnecessary to decide whether or not regs 53 and 55 are subject to this regulation.

## [¹Procedure following a referral under section 28D(1)(b) of the Child Support Act

**45.**—(1) On a referral under section 28D(1)(b) of the Child Support Act an appeal tribunal may—

    (a) consider two or more applications for a variation with respect to the same application for a maintenance calculation together, or

    (b) consider two or more applications for a variation with respect to the same maintenance calculation together.

(2) In this regulation "maintenance calculation" means a decision under section 11 or 17 of the Child Support Act, as calculated in accordance with Part I of Schedule 1 to that Act, whether as originally made or as revised under section 16 of that Act.]

3.364

### AMENDMENT

1. Regulation 13 of the Appeals Amendment Regulations 2000 (for in force date see regs 1, 14 and 15 of SI 2000/3185 below).

### DEFINITIONS

"appeal": see reg.1(3).
"referral": see reg.1(3).

3.365

### GENERAL NOTE

This regulation allows referrals of related applications for variations to be considered together. It does not apply to appeals. Subparagraph (a) applies if the applications are made under s.28A(3) of the Act and subpara.(b) applies if they are made under s.28G(1) of the Act.

3.366

## CHAPTER III

### *Striking Out Appeals*

## Appeals which may be struck out

**46.**—(1) Subject to paragraphs (2) and (3), an appeal may be struck out by the clerk to the appeal tribunal—

    (a) where it is an out of jurisdiction appeal and the appellant has been notified by the Secretary of State that an appeal brought against such a decision may be struck out;

    (b) for want of prosecution including an appeal not made within the time specified in these Regulations; [¹. . .]

    (c) [². . .] for failure of the appellant to comply with a direction given under these Regulations where the appellant has been notified that failure to comply with the direction could result in the appeal being struck out [²; or].

3.367

[³(d) for failure of the appellant to notify the clerk to the appeal tribunal, in accordance with regulation 39, whether or not he wishes to have an oral hearing of his appeal.]

(2) Where the clerk to the appeal tribunal determines to strike out the appeal, he shall notify the appellant that his appeal has been struck out and of the procedure for reinstatement of the appeal as specified in regulation 47.

(3) The clerk to the appeal tribunal may refer any matter for determination under this regulation to a legally qualified panel member for decision by the panel member rather than the clerk to the appeal tribunal.

[⁴. . .]

AMENDMENTS

1. Regulation 2(6)(a)(i) of the Social Security, Child Support and Tax Credits (Decisions and Appeals) Amendment Regulations 2004 (December 21, 2004).
2. Regulation 2(6)(a)(ii) of the Social Security, Child Support and Tax Credits (Decisions and Appeals) Amendment Regulations 2004 (December 21, 2004).
3. Regulation 2(6)(a)(iii) of the Social Security, Child Support and Tax Credits (Decisions and Appeals) Amendment Regulations 2004 (December 21, 2004).
4. Regulation 2(6)(b) of the Social Security, Child Support and Tax Credits (Decisions and Appeals) Amendment Regulations 2004 (December 21, 2004).

DEFINITIONS

3.368    "appeal": see reg.1(3).
"clerk to the appeal tribunal": see reg.1(3).
"legally qualified panel member": see reg.1(3).
"out of jurisdiction appeal": see reg.1(3).

GENERAL NOTE

There is no imbalance between this power and the more limited sanctions that a tribunal can deploy against the other parties to the proceedings who are in breach of some obligation. It is appropriate to have this power for use against appellants who do not prosecute their appeals (*CDLA 4977/01*, para.33).

*Paragraph (1)(a)*

3.369    The definition of an "out of jurisdiction appeal" does not include child support cases. See the general note to the definition in reg.1(3). There is no procedure laid down for dealing with an out of jurisdiction child support appeal or, for that matter, an out of jurisdiction child support referral. An appeal tribunal has power to decide whether a case falls within its jurisdiction and that decision is appealable to a Commissioner (*R(SB) 29/83*, para.17). It is not clear whether anyone other than an appeal tribunal has power to deal with an out of jurisdiction issue in child support.

*Paragraph (1)(d)*

This power does not extend to parties to cases referred to an appeal tribunal. The reason is that the appeal tribunal is obliged, by virtue of the Secretary of State's referral, to decide the case.

## Reinstatement of struck out appeals

**47.** [¹—(1)  The clerk to the appeal tribunal may reinstate an appeal which   3.370
has been struck out in accordance with regulation [²46(1)(d)] where—

   (a)  the appellant has made representations to him or, as the case may be,
further representations in support of his appeal with reasons why he
considers that his appeal should not have been struck out;

   (b)  the representations are made in writing within one month of the
order to strike out the appeal being issued; and

   (c)  the clerk is satisfied in the light of those representations that there are
reasonable grounds for reinstating the appeal;

but if the clerk is not satisfied that there are reasonable grounds for reinstatement a legally qualified panel member shall consider whether the
appeal should be reinstated in accordance with paragraph (2).

(2)] A legally qualified panel member may reinstate an appeal which has
been struck out in accordance with regulation 46 [³. . .] where—

   (a)  the appellant has made representations, or as the case may be, further representations in support of his appeal with reasons why he
considers that his appeal should not have been struck out, to the
clerk to the appeal tribunal, in writing within one month of the order
to strike out the appeal being issued, and the panel member is satisfied in the light of those representations that there are reasonable
grounds for reinstating the appeal;

[⁴. . .]

   (c)  the panel member is satisfied that the appeal is not an appeal which
may be struck out under regulation 46; or

   (d)  the panel member is satisfied that notwithstanding that the appeal is
one which may be struck out under regulation 46, it is not in the
interests of justice for the appeal to be struck out.

AMENDMENTS

1. Regulation 13 of the Appeals Amendment Regulations 2002 (May 20,
2002).
2. Regulation 2(7)(a) of the Social Security, Child Support and Tax Credits
(Decisions and Appeals) Amendment Regulations 2004 (December 21, 2004).
3. Regulation 2(7)(b)(i) of the Social Security, Child Support and Tax Credits
(Decisions and Appeals) Amendment Regulations 2004 (December 21, 2004).
4. Regulation 2(7)(b)(ii) of the Social Security, Child Support and Tax Credits
(Decisions and Appeals) Amendment Regulations 2004 (December 21, 2004).

DEFINITIONS

"appeal": see reg.1(3).   3.371
"clerk to the appeal tribunal": see reg.1(3)
"legally qualified panel member": see reg.1(3).

Regulation 48 is omitted by virtue of reg.2(8) of the Social Security,   3.372
Child Support and Tax Credits (Decisions and Appeals) Amendment
Regulations 2004 (December 21, 2004).

[NEXT PARAGRAPH IS 3.375]

CHAPTER IV

*Oral Hearings*

**Procedure at oral hearings**

3.375     **49.**—(1) Subject to the following provisions of this Part, the procedure for an oral hearing shall be such as the chairman, or in the case of an appeal tribunal which has only one member, such as that member, shall determine.

(2) Except where paragraph (3) applies, not less than 14 days notice (beginning with the day on which the notice is given and ending on the day before the hearing of the appeal is to take place) of the time and place of any oral hearing of an appeal shall be given to every party to the proceedings, and if such notice has not been given to a person to whom it should have been given under the provisions of this paragraph the hearing may proceed only with the consent of that person.

(3) Any party to the proceedings may waive his right to receive not less than 14 days notice of the time and place of any oral hearing by giving notice to the clerk to the appeal tribunal.

(4) If a party to the proceedings to whom notice has been given under paragraph (2) fails to appear at the hearing the chairman, or in the case of an appeal tribunal which has only one member, that member, may, having regard to all the circumstances including any explanation offered for the absence, proceed with the hearing notwithstanding his absence, or give such directions with a view to the determination of the appeal as he may think proper.

(5) If a party to the proceedings has waived his right to be given notice under paragraph (2) the chairman, or in the case of an appeal tribunal which has only one member, that member, may proceed with the hearing notwithstanding his absence.

[²(6) An oral hearing shall be in public except where the chairman, or in the case of an appeal tribunal which has only one member, that member, is satisfied that it is necessary to hold the hearing, or part of the hearing, in private—

    (a) in the interests of national security, morals, public order or children;

    (b) for the protection of the private or family life of one or more parties to the proceedings; or

    (c) in special circumstances, because publicity would prejudice the interests of justice.]

[³(7) At an oral hearing—

    (a) any party to the proceedings shall be entitled to be present and be heard; and

    (b) the following persons may be present by means of a live television link—

        (i) a party to the proceedings or his representative or both; or

        (ii) where an appeal tribunal consists of more than one member, a tribunal member other than the chairman,

    provided that the person who constitutes or is the chairman of the tribunal gives permission [⁸. . .]

(8) A person who has the right to be heard at a hearing may be accompanied and may be represented by another person whether having professional qualifications or not and, for the purposes of the proceedings at the hearing, any such representative shall have all the rights and powers to which the person whom he represents is entitled.

(9) The following persons shall also be entitled to be present at an oral hearing (whether or not it is otherwise in private) but shall take no part in the proceedings—

(a) the President;

(b) any person undergoing training as a chairman or [⁴. . .] member of an appeal tribunal or as a clerk to an appeal tribunal;

(c) any person acting on behalf of the President in the training or supervision of panel members or in the monitoring of standards of decision-making by panel members;

(d) with the leave of the chairman, or in the case of an appeal tribunal which has only one member, with the leave of that member, [⁵. . .] any other person; and

(e) a member of the Council on Tribunals or of the Scottish Committee of the Council on Tribunals.

[⁶(10) Nothing in paragraph (9) affects the rights of—

(a) any person mentioned in sub-paragraphs (a) and (b) of that paragraph where he is sitting as a member of a tribunal or acting as its clerk; or

(b) the clerk to the tribunal,

and nothing in this regulation prevents the presence at an oral hearing of any witness or of any person whom the chairman, or in the case of an appeal tribunal which has only one member, that member, permits to be present in order to assist the appeal tribunal or the clerk.]

(11) Any person entitled to be heard at an oral hearing may address the tribunal, may give evidence, may call witnesses and may put questions directly to any other person called as a witness.

(12) For the purpose of arriving at its decision an appeal tribunal shall, and for the purpose of discussing any question of procedure may, notwithstanding anything contained in these Regulations, order all persons not being members of the tribunal, other than the person acting as clerk to the appeal tribunal, to withdraw from the hearing except that—

(a) a member of the Council on Tribunals or of the Scottish Committee of the Council on Tribunals, the President or any person mentioned in paragraph (9)(c); and

(b) with the leave of the chairman, or in the case of an appeal tribunal which has only one member, with the leave of that member, any person mentioned in paragraph (9)(b) or (d),

may remain present at any such sitting.

[⁷(13) In this regulation "live television link" means a live television link or other facilities which allow a person who is not physically present at an oral hearing to see and hear proceedings and be seen and heard by those physically present.]

AMENDMENTS

2. Regulation 14(a) of the Appeals Amendment Regulations 2002 (May 20, 2002).
3. Regulation 14(b) of the Appeals Amendment Regulations 2002 (May 20, 2002).
4. Regulation 14(c)(i) of the Appeals Amendment Regulations 2002 (May 20, 2002).
5. Regulation 14(c)(ii) of the Appeals Amendment Regulations 2002 (May 20, 2002).
6. Regulation 14(d) of the Appeals Amendment Regulations 2002 (May 20, 2002).
7. Regulation 14(e) of the Appeals Amendment Regulations 2002 (May 20, 2002).
8. Regulation 2(9) of the Amendment Regulations 2005 (March 18, 2005).

DEFINITIONS

3.376 "appeal": see reg.1(3).
"clerk to the appeal tribunal: see reg.1(3).
"panel member": see reg.1(3).
"party to the proceedings": see reg.1(3).
"President": see reg.1(3).

GENERAL NOTE

3.377 It is the duty of the clerk to the appeal tribunal to summon the members under reg.37. If there is more than one member, it is the duty of the President to nominate one of the members as the chairman under s.7(3)(a) of the Social Security Act 1998. The President does not act personally, but by guidelines implemented by the clerk.

In *CCS 5230/02*, the Commissioner considered whether the tribunal had held an oral hearing. The case concerned a departure direction. The tribunal, consisting of a legally qualified panel member sitting with a financially qualified panel member, held an oral hearing and gave directions to the Secretary of State on how to calculate the non-resident parent's income, but it reserved consideration of the just and equitable requirement until that calculation had been made. When the Secretary of State provided the calculation, it was sent to the financially qualified panel member who was asked to confirm that it would be just and equitable to give a direction. The chairman then completed a decision notice to that effect. The parties were not invited to comment on the issue and there was nothing to show that the members of the tribunal had been in touch to discuss it. The Commissioner set aside the tribunal's decision for a number of procedural deficiencies and commented (para.12) that it was doubtful whether the tribunal had held an oral hearing within the meaning of this regulation. See further the *General Note on Paper Hearings* at the beginning of Ch.II of these Regulations.

*Paragraph(1)*
See also reg.38(1) under which the same power is given to a legally qualified panel member. Unlike that provision, this paragraph is limited to the procedure at an oral hearing.

The procedure must ensure that the appeal tribunal acts judicially. This is capable of referring to the personal manner and behaviour of the panel members, but more usually it refers to the basis on which the tribunal makes its decision. In that sense, it involves these requirements. The tribunal must not act capriciously (*CDLA 2986/01*, para.12). It must act rationally on evidence of probative value (*Mahon v Air New Zealand Ltd* [1984] 3 All E.R. 201 at 210, *per* Lord Diplock). It must act according to law (*R(U) 7/81*, para.8). It must act with scrupulous fairness (*R. (M) v Inner London Crown Court* [2003] 1 F.L.R. 994 at para.45). It must exercise a discretion with due regard to the purpose for which it was conferred (*South Bucks District Council v Porter* [2003] 3 All E.R. 1 at para.29 *per* Lord Bingham). A discretion must also be exercised according to common sense and justice (*Gardner v Jay* (1885) 29 Ch. D. 50 at 58 *per* Bowen L.J.). Discretion must not be exercised "subjectively or at whim or by rigid rule of thumb, but in a principled manner in accordance with reason and justice" (*United Arab Emirates v Abdeighafar* [1995] I.C.R. 65 at 70 *per* Mummery J.). Finally, the tribunal must act in compliance with natural justice and the Convention rights of the parties (*CCS 5301/02*, para.14).

It is for the chairman to determine the procedure to be followed by the tribunal. In doing so the chairman will be guided by the rules contained in the Act and the regulations made under it, as well as by the general philosophy of the tribunal. Whatever procedure is adopted, the chairman must ensure that it is fair and all the members of the tribunal, including the chairman, must give their undivided attention to the proceedings (*R. v Marylebone Magistrates' Court Ex p. Joseph, The Times,* May 7, 1993). The decision whether or not to announce the tribunal's decision orally on the day of the hearing is a matter of procedure in connection with the hearing and falls within the chairman's power under this paragraph (*CDLA 15227/96*, para.10).

In *CIB 2058/04*, para.13, the Commissioner said that the purpose of the power conferred by this paragraph is to ensure a good order and efficiency and it must be exercised in order to further that purpose. He distinguished between efficiency and effectiveness, emphasising that chairmen had to exercise their power in a way that allowed competent representatives to operate effectively. This decision is authority for the wider proposition that the power must be exercised in a way that is consistent with allowing all those present the opportunity to fulfil their proper roles.

The power to control the procedure is a case management power. It is concerned with procedure: *Care First Partnership Ltd v Roffey* [2001] I.C.R. 87.

Regulations 46 and 48 expressly provide wide powers for striking out cases, but it is not possible to avoid the procedures laid down in those regulations by acting under the general power to control the procedure at the hearing. So, the power does not confer jurisdiction to strike out a case for having no prospect of success (*ibid.*) or for want of prosecution: *Kelly v Ingersoll-Rand Co Ltd* [1982] I.C.R. 476.

*The inquisitorial approach*

The general philosophy for the conduct of tribunals is usually labelled the "inquisitorial approach." This phrase has been useful in distancing tribunal procedure from that operated in a court, but it is a misleading label in so far as it may suggest that there is a single model of inquisitorial approach which is to be applied. There is no such model, only a general descriptive phrase which reflects the broad consensus of how such tribunals should be conducted and around which chairmen have developed their own styles of procedure. The Commissioners' decisions have provided some guidance on what is involved, but this leaves ample scope for the initiative of individual chairmen.

The task for chairmen of all tribunals is to develop a procedure suited to the circumstances of the tribunals which they chair. One power which might be exercised under this approach is to order an oral hearing under reg.39(5), although this power is given to a chairman and not to the tribunal.

In *CSC 2/94*, para.20 the Commissioner decided that the procedure in a tribunal is primarily inquisitorial in so far as the issues raised are between the absent parent and the person with care, on the one hand, and the child support officer, on the other, but that the procedure might be primarily adversarial if the issues raised were primarily between the absent parent and the person with care. Unfortunately the Commissioner's reasoning depended in part on the absence in that case of any detailed notification of the basis of the child support officer's decision. This decision does, however, indicate that the procedure should be adapted to the circumstances of the appeal and provides support for the approach to procedure suggested in the preceding paragraphs.

Chairmen must work out the appropriate procedure within a threefold framework. First, there is the general philosophy set in the tribunals, second the rules laid down by the Act and the regulations, and third their views of the proper role for themselves and the tribunals which they chair. The Act and the regulations set the framework around which the general philosophy and individual procedures must be structured. Thus, for example, the power to summon witnesses and to order the production of documents provides a stronger framework for the exercise of an inquisitorial function than would otherwise be possible. However, the interpretation and application of the Act and the regulations will be informed by the general philosophy of the Service and by the individual chairman's views of the proper procedure. Thus, for example, the scope of reg.38(2) will in practice be determined in part by how chairman see the proper scope of their role in controlling the parties.

The chairman must also have regard in developing an appropriate procedure to the circumstances in which it must be applied. Again, there are differences from the social security context. There is in a child support case a greater conflict of interest between appellant and respondent than exists between the adjudication officer and the appellant in a social security tribunal. A former President of the Independent Tribunal Service, Judge Derek Holden, said that the most difficult task would be to apply an inquisitorial jurisdiction in an adversarial context. The parties are also more likely to be represented than in a social security case, so that tribunals will be able to take a more hands off approach if the parties are represented, but the chairmen will need to be alert to prevent legal representatives adopting styles or following procedures by analogy to the courts which are not appropriate in the tribunal context.

An inquisitorial approach is needed in order to ensure that all sides of a case are considered. It is not affected by the existence of a right of appeal to a higher court or by the nature of the issues that arise for consideration (*CIS 1459/03*, para.26). The procedure adopted must not be so informal as to prevent this being done. See *Dyason v Secretary of State for the Environment. The Times*, February 9, 1998.

The decisions of the courts and the Commissioners give a little guidance as to the proper exercise of the inquisitorial function. The tribunal is not entitled to sit back and act as referee between the rival contentions of the opposing parties as would be the case in a typical court procedure (*R. v Deputy Industrial Injuries Commissioner Ex p. Moore* [1965] 1 All E.R. 81 at 93, *per* Diplock L.J.) and it should disabuse representatives of any erroneous views on which their arguments are based (*Dennis v United Kingdom Central Council for Nursing, Midwifery and Health Visiting, The Times*. April 2, 1993). If it identifies a relevant point, it should be followed up and a decision reached, even if it has not been raised by the parties. A tribunal cannot limit its powers of investigation on account of the nature of the issue, for example, that it involves questioning a party about the possibility of a sexual relationship (*CIS 87/93*, para.13, also reported as *Re J (Income Support: Cohabitation)* [1995] 1 F.L.R. 660). The tribunal is also expected to pick up obvious and self evident points which arise. However, the parties are not entitled to rely upon the expertise of the tribunal to discharge the burdens of proof which properly rest on the parties themselves. Nor should a tribunal set off on a fishing expedition into the facts on the offchance that something relevant may turn up. This is especially so if the evidence has been stated with certainty (see generally *R(SB) 2/83*, paras 10–11 and *CSSB 470/89*, para.7). It is for the tribunal to reach conclusions on questions of fact and to decide whether there is sufficient evidence to do so. A Commissioner has no power to intervene unless the tribunal's decision is so unreasonable as to be perverse, and a party who choses not to attend cannot complain about the lack of oral evidence that might have been given (*CSA 1/95*, para.3). Likewise officers (and it is suggested parties with competent representatives) cannot expect to appeal successfully if they have failed to adduce the right evidence, failed to ask the right questions or failed to advance the right arguments (*CDLA 7980/95*, para.11). Despite these statements it is the consistent practice of the Commissioners to require tribunals to deal with all legal issues which are raised by the facts before them and are relevant to the decisions which they make, and decisions which fail to do so are regularly overturned on appeal. However, the duty on tribunals to exercise an inquisitorial approach is confined within sensible limits concentrating on questions which arise directly from the evidence or from further investigations which are reasonably called for by that evidence (*CIS 264/93*, para.12) and tribunals are not expected to go to absurd lengths in the exercise of this approach (*CA 60/93*, para.23). A tribunal need not go beyond what is fair and reasonable and must decide whether further investigation is likely to serve a useful purpose (*R. v National Insurance Commissioner Ex p. Viscusi* [1974] 2 All E.R. 724 at 731 and 732, *per* Lord Denning M.R. and Buckley L.J. respectively). These considerations, though, only set the bounds on the duty imposed on tribunals; they do not limit their power to investigate beyond these limits if they wish (*CIS 264/93*, para.12).

In *R(CS) 5/98* the Commissioner drew a distinction between (a) an argument in the submission that on the evidence available an officer's decision might be wrong and (b) an argument that on the evidence available it was wrong. The Commissioner criticised submissions written in the form (a) as being unhelpful to an unrepresented party iin that it did not make clear what additional evidence was required (para.8). In respect of a argument in form (a), the Commissioner held that the tribunal was not in error of law for failing to deal with the point when, in the absence of both parents, there was no evidence to justify altering the officer's decision (para.9). The Commissioner did not explain why the tribunal should not have sought further evidence directly from the the party concerned or through the child support officer. This approach is capable of being exploited by a party who believes that a decision may be incorrectly advantageous through the simple expedient of refraining from attending the tribunal. It is suggested that this aspect of this decision should be treated with caution and certainly limited to cases where the party concerned is not present at the hearing. In respect of an argument in form (b), the Commissioner held that the tribunal was under a duty to deal with it and its decision was wrong in law for failing to do so (para.11).

Commissioners speak in the context of deciding whether there has been an error of law to justify setting aside a tribunal decision. Their views set the limits within which the tribunal is expected to act if its decision is to withstand an appeal. Their views may, therefore, understate the role which tribunals should ideally play. The atmosphere should be as relaxed and informal as is consistent with the proper exercise of a judicial function and certainly more so than in a court. In particular, the tribunal is expected to fulfill an enabling role especially with an unrepresented party. This involves setting an appropriate atmosphere: the parties should feel comfortable and able to put across what they wish to say. It also involves helping the parties to understand what is required: the parties should be helped to follow the procedure, to understand the matters which are relevant to the appeal and to present the best case possible on their behalf.

In exercising the inquisitorial approach the tribunal is not limited to the terms of the appeal.

In practice the operation of the inquisitorial approach is limited where one of the parties does not attend (*CIB 17622/96*, para.8), although in such a case the tribunal will be anxious to ensure that all matters of possible benefit to that party are investigated as thoroughly as possible in his absence. Tribunals are also entitled to vary their approach according to whether or not the parties are competently represented (*CSDLA 336/00*). The approach should be more strenuously followed on behalf of a party who is unrepresented (*R(I) 6/69*, para.7). However, where parties are represented, the tribunal is entitled to take a less active role and to accept without further investigation concessions made and accepted by all parties (*CSA 2/94*, para.7; *CDLA 12150/96*, para.7). However, concessions do not bind a tribunal, unless, on the information available, they have been correctly made, and they may in any case be withdrawn (*R(IS) 14/93*, para.7). A concession may be accepted unless it is clearly bad (*CDLA 267/94*, para.8). Where the concession is one of fact rather than of law, the fact that it is made by a competent representative will be relevant in deciding whether it should be accepted. There is no need to record findings in respect of issues covered by a concession (*CDLA 12150/96*, para.8).

A tribunal is not required to embark upon an investigation merely on account of general allegations, such as to a party's dishonesty, which are frequently made on and following a marital breakup, unless there are reasons to put the tribunal on inquiry (*CCS 12/94*, para.46).

The proper implementation of the inquisitorial approach and the enabling role may mean that parties may be interrupted in the course of the presentation of their case. This does not consititute bias on the part of the tribunal (*R(SB) 6/82*, para.6). Likewise, the asking of probing questions is proper in the exercise of the tribunal's inquisitorial approach and is not of itself indicative of bias (*R(S) 4/82*, para.27).

The inquisitorial approach survives the changes made under the Social Security Act 1998, although its scope is limited by s.20(7) of the Child Support Act 1991 (*CDLA 4977/01*, paras 12–26).

*Appeal by way of rehearing*

3.378   In a broad sense every appeal is by way of rehearing with the only differences lying in the evidence and arguments that may be considered (*CIS 16701/96*, para.24). In a narrower sense the courts have distinguished two types of appeal and this distinction has been adopted in the language of the Commissioners' decisions.

The appeal strictly so called determines whether the decision under appeal was correct on the evidence before the person or body making the decision, subject perhaps to a limited right to make additional findings on the appeal. The other type of appeal is an appeal by way of rehearing (*Ponnamma v Arumogan* [1905] A.C. 383 at 390, *per* Lord Davey). Appeals before an appeal tribunal are by way of rehearing (*R(SB) 1/82*, para.10). This has not been altered by the changes made under the Social Security Act 1998 (*CDLA 4977/01*, paras 12–26). The rehearing must, subject to s.20(7) of the Act, cover all issues arising on the appeal. The case has to be proved again, so the burden of proof is as in the decision under appeal (*Rugman v Drover* [1950] 2 All E.R. 575 at 576, *per* Lord Goddard C.J.). The tribunal is not limited to the evidence, arguments and grounds that were before the Secretary of State (*R(SB) 33/83*, para.19; *CSCS 2/94*, paras 20 and 22; *CSCS 3/94*, para.14). However, the appeal must be considered in the "circumstances pertaining" at the relevant time (see s.20(7)(b) of the Act and *Northern Ireland Trailers Ltd v County Borough of Preston* [1972] 1 All E.R. 260 at 265, *per* Lord Widgery C.J., and *Rugman* above at 576, *per* Lord Goddard C.J.).

Two issues arise on the circumstances pertaining at the relevant time. The first is the scope of the issues which may be determined. This is considered in the general note to s.20(7) of the Act. The second is whether the tribunal may apply changes in the law which have occurred since the date of the original decision which was subject to the review decision on appeal before the tribunal. It is sometimes said that on appeal the tribunal should apply the substantive law as it stood at the date of the original decision but the procedural law as it stands at the date the issue is decided (*R(S) 3/93*, para.20). This, however, is an oversimplification. A new law is more likely to be applied on the appeal if it is procedural (*Att-Gen v Vernazza* [1960] 3 All E.R. 97), but less likely if it is substantive (*Wilson v Dagnall* [1972] 2 All E.R. 44 at 53 and 54, *per* Megaw and Stephenson L.JJ. respectively). However, the correct approach is not to seek to label the change in law as "procedural" or "substantive". The issue is determined by the appropriate interpretation of the relevant legislation. Difficulty can only arise where the matter is not clearly covered in the legislation. In cases where the wording is not clear due regard must be given to the common law presumption which is also contained in s.16(1)(c) Interpretation Act 1978 that clear language is necessary before legislation is interpreted to take away or impair any existing right or obligation (*Yew Bon Tew v Kenderaan Bas Mara* [1982] 3 All E.R. 833). Relevant factors to be considered will include the value of any rights affected, the potential impact on those rights of the legislation in question, the degree of fairness or unfairness of adversely affecting those rights, the clarity of the legislative language and the circumstances in which the law was enacted (*L'Office Cherifien des Phosphates v Yamashita-Shinnihon Steamship Co Ltd* [1994] 1 All E.R. 20 at 30, *per* Lord Mustill). It is unlikely that the application of any particular procedure would be of such value that a party would be held to have a vested right in that procedure being followed despite subsequent changes in the law, but the existence and extent of a person's liability to pay or receive child support maintenance as at a particular date would be likely to be sufficient to justify the presumption being applied. See also the analysis of the House of Lords in *Wilson v First County Trust Ltd* [2003] 4 All E.R. 97.

The application of the above authorities has recently been confused by *CI 337/92* where the Commissioner appears to have interpreted them in such a way that the question of the scope of the application of any particular legislative provision is to be determined according to the effect of the provision on the facts of any particular case. This approach is more akin to applying a kind of estoppel against the statute according to its operation given the facts of a particular case than to the process of statutory interpretation as normally understood. Moreover it is at variance with *L'Office Cherifien des Phosphates* above at 32 where Lord Mustill said, "we are concerned here not with the merits of the particular case, but with the generality of rights which Parliament must have contemplated would suffer if the section took effect retrospectively".

Care needs to be taken when applying social security decisions on this issue as, in the case of open-ended claims, the claim continues down to the date of the final disposal of the case, with the effect that the tribunal may take account of any changes in legislation (*R(I) 4/84*, paras 9–10, relying on the power to deal with questions first arising which tribunals do not possess, *R(I) 6/84*, paras 10–11 and *CI 309/92*).

### Evidence

The courts have said that tribunals are not bound by the strict rules on admissibility of evidence which apply in the courts, especially the criminal courts. (*R. v Deputy Industrial Injuries Commissioner Ex p. Moore* [1965] 1 All E.R. 81; *Wednesbury Corporation v Ministry of Housing and Local Government (No. 2)* [1965] 3 All E.R. 571 at 579; *T A Miller Ltd v Minister of Housing and Local Government* [1968] 2 All E.R. 633; *R. v Hull Prison Board of Visitors Ex p. St Germain (No. 2)* [1979] 3 All E.R. 545 at 552). The Commissioners themselves have repeatedly held the same (see, for example, *R(U) 5/77*, para. 3 and many of the cases cited below). As stated by Lord Widgery C.J. in *R. v Greater Birmingham Supplementary Benefit Appeal Tribunal Ex p. Khan* [1979] 3 All E.R. 759 at 763 the test is this: "It is open to the tribunal in this particular type of case to take into account all the circumstances, so far as they are probative, so far as they help to conclude proof of the truth in the individual case." In *Mahon v Air New Zealand* [1984] 3 All E.R. 201 at 210, in the context of a wholly different type of tribunal, Lord Diplock put the matter in terms of natural justice rather than in terms of evidence. The Privy Council, for which his lordship was delivering judgment, held that the tribunal was bound by the rules of natural justice and that the rules of evidence were not part of those rules. The obligation on the tribunal was that each of its findings of fact should be based on some material tending logically to show the existence of that fact. A tribunal may only rely on its own knowledge or expertise as a basis for finding a fact provided that it discloses its knowledge or expertise to the parties so that they may comment on the facts that may be founded on it (*Norbrook Laboratories (GB) Ltd v Health and Safety Executive, The Times*, February 23, 1998 and *Richardson v Solihull Metropolitan Borough Council, The Times*, April 10, 1998).

The precise limits of these statements have never been determined. It is not clear, for example, whether they are intended to override the rules on privilege. Generally, such statements identify the proper emphasis for the tribunal as being on the probative value of the evidence and its relevance to the appeal, rather than on technical rules as to admissibility. This must, though, be read subject to the limitations on the power of a chairman to summon witnesses or to order the production of documents contained in reg.43. At least four more specific things are also clear: (i) Hearsay evidence is admissible: (ii) So is evidence which was not before the Secretary of State: (iii) Tribunals are also entitled to apply presumptions (see, for example, *CM 209/87*, para.13); (iv) Opinon evidence is admissible (*CDLA 2014/04* para. 9). (i) and (ii) are considered in more detail below.

Legal professional privilege applies in adversarial jurisdictions (even those where the proceedings are conducted in a non-adversarial spirit), but in non-adversarial jurisdictions litigation privilege never arises, although the privilege between solicitor and client remains (*Re L (Police Investigation: Privilege)* [1996] 1 F.L.R. 731). Children Act proceedings are non-adversarial *(ibid.)*: judges in practice adopt an interventionist style in directions hearings and at the substantive hearing the judge has substantially greater control over the deployment of evidence and argument than a judge sitting, for example, in the Queen's Bench Division (*Oxfordshire County Council v M.* [1994] 1 F.L.R. 175 at 187–188, *per* Steyn L.J.). It is unclear (i) how, if at all, the rules of privilege apply in a jurisdiction in which the strict rules of evidence do not apply and (ii) whether or not proceedings before a tribunal are adversarial. For a further discussion of disclosure see the general note to reg.43(1).

A district chairman or an appeal tribunal may give directions for evidence to be produced within a particular timetable. If evidence if produced late, it does not follow that the tribunal is entitled to exclude that evidence. The tribunal's response to the late production of the evidence must be a proportionate one that takes account of the right to a fair hearing for all the parties to the proceedings, the purpose underlying the directions, the reasons for lateness and all the circumstances of the case (*CCS 4253/04*, paras 9–16).

The chairman should admit any evidence which has any probative value. It will then be for the tribunal as a whole to decide on the appropriate weight to be given to it. The chairman may exclude evidence which is clearly irrelevant, immaterial or repetitive (*Wednesbury Corporation*, above at 579 and *R(SB) 6/82*, para.5). One Commissioner has decided that evidence that has been used in family proceedings is admissible even if leave to disclose it has not been obtained from the court under r.4.23 of the Family Proceeding Rules 1991 (*CCS 4438/01*, paras 6–11); another Commissioner has decided that this evidence can be used if it comes from ancillary relief proceedings, but not if it comes from proceedings relating to children (*CCS 3749/03*). The fact that evidence has been excluded should be recorded by the chairman in the notes of proceedings. However, whether something is irrelevant or immaterial is not always easily judged before the evidence has been heard. In deciding whether or not to exclude evidence, chairmen should be careful not to create the impression that the party seeking to adduce the evidence has not received a fair hearing, while ensuring that other parties have no cause to feel likewise if the evidence is admitted (*R(SB) 6/82*, para.5). Wrongly excluding evidence may amount to an error of law (*ibid.* at para.4). Evidence may be excluded if it is illegible, but only after reasonable efforts have been made to obtain a legible copy (*CDLA 2880/98*, para.8).

Despite these words of caution, the courts have accepted that power is needed to control and contain proceedings. Chairmen have the power and the duty to act so as to curb prolixity and repetition and to prevent irrelevance, discursiveness and the oppression of witnesses (*R. v Whybrow, The Times*, February 14, 1994). Although they have no discretion to exclude relevant evidence, chairmen are entitled to balance the relevance of the evidence against such considerations as the need to keep the length of the hearing within reasonable bounds and to conduct the proceedings with due sensitivity to the wider public interest, and the validity of their actions will be judged by the same test as would be applied to determine the validity of the exercise of a discretion (*Vernon v Bosley, The Times*, April 8, 1994). Expert evidence to support the reliability of evidence given on oath should be excluded in all but the most exceptional cases (*R. v Robinson (Raymond)* [1994] 3 All E.R. 346). Exceptionally expert evidence may be given as to the credibility of a child as a witness, provided that the tribunal does not lose sight of the fact that the weight to be given to any piece of evidence is a matter for it to decide (*Re N (a Minor) (Child abuse: Evidence), The Times*, March 25, 1996, and *Re M and R (Child Abuse: Evidence)* [1996] 2 F.L.R. 195). For the reluctance of the courts to hold that the appearance of bias has been created by even-handed decisions relating to the management of proceedings, see the introductory general note to these Regulations.

Appeals before a tribunal are by way of a rehearing (*R(SB) 1/82*, para.10). Accordingly, evidence which was not before the Secretary of State is admissible (*R(U) 5/77*, para.3; *R(FIS) 1/82*, para.20; *R(SB) 33/83*, para.19; *CSCS 2/94*, para.20). When such evidence is presented for the first time at the hearing, the tribunal should consider whether an adjournment is necessary in order to allow the other parties to consider it and prepare themselves properly to meet it (see the approach of the Commissioner in *R(I) 6/51*, para.5). In order to avoid adjournments, it is preferable that such evidence is disclosed in advance of the hearing (*R(I) 6/51*, para.6 and *R(I) 36/56*, para.10). A chairman may wish to consider using the power to give directions under reg.5 to require any fresh evidence to be disclosed in advance. In exercising this power, care will be needed to avoid imposing an unrealistic burden on an unrepresented party. It will also be necessary to be aware of the possibility that there may not be time before the hearing to disclose evidence in rebuttal of the further evidence disclosed.

Evidence may be oral or written. Any matters of fact stated by the appellant in the grounds of appeal will constitute written evidence (*R(SB) 10/81*, para.6). If the evidence is oral, the chairman should keep a note of it. That note should distinguish clearly between evidence and other matters and should make clear who gave the evidence (*R(SB) 8/84*, para.25(2) and (6)). If the evidence is written, copies should be made available to the tribunal and all the parties. The chairman should note the receipt of the document in the record of proceedings and ensure that a copy is placed on the tribunal file. Although, in appropriate circumstances, written evidence may carry more weight than oral evidence, what a party or a witness says is nonetheless evidence. There is no rule that evidence must be written rather than oral, or that the former necessarily carries more weight than the latter. In *CCS 499/95*, para.9 the Commissioner held that only written evidence of the validity of a parent's entitlement to income support was acceptable. With respect to the Commissioner, whatever the practical benefits of evidence being in writing in such a case, the requirement that it must be in writing is pure invention.

If written evidence is put before the tribunal, its provenance should be disclosed, since this may affect the weight to be attached to it (*R(G) 1/63*, para.12). Either the identity of the author of a statement, or the fact that it is anonymous, should be disclosed (*CS 55/88*). If it is desired not to disclose the source of information, it may not be relied upon (*CDLA 14884/96*, para.10), subject of course to the cases where express legislative provision is made for this (see reg.44 and reg.8 of the Departure Regulations).

There is no requirement that evidence must be corroborated (*R(I) 2/51*, para.7 and *R(SB) 33/85*, para.14). To insist on corroboration would be impracticable (*R(U) 12/56*, para.8). The real reason for the admissibility of oral uncorroborated evidence, however, is that there is in essence nothing necessarily wrong with it. Although corroboration is not relevant to the admissibility of evidence, it may be relevant to its strength. Where evidence is weak, the presence of independent corroboration will increase its weight.

Hearsay evidence is evidence of which the witness does not have firsthand knowledge, for example, if a witness says "X told me that he earned £2000 a month," this is direct firsthand evidence of the fact that X made the statement but only hearsay evidence of X's earnings. Hearsay evidence is admissible (for example, *T A Miller Ltd*, above) and in practice plays an important role in tribunals. The fact that evidence is hearsay goes to its weight, not to its admissibility (*CI 97/49(KL)*, para.6; *R(G) 1/51*, para.5; *R(U) 12/56*, para.8 and *R(SB) 5/82*, para.9). In assessing its weight the tribunal should be aware of the limitations and dangers of hearsay evidence: the originator of the evidence is not present to be questioned and there is a risk that as information is passed from person to person it may become distorted. The tribunal will need to establish, by hearing evidence, any factors relevant to the appropriate weight to give to it. The following should be considered: (i) the reliability of the original source of the evidence; (ii) how many people it has passed through (*R(A) 7/89*, para.8); (iii) the reliability of the intervening parties; and (iv) whether more direct evidence could be obtained, bearing in mind the powers under reg.43 to summon witnesses and to order the production of documents. If the tribunal accepts hearsay evidence, it is wise for the chairman to record in the reasons for decision that the tribunal had regard to the dangers and limitations of hearsay evidence.

The evidence may be given by a party or by a witness. A tribunal member may be called as a witness and the evidence is admissible (*CIS 661/94*, para.13). However, according to the Commissioners, evidence given by a representative without personal knowledge on a *contested* matter is not evidence on which a tribunal is entitled to rely (*R(I) 36/61*, para.18; *R(I) 13/74*, para.9; *R(SB) 10/86*, para.5). This sharp distinction between the status of witness and of representative may make sense in court, but, as noted in the general note to para.(8), it is not always easy to keep the roles of witness and representative distinct in a tribunal. Moreover, there is no reason in principle why in a tribunal context the evidence of a representative should be treated any differently from that of anyone else. In practice the rulings in the above decisions are not followed. Sometimes the representative is in a position to give firsthand evidence of the relevant matters. Where the evidence is hearsay, there is no reason to treat it more harshly than any other hearsay evidence. The chairman may, as part of the enabling role, allow a representative to give the evidence in an orderly manner on behalf of a party who may be nervous or rambling and who then confirms that evidence and answers any follow up questions. This is an acceptable practice which is consistent with the spirit of *R(I) 36/61* and *R(SB) 10/86*. Moreover, it is permitted by the regulations: para.(8) provides that representatives have all the rights and powers of the person represented, which includes the right to be heard, and para.(11) provides that any person entitled to be heard may give evidence.

Unlike the position in a court, any witness can give evidence on a matter of opinion. However, tribunals are likely to give most weight to the opinion of an expert witness, for example, on whether a person is likely to suffer undue distress under s.46(3) of the Act. Expert witnesses who give written or oral evidence are under the following duties: (i) The evidence must be independent; (ii) It must be objective and unbiased; (ii) Facts or assumptions on which it is based should be stated, as should any facts which would detract from the expert's conclusion; (iv) Questions or issues which fall outside the witness's expertise should be made clear; (v) It should contain any appropriate qualifications to the opinion expressed; (vi) Any subsequent change of view after the expert's report has been written should be disclosed (*National Justice Compania Naviera SA v Prudential Assurance Co Ltd, The Times*, March 5, 1993). There is no obligation to grant a party a postponement or adjournment in order to allow expert evidence to be obtained (*Winchester Cigarette Machinery Ltd v Payne. The Times*, October 19, 1993), and a chairman has a duty to ensure that no more expert evidence is produced than is necessary (*Re G (Minors) (Medical Experts)* [1994] 2 F.L.R. 291). As to the tribunal's power to compel an expert to attend as a witness see the general note to reg.10(1) of these Regulations. For a discussion of the weight to be given to expert evidence see the following section of this note.

*Evaluation of evidence*

All evidence that is admitted must be accorded apporpriate weight in order to determine first whether it is accepted and second its significance. The task of evaluating evidence is often more difficult for a tribunal than for a court, which may be cushioned from some of the more difficult decisions by excluding certain categories of evidence. The task for the tribunal is to make a decision, however difficult that may be. Conflicts of evidence do not justify the tribunal reaching a compromise, for example, by fixing a figure between the two sums alleged to represent a parent's income (see *R(U) 2/72*, para.8). Although assessing the weight of evidence is a familiar task for lawyers, it may not be so straightforward for a lay member. While respecting each member's equal weight in the evaluation of the evidence, the chairman's experience will be helpful in assisting the other members to assess the appropriate weight to be accorded to particular pieces of evidence.

The weight to be accorded to a piece of evidence is a matter for the decision-maker (*R. v Deputy Industrial Injuries Commissioner Ex p. Moore* [1965] 1 All E.R. 81 at 94, *per* Lord Diplock) and the appropriate weight is determined by applying common sense (*Lord Advocate v Lord Blantyre (1879) 4 App. Cas. 770 at 792, per* Lord Blackburn and *R(DLA) 1/95*, para.5). The weighing of evidence always involves considering its strengths and weaknesses as against the test of balance of probabilities (*Karanakaran v Secretary of State for Home Department* [2003] 3 All E.R. 449 at 477 *per* Sedley L.J.). Where there is conflicting evidence, a comparative assessment is also involved. Where the evidence conflicts, a preference for one piece inevitably involves a rejection of another. Preference and rejection are two sides of the same coin. See *CDLA 5342/97*, para.16. There are no restrictions on the grounds on which a person's evidence may be rejected. "The tribunal never has to believe the say so of a witness before it, although they must have a reason for disbelieving" (*R. v Social Security Commissioner Ex p. Bibi*, unreported, May 23, 2000, *per* Collins J. at para.33).

The factors which would have led to the evidence being excluded at common law may be relevant when assessing the probative worth of evidence heard by a tribunal (*CDLA 2014/04* para.12).

There are no hard and fast rules and each piece of evidence must be weighed on its merits in the circumstances of a particular case. In doing so three key criteria about the witness should be considered: (i) How well placed was the witness to form an objective view of the subject matter of the evidence? (ii) How reliable is the witness's recollection? (iii) How good is the witness's capacity to convey precisely that recollection? Having considered the reliability of the witness, attention can be turned to the witness's evidence. Factors to consider include: (a) is the witness's evidence consistent; (b) how inherently credible is it; and (c) is it consistent with the other evidence before the tribunal? Other factors will also affect the weight likely to be accorded a particular piece of evidence. Thus, it is likely that direct evidence will be given more weight than hearsay (see above for the special problem of evaluating

**3.379**

hearsay evidence), that written evidence will be valued more highly than oral, that precise, specific detailed evidence will carry more weight than general evidence, and that the more contemporaneous the evidence the more highly it will be valued.

Advice on assessing the credibility of a witness's evidence was given in *Heffer v Tiffin Green (a Firm)*, *The Times*, December 28, 1998 by Henry L.J. The evidence should always be tested by reference to objective facts proved independently of the evidence, in particular by reference to any relevant documents, and particular regard should be paid to the witness's possible motives and the overall probabilities. The tribunal should also take account of the extent to which it was within a party's power to produce evidence or to contradict evidence produced by another party (*Blatch v Archer* (1774) 98 English Reports 969 at 970, quoted in *Fairchild v Glenhaven Funeral Services Ltd* [2002] 3 All E.R. 305 at para.13). The evidence of a witness must be considered realistically and as a whole, taking account of the fact that a single lie may not undermine the evidence as a whole (*EPI Environmental Technologies Inc v Symphony Plastic Technologies plc*, *The Times*, January 14, 2005).

Members of tribunals may have specialist or local knowledge. They are always entitled to rely on that knowledge, but in some circumstances it may only be used if it has been disclosed to the parties so that they may comment on it or try to refute it. Whether or not disclosure is required depends on the use that is made of the knowledge. In *Dugdale v Kraft Foods Ltd* [1977] I.C.R. 49 at 54–55 Phillips J. suggested a three-fold analysis. (i) The knowledge may be used without being disclosed in order to understand, analyse and weigh the evidence. So, a member with specialist accountancy knowledge could rely on that knowledge and experience in order to interpret a set of accounts. (ii) It may also be used without being disclosed in order to fill in uncontroversial gaps in the evidence. So, members could take account of their knowledge of council tax rates in a particular locality. (iii) However, it must be disclosed if it is to be used as evidence that is contrary to the case presented by one of the parties. So, a member's knowledge that overtime was available from a particular employer would have to be disclosed if one of the parties had given evidence to the contrary. In addition to *Dugdale*, see the decisions of the courts in *Reynolds v Llanelly Associated Tinplate Co Ltd* [1948] 1 All E.R. 140; *Metropolitan Properties Co (FGC) Ltd v Lannon* [1968] 3 All E.R. 304 at 309, *per* Lord Denning M.R.; *Wetherall v Harrision* [1976] 1 All E.R. 241; *Hammington v Berker Sportcraft Ltd* [1980] I.C.R. 248; *Norbrook Laboratories (GB) Ltd v Health and Safety Executive*, *The Times*, February 23, 1998 and *Richardson v Solihull Metropolitan Borough Council*, *The Times*, April 10, 1998. These decisions have been followed by Commissioners in *R(S) 1/94*, *CIS 278/92*, para.12 and *CS 175/92*. See also *CCS 15773/96*, para.13.

Whenever specialist or local knowledge has been disclosed the chairman's record of proceedings should note that it was done and that the parties had a chance to comment on it. Disclosure does not necessarily mean that an adjournment will be necessary so that further evidence may be produced (*R(I) 3/96*, para.8).

As often, there is a difference between law and practice. It may be wise, and will certainly remove any ground for argument, if knowledge that is relied on is disclosed in all cases.

Facts are of two kinds: primary facts and inferences. Primary facts are those matters on which the tribunal has evidence, whether direct or hearsay. The tribunal may, for example, hear evidence that a parent has been seen driving a delivery van. If it accepts this evidence, it is a primary fact. Inferences are of two kinds: evidential and forensic. Evidential inferences are those matters which the tribunal deduces from the primary facts. Thus, in the above example, it might deduce from the primary facts that the parent was employed as a delivery driver. See *British Launderers' Research Association v Central Middlesex Assessment Committee* [1949] 1 All E.R. 21 at 25, *per* Denning L.J.

Forensic inferences are those drawn as a result of a party's behaviour in relation to the proceedings. They were considered in detail by the Commissioner in *CCS*

*3757/04.* He set out a three stage process. The first issue to consider is whether an inference is necessary (*ibid.*, paras 15–18). The Commissioner explained through a series of examples that it is only necessary to draw an adverse forensic inference if there is no other way that an issue may be dealt with. It may be possible to find facts by relying on the evidence of another party or the burden of proof. Or it may be possible to make use of a default maintenance decision. An adverse inference is only necessary if none of these other possibilities is available. If an adverse inference is permissible, the second issue is how it is taken into account (paras 20–23). An inference is always a process of reasoning from evidence and conduct. The party's conduct that leads to the adverse inference is taken into account in assessing the probative worth of the evidence as a whole and in drawing inferences from the evidence available. The third issue is whether an adverse inference is permissible (paras 24–29). It is always relevant to consider all likely explanations for the failure to co-operate, as they may not all be indicative of the content of the evidence withheld. It is also relevant to consider whether the party understood the risk of not co-operating, which in some cases may require a warning to have been given by the tribunal.

If a party refuses to co-operate with the appeal tribunal, it may take that into account in deciding what inferences it was permissible to draw from the evidence. This includes: refusing to answer questions (*Re O (Care Proceedings: Evidence)* [2004] 1 F.L.R. 161 at paras 13 and 16); withholding written information in the possession of or available to the party, and failing to agree to blood or DNA testing for paternity (*Al-Khatib v Masry* [2002] 1 F.L.R. 1053 especially at paras 93–6; *Secretary of State for Work and Pensions v Jones* [2004] 1 F.L.R. 282 at paras 11–15); failing to make appropriate enquiries as to information relevant to the proceedings (*R(SB) 34/83*); and failing without good explanation to attend the hearing of an appeal or failing to arrange for witnesses to attend (*Secretary of State for Health v C (Tribunal: Failure to draw inference), The Times,* January 30, 2003).

Deciding what forensic inference to draw includes, in appropriate cases, the judgment that the person in default has made the calculation that a decision based on the evidence available will be more favourable than one that would be made on full disclosure (*Al-Khatib v Masry* [2002] 1 F.L.R. 1053 especially at paras 93–6). However, this assumes that the evidence is known to the person. If it is not given until the hearing, that will not be so. The inference must be based on a rational process of reasoning from evidence before the tribunal, including evidence of failure to make disclosure or full disclosure. There is no authority for making a finding that is purely penal (*CCS 2623/99*, para.34) or one based purely on guesswork (*CCS 7966/95*, para.11).

The findings of fact should record the tribunal's findings of primary fact relevant to the appeal. The reasons should record why evidence was rejected (*R(SB)8/84,* para:25(3)). They should also record why one piece of evidence has been preferred to another (*CSSB 212/87*, para.3). Any inferences which the tribunal drew from the primary facts should also be recorded. Failure to record any of these will amount to an error of law.

Although the weighing of evidence is a matter for the tribunal, there are occasions when the tribunal must not reject evidence without giving the party who adduced it the opportunity to present additional supporting evidence. There is no definitive statement of when this will be required. However, it will be required where evidence is adduced which is not challenged or contadicted by any other party, comes from an apparently reliable source and is an essential element in the party's case (*Kriba v Secretary of State for the Home Department, The Times,* July 18, 1997).

If a tribunal bases its decision on an adverse assessment of the honesty or integrity of one of the parties, that party must have had adequate notice that this was a possibility. Usually the question of whether or not a party's evidence is accepted is central to the issue before the tribunal and the possibility of such a finding should reasonably be appreciated. In such cases it is impossible to construct a case for the person being given an opportunity to comment on a provisional view on this issue before the final decision is made (*CI 614/93*, para.10) and it is, therefore, unnecessary for the tribunal to draw attention to the matter (*Baron v Secretary of State for Social Services, per* May L.J. reported as an Appendix to *R(M) 6/86*). However, if the circumstances are such that the person may reasonably not appreciate that the issue of honesty or integrity is in the tribunal's mind, attention should be drawn to the possibility of such a finding so that evidence or argument may be advanced on that issue (*Mahon v Air New Zealand* [1984] 3 All E.R. 201 at 210, *per* Lord Diplock). This point was considered briefly in *CI 11126/95*, para.8. The Commissioner identified the key test to be applied as that of fairness, emphasised the need for there to be a sensible limit to the tribunal's duty to put every point to a witness or party, and drew a useful distinction between what the law requires and the appropriate practice for a tribunal to follow. Having said that, having allowed the appeal on a different basis, he did not need to express a decided opinion on this point, he went on:

> "It is sometimes very difficult to say when fairness demands that a claimant be given an opportunity to meet new points against him. It is, I think, good practice for appeal tribunals to err on the safe side by ensuring that claimants and their representatives have the chance to comment on matters which tend to go against them. But the law does not require the ludicrous result that an appeal tribunal has to draw a claimant's attention to every perceived weakness in his evidence."

*R(A) 7/89*, para.12 appears to suggest a wider requirement for tribunals to draw the possibility of such an adverse finding to the party's attention if this is being considered. However, that case was special in that it involved the combination of very remote hearsay, a party who suffered a degree of confusion, a provisional view already formed by the Board and a decision to be taken on written submissions only without the possibility of an oral hearing. Nevertheless, the decision may have some application where the parties will not be present, for example where the decision is taken by a chairman alone or where an application for the setting aside of a tribunal decision is being considered. It also emphasises that the general distinction drawn in the previous paragraph must be subject to qualification in exceptional circumstances.

Although the tribunal may consider expert evidence, the decision is for the tribunal itself and not the expert (*R. v Lanfear* [1968] 1 All E.R. 683 at 684–685, *per* Diplock L.J.). The tribunal is not bound to accept the expert's opinion if there is a proper basis for rejecting it in the other evidence before the tribunal, or if the evidence is such that the tribunal does not believe it or was not convinced by it (*Walton v The Queen* [1978] 1 All E.R. 542 at 547 *per* Lord Keith and *Dover District Council v Sherred* (1997) 29 H.L.R. 864). It is an error of law for the tribunal to accept the evidence merely because it comes from an expert (*Lanfear*, above). However, the tribunal's decision must be one which is based on a rational approach to the evidence so that, if the expert evidence on a particular point is unchallenged and there are no facts or circumstances to displace or cast doubt on it, the tribunal would commit an error of law if it failed to accept it (*R. v Matheson* [1958] 2 All E.R. 87 at 90, *per* Lord Goddard C.J.).

As to the role of expert evidence in assisting the tribunal to decide on the appropriate weight to be given to any piece of evidence see *Re M and R (Child Abuse: Evidence)* [1996] 2 F.L.R. 195 referred to in the previous section of this note.

### Estoppel

Estoppel consists of a series of rules that prevent a person from proving that a particular fact exists or from raising a particular issue. The rules are designed to operate in an adversarial jurisdiction. As tribunals take an inquisitorial approach to the proceedings, estoppel does not apply *(Thoday v Thoday* [1964] 1 All E.R. 341 at 351, *per* Diplock L.J.). However, tribunals and Commissioners operate by analogy with estoppel *(R(I) 9/63,* para.24). So close has the analogy been applied that Commissioners regularly refer directly to estoppel, omitting any reference to analogy *(CCS 1535/97,* para.26).

In child support law two issues have come before Commissioners in which a principle analogous to estoppel might be developed.

The first issue is whether it is possible to prevent an officer or a tribunal from applying the legislation to the facts of the case. Commissioners have held that officers and tribunal carry out a statutory function and that nothing said or done by anyone (including an officer) can override the statutory duty to apply the law to the facts of the case *(R(CS) 2/97* and the authorities there relied on).

The second issue is whether a party may raise again an issue that has already been determined. The courts in dealing with cases involving children (in which an inquisitorial approach is taken) have developed the comments of Diplock L.J. in *Thoday,* above at 351 that similar rules to estoppel might be developed in inquisitorial jurisdictions. The courts have refused to introduce an absolute bar on an issue being considered again and have instead developed an approach based on the court's discretion as to the way the case is conducted. They seek to balance a variety of factors, such as (i) the public policy that disputes should be brought to an end, (ii) how central the issue was to the previous decision and (iii) whether it is likely that a different decision would be reached. See *Re B (Children Act Proceedings) (Issue Estoppel)* [1997] 1 F.L.R. 285 at 295–296, *per* Hale, J.

In *CCS 1535/97* paras 30–37 the Commissioner considered whether this approach should be taken in child support law, but concluded that it was neither necessary nor desirable, because there were sufficient devices available to officers, tribunals and Commissioners to confine the need to undertake a full reconsideration of a question that already been determined to those cases in which a sound and credible case has been made that the earlier decision might be wrong. In particular the Commissioner mentioned the following. (i) A party must meet the threshold in s.18(6) or s.19(1) before a review can be conducted and a sceptical attitude to changes of testimony is only to be expected and any delay in producing documents or giving oral evidence will have to be explained. The decision on the threshold and the decision on any review undertaken will be based on a consideration of the whole of the evidence available which will be weighed in the context of the history of the case. (ii) There are also procedural steps on an appeal to a tribunal which can be used. The appeal must contain a summary of the arguments relied on to support the contention that the decision was wrong: see reg.33. If the appeal is made out of time, the fact that the question raised has previously been determined by a tribunal is a relevant factor to take into account.

Any rules or approaches that are developed by tribunals and Commissioner must operate in the context of the child support legislation. Given the wide powers for decisions to be revised or superseded, including those implementing tribunal decisions, on the basis of error of fact or law, any principle developed by analogy with estoppel would have a limited application.

Lightman J. restated the principles in more general terms in *Westminster City Council v Haywood (No. 2)* [2000] 2 All E.R. 634 at 645–6, but did not take account of the family law authorities relied on in this note.

*Burdens and standard of proof*

The burden and standard of proof apply only to matters of fact, not to matters of evaluation or judgment *(Karanakaran v Secretary of State for Home Department* [2000] 3 All E.R. 449 at 477 *per* Sedley L.J.; *Secretary of State for the Home Department v Rehman* [2002] 1 All E.R. 122 at para.56 *per* Lord Hoffmann, and *R. (M) v Inner London Crown Court* [2003] 1 F.L.R. 994 at paras 41–44).

**3.380**

There are two burdens of proof. The legal burden determines which party shall bear the consequence of there being insufficient weight of evidence to establish a matter which arises for determination. The incidence of this burden, that is, the party who is to bear the burden, is ultimately a matter of policy. Although there are exceptions, the general policy underlying its incidence is to ensure the preservation of the status quo current at the time the decision is made unless a sufficient case can be made that it should be changed. (We are indebted to Terry Lynch for this insight.) The legal burden does not shift in the course of the appeal.

The incidence of the legal burden of proof in a child support appeal is as yet undecided. Reasoning from basic principles the position is as follows. Child support appeals are by way of rehearing. In such cases the incidence of the legal burden of proof is the same as in the case of the decision under appeal (*Rugman v Drover* [1950] 2 All E.R. 575 at 576, *per* Lord Goddard C.J.). Since that decision will have been a revision or supersession decision, the burden will be on the person who initiated it (*R(I) 1/71* para.16). However, in view of the similarity of a second tier review decision to an appeal, it may be that the burden will not be held to be on the party who sought the review but will remain the same as at the original decision.

The degree of certainty or probability that is necessary in order to discharge the burden of proof is determined by the standard of proof. The relevant standard is the civil standard which requires that a matter be established on the balance of probabilities (*CI 401/50(KL)*). This means that in order to prove a case the evidence must show that it is more likely than not. This is lower than the criminal standard which requires proof beyond reasonable doubt.

The balance of probabilities is not a constant, as the strength of the evidence necessary to tip the balance of probabilities varies (*Secretary of State for the Home Department v Rehman* [2002] 1 All E. R. 122 at para.55 *per* Lord Hoffmann). The position was explained by Buckley L.J. in *Thomas Bates & Son Ltd v Wyndham's (Lingerie) Ltd* [1981] 1 All E.R. 1077 at 1085:

"I think that the use of a variety of formulations used to express the degree of certainty with which a particular fact must be established in civil proceedings is not very helpful and may, indeed, be confusing. The requisite degree of cogency of proof will vary with the nature of the facts to be established and the circumstances of the case. I would say that in civil proceedings a fact must be proved with that degree of certainty which justice requires in the circumstances of the particular case. In every case the balance of probability must be discharged, but in some cases that balance may be more easily tipped than in others."

The weight of evidence needed to tip the balance will vary with the nature and seriousness of the issue to be decided (*Bater v Bater* [1950] 2 All E.R. 458 at 459, *per* Denning L.J. and *Buswell v IRC* [1974] 2 All E.R. 520 at 527, *per* Orr L.J.). Nevertheless it is necessary for the balance to be tipped and there remains a difference between the civil standard and the higher criminal standard in cases involving children (*Re U and B (Serious Injury: Standard of Proof)* [2004] 2 F.L.R. 263). Whether the balance has been tipped cannot be determined precisely or mathematically; there is scope for applying common sense and first impression (*Re A (A Minor) (Paternity: Refusal of Blood Test)* [1994] 2 F.L.R. 463 at 470 *per* Waite L.J.). There is no room for giving the benefit of a doubt (*R(I) 32/61*, para.10). In order to decide whether the evidence is such as to satisfy the necessary standard of proof in order to discharge the burden of proof it is necessary to weigh the evidence. (See previous section of this general note.)

In the great majority of cases there will be evidence which allows the tribunal to decide on the balance of probabilities. Accordingly the incidence will only be decisive in two cases: (i) where there is no relevant evidence and (ii) where the evidence is so evenly balanced that a decision on where the balance of probabilities lies cannot be made (*CIS 427/91*, paras 29–30). If the tribunal is unable to decide where the balance of probabilities lies in a particular case, no findings of fact can be recorded (*Morris v London Iron and Steel Co Ltd* [1987] 2 All E.R. 496). The proper course is to record that the tribunal was unable to decide where the balance of probabilities lay and decided the case on the burden of proof.

The legal burden does not determine the sequence of procedure. The chairman has control of the procedure and may decide to begin with the party who is in fullest possession of the facts rather than with the party who has the burden of proof on a particular matter. Moreover, the legal burden does not determine who is expected or entitled to produce evidence (*CIS 627/92*, para.7). In practice the party on whom the burden rests has an obvious interest in bringing forward evidence with which to seek to discharge that burden. However, the tribunal must not limit itself to considering the evidence of that party and must consider the evidence as a whole in order to decide whether the burden of proof has been discharged. In addition to hearing the evidence and argument presented to it, the tribunal is under an inquisitorial duty to investigate the facts and the existence of a legal burden does not relieve the tribunal of this duty (*R(IS) 21/93*, para.19).

The practical importance of the need to produce evidence is reflected in the other burden of proof, the evidentiary burden. As the hearing progresses and the evidence unfolds, the position may arise that the weight of the evidence is such that one party will lose unless further evidence, favourable to that party, emerges. In such a case, even if that party does not bear the legal burden on the issue in question, there is a risk that no other favourable evidence may emerge. In this type of case the party is said to bear an evidentiary burden. It is the nature of the evidentiary burden that it may rest on the party who bears the legal burden or on some other party and that during the hearing it may move from one party to another.

If one party alleges that an apparently genuine document produced by another party is not genuine, there is an evidentiary burden on the person making the allegation to substantiate it, although the evidence must be assessed as a whole (*Pant v Secretary of State for the Home Department* [2003] EWCA Civ 1964 at para.23).

The standard of proof has to be applied to the issue as a whole. It is not applied (a) to each individual piece of evidence, with any piece disregarded that does not satisfy the standard, or (b) to issues of evaluation rather than of fact (*Karanakaran v Secretary of State for the Home Department* [2000] 3 All E.R. 449 at 477 *per* Sedley L.J.; *Secretary of State for the Home Department v Rehman* [2002] 1 All E.R. 122 at para.56 *per* Lord Hoffmann).

Commissioners regularly refer to the burden of proof and set aside tribunal decisions which have misapplied the burden. However, there are indications that it is is misleading to think in terms of a burden of proof where a tribunal is following an inquisitorial approach (*R. v National Insurance Commissioner Ex p. Viscusi* [1974] 2 All E.R. 724 at 729 and 732, *per* Lord Denning M.R. and Buckley L.J. respectively). In line with this it has been decided that in some cases there is no burden of proof on either party. This may be because an analysis of the legislation shows that the issue has been left to be decided on the evidence available without reference to a burden (*CCR 3/93*, paras 8–12). Alternatively it may be that the nature of the issue involved is such that all relevant evidence should be available from the parties to allow a decision to be made one way or the other and, if it is not forthcoming, appropriate adverse inferences may be drawn (*CIS 317/94*, paras 11 and 12; *CCS 844/98*, paras 12–13). In *R(CS) 10/98* para.12 the Commissioner held that there was no burden of proof in relation to expenses deductible in calculating a parent's income.

Although it is important to bear in mind where the burden of proof lies, the tribunal has a duty if at all possible to make specific findings and should base its decision on the incidence on the burden of proof only where it is impossible to reach a decision on the balance of probabilities (*Morris v London Iron and Steel Co Ltd*

[1987] 2 All E.R. 496). In the Court of Appeal decision in *Crewe Services and Investment Corporation v Silk* (1997) 79 P.&C.R. 500, Robert Walker L.J., having referred to the burden of proof, said:

"The problem is in relating it to the practicalities of the disposal of business in the County Court. County Court judges constantly have to deal with cases that are inadequately prepared and presented, either as to the facts or as to the law (or both), and they must not be discouraged from doing their best to reach a fair and sensible result on inadequate materials." (page 509)

"In most cases the evidence before the court (even if imperfect and incomplete) will be more important than issues as to the burden of proof." (page 510)

These remarks are equally applicable to tribunals, subject to two safeguards. (i) First, the principles of natural justice must be observed. The parties must be told that the tribunal may take this approach and must have an opportunity to comment on its possible application. This need not result in a cumbersome procedure. The possibility of this approach being appropriate will probably be apparent on a preview of the papers and the parties can be warned at the outset that the tribunal may decide to take this approach, although they may seek to persuade the tribunal not to do so. (ii) Second, the manner in which the tribunal reached its conclusion must be explained in any statement of findings and reasons which is issued. This approach does not authorise a tribunal to make up figures or other evidence. It merely recognises that, where appropriate and in the absence of any credible evidence, matters such as a person's income may be capable of being assessed on a rational basis of reasoning from common experience and from such reliable evidence as is before the tribunal. It is in accordance with the requirement set out by Lord Diplock in giving the opinion of the Privy Council in *Mahon v Air New Zealand* [1984] 3 All E.R. 201 at 210 that its findings of fact should be based on material tending logically to show the existence of the facts found. See *CCS 1992/97*, paras 43–44.

### Use of Welsh and other languages

Generally speaking, there is no duty on the tribunal to provide an interpreter (*R(I) 11/63*, para.19). However, arrangements exist for interpreters to be supplied so that persons may speak in their own language. The tribunal has a duty to ensure that effective use is made of any interpreter present, for example that everything is translated for the party concerned (*Kunnath v The State* [1993] 4 All E.R. 30). The preferable alternative would be for all those present to speak the same language, as much can be lost in interpretation. It is sometimes possible for a tribunal to be assembled on which all the members speak the language in question. This is particularly the case in Wales.

The absence of any duty on the tribunal to provide an interpreter is subject to the specific statutory provision in the case of the use of the Welsh language. A party, witness or other person may speak in Welsh in legal proceedings in Wales and Monmouthshire (s.1(1) of the Welsh Language Act 1967). Accordingly, an oath or affirmation may also be given in Welsh. The form of oath or affirmation for use in court is laid down in a Lord Chancellor's Office circular under s.2 of the Welsh Courts Act 1942.

The Welsh Language Act 1993 has now been passed. It is gradually being brought into force and Ministers have indicated that in the meanwhile the spirit of the legislation will be implemented. It is likely that the Independent Tribunal Service will be specified as a body providing a service to the public in Wales (albeit that that service is supplied from Salford Quays), and that it will be required to prepare a scheme specifying the steps it proposes to take with regard to the use of the Welsh language so as to seek to achieve, as far as is appropriate and reasonably practicable to do so, that the English and Welsh languages are treated on a basis of equality (ss.5–7). The Commissioners also provide a service to the public in Wales.

The existing provisions with regard to proceedings *in* Wales concerning the giving of oral evidence, and the making of rules as to the form of oaths and affirmations and as to the provision and employment of interpreters, in each case in courts, are re-enacted in ss.22–24 of the 1993 Act. Additionally s.22(2) deals with written evidence by providing that any power to make rules of *court* is to include provision as to the use of documents in Welsh in proceedings *in or having a connection with* Wales (which will include a hearing before a Commissioner of an appeal from Wales). Normally a tribunal whose findings of fact are not binding (see reg.6A(2) above) would not be considered to be a court (*Shell Co of Australia v Federal Commissioner of Taxation* [1931] A.C. 275). However, in the context of this Act, it is likely that the word would be given a sufficiently broad meaning to encompass appeal tribunals.

The Welsh Language Act 1993 draws no distinction between the versions of Welsh spoken in different parts of the Principality. This could mean that a Welsh-speaking party could be faced with a Welsh-speaking tribunal whose members come from a different area and whose Welsh is such that the party is in little better position than if faced with an English-speaking tribunal. The tribunal service seeks to overcome this problem in setting up a Welsh-speaking tribunal, but this is not always possible, especially when local members are excluded as a result of adjournments, setting asides or successful appeals to a Commissioner.

There is no ground for complaint under the child support legislation that a form is invalid or ineffective merely on the basis that it is in English only and not in Welsh; any breach of the requirements of the Welsh Language Act must be remedied under the framework provided by that Act (*CCS 11728/96*, para.21).

*Role and status of presenting officer*

The presenting officer has a recognised and distinctive role at the hearing of an appeal before a tribunal. However, this role is nowhere spelt out in the legislation. The role is based in part on the provisions of the legislation, in part on the nature of the officer's function, in part on decisions of Commissioners and in part on the practice of tribunals.

The Secretary of State is a party to the proceedings

The officer is a non-partisan party (*R. v Medical Appeal Tribunal (North Midland Region) Ex p. Hubble* [1958] 2 All E.R. 374 at 379, *per* Diplock J. and *R. v National Insurance Commissioner Ex p. Viscusi* [1974] 2 All E.R. 724 at 729, *per* Lord Denning M.R.) whose only interest is to ensure that the law is properly applied.

In view of the presenting officer's non-partisan interest in the proceedings as well as the officer's knowledge and understanding of the law and access to information held by the Child Support Agency, that officer plays an important role in assisting the tribunal. (i) The officer should have previewed the papers and anticipated the needs of the tribunal. (ii) The officer should have obtained or tried to obtain information which is not contained in the papers but which will be needed by, or will assist, the tribunal. (iii) The officer should be able to provide explanations of how the law has been applied or how it might be applied in the light of the evidence before the tribunal. (iv) The officer should supplement the tribunal's questions to the parties and witnesses in order to ensure that all relevant factual issues are investigated. (v) The officer can summarise for the tribunal the issues which arise for decision. (vi) The officer may (their styles differ) provide an independent view of how the law might be applied to the case before the tribunal.

The law regarding statements made by officers including presenting officers is in an unsatisfactory state. Such statements are likely to be hearsay (*R(IS) 6/91*, para.11) and as such require to be treated with appropriate caution. However, Commissioners have gone further and suggested that more than the normal care associated with hearsay evidence is required. Statements made by officers in submissions should always be substantiated (*CSB 517/82*, para.8) and unsupported, contested statements by presenting officers should not be accepted without supporting evidence (*CSB 10/86*, para.5). Statements made by presenting officers are not evidence in the absence of personal knowledge (*R(SB) 8/84*, para.25(6)). Statements made by presenting officers should not merely be accepted, but should, if unsubstantiated, be investigated and proper findings of fact should be made (*CSB 728/84*, para.11(8)). These decisions and others were considered by the Commissioner in *CS 16448/96*, paras 17–21. The Commissioner concluded that what a child support officer or presenting officer said was evidence, although if it was not within the officer's personal knowledge it was hearsay. The extent of the enquiries that a tribunal should make in order to assess the proper weight to be given to the evidence depended on the circumstances of the case and the burden of proof.

There is no objection in principle to the presenting officer at the hearing having been involved in the handling of the case in some other capacity such as interviewing officer in relation to a possible reduced benefit direction, unless it results in some way in the hearing being unfair. It is, however, preferable for the presenting officer not to have been involved in the investigation of the case. See *CCS 1037/95*, para.16.

Tribunals should be sensitive to the position of the presenting officer. Presenting appeals is not the only duty of such officers. They may have had the papers for less time than the tribunal and other parties. They may have had to prepare for the hearing in less than satisfactory conditions and have been able to obtain only limited additional information from the file and computer system. Moreover, they may be seen by the other parties as representatives of the Child Support Agency and, therefore, as appropriate persons on whom those parties may vent their feelings. These officers should be allowed and encouraged to play an independent and constructive role in the proceedings and should not become the target for the tribunal or the other parties. Chairmen have the primary role in ensuring this.

The significance of the absence of a presenting officer at the hearing was discussed by the Commissioner in *CIB 5876/97*, para.28. The Commissioner's conclusion was that the absence of a presenting officer was not of itself a breach of natural justice and did not constitute an error of law that required the tribunal's decision to be set aside by a Commissioner on appeal. However, the absence of a presenting officer might, when coupled with other facts or circumstances in a particular case, be a contributory factor in the denial to the claimant (or any other party to the proceedings) of a fair hearing. Whether or not that was so required an analysis of the impact of the officer's absence on the fairness of the hearing. The test was not whether or not any particular party to the proceedings wanted a presenting officer to be present, but whether considered objectively the presence of such an officer was necessary in order that there be a fair hearing.

*The oral decision*

The chairman should give the decision orally on the day of the hearing.

*Contempt of tribunal*

It is undecided whether or not appeal tribunals fall within the protection of the law of contempt.

3.381  For the purposes of the Contempt of Court Act 1981, "court" is defined as including "any tribunal or body exercising the judicial power of the State" and "legal proceedings" is to be construed accordingly (s.9). In *Pickering v Liverpool Daily Post* [1990] 1 All E.R. 335 and [1991] 1 All E.R. 622 the Court of Appeal and the House of Lords each decided that a Mental Health Review Tribunal was a court within the definition of "court" in the 1981 Act. However, this case cannot be considered decisive so far as tribunals are concerned.

(i) Unfortunately, *Att-Gen v BBC* [1980] 3 All E.R. 161 was not considered in relation to the definition of "court". This case predated the 1981 Act, but discussed the meaning of court for the purposes of the common law of contempt in terms that strongly suggested that an appeal tribunal would not be within the protection of the law of contempt. Nor were other authorities discussed which consider the meaning "court" in other contexts, although admittedly they are not decisive on the question of the interpretation of s.9. One such case was *Shell Co of Australia v Federal Commissioner of Taxation* [1931] A.C. 275, which involved a discussion of whether a body was exercising the judicial power of the State. It is discussed in the context of the interpretation of the Welsh Language Act 1993 in the general note to para.(1D), and again suggests that an appeal tribunal would not be considered to be in general terms to be a court. These cases are relevant, because the definition in the 1981 Act is intended to reflect the common law concept of what constitutes a court (*Pickering*, above in the House of Lords at 630, *per* Lord Bridge).

(ii) Moreover, there are three differences between Mental Health Review Tribunals and appeal tribunals, all of which were referred to by the Court of Appeal in *Pickering* and the third of which was considered by the House of Lords to be decisive on the issue (at 630, *per* Lord Bridge). First, the decisions of the former relate to the liberty of an individual; second, they were set up in order to comply with a ruling by the European Court of Human Rights that a person had a right to test the lawfulness of detention in a court; third, they are expressly mentioned in s.12 of the Administration of Justice Act 1960 in the context of contempt (see below).

In view of the state of the authorities, the question of whether or not a tribunal is a court for the purposes of the law of contempt remains an open one. However, in favour of appeal tribunals being treated as courts are the following considerations: decisions relating to maintenance of children have previously been made exclusively by bodies who are undoubtedly courts, and proceedings relating to children have traditionally been held in private and covered by contempt. This view is supported by *Peach Grey and Co (a firm) v Sommers* [1995] 2 All E.R. 513. There the Divisional Court of Queen's Bench considered both the *BBC* case and *Pickering* in deciding that an employment tribunal was protected by the law of contempt and fell within the definition of court for the purposes of s.19 of the 1981 Act (*ibid.*, at 519–521, *per* Rose L.J.). This possibility has also been recognised by the Court of Appeal (*Bache v Essex County Council* [2000] 2 All E.R. 847).

On the basis that an appeal tribunal is a court for the purposes of the law of contempt, s.9 of the Contempt of Court Act 1981 applies to appeal tribunals. This section makes it a contempt to use, or to bring into a tribunal for use, any tape or other sound recorder, unless leave is given by the tribunal, and publication of the recording to the public or to any section of the public. It is the view of the Council on Tribunals that recording of private hearing should not be permitted and that recording of public hearings should only be permitted in the most exceptional cases (*Annual Report of the Council on Tribunals* 1981–1982, Appendix D). If someone present at the hearing insists on recording the proceedings, a number of courses are open. One approach would be to adjourn the hearing. However, as this might prejudice or inconvenience other parties, it might be better to proceed in the absence of the person concerned. A chairman could issue a direction under reg.5 forbidding the tape recording of proceedings, but see the general note to reg.5(1) for the problems of enforcement. There is support for the proposition that a tribunal may insist that its proceedings are not recorded from in the refusal by a Social Security Commissioner to grant leave to appeal in a case where, at a domiciliary hearing, the chairman insisted that a camcorder be switched off or the lens covered.

In addition to the the recording of proceedings it is necessary to consider the extent to which use may be made of information about the hearing, whatever the means by which it was acquired. This is important as proceedings before appeal tribunals are generally held in private. Section 12 of the Administration of Justice Act 1960, as amended by the Children Act 1989 is relevant to this issue. It provides that publication of any information relating to proceedings of a court (this includes a tribunal—subs.(3)) sitting in private may amount to a contempt of court where the proceedings relate wholly or mainly to the maintenance of a minor (subs.(1)(a)).

The scope of the protection afforded by s.12 has been considered in a number of cases and the general principles which emerge from the authorities are set out below. However, the matter has not been considered in the context of appeal tribunals and, if and when it is, the proper approach will be to consider the mischief at which s.12 and these Regulations are directed, rather than to concentrate on an analysis of the section and the relevant regulations, so that the privacy guaranteed by s.12 will attached to the substance of the matters with which the private hearing is concerned (*Pickering*, above in the House of Lords at 635, *per* Lord Bridge).

Turning from the general approach to the specifics of the material that is protected from publication, information about the proceedings will cover reporting of the hearing itself, including anything said or done at the hearing, together with the contents of documents (such as statements of witnesses, reports and accounts of interviews) produced at or prepared for use in the tribunal *(Re F (Otherwise A) (A Minor) (Publication of Information)* [1977] 1 All E.R. 114 at 135, *per* Geoffrey Lane L.J. and *Pickering*, above in the Court of Appeal at 344 and 347, *per* Lord Donaldson M.R. and Glidewell L.J. respectively). Information about the proceedings which is incorporated into the tribunal's reasons is also protected from publication (*Pickering*, above in the House of Lords at 636, *per* Lord Bridge). However, information which relates to the parties or to any qualifying child rather than to the proceedings is not protected (*Re F*, above at 130, *per* Scarman L.J.) and there is no protection for the fact that the proceedings have been instituted or have been taking place (*Pickering*, above in the Court of Appeal at 344, *per* Lord Donaldson M.R. and in the House of Lords at 634, *per* Lord Bridge).

The publication of the tribunal's decision is covered by s.12(2). This provides that the section does not apply to the publication of the text or a summary of the whole or part of the order, except where the tribunal, having power to do so, expressly prohibits the publication. For this purpose the order of a tribunal consists of the tribunal's decision, but not of the tribunal's reasons for decision, although if those reasons contain protected information they fall within the basic protection of the section (*Pickering*, above in the House of Lords at 635–636, *per* Lord Bridge). Subsection (2) is expressed to be without prejudice to subs. (1), so it recognises the possibility that in an exceptional case even the tribunal's decision may fall under the general protection of the section (*ibid.* at 635, *per* Lord Bridge).

As the tribunal's decision is generally only protected from publication where the tribunal, having power to do so, expressly prohibits the publication, it matters whether or not an appeal tribunal has this power. There is no express provision giving such a power and a tribunal's decision no longer states on its face that it is confidential. In *CSDLA 5/95* tribunal decisions were described as public documents, which, if correct, is fatal to them being confidential. However, this classification of tribunal decisions is questionable: see the general note to reg.13(2)–(3D) below.

Section 12(4) of the 1960 Act provides that nothing in s.12 is to be construed as implying that any publication is punishable as contempt which not be so punishable apart from the section. (Section 6(b) of the 1981 Act is in similar terms, but does not apply to s.9.) It has been held that the effect of this subsection is that the section as a whole does not create any new category of contempt (*Re F (Otherwise A) (A Minor) (Publication of Information)*, above and *Oxfordshire County Council v L and F* [1997] 1 F.L.R. 235 at 249, *per* Stuart-White J.). In *Pickering*, above in the Court of Appeal at 346 Lord Donaldson M.R. said that its sole effect was to preserve the requirement of knowledge in order for there to be a contempt and that its obscure wording could not override the plain words of s.12(1), and Farquharson L.J. said at 353 that it merely preserved the defences which could be raised by a person alleged to be in contempt. The House of Lords confirmed this interpretation, but emphasised that in the case of a novel and purely statutory jurisdiction the common law principles could only apply by analogy (above at 633, *per* Lord Bridge).

Where a contempt of court is committed in connection with tribunal proceedings, an order of committal may only be made by the Divisional Court of Queen's Bench. It may be that the Divisional Court of Queen's Bench has inherent power to punish when witnesses have been interfered with (*BBC*, above at 170 *per* Lord Scarman and *Peach Grey*, above at 520, *per* Rose L.J.).

*Paragraph (2)*

The duty only arises where an oral hearing has been requested or directed. It applies to appeals only and not to referrals, although natural justice requires the same notice to be given for both. It is subject to waiver under para.(3).

The duty relates only to the parties to the proceedings. It does not relate to a representative (*CS 113/91*, paras 10–11), although failure to notify a representative has been held to be prima facie evidence of a breach of natural justice (*ibid.*) and reg.57(1)(a) envisages that a representative is entitled to be given notice.

If a party does not attend, the tribunal should inquire whether notice was properly served and the chairman should record in the record of proceedings that the inquiry was made and its result. If the notice has not been properly served, or if the tribunal is satisfied that it did not arrive (for example, because of a change of address), the hearing should be adjourned (*R(SB) 19/83*, para.7). The tribunal must also inquire into service if a party attends a hearing but argues that notice was not given in accordance with para.(2) (*CI 4182/98*, para.10).

The notice must be of the time and place of the hearing. There is no reference to supplying the documents to be considered at the hearing, but this is required by natural justice.

If a hearing wrongly proceeds when notice has not been properly served, it is liable to be set aside under reg.57.

*Paragraph (3)*

Waiver must be based on full and informed consent. Consent under protest or in ignorance of one's rights is not sufficient. See *CI 4182/98*, para.10.

*Paragraph (6)*

It is rare in practice for anyone to want to attend a hearing who would not be entitled to be present at a private hearing under para.(8). Child support cases are likely to fall within subpara.(b). A private hearing is the normal practice where children are concerned. This is consistent with the spirit of the European Convention on Human Rights (*Re PB (Hearings in open court)* [1996] 2 F.L.R. 765 at 768, *per* Butler-Sloss, L.J.); *P v BW (Children Cases: Hearings in Public)* [2004] 1 F.L.R. 171 at para.48). In deciding whether to order a private hearing, the chairman should consider: (i) the wishes of the parties; (ii) whether information is likely to be made public which is private, intimate or embarrassing, especially if it affects a child; (iii) whether there is a public interest in the proceedings or the decision, such as if it is a test case; (iv) whether the public interest could be protected without a public hearing, such as by making the decision or its reasoning public; (v) whether it is appropriate to hold part of the hearing in public and part in private.

A public hearing means that the public must have ready access to the room used by the tribunal. A room in a secure area protected by a door with a push-button security lock is not public. It is irrelevant that no member of the public tried to attend the hearing. See *Storer v British Gas plc* [2000] 2 All E.R. 440.

*Paragraph (7)*

3.382     The right to attend and participate is qualified. The right to attend is qualified by the possibility that a request for postponement or an application for an adjournment to allow a party to attend may be refused under reg.51. The right to attend and participate is qualified by the chairman's control over the procedure under para.(1). The chairman is most likely to curtail a party's participation in order to curtail repetitious or irrelevant submissions. It may also be necessary to prevent a party attending whose behaviour towards the tribunal, the clerk or the other parties is unacceptable. However, see *Bennett v Southwark London Borough Council* [2002] I.C.R. 881 (in the general note to para.(8) below) on the need to tolerate abusive representatives.

    The power to use a live television link (defined in para.(13)) is limited. It allows a party, a representative or a panel member other than the chairman to be present by means of the link. Persons who may be present in other capacities are not included: a witness or someone falling within para.(9). The consent of the appellant is not necessary. This would be an unfortunate limitation in child support cases, as the parties may be hostile to each other and unwilling to co-operate in any step that is to the other's benefit. See the comments of the Commissioner in *CCS 4085/01*, para.6. The Commissioner hinted that the limitations on this paragraph may give rise to human rights issues. The need for the consent of the appellant will also prevent this power being used in the cases of referrals of variation applications, because there is in those cases no appellant. Perhaps, the words "if any" are implied, as in *Coates Bros plc v General Accident Life Assurance Ltd* [1991] 3 All E.R. 929 at 933.

    The consent of the tribunal's chairman or sole member of the tribunal is also needed. The discretion cannot be exercised by another legally qualified panel member, such as a full-time district chairman. No defined limit or set of circumstances must be placed on the exercise of the discretion (*Rowland v Bock* [2002] 4 All E.R. 370).

    The chairman will have to devise a means by which the person present by television link is able to participate fully in the hearing. It is not unusual, for example, for documents to be produced for the first time at the hearing. A means will have to be found for the person at the remote site to see those documents.

*Paragraph (8)*

    Parties may be accompanied by a companion and a representative. They may also bring a witness under para.(11). In the relatively informal proceedings in a tribunal these roles are not always easily distinguished. In *R(G) 1/93*, for example, the same person was representative, interpreter and witness.

    The rights and powers of a representative under this paragraph are limited to "the proceedings at the hearing", including the right to give evidence (*CDLA 2462/03*, para.11). They do not extend to the proceedings outside the hearing.

    The right to a representative is not absolute, but the tribunal and its chairman must take account of the proper role and value of a representative in exercising their discretions that may affect this right (*CIB 1009/04*; *CIB 2058/04*).

    The chairman, in determining the tribunal's procedure under para.(1), may limit the number of companions and representatives or otherwise ensure that the right under this paragraph is exercised reasonably (*CI 199/89*, para.13). Otherwise, the right to a representative is unqualified, even under the chairman's control of procedure under para.(1). In particular, there is no power to prevent a particular representative appearing for a party to the proceedings (*Bache v Essex County Council* [2000] 2 All E.R. 847) or to apply the "McKenzie friend" principles that operate in courts (*CS 1753/00*). However, in *CSHC 729/03* the Commissioner referred to other authorities and left open the issue whether a tribunal had power to prevent a representative appearing for a claimant.

    A party may be prejudiced by the acts or failings of a representative. Although an appeal tribunal would no doubt wish to minimise the impact on the party, the tribunal's decision will not be wrong in law merely because the fault of the representative is visited on the party personally (*CSB 626/88*, paras 7–8; *CI 199/89*, paras 11–12). However, in the context of limitation of actions the courts have taken a different approach, holding that once representatives have been instructed, their faults are not to be visited on the parties themselves (*Corbin v Penfold Metallising Co Ltd, The Times*, May 2, 2000).

Although an appeal tribunal may advise a party to obtain representation, there is no duty to do this (*CSIB 848/97*, para.11).

Tribunals should not abort a hearing just because a representative (or a party) makes offensive or unfounded allegations about the panel members (*Bennett v Southwark London Borough Council* [2002] I.C.R. 881).

The chairman will need to decide whether witnesses should be present throughout the entire hearing, or only when they give evidence. In doing so, matters to be considered will include whether the witness's evidence will be affected by anything that might be heard during the proceedings and whether there may be private, intimate or embarrassing matters disclosed during the hearing, especially any which affect a child, which should be given as small a circulation as possible. The presence of the witnesses is a matter for the chairman under the general rule contained in para.(ID) above (*Moore v Registrar of Lambeth County Court* [1969] 1 All E.R. 782). A representative cannot be excluded. It follows that a representative who gives evidence cannot be excluded.

The informality of the proceedings may not be used as a means of depriving one of the parties of a statutory right, such as the right to question witnesses conferred by this paragraph (*R(I) 13/74*, para.9).

*Children as witnesses*

If one of the parties seeks to call a child as a witness, a number of special considerations arise in the borderland of competence, admissibility, evaluation and the desirability of involving a child in legal proceedings between the parents. Usually, but not necessarily, the child will be the qualifying child.

*First, is it desirable that the child should give evidence?* Logically this question only arises once it is established that the child is a competent witness whose evidence could be heard by the tribunal. However, when a party wishes to call a child as a witness, it may be thought appropriate to consider this issue before coming to the legal technicalities. A child may be placed in a very difficult position if called upon to give evidence which involves taking sides with one parent against the other or which may have serious financial consequences for one or other of the parents. However, there are a number of steps which a tribunal can take if faced with a request for a child to be called as a witness. The tribunal may discuss with the parents the desirability of this action from the child's point of view. It may also ask for an indication of the facts which it is thought that the child's evidence will establish and discuss how else these matters might be established. The tribunal could then hear all the evidence except that of the child and, if satisfied that those facts have been established, the child's evidence could be excluded as unnecessary. This, however, is only possible where only one of the parties wishes the child to give evidence.

*Second, is the child a competent witness?* Children who are so young that they cannot give reliable evidence are not competent witnesses. There is no fixed age below which a child should not be allowed to give evidence. The issue can only be determined in relation to a particular child and by paying due regard to that child's maturity and the nature of the evidence which may be given. The test of competence of a child witness is whether the child was able to understand the question asked, to communicate, and to give a coherent and comprehensible account of relevant matters. This involves an ability to distinguish between truth and fiction or between fact and fantasy. This is the appropriate emphasis rather than whether the child can distinguish between truth and lies since by definition lies are intentional and are deliberate falsehoods which cannote an ability to tell the difference between lies and the truth. If the child is able to distinguish fact from fiction, it is for the tribunal to decide whether or not the evidence is true. See *R. v D, The Times*, November 11, 1995. For the use of witness summonses in the case of children see the general note to reg.10(1) above.

*Third, is the consent of a parent with parental responsibility necessary before a child may give evidence?* It seems that consent to a child appearing as a witness is an aspect of parental responsibility (*Re M (Care: Leave to Interview)* [1995] 1 F.L.R. 825 and *Re F (Specific Issues: Child Interview)* [1995] 1 F.L.R. 819). On this basis, in the case of married or divorced parent, either may consent to a child giving evidence, since parental responsibility may be exercised unilaterally (s.2(7) of the Children Act 1989). Where the parents have never been married, the tribunal must discover whether the father has acquired parental responsibility, by court order or by agreement with the mother. If so, the position is the same as for married or divorced parents. If not, only the mother has parental responsibility, and only she may decide whether the child should be a witness. In the event of a dispute as to consent, either parent may seek an order from the court.

*Fourth, should the tribunal hear the child's evidence?* In criminal cases the tendency is for the court to hear the child's evidence, subject to the question of competence. However, in family cases the courts tend to act on the principle that it is not in the best interests of the child to become embroiled in a dispute between the parents and to refuse to hear the child. In *Re M (A Minor) (Family Proceedings: Affidavits)* [1995] 2 F.L.R. 100 the Court of Appeal deprecated the attempt to involve a child aged 13 by having her swear an affidavit as to which parent she wished to live with. Applying this principle in a child support context would suggest that childrens' evidence should not be heard. This is an issue which should be decided by the chairman (*R/(SB) 1/81*, para.6).

*Fifth, should the child take the oath?* This involves establishing whether the child is able to understand not just the importance of telling the truth generally but also the particular significance of doing so to the tribunal. The test is not whether or not the child believes in the existence of God and of a divine sanction if the oath is broken, but rather "whether the child has a sufficient appreciation of the solemnity of the occasion, and the added responsibility to tell the truth, which is involved in taking an oath, over and above the duty to tell the truth which is an ordinary duty of normal social conduct" with the watershed probably falling between the ages of eight and 10 (*R. v Hayes* [1977] 2 All E.R. 288 at 291, *per* Bridge L.J.).

Under s.96(1) and (2) of the Children Act 1989 a child who does not understand the nature of the oath may give unsworn evidence, provided the child understands that there is a duty to speak the truth and has sufficient understanding to justify the evidence being heard. This provision does not apply to appeal tribunals as they are not tribunals in which the strict rules of evidence apply (s.96(7) of the 1989 Act and s.18 Civil Evidence Act 1968). However, the tribunal could apply the same principle.

*Sixth, what form should the oath take?* This is dealt with below.

*Seventh, is corroboration needed?* Corroboration is not generally required. However, the presence or absence of corroboration may be an important factor in weighing a child's evidence in the context of an individual case.

*Eighth, how is the child's evidence to be given?* If a child is to give evidence, the manner in which that evidence is given and the manner of the questioning of the child are within the control of the chairman, who may consider it appropriate that the parties should not question the child directly but that the chairman should question the child on the matters identified by the parties.

*Ninth, how is the child's evidence to be evaluated?* In addition to the usual factors which will be taken into account the tribunal will need to consider the influence which one parent may have been able to exercise over the child's evidence and the considerations which (consciously or subconsciously) may be in the child's mind whilst giving evidence (for example, a desire to help a parent who is in financial difficulty or a desire to give neutral evidence which will prevent the child appearing to take sides). As to the role of expert evidence in assisting the tribunal to decide on the appropriate weight to be given to a child's evidence see *Re M and R (Child Abuse: Evidence)* [1996] 2 F.L.R. 195 referred to in the *Evidence* section of the general note to para.(1D) above.

A Tribunal of Commissioners gave guidance on evidence from children in disability living allowance cases (*CDLA 1721/04*, para.58): (i) a tribunal should have proper regard to the wishes of a child of sufficiently mature years and understanding who wishes to give evidence, but should be very cautious before requiring any child to give evidence, and should only call for a child to give evidence if it is satisfied that a just decision cannot otherwise be made; (ii) a tribunal should be very slow to exercise its power to require a child to give evidence if that child's parent or carer takes the view that for the child to give evidence may be detrimental to the child's welfare, particularly if there is evidence from a competent professional that to do so might be harmful; (iii) even if it is one the parties who wishes to call a child as a witness, a tribunal has power to disallow the child from giving evidence if it is against the child's interests to do so; (iv) if a child is called to give evidence, the tribunal should consider how that evidence will be taken, so that the interests and welfare of the child are maintained; (v) the tribunal will also need to give consideration to practical matters such as the geography of the hearing room, having an appropriate adult in close attendance, whether any of the tribunal (including the chairman) should be selected because of experience in dealing with child witnesses and even (in appropriate cases) taking such steps as taking the child's evidence by video link if available.

## The oath

The tribunal may require a witness to give evidence on oath or affirmation. This is not a purely procedural matter which is in the hands of the chairman, but a matter for the whole tribunal to decide. This paragraph does not draw a technical distinction between a witness, on the one hand, and a party or representative, on the other. It applies to all persons who give evidence. Two questions arise with regard to the oath: (i) should it be used and (ii) if it is used, in what form should it be administered?

## Value

There are at least three reasons why the oath should either not be used at all in a tribunal or should at the very least be used only in exceptional cases. First, its use is inconsistent with the relatively informal atmosphere which should be adopted in a tribunal in comparison with a court. Second, it is nowadays unlikely in many cases to have an influence on the evidence given by the witness. Its use, therefore, creates an additional question for the tribunal: what effect has the oath had on the witness's honesty? Finally, the oath can only affect the honesty of a witness's evidence. Depending on the nature of the question in dispute, this may or may not be the central issue for the tribunal. If it is not, the tribunal will rather be concerned with the reliability of that evidence. (This has been touched on in the note on evaluation of evidence above.) The honesty of the witness will be only one factor in the evaluation of reliability. A tribunal may be reluctant to administer the oath to one person but not another at the same hearing or in relation to some aspects of a person's evidence only.

Despite the doubtful value of an oath or affirmation, it appears likely that Commissioners will set aside decisions when there has been a conflict of evidence, unless that evidence was given under oath or affirmation.

*Form*

The oath or affirmation must be given in due form. The proper form of oaths and affirmations is laid down by the Oaths Act 1978.

A person may swear by any form of oath or ceremony which he declares to be binding and is bound by this (s.4(1)). If an oath is administered it is binding regardless of whether the person has any religious belief (s.4(2)). It is usual in England, Wales and Northern Ireland that the oath is administered by the witness raising a copy of the New Testament or, if the witness is Jewish, the Old Testament (s.1(1)). In Scotland a witness swears with an uplifted hand. This form may also be used by a witness in England, Wales and Northern Ireland (s.3).

Instead of an oath a solemn affirmation may be used in two circumstances. First, if the witness objects to taking an oath (s.5(1)). In this case it is entirely a decision for the witness concerned. Secondly, if it is not reasonably practicable without inconvenience or delay to administer an oath in the manner appropriate to the witness's religious belief (s.5(2) and (3)). In this case it is a matter for the tribunal rather than for the witness concerned. In either case the affirmation is as binding as an oath (s.5(4)).

The opening words are in the case of an oath, "I swear by Almighty God that . . .", and in the case of an affirmation, "I, . . . do solemnly, sincerely and truly declare and affirm, . . ." (ss.1(1) and 6(1)). This is followed in either case by "the evidence I shall give shall be the truth, the whole truth and nothing but the truth." In the case of a child or young person under the age of 17 the proper form is to use the word "promise" instead of "swear", although either is equally valid (s.28 of the Children and Young Persons Act 1963). The use of Welsh in taking an oath or affirmation is dealt with in the general note to para.(1).

Section 1 of the Oaths Act 1978 provides that the oath is to be administered by an officer which is defined in s.1(4) as any person duly authorised to administer the oath. The Act is silent as to who is authorised to administer the oath. This is dealt with in part by s.16 of the Evidence Act 1851 which provides that "Every court, judge, . . . or other person, now or hereafter having by law . . . authority to hear, receive, and examine evidence, is hereby empowered to administer an oath to all such witnesses as are legally called before them . . .". This clearly empowers the tribunal itself, acting in practice through the chairman, to administer the oath.

There is no exhaustive statement of who may not authorise a person to administer an oath under reg.43(5). The clerks have been trained to administer the oath. Accordingly it is necessary to consider what role, if any, may properly be played by a clerk. There are three possible approaches to this question, which depend in part upon contractual and administrative considerations.

The first is that the chairman has control over procedure under para.(1) and could, therefore, authorise the clerk to administer the oath. The effectiveness of this will depend upon whether administering the oath is within the clerk's permitted duties. Presumably it is.

The second possibility is s.2 of the Commissioners for Oaths Act 1889 which provides that "Any person who, being an officer of or performing duties in relation to any court, is for the time being so authorised by a judge of the court, . . . shall have authority to administer an oath . . . for any purpose connected with his duties."

This will apply to clerks, if tribunals count as courts for the purposes of this provision. Whether or not this is so is unclear. If it does apply, and if the Guide is issued under the tribunal's judicial (as opposed to its administrative) authority, all clerks are authorised to administer the oath. In any event an individual chairman could authorise the clerk on a particular occasion. It is, therefore, arguable that the Guide contains authorisation for the clerks to administer the oath and that the tribunal or the chairman may, in any case, authorise the clerks so to do, provided that they are willing to do so within their duties.

A third approach to this problem is to consider what it means to administer an oath. It is surely not necessary for the person concerned personally to hand over the book and card. If the matter is overseen by and at the direction of the tribunal or its chairman, this could amount to the administrating of the oath by the tribunal or chairman. There is of course no power to delegate a judicial function (*Barnard v National Dock Labour Board* [1953] 1 All E.R. 1113), but it is well established that administrative aspects of a non-delegable duty may be delegated.

Chairman should not assume that clerks will always be available to administer an oath. In some places they may be clerking more than one tribunal and may, therefore, not have the time to perform this function.

If an oath is administered, or a witness is allowed to affirm, the chairman should record this fact in the notes of proceedings and should take care to ensure that a complete and accurate note of that evidence is taken. Moreover, when the oath or affirmation is being used, it will also be applied to a representative who gives evidence in the course of a presentation, for example, on the past record of violence of a spouse in a reduced benefit appeal. The tribunal will have to be alert to identify such evidence, and the chairman should record both it and the fact that it was received as evidence.

In England and Wales a person who gives evidence on oath or affirmation without believing it to be true commits the offence of perjury (ss.1(1) and (2), 15(2) and 18 of the Perjury Act 1911).

*Paragraph (11)*

In *CDLA 2462/03*, the Commissioner considered the rights and powers of a representative who wished to give evidence. The Commissioner held that a representative had the right to give evidence of matters within the representative's own knowledge (para.11). However, it was for the tribunal to decide whether a representative should be allowed to put to the tribunal a summary of the evidence of one of the parties (para.13).

*Paragraph (12)*

The clerk and anyone else allowed to remain should not only refrain from participating in the making of the decision, but should also give no cause for anyone to believe that they have participated (*R (SB) 13/83*, para.15).

## Postponement and adjournment

**51.**—(1) Where a person to whom notice of an oral hearing is given wishes to request a postponement of that hearing he shall do so in writing to the clerk to the appeal tribunal stating his reasons for the request, and the clerk to the appeal tribunal may grant or refuse the request as he thinks fit or may pass the request to a legally qualified panel member who may grant or refuse the request as he thinks fit.

(2) Where the clerk to the appeal tribunal or the panel member, as the case may be, refuses a request to postpone the hearing he shall—

(a) notify in writing the person making the request of the refusal; and

3.383

(b) place before the appeal tribunal at the hearing both the request for the postponement and notification of its refusal.

(3) A panel member or the clerk to the appeal tribunal may of his own motion at any time before the beginning of the hearing postpone the hearing.

(4) An oral hearing may be adjourned by the appeal tribunal at any time on the application of any party to the proceedings or of its own motion.

[¹. . .]

AMENDMENT

1. Regulation 15 of the Appeals Amendment Regulations 2002 (May 20, 2002).

DEFINITIONS

3.384     "appeal": see reg.1(3).
          "clerk to the appeal tribunal": see reg.1(3).
          "legally qualified panel member": see reg.1(3).
          "referral": see reg.1(3).

GENERAL NOTE

The purpose of the powers conferred by this regulation is to ensure a fair hearing and they must be exercised in order to further that purpose (*CIB 2058/04*, para.13).

*Paragraph (1)*

3.385     A request for a postponement may only be made by a person to whom notice of an oral hearing has been given. This refers to the notice of an oral hearing given under reg.49(2). Until that notice is given, there is no hearing to postpone. Delaying the listing of a case for an oral hearing is an administrative rather than a judicial matters and does not fall within this regulation. The request for a delay should be made to the clerk to the tribunal. It may be appropriate to refer the request to a legally qualified panel member who may wish to use the powers given by reg.38.

The person requesting the postponement must state reasons for the request. This is in contrast to appeals and applications which require particulars or grounds to be stated. The difference in wording reflects the fact that what is required here are factual matters rather than legal considerations.

The chairman or a clerk may grant or refuse the request "as he thinks fit." This provides an unfettered discretion. Chairmen and clerks should consider all factors relating to why the claimant is not in a position to attend or to proceed on the day set for the hearing. They will be on guard to ensure that requests for postponement are not used as a tactical device for delaying an unwanted decision. They may also be reluctant to postpone a hearing if it appears that the case could be decided in favour of the person requesting the postponement without that person being present or further prepared, especially as the hearing can be adjourned if it appears appropriate. However, the inconvenience to the other parties should be borne in mind, especially as in contrast to social security appeals there are more likely to be parties with a direct and personal interest in the hearing.

The principles governing the exercise of the discretion to postpone are very similar to those governing adjournments. The factors relevant when considering adjournments (see the general note to para.(4) will always be relevant to postponements, but other factors will also come into play in view of the earlier stage at which the decision on postponement may be made. For example, the chairman should consider the costs involved in attendance if the hearing is not postponed but has to be adjourned on the day. Alternatively, a chairman who is in doubt about whether or not to postpone may prefer to leave the hearing to take place knowing that if appropriate it can be adjourned.

The chairman or a clerk may attach such conditions as appropriate if the hearing is postponed. When making any postponement it is good practice to consider whether it is appropriate to attach any conditions or to make any directions under reg.5 which would contribute to the conduct of the proceedings.

Whenever a request for a postponement has been refused, the tribunal should always consider whether to adjourn the hearing (*CDLA 3680/97*, para.5).

*Paragraph (3)*
This is a useful power which allows a hearing to be postponed without an application being made. It gives power to deal with a request for a postponement which is not in writing and so does not comply with the requirements of para.(1). Such requests are often made by telephone shortly before the hearing.

When the hearing begins is discussed in the general note to para.(4).

*Paragraph (4)*
Once a hearing has begun, the power to postpone ceases and the power to adjourn arises. It is given to the appeal tribunal and not to the chairman. It may be exercised on application by a party to the proceedings or on the tribunal's own initiative. For the relationship between the tribunal's power to adjourn and the power to give directions under reg.38(2), see the general note to that paragraph.

When a hearing begins has never been precisely determined. It has certainly not begun before all the parties to the proceedings have entered the tribunal room and settled down. It has certainly begun by the time the appeal tribunal starts to hear evidence or submissions. The difficult area is the time spent by the chairman on an introduction. Probably, the hearing begins as soon as the chairman begins the introduction, but problems do not arise in practice and any that do are best resolved by the flexible application of common sense.

The power given to tribunals by this regulation must be interpreted and exercised in the context of the requirements of natural justice (*CDLA 5509/97*, para.12). The precise requirements of natural justice must be decided in the context of the provisions made by these Regulations: (*Russell v Duke of Norfolk* [1949] 1 All E.R. 109, *per* Tucker L.J. at page 118 and *R(SB) 55/83*, para.12). However, the Regulations will be interpreted, so far as the language allows, so as not to conflict with the requirement, in general terms, of natural justice (*John v Rees* [1969] 2 All E.R. 274 at 309, *per* Megarry J.). There will, therefore, be cases in which the circumstances that natural justice requires the tribunal to adjourn the hearing: for example *CIS 2390/97*.

There must be a good reason for a hearing to be adjourned (*Unilever Computer Services Ltd v Tiger Leasing SA* [1983] 2 All E.R. 139).

Each adjournment must be approached individually and judicially. The tribunal should seek to strike a balance between the following factors: (i) the interests of the parties to be present, and to be properly prepared to present the best case in their favour and to deal with points against them; (ii) whether the adjournment would improve the quality of the tribunal's ultimate decision; (iii) the interests of the other users of the tribunal system including the Secretary of State—adjourning one appeal delays the hearing of others; and (iv) the extent to which the case has already been adjourned or otherwise delayed. The chairman should record in the notes of proceedings all requests for adjournments, the views of the parties and the decisions on them. The tribunal should also consider the following: (i) the importance of the proceedings; (ii) the likely adverse consequences on the party seeking the adjournment; (iii) the risk of prejudice to the party seeking the adjournment if the application is refused; (iv) the risk of prejudice to any other party if the application is granted; (v) the convenience of the tribunal and the interests of justice in ensuring the efficient despatch of business so as not to delay other appeals; (vi) the extent to which the applicant was responsible for the circumstances leading to the perceived need for an adjournment (*R. v Kingston upon Thames Justices Ex p. Martin, The Times,* December 10, 1993; *R. (ota Lappin) v HM Customs and Excise* [2004] EWHC 953 (Admin)). It is always relevant to take account of the difficulties that will be caused by delay (*CDLA 13008/ 96,* para.11). The tribunal should also bear in mind that lengthy proceedings can amount to a breach of the European Convention on Human Rights (*Darnell v United Kingdom* (1994) 18 E.H.R.R. 205).

The appeal tribunals generally take a restrictive approach to adjournments. However, this is out of line with the approach of the courts. See the general note to s.24(1) of the Act and *Fox v Graham Group Ltd, The Times,* August 3, 2001, in which Neuberger J. said that a court should be very careful indeed before refusing a first request for an adjournment by an unrepresented party whose case was not plainly hopeless, even if an adjournment would result in inconvenience for another party. The tribunals' approach to adjournments must be set in the context of the power to set aside under reg.57 below, although the district chairmen also apply that provision restrictively.

The recorded reasons for refusing to adjourn need not be elaborate. It is sufficient to record the key considerations that influenced the tribunal to decide as it did, leaving them to be read against the background of the case. In the absence of any suggestion to the contrary, a Commissioner is entitled to assume that the tribunal took that background into account. See *CCS 565/99,* para.16.

Whenever a request for a postponement has been refused, the tribunal should always consider whether to adjourn the hearing (*CDLA 3680/97,* para.5).

It is only in an exceptional case that it would be an error of law for a tribunal to proceed in the absence of a party who has indicated an intention not to attend (*CDLA 4683/97,* para.23).

A party is entitled to be represented and may apply for an adjournment to allow his representative to attend. Usually this will be allowed. However, the absence of a representative does not give an automatic entitlement to an adjournment (*CI 199/89*). Nevertheless, in deciding whether to adjourn to allow a representative to attend, tribunals must take full account of the advantages that a representative brings to the party represented and to the quality of the tribunal's decision-making (*CIB 2058/04*). It is always relevant to consider whether or not there is someone who could have attended in place of a representative who is not available, but it is a mistake to assume that all members of a particular organisation are available (*CIB 1009/04*).

If a party to the proceedings claims to have evidence that is not at the hearing, the tribunal must investigate why the party was not prepared for the hearing. It may be that the more slimline submissions that are now made by the Secretary of State did not alert the party to the possible relevance of the evidence, because they no longer contain a statement of the relevant law. See *CCS 714/01*.

If an adjournment is justified by the circumstances pertaining at a particular time, it is not proper to refuse to adjourn because of something which has happened earlier (*Dick v Piller* [1943] 1 All E.R. 627 at 629, *per* Scott L.J.).

If a hearing is to be adjourned, the tribunal should consider how the best use can be made of it so as to ensure as far as possible that further adjournments are avoided. This may involve a discussion with the parties to identify other possible causes of future delay and any appropriate directions can be given to ensure that these matters are dealt with in the interim. Chairmen should also bear in mind their power to give directions under reg.38(2) and use it where appropriate if the tribunal is not minded to act. Anticipation of problems and appropriate use of the power to give directions under reg.38(2) can go a long way to avoid adjournments. If a request based on the unavailability of a representative has been made before and the appeal has already been subject to lengthy delays, refusal of a further adjournment will be a breach of natural justice (*ibid.*), but where the earlier delays have not been lengthy and the claimant has not been warned of the possibility of obtaining further adjournments, refusal to adjourn may constitute such a breach (*CSB 753/84*).

When a hearing is adjourned, any directions may be given by the tribunal or by a chairman. It is important to identify who has given the directions. The chairman's power to give directions is constrained by the terms of reg.38(2) or 49(4). The tribunal, on the other hand, has a discretion to adjourn which is fettered only by the need to act judicially. It may, therefore, adjourn on any terms it thinks appropriate, provided only that it doing so it acts judically.

This regulation only applies to adjournments from one session to a later session. Adjournments within the course of a session are within the chairman's control of procedure under reg.49(1) and are matters for the chairman rather than the tribunal. Thus, a chairman might adjourn briefly, for example, if a representative has been delayed or if a party or witness becomes distressed or in order to discuss how the tribunal should proceed (for example, whether an adjournment under this regulation is appropriate).

A tribunal may give a final decision on one aspect of an appeal and adjourn the remainder (*CSIS 118/90*, para.18), although the reasoning therein relies on considerations in social security law which have no equivalent in child support law. If this approach is permissible in child support law, any final decision made is appealable (*ibid.*). For the appropriateness of taking this approach to preliminary issues see the general note to s.24(1) of the Act. For the consequences of such a decision on the constitution of a future tribunal see the general note to para.(5) below.

If it is clear that a case will go on appeal, it is permissible to deal with it expeditiously, for example by refusing to adjourn (*Poplar Housing and Regeneration Community Association Ltd v Donoghue* [2001] 4 All E.R. 604).

For a discussion of the circumstances in which a decision to adjourn or to refuse to adjourn may be appealable, see the general note to s.24(1). In view of the existence of the alternative remedies discussed there, the adjournment decision will seldom justify a judicial review.

## At the resumed hearing

This regulation used to include a provision that if a rehearing was before a differently constituted tribunal, it had to be a completely different tribunal and the proceedings had to be by way of a complete rehearing. Those requirements were repealed from May 20, 2002.

This leaves the constitution of the tribunal for, and the proceedings at, the rehearing to be determined according to the principles of natural justice and the Convention right to a fair hearing.

It is likely that a differently constituted tribunal will be required if (a) evidence was heard at the previous hearing (*CDLA 2429/04*) and (b) a party or representative will attend the resumed hearing who was not present previously. This reflects the concern over residual knowledge noted by the Tribunal of Commissioners in *R(U) 3/88*, para.7. The panel member may have knowledge from what was said or done at the previous hearing, which may be directly relevant to the appeal as evidence or indirectly relevant to the outcome as going to the credibility of the evidence. The party or representative who did not attend that hearing will be unaware of and unable to deal with that knowledge. If the resumed hearing contains a panel member sitting in addition to the panel member from the previous hearing, there is also the risk that the members of the tribunal may not have had the same basis for decision, as in *CDLA 2429/04*.

Even if there is no actual danger of residual knowledge, there may be a suspicion in the party who did not attend before that it may exist and affect the outcome. That should be taken into account when fixing the constitution of the tribunal. If the tribunal is not differently constituted, the issue may arise whether there is a real apprehension of bias.

If a party or representative attends the rehearing who was not present at the previous hearing, the proceedings will have to be by way of a complete rehearing, regardless of whether the tribunal is differently constituted.

These considerations apply both where the adjournment is made without any final decision being made on any aspect of the case and where the tribunal makes a final decision on one aspect and adjourns the remainder. Tribunals should bear in mind that, while it may appear to be shortening the proceedings to deal with one aspect of the case, this approach is not encouraged by the law (for further discussion see the general note to reg.38(2)).

Some aspects of the procedure to be followed on a complete re-hearing were discussed by the Tribunal of Commissioners in *R(U) 3/88*, para.7. The case must be reheard afresh, unfettered by what happened at the earlier hearing. All evidence and submissions must be put to the fresh tribunal, although the notes of evidence at the previous hearing may be made use of for this purpose.

In view of the administrative problems and consequent delays that may be caused by postponement or adjournment, tribunals and chairman should make use of the devices descussed in the general notes to these regulations in order to avoid adjournments so far as that is possible and keep to a minimum those that are required. Whenever possible a hearing should be postponed rather than adjourned.

Where there is a complete re-hearing of an appeal after an adjournment, it is desirable for the chairman to record in the notes of proceedings that this is what his occurred (*C 44/87 (IVB)*).

CHAPTER V

*Decisions of Appeal Tribunals and Related Matters*

*Appeal Tribunal Decisions*

## Decisions of appeal tribunals

3.386     **53.**—(1) Every decision of an appeal tribunal shall be recorded in summary by the chairman, or in the case of an appeal tribunal which has only one member, by that member.

(2) The decision notice specified in paragraph (1) shall be in such written form as shall have been approved by the President and shall be signed by the chairman, or in the case of an appeal tribunal which has only one member, by that member.

(3) As soon as may be practicable after an appeal or referral has been decided by an appeal tribunal, a copy of the decision notice [2. . .] shall be sent or given to every party to the proceedings who shall also be informed of—

(a) his right under paragraph (4); and

(b) the conditions governing appeals to a Commissioner.

[1(4) [3Subject to paragraph 4A,] a party to the proceedings may apply in writing to the clerk to the appeal tribunal for a statement of the reasons for the tribunal's decision within one month of the sending or giving of the decision notice to every party to the proceedings or within such longer period as may be allowed in accordance with regulation 54 and following that application the chairman, or in the case of a tribunal with only one member, that member shall record a statement of the reasons and a copy of that statement shall be given to every party to the proceedings as soon as may be practicable.]

[⁴(4A) Where—

(a) the decision notice is corrected in accordance with regulation 56; or

(b) an application under regulation 57 for the decision to be set aside is refused for reasons other than a refusal to extend the time for making the application,

the period specified in paragraph (4) shall run from the date on which notice of the correction or the refusal of the application for setting aside is sent to the applicant.]

(5) If the decision is not unanimous, the decision notice specified in paragraph (1) shall record that one of the members dissented and the statement of reasons referred to in paragraph (4) shall include the reasons given by the dissenting member for dissenting.

AMENDMENTS

1. Regulation 16 of the Appeals Amendment Regulations 2002 (May 20, 2002).
2. Regulation 2(10)(a) of the Amendment Regulations 2005 (March 18, 2005).
3. Regulation 2(10)(b) of the Amendment Regulations 2005 (March 18, 2005).
4. Regulation 2(10)(c) of the Amendment Regulations 2005 (March 18, 2005).

DEFINITIONS

"appeal": see reg.1(3).      **3.387**
"clerk to the appeal tribunal": see reg.1(3).
"Commissioner": see.57B(1).
"decision": see reg.57B(1).
"decision notice": see reg.57B(2).
"party to the proceedings": see reg.1(3).
"President": see reg.1(3).
"referral": see reg.1(3).

GENERAL NOTE

As an appeal tribunal hearing a child support case may consist of two members,    **3.388** a legally qualified panel member and a financially qualified panel member, the chairman may need to use the chairman's casting vote conferred by s.7(3)(b) of the Social Security Act 1998. A member may not abstain, it is the duty of an appeal tribunal as a whole to make a decision and it is the duty of every member of the tribunal to participate in that process.

The usual procedure stated in neutral terms is as follows: (i) the tribunal makes up its mind; (ii) those present at the hearing, if any, are told; (iii) the chairman completes the written form of decision notice under para.(2); (iv) the notice is sent or given to the parties to the appeal under para.(3); (v) where appropriate reasons are written by the chairman and sent to the parties. Unfortunately, "decision" may be used in different contexts to cover any of these steps.

On general principle a decision is of no effect until it has been promulgated, *i.e.* until it has been communicated. Until that time it may be revoked or varied informally (*CSB 226/81*, para.11 and *R(1) 14/74*, para.14(a)), although there is a risk that a difference between the oral decision and that formally promulgated may lead to the decision being set aside. The need for communication in order to make a decision effective is a constitutional principle (*R. (ota Anufrijeva) v Secretary of State for the Home Department* [2003] 3 All E.R. 827). (*CM 209/87*, para.6 is in conflict with this principle in suggesting that the decision is made as soon as it is taken.) For the purposes of setting aside and appealing decisions it is suggested that the decision is promulgated at step (iv) (*CSB 226/81*). However, the decision is clearly made earlier, subject to any variation or withdrawal (*CI 141/87*, para.30). In para.(1) "decision" obviously refers to stage (i) and in para.(2) it may refer to either stage (i) or stage (ii).

The tribunal's decision will usually be given on the day of the hearing. In exceptional cases, it may be given later, but the time between the hearing and the making of the decision should be short. A lengthy delay in a case which involves the assessment of a witness's credibility may justify the setting aside of the tribunal's decision, unless (a) the tribunal's conclusion on this issue was recorded at the time of the hearing or was obvious, or (b) the appeal would be decided against the party concerned on other grounds (*Sambasivam v Secretary of State for the Home Department* [2000] 1mm. A.R. 85).

*Paragraphs (2) and (4)*

There are differences in the provisions relating to decision notice and statements. The decision notice has to be signed by the chairman, but a written statement need not be signed. The decision notice must be on a form approved by the President, but a written statement need not, although a form has been approved by the President. These contrasting provisions mean that it is possible for a decision notice to be adopted as the tribunal's statement (*CI 848/98*, para.3) and that it is impossible to argue that the lack of a signature on a statement means that it has not been supplied in proper form (*CI 1390/98*, para.23).

A signature need not be in manscript and a typed or printed name can be adopted, for example by granting leave to appeal (*R(DLA) 2/98*, para.5). Although a statement need not be signed, it is a matter of practical sense and good practice for the author of a statement to authenticate it by signing it (*CCS 14/94*, paras 15 and 17). A signature assumes greater significance where there are conflicting copies of a decision or a statement. In this case one or other will have to be authenticated, and the obvious method of doing so is by signature (*CDLA 6166/95*, para.5).

The decision notice and the statement may be written by the chairman of the tribunal or, perhaps, by another member of the tribunal, but may not be written by another chairman (*CIS 2132/98*, paras 3–8; *CCS 1664/01*), although in the case of the decision notice the chairman must sign it. A document may be produced by someone who is not authorised in law to do so, provided that it is done under the direction of the chairman or other authorised person (*CCS 14/94*, para.13). Whoever composes the documents, they must reflect the views of the tribunal the majority as a whole (*R(SB) 13/83*, paras 13–14). (The former practice of dictating the decision to the clerk (*CSB 226/81*, para.7) is now obsolete.) Usually the documents are composed by the chairman, although a member who dissents may be asked to put into words the reasons for having done so and, if a chairman dissents, the dissenting majority (as a chairman once called them) may have to put into words their reasons for decision.

In calculating the time for the purposes of para.(4), some days are disregarded: see reg.54(13).

It has been suggested that an application for leave to appeal to a Commissioner should be treated as a request for a statement, if one has not already been given (*R(IS) 11/99*, para.33), especially where the application raises an issue that is not fully explained in the decision notice (*CDLA 5793/97*, para.26).

In *CSDLA 5/95*, para.11 the Commissioner described tribunal decisions as public documents. With respect this is questionable, since tribunal decisions are not provided to persons other than the parties, although they are no longer labelled as confidential, and may not, therefore, have been "brought into existence for the purpose of its being retained indefinitely as a document of record, available for inspection by the public" (*White v Taylor* [1967] 3 All E.R. 349 at 351, *per* Buckley J.). This is not a purely academic question. Section 12(1)(a) of the Administration of Justice Act 1960 provides that publication of information relating to proceedings of any tribunal (see subs.(3)) sitting in private may amount to a contempt of court where the proceedings relate wholly or mainly to the maintenance of a minor. However, subs.(2) provides that this does not apply to the publication of the text or a summary of the whole or part of the order except where the tribunal, having power to do so, expressly prohibits the publication. It matters, therefore, whether or not a tribunal's decision is confidential.

*Paragraph (2)*

A decision in summary form must be given in all cases, even if the chairman is going to give a statement of the tribunal's findings and reasons. It may be sufficient in such a case to record the summary decision merely by referring to the statement. There is no reason in law in such a case for the decision to be placed in any particular position in the statement (*CI 199/89*, para.17). However, for the sake of clarity and the ease of implementation, the decision should be easily identifiable, and should be self-contained so as not to require the reading of the whole statement, still less its interpretation, before the decision can be identified. It is suggested that it is good practice for the decision to be placed at the beginning of the statement and so labelled as to distinguish it from the remainder of the statement by the use of a heading, the numbering of paragraphs or otherwise.

A Commissioner has decided that the tribunal's decision will be wrong in law in a case where there is no statement of reasons if the decision notice contains no reason at all, but merely a conclusion (*CIB 668/98*). With respect, this is doubtful. It is arguable that the failure to comply with the requirement to record a decision in summary form does not affect the validity of the decision, as the remedy is to obtain a statement of reasons: see the section on *Failure to comply with procedural requirements* in the introductory general note to these Regulations.

It should be obvious, but nonetheless bears emphasis and repeating, that the decision must be in a form that can be implemented. A decision which cannot be implemented is wrong in law (*CIS 5206/95*, para.12). It is acceptable to indicate to the appellant as part of the decision whether the appeal has succeeded or failed or succeeded in part. However, decisions worded solely in terms of success or failure are to be avoided. Clearly a decision which simply reads "Appeal allowed" or "Appeal allowed in part" is wholly inadequate since it gives no indication of how it has been allowed. There may seem to be less objection to a decision in the form "Appeal dismissed," but this is also capable of giving rise to problems and is better avoided. In *CS 99/93*, para.4, the Commissioner said that giving a decision in the form of dismissing the appeal or confirming the decision under appeal is better than substituting an incomplete decision for the more detailed decision of the child support officer. While it must be the case that an incomplete decision is not acceptable, the approach suggested by the Commissioner is dangerous in that it is based on the assumption that the tribunal has before it the complete and accurate text of the decision under appeal. Tribunals are, of course, entitled to the verbatim text of the decision under appeal (*CIS 137/92*, para.5), but in practice the alleged text of the decision is often clearly incomplete and in other cases neither the papers nor the information available to the presenting officer are sufficient to allow the tribunal to be sure that the exact terms of the decision under appeal are before them. The safer approach, and one which avoids an adjournment, is for the tribunal to give a complete decision itself and not to seek an easy alternative.

In view of the time constraints and other pressures on a tribunal, they are not the best bodies to undertake complex calculations unless this is unavoidable. This is especially so in view of the complexity and formulae involved in child support law. It is proper to leave the working out of the tribunal's decision to the child support officer, provided that there is power for any party to restore the case to the tribunal in the event of a dispute as to the correct calculation (*R(SB) 16/83*, para.21). "Liberty to restore" may be used, although in court terminology "liberty to apply" would be more appropriate. It should be expressly reserved, as it will not be implied into a decision which is on its face final and complete (*Penrice v Williams* (1883) 23 Ch. D. 353 at 356–357, *per* Chitty J.). Prima facie it does not allow the order to be varied (*Cristel v Cristel* [1951] 2 All E.R. 574 at 576–577, *per* Somervell L.J.). There are suggestions in *Cristel* that a change of circumstances could be taken into account so as to vary an otherwise final order under a liberty to apply, but this is an unnecessary qualification in the child support context in view of the express power to supersede contained in s.17 of the Act.

In *CIS 749/91*, para.6 the Commissioner said that "An express reference back to 'the Commissioner' would normally carry the meaning that the appeal could be referred to any person currently holding the office. . .". In other words, the reference back is not to the members who constituted the tribunal, but to the tribunal in an abstract sense. (The decision in this case was not followed in *CS 159/91*, but it does not mention this point.)

In the context of social security law the Commissioners have recognised that tribunals have power to refer a matter to be agreed between the parties and, in the failure of such agreement, for the matter to be restored for determination by a tribunal, with the decision becoming final when the issue is decided either by agreement or by a tribunal (*CIS 442/92*, para.5). It is arguable that this approach is permissible in the child support context.

The legislation contains no power for a tribunal to award costs, interest or general damages for anxiety and distress (*Jones v Department of Employment* [1988] 1 All E.R. 725 at 739, *per* Slade L.J.), although interest in respect of arrears is covered by the Arrears, Interest and Adjustment of Maintenance Assessments Regulations. Moreover, Commissioners have no power to award costs (*R(FC) 2/90*) and it must follow that tribunals also have no such power. In any event, it is not the usual practice to award costs in cases involving children (*R. v R (Costs: Child Case)* [1997] 2 F.L.R. 95 at 98, *per* Staughton L.J.).

*Paragraph (4)*

**3.389**    This paragraph applies to decisions by tribunals, but not to decisions by chairmen. Decisions by chairmen do not fall within s.10 of the Tribunals and Inquiries Act 1992 and accordingly there is no duty to give reasons under that paragraph. Indeed chairmen are under no duty to give reasons for their decisions (*R. v Social Security Appeal Tribunal Ex p. O'Hara* (1995) 92(02) L.S. Gaz. 37).

This paragraph was considered by the Court of Appeal in *Carpenter v Secretary of State for Department for Work and Pensions* reported as *R(IB) 6/03*. It decided five relevant points. First, the paragraph applies only to decisions of appeal tribunals, as opposed to determinations (para.14). For the distinction, see the *Determinations and decisions* section of the preliminary general note to these Regulations. Second, the refusal of an application for adjournment was not a decision within this paragraph so that the duty to provide a statement of reasons did not apply (para.16). Third, under general law there would be a duty to give reasons for refusing to adjourn, if the reason was not readily apparent, but those reasons need not be elaborate (paras 23–24). Fourth, Art.6(1) of the European Convention had no application to this paragraph, which was only concerned with the mechanics of obtaining written reasons (para.22). Fifth, if there was a good reason for refusing the adjournment but the reasons given were inadequate, the proper course was not to set the tribunal's decision aside on that ground, but to declare that the reasons were inadequate without granting additional relief (para.12). That approach was said to be in line with the approach of the European Court of Human Rights.

There is a duty on chairmen to record the decision of the tribunal and its reasons for that decision. The recording of reasons for decision is not optional as this paragraph is mandatory (*R(G) 1/63*, para.8). If the chairman sat with other panel members, the reasons must be those of the tribunal as a whole and not just those of the chairman (*CDLA 1807/03*). This provision displaces the general duty to supply reasons for decision pursuant to a prior request which is placed upon tribunals themselves, rather than on their chairmen, by s.10 of and Sch 1 to the Tribunals and Inquiries Act 1992 (s.10(5)(a) of that Act and *R(F) 1/70*, para.15).

The chairman may not be able to recall the reasons for decision. This is likely to occur if the application is made late or there is a delay in the application being processed by the administration. The best practice in these circumstances is for the chairman to write a short statement explaining the difficulty and adopting the decision notice as the reasons for decision. This will allow s.23A of the Act to operate and avoid the difficulties encountered in *CDLA 1685/04* in which the chairman refused to provide a statement.

Sometimes chairmen specify that the decision notice is also the statement of the tribunal's findings of fact and reasons for decision. As a practical matter, it will often not be possible to state a tribunal's findings of fact and reasons for decisions adequately and succinctly to allow this to be done (*CDLA 96/99*, para.13). As to the effectiveness of the practice in law, it is suggested that it is acceptable. The present wording does not prevent a chairman giving a statement without the need for an application in writing and there is no point in requiring the chairman to use a separate piece of paper to do this. The legal argument against the practice was based on the wording of the former regulations (*CIS 4437/98*). However, it has been confirmed under the Social Security Commissioners (Procedure) Regulations 1999 (*CSDLA 551/99*, para.6), although this does not recognise the use of the words "if separate" in the provision that the Commissioner was considering (the equivalent to reg.12(2)(b) of the Child Support Commissioners (Procedure) Regulations 1999). Chairmen may wish to use a separate form in order to avoid any possible doubt.

Failure to give adequate reasons will be an error of law (*R(SB) 26/83*, para.12). It is not every failure to give reasons that amounts to a denial of justice and an error of law. The relevant consideration is whether the reasons given are sufficient to indicate that the tribunal considered the point at issue between the parties and the evidence on which they came to their conclusions (*R. v Immigration Appeal Tribunal Ex p. Khan* [1983] 2 All E.R. 420 at 423, per Lord Lane C.J.).

The courts have laid down some general principles with regard to reasons. The Commissioners have given more detailed guidance as to what is required in particular contexts. There is a degree of conflict between the standards indicated in the court decisions on the nature and adequacy of reasons and the demands of the Commissioners who set standards which are far higher than can often realistically be achieved in the limited time available. This is made clear by the approach of the Court of Appeal in *English v Emery Reimbold and Strick Ltd* [2002] 3 All E.R. 385 (applied to tribunals by *Burns v Royal Mail Group (formerly Consignia plc), The Times*, June 24, 2004). The Court held that if reasons for decision were not stated, they must be apparent from the reasons that have been given in the context of the evidence and submissions (para.26). That is in line with the approach of the Commissioners. However, the effort to which the Court was prepared to go in the application of that principle in order to find an explanation from the context was much greater than would be undertaken in most cases by Commissioners. Their approach is evident in child support appeals. In *CSCS 2/94* the Commissioner expressed the view that a statement in a tribunal's reasons for decision that the certain expenses could not be taken into account because they were not allowable under the terms of the legislation was adequate "although barely so" (para.23). With respect to the Commissioner it is difficult to see what more could have been said or why more should have been said in a case where no arguable issue on the point arose.

The decision must be recorded on a form approved by the President. There is no express legislative power for the President to prescribe the form for the statement of findings of fact and reasons, but such a form has been approved by the President and is made available for use. It is not divided into separate boxes for findings and reasons and chairmen may welcome the freedom which this provides. However, it is nonetheless essential to make clear what findings of fact have been made and to distinguish these from other matters. The issuing of formless reasons was criticised and the use of a structured approach was recommended by the Court of Appeal in *R. v Solihull Metropolitan Borough Council Housing Benefit Review Board Ex p. Simpson* [1995] 1 F.L.R. 140 in the context of the Housing Benefit legislation.

It is seldom that such an extreme case can arise as that which came before Commissioner Heald in *CS 30/1989*, where at para.6 the Commissioner concluded as follows:

"However the absence of any note of evidence, findings, decision, or reasons therefore in respect of the period covered by the first reference must constitute an error of law. It is not strictly necessary to conclude that the tribunal did not give any attention at all to this period; the failure to make any record was a clear breach of regulation 25(2) of the Adjudication Regulations . . . Since there is no record, there is nothing to set aside consequent on the finding of error of law."

At the most basic level the test of adequacy of reasons has been stated to be one of fairness (*CM 113/91* and the cases cited therein). The reasons should fulfil three functions by providing: transparency to the decision-making process; assurance that all issues have been dealt with; and a basis on which an informed decision can be made whether or not to seek leave to appeal (*R. (O'Brien) v Independent Assessor, The Times*, May 5, 2003). The reasons should indicate why the facts were found and the decision was reached, although they need not be long and precise (*Crake v Supplementary Benefits Commission* [1982] 1 All E.R. 498 at 506 and 508, *per* Woolf J.). The reasons must be proper and adequate, being intelligible and dealing with all substantial points raised (*R(SB) 18/83*, para.10 and *Re Poyser and Mills' Arbitration* [1963] 1 All E.R. 612 at 616, *per* Megaw J.), although it is not necessary to deal with every material consideration, however insignificant, or with every argument, however peripheral (*Bolton Metropolitan Borough Council v Secretary of State for the Environment, The Times*, May 25, 1995). Whether a point is marginal or insignificant may depend on the importance attached to it by the party who raised it (*CCS 16817/96*, para.11). The reasons must be clear, but it is not necessary to produce something akin to a court judgment or to set out the relevant statutory provisions (*R(SB) 5181*, paras 7 and 10). It is not essential that every process of reasoning should be set out (*Mountview Court Properties Ltd v Devlin* (1970) 21 P.&C.R. 689 at 692, *per* Lord Parker C.J.). These principles have been regularly indorsed, including by the House of Lords in *Great Portland Estates plc v Westminster City Council* [1984] 3 All E.R. 744 at 752, *per* Lord Scarman. The record should be sufficient to show (i) that the tribunal identified the questions to be determined, (ii) that the tribunal considered all the points in dispute, (iii) the evidence relied on by the tribunal and (iv) that the tribunal acted lawfully (*Kitchen v Secretary of State for Social Services*, unreported July 30, 1993, *per* Neill L.J.). These matters may be indicated either directly or by inference (*Khan* above at 423, *per* Lord Lane C.J.).

The adequacy of a tribunal's reasons must not be considered in isolation. They must be the context of the submissions made to the tribunal, including the extent of agreement shown by those submissions and any explanation contained in the officer's submission *(CCS 10/94*, para.10). The level at which an argument was developed before the tribunal will also affect the detail to be expected from its reasons *(CCS 11729/96*, para.5). They must also be read in conjunction with the notes of proceedings and any literature referred to in the reasons (see the approach of Woolf J. in *Crake v Supplementary Benefits Commission* [1982] 1 All E.R. 498 at 508). The terms of the decision notice may be used to clarify the tribunal's reasons for decision *(CIB 1540/98*, para.23).

Where a principle is well established and well known, such as the burden and standard of proof, it may be unnecessary for the tribunal to refer to it *(Re P (Witness Summons)* [1997] 2 F.L.R. 447 at 455, *per* Wilson J.). An appeal tribunal is assumed to know the law it applies, unless the record shows that it misunderstood or misapplied it *(R(SB) 5/81*, para.7).

In the Court of Appeal decision in *B v. B (Residence Order: Reasons for Decision)* [1997] 2 F.L.R. 602 at 606 Holman J. said of the standard by which reasons are to be judged:

"a judgment is not to approached like a summing-up. It is not an assault course. Judges work under enormous time and other pressures, and it would be quite wrong for this court to interfere simply because an ex tempore judgment given at the end of a long day is not as polished as it might otherwise be."

These comments apply as much to reasons for decisions of tribunals as to judgments given in a court.

Some things are clearly inadequate. The recording of contentions and statements without findings of facts is not acceptable *(R(SB) 42/84*, para.6) and a mere restatement of the decision is not a reason for that decision *(R(SB) 23/82*, para.9 and *R. v Mental Health Review Tribunal Ex p. Clatworthy* [1985] 3 All E.R. 699 at 703, *per* Mann J.). Merely reciting the reference numbers of relevant Commissioners' Decisions is not an adequate explanation of a decision *(R(S) 2/83*, para.4). Failure to record findings of fact and the reasons is obviously unacceptable as a general principle *(R(G) 1/75*, para.2), as is failing to distinguish between evidence given and reasons *(R(F) 6/64*, para.6). More specific guidance is as follows.

The findings of fact must cover all matters material to the decision, that is, all findings necessary to support the decision and reasoning of the tribunal *(R(SB) 31/83*, para.6). The findings must be sufficiently clear to allow a child support officer to implement the tribunal's decision *(CCS 15/94*, para.10). Failure to record any findings will mean that the decision is liable to be set aside on appeal *(R(SB) 6/81*, para.14). Omissions will produce the same result. Findings of fact are not necessary in respect of matters which are not in dispute *(R(CS) 3/96*, para.13). This will include issues covered by a concession made by a competent representative, unless the concession is clearly bad *(CDLA 267/94*, para.8). A tribunal need not make findings where no evidence or totally inadequate evidence is adduced to them *(CDLA 415/94*, para.6). Care should be taken not only with the content of the findings of fact, but also with their form. The chairman should record the primary facts as found and the inferences drawn by the tribunal, not the evidence or arguments presented to the tribunal. Commissioners can be very demanding in this respect. For example, in *R(SB) 3/88*, para.8(1) the findings of fact recorded the view of a witness on a relevant matter and stated that the tribunal accepted that view. However, a Tribunal of Commissioners held that there should have been "a proper finding of fact in relation to that matter." This decision is a valuable warning of the dangers of adopting the statement of facts set out in the submission. There is no magic in any particular way of recording findings of fact. Whether a particular approach is or is not sufficient to satisfy the duty to record material findings of fact depends on the circumstances of the case. See *CI 71/97*, para.17. The comments by Commissioners about the incorporation of facts (or reasons) by reference to other documents, either in their terms or by their context, are always related to the circumstances of the case and the extent to which facts must be found or reasons given. See, for example, the points made by the Commissioner in *CSB 249/85*, para.5. In *(R(IS) 4/93*, para.11 the Commissioner set out two conditions that had to be satisfied if incorporation by reference was to be acceptable. First, the submission must record findings of fact and not arguments or assertions. Second, the findings of fact must be sufficient for the decision; any facts omitted from the submission must be added by the tribunal. The full statement of the tribunal's decision must be read as a whole and it is inappropriate to place a pedantic emphasis on the precise form of words chosen by the tribunal provided that the tribunal made it clear that it accepted those statements and found them as fact (*CDLA 5030/97*, paras 10 and 12). The source from which the facts or reasons are incorporated must be accessible to the parties to the proceedings (*CI 71/97*, para.18 and *CI 4599/97*, para.32). However, it is not adequate for a tribunal to record statements of conflicting evidence without identifying which is accepted in preference to the other (*CDLA 16313/96*, para.5). Whether or not the facts were in dispute is a relevant factor to be taken into account in deciding whether the manner in which the tribunal's findings of fact were recorded was acceptable (*CI 71/97*, para.18), although incorporation of facts by reference will seldom be sufficient if the matters of fact in dispute were of considerable contention (*CIS 548/92*, para.7). Care must also be taken in incorporating details from the chairman's notes of evidence as findings of fact *R(IS) 9/94*, para.11).

A tribunal should refrain from making findings of fact that are critical of a party to the proceedings on a matter that is not relevant to the case as put to the tribunal, and certainly should not do so without giving the party a chance to take issue with the findings (*Vogon International Ltd v Serious Fraud Office, The Times*, February 26, 2004).

This paragraph makes no mention of findings of fact, but the facts material to a decision are an essential part of the reasons for the decision and must be included (*R(I) 4/02*, para.7, qualified by the Tribunal of Commissioners in Northern Ireland in *C28/00–01 (IB)(T)*. If a tribunal decides that, even accepting the evidence presented on a particular question, the party's case is not made out, it is the assertions made that are the material facts. It is not necessary for the tribunal to reach conclusion on the assertions. See *CDLA 5787/97*, para.23. Provided that the evidence can be sufficiently identified by reference to, for example, the record of proceedings, it is not necessary for it to be set out again in the tribunal's statement (*Williams v J Walter Thompson Group Ltd, The Times*, April 5, 2005).

The reasons for decision must explain why the tribunal reached all its decisions on matters in dispute before it. This will include explanations on decisions on matters of fact, for example, why it accepted or rejected particular pieces of evidence (*R(SB) 8/84*, para.25(3)) or how it made use of its own knowledge on a particular matter, as well as how the law was applied to reach the decision. The statement should be sufficient to explain to any party why the decision was made. Every argument of any substance put forward by any party should be dealt with in the reasons (*Re B (Procedure: Family Proceedings Court)* [1993] Fam. Law 209). This is especially important in relation to matters which are emotionally charged (*ibid.*) as tribunal proceedings may be. However, where a tribunal has dealt with the case in a way that renders it unnecessary to deal with an argument, it need not deal with that argument in its reasons, even if that argument was the central one advanced by one of the parties (*The Post Office v Lewis, The Times*, April 25, 1997). In the case of a discretion, the more unusual the manner of its exercise the greater the need for a clear statement of the reasons for doing so (*Jones v Governing Body of Burdett Courts School* [1999] I.C.R. 38).

The reasons should be those that led the tribunal to its conclusion rather than a later rationalisation. In practice, these can be difficult to distinguish. In some cases, they can be. An example was *CIB 2492/04*, in which the chairman relied in part on the claimant's reaction when she received the tribunal's decision. The Commissioner held that the decision was wrong in law.

*CM 140/92*, paras 19–22 emphasises the importance of consistency as between the same parties. The issue arises when a tribunal is dealing with an issue which has already been decided in the context of an earlier assessment. If there has been no change in the facts, the tribunal should follow the earlier decision unless to do so would be perverse. If a tribunal prefers to follow this decision to *CM 20/94* (as to the difference see the general note to s.3(2) of the Act), its reasons should show that the earlier decision has been considered. Ideally, whichever decision is followed, the reasons should explain why the decision on this occasion differs from the earlier one. However, there will be no error of law if the decision does not contain such an explanation, provided that the reason for the different decision is clear.

Some chairmen may wish to follow a convenient practice and adopt the reasons in the submission as those of the tribunal. There is no objection to this approach in principle, provided that the passages adopted are sufficiently clearly and unambiguously expressed (*Givandan and Co Ltd v Minister of Housing and Local Government* [1966] 3 All E.R. 696 at 699, *per* Megaw J.). However, any chairman following this course should be aware of two dangers. First, if that submission contains any error the tribunal will have adopted that error as its own. Second, if there are any matters not dealt with in that submission, for example, why certain evidence or arguments were rejected, they must be added by the chairman (*CSB 249/85*, para.5).

Although the statement must contain the reasons for the decision, it need not go further and give the reasons for those reasons (*R. v Secretary of State for the Home Department Ex p. Swati* [1986] 1 All E.R. 717 at 728, *per* Parker L.J.). So, it is sufficient to say "we rejected this evidence because it was inherently improbable" without going on to spell out why it was inherently improbable.

It has been said that in cases involving value judgments (for example, whether persons are living together as husband and wife) clear findings on the relevant issues are all that is required by way of reasons (*CIS 87/93*, para.9), but it is wise to include some indication of the test applied by the tribunal.

The form of reasons should be user-friendly. In *Williams v J Walter Thompson Group Ltd, The Times*, April 5, 2005, extensive numbering in roman numberals caused problems for the Court of Appeal.

For a discussion of whether reasons can be supplemented, see the *Question of law* section of the general note to s.24(1) of the Act.

*Standard form reasons*

There are a number of devices that have been used to reduce the time taken in recording a full statement of the tribunal's decision. Each device is valuable in a suitable case, but only if it is used appropriately. There are three popular devices:

(i) *Specifying the decision notice as the full statement of the tribunal's decision* is appropriate if the tribunal's decision can adequately be recorded in a few short sentences, but only provided that the correct sentences are chosen.

(ii) *Adopting the Secretary of State's submission* is appropriate if the submission is accurate and deals with all the issues arising for decision. By taking this approach, the tribunal makes the mistakes or deficiencies in the submission its own.

(iii) *Using standard forms of words or standard decisions* is appropriate provided that they are used only as a model that is adapted to the facts and circumstances of the case, and the tribunal does not allow the standard terms to influence its analysis of the case.

There are three fundamental dangers in using these devices. First, they may deprive the non-resident parent and the person with care of a short statement of the reasons for decision, free of the technicality and detail of the Secretary of State's submission to the tribunal. Second, the reasons may be condensed to the extent that they are merely statements of conclusions rather than reasons. Third, the Commissioner may conclude that the tribunal did not approach the case correctly, but merely rubber stamped the Secretary of State's decision (*CSB 249/85*, para.5), began with an assumption that the Secretary of State's decision was correct and looked for reasons to show the contrary (*CP 1977/99*, para.8(2) or failed to identify or consider the issues arising for decision (*CI 5199/98*, para.6). Also, the European Court of Human Rights has decided that there was a breach of art.5(3) of the Convention, in part because the reasons given by the domestic court were in stereotyped form (*Mansur v Turkey* (1995) Series A No.319–B).

*Paragraph (5)*
A majority decision is possible, but every effort should be made to reach a unanimous decision, including delaying a decision for the minority to consider the written reasons of the majority (*Anglia Home Improvements Ltd v Kelly, The Times*, June 30, 2004).

## Late applications for a statement of reasons of tribunal decision

3.390    **54.**—(1) The time for making an application for [¹. . .] the statement of the reasons for a tribunal's decision may be extended where the conditions specified in paragraphs (2) to (8) are satisfied, but[¹, subject to [¹⁰regulation 53(4A),] no application shall in any event be brought more than three months after the date of the sending or giving of the notice of the decision of the appeal tribunal.

(2) An application for an extension of time under this regulation shall be made in writing and shall be determined by a legally qualified panel member.

(3) An application under this regulation shall contain particulars of the grounds on which the extension of time is sought, including details of any relevant special circumstances for the purposes of paragraph (4).

(4) The application for an extension of time shall not be granted unless the panel member is satisfied that it is in the interests of justice for the application to be granted.

(5) For the purposes of paragraph (4) it is not in the interests of justice to grant the application unless the panel member is satisfied that—

(a) the special circumstances specified in paragraph (6) are relevant to the application; or

(b) some other special circumstances are relevant to the application, and as a result of those special circumstances it was not practicable for the application to be made within the time limit specified in regulation 53(4).

(6) For the purposes of paragraph (5)(a), the special circumstances are that—

(a) the applicant or a [³partner] or dependant of the applicant has died or suffered serious illnes;

(b) the applicant is not resident in the United Kingdom; or

(c) normal postal services were adversely disrupted.

(7) In determining whether it is in the interests of justice to grant the application, the panel member shall have regard to the principle that the greater the amount of time that has elapsed between the expiration of the time within which the application for a copy of the statement of reasons for a tribunal's decision is to be made and the making of the application for an extension of time, the more compelling should be the special circumstances on which the application is based.

(8) In determining whether it is in the interests of justice to grant the application, no account shall be taken of the following—

(a) that the person making the application or any person acting for him was unaware of, or misunderstood, the law applicable to his case (including ignorance or misunderstanding of the time limits imposed by these Regulations); or

(b) that a Commissioner or a court has taken a different view of the law from that previously understood and applied.

(9) An application under this regulation for an extension of time which has been refused may not be renewed.

(10) The panel member who determines the application shall record a summary of his [⁴determination] in such written form as has been approved by the President.

(11) As soon as practicable after the [⁵determination] is made [⁷notice] of the [⁵determination] shall be sent or given to every party to the proceedings.

(12) Any person who under paragraph (11) receives [⁸notice] of the [⁶determination] may, within one month of the [⁶determination] being sent to him, apply in writing for a copy of the reasons for that [⁶determination] and a copy shall be supplied to him.

[⁹. . .]

AMENDMENTS

1. Regulation 29(a) of the Social Security and Child Support (Miscellaneous Amendments) Regulations 2000 (June 19, 2000).

3. Regulation 17(a) of the Appeals Amendment Regulations 2002 (May 20, 2002).

4. Regulation 17(b) of the Appeals Amendment Regulations 2002 (May 20, 2002).

5. Regulation 17(b) of the Appeals Amendment Regulations 2002 (May 20, 2002).

6. Regulation 17(b) of the Appeals Amendment Regulations 2002 (May 20, 2002).

7. Regulation 17(c) of the Appeals Amendment Regulations 2002 (May 20, 2002).

8. Regulation 17(d) of the Appeals Amendment Regulations 2002 (May 20, 2002).

9. Regulation 17(e) of the Appeals Amendment Regulations 2002 (May 20, 2002).

10. Regulation 2(11)(b) of the Amendment Regulations 2005 (March 18, 2005).

11. Regulation 2(11)(a) of the Amendment Regulations 2005 (March 18, 2005).

**3.391**    "Commissioner": see.57B(1).
"decision": see reg.57B(1).
"decision notice": see reg.57B(2).
"legally qualified panel member": see reg.1(3).
"President": see reg.1(3).

## Record of tribunal proceedings

**3.392**    **55.**—(1) A record of the proceedings at an oral hearing, which is sufficient to indicate the evidence taken, shall be made by the chairman, or in
the case of an appeal tribunal which has only one member, by that member,
in such medium as he may direct.
[¹(2) The clerk to the appeal tribunal shall preserve-
(a) the record of proceedings;
(b) the decision notice; and
(c) any statement of the reasons for the tribunal's decision,
for the period specified in paragraph (3).]
[¹(3) That period is six months from the date of-
(a) the decision made by the appeal tribunal;
(b) any statement of reasons for the tribunal's decision;
(c) any correction of the decision in accordance with regulation 56;
(d) any refusal to set aside the decision in accordance with regulation 57;
or
(e) any determination of an application under regulation 58 for leave to
appeal against the decision,
or until the date on which those documents are sent to the office of the
Social Security and Child Support Commissioners in connection with an
appeal against the decision or an application to a Commissioner for leave
to appeal, if that occurs within the six months.]
[¹(4) Any party to the proceedings may within the time specified in paragraph (3) apply in writing for a copy of the record of proceedings and a
copy shall be supplied to him.]

AMENDMENT

1. Regulation 2(12) of the Amendment Regulations 2005 (March 18, 2005).

DEFINITIONS

**3.393**    "clerk to the appeal tribunal": see reg.1(3).
"Commissioner": see.57B(1).
"decision": see reg.57B(1).
"decision notice": see reg.57B(2).
"partner": see reg.1(3)
"party to the proceedings": see reg.1(3).

GENERAL NOTE

*Paragraph (1)*
**3.394**    This paragraph imposes a duty on the chairman to make a record of proceedings.
It is best discharged by the chairman personally taking a record. Exceptionally, it

may be appropriate to delegate the duty, as when the chairman has a broken arm or is disabled. If the duty is delegated, the record should be presented as that of the person who took it, although the chairman may adopt it if satisfied that it is accurate (*R(SB) 13/83*, para.14), as may be the case if it has been dictated by the chairman. The chairman should be aware of the dangers of (i) delegating the making of the record to someone who is not experienced in the art of note-taking; (ii) relying on someone else's notes; and (iii) distracting the note-taker from other duties, especially a clerk.

*The contents of the record*

This paragraph requires the record to be "sufficient to indicate the evidence taken", but is otherwise silent on the contents.

Proceedings is used in the sense of "what took place at the hearing" (*CIB 4743/97*, para.17). The record of proceedings should a record of the evidence taken at the hearing, submissions made, and any other relevant matters. It should make clear not only what was said or done, but who said or did what. See *R(SB) 8/84*, para.25(6). The chairman's thoughts, if committed to paper, are best recorded separately.

The record should be contemporaneous (*CSB 613/83*, para.8). This does not mean that it must be made in the course of the hearing, although the closer it is made to the hearing the more likely it is to be accurate.

The National Insurance Commissioners held that the note of evidence should be complete (*R(I) 81/51*, para.23; *R(U) 16/60*, para.5). Those decisions were given at a time when an appeal to a Commissioner lay on both fact and law, so that the Commissioner needed to have all the evidence available. When an appeal to a Commissioner lay only on a question of law Commissioners no longer insisted on a verbatim record (*CSSB 212/87*, para.3). What was required was the happy mean, which chairmen regularly produced, between a verbatim record and a brief summary (*CIS 12032/96*, para.7). The specific requirement that the record be sufficient to indicate the evidence taken may lead to a higher standard of record being expected by the Commissioners.

The record of proceedings, at least as supplied to the parties, must be clear, complete, comprehensible and legible (*CDLA 16902/96*, paras 8 and 9; *CDLA 4110/97*, para.7; *CIB 3013/97*, para.10).

*Significance of the record*

Failure to make a record of proceedings may be an error of law (*R(I) 81/51*, para.23; *R(I) 42/59*, para.35). The lack of a record of proceedings before a Commissioner on appeal will be an error of law if in a particular case it is necessary to have regard to the evidence given at the hearing or to any contention put forward at the hearing in order to decide if the case falls within any of the recognised heads of error of law. The lack of any, or of an adequate, record of proceeding is not of itself and in all circumstances an error of law. The absence of, or deficiency in, the notes of proceedings is not a separate head of error of law. However, it is subsidiary to, and protective and supportive of, the recognised heads of error of law in that it will be an error of law if it prevents a Commissioner from deciding whether a particular error of law has been shown. See *CDLA 1389/97*, para.18. For example, there will be an error of law if it is necessary to refer to the record of proceedings in order to know what matters were in issue before the tribunal (*ibid.*, paras 19 and 35) or to know what evidence was before the tribunal (*CSSB 212/87*, para.3) and that it was taken into account by the tribunal (*CIS 12032/96*, para.7).

The lack of a record of proceedings will not be an error of law if no party to the proceedings requested a copy within the time limit set by para.(2) and the record was destroyed by the clerk to the appeal tribunal.

On appeal, a Commissioner is not limited the evidence appearing in the documents and the record of proceedings. As Commissioners do not insist on a verbatim note of evidence, it is inappropriate to treat the record of proceedings as a comprehensive record of the oral evidence and submissions. The position was set out in *CS 4537/98*, para.13. The chairman's record should be taken as comprehensive unless one of the parties is able to persuade the Commissioner that the record omits specific relevant evidence or submissions. The suggestion in *R(SB) 10/82*, para.15 that an agreed record should be obtained has not been followed by Commissioners. However, it would help the Commissioner if chairmen, when granting or refusing applications for leave to appeal on grounds that allege the record of proceedings was incomplete, recorded their recollections so that the Commissioner could have a relatively contemporaneous response to the allegations. In *CDLA 4879/03* para.28, the Commissioner encouraged representatives to take a record of evidence given in order to supplement, if necessary, the evidence recorded by the chairman. However, it is appropriate to treat with caution information about the evidence given, or submissions made, at the hearing before an appeal tribunal if the chairman has not commented on it.

The Commissioner in *CDLA 1389/97* did not explain how his reasoning, and that in the decisions on which he relied, related to the Commissioners' power to supplement (or overcome) the lack of a record of proceedings by reference to other sources of information about the hearing.

*Paragraphs (2) to (4)*

*The clerk's duties*

These paragraphs impose two duties on the clerk to an appeal tribunal: (i) to preverse the record of proceedings, the decision notice and any full statement of the tribunal's decision; and (ii) to supply a copy of the record to a party to the proceedings on request being made in writing.

The time limit on the duties to preserve and to supply on request a copy of the record of proceedings is set by para.(3).

The duty to supply only arises on a request in writing by a party to the proceedings. A Commissioner has suggested that an application for leave to appeal to a Commissioner should be treated as a request for a copy of the record of proceedings (*R(IS) 11/99*, para.33).

A copy is only supplied to the party to the proceedings who requested it. The other parties to the proceedings are automatically sent a copy as well.

The time limit of six months is shorter than the time limit for obtaining leave to appeal to a Commissioner.

*The clerk's powers*

This regulation is concerned with duties. It does not limit the powers of the clerk to the appeal tribunal. In particular, the clerk has power:

(i) to preserve the record of proceedings for longer than six months;

(ii) to supply a copy outside the time limit;

(iii) to supply a copy in response to an oral request;

(iv) to supply, or allow access to, the original rather than a copy of the record;

(v) to supply the original record, or a copy, to a Commissioner. A Commissioner has no power under this regulation to require the record itself or a copy. In practice, when an application for leave to appeal to a Commissioner is made, the whole file is sent to the Commissioners' Office. A Commissioner may have power to obtain the record of proceedings under reg.19(3) of the Child Support Commissioners (Procedure) Regulations 1999.

## Correction of accidental errors

**56.**—(1) The clerk to the appeal tribunal [¹or a legally qualified panel member] may at any time correct accidental errors in [²the notice of any decision] of an appeal tribunal made under . . . the Child Support Act . . .

[³(2) A correction made to a decision notice shall be deemed to be part of the decision notice and written notice of the correction shall be given as soon as practicable to every party to the proceedings.]

. . .

3.395

AMENDMENTS

1. Regulation 30 of the Social Security and Child Support (Miscellaneous Amendments) Regulations 2000 (June 19, 2000).
2. Regulation 2(13)(a) of the Amendment Regulations 2005 (March 18, 2005).
3. Regulation 2(13)(b) of the Amendment Regulations 2005 (March 18, 2005).

DEFINITIONS

"clerk to the appeal tribunal": see reg.1(3).
"decision": see reg.57B(1).
"decision notice": see reg.57B(2).
"legally qualified panel member": see reg.1(3).
"party to the proceedings": see reg.1(3).

3.396

GENERAL NOTE

*Paragraph (1)*

This regulation applies to decisions made on both appeals and on referrals. It applies only to decisions and records of decisions. It does not apply to determinations, whether by tribunals or chairmen. It does not apply to the chairman's record of proceedings made under reg.55. Correction of that record is a matter for the chairman.

The power to correct accidental errors in a decision is given to the clerk to the tribunal or to a legally qualified panel member. It is not given to the appeal tribunal or to the chairman. There will, though, be cases in which the tribunal or chairman is able to correct a decision or record of decision without reference to this regulation.

(i) This regulation does not apply until the decision is promulgated. An appeal tribunal has control over its decision until it is promulgated, which means until it is notified to the parties *(CSB 226/81)*. This may allow the tribunal time to correct its decision before this regulation begins to apply.

(ii) This regulation does not apply until the record of decision is issued. The meaning of "record of decision" is not clear. When the words were first used in reg.14 of the Child Support Appeal Tribunals (Procedure) Regulations 1992, all decisions were recorded in a record of decision that included the decision itself together with the reasons for the decision and the findings of fact material to it. This was replaced by the recording of the decision in summary form in all cases, with a full statement of the tribunal's decision and findings of fact provided only on request. The wording of reg.14 was not amended to take account of this change.

3.397

The giving of a decision in summary in all cases and the issue of a full statement of the tribunal's decision on request is embodied in reg.53. The record of decision certainly refers to the decision in summary and may also refer to the full statement of the tribunal's decision. In either case, the chairman may also have time to make corrections before the document is issued.

No application or request is necessary before a correction can be made, although in practice the issue will usually be raised by a party to the proceedings.

A decision may be corrected: (i) in order to rectify the decision as promulgated to bring it into accord with the oral decision (*Preston Banking Co v William Allsup and Sons Ltd* [1891–1894] All E.R. Rep. 688); and (ii) in order to rectify the decision as promulgated even though it accords with the decision as announced orally, provided that it is clear that the oral decision was inadvertently not what was intended (*Adam and Harvey Ltd v International Maritime Supplies Co Ltd* [1967] 1 All E.R. 533). So, there is power to correct inadvertent clerical or arithmetical errors so as to bring the decision or record of decision into line with what the tribunal intended. If, for example, the word "not" had been omitted or included in error, it could be inserted or removed as appropriate. However, there is no power, once a tribunal is *functus officio*, to alter the decision intended, as opposed to its record or expression (*Preston Banking* above at 689, *per* Lord Halsbury, *Wordingham v Royal Exchange Trust Co Ltd* [1992] 3 All E.R. 204 and *CM 209/87*, para.6.).

The approach taken by the courts when dealing with the equivalent "slip rule" is that the need for a correction must be apparent from contemporary evidence, in the form of either a contradiction between the oral and written decisions or a contradiction within the decision when taken as a whole with its reasons and supporting findings of fact. This ensures that judges do not succumb to the human failing of convincing themselves on reflection that they intended something other than they did at the time. It also takes account of the fact that the power of correction is one conferred on the court and not on the particular judge or judges who made the decision in question, and the court can only base its decision on evidence external to the minds of the members of the earlier court.

This has led the Commissioner in *CM 264/93*, para.15 to adopt the following propositions; (i) the error corrected must be contrary to the manifest intention of the tribunal on the face of the record; (ii) the error must be consistent with the stated intention of the tribunal when giving its decision; (iii) it is insufficient that the tribunal later expresses an intention that its decision should have a different meaning.

It may be, however, that the evidence on which a correction may be based is wider than the approach normally taken by the courts, provided that the evidence is sufficient to avoid the risk of reconsidering a decision rather than correcting its expression. Thus a contemporary note of the decision intended by the tribunal might suffice, as might the unanimous *and independent* recollection of all the members of the tribunal.

In practice a broader approach may be taken to the exercise of this power so as to correct a tribunal's decision if it is clearly wrong and it is clear what it should have been. However, this approach cannot be recommended, as a Commissioner may decide that the purported correction was invalid (see the general note to s.24(1) of the Act).

There is a power to correct an accidental error, but not a duty to do so. It should not be exercised if anything has occurred after the decision was notified to the parties which renders it inexpedient or inequitable to correct it (*Moore v Buchanan* [1967] 3 All E.R. 273). Thus, a correction should not be made if the decision as framed has been relied on to a party's irreversible detriment. The mere fact of delay, however, will not be a sufficient reason not to exercise the power (*Tak Ming Co Ltd v Yee Sang Metal Supplies Co* [1973] 1 All E.R. 569 at 575).

A decision made without jurisdiction cannot be corrected under either this paragraph or the inherent power (*Munks v Munks* [1985] F.L.R. 576). The proper course in such a case is for the tribunal to set aside its decision under its inherent power to do so.

No appeal lies against a correction or refusal to make a correction under this regulation (see reg.57A(2)) although a Commissioner has power to decide that a purported correction was invalid (*CM 264/93*, para.17).

By analogy with the position in employment tribunals, it is possible that if a tribunal announced an oral decision which was followed by a contradictory written decision, a Commissioner might consider that there had been a breach of natural justice (*Gutzmore v J Wardley (Holdings) Ltd* [1993] I.C.R. 581), although the tribunal does retain control over the decision until it is promulgated.

*Inherent power*

This regulation does not affect any inherent power to make corrections: see s.28ZD(2) of the Act. The inherent powers of statutory tribunals to correct slips was recognised by the Court of Appeal in *Akewushola v Secretary of State for the Home Department* [2000] 2 All E.R. 148 at 153–154.

In view of the wide terms of para.(1), the scope for this inherent power is limited. The most likely cases where the inherent power will apply are decisions by chairman, which are not covered by para.(1). Alternatively, chairmen may use their power to reconsider a decision. For a fuller discussion of the inherent power, see the general note to reg.14(1) of the Child Support Appeal Tribunals (Procedure) Regulations 1992 in the 1997 edition.

Apart from the terms of para.(1), clerks have no power to alter decisions (*Memminger-IRO GmbH v Trip-Lite Ltd (No.2)*, *The Times*, July 9, 1992).

*Paragraph (2)*

This paragraph does not apply until the decision notice or the statement of reasons has been issued to the parties to the proceedings.

## Setting aside decisions on certain grounds

**57.**—(1) On an application made by a party to the proceedings, a decision of an appeal tribunal made under . . . the Child Support Act . . . may be set aside by a legally qualified panel member in a case where it appears just to set the decision aside on the ground that—

    (a) a document relating to the proceedings in which the decision was made was not sent to, or was not received at an appropriate time by, a party to the proceedings or the party's representative or was not received at an appropriate time by the person who made the decision;

    (b) a party to the proceedings in which the decision was made or the party's representative was not present at a hearing relating to the proceedings.

    (2) In determining whether it is just to set aside a decision on the ground set out in paragraph (1)(b), the panel member shall determine whether the party making the application gave notice that he wished to have an oral hearing, and if that party did not give such notice the decision shall not be set aside unless [1. . .] that member is satisfied that the interest of justice manifestly so require.

[2(3) An application under this regulation shall—

    (a) be made within one month of the date on which—

        (i) a copy of the decision notice is sent or given to the parties to the proceedings in accordance with regulation 53(3); or

**3.398**

    (ii)  the statement of the reasons for the decision is given or sent in accordance with regulation 53(4),

    whichever is later;

  (b)  be in writing and signed by a party to the proceedings or, where the party has provided written authority to a representative to act on his behalf, that representative;

  (c)  contain particulars of the grounds on which it is made; and

  (d)  be sent to the clerk to the appeal tribunal.]

(4) Where an application to set aside a decision is entertained under paragraph (1), every party to the proceedings shall be sent a copy of the application and shall be afforded a reasonable opportunity of making representations on it before the application is determined.

[⁴(4A) Where a legally qualified panel member refuses to set aside a decision he may treat the application to set aside the decision as an application under regulation 53(4) for a statement of the reasons for the tribunal's decision, subject to the time limits set out in regulation 53(4) and (4A).]

(5) Notice in writing of a determination on an application to set aside a decision shall be sent or given to every party to the proceedings as soon as may be practicable and the notice shall contain a statement giving the reasons for the determination.

[³(6) The time within which an application under this regulation must be made may be extended by a period not exceeding one year where the conditions specified in paragraphs (7) to (11) are satisfied.

(7) An application for an extension of time shall be made in accordance with paragraph (3)(b) to (d), shall include details of any relevant special circumstances for the purposes of paragraph (9) and shall be determined by a legally qualified panel member.

(8) An application for an extension of time shall not be granted unless the panel member is satisfied that—

  (a)  if the application is granted there are reasonable prospects that the application to set aside will be successful; and

  (b)  it is in the interests of justice for the application for an extension of time to be granted.

(9) For the purposes of paragraph (8) it is not in the interests of justice to grant an application for an extension of time unless the panel member is satisfied that—

  (a)  the special circumstances specified in paragraph (10) are relevant to that application; or

  (b)  some other special circumstances exist which are wholly exceptional and relevant to that application,

and as a result of those special circumstances, it was not practicable for the application to set aside to be made within the time limit specified in paragraph (3)(a).

(10) For the purposes of paragraph (9)(a) the special circumstances are that—

  (a)  the applicant or a partner or dependant of the applicant has died or suffered serious illness;

  (b)  the applicant is not resident in the United Kingdom; or

  (c)  normal postal services were disrupted.

(11) In determining whether it is in the interests of justice to grant an application for an extension of time, the panel member shall have regard to the principle that the greater the amount of time that has elapsed between the expiry of the time within which the application to set aside is to be made and the making of the application for an extension of time, the more compelling should be the special circumstances on which the application for an extension is based.

(12) An application under this regulation for an extension of time which has been refused may not be renewed.]

AMENDMENTS

1. Regulation 18(a) of the Appeals Amendment Regulations 2002 (May 20, 2002).
2. Regulation 18(b) of the Appeals Amendment Regulations 2002 (May 20, 2002).
3. Regulation 18(c) of the Appeals Amendment Regulations 2002 (May 20, 2002).
4. Regulation 2(14) of the Amendment Regulations 2005 (March 18, 2005).

DEFINITIONS

"clerk to the appeal tribunal": see reg.1(3).                                3.399
"decision": see reg.57B(1).
"decision notice": see reg.57B(2).
"legally qualified panel member": see reg.1(3).
"partner": see reg.1(3)
"party to the proceedings": see reg.1(3).

GENERAL NOTE

This regulation provides for the decision of an appeal tribunal to be set aside by   3.400
a legally qualified panel member. This power provides a swifter and, therefore, more satisfactory remedy than an application for appeal to a Commissioner in those cases where either course would be appropriate. It should always be considered as a possible course of action in those cases.

The person dealing with the application may or may not have been a member of the tribunal whose decision is the subject of the application. Sometimes this can be an advantage as the person will know what happened at the hearing. Sometimes it would be a breach of the principles of natural justice for the same person to be involved.

The power to set aside applies only to decisions of appeal tribunals. A decision is not effective until it has been promulgated, that is, until it has been notified to the parties to the proceedings in accordance with these Regulations (*CSB 226/81*). Until then, the tribunal itself has control over the decision and may revoke it without reference to this regulation. Determinations are not decisions and cannot be set aside under this regulation.

The power under this regulation only arises on an application by a party to the proceedings. There is no provision allowing a tribunal to act on its own initiative or on the initiative of, say, a legally qualified panel member. This means, for example, that if the clerk discovers that a document sent in by a party to the proceedings was wrongly filed and not put before the appeal tribunal, the party must be invited to apply for the decision of the appeal tribunal to be set aside, unless the appeal tribunal has an inherent to act on its own initiative; see the intoductory general note to these Regulations.

No more than one application can be made, even if a different basis is identified (*CS 137188*, para.14).

There is no provision permitting or prohibiting the withdrawal of an application to set aside the decision of an appeal tribunal.

There is no express power to hold an oral hearing of an application to set aside a decision of an appeal tribunal. A legally qualified panel member has power under reg.38(1) to determine the procedure "in connection with the consideration and determination of an appeal or a referral", but it is possible that these words do not cover an application to set aside a decision so as to allow an oral hearing to be directed.

All the documents that were before the appeal tribunal should be available when the application to set aside is considered and determined (*R(S) 1/87*, para.13).

Since the determination is made by a legally qualified panel member and not by an appeal tribunal, no appeal lies to a Commissioner and the determination itself cannot be set aside, as the power to appeal lies only against a decision of an appeal tribunal and the power to set aside under para.(1) applies only to decisions of appeal tribunals. A dissatisfied applicant may apply for a judicial review of the determination (*R(SB) 55/83*, para.14) or apply for leave to appeal against the decision of the tribunal. For the possibility that a setting aside determination may be reconsidered, see the introductory general note to these Regulations.

If the decision of the appeal tribunal is set aside on grounds that fall outside this regulation and outside the inherent power (if wider), the determination will be liable to be set aside on judicial review. Until this is done, the setting aside is nonetheless binding on the Secretary of State, an appeal tribunal and a Commissioner. Neither appeal tribunals nor the Commissioners have power to carry out a judicial review (*R(G) 2/93*, para.10; *CI 79/90*, para.25). They do, however, have power to determine whether the legally qualified panel member had jurisdiction to act. The circumstances in which this will apply are very limited. They do *not* cover acting basing a decision on invalid or irrelevant considerations, failing to give an opportunity for representations to be made under para.(4) or a breach, however serious, of the principles of natural justice. See the general note to s.20 of the Act, *R(I) 7/94*, paras 25–29, 32 and 34 and *CIS 373/94*.

If the setting aside determination is set aside on judicial review, the application for the setting aside revives and must be dealt with by another legally qualified panel member.

*Paragraph (1)*

There is a discretion to set aside a decision provided that one of two requirements is satisfied. The case must first fall within the terms of subpara.(a) or (b). If it does not, the decision cannot be set aside. If it does, the decision will not automatically be set aside, but only if it appears just that this should be done.

*Subparagraph (a)*

This largely raises a question of fact, although there is a judgment involved in determining what was an appropriate time for the document to be received. In practice, the test is whether there was sufficient time to allow the party's case to be adequately prepared and for the tribunal to take account of the document. In the case of the tribunal itself, the relevant time is when the document was received by the members, not when it was received by the clerk.

The failure to refer to a chairman a request for a full statement of the tribunal's decision is a document that is covered by this provision, but it is only appropriate to set the decision aside on this ground if it is the only cause of the chairman's inability to write a statement (*CDLA 1685/04*, paras 16–17).

This subparagraph envisages that a party's representative is entitled to be sent documents relating to the proceedings, but there is no provision requiring this to be done.

*Subparagraph (b)*

This raises a question of pure fact. The reason for the party's absence is irrelevant here, although it may be relevant when determining whether it appears just to set aside the decision. A party to the proceedings does not have a licence to be absent from the hearing and then apply for the decision to be set aside if it is unfavourable (*CU 270/96*, para.12).

This is subject to para.(2).

*The discretion*

The discretion must be exercised judicially and not in an arbitrary manner (*R(U) 3/89*, para.21. The correctness of the decision is not a relevant consideration, nor is the possible impact that the person or document, if present, may have had on the decision (*ibid.*, paras 13 and 21).

*Inherent power*

This regulation does not affect any inherent power for a tribunal to set aside its decision: see s.28ZD(2) of the Act. It has been considered in relation to Commissioners and there are suggestions that the inherent power may be slightly wider than the regulation governing the setting aside of their determinations (*R(U) 3/89*, para.5(3); *CCS 910/99*, paras 11–14). However, the Court of Appeal in *Akewushola v Secretary of State for the Home Department* [2000] 2 All E.R. 148 at 153–154 considered that statutory tribunals did not have an inherent power to rescind or review their own decisions.

*Paragraph (4)*

This is in accordance with natural justice (*CU 270/86*, para.11).

*Paragraph (5)*

This paragraph makes clear that the result of an application to set aside a decision is a determination and not a decision.

## [¹Provisions common to regulations 56 and 57

**57A.**—[². . .]                                                                    3.401

(2) There shall be no appeal against a correction made under regulation 56 or a refusal to make such a correction or against a determination made under regulation 57.

(3) Nothing in this Chapter shall be construed as derogating from any power to correct errors or set aside decisions which is exercisable apart from these Regulations.]

AMENDMENTS

1. Regulation 19 of the Appeals Amendment Regulations 2002 (May 20, 2002).
2. Regulation 2(15) of the Amendment Regulations 2005 (March 18, 2005).

GENERAL NOTE

The Court of Appeal has held that a statutory tribunal has no inherent or implied power to set aside its decisions (*Akewushola v Secretary of State for the Home Department* [2000] 2 All E.R. 148 *per* Sedley L.J. at 153 and 154).

As the amending regulation was not made by the Lord Chancellor, as required by s.24(7) of the Act, it is of no effect in relation to child support cases.

## [¹Service of decision notice by electronic mail

**57AA.** For the purposes of the time limits in regulations 53 to 57, a properly addressed copy of a decision notice sent by electronic mail is effective from the date it is sent.]

AMENDMENT

1. Regulation 2(16) of the Amendment Regulations 2005 (March 18, 2005).

DEFINITION

"decision notice": see reg.57B(2).

## [¹Interpretation of Chapter V

3.402      **57B.**—(1) In Chapter V, except in regulations 58 and 58A—
"Commissioner" includes Child Support Commissioner;
"decision" includes a determination on a referral.
(2) In Chapter V—
"decision notice" has the meaning given in regulations 53(1) and (2).]

AMENDMENT

1. Regulation 2(17) of the Amendment Regulations 2005 (March 18, 2005).

PART VI

REVOCATIONS

## Revocations

3.403      **59.**—(1) The Regulations listed in column (2) of Schedule 4 are hereby revoked to the extent specified in column (3) of that Schedule.

(2) Notwithstanding their revocation for particular purposes, the Regulations listed in column (2) of Schedule 4 shall continue to have full effect up to and including 28th November 1999 in relation to any benefit to which these Regulations do not apply for the time being by virtue of regulation 1(2).

(3) So much of any document as refers expressly or by implication to any regulation revoked by paragraph (1) shall, in so far as the context permits, for the purposes of these Regulations be treated as referring to the corresponding provision of these Regulations.

DEFINITIONS

3.404      "the Act": see reg.1(3).
"appeal": see reg.1(3).
"clerk to the appeal tribunal": see reg.1(3).
"the date of notification": see reg.1(3).

"financially qualified panel member": see reg.1(3).
"legally qualified panel member": see reg.1(3).
"misconceived appeal": see reg.1(3).
"out of jurisdiction appeal": see reg.1(3).
"panel": see reg.1(3).
"panel member": see reg.1(3).
"party to the proceedings": see reg.1(3).
"president": see reg.1(3).
"referral": see reg.1(3).

### SCHEDULE 1

PROVISIONS CONFERRING POWERS EXERCISED IN MAKING THESE REGULATIONS    **3.405**

| *Column (1)* *Provision* | | *Column (2)* *Relevant Amendments* |
|---|---|---|
| Child Support Act 1991 | Section 7A91) | The Act, Section 47 |
| | Section 16(6) | The Act, Section 40 |
| | Section 20(5) and (6) | The Act, Section 42 |
| | Section 28ZA(2)(b) and (4)(c) | The Act, Section 43 |
| | Section 28ZB(6)(c) | The Act, Section 43 |
| | Section 28ZC(7) | The Act, Section 44 |
| | Section 28ZD(1) and (2) | The Act, Section 44 |
| | Section 46B | The Act, Schedule 7, paragraph 44 |
| | Section 51(2) | The Act, Schedule 7, paragraph 46 |
| | Schedule 4A, paragraph 8 | The Act, Schedule 7, paragraph 53 |

### SCHEDULE 3

Regulations 1(3) and 35
Qualifications of Persons Appointed to the Panel

*Legal qualifications*

**1.** Persons who—    **3.406**

(a)  have a general qualification (construed in accordance with section 71 of the Courts and Legal Services Act 1990); or

(b)  are advocates or solicitors in Scotland.

. . .

*Financial qualifications*

**4.** Accountants who are members of—

(a)  the Institute of Chartered Accountants in England and Wales;

(b)  the Institute of Chartered Accountants in Scotland;

(c)  the Institute of Chartered Accountants in Ireland;

[[1](cc)  the Institute of Certified Public Accountants in Ireland;]

(d)  the Association of Chartered Certified Accountants;

(e)  the Chartered Institute of Management Accountants; or

(f)  the Chartered Institute of Public Finance and Accountancy.

AMENDMENT

1. Regulation 22 of the Appeals Amendment Regulations 2002 (May 20, 2002).

DEFINITION

3.407    "panel": see reg.1(3).

GENERAL NOTE

3.408    The financially qualified panel members will be of limited relevance in child support cases. They may only sit on appeal tribunals hearing cases involving consideration of difficult issues relating to accounts. They will have a useful role in helping to interpret accounts, when this is relevant. Usually, however, when accounts have to be considered, the question for the tribunal is not what the accounts mean, but whether they are accurate. This turns on an assessment of the party presenting the accounts rather than on an analysis of the accounts. The skills involved in this assessment are not limited to those with the qualifications listed in para.4 of this Schedule and they may be better possessed by those with business experience.

In some circumstances, the presence of a financially qualified panel member is essential in order to ensure a fair hearing. Commissioners have criticised the refusal to appoint one to a tribunal (*CCS 872/00*, paras 13–14) and have directed that one is essential for a proper rehearing (*CCS 3327/99*, para.18).

## The Child Support Commissioners (Procedure) Regulations 1999

### (SI 1999/1305)

*Made by the Lord Chancellor under sections 22(3), 24(6) and (7) and 25(2), (3) and (5) of, and paragraph 4A of Schedule 4 to, the Child Support Act 1991 and of all other powers enabling him in that behalf, after consultation with the Lord Advocate and, in accordance with section 8 of the Tribunals and Inquiries Act 1992, with the Council on Tribunals.*

ARRANGEMENT OF REGULATIONS

PART I

*General Provisions*

3.409    1.  Citation and commencement.

2.  Revocation.

3.  Transitional provisions.

4.  Interpretation.

5.  General powers of a Commissioner.

6.  Transfer of proceedings between Commissioners.

7.  Delegation of functions to authorised officers.

8.  Manner of and time for service of notices, etc.

AMENDMENT

1. Regulation 3(2) of the Commissioners Procedure Amendment Regulations 2005 (February 28, 2005).

GENERAL NOTE

These Regulations apply to all child support appeals from June 1, 1999, whether or not the appeal was made before or after that date and whether it was against a decision of a child support appeal tribunal or a new appeal tribunal. They are subject to the modifications set out in reg.3, including the extraordinarily wide reg.3(3)

**3.410**

which may be too wide and too close to a sub-delegation to be authorised by the primary legislation.

These Regulations contain the procedural powers of Commissioners and their legal officers, together with provisions dealing with appeals to Commissioners against decisions of appeal tribunals and to the court against decisions of Commissioners. For the powers of a Commissioner to make findings of fact and to deal with questions first arising on an appeal, see s.24(3) and (8) of the Act, and for the power to convene a Tribunal of Commissioners, see Sch.4, para.5 to the Act.

Like the Appeals Regulations, these Regulations distinguish between determinations and decisions. See the introductory general note to those Regulations and the special provision in reg.29(1) of these Regulations.

PART I

GENERAL PROVISIONS

### Citation and commencement

3.411    **1.** These Regulations may be cited as the Child Support Commissioners (Procedure) Regulations 1999 and shall come into force on 1st June 1999.

### Revocation

3.412    **2.** The following Regulations are revoked to the extent that they relate to proceedings before the Child Support Commissioners—
- (a) the Child Support Commissioners (Procedure) Regulations 1992;
- (b) the Child Support Commissioners (Procedure) (Amendment) Regulations 1996;
- (c) the Social Security (Adjudication) and Commissioners Procedure and Child Support Commissioners (Procedure) Amendment Regulations 1997; and
- (d) the Child Support Commissioners (Procedure) (Amendment) Regulations 1997.

### Transitional provisions

3.413    **3.**—(1) Subject to paragraphs (2) and (3), these Regulations shall apply to all proceedings before the Commissioners on or after 1st June 1999.

(2) In relation to any appeal or application for leave to appeal from any child support appeal tribunal constituted under the Act, these Regulations shall have effect with the modifications that—
- (a) "appeal tribunal" includes a reference to any such tribunal;
- (b) "Secretary of State" includes a reference to a child support officer;
- (c) "three months" shall be substituted for "one month" in regulation 10(1) and "42 days" shall be substituted for "one month" in regulations 11(2) and 15(1); and
- (d) under regulation 11 a Commissioner may for special reasons accept an application for leave to appeal even though the applicant has not sought to obtain leave to appeal from the chairman.

(3) Any transitional question arising under any application or appeal in consequence of the coming into force of these Regulations shall be determined by a Commissioner who may for this purpose give such directions

as he may think just, including modifying the normal requirements of these Regulations in relation to the application or appeal.

DEFINITIONS

"the Act": see reg.4.  **3.414**
"appeal tribunal": see reg.4.
"the chairman": see reg.4.
"Commissioner": see reg.4.
"month:" see reg.4.
"proceedings": see reg.4.

GENERAL NOTE

*Paragraph (2)(d)*
An Edinburgh-based Commissioner has decided that an application for leave to  **3.415**
appeal is competent under this provision even if a full statement of the tribunal's
decision has not been provided (*CSIB 596/99*, para.8; *CSDLA 551/99*, para.9). This
removes the difference of view between the Commissioners in London and
Edinburgh that applied on the interpretation of the former Regulations.

## Interpretation

**4.** In these Regulations, unless the context otherwise requires—  **3.416**
  [1"the 1999 Regulations" means the Social Security and Child Support
    (Decisions and Appeals) Regulations 1999;]
  "the Act" means the Child Support Act 1991;
  "appeal tribunal" means an appeal tribunal constituted under Chapter 1
    of Part I of the Social Security act 1998;
  "authorised officer" means an officer authorised by the Lord
    Chancellor, or in Scotland by the Secretary of State, in accordance
    with paragraph 4A of Schedule 4 to the Act;
  "the chairman" for the purposes of regulations 10, 11 and 12 means—
    (i) the person who was the chairman or sole member of the appeal
        tribunal which gave the decision against which leave to appeal is
        being sought; [2. . .]
    (ii) any other person authorised to deal with applications for leave
         to appeal to a Commissioner against that decision under the
         Act;
  "Commissioner" means a Child Support Commissioner;
  [3"funding notice" means the notice or letter from the Legal Services
    Commission confirming that legal services are to be funded;]
  [3"legal aid certificate" means the certificate issued by the Scottish Legal
    Aid Board confirming that legal services are to be funded;]
  "legally qualified" means being a solicitor or barrister, or in Scotland, a
    solicitor or advocate;
  [4"Legal Services Commission" means the Legal Services Commission
    established under section 1 of the Access to Justice Act 1999;]
  [4"live television link" means a television link or other audio and video
    facilities which allow a person who is not physically present at an oral
    hearing to see and hear proceedings and be seen and heard by all
    others who are present (whether physically present or otherwise);]

"month" means a calendar month;

"office" means an Office of the Child Support Commissioners;

[5"panel member" means a person appointed to the panel constituted under section 6 of the Social Security Act 1998 and who—

  (i) has a general qualification (construed in accordance with section 71 of the Courts and Legal Services Act 1990);

  (ii) is a member of the Bar of Northern Ireland or a Solicitor of the Supreme Court of Northern Ireland; or

  (iii) is an advocate or solicitor in Scotland.]

"party" means a party to the proceedings;

"proceedings" means any proceedings before a Commissioner, whether by way of an application for leave to appeal to, or from, a Commissioner, by way of an appeal or otherwise;

"respondent" means any person other than the applicant or appellant who was a party to the proceedings before the appeal tribunal and any other person who, pursuant to a direction given under regulation 18 is served with notice of the appeal; [6 . . .

"Scottish Legal Aid Board" means the Scottish Legal Aid Board established under section 1 of the Legal Aid (Scotland) Act 1986; and]

"summons", in relation to Scotland, corresponds to "citation" and regulation 23 shall be construed accordingly.

AMENDMENTS

1. Regulation 3(3)(a) of the Commissioners Procedure Amendment Regulations 2005 (February 28, 2005).

2. Regulation 3(3)(d) of the Commissioners Procedure Amendment Regulations 2005 (February 28, 2005).

3. Regulation 3(3)(c) of the Commissioners Procedure Amendment Regulations 2005 (February 28, 2005).

4. Regulation 3(3)(d) of the Commissioners Procedure Amendment Regulations 2005 (February 28, 2005).

5. Regulation 3(3)(e) of the Commissioners Procedure Amendment Regulations 2005 (February 28, 2005).

6. Regulation 3(3)(f) of the Commissioners Procedure Amendment Regulations 2005 (February 28, 2005).

GENERAL NOTE

*"party"*

3.417    The parties to the proceedings are the applicant and the respondents as defined in this regulation.

*"respondent"*

This definition does not include any express power for a Commissioner to identify as a respondent someone who was not a party to the proceedings before the appeal tribunal. The power of the Commissioner under reg.18(1)(a) to give a direction specifying the parties who are to be respondents allows this.

## General powers of a Commissioner

3.418    **5.**—(1) Subject to the provisions of these Regulations, a Commissioner may adopt any procedure in relation to proceedings before him.

(2) A Commissioner may—

(a) extend or abridge any time limit under these Regulations (including, subject to regulations 11(3) and 15(2), granting an extension where the time limit has expired);

(b) expedite, postpone or adjourn any proceedings.

(3) Subject to paragraph (4), a Commissioner may, on or without the application of a party, strike out any proceedings for want of prosecution or abuse of process.

Then the information may be disclosed in the course of the proceedings

(4) Before making an order under paragraph (3), the Commissioner shall send notice to the party against whom it is proposed that it should be made giving him an opportunity to make representations why it should not be made.

(5) A Commissioner may, on application by the party concerned, give leave to reinstate any proceedings which have been struck out in accordance with paragraph (3) and, on giving leave, he may give directions as to the conduct of the proceedings.

(6) Nothing in these Regulations shall affect any power which is exercisable apart from these Regulations.

DEFINITIONS

"Commissioner": see reg.4.  
"party": see reg.4.  
"proceedings": see reg.4.

3.419

GENERAL NOTE

See the general notes to reg.51 of the Appeal Regulations for a commentary on postponement and adjournment of hearings. In contrast, para.2(b) refers to the postponement and adjournment of *proceedings*. The postponement of proceedings refers to a determination that the decision on the appeal should await the outcome of an event, such as the conclusion of an appeal in a case that might provide relevant authority (whether before a court or a Commissioner). The concept of adjournment sits easily with hearings, but less so with proceedings.

3.420

*Paragraph (2)*

The Commissioner's discretion under this paragraph is, unlike other powers such as that in reg.11(3), not subject to the need to show special reasons. The only limitation is that the discretion must be exercised judicially. See the decision of the Commissioner on the setting aside application in *CDLA 1182/97*, para.9.

*Paragraph (6)*

As far as the correction of errors and the setting aside of decisions are concerned, this paragraph is based on s.28ZD(2) of the Act.

In *CCS 910/99*, the Commissioner relied on the inherent (he preferred to call it "implied") power to set aside his earlier refusal of leave to appeal on the basis that he had given that determination under a fundamental misconception of the circumstances of the case. He disagreed with the Commissioners in *R(S) 3/89* and *R(U) 3/89*, who held that the inherent power to set aside a decision or determination was limited to procedural errors, although he accepted that the scope of the power beyond procedural error was extremely limited (*ibid*, paras

10–14). (The Commissioner did not deal with the possibility of reconsidering his determination.)

## Transfer of proceedings between Commissioners

3.421    **6.** If it becomes impractical or inexpedient for a Commissioner to continue to deal with proceedings which are or have been before him, any other Commissioner may rehear or deal with those proceedings and any related matters.

DEFINITIONS

3.422    "Commissioner": see reg.4.
"proceedings": see reg.4.

## Delegation of functions to authorised officers

3.423    **7.**—(1) The following functions of Commissioners may be exercised by legally qualified authorised officers, to be known as legal officers to the Commissioners—

(a) giving directions under regulations 8, 18 and 19;

(b) determining requests for or directing hearings under regulation 21;

(c) summoning witnesses, and setting aside a summons made by a legal officer, under regulation 23;

(d) postponing a hearing under regulation 5;

(e) giving leave to withdraw or reinstate applications or appeals under regulation 24;

(f) waiving irregularities under regulation 25 in connection with any matter being dealt with by a legal officer;

(g) extending or abridging time, directing expedition, giving notices, striking out and reinstating proceedings under regulation 5.

(2) Any party may, within 14 days of being sent notice of the direction or order of a legal officer, make a written request to a Commissioner asking him to reconsider the matter and confirm or replace the direction or order with his own, but, unless ordered by a Commissioner, a request shall not stop proceedings under the direction or order.

DEFINITIONS

3.424    "authorised officer": see reg.4.
"Commissioner": see reg.4.
"legally qualified": see reg.4.
"party": see reg.4.
"proceedings": see reg.4.
"summons": see reg.4.

## Manner of and time for service of notices, etc.

3.425    **8.**—(1) A notice to or other document for any party shall be deemed duly served if it is—

(a) delivered to him personally; or

(b) properly addressed and sent to him by prepaid post at the address last notified by him for this purpose, or to his ordinary address; or

[¹(ba) subject to paragraph (1A), sent by e-mail; or]
   (c) served in any other manner a Commissioner may direct.
[²(1A) A document may be served by e-mail on any party if the recipient has informed the person sending the e-mail in writing—
   (a) that he is willing to accept service by e-mail;
   (b) of the e-mail address to which the documents should be sent; and
   (c) if the recipient wishes to so specify, the electronic format in which documents must be sent.]
   (2) A notice to or other document for a Commissioner shall be [³—
   (a) delivered to the office in person;
   (b) sent to the office by prepaid post;
   (c) sent to the office by fax; or
   (d) where the office has given written permission in advance, sent to the office by e-mail].
   (3) For the purposes of any time limit, a properly addressed notice or other document sent by prepaid post, fax or e-mail is effective from the date it is sent.

AMENDMENTS

1. Regulation 3(4)(a) of the Commissioners Procedure Amendment Regulations 2005 (February 28, 2005).
2. Regulation 3(4)(b) of the Commissioners Procedure Amendment Regulations 2005 (February 28, 2005).
3. Regulation 3(4)(c) of the Commissioners Procedure Amendment Regulations 2005 (February 28, 2005).

DEFINITIONS

"Commissioner": see reg.4.       **3.426**
"office": see reg.4.
"party": see reg.4.

GENERAL NOTE

*Paragraph (1)*
As printed by the Stationery Office, the Statutory Instrument originally read   **3.427** "duly serviced" instead of "duly served", but this was later corrected.
A Commissioner has held that provisions do not apply if a document is never given or sent to a person, or if there is clear evidence that a document was sent to an out-of-date address and was not received, even when the whereabouts of that person are unknown (*CCS 12848/96*, para.7). If this interpretation is correct, it renders the provision ineffective when it is most needed. The power given to a Commissioner by subparagraph (c) should override this decision.

*Paragraph (3)*
A document is only sent by post if it is sent by the Royal Mail rather than by a courier or through a document exchange (*CIS 550/93*, para.6).
The proper address for a fax is the fax number and the name of the recipient.

## Confidentiality

**9.**—(1) Subject to paragraphs (3) and (4), the office shall not disclose   **3.428** information such as is mentioned in paragraph (2) except with the written consent of the person to whom the information relates to or, in the case of a child, with the written consent of the person with care of him.

(2) The information referred to in paragraph (1) is any information provided under the Act which—

(a) relates to any person whose circumstances are relevant to the proceedings; and

(b) consists of that person's address or other information which could reasonably be expected to lead to him being located.

(3) Where—

(a) the office sends a notice to a person to whom information relates stating that the information may be disclosed in the course of proceedings unless he objects within one month of the date of the notice; and

(b) written notice of that person's objection is not received at the office within one month of the date of the notice.

(4) Where the person to whom information relates is a child, the office shall send the notice referred to in paragraph (3)(a) to the person with care of the child and where written notice of that person's objection is not received at the office within one month of the date of the notice, then the information may be disclosed in the course of the proceedings.

(5) This regulation does not apply to proceedings which relate solely to a reduced benefits direction within the meaning of section 46(11) of the Act.

DEFINITIONS

**3.429**   "the Act": see reg.4.
"month": see reg.4.
"office": see reg.4.
"proceedings": see reg.4.

GENERAL NOTE

**3.430**   This regulation imposes a duty of confidentiality on the Office of the Child Support Commissioners and not on the Commissioners themselves. The Commissioners are subject to the more limited duty of confidentiality in reg.26(5). There is a possible conflict between this regulation and that provision. The Commissioner is only under a duty not to mention a child's surname and other information that could lead to the *child* being *identified*. The Office is under a duty not to disclose information that might lead to a *person* whose circumstances are relevant to the proceedings being *located*. As the Commissioner's decision will be issued by the Office, the contents of the decision may put the Office in breach of its duty.

*Paragraph (2)*

Subparagraph (a) is more uncertain, and potentially wider, in its scope than the terms of reg.44(1)(a) of the Appeals Regulations which applies to appeal tribunals.

**[¹Funding of legal services**

**9A.** If a party is granted funding of legal services at any time, he shall—

(a) where funding is granted by the Legal Services Commission, send a copy of the funding notice to the office;

(b) where funding is granted by the Scottish Legal Aid Board, send a copy of the legal aid certificate to the office; and

(c) notify every other party that funding has been granted.]

AMENDMENT

1. Regulation 3(5) of the Commissioners Procedure Amendment Regulations 2005 (February 28, 2005).

DEFINITIONS

"funding notice": see reg.4.
"legal aid certificate": see reg.4.
"Legal Services Commission": see reg.4.
"office": see reg.4.
"party": see reg.4
"Scottish Legal Aid Board": see reg.4.

PART II

APPLICATIONS FOR LEAVE TO APPEAL AND APPEALS

## Application to a Chairman for leave to appeal

**10.**—(1) [¹Subject to paragraphs (5) to (7), an application] to a chairman for leave to appeal to a Commissioner from a decision of an appeal tribunal shall be made within one month of the date the written statement of the reasons for the decision was sent to the applicant.

(2) Where an application for leave to appeal to a Commissioner is made by the Secretary of State, the clerk to an appeal tribunal shall, as soon as may be practicable, send a copy of the application to every other party.

(3) Any party who is sent a copy of an application for leave to appeal in accordance with paragraph (2) may make representations in writing within one month of the date the application is sent.

(4) A person determining an application for leave to appeal to a Commissioner shall take into account any further representations received in accordance with paragraph (3) and shall record his decision in writing and send a copy to each party.

(5) Where an applicant has not applied for leave to appeal within one month in accordance with paragraph (1), but makes an application within one year beginning on the day the one month ends, the chairman may for special reasons accept the late application.

[²(6) Where an application for leave to appeal against a decision of an appeal tribunal is made—

(a) if the chairman was a fee-paid panel member, the application may be determined by a salaried panel member; or

(b) if it is impracticable or would be likely to cause undue delay for the application to be determined by the chairman, the application may be determined by another panel member.]

[³(7) Where—

3.431

(a) any decision or the record of a decision is corrected under regulation 56 of the 1999 Regulations; or

(b) an application for a decision to be set aside under regulation 57 of the 1999 Regulations is refused for reasons other than that the application was made outside the period specified in regulation 57(3) of those Regulations,

any time limit specified by this regulation shall run from the date on which notice of the correction or refusal was sent or given to the applicant.]

AMENDMENTS

1. Regulation 3(6) of the Commissioners Procedure Amendment Regulations 2005 (February 28, 2005).
2. Regulation 3(7) of the Commissioners Procedure Amendment Regulations 2005 (February 28, 2005).
3. Regulation 3(8) of the Commissioners Procedure Amendment Regulations 2005 (February 28, 2005).

DEFINITIONS

3.432     "appeal tribunal": see reg.4.
"the chairman": see reg.4.
"Commissioner": see reg.4.
"month": see reg.4.
"panel member": see reg.4.
"party": see reg.4.

GENERAL NOTE

3.433     These Regulations use "leave" rather than "permission", the modern term used by the courts.

A party to the proceedings who wants a full statement of the tribunal's decision must apply within one month, but the time may be extended up to a maximum of three months by a legally qualified panel member. See regs 53(4) and 54(1) and (2) of the Appeals Regulations.

A grant of leave cannot be rescinded by a chairman (*CIS 2002/00*, paras 25–26).

Representatives have a wider responsibility that just to their clients. They have a duty to the tribunal and to the Commissioner not to advance arguments on application or appeal that are plainly hopeless or clearly misconceived (*CIB 908/03*, para.8).

If a chairman refuses leave to appeal to a Commissioner, there are two courses open to the applicant. One course is to apply to the Commissioner for leave under reg.11. The other course is to apply to the court for a judicial review of the refusal, although this will only be granted in the plainest cases (*R. v The Social Security Commissioner and the Social Security Appeal Tribunal Ex p. Pattni*, [1993] Fam. Law 213).

There is no power of appeal against a decision refusing leave (*Bland v Chief Supplementary Benefit Officer* [1983] 1 All E.R. 537; *Kuganathan v Chief Adjudication Officer, The Times*, March 1, 1995 and *R. v Secretary of State for Trade and Industry Ex p. Eastaway* [2001] 1 All E.R. 27). A chairman has no power to reconsider a decision on an application for leave to appeal (*CSI 559/98*, para.11) or to rescind it (*CIS 2002/00*, paras 25–26).

If the chairman purports to give leave on an application which is made outside the time limit, the grant of leave is a nullity (*R(M) 1/80*, para.5).

*Paragraph (5)*

This paragraph confers a discretion on the chairman. The chairman should first consider whether there has been a valid application for time to be extended, then whether special reasons exist and finally, if they do, whether it is a proper case in which to exercise the discretion to extend the time for appealing.

3.434

There is no valid application if the date of the decision which the applicant seeks to appeal is not identified, and if the wrong date is given any decision by the chairman is a nullity (*R(SB) 1/95*, para.12). A Commissioner has power to determine that a tribunal has acted without jurisdiction if it hears an appeal following an invalid application or a decision which is a nullity (*ibid.*, para.12). The same principle applies if in the circumstances of the case there is no application at all before the chairman (*CSB 3648/98*, paras 12–16).

The operation of the power to extend the time for appealing was considered by the Divisional Court in *R. v Social Security Appeal Tribunal Ex p. O'Hara* (1995) 92(02) L.S. Gaz. 37. The decision is authority for the following: (i) there is no specific definition of what may constitute special reasons and almost any factor may be considered; (ii) the applicant has no right to an oral hearing; (iii) the chairman has no duty to give reasons for decision (decisions by chairmen are not covered by s.10 of the Tribunals and Inquiries Act 1992); (iv) the decision can only be challenged on *Wednesbury* grounds (for the meaning of this see the general note to s.24(1) of the Act); (v) in any such challenge the court would assume that the chairman had read all the relevant documents, unless the contrary could be shown; (vi) the chairman was not under a duty to reconsider a decision (although there is power to do so: *CIS 93/92*, paras 15 and 16).

In deciding whether special reasons exist so as to justify the extension of time, the chairman is not limited to reasons relating to the delay. All of the following should ideally be considered, although in practice the information available to the chairman making the decision is limited: (i) the extent of the delay, (ii) the reasons for it, (iii) the consequences of not allowing the appeal or application to proceed, (iv) the likelihood of the appeal or application succeeding, (v) whether it is supported by the child support officer or the Secretary of State (as appropriate) and (iv) any other matter appearing to be relevant, including the amount of maintenance in issue if that is ascertainable. (See *R(U) 8/68*, para.14, *R(M) 1/87*; *CCS 2064/99* and *R. v Secretary of State for Home Department Ex p. Mehta* [1975] 1 W.L.R. 1087).

The merits of the case are relevant to any exercise of a discretion to extend time (*CCS 2064/99* and *Soinco SACl v Novokuznetsk Aluminium Plant, The Times,* December 29, 1997; *R. (Makke) v Secretary of State for the Home Department, The Times,* April 5, 2005). The merits of the case that have to be considered are not just the strength of the criticism of the decision that is subject to the application, but include the merits of the overall circumstances relating to the applicant (*Pant v Secretary of State for the Home Department* [2003] EWCA Civ 1964 at para.16).

In order that a factor may amount to a special reason it must not be common to all late appeals (*Chief Adjudication Officer v Patterson* reported as *R(I) 3/98*, a case on good cause for late claim). The fact that the law has subsequently been altered by a decision of a court or Commissioner is not of itself a ground for the *substantial* extension of time (*R(S) 8/85*, para.6). The fact that documents were despatched in good time but lost in transit will amount to a special reason provided that (at least in cases where an organisation is involved which has a system to identify the fact that no acknowledgement or response has been received) the matter is taken up within a reasonable time (*CIS 550/93*, para.9).

In the context of limitation of actions the courts have held that once representatives have been instructed their faults are not to be visited on the parties themselves (*Corbin v Penfold Metallising Co Ltd, The Times,* May 2, 2000). Commissioners have taken a different view: see the general note to reg.49(8) of the Appeals Regulations.

Delay of itself cannot justify extending the time. However, it may be that the shorter the delay that has occurred the easier it will be to justify the extension of time by reference to other factors. Certainly if the basis of the appeal is that the law has been changed by a recent decision, an application for a long extension is more likely to be successful than an application for a long extension (*R(S) 8/85*, para.6). The principles which the courts apply in striking out or refusing to strike out for want of prosecution do not apply to applications for the extension of time (*Regalbourne Ltd v East Lindsey District Council, The Times,* March 16, 1993).

Where the appeal has been grossly delayed, the chairman should seek written particulars of the reasons for lateness which go well beyond a common-form document, and the older the decision appealed against the greater should be the chairman's reluctance to exercise the discretion to extend the time for appealing (*CSB 123/93*, para.25 and *R(SB) 1/95*, paras 8 and 9). This approach was confirmed by the Court of Appeal in *Pant v Secretary of State for the Home Department* [2003] EWCA Civ 1964. The Court held that special reasons would only be found in exceptional circumstances if there had been a long, unexplained and unjustified delay, even when if it was caused by a legal representative (paras 12 and 38).

If a chairman is minded to accept the application and grant leave, the views of the potential respondents should be obtained on whether special reasons exist (*CCS 2064/99*, para.12).

The ratification of an appeal or application made without authority is not effective unless it is made within the specified time (*Presentaciones Musicales SA v Secunda* [1994] 2 All E.R. 737). If it is made outside that time, special reasons must be shown for extending the time.

*Paragraph (6)*

If an application makes allegations about the conduct of the tribunal, it is particularly important that it should be determined either by the chairman of the tribunal or only after that chairman's comments have been obtained. This practice will ensure that the chairman has a chance to comment on the allegations as close in time as possible to the events of which the applicant is complaining.

## Application to a Commissioner for leave to appeal

3.435

**11.**—(1) An application to a Commissioner for leave to appeal against the decision of an appeal tribunal may be made only where the applicant has sought to obtain leave from the chairman and leave has been refused or the application has been rejected.

(2) Subject to paragraph (3) an application to a Commissioner shall be made within one month of the date that notice of the refusal or rejection was sent to the applicant by the appeal tribunal.

(3) A Commissioner may for special reasons accept a late application or an application where the applicant failed to seek leave from the chairman within the specified time, but did so on or before the final date.

(4) In paragraph (3) the final date means the end of a period of 13 months from the date on which the decision of the appeal tribunal or, if later, any separate statement of the reasons for it, was sent to the applicant by the appeal tribunal.

DEFINITIONS

3.436
    "appeal tribunal": see reg.4.
    "the chairman": see reg.4.

"Commissioner": see reg.4.
"month": see reg.4.

GENERAL NOTE

*Paragraph (1)*

This paragraph distinguishes between a refusal of leave and a rejection of an    3.437
application for leave. An application will be rejected if (i) no full statement of the
tribunal's decision has been given or sent or (ii) the application is out of time and
the chairman refuses to extend time or it is too late to extend time. An application
will be refused if it is in time and the chairman considers it on its merits, but
determines not to grant leave to appeal.

A refusal of leave by a chairman is presumed to be valid. A defect in it does not
deprive the Commissioner of jurisdiction to consider the application. The
Commissioner is not reviewing the chairman's refusal of leave, but is concerned
with the merits of the application. See *CIS 4772/00*, paras 2–11. This is subject to
the issue of special reasons.

*Paragraph (3)*

For a discussion of special reasons see the general note to reg.10(5).

## Notice of application for leave to appeal

12.—(1) An application to a chairman or a Commissioner for leave to    3.438
appeal shall be made by notice in writing, and shall contain—
(a) the name and address of the applicant;
(b) the grounds on which the applicant intends to rely;
(c) if the application is made late, the grounds for seeking late
acceptance; and
(d) an address for sending notices and other documents to the
applicant.
(2) The notice in paragraph (1) shall have with it copies of—
(a) the decision against which leave to appeal is sought;
(b) if separate, the written statement of the appeal tribunal's reasons for
it; and
(c) if it is an application to a Commissioner, the notice of refusal or
rejection sent to the applicant by the appeal tribunal.
(3) Where an application for leave to appeal is made to a Commissioner
by the Secretary of State he shall send each respondent a copy of the notice
of application and any documents sent with it when they are sent to the
Commissioner.

DEFINITIONS

"appeal tribunal": see reg.4.    3.439
"the chairman": see reg.4.
"Commissioner": see reg.4.
"respondent": see reg.4.

GENERAL NOTE

*Paragraph (2)(b)*

3.440    For a discussion of whether the decision notice and the full statement of the tribunal's decision may be in the same document, see the general note to reg.53(4) of the Appeals Regulations. The words "if separate" in this provision recognise that they may.

The lack of a statement may, in appropriate circumstances, be waived under reg.25 (*CSDLA 536/99*).

As the applicant is required to specify grounds, the Commissioner is not required to consider any other possible ways in which the tribunal may have gone wrong in law (*R. (Makke) v Secretary of State for the Home Department, The Times*, April 5, 2005). However, in practice Commissioners take an inquisitorial approach and may grant leave for reasons not identified by the applicant.

*Paragraph (2)(c)*

An application for leave to appeal to a Commissioner must be put to the legally qualified panel member. A rejection by a clerk is not sufficient. If the application to the Commissioner is made following a rejection by a clerk, it is premature and must be returned to be put before a legally qualified panel member (*CSIS 629/98*, paras 2 and 13). If the application is rejected or leave to appeal refused by the panel member, application may then be made to the Commissioner (*ibid.*, para.14).

In *CIB 7644/99*, para.7, the Commissioner took a more practical approach to a case in which a late application had been rejected by a clerk. At the oral hearing of the application for leave to appeal, it was agreed by the parties that the decision was erroenous in law. The Commissioner admitted the application, granted leave to appeal and, with the consent of the parties, allowed the appeal. The application was not referred back. (The case was a social security case and, as the parties were agreed the decision was wrong in law, it would have had to be set aside under s.13(3) of the Social Security Act 1998. There was no equivalent to that provision in child support although see now s.23A of the Act.) This is in line with the approach in English cases of avoiding circuity of action by doing directly that which can be achieved indirectly (*Re Collard's Will Trusts* [1961] 1 All E.R. 821, approved by the House of Lords in *Pilkington v Inland Revenue Commissioners* [1962] 3 All E.R. 622).

## Determination of application

3.441    **13.**—(1) The office shall send written notice to the applicant and each respondent of any determination by a Commissioner of an application for leave to appeal to a Commissioner.

(2) Subject to a direction by a Commissioner, where a Commissioner grants leave to appeal under regulation 11—

  (a) notice of appeal shall be deemed to have been sent on the date when notice of the determination is sent to the applicant; and

  (b) the notice of application shall be deemed to be a notice of appeal sent under regulation 14.

(3) If a Commissioner grants an application for leave to appeal he may, with the consent of the applicant and each respondent, treat and determine the application as an appeal.

DEFINITIONS

3.442    "Commissioner": see reg.4.
"office": see reg.4.
"respondent": see reg.4.

GENERAL NOTE

Commissioners always give reasons for granting or refusing leave to appeal, **3.443**
although this is not required even under the Human Rights Act 1998 (*Mousaka Inc
v Golden Seagull Maritime Inc, The Times*, October 3, 2001).

## Notice of appeal

**14.**—(1) Subject to regulation 13(2), an appeal shall be made by notice **3.444**
in writing and shall contain—
  (a) the name and address of the appellant;
  (b) the date on which the appellant was notified that leave to appeal had
      been granted;
  (c) the grounds on which the appellant intends to rely;
  (d) if the appeal is made late, the grounds for seeking late acceptance;
      and
  (e) an address for sending notices and other documents to the appellant.
  (2) The notice in paragraph (1) shall have with it copies of—
  (a) the notice informing the appellant that leave to appeal has been
      granted;
  (b) the decision against which leave to appeal has been granted; and
  (c) if separate, the written statement of the appeal tribunal's reasons for it.

DEFINITION

"appeal tribunal": see reg.4. **3.445**

## Time limit for appealing after leave obtained

**15.**—(1) Subject to paragraph (2), a notice of appeal shall not be valid **3.446**
unless it is sent to a Commissioner within one month of the date on which
the appellant was sent written notice that leave to appeal had been granted.
  (2) A Commissioner may for special reasons accept a late notice of appeal.

DEFINITION

"Commissioner": see reg.4. **3.447**
"month": see reg.4.

## Acknowledgement of a notice of appeal and notification to each respondent

**16.** The office shall send— **3.448**
  (a) to the appellant, an acknowledgement of the receipt of the notice of
      appeal;
  (b) to each respondent, a copy of the notice of appeal.

DEFINITIONS

"office": see reg.4. **3.449**
"respondent": see reg.4.

PART III

PROCEDURE

## Representation

3.450    **17.** A party may conduct his case himself (with assistance from any person if he wishes) or be represented by any person whom he may appoint for the purpose.

DEFINITION

3.451    "party": see reg.4.

## Directions on Notice of Appeal

3.452    **18.**—(1) As soon as practicable after the receipt of a notice of appeal a Commissioner shall give any directions that appear to him to be necessary, specifying—

(a)  the parties who are to be respondents to the appeal; and

(b)  the order in which and the time within which any party is to be allowed to make written observations on the appeal or on the observations made by any other party.

(2) If in any case two or more persons who were parties to the proceedings before the appeal tribunal give notice of appeal to a Commissioner, a Commissioner shall direct which one of them is to be treated as the appellant and thereafter, but without prejudice to any rights or powers conferred on appellants by these Regulations, any other person who has given notice of appeal shall be treated as a respondent.

(3) Subject to an abridgement of time under regulation 5(2)(a), the time specified in directions given under paragraph (1)(b) shall not be less than one month beginning with the day on which the notice of the appeal or, as the case may be, the observations were sent to the party concerned.

DEFINITIONS

3.453    "Commissioner": see reg.4.
         "party": see reg.4.
         "respondent": see reg.4.

GENERAL NOTE

*Paragraph (1)*

3.454    Subparagraph (a) allows a Commissioner to specify as a respondent someone who was not a party to the proceedings before the appeal tribunal. Otherwise, this power would not be necessary, as the persons who would be respondents would be self-evident without the need for a direction.

## General Directions

3.455    **19.**—(1) Where a Commissioner considers that an application or appeal made to him gives insufficient particulars to enable the question at issue to be determined, he may direct the party making the application or appeal, or any respondent, to furnish any further particulars which may be reasonably required.

(2) In the case of an application for leave to appeal, or an appeal from an appeal tribunal, a Commissioner may, before determining the application or appeal, direct the tribunal to submit a statement of such facts or other matters as he considers necessary for the proper determination of that application or appeal.

(3) At any stage of the proceedings, a Commissioner may, on or without an application, give any directions as he may consider necessary or desirable for the efficient despatch of the proceedings.

(4) A Commissioner may direct any party before him to make any written observations as may seem to him necessary to enable the question at issue to be determined.

(5) An application under paragraph (3) shall be made in writing to a Commissioner and shall set out the direction which the applicant seeks.

(6) Unless a Commissioner shall otherwise determine, the office shall send a copy of an application under paragraph (3) to every other party.

DEFINITIONS

"appeal tribunal": see reg.4.  
"Commissioner": see reg.4.  
"party": see reg.4.  
"proceedings": see reg.4.  
"respondent": see reg.4.

3.456

GENERAL NOTE

*Paragraph (2)*

This power can only be used if there is a prima facie case, on the information and evidence already available to the Commissioner, that the tribunal went wrong in law (*C10/01–02(IB)(T)*, paras 35–37). Information required and provided under this paragraph is not a full statement of the tribunal's decision under reg.53(4) of the Appeals Regulations (*ibid.*, para.33).

*Paragraph (3)*

This is similar to the power given to a legally qualified panel member under reg.38(2) of the Appeals Regulations. The power under this paragraph refers to "the *efficient despatch* of the proceedings", whereas the power under reg.38(2) refers to "the *just, effective and efficient conduct* of the proceedings". This reflects the different emphasis of the Regulations and the different nature of the questions with which appeal tribunals and Commissioners are concerned.

3.457

## Procedure on linked case notice from the Secretary of State

**20.** Any notice from the Secretary of State to a Commissioner under section 28ZB of the Act (Appeal involving issues that arise on appeal in other cases) shall be sent by notice in writing signed by or on behalf of the Secretary of State and shall identify, by its file reference or the names of the parties involved, each appeal or application to which it relates.

3.458

DEFINITIONS

3.459   "Commissioner": see reg.4.
        "party": see reg.4.

## Requests for hearings

3.460   **21.**—(1) Subject to paragraphs (2), (3) and (4), a Commissioner may determine any proceedings without a hearing.

(2) Where a request for a hearing is made by any party, a Commissioner shall grant the request unless he is satisfied that the proceedings can properly be determined without a hearing.

(3) Where a Commissioner refuses a request for a hearing, he shall send written notice to the person making the request, either before or at the same time as making his determination or decision.

(4) A Commissioner may, without an application and at any stage, direct a hearing.

DEFINITIONS

3.461   "Commissioner": see reg.4.
        "party": see reg.4.
        "proceedings": see reg.4.

## Hearings

3.462   **22.**—(1) This regulation applies to any hearing of an application or appeal to which these Regulations apply.

(2) Subject to paragraph (3), the office shall give reasonable notice of the time and place of any hearing before a Commissioner.

(3) Unless all the parties concerned agree to a hearing at shorter notice, the period of notice specified under paragraph (2) shall be at least 14 days before the date of the hearing.

(4) If any party to whom notice of a hearing has been sent fails to appear at the hearing, the Commissioner may proceed with the case in that party's absence, or may give directions with a view to the determination of the case.

(5) Any hearing before a Commissioner shall be in public, unless the Commissioner for special reasons directs otherwise.

(6) Where a Commissioner holds a hearing the applicant or appellant, every respondent and, with the leave of a Commissioner, any other person, shall be entitled to be present and be heard.

[[1](6A) Subject to the direction of a Commissioner—

(a) any person or organisation entitled to be present and be heard at a hearing; and

(b) any representatives of such a person or organisation, may be present by means of a live television link.]

[[1](6B) Any provision in these Regulations which refers to a party or representative being present is satisfied if the party or representative is present by means of a live television link.]

(7) Any person entitled to be heard at a hearing may—

(a) address the Commissioner;

(b) with the leave of the Commissioner, give evidence, call witnesses and put questions directly to any other person called as a witness.

(8) Nothing in these Regulations shall prevent a member of the Council on Tribunals or of the Scottish Committee of the Council in his capacity as such from being present at a hearing before a Commissioner which is not held in public.

AMENDMENT

1. Regulation 3(9) of the Commissioners Procedure Amendment Regulations 2005 (February 28, 2005).

DEFINITIONS

"Commissioner": see reg.4.    3.463
"live television link": see reg.4.
"office": see reg.4.
"party": see reg.4.
"respondent": see reg.4.

GENERAL NOTE

Fresh points of law should not be raised after a hearing before a Commissioner    3.464
*R(IS) 14/94*, para.17). Nevertheless, in that case the Commissioner took account of the point raised as it was in the interests of the social security claimant to consider it. In child support cases, where the parties usually have competing interests, a Commissioner may be more reluctant to take account of a fresh point that is in the interests of one party to the proceedings but against the interests of another.

Once a Commissioner has investigated the alleged mistakes in the decision of an appeal tribunal and indicated acceptance of the occurring submissions of the parties that the decision should be set aside as wrong in law, a party may not advance argument in support of the decision under appeal, even if the Commissioner has issued directions relating to other matters which are to be considered before a decision is issued. This is based not on technical or doctrinal considerations, such as estoppel, but on common fairness (*CI 276/93*, para.15).

*Paragraph (5)*
A public hearing means that the public must have ready access to the room used by the Commissioner. A room in a secure area protected by a door with a push-button security lock is not public. See *Storer v British Gas plc* [2000] 2 All E.R. 440.

*Paragraph (6)*
This paragraph does not mention the rights and powers of a representative. These are conferred by reg.17 and, presumably, this paragraph is subject to that regulation.

*Paragraph (7)*
Subparagraph (b) allows questions to be asked of any person called as a witness. This must include a party who gives evidence.

## Summoning of witnesses

23.—(1) Subject to paragraph (2), a Commissioner may summon any    3.465
person to attend a hearing as a witness, at such time and place as may be

specified in the summons, to answer any questions or produce any documents in his custody or under his control which relate to any matter in question in the proceedings.

(2) A person shall not be required to attend in obedience to a summons under paragraph (1) unless he has been given at least 14 days' notice before the date of the hearing or, if less than 14 days, has informed the Commissioner that he accepts such notice as he has been given.

(3) Upon the application of a person summoned under this regulation, a Commissioner may set the summons aside.

(4) A Commissioner may require any witness to give evidence on oath and for this purpose an oath may be administered in due form.

DEFINITIONS

3.466      "Commissioner": see reg.4.
           "summons": see reg.4.

GENERAL NOTE

3.467      See the general note to reg.43 of the Appeals Regulations for a commentary on the summoning of witnesses and the administering of the oath.

## Withdrawal of application for leave to appeal and appeals.

3.468      **24.**—(1) At any time before it is determined, an applicant may withdraw an application to a Commissioner for leave to appeal against a decision of an appeal tribunal by giving written notice to a Commissioner.

(2) At any time before the decision is made, the appellant may withdraw his appeal with the leave of a Commissioner.

(3) A Commissioner may, on application by the party concerned, give leave to reinstate any application or appeal which has been withdrawn in accordance with paragraphs (1) and (2) and, on giving leave, he may make directions as to the conduct of the proceedings.

DEFINITIONS

3.469      "Commissioner": see reg.4.
           "proceedings": see reg.4.

## Irregularities

3.470      **25.** Any irregularity resulting from failure to comply with the requirements of these Regulations shall not by itself invalidate any proceedings, and the Commissioner, before reaching his decision, may waive the irregularity or take steps to remedy it.

DEFINITIONS

3.471      "Commissioner": see reg.4.
           "proceedings": see reg.4.

The Commissioners have taken a broad view of what constitutes an irregularity. For further discussion see the section on *Failure to comply with procedural requirements* in the introductory general note to the Appeals Regulations.

3.472

## PART IV

### DECISIONS

### Determinations and decisions of a Commissioner

**26.**—(1) The determination of a Commissioner on an application for leave to appeal shall be in writing and signed by him.

3.473

(2) The decision of a Commissioner on an appeal shall be in writing and signed by him and, unless it was a decision made with the consent of the parties he shall include the reasons.

(3) The office shall send a copy of the determination or decision and any reasons to each party.

(4) Without prejudice to paragraphs (2) and (3), a Commissioner may announce his determination or decision at the end of a hearing.

(5) When giving his decision on an application or appeal, whether in writing or orally, a Commissioner shall omit any reference to the surname of any child to whom the application or appeal relates and [[1], so far as practicable,] any other information which would be likely, whether directly or indirectly, to identify that child.

AMENDMENT

1. Regulation 3(10) of the Commissioners Procedure Amendment Regulations 2005 (February 28, 2005).

DEFINITIONS

"Commissioner": see reg.4.
"office": see reg.4.
"party": see reg.4.

3.474

GENERAL NOTE

*Paragraph (5)*
See the general note to reg.9.

### Correction of accidental errors in decisions

**27.**—(1) Subject to regulations 6 and 29, the Commissioner who gave the decision may at any time correct accidental errors in any decision or record of a decision.

3.475

(2) A correction made to, or to the record of, a decision shall become part of the decision or record, and the office shall send written notice of the correction to any party to whom notice of the decision has been sent.

DEFINITIONS

3.476    "Commissioner": see reg.4.
"party": see reg.4.

GENERAL NOTE

3.477    This regulation is subject to reg.29.
See the general note to reg.56 of the Appeals Regulations for a commentary on the power to correct accidental errors.

## Setting aside decisions on certain grounds

3.478    **28.**—(1) Subject to regulations 6 and 29, on an application made by any party, the Commissioner who gave the decision in proceedings may set it aside where it appears just to be do on the ground that—

(a) a document relating to the proceedings was not sent to, or was not received at an appropriate time by, a party or his representative or was not received at an appropriate time by the Commissioner; or

(b) a party or his representative was not present at a hearing before the Commissioner [[1]. . .]

(2) An application under this regulation shall be made in writing to a Commissioner within one month from the date on which the office gave written notice of the decision to the party making the application.

(3) Unless the Commissioner considers that it is unnecessary for the proper determination of an application made under paragraph (1), the office shall send a copy of it to each respondent, who shall be given a reasonable opportunity to make representations on it.

(4) The office shall send each party written notice of a determination of an application to set aside a decision and the reasons for it.

AMENDMENT

1. Regulation 3(11) of the Commissioners Procedure Amendment Regulations 2005 (February 28, 2005).

DEFINITIONS

3.479    "Commissioner": see reg.4.
"month": see reg.4.
"party": see reg.4.
"proceedings": see reg.4.

GENERAL NOTE

3.480    This regulation is subject to reg.29.
See the general note to reg.57 of the Appeals Regulations for a commentary on the power to set aside decisions.
Originally para.1(c) allowed a decision to be set aside if there had been some other procedural mishap or irregularity. This has been removed. That raises the question of whether the Commissioners have any other power to deal with deficiencies in their procedure. In *R(U) 3/89*, para.5(3), the Commissioner analysed authorities that recognised that the Commissioners had an inherent power to set

aside, which the Commissioner based on their control of their own procedure. However, the Court of Appeal has since said that statutory tribunals have no inherent power, apart from that to correct accidental slips (*Akewushola v Secretary of State for the Home Department* [2000] 2 All ER 148 at 153). It is possible to have implied powers, but it would be difficult to imply a power which had been removed by legislation and impossible to imply one that is not authorised by primary legislation. Otherwise, there is limited authority that a tribunal may have some power, additional to that conferred by legislation, to discharge orders in order to prevent injustice. An example is *R v Kensington and Chelsea Rent Tribunal, ex parte Macfarlane* [1974] 3 All ER 390, in which the Divisional Court decided that the tribunal had power to re-open a case in which the tenant had not received a notice of hearing sent in accordance with the tribunal's procedural rules. The rules contained no power for the tribunal to set aside its own decisions. This, and other scattered authority, is old and related to legislation that did not contain the detailed provision that is typical today. The scope of this power and its jurisprudential basis are unexplored. As any power that does arise under these cases must be consistent with the legislative scheme (*Wiseman v Borneman* [1971] AC 297 at 308 *per* Lord Reid), their potential effectively to replace a revoked power is doubtful.

One possible example of an additional power is that exercised by the Commissioner in *CIS 5129/97*. The Commissioner made a decision on the basis that the Secretary of State had refused to accepted certain documents as being in a proper form for a claim for social security. He expressly made his decision on the assumption that, if this was wrong, matters could be rectified by way of review or supersession, but reserved the power to substitute a different decision if the assumption proved incorrect. The Secretary of State later accepted that the documents could constistute claims. The Commissioner set his decision aside under an inherent power as (a) his earlier decision had been made on an express assumption that had proved incorrect, (b) he had reserved the power to change his decision if that assumption was not correct and (c) the claimant would otherwise suffer an irremediable injustice.

If a Commissioner rejects or refuses an application for leave to appeal, it may be set aside under this regulation. The applicant may also apply in the Administrative Court for judicial review. However, Art.6 does not give the applicant any wider powers of challenge. See *CDLA 3432/01*. The Commissioner did not refer to the possibility of reconsideration, on which see the *Reconsideration of determinations and decisions* section in the introductory general note to the Appeals Regulations.

*Subparagraph (1)(b)*
This subparagraph only applies if an oral hearing has been held (*CCS 910/99*, para.7).

## Provisions common to regulations 27 and 28

**29.**—(1) In regulations 27 and 28, the word "decision shall include determinations of applications for leave to appeal and decisions on appeals.

(2) There shall be no appeal against a correction or a refusal to correct under regulation 27 or a determination given under regulation 28.

3.481

GENERAL NOTE

The rejection of an application for leave to appeal under reg.11(3) is not a determination of the application. All that the Commissioner has done is to conclude that there are no special reasons for accepting the application. As the application was rejected, no issue of determination arose. Accordingly, there is no power to set aside

3.482

the rejection of an application, although on general principle there is power to reconsider the rejection. See *CDLA 390/01*.

## PART V

### APPLICATIONS FOR LEAVE TO APPEAL TO THE APPELLATE COURT

**Application to a Commissioner for leave to appeal to the Appellate Court**

3.483     **30.**—(1) Subject to paragraph (2), an application to a Commissioner under section 25 of the Act for leave to appeal against a decision of a Commissioner shall be made in writing, stating the grounds of the application, within three months from the date on which the applicant was sent written notice of the decision.

[[1](2) Where—

(a) any decision or record of a decision is corrected under regulation 27; or

(b) an application for a decision to be set aside under regulation 28 is refused for reasons other than that the application was made outside the period specified in regulation 28(2),

the period specified in paragraph (1) shall run from the date on which written notice of the correction or refusal of the application to set aside is sent to the applicant.]

(3) Regulations 24(1) and 24(3) shall apply to an application to a Commissioner for leave to appeal from a Commissioner's decision as they apply to the proceedings in that regulation.

AMENDMENT

1. Regulation 3(12) of the Commissioners Procedure Amendment Regulations 2005 (February 28, 2005).

DEFINITIONS

3.484     "Commissioner": see reg.4.
"month": see reg.4.
"proceedings": see reg.4.

GENERAL NOTE

3.485     It has been held by the Social Security Commissioners that grants and refusals of leave are not decisions and are not appealable. In *R(I) 14/65*, para.6, this was justified on the basis that, in the context of appeals, the only decisions which are appealable are those whereby a person's rights are determined. Grants and refusals of leave are not decisions in this sense, but merely determinations of the manner in which those rights are to be decided. This reasoning was disapproved in the decisions that hold that a decision to adjourn or to refuse to adjourn is appealable. See the general note to s.24 of the Act.

The courts have reached the same result by reference to policy considerations. In *Bland v Chief Supplementary Benefit Officer* [1983] 1 All E.R. 537, the result was explained by reference to the nature of those decisions and the need for leave to provide a filter for the higher courts. See also *Kemper Reinsurance Co v Minister of Finance (Bermuda)* [2000] 1 A.C. 1.

The standard to be applied when considering an application for leave to appeal was considered by the Court of Appeal in *Cooke v Secretary of State for Social Security* [2002] 3 All E.R. 279. When directing an oral hearing of the application in that case, Hale L.J. commented that it was possible that an application "from a second (and highly expert) judicial tier of appeal, should be regarded as akin to a second tier appeal and thus, although not technically within s.51(1) of the Access to Justice Act 1999, subject to a similar threshold test". The test that applies under s.55(1) is that permission is only given if:

    (a)  the appeal would raise an important point of principle or practice, or

    (b)  there is some other compelling reason for the Court of Appeal to hear it.

When the application was heard, permission to appeal was granted but the appeal was dismissed. The court held that although s.55(1) did not apply in its terms, its robust attitude was appropriate when considering whether an appeal had any real prospect of success.

The Court of Appeal gave guidance on the meaning and scope of s.51(1) in *Uphill v BRB (Residuary) Ltd*, [2005] 3 All E.R. 264. Permission would only be given in respect of an important point of principle or practice if it had not yet been decided. Another compelling reason meant one other than an important point of principle or practice and one which was truly exceptional.

The Court of Appeal may refuse to hear and therefore dismiss an appeal, despite the fact that a Commissioner has granted leave, if it is based on an argument that was not put to the Commissioner (*Secretary of State for Work and Pensions v Hughes (A Minor)*, reported as *R(DLA) 1/04*).

## The Social Security Act 1998 (Commencement No. 7 and Consequential and Transitional Provisions) Order 1999

### (SI 1999/1510 c.43)

*Made by the Secretary of State for Social Security under sections 79(3) and (4) and 87(2) and (3) of the Social Security Act 1998 and of all other powers enabling him in that behalf.*

GENERAL NOTE

This Order contains the transitional arrangements that were needed for the smooth transfer of functions from child support officers to the Secretary of State and from Child Support Appeal Tribunals to appeal tribunals constituted under the Social Security Act 1998.

    3.486

## PART I

### Citation and interpretation

**1.**—(1) This Order may be cited as the Social Security Act 1998 (Commencement No. 7 and Consequential and Transitional Provisions) Order 1999.

    3.487

. . .

## Date on which consequential amendments have effect

3.488    **3.**—(1) Subject to paragraph (2), Part XVIII below and the amendments made by the following provisions of this Order shall have effect on 1st June 1999.

(2) The amendment made by article 11(a)(iii) below shall have effect on 29th November 1999.

PART XVIII

TRANSITIONAL PROVISIONS

## Child Support

3.489    **48.**—(1) Any decision which fell to be made but was not made before 1st June 1999 by a child support officer shall be made by the Secretary of State.

(2) Except for the purposes of paragraph (6) below and any provision as to the time within which an appeal is to be brought, a decision of a child support officer shall be treated as a decision of the Secretary of State made under—

(a) subject to sub-paragraph (b) and paragraph (3) below, the provision under which the child support officer made the decision;

(b) section 17 of the Act where the child support officer made the decision under section 18 or 19 of the Act.

(3) A fresh maintenance assessment made pursuant to section 16(4) of the Act (periodical reviews) by virtue of the saving in article 3(4) of the Social Security Act 1998 (Commencement No. 2) Order 1998 shall be treated for the purpose of subsequent decisions as if it were made by virtue of a decision of the Secretary of State under section 17 of the Act (decisions superseding earlier decisions).

(4) For the purposes of a fresh maintenance assessment which falls to be made pursuant to section 16(4) of the Act (periodical reviews) by virtue of the saving in article 3(4) of the Social Security Act 1998 (Commencement No. 2) Order 1998, "relevant week" in the Child Support (Maintenance Assessments and Special Cases) Regulations 1992 shall mean notwithstanding regulation 1(2) of those Regulations the period of seven days immediately preceding the date on which a request for information or evidence was made under regulation 17(5) of the Child Support (Maintenance Assessment Procedure) Regulations 1992 as that provision was in force when that request was sent.

(5) The date on which the fresh maintenance assessment mentioned in paragraph (4) above made on or after 1st June 1999 takes effect shall be determined in accordance with the provisions of section 16(5) of the Act and regulations made thereunder as those provisions were in force immediately before 1st June 1999.

(6) An application which was not determined before 1st June 1999 for a review of a decision of a child support officer shall be treated—

(a) in a case where the application—

      (i)  is received within one month of the date of notification of the decision which is the subject of the application or such longer period as may be allowed by article 49 below; and

     (ii)  is made other than on the ground of a relevant change of circumstances,

    as an application to the Secretary of State for a revision of the decision under section 16 of the Act; and

  (b)  in any other case, as an application to the Secretary of State for a decision under section 17 of the Act superseding the decision.

(7) A revision under section 16 of the Act of a decision made before 22nd January 1996 to cancel a Category B interim maintenance assessment (within the meaning of regulation 8(3)(b) of the Child Support (Maintenance Assessment Procedure) Regulations 1992 shall have effect as from 22nd January 1996.

(8) For the purposes of paragraph (9) below, this paragraph applies where a decision of the Secretary of State—

  (a)  supersedes a decision of a child support officer; and

  (b)  is made on the basis of information or evidence which was not provided by a relevant person directly.

(9) Where paragraph (8) above applies, a decision which supersedes an earlier decision shall have effect as from the first day of the maintenance period in which that information or evidence was received by—

  (a)  except where sub-paragraph (b) applies, an officer of the Secretary of State exercising functions under the Act; or

  (b)  a child support officer.

(10) Where—

  (a)  a departure direction given under section 28F of the Act (departure directions) has effect on 1st June 1999;

  (b)  the applicant in response to whose application that direction was given made a later application before 1st June 1999 for a departure direction—

      (i)  on grounds additional to the grounds in respect of which the earlier direction was given; or

     (ii)  on the basis that there has been a change of circumstances in respect of any of those grounds; and

  (c)  that later application was not determined before 1st June 1999, that application shall be treated as if it were made under section 17 as extended by paragraph 2 of Schedule 4C to the Act for a decision superseding an earlier decision.

(11) A decision made by virtue of paragraph (10) above superseding an earlier, decision shall have effect as from the first day of the maintenance period in which the later application was made.

(12) A decision made—

  (a)  by the Secretary of State on his own initiative under section 17 as extended by paragraph 2 of Schedule 4C to the Act which supersedes an earlier decision with respect to a departure direction; and

  (b)  on the basis of information or evidence provided to him before 1st June 1999 by a person who is not the applicant in response to whose application the departure direction was given, shall have effect as from the first day of the maintenance period in which that information or evidence was provided to the Secretary of State.

(13) A decision—

(a) of the Secretary of State made before 1st June 1999 with respect to a departure direction; or

(b) of a child support appeal tribunal upon referral under section 28D(1)(b) of the Act,

may be revised under section 16 as extended by paragraph 1 of Schedule 4C to the Act in consequence of information or evidence—

    (i) received by the Secretary of State from a relevant person within one month of the date of notification of that decision or such longer period as may be allowed by article 49 below; and

    (ii) not acted upon before 1st June 1999.

(14) Except for the purposes of paragraph (16) below, an appeal to a child support appeal tribunal which was not determined before 1st June 1999—

(a) shall be treated as an appeal to an appeal tribunal;

(b) brought against a decision of a child support officer shall be treated as an appeal brought against a decision of the Secretary of State; and

(c) may not be withdrawn without either the consent in writing of every other party to the proceedings or the leave of a legally qualified panel member after every other party to the proceedings has been given a reasonable opportunity to make representations.

(15) In paragraph (14) above and paragraph 28 below, "party to the proceedings" means—

(a) the absent parent (within the meaning given to that expression in section 3(2) of the Act);

(b) the person with care (within the meaning given to that expression in section 3(3) of the Act);

(c) any child who has made an application for a maintenance assessment to be made under section 7 of the Act; and

(d) the Secretary of State.

(16) Regulations 3(1A) to (11B) and 15 of the Child Support Appeal Tribunals (Procedure) Regulations 1992 (in this article referred to as "the former Procedure Regulations") shall continue to apply (notwithstanding their revocation) for the purposes specified in paragraph (17) below subject to the modification to—

(a) regulation 3 specified in paragraph (18) below; and

(b) regulation 15 specified in paragraph (19) below.

(17) Paragraph (16) above applies for the purposes of—

(a) any appeal against a decision—

    (i) of the Secretary of State made before 1st June 1999 on an application for a departure direction; or

    (ii) of a child support officer; and

(b) any application to set aside a decision of a child support appeal tribunal.

(18) The modifications to regulation 3 specified in this paragraph are—

(a) in paragraph (1A), for the words "in paragraph (1)" there shall be substituted the words "in article 48(17) of the Social Security Act 1998 (Commencement No. 7 and Consequential and Transitional Provisions) Order 1999";

(b) in paragraph (3) for the words "under section 20(1) of the Act" there shall be substituted the words "against a decision of a child support officer";

(c) for paragraph (6) there shall be substituted the following paragraph—

"(6) Where an appeal or application is made—

(a) after the specified time has expired; and

(b) before 1st July 2000,

that time may for special reasons be extended by a legally qualified panel member to the date of the making of the appeal or application.";

(d) in paragraphs (7), (9A), (11) and (11A), for the word "chairman" in each place in which it occurs there shall be substituted the words "legally qualified panel member";

(e) in paragraph (8) for the words "any chairman" there shall be substituted the words "a legally qualified panel member"; and

(f) after paragraph (11B) there shall be added the following paragraph—" (11C) In this regulation—

"legally qualified panel member" has the same meaning as in regulation 1(3) of the Social Security and Child Support (Decisions and Appeals) Regulations 1999; and

"tribunal" means an appeal tribunal constituted under section 7 of the Social Security Act 1998".

(19) The modifications to regulation 15 specified in this paragraph are—

(a) in paragraph (1)—

(i) after the words "on an application made" there shall be inserted the words "before 1st July 2000"; and

(ii) for the words "the tribunal who gave the decision or by another tribunal" there shall be substituted the words "a tribunal";

(b) in paragraph (5), the words "regulation 2 and" shall be omitted; and

(c) after paragraph (5) there shall be added the following paragraph—

"(6) Except in paragraph (1)(a), "tribunal" in this regulation means an appeal tribunal constituted under section 7 of the Social Security Act 1998.".

(20) Paragraphs (21) to (24) below shall apply where—

(a) a clerk to a child support appeal tribunal gave a direction under regulation 11(1) of the former Procedure Regulations; and

(b) notification under that provision was not received by him before 1st June 1999.

(21) A notification in response to a direction given under regulation 11(1) of the former Procedure Regulations shall be in writing and shall be made within 14 days of receipt of the direction or within such other period as the clerk to an appeal tribunal may direct.

(22) An appeal may be struck out by the clerk to an appeal tribunal where a notification such as is referred to in paragraph (21) above is not received within the period specified in that paragraph.

(23) An appeal which has been struck out in accordance with paragraph (22) above shall be treated for the purpose of reinstatement as if it had been struck out under regulation 46 of the Social Security and Child Support (Decisions and Appeals) Regulations 1999.

(24) An oral hearing of the appeal shall be held where—

(a) notification is received by the clerk to the appeal tribunal under paragraph (21) above; or

(b) the chairman, or in the case of an appeal tribunal which has only one member, that member, is satisfied that such a hearing is necessary to enable the appeal tribunal to reach a decision.

(25) A legally qualified panel member may reinstate an appeal which has been struck out under regulation 6 of the former Procedure Regulations on an application made by any party to the proceedings not later than three months from the date of the order under paragraph (1) of that regulation if he is satisfied that—

(a) the applicant did not receive a notice under paragraph (2) of that regulation; and

(b) the conditions in paragraph (2A) of that regulation were not satisfied.

(26) Notwithstanding the revocation of the former Procedure Regulations, information such as was mentioned in regulation 17(2) of those Regulations shall not be disclosed if a written notification is received under that regulation within the period specified in that regulation.

(27) A copy of a statement of—

(a) the reasons for a child support appeal tribunal's decision;

(b) its findings on questions of fact material thereto; and

(c) the terms of any—

    (i) direction under section 20(4) of the Act (given before that provision was substituted); and

    (ii) decision made by the tribunal under section 28H(4)(c) of the Act (before that provision was substituted) or on a referral,

shall be supplied to each party to the proceedings if requested by any of them within 21 days of the date on which notification of the decision was given or sent.

(28) Except for the purposes of—

(a) the Child Support Commissioners (Procedure) Regulations 1999;

(b) paragraphs (16) and (27) above; or

(c) determining whether any irregularity resulted from failure to comply with the requirements of the former Procedure Regulations,

a decision of a child support appeal tribunal shall be treated as a decision of an appeal tribunal.

(29) An appeal tribunal shall completely rehear any appeal to a child support appeal tribunal which stands adjourned immediately before 1st June 1999.

(30) For the purpose of section 17(1) of the Act, a decision of a Child Support Commissioner on an appeal from a child support appeal tribunal shall be treated as a decision of a Child Support Commissioner on an appeal from an appeal tribunal.

## Late application for a revision

3.490    **49.**—(1) The period of one month specified in article 48(6)(a)(i) or (13)(i) above may be extended where the conditions specified in the following provisions of this article are satisfied.

(2) An application for an extension of time under this article shall—

(a) be made
  (i) before 1st July 2000; and
  (ii) by a relevant person or a person acting on his behalf; and
(b) contain—
  (i) particulars of the grounds on which the extension of time is sought; and
  (ii) sufficient details of the decision which it is sought to have revised to enable that decision to be identified.

(3) The application for an extension of time shall not be granted unless the person making the application or any person acting for him satisfies the Secretary of State that—

(a) it is reasonable to grant that application;
(b) the application for a decision to be revised has merit; and
(c) special circumstances are relevant to the application for an extension of time, and as a result of those special circumstances, it was not practicable for the application for a decision to be revised to be made within one month of the date of notification of the decision which it is sought to have revised.

(4) In determining whether it is reasonable to grant the application for an extension of time, no account shall be taken of the following—

(a) that the person making the application for an extension of time or any person acting for him was unaware of or misunderstood the law applicable to his case (including ignorance or misunder-standing of the time limits imposed by article 48(6)(a)(i) or (13)(i)) above; or
(b) that a Child Support Commissioner or a court has taken a different view of the law from that previously understood and applied.

(5) An application under this article for an extension of time which has been refused may not be renewed.

## Interpretation of this Part

**51.** In this Part—                                                      3.491

"the Act" means the Child Support Act 1991;
"legally qualified panel member." has the same meaning as in regulation 1(3) of the Social Security and Child Support (Decisions and Appeals) Regulations 1999; and
"maintenance period" and "relevant person" have the same meaning as in regulation 1(2) of the Child Support (Maintenance Assessment Procedure) Regulations 1992.

GENERAL NOTE

The down to the date of hearing rule continues to apply to appeals made before    3.492
May 21, 1998 and the old review procedures have to be applied by tribunals in respect of decisions made before June 1, 1999. See the principles set out in the context of Social Security Appeal Tribunals in *CIB 213/99*.

Transitional provision is made for outstanding appeals but not for outstanding referrals. This is because provision is not necessary. Unlike the making of an appeal, which is a one-off action, the making of a referral is of continuing effect, which survives the transfer of work to the new appeal tribunal under s.4(1)(a) of the Social Security Act 1998.

## The Social Security (Claims and Information) Regulations 1999

### (SI 1999/3108)

*Made by the Secretary of State for Social Security under sections 2C, 7A, 189(1), (4) and (5) and 191 of the Social Security Administration Act 1992 and sections 72 and 83(1) and (4) to (8) of the Welfare Reform and Pensions Act 1999 and all other powers enabling in that behalf.*

### Citation and commencement

3.493     **1.** These Regulations may be cited as the Social Security (Claims and Information) Regulations 1999 and shall come into force on 29th November 1999.

### Interpretation

3.494     **2.** In these Regulations,—
"the Act" means the Welfare Reform and Pensions Act 1999;
"the Child Support Acts" means the Child Support Act 1991 and the Child Support Act 1995
"relevant authority" means a person within section 72(2) of the Act.

GENERAL NOTE

3.495     Section 72(2) of the Welfare Reform and Pensions Act 1999 applies to these persons:

"(a)     a Minister of the Crown;
(b)     a person providing services to, or designated for the purposes of this section by an order of, a Minister of the Crown;
(c)     a local authority (within the meaning of the [Social Security] Administration Act [1992]); and
(d)     a person providing services to, or authorised to exercise any function of, any such authority."

### War Pensions and Child Support

3.496     **6.**—(1) Where a person resides in the area of an authority to which Part I or Part II of Schedule 1 to these Regulations refers, he may make a claim for a war pension, or submit an application under the Child Support Acts to any office displaying the <sup>one</sup> logo (whether or not that office is situated within the area of the local authority in which the person resides).

(2) Any change of circumstances arising since a claim or application was made in accordance with paragraph (1) may be reported to the office to which that claim or application was made.

(3) The areas to which this paragraph refers are those areas which are within both—

(a) the area of a local authority identified in part I or Part II of Schedule 1 to these Regulations, and

(b) a postcode area identified in Part I or Part II of Schedule 2 to these Regulations.

(4) A person making a claim or application to a participating authority in accordance with paragraph (1) shall comply with any requirements for the time being in force in relation to—

(a) claims for war pensions or applications under the Child Support Acts;

(b) the provision of information and evidence in support of such claims or applications.

(5) A participating authority shall forward to the Secretary of State—

(a) any claim for a war pension or application under the Child Support Acts made in accordance with this regulation;

(b) details of changes of circumstances reported to the authority in accordance with this regulation; and

(c) any information or evidence—

(i) given to the authority by the person making a claim or application or reporting the change of circumstances; or

(ii) which is relevant to the claim or application or the change reported and which is held by the authority.

(6) For the purposes of this regulation, a "participating authority" means any authority or person to whom a claim or application may be made or change of circumstances reported in accordance with paragraphs (1) and (2).

**Provision of information**

**8.**—(1) A relevant authority may give information or advice to any person, or to a person acting on his behalf, concerning— 3.497

(a) a claim he made, or a decision given on a claim he made, for a social security benefit or a war pension;

(b) an application he made, or a decision given on an application he made, under the Child Support Acts.

(2) For the purpose of giving information or advice in accordance with paragraph (1), a relevant authority may obtain information held by any other relevant authority.

**Information**

**13.** . . . 3.498

(4) A relevant authority which holds social security information may supply that information to any other relevant authority for the purposes of research, monitoring or evaluation in so far as it relates to any purpose specified in paragraph (5).

(5) The purposes specified in this paragraph are—

. . .

(b) any purpose for which regulations 3, 4 or 6 of these Regulations, or any regulation inserted by these Regulations, applies;

. . .

**Purposes for which information may be used**

3.499 **14.**—(1) The purposes for which information supplied in connection with matters referred to in paragraph (2) may be used are—
  (a) the processing of any claim for a social security benefit or a war pension or for an application for a maintenance assessment under the Child Support Act 1991;
  (b) the consideration of any application for employment by a person to whom information is supplied in connection with that employment opportunity;
  (c) the consideration of the training needs of the person who supplied the information;
  (d) any purpose for which a work-focused interview may be conducted;
  (e) the prevention, detection, investigation or prosecution of offences relating to social security matters.
  (2) The matters referred to in this paragraph are—
  (a) work-focused interviews; or
  (b) any other provision in or introduced by these Regulations.

**Information supplied**

3.500 **15.** Information supplied to a person or authority under these Regulations—
  (a) may be used for the purposes of amending or supplementing information held by the person or authority to whom it is supplied; and
  (b) if it is so used, may be supplied to another person or authority, and used by him or it for any purpose, to whom or for which that information could be supplied or used.

SCHEDULE 1

LOCAL AUTHORITIES ON WHICH FUNCTIONS ARE CONFERRED

PART I

*Local Authority*

3.501 **ENGLAND:**
Aylesbury Vale
Barking and Dagenham
Calderdale
Castle Point
Chelmsford
Chiltern
Epping Forest
Kirklees
Maldon
Mendip
Milton Keynes
North Warwickshire
Nuneaton and Bedworth
Redbridge
Rochford
Rugby

Sedgemoor
South Bucks
Southend-on-Sea
South Somerset
Stratford-on-Avon
Taunton Deane
Waltham Forest
Warwick
West Somerset
Wycombe

**WALES:**
Monmouthshire
Newport
Torfaen

**SCOTLAND:**
Argyll and Bute
East Renfrewshire
Inverclyde
North Ayreshire
Renfrewshire

PART II

Amber Valley                                                3.502
Ashfield
Babergh
Bassetlaw
Bolsover
East Cambridgeshire
Forest Heath
Halton
Ipswich
Leeds
Mansfield
Mid-Suffolk
North East Derbyshire
Newark and Sherwood
St. Edmundsbury
St. Helens
South Cambridge
Suffolk Coastal
Vale Royal
Warrington
Waveney
Wigan

SCHEDULE 2

POSTCODE AREAS

PART I

B37, B39, B46, B47, B49, B50, B76 to B79 and B93 to B95        3.503
BA3 to BA11, BA16, BA20 to BA22, BA24 and BA26 to BA28

CM0 to CM9
CV3, CV4, CV7 to CV12, CV21 to CV23, CV31 to CV35 and CV36 TO CV39
DT9
E4, E10, E11, E17 AND E18
EX15 AND EX16
G78
GL50 and GL55
GL56
HD1 and HD5 to HD8
HP1, HP4 to HP23 and HP27
HX1 and HX7
IG1 to IG11
KA28 to KA30
LE10
LE17
LU6 and LU7
MK1 to MK19, MK43 and MK46
NN6, NN11 and NN13
NP1
NP4
NP5
NP6
NP7
NP9, NP16, NP20, NP25, NP26 and NP44
OL14
OX5 to OX7, OXX9 and OX15
OX17
PA1 to PA17 and PA20 to PA27
RM6
RM8
RG9
SL0 to SL4 and SL6 to SL9
SS0 to SS7, SS9, SS11 and SS12
SS17
TA1 to TA24
UB9
WD3
WF12 to WF17
WO11

## PART II

3.504     BD2 to BD4, BD10, BD11, BD16, BD17 and BD20
CB1 and CB5 to CB10
CM11
CO1, CO6 and CO8 to CO11
DE5, DE55 and DE56
DN22
HG3 and HG5
IP2 to IP20, IP22 to IP24 and IP27 to IP33
LS1 to LS15 (except Bramhope), LS16, LS17, LS19, LS21, LS22, LS27 and LS28
NG14 to NG23 and NG25
NR10, NR14, NR15 and NR31 to NR35
S44, S45 and S80
WA1 to WA8 and WA11 to WA13
WF3, WF6, WF10 and WF11
YO8, YO23 and YO26

# The Child Support (Variations) (Modification of Statutory Provisions) Regulations 2000

## (SI 2000/3173)

*The Secretary of State for Social Security, in exercise of the power conferred upon him by section 28G(2) of the Child Support Act 1991, and of all other powers enabling him in that behalf, hereby makes the following Regulations:*

GENERAL NOTE

Sections 28A to 28F of, and Schs 4A and 4B to, the Act are drafted on the basis that the application for a variation was made under s.28A(3) before a decision was made on an application for a maintenance calculation. An application for a variation can also be made under s.28G(1) when a maintenance calculation is in force. These Regulations modify the Act to take account of those applications. **3.505**

## Citation, commencement and interpretation

**1.**—(1) These Regulations may be cited as the Child Support (Variations) (Modification of Statutory Provisions) Regulations 2000 and shall come into force on 31st January 2001. **3.506**

(2) In these Regulations references to "the Act" are to the Child Support Act 1991 and references to sections are to sections of, and to Schedules are to Schedules to, the Act.

## Modification of sections 28A to 28F and Schedules 4A and 4B

**2.** Where an application for a variation is made under section 28G, sections 28A to 28F, and Schedules 4A and 4B, shall apply subject to the modifications provided for in these Regulations. **3.507**

## Modification of section 28A

**3.**—(1) Section 28A (application for variation of usual rules for calculating maintenance) shall be modified by the substitution in subsection (1)— **3.508**

(a) for the words "Where an application for a maintenance calculation is made under section 4 or 7, or treated as made under section 6" by the words "Where a maintenance calculation other than an interim maintenance decision is in force"; and

(b) for the words "(in the case of an application under" by the words "(where the maintenance calculation was made following an application under".

(2) Subsection (3) shall be omitted.

## Modification of section 28B

**4.** Section 28B (preliminary consideration of applications) shall be modified—

(a) by the substitution in subsection (2) for the words "(and proceed to make his decision on the application for a maintenance calculation

553

without any variation)" by the words "(and proceed to revise or supersede a decision under section 16 or 17 respectively without taking the variation into account, or not revise or supersede a decision under section 16 or 17)"; and

(b) by the omission of paragraph (b) of subsection (2).

### Modification of section 28C

3.509  **5.**—(1) Section 28C (imposition of regular payments condition) shall be modified in accordance with the following paragraphs of this regulation and references to subsections are to subsections of that section.

(2) Subsection (1)(b) shall be omitted and in the full-out words "also" shall be omitted.

(3) In subsection (2), for the words "interim maintenance decision" there shall be substituted the words "maintenance calculation in force".

(4) In subsections (3)(c) and (7)(c), for the words "application for the maintenance calculation was" there shall be substituted the words "maintenance calculation in force was made in response to an application".

(5) For subsection (4)(a) there shall be substituted the following—

"(a) when in response to the application for a variation the Secretary of State has revised or superseded a decision under section 16 or 17 respectively (whether he agrees to a variation or not) or not revised or superseded a decision under section 16 or 17;".

(6) In subsection (5), for the words from "reach" to the end there shall be substituted "revise or supersede a decision under section 16 or 17 respectively, or not revise or supersede a decision under section 16 or 17, as if the application had failed".

### Modification of sections 28D and 28E

3.510  **6.**—(1) Section 28D (determination of applications) shall be modified by the substitution, in paragraph (a) of subsection (1), for the words "under section 11 or 12(1)" by the words "under section 16 or 17".

(2) Section 28E (matters to be taken into account) shall be modified by the substitution for paragraph (b) of subsection (3) of the following—

"(b) where the maintenance calculation in force was made in response to an application under section 7, by either of them or the child concerned.".

### Modification of section 28F

3.511  **7.** Section 28F (agreement to a variation) shall be modified—

(a) by the substitution for subsection (3) of the following—

"(3) The Secretary of State shall not agree to a variation (and shall proceed to revise or supersede a decision under section 16 or 17 respectively without taking the variation into account, or not revise or supersede a decision under section 16 or 17) if he is satisfied that prescribed circumstances apply.";

(b) by the omission in paragraph (a) of subsection (4) of the words after the word "application," where it first appears;

(c) by the substitution for subsection (4)(b) of the following—
"(b) revise or supersede a decision under section 16 or 17 respectively on that basis."; and

(d) by the omission of subsection (5).

## Modification of Schedules 4A and 4B

**8.**—(1) In paragraph 5(1) of Schedule 4A, the words [¹"application for a"] shall be omitted.

(2) In paragraphs 2(3)(a), (d) and (e) of Schedule 4B, for the words "the application for a maintenance calculation has been made (or treated as made)" there shall be substituted the words "there is a maintenance calculation in force".

(3) In paragraph 2(3)(c) of Schedule 4B, for the words "has been applied for (or treated as having been applied for)" there shall be substituted "is in force".

(4) In paragraph 3(1)(a) of Schedule 4B, for the words "the application for the maintenance calculation" there shall be substituted "the maintenance calculation in force" and for the words "that application was made" there shall be substituted "that maintenance calculation is in force".

(5) In paragraph 3(3) of Schedule 4B, for the words "the application for a maintenance calculation" there shall be substituted the words "the maintenance calculation in force".

AMENDMENT

1. Regulation 10 of the Miscellaneous Amendments Regulations 2002 (April 30, 2002).

3.512

## The Child Support (Temporary Compensation Payment Scheme) Regulations 2000

### (SI 2000/3174)

*The Secretary of State for Social Security, in exercise of the powers conferred upon him by section 27(1) to (4) and (10) of the Child Support, Pensions and Social Security Act 2000 and of all other powers enabling him in that behalf, hereby makes the following Regulations:*

### Citation, commencement and interpretation

3.513     **1.**—(1) These Regulations may be cited as the Child Support (Temporary Compensation Payment Scheme) Regulations 2000 and shall come into force on 31st January 2001.

(2) In these Regulations, unless the context otherwise requires—

"the 2000 Act" means the Child Support, Pensions and Social Security Act 2000;

"the Child Support Act" means the Child Support Act 1991 before its amendment by the 2000 Act; and

"the Social Security Act" means the Social Security Act 1998.

### Application of the Regulations

3.514     **2.**—(1) For the purposes of section 27(2) of the 2000 Act, section 27 shall have effect as if it were modified so as to apply to cases of arrears of child support maintenance which have become due under a fresh maintenance assessment made in the following circumstances:

(a) where the Secretary of State has given a departure direction under section 28F of the Child Support Act and—

(i)   the revised amount is higher than the current amount; and

(ii)  the effective date of the fresh maintenance assessment is a date before 1st June 1999; or

(b) following a review under section 18 of the Child Support Act (reviews of decisions of child support officers) or a review under section 19 of that Act (reviews at instigation of child support officers) (as those provisions had effect before their substitution by section 41 of the Social Security Act),

and the effective date of the assessment is earlier than the date on which the assessment was made; or

(c) following an appeal to a child support appeal tribunal under section 20 of the Child Support Act (as it had effect before its substitution by section 42 of the Social Security Act) against a decision of a child support officer.

(2) In this regulation—

"current amount" means the amount of child support maintenance fixed by the current assessment; and

"revised amount" means the amount of child support maintenance fixed by the fresh maintenance assessment as a result of the departure direction given by the Secretary of State.

## Prescribed date

**3.** For the purposes of section 27(1)(a) of the 2000 Act, the prescribed date is 1st April [¹2005].

3.515

AMENDMENT

1. Regulation 3 of the Child Support (Temporary Compensation Payment Scheme) (Modification and Amendment) Regulations 2002 (July 17, 2002).

## Prescribed circumstances

**4.**—(1) In relation to cases of arrears which have become due under a maintenance assessment falling within section 27(1)(a) of the 2000 Act or a fresh maintenance assessment falling within section 27(1)(b) of the 2000 Act or regulation 2(1), the prescribed circumstances for the purposes of section 27(3) of the 2000 Act are that—

3.516

  (a) more than 6 months of arrears of child support maintenance have become due under the maintenance assessment;

  (b) at least 3 months of those arrears are due to unreasonable delay due to an act or omission by the Secretary of State or a child support officer as the case may be;

  (c) the Secretary of State is authorised under section 29(1) of the Child Support Act to arrange for the collection of child support maintenance payable in accordance with the maintenance assessment;

  (d) the Secretary of State is satisfied that the absent parent is, at the time the agreement is made, making such payments as are required of him in accordance with regulations made under section 29(3)(b) or (c) of the Child Support Act;

  (e) where the absent parent is liable to make child support maintenance payments under a different maintenance assessment, there are no existing arrears in relation to any of them at the time the agreement is made, except for those arrears that the Secretary of State is satisfied have arisen through no fault of the absent parent; and

  (f) in relation to cases under section 27(1)(b) of the 2000 Act or regulation 2(1), the absent parent has paid any arrears which he has been required to pay in relation to the maintenance assessment, or has done so except in relation to—

    (i) arrears of at least 3 months which are due to unreasonable delay due to an act or omission of the Secretary of State or a child support officer as the case may be; or

    (ii) any other arrears that the Secretary of State is satisfied have arisen through no fault of the absent parent.

(2) In this regulation "agreement" means an agreement under section 27 of the 2000 Act.

## Terms of the agreement

**5.**—(1) For the purposes of section 27(4) of the 2000 Act, the terms which may be specified in the agreement are—

3.517

  (a) the period of the agreement;

    (b) payment of the child support maintenance payable in accordance with the maintenance assessment and, where relevant, the arrears, by whichever of the following methods the Secretary of State specifies as being appropriate in the circumstances—

        (i) by standing order;

        (ii) by any other method which requires one person to give his authority for payments to be made from an account of his to an account of another's on specific dates during the period for which the authority is in force and without the need for further authority from him;

        (iii) by an arrangement whereby one person gives his authority for payments to be made from an account of his, or on his behalf, to another person or to an account of that other person;

        (iv) by cheque or postal order;

        (v) in cash;

        (vi) by debit card;

        (vii) where the Secretary of State has made a deduction from earnings order under section 31 of the Child Support Act—

            (aa)  by cheque;

            (bb)  by automated credit transfer; or

            (cc)  by such other method as the Secretary of State may specify;

    (c) the amount of the arrears that the absent parent is required to pay (which shall include at least the last 6 months of the arrears due under the maintenance assessment);

    (d) the day and interval by reference to which payments of the arrears are to be made by the absent parent; and

    (e) the confirmation by the Secretary of State that he will not, while the agreement is complied with, take action to recover any of the arrears.

    (2) In this regulation "debit card" means a card, operating as a substitute for a cheque, that can be used to obtain cash or to make a payment at a point of sale whereby the card holder's bank or building society account is debited without deferment of payment.

# The Social Security (Child Maintenance Premium and Miscellaneous Amendments) Regulations 2000

## (SI 2000/3176)

*The Secretary of State for Social Security, in exercise of the powers
conferred upon him by sections 123(1)(a), (d) and (e), 136(3) and
(5)(b), 137(1) and 175(1) and (3) of the Social Security Contributions
and Benefits Act 1992, sections 12(1) and (4)(b), 35(1) and 36(1),
(2) and (4) of the Jobseekers Act 1995, sections 10 and 26(1) to (3)
of the Child Support Act 1995 and section 87(4) of the Northern
Ireland Act 1998, and of all other powers enabling him in that behalf,
after consultation, in respect of regulation 3 of these Regulations, with
organisations appearing to him to be representative of the authorities
concerned and after agreement by the Social Security Advisory
Committee that proposals in respect of these Regulations should
not be referred to it, hereby makes the following Regulations:*

## [¹Citation, commencement and interpretation

**1.**—(1) These Regulations may be cited as the Social Security (Child
Maintenance Premium and Miscellaneous Amendments) Regulations
2000 and shall come into force—

  (a) in relation to any particular case, on the date on which section 23 of
the 2000 Act comes into force in relation to that type of case ("the
commencement date");

  (b) in relation to a person who, on or after 16th February 2004—

    (i) makes a claim for income support or an income-based jobseeker's
allowance; and

    (ii) on or after the date of that claim receives any payment of child
maintenance made voluntarily,

  on 16th February 2004; or

  (c) in relation to a person who—

    (i) on 16th February 2004 is entitled to income support or an
income-based jobseeker's allowance; and

    (ii) on or after 16th February 2004 receives any payment of child
maintenance made voluntarily and that payment is the first payment of child maintenance received by that person whilst he is
entitled to income support or an income-based jobseeker's
allowance,

  on 16th February 2004 if a payment referred to in head (ii) above is
received on that day, or on the day on which such a payment is
received where it is received after 16th February 2004.

(2) In this regulation—

"the 1991 Act" means the Child Support Act 1991;

"the 2000 Act" means the Child Support, Pensions and Social Security
Act 2000;

"child maintenance" shall have the same meaning as that prescribed for
the purposes of section 74A of the Social Security Administration Act
1992;

3.518

"an income-based jobseeker's allowance" has the meaning given by section 1(4) of the Jobseekers Act 1995;

"payment of child maintenance made voluntarily" means any payment of child maintenance other than such a payment made—

(a) under a court order;

(b) under a maintenance assessment made under the 1991 Act prior to its amendment by the 2000 Act or under a maintenance calculation made under the 1991 Act after its amendment by the 2000 Act;

(c) under an agreement for maintenance;

(d) in accordance with section 28J of the 1991 Act; or

(e) by the Secretary of State in lieu of child maintenance, including any payment made by the Secretary of State under section 27 of the 2000 Act.]

AMENDMENT

1. Regulation 4 of the Social Security (Child Maintenance Premium) Amendment Regulations 2004 (February 16, 2004).

3.519 [¹4.—(1) Subject to paragraphs (2) to (8) below—

(a) regulations 2 to 13 of the Social Security (Child Maintenance Bonus) Regulations 1996 ("the Child Maintenance Bonus Regulations");

(b) the Child Maintenance Bonus (Northern Ireland Reciprocal Arrangements) Regulations 1997 ("the Reciprocal Arrangements Regulations");

(c) regulation 8 of the Social Security (Miscellaneous Amendments) Regulations 1997; and

(d) regulation 2 of the Social Security (Miscellaneous Amendments) Regulations 1998,

are hereby revoked.

(2) Subject to paragraph (6) below, the Reciprocal Arrangements Regulations and regulations 2 to 13 of the Child Maintenance Bonus Regulations shall continue to have effect as if paragraph (1) above had not been made in relation to a person—

(a) who—

(i) satisfied the requirements of regulation 10 (claiming a bonus) or, as the case may be, regulation 11(4) (claims: further provisions) of the Child Maintenance Bonus Regulations; and

(ii) satisfied the work condition in accordance with regulation 3(1)(c) of the Child Maintenance Bonus Regulations (entitlement to a bonus: the work condition),

before the commencement date, but whose claim has not been determined before that date;

(b) to whom regulation 8 (1) or (2) of the Child Maintenance Bonus Regulations (retirement) applied before the commencement date but whose entitlement has not been determined before that date;

(c) who—

(i) satisfied the requirements of regulation 10 or, as the case may be, regulation 11(4) of the Child Maintenance Bonus Regulations; and

    (ii)  satisfied the requirements of regulation 8(4) of the Child Maintenance Bonus Regulations,

before the commencement date, but whose claim has not been determined before that date; or

  (d)  who—

    (i)  satisfied the requirements of regulation 3(1)(b) to (f) of the Child Maintenance Bonus Regulations before the commencement date; and

    (ii)  satisfies the requirements of regulation 10 (claiming a bonus) or, as the case may be, regulation 11(4) (claims: further provisions) of the Child Maintenance Bonus Regulations on or after the commencement date.

(3) Subject to paragraphs (5) and (6) below, the Reciprocal Arrangements Regulations and regulations 2 to 6 and 9 to 13 of the Child Maintenance Bonus Regulations shall continue to have effect as if paragraph (1) above had not been made in relation to—

  (a)  a person who—

    (i)  satisfied the requirements of regulation 10 of the Child Maintenance Bonus Regulations before the commencement date; and

    (ii)  has not satisfied the work condition in accordance with regulation 3(1)(c) of the Child Maintenance Bonus Regulations before that date; or

  (b)  a person—

    (i)  who has not claimed a child maintenance bonus before the commencement date; and

    (ii)  to whom the provisions of paragraph (4) below apply on the day immediately before the commencement date.

(4) For the purposes of paragraph (3)(b)(ii) above, the provisions of this paragraph are that—

  (a)  the person or, where the person has a partner, her partner is entitled to, or is treated as entitled to a qualifying benefit whether it is payable or not;

  (b)  the person has residing with her a qualifying child;

  (c)  child maintenance is either—

    (i)  paid or payable to the person; or

    (ii)  retained by the Secretary of State in accordance with section 74A(3) of the Social Security Administration Act 1992; and

  (d)  the person has not satisfied the work condition in accordance with regulation 3(1)(c) of the Child Maintenance Bonus Regulations.

(5) For the purposes of paragraph (3) above, regulation 3 of the Child Maintenance Bonus Regulations shall have effect as if in paragraph (1)—

  (a)  the words "no later than the day immediately before the commencement date" were inserted after—

    (i)  "dies" in sub-paragraph (f)(i); and

    (ii)  "has" where that word first appears in sub-paragraph (f)(ii); and

  (b)  for the words "14 days" in sub-paragraph (f)(iii) there were substituted "one month".

(6) For the purposes of paragraphs (2) and (3) above, regulation 4 of the Child Maintenance Bonus Regulations (bonus period) shall have effect as if for paragraph (7) there were substituted the following paragraph—

"(7) A bonus period which would, but for this paragraph, have continued shall end—
  (a) where the applicant or, where the applicant has a partner, her partner, satisfies the work condition and claims a bonus, on the last day of entitlement to a qualifying benefit to which any award made on that claim applies;
  (b) on the date of death of a person with care of a qualifying child to whom child maintenance is payable; or
  (c) on the day immediately before the commencement date, whichever is the earlier."

(7) Nothing in this regulation shall prevent the Secretary of State from issuing a written statement pursuant to regulation 6(1) of the Child Maintenance Bonus Regulations (Secretary of State to issue estimates) to a person who appears to him to satisfy the requirements of regulation 3 of those Regulations.

(8) For the purposes of this regulation "child maintenance" has the meaning given by regulation 1(2) of the Child Maintenance Bonus Regulations (interpretation).]

AMENDMENT

1. Regulation 2 of the Social Security (Child Maintenance Premium and Miscellaneous Amendments) Amendment Regulations 2003 (in force as s.23 of the 2000 Act, which provides for s.10 of the 1995 Act to cease to have effect).

## The Child Support (Voluntary Payments) Regulations 2000

### (SI 2000/3177)

*The Secretary of State for Social Security, in exercise of the powers conferred upon him by sections 28J(5), 52(1) and (4) and 54 of the Child Support Act 1991 and of all other powers enabling him in that behalf, hereby makes the following Regulations:*

### Citation, commencement and interpretation

3.520    1.—(1) These Regulations may be cited as the Child Support (Voluntary Payments) Regulations 2000 and shall come into force on the day on which section 28J of the Act as inserted by the Child Support, Pensions and Social Security Act 2000 comes into force.

(2) In these Regulations—
  "the Act" means the Child Support Act 1991;
  "debit card" means a card, operating as a substitute for a cheque, that can be used to obtain cash or to make a payment at a point of sale

whereby the card holder's bank or building society account is debited without deferment of payment;

"the Maintenance Calculations and Special Cases Regulations" means the Child Support (Maintenance Calculations and Special Cases) Regulations 2000;

"the qualifying child's home" means the home in which the qualifying child resides with the person with care and "home" has the meaning given in regulation 1 of the Maintenance Calculations and Special Cases Regulations; and

"relevant person" means—

(a) a person with care;

(b) a non-resident parent;

(c) a parent who is treated as a non-resident parent under regulation 8 of the Maintenance Calculations and Special Cases Regulations;

(d) where the application for a maintenance calculation is made by a child under section 7 of the Act, that child,

in respect of whom a maintenance calculation has been applied for, or has been treated as applied for, under section 6(3) of the Act, or is or has been in force.

## Voluntary payment

**2.**—(1) A payment counts as a voluntary payment if it is—     3.521

(a) made in accordance with section 28J(2) and (4) of the Act;

(b) of a type to which regulation 3 applies;

(c) made on or after the effective date of the maintenance calculation made, or which would be made but for the Secretary of State's decision not to make one, and for this purpose "effective date" means the effective date as determined in accordance with the Child Support (Maintenance Calculation Procedure) Regulations 2000; and

(d) a payment in relation to which evidence or verification of a type to which regulation 4 applies is provided, if the Secretary of State so requires.

(2) Where the Secretary of State is considering whether a payment is a voluntary payment, he may invite representations from a relevant person.

## Types of payment

**3.** This regulation applies to a payment made by the non-resident parent—     3.522

(a) by any of the following methods—

(i) in cash;

(ii) by standing order;

(iii) by any other method which requires one person to give his authority for payments to be made from an account of his to an account of another on specific dates during the period for which the authority is in force and without the need for any further authority from him;

(iv) by an arrangement whereby one person gives his authority for payments to be made from an account of his, or on his behalf, to another person or to an account of that other person;

(v) by cheque or postal order; or

(vi) by debit card, and

(b) which is, or is in respect of,—

    (i) a payment in lieu of child support maintenance and which is paid to the person with care;

    (ii) a mortgage or loan taken out on the security of the property which is the qualifying child's home where that mortgage or loan was taken out to facilitate the purchase of, or to pay for essential repairs or improvements to, that property;

    (iii) rent on the property which is the qualifying child's home;

    (iv) mains-supplied gas, water or electricity charges at the qualifying child's home;

    (v) council tax payable by the person with care in relation to the qualifying child's home;

    (vi) essential repairs to the heating system in the qualifying child's home; or

    (vii) repairs which are essential to maintain the fabric of the qualifying child's home.

### Evidence or verification of payment

3.523 **4.** This regulation applies to—

(a) evidence provided by the non-resident parent in the form of—

    (i) a bank statement;

    (ii) a duplicate of a cashed cheque;

    (iii) a receipt from the payee; or

    (iv) a receipted bill or invoice; or

(b) vertification orally or in writing from the person with care.

## The Child Support (Decisions and Appeals) (Amendment) Regulations 2000

### (SI 2000/3185)

*The Secretary of State for Social Security, in exercise of the powers conferred on him by sections 16(1), (4) and (6), 17(3) and (5), 28G(2), 51 and 52(1) and (4) of the Child Support Act 1991 and of all other powers enabling him in that behalf, after consultation with the Council on Tribunals in accordance with section 8 of the Tribunals and Inquiries Act 1992, hereby makes the following Regulations*

### Citation, commencement and interpretation

3.524 **1.**—(1) These Regulations may be cited as the Child Support (Decisions and Appeals) (Amendment) Regulations 2000 and, subject to paragraph (2), shall come into force in relation to a particular case on the date on which sections 16, 17 and 20 of the Child Support Act 1991 as amended by the Child Support, Pensions and Social Security Act 2000 come into force in relation to that type of case.

(2) For the purposes of any revision, supersession or appeal in relation to a decision which is made as provided in regulation 3 of the Child

Support (Transitional Provisions) Regulations 2000 these Regulations shall come into force on the day on which section 29 of the Child Support, Pensions and Social Security Act 2000 comes fully into force.

(3) In these Regulations "the principal Regulations" means the Social Security and Child Support (Decisions and Appeals) Regulations 1999.

(4) In these Regulations any reference to a numbered regulation is to the regulation in the principal Regulations bearing that number and any reference to a numbered Part is to the Part of the principal Regulations bearing that number.

**Revocation and savings**

**14.**—(1) Subject to [¹the Child Support (Transitional Provisions) Regulations 2000 and] paragraph (2), regulations 10(2) and (3) and 11 to 17 of the Arrears, Interest and Adjustment of Maintenance Assessments Regulations are hereby revoked.     3.525

(2) Where on the commencement date—

(a) an appeal has not been decided;

(b) the time limit for lodging an appeal has not expired;

(c) the time limit for making an application for the revision of a decision has not expired; or

(d) an application for a supersession of a decision has not been decided, the provisions in regulations 10(2) and (3) and 11 to 17 of the Arrears, Interest and Adjustment of Maintenance Assessments Regulations shall continue to apply for the purposes of—

(i) the decision of the appeal tribunal referred to in sub-paragraph (a);

(ii) the ability to lodge the appeal referred to in sub-paragraph (b) and the decision of the appeal tribunal following the lodging of that appeal;

(iii) the ability to apply for the revision referred to in sub-paragraph (c) and the decision whether to revise following any such application; or

(iv) the decision whether to supersede following the application referred to in sub-paragraph (d).

(3) Where on or after the commencement date an adjustment falls to be made in relation to a maintenance assessment, these Regulations shall not apply for the purposes of making the adjustment.

(4) In this regulation—

"commencement date" means, with respect to a particular case, the date on which these Regulations come into force with respect to that type of case;

"former Act" means the Child Support Act before its amendment by the Child Support, Pensions and Social Security Act 2000; and

"maintenance assessment" has the meaning given in the former Act.

AMENDMENT

1. Regulation 2(1) and (2)(a) of the Transitional Amendments Regulations 2003 (March 3, 2003).

3.526    **15.**—[¹(Z1) This regulation is subject to the Child Support (Transitional Provisions) Regulations 2000.]

(1) Where—

(a) before the commencement date—

    (i) an application was made and not determined for a departure direction or a revision or supersession of a decision in respect of a departure direction;

    (ii) the Secretary of State had initiated but not completed a revision or supersession of a decision in respect of a departure direction; or

    (iii) any appeal was lodged in respect of a departure direction decision which, on the commencement date, had not been decided; or

(b) on the commencement date any time limit provided for in Regulations for making an application for a departure direction, or revision or, for making an appeal in respect of a departure direction decision, had not expired,

regulation 13 shall not apply for the purposes of any appeal—

    (aa) made in consequence of the decision on the application, revision or supersession referred to in paragraph (1)(a)(i);

    (bb) made in consequence of the revision or supersession referred to in paragraph (1)(a)(ii);

    (cc) referred to in paragraph (1)(a)(iii); or

    (dd) made within the time limit referred to in paragraph (1)(b) or made in consequence of a decision made on an application for a departure direction or revision made within the time limit referred to in that paragraph.

(2) In this regulation "commencement date" has the same meaning as in regulation 14.

AMENDMENT

1. Regulations 2(3) and (4)(c) of the Transitional Amendments Regulations 2003 (March 3, 2003).

## The Child Support (Transitional Provisions) Regulations 2000

### (SI 2000/3186)

ARRANGEMENT OF REGULATIONS

PART I

*General*

## Part II

*Decision Making and Appeals*

## Part III

*Amount payable following conversion decision*

## Part IV

*Court Order Phasing*

PART V

*Savings*

33 Saving in relation to revision of or appeal against a conversions or subsequent decision.

*The Secretary of State for Social Security, in exercise of the powers conferred upon him by sections 16, 17, 51(1), 52 and 54 of the Child Support Act 1991 and section 29 of the Child Support, Pensions and Social Security Act 2000 and all other powers enabling him in that behalf, hereby makes the following Regulations:*

PART I

GENERAL

**Citation and commencement**

3.528    **1.** These Regulations may be cited as the Child Support (Transitional Provisions) Regulations 2000 and shall come into force on the day on which section 29 of the 2000 Act comes fully into force.

**Interpretation**

3.529    **2.**—(1) In Parts I to III and V except where otherwise stated—
"the Act" means the Child Support Act 1991;
[⁴"the Arrears, Interest and Adjustment Regulations" means the Child Support (Arrears, Interest and Adjustment of Maintenance Assessments) Regulations 1992;]
"the Assessment Calculation Regulations" means the Child Support (Maintenance Assessments and Special Cases) Regulations 1992;
"the Assessment Procedure Regulations" means the Child Support (Maintenance Assessment Procedure) Regulations 1992;
"the 2000 Act" means the Child Support, Pensions and Social Security Act 2000;
"calculation date" means the date the Secretary of State makes a conversion decision;
"capped amount" means the amount of income for the purposes of Part I of Schedule 1 to the Act where that income is limited by the application of paragraph 10(3) of that Schedule;
"case conversion date" means the effective date for the conversion of the non-resident parent's liability to pay child support maintenance from the rate as determined under the former Act and Regulations made under that Act, as provided for in regulation 15;
"commencement date" means the date on which section 1 of the 2000 Act, which amends section 11 of the Act, comes into force for the purposes of maintenance calculations the effective date of which, were they maintenance assessments, applying [¹regulation 30 or 33(7) (but not regulation 8C or 30A) of the Assessment Procedure Regulations or regulation 3(5), (7) or (8) of the Maintenance Arrangements and Jurisdiction Regulations], and subject to paragraph (2), would be the

same as or later than the date prescribed for the purposes of section 4(10)(a) of the Act;

"conversion calculation" means the calculation made in accordance with regulation 16;

"conversion date" means the date on which section 1 of the 2000 Act, which amends section 11 of the Act, comes into force for all purposes;

"conversion decision" means the decision under regulation 3(1) or (4);

"Decisions and Appeals Regulations" means the Social Security and Child Support (Decisions and Appeals) Regulations 1999;

"departure direction" has the meaning given in section 54 of the former Act;

"Departure Regulations" means the Child Support Departure Direction and Consequential Amendments Regulations 1996;

"first prescribed amount" means the amount stated in or prescribed for the purposes of paragraph 4(1)(b) or (c) of Part I of Schedule 1 to the Act (flat rate for non-resident parent in receipt of benefit, pension or allowance);

"former Act" means the Act prior to its amendment by the 2000 Act;

"former assessment amount" means the amount of child support maintenance payable under a maintenance assessment on the calculation date excluding amounts payable in respect of arrears or reductions for overpayments;

"interim maintenance assessment" has the meaning given in section 54 of the former Act;

"Maintenance Arrangements and Jurisdiction Regulations" means the Child Support (Maintenance Arrangements and Jurisdiction) Regulations 1992 [². . .];

"maintenance assessment" has the meaning given in section 54 of the former Act other than an interim maintenance assessment;

"Maintenance Calculations and Special Cases Regulations" means the Child Support (Maintenance Calculations and Special Cases) Regulations 2000;

"maintenance period" has the meaning given in regulation 33 of the Assessment Procedure Regulations and, where in relation to a non-resident parent there is in force on the calculation date more than one maintenance assessment with more than one maintenance period, the first maintenance period to begin on or after the conversion date;

"maximum transitional amount" [³has the meaning given in regulation 25(5), (6) or (7), whichever is applicable;]

"new amount" means the amount of child support maintenance payable [⁵from the case conversion date];

"partner" there is a couple, the other member of that couple, and "couple" for this purpose has the same meaning as in paragraph 10C(5) of Part I of Schedule 1 to the Act;

"phasing amount" means the amount determined in accordance with regulation 24;

"relevant departure direction" and "relevant property transfer" have the meanings given in regulation 17;

"relevant other children" has the meaning given in paragraph 10C(2) of Part I of Schedule 1 of the Act and Regulations made under that paragraph;

"second prescribed amount" means the amount prescribed for the purposes of paragraph 4(2) of Part I of Schedule 1 to the Act (flat rate for non-resident parent who has a partner and who is in receipt of certain benefits);

"subsequent decision" means—

(a) any decision under section 16 or 17 of the Act to revise or supersede a conversion decision; or

(b) any such revision or supersession as decided on appeal, whether as originally made or as revised under section 16 of the Act or decided on appeal;

"subsequent decision amount" means the amount of child support maintenance liability resulting from a subsequent decision;

"transitional amount" means the amount of child support maintenance payable during the transitional period;

"transitional period" means—

(a) the period from the case conversion date to the end of the last complete maintenance period which falls immediately prior to the—

(i) fifth anniversary of the case conversion date; or

(ii) first anniversary of the case conversion date where regulation 12(1), (2), (4) or (5) or 13 applies; or

(b) if earlier, the period from the case conversion date up to the date when the amount of child support maintenance payable by the non-resident parent is equal to the new amount or the subsequent decision amount, as the case may be; and

"the Variations Regulations" means the Child Support (Variations) Regulations 2000.

(2) For the purposes of the definition of "commencement date" in paragraph (1)—

(a) in the application of the Assessment Procedure Regulations, where no maintenance enquiry form, as defined in those Regulations, is given or sent to the non-resident parent, the Regulations shall be applied as if references in regulation 30 of those Regulations—

(i) to the date when the maintenance enquiry form was given or sent to the non-resident parent were to the date on which the non-resident parent is first notified by the Secretary of State, orally or in writing, that an application for child support maintenance has been made in respect of which he is named as the non-resident parent; and

(ii) to the return by the non-resident parent of the maintenance enquiry form containing his name, address and written confirmation that he is the parent of the child or children in respect of whom the application was made, were to the provision of this information by the non-resident parent; or

(b) in the application of the Maintenance Arrangements and Jurisdiction Regulations, where no maintenance enquiry form, as defined in the

Assessment Procedure Regulations, is given or sent to the non-resident parent, regulation 3(8) shall apply as if the reference to the date when the maintenance enquiry form was given or sent were to the date on which the non-resident parent is first notified by the Secretary of State, orally or in writing, that an application for child support maintenance has been made in respect of which he is named as the non-resident parent.

(3) In these Regulations any reference to a numbered Part is to the Part of these Regulations bearing that number, any reference to a numbered regulation is to the regulation in these Regulations bearing that number and any reference in a regulation to a numbered paragraph is to the paragraph in that regulation bearing that number.

AMENDMENTS

1. Regulation 9(2)(a) of the Miscellaneous Amendments Regulations 2003 (February 21, 2003).
2. Regulation 9(2)(b) of the Miscellaneous Amendments Regulations 2003 (February 21, 2003).
3. Regulation 7(2) of the Miscellaneous Amendments (No.2) Regulations 2003 (November 5, 2003).
4. Regulation 8(2)(a) of the Miscellaneous Amendments Regulations 2004 (September 16, 2004).
5. Regulation 8(2)(b) of the Miscellaneous Amendments Regulations 2004 (September 16, 2004).

## PART II

### DECISION MAKING AND APPEALS

**Decision and notice of decision**

**3.**—(1) Subject to paragraph (2), a decision as to the amount of child support maintenance payable under a maintenance assessment or an interim maintenance assessment made under section 11, 12, 16, 17 or 20 of the former Act may be superseded by the Secretary of State on his own initiative under section 17 of the Act, in relation to—

(a) a maintenance assessment (whenever made) which [1. . .] is in force on the calculation date;

(b) a maintenance assessment made following an application for child support maintenance which is made or treated as made as provided for in regulation 28(1);

(c) an interim maintenance assessment [2(whenever made)] where there is sufficient information held by the Secretary of State to make a decision in accordance with this paragraph.

[3(2) Where the Secretary of State acts in accordance with paragraph (1), the information used for the purposes of that supersession will be—

(a) that held by the Secretary of State on the calculation date; or

(b) where—

(i) regulation 5(b) applies; and

3.530

(ii) the Secretary of State is unable to make the decision required to be made in accordance with that regulation on the basis of the information referred to in [⁴sub-paragraph] (a),

that which was used or considered to make the maintenance assessment to be superseded in accordance with regulation 3(1)(a) or (b).]

(3) Where a superseding decision referred to in paragraph (1) is made the Secretary of State shall—

(a) make a conversion calculation;

(b) calculate a new amount; and

(c) notify to the non-resident parent and the person with care and, where the maintenance assessment was made in response to an application under section 7 of the former Act, the child, in writing—

    (i) the new amount;

    (ii) where appropriate, the transitional amount;

    (iii) any phasing amount applied in the calculation of the transitional amount;

    (iv) the length of the transitional period;

    (v) the date the conversion decision was made;

    (vi) the effective date of the conversion decision;

    (vii) the non-resident parent's net weekly income;

    (viii) the number of qualifying children;

    (ix) the number of relevant other children;

    (x) where there is an adjustment for apportionment or shared care, or both, or under regulation 9 or 11 of the Maintenance Calculation and Special Cases Regulations, the amount calculated in accordance with Part I of Schedule 1 to the Act and those Regulations;

    (xi) any relevant departure direction or relevant property transfer taken into account in the conversion decision; and

    (xii) any apportionment carried out in accordance with regulation 25(3).

(4) Where at the calculation date there is an interim maintenance assessment in force and there is insufficient information held by the Secretary of State to make a maintenance assessment, or a decision in accordance with paragraph (1), the Secretary of State shall—

(a) supersede the interim maintenance assessment to make a default maintenance decision; and

(b) notify the non-resident parent, the person with care and, where the maintenance assessment was made in response to an application under section 7, the child, in writing, in accordance with regulation 15C(2) of the Decisions and Appeals Regulations.

(5) In a case to which paragraph (1)(c) or (4) applies, where after the calculation date information is made available to the Secretary of State to enable him to make a maintenance assessment he may—

(a) where the decision was made under paragraph (1)(c), revise the interim maintenance assessment in accordance with the Assessment Procedure Regulations, and supersede the conversion decision in accordance with the Decisions and Appeals Regulations;

(b) where the decision was made under paragraph (4), revise the interim maintenance assessment in accordance with the Assessment

Procedure Regulations, and revise the default maintenance decision in accordance with the Decisions and Appeals Regulations.

(6) A decision referred to in paragraph (1) or (4) shall take effect from the case conversion date.

AMENDMENTS

1. Regulation 9(3)(a) of the Miscellaneous Amendments Regulations 2003 (February 21, 2003).
2. Regulation 9(3)(b) of the Miscellaneous Amendments Regulations 2003 (February 21, 2003).
3. Regulation 8(3) of the Miscellaneous Amendments Regulations 2004 (September 16, 2004).
4. Regulation 7(2) of the Miscellaneous Amendments Regulations 2005 (March 16, 2005).

DEFINITIONS

"the Assessment Procedure Regulations": see reg.2(1).    3.531
"calculation date": see reg.2(1).
"commencement date": see regs 2(1) and 2(2).
"conversion calculation": see regs 2(1) and 2(2).
"conversion decision": see regs 2(1) and 2(2).
"Decisions and Appeals Regulations": see regs 2(1) and 2(2).
"former Act": see regs 2(1) and 2(2).
"interim maintenance assessment": see regs 2(1) and 2(2).
"maintenance assessment": see regs 2(1) and 2(2).
"Maintenance Calculations and Special Cases Regulations": see regs 2(1) and 2(2).
"new amount": see regs 2(1) and 2(2).
"phasing amount": see regs 2(1) and 2(2).
"relevant departure direction": see regs 2(1) and 2(2).
"relevant other children": see regs 2(1) and 2(2).
"relevant property transfer": see regs 2(1) and 2(2).
"transitional amount": see regs 2(1) and 2(2).
"transitional period": see regs 2(1) and 2(2).

## Revision, supersession and appeal of conversion decisions

4.—(1) Subject to this Part, where—    3.532
(a) an application is made to the Secretary of State or he acts on his own initiative to revise or supersede a conversion decision; or
(b) there is an appeal in respect of a conversion decision,
such application, action or appeal shall be decided under the Decisions and Appeals Regulations and except as otherwise provided in paragraph (2), notification shall be given in accordance with regulation 3(3).

(2) Where the Secretary of State acts in accordance with paragraph (1) he shall notify—
(a) in relation to regulation 3(3)(c)(i), the subsequent decision amount in place of the new amount; and
(b) where there has been agreement to a variation or a variation has otherwise been taken into account, the amounts calculated in accordance with the Child Support Variations Regulations.

(3) Where after the calculation date—

(a) an application is made to the Secretary of State or he acts on his own initiative to revise or supersede a maintenance assessment, an interim maintenance assessment or departure direction; or

(b) there is an appeal in respect of a maintenance assessment; an interim maintenance assessment or departure direction; and

(c) such application, action or appeal has been decided in accordance with regulations made under the former Act for the determination of such applications,

the Secretary of State may revise or supersede the conversion decision in accordance with the Decisions and Appeals Regulations.

[[1](4) In their application to a decision referred to in these Regulations, the Decisions and Appeals Regulations shall be modified so as to provide—

(a) on any revision or supersession of a conversion decision under section 16 or 17 respectively of the Act, that—

(i) the conversion decision may include a relevant departure direction or relevant property transfer; and

(ii) the effective date of the revision or supersession shall be as determined under the Decisions and Appeals Regulations or the case conversion date, whichever is the later;

(b) on any appeal in respect of a conversion decision under section 16 or 17 respectively of the Act, that the time within which the appeal must be brought shall be—

(i) within the time from the date of notification of the conversion decision against which the appeal is brought, to one month after the case conversion date of that decision; or

(ii) as determined under the Decisions and Appeals Regulations, whichever is the later.]

(5) In this Part, for the purposes of any revision or supersession a conversion decision shall include a subsequent decision.

AMENDMENT

1. Regulation 8(2) of the Miscellaneous Amendments Regulations 2002 (April 30, 2002).

DEFINITIONS

3.533 "the Act": see reg.2(1).
"calculation date": see reg.2(1).
"case conversion date": see reg.2(1).
"conversion decision": see reg.2(1).
"Decisions and Appeals Regulations": see reg.2(1).
"departure direction": see reg.2(1).
"former Act": see reg.2(1).
"interim maintenance assessment": see reg.2(1).
"maintenance assessment": see reg.2(1).
"new amount": see reg.2(1).
"relevant departure direction": see reg.2(1).
"relevant property transfer": see reg.2(1).

"subsequent decision": see reg.2(1).
"the Variations Regulations": see reg.2(1).

## [¹Revision and supersession of an adjustment

**4A.** Where, on or after the calculation date, an application is made to the Secretary of State or he acts on his own initiative to revise or supersede an adjustment of the amounts payable under a maintenance assessment, he may revise or supersede that adjustment in accordance with the Decisions and Appeals Regulations.]

AMENDMENT

1. Regulation 8(4) of the Miscellaneous Amendments Regulations 2004 (September 16, 2004).

DEFINITIONS

"calculation date": see reg.2(1).
"Decisions and Appeals Regulations": see reg.2(1).

## Outstanding applications at calculation date

**5.** Where at the calculation date there is outstanding an application for a maintenance assessment or a departure direction, or under section 16 or 17 of the former Act for the revision or supersession of a maintenance assessment, an interim maintenance assessment or a departure direction, the Secretary of State may—

    (a) where the application has been finally decided in accordance with Regulations made under the former Act for deciding such applications, supersede the maintenance assessment in accordance with regulation 3; or

    (b) where he is unable to make a final decision on the application for—

        (i) a departure direction; or

        (ii) a revision or supersession,

supersede the maintenance assessment or the interim maintenance assessment in accordance with regulation 3.

3.534

DEFINITIONS

"calculation date": see reg.2(1).
"departure direction": see reg.2(1).
"former Act": see reg.2(1).
"interim maintenance assessment": see reg.2(1).
"maintenance assessment": see reg.2(1).

3.535

GENERAL NOTE

See reg.5A, for the way in which this regulation applies.

## [¹Outstanding revisions and supersessions at calculation date

**5A.** Regulation 5 shall apply in the same way to a decision of the Secretary of State acting on his own initiative under section 16 or 17 of the former Act to revise or supersede a maintenance assessment, an interim maintenance assessment or a departure direction as it does to an application made for the same purpose.]

AMENDMENT

1. Regulation 8(5) of the Miscellaneous Amendments Regulations 2004 (September 16, 2004).

DEFINITIONS

"departure direction": see reg.2(1).
"former Act": see reg.2(1).
"maintenance assessment": see reg.2(1).
"interim maintenance assessment": see reg.2(1).

## Applications for a departure direction or a variation made after calculation date

3.536    **6.**—(1) Where an application for a departure direction or a variation is made after notification of the conversion decision the Secretary of State shall—

(a) where the grounds of the application are subject only to a decision under the Departure Regulations, make a decision under the Departure Regulations;

(b) where the grounds of the application are subject to a decision or determination, as the case may be, under—
   (i) the Departure Regulations; and
   (ii) the Variations Regulations,
   make a decision under the Departure Regulations; or

(c) where the grounds of the application are subject only to a determination under the Variations Regulations, treat the application as an advance application for a variation.

(2) Where the Secretary of State has made a decision or a determination in which he agrees to the departure direction or variation applied for as provided under paragraph(1) he shall—

(a) where the decision is made under paragraph (1)(a), supersede the maintenance assessment in accordance with the Assessment Procedure Regulations and the conversion decision in accordance with the Decisions and Appeals Regulations;

(b) where the decision is made under paragraph (1)(b), supersede the maintenance assessment in accordance with the Assessment Procedure Regulations and the conversion decision in accordance with the Decisions and Appeals Regulations to give effect to any relevant departure direction, and from the case conversion date any variation, in the decision; or

(c) where a determination is made under paragraph (1)(c), supersede the conversion decision in accordance with the Decisions and Appeals Regulations.

(3) Where the Secretary of State does not have the information required to make a decision under paragraph (1) he shall not revise or supersede the conversion decision.

DEFINITIONS

"the Assessment Procedure Regulations": see reg.2(1).                    3.537
"case conversion date": see reg.2(1).
"conversion decision": see reg.2(1).
"Decisions and Appeals Regulations": see reg.2(1).
"departure direction": see reg.2(1).
"Departure Regulations": see reg.2(1).
"maintenance assessment": see reg.2(1).
"relevant departure direction": see reg.2(1).
"the Variations Regulations": see reg.2(1).

## Grounds on which a conversion decision may not be revised, superseded or altered on appeal

7. A decision of the Secretary of State made under regulation 3 shall not be    3.538
revised, superseded or altered on appeal on any of the following grounds—
  (a) the use of the information held by the Secretary of State at the calculation date;
  (b) that the Secretary of State took into account a relevant departure direction in the conversion decision;
  (c) the application of the phasing amount in the calculation of the transitional amount;
  (d) the phasing amount applied to the calculation of the transitional amount;
  (e) the length of the transitional period;
  (f) that an existing departure direction has not been taken into account by the Secretary of State in the transitional amount;
  (g) that the Secretary of State took into account a relevant property transfer in the conversion decision, except where the application affects a relevant property transfer which has been included in the conversion decision on the grounds that—
    (i) where the person with care or, where the maintenance assessment was made in response to an application under section 7 of the former Act, the child applies for the relevant property transfer to be removed, that property transfer when awarded did not reflect the true nature, purpose or value of the property transfer; or
    (ii) [1. . .] the person with care, the non-resident parent or, where the maintenance assessment was made in response to an application under section 7 of the former Act, the child applies for [2. . .] a variation in relation to the same transfer.

AMENDMENTS

1. Regulation 7(3)(a) of the Miscellaneous Amendments (No.2) Regulations 2003 (November 5, 2003).
2. Regulation 7(3)(b) of the Miscellaneous Amendments (No.2) Regulations 2003 (November 5, 2003).

3.539     "calculation date": see reg.2(1).
"conversion decision": see reg.2(1).
"departure direction": see reg.2(1).
"former Act": see reg.2(1).
"maintenance assessment": see reg.2(1).
"phasing amount": see reg.2(1).
"relevant departure direction": see reg.2(1).
"relevant property transfer": see reg.2(1).
"transitional period": see reg.2(1).

## Outstanding appeals at calculation date

3.540     **8.**—(1) Where there is an appeal outstanding at the calculation date against a maintenance assessment, an interim maintenance assessment or an application for a departure direction under the former Act, the Secretary of State shall supersede the maintenance assessment in accordance with regulation 3 using the information held at that date.

(2) When the appeal is decided—

(a) it shall be put into effect in accordance with the tribunal's decision; and

(b) the conversion decision shall be superseded in accordance with the Decisions and Appeals Regulations in consequence of the implementation of the tribunal decision.

DEFINITIONS

3.541     "calculation date": see reg.2(1).
"conversion decision": see reg.2(1).
"Decisions and Appeals Regulations": see reg.2(1).
"departure direction": see reg.2(1).
"former Act": see reg.2(1).
"interim maintenance assessment": see reg.2(1).
"maintenance assessment": see reg.2(1).

PART III

AMOUNT PAYABLE FOLLOWING CONVERSION DECISION

## Amount of child support maintenance payable

3.542     **9.**—(1) [³Subject to regulation 9A, where] a decision of the Secretary of State is made as provided in regulation 3(1)(a) or (b), the amount of child support maintenance payable by the non-resident parent shall, on and from the case conversion date, including but not limited to those cases referred to in regulation 14, be the new amount, [¹unless—

(a) regulation 10 applies, in which case it shall be a transitional amount as provided for in regulations 11 and 17 to 28; or

(b) regulation 12 or 13 applies, in which case it shall be a transitional amount as provided for in those regulations.].

(2) Where a decision under regulation 3(1)(c) relates to a Category B or C interim maintenance assessment, [²regulations 10 to 14 and 16 to 28]

shall apply as if references to a maintenance assessment included references to such an interim maintenance assessment.

(3) In this regulation the reference to Category B or C interim maintenance assessments, and in regulation 14 the reference to Category A or D interim maintenance assessments, are to those assessments within the meaning given in regulation 8(3) of the Assessment Procedure Regulations.

AMENDMENTS

1. Regulation 8(3)(a) of the Miscellaneous Amendments Regulations 2002 (April 30, 2002).
2. Regulation 8(3)(b) of the Miscellaneous Amendments Regulations 2002 (April 30, 2002).
3. Regulation 8(6) of the Miscellaneous Amendments Regulations 2004 (September 16, 2004).

DEFINITIONS

"the Assessment Procedure Regulations": see reg.2(1).  3.543
"case conversion date": see reg.2(1).
"interim maintenance assessment": see reg.2(1).
"maintenance assessment": see reg.2(1).
"new amount": see reg.2(1).
"transitional amount": see reg.2(1).

## [¹Adjustment of the amount of child support maintenance payable

**9A.**—(1) Subject to paragraph (2), where—
(a) there has been an overpayment of child support maintenance under a maintenance assessment; and
(b) the amount payable under that maintenance assessment has been adjusted under regulation 10 of the Arrears, Interest and Adjustment Regulations as it applies to a maintenance assessment,
that adjustment shall apply to the new amount or the transitional amount in the conversion decision, as the case may be, if—
  (i) the overpayment remains on the case conversion date; and
  (ii) the Secretary of State considers it appropriate in all the circumstances of the case having regard to the matters set out in regulation 10(1)(b) of the Arrears, Interest and Adjustment Regulations as it applies to a conversion decision.

(2) Where the conversion decision relates to more than one parent with care, the adjustment of the amount payable under a maintenance assessment which applies to the new amount or the transitional amount, as the case may be, in accordance with paragraph (1) shall only apply in respect of the apportioned amount payable to the parent with care in relation to whom the maintenance assessment subject to the adjustment was made.

(3) In paragraph (2) the "apportioned amount" shall have the meaning given in regulation 11(4).]

AMENDMENT

1. Regulation 8(7) of the Miscellaneous Amendments Regulations 2004 (September 16, 2004).

"the Arrears, Interest and Adjustment Regulations": see reg.2(1).
"case conversion date": see reg.2(1).
"conversion decision": see reg.2(1).
"maintenance assessment: see reg.2(1).
"new amount": see reg.2(1).
"transitional amount": see reg.2(1).

## [¹Attribution of payments

**9B.**—(1) Where—

(a) there are arrears of child support maintenance under a maintenance assessment; and

(b) the Secretary of State has attributed any payment of child support maintenance made by an absent parent to child support maintenance due as he thinks fit, in accordance with regulation 9 of the Arrears, Interest and Adjustment Regulations as it applies to a maintenance assessment,

that attribution of payments shall apply to the new amount or the transitional amount in the conversion decision, as the case may be, if—

(i) the arrears remain on the case conversion date; and

(ii) the Secretary of State has made that attribution of payments as he thought fit, in accordance with regulation 9 of the Arrears, Interest and Adjustment Regulations as it applies to a conversion decision.]

AMENDMENT

1. Regulation 8(7) of the Miscellaneous Amendments Regulations 2004 (September 16, 2004).

DEFINITIONS

"the Arrears, Interest and Adjustment Regulations": see reg.2(1).
"case conversion date": see reg.2(1).
"conversion decision": see reg.2(1).
"maintenance assessment: see reg.2(1).
"new amount": see reg.2(1).
"transitional amount": see reg.2(1).

## Circumstances in which a transitional amount is payable

3.544    **10.** This regulation applies where the new amount is a basic or reduced rate [¹, an amount calculated under regulation 22] [², an amount calculated under regulation 26 of the Variations Regulations] or, except where regulation 12, 13 or 14 applies, a flat rate of child support maintenance; and

(a) the former assessment amount is greater than the new amount and when the former assessment amount is decreased by the phasing amount, the resulting figure is greater than the new amount; or

(b) the former assessment amount is less than the new amount and when the former assessment amount is increased by the phasing amount, the resulting figure is less than the new amount.

AMENDMENTS

1. Regulation 8(4) of the Miscellaneous Amendments Regulations 2002 (April 30, 2002).
2. Regulation 9(4) of the Miscellaneous Amendments Regulations 2003 (February 21, 2003).

DEFINITIONS

"former assessment amount": see reg.2(1).　　　　　　　　　　　　　　3.545
"new amount": see reg.2(1).
"phasing amount": see reg.2(1).

## Transitional amount-basic, reduced and most flat rate cases

**11.**—(1) Subject to [¹paragraphs (2) and (3)] and regulation 25, in　3.546
cases to which regulation 10 applies the transitional amount is the former assessment amount decreased, where that amount is greater than the new amount, or increased, where the latter amount is the greater, by the phasing amount.

[²(2) Subject to paragraph (3), where regulation 10 applies and there is at the calculation date more than one maintenance assessment in relation to the same absent parent, which has the meaning given in the former Act, the amount of child support maintenance payable from the case conversion date in respect of each person with care shall be determined by applying regulation 10 and paragraph (1) as if—

(a) the references to the new amount were to the apportioned amount payable in respect of the person with care; and
(b) the references to the former assessment amount were to that amount in respect of that person with care.

(3) Where regulation 10 applies and a conversion decision is made in a circumstance to which regulation 15(3C) applies, the amount of child support maintenance payable from the case conversion date—

(a) to a person with care in respect of whom an application for a maintenance calculation has been made or treated as made which is of a type referred to in regulation 15(3C)(b), shall be the apportioned amount payable in respect of that person with care; and
(b) in respect of any other person with care, shall be determined by applying regulation 10 and paragraph (1) as if the references to the new amount were to the apportioned amount payable in respect of that person with care and the references to the former assessment amount were to that amount in respect of that person with care.]

(4) In this regulation, "apportioned amount" means the amount payable in respect of a person with care calculated as provided in Part I of Schedule 1 to the Act and Regulations made under that Part and, where applicable, regulations 17 to 23 and Part IV of these Regulations.]

AMENDMENTS

1. Regulation 9(5)(a) of the Miscellaneous Amendments Regulations 2003 (February 21, 2003).
2. Regulation 9(5)(b) of the Miscellaneous Amendments Regulations 2003 (February 21, 2003).

DEFINITIONS

3.547    "the Act": see reg.2(1).
"case conversion date": see reg.2(1).
"former assessment amount": see reg.2(1).
"new amount": see reg.2(1).
"phasing amount": see reg.2(1).
"transitional amount": see reg.2(1).

## Transitional amount in flat rate cases

3.548    **12.**—(1) Except where the former assessment amount is nil, where the new amount would be the first prescribed amount but is nil owing to the application of paragraph 8 of Part I of Schedule 1 to the Act the amount of child support maintenance payable for the year commencing on the case conversion date shall be a transitional amount equivalent to the second prescribed amount and thereafter shall be the new amount [[1]. . .].

(2) Except where the former assessment amount is nil, where the new amount would be the second prescribed amount but is nil owing to the application of paragraph 8 of Part I of Schedule 1 to the Act the amount of child support maintenance payable for the year commencing on the case conversion date shall be a transitional amount equivalent to half the second prescribed amount and thereafter shall be the new amount [[2]. . .].

(3) Where—
(a) a non-resident parent has more than one qualifying child and in relation to them there is more than one person with care; and
(b) the amount of child support maintenance payable from the case conversion date to one or some of those persons with care, but not all of them, would be nil owing to the application of paragraph 8 of Part I of Schedule 1 to the Act,

the amount of child support maintenance payable by the non-resident parent from the case conversion date shall be the new amount, apportioned [[3]among the persons with care, other than any in respect of whom paragraph 8 of Part I of Schedule 1 to the Act applies, in accordance with paragraph 6(2) of that Schedule, unless paragraph (4) or (5) applies.]

(4) Subject to paragraph (6), where the former assessment amount is less than the new amount by an amount which is more than the second prescribed amount or, where paragraph 4(2) of Part I of Schedule 1 to the Act applies to the non-resident parent, half the second prescribed amount, the amount of child support maintenance payable by the non-resident parent shall be as provided in paragraph (1) where paragraph 4(1)(b) [[4]or(c)] of Part I of Schedule 1 to the Act applies, and as provided in paragraph (2) where paragraph 4(2) of that Schedule applies.

(5) Subject to paragraph (6), where the former assessment amount is greater than the new amount the amount of child support maintenance payable by the non-resident parent shall be the new amount unless the new amount is less than the second prescribed amount or, where paragraph 4(2) of Part I of Schedule 1 to the Act applies to the non-resident parent, half the second prescribed amount, in which case the amount of child support maintenance payable by the non-resident parent shall be as provided in paragraph (1) where paragraph 4(1)(b) [[5]or (c)] of Part I of Schedule 1

to the Act applies, and as provided in paragraph (2) where paragraph 4(2) of that Schedule applies.

[⁶(6) Where paragraph (4) or (5) applies, the transitional amount shall be apportioned among the persons with care, other than any in respect of whom the former assessment amount is nil and paragraph 8 of Part I of Schedule 1 to the Act applies, in accordance with paragraph 6(2) of that Schedule.]

(7) In this regulation "former assessment amount" means, in relation to a non-resident parent in respect of whom there is in force on the calculation date more than one maintenance assessment, the aggregate of the amounts payable under those assessments, and [⁷. . .] includes the amount payable where section 43 of the former Act (contribution to maintenance) applies to the non-resident parent.

AMENDMENTS

1. Regulation 8(5)(a) of the Miscellaneous Amendments Regulations 2002 (April 30, 2002).
2. Regulation 8(5)(a) of the Miscellaneous Amendments Regulations 2002 (April 30, 2002).
3. Regulation 8(5)(b) of the Miscellaneous Amendments Regulations 2002 (April 30, 2002).
4. Regulation 8(5)(c) of the Miscellaneous Amendments Regulations 2002 (April 30, 2002).
5. Regulation 8(5)(c) of the Miscellaneous Amendments Regulations 2002 (April 30, 2002).
6. Regulation 8(5)(d) of the Miscellaneous Amendments Regulations 2002 (April 30, 2002).
7. Regulation 8(5)(e) of the Miscellaneous Amendments Regulations 2002 (April 30, 2002).

DEFINITIONS

"the Act": see reg.2(1).                                                                  3.549
"case conversion date": see reg.2(1).
"first prescribed amount": see reg.2(1).
"former assessment amount": see reg.2(1) and para.(7).
"new amount": see reg.2(1) and para.(7).
"second prescribed amount": see reg.2(1) and para.(7).
"transitional amount": see reg.2(1) and para.(7).

## Transitional amount—certain flat rate cases

**13.** [¹—(1)] Where paragraph 4(2) of Part I of Schedule 1 to the Act      3.550
applies and the former assessment amount is nil, the amount of child support maintenance payable for the year beginning on the case conversion date shall be a transitional amount equivalent to half the second prescribed amount and thereafter shall not be a transitional amount but shall be the new amount.

[²(2) Where paragraph 4(1)(b) or (c) of Part I of Schedule 1 to the Act applies and the former assessment amount is nil, the amount of child support maintenance payable for the year beginning on the case conversion date shall be a transitional amount equivalent to half the first prescribed amount and thereafter shall not be a transitional amount but shall be the new amount.]

AMENDMENTS

1. Regulation 8(6) of the Miscellaneous Amendments Regulations 2002 (April 30, 2002).
2. Regulation 8(6) of the Miscellaneous Amendments Regulations 2002 (April 30, 2002).

DEFINITIONS

3.551     "the Act": see reg.2(1).
"conversion date": see reg.2(1).
"former assessment amount": see reg.2(1).
"new amount": see reg.2(1).
"second prescribed amount": see reg.2(1).
"transitional amount": see reg.2(1).

## Certain cases where the new amount is payable

3.552     **14.** The amount of child support maintenance which the non-resident parent is liable to pay on and from the case conversion date is the new amount where—

(a) the application for the maintenance assessment referred to in regulation 3(1)(a) is determined after the case conversion date, except in a case to which regulation 28(1) applies;

(b) the former assessment amount is more than nil, including where section 43 of the former Act (contribution to maintenance) applies to the non-resident parent and the new amount is the first or second prescribed amount;

(c) the new amount is the nil rate under paragraph 5 of Part I of Schedule 1 to the Act; [¹. . .]

(d) the former assessment amount is nil and the new amount is nil owing to the application of paragraph 8 of Part I of Schedule 1 (flat rate plus shared care) to the Act; or

(e) a decision under regulation 3(1)(c) relates to a Category A or D interim maintenance assessment or a decision is made under regulation 3(4).

AMENDMENT

1. Regulation 8(7) of the Miscellaneous Amendments Regulations 2002 (April 30, 2002).

DEFINITIONS

3.553     "case conversion date": see reg.2(1).
"first prescribed amount": see reg.2(1).
"former assessment amount": see reg.2(1).
"interim maintenance assessment": see reg.2(1).
"maintenance assessment": see reg.2(1).
"new amount": see reg.2(1).
"second prescribed amount": see reg.2(1).

**Case conversion date**

**15.**—(1) Subject to [³paragraphs (2) to (3G)], the case conversion date     3.554
is the beginning of the first maintenance period on or after the conversion
date.

(2) Where, on or after the commencement date, there is a maintenance
assessment in force and a maintenance calculation is made to which paragraph (3) [⁴or (3A)] applies, the case conversion date for the maintenance
assessment [⁵is] the beginning of the first maintenance period on or after
the effective date of the related maintenance calculation.

[⁶(3) This paragraph applies where the maintenance calculation is made
with respect to a relevant person who is a relevant person in relation to the
maintenance assessment whether or not with respect to a different qualifying
child.

(3A) This paragraph applies where the maintenance calculation is made
in relation to a partner ("A") of a person ("B") who is a relevant person in
relation to the maintenance assessment and—

(a) A or B is in receipt of a prescribed benefit; and
(b) either—
   (i) A is the non-resident parent in relation to the maintenance
     calculation and B is the absent parent in relation to the
     maintenance assessment; or
   (ii) A is the person with care in relation to the maintenance
     calculation and B is the person with care in relation to the
     maintenance assessment.

(3B) The case conversion date of a conversion decision made where
paragraph (3C) applies is the beginning of the first maintenance period on
or after the date of notification of the conversion decision.

(3C) This paragraph applies where on or after the commencement
date—

(a) there is a maintenance assessment in force;
(b) an application is made or treated as made which, but for the main-
    tenance assessment, would result in a maintenance calculation being
    made with an effective date before the conversion date;
(c) the non-resident parent in relation to the application referred to in
    sub-paragraph (b) is the absent parent in relation to the maintenance
    assessment referred to in sub-paragraph (a); and
(d) the person with care in relation to the application referred to in sub-
    paragraph (b) is a different person to the person with care in relation
    to the maintenance assessment referred to in sub-paragraph (a).

(3D) The case conversion date of a conversion decision made where
paragraph (3E) applies is the beginning of the first maintenance period on
or after the date on which the superseding decision referred to in paragraph
(3E)(d) takes effect.

(3E) This paragraph applies where on or after the commencement
date—

(a) a maintenance assessment is in force in relation to a person ("C")
    and a maintenance calculation is in force in relation to another
    person ("D");
(b) C or D is in receipt of a prescribed benefit;

    (c) either—
        (i) C is the absent parent in relation to the maintenance assessment and D is the non-resident parent in relation to the maintenance calculation; or
        (ii) C is the person with care in relation to the maintenance assessment and D is the person with care in relation to the maintenance calculation; and
    (d) the decision relating to the prescribed benefit referred to in sub-paragraph (b) is superseded on the ground that C is the partner of D.

(3F) The case conversion date of a conversion decision made where paragraph (3G) applies is the beginning of the first maintenance period on or after the date from which entitlement to the prescribed benefit referred to in paragraph (3G)(c) begins.

(3G) This paragraph applies where on or after the commencement date—
    (a) a person ("E") in respect of whom a maintenance assessment is in force is the partner of another person ("F") in respect of whom a maintenance calculation is in force;
    (b) either—
        (i) E is the absent parent in relation to the maintenance assessment and F is the non-resident parent in relation to the maintenance calculation; or
        (ii) E is the person with care in relation to the maintenance assessment and F is the person with care in relation to the maintenance calculation; and
    (c) E and F become entitled to a prescribed benefit as partners.]

(4) In [¹this regulation]

[⁷"absent parent" has the meaning given in the former Act;]

[²"maintenance assessment" has the meaning given in section 54 of the former Act;]

"relevant person" means, in relation to a maintenance assessment, the absent parent [⁸. . .] or person with care and, in relation to a maintenance calculation, the non-resident parent or person with care; and

"prescribed benefit" means a benefit prescribed for the purposes of paragraph 4(1)(c) of Part I of Schedule 1 to the Act.

AMENDMENTS

1. Regulation 8(8)(a) of the Miscellaneous Amendments Regulations 2002 (April 30, 2002).
2. Regulation 8(8)(b) of the Miscellaneous Amendments Regulations 2002 (April 30, 2002).
3. Regulation 9(6)(a) of the Miscellaneous Amendments Regulations 2003 (February 21, 2003).
4. Regulation 9(6)(b)(i) of the Miscellaneous Amendments Regulations 2003 (February 21, 2003).
5. Regulation 9(6)(b)(ii) of the Miscellaneous Amendments Regulations 2003 (February 21, 2003).
6. Regulation 9(6)(c) of the Miscellaneous Amendments Regulations 2003 (February 21, 2003).
7. Regulation 9(6)(d)(i) of the Miscellaneous Amendments Regulations 2003 (February 21, 2003).

8. Regulation 9(6)(d)(ii) of the Miscellaneous Amendments Regulations 2003 (February 21, 2003).

DEFINITIONS

"case conversion date": see reg.2(1).  **3.555**
"commencement date": see reg.2(1) and 2(2).
"conversion date": see reg.2(1) and 2(2).
"maintenance assessment": see reg.2(1) and 2(2).
"maintenance period": see reg.2(1) and 2(2).

## Conversion calculation and conversion decision

**16.**—(1) A conversion calculation by the Secretary of State shall be  **3.556** made—

(a)   in accordance with Part I of Schedule 1 to the Act;
[⁶(b)   taking into account the information used in accordance with regulation 3(2); and]
(c)   taking into account any relevant departure direction or any relevant property transfer as provided in regulations 17 to [¹23A].

(2) A conversion decision shall be treated for the purposes of any revision, supersession, appeal or application for a variation under sections 16, 17, 20 or 28G of the Act, and Regulations made in connection with such matters, as a decision under section 11 of the Act made with effect from the date of notification of that decision and, where a conversion decision has been made, the case shall for those purposes be treated as if there were a maintenance calculation in force.

[²(2A)  For the purposes of sections 29 to 41B of the Act and regulations made under or by virtue of those sections, a conversion decision shall be treated on or after the case conversion date as if it were a maintenance calculation.]

[⁵(2B)  For the purposes of regulation 2 of the Social Security Benefits (Maintenance Payments and Consequential Amendments) Regulations 1996 (interpretation for the purposes of section 74A of the Social Security Administration Act 1992, a conversion decision shall be treated as made on or after the case conversion date as it if were a maintenance calculation.]

[⁷(2C)  For the purposes of regulations 9 and 10 of the Arrears, Interest and Adjustment Regulations, a conversion decision shall be treated on or after the case conversion date as if it were a maintenance calculation.]

(3) A [³conversion decision] shall become a maintenance calculation when the transitional period ends or, if later, any relevant property transfer taken into account in [⁴the conversion calculation] ceases to have effect.

AMENDMENTS

1. Regulation 9(7)(a) of the Miscellaneous Amendments Regulations 2003 (February 21, 2003).
2. Regulation 9(7)(b) of the Miscellaneous Amendments Regulations 2003 (February 21, 2003).
3. Regulation 9(7)(c)(i) of the Miscellaneous Amendments Regulations 2003 (February 21, 2003).

4. Regulation 9(7)(c)(ii) of the Miscellaneous Amendments Regulations 2003 (February 21, 2003).

5. Regulation 3 of the Transitional Amendments Regulations 2003 (March 3, 2003).

6. Regulation 8(8)(a) of the Miscellaneous Amendments Regulations 2004 (September 16, 2004).

7. Regulation 8(8)(b) of the Miscellaneous Amendments Regulations 2004 (September 16, 2004).

DEFINITIONS

3.557 "the Arrears, Interest and Adjustment Regulations": see reg.2(1).
"calculation date": see reg.2(1).
"conversion calculation": see reg.2(1).
"conversion decision": see reg.2(1).
"relevant departure direction": see reg.2(1).
"relevant property transfer": see reg.2(1).
"transitional period": see reg.2(1).

## Relevant departure [¹direction] and relevant property transfer

3.558 **17.**—(1) A relevant departure direction means a departure direction given in relation to the maintenance assessment which is the subject of the conversion decision where that direction was given under the provisions of the former Act and Regulations made under that Act, and where it is one to which one of the following paragraphs of this regulation applies.

(2) This paragraph applies to a departure direction given on the special expenses grounds in paragraph 2(3)(b) (contact costs) or 2(3)(d) (debts) of Schedule 4B to the former Act where and to the extent that they exceed the threshold amount which is—

(a) £15 per week where the expenses fall within only one of those paragraphs and, where the expenses fall within both paragraphs, £15 per week in respect of the aggregate of those expenses, where the net weekly income is £200 or more; or

(b) £10 per week where the expenses fall within only one of those paragraphs and, where the expenses fall within both paragraphs, £10 per week in respect of the aggregate of those expenses, where the net weekly income is below £200,

and for this purpose "net weekly income" means the income which would otherwise be taken into account for the purposes of the conversion decision including any additional income which falls to be taken into account under regulation 20.

(3) This paragraph applies to a departure direction given on the ground in paragraph 2(3)(c) (illness and disability costs) of Schedule 4B to the former Act where the illness or disability is of a relevant other child.

(4) This paragraph applies to a departure direction given on the ground in paragraph 3 (property or capital transfer) of Schedule 4B to the former Act.

(5) Subject to paragraph (6), this paragraph applies to a departure direction given on the additional cases grounds in paragraph 5(1) of Schedule 4B to the former Act and regulation 24 (diversion of income) of the Departure Regulations or paragraph 5(2)(b) of Schedule 4B to the former

Act and regulation 25 (life-style inconsistent with declared income) of those Regulations.

[²(6) Where, but for the application of a relevant departure direction referred to in paragraph (5), the new amount would be—

(a) the first prescribed amount owing to the application of paragraph 4(1)(b) of Part I of Schedule 1 to the Act;

(b) the amount referred to in sub-paragraph (a), but is less than that amount or is nil, owing to the application of paragraph 8 of that Part; or

(c) the nil rate under paragraph 5(a) of that Part,

paragraph (5) applies where the amount of the additional income exceeds £100.]

(7) This paragraph applies to a departure direction given on the ground in paragraph 5(2)(a) of Schedule 4B to the former Act (assets capable of producing income) where the value of the assets taken into account is greater than £65,000.

(8) A relevant property transfer is a transfer which was taken into account in the decision as to the maintenance assessment in respect of which the conversion decision is made owing to the application of Schedule 3A to the Assessment Calculation Regulations.

(9) Where—

(a) a relevant departure direction is taken into account for the purposes of a conversion calculation; or

(b) a subsequent decision is made following the application of a relevant departure direction to a maintenance assessment,

the relevant departure direction shall for the purposes of any subsequent decision, including the subsequent decision in paragraph (b), be a variation as if an application had been made under section 28G of the Act for a variation in relation to the same ground and for the same amount.

[³(10) Where—

(a) a relevant property transfer is taken into account for the purposes of a conversion decision;

(b) an application is made for a variation of a type referred to in paragraph 3 of Schedule 4B to the Act and Part IV of the Variations Regulations (property or capital transfers) which relates to the same property or capital transfer as the relevant property transfer referred to in sub-paragraph (a); and

(c) the variation is agreed to,

the relevant property transfer shall cease to have effect on the effective date of the subsequent decision which resulted from the application for a variation.]

AMENDMENTS

1. Regulation 8(9)(a) of the Miscellaneous Amendments Regulations 2002 (April 30, 2002).

2. Regulation 8(9)(b) of the Miscellaneous Amendments Regulations 2002 (April 30, 2002).

3. Regulation 7(4) of the Miscellaneous Amendments (No.2) Regulations 2003 (November 5, 2003).

3.559

"the Act": reg.2(1).
"conversion calculation": see reg.2(1).
"conversion decision": see reg.2(1).
"departure direction": see reg.2(1).
"first prescribed amount": see reg.2(1).
"former Act": see reg.2(1).
"maintenance assessment": see reg.2(1).
"new amount": see reg.2(1).
"relevant departure direction": see reg.2(1).
"relevant property transfer": see reg.2(1).
"subsequent decision": see reg.2(1).
"the Variations Regulations": see reg.2(1)

### Effect on conversion calculation—special expenses

3.560

**18.**—(1) Subject to paragraph (2) and regulations 22 and 23, where the relevant departure direction is one falling within paragraph (2) or (3) of regulation 17, effect shall be given to the relevant departure direction in the conversion calculation by deducting from the net weekly income of the non-resident parent the weekly amount of that departure direction and for this purpose "net weekly income" has the meaning given in regulation 17(2).

(2) Where the income which, but for the application of this paragraph, would be taken into account in the conversion decision is the capped amount and the relevant departure direction is one falling within paragraph (2) or (3) or regulation 17 then—

(a) the weekly amount of the expenses shall first be deducted from the net weekly income of the non-resident parent which, but for the application of the capped amount, would be taken into account in the conversion decision including any additional income to be taken into account as a result of the application of paragraphs (5) or (7) of regulation 17 (additional cases);

(b) the amount by which the capped amount exceeds the figure calculated under sub-paragraph (a) shall be calculated; and

(c) effect shall be given to the relevant departure direction in the conversion calculation by deducting from the capped amount the amount calculated under sub-paragraph (b).

3.561

"capped amount": see reg.2(1).
"conversion calculation": see reg.2(1).
"conversion decision": see reg.2(1).
"relevant departure direction": see reg.2(1).

### Effect on conversion calculation—property or capital transfer

3.562

**19.** Subject to regulation 23, where the relevant departure direction is one falling within paragraph (4) of regulation 17—

(a) the conversion calculation shall be carried out in accordance with regulation 16(1) and, where there is more than one person with care in relation to the non-resident parent, the amount of child support maintenance resulting shall be apportioned among the persons with care as provided in paragraph 6 of Part I of Schedule 1 to the Act and Regulations made under that Part; and

(b) the equivalent weekly value of the transfer to which the relevant departure direction relates shall be deducted from the amount of child support maintenance which the non-resident parent would otherwise be liable to pay to the person with care with respect to whom the transfer was made.

DEFINITIONS

"the Act": see reg.2(1).
"conversion calculation": see reg.2(1).
"relevant departure direction": see reg.2(1).

3.563

## Effect on conversion calculation—additional cases

**20.** Subject to regulations 22 and 23, where the relevant departure direction is one falling within paragraph (5) or (7) of regulation 17 (additional cases), effect shall be given to the relevant departure direction in the conversion calculation by increasing the net weekly income of the non-resident parent which would otherwise be taken into account by the weekly amount of the additional income except that, where the amount of net weekly income calculated in this way would exceed the capped amount, the amount of net weekly income taken into account shall be the capped amount.

3.564

DEFINITIONS

"capped amount": see reg.2(1).
"conversion calculation": see reg.2(1).
"relevant departure direction": see reg.2(1).
"relevant property transfer": see reg.2(1).

3.565

## Effect on conversion calculation—relevant property transfer

**21.**—(1) Subject to paragraph (2) and [¹regulations 23 and 23A], a relevant property transfer shall be given effect by deducting from the net weekly income of the non-resident parent which would otherwise be taken into account the amount in relation to the relevant property transfer and for this purpose "net weekly income" has the meaning given in regulation 17(2) but after deduction in respect of any relevant departure direction falling within paragraph (2) or (3) of regulation 17 (special expenses).

3.566

(2) Where the net weekly income of the non-resident parent which is taken into account for the purposes of the conversion calculation is the capped amount, a relevant property transfer shall be given effect by deducting the amount in respect of the transfer from the capped amount.

AMENDMENT

1. Regulation 8(10) of the Miscellaneous Amendments Regulations 2002 (April 30, 2002).

3.567    "capped amount": see reg.2(1).
"conversion calculation": see reg.2(1).
"relevant departure direction": see reg.2(1).
"relevant property transfer": see reg.2(1).

## Effect on conversion calculation—maximum amount payable where relevant departure direction is on additional cases ground

3.568    **22.**—(1) Subject to regulation 23, where this regulation applies [¹the new amount] shall be whichever is the lesser of—

[²(a)  a weekly amount calculated by aggregating the first prescribed amount with the result of applying Part I of Schedule 1 to the Act to the additional income arising under the relevant departure direction; or

(b)  a weekly amount calculated by applying Part I of Schedule 1 to the Act to the aggregate of the additional income arising under the relevant departure direction and the weekly amount of any benefit, pension or allowance received by the non-resident parent which is prescribed for the purposes of paragraph 4(1)(b) of that Schedule.]

(2)  This regulation applies where the relevant departure direction is one to which paragraph (5) or (7) of regulation 17 applies (additional cases) and the non-resident parent's liability calculated as provided in Part I of Schedule 1 to the Act, and Regulations made under that Schedule, would, but for the relevant departure direction be—

(a)  the first prescribed amount;

(b)  the first prescribed amount but is less than that amount or nil, owing to the application of paragraph 8 of Part I of that Schedule; or

(c)  the first prescribed amount but for the application of paragraph 5(a) of that Schedule.

(3)  For the purposes of paragraph (1)—

(a)  "additional income" for the purposes of sub-paragraphs (a) and (b) means such income after the application of a relevant departure direction falling within paragraph (2) or (3) of regulation 17 (special expenses) [³or a relevant property transfer]; and

(b)  "weekly amount" for the purposes of sub-paragraphs (a) and (b) means the aggregate of the amounts referred to in the relevant sub-paragraph—

(i)  adjusted as provided in regulation 23(3) as if the reference in that regulation to child support maintenance were to the weekly amount; and

(ii)  after any deduction provided for in regulation 23(4) as if the reference in that regulation to child support maintenance were to the weekly amount ; [⁴and

(c)  any benefit, pension or allowance referred to in sub-paragraph (b) shall not include—

(i)  in the case of industrial injuries benefit under section 94 of the Social Security Contributions and Benefits Act 1992[38], any increase in that benefit under section 104 (constant attendance) or 105 (exceptionally severe disablement) of that Act;

(ii) in the case of a war disablement pension within the meaning in section 150(2) of that Act, any award under the following articles of the Naval, Military and Air Forces etc. (Disablement and Death) Service Pensions Order 1983 ("the Service Pensions Order"): article 14 (constant attendance allowance), 15 (exceptionally severe disablement allowance), 16 (severe disablement occupational allowance) or 26A (mobility supplement)[39] or any analogous allowance payable in conjunction with any other war disablement pension; and

(iii) any award under article 18 of the Service Pensions Order (unemployability allowances) which is an additional allowance in respect of a child of the non-resident parent where that child is not living with the non-resident parent.]

AMENDMENTS

1. Regulation 8(11) of the Miscellaneous Amendments Regulations 2002 (April 30, 2002).

2. Regulation 9(8)(a) of the Miscellaneous Amendments Regulations 2003 (February 21, 2003).

3. Regulation 9(8)(b)(i) of the Miscellaneous Amendments Regulations 2003 (February 21, 2003).

4. Regulation 9(8)(b)(ii) of the Miscellaneous Amendments Regulations 2003 (February 21, 2003).

DEFINITIONS

"the Act": reg.2(1).                                                                                   3.569
"conversion decision": see reg.2(1).
"first prescribed amount": see reg.2(1).
"maintenance assessment": see reg.2(1).
"relevant departure direction": see reg.2(1).

## Effect of relevant departure direction on conversion calculation—general

**23.**—(1) Subject to paragraphs (4) and (5), where more than one rele-   3.570
vant departure direction applies regulations 18 to 22 shall apply and the results shall be aggregated as appropriate.

(2) Paragraph 7(2) to (7) of Schedule 1 to the Act (shared care) shall apply where the rate of child support maintenance is affected by a relevant departure direction [1...] and paragraph 7(2) of that Schedule shall be read as if after the words "as calculated in accordance with the preceding paragraphs of this Part of this Schedule "there were inserted the words", the Child Support (Transitional Provision) Regulations 2000".

(3) Subject to paragraphs (4) and (5), where the non-resident parent shares the care of a qualifying child within the meaning in Part I of Schedule 1 to the Act, or where the care of such a child is shared in part by a local authority, the amount of child support maintenance the non-resident parent is liable to pay the person with care, calculated to take account of any relevant departure direction, shall be reduced in accordance with the provisions of paragraph 7 of that Part, or regulation 9 of

the Maintenance Calculations and Special Cases Regulations, as the case may be.

(4) Subject to paragraph (5), where a relevant departure direction is one falling within paragraph (4) of regulation 17 (property or capital transfer) the amount of the relevant departure direction shall be deducted from the amount of child support maintenance the non-resident parent would otherwise be liable to pay the person with care in respect of whom the transfer was made after aggregation of the effects of any relevant departure directions as provided in paragraph (1) or deduction for shared care as provided in paragraph (3).

(5) If the application of regulation 19, or paragraphs (3) or (4), would decrease the weekly amount of child support maintenance (or the aggregate of all such amounts) payable by the non-resident parent to the person with care (or all of them) to less than a figure equivalent to the first prescribed amount, the new amount shall instead be the first prescribed amount and shall be apportioned as provided in paragraph 6 of Part I of Schedule 1 to the Act, and Regulations made under that Part.

AMENDMENT

1. Regulation 8(12) of the Miscellaneous Amendments Regulations 2002 (April 30, 2002).

DEFINITIONS

3.571     "the Act": see reg.2(1).
"first prescribed amount": see reg.2(1).
"new amount": see reg.2(1).
"relevant departure direction": see reg.2(1).

## [¹Effect of a relevant property transfer and a relevant departure direction—general

**23A.** Where—
(a) more than one relevant property transfer applies; or
(b) one or more relevant property transfers and one or more relevant departure directions apply,

regulation 23 shall apply as if references to a relevant departure direction were to a relevant property transfer or to the relevant property transfers and relevant departure directions, as the case may be.]

AMENDMENT

1. Regulation 8(13) of the Miscellaneous Amendments Regulations 2002 (April 30, 2002).

DEFINITIONS

"relevant departure direction": see reg.2(1).
"relevant property transfer": see reg.2(1)

**Phasing amount**

**24.**—(1) In this Part "phasing amount" means, for the year beginning    3.572
on the case conversion date, the relevant figure provided in paragraph (2),
and for each subsequent year the phasing amount for the previous year
aggregated with the relevant figure.

(2) The relevant figure is—

(a) £2.50 where the relevant income is £100 or less;

(b) £5.00 where the relevant income is more than £100 but less than
£400; or

(c) £10.00 where the relevant income is £400 or more.

(3) [¹Subject to [³paragraphs (4)][⁵, (5) and (6)], for] the purposes of
paragraph (2), the "relevant income" is the net weekly income of the
non-resident parent taken into account in the conversion decision.

[²(4) Where the new amount is calculated under regulation 22(1), "relevant income" for the purposes of paragraph (2) is the aggregate of the
income calculated under regulation 22(1)(b).]

[⁴(5) Where the new amount is calculated under regulation [26(1) of
the Variations Regulations, the "relevant income" for the purposes of
paragraph (2) is the additional income arising under the variation.]

[⁶(6) Where a subsequent decision is made the effective date of which is
the case conversion date—

(a) the reference in paragraph (3) to the conversion decision shall apply
as if it were a reference to the subsequent decision; and

(b) the reference in paragraph (5) to the new amount shall apply as if it
were a reference to the subsequent decision amount.]

AMENDMENTS

1. Regulation 8(14)(a) of the Miscellaneous Amendments Regulations 2002
(April 30, 2002).

2. Regulation 8(14)(b) of the Miscellaneous Amendments Regulations 2002
(April 30, 2002).

3. Regulation 9(9)(a) of the Miscellaneous Amendments Regulations 2003
(February 21, 2003).

4. Regulation 9(9)(b) of the Miscellaneous Amendments Regulations 2003
(February 21, 2003).

5. Regulation 7(5)(a) of the Miscellaneous Amendments (No.2) Regulations
2003 (November 5, 2003).

6. Regulation 7(5)(b) of the Miscellaneous Amendments (No.2) Regulations
2003 (November 5, 2003).

DEFINITIONS

"case conversion date": see reg.2(1).    3.573
"conversion date": see reg.2(1).
"phasing amount": see reg.2(1).

**Maximum transitional amount**

**25.**—(1) Where a conversion decision is made in a circumstance [¹to    3.574
which regulation 15(3C)] applies (maintenance assessment and related
maintenance calculation), or a subsequent decision is made, the liability of

the non-resident parent to pay child support maintenance during the transitional period (excluding any amount payable in respect of arrears of child support maintenance and before reduction for any amount in respect of an overpayment) shall be whichever is the lesser of—

[²(a) the transitional amount payable under this Part added to, where applicable, the transitional amount payable under Part IV; and]

(b) the maximum transitional amount.

(2) Where—

(a) a conversion decision to which paragraph (1) applies, or a subsequent decision, results from an application made or treated as made for a maintenance calculation in respect of the same non-resident parent but a different qualifying child in relation to whom there is a different person with care (referred to in this regulation as "the new application"); and

(b) the amount of child support maintenance payable by the non-resident parent from the case conversion date, or the effective date of the subsequent decision, as the case may be, is the maximum transitional amount,

that amount shall be apportioned as provided in paragraph (3).

(3) The apportionment referred to in paragraph (2) shall be carried out as follows—

(a) the amount of child support maintenance payable by the non-resident parent to the person with care in relation to the new application shall be calculated as provided in Part I of Schedule 1 to the Act and Regulations made under that Part and where applicable, Part IV of these Regulations, and that amount shall be the amount payable to that person with care;

[³(aa) the amount of child support maintenance payable to a person with care in respect of whom there was a maintenance assessment in force immediately before the case conversion date and in respect of whom the amount payable is not calculated by reference to a phasing amount, shall be an amount calculated as provided in sub-paragraph (a) and, where applicable, regulations 17 to 23;]

(b) [⁴the amounts calculated as provided in sub-paragraphs (a) and (aa)] shall be deducted from the maximum transitional amount and the remainder shall be apportioned among the other persons with care so that the proportion which each receives bears the same relation to the proportions which the others receive as those proportions would have borne in relation to each other and the new amount, or the subsequent decision amount, as the case may be, if the maximum transitional amount had not been applied.

(4) Where—

(a) apportionment under paragraph (3)(b) results in a fraction of a penny, that fraction shall be treated as a penny if it is either one half or exceeds one half, otherwise it shall be disregarded; and

(b) the application of paragraph (3)(b) would be such that the aggregate amount payable by a non-resident parent would be different from the aggregate amount payable before any such apportionment, the Secretary of State shall adjust that apportionment so as to eliminate that difference and that adjustment shall be varied from time to time so as to secure that, taking one week with another and so far as is practicable, each person with care receives the amount which she would have received if no adjustment had been made under this paragraph.

[⁵(5) Subject to paragraphs (6) and (7), "maximum transitional amount" means 30% of the non-resident parent's net weekly income taken into account in the conversion decision, or the subsequent decision, as the case may be.

(6) Where the new amount is calculated under regulation 22(1), "maximum transitional amount" means 30% of the aggregate of the income calculated under regulation 22(1)(b).

(7) Where the new amount or the subsequent decision amount, as the case may be, is calculated under regulation 26(1) of the Variations Regulations "maximum transitional amount" means 30% of the additional income arising under the variation.]

AMENDMENTS

1. Regulation 9(10)(a)(i) of the Miscellaneous Amendments Regulations 2003 (February 21, 2003).
2. Regulation 9(10)(a)(ii) of the Miscellaneous Amendments Regulations 2003 (February 21, 2003).
3. Regulation 9(10)(b)(i) of the Miscellaneous Amendments Regulations 2003 (February 21, 2003).
4. Regulation 9(10)(b)(ii) of the Miscellaneous Amendments Regulations 2003 (February 21, 2003).
5. Regulation 7(6) of the Miscellaneous Amendments (No.2) Regulations 2003 (November 5, 2003).

DEFINITIONS

"the Act": see reg.2(1).     3.575
"conversion decision": see reg.2(1).
"maintenance assessment": see reg.2(1).
"maximum transitional amount": see reg.2(1).
"new amount": see reg.2(1).
"subsequent decision": see reg.2(1).
"subsequent decision amount": see reg.2(1).
"transitional amount": see reg.2(1).
"transitional period": see reg.2(1).
"the Variations Regulations": see reg.2(1)

## Subsequent decision effective on case conversion date

**26.**—(1) Where there is a subsequent decision, the effective date of   3.576 which is the case conversion date, the amount of child support maintenance payable shall be calculated as if the subsequent decision were a conversion decision.

(2) For the purposes of paragraph (1), regulations 9 to 25 shall apply as if references—

  (a) to the calculation date, including in relation to the definition of the former assessment amount, were to—

   (i)  where there has been a decision under section 16, 17 or 20 in relation to the maintenance assessment, the effective date of that decision; or

   (ii)  where sub-paragraph (i) does not apply—

     (aa)  the effective date of the subsequent decision; or

     (bb)  if earlier, the date the subsequent decision was made;

(b)  to the new amount were to the subsequent decision amount; and

(c)  to the conversion decision in regulation 24(3) were to the subsequent decision.

DEFINITIONS

3.577     "calculation date": see reg.2(1).
"case conversion date": see reg.2(1).
"conversion decision": see reg.2(1).
"former assessment amount": see reg.2(1).
"maintenance assessment": see reg.2(1)
"new amount": see reg.2(1)
"subsequent decision": see reg.2(1)

## Subsequent decision with effect in transitional period—amount payable

3.578    **27.**—(1) Subject to paragraph (6), where during the transitional period there is a subsequent decision the effective date of which is after the case conversion date, the amount of child support maintenance payable shall be the subsequent decision amount unless any of the following paragraphs applies, in which case it shall be a transitional amount as provided for in those paragraphs.

(2) Where—

(a)  the new amount was greater than the former assessment amount; and

(b)  the subsequent decision amount is greater than the new amount, the amount of child support maintenance payable shall be a transitional amount calculated as the transitional amount payable immediately before the subsequent decision ("the previous transitional amount") increased by the difference between the new amount and the subsequent decision amount and the phasing amounts shall apply to that transitional amount as they would have applied to the previous transitional amount had there been no subsequent decision.

(3) Where—

(a)  paragraph (2)(a) applies; and

(b)  the subsequent decision amount is equal to or less than the new amount, [¹and greater than the previous transitional amount,] the amount of child support maintenance payable shall be the previous transitional amount and the phasing amounts shall apply as they would have applied had there been no subsequent decision.

(4) Where—

(a)  the new amount was less than the former assessment amount; and

(b)  the subsequent decision amount is less than the new amount,

the amount of child support maintenance payable shall be a transitional amount calculated as the previous transitional amount decreased by the difference between the new amount and the subsequent decision amount and the phasing amounts shall apply to that transitional amount as they would have applied to the previous transitional amount had there been no subsequent decision.

(5) Where—

(a) paragraph (4)(a) applies; and

(b) the subsequent decision amount is equal to or more than the new amount, [²and less than the previous transitional amount,]

the amount of child support maintenance payable shall be the previous transitional amount and the phasing amounts shall apply as they would have applied had there been no subsequent decision.

(6) Paragraphs (2) to (5) shall not apply where the subsequent decision amount is the first or second prescribed amount [³, would be the first or the second prescribed amount but is less than that amount, or is nil, owing to the application of paragraph 8 of Part I of Schedule 1 to the Act, or is the nil rate.]

[⁴(7) Where paragraph (1) applies and at the date of the subsequent decision there is more than one person with care in relation to the same non-resident parent—

(a) the amount payable to a person with care in respect of whom the amount payable is calculated by reference to a phasing amount shall be determined by applying paragraphs (1) to (5) as if refer-ences to the new amount, the subsequent decision amount and the transitional amount were to the apportioned part of the amount in question; and

(b) the amount payable in respect of any other person with care shall be the apportioned part of the subsequent decision amount.]

[¹¹(7A) This paragraph applies where–

(a) paragraph (1) applies and at the date of the subsequent decision there is more than one person with care in relation to the same non-resident parent; and

(b) as a result of the subsequent decision there is one person with care in relation to that non-resident parent.]

[¹¹(7B) Where paragraph (7A) applies, the amount payable to a person with care in respect of whom the amount payable is calculated by reference to a phasing amount shall be determined by applying paragraphs (1) to (5) as if references to—

(a) the new amount and the transitional amount were to the appor-tioned part of the amount in question which had been payable immediately prior to the subsequent decision to the person with care in respect of whom the subsequent decision is made; and

(b) the subsequent decision amount were to the full amount payable under the subsequent decision.]

[⁴(8) In paragraph (7) [¹²and (7B)], "apportioned part" means the amount payable in respect of a person with care calculated as provided in Part I of Schedule 1 to the Act and Regulations made under that Part and, where applicable, Parts III and IV of these Regulations.]

⁴(9) [⁷Where] a subsequent decision is made in respect of a decision which is itself a subsequent decision, paragraphs (2) to (5) shall apply as if, except in paragraphs (2)(a) and (4)(a), references to the new amount were

to the subsequent decision amount which applied immediately before the most recent subsequent decision.]

[⁶(10) [⁸Subject to paragraph (11), where] a subsequent decision ("decision B") is made in respect of a decision which is itself a subsequent decision ("decision A") and—

(a) decision B has the same effective date as decision A; or

(b) decision B—

    (i) is a revision or alteration on appeal of decision A; and

    (ii) includes within it a determination that the effective date of decision A was incorrect,

paragraphs (2) to (5) shall apply] [⁹as if decision A had not been made.]

[¹⁰(11) In the circumstances set out in paragraph (10), paragraph (9) shall not apply where the decision in place before decision A was made was the decision which took effect from the case conversion date.]

AMENDMENTS

1. Regulation 8(15)(a) of the Miscellaneous Amendments Regulations 2002 (April 30, 2002).
2. Regulation 8(15)(b) of the Miscellaneous Amendments Regulations 2002 (April 30, 2002).
3. Regulation 8(15)(b) of the Miscellaneous Amendments Regulations 2002 (April 30, 2002).
4. Regulation 9(11) of the Miscellaneous Amendments Regulations 2003 (February 21, 2003).
5. Regulation 7(7)(b) of the Miscellaneous Amendments (No.2) Regulations 2003 (November 5, 2003).
6. Regulation 8(9)(a) of the Miscellaneous Amendments Regulations 2004 (September 16, 2004).
7. Regulation 8(9)(b)(i) of the Miscellaneous Amendments Regulations 2004 (September 16, 2004).
8. Regulation 8(9)(b)(ii) of the Miscellaneous Amendments Regulations 2004 (September 16, 2004).
9. Regulation 8(9)(c) of the Miscellaneous Amendments Regulations 2004 (September 16, 2004).
10. Regulation 7(3)(a) of the Miscellaneous Amendments Regulations 2005 (March 16, 2005).
11. Regulation 7(3)(b) of the Miscellaneous Amendments Regulations 2005 (March 16, 2005).

DEFINITIONS

3.579    "case conversion date": see reg.2(1).
"former assessment amount": see reg.2(1).
"new amount": see reg.2(1).
"phasing amount": see reg.2(1)
"subsequent decision": see reg.2(1).
"subsequent decision amount": see reg.2(1).
"transitional amount": see reg.2(1)
"transitional period": see reg.2(1)

**Linking provisions**

**28.**—(1) [¹Subject to paragraph (2A), where], after the commencement 3.580
date but before the conversion date, an application for a maintenance calculation is made or treated as made and within the relevant period a maintenance assessment was in force in relation to the same qualifying child,
non-resident parent and person with care—
   (a) the application shall be treated as an application for a maintenance
       assessment; and
   (b) any maintenance assessment made in response to the application
       shall be an assessment to which regulations 9 to 28 apply.
   (2) [²Subject to paragraph (2A), where], after the conversion date, an
application for a maintenance calculation is made or treated as made, and
within the relevant period a maintenance assessment ("the previous
assessment") had been in force in relation to the same qualifying child,
non-resident parent and person with care but had ceased to have effect—
   (a) the amount of child support maintenance payable by the non-
       resident parent from the effective date of the maintenance calcula-
       tion made in response to the application shall be calculated in the
       same way that a conversion calculation would have been made had
       the previous assessment been in force on the date the calculation is
       made; and
   (b) the provisions of regulations 9 to 28 shall apply accordingly, includ-
       ing the application where appropriate of transitional amounts, phas-
       ing amounts and a transitional period, which for this purpose shall
       begin on the date which would have been the case conversion date in
       relation to the previous assessment.
   [³(2A) Paragraph (1) or (2) shall not apply where, before any application
for a maintenance calculation of a type referred to in paragraph (1) or (2)
is made or treated as made, an application for a maintenance calculation is
made or treated as made in relation to either the person with care or the
non-resident parent (but not both of them) to whom the maintenance
assessment referred to in paragraph (1) or (2) related.]
   (3) For the purposes of paragraphs (1) and (2) "the relevant period"
means 13 weeks prior to the date that the application for the maintenance
calculation is made or treated as made.
   (4) This paragraph applies where—
   (a) the non-resident parent is liable to pay child support maintenance of
       a transitional amount and there is, during the transitional period, a
       subsequent decision (in this regulation referred to as "the first sub-
       sequent decision") as a result of which the non-resident parent is
       liable to pay child support maintenance [⁴at—
       (i) the first or second prescribed amount;
       (ii) what would be an amount referred to in head (i) but is less than
           that amount, or is nil, owing to the application of paragraph 8
           of Part I of Schedule 1 to the Act; or
       (iii) the nil rate; and]
   (b) a second subsequent decision is made with an effective date no later
       than 13 weeks after the effective date of the first subsequent decision
       the effect of which would be that the non-resident parent would be

liable to pay child support maintenance at other than [⁵a rate referred to in sub-paragraph (a)].

(5) [⁶Subject to paragraph (5A), where] paragraph (4) applies the amount of child support maintenance the non-resident parent is liable to pay from the effective date of the second subsequent decision shall be a transitional amount or, where applicable, the new amount, calculated by making a subsequent decision and, where appropriate, applying a phasing amount, as if the first subsequent decision had not occurred.

[⁷(5A) Paragraph (5) shall not apply where, before any second subsequent decision is made, an application for a maintenance calculation is made or treated as made in relation to either the person with care or the non-resident parent (but not both of them) to whom the first subsequent decision referred to in paragraph (4) related.]

(6) This paragraph applies where during the transitional period a [¹⁴conversion decision] ceases to have effect.

(7) [⁸Subject to paragraph (7A), where] paragraph (6) applies and no later than 13 weeks after the [¹⁴conversion decision] ceases to have effect [⁹an application for a maintenance calculation] is made, or treated as made, in relation to the same person with care, non-resident parent and qualifying child, the amount of child support maintenance the non-resident parent is liable to pay from the effective date of the new maintenance calculation shall be a transitional amount or, where applicable, the new amount, calculated by making a subsequent decision in relation to the [¹⁴conversion decision] as if it had not ceased to have effect, and applying a phasing amount where appropriate.

[¹⁰(7A) Paragraph (7) shall not apply where, before an application for a maintenance calculation of a type referred to in that paragraph is made or treated as made, an application for a maintenance calculation is made or treated as made in relation to either the person with care or the non-resident parent (but not both of them) to whom the [¹⁴conversion decision] referred to in that paragraph related.]

(8) [¹¹Subject to paragraph (9), where]—

[¹²(a) a [¹⁴conversion decision] is in force, or pursuant to regulation 16(3) a maintenance calculation is in force, ("the calculation") and the new amount—
   (i) is the first or second prescribed amount;
   (ii) would be an amount referred to in head (i), but is less than that amount, or is nil, owing to the application of paragraph 8 of Part I of Schedule 1 to the Act; or
   (iii) is the nil rate;]

(b) after the case conversion date a subsequent decision is made;

(c) but for the application of this regulation the subsequent decision amount would be a basic or reduced rate of child support maintenance; and

(d) within 13 weeks prior to the effective date of the subsequent decision a maintenance assessment was in force in relation to the same non-resident parent, person with care and qualifying child, under which the amount payable by the non-resident parent ("the previous assessment") was more than the amount prescribed for the purposes of paragraph 7 of Schedule 1 to the former Act;

the subsequent decision amount shall be calculated by making a subsequent decision in relation to the previous assessment as if the assessment were in force, and applying a phasing amount where appropriate.

[[13](9) Paragraph (8) shall not apply where, before a subsequent decision of a type referred to in paragraph (8)(b) is made, an application for a maintenance calculation is made or treated as made in relation to the person with care or the non-resident parent (but not both of them) to whom the calculation relates.]

AMENDMENTS

1. Regulation 8(16)(a) of the Miscellaneous Amendments Regulations 2002 (April 30, 2002).
2. Regulation 8(16)(a) of the Miscellaneous Amendments Regulations 2002 (April 30, 2002).
3. Regulation 8(16)(b) of the Miscellaneous Amendments Regulations 2002 (April 30, 2002).
4. Regulation 8(16)(c) of the Miscellaneous Amendments Regulations 2002 (April 30, 2002).
5. Regulation 8(16)(d) of the Miscellaneous Amendments Regulations 2002 (April 30, 2002).
6. Regulation 8(16)(e) of the Miscellaneous Amendments Regulations 2002 (April 30, 2002).
7. Regulation 8(16)(f) of the Miscellaneous Amendments Regulations 2002 (April 30, 2002).
8. Regulation 8(16)(g)(i) of the Miscellaneous Amendments Regulations 2002 (April 30, 2002).
9. Regulation 8(16)(g)(ii) of the Miscellaneous Amendments Regulations 2002 (April 30, 2002).
10. Regulation 8(16)(h) of the Miscellaneous Amendments Regulations 2002 (April 30, 2002).
11. Regulation 8(16)(i)(i) of the Miscellaneous Amendments Regulations 2002 (April 30, 2002).
12. Regulation 8(16)(i)(ii) of the Miscellaneous Amendments Regulations 2002 (April 30, 2002).
13. Regulation 8(16)(j) of the Miscellaneous Amendments Regulations 2002 (April 30, 2002).
14. Regulation 9(12) of the Miscellaneous Amendments Regulations 2003 (February 21, 2003).

DEFINITIONS

"case conversion date": see reg.2(1).                                    3.581
"commencement date": see reg.2(1) and 2(2)
"conversion calculation": see reg.2(1) and 2(2)
"conversion date": see reg.2(1) and 2(2)
"conversion decision": see reg.2(1) and 2(2)
"first prescribed amount": see reg.2(1) and 2(2)
"maintenance assessment": see reg.2(1) and 2(2)
"phasing amount": see reg.2(1) and 2(2)
"second prescribed amount": see reg.2(1) and 2(2)
"subsequent decision": see reg.2(1) and 2(2)
"transitional amount": see reg.2(1) and 2(2)
"transitional period": see reg.2(1) and 2(2)

PART IV

COURT ORDER PHASING

## Interpretation

3.582

**29.**—(1) In this Part—

"the Act" means the Child Support Act 1991;

"calculation amount" means the amount of child support maintenance that would, but for the provisions of this Part, be payable under a maintenance calculation which is in force;

"excess" means the amount by which the calculation amount exceeds the old amount;

"maintenance calculation" has the meaning given in section 54 of the Act the effective date of which is on or after the date prescribed for the purposes of section 4(10)(a) of the Act;

"old amount" means, subject to paragraph (2) below, the aggregate weekly amount which was payable under the orders, agreements or arrangements mentioned in regulation 30;

"subsequent decision" means—

(a) any decision under section 16 or 17 of the Act to revise or supersede a maintenance calculation to which regulation 31(1) applies; or

(b) any such revision or supersession as decided on appeal, whether as originally made or as revised under section 16 of the Act or decided on appeal;

"subsequent decision amount" means the amount of child support maintenance liability resulting from a subsequent decision;

"transitional amount" means an amount determined in accordance with regulation 31; and

"transitional period" means a period beginning on the effective date of the maintenance calculation and ending 78 weeks after that date or, if earlier, on the date on which regulation 31(3) applies.

(2) In determining the old amount the Secretary of State shall disregard any payments in kind and any payments made to a third party on behalf of or for the benefit of the qualifying child or the person with care.

## Cases to which this Part applies

3.583

**30.** This Part applies to cases where—

(a) on 4th April 1993, and at all times thereafter until the date when a maintenance calculation is made under the Act there was in force, in respect of one or more of the qualifying children in respect of whom an application for a maintenance calculation is made or treated as made under the Act and the non-resident parent concerned, one or more—

(i) maintenance orders;

(ii) orders under section 151 of the Army Act 1955 (deductions from pay for maintenance of wife or child) or section 151 of the Air Force Act 1955 (deductions from pay for maintenance of wife or child) or arrangements corresponding to such an order and made under Article 1 or 3 of the Naval and Marine Pay and Pensions (Deductions for Maintenance) Order 1959; or

    (iii) maintenance agreements (being agreements which are made or evidenced in writing);

  (b) either—

    (i) the non-resident parent was on the effective date of the maintenance calculation and continues to be a member of a family, as defined in regulation 1 of the Child Support (Maintenance Calculations and Special Cases) Regulations 2000 which includes one or more children; or

    (ii) the amount of child support maintenance payable under the maintenance calculation referred to in paragraph (a) is a basic or reduced rate under paragraph 7 of Part I of Schedule 1 to the Act (shared care-basic and reduced rate); and

  (c) the calculation amount exceeds the old amount.

DEFINITIONS

"the Act": see reg.29(1).                3.584
"calculation amount": see reg.29(1)
"maintenance calculation": see reg.29(1)
"old amount": see reg.29(1)

## Amount payable during the transitional period

**31.**—(1) In a case to which this Part applies, the amount of child sup-   3.585
port maintenance payable under a maintenance calculation during the transitional period shall, instead of being the calculation amount, be the transitional amount.

(2) The transitional amount is—

  (a) during the first 26 weeks of the transitional period, the old amount plus either 25 per cent of the excess or £20.00, whichever is the greater;

  (b) during the next 26 weeks of the transitional period, the old amount plus either 50 per cent of the excess or £40.00, whichever is the greater; and

  (c) during the last 26 weeks of the transitional period, the old amount plus either 75 per cent of the excess or £60.00, whichever is the greater.

(3) If in any case the application of the provisions of this Part would result in an amount of child support maintenance becoming payable which is greater than the calculation amount, then those provisions shall not apply or, as the case may be, shall cease to apply to that case and the amount of child support maintenance payable in that case shall be the calculation amount.

DEFINITIONS

"calculation amount": see reg.29(1).             3.586
"excess": see reg.29(1).
"maintenance calculation": see reg.29(1).
"transitional amount": see reg.29(1).
"transitional period": see reg.29(1).

**Revision and supersession**

3.587    **32.**—(1) Where the Secretary of State makes a subsequent decision in relation to a maintenance calculation to which regulation 31(1) applies, the amount of child support maintenance payable by the non-resident parent shall be—

(a) where the subsequent decision amount is more than the calculation amount, the transitional amount plus the difference between the calculation amount and the subsequent decision amount;

(b) where the subsequent decision amount is less than the calculation amount but more than the transitional amount, the transitional amount; or

(c) where the subsequent decision amount is less than the calculation amount and less than or equal to the transitional amount, the subsequent decision amount.

(2) Regulation 31(2) shall apply to cases where there has been a subsequent decision as if references to the transitional amount were to the amount resulting from the application of paragraph (1).

DEFINITIONS

3.588    "calculation amount": see reg.29(1).
"maintenance calculation": see reg.29(1).
"subsequent decision": see reg.29(1).
"subsequent decision amount": see reg.29(1).
"transitional amount": see reg.29(1).

PART V

SAVINGS

**Saving in relation to revision of or appeal against a conversion or subsequent decision**

3.589    **33.**—(1) This regulation applies where—

(a) a conversion decision has been made under regulation 3, or a subsequent decision has been made under regulation 4, in each case where regulation [¹15(2), (3B), (3D) or (3F)] applies; and

(b) in relation to the decision referred to in paragraph (a)—

(i) a revised decision is made under regulation 3A(1)(e) of the Decisions and Appeals Regulations; or

(ii) an appeal tribunal makes a decision that the conversion decision or subsequent decision was made in error, on the ground that regulation [²15(2), (3B), (3D) or (3F) as the case may be] did not apply.

(2) The provisions of the former Act and Regulations made under that Act prior to any amendments or revocations made pursuant to or in consequence of the 2000 Act shall apply, until the effective date of a further conversion decision in relation to the maintenance assessment, for the purposes of that maintenance assessment as if the decision referred to in paragraph (1)(a) had not been made, subject to any revision, supersession

or appeal having effect between the dates of the decisions in paragraph 1(a) and (b) which would have affected the maintenance assessment during that period but for the decision referred to paragraph 1(a).

AMENDMENTS

1. Regulation 9(13)(a) of the Miscellaneous Amendments Regulations 2003 (February 21, 2003).
2. Regulation 9(13)(b) of the Miscellaneous Amendments Regulations 2003 (February 21, 2003).

DEFINITIONS

"the 2000 Act": see reg.2(1).                                      **3.590**
"conversion decision": see reg.2(1).
"Decisions and Appeals Regulations": see reg.2(1).
"former Act": see reg.2(1).
"maintenance assessment": see reg.2(1).
"subsequent decision": see reg.2(1).

# The Child Support (Maintenance Calculations and Special Cases) Regulations 2000

## (SI 2001/155)

ARRANGEMENT OF REGULATIONS

PART I

*General*

PART II

*Calculation of child support maintenance*

PART III

*Special cases*

13. Child who is allowed to live with his parent under section 23(5) of the Children Act 1989
14. Person with part-time care who is not a non-resident parent

PART IV

*Revocation and savings*

15. Revocation and savings

Schedule—Net weekly income

*Whereas a draft of this Instrument was laid before Parliament in accordance with section 52(2) and (2A) of the Child Support Act 1991 and approved by a resolution of each House of Parliament:*

*Now, therefore, the Secretary of State for Social Security, in exercise of the powers conferred upon him by sections 14(1) and (1A), 42, 51, 52(4) and 54 of, and paragraphs 3(2), 4(1)(b) and (c), 4(3), 5(a), 7(3), 9, 10 and 10C(2)(b) of Schedule 1 to, the Child Support Act 1991, and of all other powers enabling him in that behalf, hereby makes the following Regulations:*

PART I

GENERAL

## Citation, commencement and interpretation

3.592     **1.**—(1) These Regulations may be cited as the Child Support (Maintenance Calculations and Special Cases) Regulations 2000.

(2) In these Regulations, unless the context otherwise requires—

"the Act" means the Child Support Act 1991;

[7"care home" has the meaning assigned to it by section 3 of the Care Standards Act 2000;

"care home service" has the meaning assigned to it by section 2(3) of the Regulation of Care (Scotland) Act 2001;]

[1"child tax credit" means a child tax credit under section 8 of the Tax Credits Act 2002;]

"Contributions and Benefits Act" means the Social Security Contributions and Benefits Act 1992;

"Contributions and Benefits (Northern Ireland) Act" means the Social Security Contributions and Benefits (Northern Ireland) Act 1992;

"couple" means a man and a woman who are—

(a) married to each other and are members of the same house-hold; or

(b) not married to each other but are living together as husband and wife;

"course of advanced education" means—

(a) a full-time course leading to a postgraduate degree or comparable qualification, a first degree or comparable qualification, a Diploma of Higher Education, a higher national diploma, a higher national diploma or higher national certificate of the Business and Technology Education Council or the Scottish Qualifications Authority or a teaching qualification; or

(b) any other full-time course which is a course of a standard above that of an ordinary national diploma, a national diploma or national certificate of the Business and Technology Education Council or the Scottish Qualifications Authority, the advanced level of the General Certificate of Education, a Scottish certificate of education (higher level), a Scottish certificate of sixth year studies or a Scottish National Qualification at Higher Level;

"day" includes any part of a day;

"day to day care" means—

(a) care of not less than 104 nights in total during the 12 month period ending with the relevant week; or

(b) where, in the opinion of the Secretary of State, a period other than 12 months is more representative of the current arrangements for the care of the child in question, care during that period of not less in total than the number of nights which bears the same ratio to 104 nights as that period bears to 12 months, and for the purpose of this definition—

    (i) where a child is a boarder at a boarding school or is a patient in a hospital or other circumstances apply, such as where the child stays with a person who is not a parent of the child, and which the Secretary of State regards as temporary, the person who, but for those circumstances, would otherwise provide day to day care of the child shall be treated as providing day to day care during the periods in question; and

    (ii) "relevant week" shall have the meaning ascribed to it in the definition in this paragraph, except that in a case where notification is given under regulation 7C of the Decisions and Appeals Regulations to the relevant persons on different dates, "relevant week" means the period of 7 days immediately preceding the date of the latest notification;

"Decisions and Appeals Regulations" means the Social Security and Child Support (Decisions and Appeals) Regulations 1999;

[². . .]

"effective date" means the date on which a maintenance calculation takes effect for the purposes of the Act;

"employed earner" has the same meaning as in section 2(1)(a) of the Contributions and Benefits Act except that it shall include—

(a) a person gainfully employed in Northern Ireland; and

(b) a person to whom section 44(2A) of the Act applies;

"family" means—

(a) a couple (including the members of a polygamous marriage) and any member of the same household for whom one or more of them is responsible and who is a child; or

(b) a person who is not a member of a couple and a member of the same household for whom that person is responsible and who is a child;

"home" means—

    (a)  the dwelling in which a person and any family of his normally live; or

    (b)  if he or they normally live in more than one home, the principal home of that person and any family of his,

and for the purpose of determining the principal home in which a person normally lives no regard shall be had to residence in [⁵a care home or an independent hospital or the provision of a care home service or an independent health care service] or a nursing home during a period which does not exceed 52 weeks or, where it appears to the Secretary of State that the person will return to his principal home after that period has expired, such longer period as the Secretary of State considers reasonable to allow for the return of that person to that home;

"Income Support Regulations" means the Income Support (General) Regulations 1987;

[⁸"independent health care service" has the meaning assigned to it by section 2(5)(a) and (b) of the Regulation of Care (Scotland) Act 2001;

"independent hospital" has the meaning assigned to it by section 2 of the Care Standards Act 2000;]

"the Jobseekers Act" means the Jobseekers Act 1995;

"Maintenance Calculation Procedure Regulations" means the Child Support (Maintenance Calculation Procedure) Regulations 2000;

"net weekly income" has the meaning given in the Schedule to these Regulations;

[⁶. . .]

"occupational pension scheme" means such a scheme within the meaning in section 1 of the Pension Schemes Act 1993 and which is approved for the purposes of Part XIV of the Income and Corporation Taxes Act 1988 [⁹or is a statutory scheme to which section 594 of that Act applies];

"partner" means—

    (a)  in relation to a member of a couple, the other member of that couple;

    (b)  in relation to a member of a polygamous marriage, any other member of that marriage with whom he lives;

"patient" means a person (other than a person who is serving a sentence of imprisonment or detention in a young offender institution within the meaning of the Criminal Justice Act 1982 or the Prisons (Scotland) Act 1989 who is regarded as receiving free in-patient treatment within the meaning of the Social Security (Hospital In-Patients) Regulations 1975;

"person" does not include a local authority;

"personal pension scheme" means such a scheme within the meaning in section 1 of the Pension Schemes Act 1993 and which is approved for the purposes of Part XIV of the Income and Corporation Taxes Act 1988;

"polygamous marriage" means any marriage during the subsistence of which a party to it is married to more than one person and in respect of which any ceremony of marriage took place under the law of a country which at the time of that ceremony permitted polygamy;

"prisoner" means a person who is detained in custody pending trial or sentence upon conviction or under a sentence imposed by a court other than a person whose detention is under the Mental Health Act 1983 or the Mental Health (Scotland) Act 1984;

"relevant week" means—

(a)  in relation to an application for child support maintenance—

    (i)  where the application is made by a non-resident parent, the period of 7 days immediately before the application is made; and

    (ii)  in any other case, the period of 7 days immediately before the date of notification to the non-resident parent and for this purpose "the date of notification to the non-resident parent" means the date on which the non-resident parent is first given notice by the Secretary of State under the Maintenance Calculation Procedure Regulations that an application for a maintenance calculation has been made, or treated as made, as the case may be, in relation to which the non-resident parent is named as the parent of the child to whom the application relates;

(b)  where a decision ("the original decision") is to be—

    (i)  revised under section 16 of the Act; or

    (ii)  superseded by a decision under section 17 of the Act on the grounds that the original decision was made in ignorance of, or was based upon a mistake as to, some material fact or was erroneous in point of law,

the period of 7 days which was the relevant week for the purposes of the original decision;

(c)  where a decision ("the original decision") is to be superseded under section 17 of the Act—

    (i)  on an application made for the purpose on the basis that a material change of circumstances has occurred since the original decision was made, the period of 7 days immediately preceding the date on which that application was made;

    (ii)  subject to sub-paragraph (b), in a case where a relevant person is given notice under regulation 7C of the Decisions and Appeals Regulations, the period of 7 days immediately preceding the date of that notification,

except that where, under paragraph 15 of Schedule 1 to the Act, the Secretary of State makes separate maintenance calculations in respect of different periods in a particular case, because he is aware of one or more changes of circumstances which occurred after the date which is applicable to that case, the relevant week for the purposes of each separate maintenance calculation made to take account of each such change of circumstances shall be the period of 7 days immediately before the date on which notification was given to the Secretary of State of the change of circumstances relevant to that separate maintenance calculations;

[6. . .]

"retirement annuity contract" means an annuity contract for the time being approved by the Board of Inland Revenue as having for its main object the provision of a life annuity in old age or the provision of an annuity for a partner or dependant and in respect of which relief from income tax may be given on any premium;

"self-employed earner" has the same meaning as in section 2(1)(b) of the Contributions and Benefits Act except that it shall include a person gainfully employed in Northern Ireland otherwise than in employed earner's employment (whether or not he is also employed in such employment);

[4"state pension credit" means the social security benefit of that name payable under the State Pension Credit Act 2002;]

"student" means a person, other than a person in receipt of a training allowance, who is aged less than 19 and attending a full-time course of advanced education or who is aged 19 or over and attending a full-time course of study at an educational establishment; and for the purposes of this definition—

(a) a person who has started on such a course shall be treated as attending it throughout any period of term or vacation within it, until the last day of the course or such earlier date as he abandons it or is dismissed from it;

(b) a person on a sandwich course (within the meaning of paragraph 1(1) of Schedule 5 to the Education (Mandatory Awards) (No. 2) Regulations 1993) shall be treated as attending a full-time course of advanced education or, as the case may be, of study;

[10"training allowance" means a payment under section 2 of the Employment and Training Act 1973 ("the 1973 Act"), or section 2 of the Enterprise and New Towns (Scotland) Act 1990 ("the 1990 Act"), which is paid—

(a) to a person for his maintenance; and

(b) in respect of a period during which that person—

(i) is undergoing training pursuant to arrangements made under section 2 of the 1973 Act or section 2 of the 1990 Act; and

(ii) has no net weekly income of a type referred to in Part II or Part III of the Schedule;]

[11"war widow's pension" means any pension or allowance payable for a widow which is—

(a) granted in respect of a death due to service or war injury and payable by virtue of the Air Force (Constitution) Act 1917, the Personal Injuries (Emergency Provisions) Act 1939, the Pensions (Navy, Army, Air Force and Mercantile Marine) Act 1939, the Polish Resettlement Act 1947 or Part VII or section 151 of the Reserve Forces Act 1980;

(b) payable under so much of any Order in Council, Royal Warrant, order or scheme as relates to death due to service in the armed forces of the Crown, wartime service in the merchant navy or war injuries;

(c) payable in respect of death due to peacetime service in the armed forces of the Crown before 3rd September 1939, and payable at rates, and subject to conditions, similar to those of a pension within sub-paragraph (b); or

(d)  payable under the law of a country other than the United Kingdom and of a character substantially similar to a pension within sub-paragraph (a), (b) or (c),

and "war widower's pension" shall be construed accordingly;]

"work-based training for young people or, in Scotland, Skillseekers training" means—

(a)  arrangements made under section 2 of the Employment and Training Act 1973 or section 2 of the Enterprise and New Towns (Scotland) Act 1990; or

(b)  arrangements made by the Secretary of State for persons enlisted in Her Majesty's forces for any special term of service specified in regulations made under section 2 of the Armed Forces Act 1966 (power of Defence Council to make regulations as to engagement of persons in regular forces),

for purposes which include the training of persons who, at the beginning of their training, are under the age of 18;

"year" means a period of 52 weeks.

[³"working tax credit" means a working tax credit under section 10 of the Tax Credits Act 2002;]

(3) The following other description of children is prescribed for the purposes of paragraph 10C(2)(b) of Schedule 1 to the Act (relevant other children)—

children other than qualifying children in respect of whom the non-resident parent or his partner would receive child benefit under Part IX of the Contributions and Benefits Act but who do not solely because the conditions set out in section 146 of that Act (persons outside Great Britain) are not met.

(4) Subject to paragraph (5), these Regulations shall come into force in relation to a particular case on the day on which Part I of Schedule 1 to the 1991 Act as amended by the Child Support, Pensions and Social Security Act 2000 comes into force in relation to that type of case.

(5) Paragraphs (1) and (2) of regulation 4 and, for the purposes of those provisions, this regulation shall come into force on 31st January 2001.

AMENDMENTS

1. Regulation 8(2)(a) of the Miscellaneous Amendments Regulations 2003 (April 6, 2003).

2. Regulation 8(2)(b) of the Miscellaneous Amendments Regulations 2003 (April 6, 2003).

3. Regulation 8(2)(c) of the Miscellaneous Amendments Regulations 2003 (April 6, 2003).

4. Regulation 27(2) of the State Pension Credit (Consequential, Transitional and Miscellaneous Provisions) Regulations 2002 (October 6, 2003).

5. Regulation 6(2)(a) of the Miscellaneous Amendments (No.2) Regulations 2003 (November 5, 2003).

6. Regulation 6(2)(b) of the Miscellaneous Amendments (No.2) Regulations 2003 (November 5, 2003).

7. Regulation 6(2)(c) of the Miscellaneous Amendments (No.2) Regulations 2003 (November 5, 2003).

8. Regulation 6(2)(d) of the Miscellaneous Amendments (No.2) Regulations 2003 (November 5, 2003).
9. Regulation 6(2)(e) of the Miscellaneous Amendments (No.2) Regulations 2003 (November 5, 2003).
10. Regulation 6(2)(f) of the Miscellaneous Amendments (No.2) Regulations 2003 (November 5, 2003).
11. Regulation 6(2)(g) of the Miscellaneous Amendments (No.2) Regulations 2003 (November 5, 2003).

GENERAL NOTE

3.593    *"unless the context otherwise requires"*
These words are not to be equated with "unless the circumstances otherwise require" (*CCS 499/95*, para.15).

*"day to day care"*
This definition is concerned with care given and not with arrangements for such care which has not in fact occurred (*CSCS 6/95*, paras 10–11; *CCS 3795/98*).
The provision of care that is relevant to this definition is the direct provision of care and not indirect provision by, for example, the placement by a local authority of a child in a boarding school and the payment of the child's fees there (*CCS 1324/97*, para.11).
A minor fluctuation in day to day care will not constitute a change of circumstances to justify a fresh calculation (*CCS 11588/95*, para.15). The legislation contemplates that the matter should be looked at over a period of one year rather than some shorter period (*ibid.*, para.15).
For the problems produced by the concentration in this definition on over-night care see the general note to s.3(3) of the Act.
The tribunal's findings of fact in relation to day to day care must specify the number of nights spent by each qualifying child with the absent parent (*CSC 7/94*, para.9). The care that is relevant is care which is provided during the night. It is not necessary that the person should provide 24 hour care (*CCS 499/95*, para.11). In determining day to day care it is not permissible to disregard any period before the child support scheme came into force (*CCS 6/94*, para.5). It is not an error of law to fail to consider whether an alternative period should be considered if there was no reason on the evidence to do so (*ibid.*, para.6). However, the written or oral evidence before the tribunal will not necessarily be given with the legal definition of day to day care in mind. The tribunal must take an inquisitorial approach to the hearing and this involves ensuring that it probes the evidence in order to determine whether there is any basis for such a consideration, unless it is clear from the evidence given or the circumstances of the case that no such possibility exists. The chairman's record of evidence and proceedings or the statement of the tribunal's reasons should make it clear that this was done. See *CCS 1992/97*, para.56.
When a child is a boarder a hypothetical decision has to be made as to where the child would have lived if not in school. It is proper to take a broad brush approach to this decision taking into account the pattern of contact when the child is not in school, although the practicalities which may influence that pattern (such as where each parent lives in relation to the school) must be considered (*R(CS) 8/98*, para.21). Which parent pays the school fees is irrelevant to the issue of day to day care (*ibid.*, para.19). A local authority does not provide day to day merely by placing a child at a boarding school and paying the fees (*CCS 1324/97*, para.11).
In *C v Secretary of State for Work and Pensions and B* [2003] 1 F.L.R. 829, the Court of Appeal considered the relevance of residence orders to the issue of where a child would be if not at boarding school. The Court held that a residence order was relevant (but not determinative) on the assumption that the parties would be

expected to comply with its terms. However, the fact that the father had been refused a shared residence order was not relevant. More important were the arrangements for contact made or approved by the court.

In making provision for boarders, the definition itself refers to "day to day care". This does not mean that, in order to apply this part of the definition, it is necessary to apply the earlier part of the definition separately to the periods when the child is at boarding school. The second part of the definition applies "for the purposes of" the earlier part. The reference to "day to day care" in the latter part of the definition as means that in determining the number of nights that a child is under the care of a particular person, the child is considered to be under the care of the person who would have care of the child for that night if the child were not a boarder. See *CCS 37/97*, para.32.

*"employed earner"*

Section 2(1)(a) of the Social Security (Contributions and Benefits) Act 1992 provides that " 'employed earner' means a person who is gainfully employed in Great Britain either under a contract of service, or in an office (including elective office) with emoluments chargeable to income tax under Schedule E". Section 122(1) provides that a contract of service "means any contract of service or apprenticeship whether written or oral and whether express or implied", and that " 'employed' has a corresponding meaning" to "employment" which "includes any trade, business, profession, office or vocation".

**3.594**

In order for there to be a contract of service the contract must require the person to perform the obligations under the contract personally. If the obligations can be carried out by someone other than the contracting party, the contract is one of services. See *Express and Echo Publications Ltd v Tanton* [1999] I.C.R. 693.

A person whose services are provided to a third party through an employment bureau may have an implied contract of employment with the third party (*Brook Street Bureau (UK) Ltd v Dacas, The Times*, March 19, 2004).

A majority shareholder in a company may be employed by the company. For a discussion of some of the relevant factors when this possibility is in issue, see *CTC 4080/02*, paras 12–14.

In deciding in a borderline case whether a particular relationship is one of employment or self-employment, the courts will take account of the label which the parties give to an arrangement. However, the parties cannot change the proper classification of an arrangement which clearly falls into one category by calling it the other (*McManus v Griffiths, The Times*, August 5, 1997).

It is perhaps unlikely that a minister of religion would be involved in an assessment of child support maintenance. Should this arise, however, ministers, including curates, do not operate under a contract of service, but are office-holders (*Diocese of Southwark v Coker* [1998] I.C.R. 140). Accordingly they fall within this definition.

A person is gainfully employed if the employment generates income, even if the expenses necessarily incurred exceed the income generated (*Vandyk v Minister of Pensions and National Insurance* [1954] 2 All E.R. 723) and regardless of whether or not that income has a contractual basis (*Benjamin v Minister of Pensions and National Insurance* [1960] 2 All E.R. 851). It may be that a person is gainfully employed if working with the hope, intention and desire of ultimate, but not immediate, gain (*ibid.* at 855–856, *per* Salmon J.).

It is possible for a person to have earnings both as an employed earner and as a self-employed earner (*CIS 14409/96*, para.13). Where the question arises whether earnings from particular activities are discrete employed earner's earnings or merely part of the person's general pool of self-employed earnings, the issue is to be decided by asking whether or not there was a contract of service in respect of the activities which generated them (*ibid.*, paras 25–32). The fact that Class I National

Insurance contributions have been deducted from particular earnings is not decisive of this issue (*ibid.*, para.22).

*"family"*

For s.22 of the Children Act 1989 see the general note to reg.51 of the Maintenance Assessment Procedure Regulations.

*"home"*

The test of which home is a person's principal home is an objective one in the sense that the person's own view is not decisive. The issue is not determined solely by reference to the number of days or nights on which the person is present at the home. As the issue is which home was the principal home as at the date the housing cost calculation is being made, some long-term considerations (such as the fact that a party's job requires occupancy of a particular home at the relevant time, but it is sensible to maintain another home for future use) may be excluded. See *R(CS) 2/96*, para.12.

If the absent parent moves to live together with the person with care while retaining another home to return to if the reconciliation is unsuccessful, the issue arises of which is the absent parent's principal home during the reconciliation. In considering the interpretation of this definition and its application to such a case, it is relevant to consider para.16(1)(d) of Sch.I to the Act, which provides that the assessment does not cease to have effect until the parties have lived together for a continuous period of six months. This suggests that child support law should be interpreted and applied so as not to hamper attempts at reconciliation, and the removal from the assessment of housing costs on the "retained" home of the absent parent could prove a powerful disincentive. This result may be unavoidable, for example where the absent parent does not retain another home, but where the facts permit it, it is suggested that short-term reconciliation should not affect a person's principal home.

*"partner"*

3.595     A person's partner is defined as the other member of a couple or another member of a polygamous marriage who is living with the person. A couple may be married or unmarried. Each is defined in reg.1(2). In the case of a married couple they must be of the opposite sex and be members of the same household. In the case of an unmarried couple they must be of the opposite sex and be living together as husband and wife. There is no reference to the need for an unmarried couple to be living in the same household. There may be exceptional cases in which a couple are not members of the same household, and there will be many cases in which a couple live together in the same household but not as husband and wife. Tribunals should, therefore, be alert to the possibility of an unusual case arising. Homosexuals are not recognised as a couple for the purposes of these definitions. Gender is fixed at birth, so a man who has changed sex and now lives with another man is not living with a partner for the purpose of this definition.

There is no single model of what constitutes a household or of what amounts to living together as husband and wife. There are nowadays a great variety of arrangements. Some allow couples a great deal of individual freedom within a relationship, while others which exist between unattached individuals are very similar to those which are often associated with couples. The proper approach to cases such as this is discussed in the general note to s.3 of the Act.

*Household*

A household is an abstract concept (*Santos v Santos* [1972] 2 All E.R. 246 at 255, *per* Sachs L.J.). It can survive changes of membership, as *R. v Birmingham Juvenile Court Ex p. N* [1984] 2 All E.R. 688 shows. The legal test concentrates on the arrangements of the persons concerned rather than the accommodation (*R. v*

*Birmingham Juvenile Court* above at 691, *per* Arnold P). It is not possible to be a member of more than one household at a time (*R(SB) 8/85*).

Whether or not a couple are living in the same household is determined by an analysis of the objective facts of their living arrangements. Findings of fact are needed on the following: (i) The nature of the accommodation; (ii) The living arrangements within it, including the distribution of domestic duties and the way they spend their leisure time; (iii) The financial arrangements between the parties; (iv) It will also frequently be useful to investigate how and why the couple came to make the living arrangements which they did. The fact that an arrangement was entered into as a result of a shortage of funds, or in an emergency or in order to secure accommodation, for example, may point towards the couple operating separate households within shared accommodation. On the other hand shift work may explain arrangements which at first sight suggest that the two people are living separate lives; (v) The relationship between the couple will also be relevant. If a couple have a close relationship but keep their financial arrangements separate, their relationship may point nonetheless to there being a single household.

Particular care is needed in applying the criteria to arrangements which are just beginning or which are coming to an end (see the comments of Woolf J., in *Crake v Supplementary Benefits Commission* [1982] 1 All E.R. 498 at 502). A couple may be unwilling to mingle their lives inextricably at first. Alternatively, a developing relationship against a constant background of living arrangements may indicate that a single household has gradually been formed. At the other end of a relationship, it may prove difficult to separate lives which have been shared for a number of years, perhaps decades. In such cases small, perhaps unilateral, alterations in a couple's arrangements will indicate that separate households have been established. Although a household is an abstract concept and the legal test is not primarily concerned with the accommodation, there are limits to the possibilities of establishing separate households in cramped accommodation and in *Adeoso v Adeoso* [1981] 1 All E.R. 107 at 110 Ormrod L.J., said that it was not possible to form separate households in a two room flat.

Absences from the shared accommodation do not necessarily indicate that a couple are no longer living together (*Re M (An Infant)* [1964] 2 All E.R. 1017 at 1024, *per* Buckley J., and *Santos* above at 251–253, *per* Sachs L.J., and *R(SB) 30/83*), nor do they indicate that there is no longer a single household. It is necessary to consider the frequency and duration of the separations as well as the reasons for them.

More than mere presence in the same place is necessary to constitute a household. There must be some collectivity, some communality and some organisation. There must also be a domestic establishment. Therefore, persons living in some form of institution such as a nursing home cannot be in the same household (*CIS 671/92*, para.4 and *CIS 81/93*, para.5).

A person may be a member of a household whilst on bail (*R(IS) 17/93*).

*Living as husband and wife*

Financial arrangements within marriage are very varied, and equal if not greater variation is to be expected among unmarried couples. It has already been said, but bears emphasising, that tribunals must be alert both to the range of possible arrangements and to the need to investigate the reason for the arrangements. Arrangements which have an arms' length or even commercial appearance may have an explanation. Neuberger J. has held that, in view of this diversity, the question to ask is whether, in the opinion of a reasonable person with normal perceptions, it could be said that the two people were living together as husband and wife, but in answering that question it was impossible to ignore the multifarious nature of marital relationships (*Re Watson (deceased)* [1999] 1 F.L.R. 878).

The fact that a couple are living in the same household is an important, perhaps essential, finding before they can be held to be living as husband and wife. However,

3.596

of itself this is not sufficient to justify such a conclusion. It is necessary to investigate how and why they share a common household (*Crake v Supplementary Benefits Commission* [1982] 1 All E.R. 498 at 502, *per* Woolf J.). A number of matters have come to be considered as relevant factors in determining whether a couple are living as husband and wife, and a CSAT should investigate each.

The essence of the decision for the tribunal is to identify the parties' general relationship and the matters considered below are only relevant in so far as they throw light on that general relationship (*CIS 87/93*, para.11). This involves taking into account the less tangible emotional aspects as well as the more concrete observable facts of the parties' relationship (*CIS 17028/96*, para.26). The mixture of factors that together give character to a relationship were listed in *Fitzpatrick v Sterling Housing Association* [1998] 1 F.L.R. 6 at 17 and 19: mutual love, faithfulness, public acknowledgement, sexual relations, shared surname, children, endurance, stability, interdependence and devotion. However, not all of these features need be present and it must be remembered that a couple may be living as husband and wife even though their relationship is unsatisfactory and unhappy. The stage of development of the relationship must be relevant when assessing the significance of a particular feature (*CIS 17028/96*, para.27).

Stability during the course of a relationship is an important indicator. Instability while not decisive against the couple living as husband and wife, would be an indicator in this direction. However stability need not and does not by itself show that a couple are living in this relationship.

How the couple are known to and seen by others is a factor to be considered. If the impression is one that has been created or encouraged by the parties (for example, by using the same surname), it will be a pointer towards the couple living as husband and wife. However, although how others view the couple is a relevant consideration (*Adeoso v Adeoso* [1981] 1 All E.R. 107 at 109, *per* Ormrod L.J.), the tribunal will need to be cautious for two reasons. First, this is less likely to be important when a relationship is first formed; according to Woolf J., in *Crake* above at 502, *Adeoso* is to be interpreted as a case concerned with the termination rather than the inception of a relationship. Second, others may not have been motivated in forming their views by the full range of factors which a tribunal is required to take into account. The fact that a couple have retained separate indentities is not so easy to interpret, since many married couples strive to retain their separate identity and do not use the same surname.

The fact that a couple have children whom they are bringing up together is a strong indication of their commitment to each other, the stability of their relationship and of how they are seen by others.

The sexual arrangements between the parties need to be investigated sensitively by the tribunal and the significance of the answers needs to be assessed carefully. It is possible, although unusual, for a married couple not to have a sexual relationship (*CIS 87/93*, para.12, also reported as *Re J (Income Support: Cohabitation)* [1995] 1 F.L.R. 660), so its absence may be a strong factor against a couple living together as husband and wife, although the age of the couple may be a factor (*Re Watson (deceased)* [1999] 1 F.L.R. 878) as well as the possibility of importance. However, the presence of a sexual relationship is by no means a decisive factor in favour of a couple living as husband and wife. It is an error of law not to investigate this aspect of a relationship, but it is an error of judgment to do so insensitively.

As with the decision whether there is a separate household so here it may be particularly difficult to analyse a relationship which is just beginning or just coming to an end. Obviously stability cannot be established at once and the parties' intentions or declared intentions will be relevant. Similarly the fact that a relationship has been stable in the past does not indicate that it has remained so.

There comes a point when the physical separation is such that the only possible conclusion can be that they are not living in the same household, for example, where they are in different countries (*CIS 508/92*, para.5).

According to the Commissioner in *CIS 317/94*, para.11, it is not appropriate to speak in terms of a burden of proof when deciding whether or not parties are living together as husband and wife, since either sufficient information will be available to make a decision one way or the other or the failure to supply such information may permit adverse inferences being drawn. However, the Commissioner does not explain how a decision is to be made if the evidence is evenly balanced on the issue.

*"personal pension scheme"*

Section 84(1) of the Social Security Act 1986 defines personal pension scheme as meaning "any scheme or arrangement which is comprised in one or more instruments or agreements and which has, or is capable of having, effect so as to provide benefits, in the form of pensions or otherwise, payable on death or retirement to or in respect of employed earners who have made arrangements with the trustees or managers of the scheme for them to become members of the scheme".

3.597

*"polygamous marriage"*

Once a person has contracted a valid polygamous marriage it is not invalidated by a change of country of residence, even if accompanied by the acquisition of a new domicile (*R(G) 1/93*).

*"prisoner"*

A person may be in custody pending trial even if no trial takes place and the person is released (*R(IS) 1/94*, para.15). A person who has been released on licence from prison is not in custody and not a prisoner for the purpose of this definition *R(IS) 20/95*, para.6).

*"relevant week"*

The relevant week is defined on the assumption that the officer will be requesting the information as soon as appropriate and making a decision reasonably quickly on its receipt. Unfortunately, there may be delays both in requesting the information and then in making the decision in the light of it. The longer the delays the more appropriate it is likely to be to use the power in the relevant provisions to take a different period and not to be tied to the relevant week. This power is even more likely to be useful on a s.18 review or on appeal when the facts can be viewed with the benefit of hindsight not given to child support officers making initial decisions.

In *CSC 5/95*, para.7 the Chief Commissioner for Northern Ireland held that the lack of any provision for fixing the relevant week with respect of earnings in relation to a change of circumstance under s.18(10) of the Act prevented such an assessment being carried out. See the general note to that subsection for a criticism of this decision.

*"self-employed earner"*

Section 2(1)(b) of the Social Security (Contributions and Benefits) Act 1992 provides that this "means a person who is gainfully employed in Great Britain otherwise than in employed earner's employment (whether or not he is also employed in such employment)". Section 122(1) provides that " 'employment' includes any trade, business, profession, office or vocation and 'employed' has a corresponding meaning".

See further in the discussion of the definition of "employed earner" above.

3.598

*"student"*

A student is first of all someone who is attending a course. A course comprises a unified sequence of study, tution and/or practical training (whether or not on a modular basis) leading on completion to one or more qualifications *(R(IS) 1/96*, para.17). It is necessary to distinguish between cases where there is practical training intermingled with tution in a single course and those where there are a series of separate courses leading to separate qualifications after each is completed.

The course must be full-time. It is the course rather than the student's attendance which must be full-time. This is a question of fact to be determined in the light of all the circumstances of the case *(CIS 152/94*, para.7). In the past an important factor has been the classification of the course by the provider, although this description could be rebutted by appropriate weightly evidence *(ibid.*, para.7). However, reference to this criterion will increasingly be of less value as institutions tailor their courses to take account of the needs, qualifications and experience of individual' students, especially through the use of modular courses *(ibid.*, para.11). Among the factors that may be helpful in deciding the appropriate classification of a course as pursued by a particular student are the number of modules being studied, the number of hours of study, the arrangements between the college and the student, the length of time it will take the student to obtain a qualification, the fees, the contents of the course prospectus *(ibid.*, para.15), the nature and amount of any grant or other financial support which the student receives, and the nature and time devoted to any work or other activities undertaken at the same time as the studies.

A person who takes time out from a course, for example, by intercalating a year, is neither in term nor vacation when doing so and is, therefore, not a student for that period *(Chief Adjudication Officer and the Secretary of State for Social Security v Clarke and Faul*, reported as *R(IS) 25/95*). A course has not been abandoned unless and until it is permanently abandoned *(ibid.*). Also a student who embarks on a full-time course of study but subsequently transfers to a part-time course is no longer attending a full-time course *(Chief Adjudication Officer v Webber*, reported as *R(IS) 15/98*).

A person may remain a student despite the fact that the end date of that course is unknown because of the requirement that the student repeat some part of the course or resit some examination *(CIS 15594/96*, paras 23–25).

*"training allowance"*

Payments which originated from the European Social Fund and were administered in this country by the Secretary of State for Employment were held to be a training allowance in *CIS 858/94*.

## PART II

### CALCULATION OF CHILD SUPPORT MAINTENANCE

#### Calculation of amounts

3.599

**2.**—(1) Where any amount is to be considered in connection with any calculation made under these Regulations or under Schedule 1 to the Act, it shall be calculated as a weekly amount and, except where the context otherwise requires, any reference to such an amount shall be construed accordingly.

(2) Subject to paragraph (3), where any calculation made under these Regulations or under Schedule 1 to the Act results in a fraction of a penny that fraction shall be treated as a penny if it is either one half or exceeds one half, otherwise it shall be disregarded.

(3) Where the calculation of the basic rate of child support maintenance or the reduced rate of child support maintenance results in a fraction of a pound that fraction shall be treated as a pound if it is either one half or exceeds one half, otherwise it shall be disregarded.

(4) In taking account of any amounts or information required for the purposes of making a maintenance calculation, the Secretary of State shall apply the dates or periods specified in these Regulations as applicable to those amounts or information, provided that if he becomes aware of a material change of circumstances occurring after such date or period, but before the effective date, he shall take that change of circumstances into account.

(5) Information required for the purposes of making a maintenance calculation in relation to the following shall be the information applicable at the effective date—

(a) the number of qualifying children;
(b) the number of relevant other children;
(c) whether the non-resident parent receives a benefit, pension or allowance prescribed for the purposes of paragraph 4(1)(b) of Schedule 1 to the Act;
(d) whether the non-resident parent or his partner receives a benefit prescribed for the purposes of paragraph 4(1)(c) of Schedule 1 to the Act; and
(e) whether paragraph 5(a) of Schedule 1 to the Act applies to the non-resident parent.

DEFINITIONS

"the Act": see reg.1(2).                                                    **3.600**
"effective date": see reg.1(2).
"partner": see reg.1(2).

GENERAL NOTE

This regulation deals with amounts and with the dates as at which calculations   **3.601**
have to be made.

*Paragraph (1)*
This paragraph provides that all amounts are to be calculated as weekly amounts

*Paragraphs (2)–(3)*
These paragraphs provide for the rounding of pennies and pounds. Paragraph (2) is subject to reg.6.

*Paragraphs (4)–(5)*
These paragraphs deal with the dates as at which amounts or information have to be taken into account.

The basic rule is that the amounts or information have to be taken into account as at the dates or periods specified in these Regulations. Paragraph (5) supplements that by specifying that the specified heads of information are those applicable at the effective date.

The basic rule is subject to the qualification in para.(4). The basic rule is overriden if the Secretary of State (not the particular decision-maker making a calculation) becomes aware that a material change of circumstances has occurred before the effective date. The application of this paragraph is obligatory. See further the general note to Sch.1, para.15 to the Act.

### Reduced Rate

**3.602**   **3.** The reduced rate is an amount calculated as follows—

$$F + (A \times T)$$

where—
F is the flat rate liability applicable to the non-resident parent under paragraph 4 of Schedule 1 to the Act;
A is the amount of the non-resident parent's net weekly income between £100 and £200; and
T is the percentage determined in accordance with the following Table—

| | 1 qualifying child of the non-resident parent | | | | 2 qualifying children of non-resident parent | | | | 3 or more qualifying children of non-resident parent | | | |
|---|---|---|---|---|---|---|---|---|---|---|---|---|
| Number of relevant other children of the non-resident parent | 0 | 1 | 2 | 3 or more | 0 | 1 | 2 | 3 or more | 0 | 1 | 2 | 3 or more |
| T(%) | 25 | 20.5 | 19 | 17.5 | 35 | 29 | 27 | 25 | 45 | 37.5 | 35 | 32.5 |

DEFINITIONS

**3.603**   "the Act": see reg.1(2).
"net weekly income": see reg.1(2).

GENERAL NOTE

This regulation prescribes the reduced rate that applies under Sch.1, para.3 to the Act.

### Flat rate

**3.604**   **4.**—(1) The following benefits, pensions and allowances are prescribed for the purposes of paragraph 4(1)(b) of Schedule 1 to the Act—
   (a) under the Contributions and Benefits Act—
      (i) bereavement allowance under section 39B;
      (ii) category A retirement pension under section 44;
      (iii) category B retirement pension under section 48C;
      (iv) category C and category D retirement pensions under section 78;
      (v) incapacity benefit under section 30A;

(vi) [⁶carer's allowance] under section 70;

(vii) maternity allowance under section 35;

(viii) severe disablement allowance under section 68;

(ix) industrial injuries benefit under section 94;

(x) widowed mother's allowance under section 37;

(xi) widowed parent's allowance under section 39A; and

(xii) widow's pension under section 38;

(b) contribution-based jobseeker's allowance under section 1 of the Jobseekers Act;

(c) a social security benefit paid by a country other than the United Kingdom;

(d) a training allowance (other than work-based training for young people or, in Scotland, Skillseekers training); [⁴. . .]

(e) a war disablement pension [². . .] within the meaning of section 150(2) of the Contributions and Benefits Act or a pension which is analogous to such a pension paid by the government of a country outside Great Britain; [³and

(f) a war widow's pension or a war widower's pension] [⁵; and

(g) a payment under a scheme mentioned in section 1(2) of the Armed Forces (Pensions and Compensation) Act 2004 (compensation schemes for armed and reserve forces).]

(2) The benefits prescribed for the purposes of paragraph 4(1)(c) of Schedule 1 to the Act are—

(a) income support under section 124 of the Contributions and Benefits Act; and

(b) income-based jobseeker's allowance under section 1 of the Jobseekers Act; [¹and

(c) state pension credit.]

(3) Where the non-resident parent is liable to a pay a flat rate by virtue of paragraph 4(2) of Schedule 1 to the Act—

(a) if he has one partner, then the amount payable by the non-resident parent shall be half the flat rate; and

(b) if he has more than one partner, then the amount payable by the non-resident parent shall be the result of apportioning the flat rate equally among him and his partners.

AMENDMENTS

1. Regulation 27(3) of the State Pension Credit (Consequential, Transitional and Miscellaneous Provisions) Regulations 2002 (October 6, 2003).

2. Regulation 6(3)(a) of the Miscellaneous Amendments (No.2) Regulations 2003 (November 5, 2003).

3. Regulation 6(3)(b) of the Miscellaneous Amendments (No.2) Regulations 2003 (November 5, 2003).

4. Regulation 6(2)(a) of the Miscellaneous Amendments Regulations 2005 (March 16, 2005).

5. Regulation 6(2)(b) of the Miscellaneous Amendments Regulations 2005 (March 16, 2005).

6. Regulation 3 of, and Sch.2 to, the Social Security Amendment (Carer's Allowance) Regulations 2002 (April 1, 2003).

DEFINITIONS

3.605    "the Act": see reg.1(2).
"Contributions and Benefits Act": see reg.1(2)
"the Jobseekers Act": see reg.1(2).
"state pension credit": see reg.1(2)
"partner": see reg.1(2).
"state pension credit": see reg.1(2).
"training allowance": see reg.1(2).
"war widow's pension": see reg.1(2)
"war widower's pension": see reg.1(2)
"work-based training for young people or, in Scotland, Skillseekers training": see
reg.1(2).

GENERAL NOTE

*Paragraph (1)*
3.606    This paragraph prescribes the benefits, pensions and allowances under Sch.1,
para.4(1)(b) to the Act.

*Paragraph (2)*
This paragraph prescribes the benefits under Sch.1, para.4(1)(c) to the Act.

*Paragraph (3)*
This paragraph prescribes the amount of the flat rate payable under Sch.1,
para.4(2) to the Act.

## Nil rate

3.607    **5.** The rate payable is nil where the non-resident parent is—
(a) a student;
(b) a child within the meaning given in section 55(1) of the Act;
(c) a prisoner;
(d) a person who is 16 or 17 years old and—
    (i) in receipt of income suport or income-based jobseeker's
    allowance; or
    (ii) a member of a couple whose partner is in receipt of income
    support or income-based jobseeker's allowance;
(e) a person receiving an allowance in respect of work-based training for
young people, or in Scotland, Skillseekers training;
(f) a person [⁷who is resident in a care home or an independent hospital or is being provided with a care home service or an independent
health care service] who—
    (i) is in receipt of a pension, benefit or allowance specified in
    regulation 4(1) or (2); or
    (ii) has the whole or part of the cost of his accommodation met by
    a local authority;
(g) a patient in hospital who is in receipt of income support whose applicable amount includes an amount under paragraph [²1(b) or 2] of
Schedule 7 to the Income Support Regulations (patient for more
than [³52] weeks);
[¹(gg) a patient in a hospital who is in receipt of state pension credit and in
respect of whom paragraph 2(1) of Schedule III to the State Pension

Credit Regulations [⁴2002] (patient for [⁵more than] 52 weeks) applies;] [⁹or]
(h) a person in receipt of a benefit specified in regulation 4(1) the amount of which has been reduced in accordance with the provisions of regulations [⁶4] and 6 of the Social Security Hospital In-Patients Regulations 1975 (circumstances in which personal benefit is to be adjusted and adjustment of personal benefit after 52 weeks in hospital); [¹⁰. . .]
[⁸. . .]

AMENDMENTS

1. Regulation 27(4) of the State Pension Credit (Consequential, Transitional and Miscellaneous Provisions) Regulations 2002 (October 6, 2003).
2. Regulation 7(a)(i) of the Social Security (Hospital In-Patients and Miscellaneous Amendments) Regulations 2003 (May 21, 2003).
3. Regulation 7(a)(ii) of the Social Security (Hospital In-Patients and Miscellaneous Amendments) Regulations 2003 (May 21, 2003).
4. Regulation 7(b)(i) of the Social Security (Hospital In-Patients and Miscellaneous Amendments) Regulations 2003 (May 21, 2003).
5. Regulation 7(b)(ii) of the Social Security (Hospital In-Patients and Miscellaneous Amendments) Regulations 2003 (May 21, 2003).
6. Regulation 7(c) of the Social Security (Hospital In-Patients and Miscellaneous Amendments) Regulations 2003 (May 21, 2003).
7. Regulation 6(4) of the Miscellaneous Amendments (No.2) Regulations 2003 (November 5, 2003).
8. Regulation 7(2) of the Miscellaneous Amendments Regulations 2004 (September 16, 2004).
9. Regulation 6(3)(a) of the Miscellaneous Amendments Regulations 2005 (March 16, 2005).
10. Regulation 6(3)(b) of the Miscellaneous Amendments Regulations 2005 (March 16, 2005).

DEFINITIONS

"the Act": see reg.1(2).                                                    3.608
"care home": see reg.1(2).
"care home service": see reg.1(2).
"couple": see reg.1(2).
"Income Support Regulations": see reg.1(2).
"independent health care service": see reg.1(2).
"independent hospital": see reg.1(2).
"net weekly income": see reg.1(2).
"partner": see reg.1(2).
"patient": see reg.1(2).
"prisoner": see reg.1(2).
"state pension credit": see reg.1(2).
"student": see reg.1(2).
"work-based training for young people or, in Scotland, Skillseekers training": see reg.1(2).

GENERAL NOTE

This regulation prescribes the descriptions of non-resident parent under Sch.1,    3.609
para.5(a) to the Act.

### Apportionment

3.610     **6.** If, in making the apportionment required by regulation 4(3) or paragraph 6 of Part I of Schedule 1 to the Act, the effect of the application of regulation 2(2) (rounding) would be such that the aggregate amount of child support maintenance payable by a non-resident parent would be different from the aggregate amount payable before any apportionment, the Secretary of State shall adjust that apportionment so as to eliminate that difference; and that adjustment shall be varied from time to time so as to secure that, taking one week with another and so far as is practicable, each person with care receives the amount which she would have received if no adjustment had been made under this paragraph.

DEFINITIONS

3.611     "the Act": see reg.1(2).
          "person": see reg.1(2).

GENERAL NOTE

3.612     The same provision is made for apportionment of the default rate by reg.7(4) of the Maintenance Calculation Procedure Regulations.

### Shared care

3.613     **7.**—(1) For the purposes of paragraphs 7 and 8 of Part I of Schedule 1 to the Act a night will count for the purposes of shared care where the non-resident parent—
          (a) has the care of a qualifying child overnight; and
          (b) the qualifying child stays at the same address as the non-resident parent.
          (2) For the purposes of paragraphs 7 and 8 of Part I of Schedule 1 to the Act, a non-resident parent has the care of a qualifying child when he is looking after the child.
          (3) Subject to paragraph (4), in determining the number of nights for the purposes of shared care, the Secretary of State shall consider the 12 month period ending with the relevant week and for this purpose "relevant week" has the same meaning as in the definition of day to day care in regulation 1 of these Regulations.
          (4) The circumstances in which the Secretary of State may have regard to a number of nights over less than a 12 month period are where there has been no pattern for the frequency with which the non-resident parent looks after the qualifying child for the 12 months preceding the relevant week, or the Secretary of State is aware that a change in that frequency is intended, and in that case he shall have regard to such lesser period as may seem to him to be appropriate, and the Table in paragraph 7(4) and the period in paragraph 8(2) of Schedule 1 to the Act shall have effect subject to the adjustment described in paragraph (5).
          (5) Where paragraph (4) applies, the Secretary of State shall adjust the number of nights in that lesser period by applying to that number the ratio which the period of 12 months bears to that lesser period.

(6) Where a child is a boarder at a boarding school, or is a patient in a hospital, the person who, but for those circumstances, would otherwise have care of the child overnight shall be treated as providing that care during the periods in question.

DEFINITIONS

"the Act": see reg.1(2).  3.614
"day to day care": see reg.1(2).
"patient": see reg.1(2).
"person": see reg.1(2).
"relevant week": see reg.1(2).

GENERAL NOTE

The Commissioner's analysis of the meaning of "care" under the previous legis-  3.615
lation (R(CS) 11/02) will not be necessary in the context of the different wording
of this legislation. Paragraphs (1)(a) and (2) make it clear that what matters is who
looks after a child overnight.

*Paragraph (1)*
This paragraph defines care for the purposes of shared care under Sch.1, paras 7
and 8 to the Act.

*Paragraph (2)*
This paragraph defines those nights that count for the purposes of shared care
under Sch.1, paras 7 and 8 to the Act.

*Paragraph (3)*
This paragraph, together with paras (4)–(6), provides for the calculation of the
number of nights for which a non-resident parent has shared care under Sch.1,
paras 7 and 8 to the Act.

Schedule 1, paras 7(3) and 8(2) provide that the starting point for the calculation
must be a prescribed 12 month period. This paragraph is made under the authority of those paragraphs. It prescribes the 12 month period as that ending with the
relevant week that applies for the purposes of day to day care.

The Secretary of State is only required to 'consider' this period. That *may* allow
some flexibility in the calculation. One approach would be purely arithmetical,
adding the number of nights in the period and converting them to a weekly number. A more flexible approach would allow unrepresentative parts of that period to
be ignored: for example, if one parent was in hospital and the other had the care of
the child for more nights than would otherwise have been the case. However, it is
suggested that the flexible approach is out of line with the detailed wording of
Sch.1, para.7(3) and 8(2) to the Act, as well as para.(5) below. Those provisions
envisage a purely arithmetical approach.

*Paragraph (4)*
Schedule 1, para.9(c) to the Act provides for the period in paras 7(3) and 8(2) to  3.616
be other than 12 months. This paragraph is made under that authority. It allows a
shorter period, but not a longer one, than 12 months to be used. The enabling provision only authorises the 12 months to be altered. It does not affect what may be prescribed under Sch.1, paras 7(3) and 8(2). In other words, it deals with the length of
the period, but not with the date on which the period must end. This is not to say
that a different end date cannot be used. It is only that this paragraph does not authorise that to be done. If a change has occurred that makes the effective date a more

appropriate end date than the relevant week, that change can be taken into account under reg.2(4) above. (The reasoning to the contrary in *CCS 128/01* does not apply under this version of the legislation, even if it was correct for the previous version.)

This paragraph does not provide a general discretion to use a period of less than 12 months whenever that would be appropriate. It only authorises it in two cases, although they cover most cases in which a lesser period is appropriate. The first case is if there was no pattern of frequency of overnight care over that period. This applies if overnight care has been random or there has been a clear change during the 12 months. The second case is where a change in that frequency is intended. That does not mean that the change is intended to take place in the future. If it did, the change would be taken into account before it occurred. It means that the evidence of recent overnight care represents an intended change of frequency and not merely a temporary variation that will be averaged out over the longer term.

If one of these cases applies, an "appropriate" and lesser period has to chosen to replace the 12 month period.

*Paragraph (6)*

It is clear from this provision that it is the school or the hospital that is actually providing the overnight care for the child. This is a deeming provision. The other person does not actually provide the overnight care for the child.

A boarding school covers any institution that is a school and that provides overnight residence for some pupils (*R(CS) 1/04*, para.24). It includes privately funded boarding and boarding that is funded by a local authority in the exercise of its social services functions (*R(CS) 1/04*, para.24) or by a local education authority (*R(CS) 2/04*, para.31).

It will usually be obvious who a child would live with if not at boarding school or in hospital. However, there are exceptional cases in which there is no clear answer. They require a careful analysis of all the circumstances of the case. It is a mistake simply to scale up the pattern of frequency that obtained when the child was boarding or in hospital. It is also a mistake to assume that circumstances, such as a parent's working arrangements, have not been affected by the fact that the child is boarding or in hospital, so that they would be different if the child had to stay instead with the non-resident parent or the person with care.

## PART III

### SPECIAL CASES

### Persons treated as non-resident parents

3.617      **8.**—(1) Where the circumstances of a case are that—

    (a) two or more persons who do not live in the same household each provide day to day care for the same [¹child, being a child in respect of whom an application for a maintenance calculation has been made or treated as made]; and

    (b) at least one of those persons is a parent of the child,

that case shall be treated as a special case for the purposes of the Act.

(2) For the purposes of this special case a parent who provides day to day care for a child of his is to be treated as a non-resident parent for the purposes of the Act in the following circumstances—

    (a) a parent who provides such care to a lesser extent than the other parent, person or persons who provide such care for the child in question; or

(b) where the persons mentioned in paragraph (1)(a) include both parents and the circumstances are such that care is provided to the same extent by both but each provides care to an extent greater than or equal to any other person who provides such care for that child—
    (i) the parent who is not in receipt of child benefit for the child in question; or
    (ii) if neither parent is in receipt of child benefit for that child, the parent who, in the opinion of the Secretary of State, will not be the principal provider of day to day care for that child.

(3) For the purposes of this regulation and regulation 10 "child benefit" means child benefit payable under Part IX of the Contributions and Benefits Act.

AMENDMENT

1. Regulation 8 (3) of the Miscellaneous Amendments Regulations 2003 (February 21, 2003).

DEFINITIONS

"the Act": see reg.1(2).                                   3.618
"Contributions and Benefits Act": see reg.1(2).
"day to day care": see reg.1(2).
"person": see reg.1(2).

GENERAL NOTE

This special case determines who is to be treated as the non-resident parent if a    3.619
child is receiving day to day care from different persons in different households. The
child support maintenance payable by the non-resident parent is adjusted under
the shared care provisions in Sch.1, paras 7 and 8 to the Act.

*Paragraph (1)*
This paragraph sets out the circumstances in which the special case applies. The
day to day care of the child must be split between persons in different households
and one of those persons must be a parent of the child. If neither parent of the child
is providing day to day care, this special case does not apply.

It is day to day care, as defined in reg.1(2) above, that is relevant, not shared care
under Sch.1, paras 7 and 8 to the Act.

There must be separate households. For the meaning of household, see the
general note to s.3(2) of the Act. This special case does not apply if the persons
providing care are members of the same household (*CCS 14625/96*, para.17).

*Paragraph (2)*
This paragraph identifies the person who is to be treated as the non-resident parent. In most cases, the care of the child will be divided between the parents and the
non-resident parent will be the parent who provides care for fewer nights than the
other or who is not in receipt of child benefit.

## Care provided in part by a local authority

**9.**—(1) This regulation applies where paragraph (2) applies and the    3.620
rate of child support maintenance payable is the basic rate, or the reduced
rate, or has been calculated following agreement to a variation where the

non-resident parent's liability would otherwise have been a flat rate or the nil rate.

(2) Where the circumstances of a case are that the care of the qualifying child is shared between the person with care and a local authority and—

(a) the qualifying child is in the care of the local authority for 52 nights or more in the 12 month period ending with the relevant week; or

(b) where, in the opinion of the Secretary of State, a period other than the 12 month period mentioned in sub-paragraph (a) is more representative of the current arrangements for the care of the qualifying child, the qualifying child is in the care of the local authority during that period for no fewer than the number of nights which bears the same ratio to 52 nights as that period bears to 12 months; or

(c) it is intended that the qualifying child shall be in the care of the local authority for a number of nights in a period from the effective date,

that case shall be treated as a special case for the purposes of the Act.

(3) In a case where this regulation applies, the amount of child support maintenance which the non-resident parent is liable to pay the person with care of that qualifying child is the amount calculated in accordance with the provisions of Part I of Schedule 1 to the Act and decreased in accordance with this regulation.

(4) First, there is to be a decrease according to the number of nights spent or to be spent by the qualifying child in the care of the local authority during the period under consideration.

(5) Where paragraph (2)(b) or (c) applies, the number of nights in the period under consideration shall be adjusted by the ratio which the period of 12 months bears to the period under consideration.

(6) After any adjustment under paragraph (5), the amount of the decrease for one child is set out in the following Table—

| Number of nights in care of local authority | Fraction to subtract |
| --- | --- |
| 52–103 | One-seventh |
| 104–155 | Two-sevenths |
| 156–207 | Three-sevenths |
| 208–259 | Four-sevenths |
| 260–262 | Five-sevenths |

(7) If the non-resident parent and the person with care have more than one qualifying child, the applicable decrease is the sum of the appropriate fractions in the Table divided by the number of such qualifying children.

(8) In a case where the amount of child support maintenance which the non-resident parent is liable to pay in relation to the same person with care is to be decreased in accordance with the provisions of both this regulation and of paragraph 7 of Part I of Schedule 1 to the Act, read with regulation 7 of these Regulations, the applicable decrease is the sum of the appropriate fractions derived under those provisions.

(9) If the application of this regulation would decrease the weekly amount of child support maintenance (or the aggregate of all such amounts) payable by the non-resident parent to less than the rate stated in or prescribed for the purposes of paragraph 4(1) of Part I of Schedule 1 to

the Act, he is instead liable to pay child support maintenance at a rate equivalent to that rate, apportioned (if appropriate) in accordance with paragraph 6 of Part I of Schedule 1 to the Act and regulation 6.

(10) Where a qualifying child is a boarder at a boarding school or is an in-patient at a hospital, the qualifying child shall be treated as being in the care of the local authority for any night that the local authority would otherwise have been providing such care.

(11) A child is in the care of a local authority for any night in which he is being looked after by the local authority within the meaning of section 22 of the Children Act 1989 or section 17(6) of the Children (Scotland) Act 1995.

DEFINITIONS

"the Act": see reg.1(2).                                                    3.621
"effective date": see reg.1(2).
"patient": see reg.1(2).
"person": see reg.1(2).
"relevant week": see reg.1(2).

GENERAL NOTE

This special case applies where the care of the child is divided between the person    3.622
with care and a local authority.

*Paragraph (1)*

The decrease in the amount of child support maintenance under this special case is not compatible with the flat rate or the nil rate. So, it only applies when one of those rates would apply, if the amount payable has been increased under a variation.

*Paragraph (2)*

Broadly, the special case only applies if the child is in the care of the local authority for at least one night a week on average. The case only applies if the child is in the care of the local authority. It is not drawn to include circumstances in which a local authority provides accommodation for a child in the exercise of one of its social services functions: see the distinction drawn in s.22(1) of the Children Act 1989.

*Paragraph (3)–(6)*

The child support maintenance payable is first calculated under Sch 1 to the Act. It is then reduced to reflect the number of nights the child spends under the care of the local authority.

## Care provided for relevant other child by a local authority

**10.** Where a child other than a qualifying child is cared for in part or in    3.623
full by a local authority and the non-resident parent or his partner receives child benefit for that child, the child is a relevant other child for the purposes of Schedule 1 to the Act.

DEFINITIONS

"the Act": see reg.1(2).                                                    3.624
"partner": see reg.1(2).

This regulation is made under the authority of Sch.1, para.10C(2)(b) to the Act.

## Non-resident parent liable to pay maintenance under a maintenance order

3.625    **11.**—(1) Subject to paragraph (2), where the circumstances of a case are that—

(a) an application for child support maintenance is made or treated as made, as the case may be, with respect to a qualifying child and a non-resident parent; and

(b) an application for child support maintenance for a different child cannot be made under the Act but that non-resident parent is liable to pay maintenance [³for that child—

    (i) under a maintenance order;

    (ii) in accordance with the terms of an order made by a court outside Great Britain; or

    (iii) under the legislation of a jurisdiction outside the United Kingdom,

that case shall be treated as a special case for the purpose of the Act.]

(2) This regulation applies where the rate of child support maintenance payable is the basic rate, or the reduced rate, or has been calculated following agreement to a variation where the non-resident parent's liablity would otherwise have been a flat rate or the nil rate.

(3) Where this regulation applies, [¹subject to paragraph (5),] the amount of child support maintenance payable by the non-resident parent shall be ascertained by—

(a) calculating the amount of maintenance payable as if the number of qualifying children of that parent included any children with respect to whom he is liable to make payments under the order referred to in paragraph (1)(b); and

(b) apportioning the amount so calculated between the qualifying children and the children with respect to whom he is liable to make payments under the order referred to in paragraph (1)(b),

and the amount payable shall be the amount apportioned to the qualifying children, and the amount payable to each person with care shall be that amount subject to the application of apportionment under paragraph 6 of Schedule 1 to the Act and the shared care provisions in paragraph 7 of Part I of that Schedule.

(4) In a case where this regulation applies paragraph 7 of Part I of Schedule 1 to the Act (shared care) and regulation 10 (care provided in part by local authority) shall not apply in relation to a child in respect of whom the non-resident parent is liable to make payments under a maintenance order as provided in paragraph (1)(b).

[²(5) If the application of paragraph (3) would decrease the weekly amount of child support maintenance (or the aggregate of all such amounts) payable by the non-resident parent to the person with care (or all of them) to an amount which is less than a figure equivalent to the flat rate of child support maintenance payable under paragraph 4(1) of Schedule 1 to the Act, the non-resident parent shall instead be liable to pay child support maintenance at a rate equivalent to that flat rate apportioned (if appropriate) as provided in paragraph 6 of Schedule 1 to the Act.]

AMENDMENTS

1. Regulation 6(5)(a) of the Miscellaneous Amendments (No.2) Regulations 2003 (November 5, 2003).
2. Regulation 6(5)(b) of the Miscellaneous Amendments (No.2) Regulations 2003 (November 5, 2003).
3. Regulation 6(4) of the Miscellaneous Amendments Regulations 2005 (March 16, 2005).

DEFINITIONS

"the Act": see reg.1(2).     **3.626**
"person": see reg.1(2).

GENERAL NOTE

*Paragraph (1)*
This special case applies if a non-resident parent is liable to pay maintenance for   **3.627** a child under a maintenance order. It provides for the child support maintenance payable for another child under the child support scheme to reflect the existence of that obligation. It does not apply if the payments for the other child are made under a maintenance agreement.

*Paragraph (2)*
The decrease in the amount of child support maintenance under this special case is not compatible with the flat rate or the nil rate. So, it only applies when one of those rates would apply, if the amount payable has been increased under a variation.

*Paragraph (3)*
The reduction reflects the existence of the obligation under the maintenance order. It does not vary according to the amount payable under the order.

## Child who is a boarder or an in-patient in hospital

**12.**—(1) Where the circumstances of the case are that—     **3.628**
  (a) a qualifying child is a boarder at a boarding school or is an inpatient in a hospital; and
  (b) by reason of those circumstances, the person who would otherwise provide day to day care is not doing so,
that case shall be treated as a special case for the purposes of the Act.

(2) For the purposes of this case, section 3(3)(b) of the Act shall be modified so that for the reference to the person who usually provides day to day care for the child there shall be substituted a reference to the person who would usually be providing such care for that child but for the circumstances specified in paragraph (1).

DEFINITIONS

"the Act": see reg.1(2).     **3.629**
"day to day care": see reg.1(2).

"patient": see reg.1(2).
"person": see reg.1(2).

GENERAL NOTE

*Paragraph (1)*

**3.630**  For the application of this paragraph, see the general note to reg.7(6) above.

*Paragraph (2)*

This paragraph limits the effect of this special case to s.3(3) of the Act. However, similar provision in made in the definition of day to day care in reg.1(2) above, for the purposes of shared care in reg.7(6) above, and in respect of care divided between the person with care and a local authority in reg.9(10) above.

## Child who is allowed to live with his parent under section 23(5) of the Children Act 1989

**3.631**  **13.**—(1) Where the circumstances of a case are that a qualifying child who is in the care of a local authority in England and Wales is allowed by the authority to live with a parent of his under section 23(5) of the Children Act 1989, that case shall be treated as a special case for the purposes of the Act.

(2) For the purposes of this case, section 3(3)(b) of the Act shall be modified so that for the reference to the person who usually provides day to day care for the child there shall be substituted a reference to the parent of the child with whom the local authority allow the child to live with under section 23(5) of the Children Act 1989.

DEFINITIONS

**3.632**  "the Act": see reg.1(2).
"day to day care": see reg.1(2).
"person": see reg.1(2).

GENERAL NOTE

**3.633**  This regulation allows a maintenance calculation to reflect the reality that the parent is providing day to day care of a child, although the child is legally in the care of a local authority. Its effect is to make that parent the person with care even though the conditions in s.3(3)(b) of the Act are not satisfied (*R(CS) 7/02*). If a child is allowed to live with one parent and then moves to live with the other parent without a fresh placement decision being made by the local authority, the other parent may be a person with care under s.3(3)(b) despite this regulation (*R(CS) 7/02*).

## Person with part-time care who is not a non-resident parent

**3.634**  **14.**—(1) Where the circumstances of a case are that—
(a) two or more persons who do not live in the same household each provide day to day care for the same qualifying child; and
(b) those persons do not include any parent who is treated as a non-resident parent of that child by regulation 8(2),
that case shall be treated as a special case for the purposes of the Act.
(2) For the purposes of this case—
(a) the person whose application for a maintenance calculation is being proceeded with shall, subject to sub-paragraph (b), be entitled to

receive all of the child support maintenance payable under the Act in respect of the child in question;

(b) on request being made to the Secretary of State by—
  (i) that person; or
  (ii) any other person who is providing day to day care for that child and who intends to continue to provide that care,
  the Secretary of State may make arrangements for the payment of any child support maintenance payable under the Act to the persons who provide such care in the same ratio as that in which it appears to the Secretary of State that each is to provide such care for the child in question;

(c) before making an arrangement under sub-paragraph (b), the Secretary of State shall consider all of the circumstances of the case and in particular the interests of the child, the present arrangements for the day to day care of the child in question and any representations or proposals made by the persons who provide such care for that child.

DEFINITIONS

"the Act": see reg.1(2).
"day to day care": see reg.1(2).
"person": see reg.1(2).

3.635

GENERAL NOTE

*Paragraph (1)*

This paragraph sets out the circumstances in which the special case applies. The day to day care of the child must be split between persons in different households and none of those persons is a parent of the child who is treated as a non-resident parent under reg.8 above:

It is day to day care, as defined in reg.1(2) above, that is relevant, not shared care under Sch.1, paras 7 and 8 to the Act.

There must be separate households. For the meaning of household, see the general note to s.3(2) of the Act. This special case does not apply if the persons providing care are members of the same household (*CCS 14625/96*, para.17).

A person who provides day to day care and who is entitled to a share of the child support maintenance under this regulation is not necessarily a person with care under s.3(3) of the Act and does not become one by virtue of this regulation. For example, the child's home need not be with the person who benefits from this regulation. The function of the regulation is to allow the Secretary of State to divert a share of the child support maintenance to someone who has day to day care of a child, but who is not a person with care and who, therefore, could not apply for a maintenance calculation.

3.636

*Paragraph (2)*

The starting point is provided by sub-para.(a): the person with care under the maintenance calculation is entitled to received all the child support maintenance payable by the non-resident parent.

On request, the Secretary of State may agree under sub-para.(b) that a share of the child support maintenance should be paid to the other person providing care. The amount is determined by the number of nights for which care is given. The wording does not allow other factors to be considered in fixing the amount, like the

3.637

respective financial burdens undertaken by the persons providing the care. These factors may, though, be relevant under sub-para.(c) to whether any arrangement should be made at all.

Sub-paragraph (c) controls the exercise of the discretion given by sub-para.(b). The discretion is limited to whether the Secretary of State should make an arrangement. It does not confer a discretion as to the terms of the arrangement. The Secretary of State must consider all the circumstances of the case, including representations made, the present arrangements for care and the interests of the child. In contrast to s.2 of the Act, it is the interests, rather than welfare, of the child that have to be considered. Also, only the child in question is mentioned in sub-para.(c), although other children could be considered as part of the circumstances of the case.

PART IV

REVOCATION AND SAVINGS

**Revocation and savings**

3.638    **15.**—(1) Subject to [¹the Child Support (Transitional Provisions) Regulations 2000 and] paragraphs (2), (3) and (4), the Child Support (Maintenance Assessments and Special Cases) Regulations 1992 ("the 1992 Regulations") shall be revoked with respect to a particular case with effect from the date that these Regulations come into force with respect to that type of case ("the commencement date").

(2) Where before the commencement date in respect of a particular case—

(a) an application was made and not determined for—
   (i) a maintenance assessment;
   (ii) a departure direction; or
   (iii) a revision or supersession of a decision;
(b) the Secretary of State had begun but not completed a revision or supersession of a decision on his own initiative;
(c) any time limit provided for in Regulations for making an application for a revision or a departure direction had not expired; or
(d) any appeal was made but not decided or any time limit for making an appeal had not expired,

the provisions of the 1992 Regulations shall continue to apply for the purposes of—

(aa) the decision on the application referred to in sub-paragraph (a);
(bb) the revision or supersession referred to in sub-paragraph (b);
(cc) the ability to apply for the revision or the departure direction referred to in sub-paragraph (c) and the decision whether to revise or to give a departure direction following any such application;
(dd) any appeal outstanding or made during the time limit referred to in sub-paragraph (d); or
(ee) any revision, supersession, appeal or application for a departure direction in relation to a decision, ability to apply or appeal referred to in sub-paragraphs (aa) to (dd) above.

(3) Where immediately before the commencement date in respect of a particular case an interim maintenance assessment was in force, the provisions of the 1992 Regulations shall continue to apply for the purposes of the decision under section 17 of the Act to make a maintenance assessment calculated in accordance with Part I of Schedule 1 to the Act before its amendment by the 2000 Act and any revision, supersession or appeal in relation to that decision.

(4) Where under regulation 28(1) of the Child Support (Transitional Provisions) Regulations 2000 an application for a maintenance calculation is treated as an application for a maintenance assessment, the provisions of the 1992 Regulations shall continue to apply for the purposes of the determination of the application and any revision, supersession or appeal in relation to any such assessment made.

(5) Where after the commencement date a maintenance assessment is revised from a date which is prior to the commencement date the 1992 Regulations shall apply for the purposes of that revision.

(6) For the purposes of this regulation—

(a) "departure direction", "maintenance assessment" and "interim maintenance assessment" have the same meaning as in section 54 of the Act before its amendment by the 2000 Act;

(b) "revision or supersession" means a revision or supersession of a decision under section 16 or 17 of the Act before their amendment by the 2000 Act; and

(c) "2000 Act" means the Child Support, Pensions and Social Security Act 2000.

AMENDMENT

1. Regulation 2(1) and (2)(c) of the Transitional Amendments Regulations 2003 (March 3, 2003).

DEFINITION

"the Act": see reg. 1(2).

3.639

SCHEDULE

NET WEEKLY INCOME

PART I

GENERAL

**Net weekly income**

1. Net weekly income means the aggregate of the net weekly income of the non-resident parent provided for in this Schedule.

3.640

**Amounts to be disregarded when calculating income**

2. The following amounts shall be disregarded when calculating the net weekly income of the non-resident parent—

3.641

(a) where a payment is made in a currency other than sterling, an amount equal to any banking charge or commission payable in converting that payment to sterling;

(b) any amount payable in a country outside the United Kingdom where there is a prohibition against the transfer to the United Kingdom of that amount.

PART II

EMPLOYED EARNER

**Net weekly income of employed earner**

3.642    **3.**(1)  The net weekly income of the non-resident parent as an employed earner shall be—

(a) his earnings provided for in paragraph 4 less the deductions provided for in paragraph 5 and calculated or estimated by reference to the relevant week as provided for in paragraph 6; or

(b) where the Secretary of State is satisfied that the person is unable to provide evidence or information relating to the deductions provided for in paragraph 5, the non-resident parent's net earnings estimated by the Secretary of State on the basis of information available to him as to the non-resident parent's net income.

(2)  Where any provision of these Regulations requires the income of a person to be estimated, and that or any other provision of these Regulations requires that the amount of such estimated income is to be taken into account for any purpose, after deducting from it a sum in respect of income tax, or of primary Class 1 contributions under the Contributions and Benefits Act or, as the case may be, the Contributions and Benefits (Northern Ireland) Act, or contributions paid by that person towards an occupational pension scheme or personal pension scheme, then,

(a) subject to sub-paragraph (c), the amount to be deducted in respect of income tax shall be calculated by applying to that income the rates of income tax applicable at the effective date less only the personal relief to which that person is entitled under Chapter I of Part VII of the Income and Corporation Taxes Act 1988 (personal relief); but if the period in respect of which that income is to be estimated is less than a year, the amount of the personal relief deductible under this paragraph shall be calculated on a pro-rata basis and the amount of income to which each tax rate applies shall be determined on the basis that the ratio of that amount to the full amount of the income to which each tax rate applies is the same as the ratio of the proportionate part of that personal relief to the full personal relief;

(b) subject to sub-paragraph (c), the amount to be deducted in respect of Class 1 contributions under the Contributions and Benefits Act or, as the case may be, the Contributions and Benefits (Northern Ireland) Act, shall be calculated by applying to that income the appropriate primary percentage applicable on the effective date;

(c) in relation to any bonus or commission which may be included in that person's income—

(i) the amount to be deducted in respect of income tax shall be calculated by applying to the gross amount of that bonus or commission the rate or rates of income tax applicable at the effective date;

(ii) the amount to be deducted in respect of primary Class 1 contributions under the Contributions and Benefits Act or, as the case may be, the Contributions and Benefits (Northern Ireland) Act, shall be calculated by applying to the gross amount of that bonus or commission the appropriate main primary percentage applicable on the effective date but no deduction shall be made in respect of the portion (if any) of the bonus or commission which, if added to the estimated income, would cause such income to exceed the upper earnings limit for Class 1 contributions as provided for in section 5(1)(b) of the Contributions and Benefits Act or, as the case may be, the Contributions and Benefits (Northern Ireland) Act;

(d) the amount to be deducted in respect of any sums or contributions towards an occupational pension scheme or personal pension scheme shall be the full amount of any such payments made or, where that scheme is intended partly to provide a capital sum to discharge a mortgage secured upon that parent's home, 75 per centum of any such payments made.

**Earnings**

**4.**—(1) Subject to sub-paragraph (2), "earnings" means, in the case of employment as an employed earner, any remuneration or profit derived from that employment and includes— **3.643**

(a) any bonus, commission, payment in respect of overtime, royalty or fees;

(b) any holiday pay except any payable more than 4 weeks after termination of the employment;

(c) any payment by way of a retainer;

(d) any statutory sick pay under Part XI of the Contributions and Benefits Act or statutory maternity pay under Part XII of the Contributions and Benefits Act; and

[15(dd) any statutory paternity pay under Part 12ZA of the Contributions and Benefits Act or any statutory adoption pay under Part 12ZB of that Act;]

(e) any payment in lieu of notice, and any compensation in respect of the absence or inadequacy of any such notice, but only in so far as such payment or compensation represents loss of income.

(2) Earnings for the purposes of this Part of Schedule 1 do not include—

(a) any payment in respect of expenses wholly, exclusively and necessarily incurred in the performance of the duties of the employment;

(b) any tax-exempt allowance made by an employer to an employee;

(c) any gratuities paid by customers of the employer;

(d) any payment in kind;

(e) any advance of earnings or any loan made by an employer to an employee;

(f) any amount received from an employer during a period when the employee has withdrawn his services by reason of a trade dispute;

(g) any payment made in respect of the performance of duties as—

(i) an auxiliary coastguard in respect of coast rescue activities;
(ii) a part-time fireman in a fire brigade maintained in pursuance of the Fire Services Acts 1947 to 1959;
[18(iia) a part-time fire-fighter employed by a fire and rescue authority;]
(iii) a person engaged part-time in the manning or launching of a lifeboat;
(iv) a member of any territorial or reserve force prescribed in Part I of Schedule 3 to the Social Security (Contributions) Regulations 1979;

(h) any payment made by a local authority to a member of that authority in respect of the performance of his duties as a member;

(i) any payment where—

(i) the employment in respect of which it was made has ceased; and
(ii) a period of the same length as the period by reference to which it was calculated has expired since that cessation but prior to the effective date; or

(j) where, in any week or other period which falls within the period by reference to which earnings are calculated, earnings are received both in respect of a previous employment and in respect of a subsequent employment, the earnings in respect of the previous employment.

**Deductions**

**5.**—(1) The deductions to be taken from gross earnings to calculate net income for the purposes of this Part of the Schedule are any amounts deducted from those earnings by way of— **3.644**

(a) income tax;

(b) primary Class 1 contributions under the Contributions and Benefits Act or under the Contributions and Benefits (Northern Ireland) Act; or

(c) any sums paid by the non-resident parent towards an occupational pension scheme or personal pension scheme or, where that scheme is intended partly to provide a capital sum to discharge a mortgage secured upon that parent's home, 75 per cent of any such sums.

(2) For the purposes of sub-paragraph (1)(a), amount deducted by way of income tax shall be the amounts actually deducted, including in respect of payments which are not included as earnings in paragraph 4.

**Calculation or estimate**

3.645    **6.**—(1) Subject to [³sub-paragraphs (3) and (4)], the amount of earnings to be taken into account for the purpose of calculating net income shall be calculated or estimated by reference to the average earnings at the relevant week having regard to such evidence as is available in relation to that person's earnings during such period as appears appropriate to the Secretary of State, beginning not earlier than 8 weeks before the relevant week and ending not later than the date of the calculation, and for the purposes of the calculation or estimate he may consider evidence of that person's cumulative earnings during the period beginning with the start of the year of assessment (within the meaning of section 832 of the Income and Corporation Taxes Act 1988) in which the relevant week falls and ending with a date no later than the date when the calculation is made.

[⁴. . .]

(3) Where a person's earnings during the period of 52 weeks ending with the relevant week include a bonus or commission made in anticipation of the calculation of profits which is paid separately from, or in relation to a longer period than, the other earnings with which it is paid, the amount of that bonus or commission shall be determined for the purposes of the calculation of earnings by aggregating any such payments received in that period and dividing by 52.

(4) Where a calculation would, but for this sub-paragraph, produce an amount which, in the opinion of the Secretary of State, does not accurately reflect the normal amount of the earnings of the person in question, such earnings, or any part of them, shall be calculated by reference to such other period as may, in the particular case, enable the normal weekly earnings of that person to be determined more accurately, and for this purpose the Secretary of State shall have regard to—

(a) the earnings received, or due to be received from any employment in which the person in question is engaged, has been engaged or is due to be engaged; and

(b) the duration and pattern, or the expected duration and pattern, of any employment of that person.

PART III

SELF-EMPLOYED EARNER

**Figures submitted to the Inland Revenue**

3.646    **7.**—(1) Subject to sub-paragraph (6) the net weekly income of the non-resident parent as a self-employed earner shall be his gross earnings calculated by reference to one of the following, as the Secretary of State may decide, less the deductions to which subparagraph (3) applies—

(a) the total taxable profits from self-employment of that earner as submitted to the Inland Revenue in accordance with their requirements by or on behalf of that earner; or

(b) the income from self-employment as a self-employed earner as set out on the tax calculation notice or, as the case may be, the revised notice.

(2) Where the information referred to in head (a) or (b) of sub-paragraph (1) is made available to the Secretary of State he may nevertheless require the information referred to in the other head from the non-resident parent and where the Secretary of State becomes aware that a revised notice has been issued he may require and use this in preference to the other information referred to in sub-paragraph (1)(a) and (b).

(3) This paragraph applies to the following deductions—

(a) any income tax relating to the gross earnings from the self-employment determined in accordance with sub-paragraph (4);

(b) any National Insurance contributions relating to the gross earnings from the self-employment determined in accordance with sub-paragraph (5); and

(c) any premiums paid by the non-resident parent in respect of a retirement annuity contract or a personal pension scheme or, where that scheme is intended partly to provide a capital sum to discharge a mortgage or a charge secured upon the parent's home, 75 per cent of the contributions payable.

(4) For the purpose of sub-paragraph (3)(a), the income tax to be deducted from the gross earnings shall be determined in accordance with the following provisions—

(a) subject to head (d), an amount of gross earnings [[17]calculated as if it were equivalent to any personal allowance which would be] applicable to the earner by virtue of the provisions of Chapter I of Part VII of the Income and Corporation Taxes Act 1988 (personal relief) shall be disregarded;

(b) subject to head (c), an amount equivalent to income tax shall be calculated in relation to the gross earnings remaining following the application of head (a) (the "remaining earnings");

(c) the tax rate applicable at the effective date shall be applied to all the remaining earnings, where necessary increasing or reducing the amount payable to take account of the fact that the earnings related to a period greater or less than one year; and

(d) the amount to be disregarded by virtue of head (a) shall be calculated by reference to the yearly rate applicable at the effective date, that amount being reduced or increased in the same proportion to that which the period represented by the gross earnings bears to the period of one year.

(5) For the purposes of sub-paragraph (3)(b), the amount to be deducted in respect of National Insurance contributions shall be the total of—

(a) the amount of Class 2 contributions (if any) payable under section 11(1) or, as the case may be, (3) of the Contributions and Benefits Act or under section 11(1) or (3) of the Contributions and Benefits (Northern Ireland) Act; and

(b) the amount of Class 4 contributions (if any) payable under section 15(2) of that Act, or under section 15(2) of the Contributions and Benefits (Northern Ireland) Act,

at the rates applicable at the effective date.

(6) The net weekly income of a self-employed earner may only be determined in accordance with this paragraph where the earnings concerned relate to a period which terminated not more than 24 months prior to the relevant week.

(7) In this paragraph—

"tax calculation notice" means a document issued by the Inland Revenue containing information as to the income of the self-employed earner; and

"revised notice" means a notice issued by the Inland Revenue where there has been a tax calculation notice and there is a revision of the figures relating to the income of a self-employed earner following an enquiry under section 9A of the Taxes Management Act 1970 or otherwise by the Inland Revenue.

(8) Any request by the Secretary of State in accordance with sub-paragraph (2) for the provision of information shall set out the possible consequences of failure to provide such information, including details of the offences provided for in section 14A of the Act for failing to provide, or providing false, information.

**Figures calculated using gross receipts less deductions**

3.647    8.—(1) Where—

(a)  the conditions of paragraph 7(6) are not satisfied; or

(b)  the Secretary of State accepts that it is not reasonably practicable for the self-employed earner to provide information relating to his gross earnings from self-employment in the forms submitted to, or as issued or revised by, the Inland Revenue; or;

(c)  in the opinion of the Secretary of State, information as to the gross earnings of the self-employed earner which has satisfied the criteria set out in paragraph 7 does not accurately reflect the normal weekly earnings of the self-employed earner,

net income means in the case of employment as a self-employed earner his earnings calculated by reference to the gross receipts [¹in respect of employment which are of a type which would be taken into account under paragraph 7(1)] less the deductions provided for in sub-paragraph (2).

(2) The deductions to be taken from the gross receipts to calculate net earnings for the purposes of this paragraph are—

(a)  any expenses which are reasonably incurred and are wholly and exclusively defrayed for the purposes of the earner's business in the period by reference to which his earnings are determined under paragraph 9(2) or (3);

(b)  any value added tax paid in the period by reference to which his earnings are determined in excess of value added tax received in that period;

(c)  any amount in respect of income tax determined in accordance with sub-paragraph (4);

(d)  any amount of National Insurance contributions determined in accordance with sub-paragraph (4); and

(e)  any premium paid by the non-resident parent in respect of a retirement annuity contract or a personal pension scheme or, where that scheme is intended partly to provide a capital sum to discharge a mortgage or a charge secured upon the parent's home, 75 per cent of contributions payable.

(3) For the purposes of sub-paragraph (2)(a)—

(a)  such expenses include—

(i)  repayment of capital on any loan used for the replacement, in the course of business, of equipment or machinery, or the repair of an existing business asset except to the extent that any sum is payable under an insurance policy for its repair;

(ii)  any income expended in the repair of an existing business asset except to the extent that any sum is payable under an insurance policy for its repair; and

(iii)  any payment of interest on a loan taken out for the purposes of the business;

(b)  such expenses do not include—

(i)  repayment of capital on any other loan taken out for the purposes of the business;

(ii)  any capital expenditure;

(iii)  the depreciation of any capital assets;

(iv)  any sum employed, or intended to be employed, in the setting up or expansion of the business;

(v)  any loss incurred before the beginning of the period by reference to which earnings are determined;

(vi)  any expenses incurred in providing business entertainment; or

(vii)  any loss incurred in any other employment in which he is engaged as a self-employed earner.

(4) For the purposes of sub-paragraph (2)(c) and (d), the amounts in respect of income tax and National Insurance contributions to be deducted from the gross receipts shall be deter-

mined in accordance with paragraph 7(4) and (5) of this Schedule as if in paragraph 7(4) references to gross earnings were references to taxable earnings and in this subparagraph "taxable earnings" means the gross receipts of the earner less the deductions mentioned in sub-paragraph (2)(a) and (b).

### Rules for calculation under paragraph 8

**9.**—(1) This paragraph applies only where the net income of a self-employed earner is calculated or estimated under paragraph 8 of this Schedule.

**3.648**

(2) Where—

(a) a non-resident parent has been a self-employed earner for 52 weeks or more, including the relevant week, the amount of his net weekly income shall be determined by reference to the average of the earnings which he has received in the 52 weeks ending with the relevant week; or

(b) a non-resident parent has been a self-employed earner for a period of less than 52 weeks including the relevant week, the amount of his net weekly income shall be determined by reference to the average of the earnings which he has received during that period.

(3) Where a calculation would, but for this sub-paragraph, produce an amount which, in the opinion of the Secretary of State, does not accurately reflect the normal weekly income of the non-resident parent in question, such earnings, or any part of them, shall be calculated by reference to such other period as may, in the particular case, enable the normal weekly earnings of the non-resident parent to be determined more accurately and for this purpose the Secretary of State shall have regard to—

(a) the earnings from self-employment received, or due to be received, by him; and

(b) the duration and pattern, or the expected duration and pattern, of any self-employment of that non-resident parent.

[⁴. . .]

### Income from board or lodging

**10.** In a case where a non-resident parent is a self-employed earner who provides board and lodging, his earnings shall include payments received for that provision where those payments are the only or main source of income of that earner.

**3.649**

PART IV

TAX CREDITS

### [⁶Working tax credit]

**11.**—(1) Subject to [⁷sub-paragraph (2)], payments by way of [⁶working tax credit] [⁸. . .], shall be treated as the income of the non-resident parent where he has qualified for them by his engagement in, and normal engagement in, remunerative work, at the rate payable at the effective date.

**3.650**

(2) Where [⁶working tax credit] is payable and the amount which is payable has been calculated by reference to [⁹the earnings] of the non-resident parent and another person—

(a) where during the period which is used by the Inland Revenue to calculate his income [¹⁰the earnings] [¹¹. . .] of that parent exceed those of the other person, the amount payable by way of [⁶working tax credit] shall be treated as the income of that parent;

(b) where during the period [¹⁰the earnings] of that parent equal those of the other person, half of the amount payable by way of [⁶working tax credit] shall be treated as the income of that parent; and

(c) where during that period [¹⁰the earnings] of that parent are less than those of that other person, the amount payable by way of [⁶working tax credit] shall not be treated as the income of that parent.

[¹²(2A) For the purposes of this paragraph, "earnings" means the employment income and the income from self-employment of the non-resident parent and the other person referred to in sub-paragraph (2), as determined for the purposes of their entitlement to working tax credit.]
[¹³. . .]

**Employment Credits**

3.651    **12.** Payments made by way of employment credits under section 2(1) of the Employment and Training Act 1973 to a non-resident parent who is participating in a scheme arranged under section 2(2) of the Employment and Training Act 1973 and known as the New Deal 50 plus shall be treated as the income of the non-resident parent, at the rate payable at the effective date.
[¹⁴. . .]

**[²Child tax credit**

3.652    **13A.** Payments made by way of child tax credit to a non-resident parent or his partner at the rate payable at the effective date.]

## PART V

### OTHER INCOME

**Amount**

3.653    **14.** The amount of other income to be taken into account in calculating or estimating net weekly income shall be the aggregate of the payments to which paragraph 15 applies, net of any income tax deducted and otherwise determined in accordance with this Part.

**Types**

3.654    **15.** This paragraph applies to any periodic payment of pension or other benefit under an occupational or personal pension scheme or a retirement annuity contract or other such scheme for the provision of income in retirement whether or not approved by the Inland Revenue.

**Calculation or estimate and period**

3.655    **16.**—(1) The amount of any income to which this Part applies shall be calculated or estimated—

(a)  where it has been received in respect of the whole of the period of 26 weeks which ends at the end of the relevant week, by dividing such income received in that period by 26;

(b)  where it has been received in respect of part of the period of 26 weeks which ends at the end of the relevant week, by dividing such income received in that period by the number of complete weeks in respect of which such income is received and for this purpose income shall be treated as received in respect of a week if it is received in respect of any day in the week in question.

(2) Where a calculation or estimate to which this Part applies would, but for this subparagraph, produce an amount which, in the opinion of the Secretary of State, does not accurately reflect the normal amount of the other income of the non-resident parent in question, such income, or any part of it, shall be calculated by reference to such other period as may, in the particular case, enable the other income of that parent to be determined more accurately and for this purpose the Secretary of State shall have regard to the nature and pattern of receipt of such income.

### [¹⁶Part VI

### BENEFITS, PENSIONS AND ALLOWANCES

**17.**—(1) Subject to paragraph (2), the net weekly income of a non-resident parent shall include payments made by way of benefits, pensions and allowances prescribed in regulation

4 for the purposes of paragraph 4(1)(b) and (c) of Schedule 1 to the Act, to a non-resident parent or his partner at the rate payable at the effective date.

(2) Paragraph (1) applies only for the purpose of establishing whether the non-resident parent is a person to whom paragraph 5(b) of Schedule 1 to the Act applies.]

AMENDMENTS

1. Regulation 7(2) of the Miscellaneous Amendments Regulations 2002 (April 30, 2002).

2. Regulation 8(4)(e) of the Miscellaneous Amendments Regulations 2003 (April 6, 2003).

3. Regulation 8(4)(a) of the Miscellaneous Amendments Regulations 2003 (April 6, 2003).

4. Regulation 8(4)(b) of the Miscellaneous Amendments Regulations 2003 (April 6, 2003).

5. Regulation 8(4)(b) of the Miscellaneous Amendments Regulations 2003 (April 6, 2003).

6. Regulation 8(4)(c)(i) of the Miscellaneous Amendments Regulations 2003 (April 6, 2003).

7. Regulation 8(4)(c)(ii)(aa) of the Miscellaneous Amendments Regulations 2003 (April 6, 2003).

8. Regulation 8(4)(c)(ii)(bb) of the Miscellaneous Amendments Regulations 2003 (April 6, 2003).

9. Regulation 8(4)(c)(iii)(aa) of the Miscellaneous Amendments Regulations 2003 (April 6, 2003).

10. Regulation 8(4)(c)(iii)(bb) of the Miscellaneous Amendments Regulations 2003 (April 6, 2003).

11. Regulation 8(4)(c)(iii)(cc) of the Miscellaneous Amendments Regulations 2003 (April 6, 2003).

12. Regulation 8(4)(c)(iv) of the Miscellaneous Amendments Regulations 2003 (April 6, 2003).

13. Regulation 8(4)(c)(v) of the Miscellaneous Amendments Regulations 2003 (April 6, 2003).

14. Regulation 8(4)(d) of the Miscellaneous Amendments Regulations 2003 (April 6, 2003).

15. Regulation 7(3) of the Miscellaneous Amendments Regulations 2004 (September 16, 2004).

16. Regulation 7(3) of the Miscellaneous Amendments Regulations 2004 (September 16, 2004).

17. Regulation 6(5) of the Miscellaneous Amendments Regulations 2005 (March 16, 2005).

18. Article 54 of the Fire and Rescue Services Act 2004 (Consequential Amendments) (England) Order 2004 (December 30, 2004)—NB applies only to England.

DEFINITIONS

"the Act": see reg.1(2).
"child tax credit": see reg.1(2)
"Contributions and Benefits Act": see reg.1(2).
"Contributions and Benefits (Northern Ireland) Act": see reg.1(2).
"day": see reg.1(2).
"effective date": see reg.1(2).
"employed earner": see reg.1(2).
"home": see reg.1(2).

3.656

"net weekly income": see reg.1(2).
"occupational pension scheme": see reg.1(2).
"partner": see reg.1(2).
"personal pension scheme": see reg.1(2).
"relevant week": see reg.1(2).
"retirement annuity contract": see reg.1(2).
"self-employed earner": see reg.1(2).
"working tax credit": see reg.1(2).
"year": see reg.1(2).

GENERAL NOTE

**3.657**    The correct approach to questions such as those which arise under this Schedule was set out in the context of income tax law by Lord Blanesburgh in *British Insulated and Helsby Cables Ltd v Atherton* [1925] All E.R. Rep. 623 at 637 as follows: "unless the context otherwise requires a different meaning to be placed upon them, such words as 'profits,' 'gains,' 'capital,' are to be construed according to their ordinary significance in commerce or accountancy." This approach has been followed and affirmed repeatedly, as in *Odeon Associated Theatres Ltd v Jones* [1972] 1 All E.R. 681 and has been applied to social security law (*R(FC) 1/91*, para.38; *CIS 5481/97*, paras 14–15). The same approach will certainly be taken in child support law. For a discussion of this approach in the context of expenses, see the note below.

*Income*
    This schedule is concerned with income. It, indeed child support law as a whole, is only concerned with capital in so far as that capital is a source or potential source of income. Accordingly, receipts are only relevant if they are income as opposed to capital receipts, except and in so far as legislation provides otherwise (*CCS 15949/96*, para.5). It is the nature of the payment as it is received that determines its proper classification as income or capital rather than its nature as paid (*Brumby v Milner* [1976] 3 All E.R. 636). The distinction is a question of fact that depends, in a commercial context, on the accepted principles of commercial accountancy (*CIS 5481/97*, paras 14–15). The treatment of a payment in a person's accounts is a relevant, but not a decisive, factor (*IRC v Land Securities Investment Trust Ltd* [1969] 2 All E.R. 430). Money received from the sale of assets which are not part of the normal subject matter of the business will be capital. In the case of drawings it is necessary to decide whether they are drawings from capital or income (*R(FC) 1/91*, para.38).
    Outside a commercial context, the distinction between income and capital was considered by the Court of Appeal in *Morrell v Secretary of State for Work and Pensions* reported as *R(IS) 6/03*. In that case, a mother had made regular payments to her daughter to meet her financial commitments following a divorce. The sums were paid on the understanding that they would be repaid as and when the daughter's circumstances allowed. The court held that the distinction depended on the ordinary and natural meaning of the words (para.31). Applying that test, the payments by the mother were income in the daughter's hands. This was not affected by the future and uncertain obligation to repay (para.33). The position would have been different if the daughter had been under a certain and immediate obligation to repay (para.33). Thorpe L.J. said (para.57): "Regular recurring payments designed to meet outgoings might serve as one definition of income." Richards J. left open the issue whether regularity or recurrence was essential (para.35). In *CH 3393/03*, the Commissioner held that regularity was to be found in the presence of a regular funding facility that could be used as and when necessary (para.9). In *CH 3013/03*, the Commissioner (without having had argument on the point) suggested that regular withdrawals under an overdraft facility were not income (para.47).

Dividend income is not income for the Schedule assessment (*CCS 2433/04*). However, the dividend arrangement may be a sham or may not have been properly authorised by the company. Another possibility is that it may be taken into account by way of a variation under reg.19 of the Variation Regulations, which has been amended to make clear that it covers income taken in the form of dividends. However, the variation route is not as satisfactory for persons with care as the Schedule assessment, because it contains discretions that do not apply under the Schedule.

*Expenses*

There is no burden of proof in relation to expenses. The tribunal should come to a common sense decision and if necessary make a fair apportion allowable and non-allowable expenses. See *R(CS) 10/98*, para.12.

**3.658**

The terms used in the provisions dealing with expenses are similar to those used in income tax law in ss.74(a) and 198(1) of the Income and Corporation Taxes Act 1988. Accordingly the authorities on the interpretation and application of those sections may be useful in the interpreting and applying the relevant provisions of this Schedule (*R(FC) 1/91*, para.30). However, as there are differences between the relevant provisions of tax and child support law, the authorities will not necessarily be relevant (*R(CS) 6/98*, para.7). (i) In the case of self-employed earners the expenses must be reasonably incurred. There is no such requirement in tax law. (ii) In both tax law and child support law the requirement that expenses of self-employed earners must be wholly and exclusively defrayed for the purposes of the business is a necessary but not a sufficient condition for the expense to be deductible. The additional condition in each case is different. In tax law the expense must be an appropriate item to set against income (*British Insulated and Helsby Cables Ltd v Atherton* [1925] All E.R. Rep. 623). This is not the case in child support law, although there are some items of expenditure which are expressly excluded from being deductible. In child support law, on the other hand, the additional condition is that the expenditure must be reasonably incurred. (iii) In tax law an employed earner's travelling expenses are subject only to the requirement that they are necessarily incurred in the performance of the employment (*MacLean v Trembath* [1956] 2 All E.R. 113 at 119, *per* Roxburgh J.), whereas in child support law they are subject to the same test as for other expenses (*i.e.* wholly, exclusively and necessarily incurred). (iv) In child support law some deductions which would be relevant in tax law are expressly excluded (*e.g.* depreciation).

Subject to the above considerations, the treatment of an alleged expense by the Inland Revenue in an individual case before a tribunal should always be considered. However, care must be taken in adopting the Revenue's approach (*R(CS) 6/98*, para.7; *CCS 2750/95*, para.22; *CCS 12073/96*, para.12; *CCS 12769/96*, para.6). (i) As explained above, there are differences between tax law and child support law which may require a different approach. (ii) The tribunal may not know the evidence upon which the income tax assessment was calculated. (iii) In so far as this is not known, the tribunal cannot be sure that the issues have been investigated by the Revenue in the way that is obligatory for a tribunal. The different evidence before a tribunal and its assessment of the weight to be given to that evidence may, even where the relevant laws are in identical terms, justify a different application. (iv) The other party will not have had an opportunity to make representations on the point to the Revenue. (v) Moreover, the decision made by the tribunal is a separate issue from the application of income tax law by the Inland Revenue and *res judicata* does not apply. (vi) It will be relevant to consider whether there is any binding case law or statute law in the income tax context in deciding whether or not to rely on the approach taken by the Revenue (*CCS 318/95* para.11). (vii) The revenue's decision may have been based on an extra-statutory concession which must be disregarded in the child support calculation. In view of all these factors the tribunal must make a decision, and not merely accept the Revenue's application of tax law, even if that decision is in the end the same as the Revenue's. See also the general warning against using tax reasoning in child support in *CCS 318/98*.

Despite all the above qualifications, there are at least two cases in which it is appropriate to follow the approach taken by the Revenue in a particular case. (a) Where the sum involved is small and the other party makes no representations on the point, the tribunal may adopt the figure used by the Revenue (*CCS 12073/96*, para.7). (b) Strictly there should be evidence from which the tribunal may calculate the actual amount spent. However, where it is obvious that there has been some expenditure and the precise amount cannot be ascertained, an estimate has to be made, and in an appropriate case the tribunal may adopt the figure used by the Revenue (*CCS 12073/96*, para.7).

Any agreement involving the employer, the Revenue and the Child Support Agency cannot bind the tribunal is not binding on the tribunal if it is in conflict with child support law (*CCS 318/95*, paras 11 and 15).

*"expenses"*

"Expenses" bears its normal meaning as understood by the accountancy and commercial worlds and the Inland Revenue (*CFC 19/93*, para.11). Only expenses of an income or revenue nature are covered except and in so far as legislation provides otherwise (*CCS 15949/96*, para.5).

Expense necessarily involves expenditure. (a) Accordingly, a loss which does not involve expenditure, such as a loss on revaluation of stock, is not an expense. (b) This also explains why depreciation is expressly excluded from consideration by para.3(4)(b)(iii). However, all or part of the expenditure incurred in replacing the asset may be allowable when it defrayed. (c) Bad debts do not involve expenditure; they merely represent money which is due but which has not been paid. If proven, the figure for bad debts should be deducted from the income figure in the accounts; these debts are not subject to the tests for deductible expenses. They are deductible despite the lack of express provision to cover them (*R(FC) 1/91*, para.37). However, the debts must relate to the current accounting period, as losses previously incurred are expressly excluded from being deductible as expenses by para.3(4)(b)(v). (d) Lost or spoilt stock is a genuine loss to the business in that the value of the stock will not be recouped through sales or work done. However, it should not be deducted as an expense. It is already covered as an expense under the figure for purchases (see below) and to include it again would be to double count it.

Expenditure on stock is an expense. The proper approach to figures relating to stock is to take the opening stock figure, add to it the purchases of stock during the period of the accounts, and then to deduct the closing stock figure (*CFC 19/93*). The closing stock figure will be the opening stock figure in the following accounting period. If it were not deducted, it would be double counted in successive accounting periods.

Income tax and interest on any money borrowed to meet liability to income tax is not an expense (*CCS 15949/96*, para.10). Rolled over liability for capital gains tax is not an allowable expense (*R2/96(CSC)*, para.13).

*Employed earners*

In the case of employed earners, payments in respect of expenses are disregarded as earnings if they were incurred wholly, exclusively and necessarily in the performance of the duties of the employment (para.4(2)(a)). The disregard applies to expenses paid by the employer, not those paid by the employee (*R(CS) 2/96*, para.15). It applies whether the expenses are reimbursed to the employee (*ibid.*, at para.15) or directly to the third party to whom they are due (*CIS 77/92*, para.5). As interpreted, the disregard prevents the amount of the expenses being double counted, once as part of the original wages and again when met by the employer. If the employer pays the expenses without being reimbursed, there is no disregard.

Commissioners have applied the reasoning in *Parsons v Hogg* [1985] 2 All E.R. 897 both to expenses wholly, exclusively and necessarily incurred in the performance of the duties of the employment and to other expenses that are deductible for tax purposes (*R(CS) 2/96* and *CCS 3882/97*, paras 29–36). *Parsons v Hogg* involved the interpretation of the brief provisions in the Family Income Supplement Regulations that governed the calculation of a claimant's income. The court used the ambiguity in the word "gross" to avoid what would otherwise have been an anomaly between the calculation of earnings from employment and other income, including income from self-employment. Gross was interpreted to mean income before the deduction of tax but after the deduction of allowable expenses. In contrast, the child support provisions are much more detailed. So far as expenses wholly, exclusively and necessarily incurred are concerned, there is specific provision and no anomaly exists between the employed and the self-employed. So far as other expenses are concerned, the question arises whether they should be added to the deductions already covered by statute by applying the reasoning in *Parsons v Hogg*. It is suggested that the reasoning in that case should not be used to extend the detailed scheme in this Schedule. This was the approach taken in *R(CS) 3/00*, para.23.

*"wholly, exclusively and necessarily"*

Each of these words covers a separate requirement. Their combined effect is so  **3.659**
strict that it has been said in the income tax context that they are "deceptive words in the sense that, when examined, they are found to come to nearly nothing at all" (*Lomax v Newton* [1952] 2 All E.R. 801 at 802, *per* Vaisey, J.). It should not, therefore, be surprising that in the child support context their scope will be equally narrow.

The words "wholly" and "exclusively" are discussed below in the context of self-employed earners. In addition the expense must be a necessary one. The fact that the expense is related to the employment and even is beneficial to the employer is not sufficient; it must also be essential to incur the expense in order to perform the duties of the employment (*Owen v Burden* [1972] 1 All E.R. 356).

These words do not involve any element of subjectivity and none is imported where, in a particular case, it is necessary to estimate the amount of expenses (*CCS 12073/96*, para.14).

*"in the performance of the duties of the employment"*

The expenses must be incurred in the performance of the duties of the employment. It is not sufficient that they are a necessary preliminary to or preparation for performing those duties (*Smith v Abbott* [1994] 1 All E.R. 673; *R(CS) 2/96*, para.27; *CCS 5352/95*, para.12; *CSC 1/96*, para.5).

It follows from this principle that the cost of travel to work is not an allowable expense (*Rickets v Colquhoun* [1926] A.C. 1), while the cost of travel in the course of work is (*Horton v Young* [1971] 3 All E.R. 412; *Owen v Pook* [1969] 2 All E.R. 1). Likewise the costs related to living in a particular place are not generally allowable. There have been decisions relating to the armed forces: expenses incurred in Army married quarters are not deductible (*R(CS) 2/96*)); a lodging allowance for an officer living in London while attached to the Ministry of Defence counted as income and was not disregarded as repayment of a deductible expense (*CCS 5352/95*, para.12). In *CCS 318/95*, para.14 payments of an allowance to a soldier relating to living abroad on service duties were disregarded as income on the basis that they were repayments of a deductible expense. In *CCS 4305/95* the Commissioner decided, without reference to any authorities other than *R(CS) 2/96* and *Parsons v Hogg* [1985] 2 All E.R. 897, that the amount spent on married quarters by an army officer posted abroad was deductible as an expense. The former case was tightly distinguished in *CCS 5352/95*, para.14 on the basis that it applied only to the special facts of a soldier living abroad. There have also been decisions relating to police officers. Police officers may be subject to one of three arrangements in respect of subsidised housing, the actual arrangement depending upon the date of their appointment. The original arrangement was for a rent allowance which attracts a tax rebate at the end of the tax year. This was replaced by a housing allowance which attracts no rebate. The most recent appointees have no housing subsidy. In *CCS 10/94*, para.13 payments of a police rent allowance were treated as income and not as repayment of a deductible expense. This decision was not followed in *CCS 12769/96*, para.9 on the ground that the additional factual information available as to the nature of the allowance showed that it was a deductible expense. However, in *R(CS) 10/98*, paras 14–17 the Commissioner held that *CCS 12769/96* was an exceptional one which turned on its own special facts and in *R(CS) 2/99*, para.20 the Commissioner reviewed various reports on housing subsidies for police officers and refused to follow *CCS 12769/96* on the ground that the appellant in that case had misunderstood the nature of the allowance. The decision in *R(CS) 2/99* was followed by a different Commissioner in *CCS 2561/98*, para.22.

### Self-employed earners

In the case of self-employed earners expenses are deducted from gross receipts in determining earnings. In order to be deductible an expenses must satisfy two tests: (i) it must have been reasonably incurred, and (ii) it must have been wholly and exclusively defrayed for the purposes of the earner's business.

The following are among the sorts of expenses which will typically be allowable in the case of self-employed earners: (i) costs related to the provision of premises—rent, rates, heating, lighting, cleaning, maintenance; (ii) wages for employees and payments to subcontractors; (iii) cost of materials; (iv) costs involved in obtaining work—advertising; (v) costs related to vehicles and travel; (vi) telephone—line rental and charges; (vii) necessary registrations such as CORGI; (viii) insurance; (ix) protective clothing; (x) accountancy fees.

In the case of a partnership, the partnership is not to be regarded (as would be a company) as a separate entity from its members nor is the position of a partner to be equated with that of an employee. The relevant purpose to be considered (see below for a discussion of purpose) is that of the individual partner who defrayed the expenditure and not the collective view of the firm as a whole or of the managing partners. See *MacKinlay v Arthur Young McClelland Moores and Co* [1990] 1 All E.R. 45.

### *"reasonably incurred"*

3.660    This is a matter of judgment (*CCS 3774/01*, para.9). There is no restriction on the factors which may be taken into account in deciding on the reasonableness of an expense. It might be considered unreasonable in view of the amount, in which case it would only be allowed in so far as it was reasonable. Another possibility is that it might be considered unreasonable on account of the nature or purpose of the expense, in which case it will be completely disallowed. Much depends on the circumstances. For example, where wages are paid to a spouse for doing the paperwork of the business, those wages might be considered too high for the work involved, in which case the amount appearing in the accounts would be reduced; or it might be that the nature and amount of the paperwork is such that the earner could cope with it without assistance, in which case no deduction would be allowed at all. Whatever its decision on reasonableness, the tribunal should explain the basis of that decision in its reasons.

### *"wholly and exclusively"*

These words are also used in relation to employed earners. However, here they are not linked to any requirement that the expense be necessarily defrayed for the purposes of the business (*Bentleys, Stokes and Lowless v Beeson* [1952] 2 All E.R. 82 at 86, *per* Romer L.J.).

The word "wholly" relates to the quantum of money spent (*Bentleys, Stokes and Lowless v Beeson* [1952] 2 All E.R. 82 at 84, *per* Romer L.J.).

The word "exclusively" further limits the words "for the purposes of the earner's business." It relates to the motive or object of the expenditure. The expense must be incurred solely in the performance of the duties. If it is defrayed solely for personal benefit, it is not allowable. The cost of personal meals while on business is not, therefore, allowable, because the expenditure is adequately and completely explained by the simple fact that a person must eat in order to live (*Caillebotte v Quinn* [1975] 2 All E.R. 412). Thus the cost of lunches taken at meetings of partners in a solicitors' firm was not deductible as an expense (*CCS 15949/96*, para.11) If the expense is defrayed for a dual purpose, it is not allowable. An expense is not, for example, allowable if it involves the cost of travel for the purpose of attending a conference and thereby also having a holiday (*Bowden v Rusell and Russell* [1965] 2 All E.R. 258). However, there is no dual purpose merely because there is some element of personal benefit necessarily inherent in what is done (*Bentleys, Stokes and Lowless v Beeson* [1952] 2 All E.R. 82). Consequently, where the sole object of undertaking an expenditure is for the purposes of the business (for example, travelling to visit a patient in the South of France), but there is an unavoidable personal benefit also involved (the earner's stay in the South of France), the expense is potentially deductible (*Mallalieu v Drummond* [1983] 2 All E.R. 1095 at 1100, *per* Lord Brightman).

The conscious motive of the earner is of vital significance (*Mallalieu v Drummond*, above at 1103 *per* Lord Brightman); it was because of the admission of the mixed motives that the expenditure incurred in *Bowden*, above was not treated as a deductible expense for income tax purposes. However, conscious motive is not necessarily the sole relevant factor. Where it is inescapable that there is some other relevant object such as the provision of clothing for warmth and decency, the object immediately in the person's mind will not be decisive of the issue (*Mallalieu v Drummond* [1983] 2 All E.R. 1095 at 1103, *per* Lord Brightman). On the other hand, where some further motive is not inescapable, such as where elective surgery is involved, a finding as to conscious motive may be decisive (*Prince v Mapp* [1970] 1 All E.R. 519 where Pennycuick J., having held that a musician had a dual business-personal motive for undergoing elective surgery on a tendon, suggested that a finding that the musician's sole motive in having the operation related to his professional rather than to his personal life might have led to the expense being deductible.) Cases in which particular attention must be paid to motivation on account of the likelihood of there being an inescapable personal object are those which involve expenditure on the provision of the everyday necessities of life required by a living human being, such as clothing suitable for everyday use for warmth and decency (*ibid.* at 1103 *per* Lord Brightman), health (*Norman v Golder* [1945] 1 All E.R. 352; *Murgatroyd v Evans-Jackson* [1967] 1 All E.R. 881), food (*Caillebotte*, above) and housing (*MacKinlay v Arthur Young McClelland Moores and Co* [1990] 1 All E.R. 45; *R(CS) 6/98*, para.8 where the Commissioner considered it to be unarguable in the context of the case that money spent on purchasing a house was deductible, although see above for some exceptional cases). However, care must be taken in analysing the facts and applying the principles which emerge from these cases. Accommodation whilst travelling, for example to a conference, is not to be confused with the provision for housing and is not required to provide for the persons' needs as human beings since they will have homes (*Watkis v Ashford Sparkes and Harward* [1985] 2 All E.R. 916 at 933 *per* Nourse, J.). There may even be special facts which make the principle inapplicable in the case of meals, as in *Horton v Young* (1930) 15 T.C. 380 (discussed in *Caillebotte*, above at 416), where the cost of meals purchased by an airline pilot while abroad and not reimbursed by the airline was allowed as a deductible expense for income tax purposes in view of the special nature of the terms of his employment.

A dual purpose is also likely to be present in the case of expenditure defrayed in pursuing professional qualification in that the qualification will probably be for the personal benefit of the earner as well as for the benefit of the business (*Lupton v Potts* [1969] 3 All E.R. 1083). Likewise action taken to protect professional standing is likely also to be concerned with the person's personal reputation which will inevitably be affected by the outcome of such proceedings (*McKnight v Sheppard, The Times*, May 12, 1997). Nevertheless, if it can be established as a fact that the sole conscious motive was the person's business standing, the expense will be deductible (*ibid.*).

Difficult issues of fact can arise when the expenses of a franchise holder are involved. In *Powell v Jackman, The Times*, April 1, 2004, the taxpayer held a franchise for milk delivery. He used his home as an office, but his round was some distance away. The Court of Appeal decided that his expenses of travelling from his home to his round were not incurred wholly and exclusively for the purposes of his trade.

*"for the purposes of the earner's business"*

**3.661**    These words are inextricably linked to the words "wholly and exclusively" which are discussed above. Expenses incurred in respect of the purchase of a share in a business are not incurred for the purposes of the business, even if that money was immediately used to purchase assets for the business (*CCS 15949/96*, para.7).

Expenditure on preventing a person being disabled from carrying on, and earnings profits from, a trade are in principle deductible (*Morgan v Tate and Lyle Ltd* [1954] 2 All E.R. 413), and such expenditure may include legal expenses (*McKnight v Sheppard, The Times*, May 12, 1997).

In *CCS 318/95*, para.13 the Commissioner expressly refrained from commenting on whether approtionment of expenses was appropriate or desirable in the child support context. However, on the basis that the position taken in income tax law and social security law will be adopted, the position is as follows. In so far as expenditure relates to both business and personal use (*R(FC) 1/91*, paras 26–35)) or to two or more businesses (*CFC 836/95*, para.11), such as a telephone line rental, it may be possible to apportion it between those uses and only the relevant business portion taken into account as an expense. Any apportionment which has been accepted by the Inland Revenue for tax purposes may be relied upon by the CSAT if there is no evidence to the contrary (*R(FC) 1/91*, para.39), but tribunals should bear in mind the comments above on the value of Inland Revenue decisions in deciding whether to investigate beyond the accepted figure. Moreover, tribunals must distinguish between cases where apportionment is appropriate and cases where there is a single expense incurred for a dual purpose such that the expense is not incurred wholly and exclusively for business purposes. The test of whether apportionment in possible is whether it is possible to apportion the expense on a time basis (*Caillebotte v Quinn* [1975] 2 All E.R. 412 at 416–417, *per* Templeman J.; *R(FC) 1/91*, para.34). If this is possible, the expense is apportionable; otherwise it is not. Whether or not apportionment is possible is a question of law (*R(FC) 1/91*, para.35), but the actual apportionment is a question of fact (*ibid.*, para.35).

Where an allowance is made in respect of the use of the home as an office, this should also be reflected in an apportionment of housing costs under Sch.3, para.5.

*Paragraph 4(1)*

This subparagraph defines the types of payment which count as earnings, subject to the exclusions in subpara.(2). The definition is in two parts. The basic definition is that earnings are any remuneration or profit derived from the employment. For doubts about the precise scope of remuneration and profit, see *CCS 284/99*, para.15. The words "derived from" are wide and mean "having their origin in"

*(R(SB) 21/86*, para.12). They apply even though the employment is a past one and where the payment is awarded by a statutory body such as an Employment Tribunal (*ibid.*, at para.12). They cover all payments whether by an employer or by a third party, such as a tip (*CCS 1992/97* paras 38–39), but not dividend income which derives not from a person's employment but from ownership of shares in the company (*CCS 2433/04*, para.90). This basic definition is expanded to include the matters set out in heads (a) to (e). These heads either cover payments which are not already covered by the basic definition or avoid argument on matters that might otherwise give rise to doubt. The list is not exhaustive, so items of income which do not fall within the precise terms of a particular head may nonetheless be caught by the generality of the basic definition. In *R(CS) 8/98*, para.24 the Commissioner, who admitted not to have seen the terms under which such allowances are paid, thought it probable that an education allowance paid to a member of the armed forces might amount to remuneration derived from the person's employment. For another example, see the general note to para.4(1)(b) below.

If an army officer retires and is then reinstated, a reduction in pay under Art.395 of the Army Pensions Warrant 1977 to reflect commutations of pension are not part of remuneration or profit derived from the officer's employment (*CCS 4144/01*).

In determining earnings the figure to be used is the amount of earnings before deduction of tax but after the deduction of expenses deductible in arriving at the taxable sum (*R(CS) 2/96*, para.17). The tribunal is not bound by any determination on this issue by the income tax authorities, but it should take such determination into account (*ibid.*, para.26).

In *CCS 4378/01*, the Commissioner held that an overpayment of salary was not remuneration that was derived from the parent's employment. The overpayment arose when the parent was transferred to a different job with the same employer at a lower salary. By mistake, his salary was not adjusted for some time. The overpayment was taken into account as his income for the purposes of child support maintenance. When the overpayment was recovered from his salary in instalments, no allowance was made for the deduction. The Commissioner considered two decisions of the Court of Appeal: *R. v Bolton Supplementary Benefits Appeal Tribunal Ex p. Fordham* [1981] 1 All E.R. 50 and *Leeves v Chief Adjudication Officer*, reported as *R(IS) 5/99*. He decided that the words "remuneration or profit derived from that employment" had to be interpreted in the context of the Schedule as a whole, specifically in the context of Pt I. The purpose of the calculation was to identify the net earnings that are available to the absent parent and from which the parent's liability for child support maintenance must be met. Given that there was no power to take account of the deduction by way of recovery, he considered that there was obvious sense in excluding the overpayment itself from the scope of the parent's earnings in order to prevent the parent incurring a double penalty. He found some, albeit limited, support for that conclusion in what is now para.4(2)(e), which excludes advances of salary from earnings. In applying that interpretation to the facts of the case, the Commissioner emphasised that the parent was aware at the time when the overpayment was made (i) that it had occurred, (ii) the amount and (iii) that he was under a duty to repay it. This brought the case within the principle in *Leeves* and outside the principle in *Bolton*, in which these matters were uncertain.

*Employment compensation*

A person may receive compensation for breach of employment rights under a variety of enactments. Some of these are covered by the individual heads of para.4(1), specifically heads (a), (b) and (e). In so far as these heads do not cover all possibilites it is necessary to consider whether the payments are caught by the opening words as being "remuneration or profit derived from . . . employment". Specifically these words will have to cover compensation under s.65(1)(b) of the Sex Discrimination Act 1975, s.56(1)(b) of the Race Relations Act 1976 and **3.662** s.8(2)(b) of the Disability Discrimination Act 1995. The opening general words are slightly different from those used in the social security legislation dealt with in the cases considered below, but it is suggested that the differences do not amount to distinctions which justify a different interpretation.

Payments of compensation are only taken into account as earnings in so far as they are income rather than capital payments. In particular a distinction is drawn between a payment which is calculated largely or exclusively by reference to past services and is, therefore, in the nature of a redundancy payment, and a payment which is calculated largely or exclusively by reference to loss of income. The former are treated as payments of capital and include a basic award for unfair dismissal under s.118(I)(a) of the Employment Rights Act 1996 (*R(SB) 21/86*, para.6), compensation for injured feelings and loss of a tax rebate under the Sex Discrimination Act 1975 (*CIS 590/93*, para.5) and severance payments which are based largely on length of service in the armed forces (*R. v National Insurance Commissioner Ex p. Stratton* [1979] 2 All E.R. 278). The latter are treated as payments of income and include a compensatory award for unfair dismissal under s.118(1)(b) of the Employment Rights Act 1996 (*R(SB) 21/86*) whether or not the contract of employment is for a fixed term (*CIS 590/93*, para.7) and compensation for loss of earnings under the Sex Discrimination Act 1975 (*CIS 590/93*, para.7). It is the essential character of the compensation which is important and this is not affected by the presence of some minor unquantified additional element (*R. v National Insurance Commissioner Ex p. Stratton* [1979] 2 All E.R. 278), although where that element is quantifiable it is severed as in *CIS 590/93*, paras 3 and 5).

In *CCS 3182/95*, paras 17–19 the Commissioner considered the treatment of a sum of money paid in relation to the termination of a person's employment, such as a payment in relation to redundancy or failure to renew the employment at the end of maternity leave, whether or not the payment is called an *ex gratia* one. It was held that the payment was not part of the normal remuneration from the employment and was only to be taken into account if and in so far as it fell within head (e). Unfortunately the Commissioner did not consider any of the above decisions which give weight to the opening words of this subparagraph. It is suggested that this decision is confined to payments or parts of payments made by employers the purpose of which cannot be ascertained so as to determine, in accordance with the principles set out above, whether they are income or capital receipts.

*Paragraph 4(1)(a)*
The inclusion of overtime is for certainty. It falls anyway within the scope of "remuneration or profit derived from that employment" in the opening words of this paragraph (*CCS 656/97*, para.26). Payments in respect of overtime amount to earnings, even if the overtime is not guaranteed (*ibid.*, para.27).

Although payments for overtime count as earnings, it is not inevitable that overtime will be taken into account in the calculation of a party's earnings for the purposes of determining net income. The calculation of earnings has to be undertaken by reference to a period. The period is fixed by reference to para.6(1) below, which provides that a period is to be selected from specified weeks in order to calculate the party's *average* earnings. Once that calculation has been performed, para.6(4) has to be considered. It provides that a different period may be used if it would allow the party's *normal* earnings to be determined more accurately. Ultimately, therefore, the purpose of the calculation to be performed is the identification of the party's *normal* earnings. If overtime payments distort the party's earnings so that the calculation carried out under para.6(1) does not reflect the party's normal earnings, a different period must be used. See *CCS 656/97*, para.28 and the general note to para.6(4) below.

The cases are likely to fall into three broad categories. (i) First, there is the case where payments for overtime are so out of the ordinary that they may be disregarded as not reflecting normal earnings. This would cover a person who received a regular basic wage, but who worked overtime on a few occasions throughout the year. (ii) Second, there is the case where payments for overtime are clustered at a particular time of the year. In this case, a separate calculation for the period when overtime was worked might be appropriate. This would cover a person who received a regular basic wage, but who worked a significant amount of overtime for several weeks, for example around Christmas. (iii) Third, there is the case where the payments for overtime are spread throughout the year. In this case, an average figure for normal earnings may be appropriate. This would cover a person whose earnings were regularly supplemented by over-time, albeit that the overtime was of varying amounts and was not guaranteed. See *CCS 656/97*, para.30.

### Paragraph 4(1)(b)

In the social security context holiday pay means pay that is dependent upon enti-   **3.663** tlement to holidays. It covers pay whilst on holiday and pay in lieu of holidays that are not taken, for example at the end of an employment. It does not cover pay which is compensation for the absence of any entitlement to holidays (*CIS 894/94*). However, such pay is undoubtedly income and is part of the remuneration or profit derived from a person's employment. It is, therefore, caught by the opening words of para.4(1)

Holiday pay becomes payable on the day on which it first becomes due to be paid (*R(SB) 11/85*, para.16(1)). This may or may not coincide with the actual date of payment (*ibid.*). The date is determined by the contract of employment. Where evidence of the express terms of the contract is not available or the contract is silent on the point, it may be possible to infer that the date of actual payment is the date when it became due (*R(SB) 33/83*, para.21(3)). This may, however, not always be possible, for example, where the practice shows no consistency.

### Paragraph 4(1)(e)

See the introductory note on employment compensation.

### Paragraph 4(2)(a)

See the introductory note on expenses.

### Paragraph 4(2)(d)

In *CCS 318/98*, para.15 the Commissioner defined a payment in kind as a payment that is made otherwise than in money, that is, otherwise than in cash or in some form that can be immediately turned into cash, such as a cheque. The Commissioner gave a number of examples of the detailed analysis needed to distinguish between three cases. One example concerned the cost of childminding: (i) if this was arranged and paid for by the employee and the cost reimbursed by the employer, the amount is part of the employee's earnings; (ii) if this was arranged by the employee but the cost was actually paid by the employer, the amount is part of the employee's earnings by indirect payment; and (iii) if this was arranged and paid for by the employer, the benefit to the employee is a payment in kind (*ibid.*, para.30).

### Paragraph 4(2)(e)

This covers, for example, loans to buy season tickets and advances of monthly salary to tide the employee over the first month of employment. Advance of earnings must mean payments of earnings before the date on which the employee is contractually entitled to them. An advance is a payment on account of future earnings and will only count as such if it is expected that it will be repaid, for example by deductions from future salary payments (*R(CS) 6/98*, para.5). It is not clear whether the sums advanced must be treated as received when they were due to be received. Producing this obvious and sensible result from the Schedule is not easy. It is difficult to avoid the conclusion that the simplest possibility of an express provision dealing with this eventuality has been overlooked. The problem could be avoided by disregarding the period covered by the advance in calculating income in reliance on the power conferred by para.6(4). Another approach would be to treat the sums as being "remuneration or profit derived from the employment" under subpara.(1) on the date they were due. This is supported by the wording which refers to "advance of earnings" which suggests sums which would otherwise fall within subpara.(1) and that the payment is only disregarded for the period of the advance. If the advances are regular it might be possible to infer that the contractual basis of payment has been changed and the practice taken as evidence of the terms of the new agreement.

When an advance of earnings is repaid, the person's income is not thereby reduced (*CCS 5352/95*, para.20 and *R(CS) 6/98*, para.10).

*Paragraph 4(2)(j)*

This express provision avoids the need to make use of para.6(4) to produce a more accurate reflection of the parent's normal income.

*Paragraph 4(3)(c)*

This provision covers contributions made under retirement annuity contracts (*R(CS) 3/00*).

*Paragraph 6(1)*

**3.664**     This subparagraph and the relationship between it and subpara.(4) raise complex issues of interpretation and application. In considering their relationship, it is also necessary to consider the effect of reg.2(4) above: see the general note to subpara.(4) below.

The calculation of income must involve reference to a period. This may be fixed under this subparagraph as an appropriate period or the period covered by the cumulative earnings, or it may be a different period fixed under subpara.(4). There must, however, be a period. The income is then fixed "having regard to", "considering" (this subparagraph) or "by reference to" (subpara.(4)) the earnings in that period. Nowhere is it required that all the income received in that period should be counted. Accordingly, it is permissible to use a particular period but to disregard certain payments if that is necessary to identify the party's average (this subparagraph) or normal earnings (subpara.(4)). Nor is it anywhere required that only income which has been disclosed should be taken into account. Furthermore, although there is no power to guess at a parent's undisclosed income, the tribunal may make an informed estimate on the basis of the evidence available, even on the basis of the evidence of one parent given at a hearing at which the other parent was not present (*CCS 7966/95*).

Where a person's pay is calculated on a daily basis, the best selection of a period is one which covers a 30 day month and a 31 day month as there are on average 30.5 days in a month (*CCS 5352/95*, para.21). Where there is no variation in income, the easiest calculation is to multiple the daily rate by seven.

This subparagraph falls into two distinct parts. The first provides for what has to be determined; the second provides for the evidence to be used in reaching that determination.

What has to be determined is the person's *average* earnings at the relevant week. However, the average earnings will not necessarily be the figure used in the child support formula, as the result is subject to the moderating influence of subpara.(4) which requires a comparison to be made with *normal* earnings. When para.6 is viewed as a whole, it is normal earnings that are the ultimate target at which the calculation is aimed. The reason for the structure of the paragraph is to give guidance to child support officers on what evidence to obtain and how to analyse it. The paragraph acts a guide and a framework rather than a straightjacket. See *CCS 84/98*, para.19.

The evidence which may be used in determing average earnings is of two types. First the CSAT must *have regard to* such evidence as is available of earnings in the appropriate period. That period must begin not earlier than eight weeks before the relevant week and end not later than the date of assessment [referred to below as the permitted period].

No criteria for fixing the appropriate period are set out, but clearly it should be the period best suited to determining the average earnings and should certainly avoid any parts of the permitted period which have any, usual features affecting earnings.

It is the earnings which must be confined to the permitted period and not the evidence of those earnings. So, for example, if the last wage slip for the permitted period is missing, regard may be had to the cumulative totals on the next wage slip which by comparison with the totals on the slip for the preceding week will allow the figures for the missing week to be identified.

The reference to "such evidence as is available" suggests that, unlike the position under the original version of this subparagraph, it is not necessary to obtain details of the earnings in the whole of the permitted period. However, the tribunal will need to have sufficient evidence of those earnings to be able to fix an appropriate period. It is also obliged to take an inquisitorial approach, and may not proceed on the basis of limited evidence that one party has produced if there are any grounds to suspect that is is unrepresentative.

The second type of evidence which may be used is the cumulative earnings from the start of the tax year containing the relevant week and ending not later than the date of assessment. This evidence must be *considered*.

There are limitations to the value of the figure for cumulative earnings and these must be investigated before the cumulative figures may be used. First, the cumulative earnings are limited to the tax year containing the relevant week. According to how the dates fall, the cumulative earnings may cover a period longer or a shorter than the permitted period. Moreover, if the relevant week falls in a different tax year from the date of assessment only the earnings in that earlier year may be considered. Second, there may have been significant changes within the period covered by the cumulative earnings, such as a pay rise or a change of duties, or they may conceal a pattern which would permit separate calculations for different periods, such as where there is a seasonal variation in earnings. Each of these points will limit the value of the cumulative figure for the purposes discussed below, and the circumstances may make it appropriate to rely on subpara.(4) in order to permit reference to the earnings in the later of the two tax years, or to permit a selection of a period or periods within the cumulative earnings period. Third, if the cumulative figure contains a bonus or commission, this must be identified and isolated for the purposes of the calculation under subpara.(3) and only the adjusted cumulative figure used.

The wording used in respect of each of the two types of evidence is different. The tribunal must "have regard to" the earnings in the appropriate period, while it "may consider" the cumulative earnings. The dictionary definitions of these words are more or less interchangeable. However the use of the two expressions suggests that there may be some difference of meaning in this context. This may merely reflect the different nature of each type of evidence. Alternatively, it may indicate that each type of evidence is to be used in a different way. For example, it might mean that the appropriate period consideration must always be undertaken, while the wording in respect of the cumulative earnings suggests a greater element of discretion in whether or not and, if so, how that figure should be used. Another possibility is that the cumulatively figures should only be used as a check on the appropriate period calculation.

It is suggested that these apparent difficulties disappear if the subparagraph is considered in the context of its actual application rather than its abstract meaning. The officer or the tribunal must begin somewhere, and the obvious place to begin is with the pay slips for the permitted period, as they will be the most contemporaneous evidence of earnings at the relevant time. The cumulative earnings may be used to supplement or to interpret the pay slips. Thus the cumulative earnings may be used to supply the figures from any missing pay-slips. They may also be used to help to interpret the pay slips by indicating whether payments of particular expenses are being taxed.

Once the figures for the permitted period have been obtained they, together with any supporting evidence, may paint a number of different pictures. The cumulative earnings may be used to check the accuracy of those pictures and to help to ensure that the period selected is indeed an appropriate one. First, the pay slips may suggest that the party concerned has a regular monthly or weekly income such that it matters not which period is taken as the appropriate period. In this case the cumulative earnings provide on a check that this is indeed the case. Second, there may be a pattern to the earnings, if the party is working, for example, a three week shift rota. Here again the cumulative earnings can be used as a check to ensure that the period selected is indeed an appropriate one. Third, there may be isolated pay slips which seem out of line. Here the cumulative earnings can be used to confirm whether it is proper to select an appropriate period which avoids these weeks.

In other cases the cumulative earnings may indicate the need to use some period other than an appropriate within the permitted period and in a suitable case that period may be the period to which the cumulative figure relates. For example, the pay slips may show no pattern. Here the cumulative earnings may suggest that no appropriate period can be found within the permitted period. It will then be necessary to decide if the period to which the cumulative earnings relate should be used instead. This will not necessarily be the case. There may have been a change within that period, in which case only some part of that period should be used. This can only be done under subpara.(4).

If the above analysis is correct, the role left for subpara.(4) is very much more limited than its role when the original version of this subparagraph was in force. It does, however, play one important role. Subparagraph (1) determines earnings at the relevant week, whereas subpara.(4) operates as at the effective date. Accordingly where there has been a change between the relevant week and the effective date, that may only be taken into account by using subpara.(4). See the reasoning in the general note to that provision below.

*Paragraph 6(3)*

**3.665**     This applies where bonus or commission is paid. However, it does not apply to any other type of payment which relates to a different period from the earnings with which it is paid. It does not, for example, apply to payments of a retainer or of expenses. The presence of such other payments may, however, make it appropriate to disregard particule payslips or payments in calculating earnings. It may be that this is an appropriate case in which to apply the constructive, purposive interpretation in order to fill the gap in the legislation as recommended by the Commissioner in *CCS 12/94*, paras 22–34.

According to *CCS 5079/95* there is no power to disregard a payment which falls to be treated under this subparagraph (*ibid.*, para.7) and the calculation is not affected by the choice of the period used to calculate the other earnings (*ibid.*, para.9). The wording of para.4(4) is arguably wide enough to permit the choice of a different period than the 52 week period stipulated here. However, unlike sub-paras (1) and (2), this subparagraph is not expressly stated to be subject to sub-para.(4), so the better interpretation is that a tribunal has no choice but to treat a bonus or commission as laid down here.

*Paragraph 6(4)*

This subparagraph applies if the calculation does not accurately reflect the normal amount of earnings. These conditions raise a number of questions.

(i) "Normal" means a level of earnings that is not extraordinary, abnormal or unusual (*Peak Trailer and Chassis, Ltd v Jackson* [1967] 1 All E.R. 172 at 176; *R. v Eastleigh Borough Council Ex p. Betts* [1983] 2 All E.R. 481 at 489–490 490 and 494; *Lowe v Rigby* [1985] 2 All E.R. 903 at 906 and 907; *CCS 656/97*, para.29).

(ii) The word "calculation" only appears in subpara.(1). As that word was not used elsewhere in para.2 at all before the amendment of subpara.(1), subpara.(4) could not initially have been limited to moderating the effect of subpara.(1), but must have applied to any calculation of employed earner's earnings under any provision in para.2 (or elsewhere). The amendment of subpara.(1) may have affected the application and operation of this subparagraph, but it cannot have affected its proper interpretation. Accordingly, this provision continues to moderate any calculation of earnings under whatever provision and not merely under subpara.(1).

(iii) The same reasoning shows that subpara.(4) is not limited to cases where earnings have been "calculated" under subpara.(1) as opposed to being "estimated".

(iv) There is no indication of the date as at which normal earnings must be determined. It is suggested that the best interpretation is that they must be determined as at the effective date rather than as at the relevant week. This must be so; if they are determined as at the relevant week, but there has been a change between then and the effective date, the provisions which allow changes of circumstances to be taken into account do not apply.

In some cases a person's income will fluctuate so widely that there is no amount that is normal by way of earnings. This possibility is reflected in the comparative terms ("more accurately") of the wording (*CCS 84/98*, para.20).

Where the Secretary of State has used this subparagraph, the tribunal must be satisfied that its use was proper (*CCS 556/95*, para.7). In theory this means that it is necessary to decide what the result of the income calculation would otherwise have been, since only then can it be known whether the approach authorised by this provision results in a more accurate determination. In practice it is permissible to move straight to para.6(4), if it is clear that any figure produced under para.6(1) will have to be departed from (*CCS 11873/96*, para.8 as qualified by *CCS 84/98*, paras 16 and 19). The need to use a different period must be established by evidence, not merely by assertion (*CCS 11873/96*, para.8). However, in practice this may be shortcircuited where this is obvious, for example, because of an exceptional payment. (*CCS 84/1998*, paras 16 and 19). **3.666**

In the particular circumstances when a change in income occurs before the effective date, this has to be taken into account by virtue of reg.6(4) above. In such a case the effect of that provision should be considered before considering the use of this subparagraph (*CCS 2750/95*, para.21).

This provision is of most assistance when special circumstances existed during the prima facie period prescribed by para.6(1), for example the period might cover the Christmas season when sales assistants earn overtime that is not available most of the year. However it has other uses and tribunal members will derive hours of harmless amusement from attempting to determine the normal earnings of an employment, such as that of a university canteen assistant, in respect of which there is no consistent normality. The purist approach is to look at the matter at the time the decision is being made and to rely on reviews under s.17 of the Act to deal with changes thereafter. This ensures a fair calculation for the parent concerned, although it is time consuming and tedious and there is an inevitable lag between the change of circumstances and the making of a fresh assessment. An alternative approach is to take the total annual income and divide it by 52 in the sure and certain hope that over the course of a year things may average out. This brings the advantages of certainty and continuity at the expense of possible financial difficulties at certain periods of the year for a parent on low income. There is some support for this latter approach in the express provision for student income in para.6(4).

In *CCS 556/95*, para.9, the Commissioner left open whether, under the original wording of para.6(1) and (4), the use of other than a single period to calculate earnings was permissible.

The period selected under this subparagraph may extend beyond the relevant week (*CCS 511/95*, para.17). Any agreement between the absent parent and the person with care as to the period over which earnings should be calculated should be given considerable weight (*ibid.*, para.21). P60s are valuable provided they are for a relevant year; they are more likely to be available when the appeal is before the tribunal than when the case is being considered by an officer (*ibid.*).

Where earnings fluctuate and are calculated over a period, there is no relevant change of circumstances every time a different amount is received. The test is whether the earnings as calculated still fairly represent the normal earnings (*CCS 511/95*, para.21).

This is the only provision under which earnings paid every four weeks could be calculated before the amendments made from April 18, 1995 (*CCS 511/95*).

When a calculation of earnings affects the amount of child support maintenance that has been payable in the past, it may be appropriate to average earnings over a lengthy period so that the effect of fluctuations may be evened out, but when a calculation affects the amount of child support maintenance payable for the future, it is appropriate to ensure as far as possible that payments may be met out of current income (*CCS 4221/98*, para.13).

*Paragraph 7(1)*

"Total taxable profits" is not defined. In *CCS 2858/02*, the Commissioner held that: (a) total taxable profits are the profits chargeable to income tax under Sch.D; (b) capital allowances are not excluded from income; and (c) nor is depreciation. However, the Court of Appeal reversed the decision, holding that the parent's capital allowances were excluded from his income (*Smith v Smith and Secretary of State for Work and Pensions* [2004] EWCA Civ 1318). The Court of Appeal's decision is under appeal to the House of Lords.

*Paragraph 7(4)*

The amendment requiring self-employed earnings to be calculated by disregarding an amount equivalent to any personal allowance that "*would be* applicable" overrides *R(CS) 1/05*.

*Paragraph 8(1)*

A person is nonetheless self-employed despite the fact that earnings are received in a lump sum (*CCS 3182/95*, paras 9 and 13) or that the employment is pursued on a speculative basis without generating commissions or remuneration (*ibid.*, para.15).

"Gross receipts" refers only to income receipts and does not include capital receipts, start up loans or the proceeds of sale of business assets (*R(FC) 1/97*).

The tribunal is not bound by any determination on this issue by the income tax authorities, but it should take such determination into account (*R(CS)2/96*, para.26).

Earnings are not to be confused with the drawings that a person makes from a business (*R(U) 3/88*, para.12).

A tribunal has no power to guess earnings, but it may make an informed estimate and may do so even on the basis of the evidence of one parent which was given at a hearing at which the other parent was not present (*CCS 7966/95*, para.11). It may also obtain evidence, for example from the Inland Revenue or the Contributions Agency, of the typical earnings to be expected from a specified location in a particular locality and use these figures if the parent concerned did not co-operate by producing credible evidence of actual earnings (*CCS 13988/96*, para.8). Other possibilites are to draw conclusions from the amount of pension contributions (*CCS 4644/98*, para.32) or from the amount of a mortgate advance. In *CCS 2901/02*, para.12, the Commissioner suggested that the tribunal could use as an objective starting point the figures from the New Earnings Survey compiled by the Office of National Statistics and published in *Facts and Figures Tables for the Calculation of Damages* for the Professional Bar Negligence Association by Sweet and Maxwell. For a further possibility see the *Burden of proof* section of the general note to reg.49(1) of the Appeals Regulations.

*Paragraph 8(2)(a)*
See the introductory note on expenses.

**3.667**

*Paragraph 8(3)(a)(iii)*
This head (unlike heads (i) and (ii)) is not specific on the purpose for which the payment must be made (*CCS 3774/01*, para.8) other than that it must be for the purposes of the business. This qualification excludes from the scope of this head interest on a liability incurred for the purchase of a share in a business (*CCS 15949/96*, para.7).

*Paragraph 8(3)(b)(vii)*
This head prevents the setting off of losses in one self-employment against gains in another. The same principle applies to prevent setting off losses in self-employment against income from employment (*R 1/96 (CSC)*, para.6).

## The Child Support (Variations) Regulations 2000

### (SI 2001/156)

*Whereas a draft of this Instrument was laid before Parliament in accordance with section 52(2) of the Child Support Act 1991 and approved by a resolution of each House of Parliament:*

**3.668**

*Now, therefore, the Secretary of State for Social Security, in exercise of the powers conferred upon him by sections 28A(5), 28B(2)(c), 28C(2)(b) and (5), 28E(1) and (5), 28F(2)(b) and (3)(b), 28G(3), 51, 52(4) and 54 of, and paragraphs 1, 2(a), 4 and 5(1) of Schedule 4A, and paragraphs 2(2) to (5), 3(1) and (2), 4, 5(1) and (3) to (5) and 6 of Schedule 4B to the Child Support Act 1991 hereby makes the following Regulations:*

ARRANGEMENT OF REGULATIONS

PART I

*General*

1. Citation, commencement and interpretation.
2. Documents.
3. Determination of amounts.

PART II

*Application and determination procedure*

PART III

*Special expenses*

PART IV

*Property or capital transfers*

PART V

*Additional cases*

PART VI

*Factors to be taken into account for the purposes of section 28F of the Act*

PART VII

*Effect of a variation on the maintenance calculation and effective dates*

PART I

GENERAL

## Citation, commencement and interpretation

**1.**—(1) These Regulations may be cited as the Child Support 3.669 (Variations) Regulations 2000 and shall come into force in relation to a particular case on the day on which section 5 of the Child Support, Pensions and Social Security Act 2000 which substitutes or amends sections 28A to 28F of the Act is commenced in relation to that type of case.

(2) In these Regulations, unless the context otherwise requires—

"the Act" means the Child Support Act 1991;

"capped amount" means the amount of income for the purposes of paragraph 10(3) of Schedule 1 to the Act;

"Contributions and Benefits Act" means the Social Security Contributions and Benefits Act 1992;

"couple" has the same meaning as in paragraph 10C(5) of Schedule 1 to the Act;

"date of notification" means the date upon which notification is given in person or communicated by telephone to the recipient or, where this is not possible, the date of posting;

"date of receipt" menas the day on which the information or document is actually received;

"home" has the meaning given in regulation 1(2) of the Maintenance Calculations and Special Cases Regulations;

"Maintenance Calculation Procedure Regulations" means the Child Support (Maintenance Calculation Procedure) Regulations 2000;

"Maintenance Calculation and Special Cases Regulations" means the Child Support (Maintenance Calculations and Special Cases) Regulations 2000;

[[1]"partner" has the same meaning as in paragraph 10C(4) of Schedule 1 to the Act;]

"qualifying child" means the child with respect to whom the maintenance calculation falls to be made;

"relevant person" means—

(a) a non-resident parent, or a person treated as a non-resident parent under regulation 8 of the Maintenance Calculations and Special Cases Regulations, whose liability to pay child support maintenance may be affected by any variation agreed;

(b) a person with care, or a child to whom section 7 of the Act applies, where the amount of child support maintenance payable by virtue of a calculation relevant to that person with care or in respect of that child may be affected by any variation agreed; and

"Transitional Regulations" means the Child Support (Transitional Provisions) Regulations 2000.

(3) In these Regulations, unless the context otherwise requires, a reference—

(a) to a numbered Part, is to the Part of these Regulations bearing that number;

(b) to the Schedule, is to the Schedule to these Regulations;

(c) to a numbered regulation, is to the regulation in these Regulations bearing that number;

(d) in a regulation, or the Schedule, to a numbered paragraph, is to the paragraph in that regulation or the Schedule bearing that number; and

(e) in a paragraph to a lettered or numbered sub-paragraph, is to the sub-paragraph in that paragraph bearing that letter or number.

AMENDMENT

1. Regulation 9(2) of the Miscellaneous Amendments Regulations 2004 (September 16, 2004).

## Documents

3.670  **2.** Except where otherwise stated, where—

(a) any document is given or sent to the Secretary of State, that document shall be treated as having been so given or sent on the date of receipt by the Secretary of State; and

(b) any document is given or sent to any other person, that document shall, if sent by post to that person's last known or notified address, be treated as having been given or sent on the date that it is posted.

DEFINITION

3.671  "date of receipt": see reg.1(2).

GENERAL NOTE

This regulation makes the usual provision favourable to the Secretary of State. For commentary, see reg.2 of the Appeals Regulations.

## Determination of amounts

**3.**—(1) Where any amount is required to be determined for the purposes of these Regulations, it shall be determined as a weekly amount and, except where the context otherwise requires, any reference to such an amount shall be construed accordingly.

(2) Where any calculation made under these Regulations results in a fraction of a penny, that fraction shall be treated as a penny if it is either one half or exceeds one half and shall be otherwise disregarded.

3.672

GENERAL NOTE

This regulation provides for amounts to be calculated as weekly amounts (para.(1)) and for rounding of fractions (para.(2)). The former is in line with all calculations under the child support scheme. The latter repeats the provision used elsewhere in the scheme.

3.673

PART II

APPLICATION AND DETERMINATION PROCEDURE

## Application for a variation

**4.**—(1) Where an application for a variation is made other than in writing and the Secretary of State directs that the application be made in writing, the application shall be made either on an application form provided by the Secretary of State and completed in accordance with the Secretary of State's instructions or in such other written form as the Secretary of State may accept as sufficient in the circumstances of any particular case.

3.674

(2) An application for a variation which is made other than in writing shall be treated as made on the date of notification from the applicant to the Secretary of State that he wishes to make such an application.

(3) Where an application for a variation is made in writing other than in the circumstances to which paragraph (1) applies, the application shall be treated as made on the date of receipt by the Secretary of State.

(4) Where paragraph (1) applies and the Secretary of State receives the application within 14 days of the date of the direction, or at a later date but in circumstances where the Secretary of State is satisfied that the delay was unavoidable, the application shall be treated as made on the date of notification from the applicant to the Secretary of State that he wishes to make an application for a variation.

(5) Where paragraph (1) applies and the Secretary of State receives the application more than 14 days from the date of the direction and in circumstances where he is not satisfied that the delay was unavoidable, the application shall be treated as made on the date of receipt.

(6) An application for a variation is duly made when it has been made in accordance with this regulation and section 28A(4) of the Act.

3.675     "the Act": see reg.1(2).
        "date of receipt": see reg.1(2).

GENERAL NOTE

3.676     This regulation provides for two matters: the date when an application is made and what constitutes a duly made application. Applications with respect to the same maintenance calculation may be considered together: see reg.9(9).

    The date when an application is made depends on how it is made. There are three possibilities. First, the application is made other than in writing and the Secretary of State accepts the application in that form. In these circumstances, the application is made on the date when the Secretary of State is notified that the applicant wishes to make an application. See para.(2). In practice, this will be when the applicant contacts the Secretary of State by telephone. Second, the application is initially made other than in writing, but the Secretary of State directs that it be made in writing. See para.(1). In these circumstances, the applicant has 14 days from the date of the direction to make an application in writing. If it is either received in that time or unavoidalby delayed, the application is made on the date when the Secretary of State was notified that the applicant wanted to make an application. If it is not received in that time and there is no unavoidable delay, it is made on the date when it is received. See paras (4) and (5). Third, the application may be made other than in writing. In these circumstances, the application is made on the date when it is received. See para.(3).

    In order to be duly made, an application must; (a) be received in accordance with paras (1) to (5); (b) be made in writing if directed by the Secretary of State; and (c) state the grounds on which it is made. See para.(6) and s.28A(4) of the Act.

## Amendment or withdrawal of application

3.677     **5.**—(1) A person who has made an application for a variation may amend or withdraw his application at any time before a decision under section 11, 16 or 17 of the Act, or a decision not to revise or supersede under section 16 or 17 of the Act, is made in response to the variation application and such amendment or withdrawal need not be in writing unless, in any particular case, the Secretary of State requires it to be.

    (2) No amendment under paragraph (1) shall relate to any change of circumstances arising after what would be the effective date of a decision in response to the variation application.

DEFINITION

3.678     "the Act": see reg.1(2).

GENERAL NOTE

    This regulation provides for the amendment and withdrawal of applications. An application may be amended or withdrawn before it is is determined. In accordance with the making of the application itself, the amendment or withdrawal need not be in writing unless the Secretary of State requires. See para.(1).

    An amendment in relation to a change of circumstances that occurred after what would be the effective date of the decision on the application, is ineffective. See para.(2). This can only be taken into account under a new application.

The effect of an amendment or withdrawal that is received after the application has been determined will depend on the circumstances. It might be treated as an appeal, as a new application or as an application for a revision or supersession. In practice, the application should be given the option of how to proceed.

## Rejection of an application following preliminary consideration

**6.**—(1) The Secretary of State may, on completing the preliminary consideration, reject an application for a variation (and proceed to make his decision on the application for a maintenance calculation, or to revise or supersede a decision under section 16 or 17 of the Act, without the variation, or not to revise or supersede a decision under section 16 or 17 of the Act, as the case may be) if one of the circumstances in paragraph (2) applies.

3.679

(2) The circumstances are—
- (a) the application has been made in one of the circumstances to which regulation 7 applies;
- (b) the application is made—
  - (i) on a ground in paragraph 2 of Schedule 4B to the Act (special expenses) and the amount of the special expenses, or the aggregate amount of those expenses, as the case may be, does not exceed the relevant threshold provided for in regulation 15;
  - (ii) on a ground in paragraph 3 of that Schedule (property or capital transfers) and the value of the property or capital transferred does not exceed the minimum value in regulation 16(4); or
  - (iii) on a ground referred to in regulation 18 (assets) and the value of the assets does not exceed the figure in regulation 18(3)(a), or on a ground in regulation 19(1) [¹ or (1A)] (income not taken into account) and the amount of the income does not exceed the figure in regulation 19(2);
- (c) a request under regulation 8 has not been complied with by the applicant and the Secretary of State is not able to determine the application without the information requested; or
- (d) the Secretary of State is satisfied, on the information or evidence available to him, that the application would not be agreed to, including where, although a ground is stated, the facts alleged in the application would not bring the case within the prescription of the relevant ground in these Regulations.

AMENDMENT

1. Regulation 8(2) of the Miscellaneous Amendments Regulations 2005 (April 6, 2005).

DEFINITION

"the Act": see reg. 1(2).

3.680

GENERAL NOTE

This regulation is made under the authority of s.28B(2)(c) of the Act. It sets out limited circumstances in which an application would be bound to fail because one of the financial restrictions is not satisfied.

**Prescribed circumstances**

3.681    7.—(1) This regulation applies where an application for a variation is made under [¹section 28A or 28G] of the Act and—

(a) the application is made by a relevant person and a circumstance set out in paragraph (2) applies at the relevant date;

(b) the application is made by a non-resident parent and a circumstance set out in paragraph (3) or (4) applies at the relevant date;

(c) the application is made by a person with care, or a child to whom section 7 of the Act applies, on a ground in paragraph 4 of Schedule 4B to the Act (additional cases) and a circumstance set out in paragraph (5) applies at the relevant date; or

(d) the application is made by a non-resident parent on a ground in paragraph 2 of Schedule 4B to the Act (special expenses) and a circumstance set out in paragraph (6) applies at the relevant date.

(2) The circumstances for the purposes of this paragraph are that—

(a) a default maintenance decision is in force with respect to the non-resident parent;

(b) the non-resident parent is liable to pay the flat rate of child support maintenance owing to the application of paragraph 4(1)(c) of Schedule 1 to the Act, or would be so liable but is liable to pay less than that amount, or nil, owing to the application of paragraph 8 of Schedule 1 to the Act, or the Transitional Regulations; or

(c) the non-resident parent is liable to pay child support maintenance at a flat rate of a prescribed amount owing to the application of paragraph 4(2) of Schedule 1 to the Act, or would be so liable but is liable to pay less than that amount, or nil, owing to the application of paragraph 8 of Schedule 1 to the Act, or the Transitional Regulations.

(3) The circumstances for the purposes of this paragraph are that the non-resident parent is liable to pay child support maintenance—

(a) at the nil rate owing to the application of paragraph 5 of Schedule 1 to the Act;

(b) at a flat rate owing to the application of paragraph 4(1)(a) of Schedule 1 to the Act, including where the net weekly income of the non-resident parent which is taken into account for the purposes of a maintenance calculation in force in respect of him is £100 per week or less owing to a variation being taken into account or to the application of regulation 18, 19 or 21 of the Transitional Regulations (reduction for relevant departure direction or relevant property transfer); or

(c) at a flat rate owing to the application of paragraph 4(1)(b) of Schedule 1 to the Act, or would be so liable but is liable to pay less than that amount, or nil, owing to the application of paragraph 8 of Schedule 1 to the Act, or the Transitional Regulations.

(4) The circumstances for the purposes of this paragraph are that the non-resident parent is liable to pay an amount of child support maintenance at a rate—

(a) of £5 per week or such other amount as may be prescribed owing to the application of paragraph 7(7) of Schedule 1 to the Act (shared care); or

668

(b) equivalent to the flat rate provided for in, or prescribed for the purposes of, paragraph 4(1)(b) of Part 1 of Schedule 1 to the Act owing to the application of—
   (i) regulation 27(5);
   (ii) regulation 9 of the Maintenance Calculation and Special Cases Regulations (care provided in part by a local authority); or
   (iii) regulation 23(5) of the Transitional Regulations.
(5) The circumstances for the purposes of this paragraph are that—
(a) the amount of the net weekly income of the non-resident parent to which the Secretary of State had regard when making the maintenance calculation was the capped amount; or
(b) the non-resident parent or a partner of his is in receipt of [⁴working tax credit under section 10 of the Tax Credits Act 2002] [⁵. . .].

(6) The circumstances for the purposes of this paragraph are that the amount of the net weekly income of the non-resident parent to which the Secretary of State would have regard after deducting the amount of the special expenses would exceed the capped amount.

(7) For the purposes of paragraph (1), the "relevant date" means the date from which, if the variation were agreed [²and the application had been made under section 28G of the Act], the decision under section 16 or 17 of the Act, as the case may be, would take effect [³and if the variation were agreed, and the application had been made under section 28A of the Act, the decision under section 11 of the Act would take effect].

AMENDMENTS

1. Regulation 9(2)(a) of the Miscellaneous Amendments Regulations 2002 (April 30, 2002).
2. Regulation 9(2)(b)(i) of the Miscellaneous Amendments Regulations 2002 (April 30, 2002).
3. Regulation 9(2)(b)(ii) of the Miscellaneous Amendments Regulations 2002 (April 30, 2002).
4. Regulation 10 of the Miscellaneous Amendments Regulations 2003 (April 6, 2003).
5. Regulation 9(3) of the Miscellaneous Amendments Regulations 2004 (September 16, 2004).

DEFINTIONS

"the Act": see reg.1(2).                                                        3.682
"capped amount": see reg.1(2).
"Maintenance Calculations and Special Cases Regulations": see reg.1(2).
"partner": see reg.1(2).
"relevant person": see reg.1(2).
"Transitional Regulations": see reg.1(2).

GENERAL NOTE

This regulation is made under the authority of s.28G(3) of the Act.

## Provision of information

8.—(1) Where an application has been duly made, the Secretary of State        3.683
may request further information or evidence from the applicant to enable

that application to be determined and any such information or evidence requested shall be provided within one month of the date of notification of the request or such longer period as the Secretary of State is satisfied is reasonable in the circumstances of the case.

(2) Where any information or evidence requested in accordance with paragraph (1) is not provided in accordance with the time limit specified in that paragraph, the Secretary of State may, where he is able to do so, proceed to determine the application in the absence of the requested information or evidence.

DEFINITIONS

3.684    "the Act": see reg.1(2).
"date of notification": see reg.1(2).

GENERAL NOTE

*Paragraph (1)*
3.685    This paragraph provides for the Secretary of State to request further information or evidence that is needed to enable the application to be determined. The power only arises if the application is duly made: see reg.4(6). So, its purpose is not to make the application effective, but to provide the Secretary of State with the information and evidence necessary to determine the application. It follows that failure to provide the information or evidence does not relieve the Secretary of State of the duty to determine the application, provided that that is possible: see para.(2).

*Paragraph (2)*
This paragraph allows the Secretary of State to determine the application, if possible, if the information or evidence is not provided. It does not authorise the Secretary of State to disregard information or evidence that is provided late but before the application is determined. However, failure to provide the information may allow the Secretary of State to reject the application on preliminary consideration: see in particular reg.6(2)(c) and (d). See also reg.9(7) on information or evidence that is received after representations have been invited from the other party.

## Procedure in relation to the determination of an application

3.686    **9.**—(1) Subject to paragraph (3), where the Secretary of State has given the preliminary consideration to an application and not rejected it he—

(a) shall give notice of the application to the relevant persons other than the applicant, informing them of the grounds on which the application has been made and any relevant information or evidence the applicant has given, except information or evidence falling within paragraph (2);

(b) may invite representations, which need not be in writing but shall be in writing if in any case he so directs, from the relevant persons other than the applicant on any matter relating to that application, to be submitted to the Secretary of State within 14 days of the date of notification or such longer period as the Secretary of State is satisfied is reasonable in the circumstances of the case; and

(c) shall set out the provisions of paragraphs (2)(b) and (c), (4) and (5) in relation to such representations.

(2) The information or evidence referred to in paragraphs (1)(a), (4)(a) and (7), are—

(a) details of the nature of the long-term illness or disability of the relevant other child which forms the basis of a variation application on the ground in regulation 11 where the applicant requests they should not be disclosed and the Secretary of State is satisfied that disclosure is not necessary in order to be able to determine the application;

(b) medical evidence or medical advice which has not been disclosed to the applicant or a relevant person and which the Secretary of State considers would be harmful to the health of the applicant or that relevant person if disclosed to him; or

(c) the address of a relevant person or qualifying child, or any other information which could reasonably be expected to lead to that person or child being located, where the Secretary of State considers that there would be a risk of harm or undue distress to that person or that child or any other children living with that person if the address or information were disclosed.

(3) The Secretary of State need not act in accordance with paragraph (1)—

(a) where regulation 29 applies (variation may be taken into account notwithstanding that no application has been made);

(b) where the variation agreed is one falling within paragraph 3 of Schedule 4B to the Act (property or capital transfer), the Secretary of State ceases to have jurisdiction to make a maintenance calculation and subsequently acquires jurisdiction in respect of the same non-resident parent, person with care and any child in respect of whom the earlier calculation was made;

(c) if he is satisfied on the information or evidence available to him that the application would not be agreed to, but if, on further consideration of the application, he is minded to agree to the variation he shall, before doing so, comply with the provisions of this regulation; or

(d) where—

(i) a variation has been agreed in relation to a maintenance calculation;

(ii) the decision as to the maintenance calculation is replaced with a default maintenance decision under section 12(1)(b) of the Act;

(iii) the default maintenance decision is revised in accordance with section 16(1B) of the Act,

and the Secretary of State is satisfied, on the information or evidence available to him, that there has been no material change of circumstances relating to the variation since the date from which the maintenance calculation referred to in head (i) ceased to have effect.

(4) Where the Secretary of State receives representations from the relevant persons—

(a) he may, if he considers it reasonable to do so, send a copy of the representations concerned (excluding material falling within paragraph (2)) to the applicant and invite any comments he may have within 14 days or such longer period as the Secretary of State is satisfied is reasonable in the circumstances of the case; and

(b) where the Secretary of State acts under sub-paragraph (a) he shall not proceed to determine the application until he has received such comments or the period referred to in that sub-paragraph has expired.

(5) Where the Secretary of State has not received representations from the relevant persons notified in accordance with paragraph (1) within the time limit specified in sub-paragraph (b) of that paragraph, he may proceed to agree or not (as the case may be) to a variation in their absence.

(6) In considering an application for a variation, the Secretary of State shall take into account any representations received at the date upon which he agrees or not (as the case may be) to the variation from the relevant persons, including any representation received in accordance with paragraphs (1)(b), [¹(4)(a)] and (7).

(7) Where any information or evidence requested by the Secretary of State under regulation 8 is received after notification has been given under paragraph (1), the Secretary of State may, if he considers it reasonable to do so, and except where such information or evidence falls within paragraph (2), send a copy of such information or evidence to the relevant persons and may invite them to submit representations, which need not be in writing unless the Secretary of State so directs in any particular case, on that information or evidence.

(8) The Secretary of State may, if he considers it appropriate, treat an application for a variation made on one ground as if it were an application made on a different ground, and, if he does intend to do so, he shall include this information in the notice and invitation to make representations referred to in paragraphs (1), (4) and (7).

(9) Two or more applications for a variation with respect to the same maintenance calculation or application for a maintenance calculation, made or treated as made, may be considered together.

AMENDMENT

1. Regulation 9(3) of the Miscellaneous Amendments Regulations 2002 (April 30, 2002).

DEFINITIONS

**3.687**  "the Act": see reg.1(2).
"date of notification": see reg.1(2).
"qualifying child": see reg.1(2).
"relevant person": see reg.1(2).
"Transitional Regulations": see reg.1(2).

GENERAL NOTE

**3.688**  This regulation deals with procedure once an application has passed the preliminary consideration under s.28B of the Act. It is largely concerned with obtaining and taking account of representations by the other party, but it also deals with treating the application as made on other grounds (para.(8)) and with considerating two or more applications with respect to the same maintenance calculation together (para.(9)). There is similar provision in reg.15B in relation to the revision or supersession of the effect of a variation.

*Paragraph (2)(b)*

This provision imposes a duty to withhold potentially harmful or distressing information or evidence. It is similar to the powers discussed in *R(A) 4/89*, paras 6 and 7 and *CSDLA 5/95*, paras 16–23. The following propositions emerge from the latter decision unless otherwise stated.

   (i) The provision prohibits disclosure, but does not operate to exclude the fundamental right for the other party to have a fair chance to comment on the issues raised by the application. The party must be told that information is being withheld.

  (ii) The evidence of advice must be "medical" and not merely factual non-medical information given by a doctor *(R(A) 4/89*, para.6).

 (iii) Disclosure must be harmful. It is not sufficient that disclosure would cause embarrassment or that it would cause difficulty. Distress in not sufficient unless it constitutes harm.

  (iv) The harm must be substantial.

  (v) If possible the gist of the information or evidence should be disclosed. The practicality of this suggestion has been doubted *(CDLA 1347/99*, para.7), but it may be possible in some cases.

  (vi) Disclosure to a representative, subject to appropriate credible undertakings not to disclose to the party, may be possible.

 (vii) This provision may be in violation of the Convention right in Art.6(1) of the European Convention on Human Rights and Fundamental Freedoms in view of *McMichael v United Kingdom* [1995] 20 E.H.R.R. 205 and *McGinley and Egan v United Kingdom, The Times*, June 15, 1998.

*Paragraph (2)(c)*

See the general notes to s.46(3) of the Act (on harm or undue distress) and reg.44 of the Appeals Regulations (on non-disclosure).

PART III

SPECIAL EXPENSES

## Special expenses—contact costs

**10.**—(1) Subject to the following paragraphs of this regulation, and to    **3.689** regulation 15, the following costs incurred or reasonably expected to be incurred by the non-resident parent, whether in respect of himself or the qualifying child or both, for the purpose of maintaining contact with that child, shall constitute expenses for the purposes of paragraph 2(2) of Schedule 4B to the Act—

  (a) the cost of purchasing a ticket for travel;

  (b) the cost of purchasing fuel where travel is by a vehicle which is not carrying fare-paying passengers;

  (c) the taxi fare for a journey or part of a journey where the Secretary of State is satisfied that the disability or long-term illness of the non-resident parent or the qualifying child makes it impracticable for any other form of transport to be used for that journey or part of that journey;

  (d) the cost of car hire where the cost of the journey would be less in total than it would be if public transport or taxis or a combination of both were used;

(e) where the Secretary of State considers a return journey on the same day is impracticable, or the established or intended pattern of contact with the child includes contact over two or more consecutive days, the cost of the non-resident parent's, or, as the case may be, the child's, accommodation for the number of nights the Secretary of State considers appropriate in the circumstances of the case; and

(f) any minor incidental costs such as tolls or fees payable for the use of a particular road or bridge incurred in connection with such travel, including breakfast where it is included as part of the accommodation cost referred to in sub-paragraph (e).

(2) The costs to which paragraph (1) applies include the cost of a person to travel with the non-resident parent or the qualifying child, if the Secretary of State is satisfied that the presence of another person on the journey, or part of the journey, is necessary including, but not limited to, where it is necessary because of the young age of the qualifying child or the disability or long-term illness of the non-resident parent or that child.

(3) The costs referred to in paragraphs (1) and (2)—

(a) shall be expenses for the purposes of paragraph 2(2) of Schedule 4B to the Act only to the extent that they are—

    (i) incurred in accordance with a set pattern as to frequency of contact between the non-resident parent and the qualifying child which has been established at or, where at the time of the variation application it has ceased, which had been established before, the time that the variation application is made; or

    (ii) based on an intended set pattern for such contact which the Secretary of State is satisfied has been agreed between the non-resident parent and the person with care of the qualifying child; and

(b) shall be—

    (i) where head (i) of sub-paragraph (a) applies and such contact is continuing, calculated as an average weekly amount based on the expenses actually incurred over the period of 12 months, or such lesser period as the Secretary of State may consider appropriate in the circumstances of the case, ending immediately before the first day of the maintenance period from which a variation agreed on this ground would take effect;

    (ii) where head (i) of sub-paragraph (a) applies and such contact has ceased, calculated as an average weekly amount based on the expenses actually incurred during the period from the first day of the maintenance period from which a variation agreed on this ground would take effect to the last day of the maintenance period in relation to which the variation would take effect; or

    (iii) where head (ii) of sub-paragraph (a) applies, calculated as an average weekly amount based on anticipated costs during such period as the Secretary of State considers appropriate.

(4) For the purposes of this regulation, costs of contact shall not include costs which relate to periods where the non-resident parent has care of a qualifying child overnight as part of a shared care arrangement for which provision is made under paragraphs 7 and 8 of Schedule 1 to the Act and regulation 7 of the Maintenance Calculations and Special Cases Regulations.

(5) Where the non-resident parent has at the date he makes the variation application received, or at that date is in receipt of, or where he will receive, any financial assistance, other than a loan, from any source to meet, wholly or in part, the costs of maintaining contact with a child as referred to in paragraph (1), only the amount of the costs referred to in that paragraph, after the deduction of the financial assistance, shall constitute special expenses for the purposes of paragraph 2(2) of Schedule 4B to the Act.

DEFINITIONS

"the Act": see reg.1(2).                                    3.690
"disability": see reg.11(2)(a).
"long-term illness": see reg.11(2)(a).
"Maintenance Calculations and Special Cases Regulations": see reg.1(2).
"qualifying child": see reg.1(2).

GENERAL NOTE

This ground of variation is made under the authority of Sch.4B, para.2(2)(a)    3.691
to the Act. It provides for a variation on the ground of special expenses in respect of maintaining contact between the non-resident parent and the qualifying child.

Generally speaking, only travel costs are taken into account, whether of the parent or the child. There are limited exceptions for overnight accommodation (para.(1)(e)) and breakfast (para.(1)(f)). Otherwise, the costs of meals and entertainment are not taken into account.

There are a number of possible expenses related to travel that may not be included. It may be sensible, for example, on a long ferry jurney to book a seat, but it may not be "minor incidental costs" under para.(1)(f). Also, the cost of a sleeper on a long rail journey or a cabin on a ferry crossing may not be "accommodation" under para.(1)(e) or "minor incidental costs" under para.(1)(f).

There is no justification for treating monthly expenses as if they were weekly (*R (Qazi) v Secretary of State*, reported as *R(CS) 5/04*, paras 24–27).

*Paragraph (2)*
The costs include those of a companion if this is necessary on account of the age of the child or the long-term illness or disability of the parent or the child.

*Paragraph (3)*
The contact on which the expenses are calculated must form an established set pattern or be a set pattern agreed between the non-resident parent and the person with care. No provision is made for a set pattern under a court order which the non-resident parent cannot afford to follow because of the amount of the maintenance calculation, unless the person with care agrees with the court so that it forms an agreed set pattern. For further commentary, see the general note to reg.15(2) and (3).

*Paragraph (4)*
This prevents a non-resident parent obtaining double advantage from both the formula allowance for shared care and the variation scheme for contact costs.

*Paragraph (5)*
Financial assistance from any source for maintaining contact is deducted. This is in addition to the thresholds in reg.15.

### Special expenses—illness or disability of relevant other child

3.692    **11.**—(1) Subject to the following paragraphs of this regulation, expenses necessarily incurred by the non-resident parent in respect of the items listed in sub-paragraphs (a) to (m) due to the long-term illness or disability of a relevant other child shall constitute special expenses for the purposes of paragraph 2(2) of Schedule 4B to the Act—

(a)  personal care and attendance;

(b)  personal communication needs;

(c)  mobility;

(d)  domestic help;

(e)  medical aids where these cannot be provided under the health service;

(f)  heating;

(g)  clothing;

(h)  laundry requirements;

(i)  payments for food essential to comply with a diet recommended by a medical practitioner;

(j)  adaptations required to the non-resident parent's home;

(k)  day care;

(l)  rehabilitation; or

(m) respite care.

(2) For the purposes of this regulation and regulation 10—

(a)  a person is "disabled" for a period in respect of which—

(i)  either an attendance allowance, disability living allowance or a mobility supplement is paid to or in respect of him;

(ii)  he would receive an attendance allowance or disability living allowance if it were not for the fact that he is a patient, though remaining part of the applicant's family; or

(iii)  he is registered blind or treated as blind within the meaning of paragraph 12(1)(a)(iii) and (2) of Schedule 2 to the Income Support (General) Regulations 1987;

and for this purpose—

(i)  "attendance allowance" means an allowance payable under section 64 of the Contributions and Benefits Act or an increase of disablement pension under section 104 of that Act, or an award under article 14 of the Naval, Military and Air Forces Etc., (Disablement and Death) Service Pensions Order 1983 or any analogous allowance payable in conjunction with any other war disablement pension within the meaning of section 150(2) of the Contributions and Benefits Act;

(ii)  "disability living allowance" means an allowance payable under section 72 of the Contributions and Benefits Act;

(iii)  "mobility supplement" means an award under article 26A of the Naval, Military and Air Forces Etc., (Disablement and Death) Service Pensions Order 1983 or any analogous allowance payable in conjunction with any other war disablement pension within the meaning of section 150(2) of the Contributions and Benefits Act; and

(iv)  "patient" means a person (other than a person who is serving a sentence of imprisonment or detention in a young offenders institution within the meaning of the Criminal Justice Act 1982) who is regarded as receiving free in-patient treatment within the meaning of the Social Security (Hospital In-Patients) Regulations 1975;

(b) "the health service" has the same meaning as in section 128 of the National Health Service Act 1977 or in section 108(1) of the National Health Service (Scotland) Act 1978;

(c) "long-term illness" means an illness from which the non-resident parent or child is suffering at the date of the application or the date from which the variation, if agreed, would take effect and which is likely to last for at least 52 weeks from that date, or, if likely to be shorter than 52 weeks, for the remainder of the life of that person; and

(d) "relevant other child" has the meaning given in paragraph 10C(2) of Schedule 1 to the Act and Regulations made under that paragraph.

[¹(3) Where, at the date on which the non-resident parent makes the variation application—

(a) he or a member of his household has received, or at that date is in receipt of, or where he or the member of his household will receive any financial assistance from any source in respect of the long-term illness or disability of the relevant other child; or

(b) a disability living allowance is received by the non-resident parent or the member of his household on behalf of the relevant other child,

only the net amount of the costs incurred in respect of the items listed in paragraph (1), after the deduction of the financial assistance or the amount of the allowance, shall constitute special expenses for the purposes of paragraph 2(2) of Schedule 4B to the Act.]

AMENDMENT

1. Regulation 8(3) of the Miscellaneous Amendments Regulations 2005 (March 16, 2005).

DEFINITIONS

"the Act": see reg.1(2).                                          **3.693**
"Contributions and Benefits Act": see reg.1(2).
"home": see reg.1(2).

GENERAL NOTE

This ground of variation is made under the authority of Sch.4B, para.2(2)(b) and       **3.694**
(4) to the Act. It provides for a variation on the ground of special expenses in respect of long-term illness or disability. They are not subject to the thresholds set by reg.15: see reg.15(1).

The limited scope of the regulation is to some extent offset by s.8(8) of the Act, which preserves the powers of the courts to make a maintenance order in respect of expenses attributable to a child's disability. This allows a parent with care, who is not covered by this regulation, to obtain maintenance in respect of the needs of a qualifying child, who is also excluded.

The expenses must be incurred by the non-resident parent: see para.(1). So, a variation can reduce the amount of a non-resident parent's liability, but it cannot be increased on the ground that the parent or other person with care incurs these expenses.

The expenses must be "necessarily incurred": see para.(1). The Commissioners will have to decide whether this is limited to those expenses that are essential or includes those that, while not essential, are reasonably necessary. This condition is linked to two other requirements. The expenses must be incurred "in respect of" the items listed in para.(1)(a)–(m) and they must be "due to" long-term illness or disability; as defined in para.(2)(a) and (c). Taken together these impose a causation requirement. They exclude costs that would be incurred even if the long-term illness or disability did not exist. This is not always easy to identify. See further the general note to para.(1)(i).

The long-term illness or disability must be that of a "relevant other child", as defined under para.(2)(d): see para.(1). This excludes qualifying children.

For practical purposes, this ground for a variation requires that an award of disability living allowance has been made for the child. For the exceptions, see para.(2)(2)(i) and (iii).

*Paragraph (1)(i) diet*

3.695    There must be a diet. There is a wide range of conditions that a doctor might impose on a person's food intake. Those conditions might significantly restrict the choice of foods allowed. The issue that arise depend on the form of the diet.

One possibility is that the person might be advised to avoid particular products, like dairy produce. That would be a diet. The food bill would be reduced by the cost of the products to be avoided, but it might be necessary to replace those products with others, such as soya products in place of dairy products. The issues will be: (a) whether the additional products were essential to comply with the diet or were merely a matter of choice; and (b) whether that results in an additional cost.

A second possibility is that the person might be advised to increase the amount of particular products, like food that is high in fibre or fruit. That would usually be called a diet. It might change the balance of products already consumed or introduce new produce into the diet. It is unlikely that there were be a compensatory saving on products that were no longer needed. The issue would be whether the change in the balance of the diet resulted in an additional cost.

A third possibility is that the person might be advised to avoid certain products which would not need to be replaced. For example, a person experiencing migraines might be advised to avoid chocolate and cheese. This might be described as a diet, but it is unlikely to result in additional cost.

The diet must be recommended by a medical practitioner. It is unlikely that the diet will have been recommended in writing, although confirmation in writing should be available as evidence. If written recommendation or confirmation is not available, the issue will be whether the available evidence is credible and reliable. If the diet is a recognised one and relates to a diagnosed condition, the evidence will be more readily accepted than if the diet is an unusal one.

The diet may have been recommended in general terms by a medical practitioner, but set out in more detail by a specialist dietician who may not fall within the meaning of "medical practitioner". It is suggested that that should be sufficient to satisfy this provision.

There is no definition of "medical practitioner". It is unfortunate that the legislation does not adopt the terminology from Sch.1 to the Interpretation Act 1978 which defines "registered medical practitioner" as meaning a fully registered person within the meaning of the Medicine Act 1983. However, it is suggested that this is how "medical practitioner" should be interpreted for two reasons. First, in dealing with the retrospective effective of the registration provisions for medical practitioners, the 1983 Act (which was a consolidation Act) provides in Sch.6, para.11(1) that:

"In any enactment passed before 1st January 1979 the expression 'legally qualified medical practitioner' or 'duly qualified medical practitioner', *or any expression importing a person recognised by law as a medical practitioner* or member of the medical profession, *shall, unless the contrary intention appears, be construed to mean a fully registered practitioner."*

The words "medical practitioner" must mean one recognised by law and it would be strange if they covered only those who were fully registered before 1979 but not subsequently. Second, although there is no general prohibition on any person practising medicine or surgery (*Younghusband v Luftig* [1949] 2 All E.R. 72 at 76, *per* Lord Goddard C.I.), it is an offence under s.49(1) of the 1983 Act to imply by the use of any name, title, addition or description that the practitioner is registered under that Act. It would, therefore, be very difficult for a person to claim to be a medical practitioner without also implying registration, with the result that, in practice, anyone claiming to be a medical practitioner would have to be registered. **3.696**

In addition to the causation requirements under the opening words of para.(1), the payments must be "essential" to comply with the diet. Implementing these provisions requires a comparison between the cost of the diet and the pre-diet food bill. There may no evidence of pre-diet costs (*e.g.* because the person has been on the diet for many years) or the evidence may be unreliable. In those circumstances, an estimate has to be made of what those costs were likely to have been. It is likely that the person may have been living on limited income and the pre-diet costs will be low. See *CCS 7522/99*, paras 24–27.

If the diet is one which leaves an element of choice in the items eaten, the test of what is essential has to be applied sensibly by asking whether the particular combination of foodstuffs eaten under the diet represents a varied and balanced application of the dietary advice. The person is not limited to the cost of large amounts of the cheapest foods on the recommended list. See *CCS 7522/99*, para.15.

*Paragraph (2)(a)(iii)*
Paragraphs 12(1)(a)(iii) of the Income Support (General) Regulations 1987 covers a person who: **3.697**

"is registered as blind in a register compiled by a local authority under section 29 of the National Assistance Act 1948 (Welfare services) or, in Scotland, has been certified as blind and in consequence he is registered as blind in a register maintained by or on behalf of a regional or islands council".

Paragraph 12(2) provides:

"For the purposes of subparagraph (1)(a)(iii), a person who has ceased to be registered as blind on regaining his eyesight shall nevertheless be treated as satisfying the additional condition set out in that subparagraph for a period of 28 weeks following the date on which he ceased to be so registered."

*Paragraph (2)(c)*
The likely duration of an illness must be determined from the point of view of the date of the application for a direction without regard to circumstances that were not obtaining at that date (*CCS 7522/99*, para.19).

## Special expenses—prior debts

**12.**—(1) Subject to the following paragraphs of this regulation and regulation 15, the repayment of debts to which paragraph (2) applies shall constitute expenses for the purposes of paragraph 2(2) of Schedule 4B to the Act where those debts were incurred— **3.698**

(a) before the non-resident parent became a non-resident parent in relation to the qualifying child; and

(b) at the time when the non-resident parent and the person with care in relation to the child referred to in sub-paragraph (a) were a couple.

(2) This paragraph applies to debts incurred—

(a) for the joint benefit of the non-resident parent and the person with care;

(b) for the benefit of the person with care where the non-resident parent remains legally liable to repay the whole or part of the debt;

(c) for the benefit of any person who is not a child but who at the time the debt was incurred—

   (i) was a child;

  (ii) lived with the non-resident parent and the person with care; and

 (iii) of whom the non-resident parent or the person with care is the parent, or both are the parents;

(d) for the benefit of the qualifying child referred to in paragraph (1); or

(e) for the benefit of any child, other than the qualifying child referred to in paragraph (1), who, at the time the debt was incurred—

   (i) lived with the non-resident parent and the person with care; and

  (ii) of whom the person with care is the parent.

(3) Paragraph (1) shall not apply to repayment of—

(a) a debt which would otherwise fall within paragraph (1) where the non-resident parent has retained for his own use and benefit the asset in connection with the purchase of which he incurred the debt;

(b) a debt incurred for the purposes of any trade or business;

(c) a gambling debt;

(d) a fine imposed on the non-resident parent;

(e) unpaid legal costs in respect of separation or divorce from the person with care;

(f) amounts due after use of a credit card;

(g) a debt incurred by the non-resident parent to pay any of the items listed in subparagraphs (c) to (f) and (j);

(h) amounts payable by the non-resident parent under a mortgage or loan taken out on the security of any property except where that mortgage or loan was taken out to facilitate the purchase of, or to pay for repairs or improvements to, any property which is the home of the person with care and any qualifying child;

(i) amounts payable by the non-resident parent in respect of a policy of insurance except where that policy of insurance was obtained or retained to discharge a mortgage or charge taken out to facilitate the purchase of, or to pay for repairs or improvements to, any property which is the home of the person with care and the qualifying child;

(j) a bank overdraft except where the overdraft was at the time it was taken out agreed to be for a specified amount repayable over a specified period;

(k) a loan obtained by the non-resident parent other than a loan obtained from a qualifying lender or the non-resident parent's current or former employer;

(l) a debt in respect of which a variation has previously been agreed and which has not been repaid during the period for which the maintenance calculation which took account of the variation was in force; or

(m) any other debt which the Secretary of State is satisfied it is reasonable to exclude.

(4) Except where the repayment is of an amount which is payable under a mortgage or loan or in respect of a policy of insurance which falls within the exception set out in sub-paragraph (h) or (i) of paragraph (3), repayment of a debt shall not constitute expenses for the purposes of paragraph (1) where the Secretary of State is satisfied that the non-resident parent has taken responsibility for repayment of that debt as, or as part of, a financial settlement with the person with care or by virtue of a court order.

(5) Where an applicant has incurred a debt partly to repay a debt repayment of which would have fallen within paragraph (1), the repayment of that part of the debt incurred which is referable to the debt repayment of which would have fallen within that paragraph shall constitute expenses for the purposes of paragraph 2(2) of Schedule 4B to the Act.

(6) For the purposes of this regulation and regulation 14—

(a) "qualifying lender" has the meaning given to it in section 376(4) of the Income and Corporation Taxes Act 1988; and

(b) "repairs or improvements" means major repairs necessary to maintain the fabric of the home and any of the following measures—

    (i) installation of a fixed bath, shower, wash basin or lavatory, and necessary associated plumbing;

    (ii) damp-proofing measures;

    (iii) provision or improvement of ventilation and natural light;

    (iv) provision of electric lighting and sockets;

    (v) provision or improvement of drainage facilities;

    (vi) improvement of the structural condition of the home;

    (vii) improvements to the facilities for the storing, preparation and cooking of food;

    (viii) provision of heating, including central heating;

    (ix) provision of storage facilities for fuel and refuse;

    (x) improvements to the insulation of the home; or

    (xi) other improvements which the Secretary of State considers reasonable in the circumstances.

## DEFINITIONS

"the Act": see reg.1(2).                                                      **3.699**
"Contributions and Benefits Act": see reg.1(2).
"home": see reg.1(2).

## GENERAL NOTE

This ground of variation is made under the authority of Sch.4B, para.2(2)(c) to     **3.700**
the Act. It provides for a variation on the ground of debts incurred by the non-resident parent while that parent and the person with care were a couple.

*Paragraph (1)*
This paragraph limits the debts by reference to the status of the non-resident parent. Debts are only relevant if they were incurred (a) before the non-resident

parent became a non-resident parent in relation to the qualifying child and (b) while the non-resident parent and the person with care were a couple. These limitations are illustrated by a debt incurred to meet the costs of the wedding of the parents of a qualifying child. If they were living together before their marriage and when the debt was incurred, this paragraph is satisfied. If they were not living together at either of those times, it is not.

### Paragraph (2)

This paragraph limits the debts by reference to the persons for whose benefit the debt was incurred.

### Paragraph (3)

This paragraph limits the debts by reference to their nature or purpose.

### Head (b)

It is unclear whether "trade and business" includes a profession. The scope of the expression depends on the context (*Stuchbery and Son v General Accident Fire and Life Assurance Corporation Ltd* [1949] 1 All E.R. 1026 at 1027–1028, *per* Lord Greene M.R. and *Rolls v Miller* (1884) 27 Ch.D 71 at 88, *per* Lindley L.D. In this context, it is suggested that profession is included; otherwise the head is anomalously restricted.

### Head (f)

3.701  Amounts due after the use of a credit card are excluded for practical considerations. It may be difficult, if not practically impossible, to identify after a period of time the amount owing that is attributable to a particular transaction. For convenience of operation, this exclusion covers all uses of a credit card, even if the amount attributable to the transaction can be identified.

There is no statutory definition of "credit card" either in the child support legislation or, despite detailed legislation regulating banking and other financial services, elsewhere. The reason lies in the fact that it is not necessary for regulatory purposes to distinguish between credit cards and other simple means of providing credit. In practice, consumers use cards with four functions, some of them combined in a single card. A cheque guarantee card provides a guarantee by a bank that a cheque will be honoured up to the maximum specified on the card. A debit card authorises the debiting of cash or payment for goods or services from the consumer's account, either immediately or after a short delay. A charge card allows short-term credit, although the whole amount must be cleared by a specified date within a month or so. Only a credit card allows long-term credit, subject to a minimum monthly payment and to the charging of interest. It is suggested that this regulation is limited to the final type of card, as it is the only one that creates difficulties in linking the current amount outstanding to a particular transaction.

The use of a credit card constitutes absolute discharge of the consumer's obligation to pay for the goods or services supplied. The supplier's only recourse is against the card provider, not against the customer. See *Re Charge Card Services Ltd* [1988] 3 All E.R. 702. The consequence of this is that it is impossible to take account of the debt underlying the credit card transaction, because it does not exist.

### Head (h)

This head does not apply if the mortgage or loan relates to the purchase, repair or improvement of the home of the person with care or the qualifying child. The relevant time at which the property must be their home is the time of the application for a variation (*CCS 1645/00*, para.15). The purpose of the loan must be judged at the date of the application (*R(CS) 5/03*, para.10).

"Repairs or improvements" is defined in para.(6)(b). See the general note to that provision.

*Head (k)*

"Qualifying lender" is defined in para.(6)(a).

"Employer" is someone who employs a person under a contract of service. It does not include a person who engages someone as an independent contractor under a contract for services (*R(CS) 3/03*, para.8).

*Head (m)*

A tribunal must make a finding on the purposes for which each debt was incurred    3.702
and make a decision whether each debt is excluded under this head. Debts cannot be excluded under this head just because the money was used on day to day living expenses, although it could be reasonable to exclude debts incurred in supporting an extravagant life-style or in purchasing items that are not reasonably required. See *R(CS) 3/02*, para.8.

*Paragraph (4)*

This paragraph excludes debts for which the non-resident parent assumed responsibility in a financial settlement with the person with care or by virtue of a court order. This ensures that the effects of settlements are only considered under Sch.4B, para.3 to the Act.

*Paragraph (5)*

This paragraph extends the scope of this regulation to debts or parts of debts that are incurred in order to discharge a debt that qualifies under this ground. It covers both (a) new debts that are incurred partly to replace the old debt and (b) new debts that are incurred solely to replace the old debt (*R(CS) 3/03*, para.17).

*Paragraph (6)*

*Head (a)*

Although the opening words of this paragraph apply the definitions to reg.14, the expression "qualifying lender" is not used there, although "lender" is. See the general note to reg.14(2).

The definition in the 1988 Act covers: (a) a building society; (b) a local authority; (c) the Bank of England; (d) the Post Office; (e) a company authorised under s.3 or s.4 of the Insurance Companies Act 1982 to carry on in the UK any of the classes of business specified in Sch.1 to that Act; (f) any company to which property and rights belonging to a trustee savings bank were transferred by s.3 of the Trustee Savings Bank Act 1985; (g) a friendly society; (h) a development corporation within the meaning of the New Towns Act 1981 or the New Towns (Scotland) Act 1968; (j) the Commission for the New Towns; (k) the Housing Corporation; (ka) Housing for Wales; (l) the Northern Ireland Housing Executive; (m) Scottish Homes; (n) the Development Board for Rural Wales; (o) the Church of England Pensions Board; (p) any of the following which is for the time being registered under s.376A of the 1988 Act—an institution authorised under the Banking Act 1987, a company authorised as mentioned in (e) above to carry in the UK any of the classes of business specified in Sch.2 to the 1982 Act, and a 90 per cent subsidiary of any such institution or company or of a company within (e) and any other body whose activities and objects appear to the Board to qualify for inclusion in the list. The definition is extended by s.376(6) of the 1988 Act, but that extension is not adopted for the purposes of this regulation.

*Head (b)*

**3.703**   This head distinguishes between repairs and other measures. The latter is defined, the former is not.

Repair covers both the remedying of defects and preventative steps taken to avoid the need for repairs in the future, such as painting a house to preserve the wood-work (*CSB 420/85*, paras 11–12). However, if it is alleged that the step taken was preventative, evidence and findings of fact will be needed on whether the work may properly be considered as undertaken as a repair or only as a cosmetic measure (*ibid.*, para.12). If, for example, the painting of a house is being considered, it will be necessary to inquire into the state of the paint work at the time and whether the work was merely to change the colour.

Repairs must be "*necessary* to maintain the fabric of the home"; a strict test. They must also be "major". Whether a repair is or is not a major repair is a question of fact (*CSB 265/87*, para.10). It is a comparative term whose meaning is bound to be somewhat fluid and imprecise, but it will always be relevant to take into account the cost as well as the nature of and the time taken for the work (*ibid.*, paras 10 and 12). Chimney sweeping cannot be a repair (*ibid.*, para.7). If the home consists of a flat or some other part of a building, repairs to the rest of the building are not repairs to the fabric of the home (*CIS 616/92*, para.16).

Most of the other "measures" are defined in terms of improvement or provision. The reasonableness of the improvement is only relevant under (xi). None of the measures is linked to the improvement of the fitness of the home for habitation or occupation, although this will be a relevant fact in determining reasonableness under (xi).

**3.704**   *Improvement* If a measure is defined in terms of improvement, it is necessary to identify the state of the home before the measure was undertaken in order to determine whether there was a deficiency to be remedied (*CSCS 3/96*, para.4).

*Provision* The Commissioners in their social security jurisdiction have held that provision can include replacement if the state of the item replaced is so bad as to affect the fitness for habitation or occupation of the home. As the child support scheme contains no reference to fitness for habitation or occupation, the social security decision do not necessarily apply.

*Reasonableness* This allows some of the limitations in the definitions of the other measures to be bypassed. For example, a sink is not within (i), but it may be a reasonable improvement under (xi). Reasonableness is not determined either subjectively or objectively. It must be determined on an overall view in the broad-est possible terms. This involves balancing the advantage of the improvement to the person carrying it out against the consequences viewed objectively. An extension to accommodate a large family, for example, might be reasonable, despite the fact that it would not be reflected in an increase in the value of the home, whereas a similar extension built when most of the family were about to leave home would not be: (*R(IS) 3/95*, para.8).

## Special expenses—boarding school fees

**3.705**   **13.**—(1) Subject to the following paragraphs of this regulation and regulation 15, the maintenance element of the costs, incurred or reason-ably expected to be incurred, by the non-resident parent for the purpose of the attendance at a boarding school of the qualifying child shall con-stitute expenses for the purposes of paragraph 2(2) of Schedule 4B to the Act.

(2) Where the Secretary of State considers that the costs referred to in paragraph (1) cannot be distinguished with reasonable certainty from other costs incurred in connection with the attendance at boarding school by the qualifying child, he may instead determine the amount of those costs and any such determination shall not exceed 35% of the total costs.

(3) Where—

(a) the non-resident parent has at the date the variation application is made, received, or at that date is in receipt of, financial assistance from any source in respect of the boarding school fees; or

(b) the boarding school fees are being paid in part by the non-resident parent and in part by another person,

a portion of the costs incurred by the non-resident parent in respect of the boarding school fees shall constitute special expenses for the purposes of paragraph 2(2) of Schedule 4B to the Act being the same proportion as the maintenance element of the costs bears to the total amount of the costs.

(4) No variation on this ground shall reduce by more than 50% the income to which the Secretary of State would otherwise have had regard in the calculation of maintenance liability.

(5) For the purposes of this regulation, "boarding school fees" means the fees payable in respect of attendance at a recognised educational establishment providing full-time education which is not advanced education for children under the age of 19 and where some or all of the pupils, including the qualifying child, are resident during term time.

Definitions

"the Act": see reg.1(2).　　　　　　　　　　　　　　　　　　　　　　**3.706**
"qualifying child": see reg.1(2).

General Note

This ground of variation is made under the authority of Sch.4B, para.2(2)(d) and　**3.707** (5) to the Act. It provides for a variation on the ground of special expenses in respect of maintaining a qualifying child at a boarding school. This may to some extent offset the effect of the power of the courts, preserved under s.8(7) of the Act, to make a maintenance order in respect of expenses incurred in connection with receiving instruction at an education establishment.

The expenses are those incurred or reasonably expected to be incurred by the non-resident parent: see para.(1). They are limited to the maintenance element of the costs: see para.(1). If that amount cannot be distinguished with reasonable certainty, the Secretary of State may determine the amount, subject to a ceiling of 35 per cent of the total costs: see para.(2). No doubt, there will be disputes about the amounts that are included in the "total costs". For example, are additional costs of school trips included?

There are a number of limitations on the financial amounts under this regulation: (a) the regulation is subject to the thresholds under reg.15; (b) the Secretary of State's determination of maintenance costs is subject to a 35 per cent ceiling under para.(2); (c) the costs are apportioned under para.(3) if the non-resident parent and another person share the costs; (d) the variation must not reduce the relevant income by more than 50 per cent.

### Special expenses—payments in respect of certain mortgages, loans or insurance policies

**3.708**   **14.**—(1) Subject to regulation 15, the payments to which paragraph (2) applies shall constitute expenses for the purposes of paragraph 2(2) of Schedule 4B to the Act.

(2) This paragraph applies to payments, whether made to the mortgagee, lender, insurer or the person with care—

(a) in respect of a mortgage or loan where—

    (i) the mortgage or loan was taken out to facilitate the purchase of, or repairs or improvements to, a property ("the property") by a person other than the non-resident parent;

    (ii) the payments are not made under a debt incurred by the non-resident parent or do not arise out of any other legal liability of his for the period in respect of which the variation is applied for;

    (iii) the property was the home of the applicant and the person with care when they were a couple and remains the home of the person with care and the qualifying child; and

    (iv) the non-resident parent has no legal or equitable interest in and no charge or right to have a charge over the property; or

(b) of amounts payable in respect of a policy of insurance taken out for the discharge of a mortgage or loan referred to in subparagraph (a), including an endowment policy, except where the non-resident parent is entitled to any part of the proceeds on the maturity of that policy.

DEFINITIONS

**3.709**   "the Act": see reg.1(2).
"couple": see reg.1(2).
"home": see reg.1(2).
"qualifying child": see reg.1(2).
"repairs or improvements": see reg.12(6)(b).

GENERAL NOTE

**3.710**   This ground of variation is made under the authority of Sch.4B, para.2(2)(e) to the Act. It provides for a variation on the ground of special expenses in respect of purchasing or maintaining the former matrimonial home. This protects the non-resident parent who is meeting all or part of the person with care's housing costs. However, it only applies if the non-resident parent has no interest in or charge over the former home and, in the case of an endowment policy, no right to any part of the proceeds on maturity. That excludes non-resident parents who have transferred their interest in the former matrimonial home to the parent with care, but who are still parties to the mortgage because the mortgagee will not agree to their release.

*Paragraph (2)*
"Lender" is not defined. However, reg.12(6)(a) contains a definition of "qualifying lender" and the opening words of that paragraph apply the definitions to reg.14. That may suggest that lender means qualifying lender.

## Thresholds for and reduction of amount of special expenses

**15.**—(1) Subject to paragraphs (2) to (4), the costs or repayments 3.711 referred to in regulations 10 and 12 to 14 shall be special expenses for the purposes of paragraph 2(2) of Schedule 4B to the Act where and to the extent that they exceed the threshold amount, which is—

   (a) £15 per week where the expenses fall within only one description of expenses and, where the expenses fall within more than one description of expenses, £15 per week in respect of the aggregate of those expenses, where the relevant net weekly income of the non-resident parent is £200 or more; or

   (b) £10 per week where the expenses fall within only one description of expenses, and, where the expenses fall within more than one description of expenses, £10 per week in respect of the aggregate of those expenses, where the relevant net weekly income is below £200.

(2) Subject to paragraph (3), where the Secretary of State considers any expenses referred to in regulations 10 to 14 to be unreasonably high or to have been unreasonably incurred he may substitute such lower amount as he considers reasonable, including an amount which is below the threshold amount or a nil amount.

(3) Any lower amount substituted by the Secretary of State under paragraph (2) in relation to contact costs under regulation 10 shall not be so low as to make it impossible, in the Secretary of State's opinion, for contact between the non-resident parent and the qualifying child to be maintained at the frequency specified in any court order made in respect of the non-resident parent and that child where the non-resident parent is maintaining contact at that frequency.

(4) For the purposes of this regulation, "relevant net weekly income" means the net weekly income taken into account for the purposes of the maintenance calculation before taking account of any variation on the grounds of special expenses.

### Definitions

"the Act": see reg.1(2). 3.712
"qualifying child": see reg.1(2).

### General Note

This regulation sets thresholds for the special expenses grounds of a variation, 3.713 except for those covered reg.11. The nature of the expenses covered by reg.11 makes further thresholds inappropriate.

There are two thresholds: (a) only expenses over a threshold amount are taken into account under para.(1); and (b) expenses may be reduced or disregarded under paras (2) and (3).

*Paragraph (1)*

Only expenses in excess of the threshold amount are taken into account: see para.(1). That amount depends on the non-resident parent's relevant weekly net income, as defined in para.(4). If it is £200 or more, the amount is £15. If the income is below £200, the amount is £10. This differential treatment according to income is authorised by Sch.4B, para.5(5) to the Act.

*Paragraphs (2) and (3)*

Expenses can be reduced or disregarded if they are unreasonably high or unreasonably incurred: see para.(2).

In the case of contact costs under reg.10, the reduction must allow the non-resident parent to continue to maintain contact at the frequency allowed by a court order: see para.(3). There is a problem for a non-resident parent who is prevented from maintaining contact at the frequency set by a court order on account of the amount of the maintenance calculation. Paragraph (3) suggests that expenses should be allowed that are sufficient for this frequency of contact to be established. However, contact that could be made under a court order can only be taken into account under reg.10 if it is actually being maintained. It seems that para.(3) does not tie in with reg.10 as intended.

## PART IV

### PROPERTY OR CAPITAL TRANSFERS

## Prescription of terms

3.714    **16.**—(1) For the purposes of paragraphs 3(1)(a) and (b) of Schedule 4B to the Act—

(a) a court order means an order made—

    (i)   under one or more of the enactments listed in or prescribed under section 8(11) of the Act; and

    (ii)  in connection with the transfer of property of a kind defined in paragraph (2); and

(b) an agreement means a written agreement made in connection with the transfer of property of a kind defined in paragraph (2).

(2) Subject to paragraphs (3) and (4), for the purposes of paragraph 3(2) of Schedule 4B to the Act, a transfer of property is a transfer by the non-resident parent of his beneficial interest in any asset to the person with care, to the qualifying child, or to trustees where the object or one of the objects of the trust is the provision of maintenance.

(3) Where a transfer of property would not have fallen within paragraph (2) when made but the Secretary of State is satisfied that some or all of the amount of that property was subsequently transferred to the person currently with care of the qualifying child, the transfer of that property to the person currently with care shall constitute a transfer of property for the purposes of paragraph 3 of Schedule 4B to the Act.

(4) The minimum value for the purposes of paragraph 3(2) of Schedule 4B to the Act is the threshold amount which is [¹£4999.99].

AMENDMENT

1. Regulation 9(4) of the Miscellaneous Amendments Regulations 2002 (April 30, 2002).

DEFINITIONS

3.715    "the Act": see reg.1(2).

"qualifying child": see reg.1(2).

See the general note to Sch.4B, para.3 to the Act.

## Value of a transfer of property–equivalent weekly value

**17.**—(1) Where the conditions specified in paragraph 3 of Schedule 4B    **3.716**
to the Act are satisfied, the value of a transfer of property for the purposes
of that paragraph shall be that part of the transfer made by the non-resident
parent (making allowances for any transfer by the person with care to the
non-resident parent) which the Secretary of State is satisfied is in lieu of
periodical payments of maintenance.

(2) The Secretary of State shall, in determining the value of a transfer of
property in accordance with paragraph (1), assume that, unless evidence to
the contrary is provided to him—

(a) the person with care and the non-resident parent had equal beneficial interests in the asset in relation to which the court order or
agreement was made;

(b) where the person with care was married to the non-resident parent,
one half of the value of the transfer was a transfer for the benefit of
the person with care; and

(c) where the person with care has never been married to the non-
resident parent, none of the value of the transfer was for the benefit
of the person with care.

(3) The equivalent weekly value of a transfer of property shall be
determined in accordance with the provisions of the Schedule.

(4) For the purposes of regulation 16 and this regulation, the term
"maintenance" means the normal day-to-day living expenses of the
qualifying child.

(5) A variation falling within paragraph (1) shall cease to have effect at
the end of the number of years of liability, as defined in paragraph 1 of the
Schedule, for the case in question.

DEFINITIONS

"the Act": see reg.1(2).    **3.717**
"qualifying child": see reg.1(2).

GENERAL NOTE

This regulation provides for the effect of satisfying the conditions set out in    **3.718**
Sch.4B, para.3 to the Act, as supplemented by reg.16.

*Paragraph (1)*
This paragraph requires that the part of the transfer that led to the reduction in
maintenance be identified. That capital sum is then converted to an equivalent
weekly value under the Schedule to these Regulations.

*Paragraph (2)*
This paragraph lays down realistic but rebuttable presumptions that assist in
identifying (a) the amount of the transfer and (b) the extent to which it was in lieu
of maintenance for the child. In practice, the value of those presumptions is likely
to be reduced by the frequency with which they are challenged.

PART V

ADDITIONAL CASES

**Assets**

3.719     **18.**—(1) Subject to paragraphs (2) and (3), a case shall constitute a case for the purposes of paragraph 4(1) of Schedule 4B to the Act where the Secretary of State is satisfied there is an asset—

(a) in which the non-resident parent [¹has a beneficial interest], or which the non-resident parent has the ability to control;

(b) which has been transferred by the non-resident parent to trustees, and the non-resident parent is a beneficiary of the trust so created, in circumstances where the Secretary of State is satisfied the non-resident parent has made the transfer to reduce the amount of assets which would otherwise be taken into account for the purposes of a variation under paragraph 4(1) of Schedule 4B to the Act; or

(c) which has become subject to a trust created by legal implication of which the non-resident parent is a beneficiary.

(2) For the purposes of this regulation "asset" means—

(a) money, whether in cash or on deposit, including any which, in Scotland, is monies due or an obligation owed, whether immediately payable or otherwise and whether the payment or obligation is secured or not and the Secretary of State is satisfied that requiring payment of the monies or implementation of the obligation would be reasonable;

(b) a legal estate or beneficial interest in land and rights in or over land;

(c) shares as defined in section 744 of the Companies Act 1985, stock and unit trusts as defined in section 6 of the Charging Orders Act 1979, gilt-edged securities as defined in Part 1 of Schedule 9 to the Taxation of Chargeable Gains Act 1992, and other similar financial instruments; or

(d) a chose in action which has not been enforced when the Secretary of State is satisfied that such enforcement would be reasonable,

and includes any such asset located outside Great Britain.

(3) Paragraph (2) shall not apply—

[⁵(a) where the total value of the assets referred to in that paragraph does not exceed £65,000 after deduction of—

(i) the amount owing under any mortgage or charge on those assets;

(ii) the value of any asset in respect of which income has been taken into account under regulation 19(1A);]

(b) in relation to any asset which the Secretary of State is satisfied is being retained by the non-resident parent to be used for a purpose which the Secretary of State considers reasonable in all the circumstances of the case;

(c) to any asset received by the non-resident parent as compensation for personal injury suffered by him;

(d) [²except where the asset is of a type specified in paragraph (2)(b) and produces income which does not form part of the net weekly income of the non-resident parent as calculated or estimated under Part III of the Schedule to the Maintenance Calculations and Special Cases Regulations,] to any asset used in the course of a trade or business; or

(e) to property which is the home of the non-resident parent or any child of his [³; or

(f) where, were the non-resident parent a claimant, paragraph 22 (treatment of payments from certain trusts) or 64 (treatment of relevant trust payments) of Schedule 10 to the Income Support (General) Regulations 1987 would apply to the asset referred to in that paragraph.]

(4) For the purposes of this regulation, where any asset is held in the joint names of the non-resident parent and another person the Secretary of State shall assume, unless evidence to the contrary is provided to him, that the asset is held by them in equal shares.

(5) Where a variation is agreed on the ground that the non-resident parent has assets for which provision is made in this regulation, the Secretary of State shall calculate the weekly value of the assets by applying the statutory rate of interest to the value of the assets and dividing by 52, and the resulting figure, aggregated with any benefit, pension or allowance [⁴prescribed for the purposes of paragraph 4(1)(b) of Schedule 1 to the Act] which the non-resident parent receives, other than any benefits referred to in regulation 26(3), shall be taken into account as additional income under regulation 25.

(6) For the purposes of this regulation, the "statutory rate of interest" means interest at the statutory rate prescribed for a judgment debt or, in Scotland, the statutory rate in respect of interest included in or payable under a decree in the Court of Session; which in either case applies on the date from which the maintenance calculation which takes account of the variation takes effect.

AMENDMENTS

1. Regulation 9(5)(a) of the Miscellaneous Amendments Regulations 2002 (April 30, 2002).
2. Regulation 9(5)(b)(i) of the Miscellaneous Amendments Regulations 2002 (April 30, 2002).
3. Regulation 9(5)(b)(ii) of the Miscellaneous Amendments Regulations 2002 (April 30, 2002).
4. Regulation 9(6) of the Miscellaneous Amendments Regulations 2002 (April 30, 2002).
5. Regulation 8(4) of the Miscellaneous Amendments Regulations 2005 (April 6, 2005).

DEFINITIONS

"the Act": see reg.1(2).                                                                   3.720
"home": see reg.1(2)
"Maintenance Calculations and Special Cases Regulations": see reg.1(2)

GENERAL NOTE

This ground of variation is made under the authority of Sch.4B, para.4(2)(a) to    3.721
the Act. In effect, this regulation provides for a notional income to be attributed to

a non-resident parent's specified capital assets that in aggregate exceed a minimum value.

The application of this regulation may vary according to how the items under consideration are viewed. Some may be viewed individually as a parcel. For example, a farm may be viewed as a single asset or as a parcel consisting of a number of assets, like the farmhouse and land. The Secretary of State and the appeal tribunal are entitled to treat the items individually or collectively if both views are appropriate. See *CCS 8/00*, para.16.

*Paragraph (1)*

This paragraph defines the legal relationships that must exist between the non-resident parent and the assets.

*Head (a)*

This head and para.(2)(b) below cannot be read together literally. If they were, the Secretary of State would have to be satisfied that the non-resident parent had a beneficial interest in a beneficial interest in land. That is nonsense. The provision has to be interpreted to mean that the Secretary of State must be satisfied that the non-resident parent has a beneficial interest in land. See *CCS 8/00*, para.24.

Control may exist in law, as in the case of a director's control over the activities of a company, or in practice, as in the case of one spouse's control over the other or a parent's control over a child.

In the case of control in law, its existence is easily shown and its exercise readily appears from the decisions taken.

Control in practice is more difficult to prove. The word "ability" indicates that it is the reality of control that is important. Control is stronger than influence. The difference is one of fact and degree. In practice, it may be difficult to investigate sufficiently to show whether the degree of influence that one person exercises over another amounts to control.

It may be necessary to distinguish between control for different purposes. This is especially so in the case of a registered company, because different decisions may in law be made by different organs of the company and each organ may be subject to control or influence by others. So, the salary of the directors may be controlled in law by the board, which may be controlled in practice by one or more actual or shadow directors or shareholders, while dividends may be controlled, at least to the extent of approval, by the general meeting, which in turn may control or be controlled by the board.

If the persons involved do not co-operate in investigating the location of real control, it is necessary to proceed by inferences based on the probabilities and taking account of the likely reasons for refusing to co-operate.

Often the non-resident parent may only own an asset jointly with a partner. There may be evidence that the partner will not co-operate in a sale. That is not conclusive of the issue. The Secretary of State or the appeal tribunal must decide whether to accept that evidence (*CCS 8/00*, para.33). The non-resident parent may be able to apply for an order for sale under ss.14 and 15 of the Trusts of Land and Appointment of Trustees Act 1996, but it is not inevitable that the court would make an order (*CCS 8/00*, paras 32–34).

*Paragraph (2)*

3.722    This paragraph defines the assets that are covered by this regulation.

*Head (c)*

Section 744 of the Companies Act 1985 provides that "'share' means share in the capital of a company, and includes stock except where such a distinction between stock and share is expressed or implied."

In valuing shares, it is the shares themselves that have to be valued, not the assets or any particular asset owned by the company *(R(IS) 13/93)*. In valuing shares in a public company, the bid price must be used rather than the offer price or the averaged prices which are published in the press, although in line with Inland Revenue practice it may be permissible to take the lowest bid price on a particular day and add to it one-quarter of the difference between the lowest and highest prices *(R(IS) 18/95,* paras 9 and 10).

*Paragraph (3)*
This paragraph contains the exceptions. Only head (b) contains a discretionary element.

*Head (b)*
This exception confers a discretion on the Secretary of State to disregard an asset. It is an all or nothing exception. Only the whole of the asset can be disregarded; there is no scope for apportionment.

The test is whether the asset has been retained to be used for a purpose that is reasonable. It is the purpose that must be reasonable, not the retention. Use and purpose will usually be two sides of the same coin. A pension fund is an obvious example of an asset which will be excluded under this exception. Non-resident parents may argue that assets not held in a fund are in fact intended to be retained to provide for retirement. Whether or not that is the case is a question of fact.

*Head (d)*
See the general note to reg. 12(3)(b)

## Income not taken into account and diversion of income

**19.**—(1) Subject to paragraph (2), a case shall constitute a case for the purposes of paragraph 4(1) of Schedule 4B to the Act where— 3.723

- (a) the non-resident parent's liability to pay child support maintenance under the maintenance calculation which is in force or has been applied for or treated as applied for, is, or would be, as the case may be—
  - (i) the nil rate owing to the application of paragraph 5(a) of Schedule 1 to the Act; or
  - (ii) a flat rate, owing to the application of paragraph 4(1)(b) of Schedule 1 to the Act, or would be a flat rate but is less than that amount, or nil, owing to the application of paragraph 8 of Schedule 1 to the Act; and
- (b) the Secretary of State is satisfied that the non-resident parent is in receipt of income which would fall to be taken into account under the Maintenance Calculations and Special Cases Regulations but for the application to the non-resident parent of paragraph 4(1)(b) or 5(a) of Schedule 1 to the Act.

[²(1A) Subject to paragraph (2), a case shall constitute a case for the purposes of paragraph 4(1) of Schedule 4B to the Act where—
- (a) the non-resident parent has the ability to control the amount of income he receives from a company or business, including earnings from employment or self-employment; and
- (b) the Secretary of State is satisfied that the non-resident parent is receiving income from that company or business which would not

otherwise fall to be taken into account under the Maintenance Calculations and Special Cases Regulations.]

[³(2) Paragraphs (1) and (1A) shall apply where—
- (a) the income referred to in paragraph (1)(b) is net weekly income of over £100; or
- (b) the income referred to in paragraph (1A)(b) is over £100; or
- (c) the aggregate of the net weekly income referred to in sub-paragraph (a) and the income referred to in sub-paragraph (b) is over £100,

as the case may be.]

(3) Net weekly income for the purposes of paragraph (2), in relation to earned income of a non-resident parent who is a student, shall be calculated by aggregating the income for the year ending with the relevant week (which for this purpose shall have the meaning given in the Maintenance Calculations and Special Cases Regulations) and dividing by 52, or, where the Secretary of State does not consider the result to be representative of the student's earned income, over such other period as he shall consider representative and dividing by the number of weeks in that period.

(4) A case shall constitute a case for the purposes of paragraph 4(1) of Schedule 4B to the Act where—
- (a) the non-resident parent has the ability to control the amount of income he receives, including earnings from employment or self-employment, whether or not the whole of that income is derived from the company or business from which his earnings are derived, and
- (b) the Secretary of State is satisfied that the non-resident parent has unreasonably reduced the amount of his income which would otherwise fall to be taken into account under the Maintenance Calculations and Special Cases Regulations [⁴or paragraph (1A)] by diverting it to other persons or for purposes other than the provision of such income for himself [⁵. . .].

(5) Where a variation on this ground is agreed to—
- (a) in a case to which paragraph (1) applies, the additional income taken into account under regulation 25 shall be the whole of the income referred to in paragraph (1)(b), aggregated with any benefit, pension or allowance [¹ prescribed for the purposes of paragraph 4(1)(b) of Schedule 1 to the Act] which the non-resident parent receives other than any benefits referred to in regulation 26(3); and
- (b) in a case to which paragraph (4) applies, the additional income taken into account under regulation 25 shall be the whole of the amount by which the Secretary of State is satisfied the non-resident parent has unreasonably reduced his income [⁶; and
- (c) in a case to which paragraph (1A) applies, the additional income taken into account under regulation 25 shall be the whole of the income referred to in paragraph (1A)(b).]

AMENDMENTS

1. Regulation 9(6) of the Miscellaneous Amendments Regulations 2002 (April 30, 2002).

2. Regulation 8(5)(a) of the Miscellaneous Amendments Regulations 2005 (April 6, 2005).

3. Regulation 8(5)(b) of the Miscellaneous Amendments Regulations 2005 (April 6, 2005).

4. Regulation 8(5)(c)(i) of the Miscellaneous Amendments Regulations 2005 (April 6, 2005).

5. Regulation 8(5)(c)(ii) of the Miscellaneous Amendments Regulations 2005 (April 6, 2005).

6. Regulation 8(5)(d) of the Miscellaneous Amendments Regulations 2005 (April 6, 2005).

DEFINITIONS

"the Act": see reg.1(2).                                                                                        **3.724**
"Maintenance Calculations and Special Cases Regulations": see reg.1(2).

GENERAL NOTE

This ground of variation is made under the authority of Sch.4B, para.4(2)(c) and   **3.725**
(d) to the Act. It covers three types of case: paras (1), (1A) and (4).

*Paragraph (1)*
This paragraph, supplemented by paras (2) and (3), covers cases where a non-resident parent has income which is not taken into account under Sch.1 to the Act. The effect of this type of variation is specified in para.5(a).

This type of variation only applies to non-resident parents who would otherwise pay a flat or nil, but only because income is excluded under para.4(1)(b) or 5(a) of Sch.1 to the Act.

*Paragraph 1A*
This paragraph complements para.(4). That paragraph deals with the case in which the non-resident parent reduces income that would otherwise be taken into account under the Maintenance Calculations and Special Cases Regulations. This paragraph deals with the case in which the non-resident parent organises the financial affairs of the business or company in order to take income in a form that would not be taken into account under the Maintenance Calculations and Special Cases Regulations. In doing so, it catches directors who take income as dividends, which are outside an assessment under those Regulations, instead of as wages or salary, which are covered by the Schedule assessment.

*Paragraph (2)*
Paragraph (1) only applies if the amount of the net weekly income excluded under Sch.1 to the Act is over £100. This is subject to para.(3).

*Paragraph (3)*
This paragraph governs the calculation of net weekly income of a student.

*Paragraph (4)*
This paragraph covers a case where a non-resident parent is able to control earn-   **3.726**
ings and has unreasonably reduced them, in whole or in part. The effect of this type of variation is specified in para.5(b).

For a discussion of "ability to control", see the general note to reg.18(1)(a).

Businesses that are run on sound lines in accordance with recognised business and accounting practices are unlikely to be caught by this paragraph. However, many small business are not run in that way and, in the case of registered companies, are run without any clear understanding of the separate existence in law of the company and its owners and without regard to the proper functions of the different organs of the company.

In practice, the key issue will often be the reasonableness of the reduction. If the spouse of a non-resident parent is paid for work in a business, this will largely depend on the relationship between the wages paid and the spouse's contribution to the business. Cases where money is retained in a company or paid as dividends instead of paid as wages to a non-resident parent cause difficulties. It is legitimate and reasonable for a business to make profits and to retain all or part of them to help in growth. However, retained profits are not the only source of funds. A company could issue more shares to raise capital or borrow. In considering whether retention was reasonable, interest rates, tax regimes and the stage of the company's development will all be relevant. Motivation and intention is not directly relevant, but if they can be proved they may be indirectly relevant to reasonableness.

It is the reduction in the non-resident parent's income that is relevant, not the amount by which anyone else benefits. Suppose that a non-resident parent's income from a company is reduced and diverted to that parent's spouse who is also employed by the company, the amount that the spouse receives may be greater than the reduction in the parent's income, after tax and national insurance contributions are taken into account. It is the reduction that is relevant. The relevant figure is the amount of income that the non-resident parent could *receive*, but does not. When this is read in conjunction with para.(5)(b) and reg.25, it is clear that it is the net amount that is relevant.

Merely withdrawing money from an account is not a diversion or reduction of income in the context of this provision (*CCS 2861/02*, para.9). Taking a benefit in kind (as, for example, a company car) instead of in cash is diverting income for another purpose (*CCS 3757/04*, para.34).

For the case in which the non-resident parent reorganises the finances of a business or company in order to take income in a form that is outside the scope of the Maintenance Calculations and Special Cases Regulations, see para.(1A).

## Life-style inconsistent with declared income

3.727    **20.**—(1) Subject to paragraph (3), a case shall constitute a case for the purposes of paragraph 4(1) of Schedule 4B to the Act where—

  (a) the non-resident parent's liability to pay child support maintenance under the maintenance calculation which is in force, or which has been applied for or treated as applied for, is, or would be, as the case may be—

  (i) the basic rate,

  (ii) the reduced rate,

  (iii) a flat rate owing to the application of paragraph 4(1)(a) of Schedule 1 to the Act, including where the net weekly income of the non-resident parent taken into account for the purposes of the maintenance calculation is, or would be, £100 per week or less owing to a variation being taken into account, or to the application of regulation 18, 19 or 21 of the Transitional Regulations (deduction for relevant departure direction or relevant property transfer);

  (iv) £5 per week or such other amount as may be prescribed owing to the application of paragraph 7(7) of Schedule 1 to the Act (shared care);

  (v) equivalent to the flat rate provided for in, or prescribed for the purposes of, paragraph 4(1)(b) of Schedule 1 to the Act owing to the application of—

(aa) regulation 27(5);

(bb) regulation 9 of the Maintenance Calculations and Special Cases Regulations (care provided in part by a local authority); or

(cc) regulation 23(5) of the Transitional Regulations; or

(vi) the nil rate owing to the application of paragraph 5(b) of Schedule 1 to the Act; and

(b) the Secretary of State is satisfied that the income which has been, or would be, taken into account for the purposes of the maintenance calculation is substantially lower than the level of income required to support the overall life-style of the non-resident parent.

(2) Subject to paragraph (4), a case shall constitute a case for the purposes of paragraph 4(1) of Schedule 4B to the Act where the non-resident parent's liability to pay child support maintenance under the maintenance calculation which is in force, or which has been applied for or treated as applied for, is, or would be, as the case may be—

(a) a flat rate owing to the application of paragraph 4(1)(b) of Schedule 1 to the Act, or would be a flat rate but is less than that amount, or nil, owing to the application of paragraph 8 of Schedule 1 to the Act; or

(b) the nil rate owing to the application of paragraph 5(a) of Schedule 1 to the Act,

and the Secretary of State is satisfied that the income which would otherwise be taken into account for the purposes of the maintenance calculation is substantially lower than the level of income required to support the overall life-style of the non-resident parent.

(3) Paragraph (1) shall not apply where the Secretary of State is satisfied that the life-style of the non-resident parent is paid for from—

(a) income which is or would be disregarded for the purposes of a maintenance calculation under the Maintenance Calculations and Special Cases Regulations;

[²(aa) income which falls to be considered under regulation 19(1A) (income not taken into account);

(b) income which falls to be considered under regulation 19(4) (diversion of income);

(c) assets as defined for the purposes of regulation 18, or income derived from those assets;

(d) the income of any partner of the non-resident parent, except where the non-resident parent is able to influence or control the amount of income received by that partner; or

(e) assets as defined for the purposes of regulation 18 of any partner of the non-resident parent, or any income derived from such assets, except where the non-resident parent is able to influence or control the assets, their use, or income derived from them.

(4) Paragraph (2) shall not apply where the Secretary of State is satisfied that the life-style of the non-resident parent is paid for—

(a) from a source referred to in paragraph (3);

(b) from net weekly income of £100 or less; or

(c) from income which falls to be considered under regulation 19(1).

(5) Where a variation on this ground is agreed to, the additional income taken into account under regulation 25 shall be the difference between the income which the Secretary of State is satisfied the non-resident parent

requires to support his overall life-style and the income which has been or, but for the application of paragraph 4(1)(b) or 5(a) of Schedule 1 to the Act, would be taken into account for the purposes of the maintenance calculation, aggregated with any benefit, pension or allowance [¹ prescribed for the purposes of paragraph 4(1)(b) of Schedule 1 to the Act] which the non-resident parent receives other than any benefits referred to in regulation 26(3).

AMENDMENTS

1. Regulation 9(6) of the Miscellaneous Amendments Regulations 2002 (April 30, 2002).
2. Regulation 8(6) of the Miscellaneous Amendments Regulations 2005 (April 6, 2005).

DEFINITIONS

3.728 "the Act": see reg.1(2).
"Maintenance Calculations and Special Cases Regulations": See reg.1(2).
"partner": see reg.1(2).

GENERAL NOTE

3.729 This ground of variation is made under the authority of Sch.4B, para.4(2)(b) to the Act. It allows income to be determined by inference from life-style rather than by more direct evidence (*CCS 2230/01*, para.19).

This ground of variation has an uneasy relationship with the Schedule assessment. Commissioners criticised the equivalent head of departure dirrection as being unnecessary (*CCS 6282/99*, para.9).

The relationship between this head and a Schedule assessment of income was considered by the Commissioner in *R(CS) 3/01*, paras 25–34. He noted that a parent's life-style could be used as evidence for a Schedule assessment or as evidence of additional income for a variation. In the case of an overlap, an appeal tribunal should deal with the evidence in the context of the case before it. If the case is a Schedule case, it is mandatory to take account of income, however it is proved. If it has been taken into account under the Schedule, it cannot be relied on again under this regulation. If for some reason it has not been taken into account under the Schedule, it can be considered under this regulation. If it is taken into account under this regulation, the next time that the application of the Schedule is reconsidered, it can be taken directly into account so that the variation is no longer needed. In *CCS 821/03*, the Commissioner emphasised at para.14 that he was in that case concerned with income that was proved by inference. If the income was proved by direct evidence and was assessed by reference to a past accounting period, it was inherent that the calculation might be out of date to the advantage of either the non-resident parent or the person with care. In those circumstances, it was better to leave the Schedule assessment of income to catch up with reality over time rather than to disrupt it by the variation scheme.

Before an appeal tribunal can apply this head, it needs to know the income on which the Schedule assessment was based, its source and the nature of any deductions from it (*CCS 3331/99*, para.10).

In principle, it should not be possible to have a life-style the funding of which cannot be accounted for if there has been full disclosure of income. If the tribunal considers that there has been full disclosure, but that nonetheless it cannot account for the evidence of life-style, the tribunal should investigate further to try to reconcile this apparent inconsistency. See *CCS 821/03*, paras 18–20.

*Subparagraph (1)(b)*

"Overall life-style" is wide enough to cover all aspects of personal behaviour, activities, interests and choices. "Substantially" is an ordinary word with no technical meaning; a definition is not necessary and might improperly limit its scope. See *CCS 4247/99*, para.32 and *CSC6/03–04(T)*, paras 46–49).

The relevant time at which this regulation has to be applied is the effective date of the variation that might be agreed. The tribunal must inevitably rely on evidence from the past to prove both the life-style and how that life-style is funded. However, that evidence must be related to the relevant time. See *CCS 821/03*, paras 10–13. If the Schedule assessment was based on income at a much earlier time, the just and equitable requirement should be used to prevent inappropriate comparisons being used between income at one date and life-style at another. See *CCS 821/03*, para.13.

An amount paid by way of a pension premium in excess of the amounts laid down in the income tax legislation may be evidence of the level of life-style enjoyed by a parent (*CCS 4666/99*, para.16).

3.730

The lack of sufficient findings of fact on life-style under this regulation does not justify an appeal tribunal taking a wider approach to the calculation of income than is authorised by subpara.(5) (*CCS 3927/99*, para.20).

The Secretary of State regularly relied in departure direction cases on a ministerial statement in the House of Commons on the importance of discretion in view of the difficulties of producing direct or conclusive evidence to support an application. In *CCS 7411/99*, paras 13–15, the Commissioner rejected this suggestion. He recognised that many applicants would have to rely heavily on the drawing of inferences and that tribunals would bear in mind the difficulties facing applicants, but nonetheless there must be a rational basis for drawing the inferences and non-applicants must not be prejudiced by drawing inferences that are not based on a rational analysis of the evidence. No special discretionary approach was required, as both parties could be adequately protected by concentrating on the issues identified as relevant by the legislation and by applying the civil burden and standard of proof to those issues.

The standard of proof is the usual balance of probabilities. That is a variable standard in that the persuasiveness of the evidence needed to tip the balance varies with the seriousness of the allegation. See the *Burdens and standard of proof* section of the general note to reg.49(1) of the Appeals Regulations. An allegation under this provision is not tantamount to an allegation of fraud (*CCS 2623/99*).

*Paragraph (2)*

This paragraph covers cases where the non-resident parent falls within para.4(1)(b) or 5(a) of Sch.1 to the Act.

See the general note to para.(1)(b) above.

*Paragraph (3)*

This contains exceptions to the scope of para.(1). They are not exhaustive of the possibilities. A common explanation for an inconsistency between a parent's lifestyle and disclosed income is that it is supported by debt. Other sources of support for the life-style are not irrelevant. They must be taken into account in applying the just and equitable test. In *CCS 2230/01*, para.19, the Commissioner was concerned with a case in which the tribunal had found that the non-resident parent's life-style was supported by contributions from a lady friend who was not living with him. As she was not his partner, this provision did not apply. However, the Commissioner held that the source was relevant to the application of the just and equitable test. He did not rule out the possibility that it might be just and equitable to agree to a variation on the basis that a contribution from someone who was not covered by this provision should be treated as part of the non-resident parent's

3.731

income for the purposes of child support, but did not accept that such a contribution must always be taken into account (para.19).

This paragraph only applies if the whole of the additional income needed to support the life-style comes from one or more of the sources listed: *R(CS) 6/02*. If it comes only partly from those sources, this paragraph does not apply, but the fact that some of it comes from those sources provides a strong case for not agreeing to a variation in respect of it (*R(CS) 6/02*).

Subparagraph (c) refers to reg.18. However, only reg.18(2) is relevant. Subparagraph (c) refers to types of asset and the only place where they are defined in reg.18 is in para.(2). The general reference to reg.18 does not import all the provisions of that regulation, including para.(3).

*Paragraph (4)*

This contains the exceptions to the scope of para.(4) by extending the scope of para.(3).

*Paragraph (5)*

The calculation set out in this paragraph is mandatory. It is not permissible simply to determine the parent's total income. Only the level of income necessary to support the overall life-style may be taken into account: *R(CS) 3/01* para.21; *CCS 1840/99*, para.12; *CCS 3927/99*, paras 14–15.

However, the calculation required by this paragraph cannot be made with precision. In practice, there is likely to be a range of incomes that could support the life-style. This allows a tribunal, in an exceptional case, to use a parent's total income as a guide to the level of income necessary to support the parent's life-style. There may be sufficient evidence to allow a fairly accurate determination of a parent's total income. If that amount is within the range of incomes that would be needed to support the life-style, it is proper to treat that income as the level needed to support the life-style. See *CCS 3927/99*, para.19.

The lack of sufficient findings of fact on life-style does not justify an appeal tribunal taking a wider approach to the calculation of income than is authorised by this paragraph (*CCS 3927/99*, para.20).

PART VI

FACTORS TO BE TAKEN INTO ACCOUNT FOR THE PURPOSES OF SECTION 28F OF THE ACT

## Factors to be taken into account and not to be taken into account

3.732     **21.**—(1) The factors to be taken into account in determining whether it would be just and equitable to agree to a variation in any case shall include—

    (a) where the application is made on any ground—

        (i) whether, in the opinion of the Secretary of State, agreeing to a variation would be likely to result in a relevant person ceasing paid employment;

        (ii) if the applicant is the non-resident parent, the extent, if any, of his liability to pay child maintenance under a court order or agreement in the period prior to the effective date of the maintenance calculation; and

(b) where an application is made on the ground that the case falls within regulations 10 to 14 (special expenses), whether, in the opinion of the Secretary of State—

    (i) the financial arrangements made by the non-resident parent could have been such as to enable the expenses to be paid without a variation being agreed; or

    (ii) the non-resident parent has at his disposal financial resources which are currently utilised for the payment of expenses other than those arising from essential everyday requirements and which could be used to pay the expenses.

(2) The following factors are not to be taken into account in determining whether it would be just and equitable to agree to a variation in any case—

(a) the fact that the conception of the qualifying child was not planned by one or both of the parents;

(b) whether the non-resident parent or the person with care of the qualifying child was responsible for the breakdown of the relationship between them;

(c) the fact that the non-resident parent or the person with care of the qualifying child has formed a new relationship with a person who is not a parent of that child;

(d) the existence of particular arrangements for contact with the qualifying child, including whether any arrangements made are being adhered to;

(e) the income or assets of any person other than the non-resident parent, other than the income or assets of a partner of the non-resident parent taken into account under regulation 20(3);

(f) the failure by a non-resident parent to make payments of child support maintenance, or to make payments under a maintenance order or a written maintenance agreement; or

(g) representations made by persons other than the relevant persons.

DEFINITIONS

"partner": see reg.1(2).        3.733
"qualifying child": see reg.1(2).
"relevant person": see reg.1(2).

GENERAL NOTE

This regulation is made under the authority of s.28F(2)(b) of the Act. It contains   3.734
the prescribed circumstances that must, or must not, be taken into account in determining whether it would be just and equitable to agree to a variation.

*Paragraph (1)*
This sets out the factors that must be taken into account.

*Subparagraph (a)*
These factors apply in all cases. None is decisive. They are additional to the factors that are relevant under the general principle in s.28E(1)(b) of the Act and the duty in s.28F(2)(a) of the Act.

*Head (i)*

Non-resident parents often threaten to give up work, but that it is not decisive. It may not be a real threat. Even if it is, it only has to be taken into account and balanced with all other relevant factors. It must be seen not as a blackmailer's charter, but as part of the reality that the child support maintenance payable depends on the continuing viability of the non-resident parent's employment. A variation should not be agreed to if its effect would be to place such a financial burden on a non-resident parent that the best option would be to cease paid employment.

This factor is most likely to arise as a live issue if the variation might lead to the non-resident parent giving up work, but it is not so limited. It applies also if the increase in child support maintenance would allow the person with care to cease employment.

It is the agreeing to the variation that must create the risk. It is irrelevant that the refusal to agree might produce this outcome, although that would be relevant under the general requirement in s.28F(1)(b).

Appeal tribunals must be careful to distinguish between this factor and s.28E(4)(a) of the Act.

*Head (ii)*

3.735      This factor may support a variation by reducing the amount of child support maintenance payable in order to ease the burden of the transition from a relatively low amount under an order or agreement to a higher amount of child support maintenance. It may also have the opposite effect if the amount previously payable was unrealistically low given what the non-resident parent could afford.

Although it does not expressly say so, this head must be limited to cases where (a) the maintenance was payable to or for the qualifying child and (b) immediately before the effective date of the maintenance calculation.

*Subparagraph (b)*

These factors only apply to the special cases heads of a variation. They are effectively anti-avoidance measures.

*Paragraph (2)*

This sets out the factors that must not be taken into account. See also the factors in s.28E(4) of the Act.

*Head (c)*

It is the fact of the new relationship that has to be disregarded, not facts that follow from it, such as additional income available to support the non-resident parent's new family from the partner (*CSCS 16/03*, paras 16–17).

*Head (d)*

The costs of maintaining contact are relevant under reg.10. This head limits the existence and honouring of contact arrangements to that provision.

*Head (e)*

This excludes the income and assets of anyone other than the non-resident parent. The income and assets of the person with care are therefore irrelevant. This is not surprising, as the focus of the new child support scheme is on making a share of the non-resident parent's income available for the benefit of the child. The focus is no longer on sharing the costs of bringing up a child.

*Head (f)*

This head only operates if an application for a variation is being considered. If a regular payments condition has been imposed under s.28C of the Act, failure to comply may lead to the application not being considered under s.28C(5).

The emphasis in an application for a variation is on the future. Hence past failure is irrelevant once the just and equitable stage has been reached.

*Head (g)*

This complements s.28E(3) of the Act. That subsection applies generally and is not limited to the just and equitable requirement. It does not prevent the Secretary of State making submissions to an appeal tribunal on appeal.

## PART VII

### EFFECT OF A VARIATION ON THE MAINTENANCE CALCULATION AND EFFECTIVE DATES

## Effective dates

**22.**—(1) Subject to paragraph (2), where the application for a variation is made in the circumstances referred to in section 28A(3) of the Act (before the Secretary of State has reached a decision under section 11 or 12(1) of the Act) and the application is agreed to, the effective date of the maintenance calculation which takes account of the variation shall be—

    (a) where the ground giving rise to the variation existed from the effective date of the maintenance calculation as provided for in the Maintenance Calculation Procedure Regulations, that date; or

    (b) where the ground giving rise to the variation arose after the effective date referred to in sub-paragraph (a), the first day of the maintenance period in which the ground arose.

(2) Where the ground for the variation applied for under section 28A(3) of the Act is a ground in regulation 12 (prior debts) or 14 (special expenses-payments in respect of certain mortgages, loans or insurance policies) and payments falling within regulation 12 or 14 which have been made by the non-resident parent constitute voluntary payments for the purposes of section 28J of the Act and Regulations made under that section, the date from which the maintenance calculation shall take account of the variation on this ground shall be the date on which the maintenance period begins which immediately follows the date on which the non-resident parent is notified under the Maintenance Calculation Procedure Regulations of the amount of his liability to pay child support maintenance.

(3) Where the ground for the variation applied for under section 28A(3) of the Act has ceased to exist by the date the maintenance calculation is made, that calculation shall take account of the variation for the period ending on the last day of the maintenance period in which the ground existed.

DEFINITION

"Maintenance Calculation Procedure Regulations": see reg.1(2).

**3.736**

**3.737**

GENERAL NOTE

**3.738**    Paragraphs (1) and (2) of this regulation determines the effective date of a variation if the application for a variation is considered together with an application for a maintenance calculation. Despite the heading of the regulation, para.(3) deals with the termination of a variation.

*Paragraph (1)*
    This paragraph contains a basic rule and an exception. The basic rule is that the effective date of the variation is the same as that of the calculation. The exception applies if the variation is based on a change that occurred after that date. In that case, the effective date is the first day of the maintenance period in which the change occurred.

*Paragraph (2)*
    This paragraph applies if payments made under reg.12 or 14 were voluntary payments under s.28J of the Act. In that case, the effective date is the first day of the maintenance period following the notification of the amount of the non-resident parent's liability to child support maintenance. For the date of notification, see the definition in reg.1(2).

*Paragraph (3)*
    This paragraph applies if the ground for a variation has ceased to exist by the date when the maintenance calculation is made. In that case, it runs only until the last day of the maintenance period in which it ceased to exist.

### Effect on maintenance calculation—special expenses

**3.739**    **23.**—(1) Subject to paragraph (2) and regulations 26 and 27, where the variation agreed to is one falling within regulation 10 to 14 (special expenses) effect shall be given to the variation in the maintenance calculation by deducting from the net weekly income of the non-resident parent the weekly amount of those expenses.
    (2) Where the income which is taken into account in the maintenance calculation is the capped amount and the variation agreed to is one falling within regulation 10 to 14 then—
    (a) the weekly amount of the expenses shall first be deducted from the actual net weekly income of the non-resident parent;
    (b) the amount by the which the capped amount exceeds the figure calculated under sub-paragraph (a) shall be calculated; and
    (c) effect shall be given to the variation in the maintenance calculation by deducting from the capped amount the amount calculated under sub-paragraph (b).

DEFINITION

    "capped amount": see reg.1(2).
    "net weekly income": see reg.27(7).

GENERAL NOTE

**3.740**    This regulation, together with regs 26 and 27, specifies the effect of a variation on the ground of a special expense under regs 10 to 14:

*Paragraph (1)*

The effect of a variation is to reduce the net weekly income by the amount of the    **3.741**
expenses. This is subject to para.(2).

*Paragraph (2)*

If the income under the maintenance calculation is the capped amount, this paragraph applies. (a) The special expenses are first deducted from the actual net weekly income. (b) The amount by which the capped amount exceeds that figure is then calculated. (c) Finally, that amount is then deduced from the capped amount. The effect of this paragraph is to ensure that any excess in the non-resident parent's actual net weekly income over the capped amount is used to meet special expenses before the maintenance calculation is reduced.

Take this example. The non-resident parent's actual net weekly income is £2,200 and is capped at £2,000. The special expenses are £250. The effect of this paragraph is to reduce the capped amount to £1,950. (a) £2,200−£250 = £1,950. (b) £2,000−£1,950 = £50. (c) £2,000−£50 = £1,950.

## Effect on maintenance calculation—property or capital transfer

**24.** Subject to regulation 27, where the variation agreed to is one falling    **3.742**
within regulation 16 (property or capital transfers)—

   (a)  the maintenance calculation shall be carried out in accordance with
        Part 1 of Schedule 1 to the Act and Regulations made under that
        Part; and
   (b)  the equivalent weekly value of the transfer calculated as provided in
        regulation 17 shall be deducted from the amount of child support
        maintenance which he would otherwise be liable to pay to the person
        with care with respect to whom the transfer was made.

DEFINITIONS

   "the Act": see reg.1(2).    **3.743**

## Effect on maintenance calculation—additional cases

**25.** Subject to regulations 26 and 27, where the variation agreed to is    **3.744**
one falling within regulations 18 to 20 (additional cases), effect shall be given to the variation in the maintenance calculation by increasing the net weekly income of the non-resident parent which would otherwise be taken into account by the weekly amount of the additional income except that, where the amount of net weekly income calculated in this way would exceed the capped amount, the amount of net weekly income taken into account shall be the capped amount.

DEFINITION

   "capped amount": see reg.1(2).    **3.745**
   "net weekly income": see reg.27(7).

GENERAL NOTE

   This regulation, together with regs 26 and 27, specifies the effect of a variation    **3.746**
on the ground of an additional case: regs 18 to 20.

The effect of a variation is to increase the net weekly income by the amount identified in the relevant regulation. If this would exceed the capped amount, the amount payable is the capped amount.

## Effect on maintenance calculation—maximum amount payable where the variation is on additional cases ground

**3.747**

**26.**—(1) Subject to regulation 27, where this regulation applies the amount of child support maintenance which the non-resident parent shall be liable to pay shall be whichever is the lesser of—

(a) a weekly amount calculated by aggregating an amount equivalent to the flat rate stated in or prescribed for the purposes of paragraph 4(1)(b) of Schedule 1 to the Act with the amount calculated by applying that Schedule to the Act to the additional income arising under the variation, other than the weekly amount of any benefit, pension or allowance the non-resident parent receives which is prescribed for the purposes of that paragraph; or

(b) a weekly amount calculated by applying Part 1 of Schedule 1 to the Act to the additional income arising under the variation.

(2) This regulation applies where the variation agreed to is one to which regulation 25 applies and the non-resident parent's liability calculated as provided in Part 1 of Schedule 1 to the Act and Regulations made under that Schedule would, but for the variation, be—

(a) a flat rate under paragraph 4(1)(b) of that Schedule;

(b) a flat rate but is less than that amount or nil, owing to the application of paragraph 8 of that Schedule; or

(c) a flat rate under paragraph 4(1)(b) of that Schedule but for the application of paragraph 5(a) of that Schedule.

(3) For the purposes of paragraph (1)—

(a) any benefit, pension or allowance taken into account in the additional income referred to in sub-paragraph (b) shall not include—

(i) in the case of industrial injuries benefit under section 94 of the Contributions and Benefits Act, any increase in that benefit under section 104 (constant attendance) or 105 (exceptionally severe disablement) of that Act;

(ii) in the case of a war disablement pension within the meaning in section 150(2) of the Contributions and Benefits Act, any award under the following articles of the Naval, Military and Air Forces Etc., (Disablement and Death) Service Pensions Order 1983 ("the Service Pensions Order"): article 14 (constant attendance allowance), 15 (exceptionally severe disablement allowance), 16 (severe disablement occupational allowance) or 26A (mobility supplement) or any analogous allowances payable in conjunction with any other war disablement pension; and

(iii) any award under article 18 of the Service Pensions Order (unemployability allowances) which is an additional allowance in respect of a child of the non-resident parent where that child is not living with the non-resident parent;

(b) "additional income" for the purposes of sub-paragraphs (a) and (b) means such income after the application of a variation falling within regulations 10 to 14 (special expenses); and

(c) "weekly amount" for the purposes of sub-paragraphs (a) and (b) means the aggregate of the amounts referred to in the relevant sub-paragraph—

    (i) adjusted as provided in regulation 27(3) as if the reference in that regulation to child support maintenance were to the weekly amount; and

    (ii) after any deduction provided for in regulation 27(4) as if the reference in that regulation to child support maintenance were to the weekly amount.

DEFINITIONS

"the Act": see reg.1(2).        **3.748**
"Contributions and Benefits Act": see reg.1(2).

GENERAL NOTE

This regulation fixes the maximum amount of child support maintenance payable   **3.749**
as a result of a variation.

## Effect on maintenance calculation—general

**27.**—(1) Subject to paragraphs (4) and (5), where more than one varia-   **3.750**
tion is agreed to in respect of the same period regulations 23 to 26 shall apply and the results shall be aggregated as appropriate.

(2) Paragraph 7(2) to (7) of Schedule 1 to the Act (shared care) shall apply where the rate of child support maintenance is affected by a variation which is agreed to and paragraph 7(2) shall be read as if after the words "as calculated in accordance with the preceding paragraphs of this Part of this Schedule" there were inserted the words ", Schedule 4B and Regulations made under that Schedule".

(3) Subject to paragraphs (4) and (5), where the non-resident parent shares the care of a qualifying child within the meaning in Part 1 of Schedule 1 to the Act, or where the care of such a child is shared in part by a local authority, the amount of child support maintenance the non-resident parent is liable to pay the person with care, calculated to take account of any variation, shall be reduced in accordance with the provisions of paragraph 7 of that Part or regulation 9 of the Maintenance Calculations and Special Cases Regulations, as the case may be.

(4) Subject to paragraph (5), where the variation agreed to is one falling within regulation 16 (property or capital transfers) the equivalent weekly value of the transfer calculated as provided in regulation 17 shall be deducted from the amount of child support maintenance the non-resident parent would otherwise be liable to pay the person with care in respect of whom the transfer was made after aggregation of the effects of any other variations as provided in paragraph (1) or deduction for shared care as provided in paragraph (3).

(5) If the application of regulation 24, or paragraph (3) or (4), would decrease the weekly amount of child support maintenance (or the aggregate

of all such amounts) payable by the non-resident parent to the person with care (or all of them) to less than a figure equivalent to the flat rate of child support maintenance payable under [¹paragraph 4(1)] of Schedule 1 to the Act, he shall instead be liable to pay child support maintenance at a rate equivalent to that rate apportioned (if appropriate) as provided in paragraph 6 of Schedule 1 to the Act.

(6) The effect of a variation shall not be applied for any period during which a circumstance referred to in regulation 7 applies.

(7) For the purposes of regulations 23 and 25 "net weekly income" means as calculated or estimated under the Maintenance Calculations and Special Cases Regulations.

AMENDMENT

1. Regulation 9(4) of the Miscellaneous Amendments Regulations 2004 (September 16, 2004).

DEFINITIONS

3.751    "the Act": see reg.1(2).
"Maintenance Calculations and Special Cases Regulations": see reg.1(2).
"qualifying child": see reg.1(2).

GENERAL NOTE

3.752    This regulation qualifies regs 23 to 25.

*Paragraph (1)*
Variations agreed to in respect of the same period are aggregated.

*Paragraph (2)*
This deals with shared care when a variation is agreed to by modifying the wording of para.7(2) of Sch.1 to the Act.

*Paragraph (3)*
This deals with cases where care of the child is shared by the non-resident parent and the person with care (para.7 of Sch.1 to the Act) or a local authority (reg.9 of the Maintenance Calculations and Special Cases Regulations).

*Paragraph (4)*
This governs the order of calculations in cases that fall within reg.16.

*Paragraph (5)*
If this paragraph applies, a variation may not reduce the amount of child support maintenance below the flat rate. The evidence purpose of this provision is to ensure that a non-resident parent makes some contribution, however small.

*Paragraph (6)*
This paragraph effectively suspends the operation of a variation during any period in which one of the circumstances specified in reg.7 applies.

*Paragraph (7)*

This definition is included here rather than with the other definitions in reg.1(2), because it has a limited application.

## Transitional provisions—conversion decisions

**28.** [¹Subject to regulation 17(10) of the Transitional Regulations, where] the variation is being applied for in connection with a subsequent decision within the meaning given in the Transitional Regulations, and the decision to be revised or superseded under section 16 or 17 of the Act, as the case may be, takes into account a relevant property transfer as defined and provided for in those Regulations—

    (a) for the purposes of regulations 23 and 25 "capped amount" shall mean the income for the purposes of paragraph 10(3) of Schedule 1 to the Act less any deduction in respect of the relevant property transfer;

    (b) for the purposes of regulation 26(3)(b) the additional income for the purposes of paragraph (1) of that regulation shall be after deduction in respect of the relevant property transfer;

    (c) regulation 27(4) shall be read as if the aggregation referred to included any deduction in respect of the relevant property transfer; and

    (d) regulation 27(5) shall be read as if after the reference to paragraph (3) or (4) there were a reference to any deduction in respect of the relevant property transfer.

3.753

AMENDMENT

1. Regulation 8 of the Miscellaneous Amendments (No.2) Regulations 2003 (November 5, 2003).

DEFINITIONS

"the Act": see reg.1(2).
"capped amount": see reg.1(2).
"Transitional Regulations": see reg.1(2).

3.754

## Situations in which a variation previously agreed to may be taken into account in calculating maintenance liability

**29.**—(1) This regulation applies where a variation has been agreed to in relation to a maintenance calculation.

(2) In the circumstances set out in paragraph (3), the Secretary of State may take account of the effect of such a variation upon the rate of liability for child support maintenance notwithstanding the fact that an application has not been made.

(3) The circumstances are—

    (a) that the decision as to the maintenance calculation is superseded under section 17 of the Act on a change of circumstances so that the non-resident parent becomes liable to pay child support maintenance at the nil rate, or another rate which means that the variation cannot be taken into account; and

    (b) that the superseding decision referred to in sub-paragraph (a) is itself superseded under section 17 of the Act on a change of circumstances

3.755

so that the non-resident parent becomes liable to pay a rate of child support maintenance which can be adjusted to take account of the variation.

DEFINITION

3.756    "the Act": see reg.1(2).

GENERAL NOTE

This regulation applies when successive supersessions on a change of circumstances affect the implementation of a variation that has been agreed to. It provides for the effect of a variation to be suspended while it cannot be taken into account following a supersession, but to revive without an application when a further supersession allows it to be taken into account.

## Circumstances for the purposes of section 28F(3) of the Act

3.757    **30.** The circumstances prescribed for the purposes of section 28F(3) of the Act (Secretary of State shall not agree to a variation) are—
  (a)  the prescribed circumstances in regulation 6(2) or 7; and
  (b)  where the Secretary of State considers it would not be just and equitable to agree to the variation having regard to any of the factors referred to in regulation 21.

DEFINITION

3.758    "the Act": see reg.1(2).

PART VIII

MISCELLANEOUS

## Regular payments condition

3.759    **31.**—(1) For the purposes of section 28C(2)(b) of the Act (payments of child support maintenance less than those specified in the interim maintenance decision) the payments shall be those fixed by the interim maintenance decision or the maintenance calculation in force, as the case may be, adjusted to take account of the variation applied for by the non-resident parent as if that variation had been agreed.

(2) The Secretary of State may refuse to consider the application for a variation where a regular payments condition has been imposed and the non-resident parent has failed to comply with it in the circumstances to which paragraph (3) applies.

(3) This paragraph applies where the non-resident parent has failed to comply with the regular payments condition and fails to make such payments which are due and unpaid within one month of being required to do so by the Secretary of State or such other period as the Secretary of State may in the particular case decide.

DEFINITION

"the Act": see reg.1(2). 3.760

GENERAL NOTE

Paragraph (1) applies to both applications for variations (a) made before a decision on an application for a maintenance calculation has been determined (when an interim maintenance decision may be made under s.12(2) of the Act) and (b) made when a maintenance calculation is in force.

Paragraphs (2) and (3) are made under the authority of s.28C(5) of the Act.

## Meaning of "benefit" for the purposes of section 28E of the Act

**32.** For the purposes of section 28E of the Act, "benefit" means income 3.761 support, income-based jobseeker's allowance, housing benefit and council tax benefit.

DEFINITION

"the Act": see reg.1(2). 3.762

PART IX

REVOCATION

**Revocation and savings**

**33.**—(1) Subject to [¹the Transitional Regulations and] paragraph (2), 3.763 the Child Support Departure Direction and Consequential Amendments Regulations 1996 shall be revoked with respect to a particular case with effect from the date that these Regulations come into force with respect to that type of case ("the commencement date").

(2) Where before the commencement date in respect of a particular case—

(a) an application was made and not determined for—
  (i) a maintenance assessment;
  (ii) a departure direction; or
  (iii) a revision or supersession of a decision;
(b) the Secretary of State had begun but not completed a revision or supersession of a decision on his own initiative;
(c) any time limit provided for in Regulations for making an application for a revision or a departure direction had not expired; or
(d) any appeal was made but not decided or any time limit for making an appeal had not expired,

the provisions of the Child Support Departure Direction and Consequential Amendments Regulations 1996 shall continue to apply for the purposes of—

  (aa) the decision on the application referred to in sub-paragraph (a);
  (bb) the revision or supersession referred to in sub-paragraph (b);

(cc) the ability to apply for the revision or the departure direction referred to in sub-paragraph (c) and the decision whether to revise or to give a departure direction following any such application;

(dd) any appeal outstanding or made during the time limit referred to in sub-paragraph (d); or

(ee) any revision, supersession or appeal or application for a departure direction in relation to a decision, ability to apply or appeal referred to in subparagraphs (aa) to (dd).

(3) Where, after the commencement date, a decision with respect to a departure direction is revised from a date which is prior to the commencement date, the provisions of the Child Support Departure Direction and Consequential Amendments Regulations 1996 shall continue to apply for the purposes of that revision.

(4) Where, under regulation 28(1) of the Transitional Regulations, an application for a maintenance calculation is treated as an application for a maintenance assessment, the provisions of the Child Support Departure Direction and Consequential Amendments Regulations 1996 shall continue to apply for the purposes of an application for a departure direction in relation to any such assessment made.

(5) For the purposes of this regulation—

(a) "departure direction" and "maintenance assessment" means as provided in section 54 of the Act before its amendment by the 2000 Act;

(b) "revision or supersession" means a revision or supersession of a decision under section 16 or 17 of the Act before its amendment by the 2000 Act and "any time limit for making an application for a revision" means any time limit provided for in Regulations made under section 16 of the Act; and

(c) "2000 Act" means the Child Support, Pensions and Social Security Act 2000.

AMENDMENT

1. Regulation 2(5) of the Transitional Amendments Regulations 2003 (March 3, 2003).

DEFINITIONS

**3.764**   "the Act": see reg.1(2).
"Transitional Regulations": see reg.1(2).

SCHEDULE

EQUIVALENT WEEKLY VALUE OF A TRANSFER OF PROPERTY

**3.765**   **1.**—(1) Subject to paragraph 3, the equivalent weekly value of a transfer of property shall be calculated by multiplying the value of a transfer of property determined in accordance with regulation 17 by the relevant factor specified in the Table set out in paragraph 2 ("the Table").

(2) For the purposes of sub-paragraph (1), the relevant factor is the number in the Table at the intersection of the column for the statutory rate and of the row for the number of years of liability.

(3) In sub-paragraph (2)—

(a) "the statutory rate" means interest at the statutory rate prescribed for a judgment debt or, in Scotland, the statutory rate in respect of interest included in or payable under a decree in the Court of Session, which in either case applies at the date of the court order or written agreement relating to the transfer of the property;

(b) "the number of years of liability" means the number of years, beginning on the date of the court order or written agreement relating to the transfer of property and ending on—

(i) the date specified in that order or agreement as the date on which maintenance for the youngest child in respect of whom that order or agreement was made shall cease; or

(ii) if no such date is specified, the date on which the youngest child specified in the order or agreement reaches the age of 18,

and where that period includes a fraction of a year, that fraction shall be treated as a full year if it is either one half or exceeds one half of a year, and shall otherwise be disregarded.

**2.** The Table referred to in paragraph 1(1) is set out below—                    **3.766**

### THE TABLE

| Number of years of liability | Statutory Rate | | | | | | | |
| --- | --- | --- | --- | --- | --- | --- | --- | --- |
| | 7.0% | 8.0% | 10.0% | 11.0% | 12.0% | 12.5% | 14.0% | 15.0% |
| 1. | .02058 | .02077 | .02115 | .02135 | .02154 | .02163 | .02192 | .02212 |
| 2. | .01064 | .01078 | .01108 | .01123 | .01138 | .01145 | .01168 | .01183 |
| 3. | .00733 | .00746 | .00773 | .00787 | .00801 | .00808 | .00828 | .00842 |
| 4. | .00568 | .00581 | .00607 | .00620 | .00633 | .00640 | .00660 | .00674 |
| 5. | .00469 | .00482 | .00507 | .00520 | .00533 | .00540 | .00560 | .00574 |
| 6. | .00403 | .00416 | .00442 | .00455 | .00468 | .00474 | .00495 | .00508 |
| 7. | .00357 | .00369 | .00395 | .00408 | .00421 | .00428 | .00448 | .00462 |
| 8. | .00322 | .00335 | .00360 | .00374 | .00387 | .00394 | .00415 | .00429 |
| 9. | .00295 | .00308 | .00334 | .00347 | .00361 | .00368 | .00389 | .00403 |
| 10. | .00274 | .00287 | .00313 | .00327 | .00340 | .00347 | .00369 | .00383 |
| 11. | .00256 | .00269 | .00296 | .00310 | .00324 | .00331 | .00353 | .00367 |
| 12. | .00242 | .00255 | .00282 | .00296 | .00310 | .00318 | .00340 | .00355 |
| 13. | .00230 | .00243 | .00271 | .00285 | .00299 | .00307 | .00329 | .00344 |
| 14. | .00220 | .00233 | .00261 | .00275 | .00290 | .00298 | .00320 | .00336 |
| 15. | .00211 | .00225 | .00253 | .00267 | .00282 | .00290 | .00313 | .00329 |
| 16. | .00204 | .00217 | .00246 | .00261 | .00276 | .00283 | .00307 | .00323 |
| 17. | .00197 | .00211 | .00240 | .00255 | .00270 | .00278 | .00302 | .00318 |
| 18. | .00191 | .00205 | .00234 | .00250 | .00265 | .00273 | .00297 | .00314 |

**3.** The Secretary of State may determine a lower equivalent weekly value than that determined in accordance with paragraphs 1 and 2 where the amount of child support maintenance that would be payable in consequence of agreeing to a variation of that value is lower than the amount of the periodical payments of maintenance which were payable under the court order or written agreement referred to in regulation 16.

GENERAL NOTE

3.767    The statutory rate of interest in England and Wales was:

| From and including | rate of interest |
|---|---|
| April 20, 1971 | 7.5% |
| March 1, 1977 | 10% |
| December 3, 1979 | 12.5% |
| June 9, 1980 | 15% |
| June 8, 1982 | 14% |
| November 10, 1982 | 12% |
| April 16, 1985 | 15% |
| April 1, 1993 | 8% |

The statutory rate of interest in Scotland was:

| From and including | rate of interest |
|---|---|
| January 6, 1970 | 7% |
| January 7, 1975 | 11% |
| April 6, 1983 | 12% |
| August 16, 1985 | 15% |
| April 1, 1993 | 8% |

# The Child Support (Maintenance Calculation Procedure) Regulations 2000

## (SI 2001/157)

### ARRANGEMENT OF REGULATIONS

#### PART I

#### GENERAL

#### PART II

#### APPLICATIONS FOR A MAINTENANCE CALCULATION

#### PART III

#### DEFAULT MAINTENANCE DECISIONS

## Part IV

### Reduced Benefit Decisions

## Part V

### Miscellaneous Provisions

## Part VI

### Notifications following Certain Decisions

## Part VII

### Effective Dates of Maintenance Calculations.

PART VIII

REVOCATION, SAVINGS AND TRANSITIONAL PROVISIONS

30. Revocation and savings.
31. Transitional provision—effective dates and reduced benefit decisions.

SCHEDULES

Schedule 1—Meaning of "child" for the purposes of the Act.
Schedule 2—Multiple applications.

*Whereas a draft of this instrument was laid before Parliament in accordance with section 52(2) of the Child Support Act 1991 and approved by a resolution of each House of Parliament:*
*Now, therefore, the Secretary of State for Social Security, in exercise of the powers conferred upon him by sections 3(3), 5(3), 12(4) and (5)(b), 46(2), (5), (8) and (10), 51, 52(4), 54 and 55 of, and paragraphs 11 and 14 of Schedule 1 to, the Child Support Act 1991 and of all other powers enabling him in that behalf, hereby makes the following Regulations:*

PART I

GENERAL

## Citation, commencement and interpretation

3.769    **1.**—(1) These Regulations may be cited as the Child Support (Maintenance Calculation Procedure) Regulations 2000.

(2) In these Regulations, unless the context otherwise requires—
"the Act" means the Child Support Act 1991;
"date of notification to the non-resident parent" means the date on which the non-resident parent is first given notice of a maintenance application;
"effective application" means as provided for in regulation 3;
"date of receipt" means the date on which the information or document is actually received;
"effective date" means the date on which a maintenance calculation takes effect for the purposes of the Act;
"notice of a maintenance application" means notice by the Secretary of State under regulation 5(1) that an application for a maintenance calculation has been made, or treated as made, in relation to which the non-resident parent is named as a parent of the child to whom the application relates;
"Maintenance Calculations and Special Cases Regulations" means the Child Support (Maintenance Calculations and Special Cases) Regulations 2000;
"maintenance period" has the same meaning as in section 17(4A) of the Act;
"relevant person" means—

    (a)   a person with care;

    (b)   a non-resident parent;

    (c)   a parent who is treated as a non-resident parent under regulation 8 of the Maintenance Calculations and Special Cases Regulations;

    (d)   where the application for a maintenance calculation is made by a child under section 7 of the Act, that child,

in respect of whom a maintenance calculation has been applied for, or has been treated as applied for under section 6(3) of the Act, or is or has been in force.

(3) The provisions in Schedule 1 shall have effect to supplement the meaning of "child" in section 55 of the Act.

(4) In these Regulations, unless the context otherwise requires, a reference—

    (a)   to a numbered Part is to the Part of these Regulations bearing that number;

    (b)   to a numbered Schedule is to the Schedule to these Regulations bearing that number;

    (c)   to a numbered regulation is to the regulation in these Regulations bearing that number;

    (d)   in a regulation or Schedule to a numbered paragraph is to the paragraph in that regulation or Schedule bearing that number; and

    (e)   in a paragraph to a lettered or numbered sub-paragraph is to the sub-paragraph in that paragraph bearing that letter or number.

(5) These Regulations shall come into force in relation to a particular case on the day on which the amendments to sections 5, 6, 12, 46, 51 [¹and 54] of the Act made by the Child Support, Pensions and Social Security Act 2000 come into force in relation to that type of case.

AMENDMENT

1. Regulation 6(2) of the Miscellaneous Amendments Regulations 2002 (April 30, 2002).

## Documents

**2.** Except where otherwise stated, where—                3.770

    (a)   any document is given or sent to the Secretary of State, that document shall be treated as having been so given or sent on the day that it is received by the Secretary of State; and

    (b)   any document is given or sent to any other person, that document shall, if sent by post to that person's last known or notified address, be treated as having been given or sent on the day that it is posted.

GENERAL NOTE

This regulation provides for the date when a document is given or sent. It makes    3.771
different provision according to whether the document is sent to the Secretary of State or someone else. It is possible that this difference, and in particular the deemed service provision in head (b), is not authorised by statute: see the general note to reg.2(b) of the Appeals Regulations.

*Head (a)*

The opening of mail may have been privatised. The Secretary of State has power to authorise post to be opened, but this head gives no power to authorise anyone other than the Secretary of State to receive the contents of it. However, it is receipt of the document that is relevant, not receipt of the information contained in it. So, it is important to know the date when it is opened. That may not be the date stamped on it, as the stamp may show either the date when the post was actually opened or the date when it was due to be delivered to the addressee.

*Head (b)*

A document is only posted when it is sent by the Royal Mail and not by courier or through a document exchange system (*CIS 550/93*, para.6). This head does not apply to a document that is never sent or given, even if the whereabouts of the person are unknown (*CCS 1284/96*, para.7).

## PART II

### APPLICATIONS FOR A MAINTENANCE CALCULATION

**Applications under section 4 or 7 of the Act**

3.772
**3.**—(1) A person who applies for a maintenance calculation under section 4 or 7 of the Act need not normally do so in writing, but if the Secretary of State directs that the application be made in writing, the application shall be made either by completing and returning, in accordance with the Secretary of State's instructions, a form provided for that purpose, or in such other written form as the Secretary of State may accept as sufficient in the circumstances of any particular case.

(2) An application for a maintenance calculation is effective if it complies with paragraph (1) and, subject to paragraph (4), is made on the date it is received.

(3) Where an application for a maintenance calculation is not effective the Secretary of State may request the person making the application to provide such additional information or evidence as the Secretary of State may specify and, where the application was made on a form, the Secretary of State may request that the information or evidence be provided on a fresh form.

(4) Where the additional information or evidence requested is received by the Secretary of State within 14 days of the date of his request, or at a later date in circumstances where the Secretary of State is satisfied that the delay was unavoidable, he shall treat the application as made on the date on which the earlier or earliest application would have been treated as made had it been effective.

(5) Where the Secretary of State receives the additional information or evidence requested by him more than 14 days from the date of the request and in circumstances where he is not satisfied that the delay was unavoidable, the Secretary of State shall treat the application as made on the date of receipt of the information or evidence.

(6) Subject to paragraph (7), a person who has made an effective application may amend or withdraw the application at any time before a maintenance calculation is made and such amendment or withdrawal need not

be in writing unless, in any particular case, the Secretary of State requires it to be.

(7) No amendment made under paragraph (6) shall relate to any change of circumstances arising after the effective date of a maintenance calculation resulting from an effective application.

DEFINITIONS

"the Act": see reg.1(2).  3.773
"date of receipt": see reg.1(2).
"effective application": see reg.1(2).
"effective date": see reg.1(2).

GENERAL NOTE

*Paragraph (1)*
An application for a maintenance calculation will not normally have to be made  3.774
in writing, but the Secretary of State has a reserve power to require it to be made in writing, most likely by completing a form. This only applies to applications under ss.4 and 7; if a case falls under s.6, an application is treated as made.

*Paragraph (2)*
This paragraph defines an effective application. An effective application is one that complies with formal requirements (*R(CS) 1/96*, para.11; *R(CS) 3/97*). It is not necessary for the information supplied to be accurate in all particulars (*CCS 2626/99*, para.15). If the Secretary of State requires the application to be made by completing and returning a form, it must comply, or substantially comply, with the instructions given by the Secretary of State for completion and return of the form (*CCS 2626/99*, para.15).

If an application is effective, it must be referred to a decision-maker to be dealt with under s.11 of the Act. It is then that officer's duty to determine whether the application has been properly made and, if it has, to make a calculation (*R(CS) 1/96*, paras 12–13).

*Paragraphs (3)–(5)*
These paragraphs provide for the remedying of ineffective applications and for the date when they become effective.

*Paragraph (6)*
This paragraph allows amendments to an effective application. It does not deal  3.775
with amendments to an ineffective application made with a view to it becoming effective. It is a permissible amendment to withdraw a child from an application (*CCS 8065/95*, paras 11–12).

This paragraph does not prevent some parts of an effective application being rejected and the application processed with respect to the remainder (*CCS 2626/99*, para.15).

*Paragraph (7)*
Changes of circumstances that will occur after the effective date of a maintenance calculation cannot be added by way of amendment under para.(6). They must be made the subject of an application for revision or supersession.

This only prevents changes being added by way of amendment. It does not prevent changes being identified in the application as originally made; they may be taken into account under Sch.1, para.15 to the Act.

**Multiple applications**

3.776     **4.**—(1) The provisions of Schedule 2 shall apply in cases where there is more than one application for a maintenance calculation.

(2) The provisions of paragraphs 1, 2 and 3 of Schedule 2 relating to the treatment of two or more applications as a single application shall apply where no request is received for the Secretary of State to cease acting in relation to all but one of the applications.

(3) Where, under the provisions of paragraph 1, 2 or 3 of Schedule 2, two or more applications are to be treated as a single application, that application shall be treated as an application for a maintenance calculation to be made with respect to all of the qualifying children mentioned in the applications, and the effective date of that maintenance calculation shall be determined by reference to the earlier or earliest application.

DEFINITION

3.777     "effective date": see reg.1(2).

**Notice of an application for a maintenance calculation**

3.778     **5.**—(1) Where an effective application has been made under section 4 or 7 of the Act, or [¹an application] is treated as made under section 6(3) of the Act, as the case may be, the Secretary of State shall as soon as is reasonably practicable notify, orally or in writing, the non-resident parent and any other relevant persons (other than the person who has made, or is treated as having made, the application) of that application and request such information as he may require to make the maintenance calculation in such form and manner as he may specify in the particular case.

(2) Where the person to whom notice is being given under paragraph (1) is a non-resident parent, that notice shall specify the effective date of the maintenance calculation if one is to be made, and the ability to make a default maintenance decision.

(3) Subject to paragraph (4), a person who has provided information under paragraph (1) may amend the information he has provided at any time before a maintenance calculation is made and such information need not be in writing unless, in any particular case, the Secretary of State requires it to be.

(4) No amendment under paragraph (3) shall relate to any change of circumstances arising after the effective date of any maintenance calculation made in response to the application in relation to which the information was requested.

AMENDMENT

1. Regulation 7(2) of the Miscellaneous Amendments Regulations 2003 (February 21, 2003).

DEFINITIONS

3.779     "the Act": see reg.1(2).
    "effective application": see reg.1(2).

"effective date": see reg.1(2).
"relevant person": see reg.1(2).

GENERAL NOTE

This regulation provides for notice of an application that is made or treated as made and for the obtaining of information relevant to the calculation. Neither the notice nor the provision need be in writing, although the Secretary of State may require information to be provided in writing. Paragraph (4) reflects and is a necessary companion to reg.3(7).

**3.780**

## Death of a qualifying child

**6.**—(1) Where the Secretary of State is informed of the death of a qualifying child with respect to whom an application for a maintenance calculation has been made or has been treated as made, he shall—

(a) proceed with the application as if it had not been made with respect to that child if he has not yet made a maintenance calculation;

(b) treat any maintenance calculation already made by him as not having been made if the relevant persons have not been notified of it and proceed with the application as if it had not been made with respect to that child.

(2) Where all of the qualifying children with respect to whom an application for a maintenance calculation has been made have died, and either the calculation has not been made or the relevant persons have not been notified of it, the Secretary of State shall treat the application as not having been made.

**3.781**

DEFINITION

"relevant person": see reg.1(2).

**3.782**

GENERAL NOTE

The effect of this regulation is that an no maintenance calculation is made in respect of a child who dies before the calculation is both made and notified.

PART III

DEFAULT MAINTENANCE DECISIONS

## Default rate

**7.**—(1) Where the Secretary of State makes a default maintenance decision under section 12(1) of the Act (insufficient information to make a maintenance calculation or to make a decision under section 16 or 17 of the Act) the default rate is as set out in paragraph (2).

(2) The default rate for the purposes of section 12(5)(b) of the Act shall be—

£30 where there is one qualifying child of the non-resident parent;

£40 where there are two qualifying children of the non-resident parent;

£50 where there are three or more qualifying children of the non-resident parent,

**3.783**

apportioned, where the non-resident parent has more than one qualifying child and in relation to them there is more than one person with care, as provided in paragraph 6(2) of Part I of Schedule I to the Act.

(3) Subject to paragraph (4), where any apportionment made under this regulation results in a fraction of a penny that fraction shall be treated as a penny if it is either one half or exceeds one half, otherwise it shall be disregarded.

(4) If, in making the apportionment required by this regulation, the effect of the application of paragraph (3) would be such that the aggregate amount of child support maintenance payable by a non-resident parent would be different from the aggregate amount payable before any apportionment, the Secretary of State shall adjust that apportionment so as to eliminate that difference; and that adjustment shall be varied from time to time so as to secure that, taking one week with another and so far as is practicable, each person with care receives the amount which she would have received if no adjustment had been made under this paragraph.

DEFINITION

3.784    "the Act": see reg.1(2).

GENERAL NOTE

This regulation sets the amount payable under a default maintenance decision, which is made if the Secretary of State has insufficient information to make a maintenance calculation or a revision or suprsession decision.

*Paragraph (4)*
The same provision is made for apportionment of the maintenance calculation by reg.6 of the Maintenance Calculations and Special Cases Regulations.

PART IV

REDUCED BENEFIT DECISIONS

## Interpretation of Part IV

3.785    **8.**—(1)  For the purposes of this Part—
"applicable amount" is to be construed in accordance with Part IV of the Income Support Regulations and regulations 83 to 86 of the Jobseeker's Allowance Regulations;
"benefit week", in relation to income support has the same meaning as in the Income Support Regulations, and in relation to jobseeker's allowance has the same meaning as in the Jobseeker's Allowance Regulations;
"Income Support Regulations" means the Income Support (General) Regulations 1987;
"Jobseeker's Allowance Regulations" means the Jobseeker's Allowance Regulations 1996; "parent concerned" means the parent with respect to whom a reduced benefit decision is given;

"reduced benefit decision" has the same meaning as in section 46(10)(b) of the Act; and

"relevant benefit" has the same meaning as in section 46(10)(c) of the Act.

(2) In this Part references to a reduced benefit decision as being "in operation", "suspended" or "in force" shall be construed as follows—

(a) a reduced benefit decision is "in operation" if, by virtue of that decision, relevant benefit is currently being reduced;

(b) a reduced benefit decision is "suspended" if—

(i) after that decision has been given, relevant benefit ceases to be payable, or [¹the circumstances in regulation 14(4) or 15(4), as the case may be, apply;]

(ii) at the time the reduced benefit decision is given, [²the circumstances in regulation 14(4) or 15(4), as the case may be, apply,] and these Regulations provide for relevant benefit payable from a later date to be reduced by virtue of the same reduced benefit decision; and

(c) a reduced benefit decision is "in force" if it is either in operation or suspended and cognate terms shall be construed accordingly.

AMENDMENTS

1. Regulation 5(2)(a) of the Miscellaneous Amendments (No.2) Regulations 2003 (November 5, 2003).

2. Regulation 5(2)(b) of the Miscellaneous Amendments (No.2) Regulations 2003 (November 5, 2003).

DEFINITION

"the Act": see reg.1(2).                                                    3.786

## Period within which reasons are to be given

**9.** The period specified for the purposes of section 46(2) of the Act (for    3.787
the parent to supply her reasons) is 4 weeks from the date on which the
Secretary of State serves notice under that subsection.

DEFINITION

"the Act": see reg.1(2).                                                    3.788

## [¹Period for parent to state if request still stands

**9A.** The period to be specified for the purposes of section 46(6) of the Act
(period for the parent to state if her request still stands) is 4 weeks from the
date on which the Secretary of State serves notice under that subsection.]

AMENDMENT

1. Regulation 6(3) of the Miscellaneous Amendments Regulations 2002 (April 30, 2002).

"the Act": see reg.1(2).

## Circumstances in which a reduced benefit decision shall not be given

3.789    **10.** [²−(1)] The Secretary of State shall not give a reduced benefit decision where—

  (a) income support is paid to, or in respect of, the parent in question and the applicable amount of the claimant for income support includes one or more of the amounts set out in paragraph 15(3), (4) or (6) of Part IV of Schedule 2 to the Income Support Regulations; or

  (b) an income-based jobseeker's allowance is paid to, or in respect of, the parent in question and the applicable amount of the claimant for an income-based jobseeker's allowance includes one or more of the amounts set out in paragraph 20(4), (5) or (7) of Schedule 1 to the Jobseeker's Allowance Regulations; [¹or

  (c) an amount prescribed under section 9(5)(c) of the Tax Credits Act 2002 (increased elements of child tax credit for children or young persons with a disability) is included in an award of child tax credit payable to the parent in question or a member of that parent's family living with him.]

[³(2) In paragraph (1)(c), "family" has the same meaning as in the Maintenance Calculations and Special Cases Regulations.]

AMENDMENTS

1. Regulation 7(3) of the Miscellaneous Amendments Regulations 2003 (April 6, 2003).
2. Regulation 5(1) of the Miscellaneous Amendments Regulations 2005 (March 16, 2005).
3. Regulation 5(2) of the Miscellaneous Amendments Regulations 2005 (March 16, 2005).

DEFINITIONS

3.790    "applicable amount": see reg.8(1).
"Income Support Regulations": see reg.8(1).
"Jobseeker's Allowance Regulations": see reg.8(1).
"reduced benefit decision": see reg.8(1).

## Amount of and period of reduction of relevant benefit under a reduced benefit decision

3.791    **11.**—(1) The reduction in the amount payable by way of a relevant benefit to, or in respect of, the parent concerned and the period of such reduction by virtue of a reduced benefit decision shall be determined in accordance with paragraphs (2) to (8) below.

(2) Subject to paragraph (6) and regulations 12, 13, 14, and 15, there shall be a reduction for a period of 156 weeks from the day specified in the reduced benefit decision under the provisions of section 46(8) of the Act in respect of each such week equal to—

$$0.4 \times B$$

where B is an amount equal to the weekly amount in relation to the week in question, specified in column (2) of paragraph 1(1) (e) of Schedule 2 to the Income Support Regulations.

(3) Subject to paragraph (4), a reduced benefit decision shall come into operation on the first day of the second benefit week following the date of the reduced benefit decision.

(4) Subject to paragraph (5), where a reduced benefit decision ("the subsequent decision") is made on a day when a reduced benefit decision ("the earlier decision") is in force in respect of the same parent, the subsequent decision shall come into operation on the day immediately following the day on which the earlier decision ceased to be in force.

(5) Where the relevant benefit is income support and the provisions of regulation 26(2) of the Social Security (Claims and Payments) Regulations 1987 (deferment of payment of different amount of income support) apply, a reduced benefit decision shall come into operation on such later date as may be determined by the Secretary of State in accordance with those provisions.

(6) Where the benefit payable is income support or an income-based jobseeker's allowance and there is a change in the benefit week whilst a reduced benefit decision is in operation, the period of the reduction specified in paragraph (2) shall be a period greater than 155 weeks but less than 156 weeks and ending on the last day of the last benefit week falling entirely within the period of 156 weeks specified in that paragraph.

(7) Where the weekly amount specified in column (2) of paragraph 1(1)(e) of Schedule 2 to the Income Support Regulations changes on a day when a reduced benefit decision is in operation, the amount of the reduction of income support or income-based jobseeker's allowance shall be changed from the first day of the first benefit week to commence for the parent concerned on or after the day that weekly amount changes.

(8) Only one reduced benefit decision in relation to a parent concerned shall be in force at any one time.

DEFINITIONS

"the Act": see reg.1(2).  3.792
"benefit week": see reg.8(1).
"in force": see reg.8(2).
"in operation": see reg.8(2).
"Income Support Regulations": see reg.8(1).
"parent concerned": see reg.8(1).
"reduced benefit decision": see reg.8(1).
"relevant benefit": see reg.8(1).

## Modification of reduction under a reduced benefit decision to preserve minimum entitlement to relevant benefit

**12.** Where in respect of any benefit week the amount of the relevant  3.793
benefit that would be payable after it has been reduced following a reduced benefit decision would, but for this regulation, be nil or less than the minimum amount of that benefit that is payable as determined—
 (a) in the case of income support, by regulation 26(4) of the Social Security (Claims and Payments) Regulations 1987;

    (b) in the case of an income-based jobseeker's allowance, by regulation 87A of the Jobseeker's Allowance Regulations,
the amount of that reduction shall be decreased to such extent as to raise the amount of that benefit to the minimum amount that is payable.

DEFINITIONS

3.794    "benefit week": see reg.8(1).
"Jobseeker's Allowance Regulations": see reg.8(1).
"reduced benefit decision": see reg.8(1).
"relevant benefit": see reg.8(1).

## Suspension of a reduced benefit decision when relevant benefit ceases to be payable

3.795    **13.**—(1) Where relevant benefit ceases to be payable to, or in respect of, the parent concerned at a time when a reduced benefit decision is in operation, that reduced benefit decision shall, subject to paragraph (2), be suspended for a period of 52 weeks from the date the relevant benefit ceases to be payable.

    (2) Where a reduced benefit decision has been suspended for a period of 52 weeks and no relevant benefit is payable at the end of that period, it shall cease to be in force.

    (3) Where a reduced benefit decision is suspended and relevant benefit again becomes payable to, or in respect of, the parent concerned, the amount payable by way of that benefit shall, subject to regulations 14 and 15, be reduced in accordance with that reduced benefit decision for the balance of the reduction period.

    (4) The amount or, as the case may be, the amounts of that reduction to be made during the balance of the reduction period shall be determined in accordance with regulation 11(2).

    (5) No reduction in the amount of benefit under paragraph (3) shall be made before the expiry of a period of 14 days from service of the notice specified in paragraph (6), and the provisions of regulation 11(3) shall apply as to the date the reduced benefit decision again comes into operation.

    (6) Where relevant benefit again becomes payable to, or in respect of, a parent with respect to whom a reduced benefit decision is suspended, she shall be notified in writing by the Secretary of State that the amount of relevant benefit paid to, or in respect of, her will again be reduced, in accordance with the provisions of paragraph (3), if she falls within section 46(1) of the Act.

DEFINITIONS

3.796    "the Act": see reg.1(2).
"in force": see reg.8(2).
"in operation": see reg.8(2).
"parent concerned": see reg.8(1).
"reduced benefit decision": see reg.8(1).
"relevant benefit": see reg.8(1).
"suspended": see reg.8(2).

## Suspension of a reduced benefit decision [¹. . .] (income support)

**14.**—(1) Where a reduced benefit decision is given or is in operation at a time when income support is payable to, or in respect of, the parent concerned [²but the circumstances in paragraph (4) apply to her], that decision shall be suspended for so long as [³those circumstances apply], or 52 weeks, whichever period is the shorter.

[⁴. . .]

(3) Where a case falls within paragraph (1) [⁵. . .] and a reduced benefit decision has been suspended for 52 weeks, it shall cease to be in force.

[⁶(4) The circumstances referred to in paragraph (1) are that—

(a) she is resident in a care home or an independent hospital;

(b) she is being provided with a care home service or an independent health care service; or

(c) her applicable amount falls to be calculated under regulation 21 of and any of paragraphs 1 to 3 of Schedule 7 to the Income Support Regulations (patients).

(5) In paragraph (4)—

"care home" has the meaning assigned to it by section 3 of the Care Standards Act 2000;

"care home service" has the meaning assigned to it by section 2(3) of the Regulation of Care (Scotland) Act 2001;

"independent health care service" has the meaning assigned to it by section 2(5)(a) and (b) of the Regulation of Care (Scotland) Act 2001; and

"independent hospital" has the meaning assigned to it by section 2 of the Care Standards Act 2000.]

AMENDMENTS

1. Regulation 5(3)(a) of the Miscellaneous Amendments (No.2) Regulations 2003 (November 5, 2003).

2. Regulation 5(3)(b)(i) of the Miscellaneous Amendments (No.2) Regulations 2003 (November 5, 2003).

3. Regulation 5(3)(b)(ii) of the Miscellaneous Amendments (No.2) Regulations 2003 (November 5, 2003).

4. Regulation 5(3)(c) of the Miscellaneous Amendments (No.2) Regulations 2003 (November 5, 2003).

5. Regulation 5(3)(d) of the Miscellaneous Amendments (No.2) Regulations 2003 (November 5, 2003).

6. Regulation 5(3)(e) of the Miscellaneous Amendments (No.2) Regulations 2003 (November 5, 2003).

DEFINITIONS

"in force": see reg.8(2).
"in operation": see reg.8(2).
"Income Support Regulations": see reg.8(1).
"parent concerned": see reg.8(1).
"reduced benefit decision": see reg.8(1).
"suspended": see reg.8(2).

### Suspension of a reduced benefit decision [¹. . .] (income-based jobseeker's allowance)

3.799    **15.**—(1) Where a reduced benefit decision is given or is in operation at a time when an income-based jobseeker's allowance is payable to, or in respect of, the parent concerned [²but the circumstances in paragraph (4) apply to her], that reduced benefit decision shall be suspended for so long as [³those circumstances apply], or 52 weeks whichever is the shorter.

[⁴. . .]

(3) Where a case falls within paragraph (1) [⁵. . .] and a reduced benefit decision has been suspended for 52 weeks, it shall cease to be in force.

[⁶(4) The circumstances referred to in paragraph (1) are that—

(a) she is resident in a care home or an independent hospital;

(b) she is being provided with a care home service or an independent health care service; or

(c) her applicable amount falls to be calculated under regulation 85 of and paragraph 1 or 2 of Schedule 5 to the Jobseeker's Allowance Regulations (patients).

(5) In paragraph (4)—

"care home" has the meaning assigned to it by section 3 of the Care Standards Act 2000;

"care home service" has the meaning assigned to it by section 2(3) of the Regulation of Care (Scotland) Act 2001;

"independent health care service" has the meaning assigned to it by section 2(5)(a) and (b) of the Regulation of Care (Scotland) Act 2001; and

"independent hospital" has the meaning assigned to it by section 2 of the Care Standards Act 2000.]

AMENDMENTS

1. Regulation 5(4)(a) of the Miscellaneous Amendments (No.2) Regulations 2003 (November 5, 2003).
2. Regulation 5(4)(b)(i) of the Miscellaneous Amendments (No.2) Regulations 2003 (November 5, 2003).
3. Regulation 5(4)(b)(ii) of the Miscellaneous Amendments (No.2) Regulations 2003 (November 5, 2003).
4. Regulation 5(4)(c) of the Miscellaneous Amendments (No.2) Regulations 2003 (November 5, 2003).
5. Regulation 5(4)(d) of the Miscellaneous Amendments (No.2) Regulations 2003 (November 5, 2003).
6. Regulation 5(4)(e) of the Miscellaneous Amendments (No.2) Regulations 2003 (November 5, 2003).

DEFINITIONS

3.800    "in force": see reg.8(2).

"in operation": see reg.8(2).

"Jobseeker's Allowance Regulations": see reg.8(1).

"parent concerned": see reg.8(1).

"reduced benefit decision": see reg.8(1).

"suspended": see reg.8(2).

**Termination of a reduced benefit decision**

**16.** A reduced benefit decision shall cease to be in force—
  (a) where the parent concerned—
     (i) withdraws her request under section 6(5) of the Act;
     (ii) complies with her obligation under section 6(7) of the Act; or
     (iii) consents to take a scientific test (within the meaning of section 27A of the Act);
  (b) where following written notice under section 46(6)(b) of the Act, the parent concerned responds to such notice and the Secretary of State considers there are reasonable grounds;
  (c) subject to regulation 13, where relevant benefit ceases to be payable to, or in respect of, the parent concerned; or
  (d) where a qualifying child with respect to whom a reduced benefit decision is in force applies for a maintenance calculation to be made with respect to him under section 7 of the Act and a calculation is made in response to that application in respect of all the qualifying children in relation to whom the parent concerned falls within section 46(1) of the Act.

3.801

DEFINITIONS

"the Act": see reg.1(2).
"in force": see reg.8(2).
"parent concerned": see reg.8(1).
"reduced benefit decision": see reg.8(1).
"relevant benefit": see reg.8(1).

3.802

## Reduced benefit decisions where there is an additional qualifying child

**17.**—(1) Where a reduced benefit decision is in operation, or would be in operation but for the provisions of regulations 14 and 15, and the Secretary of State gives a further reduced benefit decision with respect to the same parent concerned in relation to an additional qualifying child of whom she is a parent with care, the earlier reduced benefit decision shall cease to be in force.

3.803

(2) Where a further reduced benefit decision comes into operation in a case falling within paragraph (1), the provisions of regulation 11 shall apply to it.

  (3) Where—
  (a) a reduced benefit decision ("the earlier decision") has ceased to be in force by virtue of regulation 13(2); and
  (b) the Secretary of State gives a further reduced benefit decision ("the further decision") with respect to the same parent concerned where that parent falls within section 46(1) of the Act,
as long as the further decision remains in force, no additional reduced benefit decision shall be brought into force with respect to that parent in relation to one or more children to whom the earlier decision was given.

(4) Where a case falls within paragraph (1) or (3) and the further deci-sion, but for the provisions of this paragraph, would cease to be in force by

virtue of the provisions of regulation 16, but the earlier decision would not have ceased to be in force by virtue of the provisions of regulation 16, the further reduced benefit decision shall remain in force for a period calculated in accordance with regulation 11.

(5) In this regulation "additional qualifying child" means a qualifying child of whom the parent concerned is a parent with care and who was either not such a qualifying child at the time the earlier decision was given or had not been born at the time the earlier decision was given.

DEFINITIONS

3.804    "the Act": see reg.1(2).
"in force": see reg.8(1).
"in operation": see reg.8(1).
"parent concerned": see reg.8(1).
"reduced benefit decision": see reg.8(1).

### Suspension and termination of a reduced benefit decision where the sole qualifying child ceases to be a child or where the parent concerned ceases to be a person with care

3.805    **18.**—(1) Where a reduced benefit decision is in operation and—
(a) there is, in relation to that decision, only one qualifying child, and that child ceases to be a child within the meaning of the Act; or
(b) the parent concerned ceases to be a person with care, the decision shall be suspended from the last day of the benefit week during the course of which the child ceases to be a child within the meaning of the Act, or the parent concerned ceases to be a person with care, as the case may be.

(2) Where, under the provisions of paragraph (1), a decision has been suspended for a period of 52 weeks and no relevant benefit is payable at that time, it shall cease to be in force.

(3) If during the period specified in paragraph (2) the former child again becomes a child within the meaning of the Act or the parent concerned again becomes a person with care and relevant benefit is payable to, or in respect of, that parent, a reduction in the amount of that benefit shall be made in accordance with the provisions of paragraphs (3) to (6) of regulation 13.

DEFINITIONS

3.806    "the Act": see reg.1(2).
"benefit week": see reg.8(1).
"in force": see reg.8(2).
"in operation": see reg.8(2).
"parent concerned": see reg.8(1).
"reduced benefit decision": see reg.8(1).
"relevant benefit": see reg.8(1).
"suspended": see reg.8(2).

### Notice of termination of a reduced benefit decision

3.807    **19.** Where a reduced benefit decision ceases to be in force under the provisions of regulation 16, 17 or 18 the Secretary of State shall serve notice of this on the parent concerned and shall specify the date on which the reduced benefit decision ceases to be in force.

DEFINITIONS

"in force": see reg.8(2).　　　　　　　　　　　　　　　　　　　**3.808**
"parent concerned": see reg.8(1).
"reduced benefit decision": see reg.8(1).

## Rounding provisions

**20.** Where any calculation made under this Part results in a fraction of　　**3.809** a penny, that fraction shall be treated as a penny if it exceeds one half and shall otherwise be disregarded.

### PART V

### MISCELLANEOUS PROVISIONS

## Persons who are not persons with care

**21.**—(1) For the purposes of the Act the following categories of person　　**3.810** shall not be persons with care—

(a) a local authority;

(b) a person with whom a child who is looked after by a local authority is placed by that authority under the provisions of the Children Act 1989, except where that person is a parent of such a child and the local authority allow the child to live with that parent under section 23(5) of that Act;

(c) in Scotland, a family or relative with whom a child is placed by a local authority under the provisions of section 26 of the Children (Scotland) Act 1995.

(2) In paragraph (1) above—

"family" means family other than such family defined in section 93(1) of the Children (Scotland) Act 1995;

"local authority" means, in relation to England, a county council, a district council, a London borough council, the Common Council of the City of London or the Council of the Isles of Scilly and, in relation to Wales, a county council or a county borough council, and, in relation to Scotland, a council constituted under section 2 of the Local Government etc (Scotland) Act 1994; and

"a child who is looked after by a local authority" has the same meaning as in section 22 of the Children Act 1989 or section 17(6) of the Children (Scotland) Act 1995 as the case may be.

DEFINITION

"the Act": see reg.1(2).　　　　　　　　　　　　　　　　　　　　**3.811**

GENERAL NOTE

Persons in these prescribed categories are not able to be persons with care. This provision would not be necessary if they did not provide day to day care. As they cannot be persons with care, they cannot apply for a maintenance calculation or be paid child support maintenance. If they usually provide day to day care, there is no one who can be a person with care and the child is thereby excluded from the scope of the child support scheme.

The fact that these persons cannot be persons with care does not mean that they cannot provide day to day care. This possibility is reflected in reg.9 of the Maintenance Calculations and Special Cases Regulations. This provides for a special case if the local authority is in the care of the local authority for part of the time.

The reference to a local authority in subpara.(1)(a) does not include the local authority in its capacity as a local education authority, because that authority cannot provide day to day care of a child within the meaning of the child support legislation (*R(CS) 2/04*).

Section 22 of the Children Act 1989 defines "a child who is looked after by a local authority" as a child who is in the local authority's care or for whom the authority provides accommodation for a continuous period of more than 24 hours in the exercise of any function (in particular those under the Children Act itself) which stand referred to their social services committee under the Local Authority Social Services Act 1970.

A parent may be liable to contribute to a child's maintenance in local authority care under Pt III of Sch.2 to the Children Act 1989. For guidance on how the amount to be paid should be fixed, see *Re C (A Minor: Contribution Notice)* [1994] 1 F.L.R. 111.

Subparagraph (1)(b) draws a distinction between *placing* a child and *allowing* a child to live with a parent. If a child is placed with someone, the local authority has the care of the child and cannot be a person with care. However, if a child is allowed to live with a parent, the parent may be a person with care by virtue of the special case in reg.13 of the Maintenance Calculations and Special Cases.

## Authorisation of representative

3.812     **22.**—(1) A person may authorise a representative, whether or not legally qualified, to receive notices and other documents on his behalf and to act on his behalf in relation to the making of applications and the supply of information under any provisions of the Act or these Regulations.

(2) Where a person has authorised a representative for the purposes of paragraph (1) who is not legally qualified, he shall confirm that authorisation in writing to the Secretary of State.

DEFINITION

3.813     "the Act": see reg.1(2).

GENERAL NOTE

A person may be represented in dealings with the Child Support Agency. The representative need not be legally qualified, but the authority of a representative who is not legally qualified must be confirmed in writing.

## Part VI

### Notifications Following Certain Decisions

### Notification of a maintenance calculation

**23.**—(1) A notification of a maintenance calculation made under section 11 or 12(2) of the Act (interim maintenance decision) shall set out, in relation to the maintenance calculation in question—

    3.814

(a) the effective date of the maintenance calculation;

(b) where relevant, the non-resident parent's net weekly income;

(c) the number of qualifying children;

(d) the number of relevant other children;

(e) the weekly rate;

(f) the amounts calculated in accordance with Part I of Schedule 1 to the Act and, where there has been agreement to a variation or a variation has otherwise been taken into account, the Child Support (Variations) Regulations 2000;

(g) where the weekly rate is adjusted by apportionment or shared care, or both, the amount calculated in accordance with paragraph 6, 7 or 8, as the case may be, of Part I of Schedule 1 to the Act; and

(h) where the amount of child support maintenance which the non-resident parent is liable to pay is decreased in accordance with regulation 9 or 11 of the Maintenance Calculations and Special Cases Regulations (care provided in part by local authority and non-resident parent liable to pay maintenance under a maintenance order), the adjustment calculated in accordance with that regulation.

(2) A notification of a maintenance calculation made under section 12(1) of the Act (default maintenance decision) shall set out the effective date of the maintenance calculation, the default rate, the number of qualifying children on which the rate is based, whether any apportionment has been applied under regulation 7 and shall state the nature of the information required to enable a decision under section 11 of the Act to be made by way of section 16 of the Act.

(3) Except where a person gives written permission to the Secretary of State that the information in relation to him, mentioned in subparagraphs (a) and (b) below, may be conveyed to other persons, any document given or sent under the provisions of paragraph (1) or (2) shall not contain—

(a) the address of any person other than the recipient of the document in question (other than the address of the office of the officer concerned who is exercising functions of the Secretary of State under the Act) or any other information the use of which could reasonably be expected to lead to any such person being located;

(b) any other information the use of which could reasonably be expected to lead to any person, other than a qualifying child or a relevant person, being identified.

(4) Where a decision as to a maintenance calculation is made under section 11 or 12 of the Act, a notification under paragraph (1) or (2) shall include information as to the provisions of sections 16, 17 and 20 of the Act.

DEFINITIONS

**3.815**
"the Act": see reg.1(2).
"effective date": see reg.1(2).
"Maintenance Calculations and Special Cases Regulations": see reg.1(2).
"relevant person": see reg.1(2).

GENERAL NOTE

*Paragraphs (1)–(2)*
**3.816**
These paragraphs provide for notification of a maintenance calculation or of a default maintenance decision or an interim maintenance decision. The matters listed are the minimum that must be provided. Other matters may also be notified and natural justice requires that any information needed to explain the assessment to the parties must be included (*Huxley v Child Support Officer and Huxley* [2000] 1 F.L.R. 898 at 906 *per* Hale L.J.).

*Paragraph (3)*
This paragraph contains a confidentiality provision.

## Notification when an applicant under section 7 of the Act ceases to be a child

**3.817**
**24.** Where a maintenance calculation has been made in response to an application by a child under section 7 of the Act and that child ceases to be a child for the purposes of the Act, the Secretary of State shall immediately notify, so far as that is reasonably practicable—

(a) the other qualifying children who have attained the age of 12 years and the non-resident parent with respect to whom that maintenance calculation was made; and

(b) the person with care.

DEFINITION

**3.818**
"the Act": see reg.1(2).

PART VII

EFFECTIVE DATES OF MAINTENANCE CALCULATIONS

## Effective dates of maintenance calculations

**3.819**
**25.**—(1) Subject to regulations 26 to 29 [¹and 31], where no maintenance calculation is in force with respect to the person with care or the non-resident parent, the effective date of a maintenance calculation following an application made under section 4 or 7 of the Act, or treated as made under section 6(3) of the Act, as the case may be, shall be the date determined in accordance with paragraphs (2) to (4) below.

(2) Where the application for a maintenance calculation is made under section 4 of the Act by a non-resident parent, the effective date of the maintenance calculation shall be the date that an effective application is made or treated as made under regulation 3.

(3) Where the application for a maintenance calculation is—

(a) made under section 4 of the Act by a person with care;

(b) treated as made under section 6(3) of the Act; or

(c) made by a child under section 7 of the Act, the effective date of the maintenance calculation shall be the date of notification to the non-resident parent.

(4) For the purposes of this regulation, where the Secretary of State is satisfied that a non-resident parent has intentionally avoided receipt of a notice of a maintenance application he may determine the date of notification to the non-resident parent as the date on which the notification would have been given to him but for such avoidance.

(5) Where in relation to a decision made under section 11 of the Act a maintenance calculation is made to which paragraph 15 of Schedule 1 to the Act applies, the effective date of the calculation shall be the beginning of the maintenance period in which the change of circumstance to which the calculation relates occurred or is expected to occur.

AMENDMENT

1. Regulation 7(4) of the Miscellaneous Amendments Regulations 2003 (February 21, 2003).

DEFINITIONS

"the Act": see reg.1(2).                                                3.820
"date of notification to the non-resident parent": see reg.1(2).
"effective application": see reg.1(2).
"effective date": see reg.1(2).
"maintenance period": see reg.1(2).
"notice of a maintenance application": see reg.1(2).

GENERAL NOTE

This regulation contains the basic provisions for determining the effective date if    3.821
a maintenance calculation is not in force.

*Paragraph (2)*

If a maintenance calculation is made on the application of the non-resident parent, the effective date is the date of the parent's effective application.

*Paragraph (3)*

If a maintenance calculation is made otherwise than on the application of the non-resident parent, the effective date is the date on which that parent was given notice that an application has been made or treated as made. This is subject to the anti-provision in para.(4).

*Paragraph (5)*

If a series of maintenance calculations is made under Sch.1, para.15 to the Act, the effective date of the first calculation is made under paras (2)–(4) and the effective dates of the subsequent assessments are the first day of the maintenance periods in which the relevant changes of circumstances occur.

### Effective dates of maintenance calculations—maintenance order and application under section 4 or 7

3.822

**26.**—(1) This regulation applies, subject to regulation 28, where—

(a) no maintenance calculation is in force with respect to the person with care or the non-resident parent;

(b) an application for a maintenance calculation is made under section 4 or 7 of the Act; and

[¹(c) there is a maintenance order which—

   (i) is in force and was made on or after the date prescribed for the purposes of section 4(10)(a) of the Act;

   (ii) relates to the person with care, the non-resident parent and all the children to whom the application referred to in sub-paragraph (b) relates; and

   (iii) has been in force for at least one year prior to the date of the application referred to in sub-paragraph (b).]

(2) The effective date of the maintenance calculation shall be two months and two days after the application is made.

AMENDMENT

1. Regulation 6(4) of the Miscellaneous Amendments Regulations 2002 (April 30, 2002).

DEFINITIONS

3.823

"the Act": see reg.1(2).
"effective date": see reg.1(2)

GENERAL NOTE

3.824

This regulation, together with regs 27 and 28, deals the effective date in cases in which a maintenance order is in force before a maintenance calculation is made.

*Paragraph (1)*

This paragraphs set out the conditions that must be satisfied: a maintenance order has been in force in relation to the person with care and the non-resident parent for at least one year before the date of an application under s.4 or s.7 of the Act.

*Paragraph (2)*

If the conditions in para.(1) are satisfied, the effective date is two months and two days after the date of the application. Unlike under reg.27, the date when the maintenance calculation is made is irrelevant. This paragraph and head (c) refer to the date on which the application was made. They do not refer to an *effective* application or to the date on which the application was made or was treated as made under reg.3. Contrast regs 25(2) and 29(a).

## Effective dates of maintenance calculations—maintenance order and application under section 6

**27.**—(1) This regulation applies, subject to regulation 28, where—     **3.825**
(a) the circumstances set out in regulation 26(1)(a) apply;
(b) an application for a maintenance calculation is treated as made under section 6(3) of the Act; and
(c) there is a maintenance order in force in relation to the person with care [¹, the non-resident parent and all the children to whom the application referred to in sub-paragraph (b) relates].
(2) The effective date of the maintenance calculation shall be 2 days after the maintenance calculation is made.

AMENDMENT

1. Regulation 6(5) of the Miscellaneous Amendments Regulations 2002 (April 30, 2002).

DEFINITIONS

"the Act": see reg.1(2).     **3.826**
"effective date": see reg.1(2).

GENERAL NOTE

This regulation, together with regs 26 and 28, deals the effective date in cases     **3.827**
in which a maintenance order is in force before a maintenance calculation is
made.

*Paragraph (1)*
This paragraphs set out the conditions that must be satisfied: a maintenance
order is in force in relation to the person with care and the non-resident parent
when an application is treated as made under s.6(3) of the Act.

*Paragraph (2)*
If the conditions in para.(1) are satisfied, the effective date is two days after the
maintenance calculation is made. Unlike under reg.26, the date of the application
is irrelevant.

## Effective dates of maintenance calculations—maintenance order ceases

**28.** Where—     **3.828**
(a) a maintenance calculation is made; and
(b) there was a maintenance order in force in relation to the person with care and the non-resident parent which ceased to have effect after the date on which the application for the maintenance calculation was made but before the effective date provided for in regulation [¹26 or 27] as the case may be, the effective date of the maintenance calculation shall be the day following that on which the maintenance order ceased to have effect.

AMENDMENT

1. Regulation 6(6) of the Miscellaneous Amendments Regulations 2002 (April 30, 2002).

DEFINITION

3.829 "effective date": see reg.1(2).

GENERAL NOTE

This regulation, together with regs 26 and 27, deals the effective date in cases in which a maintenance order is in force before a maintenance calculation is made.

*The conditions*

Heads (a) and (b) set out the conditions that must be satisfied: a maintenance order was in force in relation to the person with care and the non-resident parent when an application was made under s.4 or s.7 of the Act, but had ceased to have effect before the effective date as determined by reg.26 or reg.27.

Head (b) refers to the date on which the application was made. It does not refer to an *effective* application or to the date on which the application was made or was treated as made under reg.3. Contrast regs 25(2) and 29(a).

*The effective date*

If the conditions in heads (a) and (b) are satisfied, the effective date is the day after the maintenance order ceased to have effect.

## Effective dates of maintenance calculations in specified cases

3.830 **29.**—[²(1)] Where an application for a maintenance calculation is made under section 4 or 7 of the Act, or treated as made under section 6(3) of the Act—

(a) except where the parent with care has made a request under section 6(5) of the Act, where in the period of 8 weeks immediately preceding the date the application is made, or treated as made under regulation 3, there has been in force a maintenance calculation in respect of the same non-resident parent and child but a different person with care, the effective date of the maintenance calculation made in respect of the application shall be [³the date] on which the previous maintenance calculation ceased to have effect;

(b) where a maintenance calculation ("the existing calculation") is in force with respect to the person who is the person with care in relation to the application but who is the non-resident parent in relation to the existing calculation, the effective date of the calculation shall be a date not later than 7 days after the date of notification to the non-resident parent which is the day on which a maintenance period in respect of the existing calculation begins;

[¹(c) except where the parent with care has made a request under section 6(5) of the Act, where—

(i) in the period of 8 weeks immediately preceding the date the application is made, or treated as made under regulation 3, a maintenance calculation ("the previous maintenance calculation") has been in force and has ceased to have effect;

(ii) the parent with care in respect of the previous maintenance calculation is the non-resident parent in respect of the application;

(iii) the non-resident parent in respect of the previous maintenance calculation is the parent with care in respect of the application; and

(iv) the application relates to the same qualifying child, or all of the same qualifying children, and no others, as the previous maintenance calculation,

the effective date of the maintenance calculation to which the application relates shall be the date on which the previous maintenance calculation ceased to have effect.]

[⁵(d) except where the parent with care has made a request under section 6(5) of the Act, where on the date the application is made, or treated as made under regulation 3, there is in force a maintenance calculation in relation to the same non-resident parent and a different person with care, and the maintenance calculation in force when the application was made has ceased to have effect before a decision has been made in respect of that application, the effective date of the maintenance calculation made in response to the application shall be—

(i) where the date of notification to the non-resident parent is before the date on which the maintenance calculation in force has ceased to have effect, the day following the day on which that maintenance calculation ceases to have effect;

(ii) where the date of notification to the non-resident parent is after the date on which the maintenance calculation in force has ceased to have effect, the date of notification to the non-resident parent.]

[⁴(2) Where an application is treated as made under section 6(3) of the Act, references in sub-paragraphs (a) and (c) of paragraph (1) to "the date the application is made" shall mean whichever is the later of—

(a) the date of the claim for a prescribed benefit made by or in respect of the parent with care, as determined by regulation 6 of the Social Security (Claims and Payments) Regulations 1987; and

(b) the date on which the parent with care or her partner in the claim reports to the Secretary of State (in respect of a claim for a prescribed benefit) or to the Commissioners of Inland Revenue (in respect of a claim for a tax credit) a change of circumstances, which change—

(i) relates to an existing claim, in respect of the parent with care, for a prescribed benefit; and

(ii) has the effect that the parent with care is treated as applying for a maintenance calculation under section 6(1) of the Act (whether or not that section already applied to that parent with care).

(3) For the purposes of—

(a) paragraph (1), "ceased to have effect" means ceased to have effect under paragraph 16 of Schedule 1 to the Act; and

(b) paragraph (2), "prescribed benefit" means a benefit referred to in section 6(1) of the Act or prescribed in regulations made under that section.]

1. Regulation 6(7) of the Miscellaneous Amendments Regulations 2002 (April 30, 2002).
2. Regulation 7(5) of the Miscellaneous Amendments Regulations 2003 (February 21, 2003).
3. Regulation 7(5)(a) of the Miscellaneous Amendments Regulations 2003 (February 21, 2003).
4. Regulation 7(5)(b) of the Miscellaneous Amendments Regulations 2003 (February 21, 2003).
5. Regulation 6(2) of the Miscellaneous Amendments Regulations 2004 (September 16, 2004).

DEFINITIONS

**3.831**    "the Act": see reg.1(2).
"date of notification to the non-resident parent": see reg.1(2).
"effective date": see reg.1(2).
"maintenance period": see reg.1(2).

GENERAL NOTE

**3.832**    This regulation deals with cases in which a new person becomes a person with care.

*Paragraph (1)—head (a)*
This head applies if another person becomes the person with care other than the non-resident parent. The effective date of the maintenance calculation in respect of the new person with care is the date of the calculation in respect of the former person with care ceased to have effect. This is subject to two conditions. First, an application must not have been made under s.6(5) of the Act. Second, the application in respect of the new person with care must have been made within eight weeks of the previous calculation being in force.

*Paragraph (1)—head (b)*
This head applies if a non-resident parent becomes the person with care. The maintenance calculation in respect of that parent as the non-resident parent continues for the remainder of the maintenance period in which the application for a replacement maintenance calculation is made. The effective date of replacement calculation is the following day.

PART VIII

REVOCATION, SAVINGS AND TRANSITIONAL PROVISIONS

**Revocation and savings**

**3.833**    **30.**—(1) Subject to [¹the Child Support (Transitional Provisions) Regulations 2000 and] paragraph (2), the Child Support (Maintenance Assessment Procedure) Regulations 1992 shall be revoked with respect to a particular case with effect from the date that these Regulations come into force with respect to that type of case ("the commencement date").

(2) Subject to [²regulation 31(1C)(b) and (2)], where before the commencement date in respect of a particular case—
  (a) an application was made and not determined for—
      (i) a maintenance assessment;
      (ii) a departure direction; or
      (iii) a revision or supersession of a decision;
  (b) the Secretary of State had begun but not completed a revision or supersession of a decision on his own initiative;
  (c) any time limit provided for in Regulations for making an application for a revision or a departure direction had not expired; or
  (d) any appeal was made but not decided or any time limit for making an appeal had not expired,
the provisions of the Child Support (Maintenance Assessment Procedure) Regulations 1992 shall continue to apply for the purposes of—
          (aa) the decision on the application referred to in sub-paragraph (a);
          (bb) the revision or supersession referred to in sub-paragraph (b);
          (cc) the ability to apply for the revision or the departure direction referred to in sub-paragraph (c) and the decision whether to revise or to give a departure direction following any such application;
          (dd) any appeal outstanding or made during the time limit referred to in sub-paragraph (d); or
          (ee) any revision, supersession, appeal or application for a departure direction in relation to a decision, ability to apply or appeal referred to in sub-paragraphs (aa) to (dd) above.
(3) Where immediately before the commencement date in respect of a particular case an interim maintenance assessment was in force, the provisions of the Child Support (Maintenance Assessment Procedure) Regulations 1992 shall continue to apply for the purposes of the decision under section 17 of the Act to make a maintenance assessment calculated in accordance with Part I of Schedule 1 to the 1991 Act before its amendment by the 2000 Act and any revision, supersession or appeal in relation to that decision.
(4) Where after the commencement date a maintenance assessment is revised, cancelled or ceases to have effect from a date which is prior to the commencement date, the Child Support (Maintenance Assessment Procedure) Regulations 1992 shall apply for the purposes of that cancellation or cessation.
(5) Where under regulation 28(1) of the Child Support (Transitional Provisions) Regulations 2000 an application for a maintenance calculation is treated as an application for a maintenance assessment, the provisions of the Child Support (Maintenance Assessment Procedure) Regulations 1992 shall continue to apply for the purposes of the determination of the application and any revision, supersession or appeal in relation to any such assessment made.
(6) For the purposes of this regulation—
  (a) "departure direction", "maintenance assessment" and "interim maintenance assessment" have the same meaning as in section 54 of the Act before its amendment by the 2000 Act;

(b) "revision or supersession" means a revision or supersession of a decision under section 16 or 17 of the Act before their amendment by the 2000 Act;

(c) "2000 Act" means the Child Support, Pensions and Social Security Act 2000.

AMENDMENTS

1. Regulation 2(1) and (2)(b) of the Transitional Amendments Regulations 2003 (March 3, 2003).
2. Regulation 7(8) of the Miscellaneous Amendments Regulations 2003 (February 21, 2003).

DEFINITION

3.834   "the Act": see reg.1(2).

## Transitional provision—effective dates and reduced benefit decisions

3.835   **31.**—[²(1) Where a maintenance assessment is, or has been, in force and an application to which regulation 29 applies is made, or is treated as made under section 6(3) of the Act, that regulation shall apply as if in paragraph (1) references to—

(a) a maintenance calculation in force were to a maintenance assessment in force;

(b) a maintenance calculation having been in force were to a maintenance assessment having been in force; and

(c) a non-resident parent in sub-paragraph (a), the first time it occurs in sub-paragraph (b)[⁶, in sub-paragraph (c)(iii) and the first time it occurs in sub-paragraph (d)], were to an absent parent.

(1A) Where regulation 28(7) of the Child Support (Transitional Provisions) Regulations 2000 (linking provisions) applies, the effective date of the maintenance calculation shall be the date which would have been the beginning of the first maintenance period in respect of the conversion decision on or after what, but for this paragraph, would have been the relevant effective date provided for in regulation 25(2) to (4).

(1B) The provisions of Schedule 3 shall apply where—

(a) an effective application for a maintenance assessment has been made under the former Act ("an assessment application"); and

(b) an effective application for a maintenance calculation is made or an application for a maintenance calculation is treated as made under the Act ("a calculation application").

(1C) Where the provisions of Schedule 3 apply and, by virtue of regulation 4(3) of the Assessment Procedure Regulations, the relevant date would be—

(a) before the prescribed date, the application to be proceeded with shall be treated as an application for a maintenance assessment;

(b) on or after the prescribed date, that application shall be treated as an application for a maintenance calculation and the effective date of that maintenance calculation shall be the date which would be the assessment effective date if a maintenance assessment were to be made.

(2) Where—

(a) an application for a maintenance assessment was made before the prescribed date; and

(b) the assessment effective date of that application would be on or after the prescribed date,

the application shall be treated as an application for a maintenance calculation and the effective date of that maintenance calculation shall be the date which would be the assessment effective date if a maintenance assessment were to be made.]

(3) Paragraphs (4) to (7) shall apply where, [¹immediately before] the commencement date, section 6 of the former Act applied to the parent with care.

(4) [³Where the assessment effective date] is before the prescribed date and on or after the commencement date the parent with care notifies the Secretary of State that she is withdrawing her authorisation under subsection (1) of that section, these Regulations shall apply as if the notification were a request not to act under section 6(5) of the Act.

(5) Where a maintenance assessment was not made because section 6(2) of the former Act applied, these Regulations shall apply as if section 6(5) of the Act applied.

(6) Where a maintenance assessment was not made, section 6(2) of the former Act did not apply and a reduced benefit direction was given under section 46(5) of the former Act, these Regulations shall apply as if the reduced benefit direction were a reduced benefit decision made under section 46(5) of the Act, from the same date and with the same effect as the reduced benefit direction.

(7) Where a maintenance assessment was not made, the parent with care failed to comply with a requirement imposed on her under section 6(1) of the former Act and the Secretary of State was in the process of serving a notice or considering reasons given by the parent with care under section 46(2) or (3) of the former Act, these Regulations shall apply as if the Secretary of State was in the process of serving a notice or considering reasons under section 46(2) or (3) of the Act.

(8) For the purposes of this regulation—

(a) "2000 Act" means the Child Support, Pensions and Social Security Act 2000;

[⁴"absent parent" has the meaning given in section 3(2) of the former Act;

"assessment effective date" means the effective date of the maintenance assessment under regulation 30 or 33(7) of the Assessment Procedure Regulations or regulation 3(5), (7) or (8) of the Maintenance Arrangements and Jurisdiction Regulations, whichever applied to the maintenance assessment in question or would have applied had the effective date not been determined under regulation 8C or 30A of the Assessment Procedure Regulations;]

"Assessment Procedure Regulations" means the Child Support (Maintenance Assessment Procedure) Regulations 1992;

"commencement date" means with respect to a particular case the date these Regulations come into force with respect to that type of case;

"former Act" means the Act before its amendment by the 2000 Act;

"Maintenance Arrangements and Jurisdiction Regulations" means the Child Support (Maintenance Arrangements and Jurisdiction) Regulations 1992;

"maintenance assessment" has the meaning given in the former Act; and

"prescribed date" means the date prescribed for the purposes of section 4(10)(a) of the Act; [⁵and

"relevant date" means the date which would be the assessment effective date of the application which is to be proceeded with in accordance with Schedule 3, if a maintenance assessment were to be made.]

(b) references in paragraphs (4) to (7) to sections 6(5), 46(5) and 46(2) and (3) of the Act mean those provisions as substituted by the 2000 Act; and

(c) in the application of the Assessment Procedure Regulations for the purposes of paragraph (4) where, on or after the prescribed date, no maintenance enquiry form, as defined in those Regulations, is given or sent to the absent parent, the Regulations shall be applied as if references in regulation 30—

    (i) to the date when the maintenance enquiry form was given or sent to the absent parent were to the date of notification to the non-resident parent;

    (ii) to the return by the absent parent of the maintenance enquiry form containing his name, address and written confirmation that he is the parent of the child or children in respect of whom the application was made were to the provision of this information by the non-resident parent; and

(d) in the application of the Maintenance Arrangements and Jurisdiction Regulations for the purposes of paragraph (4), where, on or after the prescribed date no maintenance enquiry form, as defined in the Assessment Procedure Regulations, is given or sent to the absent parent, regulation 3(8) shall be applied as if the reference to the date when the maintenance enquiry form was given or sent were a reference to the date of notification to the non-resident parent.

AMENDMENTS

1. Regulation 6(8) of the Miscellaneous Amendments Regulations 2002 (April 30, 2002).

2. Regulation 7(7)(a) of the Miscellaneous Amendments Regulations 2003 (February 21, 2003).

3. Regulation 7(7)(b) of the Miscellaneous Amendments Regulations 2003 (February 21, 2003).

4. Regulation 7(7)(c)(i) of the Miscellaneous Amendments Regulations 2003 (February 21, 2003).

5. Regulation 7(7)(c)(ii) of the Miscellaneous Amendments Regulations 2003 (February 21, 2003).

6. Regulation 6(3) of the Miscellaneous Amendments Regulations 2004 (September 16, 2004).

DEFINITIONS

"the Act": see reg.1(2).

"date of notification to the non-resident parent": see reg.1(2).

3.836

### SCHEDULE 1

MEANING OF "CHILD" FOR THE PURPOSES OF THE ACT

**Persons of 16 or 17 years of age who are not in full-time non-advanced education**

1.—(1) Subject to sub-paragraph (3), the conditions which must be satisfied for a person to be a child within section 55(1)(c) of the Act are—

3.837

(a) the person is registered for work or for training under work-based training for young people or, in Scotland, Skillseekers training with—

    (i) the Department for Education and Employment;

    (ii) the Ministry of Defence;

    (iii) in England and Wales, a local education authority within the meaning of the Education Acts 1944 to 1992;

    (iv) in Scotland, an education authority within the meaning of section 135(1) of the Education (Scotland) Act 1980 (interpretation); or

    (v) for the purposes of applying Council Regulation (EEC) No.1408/71, any corresponding body in another member State;

(b) the person is not engaged in remunerative work, other than work of a temporary nature that is due to cease before the end of the extension period which applies in the case of that person;

(c) the extension period which applies in the case of that person has not expired; and

(d) immediately before the extension period begins, the person is a child for the purposes of the Act without regard to this paragraph.

(2) For the purposes of heads (b), (c) and (d) of sub-paragraph (1), the extension period—

(a) begins on the first day of the week in which the person would no longer be a child for the purposes of the Act but for this paragraph; and

(b) where a person ceases to fall within section 55(1)(a) of the Act or within paragraph 5—

    (i) on or after the first Monday in September, but before the first Monday in January of the following year, ends on the last day of the week which falls immediately before the week which includes the first Monday in January in that year;

    (ii) on or after the first Monday in January but before the Monday following Easter Monday in that year, ends on the last day of the week which falls 12 weeks after the week which includes the first Monday in January in that year;

    (iii) at any other time of the year, ends on the last day of the week which falls 12 weeks after the week which includes the Monday following Easter Monday in that year.

(3) A person shall not be a child for the purposes of the Act under this paragraph if—

(a) he is engaged in training under work-based training for young people or, in Scotland, Skillseekers training; or

(b) he is entitled to income support or an income-based jobseeker's allowance.

**Meaning of "advanced education" for the purposes of section 55 of the Act**

3.838     **2.** For the purposes of section 55 of the Act "advanced education" means education of the following description—

(a)  a course in preparation for a degree, a Diploma of Higher Education, a higher national diploma, a higher national diploma or higher national certificate of the Business and Technology Education Council or the Scottish Qualifications Council or a teaching qualification; or

(b)  any other course which is of a standard above that of an ordinary national diploma, a national diploma or a national certificate of the Business and Technology Education Council or the Scottish Qualifications Authority, the advanced level of the General Certificate of Education, a Scottish certificate of education (higher level), a Scottish certificate of sixth year studies, or a Scottish National Qualification at Higher Level.

**Circumstances in which education is to be treated as full-time education**

**3.** For the purposes of section 55 of the Act education shall be treated as being full-time if it is received by a person attending a course of education at a recognised educational establishment and the time spent receiving instruction or tuition, undertaking supervised study, examination of practical work or taking part in any exercise, experiment or project for which provision is made in the curriculum of the course, exceeds 12 hours per week, so however that in calculating the time spent in pursuit of the course, no account shall be taken of time occupied by meal breaks or spent on unsupervised study, whether undertaken on or off the premises of the educational establishment.

**Interruption of full-time education**

3.839     **4.**—(1) Subject to sub-paragraph (2), in determining whether a person falls within section 55(1)(b) of the Act no account shall be taken of a period (whether beginning before or after the person concerned attains age 16) of up to 6 months of any interruption to the extent to which it is accepted that the interruption is attributable to a cause which is reasonable in the particular circumstances of the case; and where the interruption or its continuance is attributable to the illness or disability of mind or body of the person concerned, the period of 6 months may be extended for such further period as the Secretary of State considers reasonable in the particular circumstances of the case.

(2) The provisions of sub-paragraph (1) shall not apply to any period of interruption of a person's full-time education which is likely to be followed immediately or which is followed immediately by a period during which—

(a)  provision is made for the training of that person, and for an allowance to be payable to that person, under work-based training for young people or, in Scotland, Skillseekers training; or

(b)  he is receiving education by virtue of his employment or of any office held by him.

**Circumstances in which a person who has ceased to receive full-time education is to be treated as continuing to fall within section 55(1) of the Act**

**5.**—(1) Subject to sub-paragraphs (2) and (5), a person who has ceased to receive full-time education (which is not advanced education) shall, if—

(a)  he is under the age of 16 when he so ceases, from the date on which he attains that age; or

(b)  he is 16 or over when he so ceases, from the date on which he so ceases,

be treated as continuing to fall within section 55(1) of the Act up to and including the week including the terminal date, or if he attains the age of 19 on or before that date, up to and including the week including the last Monday before he attains that age.

(2) In the case of a person specified in sub-paragraph (1)(a) or (b) who had not attained the upper limit of compulsory school age when he ceased to receive full-time education, the

terminal date shall be that specified in head (a), (b) or (c) of sub-paragraph (3), whichever next follows the date on which he would have attained that age.

(3) In this paragraph the "terminal date" means—

(a)  the first Monday in January; or

(b)  the Monday following Easter Monday; or

(c)  the first Monday in September,

whichever first occurs after the date on which the person's said education ceased.

(4) In this paragraph "compulsory school age" means—

(a)  in England and Wales, compulsory school age as determined in accordance with section 9 of the Education Act 1962;

(b)  in Scotland, school age as determined in accordance with sections 31 and 33 of the Education (Scotland) Act 1980.

(5) A person shall not be treated as continuing to fall within section 55(1) of the Act under this paragraph if he is engaged in remunerative work, other than work of a temporary nature that is due to cease before the terminal date.

(6) Subject to sub-paragraphs (5) and (8), a person whose name was entered as a candidate for any external examination in connection with full-time education (which is not advanced education), which he was receiving at the time, shall so long as his name continued to be so entered before ceasing to receive such education be treated as continuing to fall within section 55(1) of the Act for any week in the period specified in sub-paragraph (7).

(7) Subject to sub-paragraph (8), the period specified for the purposes of sub-paragraph (6) is the period beginning with the date when that person ceased to receive such education ending with—

(a)  whichever of the dates in sub-paragraph (3) first occurs after the conclusion of the examination (or the last of them, if there is more than one); or

(b)  the expiry of the week which includes the last Monday before his 19th birthday,

whichever is the earlier.

(8) The period specified in sub-paragraph (7) shall, in the case of a person who had not attained the age of 16 when he so ceased, begin with the date on which he did attain that age.

### Interpretation

**6.** In this Schedule—

"Education Acts 1944 to 1992" has the meaning prescribed in section 94(2) of the Further and Higher Education Act 1992;

"remunerative work" means work of not less than 24 hours a week—

3.840

(a)  in respect of which payment is made; or

(b)  which is done in expectation of payment;

"week" means a period of 7 days beginning with a Monday;

"work-based training for young people or, in Scotland, Skillseekers training" means—

(a)  arrangements made under section 2 of the Employment and Training Act 1973 (functions of the Secretary of State) or section 2 of the Enterprise and New Towns (Scotland) Act 1990;

(b)  arrangements made by the Secretary of State for the persons enlisted in Her Majesty's forces for any special term of service specified in regulations made under section 2 of the Armed Forces Act 1966 (power of Defence Council to make regulations as to engagement of persons in regular forces); or

(c) for the purposes of the applications of Council Regulation (EEC) No. 1408/71, any corresponding provisions operated in another member State, for purposes which include the training of persons who, at the beginning of their training, are under the age of 18.

DEFINITION

3.841     "the Act": see reg.1(2).

## SCHEDULE 2

MULTIPLE APPLICATIONS

**No maintenance calculation in force: more than one application for a maintenance calculation by the same person under section 4 or 6 or under sections 4 and 6 of the Act**

3.842     **1.**—(1) Where an effective application is made or treated as made, as the case may be, for a maintenance calculation under section 4 or 6 of the Act and, before that calculation is made, the applicant makes a subsequent effective application under that section with respect to the same non-resident parent or person with care, as the case may be, those applications shall be treated as a single application.

(2) Where an effective application for a maintenance calculation is made, or treated as made, as the case may be, by a person with care—

(a) under section 4 of the Act; or

(b) under section 6 of the Act,

and, before that maintenance calculation is made, the person with care—

(i) in a case falling within head (a), is treated as making an application under section 6 of the Act; or

(ii) in a case falling within head (b), makes a subsequent effective application under section 4 of the Act,

with respect to the same non-resident parent, those applications shall, if the person with care does not cease to fall within section 6(1) of the Act, be treated as a single application under section 6 of the Act, and shall otherwise be treated as a single application under section 4 of the Act.

**No maintenance calculation in force: more than one application by a child under section 7 of the Act**

**2.** Where a child makes an effective application for a maintenance calculation under section 7 of the Act and, before that calculation is made, makes a subsequent effective application under that section with respect to the same person with care and non-resident parent, both applications shall be treated as a single application for a maintenance calculation.

**No maintenance calculation in force: applications by different persons for a maintenance calculation**

3.843     **3.**—(1) Where the Secretary of State receives more than one effective application for a maintenance calculation with respect to the same person with care and non-resident parent, he shall, if no maintenance calculation has been made in relation to any of the applications, determine which application he shall proceed with in accordance with sub-paragraphs (2) to (11).

(2) Where an application by a person with care is made under section 4 of the Act or is treated as made under section 6 of the Act, and an application is made by a non-resident parent under section 4 of the Act, the Secretary of State shall proceed with the application of the person with care.

(3) Where there is an application for a maintenance calculation by a qualifying child under section 7 of the Act and a subsequent application is made with respect to that child by a person who is, with respect to that child, a person with care or a non-resident parent, the Secretary of State shall proceed with the application of that person with care or non-resident parent, as the case may be.

(4) Where, in a case falling within sub-paragraph (3), there is made more than one subsequent application, the Secretary of State shall apply the provisions of sub-paragraphs (2), (7), (8), or (10), as is appropriate in the circumstances of the case, to determine which application he shall proceed with.

(5) Where there is an application for a maintenance calculation by more than one qualifying child under section 7 of the Act in relation to the same person with care and non-resident parent, the Secretary of State shall proceed with the application of the elder or, as the case may be, eldest of the qualifying children.

(6) Where there are two non-resident parents in respect of the same qualifying child and an effective application is received from each such person, the Secretary of State shall proceed with both applications, treating them as a single application for a maintenance calculation.

(7) Where an application is treated as having been made by a parent with care under section 6 of the Act and there is an application under section 4 of the Act by another person with care who has parental responsibility for (or, in Scotland, parental rights over) the qualifying child or qualifying children with respect to whom the application under section 6 of the Act was treated as made, the Secretary of State shall proceed with the application under section 6 of the Act by the parent with care.

(8) Where—

(a) more than one person with care makes an application for a maintenance calculation under section 4 of the Act in respect of the same qualifying child or qualifying children (whether or not any of those applications is also in respect of other qualifying children);

(b) each such person has parental responsibility for (or, in Scotland, parental rights over) that child or children; and

(c) under the provisions of regulation 8 of the Maintenance Calculations and Special Cases Regulations one of those persons is to be treated as a non-resident parent,

the Secretary of State shall proceed with the application of the person who does not fall to be treated as a non-resident parent under the provisions of regulation 8 of those Regulations.

(9) Where, in a case falling within sub-paragraph (8), there is more than one person who does not fall to be treated as a non-resident parent under the provisions of regulation 8 of those Regulations, the Secretary of State shall apply the provisions of paragraph (10) to determine which application he shall proceed with.

(10) Where—

(a) more than one person with care makes an application for a maintenance calculation under section 4 of the Act in respect of the same qualifying child or qualifying children (whether or not any of those applications is also in respect of other qualifying children); and

(b) either—

(i) none of those persons has parental responsibility for (or, in Scotland, parental rights over) that child or children; or

(ii) the case falls within sub-paragraph (8)(b) but the Secretary of State has not been able to determine which application he is to proceed with under the provisions of sub-paragraph (8),

the Secretary of State shall proceed with the application of the principal provider of day to day care, as determined in accordance with sub-paragraph (11).

(11) Where—

(a) the applications are in respect of one qualifying child, the application of that person with care to whom child benefit is paid in respect of that child;

(b)  the applications are in respect of more than one qualifying child, the application of that person with care to whom child benefit is paid in respect of those children;

(c)  the Secretary of State cannot determine which application he is to proceed with under head (a) or (b) the application of that applicant who in the opinion of the Secretary of State is the principal provider of day to day care for the child or children in question.

(12)  Subject to sub-paragraph (13), where, in any case falling within sub-paragraphs (2) to (10), the applications are not in respect of identical qualifying children, the application that the Secretary of State is to proceed with as determined by those sub-paragraphs shall be treated as an application with respect to all of the qualifying children with respect to whom the applications were made.

(13)  Where the Secretary of State is satisfied that the same person with care does not provide the principal day to day care for all of the qualifying children with respect to whom an application would but for the provisions of this paragraph be made under sub-paragraph (12), he shall make separate maintenance calculations in relation to each person with care providing such principal day to day care.

(14)  For the purposes of this paragraph "day to day care" has the same meaning as in the Maintenance Calculations and Special Cases Regulations.

**Maintenance calculation in force: subsequent application with respect to the same persons**

3.844      4.  Where a maintenance calculation is in force and a subsequent application is made or treated as made, as the case may be, under the same section of the Act for a maintenance calculation with respect to the same person with care, non-resident parent, and qualifying child or qualifying children as those with respect to whom the maintenance calculation in force has been made, that application shall not be proceeded with.

DEFINITIONS

3.845      "the Act": see reg.1(2).
           "effective application": see reg.1(2).
           "Maintenance Calculations and Special Cases Regulations": see reg.1(2).


['SCHEDULE 3                              **Regulation 31(1B)**

MULTIPLE APPLICATIONS—TRANSITIONAL PROVISIONS

**No maintenance assessment or calculation in force: more than one application for maintenance by the same person under section 4 or 6, or under sections 4 and 6, of the former Act and of the Act.**

3.846      1.—(1)  Where an assessment application is made and, before a maintenance assessment under the former Act is made, the applicant makes or is treated as making, as the case may be, a calculation application under section 4 or 6 of the Act, with respect to the same person with care or with respect to a non-resident parent who is the absent parent with respect to the assessment application, as the case may be, those applications shall be treated as a single application.

(2)  Where an assessment application is made by a person with care—

(a)  under section 4 of the former Act; or

(b)  under section 6(1) of the former Act,

and, before a maintenance assessment under the former Act is made, the person with care—

(i)  in a case falling within head (a), is treated as making a calculation application under section 6(1) of the Act; or

(ii)  in a case falling within head (b), makes a calculation application under section 4 of the Act, with respect to a non-resident parent who is the absent parent with respect to the assessment application, those applications shall, if the person with care does not cease to fall within section 6(1) of the Act, be treated as a single application under section 6(1) of the former Act or of the Act, as the case may be, and shall otherwise be treated as a single application under section 4 of the former Act or of the Act, as the case may be.

### No maintenance assessment or calculation in force: more than one application for maintenance by a child under section 7 of the former Act and of the Act

**2.** Where a child makes an assessment application under section 7 of the former Act and, **3.847** before a maintenance assessment under the former Act is made, makes a calculation application under section 7 of the Act with respect to the same person with care and a non-resident parent who is the absent parent with respect to the assessment application, both applications shall be treated as a single application.

### No maintenance assessment or calculation in force: applications by different persons for maintenance

**3.**—(1) Where the Secretary of State receives more than one application for maintenance **3.848** with respect to the same person with care and absent parent or non-resident parent, as the case may be, he shall, if no maintenance assessment under the former Act or maintenance calculation under the Act, as the case may be, has been made in relation to any of the applications, determine which application he shall proceed with in accordance with sub-paragraphs (2) to (11).

(2) Where an application by a person with care is made under section 4 of the former Act or of the Act, or is made under section 6 of the former Act, or is treated as made under section 6 of the Act, and an application is made by an absent parent or non-resident parent under section 4 of the former Act or of the Act, as the case may be, the Secretary of State shall proceed with the application of the person with care.

(3) Where there is an assessment application by a qualifying child under section 7 of the former Act and a calculation application is made with respect to that child by a person who is, with respect to that child, a person with care or a non-resident parent, the Secretary of State shall proceed with the application of that person with care or non-resident parent, as the case may be.

(4) Where, in a case falling within sub-paragraph (3), there is made more than one subsequent application, the Secretary of State shall apply the provisions of sub-paragraphs (2), (7), (8) or (10), as appropriate in the circumstances of the case, to determine which application he shall proceed with.

(5) Where there is an assessment application and a calculation application by more than one qualifying child under section 7 of the former Act or of the Act, in relation to the same person with care and absent parent or non-resident parent, as the case may be, the Secretary of State shall proceed with the application of the elder or, as the case may be, eldest of the qualifying children.

(6) Where there is one absent parent and one non-resident parent in respect of the same qualifying child and an assessment application and a calculation application is received from each such person respectively, the Secretary of State shall proceed with both applications, treating them as a single application.

(7) Where a parent with care is required to authorise the Secretary of State to recover child support maintenance under section 6 of the former Act and there is a calculation application under section 4 of the Act by another person with care who has parental responsibility for (or, in Scotland, parental rights over) the qualifying child or qualifying children with respect to whom the application was made under section 6 of the former Act, the Secretary of State shall proceed with the assessment application under section 6 of the former Act by the parent with care.

(8) Where—

(a) a person with care makes an assessment application under section 4 of the former Act and a different person with care makes a calculation application under section 4 of the Act and those applications are in respect of the same qualifying child or qualifying children (whether or not any of those applications is also in respect of other qualifying children);

(b) each such person has parental responsibility for (or, in Scotland, parental rights over) that child or children; and

   (c)   under regulation 20 of the Child Support (Maintenance Assessments and Special Cases) Regulations 1992 ("the Maintenance Assessments and Special Cases Regulations") one of those persons is to be treated as an absent parent or under the provisions of regulation 8 of the Maintenance Calculations and Special Cases Regulations one of those persons is to be treated as a non-resident parent, as the case may be,

the Secretary of State shall proceed with the application of the person who does not fall to be treated as an absent parent under regulation 20 of the Maintenance Assessments and Special Cases Regulations, or as a non-resident parent under regulation 8 of the Maintenance Calculations and Special Cases Regulations, as the case may be.

(9) Where, in a case falling within sub-paragraph (8), there is more than one person who does not fall to be treated as an absent parent under regulation 20 of the Maintenance Assessments and Special Cases Regulations or as a non-resident parent under regulation 8 of the Maintenance Calculations and Special Cases Regulations, as the case may be, the Secretary of State shall apply the provisions of paragraph (10) to determine which application he shall proceed with.

   (10)  Where—

   (a)   a person with care makes an assessment application under section 4 of the former Act and a different person with care makes a calculation application under section 4 of the Act and those applications are in respect of the same qualifying child or qualifying children (whether or not any of those applications is also in respect of other qualifying children); and

   (b)  either—

      (i)   none of those persons has parental responsibility for (or, in Scotland, parental rights over) that child or children; or

     (ii)  the case falls within sub-paragraph (8)(b) but the Secretary of State has not been able to determine which application he is to proceed with under the provisions of sub-paragraph (8),

the Secretary of State shall proceed with the application of the principal provider of day to day care, as determined in accordance with sub-paragraph (11).

(11) For the purposes of sub-paragraph (10), the application of the principal provider is, where—

   (a)   the applications are in respect of one qualifying child, the application of that person with care to whom child benefit is paid in respect of that child;

   (b)   the applications are in respect of more than one qualifying child, the application of that person with care to whom child benefit is paid in respect of those children;

   (c)   the Secretary of State cannot determine which application he is to proceed with under head (a) or (b), the application of that applicant who in the opinion of the Secretary of State is the principal provider of day to day care for the child or children in question.

(12) Subject to sub-paragraph (13), where, in any case falling within sub-paragraphs (2) to (10), the applications are not in respect of identical qualifying children, the application that the Secretary of State is to proceed with as determined by those sub-paragraphs shall be treated as an application with respect to all of the qualifying children with respect to whom the applications were made.

(13) Where the Secretary of State is satisfied that the same person with care does not provide the principal day to day care for all of the qualifying children with respect to whom an application would but for the provisions of this paragraph be made under sub-paragraph (12), he shall make separate maintenance assessments under the former Act or maintenance calculations under the Act, as the case may be, in relation to each person with care providing such principal day to day care.

(14) For the purposes of this paragraph "day to day care" has the same meaning as in the Maintenance Assessments and Special Cases Regulations or the Maintenance Calculations and Special Cases Regulations, as the case may be.

**Maintenance assessment in force: subsequent application with respect to the same persons**

4. Where—  **3.849**

(a)  a maintenance assessment is in force under the former Act;

(b)  a calculation application is made or treated as made under the section of the Act which is the same section as the section of the former Act under which the assessment application was made; and

(c)  the calculation application relates to—

(i)  the same person with care and qualifying child or qualifying children as the maintenance assessment; and

(ii)  a non-resident parent who is the absent parent with respect to the maintenance assessment,

the calculation application shall not be proceeded with.

**Interpretation**

5. In this Schedule, "absent parent", "former Act" and "maintenance assessment" have the  **3.850**
meanings given in regulation 31(8)(a).]

AMENDMENT

1. Regulation 7(8) of, and the Schedule to, the Miscellaneous Amendments Regulations 2003 (February 21, 2003).

DEFINITIONS

"the Act": see reg.1(2).
"Maintenance Calculations and Special Cases Regulations": see reg.1(2)

# The Child Support (Consequential Amendments and Transitional Provisions) Regulations 2001

## (SI 2001/158)

*Made by the Secretary of State for Social Security, in exercise of the powers conferred upon him by section 29(2) of the Child Support, Pensions and Social Security Act 2000, and of all other powers enabling him in that behalf.*

## Citation and commencement

1.—(1) These Regulations may be cited as the Child Support  **3.851**
(Consequential Amendments and Transitional Provisions) Regulations
2001.

(2) Regulation 11 and, for the purposes of that provision, this regulation
and regulation 2, shall come into force on 15th February 2001.

(3) The remainder of these Regulations shall come into force in relation
to a particular case on the date on which section 1 of the 2000 Act comes
into force in relation to that type of case.

**Interpretation**

3.852    **2.** In these Regulations—
"the 2000 Act" means the Child Support, Pensions and Social Security
        Act 2000;
"the Act" means the Child Support Act 1991;
. . .
"the former Act" means the Act prior to its amendment by the 2000 Act;
. . .

PART IV

TRANSITIONAL PROVISION

**Transitional provision—redetermination of appeals**

3.853    **11.** In relation to any particular case, before the date on which these
Regulations, except for this regulation, come into force for the purposes
of that case, in section 23A(4)(b) of the Act the reference to "qualifying
persons" shall be treated as a reference to any person referred to in section 20 of the former Act with a right of appeal under that section and the
reference in section 23A(3) to "the principal parties" shall be construed
accordingly.

**The Child Support (Information, Evidence and Disclosure and
Maintenance Arrangements and Jurisdiction) (Amendment)
Regulations 2000**

(SI 2001/161)

*The Secretary of State for Social Security, in exercise of the powers conferred
upon him by sections 4(4), 6(7), 7(5), 10(1), (2) and (4), 14(1), (1A)
and (3), 44(2A), 51, 52(1) and (4), 54 and 57 of the Child Support
Act 1991, and of all other powers enabling him in that behalf, hereby
makes the following Regulations:*

**Citation, commencement and interpretation**

3.854    **1.**—(1) These Regulations may be cited as the Child Support
(Information, Evidence and Disclosure and Maintenance Arrangements
and Jurisdiction) (Amendment) Regulations 2000.
. . .
(3) These Regulations shall come into force as follows—
. . .
(d) the remainder of these Regulations shall come into force in relation
to a particular case on the day on which sub-paragraphs (19) and (20) of
paragraph 11 of Schedule 3 to the Child Support, Pensions and Social
Security Act 2000, which respectively amend sections 51 and 54 of the Act,
come into force for the purposes of that type of case.

**Transitional provisions and savings**

**10.**—[¹(Z1) This regulation is subject to the Child Support     3.855
(Transitional Provisions) Regulations 2000.]

(1) Where in respect of a particular case before the date that these
Regulations come into force with respect to that type of case ("the
commencement date")—

  (a) an application was made and not determined for—
    (i) a maintenance assessment;
    (ii) a departure direction; or
    (iii) a revision or supersession of a decision;
  (b) the Secretary of State had begun but not completed a revision or
      supersession of a decision on his own initiative;
  (c) any time limit provided for in Regulations for making an application
      for a revision or a departure direction had not expired; or
  (d) any appeal was made but not decided or any time limit for making
      an appeal had not expired,

regulations 2, 3, 5 (except for sub-paragraphs (2)(b), (d) and (e)), 6(1) and
(2), 7(2) and (3), 8(1) and (2) and 9 shall not apply for the purposes of—

    (aa) the decision on the application referred to in sub-paragraph (a);
    (bb) the revision or supersession referred to in sub-paragraph (b);
    (cc) the ability to apply for the revision or the departure direction
         referred to in sub-paragraph (c) and the decision whether to
         revise or to give a departure direction following any such
         application;
    (dd) any appeal outstanding or made during the time limit referred
         to in sub-paragraph (d); or
    (ee) any revision, supersession or appeal or application for a depar-
         ture direction in relation to a decision, ability to apply or appeal
         referred to in sub-paragraphs (aa) to (dd) above.

(2) Where after the commencement date a maintenance assessment
falls to be cancelled on grounds of lack of jurisdiction with effect from
before the commencement date, regulation 8(2) shall not apply for that
purpose.

(3) For the purposes of this regulation—

  (a) "departure direction" and "maintenance assessment" have the same
      meaning as in section 54 of the Act before its amendment by the
      2000 Act;
  (b) "revision or supersession" means a revision or supersession of a deci-
      sion under section 16 or 17 of the Act before its amendment by the
      2000 Act; and
  (c) "2000 Act" means the Child Support, Pensions and Social Security
      Act 2000.

AMENDMENT

1. Regulation 2(3) and (4)(d) of the Transitional Amendments Regulations 2003
(March 3, 2003).

## The Child Support (Collection and Enforcement and Miscellaneous Amendments) Regulations 2000

### (SI 2001/162)

*The Secretary of State for Social Security, in exercise of the powers conferred upon him by sections 28J(3), 29(2) and (3), 30(1), (4) and (5), 32(1) to (5) and (7) to (9), 34(1), 35(7) and (8), 39(1), (3) and (4), 40(11), 40B(11), 41(2), 41A(1) and (4), 47(1) to (3), 51, 52(4) and 54 of the Child Support Act 1991 and of all other powers enabling him in that behalf, hereby makes the following Regulations:*

### Citation, commencement and interpretation

3.856

**1.**—(1) These Regulations may be cited as the Child Support (Collection and Enforcement and Miscellaneous Amendments) Regulations 2000.

(2) Regulations 4 and 6(3), and, for the purposes of those provisions, this regulation, shall come into force on 2nd April 2001 and regulation 2(6)(c) and (9), and, for the purposes of those provisions, this regulation, shall come into force on the day on which section 16 of the 2000 Act comes into force.

[¹(2A) Regulation 2(6)(b) and, for the purposes of that provision, this regulation, shall come into force on 31st May 2001.]

(3) The remainder of these Regulations shall come into force in relation to a particular case on the day on which sections 1(2) and (3), 4, 18(1) and (2), and 20(1) of and Schedule 3 paragraph 11(2) and (16) to the 2000 Act come into force for the purposes of that type of case.

(4) In these Regulations, unless the context otherwise requires—
"the Act" means the Child Support Act 1991;
"the Fees Regulations" means the Child Support Fees Regulations 1992.

AMENDMENT

1. Regulation 2 of the Child Support (Miscellaneous Amendments) Regulations 2001 (May 31, 2001).

### Savings

3.857

**6.**—[¹(Z1) This regulation is subject to the Child Support (Transitional Provisions) Regulations 2000.]

(1) Where, in respect of a particular case before the date that these Regulations come into force with respect to that type of case,—
(a) interest has become due but has not been paid;
(b) the Secretary of State has made a payment by way of reimbursement under section 41B(2) of the Act; or
(c) arrears of child support maintenance have not been paid, these Regulations shall not apply for the purposes of—
(i) the recovery of the interest referred to in sub-paragraph (a);
(ii) the repayment to the Secretary of State of the whole, or part, of the sum reimbursed referred to in sub-paragraph (b); or

(iii) the collection and enforcement of the arrears referred to in sub-paragraph (c).

(2) Where in respect of a particular case after the date that these Regulations come into force with respect to that type of case an adjustment falls to be made in relation to a maintenance assessment, these Regulations shall not apply for the purposes of making the adjustment.

(3) Where, before the coming into force of regulation 4 of these Regulations, fees have become due but have not been paid, the Fees Regulations shall have effect as if regulation 4 of these Regulations had not been made.

AMENDMENT

1. Regulations 2(3) and (4)(a) of the Transitional Amendments Regulations 2003 (March 3, 2003).

## The Child Support (Civil Imprisonment) (Scotland) Regulations 2001

### (SI 2001/1236 (S.3))

*The Secretary of State for Social Security, in exercise of the powers conferred upon him by section 40A of the Child Support Act 1991 and of all other powers enabling him in that behalf, hereby makes the following Regulations:*

### Citation, commencement and interpretation

**1.**—(1) These Regulations may be cited as the Child Support (Civil Imprisonment) (Scotland) Regulations 2001 and shall come into force on 24th April 2001.

(2) In these Regulations the "1991 Act" means the Child Support Act 1991.

**3.858**

### Expenses of commitment to prison

**2.** The amount to be included in the warrant under section 40A(2)(ii) of the 1991 Act (sheriff's warrant for committal to prison of liable person) in respect of the expenses of commitment shall be such amount as, in the view of the sheriff, is equal to the expenses reasonably incurred by the Secretary of State in respect of the expenses of commitment.

**3.859**

### Reduction of period of imprisonment

**3.**—(1) For the purposes of subsection (6) of section 40A of the 1991 Act (reduction of period of imprisonment for part payment) the following paragraphs shall apply.

(2) Where, after the sheriff has issued a warrant for committal to prison under section 40A of the 1991 Act, part payment of the amount stated in the warrant is made, the period of imprisonment specified in the warrant shall be reduced proportionately so that for the period of imprisonment

**3.860**

specified in the warrant, there shall be substituted a period of imprisonment of such number of days as bears the same proportion to the number of days specified in the warrant as the amount remaining unpaid under the warrant bears to the amount specified in the warrant.

(3) Where the part payment is of such an amount as would, under paragraph (2) above, reduce the period of imprisonment to such number of days as have already been served (or would be so served in the course of the day of payment) the period of imprisonment shall be reduced to the period already served plus one day.

## The Child Support Appeals (Jurisdiction of Courts) Order 2002

### (SI 2002/1915 (L.9))

*Whereas a draft of this Order has been laid before and approved by a resolution of each House of Parliament:*
*Now, therefore, the Lord Chancellor in exercise of the power conferred upon him by section 45(1) and (7) of the Child Support Act 1991 hereby makes the following Order:*

### Citation, commencement, interpretation and extent

3.861      **1.**—(1) This Order may be cited as the Child Support Appeals (Jurisdiction of Courts) Order 2002.

(2) Subject to paragraph (3) this Order shall come into force on the day after the date on which it is made.

(3) This Order shall not have effect in relation to a particular type of case until the day on which section 10 of the Child Support, Pensions and Social Security Act 2000 comes into force for the purposes of that type of case.

(4) In this Order—

(a) "the Act" means the Child Support Act 1991; and

(b) "the Regulations" means the Social Security and Child Support (Decisions and Appeals) Regulations 1999.

(5) This Order extends to England and Wales only.

GENERAL NOTE

For equivalent provision for Scotland, see the Child Support Appeals (Jurisdiction of Courts) (Scotland) Order 2003.

Section 10 of the 2000 Act introduced a new version of s.20 of the Act. For its commencement, see that section.

### Revocation

3.862      **2.** The Child Support Appeals (Jurisdiction of Courts) Order 1993, to the extent to which it applies in England and Wales, is revoked.

### Parentage appeals to be made to courts

3.863      **3.** An appeal under section 20 of the Act shall be made to a court instead of to an appeal tribunal in the circumstances mentioned in article 4.

**4.** The circumstances are that—

(a) the appeal will be an appeal under section 20(1)(a) or (b) of the Act;

(b) the determination made by the Secretary of State in making the decision to be appealed against included a determination that a particular person (whether the applicant or some other person) either was, or was not, a parent of the qualifying child in question ("a parentage determination"); and

(c) the ground of the appeal will be that the decision to be appealed against should not have included that parentage determination.

GENERAL NOTE

An appeal tribunal has jurisdiction unless the circumstances set out in this article   **3.864**
apply *(R(CS) 13/98*, para.6).

Parentage may be disputed at various stages. This article only applies if the issue of parentage is raised on the appeal. If it is, it deprives the appeal tribunal of jurisdiction. If it is raised at an earlier stage, s.27 of the Act applies. If parentage is disputed in the letter of appeal, the case should be transferred to the court without the case coming before an appeal tribunal. However, if a case does slip through and come before an appeal tribunal, it must declare that it has no jurisdiction to hear the appeal. It has been held in Northern Ireland that if parentage is disputed for the first time at the hearing, this article does not apply. The tribunal should deal with the other grounds of appeal and leave the issue to be dealt with as a revision or supersession. See *CSC 1/94*, paras 5 and 8(d)(iv) and *CSC 3/94*, para.9. However, it is possible that this view is not correct and that any parentage challenge during the appeal is covered by this article.

An appeal tribunal is only deprived of jurisdiction, if the argument is put that the person is not a parent of the qualifying child. If the lesser argument is put that the person may not be the parent or does not admit to being the parent, this article is not satisfied and the tribunal retains jurisdiction. If an argument is put in this form, the tribunal must require the person to state unequivocally whether parentage is denied. If it is, then the tribunal loses jurisdiction.

If a tribunal is deprived of jurisdiction in these circumstances, it may wish to remind the person concerned (a) that the appeal remains in existence but will be transferred to the court, (b) which has power to order a test to be carried out to determine parentage and (c) that the normal court rules as to public funding and costs apply.

Sometimes arguments are put to a tribunal in the alternative, so that parentage is not the only issue raised on the appeal. It is not clear how this article applies in those circumstances. Its wording assumes that it only applies if parentage is the only issue on the appeal. One possible interpretation is that the issues are severed with the parentage issue going to the court while the tribunal retains jurisdiction to deal with the other issues. If this is correct, the tribunal might consider it appropriate to adjourn the hearing on the other issues until the outcome of the parentage challenge is known.

It has been held in Northern Ireland that a calculation should be put into abeyance once parentage is challenged *(CSC 3/94*, para.10), but the Commissioner left open the issue of recoupment of child support maintenance if the parentage issue was decided in favour of the person concerned *(ibid.)*. However, a different view has been taken in the UK. It has been held that the denial of parentage does not suspend or stop proceedings leading to a maintenance calculation or its implementation or enforcement *(CCS 11586/95*, para.13). However, it has also been said that an interim maintenance assessment (comparable to a default maintenance decision) should remain in force but not be enforced pending resolution of the parentage issue (*R(CS) 2/98*, para.22). The Commissioner in that case did not refer to *CCS 11586/95* and did not have to decide the issue. If a person was seeking to set aside a finding of parentage in circumstances that fell within Case F of s.26(2) of the Act, it might be appropriate to collect information necessary to make a maintenance calculation, but to delay the making of the calculation until the issues was resolved (*ibid.*, para.24). If the case does not fall within s.26 of the Act, the Secretary of State should consider applying or offer the parent with care the chance of applying under s.27 of the Act before refusing to make a maintenance calculation (*ibid.*, para.25).

**5.** Regulations 31 and 32 of the Regulations shall apply to appeals brought under this Order with the following modifications—

(a) for the words "an appeal tribunal" shall be substituted "a court";

(b) for the words "legally qualified panel member" and "panel member" shall be substituted "justices' clerk or the court"; and

(c) in regulation 32(10) for the words "such written form as has been approved by the President" shall be substituted "written form".

## Child Support Appeals (Jurisdiction of Courts) (Scotland) Order 2003

### (SSI 2003/96)

*The Scottish Ministers, in exercise of the powers conferred by sections 45(1) and (7) and 58(7) of the Child Support Act 1991 and of all other powers enabling them in that behalf, hereby make the following Order, a draft of which has, in accordance with section 52(2) of that Act, been laid before and approved by resolution of the Scottish Parliament:*

### Citation, commencement, interpretation and extent

3.865     **1.**—(1) This Order may be cited as the Child Support Appeals (Jurisdiction of Courts) (Scotland) Order 2003.

(2) This Order shall come into force in relation to a particular type of case on the date on which section 10 of the Child Support, Pensions and Social Security Act 2000 comes into force for the purposes of that type of case.

(3) In this Order—

(a) "the Act" means the Child Support Act 1991; and

(b) "the Regulations" means the Social Security and Child Support (Decisions and Appeals) Regulations 1999.

(4) This Order extends to Scotland only.

GENERAL NOTE

For equivalent provision for England and Wales, see the Child Support Appeals (Jurisdiction of Courts) Order 2002.

Section 10 of the 2000 Act introduced a new version of s.20 of the Act. For its commencement, see that section.

## Parentage appeals to be made to courts

**2.** An appeal under section 20 of the Act shall be made to a court 3.866
instead of to an appeal tribunal in the circumstances mentioned in article
3.

**3.** The circumstances are that-
(a) the appeal will be an appeal under section 20(1)(a) or (b) of the Act;
(b) the decision by the Secretary of State against which the appeal is
brought was made on the basis that a particular person (whether the
applicant or some other person) either was, or was not, a parent of
the qualifying child in question ("a parentage determination"); and
(c) the ground of appeal will be that, the parentage determination being
unfounded in fact, the decision should not have been made on that
basis.

GENERAL NOTE

For a commentary, see the general note to art.4 of the Child Support Appeals 3.867
(Jurisdiction of Courts) Order 2002, which applies to England and Wales.

**4.**—(1) For the purposes of article 2, an appeal may be made to a court
in Scotland if—
(a) the child in question was born in Scotland; or
(b) the child, the non-resident parent or the person with care of the child
is domiciled in Scotland on the date when the appeal is made or is
habitually resident in Scotland on that date.
(2) Where an appeal to a court in Scotland is to be made to the sheriff,
it shall be to the sheriff of the sheriffdom where—
(a) the child in question was born; or
(b) the child, the non-resident parent or the person with care of the child
is habitually resident on the date when the appeal is made.

## Modifications to the Social Security and Child Support (Decisions and Appeals) Regulations 1999

**5.** Regulations 31 and 32 of the Regulations shall apply to appeals 3.868
brought under this Order with the following modifications—
(a) in regulation 31(1), for "an appeal tribunal" substitute "a court";
(b) wherever they appear, for "legally qualified panel member" or "panel
member" substitute "the court";
(c) in regulation 32(10) for "such written form as has been approved by
the President" substitute "written form".

## Revocation

**6.** The Child Support Appeals (Jurisdiction of Courts) Order 1993, to 3.869
the extent that it applies to Scotland, is revoked.

## Amendment of the Law Reform (Parent and Child) (Scotland) Act 1986

**7.** In section 8 (Interpretation) of the Law Reform (Parent and Child) 3.870
(Scotland) Act 1986 at the end of the definition of "action for declarator"

there shall be inserted the words "but does not include an appeal under section 20(1)(a) or (b) (Appeals) of the Child Support Act 1991 made to the court by virtue of an order made under section 45 (jurisdiction of the courts in certain proceedings) of that Act:".

### The Child Support (Information, Evidence and Disclosure) Amendment Regulations 2003

#### (SI 2003/3206)

*Made by the Secretary of State for Work and Pensions, in exercise of the powers conferred upon him by sections 14(1), 51(1) and (2)(g), 52(4), 54 and 57(1) of the Child Support Act 1991 and of all other powers enabling him in that behalf, hereby makes the following Regulations*

### Citation, commencement and effect

3.871    **1.**—(1) These Regulations may be cited as the Child Support (Information, Evidence and Disclosure) Amendment Regulations 2003.

(2) Subject to paragraph (3), these Regulations shall come into force on 7th January 2004.

(3) These Regulations shall have effect only for the purposes of any case in respect of which section 12 of the Child Support, Pensions and Social Security Act 2000 (information required by the Secretary of State) has not come into force and for so long as that section is not in force for the purposes of such a case.

### Amendment of the Child Support (Information, Evidence and Disclosure) Regulations 1992

3.872    **2.**—(1) The Child Support (Information, Evidence and Disclosure) Regulations 1992 shall be amended in accordance with the following paragraphs.

(2) In regulation 2 (persons under a duty to furnish information or evidence)—

(a) in paragraph (1), for "to enable a decision to be made under section 11, 12, 16 or 17 of the Act" substitute "and is needed for any of the purposes specified in regulation 3(1)"; and

(b) for paragraph (1A), substitute—

" (1A) In such cases as the Secretary of State may determine, a person falling within a category listed in paragraph (2) shall furnish such information or evidence as the Secretary of State may determine which is information or evidence—

(a)   with respect to the matter or matters specified in that paragraph in relation to that category;

(b)   needed by the Secretary of State for the purpose specified in regulation 3(1A); and

(c)   in that person's possession or which that person can reasonably be expected to acquire.".

(3) In regulation 3 (purposes for which information or evidence may be required), after paragraph (1) insert—

"(1A) The Secretary of State may require information or evidence to be provided under the provisions of regulation 2(1A) only for the purpose of verifying whether information or evidence which he holds, or has held, is correct.".

## COMMENCEMENT

### The Child Support, Pensions and Social Security Act 2000 (Commencement No.12) Order 2003

### (SI 2003/192 (C.11))

*Made by the Secretary of State for Work and Pensions, in exercise of the powers conferred upon him by section 86(2) of the Child Support, Pensions and Social Security Act 2000 and of all other powers enabling him in that behalf.*

### Citation and interpretation

1.—(1) This Order may be cited as the Child Support, Pensions and Social Security Act 2000 (Commencement No.12) Order 2003.

3.873

(2) In this Order—

(a) "the Act" means the Child Support, Pensions and Social Security Act 2000 and, except where otherwise stated, references to sections and Schedules are references to sections of, and Schedules to, the Act;

(b) "the 1991 Act" means the Child Support Act 1991;

(c) "absent parent" has the meaning given in the 1991 Act before its amendment by the Act;

(d) "the Arrangements and Jurisdiction Regulations" means the Child Support (Maintenance Arrangements and Jurisdiction) Regulations 1992 as in force immediately before 3rd March 2003;

(e) "the Assessment Procedure Regulations" means the Child Support (Maintenance Assessment Procedure) Regulations 1992 as in force immediately before 3rd March 2003;

(f) "effective date", in relation to a maintenance assessment or a maintenance calculation, has the meaning given in article 8 of this Order;

(g) "existing assessment" means a maintenance assessment which is in force with an effective date which is before 3rd March 2003;

(h) "maintenance assessment" has the meaning given in the 1991 Act before its amendment by the Act;

(i) "maintenance calculation" has the meaning given in the 1991 Act as amended by the Act;

(j) "non-resident parent" has the meaning given in the 1991 Act as amended by the Act;

(k) "partner" has the meaning given in paragraph 10C(4) of Part I of Schedule 1 to the 1991 Act as amended by the Act;

(l) "person with care" has the meaning given in the 1991 Act;
(m) "prescribed benefit" means a benefit prescribed for the purposes of paragraph 4(1)(c) of Part I of Schedule 1 to the 1991 Act as amended by the Act;
(n) "qualifying child" has the meaning given in the 1991 Act; and
(o) "relevant person" means, in relation to a maintenance assessment, the absent parent or person with care and, in relation to a maintenance calculation, the non-resident parent or person with care.

### Appointed day for purpose of making regulations

3.874    **2.** 4th February 2003 is the day appointed for the coming into force of—
(a) section 2(1) and (2) (applications under section 4 of the 1991 Act); and
(b) paragraph 11(4)(b)(i) and (ii) of Schedule 3 (right of a child in Scotland to apply for maintenance calculation), and section 26 so far as it relates to that provision,
for the purpose of the exercise of the power to make regulations.

DEFINITIONS

"the 1991 Act": see art.1(2).
"maintenance calculation": see art.1(2)

### Appointed day for the provisions specified in the Schedule to this Order

3.875    **3.**—(1) 3rd March 2003 is the day appointed for the coming into force of the provisions of the Act specified in the Schedule to this Order, in so far as those provisions are not already in force, for the purpose of—
(a) cases where an application for child support maintenance is made to the Secretary of State (whether or not in writing) and the effective date would be on or after 3rd March 2003;
(b) cases where there is an existing assessment and a related decision falls to be made; and
(c) cases where there is an existing assessment and where—
   (i) an application is made or treated as made which would but for that assessment result in a maintenance calculation being made,
   (ii) the non-resident parent in relation to the application referred to in paragraph (i) is the absent parent in relation to the existing assessment, and
   (iii) the person with care in relation to the application referred to in paragraph (i) is a different person to the person with care in relation to the existing assessment.
(2) For the purposes of paragraph (1)(b), "a related decision" is—
(a) a maintenance calculation which falls to be made with respect to a person who is a relevant person in relation to the existing assessment, whether or not with respect to a different qualifying child;
(b) a maintenance calculation which falls to be made with respect to the partner ("A") of a person ("B") who is a relevant person in relation to the existing assessment, where A or B is in receipt of a prescribed benefit and either—

(i) A is the non-resident parent in relation to the maintenance calculation and B is the absent parent in relation to the existing assessment, or

(ii) A is the person with care in relation to the maintenance calculation and B is the person with care in relation to the existing assessment;

(c) a decision which falls to be made in a case where—

    (i) the existing assessment is in force in relation to a person ("C") and a maintenance calculation is in force in relation to another person ("D"),

    (ii) C or D is in receipt of a prescribed benefit,

    (iii) either—

        (aa) C is the absent parent in relation to the existing assessment and D is the non-resident parent in relation to the maintenance calculation, or

        (bb) C is the person with care in relation to the existing assessment and D is the person with care in relation to the maintenance calculation, and (iv) a decision relating to the prescribed benefit referred to in paragraph (ii) is superseded on the ground that C is the partner of D; or

(d) a decision which falls to be made in a case where a person ("E") and another person ("F") become entitled to a prescribed benefit as partners, and where—

    (i) E is the absent parent in relation to the existing assessment and F is the non-resident parent in relation to a maintenance calculation, or

    (ii) E is the person with care in relation to the existing assessment and F is the person with care in relation to a maintenance calculation.

DEFINITIONS

"the Act": see art.1(2).
"absent parent": see art.1(2).
"effective date": see art.1(2).
"existing assessment": see art.1(2).
"maintenance calculation": see art.1(2).
"non-resident parent": see art.1(2).
"partner": see art.1(2).
"person with care": see art.1(2).
"prescribed benefit": see art.1(2).
"qualifying child": see art.1(2).
"relevant person": see art.1(2).

## Appointed day for sections 3 and 19

**4.** 3rd March 2003 is the day appointed for the coming into force of sections 3 and 19, in so far as those provisions are not already in force, for the purpose of the following cases—

    (a) where, on or after 3rd March 2003, income support, an income-based jobseeker's allowance or any other benefit prescribed for the purposes of section 6 of the 1991 Act as substituted by section 3 is

**3.876**

claimed by or in respect of, or paid to or in respect of, the parent of a qualifying child who is also the person with care of the child, and when the claim is made—

  (i) there is no maintenance assessment or maintenance calculation in force in respect of that parent, and

  (ii) there has been no maintenance assessment in force during the previous 8 weeks in respect of that child;

(b) where—

  (i) before 3rd March 2003, section 6(1) of the 1991 Act, before its substitution by the Act, applied to the parent with care,

  (ii) a maintenance assessment has been made with an effective date which is before 3rd March 2003, and

  (iii) on or after 3rd March 2003 the parent with care withdraws her authorisation under that section 6(1) at a date when she continues to fall within that section 6(1);

(c) where, immediately before 3rd March 2003, subsection (1) of section 6 of the 1991 Act, before its substitution by the Act, applied to the parent with care, and a maintenance assessment has not been made because—

  (i) the Secretary of State was in the process of considering whether the parent with care should be required to give the authorisation referred to in that subsection;

  (ii) subsection (2) of that section applied;

  (iii) subsection (2) of that section did not apply and a reduced benefit direction was given under section 46(5) of the 1991 Act before its substitution by the Act; or

  (iv) the parent with care failed to comply with a requirement imposed on her under subsection (1) of that section 6 and the Secretary of State was in the process of serving a notice or considering reasons given by the parent with care under section 46(2) or (3) of the 1991 Act before its substitution by the Act.

DEFINITIONS

"the Act": see art.1(2).
"the 1991 Act": see art.1(2).
"effective date": see art.1(2).
"maintenance assessment": see art.1(2).
"maintenance calculation": see art.1(2).
"prescribed benefit": see art.1(2).
"qualifying child": see art.1(2).

## Appointed day for section 20

3.877   **5.** 3rd March 2003 is the day appointed for the coming into force of section 20, in so far as that section is not already in force, for the purposes of cases where an application for child support maintenance is made to the Secretary of State (whether or not in writing) and the effective date would be on or after 3rd March 2003.

"effective date": see art.1(2).

[¹**Appointed day for section 23 and associated repeal**

**6.**—(1) The day appointed for the coming into force of the provisions    3.878
specified in paragraph (2) for the purposes of cases specified in paragraph
(3) is—

(a) as respects any case specified in paragraph (3)(a) where, before 3rd
March 2003, relevant maintenance is paid or payable—
  (i) where 3rd March 2003 is the day on which the maintenance
  calculation in relation to that case takes effect, 3rd March 2003,
  (ii) where the maintenance calculation in relation to that case takes
  effect on a day later than 3rd March 2003, that later day;

(b) as respects any other case specified in paragraph (3)(a), 3rd March
2003;

(c) as respects any case which is specified in paragraph (3)(b)—
  (i) where 3rd March 2003 is the case conversion date in relation to
  that case, 3rd March 2003,
  (ii) where a day later than 3rd March 2003 is the case conversion
  date in relation to that case, that later day;

(d) as respects any case specified in paragraph (3)(c) which is referred
to—
  (i) in paragraph (a) of article 4, the day on which the claim for the
  benefit mentioned in that paragraph is made,
  (ii) in paragraph (b) of that article, the day on which the Secretary
  of State is notified that the authorisation mentioned in sub-
  paragraph (iii) of that paragraph is withdrawn,
  (iii) in paragraph (c) of that article, 3rd March 2003;

(e) as respects any case which is specified in sub-paragraph (d) of
paragraph (3), the day on which the maintenance referred to in that
sub-paragraph is first paid.

(2) The provisions mentioned in paragraph (1) are—

(a) section 23 (section 10 of the Child Support Act 1995 to cease to
have effect); and

(b) Part I of Schedule 9 in so far as it relates to the repeal of section 10
of the Child Support Act 1995.

(3) The cases mentioned in paragraph (1) are—

(a) cases referred to in sub-paragraph (a) of article 3(1);

(b) cases referred to in sub-paragraph (b) or (c) of article 3(1);

(c) cases referred to in paragraph (a), (b) or (c) of article 4;

(d) cases to which sub-paragraphs (a) to (c) do not apply where, on or
after 3rd March 2003, relevant maintenance is first paid.

(4) For the purposes of sub-paragraph (d) of paragraph (3), a case shall
not be regarded as one to which that sub-paragraph does not apply by
reason only of the fact that relevant maintenance was paid or payable
before 3rd March 2003—

(a) in respect of the care of a different child;

(b) under an earlier agreement; or

(c) by virtue of an earlier order of the court.

(5) In this article—

"case conversion date" means the date which is, by virtue of regulation 15 of the Child Support (Transitional Provisions) Regulations 2000, the case conversion date in relation to that case; and

"relevant maintenance" means maintenance, other than child support maintenance, which is paid or payable—

(a) to a person who has the care of a child in the United Kingdom;

(b) in respect of the care of the child; and

(c) under an agreement (whether enforceable or not) between that person and the person by whom the maintenance is payable, or by virtue of an order of the court.]

AMENDMENT

3.879     1. Article 2 of the Child Support, Pensions and Social Security Act 2000 (Commencement No.13) Order 2003.

DEFINITION

"maintenance calculation": see art.1(2).

### Appointed day for coming into force of section 29, and Schedule 3, paragraph 11(15)

3.880     7. 3rd March 2003 is the day appointed for the coming into force of—

(a) section 29 (interpretation, transitional provisions, savings, etc.) in so far as it is not already in force; and

(b) paragraph 11(15) of Schedule 3 (which substitutes subsection (2) in section 30 of the 1991 Act, and section 26 so far as it relates to that paragraph 11(15).

DEFINITION

"the 1991 Act": see art.1(2).

### The effective date

3.881     8.—(1) For the purposes of this Order, "the effective date" means, in relation to any case, the date which would be the effective date of a maintenance assessment under regulation 30 or 33(7) of the Assessment Procedure Regulations (effective dates of new maintenance assessments, and maintenance periods) or regulation 3(5), (7) or (8) of the Arrangements and Jurisdiction Regulations (relationship between maintenance assessments and certain court orders), whichever would apply to the case in question, or would have applied had the effective date not fallen to be determined under regulation 8C or 30A of the Assessment Procedure Regulations; and paragraphs (2) and (3) shall apply in relation to the application of those Regulations for this purpose.

(2) In the application of the Assessment Procedure Regulations for the purposes of paragraph (1), where, on or after 3rd March 2003, no maintenance enquiry form, as defined in those Regulations, is given or sent to

the absent parent, those Regulations shall be applied as if references in regulation 30—

(a) to the date when the maintenance enquiry form was given or sent to the absent parent were references to the date on which the absent parent is first notified by the Secretary of State (whether or not in writing) that an application for child support maintenance has been made in respect of which he is named as the absent parent; and

(b) to the return by the absent parent of the maintenance enquiry form containing his name, address and written confirmation that he is the parent of the child or children in respect of whom the application was made were references to the provision of this information by the absent parent.

(3) In the application of the Arrangements and Jurisdiction Regulations for the purposes of paragraph (1), where, on or after 3rd March 2003, no maintenance enquiry form, as defined in the Assessment Procedure Regulations, is given or sent to the absent parent, regulation 3(8) shall be applied as if the reference to the date when the maintenance enquiry form was given or sent to the absent parent were to the date on which the absent parent is first notified by the Secretary of State (whether or not in writing) that an application for child support maintenance has been made in respect of which he is named as the absent parent.

DEFINITIONS

"absent parent": see art.1(2).
"the Arrangements and Jurisdiction Regulations": see art.1(2).
"the Assessment Procedure Regulations": see art.1(2).
"effective date": see art.1(2).

SCHEDULE

PROVISIONS BOUGHT INTO FORCE AS PROVIDED IN ARTICLE 3

| Provision of the Act | Subject Matter | |
|---|---|---|
| Section 1(1) and (2) | Maintenance calculations and terminology | **3.882** |
| Section 2 | Applications under section 4 of the 1991 Act | |
| Section 4 | Default and interim maintenance decisions | |
| Section 5 | Departure from usual rules for calculating maintenance | |
| Section 7 | Variations: revision and supersession | |
| Section 8 | Revision of decisions | |
| Section 9 | Decisions superseding earlier decisions | |
| Section 10 | Appeals to appeal tribunals | |
| Section 12 | Information required by Secretary of State | |
| Section 18 | Financial penalties | |

| Provision of the Act | Subject Matter |
|---|---|
| Section 21 | Recovery of child support maintenance by deduction from benefit |
| Section 22(4) | Jurisdiction |
| Section 25 | Regulations |
| Schedule 1 and section 1(3) | Substituted Part I of Schedule 1 to the 1991 Act |
| Schedule 2 and section 6 | Substituted Schedules 4A and 4B to the 1991 Act |
| Schedule 3, except for paragraph 11(15), and section 26 | Amendment of enactments relating to child support |
| Part I of Schedule 9, except as respects the repeal of section 10 of the Child Support Act 1995, and section 85 so far as it relates to that Part I | Repeals and revocations (child support) |

## The Child Support (Miscellaneous Amendments) (No. 2) Regulations 2003

### (SI 2003/2779)

*Whereas a draft of this instrument was laid before Parliament in accordance with section 52(2) of the Child Support Act 1991 and approved by resolution of each House of Parliament:*

*Now, therefore, the Secretary of State for Work and Pensions, in exercise of the powers conferred upon him by sections 12(2), 16(1), 17(3), 28E(5), 42, 46, 51, 52 and 54 of, and paragraphs 4, 5, 6, 10(1) and 11 of Schedule 1 and paragraphs 2, 3(1)(b), 4(1)(b) and 5 of Schedule 4B to, the Child Support Act 1991 and section 29 of the Child Support, Pensions and Social Security Act 2000 and of all other powers enabling him in that behalf, hereby makes the following Regulations:*

*Made        4th November 2003*

### Citation and commencement

3.883    **1.** These Regulations may be cited as the Child Support (Miscellaneous Amendments) (No. 2) Regulations 2003 and shall come into force on the day after the day that they are made.

. . .

**Savings**

**9.** Regulations 1(3), 40 and 40ZA of the Child Support (Maintenance    **3.884**
Assessment Procedure) Regulations 1992 and regulations 8(2)(b), 14 and
15 of the Child Support (Maintenance Calculation Procedure) Regulations
2000 shall continue to have effect in relation to a person to whom any of
those provisions applied before the date these Regulations come into force
as if regulations 3(2), (4) and (5) and 5 of these Regulations had not come
into force.

# MATERIAL AND COMMENTARY
# FOR THE ORIGINAL SCHEME

# Child Support Act 1991

## SCHEDULE 1

## MAINTENANCE ASSESSMENTS

### Part I

## CALCULATION OF CHILD SUPPORT MAINTENANCE

### *The Maintenance Requirement*

**1.**—(1) In this Schedule "the maintenance requirement" means the amount, calculated in accordance with the formula set out in subparagraph (2), which is to be taken as the minimum amount necessary for the maintenance of the qualifying child or, where there is more than one qualifying child, all of them.

(2) The formula is—

$$MR = AG - CB$$

where—

MR is the amount of the maintenance requirement;

AG is the aggregate of the amounts to be taken into account under sub-paragraph (3); and

CB is the amount payable by way of child benefit (or which would be so payable if the person with care of the qualifying child were an individual) or, where there is more than one qualifying child, the aggregate of the amounts so payable with respect to each of them.

(3) The amounts to be taken into account for the purpose of calculating AG are—

(a) such amount or amounts (if any), with respect to each qualifying child, as may be prescribed;

(b) such amount or amounts (if any), with respect to the person with care of the qualifying child or qualifying children, as may be prescribed; and

(c) such further amount or amounts (if any) as may be prescribed.

(4) For the purposes of calculating CB it shall be assumed that child benefit is payable with respect to any qualifying child at the basic rate.

(5) In subparagraph (4) "basic rate" has the meaning for the time being prescribed.

*The general rule*

4.2     **2.**—(1) In order to determine the amount of any maintenance assessment, first calculate—

$$(A + C) \times P$$

where—

A is the absent parent's assessable income;

C is the assessable income of the other parent, where that parent is the person with care, and otherwise has such value (if any) as may be prescribed; and

P is such number greater than zero but less than 1 as may be prescribed.

(2) Where the result of the calculation made under subparagraph (1) is an amount which is equal to, or less than, the amount of the maintenance requirement for the qualifying child or qualifying children, the amount of maintenance payable by the absent parent for that child or those children shall be an amount equal to—

$$A \times P$$

where A and P have the same values as in the calculation made under subparagraph (1).

(3) Where the result of the calculation made under subparagraph (1) is an amount which exceeds the amount of the maintenance requirement for the qualifying child or qualifying children, the amount of maintenance payable by the absent parent for that child or those children shall consist of—

    (a) a basic element calculated in accordance with the provisions of paragraph 3; and

    (b) an additional element calculated in accordance with the provisions of paragraph 4.

*The basic element*

4.3     **3.**—(1) The basic element shall be calculated by applying the formula—

$$BE = A \times G \times P$$

where—

BE is the amount of the basic element;

A and P have the same values as in the calculation made under paragraph 2(1); and

G has the value determined under subparagraph (2).

(2) The value of G shall be determined by applying the formula—

$$G = \frac{MR}{(A + C) \times P}$$

where—

MR is the amount of the maintenance requirement for the qualifying children; and

A, C and P have the same values as in the calculation made under paragraph 2(1).

*The additional element*

4.4     **4.**—(1) Subject to subparagraph (2), the additional element shall be calculated by applying the formula—

$AE = (1–G) \times A \times R$ where—

AE is the amount of the additional element;

A has the same value as in the calculation made under paragraph 2(1);

G has the value determined under paragraph 3(2); and

R is such number greater than zero but less than 1 as may be prescribed.

(2) Where applying the alternative formula set out in subparagraph (3) would result in a lower amount for the additional element, that formula shall be applied in place of the formula set out in subparagraph (1).

(3) The alternative formula is—

$$AE = Z \times Q \times \left\{ \frac{A}{A + C} \right\}$$

where—

A and C have the same values as in the calculation made under paragraph 2(1);

Z is such number as may be prescribed; and

Q is the aggregate of—

(a) any amount taken into account by virtue of paragraph 1(3)(a) in calculating the maintenance requirement; and

(b) any amount which is both taken into account by virtue of paragraph 1(3)(c) in making that calculation and is an amount prescribed for the purposes of this paragraph.

*Assessable income*

**5.**—(1) The assessable income of an absent parent shall be calculated by applying the formula—

$A = N - E$

where—

A is the amount of that parent's assessable income;

N is the amount of that parent's net income, calculated or estimated in accordance with regulations made by the Secretary of State for the purposes of this subparagraph; and

E is the amount of that parent's exempt income, calculated or estimated in accordance with regulations made by the Secretary of State for those purposes.

(2) The assessable income of a parent who is a person with care of the qualifying child or children shall be calculated by applying the formula—

$C = M - F$

where—

C is the amount of that parent's assessable income;

M is the amount of that parent's net income, calculated or estimated in accordance with regulations made by the Secretary of State for the purposes of this subparagraph; and

F is the amount of that parent's exempt income, calculated or estimated in accordance with regulations made by the Secretary of State for those purposes.

4.5

(3) Where the preceding provisions of this paragraph would otherwise result in a person's assessable income being taken to be a negative amount his assessable income shall be taken to be nil.

(4) Where income support [³, an income-based jobseeker's allowance] or any other benefit of a prescribed kind is paid to or in respect of a parent who is an absent parent or a person with care that parent shall, for the purposes of this Schedule, be taken to have no assessable income.

*Protected income*

4.6

**6.**—(1) This paragraph applies where—

(a) one or more maintenance assessments have been made with respect to an absent parent; and

(b) payment by him of the amount, or the aggregate of the amounts, so assessed would otherwise reduce his disposable income below his protected income level.

(2) The amount of the assessment, or (as the case may be) of each assessment, shall be adjusted in accordance with such provisions as may be prescribed with a view to securing so far as is reasonably practicable that payment by the absent parent of the amount, or (as the case may be) aggregate of the amounts, so assessed will not reduce his disposable income below his protected income level.

(3) Regulations made under subparagraph (2) shall secure that, where the prescribed minimum amount fixed by regulations made under paragraph 7 applies, no maintenance assessment is adjusted so as to provide for the amount payable by an absent parent in accordance with that assessment to be less than that amount.

(4) The amount which is to be taken for the purposes of this paragraph as an absent parent's disposable income shall be calculated, or estimated, in accordance with regulations made by the Secretary of State.

(5) Regulations made under sub-paragraph (4) may, in particular, provide that, in such circumstances and to such extent as may be prescribed—

(a) income of any child who is living in the same household with the absent parent; and

[¹²(b) where the absent parent—

(i) is living together in the same household with another adult of the opposite sex (regardless of whether or not they are married),

(ii) is living together in the same household with another adult of the same sex who is his civil partner,

(iii) is living together in the same household with another adult of the same sex as if they were civil partners,

income of that other adult,]

is to be treated as the absent parent's income for the purposes of calculating his disposable income.

[¹³(5A) For the purposes of this paragraph, two adults of the same sex are to be regarded as living together as if they were civil partners if, but only if, they would be regarded as living together as husband and wife were they instead two adults of the opposite sex.]

(6) In this paragraph the "protected income level" of a particular absent parent means an amount of income calculated, by reference to the circum-

stances of that parent, in accordance with regulations made by the
Secretary of State.

### *The minimum amount of child support maintenance*

**7.**—(1) The Secretary of State may prescribe a minimum amount for
the purposes of this paragraph.

(2) Where the amount of child support maintenance which would be
fixed by a maintenance assessment but for this paragraph is nil, or less than
the prescribed minimum amount, the amount to be fixed by the assessment
shall be the prescribed minimum amount.

(3) In any case to which section 43 applies, and in such other cases (if
any) as may be prescribed, subparagraph (2) shall not apply.

### *Housing costs*

**8.** Where regulations under this Schedule require [⁴the Secretary of
State] to take account of the housing costs of any person in calculating, or
estimating, his assessable income or disposable income, those regulations
may make provision—

(a) as to the costs which are to be treated as housing costs for the
purpose of the regulations;

(b) for the apportionment of housing costs; and

(c) for the amount of housing costs to be taken into account for
prescribed purposes not to exceed such amount (if any) as may be
prescribed by, or determined in accordance with, the regulations.

### *Regulations about income and capital*

**9.** The Secretary of State may by regulations provide that, in such
circumstances and to such extent as may be prescribed—

(a) income of a child shall be treated as income of a parent of his;

(b) where [⁵the Secretary of State] is satisfied that a person has intentionally deprived himself of a source of income with a view to reducing the amount of his assessable income, his net income shall be
taken to include income from that source of an amount estimated by
[⁵the Secretary of State];

(c) a person is to be treated as possessing capital or income which he
does not possess;

(d) capital or income which a person does possess is to be disregarded;

(e) income is to be treated as capital;

(f) capital is to be treated as income.

### *References to qualifying children*

**10.** References in this Part of this Schedule to "qualifying children"
are to those qualifying children with respect to whom the maintenance
assessment falls to be made.

PART II

GENERAL PROVISIONS ABOUT MAINTENANCE
ASSESSMENTS

*Effective date of assessment*

4.11     **11.**—(1) A maintenance assessment shall take effect on such date as may be determined in accordance with regulations made by the Secretary of State.

(2) That date may be earlier than the date on which the assessment is made.

*Form of assessment*

4.12     **12.** Every maintenance assessment shall be made in such form and contain such information as the Secretary of State may direct.

*Assessments where amount of child support is nil*

4.13     **13.** [⁶The Secretary of State] shall not decline to make a maintenance assessment only on the ground that the amount of the assessment is nil.

*Consolidated applications and assessments*

4.14     **14.** The Secretary of State may by regulations provide—
          (a) for two or more applications for maintenance assessments to be treated, in prescribed circumstances, as a single application; and
          (b) for the replacement, in prescribed circumstances, of a maintenance assessment made on the application of one person by a later maintenance assessment made on the application of that or any other person.

*Separate assessments for different periods*

4.15     **15.** Where [⁷the Secretary of State] is satisfied that the circumstances of a case require different amounts of child support maintenance to be assessed in respect of different periods, he may make separate maintenance assessments each expressed to have effect in relation to a different specified period.

*Termination of assessments*

4.16     **16.**—(1) A maintenance assessment shall cease to have effect—
          (a) on the death of the absent parent, or of the person with care, with respect to whom it was made;
          (b) on there no longer being any qualifying child with respect to whom it would have effect;
          (c) on the absent parent with respect to whom it was made ceasing to be a parent of—

     (i)   the qualifying child with respect to whom it was made; or

    (ii)  where it was made with respect to more than one qualifying child, all of the qualifying children with respect to whom it was made;

  (d)  where the absent parent and the person with care with respect to whom it was made have been living together for a continuous period of six months;

  (e)  where a new maintenance assessment is made with respect to any qualifying child with respect to whom the assessment in question was in force immediately before the making of the new assessment.

(2) A maintenance assessment made in response to an application under section 4 or 7 shall be cancelled by [8the Secretary of State] if the person on whose application the assessment was made asks him to do so.

(3) A maintenance assessment made in response to an application under section 6 shall be cancelled by [8the Secretary of State] if—

  (a)  the person on whose application the assessment was made ("the applicant") asks him to do so; and

  (b)  he is satisfied that the applicant has ceased to fall within subsection (1) of that section.

(4) Where [8the Secretary of State] is satisfied that the person with care with respect to whom a maintenance assessment was made has ceased to be a person with care in relation to the qualifying child, or any of the qualifying children, with respect to whom the assessment was made, he may cancel the assessment with effect from the date on which, in his opinion, the change of circumstances took place.

[1(4A) A maintenance assessment may be cancelled by [8the Secretary of State] if he is [9proposing to make a decision under section 16 or 17] and it appears to him—

  (a)  that the person with care with respect to whom the maintenance assessment in question was made has failed to provide him with sufficient information to enable him to [9make the decision] ; and

  (b)  where the maintenance assessment in question was made in response to an application under section 6, that the person with care with respect to whom the assessment was made has ceased to fall within subsection (1) of that section.]

(5) Where—

  (a)  at any time a maintenance assessment is in force but [8the Secretary of State] would no longer have jurisdiction to make it if it were to be applied for at that time; and

  (b)  the assessment has not been cancelled, or has not ceased to have effect, under or by virtue of any other provision made by or under this Act,

it shall be taken to have continuing effect unless cancelled by [8the Secretary of State] in accordance with such prescribed provision (including provision as to the effective date of cancellation) as the Secretary of State considers it appropriate to make.

(6) Where both the absent parent and the person with care with respect to whom a maintenance assessment was made request [8the Secretary of State] to cancel the assessment, he may do so if he is satisfied that they are living together.

(7) Any cancellation of a maintenance assessment under subparagraph [² 4(A),] (5) or (6) shall have effect from such date as may be determined by [⁸the Secretary of State].

(8) Where [⁸the Secretary of State] cancels a maintenance assessment, he shall immediately notify the absent parent and person with care, so far as that is reasonably practicable.

(9) Any notice under subparagraph (8) shall specify the date with effect from which the cancellation took effect.

(10) A person with care with respect to whom a maintenance assessment is in force shall provide the Secretary of State with such information, in such circumstances, as may be prescribed, with a view to assisting the Secretary of State [¹¹. . .] in determining whether the assessment has ceased to have effect, or should be cancelled.

(11) The Secretary of State may be regulations make such supplemental, incidental or transitional provision as he thinks necessary or expedient in consequence of the provisions of this paragraph.

AMENDMENTS

1. Section 14(2) of the 1995 Act (January 22, 1996).
2. Section 14(3) of the 1995 Act (January 22, 1996).
3. Paragraph 20(7) of Sched.2 to the Jobseekers Act 1995 (October 7, 1996).
4. Paragraph 48(1) of Sched.7 to the Social Security Act 1998 (June 1, 1999).
5. Paragraph 48(2) of Sched.7 to the Social Security Act 1998 (June 1, 1999).
6. Paragraph 48(3) of Sched.7 to the Social Security Act 1998 (June 1, 1999).
7. Paragraph 48(4) of Sched.7 to the Social Security Act 1998 (June 1, 1999).
8. Paragraph 48(5)(a) of Sched.7 to the Social Security Act 1998 (June 1, 1999).
9. Paragraph 48(5)(b) of Sched.7 to the Social Security Act 1998 (June 1, 1999).
10. Paragraph 48(5)(c) of Sched.7 to the Social Security Act 1998 (June 1, 1999).
11. Paragraph 48(5)(d) of Sched.7 to the Social Security Act 1998 (June 1, 1999).
12. Paragraph 4 of Sched.24 to the Civil Partnership Act 2004.
13. Paragraph 5 of Sched.24 to the Civil Partnership Act 2004.

4.17   DEFINITIONS

"absent parent": see s.3(2).
"child": see s.55.
"child benefit": see s.54.
"income support": see s.54.
"maintenance assessment": see s.54.
"parent": see s.54.
"person with care": see s.3(3).
"prescribed": see s.54.
"qualifying child": see s.3(l).

4.18   GENERAL NOTE

*Overview of Part I*
Part I of this Schedule contains the core provisions which deal with the calculation of maintenance assessments. It must be read in conjunction with the Maintenance Assessments and Special Cases Regulations. The calculations which must be made are expressed as formulae; this makes it easy to state the calculation which must be made, but not necessarily easy to understand why the calculation is

relevant or what its effect will be. It is helpful to have an overview of the structure and terminology in order better to understand the details. The following paragraphs provide this overview.

There are broadly two types of calculation which have to be made in order to calculate a maintenance assessment. One is based on the actual financial circumstances of the person concerned. The other is based on figures from income support law (supplemented sometimes by an element based on the party's actual financial circumstances). These figures are used for the purpose of the calculation only. It is not necessary that any party should be in receipt of, or entitled to, income support. As the income support figures increase each year in the annual uprating of benefits, so the figures used for child support purposes increase, although they are only be fed into an existing maintenance assessment when it is reviewed.

Child support law is concerned with the financial responsibility of parents for their children (s.l). In this context "parent" means the parent in law (s.54) and covers natural parents, parents by virtue of adoption and parents by virtue of the operation of the Human Fertility and Embryology Act 1990.

Accordingly, child support law has no relevance where (a) a child has no parents, or (b) the child is living in a single household which includes both parents or the only parent.

In all other cases child support law provides that each parent is responsible for maintaining a child (s.l). Parents who are looking after their children must meet all or part of the costs from their income, including benefit income. Parents who are absent must usually pay child support maintenance to the person with care of the child, whether or not that person is also a parent of the child.

The law does not identify the actual cost of maintaining a child. (There is a *maintenance requirement* which may approach the minimum cost, but it is too simple to see that as the actual cost of bringing up a child. See below.) Rather it concentrates on how much an absent parent is required to pay towards maintaining a child.

The extent to which each parent is expected to meet the cost of maintaining a child depends on that parent's available income. "Available income" is not a term that is used in the child support legislation. It is used here to capture the essence of a series of complex calculations which have to be made, but whose overall purpose is to identify the pot of money from which an absent parent is expected to contribute towards a child's maintenance. Where the other parent is also involved in the calculation, the size of the pot will be fixed by taking into account the other parent's available income.

Where both parents are involved in maintaining their child, the respective levels of their income are relevant in fixing the amount of child support maintenance to be paid by the absent parent However, where the person with care is not a parent of the child and the child support calculation only concerns one parent, only that person's available income is taken into account.

The first stage of a maintenance assessment is to calculate the *maintenance requirement*. This is based on income support allowances and premiums minus child benefit payments. It varies according to the following factors:

(a) the number of children concerned;
(b) their ages;
(c) whether the person with care has a partner; and
(d) the rate of child benefit payable in respect of each child.

In essence the maintenance requirement consists of the additional amount of **4.19** income support which would be paid to the person with care on account of the presence of the child in that person's household plus an allowance to reflect the care provided by that person. However, it does not represent even the minimum cost of maintaining a child, as it excludes the additional housing costs attributable to the child's presence in the household as well as the services which are provided free to a person with care who is in receipt of income support.

The maintenance requirement fulfils two functions. First, it provides a yardstick by reference to which the level of child support maintenance is set. Second, given that one of the policies underlying the child support scheme is that parents rather than the State should bear the cost of bringing up their children, it sets as a target the amount of income support attributable to the child's presence and therefore to be recouped from the absent parent.

The second stage of a maintenance assessment is to determine the available income of the absent parent, and also of the person with care if that person is also a parent of the child. This involves a number of separate steps.

(a) First, the parent's income has to be determined. This consists mostly of the parent's actual income, such as earnings, interest on savings, dividends from shares and so on. However, some income is attributed to the parent and some income is disregarded.

(b) From this is deducted key work-related costs, such as income tax, national insurance, half of any pension contributions and essential expenses.

(c) The result is the parent's *net income*. In simple terms this is the money in the parent's pocket.

(d) The next step is to make allowance for the key living expenses such as food, clothing and housing. This is called the parent's *exempt income*. It is based in part on income support allowances and premiums and in part on the parent's actual expenses, particularly housing (capped if excessive). Allowances are also made in respect of travel to work costs and to compensate for a clean break settlement. Some of the income support premiums are reduced if the parent has a child who lives as part of the household for only part of the week. Some are also reduced if the parent has a partner and a child, and the partner's income exceeds a threshold.

(e) The exempt income is deducted from the net income to produce the *assessable income*.

4.20    The result of the maintenance assessment so far has been to identify the amount of child support maintenance that is prima facie payable. However, this amount may be reduced in order to preserve a minimum level of income available to the absent parent's household. This is the *protected income* calculation. It looks at the effect of the prima facie child support maintenance figure not just on the absent parent's net income, but on the combined net incomes of the absent parent and that parent's current partner (if any). This (combined) total is called the *disposable income*. Part of this income is ring fenced. This ring fence is known as the *protected income level*. If the result of paying the prima facie figure would be to reduce the household's disposable income below this level, the child support maintenance payable is capped to prevent this occurring. The protected income level is a minimum of 70 per cent of the absent parent's net income. It will be more if the alternative calculation produces a higher figure. The alternative calculation is in some respects very similar to that for exempt income. It is based in part on income support allowances and premiums and in part on the actual expenses, particularly housing costs (an allowance is made if the housing costs are treated as nil) and council tax. Allowance is also made in respect of travel to work costs. Some of the income support premiums are reduced if the parent has a child who lives as part of the household for only part of the week. There is included a flat rate amount and an additional percentage of the household's income in excess of the remainder of the calculation, the latter being an incentive to increase the household's income by ensuring that any increase in low income families is not lost pound for pound by an increase in the amount of child support maintenance payable. It is important to distinguish between the exempt income and the income disregarded in determining the net income. The former is a figure largely derived from income support figures, while the latter is actual income from specified sources. They must not be confused, as the net income figure (which excludes disregarded income but not exempt income) is used for another purpose (see below).

Now that the assessable income of the parents has been calculated, it is possible to move to the third stage and calculate the prima facie amount of child support maintenance payable. As a minimum, the parents are expected to put up to one half of their assessable incomes towards meeting the maintenance requirement for their child (para.2). They contribute in proportion to their respective incomes. If their joint assessable incomes exceed the maintenance requirement, a greater contribution to the cost of the child's upbringing is expected. If this is the case, any maintenance payable by an absent parent will be made up of two elements, a *basic element* and an *additional element*. The basic element is a percentage of half of the absent parent's assessable income (para.3). It will either be equal to the maintenance requirement or, if the person with care is a parent who has income as well as the absent parent, it will be the same percentage of the maintenance requirement as the absent parent's income represents of the parents' joint incomes. The additional element reflects the fact that there are extra resources for the parents to devote to the child. It is a percentage of one-quarter of the absent parent's assessable income (or less if there are fewer than three children) and is subject to a ceiling (para.4).

The figure produced by these formulae is not necessarily the amount of child support maintenance that will be paid. The Schedule contains two longstops which provide a measure of protection for the child and the absent parent. The protection for the child is found in para.7, which provides that in most cases there is a minimum amount of child support maintenance which must be paid, regardless both of the results of the calculations in the third step and of the respective incomes of the absent parent and the person with care. This is known as the *prescribed minimum amount* and is fixed at a percentage of an income support figure. The protection for the absent parent is found in para.6 which provides that as far as possible the amount of child support maintenance payable should not reduce the parent's *disposable income* below the *protected income level*. The calculation of disposable income takes account of the income of the absent parent and of any partner as well as of any children living with them. It is calculated in very much the same way as the net income (hence the importance of distinguishing between disregarded income and exempt income). The protected income level is fixed by reference to income support figures supplemented by some elements of the family's actual financial circumstances. If there is a conflict between these two protections, the protection for the child has priority and the prescribed minimum amount is payable, even if the result is to reduce the absent parent's disposable income below the protected income level. 4.21

Although child support maintenance only determines the maintenance payable for the child, its receipt may increase the person with care's family income above the income support applicable amount. If this is the case, the person with care may have only the child support maintenance on which to support the whole family. When the loss of the fringe benefits associated with income support is also taken into account, the result of a child support maintenance assessment may be to reduce the carer family's income, although in the case of a s.6 application the burden on the public purse will have been removed.

*Special Cases* 4.22

Where the case is a special case within Part III of the Maintenance Assessments and Special Cases Regulations, the provisions of this Schedule may be modified. Modifications which are relevant to a particular paragraph of this Schedule are noted either in the general note to that paragraph or in the general note to the relevant regulation thereunder. The modifications which are of general application are as follows:

Where both parents of a qualifying child are absent parents and an application is made in relation to them both, separate assessments must be made in respect of each (reg.19(2)(a) of the Maintenance Assessments and Special Cases Regulations).

Where one parent is an absent parent and the other is *treated as* an absent parent under reg.20 of the Maintenance Assessments and Special Cases Regulations, references in this Schedule to a parent who is a person with care should be read as references to the person who is treated as an absent parent under reg.20 (reg.21).

Where two or more persons who do not live in the same household each provide day to day care for the same qualifying child and none of those persons is a parent who is treated as an absent parent under reg.20 of the Maintenance Assessments and Special Cases Regulations, the case is a special one by virtue of reg.24 of those Regulations. The person whose application is being dealt with is entitled to receive the whole of the child support maintenance payable, subject to the Secretary of State's right to apportion the payment in proportion to the provision of care (reg.24(2)). As this is a decision which relates to payment rather than calculation, it is not a matter for a decision-maker. Consequently, no appeal lies to a tribunal.

Where a local authority and a person each provide day to day care for a qualifying child, the case is a special case by virtue of reg.25 of the Maintenance Assessments and Special Cases Regulations. If this case applies, the child support maintenance is calculated in accordance with this Schedule. It is then divided by seven in order to find a daily amount. The daily amount is paid for each night in respect of which the person other than the local authority provides day to day care. Maintenance is not payable in respect of any night for which the local authority provides day to day care. See reg.25(2). Special provision is made for the case where more than one child is included in an assessment (reg.25(3)).

4.23    *Paragraph 1*

This paragraph provides for the calculation of the maintenance requirement for a qualifying child The maintenance requirement is not necessarily the amount of maintenance which will become payable. That figure may be either more or less than the requirement. The significance of the maintenance requirement is that it provides a figure which is the minimum desirable maintenance payment, although it will not always be attained. For the significance of the maintenance requirement in other calculations see para.2(2) and (3). It is also used to fix the amount of a Category A interim maintenance assessment (see the original s.12 of the Act and the regulations made thereunder).

The maintenance requirement is the total of certain amounts derived from income support law (AG in the formula) less the amount of child benefit in respect of the child (CB in the formula).

The words "person with care" in para.1(3)(b) include a parent of the qualifying child (*R(CS) 2/95*, para.17).

AG is prescribed by reg.3 of the Maintenance Assessments and Special Cases Regulations. It is the total of the following amounts fixed by reference to the Income Support Schedule. The appropriate amounts are those applicable on the effective date (reg.3(2)).

- (a) The personal allowance for a child of the age of each qualifying child. The age is that of the child on the effective date.
- (b) If the child is aged less than 16 all or part of the personal allowance for a single claimant aged not less than 25. The age of the child is determined at the effective date. Although the personal allowance is that of an adult aged not less than 25, the age of the person with care is irrelevant and will apply even if that person is aged less than 25.
- (c) The family premium.
- (d) If the person with care has no partner, the amount appropriate to a lone parent. This does not apply if both parents are absent parents and the person

with care is a body of persons corporate or unincorporate (reg.19 of the Maintenance Assessments and Special Cases Regulations).

The amounts under (b), (c), and (d) need to be modified if the case is a special case by virtue of reg.23 of the Maintenance Assessments and Special Cases Regulations. See the general note to reg.3.

CB is prescribed by reg.4 of the Maintenance Assessments and Special Cases Regulations. It is the rate of child benefit applicable to the child in question at the effective date.

*Paragraph 2*                                                                                            **4.24**

The first step in applying this paragraph is to decide whose assessable incomes are to be taken into account for the purpose of this paragraph. If the person with care is not a parent of the child, only the assessable income of the absent parent is taken into account under this paragraph. This is the effect of reg.5(a) of the Maintenance Assessments and Special Cases Regulations. If the person with care is a parent of the child, the joint assessable incomes of the absent parent and the person with care are taken into account. There is a special case if both parents are absent parents. In this case if the application has been made in respect of both absent parents, the joint assessable incomes of both parents are considered (reg.19(2)(b) of the Maintenance Assessments and Special Cases Regulations). However, if there is information about the income of one parent but not about the other's, the maintenance assessment in relation to the first parent is calculated on the basis that the income of the other parent is nil and a fresh assessment is made when the information about the other parent's income becomes available (reg.19(3) and (4)). These special provisions do not apply if the application for a maintenance assessment has been made in respect of only one parent. In this case that parent's assessable income is the only relevant income for the purposes of this paragraph.

The second step is to determine the assessable income of each relevant parent under para.5 of this Schedule. This income is usually applied directly in the formula. However, in two special cases only a proportion is fed into the formula. Since this may be relevant to the calculation under both this and some subsequent paragraphs, the third step is to decide if either of these special cases applies and if so, its effect. The first special case arises where two or more applications for maintenance assessments have been made in respect of the same person who is, or who is treated as, an absent parent but those applications relate to different children (reg.22 of the Maintenance Assessments and Special Cases Regulations). In this case the proportion of the absent parent's assessable income that is taken into account is determined by the formula in reg.22(2). The amount treated as the absent parent's assessable income for this purpose is the same proportion of the total of the absent parent's assessable income and all allowances for qualifying transfers as the maintenance requirement for the application being considered represents of the total of the maintenance requirements for all the applications in question less the value of the qualifying transfer in respect of the assessment in question. The second special case is where the person with care is the person with care of two or more qualifying children and there are different persons who are, or who are treated as, absent parents in relation to at least two of those children (reg.23(4)). In this case, if the person with care is the parent of any of the children, the proportion of the parent with care's assessable income which is taken into account is determined by the formula in reg.22(2). In other words, the amount of assessable income taken into account in this case is the same proportion as the maintenance requirement for the application being considered represents of the total of the maintenance requirements for all the applications made by the person with care.

The amount of the assessable income which is taken into account for the purposes of this paragraph may therefore be 100 per cent or, if one of the special cases                **4.25** applies, less. In either case it will be referred to as "the relevant income." The relevant incomes fixed under this paragraph will also be used in paras 3 and 4.

When the relevant incomes to be used in the formula have been assessed, the fourth step is to multiply those incomes by P. P is prescribed by reg.5(b) of the Maintenance Assessments and Special Cases Regulations. It is 0.5. Thus the result of the calculation will be half of the total of the relevant incomes.

The fifth step is to compare this figure with the maintenance requirement fixed under para.1. If it is equal to or less than the maintenance requirement, the maintenance payable by the absent parent for that child is half of the absent parent's relevant income (para.2(2)). The effect is that the maintenance payable is half of the absent parent's relevant income regardless of the person with care's relevant income. It is the person with care who must bear the consequences of the shortfall. This is all subject to paras 6 and 7 (see below).

If the figure produced by the formula is more than the maintenance requirement, it is necessary to make further calculations in order to decide the maintenance payable. The amount payable will consist of two elements: a basic element and an additional element (para.2(3)). The calculation of the basic element is governed by para.3 and the calculation of the additional element is governed by para.4. The essence of these calculations is that half of the absent parent's relevant income is used in calculating the basic element, up to a quarter is used in calculating the additional element and the remainder is not used at all.

4.26    *Paragraph 3*

This paragraph provides for the fixing of the basic element of maintenance which is payable. It only applies if the calculation under para.2(1) results in a figure which is higher than the maintenance requirement. The relevant formula is set out in para.3(1). At first sight the formula may appear complicated. However its effect is simple. If the person with care is either not a parent of the child or is a parent but has no relevant income, the basic element is equal to the maintenance requirement. In any other case the basic element is the same percentage of the maintenance requirement as the absent parent's relevant income represents of the joint relevant incomes of the parents. It is only in this latter case that it is necessary to work through the formula.

The formula starts with the absent parent's relevant income. It then takes half (*i.e.* the value of P) of this and further reduces it by the value of G. The formula for calculating G is in para.3(2). It is found by dividing the result of the calculation made under para.2(1) (half of the relevant incomes) into the maintenance requirement fixed under para.1. The figure produced when the formula has been applied is equal to that proportion of the maintenance requirement which is equivalent to the absent parent's share of the joint relevant incomes. The effect is that as the absent parent's relevant income rises in relation to the parent with care's relevant income, so the percentage represented by G goes up and the higher the amount of the maintenance requirement which is payable as the basic element. The proportion of the maintenance requirement which the parent with care is expected to bear correspondingly reduces.

With the maintenance requirement covered, the calculation goes on to fix an additional amount. This reflects the fact that the absent parent alone or in conjunction with the parent with care can afford to contribute more than the maintenance requirement towards the child's maintenance.

*Paragraph 4*

This paragraph provides for two different formulae which may be used for setting the additional element of maintenance which is payable. They only apply if the calculation under para.2(1) results in a figure which is higher than the maintenance requirement. The so-called "alternative formula" in para.4(3) sets the ceiling on the amount of additional element which an absent parent will be expected to pay. The other formula, which is set out in para.4(1), will be used if it produces a lower figure than the alternative formula (para.4(2)).

*Subparagraph 4(1)*

The formula in para.4(1) fixes a percentage of the absent parent's relevant income. It starts with the absent parent's relevant income. It then takes a percentage (i.e. the value of R set by reg.6(1) of the Maintenance Assessments and Special Cases Regulations) of this and further reduces it. The proportion of the absent parent's relevant income which is, subject to the overall ceiling, to form the additional element is found by deducting the figure for G (which was fixed under para.3(2)) from 1.

*Subparagraph 4(3)*                                                                    4.27

The alternative formula sets the maximum amount of additional element which will be payable. The formula for the additional element which is used in para.4(1) fixes the additional element as a percentage of the absent parent's relevant income. However, the alternative formula in para.4(3) sets the ceiling on the amount of additional element by reference to figures from income support law, although relevant incomes do have a part to play.

The alternative formula is fixed as follows. Start with the relevant income support personal allowance figures for the children. They were used in the calculation of the maintenance requirement under para.1. Then add to these an amount equal to the income support family premium for *each* child (reg.6(2)(b) of the Maintenance Assessments and Special Cases Regulations). The total is Q. Next multiply this by Z which is 1.5 (reg.6(2)(a) of the Maintenance Assessments and Special Cases Regulations). The final step is only necessary if the person with care is a parent of the child and has relevant income. This step fixes a proportion of the $Q \times Z$ calculation. This proportion is equal to the percentage which the absent parent's relevant income presents of the total relevant incomes. It is found by dividing the latter into the former.

Assuming that no special case applies, the overall effect of this calculation is as follows: If the person with care is the other parent of the child, the higher the absent parent's relevant income in relation to the parent with care's relevant income, the higher the percentage of the $Q \times Z$ calculation that is taken into account and therefore the higher the maximum amount of additional element payable. If the person with care is not the other parent of the child, the ceiling on the additional amount is simply Q multiplied by 1.5.

*Paragraph 5*

This paragraph is extended by reg.10A of the Maintenance Assessment and Special Cases Regulations by adding working tax credit to the benefits payment of which results in a parent with care or, to the limited extent allowed by reg.10A(2), an absent parent being treated as having no assessable income.

The assessable income of the absent parent and of any parent with care is determined by reference to regs 7 to 10 of, and Scheds 1, 2, 3A and 3B to, the Maintenance Assessments and Special Cases Regulations.

The Court of Appeal decided that the reference in subpara.(4) to payment of benefit means actual, not lawful, payment (*Secretary of State for Social Security v. Harmon, Carter and Cocks* [1998] 2 F.L.R. 598). A Tribunal of Commissioners was appointed to consider whether this decision is still good law, but the issue was not decided because it was discovered at the last moment that the case involved contribution-based jobseeker's allowance and not income-based jobseeker's allowance (*CCS 2725/04*). The issue remains to be determined in an appropriate case. The Court of Appeal for Northern Ireland confirmed *Harmon* in *Department for Social Development v MacGeagh* [2005] NICA 28(1).

**4.28**     *Paragraph 6*

"Maintenance assessment" refers to any stage of the calculation undertaken with respect ot he remaining provisions of para.6 (*Huxley v Child Support Officer* reported as *R(CS) 1/00 per* Hale L.J.).

The absent parent's protected income level must be calculated in accordance with reg.11 of the Maintenance Assessments and Special Cases Regulations. It is the total of the following amounts fixed by reference to the Income Support Schedule. The appropriate amounts are those applicable on the effective date (reg.11(5)). The effective date is determined under para.11. In summary the amounts to be added together are as follows. Any Income Support premiums are only taken into account if the conditions of entitlement would be satisfied.

  (i)     Appropriate Income Support premium for the absent parent according to whether or not there is a partner,

 (ii)     Housing costs,

(iii)     The Income Support lone parent rate of the family premium but only if the conditions are satisfied.

 (iv)     The Income Support disability premium.

  (v)     The Income Support severe disability premium and/or the carer premium,

 (vi)     The Income Support family premium,

 (vi)     The relevant Income Support personal allowances for each child who is a member of the absent parent's family and the disabled child premium for each relevant child,

(viii)     Any other Income Support premium, the conditions for which would be satisfied by the absent parent or his family if that parent were a claimant.

 (ix)     Fees payable for living in accommodation provided under the National Assistance Act 1948 or the National Health Service Act 1977 or in a nursing or residential care home,

  (x)     Council tax less any council tax benefit.

 (xi)     £30.00.

(xii)     Travelling costs.

(xiii)     If the total of the income of the absent parent, of any partner of the absent parent and of any child who is a member of the absent parent's family exceeds the total of (i) to (xi) 15 per cent of the excess. For this purpose the income of the absent parent and of any partner is calculated as follows: Take their net income as calculated under reg.7. Add to this the basic rate of child benefit and any maintenance payable in respect of any member of the family. Then deduct any maintenance payments by the absent parent or the partner under a maintenance order where a maintenance assessment could not be made.

Where there are two or more applications for a maintenance assessment in respect of the same person who is, or who is treated as, an absent parent but those applications relate to different qualifying children, the case is a special case by virtue of reg.22 of the Maintenance Assessments and Special Cases Regulations. In this case if the total of the assessments made would reduce the disposable income of that absent parent below the protected income level, the total is reduced by the minimum necessary to prevent this occurring. However, the total must not be reduced below the minimum amount of child support maintenance under para.7 below. The individual assessments are reduced in the same proportion as they bear to each other (see reg.22(3)).

If there is a person who is treated as an absent parent under reg.20 of the Maintenance Assessments and Special Cases Regulations, the provisions of this paragraph are only applied after the application of the effect of the formula in reg.20(4) has been calculated (reg.20(6)).

*Minimum amount*

In most cases an absent parent will be required to pay a minimum amount of child support maintenance even if the maintenance assessment as calculated under this Schedule would otherwise be lower. The minimum amount is fixed by reg.13 of the Maintenance Assessments and Special Cases Regulations. It is 10 per cent of the income support allowance for a single claimant aged not less than 25. If the figure is not a multiple of 5, it is rounded up to the next higher multiple of 5 pence.

*Nil assessment*

In some cases the minimum amount does not apply and the child support maintenance is fixed at nil. This is the position in those cases which are special cases by virtue of reg.26 of the Maintenance Assessments and Special Cases Regulations. In order to come within this regulation, the circumstances must be such that the minimum amount fixed under this paragraph would otherwise be payable and one of certain additional factors applies. These factors are in summary:

    (i) the absent parent's income includes one or more of the items listed in Schedule 4 to the Maintenance Assessments and Special Cases Regulations;

    (ii) the absent parent is a member of a family of which at least one member is a child or young person;

    (iii) the absent parent is a child;

    (iv) the absent parent is a prisoner;

    (v) the absent parent's net income is less than the minimum amount of child support maintenance.

*Payments in place of child support maintenance*                            4.30

In some cases no child support maintenance is payable, but payments in place of child support maintenance may be deducted from the parent's benefit. This is governed by s.43 above and reg.28 of, and Sched.5 to, the Maintenance Assessments and Special Cases Regulations. Such payments may have to be made if the following conditions are satisfied in respect of the absent parent:

    (i) the absent parent is taken to have no assessable income by virtue of income support or an income-based jobseeker's allowance being paid to or in respect of that parent;

    (ii) the absent parent is aged 18 or over;

    (iii) the absent parent is not a member of a family containing a child or young person;

    (iv) the absent parent does not have day-to-day care of *any* child;

    (v) the absent parent is not in receipt of any listed income relating to disability.

*Special provision*                                                          4.31

Where there are two or more applications for a maintenance assessment in respect of the same person who is, or who is treated as, an absent parent but those applications relate to different qualifying children, the case is a special case by virtue of reg.22 of the Maintenance Assessments and Special Cases Regulations. In this case the minimum amount of child support maintenance is payable and is apportioned between the individual assessments in the same ratio as the maintenance requirements bear to each other (reg.22(4)).

If there is a person who is treated as an absent parent under reg.20 of the Maintenance Assessments and Special Cases Regulations, the provisions of this paragraph are only applied after the application of the effect of the formula in reg.20(4) has been calculated (reg.20(6)). There is no apportionment of the minimum amount. There is no provision expressly permitting such an apportionment. Moreover, the wording of para.7(2) requires a knowledge of the assessment that would otherwise be made apart from the minimum payment provision, thereby making it clear that the minimum payment provision operates at the end of the calculation after any apportionment has been made.

*Paragraph 11*

There are some cases in respect of which no provision is made for fixing the effective date.

(i) There is no general provision for the fixing of the effective date of an assessment made under para.15 of this Schedule, whether on a review under the original s.18(10) or otherwise. The provisions relating to changes of circumstances taken into account on reviews under the original s.17 or s.19 do not apply. There are three possible approaches:

(a) One approach is to fix the effective date as the day on which the relevant change occurred.

(b) Another approach is to fix the effective date as the first day of the maintenance period in which the change occurred. This approach is more consistent with the express provisions in the Maintenance Assessment Procedure Regulations.

(c) The third possibility is to fix the effective date as the first day of the maintenance period following that in which the change occurred. This is in line with reg.9(2) of the Maintenance Assessment Procedure Regulations and reg.32(1)(b) of the Departure Regulations which fixes this date in respect of changes occurring before the date of the current assessment while taking approach (b) in respect of changes after that date.

Either of these last two approaches could be justified under the purposive approach to interpretation of the child support legislation advocated by the Commissioner in *CCS 12/94*. The general approach to follow is that suggested under (b) above (*CCS 1992/97*, para.59). However, any such general approach must be taken as subject to the following qualifications:

(a) The legislation may specify a day as the effective date, as in reg.63(5) of the Amendment Regulations 1995.

(b) The legislation may provide that the effective date may not be before a specified day, as in reg.30A(3) of the Maintenance Assessment Procedure Regulations.

(c) Where the change of circumstances results from a change in the legislation, it can be argued that it is not permissible to fix an effective date before the commencement date of the legislation as this would be to make the legislation retrospective contrary to express provision.

(d) Where the legislation specifies that the facts are to be determined on the effective date, it is by definition impossible to fix an earlier date when the facts were different. For example, Sched.1, para.6(3) to the Maintenance Assessments and Special Cases Regulations provides that amount of any benefit payment taken into account shall be that payable on the effective date. Any fresh assessment which involves a change in the amount of a benefit payment cannot, therefore, predate the change. Likewise reg.16 of those Regulations provides that the housing costs shall be those payable at the effective, so that date cannot pre-date the change.

4.32    Qualification such as these will apply to any general rule on the fixing of the effective date, so their existence is not an argument against having a general rule or against any particular version of a general rule.

(ii) There is also no provision permitting the fixing of an effective date later than that which would otherwise be applicable if jurisdiction to make an assessment did not exist until a later date. This may arise, for example, because a parent is still living in the same household as the other parent and the qualifying child at the time of the application and of the issue of the Maintenance Enquiry Form, only leaving at a later date. If the tribunal allows the appeal on this basis, it cannot substitute a later effective date for the assessment. It must hold that the Secretary of State did not have jurisdiction to make the assessment. No assessment is then permissible until a fresh application has been made. These circumstances arose in *CCS 14625/96,* para.10. The child support officer made an assessment on the basis that the father was at all relevant times an absent parent. The Commissioner decided that he had only become an absent parent at a later date. The Commissioner discharged the assessment that should not have been made, but directed the child support officer to calculate an assessment in respect of the father from the time when he became an absent parent, the effective date being fixed on the basis that the child support officer was making *a fresh* assessment under s.18. The Commissioner did not examine the arguments for and against treating the assessment to be made as a fresh one. The result achieved has the benefit of avoiding the need for a fresh application for an assessment. *If* this is the solution to this apparent deficiency in the effective date provisions, the decision highlights an anomaly in its operation which can be seen by changing the facts. If the child support officer had correctly declined initially to make an assessment on the basis that the father was not an absent father, the approach taken in this case would not allow an assessment to be made from the date when the parent became an absent parent. In this case a fresh application would have to be made.

(iii) If the Maintenance Enquiry Form is returned promptly and the assessment is made soon after its receipt, the date of the assessment may be before the effective date determined under reg.30(2)(a)(i) of the Maintenance Assessment Procedure Regulations. If a change of circumstances occurs between the date of the assessment and the effective date, it must be dealt with under an original s.17 review. An application for a s.17 review can only be made where a maintenance assessment is in force (see the wording of s.17(1)). The words "in force" are not defined. If the assessment does not come into force until the effective date, no problem arises since any application made before that date can be treated as made as soon as the assessment comes into force and the effective date of any change will be the first day of the maintenance period in which the application was made (reg.31(3) of the Maintenance Assessment Procedure Regulations), which will be the same as the effective date. However, if an assessment is in force as soon as it is made, any application under s.17 which is made before the effective date will not be in a maintenance period and there is no provision under which an effective date for the change may be fixed.

*Departure Directions*                                                                                    **4.33**

The effective date of decisions relating to departure directions are governed by Part VII of the Departure Regulations and, in the case of transitional cases, by regs 48 and 49 of those Regulations.

*Paragraph 15*                                                                                            **4.34**

The use of this provision is mandatory and not discretionary (*CCS 2657/98,* para.9).

At the time an assessment is made it may be certain that changes (e.g. a new job, a pay rise, a change in mortgage interest rate, a change in benefit rates) will shortly occur. These may be taken into account under this paragraph. When relying on this provision the decision-maker makes a series of separate assessments and not a single stepped assessment (see the wording of the original s.19(6) and of reg.8C(4) of the Maintenance Assessment Procedure Regulations as well as the wording of this paragraph).

As by definition the period of at least one of the assessments will have expired before the application for an original s.18 review has been made, that assessment will no longer be in force and it does not fall within the wording of s.18(2).

However, the scope of that subsection is extended by reg.29 of the Maintenance Assessment Procedure Regulations to cover such cases. If the case does not fall within reg.29, there can be no appeal in respect of that assessment. The origninal s.18(6A) cannot be used to overcome this because it only applies when a review is being conducted. The original s.19(1)(c) can be used, but unless this gives rise to an assessment in force an appeal is only possible if reg.29 applies.

A periodical review can be undertaken only in respect of the last assessment in the series which is still in effect and the effective date of that periodical review must be fixed by reference to the effective date of that last assessment and not by reference to the first assessment of the series.

The minimum change provisions which normally constrain reviews on the basis of a change of circumstance do not usually apply to assessments made under Sched.1, para.15. They are expressed to apply to reviews under s.17 (regs 20—22 of the Maintenance Assessment Procedure Regulations). They also apply to s.19 reviews which are conducted as if an application for a s.17 review had been made (reg.23 of those Regulations). They only apply to s.18 (and s.19) reviews where the review is of the refusal of an application for a s.17 review (regs 27 and 28 of those Regulations).

If the series of assessments was made under s.18, it is possible to appeal all or only some of them. Usually, the person making the appeal will not be aware of this and will simply appeal the officer's "decision", in which case the appeal will be against all the assessments, but the letter of appeal may be so worded as to identify only one of the series of assessments. If there is an appeal against a series of assessments, the tribunal must (subject to s.20(2A)) find an error in every assessment during which a change of circumstances occurred and may not open one assessment in the series on the basis of an error in another of the assessments in the series. The task may be made easier by the possibility that an error in one of the assessments will have a knock-on effect on later assessments in the series, although an error in later assessment can never affect earlier ones in the series.

As to the effective date of an assessment made under this paragraph, see the general note to Sched.1, para.11 above.

4.35 *Paragraph 16*

Although subpara.(1) is worded as having automatic effect, heads (a) to (d) are given effect to by a termination decision under reg.52 of the Maintenance Assessment Procedure Regulations.

If a decision-maker acting under the original s.18 or a tribunal on appeal makes a fresh assessment, the assessment under review does not cease to have effect nor is it cancelled under this paragraph (*CCS 3/93*, para.4). However, where a tribunal decides that a maintenance assessment should never have been made, it should direct that the assessment be cancelled despite the lack of any express power to do so (*CCS 7062/95*, paras 11 and 12). In *CCS 14625/96*, para.1, the Commissioner used the word "discharged" rather than "cancelled".

Where a person with care believes that an assessment has ceased to have effect or should be cancelled, that person is under a duty to notify the Secretary of State of this belief and the reasons for it, and to provide the Secretary of State with such information as he reasonably requires to allow a determination to be made as to whether the assessment has ceased to have effect or should be cancelled (reg.6 of the Information, Evidence and Disclosure Regulations).

If the absent parent returns to live with the person with care and the qualifying child, the child ceases to be a qualifying child under s.3(l) as there is no longer an absent parent. The case then falls within subpara.(l)(b). See *R(CS) 8/99*, para.16. The Commissioner considered the suggestion (set out in the 1997 edition) that in this subparagraph "qualifying child" concentrated on the person's status as a child, but rejected it on the ground that it was not appropriate in the context of the Act as a whole (paras 17—18). The Commissioner recognised that the effect of his decision was to leave little or no scope for subpara.(l)(d) (para.16). It was to avoid rendering this provision redundant that it was suggested that "qualifying child" must bear a different meaning in subpara.(l)(b).

The date from which cancellation under subparagraph (3) takes effect is determined under reg.32 of the Maintenance Assessment Procedure Regulations. Cancellation of assessments when an absent parent, person with care or qualifying child ceases to be habitually resident in the jurisdiction is covered by reg.32A of those Regulations and reg.7 of the Maintenance Arrangements and Jurisdiction Regulations. The date of cancellation varies according to the relevant provision. Cancellation under subparas (2) and (3) takes effect on the day of receipt of the application or such later date as the decision-maker determines, whereas cancellation under subpara.(4) takes effect on the date of the relevant change, as does cancellation where a person ceases to be habitually resident in the jurisdiction. This reflects the difference that in the former case the Agency's involvement is dependent upon the continuing consent of the applicant for a maintenance assessment and cancellation is not appropriate until that consent is withdrawn, which occurs on the making of the request, while in the latter cases the child support authorities no longer have jurisdiction and the cancellation is merely recognising this fact.

## The Child Support (Maintenance Assessment Procedure) Regulations 1992

### (SI 1992/1813)

*Made by the Secretary of State for Social Secretary under sections 3(3), 5(3), 6(1), 12, 16, 17, 18, 42(3), 46(11), 51, 52(4), 54 and 55 of, and paragraphs 11, 14 and 16 of Schedule 1 to, the Child Support Act 1991 and all other powers enabling him in that behalf.*

ARRANGEMENT OF REGULATIONS

PART I

*General*                                                              4.36

1. Citation, commencement and interpretation

PART II                                                                 4.37

*Applications for a maintenance assessment*

2. Applications under section 4, 6 or 7 of the Act.
3. Applications on the termination of a maintenance assessment.
4. Multiple applications.
5. Notice to other persons of an application for a maintenance assessment.
6. Response to notification of an application for a maintenance assessment.
7. Death of a qualifying child.

PART I

GENERAL

**Citation, commencement and interpretation**

**1.**—(1) These Regulations may be cited as the Child Support      **4.44**
(Maintenance Assessment Procedure) Regulations 1992 and shall come
into force on 5th April 1993.

(2) In these Regulations, unless the context otherwise requires—

"the Act" means the Child Support Act 1991;

"applicable amount"[⁶, except in regulation 40ZA,] is to be construed in accordance with Part IV of the Income Support Regulations;

"applicable amounts Schedule" means Schedule 2 to the Income Support Regulations;

"award period" means a period in respect of which an award of family credit or disability working allowance is made;

"balance of the reduction period" means, in relation to a direction that is or has been in force, the portion of the period specified in a direction in respect of which no reduction of relevant benefit has been made;

"benefit week" in relation to income support, has the same meaning as in the Income Support Regulations, [⁷in relation to jobseeker's allowance has the same meaning as in the Jobseeker's Allowance Regulations,] and, in relation to family credit and disability working allowance, is to be construed in accordance with the Social Security (Claims and Payments) Regulations 1987;

[¹⁸"designated authority" has the meaning it has in regulation 2(1) of the Social Security (Work-focused Interviews) Regulations 2000;]

"direction" means reduced benefit direction;

[¹⁵"disability working allowance" means an award of disability working allowance under section 129 of the Social Security Contributions and Benefits Act 1992 which was awarded with effect from a date falling before 5th October 1999;]

"day to day care" has the same meaning as in the Maintenance Assessments and Special Cases Regulations;

"effective application" means any application that complies with the provisions of regulation 2;

"effective date" means the date on which a maintenance assessment takes effect for the purposes of the Act;

[²²"family" has the same meaning as in the Maintenance Assessments and Special Cases Regulations;]

[¹⁶"family credit" means an award of family credit under section 128 of the Social Security Contributions and Benefits Act 1992 which was awarded with effect from a date falling before 5th October 1999;]

"Income Support Regulations" means the Income Support (General) Regulations 1987;

"Information, Evidence and Disclosure Regulations" means the Child Support (Information, Evidence and Disclosure) Regulations 1992;

[⁸"the Jobseeker's Allowance Regulations" means the Jobseeker's Allowance Regulations 1996;]

[¹Maintenance Arrangements and Jurisdiction Regulations" means the Child Support (Maintenance Arrangements and Jurisdiction) Regulations 1992;]

"Maintenance Assessments and Special Cases Regulations" means the Child Support (Maintenance Assessments and Special Cases) Regulations 1992;

"maintenance period" has the meaning prescribed in regulation 33;

"obligation imposed by section 6 of the Act" is to be construed in accordance with section 46(1) of the Act;

[¹³"official error" means an error made by—

    (a)    an officer of the Department of Social Security acting as such which no person outside that Department caused or to which no person outside that Department materially contributed;]

    [¹⁹(b)  a person employed by a designated authority acting on behalf of the authority, which no person outside that authority caused or to which no person outside that authority materially contributed,

but excludes any error of law which is only shown to have been an error by virtue of a subsequent decision of a Child Support Commissioner or the court;]

"parent with care" means a person who, in respect of the same child children, is both a parent and a person with care;

"the parent concerned" means the parent with respect to whom a direction is given;

"protected income level" has the same meaning as in paragraph 6(6) of Schedule 1 to the Act;

[²³"partner" has the same meaning as in the Maintenance Assessments and Special Cases Regulations;]

"relevant benefit" means income support, [⁹income-based jobseeker's allowance,] [¹⁷or an award of family credit or disability working allowance which was awarded with effect from a date falling before 5th October 1999];

"relevant person" means—

    (a)  a person with care;

    (b)  an absent parent;

    (c)  a parent who is treated as an absent parent under regulation 20 of the Maintenance Assessments and Special Cases Regulations;

    (d)  where the application for an assessment is made by a child under section 7 of the Act, that child,

in respect of whom a maintenance assessment has been applied for or is or has been in force.

(3) In these Regulations, references to a direction as being "in operation", "suspended", or "in force" shall be construed as follows—

a direction is "in operation" if, by virtue of that direction, relevant benefit is currently being reduced;

a direction is "suspended" if [². . .]—

    (a)  after that direction has been given, relevant benefit ceases to be payable, or [²⁰the circumstances in regulation 40(3) or regulation 40ZA(4), as the case may be, apply;]

    (b)  at the time that the direction is given[²¹, the circumstances in regulation 40(3) or regulation 40ZA(4), as the case may be, apply; or]

    [⁵(c)  at the time that the direction is given one or more of the deductions set out in regulation 40A is being made from the income support [¹¹or income-based jobseeker's allowance] payable to or in respect of the parent concerned,]

and these Regulations provide for relevant benefit payable from a later date to be reduced by virtue of the same direction;

4.45

a direction is "in force" if it is either in operation or is suspended, and cognate terms shall be construed accordingly.

(4) The provisions of Schedule 1 shall have effect to supplement the meaning of "child" in section 55 of the Act.

(5) The provisions of these Regulations shall have general application to cases prescribed in regulations 19 to 26 of the Maintenance Assessments and Special Cases Regulations as cases to be treated as special cases for the purposes of the Act, and the terms "absent parent" and "person with care" shall be construed accordingly.

(6) Except where express provision is made to the contrary, where, by any provision of the Act or of these Regulations—

(a) any document is given or sent to the Secretary of State, that document shall, subject to paragraph (7), be treated as having been so given or sent on the day it is received by the Secretary of State; and

(b) any document is given or sent to any [¹²other] person, that document shall, if sent by post to that person's last known or notified address, and subject to paragraph (8), be treated as having been given or sent on the second day after the day of posting, excluding any Sunday or any day which is a bank holiday in England, Wales, Scotland or Northern Ireland under the Banking and Financial Dealings Act 1971.

(7) Except where the provisions of regulation [¹⁴9(1) or 18(4)] apply, the Secretary of State may treat a document given or sent to him as given or sent on such day, earlier than the day it was received by him, as he may determine, if he is satisfied that there was unavoidable delay in his receiving the document in question.

(8) Where, by any provision of the Act or of these Regulations, and in relation to a particular application, notice or notification—

(a) more than one document is required to be given or sent to a person, and more than one such document is sent by post to that person but not all the documents are posted on the same day; or

(b) documents are required to be given or sent to more than one person, and not all such documents are posted on the same day, all those documents shall be treated as having been posted on the later or, as the case may be, the latest day of posting.

(9) In these Regulations, unless the context otherwise requires, a reference—

(a) to a numbered Part is to the Part of these Regulations bearing that number;

(b) to a numbered Schedule is to the Schedule to these Regulations bearing that number;

(c) to a numbered regulation is to the regulation in these Regulations bearing that number;

(d) in a regulation or Schedule to a numbered paragraph is to the paragraph in that regulation or Schedule bearing that number;

(e) in a paragraph to a lettered or numbered sub-paragraph is to the sub-paragraph in that paragraph bearing that letter or number.

AMENDMENTS

1. Regulation 4 of the Miscellaneous Amendments Regulations 1995 (February 16, 1995).

2. Regulation 15(i) of the Miscellaneous Amendments (No. 2) Regulations 1995 (January 22, 1996).

5. Regulation 15(iv) of the Miscellaneous Amendments (No. 2) Regulations 1995 (January 22, 1996).

6. Regulation 5(2)(a)(i) of the Jobseekers Amendment Regulations (October 7, 1996).

7. Regulation 5(2)(a)(ii) of the Jobseekers Amendment Regulations (October 7, 1996).

8. Regulation 5(2)(a)(iii) of the Jobseekers Amendment Regulations (October 7, 1996).

9. Regulation 5(2)(a)(iv) of the Jobseekers Amendment Regulations (October 7, 1996).

11. Regulation 5(2)(b)(ii) of the Jobseekers Amendment Regulations (October 7, 1996).

12. Regulation 5 of the Miscellaneous Amendments (No. 2) Regulations 1996 (January 13, 1997).

13. Regulation 16(5) of, and para.8(a) of Sched.6 to, the Social Security (Work-focused Interviews) Regulations 2000 (April, 3, 2000).

14. Regulation 2(b) of the Miscellaneous Amendments (No. 2) Regulations 1999 (June 1, 1999).

15. Regulation 5(2) of the Tax Credits Amendments Regulations 1999 (October 5, 1999).

16. Regulation 5(3) of the Tax Credits Amendments Regulations 1999 (October 5, 1999).

17. Regulation 5(4) of the Tax Credits Amendments Regulations 1999 (October 5, 1999).

18. Regulation 16(5) of, and para.8(b) of Sched.6 to, the Social Security (Work-focused Interviews) Regulations 2000 (April, 3, 2000).

19. Regulation 6 of the Miscellaneous Amendments Regulations 2000 (June 19, 2000).

20. Regulation 3(2)(a) of the Miscellaneous Amendments (No. 2) Regulations 2003 (November 5, 2003).

21. Regulation 3(2)(b) of the Miscellaneous Amendments (No. 2) Regulations 2003 (November 5, 2003).

22. Regulation 3(2) of the Miscellaneous Amendments Regulations 2005 (March 16, 2005).

23. Regulation 3(2) of the Miscellaneous Amendments Regulations 2005 (March 16, 2005).

## PART II

APPLICATIONS FOR A MAINTENANCE ASSESSMENT

### Applications under section 4, 6 or 7 of the Act

**2.**—(1) Any person who applies for a maintenance assessment under section 4 or 7 of the Act shall do so on a form (a "maintenance application form") provided by the Secretary of State.

4.46

(2) Maintenance application forms provided by the Secretary of Slate under section 6 of the Act or under paragraph (1) shall be supplied without charge by such persons as the Secretary of Slate appoints or authorises for that purpose.

(3) A completed maintenance application form shall be given or sent to the Secretary of State.

(4) Subject to paragraph (5), an application for a maintenance assessment under the Act shall be an effective application if it is made on a maintenance application form and that form has been completed in accordance with the Secretary of Slate's instructions.

(5) Where an application is not effective under the provisions of paragraph (4), the Secretary of State may—

(a) give or send the maintenance application form to the person who made the application, together, if he thinks appropriate, with a fresh maintenance application form, and request (hat the application be re-submitted so as to comply with the provisions of that paragraph; or

(b) request the person who made the application to provide such additional information or evidence as the Secretary of Slate specifies, and if a completed application form or, as the case may be, the additional information or evidence requested is received by the Secretary of State within 14 days of the date of his request, he shall treat the application as made on the date on which the earlier or earliest application would have been treated as made had it been effective under the provisions of paragraph (4).

(6) Subject to paragraph (7), a person who has made an effective application may amend his application by notice in writing to the Secretary of State at any time before a maintenance assessment is made.

(7) No amendment under paragraph (6) shall relate to any change of circumstances arising after the effective date of a maintenance assessment resulting from an effective application.

**4.47**  DEFINITIONS

"the Act": see reg.1(2).
"effective application": see reg.1(2).

## Applications on the termination of a maintenance assessment

**4.48**  **3.**—(1) Where a maintenance assessment has been in force with respect to a person with care and a qualifying child and that person is replaced by another person with care, an application for a maintenance assessment with respect to that person with care and that qualifying child may for the purposes of regulation 30(2)(b)(ii) and subject to paragraph (3) be treated as having been received on a date earlier than that on which it was received.

(2) Where a maintenance assessment has been made in response to an application by a child under section 7 of the Act and either—

(a) [¹the Secretary of State] cancels that assessment following a request from that child; or

(b) that child ceases to be a child for the purposes of the Act, any application for a maintenance assessment with respect to any other children who were qualifying children with respect to the earlier maintenance assessment may for the purposes of regulation 30(2)(b)(ii) and subject to paragraph (3) be treated as having been received on a date earlier than that on which it was received.

(3) No application for a maintenance assessment shall be treated as having been received under paragraph (1) or (2) on a date—

(a) more than 8 weeks earlier than the date on which the application was received; or

(b) on or before the first day of the maintenance period in which the earlier maintenance assessment ceased to have effect.

AMENDMENT

1. Regulation 3 of the Miscellaneous Amendments (No. 2) Regulations 1999 (June 1, 1999).

DEFINITIONS

"the Act": see reg.1(2).                                                      **4.49**
"maintenance period": see reg.1(2).
"person with care": see reg.1(5).

## Multiple applications

**4.**—(1) The provisions of Schedule 2 shall apply in cases where there is    **4.50**
more than one application for a maintenance assessment.

(2) The provisions of paragraphs 1, 2 and 3 of Schedule 2 relating to the treatment of two or more applications as a single application, shall apply where no request is received by the Secretary of State to cease acting in relation to all but one of the applications.

(3) Where, under the provisions of paragraph 1, 2 or 3 of Schedule 2, two or more applications are to be treated as a single application, that application shall be treated as an application for a maintenance assessment to be made with respect to all of the qualifying children mentioned in the applications, and the effective date of that assessment shall be determined by reference to the earlier, or earliest application.

DEFINITION

"effective date": see reg.1(2).                                               **4.51**

## Notice to other persons of an application for a maintenance assessment

**5.**—(1) [¹Subject to paragraph (2A), where] an effective application for    **4.52**
a maintenance assessment has been made the Secretary of State shall as soon as is reasonably practicable give notice in writing of that application to the relevant persons other than the applicant.

(2) The Secretary of State shall [²subject to paragraph (2A),] give or send to any person to whom notice has been given under paragraph (1) a form (a "maintenance enquiry form") and a written request that the form be completed and returned to him for the purpose of enabling the application for the maintenance assessment to be proceeded with.

[³(2A) The provisions of paragraphs (1) and (2) shall not apply where the Secretary of State is satisfied that an application for a maintenance assessment can be dealt with in the absence of a completed and returned maintenance enquiry form.]

(3) Where the person to whom notice is being given under paragraph (1) is an absent parent, that notice shall specify the effective date of the maintenance assessment if one is to be made, and set out in general terms the provisions relating to interim maintenance assessments.

AMENDMENTS

1. Regulation 2(2) of the Amendment Regulations (April 5, 1993).
2. Regulation 2(3) of the Amendment Regulations (April 5, 1993).
3. Regulation 2(4) of the Amendment Regulations (April 5, 1993).

DEFINITIONS

4.53    "absent parent": see reg.1(5).
"effective date": see reg.1(2).
"relevant person": see reg.1(2).

## Response to notification of an application for a maintenance assessment

4.54    6.—(1) Any person who has received a maintenance enquiry form given or sent under regulation 5(2) shall complete that form in accordance with the Secretary of State's instructions and return it to the Secretary of State within 14 days of its having been given or sent.

(2) Subject to paragraph (3), a person who has returned a completed maintenance enquiry form may amend the information he has provided on that form at any time before a maintenance assessment is made by notifying the Secretary of State in writing of the amendments.

(3) No amendment under paragraph (2) shall relate to any change of circumstances arising after the effective date of any maintenance assessment made in response to the application in relation to which the maintenance enquiry form was given or sent.

DEFINITION

4.55    "effective date": see reg.1(2).

## Death of a qualifying child

4.56    7.—(1) Where [¹the Secretary of State] is informed of the death of a qualifying child with respect to whom an application for a maintenance assessment has been made, he shall—

(a) proceed with the application as if it had not been made with respect to that child if he has not yet made an assessment;

(b) treat any assessment already made by him as not having been made if the relevant persons have not been notified of it and proceed with the application as if it had not been made with respect to that child.

(2) Where all of the qualifying children with respect to whom an application for a maintenance assessment has been made have died, and either

the assessment has not been made or the relevant persons have not been notified of it, [²the Secretary of State] shall treat the application as not having been made.

AMENDMENTS

1. Regulation 4(a) of the Miscellaneous Amendments (No. 2) Regulations 1999 (June 1, 1999).
2. Regulation 4(b) of the Miscellaneous Amendments (No. 2) Regulations 1999 (June 1, 1999).

DEFINITION

"relevant person": see reg.1(2).                                          4.57

PART III

INTERIM MAINTENANCE ASSESSMENTS

[¹**Categories of interim maintenance assessment**

**8.**—(1) Where [²the Secretary of State] serves notice under section    4.58
12(4) of the Act of his intention to make an interim maintenance assessment, he shall not make that interim assessment before the end of a period of 14 days, commencing with the date that notice was given or sent.

(2) There shall be four categories of interim maintenance assessment, Category A, Category B, Category C and Category D interim maintenance assessments.

(3) An interim maintenance assessment made by [⁵the Secretary of State] shall be—

(a) a Category A interim maintenance assessment, where any information, other than information referred to in subparagraph (b), that is required by him to enable him to make an assessment in accordance with the provisions of Part I of Schedule 1 to the Act has not been provided by that absent parent, and that parent has that information in his possession or can reasonably be expected to acquire it;

(b) a Category B interim maintenance assessment, where the information that is required by him as to the income of the partner or other member of the family of the absent parent or parent with care for the purposes of the calculation of the income of that partner or other member of the family under regulation 9(2), 10, 11(2) or 12(1) of the Maintenance Assessments and Special Cases Regulations—

(i) has not been provided by that partner or other member of the family, and that partner or other member of the family has that information in his possession or can reasonably be expected to acquire it; or

(ii) has been provided by that partner or other member of the family to the absent parent or parent with care, but the absent parent or parent with care has not provided it to the Secretary of State [⁴. . .];

805

    (c)  a Category C interim maintenance assessment where—

        (i)  the absent parent is a self-employed earner as defined in regulation 1(2) of the Maintenance Assessments and Special Cases Regulations; and

       (ii)  the absent parent is currently unable to provide, but has indicated that he expects within a reasonable time to be able to provide, information to enable [³the Secretary of State] to determine the earnings of that absent parent in accordance with paragraphs 3 to 5 of Schedule 1 to the Maintenance Assessments and Special Cases Regulations; and

      (iii)  no maintenance order as defined in section 8(11) of the Act or written maintenance agreement as defined in section 9(1) of the Act is in force with respect to children in respect of whom the Category C interim maintenance assessment would be made; or

    (d)  a Category D interim maintenance assessment where it appears to [³the Secretary of State], on the basis of information available to him as to the income of the absent parent, that the amount of any maintenance assessment made in accordance with Part I of Schedule 1 to the Act applicable to that absent parent may be higher than the amount of Category A interim maintenance assessment in force in respect of him.

    [⁵. . .]

AMENDMENTS

    1.  Regulation 16 of the Miscellaneous Amendments (No. 2) Regulations 1995 (January 22, 1996).

    2.  Regulation 5(a) of the Miscellaneous Amendments (No. 2) Regulations 1999 (June 1, 1999).

    3.  Regulation 5(b)(i) of the Miscellaneous Amendments (No. 2) Regulations 1999 (June 1, 1999).

    4.  Regulation 5(b)(ii) of the Miscellaneous Amendments (No. 2) Regulations 1999 (June 1, 1999).

    5.  Regulation 3(3) of the Miscellaneous Amendments Regulations 2005 (March 16, 2005).

DEFINITIONS

4.59      "absent parent": see reg.1(5).
      "the Act": see reg.1(2).
      "Maintenance Assessments and Special Cases Regulations": see reg.1(2).
      "parent with care": see reg.1(5).

## [¹Amount of an interim maintenance assessment

4.60      **8A.**—(1) The amount of child support maintenance fixed by a Category A interim maintenance assessment shall be 1.5 multiplied by the amount of the maintenance requirement in respect of the qualifying child or qualifying children concerned calculated in accordance with the provisions of paragraph 1 of Schedule 1 to the Act, and paragraphs 2 to 9 of that Schedule shall not apply to Category A interim maintenance assessments.

(2) Subject to paragraph (5), the amount of child support maintenance fixed by a Category B interim maintenance assessment shall be determined in accordance with paragraphs (3) and (4).

(3) Where [³the Secretary of State] is unable to determine the exempt income—

(a) of an absent parent under regulation 9 of the Maintenance Assessments and Special Cases Regulations because he is unable to determine whether regulation 9(2) of those Regulations applies;

(b) of a parent with care under regulation 10 of those Regulations because he is unable to determine whether regulation 9(2) of those Regulations, as modified by and applied by regulation 10 of those Regulations, applies,

the amount of the Category B interim maintenance assessment shall be the maintenance assessment calculated in accordance with Part I of Schedule 1 to the Act on the assumption that—

(i) in a case falling within subparagraph (a), regulation 9(2) of those Regulations does apply;

(ii) in a case falling within subparagraph (b), regulation 9(2) of those Regulations as modified by and applied by regulation 10 of those Regulations does apply.

[²(4) Where [³the Secretary of State] is unable to ascertain the income of other members of the family of an absent parent so that the disposable income of that absent parent can be calculated in accordance with regulation 12(1)(a) of the Maintenance Assessments and Special Cases Regulations, the amount of the Category B interim maintenance assessment shall be the maintenance assessment calculated in accordance with Part I of Schedule 1 to the Act on the assumption that the provisions of paragraph 6 of that Schedule do not apply to the absent parent.]

(5) Where the application of the provisions of paragraph (3) or (4) would result in the amount of a Category B interim maintenance assessment being more than 30 per centum of the net income of the absent parent as calculated in accordance with regulation 7 of the Maintenance Assessments and Special Cases Regulations, those provisions shall not apply to that absent parent and instead, the amount of that Category B interim maintenance assessment shall be 30 per centum of his net income as so calculated and where that calculation results in a fraction of a penny, that fraction shall be disregarded.

(6) The amount of child support maintenance fixed by a Category C interim maintenance assessment shall be £30.00 but [³the Secretary of State] may set a lower amount, including a nil amount, if he thinks it reasonable to do so in all the circumstances of the case.

(7) Paragraph 6 of Schedule 1 to the Act shall not apply to Category C interim maintenance assessments.

(8) [³The Secretary of State] shall notify the person with care where he is considering setting a lower amount for a Category C interim maintenance assessment in accordance with paragraph (6) and shall take into account any relevant representations made by that person with care in deciding the amount of that Category C interim maintenance assessment.

(9) The amount of child support maintenance fixed by a Category D interim maintenance assessment shall be calculated or estimated by

applying to the absent parent's income, in so far as [³the Secretary of State] is able to determine it at the time of the making of the Category D interim maintenance assessment the provisions of Part I of Schedule 1 to the Act and regulations made under it, subject to the modification that—

(a) paragraphs 6 and 8 of that Schedule shall not apply;

(b) only paragraphs (l)(a) and (5) of regulation 9 of the Maintenance Assessments and Special Cases Regulations shall apply; and

(c) heads (b) and (c) of subparagraph (3) of paragraph 1 of Schedule 1 to the Maintenance Assessments and Special Cases Regulations shall not apply.

(10) Where the absent parent referred to in paragraph (9) is an employed earner as defined in regulation 1 of the Maintenance Assessments and Special Cases Regulations and [³the Secretary of State] is unable to calculate the net income of that absent parent, his net income shall be estimated under the provisions of paragraph (2A)(a) and (b) of that regulation.]

AMENDMENTS

1. Regulation 16 of the Miscellaneous Amendments (No. 2) Regulations 1995 (January 22, 1996).

2. Regulation 35 of the Miscellaneous Amendments Regulations 1998 (January 19, 1998).

3. Regulation 6 of the Miscellaneous Amendments (No. 2) Regulations 1999 (June 1, 1999).

DEFINITIONS

4.61     "absent parent": see reg.1(5).
"the Act": see reg.1(2).
"family": see reg.8(3)(e).
"Maintenance Assessments and Special Cases Regulations": see reg.1(2).
"parent with care": see reg.1(5).
[Regulation 8B is revoked by reg.7 of the Miscellaneous Amendments (No. 2) Regulations 1999 with effect from June 1, 1999.]

## [¹Effective date of an interim maintenance assessment

4.62     **8C.**—(1) Except where regulation 3(5) of the Maintenance Arrangements and Jurisdiction Regulations (effective date of maintenance assessment where court order in force), regulation [². . .] 33(7) or paragraph (2) applies, the effective date of an interim maintenance assessment shall be—

(a) in respect of a Category A interim maintenance assessment, subject to [³. . .] subparagraph (d), such date, being not earlier than the first and not later than the seventh day following the date upon which that interim maintenance assessment was made, as falls on the same day of the week as the date determined in accordance with regulation 30(2)(a)(ii) or (b)(ii) as the case may be;

(b) in respect of a Category B interim maintenance assessment made after 22nd January 1996, subject to subparagraph (d) [⁴. . .], the date specified in regulation 30(2)(a)(ii) or (b)(ii) as the case may be;

(c) in respect of a Category C interim maintenance assessment, subject to subparagraph (d) [⁵. . .], the date set out in subparagraph (a);

(d) in respect of a Category A, Category B or Category C interim maintenance assessment, where the application of the provisions of subparagraph (a), (b) or (c) would otherwise set an effective date for an interim maintenance assessment earlier than the end of a period of eight weeks from the date upon which—

(i) the maintenance enquiry form referred to in regulation 30(2)(a)(i) was given or sent to an absent parent; or

(ii) the application made by an absent parent referred to in regulation 30(2)(b)(i) was received by the Secretary of State,

in circumstances where that absent parent has complied with the provisions of regulation 30(2)(a)(i) or (b)(i) or paragraph (2A) of that regulation applies, the date determined in accordance with regulations 30(2)(a)(i) or (b)(i).

(2) [⁶The effective date of an interim maintenance assessment made under section 12(1)(b) of the Act shall, subject to regulation 33(7)], be such date, not earlier than the first and not later than the seventh day following the date upon which that interim maintenance assessment was made, as falls on the same day of the week as the effective date of the maintenance assessment calculated in accordance with Part I of Schedule 1 to the Act which [⁷the Secretary of State is proposing to supersede with a decision under section 17 of the Act].

(3) In cases where the effective date of an interim maintenance assessment is determined under paragraph (1) [⁸. . .], where a maintenance assessment, except a maintenance assessment falling within regulation 8D(7), is made after an interim maintenance assessment has been in force, child support maintenance calculated in accordance with Part I of Schedule 1 to the Act shall be payable in respect of the period preceding that during which the interim maintenance assessment was in force.

(4) The child support maintenance payable under the provisions of paragraph (3) shall be payable in respect of the period between the effective date of the assessment (or, where separate assessments are made for different periods under paragraph 15 of Schedule 1 to the Act, the effective date of the assessment in respect of the earliest such period) and the effective date of the interim maintenance assessment.]

AMENDMENTS

1. Regulation 16 of the Miscellaneous Amendments (No. 2) Regulations 1995 (January 22, 1996).

2. Regulation 8(a) of the Miscellaneous Amendments (No. 2) Regulations 1999 (June 1, 1999).

3. Regulation 8(b) of the Miscellaneous Amendments (No. 2) Regulations 1999 (June 1, 1999).

4. Regulation 8(c) of the Miscellaneous Amendments (No. 2) Regulations 1999 (June 1, 1999).

5. Regulation 8(d) of the Miscellaneous Amendments (No. 2) Regulations 1999 (June 1, 1999).

6. Regulation 8(e)(i) of the Miscellaneous Amendments (No. 2) Regulations 1999 (June 1, 1999).

7. Regulation 8(e)(ii) of the Miscellaneous Amendments (No. 2) Regulations 1999 (June 1, 1999).

8. Regulation 8(f) of the Miscellaneous Amendments (No. 2) Regulations 1999 (June 1, 1999).

DEFINITIONS

4.63    "absent parent": see reg.1(5).
"the Act": see reg.1(2).
"effective date": see reg.1(2).
"Maintenance Arrangements and Jurisdiction Regulations": see reg.1(2).

## [¹Miscellaneous provisions in relation to interim maintenance assessments

4.64    **8D.**—(1) Subject to paragraph (2), where a maintenance assessment calculated in accordance with Part I of Schedule 1 to the Act is made following an interim maintenance assessment, the amount of child support maintenance payable in respect of the period after 18th April 1995, during which that interim maintenance assessment was in force, shall be that fixed by the maintenance assessment.

[³(1A) The reference in paragraph (1) to a maintenance assessment calculated in accordance with Part I of Schedule 1 to the Act shall include a maintenance assessment falling within regulation 30A(2).]

(2) Paragraph (1) shall not apply where a maintenance assessment calculated in accordance with Part I of Schedule 1 to the Act falls within paragraph (7).

[⁴. . .]

(4) The provisions of regulations [⁵32 and 33(5)] shall not apply to a Category A or Category D interim maintenance assessment.

(5) Subject to paragraph (6) [⁶. . .], an interim maintenance assessment shall cease to have effect on the first day of the maintenance period during which the Secretary of State receives the information which enables [⁷him] to make the maintenance assessment or assessments in relation to the same absent parent, person with care and qualifying child or qualifying children, calculated in accordance with Part I of Schedule 1 to the Act.

(6) [⁸. . .] Where [⁹the Secretary of State] has insufficient information or evidence to enable him to make a maintenance assessment calculated in accordance with Part I of Schedule 1 to the Act for the whole of the period beginning with the effective date applicable to a particular case, an interim maintenance assessment made in that case shall cease to have effect—

(a) on 18th April 1995 where by that date the Secretary of State has received the information or evidence set out in paragraph (7); or

(b) on the first day of the maintenance period after 18th April 1995 in which the Secretary of State has received that information or evidence.

(7) The information or evidence referred to in paragraph (6) is information or evidence enabling [¹⁰the Secretary of State] to make a maintenance assessment calculated in accordance with Part I of Schedule 1 to the Act, for a period beginning after the effective date applicable to that case, in respect of the absent parent, parent with care and qualifying child or

qualifying children in respect of whom the interim maintenance assessment referred to in paragraph (6) was made.]

[²(8) Where the information or evidence referred to in paragraph (6)(a) or (b) is that there has been an award of income support[¹¹, state pension credit] or an income-based jobseeker's allowance, the Secretary of State shall be treated as having received that information or evidence on the first day in respect of which income support[¹¹, state pension credit] or an income-based jobseeker's allowance was payable under that award.]

AMENDMENTS

1. Regulation 16 of the Miscellaneous Amendments (No. 2) Regulations 1995 (January 22, 1996).
2. Regulation 6 of the Miscellaneous Amendments (No. 2) Regulations 1996 (January 13, 1997).
3. Regulation 36 of the Miscellaneous Amendments Regulations 1998 (January 19, 1998).
4. Regulation 9(a) of the Miscellaneous Amendments (No. 2) Regulations 1999 (June 1, 1999).
5. Regulation 9(b) of the Miscellaneous Amendments (No. 2) Regulations 1999 (June 1, 1999).
6. Regulation 9(c)(i) of the Miscellaneous Amendments (No. 2) Regulations 1999 (June 1, 1999).
7. Regulation 9(c)(ii) of the Miscellaneous Amendments (No. 2) Regulations 1999 (June 1, 1999).
8. Regulation 9(d)(i) of the Miscellaneous Amendments (No. 2) Regulations 1999 (June 1, 1999).
9. Regulation 9(d)(ii) of the Miscellaneous Amendments (No. 2) Regulations 1999 (June 1, 1999).
10. Regulation 9(e) of the Miscellaneous Amendments (No. 2) Regulations 1999 (June 1, 1999).
11. Regulation 3(3) of the Miscellaneous Amendments (No. 2) Regulations 2003 (November 5, 2003).

DEFINITIONS

"absent parent": see reg.1(5).          **4.65**
"the Act": see reg.1(2).
"parent with care": see reg.1(5).

## [¹Interim maintenance assessments which follow other interim maintenance assessments

**9.**—(1) Where an interim maintenance assessment is being revised on **4.66** the ground specified in regulation 17(l)(b) and the Secretary of State is satisfied—

 (a) that another Category A, Category B or Category D maintenance assessment should be made, and
 (b) that there has been unavoidable delay for part of the period during which the assessment which is being revised was in force,
the effective date of that other—

  (i) Category A or Category D interim maintenance assessment shall be the first day of the maintenance period following the date upon which, in the opinion of the Secretary of State, the delay became avoidable;

    (ii)  Category B interim maintenance assessment shall be the date set out in regulation 8C(l)(b).

(2) Where an interim maintenance assessment is revised on either of the grounds set out in regulation 17(4) or (5), payments made under that interim maintenance assessment before the revision shall be treated as payments made under the Category B interim maintenance assessment which replaces it.

(3) Subject to paragraphs (5) and (6), where the Secretary of State makes a Category B interim maintenance assessment following the revision of an interim maintenance assessment in accordance with regulation 17(4), the effective date of that Category B interim maintenance assessment shall be the date determined in accordance with regulation 8C(l)(b).

(4) Where the Secretary of State makes a fresh interim maintenance assessment following the supersession of an interim maintenance assessment in accordance with regulation 20(7), the effective date of that fresh interim maintenance assessment shall be the date from which that supersession took effect.

(5) Where the Secretary of State cancels upon a revision an interim maintenance assessment in accordance with regulation 17(4) which caused a court order to cease to have effect in accordance with regulation 3(6) of the Maintenance Arrangements and Jurisdiction Regulations, the effective date of the Category B interim maintenance assessment referred to in regulation 17(4) shall be the date on which that revision took effect.

(6) Where the revision of an interim maintenance assessment in accordance with regulation 17(5) caused a court order to cease to have effect in accordance with regulation 3(6) of the Maintenance Arrangements and Jurisdiction Regulations, the effective date of the Category B interim maintenance assessment referred to in regulation 17(4) shall be the date on which that revision took effect.]

AMENDMENT

1. Regulation 10 of the Miscellaneous Amendments (No. 2) Regulations 1999 (June 1, 1999).

PART IV

NOTIFICATIONS FOLLOWING CERTAIN DECISIONS
BY CHILD SUPPORT OFFICERS

**Notification of a new or a fresh maintenance assessment**

4.67    **10.**—[20(1) A person with a right of appeal to an appeal tribunal under—

    (a)  section 20 of the Act; and

    (b)  section 20 of the Act as extended by paragraph 3(l)(b) of Schedule 4C to the Act, shall be given notice of that right and of the decision to which that right relates.]

(2) [³Subject to paragraphs (2A) and 2B)], a notification under paragraph (1)] [²²of a new or fresh maintenance assessment made under section 11, 16 or 17] shall set out, in relation to the maintenance assessment in question—

(a)     the maintenance requirement;

(b)     the effective date of the assessment;

[¹²(c)  the net and assessable income of the absent parent and, where relevant, the amount determined under regulation 9(l)(b) of the Maintenance Assessments and Special Cases Regulations (housing costs);]

[¹³(cc) where relevant, the absent parent's protected income level and the amount of the maintenance assessment before the adjustment in respect of protected income specified in paragraph 6(2) of Schedule 1 to the Act was carried out;]

[¹⁴(d)  the net and assessable income of the parent with care and, where relevant, an amount in relation to housing costs determined in the manner specified in regulation 10 of the Maintenance Assessments and Special Cases Regulations (calculation of exempt income of parent with care;]

(e)     details as to the minimum amount of child support maintenance payable by virtue of regulations made under paragraph 7 of Schedule 1 to the Act; and

(f)     details as to apportionment where a case is to be treated as a special case for the purposes of the Act under section 42 of the Act.

[(g)    not reproduced here—refer to para.10 to the Schedule to the Transitional Provisions Order.]

[¹⁵(h)  any amount determined in accordance with Schedule 3A or 3B to the Maintenance Assessments and Special Cases Regulations (qualifying transfer or property and travel costs).]

[¹⁷(i)  where the notification under paragraph (l)(a) [²³. . .] follows the giving, or cancellation of a departure direction, the amounts calculated in accordance with Part I of Schedule 1 to the Act, or in accordance with regulation 8A, which have been changed as a result of the giving or cancellation of that departure direction.]

[⁵(2A) Where a new Category A, [⁶Category C or Category D] interim maintenance assessment is made, or a fresh Category A, [⁶Category C or Category D] interim maintenance assessment is made following [²⁴a revision of a maintenance assessment under section 16 of the Act or a supersession of a maintenance assessment under section 17] of the Act, a notification under paragraph (1) shall set out, in relation to that interim maintenance assessment, the maintenance requirement and the effective date.]

[¹⁸(2AA) Where a fresh Category D interim maintenance assessment is made following the giving or cancellation of a departure direction, a notification under paragraph (1) shall set out in relation to that interim maintenance assessment the amounts calculated in accordance with regulation 8A which have changed as a result of the giving or cancellation of that departure direction.]

[⁷(2B) A notification under paragraph (1) in relation to a Category B interim maintenance assessment shall set out in relation to it—]

[¹⁹(a) the matters listed in sub-paragraphs (a), (b) and (d) to (f) of paragraph (2);

(b) where known, the absent parent's assessable income; and

(c) where the Category B interim maintenance assessment is made following the giving or cancellation of a departure direction, the amounts calculated in accordance with regulation 8A which have changed as a result of the giving or cancellation of that departure direction.]

(3) Except where a person gives written permission to the Secretary of State that the information, in relation to him, mentioned in subparagraphs (a) and (b) below may be conveyed to other persons, any document given or sent under the provisions of paragraph (1) or (2) shall not contain—

(a) the address of any person other than the recipient of the document in question (other than the address of the office [²⁵of the officer concerned who is exercising functions of the Secretary of State under the Act]) or any other information the use of which could reasonably be expected to lead to any such person being located;

(b) any other information the use of which could reasonably be expected to lead to any person, other than a qualifying child or a relevant person, being identified.

[²⁶(4) Where a decision as to a maintenance assessment is made under section 11, 12, 16 or 17 of the Act, a notification under paragraph (1) shall include information as to the provisions of sections 16 and 17 of the Act.]

AMENDMENTS

3. Regulation 6(2) of the Miscellaneous Amendments Regulations 1995 (February 16, 1995).

4. Regulation 30(3) of the Amendment Regulations 1995 (April 18, 1995).

5. Regulation 6(3) of the Miscellaneous Amendments Regulations 1995 (February 16, 1995).

6. Regulation 30(4) of the Amendment Regulations 1995 (April 18, 1995).

7. Regulation 30(5) of the Amendment Regulations 1995 (April 18, 1995).

12. Regulation 18(3) of the Miscellaneous Amendments (No. 2) Regulations 1995 (January 22, 1996).

13. Regulation 18(4) of the Miscellaneous Amendments (No. 2) Regulations 1995 (January 22, 1996).

14. Regulation 18(5) of the Miscellaneous Amendments (No. 2) Regulations 1995 (January 22, 1996).

15. Regulation 18(6) of the Miscellaneous Amendments (No. 2) Regulations 1995 (January 22, 1996).

17. Regulation 67(3) of the Departure Regulations (December 2, 1996).

18. Regulation 67(4) of the Departure Regulations (December 2, 1996).

19. Regulation 67(5) of the Departure Regulations (December 2, 1996).

20. Regulation 11 (a) of the Miscellaneous Amendments (No. 2) Regulations 1999 (June 1, 1999).

21. Regulation 11(b) of the Miscellaneous Amendments (No. 2) Regulations 1999 (June 1, 1999).

22. Regulation 11(c)(i) of the Miscellaneous Amendments (No. 2) Regulations 1999 (June 1, 1999).

23. Regulation 11(c)(ii) of the Miscellaneous Amendments (No. 2) Regulations 1999 (June 1, 1999).

24. Regulation 11(d) of the Miscellaneous Amendments (No. 2) Regulations 1999 (June 1, 1999).

25. Regulation 11(e) of the Miscellaneous Amendments (No. 2) Regulations 1999 (June 1, 1999).

26. Regulation 11 (f) of the Miscellaneous Amendments (No. 2) Regulations 1999 (June 1, 1999).

DEFINITIONS

"absent parent": see reg.1(5).　　　　　　　　　　　　　　　　　　　　**4.68**
"the Act": see reg.1(2).
"effective date": see reg.1(2).
"Maintenance Assessments and Special Cases Regulations": see reg.1(2).
"parent with care": see reg.1(2).
"protected income level": see reg.1(2).
"relevant person": see reg.1(2).

## [¹Notification of increase or reduction in the amount of a maintenance assessment

**10A.**—(1) Where, in a case falling within paragraph (2B) of regulation　**4.69** 22 of the Maintenance Assessments and Special Cases Regulations (multiple applications relating to an absent parent), [²the Secretary of State] has increased or reduced one or more of the other maintenance assessments referred to in that paragraph following the making of the fresh assessment referred to in sub-paragraph (c) of that paragraph, he shall, so far as that is reasonably practicable, immediately notify the relevant persons in respect of whom each maintenance assessment so increased or reduced was made of—

(a) the making of that fresh assessment;

(b) the amount of the increase or reduction in that maintenance assessment; and

(c) the date on which that increase or reduction shall take effect, and the notification shall include information as to the provisions of [³sections 16 and 17] of the Act.

(2) Except where a person gives written permission to the Secretary of State that the information in relation to him mentioned in sub-paragraphs (a) and (b) below may be conveyed to other persons, any document given or sent under the provisions of paragraph (1) shall not contain—

(a) the address of any person other than the recipient of the document in question (other than the address of the office [⁴of the officer concerned who is exercising functions of the Secretary of State under the Act]) or any other information the use of which could reasonably be expected to lead to any such person being located;

(b) any other information the use of which could reasonably be expected to lead to any person, other than a qualifying child or a relevant person, being identified.]

AMENDMENTS

1. Regulation 30 of the Miscellaneous Amendments Regulations 1998 (January 19, 1998).
2. Regulation 12(a)(i) of the Miscellaneous Amendments (No. 2) Regulations 1999 (June 1, 1999).
3. Regulation 12(a)(ii) of the Miscellaneous Amendments (No. 2) Regulations 1999 (June 1, 1999).
4. Regulation 12(b) of the Miscellaneous Amendments (No. 2) Regulations 1999 (June 1, 1999).

DEFINITIONS

4.70    "the Act": see reg.1(2).
"Maintenance Assessments and Special Cases Regulations": see reg.1(2).
"relevant person": see reg.1(2).
[Regulations 11 to 15A are revoked by reg.13 of the Miscellaneous Amendments (No. 2) Regulations 1999 with effect from June 1, 1999.]

## Notification when an applicant under section 7 of the Act ceases to be a child

4.71    **16.** Where a maintenance assessment has been made in response to an application by a child under section 7 of the Act and that child ceases to be a child for the purposes of the Act, [²the Secretary of State] shall immediately notify, so far as that is reasonably practicable—
   (a)  the other qualifying children [¹who have attained the age of 12 years] and the absent parent with respect to whom that maintenance assessment was made; and
   (b)  the person with care.

AMENDMENTS

1. Regulation 6 of the Amendment Regulations (April 5, 1993).
2. Regulation 14 of the Miscellaneous Amendments (No. 2) Regulations 1999 (June 1, 1999).

DEFINITIONS

4.72    "absent parent": see reg.1(5).
"the Act": see reg.1(2).
"person with care": see reg.1(5).

## [¹Notification that an appeal has lapsed

4.73    **16A.** Where an appeal lapses in accordance with section 16(6) of the Act, the Secretary of State shall, so far as is reasonably practicable, notify the relevant persons that that appeal has lapsed.]

AMENDMENT

1. Regulation 15 of the Miscellaneous Amendments (No. 2) Regulations 1999 (June 1, 1999).

"the Act": reg.1(2).                                                                      **4.74**
"relevant person": see reg.1(2).

[¹PART V

REVISIONS AND SUPERSESSIONS

**Revision of decisions**

**17.**—(1) Subject to paragraphs (6) and (8), any decision may be revised    **4.75**
by the Secretary of State—

(a) if the Secretary of State receives an application for the revision of a
decision under section 16 of the Act within one month of the date of
notification of the decision or within such longer time as may be
allowed by regulation 18;

(b) if—

(i) the Secretary of State notifies a person, who applied for a decision to be revised within the period specified in subparagraph
(a), that the application is unsuccessful because the Secretary of
State is not in possession of all of the information or evidence
needed to make a decision; and

(ii) that person reapplies for a decision to be revised within one
month of the notification described in head (i) above, or such
longer period as the Secretary of State is satisfied is reasonable in
the circumstances of the case, and provides in that application sufficient evidence or information to enable a decision to be made;

(c) if the decision arose from an official error;

(d) if the Secretary of State is satisfied that the original decision was
erroneous due to a misrepresentation of, or failure to disclose, a
material fact and that the decision was more advantageous to the
person who misrepresented or failed to disclose that fact than it
would otherwise have been but for that error; [³. . .]

(e) if the Secretary of State commences action leading to the revision
of a decision within one month of the date of notification of the
decision; [⁴or

(f) if an appeal is made under section 20 of the Act against a decision
within the time prescribed in regulation 31 of the Social Security and
Child Support (Decisions and Appeals) Regulations 1999, or in a
case to which regulation 32 of those Regulations applies within the
time prescribed in that regulation, but the appeal has not been
determined.]

(2) A decision may be revised by the Secretary of State in consequence
of a departure direction where that departure direction takes effect on the
effective date.

(3) Subject to regulation 20(6) a decision of the Secretary of State under
section 12 of the Act may be revised where—

(a) the Secretary of State receives information which enables him to
make a maintenance assessment calculated in accordance with Part

I of Schedule 1 to the Act for the whole of the period beginning with the effective date applicable to a particular case; or
(b)  the Secretary of State is satisfied that there was unavoidable delay by the absent parent in—
   (i)  completing and returning a maintenance enquiry form under the provisions of regulation 6(1);
   (ii)  providing information or evidence that is required by him for the determination of an application for a maintenance assessment; or
   (iii)  providing information or evidence that is required by him to enable him to revise a decision under section 16 of the Act or supersede a decision under section 17 of the Act.

(4) Where an interim maintenance assessment is in force which is not a Category B interim maintenance assessment and the Secretary of State is satisfied that it would be appropriate to make a Category B interim maintenance assessment, he may revise the interim maintenance assessment which is in force.

(5) Where the Secretary of State revises an interim maintenance assessment in accordance with paragraph (4) and that interim maintenance assessment was made immediately following a previous interim maintenance assessment, he may also revise that previous interim maintenance assessment.

(6) Paragraph (1) shall apply neither—
(a)  in respect of a material change of circumstances which—
   (i)  occurred since [²the date on which the decision was made]; or
   (ii)  is expected, according to information or evidence which the Secretary of State has, to occur; nor
(b)  where—
   (i)  an appeal against a decision has been brought but not determined; and
   (ii)  from the point of view of the appellant, a revision of that decision, if made, would be less to his advantage than the original decision.

(7) In paragraphs (1), (2) and (6) and regulation 18(3) "decision" means a decision of the Secretary of State under section 11 or 12 of the Act and any supersession of such a decision.

(8) Paragraph (1) shall apply in relation to—
(a)  any decision of the Secretary of State with respect to a reduced benefit direction or a person's liability under section 43 of the Act; and
(b)  the supersession of any such decision under section 17 as extended by paragraph 2 of Schedule 4C to the Act,
as it applies in relation to any decision of the Secretary of State under sections 11, 12 or 17 of the Act.]

AMENDMENTS

1. Regulation 16 of the Miscellaneous Amendments (No. 2) Regulations 1999 (June 1, 1999).
2. Regulation 7 of the Miscellaneous Amendments Regulations 2000 (June 19, 2000).

3. Regulation 4(a) of the Miscellaneous Amendments Regulations 2004 (September 16, 2004).

4. Regulation 4(b) of the Miscellaneous Amendments Regulations 2004 (September 16, 2004).

## [¹Late applications for a revision

**18.**—(1) The period of one month specified in regulation 17(l)(a) may be extended where the requirements specified in the following provisions of (his regulation are met.

4.76

(2) An application for an extension of time shall be made by a relevant person or a person acting on his behalf.

(3) An application for an extension of time under this regulation shall—

(a) be made within 13 months of the date on which notification of the decision which it is sought to have revised was given or sent; and

(b) contain particulars of the grounds on which the extension of time is sought and shall contain sufficient details of the decision which it is sought to have revised to enable that decision to be identified.

(4) The application for an extension of time shall not be granted unless the person making the application or any person acting for him satisfies the Secretary of State that—

(a) it is reasonable to grant that application;

(b) the application for a decision to be revised has merit; and

(c) special circumstances are relevant to the application for an extension of time,

and as a result of those special circumstances, it was not practicable for the application for a decision to be revised to be made within one month of the date of notification of the decision which it is sought to have revised.

(5) In determining whether it is reasonable to grant an application for an extension of time, the Secretary of State shall have regard to the principle that the greater the time that has elapsed between the expiration of the period of one month described in regulation 17(l)(a) from the date of notification of the decision which it is sought to have revised and the making of the application for an extension of time, the more compelling should be the special circumstances on which the application is based.

(6) In determining whether it is reasonable to grant the application for an extension of time, no account shall be taken of the following—

(a) that the person making the application for an extension of time or any person acting for him was unaware of or misunderstood the law applicable to his case (including ignorance or misunderstanding of the time limits imposed by these Regulations); or

(b) that a Child Support Commissioner or a court has taken a different view of the law from that previously understood and applied.

(7) An application under this regulation for an extension of time which has been refused may not be renewed.]

AMENDMENT

1. Regulation 16 of the Miscellaneous Amendments (No. 2) Regulations 1999 (June 1, 1999).

## [¹Date from which revised decision takes effect

4.77    **19.** Where the date from which a decision took effect is found to be erroneous on a revision under section 16 of the Act, the revision shall take effect from the date on which the revised decision would have taken effect had the error not been made.]

AMENDMENT

1. Regulation 16 of the Miscellaneous Amendments (No. 2) Regulations 1999 (June 1, 1999).

## [¹Supersession of decisions

4.78    **20.**—(1) Subject to paragraphs (9) and (10), for the purposes of section 17 of the Act, the cases and circumstances in which a decision ("a superseding decision") may be made under that section are set out in paragraphs (2) to (7).

(2) A decision may be superseded by a decision made by the Secretary of State acting on his own initiative—

(a) where he is satisfied that the decision is one in respect of which there has been a material change of circumstances since the decision was made—

(b) where he is satisfied that the decision was made in ignorance of, or was based upon a mistake as to, some material fact; or

(c) in consequence of a departure direction or of a revision or supersession of a decision with respect to a departure direction.

(3) Except where paragraph (8) applies, [⁴but subject to regulation 23(22)] a decision may be superseded by a decision made by the Secretary of State where—

(a) an application is made on the basis that—

(i) there has been a change of circumstances [²since the date from which the decision had effect]; or

(ii) it is expected that a change of circumstances will occur; and

(b) the Secretary of State is satisfied that the change of circumstances is or would be material.

(4) A decision may be superseded by a decision made by the Secretary of State where—

(a) an application is made on the basis that the decision was made in ignorance of, or was based upon a mistake as to, a fact; and

(b) the Secretary of State is satisfied that the fact is or would be material.

[³(4A) A decision may be superseded by a decision made by the Secretary of State—

(a) where an application is made on the basis that; or

(b) acting on his own initiative where,

the decision to be superseded is a decision of an appeal tribunal or of a Child Support Commissioner that was made in accordance with section 28ZB(4)(b) of the Act, in a case where section 28ZB(5) of the Act applies.]

(5) A decision, other than a decision given on appeal, may be superseded by a decision made by the Secretary of State—

(a) acting on his own initiative where he is satisfied that the decision was erroneous in point of law; or

(b) where an application is made on the basis that the decision was erroneous in point of law.

(6) An interim maintenance assessment may be superseded by a decision made by the Secretary of State where he receives information which enables him to make a maintenance assessment calculated in accordance with Part I of Schedule 1 to the Act for a period beginning after the effective date of that interim maintenance assessment.

(7) Subject to paragraphs (4) and (5) of regulation 17, where the Secretary of State is satisfied that it would be appropriate to make an interim maintenance assessment the category of which is different from (hat of the interim maintenance assessment which is in force, he may make a decision which supersedes the interim maintenance assessment which is in force.

(8) This paragraph applies—

(a) where any paragraph of regulation 21 applies; and

(b) in the case of a Category A or Category D interim maintenance assessment.

(9) The cases and circumstances in which a decision may be superseded shall not include any case or circumstance in which a decision may be revised.

(10) Paragraphs (2) to (6) shall apply neither in respect of—

(a) a decision to refuse an application for a maintenance assessment; nor

(b) a decision to cancel a maintenance assessment.

(11) For the purposes of section 17 of the Act as extended by paragraph 2 of Schedule 4C (o the Act, paragraphs (2) to (5) shall apply in relation to—

(a) a decision with respect to a reduced benefit direction or a person's liability under section 43 of the Act; and

(b) any decision of the Secretary of State under section 17 of the Act as extended by paragraph 2 of Schedule 4C to the Act, whether as originally made or as revised under section 16 of the Act as extended by paragraph 1 of Schedule 4C to the Act, as they apply in relation to any decision as to a maintenance assessment save that paragraph (8) shall not apply in respect of such a decision.

whether as originally made or as revised under section 16 of the Act as extended by paragraph 1 of Schedule 4C to the Act, as they apply in relation to any decision as to a maintenance assessment save that paragraph (8) shall not apply in respect of such a decision.]

AMENDMENTS

1. Regulation 16 of the Miscellaneous Amendments (No. 2) Regulations 1999 (June 1, 1999).

2. Regulation 8 of the Miscellaneous Amendments Regulations 2000 (June 19, 2000).

3. Regulation 5(1) of the Social Security and Child Support (Miscellaneous Amendments) Regulations 2003 (May 5, 2003).

4. Regulation 3(4) of the Miscellaneous Amendments Regulations 2005 (March 16, 2005).

DEFINITION

4.79    "the Act": see reg.1(2).

## [¹Circumstances in which a decision may not be superseded

4.80    **21.**—(1) A decision of the Secretary of State shall not be superseded in any of the circumstances specified in the following paragraphs of this regulation.

(2) Except where paragraph (3) or (4) applies and subject to paragraph (5) and regulation 22, this paragraph applies where the difference between—

(a) the amount of child support maintenance (' 'the amount") fixed in accordance with the original decision; and

(b) the amount which would be fixed in accordance with a superseding decision,

is less than £10.00 per week.

(3) Subject to paragraph (5), this paragraph applies where the circumstances of the absent parent are such that the provisions of paragraph 6 of Schedule 1 to the Act would apply and either—

(a) the amount fixed in accordance with the original decision is less than the amount that would be fixed in accordance with a superseding decision and the difference between the two amounts is less than £5.00 per week; or

(b) the amount fixed in accordance with the original decision is more than the amount that would be fixed in accordance with the superseding decision and the difference between the two amounts is less than £1.00 per week.

(4) Subject to paragraph (5), this paragraph applies where—

(a) the children, in respect of whom child support maintenance would be fixed in accordance with a superseding decision, are not the same children for whom child support maintenance was fixed in accordance with the original decision; and

(b) the difference between—

(i) the amount of child support maintenance ("the amount") fixed in accordance with the original decision; and

(ii) the amount which would be fixed in accordance with a superseding decision,

is less than £1.00 per week.

(5) This regulation shall not apply where—

(a) the absent parent is, by virtue of paragraph 5(4) of Schedule 1 to the Act, to be taken for the purposes of that Schedule to have no assessable income;

(b) the case falls within paragraph 7(2) of Schedule 1 to the Act; or

(c) it appears to the Secretary of State that the case no longer falls within paragraph 5(4) of Schedule 1 to the Act.

(6) In this regulation—

"original decision" means the decision which would be superseded but for the application of this regulation; and

"superseding decision" means a decision which would supersede the original decision but for the application of this regulation.]

1. Regulation 16 of the Miscellaneous Amendments (No. 2) Regulations 1999 (June 1, 1999).

## [¹Special cases and circumstances for which regulation 21 is modified

**22.** Where an application is made for a supersession on the basis of a change of circumstances which is relevant to more than one maintenance assessment, regulation 21 shall apply with the following modifications—

    (a) before the word "amount" in each place it occurs there shall be inserted the word "aggregate"; and

    (b) for the word "decision" in each place it occurs there shall be substituted the word "decisions".]

4.81

AMENDMENT

1. Regulation 16 or the Miscellaneous Amendments (No. 2) Regulations 1999 (June 1, 1999).

## [¹Date from which a decision is superseded

**23.**—(1) Except in a case to which paragraph (2) applies, where notice is given under regulation 24 in the period which begins 28 days before an application for a supersession is made and ends 28 days after that application is made, the superseding decision of which notice was given under regulation 24 shall take effect as from (he first day of the maintenance period in which that application was made.

    (2) [²Subject to paragraph (19), where a decision is superseded] by a decision made by the Secretary of Stale in a case to which regulation 20(2)(a) applies on the basis of evidence or information which was also the basis of a decision made under section 9 or 10 of the Social Security Act 1998 the superseding decision under section 17 shall take effect as from the first day of the maintenance period in which that evidence or information was first brought to the attention of an officer exercising the functions of the Secretary of State under the Act.

    (3) Where a superseding decision is made in a case to which either paragraph (2)(b) or (5)(a) of regulation 20 applies, the decision shall take effect as from the first day of the maintenance period in which the decision was made.

    (4) Where a superseding decision is made in a case to which regulation 20(3)(a)(i), (4) or (5)(b) applies, the decision shall take effect as from the first day of the maintenance period in which the application for a supersession was made.

    (5) [³Subject to paragraph (19), where a superseding decision is made] in a case to which regulation 20(3)(a)(ii) applies, the decision shall take effect as from the first day of the maintenance period in which the change of circumstances is due to occur.

    (6) Subject to paragraphs (1), (3) and (14), in a case to which regulation 24 applies, a superseding decision shall take effect as from the first day of

4.82

the maintenance period in which falls the date which is 28 days after the date on which the Secretary of State gave notice to the relevant persons under that regulation.

(7) For the purposes of paragraph (6), where the relevant persons are notified on different dates, the period of 28 days shall be counted from the date of the latest notification.

(8) For the purposes of paragraphs (6) and (7)—

(a) notification includes oral and written notification;

(b) where a person is notified in more than one way, the date on which he is notified is the date on which he was first given notification; and

(c) the date of written notification is the date on which it was handed or sent to the person.

(9) Regulation 1(6) shall not apply in a case to which paragraph (8)(c) applies.

(10) Where—

(a) a decision made by an appeal tribunal under section 20 of the Act or by a Child Support Commissioner is superseded on the ground that it was erroneous due to a misrepresentation of, or that there was a failure to disclose, a material fact; and

(b) the Secretary of State is satisfied that the decision was more advantageous to the person who misrepresented or failed to disclose that fact than it would otherwise have been but for that error,

the superseding decision shall take effect as from the date the decision of the appeal tribunal or, as the case may be, the Child Support Commissioner took, or was to take effect.

(11) Any decision given under section 17 of the Act in consequence of a determination which is a relevant determination for the purposes of section 28ZC of the Act (restrictions on liability in certain cases of error) shall take effect as from the date of the relevant determination.

(12) Where the Secretary of State supersedes a decision in accordance with regulation 20(6), the superseding decision shall take effect as from the first day of the maintenance period in which the Secretary of State has received the information referred to in that paragraph.

(13) Where the Secretary of State supersedes a decision in accordance with regulation 20(7), the superseding decision shall take effect as from the first day of the maintenance period in which the Secretary of State became satisfied that it would be appropriate to make an interim maintenance assessment the category of which is different from that of the maintenance assessment which is in force.

(14) Where a decision is superseded in consequence of a departure direction or a revision or supersession of a decision with respect to a departure direction—

(a) paragraph (6) above shall not apply; and

(b) the superseding decision shall take effect as from the date on which the departure direction or, as the case may be, the revision or supersession, took effect.

(15) Where a decision with respect to a reduced benefit direction is superseded because the direction ceases to be in force in accordance with regulation 41(a), the superseding decision shall have effect as from—

(a) where the direction is in operation immediately before it ceases to be in force, the last day of the benefit week during the course of which the parent concerned complied with the obligations imposed by section 6 of the Act; or

(b) where the direction is suspended immediately before it ceases to be in force, the date on which the parent concerned complied with the obligations imposed by section 6 of the Act.

(16) Where a decision with respect to a reduced benefit direction is superseded because the direction ceases to be in force in accordance with regulation 41(b), the superseding decision shall have effect as from—

(a) where the direction is in operation immediately before it ceases to be in force, the last day of the benefit week during the course of which the application under regulation 41(b) was made; or

(b) where the direction is suspended immediately before it ceases to be in force, the date on which the application under regulation 41 (b) was made.

(17) Where a decision with respect to a reduced benefit direction is superseded because the direction ceases to be in force in accordance with regulation 41(c) or (d), the superseding decision shall have effect as from—

(a) where the direction is in operation immediately before it ceases to be in force, the last day of the benefit week during the course of which the Secretary of State is supplied with information that enables him to make the assessment;

(b) where the direction is suspended immediately before it ceases to be in force, the date on which the Secretary of State is supplied with information that enables him to make the assessment.

(18) Where a decision with respect to a reduced benefit direction is superseded because the direction ceases to be in force in accordance with regulation 47(1), the superseding decision shall have effect as from the last day of the benefit Week preceding the benefit week on the first day of which, in accordance with the provisions of regulation 36(4), the further direction comes into operation, or would come into operation but for the provisions of regulation 40 or 40ZA.]

[⁴(19) Where a superseding decision is made in a case to which regulation 20(2)(a) or (3) applies and the material circumstance is the death of a qualifying child or a qualifying child ceasing to be a qualifying child, the decision shall take effect as from the first day of the maintenance period in which the change occurred.]

[⁵(20) Where a superseding decision is made in a case to which regulation 20(4A) applies that decision shall take effect from the first day of the maintenance period following the date on which the appeal tribunal or the Child Support Commissioner's decision would have taken effect had it been decided in accordance with the determination of the Child Support Commissioner or the court in the appeal referred to in section 28ZB(1)(b) of the Act.]

[⁶(21) Where a superseding decision is made in a case to which regulation 20(2)(a) or (3) applies, and the relevant circumstance is that a person has ceased to be a person with care in relation to a qualifying child in respect of whom the maintenance assessment was made, the decision shall take effect from the first day of the maintenance period in which that person ceased to be that person with care in relation to that qualifying child.

(22) Regulation 21 shall not apply where a superseding decision is made under regulation 20(3) in the circumstances set out in paragraph (19) or (21).]

AMENDMENTS

1. Regulation 16 of the Miscellaneous Amendments (No. 2) Regulations 1999 (June 1, 1999).
2. Regulation 9(a) of the Miscellaneous Amendments Regulations 2000 (June 19, 2000).
3. Regulation 9(b) of the Miscellaneous Amendments Regulations 2000 (June 19, 2000).
4. Regulation 9(c)of the Miscellaneous Amendments Regulations 2000 (June 19, 2000).
5. Regulation 5(2) of the Social Security and Child Support (Miscellaneous Amendments) Regulations 2003 (May 5, 2003).
6. Regulation 3(5) of the Miscellaneous Amendments Regulations 2005 (March 16, 2005).

## [¹Procedure where the Secretary of State proposes to supersede a decision on his own initiative

4.83    **24.** Where the Secretary of State on his own initiative proposes to make a decision superseding a decision other than in consequence of a decision with respect to a departure direction or a revision or supersession of such a decision he shall notify the relevant persons who could be materially affected by the decision of that intention.]

AMENDMENT

1. Regulation 16 of the Miscellaneous Amendments (No. 2) Regulations 1999 (June 1, 1999).

[Regulations 25 to 29 were effectively revoked by the Miscellaneous Amendments (No. 2) regulations 1995 with effect from June 1, 1999.]

PART VIII

## COMMENCEMENT AND TERMINATION OF MAINTENANCE ASSESSMENTS AND MAINTENANCE PERIODS

### Effective dates of new maintenance assessments

4.84    **30.**—(1) Subject to [⁵regulations 8C (effective dates of interim maintenance assessments), 30A (effective dates in particular cases), 33(7) (maintenance periods)] [¹and to regulation 3(5) [²(7) and (8)] of the Maintenance Arrangements and Jurisdiction Regulations (maintenance assessments where court order in force),] the effective date of a new maintenance assessment following an application under section 4, 6 or 7 of the Act shall be the date determined in accordance with paragraphs (2) to (4).

[³(2) Where no maintenance assessment made in accordance with Part I of Schedule 1 to the Act is in force with respect to the person with care and absent parent, the effective date of a new assessment shall be—

(a) in a case where the application for a maintenance assessment is made by a person with care or by a child under section 7 of the Act—

    (i) eight weeks from the date on which a maintenance enquiry form has been given or sent to an absent parent, where such date is on or after 18th April 1995 and where within four weeks of the date that form was given or sent, it has been returned by the absent parent to the Secretary of State and it contains his name, address and written confirmation that he is the parent of the child or children in respect of whom the application for a maintenance assessment was made;

    (ii) in all other circumstances, the date a maintenance enquiry form is given or sent to an absent parent;

(b) in a case where the application for a maintenance assessment is made by an absent parent—

    (i) eight weeks from the date on which an application made by an absent parent was received by the Secretary of State, where such date is on or after 18th April 1995 and where, on, or within four weeks of, the date of receipt of that maintenance application, the absent parent has provided his name, address and written confirmation that he is the parent of the child or children in respect of whom the application was made;

    (ii) in all other circumstances, the date an effective maintenance application form is received by the Secretary of State];

[⁶(c) in a case where the application for a maintenance assessment is an application in relation to which the provisions of regulation 3 have been applied, the date an effective maintenance application form is received by the Secretary of State.]

[⁴(2A) Where [⁷the Secretary of State] is satisfied that there was unavoidable delay by the absent parent in providing the information listed in sub-paragraphs (a)(i) or (b)(i) of paragraph (2) within the time specified in those subparagraphs, he may apply the provisions of those subparagraphs for the purpose of setting the effective date of a maintenance assessment even though that information was not provided within the time specified in those subparagraphs.]

(3) The provisions of regulation 1(6)(b) shall not apply to paragraph (2)(a).

(4) Where [⁸the Secretary of State] is satisfied that an absent parent has deliberately avoided receipt of a maintenance enquiry form, he may determine the date on which the form would have given or sent but for such avoidance, and that date shall be the relevant date for the purposes of paragraph (2)(a).

AMENDMENTS

1. Regulation 7 of the Miscellaneous Amendments Regulations 1995 (February 16, 1995).
2. Regulation 36(2) of the Amendment Regulations 1995 (April 18, 1995).

3. Regulation 36(3) of the Amendment Regulations 1995 (April 18, 1995).

4. Regulation 36(4) of the Amendment Regulations 1995 (April 18, 1995).

5. Regulation 32(2) of the Miscellaneous Amendments (No. 2) Regulations 1995 (January 22, 1996).

6. Regulation 32(3) of the Miscellaneous Amendments (No. 2) Regulations 1995 (January 22, 1996).

7. Regulation 17 of the Miscellaneous Amendments (No. 2) Regulations 1999 (June 1, 1999).

8. Regulation 17 of the Miscellaneous Amendments (No. 2) Regulations 1999 (June 1, 1999).

DEFINITIONS

**4.85**    "absent parent": see reg.1(5).
"the Act": see reg.1(2).
"effective date": see reg.1(2).
"person with care": see reg.1(5).

## [¹Effective dates of new maintenance assessments in particular cases

**4.86**    **30A.**—(1) Subject to regulation 33(7), where a new maintenance assessment is made in accordance with Part I of Schedule 1 to the Act following an interim maintenance assessment which has ceased to have effect in the circumstances set out in regulation 8D(6), the effective date of that maintenance assessment shall be the date upon which that interim maintenance assessment ceased to nave effect in accordance with that regulation.]

[²(2) Where [⁴the Secretary of State] receives the information or evidence to enable him to make a maintenance assessment, calculated in accordance with the provisions of Part I of Schedule 1 to the Act, for the period from the date set by regulation 3(7) of the Maintenance Arrangements and Jurisdiction Regulations or regulation 30(2)(a) or (b), as me case may be, to the effective date of the maintenance assessment referred to in paragraph (1), the maintenance assessment first referred to in this paragraph shall, subject to regulation 33(7), have effect for that period.]

[³(3) The effective date of a new maintenance assessment made in respect of a person with care and an absent parent shall, where the circumstances set out in paragraph (4) apply, be the first day of the maintenance period after the child support officer has received the information or evidence referred to in paragraph (4)(c) or 13th January 1997, whichever is the later.

(4) The circumstances referred to in paragraph (3) are where—

(a) paragraphs (1) and (2) do not apply to that person with care and that absent parent;

(b) no maintenance assessment made in accordance with the provisions of Part I of Schedule 1 to the Act is in force in relation to that person with care and that absent parent; and

(c) on or after 13th January 1997, ^Secretary of Stale] has sufficient information or evidence to enable him to make a new maintenance assessment, calculated in accordance with Part I of Schedule 1 to the Act, in relation to that person with are and that absent parent but in respect only of a period beginning after the effective date applicable in their case by virtue of regulation 30(2).

(5) Where the information or evidence referred to in paragraph (3) is that there has been an award of income support[⁶, state pension credit] or an income-based jobseeker's allowance, the Secretary of State shall be treated as having received the information or evidence which enables [⁵him] to make the assessment referred to in that paragraph on the first day in respect of which income support[⁶, state pension credit] or an income-based jobseeker's allowance was payable under that award.

(6) Where, in a case falling with paragraph (3), [⁴Secretary of State] receives the information or evidence to enable him to make a maintenance assessment calculated in accordance with the provisions of Part 1 of Schedule 1 to the Act, for the period from the effective date applicable to that case under regulation 30(2)(a) or (b), as the case may be, to the effective date of the assessment referred to in paragraph (3), the maintenance assessment first referred to in this paragraph shall have effect for that period.

(7) Paragraphs (3) to (6) shall not apply where a case falls with regulation 33(7), or regulation 3 of the Maintenance Arrangements and Jurisdiction Regulation (relationship between maintenance assessments and certain court orders).]

AMENDMENTS

1. Regulation 33 of the Miscellaneous Amendments (No. 2) Regulations 1995 (January 22. 1996).
2. Regulation 8(2) of the Miscellaneous Amendments (No. 2) Regulations 1996 (January 13. 1997).
3. Regulation 8(3) of the Miscellaneous Amendments (No. 2) Regulations 1996 (January 13, 1997).
4. Regulation I8(a) of the Miscellaneous Amendment {No. 2) Regulations 1999 (June I. 1999).
5. Regulation 18(b) of the Miscellaneous Amendment (No. 2) Regulations 1999 (June 1. 1999).
6. Regulation 3(3) of the Miscellaneous Amendments (No. 2) Regulations 2003 (November 5, 2003).

DEFINITIONS

"the Act": see reg.1(2).                                                    4.87
"effective date": see reg.1(2).
"Maintenance Arrangements and Jurisdiction Regulations"; see reg.1(2).
[Regulations 31 to 31C are revoked by reg.19 of the Miscellaneous Amendments (No. 2) Regulations 1999 with effect from June 1. I999.|

## Cancellation of a maintenance assessment

**32.** Where [¹the Secretary of State] cancels a maintenance assessment   4.88
under paragraph 16(2) or (3) of Schedule 1 to the Act, the assessment shall cease to have effect from the date of receipt of the request for the cancellation of the assessment or from such later date as [²he] may determine.

AMENDMENTS

1. Regulation 20(a) of the Miscellaneous Amendments (No. 2) Regulations 1999 (June 1, 1999).
2. Regulation 20(b) of the Miscellaneous Amendments (No. 2) Regulations 1999 (June 1, 1999).

DEFINITION

4.89    "the Act": see reg.1(2).

## [¹Cancellation of maintenance assessments made under section 7 of the Act where the child is no longer habitually resident in Scotland]

4.90    **32A.**—(1) Where a maintenance assessment made in response to an application by a child under section 7 of the Act is in force and that child ceases to be habitually resident in Scotland, [²the Secretary of State] shall cancel that assessment.

(2) In any case where paragraph (1) applies, the assessment shall cease to have effect from the date that [³Secretary of State] determines is the date on which the child concerned ceased to be habitually resident in Scotland.]

AMENDMENTS

1. Regulation 12 of the Amendment Regulations (April 5, 1993).
2. Regulation 21(a) of the Miscellaneous Amendments (No. 2) Regulations 1999 (June 1, 1999).
3. Regulation 21(b) of the Miscellaneous Amendments (No. 2) Regulations 1999 (June 1, 1999).

DEFINITION

4.91    "the Act": see reg.1(2).

## [¹Notification of intention to cancel a maintenance assessment under paragraph 16(4A) of Schedule 1 to the Act

4.92    **32B.**—(1) [²The Secretary of State] shall, if it is reasonably practicable to do so, give written notice to the relevant persons of his intention to cancel a maintenance assessment under paragraph 16(4A) of Schedule 1 to the Act.

(2) Where a notice under paragraph (1) has been given, [²the Secretary of State] shall not cancel that maintenance assessment before the end of a period of 14 days commencing with the date on which the notice was given or sent.]

AMENDMENTS

1. Regulation 35 of the Miscellaneous Amendments (No. 2) Regulations 1995 and regulation 2 of the Miscellaneous Amendments (No. 3) Regulations 1995 (January 22, 1996).
2. Regulation 22 of the Miscellaneous Amendments (No. 2) Regulations 1999 (June 1, 1999).

DEFINITIONS

"the Act": reg.1(2).     **4.93**
"relevant person": see reg.1(2).

## Maintenance periods

**33.**—(1) The child support maintenance payable under a maintenance     **4.94** assessment shall be calculated at a weekly rate and be in respect of successive maintenance periods, each such period being a period of 7 days.

(2) Subject to paragraph (6), the first maintenance period shall commence on the effective date of the first maintenance assessment, and each succeeding maintenance period shall commence on the day immediately following the last day of the preceding maintenance period.

(3) The maintenance periods in relation to a fresh maintenance assessment [⁴made upon the supersession of a decision under section 17 of the Act] shall coincide with the maintenance periods in relation to the earlier assessment, had it continued in force, and the first maintenance period in relation to a fresh assessment shall commence on the day following the last day of the last maintenance period in relation to the earlier assessment.

(4) The amount of child support maintenance payable in respect of a maintenance period which includes the effective date of a fresh maintenance assessment shall be the amount of maintenance payable under that fresh assessment.

(5) The amount of child support maintenance payable in respect of a maintenance period during the course of which a cancelled maintenance assessment ceases to have effect shall be the amount of maintenance payable under that assessment.

[²(6) Where a case is to be treated as a special case for the purposes of the Act by virtue of regulation 22 of the Maintenance Assessments and Special Cases Regulations (multiple applications relating to an absent parent) and an application is made by a person with care in relation to an absent parent where—

(a) there is already a maintenance assessment in force in relation to that absent parent and a different person with care; or

(b) subparagraph (b) does not apply, but before a maintenance assessment is made in relation to that application, a maintenance assessment is made in relation to that absent parent and a different person with care,

the maintenance periods in relation to an assessment made in response to that application shall coincide with the maintenance periods in relation to the earlier maintenance assessment, except where regulation 3(7) of the Maintenance Arrangements and Jurisdiction Regulations or paragraph (8) applies, and the first such period shall, subject to paragraph (9), commence not later than 7 days after the date of notification to the relevant persons of the later maintenance assessment.]

[¹(7) Subject to regulation 3(7), of the Maintenance Arrangements and Jurisdiction Regulations and to paragraph (8), the effective date of a maintenance assessment made in response to an application falling within paragraph (6) shall be the date upon which the first maintenance period in relation to that application commences in accordance with that paragraph.

(8) The first maintenance period in relation to a maintenance assessment which is made in response to an application falling within paragraph (6) and which immediately follows an interim maintenance assessment shall commence on the effective date of that interim maintenance assessment or 22nd January 1996, whichever is the later, and the effective date of that maintenance assessment shall be the date upon which that first maintenance period commences.]

[³(9) Where the case is one to which, if paragraphs (6) and (7) did not apply, regulation 30(2)(a)(i) or (b)(i) would apply, and the first maintenance period would, under the provisions of paragraphs (6), commence during the 8-week period referred to in subparagraph (a) or (b) of that regulation, the first maintenance period shall commence not later than 7 days after the expiry of that period of 8 weeks.]

AMENDMENTS

1. Regulation 36(2) of the Miscellaneous Amendments (No. 2) Regulations 1995 (January 22, 1996).
2. Regulation 12(2) of the Miscellaneous Amendments Regulations 1996 (August 5, 1996).
3. Regulation 12(3) of the Miscellaneous Amendments Regulations 1996 (August 5, 1996).
4. Regulation 23 of the Miscellaneous Amendments (No. 2) Regulations 1999 (June 1, 1999).

DEFINITIONS

4.95    "absent parent": see reg.1(5).
"the Act": see reg.1(2).
"effective date": see reg.1(2).
"Maintenance Arrangements and Jurisdiction Regulations": see reg.1(2).
"maintenance period": see reg.1(2).
"person with care": see reg.1(5).
"relevant person": see reg.1(2).

PART IX

REDUCED BENEFIT DIRECTIONS

**Prescription of disability working allowance for the purposes of section 6 of the Act**

4.96    **34.** Disability working allowance shall be a benefit of a prescribed kind for the purposes of section 6 of the Act.

DEFINITIONS

"the Act": see reg.1(2).
"disability working allowance": see reg.1(2).

## [¹Periods for compliance with obligations imposed by section 6 of the Act

**35.** The period specified for the purposes of section 46(2) of the Act is—
(a) except where paragraph (b) applies, four weeks from the date on which the Secretary of State serves notice under that subsection; or
(b) eight weeks from that date where the Secretary of State has received, within two weeks of serving that notice, a statement in writing from the parent with care which sets out the reasons why she believes that, if she were to be required to comply with an obligation imposed by section 6 of the Act, there would be a risk, as a result of that compliance, of her or any child or children living with her suffering harm or undue distress.]

4.97

AMENDMENT

1. Regulation 24 of the Miscellaneous Amendments (No. 2) Regulations 1999 (June 1, 1999).

DEFINITIONS

"the Act": see reg.1(2).
"obligation imposed under section 6 of the Act": see reg.1(2).

4.98

## [¹Circumstances in which a reduced benefit direction shall not be given

**35A.** [³The Secretary of State] shall not after 22nd January 1996 give a reduced benefit direction where—
(a) income support is paid to or in respect of the parent in question and the applicable amount of the claimant for income support includes one or more of the amounts set out in paragraph 15(3), (4) or (6) of Part IV of Schedule 2 to the Income Support (General) Regulations 1987;
[²(aa) income-based jobseeker's allowance is paid to or in respect of the parent in question and the applicable amount of the claimant for income-based jobseeker's allowance includes one or more of the amounts set out in paragraph 20(4), (5) or (7) of Schedule 1 to the Jobseeker's Allowance Regulations; or]
(b) an amount equal to one or more of the amounts specified in subparagraph (a) is included, by virtue of regulation 9 of the Maintenance Assessments and Special Cases Regulations, in the exempt income of the parent in question and family credit or disability working allowance is paid to or in respect of that parent]; [⁴or
(c) an amount prescribed under section 9(5)(c) of the Tax Credits Act 2002 (increased elements of child tax credit for children or young persons with a disability) is included in an award of child tax credit payable to the parent in question or a member of that parent's family living with him.]

4.99

AMENDMENTS

1. Regulation 37 of the Miscellaneous Amendments (No. 2) Regulations 1995 (January 22, 1996).
2. Regulation 5(5) of the Jobseekers Amendment Regulations (October 7, 1996).
3. Regulation 25 of the Miscellaneous Amendments (No. 2) Regulations 1999 (June 1, 1999).
4. Regulation 5 of the Miscellaneous Amendments Regulations 2003 (April 6, 2003).

DEFINITIONS

4.100    "family credit": see reg.1(2).
"Maintenance Assessments and Special Cases Regulations": reg.1(2).
"the Jobseeker's Allowance Regulations": see reg.1(2).

## Amount of and period of reduction of relevant benefit under a reduced benefit direction

4.101    **36.**—(1) The reduction in the amount payable by way of a relevant benefit to, or in respect of, the parent concerned and the period of such reduction by virtue of a direction shall be determined in accordance with paragraphs (2) to (9).

(2) Subject to paragraph (6) and regulations 37, 38(7)[³, 40 and 40ZA], there shall be a reduction for a period of [⁹156 weeks] from the day specified in the direction under the provisions of section 46(9) of the Act in respect of each such week equal to

$$[^9 0.4 \times B]$$

where B is an amount equal to the weekly amount, in relation to the week in question, specified in column (2) of paragraph 1(l)(e) of the applicable amounts Schedule.

[¹⁰...]

(4) [¹Subject to paragraphs ["(4A),] (5), (5A) and (5B)], a direction shall come into operation on the first day of the second benefit week following the review, carried out by [¹⁴the Secretary of State] in consequence of the direction, of the relevant benefit that is payable.

[¹²(4A) Subject to paragraphs (5), (5A) and (5B), where a reduced benefit direction ("the subsequent direction") is made on a day when a reduced benefit direction ("the earlier direction") is in force in respect of the same parent, the subsequent direction shall come into operation on the day immediately following the day on which the earlier direction ceased to be in force.]

(5) Where the relevant benefit is income support and the provisions of regulation 26(2) of the Social Security (Claims and Payments) Regulations 1987 (deferment of payment of different amount of income support) apply, a direction shall come into operation on such later date as may be determined by the Secretary of State in accordance with those provisions.

[²(5A) Where the relevant benefit is family credit or disability working allowance and, at the time a direction is given, a lump sum payment has already been made under the provisions of regulation 27(1A) of the Social

Security (Claims and Payments) Regulations 1987 (payment of family credit or disability working allowance by lump sum) the direction shall, subject to paragraph (5B), come into operation on the first day of any benefit week which immediately follows the period in respect of which the lump sum payment was made, or the first day of any benefit week which immediately follows 18th April 1995 if later.

(5B) Where the period in respect of which the lump sum payment was made is not immediately followed by a benefit week, but family credit or disability working allowance again becomes payable, or income support [⁴or income-based jobseeker's allowance] becomes payable, during a period of 52 weeks from the date the direction was given, the direction shall come into operation on the first day of the second benefit week which immediately follows the expiry of a period of 14 days from service of the notice specified in paragraph (5C).

(5C) Where paragraph (5B) applies, the parent to or in respect of whom family credit or disability working allowance has again become payable, or income support [⁵or income-based jobseeker's allowance] has become payable, shall be notified in writing by [¹⁵the Secretary of State] that the amount of family credit, disability working allowance [⁶, income support or income-based job-seeker's allowance] paid to or in respect of her will be reduced in accordance with the provisions of paragraph (5B) if she continues to fail to comply with the obligations imposed by section 6 of the Act.

(5D) Where—

(a) family credit or disability working allowance has been paid by lump sum under the provisions of regulation 27(1A) of the Social Security (Claims and Payments) Regulations 1987 (whether or not a benefit week immediately follows the period in respect of which the lump sum payment was made); and

(b) where income support [⁷or income-based jobseeker's allowance] becomes payable to or in respect of a parent to or in respect of whom family credit or disability working allowance was payable at the time the direction referred to in paragraph (5A) was made,

income support [⁸or, as the case may be, income-based jobseeker's allowance] shall become a relevant benefit for the purposes of that direction and the amount payable by way of income support [⁸or, as the case may be, income-based jobseeker's allowance] shall be reduced in accordance with that direction.

(5E) In circumstances to which paragraph (5A) or (5B) applies, where no relevant benefit has become payable during a period of 52 weeks from the date °n which a direction was given, it shall lapse.]

[¹³(6) Where the benefit payable is income support or income-based job-seeker's allowance and there is a change in the benefit week whilst a direction is in operation, the period of the reduction specified in paragraph (2) shall be a period greater than 155 weeks but less than 156 weeks and ending on the last day of the last benefit week falling entirely within the period of 156 weeks specified in that paragraph.]

(7) Where the weekly amount specified in column (2) of paragraph (1)(1)(e) of the applicable amounts Schedule changes on a day when a direction is in operation, the amount of the reduction of the relevant benefit shall be changed—

(a) where the benefit is income support [⁴or income-based jobseeker's allowance], from the first day of the first benefit week to commence for the parent concerned on or after the day that weekly amount changes;

(b) where the benefit is family credit or disability working allowance, from the first day of the next award period of that benefit for the parent concerned commencing on or after the day that weekly amount changes.

(8) Only one direction in relation to a parent shall be in force at any one time.

[¹⁰. . .]

AMENDMENTS

1. Regulation 38(2) of the Amendment Regulations 1995 (April 18, 1995).
2. Regulation 38(3) of the Amendment Regulations 1995 (April 18, 1995).
3. Regulation 5(6)(a) of the Jobseekers Amendment Regulations (October 7, 1996).
4. Regulation 5(6)(b) of the Jobseekers Amendment Regulations (October 7, 1996).
5. Regulation 5(6)(c)(i) of the Jobseekers Amendment Regulations (October 7, 1996).
6. Regulation 5(6)(c)(ii) of the Jobseekers Amendment Regulations (October 7, 1996).
7. Regulation 5(6)(d)(i) of the Jobseekers Amendment Regulations (October 7, 1996).
8. Regulation 5(6)(d)(ii) of the Jobseekers Amendment Regulations (October 7, 1996).
9. Regulation 14(2) of the Miscellaneous Amendment Regulations 1996 (October 7, 1996).
10. Regulation 14(3) of the Miscellaneous Amendment Regulations 1996 (October 7, 1996, immediately following the coming into force of regulation 5 of the Jobseekers Amendment Regulations).
11. Regulation 14(4) of the Miscellaneous Amendment Regulations 1996 (October 7, 1996).
12. Regulation 14(5) of the Miscellaneous Amendment Regulations 1996 (October 7, 1996).
13. Regulation 14(6) of the Miscellaneous Amendments Regulations 1996 (October 7, 1996, immediately following the coming into force of regulation 5 of the Jobseekers Amendment Regulations).
14. Regulation 26(a) of the Miscellaneous Amendments (No. 2) Regulations 1999 (November 29, 1999).
15. Regulation 26(b) of the Miscellaneous Amendments (No. 2) Regulations 1999 (June 1, 1999).

DEFINITIONS

4.102      "the Act": see reg.1(2).
"applicable amounts Schedule": see reg.1(2).
"benefit week": see reg.1(2).
"direction": see reg.1(2).
"disability working allowance": see reg.1(2).
"family credit": see reg.1(2).
"in force": see reg.1(3).

"in operation": see reg.1(3).
"parent concerned": see reg.1(2).
"relevant benefit": see reg.1(2).

## Modification of reduction under a reduced benefit direction to preserve minimum entitlement to relevant benefit

**37.** Where in respect of any benefit week the amount of the relevant ben- **4.103**
efit that would be payable after it has been reduced following a direction
would, but for this regulation, be nil or less than the minimum amount of
that benefit that is payable as determined—

(a) in the case of income support, by regulation 26(4) of the Social
    Security (Claims and Payments) Regulations 1987;

[¹(aa) in the case of jobseeker's allowance, by regulation [²87A of the
    Jobseeker's Allowance Regulations 1996];

(b) in the case of family credit and disability working allowance, by
    regulation 27(2) [²of the Social Security (Claims and Payments)
    Regulations 1987].

the amount of that reduction shall be decreased to such extent as to raise
the amount of that benefit to the minimum amount that is payable.

AMENDMENTS

1. Regulation 5(7) of the Jobseekers Amendment Regulations (October 7,
1996).
2. Regulation 6(2) of the Jobseekers Miscellaneous Amendments Regulations
(October 28, 1996).

DEFINITIONS

"benefit week": see reg.1(2).                                          **4.104**
"direction": see reg.1(2).
"disability working allowance": see reg.1(2).
"family credit": see reg.1(2).
"relevant benefit": see reg.1(2).

## Suspension of a reduced benefit direction when relevant benefit ceases to be payable

**38.**—(1) Where relevant benefit ceases to be payable to, or in respect of, **4.105**
the parent concerned at a time when a direction is in operation, that direction shall, subject to paragraph (2), be suspended for a period of 52 weeks
from the date the relevant benefit has ceased to be payable.

(2) Where a direction has been suspended for a period of 52 weeks and
no relevant benefit is payable at the end of that period, it shall cease to be
in force.

(3) Where a direction is suspended and relevant benefit again becomes
payable to or in respect of the parent concerned, the amount payable by
way of that benefit shall, subject to regulations 40, [¹40ZA,] 41 and 42, be
reduced in accordance with that direction for the balance of the reduction
period.

(4) The amount or, as the case may be, amounts of the reduction to be made during the balance of the reduction period shall be determined in accordance with regulation 36(2) [². . .].

(5) No reduction in the amount of benefit under paragraph (3) shall be made before the expiry of a period of 14 days from service of the notice specified in paragraph (6), and the provisions of regulation 36(4) shall apply as to the date when the direction again comes into operation.

(6) Where relevant benefit again becomes payable to or in respect of a parent with respect to whom a direction is suspended she shall be notified in writing by [³the Secretary of State] that the amount of relevant benefit paid to or in respect of her will again be reduced, in accordance with the provisions of paragraph (3), if she continues to fail to comply with the obligations imposed by section 6 of the Act.

(7) Where a direction has ceased to be in force by virtue of the provisions of paragraph (2), a further direction in respect of the same parent given on account of that parent's failure to comply with the obligations imposed by section 6 of the Act in relation to one or more of the same qualifying children shall, unless it also ceases to be in force by virtue of the provisions of paragraph (2), be in operation for the balance of the reduction period relating to the direction that has ceased to be in force, and the provisions of paragraph (4) shall apply to it.

AMENDMENTS

1. Regulation 5(8) of the Jobseekers Amendment Regulations (October 7, 1996).
2. Regulation 15 of the Miscellaneous Amendments Regulations 1996 (October 7, 1996).
3. Regulation 27 of the Miscellaneous Amendments (No. 2) Regulations 1999 (June 1, 1999).

DEFINITIONS

4.106     "the Act": see reg.1(2).
"balance of the reduction period": see reg.1(2).
"direction": see reg.1(2).
"in force": see reg.1(3).
"in operation": see reg.1(3).
"obligation imposed by section 6 of the Act": see reg.1(2).
"parent concerned": see reg.1(2).
"relevant benefit": see reg.1(2).
"suspended": see reg.1(3).

## Reduced benefit direction where family credit or disability working allowance is payable and income support becomes payable

4.107     **39.**—(1) Where a direction is in operation in respect of a parent to whom or in respect of whom family credit or disability working allowance is payable, and income support [¹or income-based jobseeker's allowance] becomes payable to or in respect of that parent, income support [²or, as the case may be, income-based jobseeker's allowance] shall become a relevant benefit for the purposes of that direction, and the amount payable by way of income support [²or, as the case may be, income-based jobseeker's allowance] shall be reduced in accordance with that direction for the balance of the reduction period.

(2) The amount or, as the case may be, the amounts of the reduction to be made during the balance of the reduction period shall be determined in accordance with regulation 36(2) [³. . . ].

AMENDMENTS

1. Regulation 5(9)(a) of the Jobseekers Amendment Regulations (October 7, 1996).
2. Regulation 5(9)(b) of the Jobseekers Amendment Regulations (October 7, 1996).
3. Regulation 16 of the Miscellaneous Amendments Regulations 1996 (October 7, 1996).

DEFINITIONS

"balance of the reduction period": see reg.1(2).                                      **4.108**
"direction": see reg.1(2).
"disability working allowance": see reg.1(2).
"family credit": see reg.1(2).
"in operation": see reg.1(3).
"relevant benefit": see reg.1(2).

## Suspension of a reduced benefit direction [(⁴income support)]

**40.**—(1) Where a direction is given or is in operation at a time when     **4.109**
income support is payable to or in respect of the parent concerned [⁵but the circumstances in paragraph (3) apply to her], that direction shall be suspended for so long as [⁶those circumstances apply], or 52 weeks, whichever period is the shorter.

[⁷. . .]

(2) Where a case falls within paragraph (1) [⁸. . .] and a direction has been suspended for a period of 52 weeks, it shall cease to be in force.

[⁹(3) The circumstances referred to in paragraph (1) are that—
(a) she is resident in a care home or an independent hospital;
(b) she is being provided with a care home service or an independent health care service; or
(c) her applicable amount falls to be calculated under regulation 21 of and any of paragraphs 1 to 3 of Schedule 7 to the Income Support Regulations (patients).

(4) In paragraph (3)—
"care home" has the meaning assigned to it by section 3 of the Care Standards Act 2000;
"care home service" has the meaning assigned to it by section 2(3) of the Regulation of Care (Scotland) Act 2001;
"independent health care service" has the meaning assigned to it by section 2(5)(a) and (b) of the Regulation of Care (Scotland) Act 2001; and
"independent hospital" has the meaning assigned to it by section 2 of the Care Standards Act 2000.]

AMENDMENTS

4. Regulation 3(4)(a) of the Miscellaneous Amendments (No. 2) Regulations 2003 (November 5, 2003).
5. Regulation 3(4)(b)(i) of the Miscellaneous Amendments (No. 2) Regulations 2003 (November 5, 2003).
6. Regulation 3(4)(b)(ii) of the Miscellaneous Amendments (No. 2) Regulations 2003 (November 5, 2003).
7. Regulation 3(4)(c) of the Miscellaneous Amendments (No. 2) Regulations 2003 (November 5, 2003).
8. Regulation 3(4)(d) of the Miscellaneous Amendments (No. 2) Regulations 2003 (November 5, 2003).
9. Regulation 3(4)(e) of the Miscellaneous Amendments (No. 2) Regulations 2003 (November 5, 2003).

DEFINITIONS

4.110     "applicable amount": see reg.1(2).
"direction": see reg.1(2).
"in force": see reg.1(3).
"in operation": see reg.1(3).
"Income Support Regulations": see reg.1(2).
"parent concerned": see reg.1(2).
"suspended": see reg.1(3).

## [¹Suspension of a reduced benefit direction [²(income-based jobseeker's allowance)]

4.111     **40ZA.**—(1) Where a direction is given or is in operation at a time when income-based jobseeker's allowance is payable to or in respect of the parent concerned [³but the circumstances in paragraph (4) apply to her], that direction shall be suspended for so long as [⁴those circumstances apply], or 52 weeks, whichever period is the shorter.

[⁵. . .]

(3) Where a case falls within paragraph (1) [⁶. . .] and a direction has been suspended for a period of 52 weeks, it shall cease to be in force.

[⁷(4) The circumstances referred to in paragraph (1) are that—

(a) she is resident in a care home or an independent hospital;
(b) she is being provided with a care home service or an independent health care service; or
(c) her applicable amount falls to be calculated under regulation 85 of and paragraph 1 or 2 of Schedule 5 to the Jobseeker's Allowance Regulations (patients).

(5) In paragraph (4)—

"care home" has the meaning assigned to it by section 3 of the Care Standards Act 2000;

"care home service" has the meaning assigned to it by section 2(3) of the Regulation of Care (Scotland) Act 2001;

"independent health care service" has the meaning assigned to it by section 2(5)(a) and (b) of the Regulation of Care (Scotland) Act 2001; and

"independent hospital" has the meaning assigned to it by section 2 of the Care Standards Act 2000.]

AMENDMENTS

1. Regulation 5(10) of the Jobseekers Amendment Regulations (October 7, 1996).
2. Regulation 3(5)(a) of the Miscellaneous Amendments (No. 2) Regulations 2003 (November 5, 2003).
3. Regulation 3(5)(b)(i) of the Miscellaneous Amendments (No. 2) Regulations 2003 (November 5, 2003).
4. Regulation 3(5)(b)(ii) of the Miscellaneous Amendments (No. 2) Regulations 2003 (November 5, 2003).
5. Regulation 3(5)(c) of the Miscellaneous Amendments (No. 2) Regulations 2003 (November 5, 2003).
6. Regulation 3(5)(d) of the Miscellaneous Amendments (No. 2) Regulations 2003 (November 5, 2003).
7. Regulation 3(5)(e) of the Miscellaneous Amendments (No. 2) Regulations 2003 (November 5, 2003).

DEFINITIONS

"applicable amount": see reg.1(2).     **4.112**
"direction": see reg.1(2).
"in force": see reg.1(3).
"in operation": see reg.1(3).
"the Jobseeker's Allowance Regulations": see reg.1(2).
"parent concerned": see reg.1(2).
"suspended": see reg.1(3).
[Regulation 40A was revoked by reg.9 of the Miscellaneous Amendments (No. 2) Regulations 1996 from January 13, 1997, subject to reg.16(3) of those Regulations.]

## [¹Termination of reduced benefit direction

**41.** A reduced benefit direction shall cease to be in force—     **4.113**
  (a) where a parent with care, with respect to whom such a direction is in force, complies with the obligations imposed by section 6 of the Act;
  (b) upon an application made for the purpose where the Secretary of State is satisfied that a parent with care, with respect to whom such a direction is in force, should not be required to comply with the obligations imposed by section 6 of the Act;
  (c) where a qualifying child of a parent with respect to whom a direction is in force applies for a maintenance assessment to be made with respect to him under section 7 of the Act and an assessment is made in response to that application in respect of all of the qualifying children in relation to whom the parent concerned failed to comply with the obligations imposed by section 6 of the Act; or
  (d) where—
    (i) an absent parent applies for a maintenance assessment to be made under section 4 of the Act with respect to all of his qualifying children in relation to whom the other parent of those children is a person with care;
    (ii) a direction is in force with respect to that other parent following her failure to comply with the obligations imposed by section 6 of the Act in relation to those qualifying children; and

841

(iii) an assessment is made in response to that application by the absent parent for a maintenance assessment.]

AMENDMENT

1. Regulation 28 of the Miscellaneous Amendments (No. 2) Regulations 1999 (June 1, 1999).

[Regulations 42 to 46 were revoked by reg.28 of the Miscellaneous Amendments (No. 2) Regulations 1999 with effect from June 1, 1999.]

## Reduced benefit directions where there is an additional qualifying child

4.114    **47.**—(1) Where a direction is in operation or would be in operation but for the provisions of regulation 40 [¹or 40ZA] and [⁶the Secretary of State] gives a further direction with respect to the same parent on account of that parent failing to comply with the obligations imposed by section 6 of the Act in relation to an additional qualifying child of whom she is a person with care, the earlier direction shall cease to be in force [⁷. . .].

(2) Where a further direction comes into operation in a case falling within paragraph (1), the provisions of regulation 36 shall apply to it.

[²(3) Where—

(a) a direction ("the earlier direction") has ceased to be in force by virtue of regulation 38(2); and

(b) [⁸the Secretary of State] gives a direction ("the further direction") with respect to the same parent on account of that parent's failure to comply with the obligations imposed by section 6 of the Act in relation to an individual qualifying child,

as long as that further direction remains in force, no additional direction shall be brought into force with respect to that parent on account of her failure to comply with the obligations imposed by section 6 of the Act in relation to one or more children in relation to whom the earlier direction was given.]

(4) Where a case falls within paragraph (1) or (3) and the further direction, but for the provisions of this paragraph would cease to be in force by virtue of the provisions of regulation 41 or 42, but the earlier direction would not have ceased to be in force by virtue of the provisions of those regulations, the later direction shall continue in force for a period ("the extended period") calculated in accordance with the provisions of paragraph (5) and the reduction of relevant benefit [³for the extended period shall be determined in accordance with regulation 36(2).]

(5) The extended period for the purposes of paragraph (4) shall be [⁴(156–F–S) weeks]

where—

F is the number of weeks for which the earlier direction was in operation; and

S is the number of weeks for which the later direction has been in operation.

[⁵. . .]

(8) In this regulation "an additional qualifying child" means a qualifying child of whom the parent concerned is a person with care and who was

either not such a qualifying child at the time the earlier direction was given or had not been born at the time the earlier direction was given.

AMENDMENTS

1. Regulation 5(11) of the Jobseekers Amendment Regulations (October 7, 1996).
2. Regulation 17(2) of the Miscellaneous Amendments Regulations 1996 (October 7, 1996).
3. Regulation 17(3) of the Miscellaneous Amendments Regulations 1996 (October 7, 1996).
4. Regulation 17(4) of the Miscellaneous Amendments Regulations 1996 (October 7, 1996).
5. Regulation 17(5) of the Miscellaneous Amendments Regulations 1996 (October 7, 1996).
6. Regulation 29(a)(i) of the Miscellaneous Amendments (No. 2) Regulations 1999 (June 1, 1999).
7. Regulation 29(a)(ii) of the Miscellaneous Amendments (No. 2) Regulations 1999 (June 1, 1999).
8. Regulation 29(b) of the Miscellaneous Amendments (No. 2) Regulations 1999 (June 1, 1999).

DEFINITIONS

"the Act": see reg.1(2)  **4.115**
"benefit week": see reg.1(2).
"direction": see reg.1(2).
"in force": see reg.1(3).
"in operation": see reg.1(3).
"obligation imposed by section 6 of the Act": see reg.1(2).
"parent concerned": see reg.1(2).
"person with care": see reg.1(5).
"relevant benefit": see reg.1(2).

## Suspension and termination of a reduced benefit direction where the sole qualifying child ceases to be a child or where the parent concerned ceases to be a person with care

**48.**—(1) Where, whilst a direction is in operation—  **4.116**
(a) there is, in relation to that direction, only one qualifying child, and that child ceases to be a child within the meaning of the Act; or
(b) the parent concerned ceases to be a person with care,
the direction shall be suspended from the last day of the benefit week during the course of which the child ceases to be a child within the meaning of the Act, or the parent concerned ceases to be a person with care, as the case may be.

(2) Where, under the provisions of paragraph (1), a direction has been suspended for a period of 52 weeks and no relevant benefit is payable at that time, it shall cease to be in force.

(3) If during the period specified in paragraph (1) the former child again becomes a child within the meaning of the Act or the parent concerned again becomes a person with care and relevant benefit is payable to or in respect of that parent, a reduction in the amount of that benefit

shall be made in accordance with the provisions of paragraphs (3) to (7) of regulation 38.

DEFINITIONS

**4.117**    "the Act": see reg.1(2).
"direction": see reg.1(2).
"in operation": see reg.1(3).
"parent concerned"; see reg.1(2).
"person with care": see reg.1(5).
"relevant benefit": see reg.1(2).
"suspended": see reg.1(3).

## [¹Notice of termination of a reduced benefit direction

**4.118**    **49.** Where a direction ceases to be in force under the provisions of regulations 41, 47 or 48, or is suspended under the provisions of regulation 48, the Secretary of State shall serve notice of such a termination or suspension, as the case may be, on the parent concerned and shall specify the date on which the direction ceases to be in force or is suspended, as the case may be.]

AMENDMENT

1. Regulation 30 of the Miscellaneous Amendments (No. 2) Regulations 1999 (June 1, 1999).

DEFINITIONS

**4.119**    "direction": see reg.1(2).
"in force": see reg.1(3)
"parent concerned": see reg.1(2).
"suspended": see reg.1(3).
[Regulation 49A was revoked by reg.9 of the Miscellaneous Amendments (No. 2) Regulations 1996 from January 13, 1997, subject to reg.16(3) of those Regulations.]

## Rounding provisions

**4.120**    **50.** Where any calculation made under this Part of these Regulations results in a fraction of a penny, that fraction shall be treated as a penny if it exceeds one half, and shall otherwise be disregarded.

PART X

MISCELLANEOUS PROVISIONS

## Persons who are not persons with care

**4.121**    **51.**—(1) For the purposes of the Act the following categories of person shall not be persons with care—
  (a) a local authority;
  (b) a person with whom a child who is looked after by a local authority
     is placed by that authority under the provisions of the Children Act

1989, [¹except where that person is a parent of such a child and the local authority allow the child to live with that parent under section 23(5) of that Act;]

(c) in Scotland, a person with whom a child is boarded out by a local authority under the provisions of section 21 of the Social Work (Scotland) Act 1968.

(2) In paragraph (1) above—

"local authority" means, in relation to England and Wales, the council of a county, a metropolitan district, a London Borough or the Common Council of the City of London and, in relation to Scotland, a regional council or an islands council;

"a child who is looked after by a local authority" has the same meaning as in section 22 of the Children Act 1989.

AMENDMENT

1. Regulation 15 of the Amendment Regulations (April 5, 1993).

DEFINITIONS

"the Act": see reg.1(2).                                                      4.122
"person with care": see reg.1(5).

[Regulations 52 was revoked by reg.31 of the Miscellaneous Amendments (No. 2) Regulations 1999 with effect from June 1, 1999.]

## Authorisation of representative

**53.**—(1) A person may authorise a representative, whether or not legal-    4.123
ly qualified, to receive notices and other documents on his behalf and to act on his behalf in relation to the making of applications and the supply of information under any provision of the Act or these Regulations.

(2) Where a person has authorised a representative for the purposes of paragraph (1) who is not legally qualified, he shall confirm that authorisation in writing to the Secretary of State.

DEFINITION

"the Act": see reg.1(2).                                                      4.124

[Regulations 52 to 57 were revoked by reg.31 the Miscellaneous Amendments (No. 2) Regulations 1999 with effect from June 1, 1999.]

SCHEDULE 1                                  **Regulation 1(4)**

MEANING OF "CHILD" FOR THE PURPOSES OF THE ACT

## Persons of 16 or 17 years of age who are not in full-time non-advanced education

**1.**—(1) Subject to subparagraph (3), the conditions which must be          4.125
satisfied for a person to be a child within section 55(1)(c) of the Act are—

(a) The person is registered for work or for training under [³work-based training for young people or, in Scotland, Skillseekers training] with—

    (i)  the Department of Employment;

   (ii)  the Ministry of Defence;

  (iii)  in England and Wales, a local education authority within the meaning of the Education Acts 1944 to 1992;

  (iv)  in Scotland, an education authority within the meaning of section 135(1) of the Education (Scotland) Act 1980 (interpretation); or

   (v)  for the purposes of applying Council Regulation (EEC) No. 1408/71, any corresponding body in another Member State;

  (b)  the person is not engaged in remunerative work, other than work of a temporary nature that is due to cease before the end of the extension period which applies in the case of that person;

  (c)  the extension period which applies in the case of that person has not expired; and

  (d)  immediately before the extension period begins, the person is a child for the purposes of the Act without regard to this paragraph.

(2) For the purposes of paragraphs (b), (c) and (d) of sub-paragraph (1), the extension period—

  (a)  begins on the first day of the week in which the person would no longer be a child for the purposes of the Act but for this paragraph; and

  (b)  where a person ceases to fall within section 55(1)(a) of the Act or within paragraph 5—

    (i)  on or after the first Monday in September, but before the first Monday in January of the following year, ends on the last day of the week which falls immediately before the week which includes the first Monday in January in that year;

   (ii)  on or after the first Monday in January but before the Monday following Easter Monday in that year, ends on the last day of the week which falls 12 weeks after the week which includes the first Monday in January in that year;

  (iii)  at any other time of the year, ends on the last day of the week which falls 12 weeks after the week which includes the Monday following Easter Monday in that year.

(3) A person shall not be a child for the purposes of the Act under this paragraph if—

  (a)  he is engaged in training under [³work-based training for young people or, in Scotland, Skillseekers training]; or

  (b)  he is entitled to income support [²or income-based jobseeker's allowance].

### Meaning of "advanced education" for the purposes of section 55 of the Act

4.126    **2.** For the purposes of section 55 of the Act "advanced education" means education of the following description—

  (a)  a course in preparation for a degree, a Diploma of Higher Education, a higher national diploma, a higher national diploma or higher national certificate of the Business and [¹Technology] Education Council or the Scottish Vocational Education Council or a teaching qualification; or

(b) any other course which is of a standard above that of an ordinary national diploma, a national diploma or national certificate of the Business and [¹Technology] Education Council or the Scottish Vocational Education Council, the advanced level of the General Certificate of Education, a Scottish certificate of education (higher level) or a Scottish certificate of sixth year studies.

## Circumstances in which education is to be treated as full-time education

**3.** For the purposes of section 55 of the Act education shall be treated as being full-time if it is received by a person attending a course of education at a recognised educational establishment and the time spent receiving instruction or tuition, undertaking supervised study, examination or practical work or taking part in any exercise, experiment or project for which provision is made in the curriculum of the course, exceeds 12 hours per week, so however that in calculating the time spent in pursuit of the course, no account shall be taken of time occupied by meal breaks or spent on unsupervised study, whether undertaken on or off the premises of the educational establishment.

**4.127**

## Interruption of full-time education

**4.**—(1) Subject to sub-paragraph (2), in determining whether a person falls within section 55(l)(b) of the Act no account shall be taken of a period (whether beginning before or after the person concerned attains age 16) of up to 6 months of any interruption to the extent to which it is accepted that the interruption is attributable to a cause which is reasonable in the particular circumstances of the case; and where the interruption or its continuance is attributable to the illness or disability of mind or body of the person concerned, the period of 6 months may be extended for such further period as [⁴the Secretary of State] considers reasonable in the particular circumstances of the case.

**4.128**

(2) The provisions of subparagraph (1) shall not apply to any period of interruption of a person's full-time education which is likely to be followed immediately or which is followed immediately by a period during which—
(a) provision is made for the training of that person, and for an allowance to be payable to that person, under [³work-based training for young people or, in Scotland, Skillseekers training]; or
(b) he is receiving education by virtue of his employment or of any office held by him.

## Circumstances in which a person who has ceased to receive full-time education is to be treated as continuing to fall within section 55(1) of the Act

**5.**—(1) Subject to subparagraphs (2) and (5), a person who has ceased to receive full-time education (which is not advanced education) shall, if—
(a) he is under the age of 16 when he so ceases, from the date on which he attains that age; or

**4.129**

(b) he is 16 or over when he so ceases, from the date on which he so ceases, be treated as continuing to fall within section 55(1) of the Act up to and including the week including the terminal date or if he attains the age of 19 on or before that date up to and including the week including the last Monday before he attains that age.

(2) In the case of a person specified in sub-paragraph (l)(a) or (b) who had not attained the upper limit of compulsory school age when he ceased to receive full-time education, the terminal date in his case shall be that specified in paragraph (a), (b) or (c) of subparagraph (3), whichever next follows the date on which he would have attained that age.

(3) In this paragraph the "terminal date" means—
(a) the first Monday in January; or
(b) the Monday following Easter Monday; or
(c) the first Monday in September, whichever first occurs after the date on which the person's said education ceased.

(4) In this paragraph "compulsory school age" means—
(a) in England and Wales, compulsory school age as determined in accordance with section 9 of the Education Act 1962;
(b) in Scotland, school age as determined in accordance with sections 31 and 33 of the Education (Scotland) Act 1980.

(5) A person shall not be treated as continuing to fall within section 55(1) of the Act under this paragraph if he is engaged in remunerative work, other than work of a temporary nature that is due to cease before the terminal date.

(6) Subject to subparagraphs (5) and (8), a person whose name was entered as a candidate for any external examination in connection with full-time education (which is not advanced education), which he was receiving at that time, shall so long as his name continued to be so entered before ceasing to receive such education be treated as continuing to fall within section 55(1) of the Act for any week in the period specified in subparagraph (7).

(7) Subject to subparagraph (8), the period specified for the purposes of subparagraph (6) is the period beginning with the date when that person ceased to receive such education ending with—
(a) whichever of the dates in sub-paragraph (3) first occurs after the conclusion of the examination (or the last of them, if there are more than one); or
(b) the expiry of the week which includes the last Monday before his 19th birthday, whichever is the earlier.

(8) The period specified in subparagraph (7) shall, in the case of a person who has not attained the age of 16 when he so ceased, begin with the date on which he attained that age.

**Interpretation**

4.130    **6.** In this Schedule—
"Education Acts 1944 to 1992" has the meaning prescribed in section 94(2) of the Further and Higher Education Act 1992;
"remunerative work" means work of not less than 24 hours a week—
(a) in respect of which payment is made; or

(b) which is done in expectation of payment;

"week" means a period of 7 days beginning with a Monday;

"[³work-based training for young people or, in Scotland, Skillseekers training]" means—

(a) arrangements made under section 2 of the Employment and Training Act 1973 (functions of the Secretary of State) or section 2 of the Enterprise and New Towns (Scotland) Act 1990;

(b) arrangements made by the Secretary of State for persons enlisted in Her Majesty's forces for any special term of service specified in regulations made under section 2 of the Armed Forces Act 1966 (power of Defence Council to make regulations as to engagement of persons in regular forces); or

(c) for the purposes of the application of Council Regulation (EEC) No. 1408/71, any corresponding provisions operated in another Member State,

for purposes which include the training of persons who, at the beginning of their training, are under the age of 18.

AMENDMENTS

1. Regulation 17 of the Amendment Regulations (April 5, 1993).

2. Regulation 5(12) of the Jobseekers Amendment Regulations (October 7, 1996).

3. Regulation 5 of the Miscellaneous Amendments Regulations 1999 (April 6, 1999).

4. Regulation 32 of the Miscellaneous Amendments (No. 2) Regulations 1999 (June 1, 1999).

DEFINITION

"the Act": see reg.1(2).                                                      4.131

SCHEDULE 2                                    **Regulation 4**

MULTIPLE APPLICATIONS

## No maintenance assessment in force: more than one application for a maintenance assessment by the same person under section 4 or 6 or under sections 4 and 6 of the Act

**1.**—(1) Where a person makes an effective application for a mainte-    4.132
nance assessment under section 4 or 6 of the Act and, before that assessment is made, makes a subsequent effective application under that section with respect to the same absent parent or person with care, as the case may be, those applications shall be treated as a single application.

(2) Where a parent with care makes an effective application for a maintenance assessment—

(a) under section 4 of the Act; or

(b) under section 6 of the Act,

and, before that assessment is made, makes a subsequent effective application—

849

(c) in a case falling within paragraph (a), under section 6 of the Act; or

(d) in a case falling within paragraph (b), under section 4 of the Act,

with respect to the same absent parent, those applications shall, if the parent with care does not cease to fall within section 6(1) of the Act, be treated as a single application under section 6 of the Act, and shall otherwise be treated as a single application under section 4 of the Act.

### No maintenance assessment in force: more than one application by a child under section 7 of the Act

4.133

**2.** Where a child makes an effective application for a maintenance assessment under section 7 of the Act and, before that assessment is made, makes a subsequent effective application under that section with respect to the same person with care and absent parent, both applications shall be treated as a single application for a maintenance assessment.

### No maintenance assessment in force: applications by different persons for a maintenance assessment

4.134

**3.**—(1) Where the Secretary of State receives more than one effective application for a maintenance assessment with respect to the same person with care and absent parent, he shall[⁵, if no maintenance assessment has been made in relation to any of the applications,] determine which application he shall proceed with in accordance with subparagraphs (2) to (11).

(2) Where there is an application by a person with care under section 4 or 6 of the Act and an application by an absent parent under section 4 of the Act, [⁶the Secretary of State] shall proceed with the application of the person with care.

(3) Where there is an application for a maintenance assessment by a qualifying child under section 7 of the Act and a subsequent application is made with respect to that child by a person who is, with respect to that child, a person with care or an absent parent, [⁶the Secretary of State] shall proceed with the application of that person with care or absent parent, as the case may be.

(4) Where, in a case falling within subparagraph (3), there is more than one subsequent application, [⁶the Secretary of State] shall apply the provisions of sub-paragraph (2), (8), (9) or (11), as is appropriate in the circumstances of the case, to determine which application he shall proceed with.

(5) Where there is an application for a maintenance assessment by more than one qualifying child under section 7 of the Act in relation to the same person with care and absent parent, [⁶the Secretary of State] shall proceed with the application of the elder or, as the case may be, eldest of the qualifying children.

(6) Where a case is to be treated as a special case for the purposes of the Act under regulation 19 of the Maintenance Assessments and Special Cases Regulations (both parents are absent) and an effective application is received from each absent parent, [⁶the Secretary of State] shall proceed with both applications, treating them as a single application for a maintenance assessment.

(7) Where, under the provisions of regulation 20 of the Maintenance Assessments and Special Cases Regulations (persons treated as absent parents), two persons are to be treated as absent parents and an effective application is received from each such person, [⁶the Secretary of State] proceed with both applications, treating them as a single application for a maintenance assessment.

(8) Where there is an application under section 6 of the Act by a parent with care and an application under section 4 of the Act by another person with care who has parental responsibility for (or, in Scotland, parental rights over) the qualifying child or qualifying children with respect to whom the application under section 6 of the Act was made, [⁶the Secretary of State] shall proceed with the application under section 6 of the Act by the parent with care.

(9) Where—

(a) more than one person with care makes an application for a maintenance assessment under section 4 of the Act in respect of the same qualifying child or qualifying children (whether or not any of those applications is also in respect of other qualifying children);

(b) each such person has parental responsibility for (or, in Scotland, parental rights over) that child or children; and

(c) under the provisions of regulation 20 of the Maintenance Assessments and Special Cases Regulations one of those persons is to be treated as an absent parent,

[⁶the Secretary of State] shall proceed with the application of the person who does not fall to be treated as an absent parent under the provisions of regulation 20 of those Regulations.

(10) Where, in a case falling within sub-paragraph (9), there is more than one person who does not fall to be treated as an absent parent under the provisions of regulation 20 of those Regulations, [⁶the Secretary of State] shall apply the provisions of paragraph (11) to determine which application he shall proceed with.

(11) Where—

(a) more than one person with care makes an application for a maintenance assessment under section 4 of the Act in respect of the same qualifying child or qualifying children (whether or not any of those applications is also in respect of other qualifying children); and

(b) either—

(i) none of those persons has parental responsibility for (or, in Scotland, parental rights over) that child or children; or

(ii) the case falls within subparagraph (9)(b) but the [⁶Secretary of State] has not been able to determine which application he is to proceed with under the provisions of subparagraph (9),

[⁶the Secretary of State] shall proceed with the application of the principal provider of day to day care, as determined in accordance with subparagraph (12).

(12) Where—

(a) the applications are in respect of one qualifying child, the application of that person with care with whom the child spends the greater or, as the case may be, the greatest proportion of his time;

(b) the applications are in respect of more than one qualifying child, the application of that person with care with whom the children spend the greater or, as the case may be, the greatest proportion of their time, taking account of the time each qualifying child spends with each of the persons with care in question;

(c) [⁶the Secretary of State] cannot determine which application he is to proceed with under paragraph (a) or (b), and child benefit is paid in respect of the qualifying child or qualifying children to one but not any other of the applicants, the application of the applicant to whom child benefit is paid;

(d) [⁶the Secretary of State] cannot determine which application he is to proceed with under paragraph (a), (b) or (c), the application of that applicant who in the opinion of the [⁶Secretary of State] is the principal provider of day to day care for the child or children in question.

(13) Subject to subparagraph (14), where, in any case falling within subparagraphs (2) to (11), the applications are not in respect of identical qualifying children, the application that the [⁶Secretary of State] is to proceed with as determined by those paragraphs shall be treated as an application with respect to all of the qualifying children with respect to whom the applications were made.

(14) Where the [⁶Secretary of State] is satisfied that the same person with care does not provide the principal day to day care for all of the qualifying children with respect to whom an assessment would but for the provisions of this paragraph be made under subparagraph (13), he shall make separate assessments in relation to each person with care providing such principal day to day care.

### Maintenance assessment in force: subsequent application for a maintenance assessment with respect to the same persons

4.135    **4.** Where a maintenance assessment is in force and a subsequent application is made under the same section of the Act for an assessment with respect to the same person with care, absent parent, and qualifying child or qualifying children as those with respect to whom the assessment in force has been made, that application shall not be proceeded with [⁷. . .].

### Maintenance assessment in force: subsequent application for a maintenance assessment under section 6 of the Act

4.136    **5.** Where a maintenance assessment is in force following an application under section 4 or 7 of the Act and the person with care makes an application under section 6 of the Act, any maintenance assessment made in response to that application shall replace the assessment currently in force.

### Maintenance assessment in force: subsequent application for a maintenance assessment in respect of additional children

4.137    **6.**—[²(1) Where there is in force a maintenance assessment made in response to an application under section 4 of the Act by an absent parent or person with care and that assessment is not in respect of all of the absent parent's children who are in the care of the person with care with respect to whom that assessment was made—

(a) if that absent parent or that person with care makes an application under section 4 of the Act with respect to the children in respect of whom the assessment currently in force was made and the additional child or one or more of the additional children in the care of that person with care who are children of that absent parent, an assessment made in response to that application shall replace the assessment currently in force;

(b) if that absent parent or that person with care makes an application under section 4 of the Act in respect of an additional qualifying child or additional qualifying children of that absent parent in the care of that person with care, that application shall be treated as an application for a maintenance assessment in respect of all the qualifying children concerned and the assessment made shall replace the assessment currently in force.]

(3) Where a maintenance assessment made in response to an application by a child under section 7 of the Act is in force and the person with care [³or the absent parent] application for a maintenance assessment under section 4 of the Act in respect of [¹one or more [⁴children of that absent parent who are in the care of that person with care], that application shall be treated as an application for a maintenance with respect to all the children of the absent parent who are in her care, and] that assessment shall replace the assessment currently in force.

AMENDMENTS

1. Regulation 18 of the Amendment Regulations (April 5, 1993).

2. Regulation 41(2) of Miscellaneous Amendments Regulations 1998 (January 19, 1998).

3. Regulation 41(3)(a) of Miscellaneous Amendments Regulations 1998 (January 19, 1998).

4. Regulation 41(3)(b) of Miscellaneous Amendments Regulations 1998 (January 19, 1998).

5. Regulation 33(a) of the Miscellaneous Amendments (No. 2) Regulations 1999 (June 1, 1999).

6. Regulation 33(b) of the Miscellaneous Amendments (No. 2) Regulations 1999 (June 1, 1999).

7. Regulation 33(b) of the Miscellaneous Amendments (No. 2) Regulations 1999 (June 1, 1999).

DEFINITIONS

"absent parent": see reg.1(5).                                    **4.138**
"the Act": see reg.1(2).
"day to day care": see reg.1(2).
"effective application": see reg.1(2).
"parent with care": see reg.1(2).
"person with care": see reg.1(5).

**The Child Support (Maintenance Assessments and Special Cases) Regulations 1992**

(SI 1992/1815)

*Made by the Secretary of State for Social Security under sections 42, 43, 51, 52(4) and 54 of, and paragraphs 1, 2 and 4 to 9 of Schedule 1 to, the Child Support Act 1991 and all other powers enabling him in that behalf*

ARRANGEMENT OF REGULATIONS

PART I

24.　Persons with part-time care—not including a person treated as an absent parent.
25.　Care provided in part by a local authority.
26.　Cases where child support maintenance is not payable.
27.　Child who is a boarder or an in-patient.
27A.　Child who is allowed to live with his parent under section 23(5) of the Children Act 1989.
28.　Amount payable where absent parent is in receipt of income support or other prescribed benefit.

SCHEDULES

Schedule 1—Calculation of N and M.
Schedule 2—Amounts to be disregarded when calculating or estimating N and M.
Schedule 3—Eligible housing costs.
Schedule 3A—Amount to be allowed in respect of transfers of property.
Schedule 3B—Amount to be allowed in respect of travelling costs.
Schedule 4—Cases where child support maintenance is not to be payable.
Schedule 5—Provisions applying to cases to which section 43 of the Act and regulation 28 apply.

PART 1

GENERAL

**Citation, commencement and interpretation**

1.—(1) These Regulations may be cited as the Child Support (Maintenance Assessments and Special Cases) Regulations 1992 and shall come into force on 5th April 1993.　　　　　　　　　　　　　　4.141
(2) In these Regulations unless the context otherwise requires—
"the Act" means the Child Support Act 1991;
[48"care home" has the meaning assigned to it by section 3 of the Care Standards Act 2000;]
[48"care home service" has the meaning assigned to it by section 2(3) of the Regulation of Care (Scotland) Act 2001;]
[42"child tax credit" means a child tax credit undre section 8 of the Tax Credits Act 2002;]
[19"Child Benefit Rates Regulations" means the Child Benefit and Social Security (Fixing and Adjustment of Rates) Regulations 1976;]
"claimant" means a claimant for income support;
"Contributions and Benefits Act" means the Social Security Contributions and Benefits Act 1992;
[25"Contributions and Benefits (Northern Ireland) Act" means the Social Security Contributions and Benefits (Northern Ireland) Act 1992;]
"council tax benefit" has the same meaning as in the Local Government Finance Act 1992;

[¹"couple" means a married or unmarried couple;]
"course of advanced education" means—
(a) a full-time course leading to a postgraduate degree or comparable qualification, a first degree or comparable qualification, a Diploma of Higher Education, a higher national diploma, a higher national diploma or higher national certificate of the Business and [²Technology] Education Council or the Scottish Vocational Education Council or a teaching qualification; or
(b) any other full-time course which is a course of a standard above that of an ordinary national diploma, a national diploma or national certificate of the Business and [²Technology] Education Council or the Scottish Vocational Education Council, the advanced level of the General Certificate of Education, a Scottish certificate of education (higher level) or a Scottish certificate of sixth year studies;
"covenant income" means the gross income payable to a student under a Deed of Covenant by a parent;
"day" includes any part of a day;
[⁷"day to day care" means—
(a) care of not less than 104 nights in total during the 12 month period ending with the relevant week; or
(b) where, in the opinion of the [³⁵Secretary of State, a period other than 12 months] is more representative of the current arrangements for the care of the child in question, care during that period of not less in total than the number of nights which bears the same ratio to 104 nights as that period bears to 12 months,
and for the purpose of this definition—
  (i) where a child is a boarder at a boarding school, or is an inpatient in a hospital, the person who, but for those circumstances, would otherwise provide day to day care of the child shall be treated as providing day to day care during the periods in question;]
  [¹⁴(ii) in relation to an application for child support maintenance, "relevant week" shall have the meaning ascribed to it in head (ii) of sub-paragraph (a) of the definition of "relevant week" in this paragraph;]
  [³⁶(iii) in a case where notification is given under regulation 24 of the Maintenance Assessment Procedure Regulations to the relevant persons on different dates, "relevant week" means the period of seven days immediately preceding the date of the latest notification;]
[²²"Departure Direction and Consequential Amendments Regulations" means the Child Support Departure Direction and Consequential Amendments Regulations 1996;]
[⁴³ . . .]
"earnings" has the meaning assigned to it by paragraph [³⁷1, 2A or 3], as the case may be, of Schedule 1;
[²⁰"earnings top-up" means the allowance paid by the Secretary of State under the rules specified in the Earnings Top-up Scheme;]
[²⁰"The Earnings Top-up Scheme" means the Earnings Top-up Scheme 1996;]

"effective date" means the date on which a maintenance assessment takes effect for the purposes of the Act;

"eligible housing costs" shall be construed in accordance with Schedule 3;

"employed earner" has the same meaning as in section 2(l)(a) of the Contributions and Benefits Act [30except that it shall include a person gainfully employed in Northern Ireland],

[21"family" means—

(a) a married or unmarried couple including the members of a polygamous marriage);

(b) a married or unmarried couple (including the members of a polygamous marriage) and any child or children living with them for whom at least one member of that couple has day to day care;

(c) where a person who is not a member of a married or unmarried couple has day to day care of any child or children, that person and any such child or children;

and for the purposes of this definition a person shall not be treated as having day to day care of a child who is a member of that person's household where the child in question is being looked after by a local authority within the meaning of section 22 of the Children Act 1989 or, in Scotland, where the child is boarded out with that person by a local authority under the provisions of section 21 of the Social Work (Scotland) Act 1968;]

[43. . .]

"grant" means any kind of educational grant or award and includes any scholarship, exhibition, allowance or bursary but does not include a payment made under section 100 of the Education Act 1944 or section 73 of the Education (Scotland) Act 1980;

"grant contribution" means any amount which a Minister of the Crown or an education authority treats as properly payable by another person when assessing the amount of a student's grant and by which that amount is, as a consequence, reduced;

"home" means—

(a) the dwelling in which a person and any family of his normally live; or
(b) if he or they normally live in more than one home, the principal home of that person and any family of his,

4.142

and for the purpose of determining the principal home in which a person normally lives no regard shall be had to residence in [45a care home or an independent hospital or to the provision of a care home service or an independent health care service] during a period which does not exceed 52 weeks or, where it appears to the [39Secretary of State] that the person will return to his principal home after that period has expired, such longer period as [40the Secretary of State] considers reasonable to allow for the return of that person to that home;

"housing benefit" has the same meaning as in section 130 of the Contributions and Benefits Act;

"Housing Benefit Regulations" means the Housing Benefit (General) Regulations 1987;

[49"independent health care service" has the meaning assigned to it by section 2(5)(a) and (b) of Tthe Regulation of Care (Scotland) Act 2001;]

[49"independent hospital" has the meaning assigned to it by section 2 of the Care Standards Act 2000;]

"Income Support Regulations" means the Income Support (General) Regulations 1987;

[3"Independent Living (1993) Fund" means the charitable trust of that name established by a deed made between the Secretary of State for Social Security of the one part and Robin Glover Wendt and John Fletcher Shepherd of the other part;]

[3"Independent Living (Extension) Fund" means the charitable trust of that name established by a deed made between the Secretary of State for Social Security of the one part and Robin Glover Wendt and John Fletcher Shepherd of the other part;]

[18"the Jobseekers Act" means the Jobseekers Act 1996;]

"Maintenance Assessment Procedure Regulations" means the Child Support (Maintenance Assessment Procedure) Regulations 1992;

"married couple" means a man and a woman who are married to each other and are members of the same household;

"non-dependant" means a person who is a non-dependant for the purposes of either—

(a) regulation 3 of the Income Support Regulations; or

(b) regulation 3 of the Housing Benefit Regulations,

or who would be a non-dependant for those purposes if another member of the household in which he is living were entitled to income support or housing benefit as the case may be;

[46. . .]

"occupational pension scheme" has the same meaning as in [31section 1 of the Pension Schemes Act 1993];

"ordinary clothing or footwear" means clothing or footwear for normal daily use, but does not include school uniforms, or clothing or footwear used solely for sporting activities;

"parent with care" means a person who, in respect of the same child or children, is both a parent and a person with care;

"partner" means—

(a) in relation to a member of a married or unmarried couple who are living together, the other member of that couple;

(b) in relation to a member of a polygamous marriage, any other member of that marriage with whom he lives;

"patient" means a person (other than a person who is serving a sentence of imprisonment or detention in a young offender institution within the meaning of the Criminal Justice Act 1982 as amended by the Criminal Justice Act 1988) who is regarded as receiving free in-patient treatment within the meaning of the Social Security (Hospital In-Patients) Regulations 1975;

"person" does not include a local authority;

"personal pension scheme" has the same meaning as in [26section 1 of the Pensions Schemes Act 1993] and, in the case of a self-employed earner, includes a scheme approved by the Inland Revenue under Chapter IV of Part XIV of the Income and Corporation Taxes Act 1988;

"polygamous marriage" means any marriage during the subsistence of which a party to it is married to more than one person and in respect of which any ceremony of marriage took place under the law of a country which at the time of that ceremony permitted polygamy;

"prisoner" means a person who is detained in custody pending trial or sentence upon conviction or under a sentence imposed by a court other than a person whose detention is under the Mental Health Act 1983 or the Mental Health (Scotland) Act 1984;

[27"profit-related pay" means any payment by an employer calculated by reference to actual or anticipated profits;]

[8"qualifying transfer" has the meaning assigned to it in Schedule 3A;]

"relevant child" means a child of an absent parent or a parent with care who is a member of the same family as that parent;

"relevant Schedule" means Schedule 2 to the Income Support Regulations (income support applicable amounts);

[41"relevant week" means—

(a) in relation to an application for child support maintenance—

    (i) in the case of the applicant, the period of seven days immediately preceding the date on which the appropriate maintenance assessment application form (being an effective application within the meaning of regulation 2(4) of the Maintenance Assessment Procedure Regulations) is submitted to the Secretary of State;

    (ii) in the case of a person to whom a maintenance assessment enquiry form is given or sent as the result of such an application, the period of seven days immediately preceding the date on which that form is given or sent to him or, as the case may be, the date on which it is treated as having been given or sent to him under regulation 1(6)(b) of the Maintenance Assessment Procedure Regulations;

(b) where a decision ("the original decision") is to be—

    (i) revised under section 16 of the Act; or

    (ii) superseded by a decision under section 17 of the Act on the basis that the original decision was made in ignorance of, or was based upon a mistake as to some material fact or was erroneous in point of law,

the period of seven days which was the relevant week for the purposes of the original decision;

(c) where a decision ("the original decision") is to be superseded by a decision under section 17 of the Act—

    (i) on an application made for the purpose on the basis that a material change of circumstances has occurred since the original decision was made, the period of seven days immediately preceding the date on which that application was made;

    (ii) subject to paragraph (b), in a case where a relevant person is given notice under regulation 24 of the Maintenance Assessment Procedure Regulations, the period of seven days immediately preceding the date of that notification;

except that where, under paragraph 15 of Schedule 1 to the Act, the Secretary of State makes separate maintenance assessments in respect of different periods in a particular case, because he is aware of one or more changes of circumstances which occurred after the date which is applicable

4.143

to that case under paragraph (a), (b) or (c) the relevant week for the purposes of each separate assessment made to take account of each such change of circumstances, shall be the period of seven days immediately preceding the date on which notification was given to the Secretary of State of the change of circumstances relevant to that separate maintenance assessment;]

[⁴⁷. . .]

"retirement annuity contract" means an annuity contract for the time being approved by the Board of Inland Revenue as having for its main object the provision of a life annuity in old age or the provision of an annuity for a partner or dependant and in respect of which relief from income tax may be given on any premium;

"self-employed earner" has the same meaning as in section 2(1 )(b) of the Contributions and Benefits Act ["except that it shall include a person gainfully employed in Northern Ireland otherwise than in employed earner's employment (whether or not he is also employed in such employment)];

[⁵⁰"state pension credit" means the social security benefit of that name payable under the State Pension Credit Act 2002;]

"student" means a person, other than a person in receipt of a training allowance, who is aged less than 19 and attending a full-time course of advanced education or who is aged 19 or over and attending a full-time course of study at an educational establishment; and for the purposes of this definition—

(a) a person who has started on such a course shall be treated as attending it throughout any period of term or vacation within it, until the last day of the course or such earlier date as he abandons it or is dismissed from it;

(b) a person on a sandwich course (within the meaning of paragraph 1(1) of Schedule 5 to the [^Education (Mandatory Awards) (No. 2) Regulations 1993] shall be treated as attending a full-time course of advanced education or, as the case may be, of study;

"student loan" means a loan which is made to a student pursuant to arrangements made under section 1 of the Education (Student Loans) Act 1990;

[⁵. . .]

"training allowance" has the same meaning as in regulation 2 of the Income Support Regulations;

"unmarried couple" means a man and a woman who are not married to each other but are living together as husband and wife;

"weekly council tax" means the annual amount of the council tax in question payable in respect of the year in which the effective date falls, divided by 52;

[⁴⁴"working tax credit" means a working tax credit under section 10 of the Tax Credits Act 2002;]

"year" means a period of 52 weeks;

[³⁸"work-based training for young people or, in Scotland, Skillseekers training]" means—

(a) arrangements made under section 2 of the Employment and Training Act 1973 or section 2 of the Enterprise and New Towns (Scotland) Act 1990;

(b) arrangements made by the Secretary of State for persons enlisted in Her Majesty's forces for any special term of service specified in regulations made under section 2 of the Armed Forces Act 1966 (power of Defence Council to make regulations as to engagement of persons in regular forces);

for purposes which include the training of persons who, at the beginning of their training, are under the age of 18.

[6(2A) Where any provision of these Regulations requires the income of a person to be estimated and that or any other provision of these Regulations requires that the amount of such estimated income is to be taken into account for any purpose after deducting from it a sum in respect of income tax or of primary Class 1 contributions under the Contributions and Benefits Act [28or, as the case may be, the Contributions and Benefits (Northern Ireland) Act] or of contributions paid by that person towards an occupational or personal pension scheme, then [10subject to subparagraph (e)]—

4.144

(a) the amount to be deducted in respect of income tax shall be calculated by applying to that income the rates of income tax applicable at the [11relevant week] less only the personal relief to which that person is entitled under Chapter 1 of Part VII of the Income and Corporations Taxes Act 1988 (personal relief); but if the period in respect of which that income is to be estimated is less than a year, the amount of the personal relief deductible under this subparagraph shall be calculated on a pro rata basis [34and the amount of income to which each tax rate applies shall be determined on the basis that the ratio of that amount to the full amount of the income to which each tax rate applies is the same as the ratio of the proportionate part of that personal relief to the full personal relief];

(b) the amount to be deducted in respect of Class 1 contributions under the Contributions and Benefits Act [28or, as the case may be, the Contributions and Benefits (Northern Ireland) Act] shall be calculated by applying to that income the appropriate primary percentage applicable in the relevant week; and

(c) the amount to be deducted in respect of contributions paid by that person towards an occupational [12. . .] pension scheme shall be one-half of the sums so [13paid; and

(d) the amount to be deducted in respect of contributions towards a personal pension scheme shall be one half of the contributions paid by that person or, where that scheme is intended partly to provide a capital sum to discharge a mortgage secured on that person's home, 37.5 per centum of those contributions;

(e) in relation to any bonus or commission which may be included in that person's income—

(i) the amount to be deducted in respect of income tax shall be calculated by applying to the gross amount of that bonus or commission the rate or rates of income tax applicable in the relevant week;

(ii) the amount to be deducted in respect of primary Class 1 contributions under the Contributions and Benefits Act or [28or, as the case may be, the Contributions and Benefits (Northern

Ireland) Act][29. . .] shall be calculated by applying to the gross amount of that bonus or commission the appropriate main primary percentage applicable in the relevant week [17but no deduction shall be made in respect of the portion (if any) of the bonus or commission which, if added to the estimated income, would cause such income to exceed the upper earnings limit for Class 1 contributions as provided for in section 5(1)(b) of the Contributions and Benefit Act] [28or, as the case may be, the Contributions and Benefits (Northern Ireland) Act]; and

(iii) the amount to be deducted in respect of contributions paid by that person in respect of the gross amount of that bonus or commission towards an occupational pension scheme shall be one half of any sum so paid.]

(3) In these Regulations, unless the context otherwise requires, a reference—

(a) to a numbered Part is to the Part of these Regulations bearing that number;

(b) to a numbered Schedule is to the Schedule to these Regulations bearing that number;

(c) to a numbered regulation is to the regulation in these Regulations bearing that number;

(d) in a regulation or Schedule to a numbered paragraph is to the paragraph in that regulation or Schedule bearing that number;

(e) in a paragraph to a lettered or numbered sub-paragraph is to the subpara-graph in that paragraph bearing that letter or number.

(4) [23These Regulations are subject to the provisions of Parts VIII and IX of the Departure Direction and Consequential Amendments Regulations and] the regulations in Part II and the provisions of the Schedules to these Regulations are subject to the regulations relating to special cases in Part III.

AMENDMENTS

1. Regulation 19(2)(b) of the Amendment Regulations (April 5, 1993).
2. Regulation 19(2)(a) of the Amendment Regulations (April 5, 1993).
3. Regulation 19(2)(c) of the Amendment Regulations (April 5, 1993).
4. Regulation 19(2)(d) of the Amendment Regulations (April 5, 1993).
5. Regulation 19(2)(e) of the Amendment Regulations (April 5, 1993).
6. Regulation 19(3) of the Amendment Regulations (April 5, 1993).
7. Regulation 41(2)(i) of the Amendment Regulations 1995 (April 18, 1995).
8. Regulation 41(2)(ii) of the Amendment Regulations 1995 (April 18, 1995).
9. Regulation 41(2)(iii) of the Amendment Regulations 1995 (April 18, 1995).
10. Regulation 41(3)(a) of the Amendment Regulations 1995 (April 18, 1995).
11. Regulation 41(3)(b) of the Amendment Regulations 1995 (April 18, 1995).
12. Regulation 41(3)(c) of the Amendment Regulations 1995 (April 18, 1995).
13. Regulation 41(3)(c) and (d) of the Amendment Regulations 1995 (April 18, 1995).
17. Regulation 40(3) of the Miscellaneous Amendments (No. 2) Regulations 1995 (January 22, 1996).
18. Regulation 6(2) of the Jobseekers Amendment Regulations (October 7, 1996).

19. Regulation 7 of the Child Benefit Amendment Regulations (April 7, 1997).

20. Regulation 18(2) of the Miscellaneous Amendments Regulations 1996 (October 7, 1996).

21. Regulation 18(3) of the Miscellaneous Amendments Regulations 1996 (August 5, 1996).

22. Regs 30 and 42(2)(a) of Miscellaneous Amendments Regulations 1998 (January 19, 1998).

23. Regulation 68(3) of the Departure Regulations (December 2, 1996).

25. Regulation 10(2)(b) of the Miscellaneous Amendments (No. 2) Regulations 1996 (January 13, 1997).

26. Regulation 10(2)(c) of the Miscellaneous Amendments (No. 2) Regulations 1996 (January 13, 1997).

27. Regulation 10(2)(d) of the Miscellaneous Amendments (No. 2) Regulations 1996 (January 13, 1997).

28. Regulation 10(3)(a) of the Miscellaneous Amendments (No. 2) Regulations 1996 (January 13, 1997).

29. Regulation 10(3)(b) of the Miscellaneous Amendments (No. 2) Regulations 1996 (January 13, 1997).

30. Regulation 42(2)(b) of the Miscellaneous Amendments Regulations 1998 (January 19, 1998).

31. Regulation 42(2)(c) of the Miscellaneous Amendments Regulations 1998 (January 19, 1998).

33. Regulation 42(2)(e) of the Miscellaneous Amendments Regulations 1998 (January 19, 1998).

34. Regulation 42(3) of the Miscellaneous Amendments Regulations 1998 (January 19, 1998).

35. Article 14(a)(i) of the Commencement No. 7 Order 1999 (June 1, 1999).

36. Article 14(a)(ii) of the Commencement No. 7 Order 1999 (June 1, 1999).

37. Regulation 6(2)(a) of the Miscellaneous Amendments Regulations 1999 (October 4, 1999).

38. Regulation 6(2)(b) of the Miscellaneous Amendments (No. 2) Regulations 1999 (June 1. 1999).

39. Article 14(b)(i) of the Commencement No. 7 Order 1999 (June 1, 1999).

40. Article 14(b)(ii) of the Commencement No. 7 Order 1999 (June 1. 1999).

41. Article 14(c) of the Commencement No. 7 Order 1999 (June 1, 1999).

42. Regulation 6(2)(a) of the Miscellaneous Amendments Regulations 2003 (April 6, 2003).

43. Regulation 6(2)(b) of the Miscellaneous Amendments Regulations 2003 (April 6, 2003).

44. Regulation 6(2)(c) of the Miscellaneous Amendments Regulations 2003 (April 6, 2003).

45. Regulation 4(2)(a) of the Miscellaneous Amendments (No. 2) Regulations 2003 (November 5, 2003).

46. Regulation 4(2)(b) of the Miscellaneous Amendments (No. 2) Regulations 2003 (November 5, 2003).

47. Regulation 4(2)(b) of the Miscellaneous Amendments (No. 2) Regulations 2003 (November 5, 2003).

48. Regulation 4(2)(c) of the Miscellaneous Amendments (No. 2) Regulations 2003 (November 5, 2003).

49. Regulation 4(2)(d) of the Miscellaneous Amendments (No. 2) Regulations 2003 (November 5, 2003).

50. Regulation 4(2)(e) of the Miscellaneous Amendments (No. 2) Regulations 2003 (November 5, 2003).

PART II

## CALCULATION OR ESTIMATION OF CHILD SUPPORT MAINTENANCE

### Calculation or estimation of amounts

4.145     **2.**—(1) Where any amount [³is to be considered in connection with any calculation made under these Regulations], it shall be calculated or estimated as a weekly amount and, except where the context otherwise requires, any reference to such an amount shall be construed accordingly.

(2) Subject to [¹regulations 11(6) and (7) and 13(2) and [²regulation 8A(5)] of the Maintenance Assessment Procedure Regulations] where any calculation made under [¹the Act or] these Regulations results in a fraction of a penny that fraction shall be treated as a penny if it is either one half pr-exceeds one half, otherwise it shall be disregarded.

(3) [⁴The Secretary of State] shall calculate the amounts to be taken into account for the purposes of these Regulations by reference, as the case may be, to the dates, weeks, months or other periods specified herein provided that if he becomes aware of a material change of circumstances occurring after such date, week, month or other period but before the effective date, he shall take that change of circumstances into account.

AMENDMENTS

    1. Regulation 42 of the Amendment Regulations 1995 (April 18, 1995).

    2. Regulation 41 of the Miscellaneous Amendments (No. 2) Regulations 1995 and reg.3 of the Miscellaneous Amendments (No. 3) Regulations 1995 (January 22, 1996).

    3. Regulation 43 of Miscellaneous Amendments Regulations 1998 (January 19, 1998).

    4. Article 15 of the Commencement No.7 Order 1999 (June 1, 1999).

DEFINITIONS

4.146     "the Act: see reg.1(2).
"effective date': see reg.1(2).
"Maintenance Assessment Procedure Regulations": see reg.1(2).

### Calculation of AG

4.147     **3.**—(1) The amounts to be taken into account for the purposes of calculating AG in the formula set out in paragraph 1(2) of Schedule 1 to the Act are—

    (a) with respect to each qualifying child, an amount equal to the amount specified in column (2) of paragraph 2 of the relevant Schedule for a person of the same age (income support personal allowance for child or young person);

    [¹(b) with respect to a person with care of one or more qualifying children—

        (i) where one or more of those children is aged less than 11, an amount equal to the amount specified in column (2) of para-

graph 1(l)(e) of the relevant Schedule (income support personal allowance for a single claimant aged not less than 25);
(ii) where none of those children are aged less than 11 but one or more of them is aged less than 14, an amount equal to 75 per centum of the amount specified in head (i) above; and
(iii) where none of those children are aged less than 14 but one or more of them is aged less than 16, an amount equal to 50 per centum of the amount specified in head (i) above;]
[²(c) an amount equal to the amount specified in paragraph 3(l)(b) of the relevant Schedule.]
[³..]
(2) The amounts referred to in paragraph (1) shall be the amounts applicable at the effective date.

AMENDMENTS

1. Regulation 4(2) of the Miscellaneous Amendments Regulations 1994 (February 7, 1994).
2. Regulation 44 of Miscellaneous Amendments Regulations 1998 (April 6, 1998).
3. Regulation 8(b) of the Child Benefit Amendment Regulations (April 7, 1997).

DEFINITIONS

"the Act": see reg.1(2).                                                    **4.148**
"effective date": see reg.1(2).
"Income Support Regulations": see reg.1(2).
"partner": see reg.1(2).
"relevant Schedule": see reg.1(2).

## Basic rate of child benefit

**4.** For the purposes of paragraph 1(4) of Schedule 1 to the Act "basic    **4.149**
rate" means the rate of child benefit which is specified in [¹regulation 2(l)(a)(i) or 2(l)(b) of the Child Benefit Rates Regulations (weekly rate for only, elder or eldest child and for other children)] applicable to the child in question at the effective date.

AMENDMENT

1. Regulation 9 of the Child Benefit Amendment Regulations (April 7, 1997).

DEFINITIONS

"the Act": see reg.1(2).                                                    **4.150**
"Child Benefit Rates Regulations": see reg.1(2).
"effective date": see reg.1(2).

## The general rule

**5.** For the purposes of paragraph 2(1) of Schedule 1 to the Act—        **4.151**
(a) the value of C, otherwise than in a case where the other parent is the person with care, is nil; and
(b) the value of P is 0.5.

4.152 "the Act": see reg.1(2).

## The additional element

4.153 **6.**—[[1](1) For the purposes of the formula in paragraph 4(1) of Schedule 1 to the Act, the value of R is—

(a) where the maintenance assessment in question relates to one qualifying child, 0.15;

(b) where the maintenance assessment in question relates to two qualifying children, 0.20; and

(c) where the maintenance assessment in question relates to three or more qualifying children, 0.25.]

(2) For the purposes of the alternative formula in paragraph 4(3) of Schedule 1 to the Act—

(a) the value of Z is [[2]1.5];

(b) the amount for the purposes of paragraph (b) of the definition of Q is the same as the amount specified in [[3]regulation] [[4]3(l)(c)] (income support family premium) in respect of each qualifying child.

AMENDMENTS

1. Regulation 4(3) of the Miscellaneous Amendments Regulations 1994 (February 7, 1994).
2. Regulation 43 of the Amendment Regulations 1995 (April 18, 1995).
3. Regulation 10 of the Child Benefit Amendment Regulations (April 7, 1997).
4. Regulation 45 of Miscellaneous Amendments Regulations 1998 (April 6, 1998).

DEFINITION

4.154 "the Act": see reg.1(2).

## Net income: calculation or estimation of N

4.155 **7.**—(1) Subject to the following provisions of this regulation, for the purposes of the formula in paragraph 5(1) of Schedule 1 to the Act, the amount of N (net income of absent parent) shall be the aggregate of the following amounts—

(a) the amount, determined in accordance with Part I of Schedule 1, of any earnings of the absent parent;

(b) the amount, determined in accordance with Part II of Schedule 1, of any benefit payments under the Contributions and Benefits Act [[1]or the Jobseekers Act] paid to or in respect of the absent parent;

(c) the amount, determined in accordance with Part III of Schedule 1, of any other income of the absent parent;

(d) the amount, determined in accordance with Part IV of Schedule 1, of any income of a relevant child which is treated as the income of the absent parent;

(e) any amount, determined in accordance with Part V of Schedule 1, which is treated as the income of the absent parent.

(2) Any amounts referred to in Schedule 2 shall be disregarded.

(3) Where an absent parent's income consists—

(a) only of a [²work-based training for young people or, in Scotland, Skillseekers training] allowance; or

(b) in the case of a student, only of grant, an amount paid in respect of grant contribution or student loan or any combination thereof; or

(c) only of prisoner's pay,

then for the purposes of determining N such income shall be disregarded.

(4) Where a parent and any other person are beneficially entitled to any income but the shares of their respective entitlements are not ascertainable the [³Secretary of State] shall estimate their respective entitlements having regard to such information as is available but where sufficient information on which to base an estimate is not available the parent and that other person shall be treated as entitled to that income in equal shares.

(5) Where any income normally received at regular intervals has not been received it shall, if it is due to be paid and there are reasonable grounds for believing it will be received, be treated as if it had been received.

AMENDMENTS

1. Regulation 6(6) and (7)(a) of the Jobseekers Amendment Regulations (October 7, 1996).

2. Regulation 6(3) of the Miscellaneous Amendments Regulations 1999 (April 6, 1999).

3. Article 16 of the Commencement No. 7 Order 1999 (June 1, 1999).

DEFINITIONS

"the Act": see reg.1(2).                                                           **4.156**
"Contributions and Benefits Act": see reg.1(2).
"earnings": see reg.1(2).
"effective date": see reg.1(2).
"grant": see reg.1(2).
"grant contribution": see reg.1(2).
"the Jobseekers Act": see reg.1(2).
"person": see reg.1(2).
"prisoner": see reg.1(2).
"student": see reg.1(2).
"student loan": see reg.1(2).
"training allowance": see reg.1(2).

## Net income: calculation or estimation of M

**8.** For the purposes of paragraph 5(2) of Schedule 1 to the Act, the      **4.157**
amount of M (net income of the parent with care) shall be calculated in
the same way as N is calculated under regulation 7 but as if references to
the absent parent were references to the parent with care.

DEFINITIONS

"the Act": see reg.1(2).                                                           **4.158**
"parent with care": see reg.1(2).

### Exempt income: calculation or estimation of E

4.159    **9.**—(1) For the purposes of paragraph 5(1) of Schedule 1 to the Act, the amount of E (exempt income of absent parent) shall subject to paragraphs (3) and (4), be the aggregate of the following amounts—

(a) an amount equal to the amount specified in column (2) of paragraph 1(1)(e) of the relevant Schedule (income support personal allowance for a single claimant aged not less than 25);

(b) an amount in respect of housing costs determined in accordance with regulations 14 to [¹⁴16 and 18];

[²(bb) where applicable, an amount in respect of a qualifying transfer of property determined in accordance with Schedule 3A;]

[⁷. . .]

(d) where, if the parent were a claimant aged less than 60, the conditions in paragraph 11 of the relevant Schedule (income support disability premium) would be satisfied in respect of him, an amount equal to the amount specified in column (2) of paragraph 15(4)(a) of that Schedule (income support disability premium);

(e) where—

   (i) if the parent were a claimant, the conditions in paragraph 13 of the relevant Schedule (income support severe disability premium) would be satisfied, an amount equal to the amount specified in column (2) of paragraph 15(5)(a) of that Schedule (except that no such amount shall be taken into account in the case of an absent parent in respect of whom [¹⁹a carer's care allowance] under section 70 of the Contributions and Benefits Act is payable to some other person);

   (ii) if the parent were a claimant, the conditions in paragraph 14ZA of the relevant Schedule (income support carer premium) would be satisfied in respect of him, an amount equal to the amount specified in column (2) of paragraph 15(7) of that Schedule;

  [¹⁷(iii) if the parent were a claimant, the conditions set out in paragraph 13A of the relevant Schedule (income support enhanced disability premium) would be satisfied in respect of him, an amount equal to the amount specified in paragraph 15(8)(b) of that Schedule;]

(f) where, if the parent were a claimant, the conditions in paragraph 3 of the relevant Schedule (income support family premium) would be satisfied in respect of a relevant child of that parent, [⁹. . .] the amount specified in [¹⁰subparagraph (b) of] that paragraph or, where those conditions would be satisfied only by virtue of the case being one to which paragraph (2) applies, half that amount;

(g) in respect of each relevant child—

   (i) an amount equal to the amount of the personal allowance for that child, specified in column (2) of paragraph 2 of the relevant Schedule (income support personal allowance) or, where paragraph (2) applies, half that amount;

   (ii) if the conditions set out in paragraph 14(b) and (c) of the relevant Schedule (income support disabled child premium) are satisfied in respect of that child, an amount equal to the amount specified in column (2) of paragraph 15(6) of the relevant Schedule or, where paragraph (2) applies, half that amount;

[¹⁸(iii) if the parent were a claimant, the conditions set out in paragraph 13A of the relevant Schedule (income support enhanced disability premium) are satisfied in respect of that child, an amount equal to the amount specified in paragraph 15(8)(a) of that Schedule or, where paragraph (2) applies, half that amount];]

[²⁰(h) where the absent parent or his partner is resident in a care home or an independent hospital or is being provided with a care home service or an independent health care service, the amount of fees paid in respect of that home, hospital or service, as the case may be, but where it has been determined that the absent parent in question or his partner is entitled to housing benefit in respect of fees for that home, hospital or service, as the case may be, the net amount of such fees after deduction of housing benefit;]

[³(i) where applicable, an amount in respect of travelling costs determined in accordance with Schedule 3B.]

(2) This paragraph applies where—

(a) the absent parent has a partner;

(b) the absent parent and the partner are parents of the same relevant child; and

(c) the income of the partner, calculated under regulation 7(1) [¹(but excluding the amount mentioned in subparagraph (d) of that regulation)] as if that partner were an absent parent to whom that regulation applied, exceeds the aggregate of—

    (i) the amount specified in column 2 of paragraph 1(l)(e) of the relevant Schedule (income support personal allowance for a single claimant aged not less than 25);

  (ii) half the amount of the personal allowance for that child specified in column (2) of paragraph 2 of the relevant Schedule (income support personal allowance);

 (iii) half the amount of any income support disabled child premium specified in column (2) of paragraph 15(6) of that Schedule in respect of that child; [⁴and]

 (iv) half the amount of any income support family premium specified in paragraph [¹¹3[¹⁶(l)](b) of the relevant Schedule] except where such premium is payable irrespective of that child [⁵ . . .]

[¹⁵(v) where a departure direction has been given on the grounds that a case falls within regulation 27 of the Departure Direction and Consequential Amendments Regulations (partner's contribution to housing costs), the amount of the housing costs which corresponds to the percentage of the housing costs mentioned in regulation 40(7) of those Regulations.]

(3) Where an absent parent does not have day to day care of any relevant child for 7 nights each week but does have day to day care of one or more such children for fewer than 7 nights each week, [¹²any amount] to be taken into account under subparagraphs (l)(c) [¹³or (f)] shall be reduced

4.160

so that they bear the same proportion to the amounts referred to in those sub-paragraphs as the average number of nights each week in respect of which such care is provided has to 7.

(4) Where an absent parent has day to day care of a relevant child for fewer than 7 nights each week, any amounts to be taken into account under subpara-graph (l)(g) in respect of such a child shall be reduced so that they bear the same proportion to the amounts referred to in that sub-paragraph as the average number of nights each week in respect of which such care is provided has to 7.

(5) The amounts referred to in paragraph (1) are the amounts applicable at the effective date.

AMENDMENTS

1. Regulation 20 of the Amendment Regulations (April 5, 1993).
2. Regulation 44(2)(a) of the Amendment Regulations 1995 (April 18, 1995).
3. Regulation 44(2)(b) of the Amendment Regulations 1995 (April 18, 1995).
4. Regulation 44(3)(i) of the Amendment Regulations 1995 (April 18, 1995).
5. Regulation 44(3)(ii) of the Amendment Regulations 1995 (April 18, 1995).
7. Regulation 47(2)(a) of Miscellaneous Amendments Regulations 1998 (April 6, 1998).
9. Regulation 47(2)(b) of Miscellaneous Amendments Regulations 1998 (April 6, 1998).
10. Regulation 11(2)(b)(ii) of the Child Benefit Amendment Regulations (April 7, 1997).
11. Regulation 11(3) of the Child Benefit Amendment Regulations (April 7, 1997).
12. Regulation 11(4)(a) of the Child Benefit Amendment Regulations (April 7, 1997).
13. Regulation 11(4)(b) of the Child Benefit Amendment Regulations (April 7, 1997).
14. Regulation 19 of the Miscellaneous Amendments Regulations 1996 (October 7, 1996).
15. Regulation 68(4) of the Departure Regulations (December 2, 1996).
16. Regulation 47(3) of Miscellaneous Amendments Regulations 1998 (April 6, 1998).
17. Regulation 5(a) of the Miscellaneous Amendments Regulations 2002 (April 30, 2002).
18. Regulation 5(b) of the Miscellaneous Amendments Regulations 2002 (April 30, 2002).
19. Regulation 6(3) of the Miscellaneous Amendments Regulations 2003 (April 1, 2003).
20. Regulation 4(3) of the Miscellaneous Amendments (No. 2) Regulations 2003 (November 5, 2003).

DEFINITIONS

**4.161**     "the Act": see reg.1(2).
"care home": see reg.1(2).
"care home service": see reg.1(2).
"claimant": see reg.1(2).
"Contributions and Benefits Act": see reg.1(2).
"day to day care": see reg.1(2).

"Departure Direction and Consequential Amendments Regulations": see reg.1(2).
"effective date": see reg.1(2).
"housing benefit": see reg.1(2).
"Income Support Regulations": see reg.1(2).
"independent health care service": see reg.1(2).
"independent hospital": see reg.1(2).
"partner": see reg.1(2).
"relevant child": see reg.1(2).
"relevant Schedule": see reg.1(2).

## Exempt income: calculation or estimation of F

**10.** For the purposes of paragraph 5(2) of Schedule 1 to the Act, the amount of F (exempt income of parent with care) shall be calculated in the same way as E is calculated under regulation 9 but as if references to the absent parent were references to the parent with care [¹except that—
  (a) subparagraph (bb) of paragraph (1) of that regulation shall not apply unless at the time of the making of the qualifying transfer the parent with care would have been the absent parent had the Child Support Act 1991 been in force at the date of the making of the transfer; and
  (b) paragraph (3) and (4) of that regulation shall apply only where the parent with care shares day to day care of the child mentioned in those paragraphs with one or more other persons.]

4.162

AMENDMENT

1. Regulation 45 of the Amendment Regulations 1995 (April 18, 1995).

DEFINITIONS

"the Act": see reg.1(2).
"day to day care": see reg.1(2).
"parent with care": see reg.1(2).

4.163

## [¹Assessable income: [³working tax credit] paid to or in respect of a parent with care or an absent parent

**10A.**—(1) Subject to paragraph (2), where [³working tax credit] is paid to or in respect of a parent with care or an absent parent, that parent shall, for the purposes of Schedule 1 to the Act, be taken to have no assessable income.
  (2) Paragraph (1) shall apply to an absent parent only if—
  (a) he is also a parent with care; and
  (b) either—
    (i) a maintenance assessment in respect of a child in relation to whom he is a parent with care is in force; or
    (ii) the [²Secretary of State] is considering an application for such an assessment to be made.]

4.164

AMENDMENTS

1. Regulation 11 of the Miscellaneous Amendments (No. 2) Regulations 1996 (January 13, 1997).
2. Article 16 of the Commencement No. 7 Order 1999 (June 1, 1999).
3. Regulation 6(4) of the Miscellaneous Amendments Regulations 2003 (April 6, 2003).

DEFINITIONS

**4.165**  "the Act": see reg.1(2).
"working credit": see reg.1(2).

## [¹Assessable income: state pension credit paid to or in respect of a parent with care or an absent parent

**4.166**  **10B.** Where state pension credit is paid to or in respect of a parent with care or an absent parent, that parent shall, for the purposes of Schedule 1 to the Act, be taken to have no assessable income.]

AMENDMENT

1. Regulation 4(4) of the Miscellaneous Amendments (No. 2) Regulations 2003 (November 5, 2003).

DEFINITION

**4.167**  "state pension credit": see reg.1(2).

## Protected income

**4.168**  **11.**—(1) For the purposes of paragraph 6 of Schedule 1 to the Act the protected income level of an absent parent shall, [¹subject to paragraphs (3), (4)[²², (6) and (6A)]] be the aggregate of the following amounts—
   (a) where—
      (i) absent parent does not have a partner, an amount equal to the amount specified in column (2) of paragraph 1(1)(e) of the relevant Schedule (income support personal allowance for a single claimant aged not less than 25 years);
      (ii) the absent parent has a partner, an amount equal to the amount specified in column (2) of paragraph 1(3)(c) of the relevant Schedule (income support personal allowance for a couple where both members are aged not less than 18 years);
      (iii) the absent parent is a member of a polygamous marriage, an amount in respect of himself and one of his partners, equal to the amount specified in subparagraph (ii) and, in respect of each of his other partners, an amount equal to the difference between the amounts specified in subparagraph (ii) and subparagraph (i);
   (b) an amount in respect of housing costs determined in accordance with regulations 14, 15, 16 and 18, or, in a case where the absent parent is a non-dependant member of a household who is treated as having no housing costs by [¹²regulation 15(4)], the non-dependant

amount which would be calculated in respect of him under [²paragraphs (1), (2) and (9) of regulation 63 of the Housing Benefit Regulations (non-dependant deductions) if he were a non-dependant in respect of whom a calculation were to be made under those paragraphs (disregarding any other provision of that regulation)] ]

[¹⁶. . .]

(d) where, if the parent were a claimant, the conditions in paragraph 11 of the relevant Schedule (income support disability premium) would be satisfied, an amount equal to the amount specified in column (2) of paragraph 15(4) of that Schedule (income support disability premium);

(e) where, if the parent were a claimant, the conditions in paragraph 13 or 14ZA of the relevant Schedule (income support severe disability and carer premiums) would be satisfied in respect of either or both premiums, an amount equal to the amount or amounts specified in column (2) of paragraph 15(5) or, as the case may be, (7) of that Schedule in respect of that or those premiums (income support premiums);

(f) where, if the parent were a claimant, the conditions in paragraph 3 of the relevant Schedule (income support family premium) would be satisfied [¹⁷. . .], the amount specified in [¹⁸sub-paragraph (b) of] that paragraph;

(g) in respect of each child who is a member of the family of the absent parent—

    (i) an amount equal to the amount of the personal allowance for that child, specified in column (2) of paragraph 2 of the relevant Schedule (income support personal allowance);

    (ii) if the conditions set out in paragraphs 14(b) and (c) of the relevant Schedule (income support disabled child premium) are satisfied in respect of that child, an amount equal to the amount specified in column (2) of paragraph 15(6) of the relevant Schedule;

(h) where, if the parent were a claimant, the conditions specified in Part III of the relevant Schedule would be satisfied by the absent parent in question or any member of his family in relation to any premium not otherwise included in this regulation, an amount equal to the amount specified in Part IV of that Schedule (income support premiums) in respect of that premium;

[²⁶(i) where the absent parent or his partner is resident in a care home or an independent hospital or is being provided with a care home service or an independent health care service, the amount of fees paid in respect of that home, hospital or service, as the case may be, but where it has been determined that the absent parent in question or his partner is entitled to housing benefit in respect of fees for that home, hospital or service, as the case may be, the net amount of such fees after deduction of housing benefit;]

[³(j) where—

    (i) the absent parent is, or that absent parent and any partner of his are, the only person or persons resident in, and liable to pay council tax in respect of, the home for which housing costs are included under subparagraph (b), the amount of weekly council tax for which he is liable in respect of that home, less any applicable council tax benefit;

(ii) where other persons are resident with the absent parent in, and liable to pay council tax in respect of, the home for which housing costs are included under subparagraph (b), an amount representing the share of the weekly council tax in respect of that home applicable to the absent parent, determined by dividing the total amount of council tax due in that week by the number of persons liable to pay it, less any council tax benefit applicable to that share, provided that, if the absent parent is required to pay and pays more than that share because of default by one or more of those other persons, the amount for the purposes of this regulation shall be the amount of weekly council tax the absent parent pays, less any council tax benefit applicable to such amount;]

(k) an amount of [⁴£30.00;

[⁵(kk) an amount in respect of travelling costs determined in accordance with Schedule 3B;]

(l) where the income of—
  (i) the absent parent in question;
  (ii) any partner of his; and
  (iii) any child or children for whom an amount is included under subparagraph (g)(i);

exceeds the sum of the amounts to which reference is made in subparagraphs [⁶(a) to (kk)], [⁷15 per centum] of the excess.

**4.169**
(2) For the purposes of subparagraph (1) of paragraph (1) "income" shall be calculated—

(a) in respect of the absent parent in question or any partner of his, in the same manner as N (net income of absent parent) is calculated under regulation 7 except—

  (i) there shall be taken into account the basic rate of any child benefit and any maintenance which in either case is in payment in respect of any member of the family of the absent parent;

  (ii) there shall be deducted the amount of any maintenance under a maintenance order which the absent parent or his partner is paying in respect of a child in circumstances where an application for a maintenance assessment could not be made in accordance with the Act in respect of that child; [⁸ . . .]

  [⁹(iii) to the extent that it falls under subparagraph (b), the income of any child in that family shall not be treated as the income of the parent or his partner and Part IV of Schedule 1 shall not apply;] [¹⁴. . .]

  [¹⁵(iv) paragraph 27 of Schedule 2 shall apply as though the reference to paragraph 3(2) and (4) of Schedule 3 were omitted;

  (v) there shall be deducted the amount of any maintenance which is being paid in respect of a child by the absent parent or his partner under an order requiring such payment made by a court outside Great Britain; and]

[<sup>25</sup>(v) there shall be taken into account any child tax credit which is payable to the absent parent or his partner; and]

(b) in respect of any child in that family, as being the total of [<sup>10</sup>that child's relevant income (within the meaning of paragraph 23 of Schedule 1), there being disregarded any maintenance in payment to or in respect of him,] but only to the extent that such income does not exceed the amount included under subparagraph (g) of paragraph (1) (income support personal allowance for a child and income support disabled child premium) reduced, as the case may be, under paragraph (4).

(3) Where an absent parent does not have day to day care of any child (whether or not a relevant child) for 7 nights each week but does have day to day care of one or more such children for fewer than 7 nights each week, [<sup>19</sup>any amount] to be taken into account under [<sup>20</sup>sub-paragraph (f)] of paragraph (1) [<sup>21</sup>. . .] (income support family premium) shall be reduced so that they bear the same proportion to the amounts referred to in those subparagraphs as the average number of nights each week in respect of which such care is provided has to 7.

(4) Where an absent parent has day to day care of a child (whether or not a relevant child) for fewer than 7 nights each week any amounts in relation to that child to be taken into account under subparagraph (g) of paragraph (1) (income support personal allowance for child and income support disabled child premium) shall be reduced so that they bear the same proportion to the amounts referred to in that subparagraph as the average number of nights in respect of which such care is provided has to 7.

(5) The amounts referred to in paragraph (1) shall be the amounts applicable at the effective date.

[<sup>11</sup>(6) If the application of the above provisions of this regulation would result in the protected income level of an absent parent being less than 70 per centum of his net income, as calculated in accordance with regulation 7, those provisions shall not apply in his case and instead his protected income level shall be 70 per centum of his net income as so calculated.]

[<sup>23</sup>(6A) In a case to which paragraph (6) does not apply, if the application of paragraphs (1) to (5) and of regulation 12(l)(a) would result in the amount of child support maintenance payable being greater than 30 per centum of the absent parent's net income calculated in accordance with regulation 7, paragraphs (1) to (5) shall not apply in his case and instead his protected income shall be 70 per centum of his net income as so calculated.]

[<sup>11</sup>(7) Where any calculation under paragraph (6) [<sup>24</sup>or (6A)] results in a fraction of a penny, that fraction shall be treated as a penny.]

AMENDMENTS

1. Regulation 46(2)(a) of the Amendment Regulations 1995 (April 18, 1995).
2. Regulation 46(2)(b) of the Amendment Regulations 1995 (April 18, 1995).
3. Regulation 46(2)(c) of the Amendment Regulations 1995 (April 18, 1995).

4. Regulation 4(4) of the Miscellaneous Amendments Regulations 1994 (February 7, 1994).

5. Regulation 46(2)(d) of the Amendment Regulations 1995 (April 18, 1995).

6. Regulation 46(2)(e) of the Amendment Regulations 1995 (April 18, 1995).

7. Regulation 4(5) of the Miscellaneous Amendments Regulations 1994 (February 7, 1994).

8. Regulation 46(3) of the Amendment Regulations 1995 (April 18, 1995).

9. Regulation 46(4) of the Amendment Regulations 1995 (April 18, 1995).

10. Regulation 46(5) of the Amendment Regulations 1995 (April 18, 1995).

11. Regulation 46(6) of the Amendment Regulations 1995 (April 18, 1995).

12. Regulation 43(2) of the Miscellaneous Amendments (No. 2) Regulations 1995 (January 22, 1996).

14. Regulation 43(4) of the Miscellaneous Amendments (No. 2) Regulations 1995 (January 22, 1996).

15. Regulation 43(5) of the Miscellaneous Amendments (No. 2) Regulations 1995 (January 22, 1996).

16. Regulation 49(2)(a) of Miscellaneous Amendments Regulations 1998 (April 6, 1998).

17. Regulation 49(2)(b) of Miscellaneous Amendments Regulations 1998 (April 6, 1998).

18. Regulation 12(2)(b)(ii) of the Child Benefit Amendment Regulations (April 7, 1997).

19. Regulation 12(3)(a) of the Child Benefit Amendment Regulations (April 7, 1997).

20. Regulation 49(3) of Miscellaneous Amendments Regulations 1998 (April 6, 1998).

21. Regulation 12(3)(c) of the Child Benefit Amendment Regulations (April 7, 1997).

22. Regulation 20(2) of the Miscellaneous Amendments Regulations 1996 (August 5, 1996).

23. Regulation 20(3) of the Miscellaneous Amendments Regulations 1996 (August 5, 1996).

24. Regulation 20(4) of the Miscellaneous Amendments Regulations 1996 (August 5, 1996).

25. Regulation 6(5) of the Miscellaneous Amendments Regulations 2003 (April 6, 2003).

26. Regulation 4(5) of the Miscellaneous Amendments (No. 2) Regulations 2003 (November 5, 2003).

DEFINITIONS

**4.170**    "the Act": see reg.1(2).
"care home": see reg.1(2).
"care home service": see reg.1(2).
"child tax credit": se reg.1(2).
"claimant": see reg.1(2).
"council tax benefit": see reg.1(2).
"couple": see reg.1(2).
"effective date": see reg.1(2).
"family": see reg.1(2).
"Housing Benefit Regulations": see reg.1(2).
"Income Support Regulations": see reg.1(2).
"independent health care service": see reg.1(2).
"independent hospital": see reg.1(2).
"non-dependant": see reg.1(2).

"partner": see reg.1(2).
"polygamous marriage": see reg.1(2).
"relevant Schedule": see reg.1(2).

## Disposable income

**12.**—[¹(1) For the purposes of paragraph 6(4) of Schedule 1 to the Act
(protected income), the disposable income of an absent parent shall be—

    (a)    except in a case to which regulation 11(6) [²or (6A)] applies, the
aggregate of his income and any income of any member of his family calculated in like manner as under regulation 11(2); [³. . .]

    (b)    [⁴subject to sub-paragraph (c),] in a case to which regulation 11(6)
[²or (6A)] applies, his net income as calculated in accordance with
regulation 7 [⁵; and]

    [⁶(c)    in a case to which regulation 11 (6) applies and the absent parent
is paying maintenance under an order of a kind mentioned in
regulation 1 1(2)(a)(ii) or (v), his net income as calculated in accordance with regulation 7 less the amount of maintenance he is
paying under that order.]

(2) Subject to paragraph (3), where a maintenance assessment has been
made with respect to the absent parent and payment of the amount of that
assessment would reduce his disposable income below his protected
income level the amount of the assessment shall be reduced by the minimum amount necessary to prevent his disposable income being reduced
below his protected income level.

(3) Where the prescribed minimum amount fixed by regulations under
paragraph 7 of Schedule 1 to the Act is applicable (such amount being
specified in regulation 13) the amount payable under the assessment shall
not be reduced to less than the prescribed minimum amount.]

**4.171**

AMENDMENTS

1. Regulation 47 of the Amendment Regulations 1995 (April 18, 1995).
2. Regulation 21 of the Miscellaneous Amendments Regulations 1996 (August
5, 1996).
3. Regulation 12(2) of the Miscellaneous Amendments (No. 2) Regulations
1996 (January 13, 1997).
4. Regulation 12(3)(a) of the Miscellaneous Amendments (No. 2) Regulations
1996 (January 13, 1997).
5. Regulation 12(3)(b) of the Miscellaneous Amendments (No. 2) Regulations
1996 (January 13, 1997).
6. Regulation 12(4) of the Miscellaneous Amendments (No. 2) Regulations
1996 (January 13, 1997).

DEFINITIONS

"the Act": see reg.1(2).
"family": see reg.1(2).

**4.172**

## The minimum amount

**13.**—(1) Subject to regulation 26, for the purposes of paragraph 7(1) of
Schedule 1 to the Act the minimum amount shall be [¹2 multiplied by] 5

**4.173**

per centum of the amount specified in paragraph 1(1) (e) of the relevant Schedule (income support personal allowance for single claimant aged not less than 25).

(2) Where [²the 5 per centum amount] calculated under paragraph (1) results in a sum other than a multiple of 5 pence, it shall be treated as the sum which is the next higher multiple of 5 pence.

AMENDMENTS

1. Regulation 2(2) of the Child Support (Maintenance Assessments and Special Cases) and Social Security (Claims and Payments) Regulations 1996 (April 8, 1996)

2. Regulation 2(3) of the Child Support (Maintenance Assessments and Special Cases) and Social Security (Claims and Payments) Regulations 1996 (April 8, 1996)

DEFINITION

4.174     "the Act": see reg.1(2).

### Eligible housing costs

4.175     **14.** Schedule 3 shall have effect for the purpose of determining the costs which are eligible to be taken into account as housing costs for the purposes of these Regulations.

GENERAL NOTE

There is an allowance for an amount in respect of housing costs in both assessable income and protected income (regs 9(l)(b), 10 and 11(1) (b)). This figure will not necessarily be the same for each type of income, nor will it necessarily be the same as the parent's actual housing costs. In this note that amount will be referred to as the allowable housing costs. The tribunal should approach the question of allowable housing costs in the following stages.

First, identify the parent's home, as defined in reg.1(2). The only allowable housing costs are those in respect of that home (reg.15(1)).

Second, identify the housing costs in respect of that home. The costs must be determined at the effective date (reg.16). The approach to this stage depends upon whether the parent has been determined by the local authority to be entitled to housing benefit. If so, the parent's housing costs are the weekly rent for the purposes of regs 10 and 69 of the Housing Benefit (General) Regulations less the housing benefit and the non-dependant deductions discussed below (reg.15(2)). If the parent has not been determined to be entitled to housing benefit, the calculation is more complicated, (i) Begin by determining the types of eligible housing costs incurred in respect of the parent's home from those listed in Sched.3, paras 1, 2 and (for assessable income purposes only) 3 (regs 14 and 15(1)). (ii) Then decide whether the general conditions of entitlement for those costs to be taken into account have been met (Sched.3, para.4). (iii) If so, make the following deductions: where those costs are shared with someone other than a member of the parent's family, the share of those costs applicable to the other person (reg.15(3)); apportionment for non-residential accommodation covered by the payments under (i) above (Sched.3, para.5); deductions for ineligible service charges, fuel charges and water and allied environmental services (Sched.3, para.6). The result is the parent's housing costs.

Third, if the parent has housing costs, the tribunal must determine to whom those costs are paid. If the parent is a non-dependant member of a household and pays housing costs only to another member or members of that household, the parent is treated as having no housing costs (reg.15(10)). This only applies for the purposes of calculating assessable income (regs 9(l)(b) and 10) and does not apply for the purposes of the protected income calculation in respect of which a notional allowance is made for housing costs (reg.ll(l)(b)).

Fourth, if the parent has housing costs, these must be converted to a weekly figure under reg.16.

Fifth, the tribunal should determine whether the costs exceed the ceiling imposed by reg.18. If they do, no costs are allowed over the ceiling.

The result is the allowable housing costs.

## Amount of housing costs

**15.**—(1) Subject to the provisions of this regulation and [¹regulations 16 and 18], a parent's housing costs shall be the aggregate of the eligible housing costs payable in respect of his home.

(2) Where a local authority has determined that a parent is entitled to housing benefit, the amount of his housing costs shall, subject to paragraphs (4) to (9), be the weekly amount treated as rent under regulations 10 and 69 of the Housing Benefit Regulations (rent and calculation of weekly amounts) less the amount of housing benefit.

(3) Where a parent has eligible housing costs and another person who is not a member of his family is also liable to make payments in respect of the home, the amount of the parent's housing costs shall be his share of those costs.

[² . . .]

[³[⁴(4)] A parent shall be treated as having no housing costs where he is a non-dependant member of a household and is not responsible for meeting housing costs except to another member, or other members, of that household[⁵, but, where that other person does not make those payments in circumstances where head (a) of paragraph 4(2) of Schedule 3 applies, the eligible housing costs of that parent shall include the housing costs for which, because of that failure to pay, that parent is treated as responsible under that head.]

4.176

AMENDMENTS

1. Regulation 48(2) of the Amendment Regulations 1995 (April 18, 1995).
2. Regulation 48(3) of the Amendment Regulations 1995 (April 18, 1995).
3. Regulation 48(4) of the Amendment Regulations 1995 (April 18, 1995).
4. Regulation 44 of the Miscellaneous Amendments (No. 2) Regulations 1995 (January 22, 1996).
5. Regulation 50 of Miscellaneous Amendments Regulations 1998 (January 19, 1998).

DEFINITIONS

"eligible housing costs": see reg.1(2).
"family": see reg.1(2).
"home": see reg.1(2).
"housing benefit": see reg.1(2).

4.177

"Housing Benefit Regulations": see reg.1(2).
"non-dependant": see reg.1(2).

**4.178** GENERAL NOTE

*Paragraph (3)*

As a result of this provision only half of the housing costs is to be taken into account as an eligible housing cost where the parent whose home the property is is not solely liable for those costs (*CSCS 8/95*, para.15 and *CCS 8189/95*). In the latter decision the Commissioner refers throughout to reg.50 of these Regulations. There is no such regulation and the words quoted by the Commissioner are those of this paragraph.

If the parent occupying the home has to pay the whole of the costs, the case falls within Sched.3, para.4(2)(a) below (*CCS 13698/96*, para.7).

**[¹Weekly amount of housing costs**

**4.179** **16.**—(1) [²Where housing costs are payable by a parent]—
(a) on a weekly basis, the amount of such housing costs shall, subject to paragraph (2), be the weekly rate payable at the effective date;
(b) on a monthly basis, the amount of such housing costs shall, subject to paragraph (2), be the monthly rate payable at the effective date, multiplied by 12 and divided by 52;
(c) by way of rent to a housing association, as defined in section 1(1) of the Housing Associations Act 1985 which is registered in accordance with section 5 of that Act, or to a local authority, on a free week basis, that is to say the basis that he pays an amount by way of rent for a given number of weeks in a 52–week period, with a lesser number of weeks in which there is no liability to pay ("free weeks"), the amount of such housing costs shall be [³the amount payable]—
(i) in the relevant week if it is not a free week; or
(ii) in the last week before the relevant week which is not a free week, if the relevant week is a free week;
(d) on any other basis, the amount of such housing costs shall, subject to paragraph (2), be the rate payable at the effective date, multiplied by the number of payment periods, or the nearest whole number of payment periods (any fraction of one-half being rounded up), falling within a period of 365 days and divided by 52.

(2) Where housing costs consist of payments on a repayment mortgage and the absent parent or parent with care has not provided information or evidence as to the rate of repayment of the capital secured and the interest payable on that mortgage at the effective date and that absent parent or parent with care has provided a statement from the lender, in respect of a period ending not more than 12 months prior to the first day of the relevant week, for the purposes of the calculation of exempt income under regulation 9 and protected income under regulation 11—
(a) if the amount of capital repaid for the period covered by that statement is shown on it, the rate of repayment of capital owing under that mortgage shall be calculated by reference to that amount; and
(b) if the amount of capital owing and the interest rate applicable at the end of the period covered by that statement are shown on it, the

interest payable on that mortgage shall be calculated by reference to that amount and that interest rate.]

AMENDMENTS

1. Regulation 22 of the Miscellaneous Amendments Regulations 1996 (August 5, 1996).
2. Regulation 51(a) of Miscellaneous Amendments Regulations 1998 (January 19, 1998).
3. Regulation 51(b) of Miscellaneous Amendments Regulations 1998 (January 19, 1998).

DEFINITIONS

"effective date": see reg.1(2).                                                    **4.180**
"relevant week": see reg.1(2).

GENERAL NOTE                                                                        **4.181**

Although this regulation provides that the housing costs shall be those payable at the effective date, some of the provisions which determine the effective date have the effect that the effective date may pre-date the change in the housing costs. For example, a change in housing costs which occurs on the second day of a maintenance period and which is notified to the officer on the following day will result in a fresh assessment of which the effective date is the first day of the maintenance period (reg.31(3) of the Maintenance Assessment Procedure Regulations).
[Regulation 17 was revoked by reg.50 of the Amendment Regulations 1995 from April 18, 1995.]

## Excessive housing costs

**18.**—(1) Subject to paragraph (2), the amount of the housing costs of   **4.182**
an absent parent which are to be taken into account—
 (a) under regulation 9(l)(b) shall not exceed the greater of £80.00 or half the amount of N as calculated or estimated under regulation 7;
 (b) under regulation ll(l)(b) shall not exceed the greater of £80.00 or half of the amount calculated in accordance with regulation 11(2).
 (2) The restriction imposed by paragraph (1) shall not apply where—
 (a) the absent parent in question—
    (i) has been awarded housing benefit (or is awaiting the outcome of a claim to that benefit);
    (ii) has the day to day care of any child; or
    (iii) is a person to whom a disability premium under paragraph 11 of the relevant Schedule applies in respect of himself or his partner or would so apply if he were entitled to income support and were aged less than 60;
 (b) the absent parent in question, following a divorce from, or the breakdown of his relationship with, his former partner, remains in the home he occupied with his former partner;
 (c) the absent parent in question has paid the housing costs under the mortgage, charge or agreement in question for a period in excess of 52 weeks before the date of the first application for child support maintenance in relation to a qualifying child of his and there has

been no increase in those costs other than an increase in the interest payable under the mortgage or charge or, as the case may be, in the amount payable under the agreement under which the home is held;

(d) the housing costs in respect of the home in question would not exceed the amount set out in paragraph (1) but for an increase in the interest payable under a mortgage or charge secured on that home or, as the case may be, in the amount payable under any agreement under which it is held; or

(e) the absent parent is responsible for making payments in respect of housing costs which are higher than they would be otherwise by virtue of the unavailability of his share of the equity of the property formerly occupied with his partner and which remains occupied by that former partner.

DEFINITIONS

4.183    "day to day care": see reg.1(2).
"home": see reg.1(2).
"housing benefit": see reg.1(2).
"partner": see reg.1(2).
"relevant Schedule": see reg.1(2).

4.184    GENERAL NOTE

*Subparagraph (2)(b)*
The partner referred to in this subparagraph need not be the person with care of the qualifying child (*CCS 12769/96*, para.11).

PART III

SPECIAL CASES

**Both parents are absent**

4.185    **19.**—(1) Subject to regulation 27, where the circumstances of a case are that each parent of a qualifying child is an absent parent in relation to that child (neither being a person who is treated as an absent parent by regulation 20(2)) that case shall be treated as a special case for the purposes of the Act.

(2) For the purposes of this case—

(a) where the application is made in relation to both absent parents, separate assessments shall be made under Schedule 1 to the Act in respect of each so as to determine the amount of child support maintenance payable by each absent parent;

(b) subject to paragraph (3), where the application is made in relation to both absent parents, the value of C in each case shall be the assessable income of the other absent parent and where the application is made in relation to only one the value of C in the case of the other shall be nil;

[¹. . .]

[²(d) where the application is made in relation to one absent parent only, the amount of the maintenance requirement applicable in that case shall be one-half of the amount determined in accordance with paragraph 1(2) of Schedule 1 to the Act or, where regulation 23 applies (person caring for children of more than one absent parent), of the amount determined in accordance with paragraphs (2) to (3) of that regulation.]

(3) Where, for the purposes of paragraph (2)(b), information regarding the income of the other absent parent has not been submitted to the Secretary of State [³. . .] within the period specified in regulation 6(1) of the Maintenance Assessment Procedure Regulations then until such information is acquired the value of C shall be nil.

(4) When the information referred to in paragraph (3) is acquired the [⁴Secretary of State] shall make a fresh assessment which shall have effect from the effective date in relation to that other absent [⁵parent, or, from the effective date as determined by paragraph (2) of regulation 30 of the Maintenance Assessment Procedure Regulations, whichever is the later.]

AMENDMENTS

1. Regulation 52 of Miscellaneous Amendments Regulations 1998 (April 6, 1998).
2. Regulation 23 of the Miscellaneous Amendments Regulations 1996 (October 7, 1996).
3. Article 17(a) of the Commencement No. 7 Order 1999 (June 1, 1999).
4. Article 17(b) of the Commencement No. 7 Order 1999 (June 1, 1999).
5. Regulation 6(4) of the Miscellaneous Amendments Regulations 1999 (April 6, 1999).

DEFINITIONS

"the Act": see reg.1(2).	**4.186**
"effective date": see reg.1(2).
"Maintenance Assessment Procedure Regulations": see reg.1(2).
"person": see reg.1(2).

## Persons treated as absent parents

**20.**—(1) Where the circumstances of a case are that—	**4.187**
(a) two or more persons who do not live in the same household each provide day to day care for the same qualifying child; and
(b) at least one of those persons is a parent of that child,
that case shall be treated as a special case for the purposes of the Act.

(2) For the purposes of this case a parent who provides day to day care for a child of his in the following circumstances is to be treated as an absent parent for the purposes of the Act and these Regulations—
(a) a parent who provides such care to a lesser extent than the other parent, person or persons who provide such care for the child in question;
(b) where the persons mentioned in paragraph (1)(a) include both parents and the circumstances are such that care is provided to the same

extent by both but each provides care to a greater or equal extent than any other person who provides such care for that child—

  (i) the parent who is not in receipt of child benefit for the child in question; or

  (ii) if neither parent is in receipt of child benefit for that child, the parent who, in the opinion of the [1Secretary of State], will not be the principal provider of day to day care for that child.

(3) Subject to paragraphs (5) and (6), where a parent is treated as an absent parent under paragraph (2) child support maintenance shall be payable by that parent in respect of the child in question and the amount of the child support maintenance so payable shall be calculated in accordance with the formula set out in paragraph (4).

(4) The formula for the purposes of paragraph (3) is—

$$T = X - \left\{ X + Y \times \frac{J}{7 \times L} \right\}$$

where—

T is the amount of child support maintenance payable;

X is the amount of child support maintenance which would be payable by the parent who is treated as an absent parent, assessed under Schedule 1 to the Act as if paragraphs 6 and 7 of that Schedule did not apply, and, where the other parent is an absent parent as if the value of C was the assessable income of the other parent;

Y is—

  (i) the amount of child support maintenance assessed under Schedule 1 to the Act payable by the other parent if he is an absent parent or which would be payable if he were an absent parent, and for the purposes of such calculation the value of C shall be the assessable income of the parent treated as an absent parent under subparagraph (2); or,

  (ii) if there is no such other parent, shall be nil;

J is the total of the weekly average number of nights for which day to day care is provided by the person who is treated as the absent parent in respect of each child included in the maintenance assessment and shall be calculated to 2 decimal places;

L is the number of children who are included in the maintenance assessment in question.

(5) Where the value of T calculated under the provisions of paragraph (4) is less than zero, no child support maintenance shall be payable.

(6) The liability to pay any amount calculated under paragraph (4) shall be subject to the provision made for protected income and minimum payments under paragraphs 6 and 7 of Schedule 1 to the Act.

AMENDMENT

1. Article 16 of the Commencement No. 7 Order 1999 (June 1, 1999).

DEFINITIONS

**4.188**       "the Act": see reg.1(2).
"day to day care": see reg.1(2).
"person": see reg.1(2).

## One parent is absent and the other is treated as absent

**21.**—(1) Where the circumstances of a case are that one parent is an absent parent and the other parent is treated as an absent parent by regulation 20(2), that case shall be treated as a special case for the purposes of the Act.

4.189

(2) For the purpose of assessing the child support maintenance payable by an absent parent where this case applies, each reference in Schedule 1 to the Act to a parent who is a person with care shall be treated as a reference to a person who is treated as an absent parent by regulation 20(2).

DEFINITION

"the Act": see reg.1(2).

4.190

## Multiple applications relating to an absent parent

**22.**—[³(1) Where an application for a maintenance assessment has been made in respect of an absent parent and—

4.191

(a) at least one other application for a maintenance assessment has been made in relation to the same absent parent (or a person who is treated as an absent parent by regulation 20(2)) but to different children; or

(b) at least one maintenance assessment is in force in relation to the same absent parent or a person who is treated as an absent parent by regulation 20(2) but to different children, that case shall be a special case for the purposes of the Act.]

[²(2) For the purposes of assessing the amount of child support maintenance payable in respect of each application where [⁴paragraph (1)(a)] applies [⁴or in respect of the application made in circumstances where paragraph (1)(b) applies], for references to the assessable income of an absent parent in the Act and in these Regulations [⁶, and subject to paragraph (2ZA),] there shall be substituted references to the amount calculated by the formula—

$$\left\{ (A + T) \times \frac{B}{D} \right\} - CS$$

where—

A is the absent parent's assessable income;

T is the sum of the amounts allowable in the calculation or estimation of his exempt income by virtue of Schedule 3A;

B is the maintenance requirement calculated in respect of the application in question;

D is the sum of the maintenance requirements as calculated for the purposes of each assessment relating to the absent parent in question; and

CS is the amount (if any) allowable by virtue of Schedule 3A in calculating or estimating the absent parent's exempt income in respect of a relevant qualifying transfer of property in respect of the assessment in question.]

[⁷(2ZA) Where a case falls within regulation 39(1)(a) of the Departure Direction and Consequential Amendments Regulations, for the purposes of assessing the amount of child support maintenance payable in respect of an application for child support maintenance before a departure direction in respect of the maintenance assessment in question is given, for references to the assessable income of an absent parent in the Act and in these Regulations there shall be substituted references to the amount calculated by the formula

$$(A + T) \times \frac{B}{D}$$

where A, T, B and D have the same meanings as in paragraph (2).]

[5(2A) Where paragraph (l)(b) applies, and a maintenance assessment has been made in respect of the application referred to in paragraph (1), each maintenance assessment in force at the time of that assessment shall be reduced using the formula for calculation of assessable income set out in paragraph (2) and each reduction shall take effect on the date specified in regulation 33(7) of the Maintenance Assessment Procedure Regulations.]

[8(2B) Where—

(a)   a case is treated as a special case for the purposes of the Act by virtue of paragraph (1);

(b)   more than one maintenance assessment is in force in respect of the absent parent; and

[9(c)   any of those assessments falls to be replaced by a fresh assessment to be made by virtue of a revision under section 16 of the Act or a decision under section 17 of the Act superseding an earlier decision,]

the formula set out in paragraph (2) or, as the case may be, paragraph (2ZA) shall be applied to calculate or estimate the amount of child support maintenance payable under that fresh assessment.]

[8(2C) Where a maintenance assessment falls within subparagraph (b) of paragraph (2B) but [10not within] subparagraph (c) of that paragraph, the formula set out in paragraph (2) or, as the case may be, paragraph (2ZA) shall be applied to determine whether that maintenance assessment should be increased or reduced as a result of the making of a fresh assessment under sub-paragraph (c) and any increase or reduction shall take effect from the effective date of that fresh assessment.]

(3) When more than one maintenance assessment has been made with respect to the absent parent and payment by him of the aggregate of the amounts of those assessments would reduce his disposable income below his protected income-level, the aggregate amount of those assessments shall be reduced (each being reduced by reference to the same proportion as those assessments bear to each other) by the minimum amount necessary to prevent his disposable income being reduced below his protected income level provided that the aggregate amount payable under those assessments shall not be reduced to less than the minimum amount prescribed in regulation 13(1).

[1(4) Where the aggregate of the child support maintenance payable by the absent parent is less than the minimum amount prescribed in regulation 13(1), the child support maintenance payable shall be—

(i)   that prescribed minimum amount apportioned between the two or more applications in the same ratio as the maintenance requirements in question bear to each other; or

(ii) where, because of the application of regulation 2(2), such an apportionment produces an aggregate amount which is different from that prescribed amount, that different amount.]

(5) Payment of each of the maintenance assessments calculated under this regulation shall satisfy the liability of the absent parent (or a person treated as such) to pay child support maintenance.

AMENDMENTS

1. Regulation 23 of the Amendment Regulations (April 5, 1993).
2. Regulation 51 of the Amendment Regulations 1995 (April 18, 1995).
3. Regulation 45(2) of the Miscellaneous Amendments (No. 2) Regulations 1995 (January 22, 1996).
4. Regulation 45(3) of the Miscellaneous Amendments (No. 2) Regulations 1995 (January 22, 1996).
5. Regulation 45(4) of the Miscellaneous Amendments (No. 2) Regulations 1995 (January 22, 1996).
6. Regulation 68(5)(a) of the Departure Regulations (December 2, 1996).
7. Regulation 68(5)(b) of the Departure Regulations (December 2, 1996).
8. Regulation 53 of the Miscellaneous Amendments Regulations 1998 (January 19, 1998).
9. Article 18(a) of the Commencement No. 7 Order 1999 (June 1, 1999).
10. Article 18(b) of the Commencement No. 7 Order 1999 (June 1, 1999).

DEFINITIONS

"the Act": see reg.1(2).　　　　　　　　　　　　　　　　　　　　　4.192
"Departure Direction and Consequential Amendments Regulations": see reg.1(2).
"Maintenance Assessment Procedure Regulations": see reg.1(2).
"qualifying transfer": see reg.1(2).

## Person caring for children of more than one absent parent

**23.**—(1) Where the circumstances of a case are that—　　　　　　4.193
(a) a person is a person with care in relation to two or more qualifying children; and
(b) in relation to at least two of those children there are different persons who are absent parents or persons treated as absent parents by regulation 20(2);
that case shall be treated as a special case for the purposes of the Act.

(2) [¹Subject to paragraph (2A)] in calculating the maintenance requirements for the purposes of this case, for any amount which (but for this paragraph) would have been included under regulation 3(1)(b) [³or (c)] (amounts included in the calculation of AG) there shall be substituted an amount calculated by dividing the amount which would have been so included by the relevant number.

[¹(2A) In applying the provisions of paragraph (2) to the amount which is to be included in the maintenance requirements under regulation 3(l)(b)—
(a) first take the amount specified in head (i) of regulation 3(1)(b) and divide it by the relevant number;

(b) then apply the provisions of regulation 3(1)(b) as if the references to the amount specified in column (2) of paragraph 1(l)(e) of the relevant Schedule were references to the amount which is the product of the calculation required by head (a) above, and as if, in relation to an absent parent, the only qualifying children to be included in the assessment were those qualifying children in relation to whom he is the absent parent.]

(3) [²In paragraph (2) and (2A)] "the relevant number" means the number equal to the total number of persons who, in relation to those children, are either absent parents or persons treated as absent parents by regulation 20(2) except that where in respect of the same child both parents are persons who are either absent parents or persons who are treated as absent parents under that regulation, they shall count as one person.

(4) Where the circumstances of a case fall within this regulation and the person with care is the parent of any of the children, for C in paragraph 2(1) of Schedule 1 to the Act (the assessable income of that person) there shall be substituted the amount which would be calculated under regulation 22(2) if the references therein to an absent parent were references to a parent with care.

AMENDMENTS

1. Regulation 4(6) of the Miscellaneous Amendments Regulations 1994 (February 7, 1994).
2. Regulation 4(7) of the Miscellaneous Amendments Regulations 1994 (February 7, 1994).
3. Regulation 14 of the Child Benefit Amendment Regulations (April 7, 1997).

DEFINITIONS

4.194    "the Act": see reg.1(2).
"person": see reg.1(2).


**Persons with part-time care—not including a person treated as an absent parent**

4.195    **24.**—(1) Where the circumstances of a case are that—
(a) two or more persons who do not live in the same household each provide day to day care for the same qualifying child; and
(b) those persons do not include any parent who is treated as an absent parent of that child by regulation 20(2),
that case shall be treated as a special case for the purposes of the Act.
(2) For the purposes of this case—
(a) the person whose application for a maintenance assessment is being proceeded with shall, subject to paragraph (b), be entitled to receive all the child support maintenance payable under the Act in respect of the child in question;
(b) on request being made to the Secretary of State by—
  (i) that person; or
  (ii) any other person who is providing day to day care for the child and who intends to continue to provide that care,

the Secretary of State may make arrangements for the payment of any child support maintenance payable under the Act to the persons who provide such care in the same ratio as that in which it appears to the Secretary of State, that each is to provide such care for the child in question;

(c) before making an arrangement under subparagraph (b), the Secretary of State shall consider all of the circumstances of the case and in particular the interests of the child, the present arrangements for the day to day care of the child in question and any representations or proposals made by the persons who provide such care for that child.

DEFINITIONS

"the Act": see reg.1(2).  4.196
"day to day care": see reg.1(2).
"person": see reg.1(2).

## Care provided in part by a local authority

**25.**—(1) Where the circumstances of a case are that a local authority  4.197
and a person each provide day to day care for the same qualifying child, that case shall be treated as a special case for the purposes of the Act.

(2) [¹Subject to paragraph 3, in a case where this regulation applies]—

(a) child support maintenance shall be calculated in respect of that child as if this regulation did not apply;

(b) the amount so calculated shall be divided by 7 so as to produce a daily amount;

(c) in respect of each night for which day to day care for that child is provided by a person other than the local authority, the daily amount relating to that period shall be payable by the absent parent (or, as the case may be, by the person treated as an absent parent under regulation 20(2));

(d) child support maintenance shall not be payable in respect of any night for which the local authority provides day to day care for that qualifying child.

[²(3) In a case where more than one qualifying child is included in a child support maintenance assessment application and where this regulation applies to at least one of those children, child support maintenance shall be calculated by applying the formula—

$$S \times \left\{ \frac{A}{7 \times B} \right\}$$

where—

S is the total amount of child support maintenance in respect of all qualifying children included in that maintenance assessment application, calculated as if this regulation did not apply;

A is the aggregate of the number of nights of day to day care for all qualifying children included in that maintenance assessment application provided in each week by a person other than the local authority;

B is the number of qualifying children in respect of whom the maintenance assessment application has been made.]

1. Regulation 52(2) of the Amendment Regulations 1995 (April 18, 1995).
2. Regulation 52(3) of the Amendment Regulations 1995 (April 18, 1995).

DEFINITIONS

4.198     "the Act": see reg.1(2).
"day to day care": see reg.1(2).
"person": see reg.1(2).

## Cases where child support maintenance is not to be payable

4.199     **26.**—(1) Where the circumstances of a case are that—
  (a) but for this regulation the minimum amount prescribed in regulation 13(1) would apply; and
  (b) any of the following conditions are satisfied—
    (i) the income of the absent parent includes one or more of the payments or awards specified in Schedule 4 or would include such a payment but for a provision preventing the receipt of that payment by reason of it overlapping with some other benefit payment or would, in the case of the payments referred to in paragraph (a) (i) or (iv) of that Schedule, include such a payments if the relevant contribution conditions for entitlement had been satisfied;
    (ii) an amount to which regulation [$^2$11(1) (f)] applies (protected income: income support family premium) is taken into account in calculating or estimating [$^1$under paragraphs (1) to (5) of regulation 11,] the protected income of the absent parent;
    (iii) the absent parent is a child within the meaning of section 55 of the Act;
    (iv) the absent parent is a prisoner; or
    (v) the absent parent is a person in respect of whom N (as calculated or estimated under regulation 7(1)) is less than the minimum amount prescribed by regulation 13(1),
the case shall be treated as a special case for the purposes of the Act.
  (2) For the purposes of this case—
  (a) the requirement in paragraph 7(2) of Schedule 1 to the Act (minimum amount of child support maintenance fixed by an assessment to be the prescribed minimum amount) shall not apply;
  (b) the amount of the child support maintenance to be fixed by the assessment shall be nil.

AMENDMENTS

1. Regulation 53 of the Amendment Regulations 1995 (April 18, 1995).
2. Regulation 54 of Miscellaneous Amendments Regulations 1998 (April 6, 1998).

DEFINITIONS

"the Act": see reg.1(2).    4.200
"person": see reg.1(2).
"prisoner": see reg.1(2).

## Child who is a boarder or an in-patient

**27.**—(1) Where the circumstances of a case are that—    4.201
(a) a qualifying child is a boarder at a boarding school or is an in-patient
  in a hospital; and
(b) by reason of those circumstances, the person who would otherwise
  provide day to day care is not doing so,
that case shall be treated as a special case for the purposes of the Act.

(2) For the purposes of this case, section 3(3)(b) of the Act shall be
modified so [¹that] for the reference to the person who usually provides day
to day care for the child there shall be substituted a reference to the person
who would usually be providing such care for that child but for the
circumstances specified in paragraph (1).

AMENDMENT

1. Regulation 24 of the Amendment Regulations (April 5, 1993).

DEFINITIONS

"the Act": see reg.1(2).    4.202
"day to day care": see reg.1(2).
"person": see reg.1(2).

## [¹Child who is allowed to live with his parent under section 23(5) of the Children Act 1989

**27A.**—(1) Where the circumstances of a case are that a qualifying child
who is in the care of a local authority in England and Wales is allowed by
the authority to live with a parent of his under section 23(5) of the Children
Act 1989, that case shall be treated as a special case for the purposes of the
Act.

(2) For the purposes of this case, section 3(3)(b) of the Act shall be
modified so that for the reference to the person who usually provides day
to day care for the child there shall be substituted a reference to the parent
of a child whom the local authority allow the child to live with under
section 23(5) of the Children Act 1989.]

AMENDMENT

1. Regulation 25 of the Amendment Regulations (April 5, 1993).

DEFINITIONS

"the Act": see reg.1(2).    4.203
"day to day care": see reg.1(2).

### Amount payable where absent parent is in receipt of income support or other prescribed benefit

4.204    **28.**—(1) Where the condition specified in section 43(1)(a) of the Act is satisfied in relation to an absent parent (assessable income to be nil where income support[⁵, income-based jobseeker's allowance] or other prescribed benefit is paid), the prescribed conditions for the purposes of section 43(l)(b) of the Act are that—

(a) the absent parent is aged 18 or over;

(b) he does not satisfy the conditions in paragraph [⁶3(i)(a) or (b)] of the relevant Schedule (income support family premium) [¹and does not have day to day care of any child (whether or not a relevant child)]; and

(c) [²his income does not include] one or more of the payments or awards specified in Schedule 4 (other than by reason of a provision preventing receipt of overlapping benefits or by reason of a failure to satisfy the relevant contribution conditions).

(2) For the purposes of section 43(2)(a) of the Act, the prescribed amount shall be equal to the minimum amount prescribed in regulation 13(1) for the purposes of paragraph 7(1) of Schedule 1 to the Act.

[³(3) Subject to paragraph (4), where—

(a) an absent parent is liable under section 43 of the Act and this regulation to make payments in place of payments of child support maintenance with respect to two or more qualifying children in relation to whom there is more than one parent with care; or

(b) that absent parent and his partner (within the meaning of regulation 2(1) of the Social Security (Claims and Payments) Regulations 1987) are both liable to make such payments,

the prescribed amount mentioned in paragraph (2) shall be apportioned between the persons with care in the same ratio as the maintenance requirements of the qualifying child or children in relation to each of those persons with care bear to each other.]

[⁴(4) If, in making the apportionment required by paragraph (3), the effect of the application of regulation 2(2) would be such that the aggregate amount payable would be different from the amount prescribed in paragraph (2) the Secretary of State shall adjust the apportionment so as to eliminate that difference; and that adjustment shall be varied from time to time so as to secure that, taking one week with another and so far as is practicable, each person with care receives the amount which she would have received if no adjustment had been made under this paragraph.

(5) The provisions of Schedule 5 shall have effect in relation to cases to which section 43 of the Act and this regulation apply.]

AMENDMENTS

1. Regulation 26(l)(a) of the Amendment Regulations (April 5, 1993).
2. Regulation 26(l)(b) of the Amendment Regulations (April 5, 1993).
3. Regulation 2(2) of the Child Support (Maintenance Assessments and Special Cases) Amendment Regulations 1993 (April 26, 1993).
4. Regulation 26(2) of the Amendment Regulations (April 5, 1993).

5. Regulation 6(3) of the Jobseekers Amendment Regulations (October 7, 1996).

6. Regulation 55 of Miscellaneous Amendments Regulations 1998 (April 6, 1998).

DEFINITIONS

"the Act": see reg.1(2).  4.205
"day to day care": see reg.1(2).
"relevant Schedule": see reg.1(2).


SCHEDULE 1

CALCULATION OF N AND M

PART I

EARNINGS

CHAPTER 1

*Earnings of an employed earner*

**1.**—(1) Subject to sub-paragraphs (2) and (3), "earnings" means in the  4.206
case of employment as an employed earner, any remuneration or profit
derived from that employment and includes—

(a) any bonus, commission, [⁵payment in respect of overtime,] royalty or
fee; [³³(aa) any profit-related pay, whether paid in anticipation of, or
following, the calculation of profits;]

(b) any holiday pay except any payable more than 4 weeks after
termination of the employment;

(c) any payment by way of a retainer;

[²⁹(d) any payment made by the parent's employer in respect of any
expenses not wholly, exclusively and necessarily incurred in the performance of the duties of the employment, including any payment
made by the parent's employer in respect of—

(i) travelling expenses incurred by the parent between his home
and place of employment; and

(ii) expenses incurred by that parent under arrangements made for
the care of a member of his family owing to that parent's
absence from home;]

(e) any award of compensation made under section 68(2) or 71(2)(a) of
the Employment Protection (Consolidation) Act 1978 (remedies
and compensation for unfair dismissal);

(f) any such sum as is referred to in section 112 of the Contributions
and Benefits Act (certain sums to be earnings for social security purposes);

(g) any statutory sick pay under Part I of the Social Security and
Housing Benefits Act 1982 or statutory maternity pay under Part V
of the Social Security Act 1986;

[<sup>81</sup>(gg) any statutory paternity pay under Part 12ZA of the Contributions and Benefits Act or any statutory adoption pay under Part 12ZB of that Act;]

(h) any payment in lieu of notice and any compensation in respect of the absence or inadequacy of any such notice but only insofar as such payment or compensation represents loss of income;

(i) any payment relating to a period of less than a year which is made in respect of the performance of duties as—

(i) an auxiliary coastguard in respect of coast rescue activities;

(ii) a part-time fireman in a fire brigade maintained in pursuance of the Fire Services Acts 1947 to 1959;

[<sup>78</sup>(iia) a part-time fire-fighter employed by a fire and rescue authority;]

(iii) a person engaged part-time in the manning or launching of a lifeboat;

(iv) a member of any territorial or reserve force prescribed in Part I of Schedule 3 to the Social Security (Contributions) Regulations 1979;

(j) any payment made by a local authority to a member of that authority in respect of the performance of his duties as a member, other than any expenses wholly, exclusively and necessarily incurred in the performance of those duties.

(2) Earnings shall not include—

(a) any payment in respect of expenses wholly, exclusively and necessarily incurred in the performance of the duties of the employment [<sup>41</sup> except any such payment which is made in respect of housing costs and those housing costs are included in the calculation of the exempt or protected income of the absent parent under regulation 9(1) (b) or, as the case may be, regulation 11(1) (b)];

(b) any occupational pension;

(c) any payment where—

(i) the employment in respect of which it was made has ceased; and

(ii) a period of the same length as the period by reference to which it was calculated has expired since that cessation but prior to the effective date;

(d) any advance of earnings or any loan made by an employer to an employee;

(e) any amount received from an employer during a period when the employee has withdrawn his services by reason of a trade dispute;

(f) any payment in kind;

(g) where, in any week or other period which falls within the period by reference to which earnings are calculated, earnings are received both in respect of a previous employment and in respect of a subsequent employment, the earnings in respect of the previous employment;

[<sup>34</sup>(h) any tax-exempt allowance made by an employer to an employee [<sup>42</sup>except any such allowance which is made in respect of housing costs and those housing costs are included in the calculation of the exempt or protected income of the absent parent under regulation 9(1)(b) or, as the case may be, regulation 11(1)(b)].]

(3) The earnings to be taken into account for the purposes of calculating N and M shall be gross earnings less—

(a) any amount deducted from those earnings by way of—

    (i) income tax;

    (ii) primary Class 1 contributions under the Contributions and Benefits Act [6or under the Social Security Contributions and Benefits (Northern Ireland) Act 1992], and

(b) one half of any sums paid by the parent towards an ['occupational pension scheme];

[8(c) one half of any sums paid by the parent towards a personal pension scheme, or, where that scheme is intended partly to provide a capital sum to discharge a mortgage secured upon the parent's home, 37.5 per centum of any such sums.]

**2.** [9(1) Subject to subparagraphs [35(1A)] to (4), the amount of the earnings to be taken into account for the purpose of calculating N and M shall be calculated or estimated by reference to the average earnings at the relevant week having regard to such evidence as is available in relation to that person's earnings during such period as appears appropriate to the [56Secretary of State] beginning not earlier than eight weeks before the relevant week and ending not later than the date of the assessment and for the purpose of that calculation or estimate he may consider evidence of that person's cumulative earnings during the period beginning with the start of the year of assessment (within the meaning of section 832 of the Income and Corporation Taxes Act 1988) in which the relevant week falls and ending with a date no later than the date of the assessment.]

                                          4.207

[36(1A) Subject to sub-paragraph (4), where a person has claimed, or has been paid, [71working tax credit or child tax credit] on any day during the period beginning not earlier than eight weeks before the relevant week and ending not later than the date on which the assessment is made, [57Secretary of State] may have regard to the amount of earnings taken into account in determining entitlement to those benefits in order to calculate or estimate the amount of earnings to be taken into account for the purposes of calculating N and M, notwithstanding the fact that entitlement to those benefits may have been determined by reference to earnings attributable to a period other than that specified in sub-paragraph (1).]

[37(2) Where a person's earnings during the period of 52 weeks ending with the relevant week include—

(a) a bonus, commission or payment of profit-related pay made in anticipation of the calculation of profits which is paid separately from or in relation to a longer period than, the other earnings with which it is paid; or

(b) a payment in respect of profit-related pay made following the calculation of the employer's profits,

the amount of that bonus, commission or profit-related pay shall be determined for the purposes of the calculation of earnings by aggregating any such payments received in that period and dividing by 52.]

(3) Subject to subparagraph (4), the amount of any earnings of a student shall be determined by aggregating the amount received in the year ending with the relevant week and dividing by 52 or, where the person in question has been a student for less than a year, by aggregating the amount received

in the period starting with his becoming a student and ending with the relevant week and dividing by the number of complete weeks in that period.

[38(3A) Where a case is one to which regulation 30A(1) or (3) of the Maintenance Assessment Procedure Regulations applies (effective dates of new maintenance assessments in particular cases), the term "relevant week" shall, for the purposes of this paragraph, mean the period of seven days immediately preceding the date on which the information or evidence is received which enables [59the Secretary of State] to make a new maintenance assessment calculated in accordance with the provisions of Part I of Schedule 1 to the Act in respect of that case for a period beginning after the effective date applicable to that case.]

(4) Where a calculation would, but for this sub-paragraph, produce an amount which, in the opinion of the [58Secretary of State], does not accurately reflect the normal amount of the earnings of the person in question, such earnings, or any part of them, shall be calculated by reference to such other period as may, in the particular case, enable the normal weekly earnings of that person to be determined more accurately and for this purpose the [58Secretary of State] shall have regard to—

(a) the earnings received, or due to be received, from any employment in which the person in question is engaged, has been engaged or is due to be engaged;

(b) the duration and pattern, or the expected duration and pattern, of any employment of that person.

## CHAPTER 2

### *Earnings of a self-employed earner*

4.208 [462A.—(1) Subject to paragraphs 2B, 2C, 4 and 5A, "earnings" in the case of employment as a self-employed earner shall have the meaning given by the following provisions of this paragraph.

(2) "Earnings" means the total taxable profits from self-employment of that earner as submitted to the Inland Revenue, less the following amounts—

(a) any income tax relating to the taxable profits from the self-employment determined in accordance with subparagraph (3);

(b) any National Insurance Contributions relating to the taxable profits from the self-employment determined in accordance with subparagraph (4);

(c) one half of any premium paid in respect of a retirement annuity contract or a personal pension scheme or, where that scheme is intended partly to provide a capital sum to discharge a mortgage or charge secured upon the self-employed earner's home, 37.5 per centum of the contributions payable.

(3) For the purposes of subparagraph (2)(a) the income tax to be deducted from the total taxable profits shall be determined in accordance with the following provisions—

(a) subject to head (d), an amount of earnings [82calculated as if were equivalent to any personal allowance which would be] applicable to the earner by virtue of the provisions of Chapter 1 of Part VII of the Income and Corporation Taxes Act 1988 (personal reliefs) shall be disregarded;

(b) subject to head (c), an amount equivalent to income tax shall be calculated in relation to the earnings remaining following the application of head (a) (the "remaining earnings");

(c) the tax rate applicable at the effective date shall be applied to all the remaining earnings, where necessary increasing or reducing the amount payable to take account of the fact that the earnings relate to a period greater or less than one year;

(d) the amount to be disregarded by virtue of head (a) shall be calculated by reference to the yearly rate applicable at the effective date, that amount being reduced or increased in the same proportion to that which the period represented by the taxable profits bears to the period of one year.

(4) For the purposes of subparagraph (2)(b) above, the amount to be deducted in respect of National Insurance Contributions shall be the total of—

(a) the amount of Class 2 contributions (if any) payable under section 11(1) or, as the case may be, (3), of the Contributions and Benefits Act; and

(b) the amount of Class 4 contributions (if any) payable under section 15(2) of that Act,

at the rates applicable at the effective date.]

[[46]**2B.**—(1) Where—    4.209

(a) a self-employed earner cannot provide the [Secretary of State] with the total taxable profit figure from self-employment for the period concerned as submitted to the Inland Revenue, but can provide a copy of his tax calculation notice; or

(b) the [[84]Secretary of State] becomes aware that the total taxable profit figure from the self-employment submitted by the self-employed earner has been revised by the Inland Revenue,

the earnings of that earner shall be calculated by reference to the income from employment as a self-employed earner as set out in the tax calculation notice issued in relation to his case, and if a revision of the figures included in that notice has occurred, by reference to the revised notice.

(2) In this paragraph and elsewhere in this Schedule—

"submitted to" means submitted to the Inland Revenue in accordance with their requirements by or on behalf of the self-employed earner; and

a "tax calculation notice" means a document issued by the Inland Revenue containing information as to the income of a self-employed earner;

a "revision of the figures" means the revision of the figures relating to the total taxable profit of a self-employed earner following an enquiry under section 9A of the Taxes Management Act 1970 or otherwise by the Inland Revenue.]

[[46]**2C.**—Where the [[84]Secretary of State] accepts that it is not reasonably    4.210 practicable for the self-employed earner to provide information relating to his total taxable profits from self-employment in the form submitted to, or (where paragraph 2B applies) as issued or revised by, the Inland Revenue, "earnings" in relation to that earner shall have the meaning given by paragraph 3 of this Schedule.]

4.211      **3.**—(1) [⁴⁷Where paragraph 2C applies, and subject] to subparagraphs (2) and (3) and to paragraph 4, "earnings" in the case of employment as a self-employed earner means the gross receipts of the employment including, where an allowance in the form of periodic payments is paid under section 2 of the Employment and Training Act 1973 or section 2 of the Enterprise and New Towns (Scotland) Act 1990 in respect of the relevant week for the purpose of assisting him in carrying on his business, the total of those payments made during the period by reference to which his earnings are determined under paragraph 5.

(2) Earnings shall not include—

(a) any allowance paid under either of those sections in respect of any part of the period by reference to which his earnings are determined under paragraph 5 if no part of that allowance is paid in respect of the relevant week;

(b) any income consisting of payments received for the provision of board and lodging accommodation unless such payments form the largest element of the recipient's income.

(3) [¹Subject to subparagraph (7),] there shall be deducted from the gross receipts referred to in subparagraph (1)—

(a) [²except in a case to which paragraph 4 applies,] any expenses which are reasonably incurred and are wholly and exclusively defrayed for the purposes of the earner's business in the period by reference to which his earnings are determined under paragraph 5(1) or, where paragraph 5(2) applies, any such expenses relevant to the period there mentioned (whether or not defrayed in that period);

(b) [²except in a case to which paragraph 4 [¹⁰or 5(2)] applies, any value added tax paid in the period by reference to which earnings are determined in excess of value added tax received in that period;

(c) any amount in respect of income tax determined in accordance with subparagraph (5);

(d) any amount in respect of National Insurance contributions determined in accordance with subparagraph (6);

(e) one half of any premium paid in respect of a retirement annuity contract or a personal pension scheme[¹¹, or, where that scheme is intended partly to provide a capital sum to discharge a mortgage or charge secured upon the parent's home, 37.5 per centum of the contributions payable].

(4) For the purposes of subparagraph (3)(a)—

(a) such expenses include—

(i) repayment of capital on any loan used for the replacement, in the course of business, of equipment or machinery, or the repair of an existing business asset except to the extent that any sum is payable under an insurance policy for its repair;

(ii) any income expended in the repair of an existing business asset except to the extent that any sum is payable under an insurance policy for its repair;

     (iii)  any payment of interest on a loan taken out for the purposes of the business;

  (b)  such expenses do not include—

     (i)  repayment of capital on any other loan taken out for the purposes of the business;

     (ii)  any capital expenditure;

     (iii)  the depreciation of any capital asset;

     (iv)  any sum employed, or intended to be employed, in the setting up or expansion of the business;

     (v)  any loss incurred before the beginning of that period by reference to which earnings are determined;

     (vi)  any expenses incurred in providing business entertainment; (vii) any loss incurred in any other employment in which he is engaged as a self-employed earner.

[³⁹(5)  For the purposes of sub-paragraph (3)(c), the amount in respect of income tax shall be determined in accordance with the following provisions—

  (a)  subject to head (c), an amount of chargeable earnings [⁸³calculated as if were equivalent to any personal allowance which would be] applicable to the earner by virtue of the provisions of Chapter 1 of Part VII of the Income and Corporation Taxes Act 1988 (personal reliefs) shall be disregarded;

  (b)  [⁴³subject to head (bb),] an amount equivalent to income tax shall be calculated with respect to taxable earnings at the rates applicable at the effective date;

[⁴⁴(bb)  where taxable earnings are determined over a period of less or more than one year, the amount of earnings to which each tax rate applies shall be reduced or increased in the same proportion to that which the period represented by the chargeable earnings bears to the period of one year;]

  (c)  the amount to be disregarded by virtue of head (a) shall be calculated be reference to the yearly rate applicable at the effective date, that amount being reduced or increased in the same proportion to that which the period represented by the chargeable earnings bears to the period of one year;

  (d)  in this sub-paragraph, "taxable earnings" means the chargeable earnings of the earner following the disregard of any applicable personal allowances.]

(6)  For the purposes of subparagraph (3)(d), the amount to be deducted in respect of National Insurance contributions shall be the total of—

  (a)  the amount of Class 2 contributions (if any) payable under section 11(1) or, as the case may be, [¹³(3)] of the Contributions and Benefits Act; and

  (b)  the amount of Class 4 contributions (if any) payable under section 15(2) of that Act, at the rates applicable [⁴to the chargeable earnings] at the effective date.

[¹⁴(7)  In the case of a self-employed earner whose employment is carried on in partnership or is that of a share fisherman within the meaning of the Social Security (Mariners' Benefits) Regulations 1975, subparagraph (3) shall have effect as though it requires—

    (a) a deduction from the earner's estimated or, where appropriate, actual share of the gross receipts of the partnership or fishing boat, of his share of the sums likely to be deducted or, where appropriate, deducted from those gross receipts under heads (a) and (b) of that subparagraph; and

    (b) a deduction from the amount so calculated of the sums mentioned in heads (c) to (e) of that subparagraph.]

[⁴(8) In subparagraphs (5) and (6) "chargeable earnings" means the gross receipts of the employment less any deductions mentioned in subparagraph (3) (a) and (b).]

**4.** In a case where a person is self-employed as a childminder the amount of earnings referable to that employment shall be one-third of the gross receipts.

4.212 **5.**—(1) Subject to subparagraphs [¹⁵(2) to (3)]—

    (a) where a person has been a self-employed earner for 52 weeks or more including the relevant week, the amount of his earnings shall be determined by reference to the average of the earnings which he has received in the 52 weeks ending with the relevant week;

    (b) where the person has been a self-employed earner for a period of less than 52 weeks including the relevant week, the amount of his earnings shall be determined by reference to the average of the earnings which he has received during that period.

(2) [¹⁶Subject to subparagraph (2A), where] a person who is a self-employed earner provides in respect of the employment a profit and loss account and, where appropriate, a trading account or a balance sheet or both, and the profit and loss account is in respect of a period at least 6 months but not exceeding 15 months and that period terminates within the [¹⁷24 months] immediately preceding the effective date, the amount of his earnings shall be determined by reference to the average of the earnings over the period to which the profit and loss account relates and such earnings shall include receipts relevant to that period (whether or not received in that period).

[¹⁸(2A) Where the [⁶¹Secretary of State] is satisfied that, in relation to the person referred to in subparagraph (2) there is more than one profit and loss account, each in respect of different periods, both or all of which satisfy the conditions mentioned in that subparagraph, the provisions of that subparagraph shall apply only to the account which relates to the latest such period, unless [⁶⁰the Secretary of State] is satisfied that the latest such account is not available for reasons beyond the control of that person, in which case he may have regard to any such other account which satisfies the requirements of that subparagraph.]

(3) Where a calculation would, but for this subparagraph, produce an amount which, in the opinion of the [⁶²Secretary of State], does not accurately reflect the normal amount of the earnings of the person in question, such earnings, or any part of them, shall be calculated by reference to such other period as may, in the particular case, enable the normal weekly earnings of that person to be determined more accurately and for this purpose the [⁶²Secretary of State] shall have regard to—

(a) the earnings received, or due to be received, from any employment in which the person in question is engaged, or has been engaged or is due to be engaged;

(b) the duration and pattern, or the expected duration and pattern, of any employment of that person.

(4) In subparagraph (2)—

(a) "balance sheet" means a statement of the financial position of the employment disclosing its assets, liabilities and capital at the end of the period in question;

(b) "profit and loss account" means a financial statement showing net profit or loss of the employment for the period in question; and

(c) "trading account" means a financial statement showing the revenue from sales, the cost of those sales and the gross profit arising during the period in question.

[⁴⁰(5) Subject to subparagraph (3), where a person has claimed, or has been paid, [⁷²working tax credit or child tax credit] on any day during the period beginning not earlier than eight weeks before the relevant week and ending not later than the date on which the assessment is made, the [⁶³Secretary of State] may have regard to the amount of earnings taken into account in determining entitlement to those benefits in order to calculate or estimate the amount of earnings to be taken into account for the purposes of calculating N and M, notwithstanding the fact that entitlement to those benefits may have been determined by reference to earnings attributable to a period other than that specified in subparagraph (1).]

[⁴⁸(6) This paragraph applies only where the earnings of a self-employed earner have the meaning given by paragraph 3 of this Schedule.]

[⁴⁹**5A.**—(1) Subject to subparagraph (2) of this paragraph, the earnings of a self-employed earner may be determined in accordance with the provisions of paragraph 2A only where the total taxable profits concerned relate to a period of not less than 6, and not more than 15 months, which terminated not more than 24 months prior to the relevant week;

4.213

(2) Where there is more than one total taxable profit figure which would satisfy the conditions set out in subparagraph (1), the earnings calculation shall be based upon the figure pertaining to the latest such period.

(3) Where, in the opinion of the [⁸⁴Secretary of State], information as to the total taxable profits of the self-employed earner which would satisfy the criteria set out in subparagraphs (1) and (2) of this paragraph does not accurately reflect the normal weekly earnings of the self-employed earner, the earnings of that earner can be calculated by reference to the provisions of paragraphs 3 and 5 of this Schedule.]

## PART II

## BENEFIT PAYMENTS

**6.**—(1) The benefit payments to be taken into account in calculating or estimating N and M shall be determined in accordance with this Part.

4.214

(2) "Benefit payments" means any benefit payments under the Contributions and Benefits Act [²⁴or the Jobseekers Act] except amounts to be disregarded by virtue of Schedule 2.

(3) The amount of any benefit payment to be taken into account shall be determined by reference to the rate of that benefit applicable at the effective date.

**7.**—(1) Where a benefit payment under the Contributions and Benefits Act includes an adult or child dependency increase—

(a) if that benefit is payable to a parent, the income of that parent shall be calculated or estimated as if it did not include that amount;

(b) if that benefit is payable to some other person but includes an amount in respect of the parent, the income of the parent shall be calculated or estimated as if it included that amount.

[²¹(1A) For the purposes of subparagraph (1), an addition to a contribution-based job-seeker's allowance under [⁵⁰regulation 10(4)] of the Jobseeker's Allowance (Transitional Provisions) Regulations [⁵¹1996] shall be treated as a dependency increase included with a benefit under the Contributions and Benefits Act.]

[⁷³. . .]

[²⁵(6) Where child benefit in respect of a relevant child is in payment at the rate specified in regulation 2(l)(a)(ii) of the Child Benefit Rates Regulations, the difference between that rate and the basic rate applicable to that child, as defined in regulation 4.]

## PART III

## OTHER INCOME

4.215  **8.** The amount of the other income to be taken into account in calculating or estimating N and M shall be the aggregate of the following amounts determined in accordance with this Part.

4.216  **9.** Any periodic payment of pension or other benefit under an occupational or personal pension scheme or a retirement annuity contract or other such scheme for the provision of income in retirement.

[⁵²**9A.**—(1) Where a war disablement pension includes an adult or child dependency increase—

(a) if that pension, including the dependency increase, is payable to a parent, the income of that parent shall be calculated or estimated as if it did not include that amount;

(b) if that pension, including the dependency increase, is payable to some other person but includes an amount in respect of the parent, the income of the parent shall be calculated or estimated as if it included that amount.

(2) For the purposes of this paragraph, a "war disablement pension" includes a war widow's pension [⁷⁹and a war widower's pension], a payment made to compensate for non-payment of such a pension, and a pension or payment analogous to such a pension or payment paid by the government of a country outside Great Britain.]

4.217  **10.** Any payment received on account of the provision of board and lodging which does not come within Part I of this Schedule.

4.218  **11.** Subject to regulation 7(3)(b) and paragraph 12, any payment to a student of—

(a) a grant;

(b) an amount in respect of grant contribution;

(c) covenant income except to the extent that it has been taken into account under subparagraph (b);

(d) a student loan.

**12.** The income of a student shall not include any payment—

(a) intended to meet tuition fees or examination fees;

(b) intended to meet additional expenditure incurred by a disabled student in respect of his attendance on a course;

(c) intended to meet additional expenditure connected with term time residential study away from the student's educational establishment;

(d) on account of the student maintaining a home at a place other than at which he resides during his course;

(e) intended to meet the cost of books, and equipment (other than special equipment) or, if not so intended, an amount equal to the amount allowed under [$^{74}$regulation 62(2A)(b) of the Income Support (General) Regulations 1987 towards such costs;]

(f) intended to meet travel expenses incurred as a result of his attendance on the course.

**13.** Any interest, dividend or other income derived from capital.

**14.** Any maintenance payments in respect of a parent.

[$^{31}$**14A.**—(1) Subject to subparagraph (2), the amount of any earnings top-up paid to or in respect of the absent parent or the parent with care.

(2) Subject to subparagraphs (3) and (4), where earnings top-up is payable and the amount which is payable has been calculated by reference to the weekly earnings of either the absent parent and another person or the parent with care and another person—

(a) if during the period which is used to calculate his weekly earnings under paragraph 2 or, as the case may be, paragraph 5, the normal weekly earnings of that parent exceed those of the other person, the amount payable by way of earnings top-up shall be treated as the income of that parent;

(b) if during that period, the normal weekly earnings of that parent equal those of the other person, half of the amount payable by way of earnings top-up shall be treated as the income of that parent;

(c) if during that period, the normal weekly earnings of that parent are less than those of the other person, the amount payable by way of earnings top-up shall be not treated as the income of that parent.

(3) Where any earnings top-up is in payment and, not later than the effective date, the person, or, if more than one, each of the persons by reference to whose engagement and normal engagement in remunerative work that payment has been calculated is no longer the partner of the person to whom the payment is made, the payment in question shall be treated as the income of the parent in question only where that parent is in receipt of it.

(4) Where any earnings top-up is in payment and, not later than the effective date, either or both of the persons by reference to whose engagement and normal engagement in remunerative work that payment has been calculated has ceased to be employed, half of the amount payable by way of earnings top-up shall be treated as the income of the parent in question.]

4.219

4.220

4.221

4.222

4.223     [⁷⁵**14B.**—(1) Subject to sub-paragraph (2), payments to a person of working tax credit shall be treated as the income of the parent who has qualified for them by his normal engagement in remunerative work at the rate payable at the effective date.

(2) Where working tax credit is payable and the amount which is payable has been calculated by reference to the earnings of the absent parent and another person—

  (a) if during the period which is used to calculate his earnings under paragraph 2 or, as the case may be, paragraph 5, the normal weekly earnings of that parent exceed those of the other person, the amount payable by way of working tax credit shall be treated as the income of that parent;

  (b) if during that period the normal weekly earnings of that parent equal those of the other person, half of the amount payable by way of working tax credit shall be treated as the income of that parent; and

  (c) if during that period the normal weekly earnings of that parent are less than those of that other person, the amount payable by way of working tax credit shall not be treated as the income of that parent.]

4.224     **15.** Any other payments or other amounts received on a periodical basis which are not otherwise taken into account under Part I, II, IV or V of this Schedule [³²except payments or other amounts which—

  (a) are excluded from the definition of "earnings" by virtue of paragraph 1(2);

  (b) are excluded from the definition of "the relevant income of a child" by virtue of paragraph 23; or

  (c) are the share of housing costs attributed by virtue of paragraph (3) of regulation 15 to any former partner of the parent of the qualifying child in respect of whom the maintenance assessment is made and are paid to that parent.]

4.225     **16.**—(1) Subject to subparagraphs (2) to [⁷⁶(7)] the amount of any income to which this Part applies shall be calculated or estimated—

  (a) where it has been received in respect of the whole of the period of 26 weeks which ends at the end of the relevant week, by dividing such income received in that period by 26;

  (b) where it has been received in respect of part of the period of 26 weeks which ends at the end of the relevant week, by dividing such income received in that period by the number of complete weeks in respect of which such income is received and for this purpose income shall be treated as received in respect of a week if it is received in respect of any day in the week in question.

  (2) The amount of maintenance payments made in respect of a parent—

  (a) where they are payable weekly and have been paid at the same amount in respect of each week in the period of 13 weeks which ends at the end of the relevant week, shall be the amount equal to one of those payments;

  (b) in any other case, shall be the amount calculated by aggregating the total amount of those payments received in the period of 13 weeks which ends at the end of the relevant week and dividing by the number of weeks in that period in respect of which maintenance was due.

  (3) In the case of a student—

(a) the amount of any grant and any amount paid in respect of grant contribution shall be calculated by apportioning it equally between the weeks in respect of which it is payable;

(b) the amount of any covenant income shall be calculated by dividing the amount payable in respect of a year by 52 (or, where such amount is payable in respect of a lesser period, by the number of complete weeks in that period) and, subject to subparagraph (4), deducting £5.00;

(c) the amount of any student loan shall be calculated by apportioning the loan equally between the weeks in respect of which it is payable and, subject to subparagraph (4), deducting £10.00.

(4) For the purposes of subparagraph (3)—

(a) not more than £5.00 shall be deducted under subparagraphs (3)(b);

(b) not more than £10.00 in total shall be deducted under subparagraphs (3) (b) and (c).

(5) Where in respect of the period of 52 weeks which ends at the end of the relevant week a person is in receipt of interest, dividend or other income which has been produced by his capital, the amount of that income shall be calculated by dividing the aggregate of the income so received by 52.

(6) Where a calculation would, but for this subparagraph, produce an amount which, in the opinion of the [⁶⁴Secretary of State], does not accurately reflect the normal amount of the other income of the person in question, such income, or any part of it, shall be calculated by reference to such other period as may, in the particular case, enable the other income of that person to be determined more accurately and for this purpose the [⁶⁴Secretary of State] shall have regard to the nature and pattern of receipt of such income.

[⁷⁷(7) This paragraph shall not apply to payments of working tax credit referred to in paragraph 14B.]

## PART IV

## INCOME OF CHILD TREATED AS INCOME OF PARENT

**17.** The amount of any income of a child which is to be treated as the income of the parent in calculating or estimating N and M shall be the aggregate of the amounts determined in accordance with this Part.

4.226

**18.** Where a child has income which falls within the following paragraphs of this Part and that child is a member of the family of his parent (whether that child is a qualifying child in relation to that parent or not), the relevant income of that child shall be treated as that of his parent.

4.227

**19.** Where child support maintenance is being assessed for the support of only one qualifying child, the relevant income of that child shall be treated as that of the parent with care.

4.228

**20.** Where child support maintenance is being assessed to support more than one qualifying child, the relevant income of each of those children shall be treated as that of the parent with care to the extent that it does not exceed the aggregate of—

4.229

(a) the amount determined under—

    (i)   regulation 3(1 )(a) (calculation of AG) in relation to the child in question; and

    (ii)  the total of any other amounts determined under regulation 3(1)(b) [26and (c)] which are applicable in the case in question divided by the number of children for whom child support maintenance is being calculated,

less the basic rate of child benefit (within the meaning of regulation 4) for the child in question; and

(b)  [19one-and-a-half times] the total of the amounts calculated under regulation 3(l)(a) (income support personal allowance for child or young person) in respect of that child and regulation [273(l)(c)] (income support family premium).

**4.230**     **21.** Where child support maintenance is not being assessed for the support of the child whose income is being calculated or estimated, the relevant income of that child shall be treated as that of his parent to the extent that it does not exceed the amount determined under regulation 9(l)(g).

**4.231**     **22.**[22—(1)] Where a benefit under the Contributions and Benefits Act includes an adult or child dependency increase in respect of a relevant child, the relevant income of that child shall be calculated or estimated as if it included that amount.

[22(1A) For the purposes of subparagraph (1), an addition to a contribution-based job-seeker's allowance under [53regulation 10(4)] of the Jobseeker's Allowance (Transitional Provisions) Regulations [541996] shall be treated as a dependency increase included with a benefit under the Contributions and Benefits Act.]

[5522(lB).—(1) Where a war disablement pension includes a dependency allowance paid in respect of a relevant child, the relevant income of that child shall be calculated or estimated as if it included that amount.

(2) For the purposes of this paragraph, a "war disablement pension" includes a war widow's pension [80and a war widower's pension], a payment made to compensate for non-payment of such a pension, and a pension or payment analogous to such a pension or payment paid by the government of a country outside Great Britain.]

**4.232**     **23.** For the purposes of this Part, "the relevant income of a child" does not include—

(a)  any earnings of the child in question;

(b)  payments by an absent parent [45to] the child for whom maintenance is being assessed;

(c)  where the class of persons who are capable of benefiting from a discretionary trust include the child in question, payments from that trust except in so far as they are made to provide for food, ordinary clothing and footwear, gas, electricity or fuel charges or housing costs; or

(d)  any interest payable on arrears of child support maintenance for that child [20;

(e)  the first £10 of any other income of that child].

**4.233**     **24.** The amount of the income of a child which is treated as the income of the parent shall be determined in the same way as if such income were the income of the parent.

PART V

AMOUNTS TREATED AS THE INCOME OF A PARENT

**25.** The amounts which fall to be treated as income of the parent in cal-    4.234
culating or estimating N and M shall include amounts to be determined in
accordance with this Part.

**26.** Where [65the Secretary of State] is satisfied—    4.235
- (a) that a person has performed a service either—
  - (i) without receiving any remuneration in respect of it; or
  - (ii) for remuneration which is less than that normally paid for that
    service;
- (b) that the service in question was for the benefit of—
  - (i) another person who is not a member of the same family as the
    person in question; or
  - (ii) a body which is neither a charity nor a voluntary organisation;
- (c) that the service in question was performed for a person who, or as
  the case may be, a body which was able to pay remuneration at the
  normal rate for the service in question;
- (d) that the principal purpose of the person undertaking the service
  without receiving any or adequate remuneration is to reduce his
  assessable income for the purposes of the Act; and
- (e) that any remuneration foregone would have fallen to be taken into
  account as earnings,

the value of the remuneration foregone shall be estimated by a [65the
Secretary of State] and an amount equal to the value so estimated shall be
treated as income of the person who performed those services.

**27.** Subject to paragraphs 28 to 30, where the [68Secretary of State] is    4.236
satisfied that, otherwise than in the circumstances set out in paragraph 26,
a person has intentionally deprived himself of—
- (a) any income or capital which would otherwise be a source of income;
- (b) any income or capital which it would be reasonable to expect would
  be secured by him,

with a view to reducing the amount of his assessable income, his net
income shall include the amount estimated by [66the Secretary of State] as
representing the income which that person would have had if he had not
deprived himself of or failed to secure that income, or as the case may be,
that capital.

**28.** No amount shall be treated as income by virtue of paragraph 27 in    4.237
relation to—
- [28(a) if the parent satisfies the conditions for payment at the rate of
  child benefit specified in regulation 2(l)(a)(ii) of the Child Benefit
  Rates Regulations, an amount representing the difference between
  that rate and the basic rate, as defined in regulation 4;]
- (b) if the parent is a person to, or in respect of, whom income support
  is payable, [23a contribution-based jobseeker's allowance].
- (c) a payment from a discretionary trust or a trust derived from a
  payment made in consequence of a personal injury.

**29.** Where an amount is included in the income of a person under para-    4.238
graph 27 in respect of income which would become available to him on

907

application, the amount included under that paragraph shall be included from the date on which it could be expected to be acquired.

4.239    **30.** Where [<sup>67</sup>the Secretary of State] determines under paragraph 27 that a person has deprived himself of capital which would otherwise be a source of income, the amount of that capital shall be reduced at intervals of 52 weeks, starting with the week which falls 52 weeks after the first week in respect of which income from it is included in the calculation of the assessment in question, by an amount equal to the amount which the [<sup>69</sup>the Secretary of State] estimates would represent the income from that source in the immediately preceding period of 52 weeks.

**31.** Where a payment is made on behalf of a parent or a relevant child in respect of food, ordinary clothing or footwear, gas, electricity or fuel charges, housing costs or council tax, an amount equal to the amount which the [<sup>70</sup>Secretary of State] estimates represents the value of that payment shall be treated as the income of the parent in question except to the extent that such amount is—

(a) disregarded under paragraph 38 of Schedule 2;

(b) a payment of school fees paid by or on behalf of someone other than the absent parent.

4.240    **32.** Where paragraph 26 applies the amount to be treated as the income of the parent shall be determined as if it were earnings from employment as an employed earner and in a case to which paragraph 27 or 31 applies the amount shall be determined as if it were other income to which Part III of this Schedule applies.

AMENDMENTS

1. Regulation 27(l)(a) of the Amendment Regulations (April 5, 1993).
2. Regulation 27(l)(b) of the Amendment Regulations (April 5, 1993).
3. Regulation 27(3) of the Amendment Regulations (April 5, 1993).
4. Regulation 27(4) of the Amendment Regulations (April 5, 1993).
5. Regulation 54(2) of the Amendment Regulations 1995 (April 18, 1995).
6. Regulation 54(3)(a) of the Amendment Regulations 1995 (April 18, 1995).
7. Regulation 54(3)(b) of the Amendment Regulations 1995 (April 18, 1995).
8. Regulation 54(3)(c) of the Amendment Regulations 1995 (April 18, 1995).
9. Regulation 54(4) of the Amendment Regulations 1995 (April 18, 1995).
10. Regulation 54(5)(a) of the Amendment Regulations 1995 (April 18, 1995).
11. Regulation 54(5)(b) of the Amendment Regulations 1995 (April 18, 1995).
12. Regulation 54(6) of the Amendment Regulations 1995 (April 18, 1995).
13. Regulation 54(7) of the Amendment Regulations 1995 (April 18, 1995).
14. Regulation 54(8) of the Amendment Regulations 1995 (April 18, 1995).
15. Regulation 54(9)(a) of the Amendment Regulations 1995 (April 18, 1995).
16. Regulation 54(9)(b)(i) of the Amendment Regulations 1995 (April 18, 1995).
17. Regulation 54(9)(b)(ii) of the Amendment Regulations 1995 (April 18, 1995).
18. Regulation 54(9)(c) of the Amendment Regulations 1995 (April 18, 1995).
19. Regulation 54(10) of the Amendment Regulations 1995 (April 18, 1995).
20. Regulation 54(11) of the Amendment Regulations 1995 (April 18, 1995).
21. Regulation 6(4)(a) of the Jobseekers Amendment Regulations (October 7, 1996).
22. Regulation 6(4)(b) of the Jobseekers Amendment Regulations (October 7, 1996).

23. Regulation 6(4)(c) of the Jobseekers Amendment Regulations (October 7, 1996).

24. Regulation 6(6) and (7)(b) of the Jobseekers Amendment Regulations (October 7, 1996).

25. Regulation 17(2) of the Child Benefit Amendment Regulations (April 7, 1997).

26. Regulation 17(3)(a) of the Child Benefit Amendment Regulations (April 7, 1997).

27. Regulation 56(5) of Miscellaneous Amendments Regulations 1998 (April 6, 1998).

28. Regulation 17(4) of the Child Benefit Amendment Regulations (April 7, 1997).

29. Regulation 24(2) of the Miscellaneous Amendments Regulations 1996 (October 7, 1996).

31. Regulation 24(4) of the Miscellaneous Amendments Regulations 1996 (October 7, 1996).

32. Regulation 56(4) of Miscellaneous Amendments Regulations 1998 (January 19, 1998).

33. Regulation 13(2)(a) of the Miscellaneous Amendments (No. 2) Regulations 1996 (January 13, 1997).

34. Regulation 13(2)(b) of the Miscellaneous Amendments (No. 2) Regulations 1996 (January 13, 1997).

35. Regulation 13(3)(a) of the Miscellaneous Amendments (No. 2) Regulations 1996 (January 13, 1997).

36. Regulation 13(3)(b) of the Miscellaneous Amendments (No. 2) Regulations 1996 (January 13, 1997).

37. Regulation 13(3)(c) of the Miscellaneous Amendments (No. 2) Regulations 1996 (January 13, 1997).

38. Regulation 13(3)(d) of the Miscellaneous Amendments (No. 2) Regulations 1996 (January 13,1997).

39. Regulation 13(4) of the Miscellaneous Amendments (No. 2) Regulations 1996 (January 13, 1997).

40. Regulation 13(5) of the Miscellaneous Amendments (No. 2) Regulations 1996 (January 13, 1997).

41. Regulation 56(2)(a) of Miscellaneous Amendments Regulations 1998 (January 19, 1998).

42. Regulation 56(2)(b) of Miscellaneous Amendments Regulations 1998 (January 19, 1998).

43. Regulation 56(3)(a) of Miscellaneous Amendments Regulations 1998 (January 19, 1998).

44. Regulation 56(3)(b) of Miscellaneous Amendments Regulations 1998 (January 19, 1998).

45. Regulation 56(6) of Miscellaneous Amendments Regulations 1998 (January 19, 1998).

46. Regulation 6(5)(a) of the Miscellaneous Amendments Regulations 1999 (October 4, 1999).

47. Regulation 6(5)(b) of the Miscellaneous Amendments Regulations 1999 (October 4, 1999).

48. Regulation 6(5)(c) of the Miscellaneous Amendments Regulations 1999 (October 4, 1999).

49. Regulation 6(5)(d) of the Miscellaneous Amendments Regulations 1999 (October 4, 1999).

50. Regulation 6(5)(e)(i) of the Miscellaneous Amendments Regulations 1999 (April 6, 1999).

51. Regulation 6(5)(e)(ii) of the Miscellaneous Amendments Regulations 1999 (April 6, 1999).

52. Regulation 6(5)(f) of the Miscellaneous Amendments Regulations 1999 (April 6, 1999).

53. Regulation 6(5)(g)(i) of the Miscellaneous Amendments Regulations 1999 (April 6, 1999).

54. Regulation 6(5)(g)(ii) of the Miscellaneous Amendments Regulations 1999 (April 6, 1999).

55. Regulation 6(5)(h) of the Miscellaneous Amendments Regulations 1999 (April 6, 1999).

56. Article 19(a)(i) of the Commencement No. 7 Order 1999 (June 1, 1999).

57. Article 19(a)(i) of the Commencement No. 7 Order 1999 (June

58. Article 19(a)(i) of the Commencement No. 7 Order 1999 (June 1, 1999).

59. Article 19(a)(ii) of the Commencement No. 7 Order 1999 (June 1, 1999).

60. Article 19(b)(i) of the Commencement No. 7 Order 1999 (June 1, 1999).

61. Article 19(b)(ii) of the Commencement No. 7 Order 1999 (June 1, 1999).

62. Article 19(b)(ii) of the Commencement No. 7 Order 1999 (June 1, 1999).

63. Article 19(b)(ii) of the Commencement No. 7 Order 1999 (June 1, 1999).

64. Article 19(c) of the Commencement No. 7 Order 1999 (June 1, 1999).

65. Article 19(d) of the Commencement No. 7 Order 1999 (June 1, 1999)

66. Article 19(d) of the Commencement No. 7 Order 1999 (June 1, 1999)

67. Article 19(d) of the Commencement No. 7 Order 1999 (June 1, 1999)

68. Article 19(e) of the Commencement No. 7 Order 1999 (June 1, 1999).

69. Article 19(e) of the Commencement No. 7 Order 1999 (June 1, 1999).

70. Article 19(e) of the Commencement No. 7 Order 1999 (June 1, 1999).

71. Regulation 6(6)(a) of the Miscellaneous Amendments Regulations 2003 (April 6, 2003).

72. Regulation 6(6)(a) of the Miscellaneous Amendments Regulations 2003 (April 6, 2003).

73. Regulation 6(6)(b) of the Miscellaneous Amendments Regulations 2003 (April 6, 2003).

74. Regulation 6(6)(c) of the Miscellaneous Amendments Regulations 2003 (April 6, 2003).

75. Regulation 6(6)(d) of the Miscellaneous Amendments Regulations 2003 (April 6, 2003).

76. Regulation 6(6)(e)(i) of the Miscellaneous Amendments Regulations 2003 (April 6, 2003).

77. Regulation 6(6)(e)(ii) of the Miscellaneous Amendments Regulations 2003 (April 6, 2003).

78. Article 28 of the Fire and Rescue Services Act 2004 (Consequential Amendments) (England) Order 2004 (December 30, 2004)—NB applies only to England.

79. Regulation 4(6)(a) of the Miscellaneous Amendments (No. 2) Regulations 2003 (November 5, 2003).

80. Regulation 4(6)(b) of the Miscellaneous Amendments (No. 2) Regulations 2003 (November 5, 2003).

81. Regulation 5(2) of the Miscellaneous Amendments Regulations 2004 (September 16, 2004).

82. Regulation 4(2)(a) of the Miscellaneous Amendments Regulations 2005 (March 16, 2005).

83. Regulation 4(2)(b) of the Miscellaneous Amendments Regulations 2005 (March 16, 2005).

84. Article 46 of the Commencement No. 7 Order 1999 (June 1, 1999).

DEFINITIONS

"the Act": See reg.1(2).                                                    4.241
"child tax credit": see reg.1(2).
"Child Benefit Rates Regulations": see reg.1(2).
"Contributions and Benefits Act": see reg.1(2)..
"covenant income": see reg.1(2).
"earnings": see reg.1(2).
"earnings top-up": see reg.1(2).
"effective date": see reg.1(2).
"employed earner": see reg.1(2).
"family": see reg.1(2).
"grant": see reg.1(2).
"grant contribution": see reg.1(2).
"Maintenance Assessment Procedure Regulations": see reg.1(2).
"the Jobseekers Act": see reg.1(2).
"occupational pension scheme": see reg.1(2).
"parent with care": see reg.1(2).
"partner": see reg.1(2).
"person": see reg.1(2).
"personal pension scheme": see reg.1(2).
"profit-related pay": see reg.1(2).
"relevant week": see reg.1(2).
"retirement annuity contract": see reg.1(2).
"self-employed earner": see reg.1(2).
"student": see reg.1(2).
"student loan": see reg.1(2).
"working tax credit": see reg.1(2).
"year": see reg.1(2).

GENERAL NOTE                                                                4.242

*Paragraph 6*
The amount of a benefit payment is the amount actually received, not the amount that should have been paid if entitlement had been correctly determined (*CCS 1039/97*, paras 12–13). Subparagraph (3) identifies the date on which the amount of the payment to be taken into account is determined. If it is later decided that the amount should not have been paid, that cannot alter the fact that at that date that was the amount in payment (*ibid.*, para.14).

*Paragraph 9*
In *R(CS) 2/00*, the Commissioner decided that payments of an injury pension paid to a firefighter following an injury on duty fall within this paragraph and are not disregarded under Sch.2, para.5. An appeal against this decision was dismissed by the Court of Appeal in *Wakefield v Secretary of State for Social Security* also reported as *R(CS) 2/00*.

*Paragraph 14*
Tribunals should make adequate findings of fact to indicate whether maintenance is paid as spousal maintenance to the parent with care or maintenance for the qualifying child (*R2/96(CSC)*, paras 5 and 13). Clearly child support maintenance payments do not fall within this paragraph as they are defined by s.1(2) of the Act as being payments with respect to the child rather than the parent.
In *CCS 13698/96*, paras 11–12 and *CCS 13923/96*, para.8 it was held that this paragraph did not apply to maintenance paid by the absent parent to the parent

with care or vice versa and that a similar qualification was to be implied elsewhere in the Schedule with no distinction being drawn between one parent paying cash to the other and one parent settling a liability of the other. On this view, this paragraph only covers payments of maintenance by a person who is not a parent of the qualifying child. There was unanimity among the Commissioners that these two decisions should not be reported.

*Paragraph 15*

In the case of rental income, the only amounts that may be deducted from the gross rental income are those authorised by Sch.2, especially para.23 (*R(CS) 3/00*, para. 23).

It is suggested that this paragraph does not cover child support maintenance payments received by a parent in respect of any child, whether or not a qualifying child. See the general note to Sch.2, para.44 below.

Regular payments made by a person other than a parent which are intended and used for the payment of school fees are subject to a trust or equity and are not to be regarded as income of either parent or of the child (*CCS 15/94*, paras 6–8).

*Paragraphs 17–24*

These paragraphs provide for income of a child who is living as member of a parent's family to be treated as income of a parent. First it is necessary to identify the child's income. This is done on normal principles. Where benefit is paid (to whom is not specified) which includes an increase in respect of the child, this is counted as the child's income (para.22). Certain items of income are then disregarded under para.23. The overall result is the relevant income of the child. The amount of this income is then determined as provided in para.24. This amount is then attributed by virtue of para.18 to the parent who is identified under paras 19–21, subject to any limits set therein. In the case of the income of a qualifying child, the income is attributed to the parent with care (paras 19–20). This provision is necessary as, where each parent has day to day care of the child, the child will be a member of the family of each.

It is suggested that any income of a child which derives from the parent with care should be disregarded. If it is not the following anomaly can result. Imagine that a parent with care earns a small wage and pays the qualifying child £15 per week pocket money. £10 of that is disregarded under para.23(e). This leaves £5 which is treated as the income of the parent with care. However, if this £5 is so treated, the parent with care will have that sum double counted in the assessable income calculation.

*Paragraph 22*

The amendments to this paragraph have been appallingly drafted. Original there were no subparagraphs. Then the original paragraph was numbered as subpara.(1) and subpara.(1A) added. Why was it not numbered.(2)? Then the rest was added. The obvious intention was to add subparas (1B) and (2), but that is not how they were numbered in the amending legislation. A superfluous "22" was included for some reason and there seems no reason why subpara.(1B) could not be numbered as (2) and subpara.(2) as (3). Be that as it may, the legislation as printed is as set out in the amending legislation.

*Paragraph 23*

All payments by an absent parent to the child are disregarded under head (b).

Previously all payments "in respect of" the child were disregarded. This would include child support maintenance, which by virtue of s.1(2) of the Act is defined as being paid with respect to the child. It would also include any other payments in respect of the child such as those which are covered by para.31. If payments covered by para.31 were not excluded by this head, they would be double counted. If the absent parent paid pocket money to a qualifying child, in so far as it was not disregarded under para.23(e) it would be treated as income of the parent with care. Where the person with care was treated as having no assessable income (because the person is not a parent of the child or because the person is in receipt of a relevant benefit under Sch.1, para.5(4) to the Act), the pocket money could not be taken into account under the formula assessment and could only be taken into account by the Secretary of State in reduction of money owed by the absent parent (*R(CS) 9/98*, para.9).

*Paragraphs 25–32*                                                                                              **4.243**
    These paragraphs only apply to amounts that would not otherwise be treated as income (*CCS 318/98*, para.26).

*Paragraph 26*
    Tribunals will in particular need to pay careful attention to the following points:
    (i) The precise nature of the service needs to be identified. Until this has been done it is impossible to decide the normal rate for the service. Merely identifying a job by a title such as shop assistant will often be insufficient since there will be a range of work and of remuneration associated with such broad descriptions.
    (ii) Evidence will be needed of the normal rate for the services identified. This will need to be examined to ensure that it relates to work of the same description as that performed by the person. Again reliance on job titles may mislead.
    (iii) The paragraph presupposes that the services are such that there is a normal rate for them. This gives rise to a number of problems. The first is that there will often not be a rate for a particular job but a range of payments. Actual payment will depend on a number of factors. The service performed will be one, but others will include the locality where the work is undertaken, the state of the job market at the time, the employee's qualifications and experience, and the ability of the employer to pay. The emphasis in this paragraph is on remuneration that has been foregone and that will require all factors relevant to the level of that remuneration to be considered. Second, it may well be that quite apart from the matters just considered there is a range of payments for the work with some employers paying better than others. If the payment falls outside that range there will be no difficulty in applying subpara.(a)(ii), although the possible application of subpara.(c) will then have to be considered. Otherwise an estimate will have to be made of the payment which the employer in question was likely to make. A third problem is that the services may be unique; for example a person may be assisting in the running of a business by performing a combination of duties which do not correspond to any single job in the job market. In such a case the tribunal must undertake a more hypothetical exercise and attribute an appropriate income to the work. The alternative approach would be to hold that if there is no equivalent job with which to compare the work in question, the paragraph does not apply and no earnings are attributed to the person in respect of it. This approach cannot be right; it amounts to saying that the more unique and therefore in a sense the more valuable the work to an employer, the less likely it is that earnings will be attributed in respect of it.
    (iv) It is essential to establish that the principal purpose of undertaking the service without appropriate remuneration is to reduce the person's assessable income. This is a subjective test. Often the In contrast to para.26, it is only necessary to establish that the deprivation or failure to secure was "with a view to" reducing assessable income. It is not necessary to show that this was

its principal purpose. It may therefore be possible to catch cases under this paragraph which fail to satisfy the principal purpose test for para.26.

Income which falls within this paragraph is treated as other income to which Part III of this Schedule applies (para.32).

Where a person is paid wholly or partly in kind the value of the payment in kind is disregarded in deciding whether the person has been paid less than the amount normally paid for the service provided (*CIS 11482/95*, paras 11–12). Where there has been a payment partly in kind and partly in cash, it is clear from the wording of this paragraph that only the value of the remuneration foregone is to be attributed to the person concerned. In other words, the value of the cash payment is taken into account as actual earnings and the remuneration forgone is added to it. The wording of this paragraph avoids the contortions of interpretation and application that were found necessary in such circumstances on the wording of the income support provision in *CIS 11482/95*.

In *CCS 4912/98*, the Commissioner interpreted this paragraph broadly and controversially, producing the same effect as if the veil of incorporation had been lifted from a personal service company. The same result can be achieved more satisfactorily by using a departure direction under reg.24 of the Departure Direction Regulations on the basis of diversion of income or under reg.25 of those Regulations on the basis of life-style inconsistent with declared income.

4.244   *Paragraph 27*

This paragraph is the companion to para.26. It deals with disposals of and failures to obtain income or income-earning capital whereas para.26 deals with services. Paragraph 27 is unhappily worded. At one point it refers to the intentional deprivation of something a person has never had. The wording used later in the paragraph is better in referring to deprivation or failure to secure.

Subparagraph (a) applies where a person has had income or capital but no longer has it. It only deals with deprivation of income or capital. The test to apply is whether the person's dominant intention was to reduce income which might be relevant to the child support assessment which is being made or is reasonably expected to be made (*R(CS) 3/00*, para. 19). It is for the person to prove that the income or capital has been disposed of (*R(SB) 38/85*, para.18). If this cannot be proved the person must be taken as still in possession of the income or capital. No question of applying this paragraph then arises and the person will be unable to claim any benefit that might otherwise be derived from para.30. If deprivation is proved, it is necessary to investigate whether it was done intentionally with a view to reducing assessable income. The test is a subjective one, although the reasonableness of a person's action will be a relevant factor in assessing any evidence by that person on the reasons for so acting. Usually the tribunal will have to infer the purpose for the deprivation (see the general note to para.26 on inferences of intention). A person is deprived of capital even if it is replaced by something else (*R(SB) 40/85*, para.8). So a person who spends money on the purchase of an item of equal value is still deprived of that money. However, the fact that something is acquired in exchange will be relevant to the question whether the deprivation was effected with a view to reducing the assessable income. Since there is no discretion in this paragraph, it is only through this reasoning that the expenditure of capital on the purchase of non-income producing assets can escape this paragraph. If an income producing resource is disposed of and replaced by a lower income producing resource it will be possible to apply this paragraph to the difference.

Subparagraph (b) applies where a person has never had the income or capital in question but has failed to secure it in circumstances in which it would be reasonable to expect that it would be secured. Whether securing the income or capital was to be expected is an objective consideration, but it is still necessary to establish an intention to deprive with a view to reducing assessable income. The application of this paragraph will give rise to difficult decisions for tribunals. Some cases of failure to secure income will be relatively straightforward: the person may have failed to cash a cheque (*CSB 598/89*, para.11), to claim a benefit (subject to para.28) or to put money in an account bearing as high a rate of interest as possible. In other cases detailed consideration of evidence will be needed before a tribunal can decide whether it was reasonable to expect the income to be secured. For example, a dividend may not have been declared by a company in which a person has an interest. It is obvious that a dividend should have been declared if that person had such control over the company as to be able to determine or influence the dividend provided that it would be appropriate to declare a dividend given the financial position and the plans of the company. Evidence on each of these matters will need to be considered. Yet other cases will present difficult decisions on how far a person can be expected to act in securing income: for example, the chances of a person securing a particular job or type of job. Decisions on failure to secure capital will almost always be difficult. Capital here must mean capital which produces income. A person with sufficient cash may be expected to subscribe to a rights issue, but a tribunal cannot be expected to decide which shares a stock market investor could reasonably be expected to purchase. Moreover, the concern with this paragraph is with income which will be derived from the capital that should have been secured. There will, however, often be a risk attached to capital investment and this will need to be taken into account in deciding whether or not it was reasonable to expect a particular investment to be secured. In practice it is unlikely that a tribunal will be willing to second-guess investment decisions even with the benefit of hindsight except in blatant cases.

In contrast to para.26, it is only necessary to establish that the deprivation or failure to secure was "with a view to" reducing assessable income. It is not necessary to show that this was its principal purpose. It may therefore be possible to catch cases under this paragraph which fail to satisfy the principal purpose test for para.26.

Income attributed under this paragraph is part of the parent's net income and is treated as other income to which Part III of this Schedule applies (para.32). Net income is calculated under regs 7 and 8. It includes income determined in accordance with Part III. It excludes any amount specified in Sch.2 and para.2 It follows that income tax should be deducted from the income attributed. This makes sense, as income tax would be deducted if the were actually received. See *CCS 185/05*, para.15.

In *CCS 4912/98*, the Commissioner interpreted this paragraph broadly and controversially, producing the same effect as if the veil of incorporation had been lifted from a personal service company. The same result can be achieved more satisfactorily by using a departure direction under reg.24 of the Departure Direction Regulations on the basis of diversion of income or under reg.25 of those Regulations on the basis of life-style inconsistent with declared income.

*Paragraph 28(c)*                                                                                      4.245
Personal injury in the form of a disease also covers injuries suffered as a result of the disease such as an amputation necessary as a result of contracting meningitis and septicaemia (*R(SB) 2/89*, para.15). The key factor is the nature of the injury and not the particular loss for which the income from the trust is compensation. It would therefore cover financial loss as a result of an injury (such as loss of earnings) as much as the loss of amenity or the pain and suffering associated with the injury.

*Paragraph 31*
This provision only applies where a payment is made on behalf of a parent or child. It does not, therefore, cover cases where an item is bought by one parent as a present for a child or out of a sense of responsibility. It is not sufficient that the

payment should be for the benefit of the parent or child. There must be evidence which shows that the purchase was on behalf of the other parent or child. This evidence might take the form of a request that the item be purchased. The most obvious cases where this provision will apply are those where the clear legal responsibility is that of the parent with care (for example, to pay rent or an electricity bill), but payment is made by someone else such as a former partner under a divorce settlement or by a grandparent.

The treatment of payment by one parent of the housing costs in respect of the home occupied by the other but for which both are liable is unclear. According to *CSCS 8/95*, para.16 and *CCS 8189/95*, para.9 the amount by which the payment exceeds that person's share of the housing costs falls to be treated as income under this paragraph. However, in *CCS 13698/96*, paras 11–12 the Commissioner decided that payments of maintenance by the absent parent to the parent with care fell outside Sch.1, even though the result is to render the concluding words of head (b) otiose. Accordingly payments by the absent parent of the parent with care's share of the housing costs are not to be taken into account as the parent with care's income. On this view the Commissioner did not have to decide whether the payments should be treated as for the joint benefit of the parent with care and the child (*ibid.*, para.10). *CCS 13923/96*, para.8 is to the same effect as *CCS 13698/96*, paras 11–12. There was unanimity among the Commissioners that these two decisions should not be reported. On housing costs see further reg.15(3) above and the general note thereto.

This paragraph first lists items expenditure on which may be attributed to a parent, and then exempts from its scope certain payments. One of these is school fees. As this is an exemption for an item which would otherwise fall within this paragraph, the reference to school fees cannot include tuition fees, which would not fall within any of the items listed earlier. The school fees which are not to be treated as the parent's income must be those related to accommodation and board rather than tuition. The exemption does not apply when the fees are paid by the absent parent, although according to *CCS 13698/96*, para.12 the reference to the absent parent is otiose.

A payment is made "on behalf of " a parent or a child if the person making payment undertakes liability as agent of the parent or child or discharges a liability of the parent or child as their agent (*CCS 1318/97*, para.16, approved in *CCS/318/98*, para.27).

SCHEDULE 2

## AMOUNTS TO BE DISREGARDED WHEN CALCULATING OR ESTIMATING N AND M

4.246    **1.** The amounts referred to in this Schedule are to be disregarded when calculating or estimating N and M (parent's net income).

**2.** An amount in respect of income tax applicable to the income in question where not otherwise allowed for under these Regulations.

**3.** Where a payment is made in a currency other than sterling, an amount equal to any banking charge or commission payable in converting that payment to sterling.

**4.** Any amount payable in a country outside the United Kingdom where there is a prohibition against the transfer to the United Kingdom of that amount.

**5.** Any compensation for personal injury and any payments from a trust fund set up for that purpose.

**6.** Any advance of earnings or any loan made by an employer to an employee.

**7.** Any payment by way of, or any reduction or discharge of liability resulting from entitlement to, housing benefit or council tax benefit.

**8.** Any disability living allowance, mobility supplement or any payment intended to compensate for the non-payment of any such allowance or supplement.

**9.** Any payment which is—

(a) an attendance allowance under section 64 of the Contributions and Benefits Act;

(b) an increase of disablement pension under section 104 or 105 of that Act (increases where constant attendance needed or for exceptionally severe disablement);

(c) a payment made under regulations made in exercise of the power conferred by Schedule 8 to that Act (payments for pre-1948 cases);

(d) an increase of an allowance payable in respect of constant attendance under that Schedule;

(e) payable by virtue of articles 14, 15, 16, 43 or 44 of the Personal Injuries (Civilians) Scheme 1983 (allowances for constant attendance and exceptionally severe disablement and severe disablement occupational allowance) or any analogous payment; or

(f) a payment based on the need for attendance which is paid as part of a war disablement pension.

**10.** Any payment under section 148 of the Contributions and Benefits Act (pensioners' Christmas bonus).

**11.** Any social fund payment within the meaning of Part VIII of the Contributions and Benefits Act.

**12.** Any payment made by the Secretary of State to compensate for the loss (in whole or part) of entitlement to housing benefit.

**13.** Any payment made by the Secretary of State to compensate for loss of housing supplement under regulation 19 of the Supplementary Benefit (Requirements) Regulations 1983.

**14.** Any payment made by the Secretary of State to compensate a person who was entitled to supplementary benefit in respect of a period ending immediately before 11th April 1988 but who did not become entitled to income support in respect of a period beginning with that day.

**15.** Any concessionary payment made to compensate for the non-payment of income support[21, state pension credit], [12income-based jobseeker's allowance] disability living allowance, or any payment to which paragraph 9 applies.

**16.** Any payments of child benefit to the extent that they do not exceed the basic rate of that benefit as defined in regulation 4.

**17.** Any payment made under regulations 9 to 11 or 13 of the Welfare Food Regulations 1988 (payments made in place of milk tokens or the supply of vitamins).

**18.** Subject to paragraph 20 and to the extent that it does not exceed £10.00—

(a) war disablement pension or war widow's pension [22or war widower's pension] or a payment made to compensate for non-payment of such a pension;

4.247

(b) a pension paid by the government of a country outside Great Britain and which either—
  (i) is analogous to a war disablement pension; or
  (ii) is analogous to a war widow's pension[23or war widower's pension].

[26**18A.** Subject to paragraph 20, and to the extent that it does not exceed £10.00, a payment made in respect of a parent under a scheme mentioned in section 1(2) of the Armed Forces (Pensions and Compensation) Act 2004 (compensation schemes for armed and reserve forces).]

**19.**—(1) Except where subparagraph (2) applies and subject to subparagraph (3) and paragraphs 20, 38 and 47, [10up to £20.00] of any charitable or voluntary payment made, or due to be made, at regular intervals.

(2) Subject to subparagraph (3) and paragraphs 38 and 47, any charitable or voluntary payment made or due to be made at regular intervals which is intended and used for an item other than food, ordinary clothing or footwear, gas, electricity or fuel charges, housing costs of any member of the family or the payment of council tax.

(3) Subparagraphs (1) and (2) shall not apply to a payment which is made by a person for the maintenance of any member of his family or of his former partner or of his children.

(4) For the purposes of subparagraph (1) where a number of charitable or voluntary payments fall to be taken into account they shall be treated as though they were one such payment.

4.248

**20.**—(1) Where, but for this paragraph, more than [11£20.00] would be disregarded under paragraphs [2718 to 19(1)] in respect of the same week, only ["£20.00] in aggregate shall be disregarded and where an amount falls to be deducted from the income of a student under paragraph 16(3)(b) or (c) of Schedule 1, that amount shall count as part of the [11£20.00] disregard allowed under this paragraph.

(2) Where any payment which is due to be paid in one week is paid in another week, subparagraph (1) and paragraphs [2718 to 19(1)] shall have effect as if that payment were received in the week in which it was due.

**21.** In the case of a person participating in arrangements for training made under section 2 of the Employment and Training Act 1973 or section 2 of the Enterprise and New Towns (Scotland) Act 1990 (functions in relation to training for employment etc.) or attending a course at an employment rehabilitation centre established under section 2 of the 1973 Act—
  (a) any travelling expenses reimbursed to the person;
  (b) any living away from home allowance under section 2(2)(d) of the 1973 Act or section 2(4)(c) of the 1990 Act;
  (c) any training premium,
but this paragraph, except in so far as it relates to a payment mentioned in subparagraph (a), (b) or (c), does not apply to any part of any allowance under section 2(2)(d) of the 1973 Act or section 2(4)(c) of the 1990 Act.

**22.** Where a parent occupies a dwelling as his home and that dwelling is also occupied by a person, other than a non-dependant or a person who is provided with board and lodging accommodation, and that person is contractually liable to make payments in respect of his occupation of the dwelling to the parent, the amount or, as the case may be, the amounts specified in [¹⁸paragraph 19 of Schedule 9 to the Income Support (General) Regulations 1987 which would have applied if he had not been in receipt of income support.]

**23.** Where a parent, who is not a self-employed earner, is in receipt of rent or any other money in respect of the use and occupation of property other than his home, that rent or other payment to the extent of any sums which that parent is liable to pay by way of—

[¹(a)  payments which are to be taken into account as eligible housing costs under subparagraphs (b), (c), (d) and (t) of paragraph 1 of Schedule 3 (eligible housing costs for the purposes of determining exempt income and protected income) and paragraph 3 of that Schedule (exempt income: additional provisions relating to housing costs);]

(b)  council tax payable in respect of that property;

(c)  water and sewerage charges in respect of that property.

**24.** [⁶For each week in which a parent provides] board and lodging accommodation in his home otherwise than as a self-employed earner—

(a)  £20.00 of any payment for that accommodation made by [⁷, on behalf or in respect of] the person to whom that accommodation is provided; and

(b)  where any such payment exceeds £20.00, 50 per centum of the excess.

**25.** Any payment made to a person in respect of an adopted child who is a member of his family that is made in accordance with any regulations made under section 57A or pursuant to section 57A(6) of the Adoption Act 1976 (permitted allowances) [²⁸or paragraph 3 of Schedule 4 to the Adoption and Children Act 2002] or, as the case may be, [¹⁷section 51A] of the Adoption (Scotland) Act 1978 (schemes for the payment of allowances to adopters)—

(a)  where the child is not a child in respect of whom child support maintenance is being assessed, to the extent that it exceeds [²the aggregate of the amounts to be taken into account in the calculation of E under regulation 9(l)(g)], reduced, as the case may be, under regulation 9(4);

(b)  in any other case, to the extent that it does not exceed the amount of the income of a child which is treated as that of his parent by virtue of Part IV [¹⁵of Schedule 1].

[²⁹**25A.** Any payment made to a person in accordance with regulations made pursuant to section 14F of the Children Act 1989 (special guardianship support services) in respect of a child who is a member of his family.]

**26.** Where a local authority makes a payment in respect of the accommodation and maintenance of a child in pursuance of paragraph 15 of Schedule 1 to the Children Act 1989 (local authority contribution to child's maintenance) to the extent that it exceeds the amount referred to in [³regulation 9(1)(g)] (reduced, as the case may be, under regulation 9(4)).

**27.** Any payment received under a policy of insurance taken out to insure against the risk of being unable to maintain repayments on a loan taken out to acquire an interest in, or to meet the cost of repairs or improvements to, the parent's home and used to meet such repayments, to the extent that the payment received under that policy [⁸exceeds] [⁹the total of the amount of the payments set out in paragraphs l(b), 3(2), and (4) of Schedule 3 as modified, where applicable, by regulation 18.]

**28.** In the calculation of the income of the parent with care, any maintenance payments made by the absent parent in respect of his qualifying child.

**29.** Any payment made by a local authority to a person who is caring for a child under section 23(2)(a) of the Children Act 1989 (provision of accommodation and maintenance by a local authority for children whom the authority is looking after), or, as the case may be, section 21 of the Social Work (Scotland) Act 1968 or by a voluntary organisation under section 59(1 )(a) of the Children Act 1989 (provision of accommodation by voluntary organisations) or by a care authority under regulation 9 of the Boarding Out and Fostering of Children (Scotland) Regulations 1985 (provision of accommodation and maintenance for children in care).

4.249

**30.** Any payment made by a health authority, local authority or voluntary organisation in respect of a person who is not normally a member of the household but is temporarily in the care of a member of it.

**31.** Any payment made by a local authority under section 17 or 24 of the Children Act 1989 or, as the case may be, section 12, 24 or 26 of the Social Work (Scotland) Act 1968 (local authorities' duty to promote welfare of children and powers to grant financial assistance to persons looked after, or in, or formerly in, their care).

**32.** Any resettlement benefit which is paid to the parent by virtue of regulation 3 of the Social Security (Hospital In-Patients) Amendment (No. 2) Regulations 1987 (transitional provisions).

**33.**—(1) Any payment or repayment made—
  (a) as respects England and Wales, under regulation 3, 5 or 8 of the National Health Service (Travelling Expenses and Remission of Charges) Regulations 1988 (travelling expenses and health service supplies);
  (b) as respects Scotland, under regulation 3, 5 or 8 of the National Health Service (Travelling Expenses and Remission of Charges) (Scotland) Regulations 1988 (travelling expenses and health service supplies).

(2) Any payment or repayment made by the Secretary of State for Health, the Secretary of State for Scotland or the Secretary of State for Wales which is analogous to a payment or repayment mentioned in subparagraph (1).

**34.** Any payment made (other than a training allowance), whether by the Secretary of State or any other person, under the Disabled Persons Employment Act 1944 or in accordance with arrangements made under section 2 of the Employment and Training Act 1973 to assist disabled persons to obtain or retain employment despite their disability.

**35.** Any contribution to the expenses of maintaining a household which is made by a non-dependant member of that household.

**36.** Any sum in respect of a course of study attended by a child payable by virtue of regulations made under section 81 of the Education Act 1944 (assistance by means of scholarship or otherwise), or by virtue of section 2(1) of the Education Act 1962 (awards for courses of further education) or section 49 of the Education (Scotland) Act 1980 (power to assist persons to take advantage of educational facilities).

[²⁵**36A.** Any sum in respect of financial assistance given, or given under arrangements made, by the Secretary of State (in relation to England) or the National Assembly for Wales (in relation to Wales) under section 14 of the Education Act 2002 (power of Secretary of State and National Assembly for Wales to give financial assistance for purposes related to education), to a child.]

**37.** Where a person receives income under an annuity purchased with a loan which satisfies the following conditions—

(a) that loan was made as part of a scheme under which not less than 90 per centum of the proceeds of the loan were applied to the purchase by the person to whom it was made of an annuity ending with his life or with the life of the survivor of two or more persons (in this paragraph referred to as "the annuitants") who include the person to whom the loan was made;

(b) that the interest on the loan is payable by the person to whom it was made or by one of the annuitants;

(c) that at the time the loan was made the person to whom it was made or each of the annuitants had attained the age of 65;

(d) that the loan was secured on a dwelling in Great Britain and the person to whom the loan was made or one of the annuitants owns an estate or interest in that dwelling; and

(e) that the person to whom the loan was made or one of the annuitants occupies the dwelling on which it was secured as his home at the time the interest is paid, the amount, calculated on a weekly basis equal to—

  (i) where, or insofar as, section 26 of the Finance Act 1982 (deduction of tax from certain loan interest) applies to the payments of interest on the loan, the interest which is payable after the deduction of a sum equal to income tax on such payments at the basic rate for the year of assessment in which the payment of interest becomes due;

  (ii) in any other case the interest which is payable on the loan without deduction of such a sum.

**38.** Any payment of the description specified in paragraph 39 of Schedule 9 to the Income Support Regulations (disregard of payments made under certain trusts and disregard of certain other payments) and any income derived from the investment of such payments.

**39.** Any payment made to a juror or witness in respect of attendance at court other than compensation for loss of earnings or for loss of a benefit payable under the Contributions and Benefits Act [¹³or the Jobseekers Act].

**40.** Any special war widows' payment made under—

(a) the Naval and Marine Pay and Pensions (Special War Widows Payment) Order 1990 made under section 3 of the Naval and Marine Pay and Pensions Act 1865;

(b) the Royal Warrant dated 19th February 1990 amending the Schedule to the Army Pensions Warrant 1977 (Army Code No. 13045);

(c) the Queen's Order dated 26th February 1990 made under section 2 of the Air Force (Constitution) Act 1917;

4.250

(d) the Home Guard War Widows Special Payments Regulations 1990 made under section 151 of the Reserve Forces Act 1980;

(e) the Orders dated 19th February 1990 amending Orders made on 12th December 1980 concerning the Ulster Defence Regiment made in each case under section 140 of the Reserve Forces Act 1980 (Army Code No. 60589),

and any analogous payment by the Secretary of State for Defence to any person who is not a person entitled under the provisions mentioned in subparagraphs (a) to (e).

**41.** Any payment to a person as holder of the Victoria Cross or the George Cross or any analogous payment.

**42.** Any payment made either by the Secretary of State for the Home Department or by the Secretary of State for Scotland under a scheme established to assist relatives and other persons to visit persons in custody.

**43.** Any amount by way of a refund of income tax deducted from profits or emoluments chargeable to income tax under Schedule D or Schedule E.

**44.** Maintenance payments (whether paid under the Act or otherwise) insofar as they are not treated as income under Part III or IV [[16]of Schedule 1].

**45.** Where following a divorce or separation—

(a) capital is divided between the parent and the person who was his partner before the divorce or separation; and

(b) that capital is intended to be used to acquire a new home for that parent or to acquire furnishings for a home of his,

income derived from the investment of that capital for one year following the date on which that capital became available to the parent.

[[4]**46.** Except in the case of a self-employed earner, payments in kind.]

**47.** Any payment made by the Joseph Rowntree Memorial Trust from money provided to it by the Secretary of State for Health for the purpose of maintaining a family fund for the benefit of severely handicapped children.

**48.** Any payment of expenses to a person who is—

(a) engaged by a charitable or voluntary body; or

(b) a volunteer,

if he otherwise derives no remuneration or profit from the body or person paying those expenses.

[[5]**48A.** Any guardian's allowance under Part III of the Contributions and Benefits Act.]

[[5]**48B.** Any payment in respect of duties mentioned in paragraph 1(l)(i) of Chapter 1 of Part 1 of Schedule 1 relating to a period of one year or more.]

[[14]**48C.** Any payment to a person under section 1 of the Community Care (Direct Payments) Act 1996 or section 12B of the Social Work (Scotland) Act 1968 in respect of his securing community care services, as defined in section 46 of the National Services and Community Care Act 1990.]

[[19]**48D.** Any payment of child tax credit.]

[[20]**48E.** Any payment made by a local authority, or by the National Assembly for Wales, to a person relating to a service which is provided to develop or sustain the capacity of that person to live independently in his accommodation.]

[²⁴**48F.** Any supplementary pension under article 29(1A) of the Naval, Military and Air Forces etc. (Disablement and Death) Service Pensions Order 1983 (pensions to widows and widowers) or under article 27(3) of the Personal Injuries (Civilians) Scheme 1983 (pensions to widows and widowers).]

**49.** In this Schedule—

"concessionary payment" means a payment made under arrangements made by the Secretary of State with the consent of the Treasury which is charged either to the National Insurance Fund or to a Departmental Expenditure Vote to which payments of benefit under the Contributions and Benefits Act [¹³or the Jobseekers Act] are charged;

"health authority" means a health authority established under the National Health Service Act 1977 or the National Health Service (Scotland) Act 1978;

"mobility supplement" has the same meaning as in regulation 2(1) of the Income Support Regulations;

"war disablement pension" and "war widow" have the same meanings as in section 150 (2) of the Contributions and Benefits Act.

AMENDMENTS

1. Regulation 28 of the Amendment Regulations (April 5, 1993).
2. Regulation 29 of the Amendment Regulations (April 5, 1993).
3. Regulation 30 of the Amendment Regulations (April 5, 1993).
4. Regulation 31 of the Amendment Regulations (April 5, 1993).
5. Regulation 32 of the Amendment Regulations (April 5, 1993).
6. Regulation 55(2) of the Amendment Regulations 1995 (April 18, 1995).
7. Regulation 55(3) of the Amendment Regulations 1995 (April 18, 1995).
8. Regulation 55(4) of the Amendment Regulations 1995 (April 18, 1995).
9. Regulation 46 of the Miscellaneous Amendments (No. 2) Regulations 1995 (January 22, 1996).
10. Regulation 3(2) of the Child Support (Maintenance Assessments and Special Cases) and Social Security (Claims and Payments) Regulations 1996 (for commencement see regs 1(1) and 4 of those regulations).
11. Regulation 3(3) of the Child Support (Maintenance Assessments and Special Cases) and Social Security (Claims and Payments) Regulations 1996 (for commencement see regs 1(1) and 4 of those regulations).
12. Regulation 6(5) of the Jobseekers Amendment Regulations (October 7, 1996).
13. Regulation 6(6) and (7)(c) of the Jobseekers Amendment Regulations (October 7, 1996).
14. Regulation 14 of the Miscellaneous Amendments (No. 2) Regulations 1996 (January 13, 1997).
15. Regulation 57 of the Miscellaneous Amendments Regulations 1998 (January 1998).
16. Regulation 57 of the Miscellaneous Amendments Regulations 1998 (January 1998).
17. Regulation 6(6) of the Miscellaneous Amendments Regulations 1999 (April 6, 1999).
18. Regulation 6(7)(a) of the Miscellaneous Amendments Regulations 2003 (April 6, 2003).
19. Regulation 6(7)(b) of the Miscellaneous Amendments Regulations 2003 (April 6, 2003).

20. Regulation 4(7)(c) of the Miscellaneous Amendments (No. 2) Regulations 2003 (November 5, 2003).

21. Regulation 4(7)(a) of the Miscellaneous Amendments (No. 2) Regulations 2003 (November 5, 2003).

22. Regulation 4(7)(b) of the Miscellaneous Amendments (No. 2) Regulations 2003 (November 5, 2003).

23. Regulation 4(7)(b) of the Miscellaneous Amendments (No. 2) Regulations 2003 (November 5, 2003).

24. Regulation 4(7)(d) of the Miscellaneous Amendments (No. 2) Regulations 2003 (November 5, 2003).

25. Regulation 5(3) of the Miscellaneous Amendments Regulations 2004 (September 16, 2004).

DEFINITIONS

4.251    "child tax credit": see reg.1(2).
"Contributions and Benefits Act": see reg.1(2).
"council tax benefit": see reg.1(2)
"earnings": see reg.1(2)
"family": see reg.1(2)
"home": see reg.1(2)
"housing benefit": see reg.1(2)
"the Jobseekers Act": see reg.1(2)
"non-dependant": see reg.1(2)
"ordinary clothing or footwear": see reg.1(2)
"parent with care": see reg.1(2)
"partner": see reg.1(2)
"person": see reg.1(2)
"self-employed earner": see reg.1(2)
"state pension credit": see reg.1(2)
"student": see reg.1(2)
"training allowance": see reg.1(2)

4.252    GENERAL NOTE

*Paragraph 5*

This paragraph applies to compensation for "personal injury". A personal injury may be physical or mental. In the latter case there must be a recognisable psychiatric illness (*McLoughlin v. O'Brian*, [1983] 1 A.C. 410). It may also take the form of a disease (*R(SB) 2/89*, para.11) and will include any injuries sustained as a result of the disease, such as an amputation following meningitis and septicaemia (*ibid.*, para.15).

The compensation must be paid *for* the personal injury and not merely because of it. Strictly, compensation is not paid for an injury, but for the consequences of the injury (*Baker v. Willoughby* [1969] 3 All E.R. 1528 at 1532, *per* Lord Reid). This is true not only of a civil claim for damages, but also a claim for Disablement Benefit under which entitlement depends on the degree of the resulting disablement. The paragraph cannot, therefore, be read literally.

In *R(CS) 2/00*, para.16 the Commissioner held that "compensation for personal injury" only covers payment to an injured party by the person who was liable in tort to make reparation for the injury or who accepted such liability. Any other interpretation would render the reference to a trust fund superfluous as cases where a trust fund was set up would be covered by the earlier words of the paragraph. On this reasoning, the paragraph covers all compensation paid on a civil claim for damage, including compensation for the loss of earnings as a result of the injury. It is arguable that, in the context of child support and having regard to the nature of the type of exclusion covered by this Schedule, compensation should not include compensation for loss of future income, as compensation which replaces income that would otherwise have been received is out of step with the character of the contents of the Schedule. On this reasoning, payments of disablement benefit will not count as compensation for the purposes of this paragraph. This also would be out of step with the character of the contents of the Schedule. An appeal against the Commissioner's decision was dismissed by the Court of Appeal in *Wakefield v Secretary of State for Social Security* , also reported as *R(CS) 2/00.*

*Paragraph 6*
This paragraph is in the same terms as Sched.1, para.l(2)(d) above.

*Paragraph 19*
Whether a payment is voluntary is judged by looking at the payer and not the payee. Consequently a payment by British Coal to a miner's widow in lieu of concessionary coal is not a voluntary payment (*R. v. Doncaster Metropolitan Borough Council, ex p. Boulton* (1992) 25 H.L.R. 195 and *R(IS) 4/94*). It is irrelevant whether or not the payment in question was legally enforceable (*ibid.*). Where payments are made under an annuity which was purchased with money given for the purpose, they are not voluntary since they are made under the terms of the annuity which is a form of contract (*CIS 702/91*, para.15).

*Paragraph 23*
This paragraph is not comprehensive of the disregards for parents that fall within it. In particular it does not displace the disregard in para.2 (*CCS 185/05*, para.16).

*Paragraph 44*
The question arises of whether or not child support maintenance payments received by a parent, whether or not in respect of a qualifying child, are to be disregarded under this paragraph. Maintenance payments in respect of a parent are covered by Sched.1, para.14, but there is no express reference to child support maintenance payments in Part III or IV of Sched.1. However, Sched.1, para.15 covers any other payments or amounts received on a periodical basis. This wording is wide enough to cover payments of child support maintenance, but the never ending circles of calculations involved in doing so point to these payments not falling within the words of para.15. Take as an example the case of a mother with care of a child whose child support maintenance is being calculated on review. The child support maintenance ultimately payable would have to be taken into account before it was fixed, a plain impossibility. There would be even greater complexities if the mother had care of two children by different fathers and received child support maintenance payments in respect of each. The only way to avoid these circles is by interpreting para.15 as not covering payments of child support maintenance.

*Paragraph 45*
Capital earmarked for the purpose or acquiring a new home falls within this paragraph for as long as it remains earmarked, although the parent could have used it for another purpose (*CCS 4923/95*, para.5).

*Paragraph 49*
Concessionary payments are only made to compensate for the effects of defective legislation and do not include *ex gratia* payments for the loss of statutory entitlement, for example was a result of maladministration (*CIS 2285/99*).

SCHEDULE 3

ELIGIBLE HOUSING COSTS

**Eligible housing costs for the purposes of determining exempt income and protected income**

4.253     **1.** Subject to the following provisions of this Schedule, [²²the following amounts payable] in respect of the provision of a home shall be eligible to be taken into account as housing costs for the purposes of these Regulations—

(a)  [²³amounts payable by way of] rent;

[²⁵(b) amounts payable by way of mortgage interest;]

(c)  [²⁶amounts payable by way of interest] under a hire purchase agreement to buy a home;

(d)  [²⁷amounts payable by way of interest] on loans for repairs and improvements to the home[¹, including interest on a loan for any service charge imposed to meet the cost of such repairs and improvements;]

(e)  [²⁸amounts payable] by way of ground rent or in Scotland, payments by way of feu duty;

(f)  [²⁹amounts payable] under a co-ownership scheme;

(g)  [³⁰amounts payable] in respect of, or in consequence of, the use and occupation of the home;

(h)  where the home is a tent, [³¹amounts payable] in respect of the tent and the site on which it stands;

(i)  [³²amounts payable] in respect of a licence or permission to occupy the home (whether or not board is provided);

(j)  [³³amounts payable] by way of mesne profits or, in Scotland, violent profits;

(k)  [²⁴amounts payable by way of] of, or by way of, service charges, the payment of which is a condition on which the right to occupy the home depends;

(l)  [³⁵amounts payable] under or relating to a tenancy or licence of a Crown tenant;

(m) mooring charges payable for a houseboat;

(n)  where the home is a caravan or a mobile home, [³⁵amounts payable] in respect of the site on which it stands;

(o)  any contribution payable by a parent resident in an almshouse provided by a housing association which is either a charity of which particulars are entered in the register of charities established under section 4 of the Charities Act 1960 (register of charities) or an exempt charity within the meaning of that Act, which is a contribution towards the cost of maintaining that association's almshouses and essential services in them;

(p)  [³⁶amounts payable] under a rental purchase agreement, that is to say an agreement for the purchase of a home under which the whole or part of the purchase price is to be paid in more than one instalment and the completion of the purchase is deferred until the whole or a specified part of the purchase price has been paid;

    (q) where, in Scotland, the home is situated on or pertains to a croft within the meaning of section 3(1) of the Crofters (Scotland) Act 1955, the [³⁷amount payable] in respect of the croft land;

    (r) where the home is provided by an employer (whether under a condition or term in a contract of service or otherwise), [³⁸amounts payable] to that employer in respect of the home, including [³⁹any amounts deductible by the employer] from the remuneration of the parent in question;

[². . .]

[¹⁶(t) amounts payable in respect of a loan taken out to pay off another loan but only to the extent that it was incurred in respect of amounts eligible to be taken into account as housing costs by virtue of other provisions of this Schedule.]

### Loans for repairs and improvements to the home

**2.** [⁵Subject to paragraph 2A (loans for repairs and improvements in transitional cases), for the purposes of] paragraph 1(d) "repairs and improvements" means major repairs necessary to maintain the fabric of the home and any of the following measures undertaken with a view to improving its fitness for occupation—

    (a) installation of a fixed bath, shower, wash basin or lavatory, and necessary associated plumbing;

    (b) damp proofing measures;

    (c) provision or improvement of ventilation and natural lighting;

    (d) provision of electric lighting and sockets;

    (e) provision or improvement of drainage facilities;

    (f) improvement of the structural condition of the home;

    (g) improvements to the facilities for the storing, preparation and cooking of food;

    (h) provision of heating, including central heating; (i) provision of storage facilities for fuel and refuse; (j) improvements to the insulation of the home;

    (k) other improvements which the [⁴⁷Secretary of State] considers reasonable in the circumstances.

### [⁶Loans for repairs and improvements in transitional cases

**2A.** In the case of a loan entered into before the first date upon which a maintenance application or enquiry form is given or sent or treated as given or sent to the relevant person, for the purposes of paragraph 1(d) "repairs and improvements" means repairs and improvements of any description whatsoever.]

### Exempt income: additional provisions relating to eligible housing costs

**3.**—(1) The additional provisions made by this paragraph shall have effect only for the purposes of calculating or estimating exempt income.

(2) Subject to subparagraph (6), where the home of an absent parent or, as the case may be, a parent with care, is subject to a mortgage or charge

4.254

4.255

4.256

and that parent [⁴⁰is liable to make periodical payments] to reduce the capital secured by that mortgage or charge of an amount provided for in accordance with the terms thereof, [⁴⁰those amounts payable] shall be eligible to be taken into account as the housing costs of that parent.

[¹¹(2A) Where an absent parent or as the case may be a parent with care has entered into a loan for repairs or improvements of a kind referred to in paragraph 1(4) and that parent [⁴¹is liable to make periodical payments] of an amount provided for in accordance with the terms of that loan to reduce the amount of that loan, [⁴¹those amounts payable] shall be eligible to be taken into account as housing costs of that parent.]

(3) Subject to subparagraph (6), where the home of an absent parent or, as the case may be, a parent with care, is held under an agreement and [⁴²certain amounts payable] under that agreement are included as housing costs by virtue of paragraph 1 of this Schedule, [⁴³any other amounts payable] in accordance with that agreement by the parent in order either—

(a) to reduce his liability under that agreement; or
(b) to acquire the home to which it relates, shall also be eligible to be taken into account as housing costs.

(4) Where a policy of insurance has been obtained and retained for the purpose of discharging a mortgage or charge on the home of the parent in question, the amount of the [⁴⁴permiums payable] under that policy shall be eligible to be taken into account as a housing cost ['including for the avoidance of doubt such a policy of insurance whose purpose is to secure the payment of monies due under the mortgage or charge in the event of the unemployment, sickness or disability of the insured.]

[¹⁷(4A) Where—

(a) an absent parent or parent with care has obtained which constitutes an eligible housing cost falling within sub-paragraph (d) or (t) of paragraph 1; and
(b) a policy of insurance has been obtained and retained, the purpose of which is solely to secure the payment of monies due under that loan in the event of unemployment, sickness or disability of the insured person,

the amount of the premiums payable under that policy shall be eligible to be taken into account as housing costs.]

[³(5) Where a policy of insurance has been obtained and retained for the purpose of discharging a mortgage or charge on the home of the parent in question and also for the purpose of accruing profits on the maturity of the policy, there shall be eligible to be taken into account as a housing cost—

(a) where the sum secured by the mortgage or charge does not exceed £60,000, the whole of the [⁴⁵premiums payable] under that policy; and
(b) where the sum secured by the mortgage or charge exceeds £60,000, the part of the [⁴⁵premiums payable] under that policy which are necessarily incurred for the purpose of discharging the mortgage or charge or, where that part cannot be ascertained, 0.0277 per centum of charge.]

[⁸(5A) Where a plan within the meaning of regulation 4 of the Personal Equity Plans Regulations 1989 has been obtained and retained for the purpose of discharging a mortgage or charge on the home of the parent in question and also for the purpose of accruing profits upon the realisation of the plan, there shall be eligible to be taken into account as a housing cost—

(a) where the sum secured by the mortgage or charge does not exceed £60,000, the whole of the premiums payable in respect of the plan; and

(b) where the sum secured by the mortgage or charge exceeds £60,000, that part of the premiums payable in respect of the plan which is necessarily incurred for the purpose of discharging the mortgage or charge or, where that part cannot be ascertained, 0.0277 per centum of the amount secured by the mortgage or charge.

(5B) Where a personal pension plan [18derived from a personal pension scheme] has been obtained and retained for the purpose of discharging a mortgage or charge on the home of the parent in question and also for the purpose of securing the payment of a pension to him, there shall be eligible to be taken into account as a housing cost 25 per centum of the contributions payable in respect of that personal pension plan.]

(6) For the purposes of subparagraphs (2) and (3), housing costs shall not include—

(a) [9any payments in excess of those required] to be made under or in respect of a mortgage, charge or agreement to which either of those subparagraphs relate;

(b) [46amounts payable] any second or subsequent mortgage on the home to the extent that [10they would not be eligible] to be taken into account as housing costs;

(c) premiums payable in respect of any policy of insurance against loss caused by the destruction of or damage to any building or land.

### Conditions relating to eligible housing costs

**4.**—(1) Subject to the following provisions of this paragraph the housing costs referred to in this Schedule shall be included as housing costs only where—

4.257

[19(a) they are necessarily incurred for the purpose of purchasing, renting or otherwise securing possession of the home for the parent and his family, or for the purpose of carrying out repairs and improvements to that home;]

(b) the parent or, if he is one of a family, he or a member of his family, is responsible for those costs; and

(c) the liability to meet those costs is to a person other than a member of the same household.

[20(1A) For the purposes of sub-paragraph (l)(a) "repairs and improvements" shall have the meaning given in paragraph 2 of this Schedule.]

(2) For the purposes of subparagraph (l)(b) a parent shall be treated as responsible for housing costs where—

(a) because the person liable to meet those costs is not doing so, he has to meet those costs in order to continue to live in the home and either he was formerly the partner of the person liable, or he is some other person whom it is reasonable to treat as liable to meet those costs; or

  (b) he pays a share of those costs in a case where—

    (i) he is living in a household with other persons;

    (ii) those other persons include persons who are not close relatives of his or his partner;

    (iii) a person who is not such a close relative is responsible for those costs under the preceding provisions of this paragraph or has an equivalent responsibility for housing expenditure; and

    (iv) it is reasonable in the circumstances to treat him as sharing that responsibility.

[21(3) Subject to sub-paragraph (4), payments on a loan shall constitute an eligible housing cost only if that loan has been obtained for the purposes specified in sub-paragraph (l)(a).

(4) Where a loan has been obtained only partly for the purposes specified in sub-paragraph (l)(a), the eligible housing cost shall be limited to that part of the payment attributable to those purposes.]

## Accommodation also used for other purposes

4.258    **5.** Where amounts are payable in respect of accommodation which consists partly of residential accommodation and partly of other accommodation, only such proportion thereof as is attributable to residential accommodation shall be eligible to be taken into account as housing costs.

## Ineligible service and fuel charges

4.259    **6.** Housing costs shall not include—

  [12(a) where the costs are inclusive of ineligible service charges within the meaning of paragraph l(a)(i) of Schedule 1 to the Housing Benefit (General) Regulations 1987 (ineligible service charges), the amounts specified as ineligible in paragraph 1A of that Schedule;]

  [13. . .]

  (b) where the costs are inclusive of any of the items mentioned in paragraph 5(2) of Schedule 1 to the Housing Benefit (General) Regulations 1987 (payment in respect of fuel charges), the deductions prescribed in that paragraph unless the parent provides evidence on which the actual or approximate amount of the service charge for fuel may be estimated, in which case the estimated amount; [14. . .]

  (c) charges for water, sewerage or allied environmental services and where the amount of such charges is not separately identified, such part of the charges in question as is attributable to those services. [15and

  (d) where the costs are inclusive of charges, other than those which are not to be included by virtue of sub-paragraphs (a) to (c), that part of those charges which exceeds the greater of the following amounts—

    (i) the total of the charges other than those which are ineligible service charges within the meaning of paragraph 1 of Schedule 1 to the Housing Benefit Regulations (housing costs);

    (ii) 25 per centum of the total amount of eligible housing costs, and for the purposes of this sub-paragraph, where the amount of those charges is not separately identifiable, that amount shall be such amount as is reasonably attributable to those charges.]

**Interpretation**

7. In this Schedule except where the context otherwise requires—  4.260
"close relative" means a parent, parent-in-law, son, son-in-law, daughter, daughter-in-law, step-parent, step-son, step-daughter, brother, sister, or the spouse of any of the preceding persons or, if that person is one of an unmarried couple, the other member of that couple;
"co-ownership scheme" means a scheme under which the dwelling is let by a housing association and the tenant, or his personal representative, will, under the terms of the tenancy agreement or of the agreement under which he became a member of the association, be entitled, on his ceasing to be a member and subject to any conditions stated in either agreement, to a sum calculated by reference directly or indirectly to the value of the dwelling.
"housing association" has the meaning assigned to it by section 1(1) of the Housing Association Act 1985.

AMENDMENTS

1. Regulation 33(a) of the Amendment Regulations (April 5, 1993).
2. Regulation 33(b) of the Amendment Regulations (April 5, 1993).
3. Regulation 4(8) of the Miscellaneous Amendments Regulations 1994 (February 7, 1994).
5. Regulation 56(3) of the Amendment Regulations 1995 (April 18, 1995).
6. Regulation 56(4) of the Amendment Regulations 1995 (April 18, 1995).
7. Regulation 56(5)(a) of the Amendment Regulations 1995 (April 18, 1995).
8. Regulation 56(5)(b) of the Amendment Regulations 1995 (April 18, 1995).
9. Regulation 56(5)(c)(i) of the Amendment Regulations 1995 (April 18, 1995).
10. Regulation 56(5)(c)(ii) of the Amendment Regulations 1995 (April 18, 1995).
11. Regulation 47(2) of the Miscellaneous Amendments (No. 2) Regulations 1995 (January 22, 1996).
12. Regulation 47(3)(i) of the Miscellaneous Amendments (No. 2) Regulations 1995 (January 22, 1996).
13. Regulation 47(3)(ii) of the Miscellaneous Amendments (No. 2) Regulations 1995 (January 22, 1996).
14. Regulation 47(3)(iii) of the Miscellaneous Amendments (No. 2) Regulations 1995 (January 22, 1996).
15. Regulation 47(3)(iv) of the Miscellaneous Amendments (No. 2) Regulations 1995 (January 22, 1996).
16. Regulation 58(2)(h) of the Miscellaneous Amendments Regulation 1998 (January 19, 1998).
17. Regulation 15(3)(a) of the Miscellaneous Amendments (No. 2) Regulations 1996 (January 13, 1997).
18. Regulation 15(3)(b) of the Miscellaneous Amendments (No. 2) Regulations 1996 (January 13, 1997).
19. Regulation 15(4)(a) of the Miscellaneous Amendments (No. 2) Regulations 1996 (January 13, 1997).

20. Regulation 15(4)(b) of the Miscellaneous Amendments (No. 2) Regulations 1996 (January 13, 1997).
21. Regulation 15(4)(c) of the Miscellaneous Amendments (No. 2) Regulations 1996 (January 13, 1997).
22. Regulation 58(2)(a) of Miscellaneous Amendments Regulations 1998 (January 19, 1998).
23. Regulation 58(2)(b) of Miscellaneous Amendments Regulations 1998 (January 19, 1998).
24. Regulation 58(2)(b) of Miscellaneous Amendments Regulations 1998 (January 19, 1998).
25. Regulation 58(2)(c) of Miscellaneous Amendments Regulations 1998 (January 19, 1998).
26. Regulation 58(2)(d) of Miscellaneous Amendments Regulations 1998 (January 19, 1998).
27. Regulation 58(2)(e) of Miscellaneous Amendments Regulations 1998 (January 19, 1998).
28. Regulation 58(2)(e) of Miscellaneous Amendments Regulations 1998 (January 19, 1998).
29. Regulation 59(2)(e) of Miscellaneous Amendments Regulations 1998 (January 19, 1998).
30. Regulation 58(2)(e) of Miscellaneous Amendments Regulations 1998 (January 19, 1998).
31. Regulation 58(2)(e) of Miscellaneous Amendments Regulations 1998 (January 19, 1998).
32. Regulation 58(2)(e) of Miscellaneous Amendments Regulations 1998 (January 19, 1998).
33. Regulation 58(2)(e) of Miscellaneous Amendments Regulations 1998 (January 19, 1998).
34. Regulation 58(2)(e) of Miscellaneous Amendments Regulations 1998 (January 19, 1998).
35. Regulation 58(2)(e) of Miscellaneous Amendments Regulations 1998 (January 19, 1998).
36. Regulation 58(2)(e) of Miscellaneous Amendments Regulations 1998 (January 19, 1998).
37. Regulation 58(2)(f) of Miscellaneous Amendments Regulations 1998 (January 19, 1998).
38. Regulation 58(2)(g)(i) of Miscellaneous Amendments Regulations 1998 (January 19, 1998).
39. Regulation 58(2)(g)(ii) of Miscellaneous Amendments Regulations 1998 (January 19, 1998).
40. Regulation 58(3)(a) of Miscellaneous Amendments Regulations 1998 (January 19, 1998).
41. Regulation 58(3)(a) of Miscellaneous Amendments Regulations 1998 (January 19, 1998).
42. Regulation 58(3)(b)(i) of Miscellaneous Amendments Regulations 1998 (January 19, 1998).
43. Regulation 58(3)(b)(ii) of Miscellaneous Amendments Regulations 1998 (January 19, 1998).
44. Regulation 58(3)(c) of Miscellaneous Amendments Regulations 1998 (January 19, 1998).
45. Regulation 58(3)(c) of Miscellaneous Amendments Regulations 1998 (January 19, 1998).
46. Regulation 58(3)(d) of Miscellaneous Amendments Regulations 1998 (January 19, 1998).
47. Article 20 of the Commencement No. 7 Order 1999 (June 1, 1999).

DEFINITIONS

"family": see reg.1(2).  4.261
"home": see reg.1(2)
"Housing Benefit Regulations": see reg.1(2)
"parent with care": see reg.1(2)
"partner": see reg.1(2)
"person": see reg.1(2)
"personal pension scheme": see reg.1(2)

GENERAL NOTE  4.262

The provisions dealing with housing costs are mandatory and contain no element of discretion. Accordingly s.2 of the Act has no application to them (*CCS 9/95*, para.8).

*Paragraph 1*

This paragraph lays down the eligible housing costs for all purposes except the calculation of exempt income where the provisions are supplemented by para.3. Where repayment of a loan or credit is concerned, only interest payments are included and not capital payments. Housing costs are not defined. They bear their normal meaning of costs associated with the provision of housing for an individual or a family (Common Appendix to *R(IS) 3/91* and *R(IS) 4/91*, para.10). This is subject to para.4 below. The housing costs allowable are those which are reasonably necessary for providing a home or repairs or improvements to it, and do not include other costs which happen to be secured upon it (*CCS 12/94*, para.35), even if those costs were incurred in order to avoid loss of the home (*ibid.*, para.39). They do, however, include loans to a partner to purchase the other partner's former interest in the property from the partner's trustee in bankruptcy (*R(IS) 6/94*). As a result of the Amendment Regulations, payments analogous to those listed are not within the scope of the paragraph.

In *R(CS) 6/98*, para.12 the Commissioner declined to express a view on whether the "home" in question was the home at the time in respect of which maintenance is being assessed or the home at the time the expenditure was incurred, although he did say that the former might be the case.

For the significance of the reference to the *provision* of a home see the general note to para.4 below.

The language of "costs" and "payments" makes it clear that housing costs only include actual expenditure and not cases where there is liability but no payment, for example in a deferred repayment mortgage (*CIS 636/92*, para.8).

There is no power for decision-makers, tribunals or Commissioners to make allowance for voluntary payments by an absent parent towards housing costs of the former matrimonial home now occupied by the parent with care and the qualifying child (*CCS 12/95*, para.5; *R(CS) 9/98*, para.8). The giving of credit for such payments is relevant only to recovery of child support maintenance and not to its assessment, and is a matter for the Secretary of State alone (*ibid.*).

*Subparagraph (b)*

An Islamic Trust Funding Arrangement to facilitate the acquisition of a home under which the property is conveyed into the name of the parent to be held on trust in unequal shares for that parent and the funding provider with the former required to buy shares from the latter by way of payments which are called mesne profits but calculated by reference to interest rates, is not to be equated with a mortgage under which interest payments are made (*CIS 14483/96*, para.10). Since the Commissioner looked at the legal form of the arrangement rather than its economic substance, it is likely that in child support law the arrangement would fall within subpara.(j) below.

In *CCS 1049/04*, the Commissioner decided that for a current account mortgage the eligible housing costs are limited to the minimum amounts that have to be paid under the terms of the loans. Additional payments that were made in order to reduce the outstanding balance and thereby save interest did not count.

*Subparagraph (d)*

If this head is to be satisfied there must be a loan. It is not sufficient that a debt, for example to cover private street works, is deferred and paid in instalments with interest (*R(SB) 3/87*, para.7). It is undecided whether loans taken out in respect of work already undertaken are within this head (*CIS 264/93*, para.13). Repairs and improvements are defined in paras 2 and 2A.

Tribunals have to consider three matters: (i) the basis upon which the loan was made; (ii) the nature of the works for which the money was borrowed; (iii) the use to which the money was put. In the case of a loan from a commercial lender, its basis is to be found either (a) in a term of the contract of loan requiring that the money be used for a specified purpose or (b) in the representation by the absent parent to the lender of the reason why the money was needed. The basis on which the loan was entered into is likely to be stated in general terms that are not sufficiently detailed and precise to show whether the other conditions are satisfied. So, it is necessary to identify the nature of the work for which the money was borrowed in order to check if the conditions in paras 2 or 2A are satisfied. Interest on money which is borrowed for repairs or improvements, but put to other use, is not a payment in respect of the home for the purposes of the opening words of para.1. See *CCS 349/97*, paras 9–11. The person's motive in carrying out the repairs or improvements is irrelevant (*ibid.*, para.12).

**4.263** *Subparagraph (f)*

This provision does not apply where possession proceedings have been brought by a lender against the borrower, since in due course the whole of the lender's interest may pass to the borrower, but at no stage will there be joint ownership between lender and borrower (*CIS 392/94*, para.9).

*Subparagraph (g)*

The common law meaning of "use and occupation" is a payment for the use and occupation of land which is made where a person has been given permission to occupy the land of another without any binding terms being agreed about payment, and the words "in respect of, or in consequence of" are restrictive (*R v Bristol City Council, ex parte Jacobs* (1999) 32 H.L.R. 841).

The Commissioners have decided that the extent of the provision is uncertain (*R(CS) 3/96*, para.23). It does not cover capital repayments as they are the subject of special provision in para.3 which would be anomalous and unnecessary if such repayments fell within this subparagraph. The following do not fall within this provision: premiums on contents and property insurance, because they are also covered by para.3 and anomalies would arise if this subparagraph were interpreted so as to cover them (*R(CS) 3/96*, paras 20–23 and *R 1/94 (CSC)*); payments in respect of the purchase of a home (*R(CS) 6/98*, para.12); repayments on a loan to restock a home with items taken by the other partner on separation (*CSC 2/96*, para.5); water rates (*CSC 3/96*, para.5); council tax (*R(CS) 11/98*, paras 9–10). Payments in respect of road charges and interest paid on them are charges in respect of a home (*R(SB) 3/87*, para.8).

*Subparagraph (j)*

The decision in *CIS 14483/96* dealing with an Islamic Trust Funding Arrangement is explained in the general note to subpara.(b) above. On the basis of the Commissioner's reasoning it is likely that such an arrangement will fall within this subparagraph.

*Subparagraph (k)*

Service charges are not defined. Their meaning was discussed by the Tribunal of Commissioners whose decision appears in the Common Appendix to *R(IS) 3/91* and *R(IS) 4/91*, paras 11 and 15. The words are to be interpreted liberally and mean charges made for services provided in connection with housing. They must be charges which involve the determination and arrangement of a service, which would otherwise be for the occupier to decide on and arrange, in a manner binding on the occupier and which cannot be withdrawn from at leisure. They must bind all those with the same interest in the property or they must run with the land so as to bind successors in occupancy. Buildings insurance is not a service charge (*Dunne v. Department of Health and Social Security*, unreported, Court of Appeal in Northern Ireland, January 22, 1992 and *CSIS 4/90*, para.8), but counselling and other support services can be (*R v North Cornwall District Council, ex p. Singer*, The Times, January 12, 1994). The service charges which are covered are limited by para.6.

*Paragraph 2*                                                                                                    4.264

This paragraph defines repairs and improvements for the purposes of para.1(d). Repair covers both the remedying of defects and steps taken to prevent these, such as the painting of a house to preserve the woodwork (*CSB 420/85*, paras 11–12). However, where the alleged repair is of the preventive kind, evidence and findings of fact will be needed on whether the work may properly be considered to have been undertaken as a repair or only for cosmetic reasons (*ibid.*, at para.12). It would, for example, if the painting of a house were being considered, be necessary to inquire into the state of the paint work at the time and whether the change was merely to change the colour.

Repairs must be "necessary to maintain the fabric of the home", a strict test. They must also be "major." Whether a repair is or is not major is a question of fact (*CSB 265/87*, para.10). It is a comparative term whose meaning is bound to be somewhat fluid and imprecise, but it will always be relevant to take into account the cost as well as the nature of and the tune taken for the work (*ibid.*, at paras 10 and 12). Chimney-sweeping cannot be a repair (*ibid.*, at para.7). Where the home consists of a flat or some other part of the building, repairs to some other part of the building than the flat itself are not repairs to the fabric of the home (*CIS 616/92*, para.16).

The proper approach to improvements was exemplified by the Commissioner in *CSCS 3/96*, para.4 as follows. First facts have to be found as to the previous state of the home so that it can be seen that the work led to an improvement. Then it has to be shown that the improvement was properly undertaken in order to improve the fitness for occupation of the home. The facts, in other words, must show that there was some existing unfitness to be remedied.

Improvements need not be major but they must fall within one of the categories listed and they must be undertaken with a view to improving the fitness of the home for occupation. The reasonableness of the improvements is not a factor except under (k) but this will be a relevant consideration in assessing the credibility of the evidence on this issue. Moreover the work must be undertaken with a view not just to improving the home but to improving its fitness for occupation. The paragraph assumes that there should be a minimum standard of accommodation and allows the cost of bring the home up to that standard to be taken into account as eligible housing costs. So the test is whether the work is carried out with a view to bringing the home up to a standard above the minimum in a particular respect. This provision is not a licence to install a replacement or additional bathroom or further electric sockets where the current provision is adequate. Care is also needed with self-build homes to ensure that this paragraph is not used to cover the costs of completion rather than of the improvement of a home.

The improvements must be improvements to the home (in other words, to the dwelling—reg.1(2)), although they need not be to the fabric of the home (*CIS 264/93*, paras 15 and 16).

*Subparagraph (a)*

Unlike its social security counterpart, this sub-paragraph does not cover sinks.

*Subparagraph (k)*

The improvements must be made with a view to improving the home's fitness for occupation, which is wider than fitness for habitation and would cover access to the premises (*R(SB) 3/87*, para.10). The improvement must not be viewed from either a subjective or an objective viewpoint, but overall in the broadest possible terms. The tribunal should balance the advantage of the improvement to the person carrying it out against the consequences viewed objectively. An extension to accommodate a large young family, for example, would be reasonable, despite the fact that it was not reflected in any comparable increase in the value of the property, whereas a similar extension built when most of the family were about to leave home would not be (*CIS 453/93*, para.8).

*Paragraph 2A*

Improvements bears its ordinary meaning (*CCS 349/97*, para.10.1).

*Paragraph 3*

The terms of this paragraph are useful not only in their own right but also for the light they shed on the scope of some of the subparagraphs in paragraph 1. It makes special provision for the purposes of calculating exempt income by extending the eligible housing costs under para.1 to include capital repayments and endowment policy premiums in so far as they cover the capital repayments. Where the policy is designed to produce a profit as well as to cover the capital, for example in a with profits endowment or a pension mortgage, the part of the premiums necessarily incurred for the purpose of discharging a mortgage or charge should be identifiable by expert evidence. Where this is not possible or the evidence is not available, 0.0277 per cent, of the sum secured is used as the eligible housing cost. This figure is sufficient to ensure that the capital would be covered assuming an annual rate of return of 8 per cent over 25 years. Payments of arrears or voluntary additional payments of capital are not covered, nor is the cost of insurance against loss of or damage to the building or land.

This paragraph, like para.1, is limited to costs incurred for the provision of a home or for repairs or improvements to it (*CCS 12/94*, para.43).

This paragraph is not restricted to policies that are obtained at a time when the mortgage to be secured has already been obtained (*CCS 1321/97*, para.13).

In *CCS 2750/95*, para.18 the Commissioner held that subpara.(4) applied to term assurances while subpara.(5) applied to endowment policies. He held that both types of policy, if taken out and retained for the purpose of discharging the loan, were allowable, although the reason for the retention of both policies would require investigation in order to be sure that they were being retained for the specified purpose. With respect to the Commissioner, it is doubtful whether his analysis of the relationship of these two subparagraphs is correct. It is suggested that subpara.(4) is the general provision which catches any type of assurance or insurance, while subpara.(5) provides for a limit on the amount where there is a with-profits element in the arrangement. This does not, however, detract from the need to investigate any apparent over-provision in the finance arrangements.

Without expressing a concluded opinion on the point, the Commissioner in *CCS 2750/95*, para.29 said that where only a proportion of a loan is eligible as housing costs, the allowable portion will determine whether the case falls under head (a) or (b).

*Subparagraph (2)*

This subparagraph covers an equitable mortgage by deposit of title deeds or certificate (*CCS 9/95*, para.12). It covers payments which are not fixed at the outset but are subsequently provided for by variation or novation (*ibid.*, para.17).

*Subparagraphs (4) and (5)*                                              4.265

There is no need for the policy to be tied to the mortgage or charge as part of an endowment mortgage. An endowment policy taken out for the purpose of discharging early a repayment mortgage (such an arrangement might be used by a person in poor health in order to avoid the high life premiums involved in an endowment mortgage) is within the wording of these paragraphs with the result that both the premiums on the policy and the capital repayments under the mortgage are eligible housing costs for the purpose of exempt income.

The purpose of the policy must be the discharge of the mortgage or charge. It is not sufficient for the purpose to be to reduce the outstanding capital, as it is only when the whole of the balance of the loan is repaid that the mortgage or charge will be discharged.

In the case of a mortgage which is part repayment and part endowment, the endowment element is within these paragraphs as it is intended that the policy will discharge the outstanding balance at the date of maturity.

The amendment to subpara.(4) is made "for the avoidance of doubt" which shows that it is retrospective in its effect. However, in its terms it only applies to policies which secure payment of monies due under the mortgage or charge. The words "monies due" are in contrast to "discharging the mortgage or charge" and suggest that the amendment applies to periodical payments only. Policies which provide for repayment of the capital were considered in *R(CS) 10/98*. This case concerned an assessment for a period before the amendment came into force. The policy concerned was one which secured the payment of all or part of the mortgage capital in the event of death or serious illness. The Commissioner held, at para.18, that this fell within the subparagraph as it stood at the relevant time. He did not mention the amendment, nor did he consider whether or not it was necessary, as is suggested above, for the policy to provide for the payment of all, rather than merely part, of the sum secured.

*Subparagraph (5B)*

The words "personal pension plan" are not defined. The words "personal pension scheme" are used elsewhere in these Regulations, so the choice of different wording must be significant. Technically, a personal pension plan could not be made under the pre-1988 legislation. However, it would be anomalous if this subparagraph were interpreted to exclude these earlier arrangements. Accordingly, it is suggested that the words should be interpreted generally and not limited to any technical meaning.

The plan must have been obtained and retained for the purpose of discharging a mortgage or charge. That purpose need not have been an absolute one, as it is the nature of things that a person might well wish to have as large a pension as possible and intend to resort to the plan only if some other source of finance was not available.

*Subparagraph (6)(a)*

This provision may not cover the type of mortgage considered in *CIS 141/93* in which the mortgagor had the option at each interest rate increase of continuing with the existing level of payments, with the capital being increased and the term of the mortgage extended. In such a case there are never arrears owing under the terms of the mortgage.

*Paragraph 4(1)*

This subparagraph lays down three conditions all of which must be satisfied in order for the housing costs to be eligible for child support purposes. First, the costs must be necessarily incurred for the purchasing, renting or otherwise securing the possession of the home or carrying out repairs and improvements to it. The requirement of necessity must be interpreted and applied sensibly with appropriate regard to the realities of property acquisition and of the mortgage market (*Pabari v Secretary of State for Work and Pensions* [2005] 1 All E.R. 287). The costs must relate to the parent's own home; costs which are met, for example, in respect of the home of a relative or a divorced spouse are not covered. In *CCS 2750/95*, para.14 the Commissioner held that the former version of this head was concerned solely with limiting eligible housing costs to the home of the parent concerned. Clearly in its present form it has a wider function of additionally emphasising the essential purpose of the expenditure. Second, the parent or a member of the parent's family must be responsible for them. It is clear from para.4(1)(c) and (2) that what matters is legal responsibility rather than a voluntary assumption of payment. However, in two cases persons are treated as responsible for costs which they are not legally liable to meet: see subpara.(2). What matters is legal liability and not whether the person liable is paying the costs. It will not be unusual for example for spouses or partners to be jointly and severally liable on a mortgage but for the payments to be met by only one of them. Third, the liability must be to someone who is not a member of the same household. This goes some way to prevent collusion between members of a household. It may be possible for parties to arrange their affairs so that there are separate households, and tribunals will need to be astute to distinguish genuine arrangements which do result in separate households, even if those arrangements are made in order to fall within subpara.(1), and shams.

In order to amount to an eligible housing cost the payment must be made in respect of the provision of the home under para.1 above and must additionally fall within the terms of head (a) of this subparagraph. The terms used in para.1 and head (a) are narrower than "acquiring an interest in the dwelling" which is the equivalent phrase in income support law. The meaning of "provision of a home" was discussed in *R(CS) 12/98*, paras 9–14. According to that decision it covers the initial acquisition of the person's interest in the home and matters which serve to preserve the home, such as repairs and improvements to it. Whether or not it covers the acquisition of a higher or further interest in the home, such as the purchase by a lessee of the freehold or the purchase of one joint owner of the other's share, is a matter of degree. For example, in the case of the purchase of the freehold, it will be relevant to consider how long the lease has to run, and in the case of the purchase of a joint owner's interest, it will be relevant to consider how secure the person's occupancy is in view of the possibility of the other owner obtaining an order for sale. This interpretation is reinforced by head (a) which requires that the costs be "necessarily incurred" and uses the phrase "otherwise securing possession of the home" in head (a). However, with respect it is doubtful whether this interpretation gives sufficient weight to the complexities of the analysis which it requires of the child support officers who will have to implement it. In this respect it is in contrast to the approach taken in *R(CS) 14/98*, para.16 where the Commissioner declined to distinguish between living with and staying with, commenting that "it is inconceivable that the Secretary of State intended that such fine distinctions should be drawn when they would, in many cases, be highly contentious. No-one could describe this legislation as simple, but it does seem designed to produce fairly clear-cut answers to most cases so that a relatively junior child support officer is able to apply the law."

Where a person is on a low income but has a partner with a higher income which can support the family's relatively high housing costs, the person is treated as responsible for those costs, thereby significantly reducing or even eliminating the person's assessable income, although the costs are met in practice by the partner. This is subject to the possibility of a departure direction.

*Paragraph 4(2)*                                                                                    4.266

This subparagraph provides for two cases in which persons who are paying housing costs for which they are not liable are treated as if they were responsible for those costs. The first is where the person who is liable is not paying and the parent is making payments in order to continue to live in the home. It must be necessary for the parent to meet the costs in order to continue to live in the home. Failure must therefore put the home at risk. So failure to pay a loan which is not secured on the home will not be sufficient. In practice even if the loan is secured on the home eviction for non-payment is a difficult and lengthy process. However tribunals are likely to regard all cases in which the risk of eviction may arise in the event of non-payment as falling within this head. The typical case covered will be where the parent has been deserted by a former partner who is liable for housing costs but is refusing to pay them. If this is the case then the parent is treated as responsible for the costs. The parent may also be treated as responsible in other cases, for example if a grandparent was meeting the costs. In these other cases however it must be reasonable to treat the parent as liable; no issue of reasonableness arises if the person liable was a former partner. The second case covered is where the parent is sharing housing costs with others who also live in the accommodation of whom at least one who is not a close relative is liable or treated as liable for those costs, provided that it is reasonable to treat the parent as sharing the responsibility for the costs. The wording speaks of others in the plural, but by virtue of s.6(c) of the Interpretation Act 1978 this will include the singular. Findings of fact on each element of each case will be necessary and decisions on reasonableness will need to be justified in the reasons for decision.

Subparagraph (2)(a) will apply where a parent is occupying the former joint home in respect of which there is shared liability for the housing costs, but is having to meet the whole of those costs the former partner's share of those costs is not being paid (*CCS 13698/96*, para.7).

*Paragraph 5*

This allows costs to be apportioned in cases where premises are used for a dual purpose. However it only covers cases where there is separate accommodation which is put to each use, such as where living accommodation is connected to retail premises or where a business is run from a distinct and separate part of accommodation. It does not cover cases where a business is run from a part of a person's home which is also used for other purposes, such as a business run from a desk in the corner of the living room.

*Paragraph 6*                                                                                    4.267

This paragraph contains conditions for those service charges which are to be eligible as housing costs. The conditions are additional to the requirement in para.1(k) that the charge should be a condition on which the right to occupy the home depends.

Paragraph 1 of the Schedule reads as follows.

"**1.** The following service charges shall not be eligible to be met by housing benefit—

(a) charges in respect of day-to-day living expenses including, in particular, all provision of—

   (i) subject to paragraph 1A meals (including the preparation of meals or provision of unprepared food);

   (ii) laundry (other than the provision of premises or equipment to enable a person to do his own laundry);

   (iii) leisure items such as either sports facilities (except a children's play area), or television rental and licence fees (except radio relay charges, charges made in respect of the conveyance and the installation and maintenance of equipment for such conveyance of a television broadcasting service which is not a domestic satellite service, or charges made in respect of the conveyance and the installation and maintenance of equipment for such conveyance of a television programme service where in respect of the claimant's dwelling the installation of such equipment is the only practicable means of conveying satisfactorily a television broadcasting service which is not a domestic satellite service, as these services are defined in the Broadcasting Act 1990);

   (iv) cleaning of rooms and windows except cleaning of—

     (aa) communal areas; or

     (bb) the exterior of any windows where neither the claimant nor any member of his household is able to clean them himself,

    where a payment is not made in respect of such cleaning by a local authority (including, in relation to England, a county council) or the National Assembly of Wales to the claimant or his partner, or to another person on their behalf; and

   (v) transport;

(b) charges in respect of—

   (i) the acquisition of furniture or household equipment, and

   (ii) the use of furniture or equipment where that furniture or household equipment will become the property of the claimant by virtue of an agreement with the landlord;

(c) charges in respect of the provision of an emergency alarm system;

(d) charges in respect of medical expenses (including the cost of treatment or counselling related to mental disorder, mental handicap, physical disablement or past or present alcohol or drug dependence);

(e) charges in respect of the provision of nursing care or personal care (including assistance at mealtimes or with personal appearance or hygiene);

(f) charges in respect of general counselling or of any other support services whoever provides those services;

(g) charges in respect of any services not specified in sub-paragraphs (a) to (f) which are not connected with the provision of adequate accommodation."

Para.5(2) of the Schedule in so far as it is relevant reads as follows.

"(a) for heating (other than hot water)
(b) for hot water
(c) for lighting
(d) for cooking"

A service charge may be fixed, in which case the amount changes only when the rent is changed, or variable, in which case the amount varies as the costs to which the charge relates varies. A service charge may be difficult to identify as the landlord may merely quote a figure for "rent" without specifying any amount as relating, for example, to water rates. Child support law has adopted provisions from the Housing Benefit (General) Regulations. They seek to distinguish costs which relate to the provision of adequate housing from other costs, thereby placing tenants and homeowners on an equal footing. The standard deduction approach is convenient in the context of a formula assessment, but the deduction used can be unrealistically low when compared to the costs which would be allowed by a rent officer. The law is in such cases generous to the parent concerned, and fails to provide equal treatment as between tenants and homeowners.

The essence of a service charge is that it consists of an arrangement for determining whether a particular service, such as redecoration, is required and, if so, for providing the service or arranging for it to be provided. The arrangement must not only be binding, but be binding on all those with the same interest in the property. See the Common Appendix to *R(IS) 3/91* and *R(IS) 4/91*, para.15. This draws a clear and logical distinction between charges which are payable as an incident of the owner's estate or interest in the property and those which arise in some other way such as under a personal contract with the tenant or owner (*R(IS) 19/93*, para.12). Paragraphs 1(a)-(f) exclude particular service charges, while para.1(g) contains a general exclusion for other service charges which are not connected with the provision of adequate accommodation.

Payments required to be made under the terms of a lease for repairs, redecoration, renewal or insurance are service charges and are connected with the provision of adequate accommodation (Common Appendix, para.18, and *R(IS) 4/92*, paras 12—15). Payment of premiums for insurance required under the terms of mortgage is not a service charge since the obligation arises not from the borrower's interest or estate in the property but from the mortgage. In other words, it arises from the financial arrangements for purchase and not out of the ownership of the property itself *R(IS) 19/93*, para.14). Likewise, insurance premiums effected between an owner-occupier and an insurance company are not a service charge (*CIS 17/88*, approved in *R(IS) 4/92*, para.15, and *R(IS) 19/93*, para.15), although they are connected with the provision of adequate accommodation (*R(IS) 4/92*, para.15, and *R(IS) 19/93*, para.15). Payments of administration and other charges related to arrears of mortgage payments are not service charges connected to the adequacy of the accommodation (*CIS 392/94*, para.7).

In order to fall within subpara.(f) the services must relate to preserving the fabric of the accommodation rather than to maintaining the person in the accommodation, for example by ensuring that the rent is paid (*R v Sutton London Borough Council, ex p. Harrison,* The Times, August 22, 1997). Paragraph 1A is set out below.

4.268 "**1A.**—(1) Where a charge for meals is ineligible to be met by housing benefit under paragraph 1. the amount ineligible in respect of each week shall be the amount specified in the following provisions of this paragraph.

(2) Subject to sub-paragraph (3A) where the charge includes provisions for at least three meals a day, the amount shall be—

(a) for a single claimant,

(b) if the claimant is a member of a family

(i) for the claimant and for each member of his family aged 16 or over,

(ii) for each member of his family under age 16,

(3) Except where subparagraph (4) applies and subject to sub-paragraph (3A), where the charge includes provision for less than three meals a day, the amount shall be—

(a) for a single claimant,

(b) if the claimant is a member of a family—

(i) for the claimant and for each member of his family aged 16 or over,

(ii) for each member of his family under age 16,

(3A) For the purposes of sub-paragraphs (2)(b) and (3)(b), a person attains the age of 16 on the first Monday in September following his 16th birthday.

(4) Where the charge for meals includes the provision of breakfast only, the amount for the claimant and, if he is a member of a family, for the claimant and for each member of his family, shall be . . .

(5) Where a charge for meals includes provision for meals for a person who is not a member of the claimant's family subparagraphs (2) to (4) shall apply as if that person were a member of the claimant's family.

(6) For the avoidance of doubt where the charge does not include provision for meals for a claimant or, as the case may be, a member of his family, subparagraphs (2) to (4) shall not apply in respect of that person."

[¹SCHEDULE 3A

## AMOUNT TO BE ALLOWED IN RESPECT OF TRANSFERS OF PROPERTY

**Interpretation**

4.269 **1.**—(1) In this Schedule—

"property" means—

(a) a legal estate or an equitable interest in land; or

(b) a sum of money which is derived from or represents capital, whether in cash or in the form of a deposit with—

(i) the Bank of England;

(ii) an authorised institution or an exempted person within the meaning of the Banking Act 1987;

(iii) a building society incorporated or deemed to be incorporated under the Building Societies Act 1986;

(c) any business asset as defined in subparagraph (2) (whether in the form of money or an interest in land or otherwise);

(d) any policy of insurance which has been obtained and retained for the purpose of providing a capital sum to discharge a mortgage or charge secured upon an estate or interest in land which is also the subject of the transfer (in this Schedule referred to as an endowment policy);

"qualifying transfer" means a transfer of property—

(a) which was made in pursuance of a court order made, or a written maintenance agreement executed, before 5th April 1993;

(b) which was made between the absent parent and either the parent with care or a relevant child [⁴, or both whether jointly or otherwise including, in Scotland, in common property];

(c) which was made at a time when the absent parent and the parent with care were living separate and apart;

[⁵(d) the effect of which is that (subject to any mortgage or charge) the parent with care or a relevant child is solely beneficially entitled to the property of which the property transferred forms the whole or part, or the business asset, or the parent with care is beneficially entitled to that property or that asset together with the relevant child or absent parent or both, jointly or otherwise or, in Scotland, in common property, or the relevant child is so entitled together with the absent parent;]

[⁶(e) which was not made for the purpose only of compensating the parent with care either for the loss of a right to apply for, or receive, periodical payments or a capital sum in respect of herself, or for any reduction in the amount of such payments or sum;]

"compensating transfer" means a transfer of property which would be a qualifying transfer (disregarding the requirement of paragraph (e) of the definition of "qualifying transfer") if it were made by the absent parent, but which is made by the parent with care in favour of the absent parent f, or] or a relevant child for both jointly or otherwise, or, in Scotland, in common property];

"relevant date" means the date of the making of the court order execution of the written maintenance agreement in pursuance of which the qualifying transfer was made.

(2) For the purposes of subparagraph (1) "business asset" means an asset, whether in the form of money or an interest in land or otherwise which, prior to the date of transfer was used in the course of a trade or business carried on—

(a) by the absent parent as a sole trader;

(b) by the absent parent in partnership, whether with the parent with care or not;

(c) by a close company within the meaning of sections 414 and 415 of the Income and Corporation Taxes Act 1988 in which the absent parent was a participator at the date of the transfer.

(3) Where the condition specified in regulation 10(a) is satisfied this Schedule shall apply as if references—

(a) to the parent with care were references to the absent parent; and

(b) to the absent parent were references to the parent with care.

**Evidence to be produced in connection with the allowance for transfers of property**

4.270    **2.**—(1) Where the absent parent produces to the Secretary of State—
(a) contemporaneous evidence in writing of the making of a court order or of the execution of a written maintenance agreement, which requires the relevant person to make a qualifying transfer of property;
(b) evidence in writing and whether contemporaneous or not as to—
(i) the fact of the transfer;
(ii) the value of the property transferred at the relevant date;
(iii) the amount of any mortgage or charge outstanding at the relevant date,

an amount in respect of the relevant value of the transfer determined in accordance with the following provisions of this Schedule shall be allowed in calculating or estimating the exempt income of the absent parent.

(2) Where the evidence specified in subparagraph (1) is not produced within a reasonable time after the Secretary of State has been notified of the wish of the absent parent that [$^{16}$the Secretary of State] consider the question, [$^{17}$he] shall determine the question on the basis that the relevant value of the transfer is nil.

**Consideration of evidence produced by other parent**

4.271    [$^{18}$**3.**—(1) Where an absent parent has notified the Secretary of State that he wishes him to consider whether an amount should be allowed in respect of the relevant value of a qualifying transfer, the Secretary of State shall—
(a) give notice to the other parent of that application; and
(b) have regard in determining the application to any representations made by the other parent which are received within the period specified in subparagraph (2).

(2) The period specified in this subparagraph is one month from the date on which the notice referred to in subparagraph (1)(a) above was sent or such longer period as the Secretary of State is satisfied is reasonable in the circumstances of the case.]

**Computation of qualifying value—business assets and land**

4.272    **4.**—(1) Subject to paragraph 6, where the property [$^9$transferred] by the absent parent is, or includes, an estate or interest in land, or a business asset, the qualifying value of that estate, interest or asset shall be determined in accordance with the formula—

$$[^{10}QV = \frac{(VP\text{-}MCP)}{2} - (VAP\text{-}MCR) - VCR$$

where—
QV is the qualifying value,
VP is the value at the relevant date of the business asset or the property of which the estate or interest forms the whole or part, and for the purposes of this calculation it is assumed that the estate, interest or asset held on the relevant date by the absent parent or by the absent parent and the par-

944

ent with care is held by them jointly in equal shares or, in Scotland, in common property;

MCP is the amount of any mortgage or charge outstanding immediately prior to the relevant date on the business asset or on the property of which the estate or interest forms the whole or part;

VAP is the value calculated at the relevant date of the business asset or of the property of which the estate or interest forms the whole or part beneficially owned by the absent parent immediately following the transfer (if any);

MCR is, where immediately after the transfer the absent parent is responsible for discharging a mortgage or charge on the business asset or on the property of which the estate or interest forms the whole or part, the amount calculated at the relevant date which is a proportion of any such mortgage or charge outstanding immediately following the transfer, being the same percentage as VAP bears to that property as a whole; and

VCR is the value of any charge in favour of the absent parent on the business asset or on the property of which the estate or interest forms the whole or part, being the amount specified in the court order or written maintenance agreement in relation to the charge, or the amount of a proportion of the value of the business asset or the property on the relevant date specified in the court order or written maintenance agreement.]

(2) For the purposes of subparagraph (1) the value of an estate or interest in land is to be determined upon the basis that the parent with care and any relevant child, if in occupation of the land, would quit on completion of the sale.

## Computation of qualifying value—cash, deposits and endowment policies

5.—(1) Subject to paragraph 6, where the property which is the subject    4.273
of the qualifying transfer is, or includes—

  (i) a sum of money whether in cash or in the form of a deposit with the Bank of England, an authorised institution or exempted person within the meaning of the Banking Act 1987, or a building society incorporated or deemed to be incorporated under the Building Societies Act 1986, derived from or representing capital; or

 (ii) an endowment policy,

the amount of the qualifying value shall be determined by applying the formula—

$$QV = \frac{VT}{2}$$

where—

  (a) QV is the qualifying value; and

  (b) VT is the amount of cash, the balance of the account or the surrender value of the endowment policy on the relevant date [[11]and for the purposes of this calculation it is assumed that the cash, balance or policy held on the relevant date by the absent parent and the parent with care is held by them jointly in equal shares or, in Scotland, in common property.]

### Transfers wholly in lieu of periodical payments for relevant child

4.274    **6.** Where the evidence produced in relation to a transfer to, or in respect of, a relevant child, shows expressly that the whole of that transfer was made exclusively in lieu of periodical payments in respect of that child—

(a) in a case to which paragraph 4 applies, [¹²the qualifying value shall be treated as being twice the qualifying value calculated in accordance with that paragraph]; and

(b) in a case to which paragraph 5 applies, the qualifying value shall be [¹³treated as being twice the qualifying value calculated in accordance with that paragraph.]

### Multiple transfers to related persons

4.275    **7.**—(1) Where there has been more than one qualifying transfer from the absent parent—

(a) to the same parent with care;

(b) to or for the benefit of the same relevant child;

(c) to or for the benefit of two or more relevant children with respect to all of whom the same persons are respectively the parent with care and the absent parent;

or any combination thereof, the relevant value by reference to which the allowance is to be calculated in accordance with paragraph 10 shall be the aggregate of the qualifying transfers calculated individually in accordance with the preceding paragraphs of this Schedule, less the value of any compensating transfer or where there has been more than one, the aggregate of the values of the compensating transfers so calculated.

(2) Except as provided by subparagraph (1), the values of transfers shall not be aggregated for the purposes of this Schedule.

### Computation of the value of compensating transfers

4.276    **8.** [²Subject to paragraph 8A, the value of] a compensating transfer shall be determined in accordance with paragraph 4 to 7 above, but as if any reference in those paragraphs—

(a) to the absent parent were a reference to the parent with care;

(b) to the parent with care were a reference to the absent parent; and

(c) to a qualifying transfer were a reference to a compensating transfer.

4.277    [³**8A.**—(1) This paragraph applies where—

(a) the property which is the subject of a compensating transfer is or includes cash or deposits as defined in paragraph 5(i);

(b) that property was acquired by the parent with care after the relevant date;

(c) the absent parent has no legal interest in that property;

(d) if that property is or includes cash obtained by a mortgage or charge, that mortgage or charge was executed by the parent with care after the relevant date and was of property to the whole of which she is legally entitled; and

(e) the effect of the compensating transfer is that the parent with care or a relevant child is beneficially entitled (subject to any mortgage or charge) to the whole of the absent parent's legal estate in the land which is the subject of the qualifying transfer.

(2) Where subparagraph (1) applies, the qualifying value of the compensating transfer shall be the amount of the cash or deposits transferred pursuant to the court order or written maintenance agreement referred to in head (a) of the definition of "qualifying transfer" in paragraph 1(1).]

### Computation of relevant value of a qualifying transfer

**9.** The relevant value of a qualifying transfer shall be calculated by deducting from the qualifying value of the qualifying transfer the qualifying value of any compensating transfer between the same persons as are parties to the qualifying transfer.

**4.278**

### Amount to be allowed in respect of a qualifying transfer

**10.** For the purposes of regulation 9(l)(bb), the amount to be allowed in the computation of E, or in case where regulation 10(a) applies, F, shall be—

**4.279**

(a) where the relevant value calculated in accordance with paragraph 9 is less than £5,000, nil;

(b) where the relevant value calculated in accordance with paragraph 9 is at least £5,000, but less than £10,000, £20.00 per week;

(c) where the relevant value calculated in accordance with paragraph 9 is at least £10,000, but less than £25,000, £40.00 per week;

(d) where the relevant value calculated in accordance with paragraph 9 is not less than £25,000, £60.00 per week.

**11.** This Schedule in its application to Scotland shall have effect as if—

**4.280**

(a) in paragraph 1 for the words "legal estate or equitable interest in land" [$^{14}$and in head (e) of paragraph 8A(1), for the words "legal estate in the land"] there were substituted the words "an interest in land within the meaning of section 2(6) of the Convincing and Feudal Reform (Scotland) Act 1970";

(b) in paragraph 4 the word "estate," and the words "estate or" in each place where they respectively occur were omitted [$^{15}$(c) in paragraphs 1, 2, 4 and 8A for the word "mortgage" there were substituted the words "heritable security".]

AMENDMENTS

1. Regulation 57 of and Sched.1 to the Amendment Regulations 1995 (April 18, 1995).

2. Regulation 48(1) of the Miscellaneous Amendments (No. 2) Regulations 1995 (December 18, 1995).

3. Regulation 48(2) of the Miscellaneous Amendments (No. 2) Regulations 1995 (December 18, 1995).

4. Regulation 6(7)(a)(i) of the Miscellaneous Amendments Regulations 1999 (April 6, 1999).

5. Regulation 6(7)(a)(ii) of the Miscellaneous Amendments Regulations 1999 (April 6, 1999).

6. Regulation 6(7)(a)(iii) of the Miscellaneous Amendments Regulations 1999 (April 6, 1999).

7. Regulation 6(7)(b)(i) of the Miscellaneous Amendments Regulations 1999 (April 6, 1999).

8. Regulation 6(7)(b)(ii) of the Miscellaneous Amendments Regulations 1999 (April 6, 1999).

9. Regulation 6(7)(c)(i) of the Miscellaneous Amendments Regulations 1999 (April 6, 1999).

10. Regulation 6(7)(c)(ii) of the Miscellaneous Amendments Regulations 1999 (April 6, 1999).

11. Regulation 6(7)(d) of the Miscellaneous Amendments Regulations 1999 (April 6, 1999).

12. Regulation 6(7)(e)(i) of the Miscellaneous Amendments Regulations 1999 (April 6, 1999).

13. Regulation 6(7)(e)(ii) of the Miscellaneous Amendments Regulations 1999 (April 6, 1999).

14. Regulation 6(7)(f)(i) of the Miscellaneous Amendments Regulations 1999 (April 6, 1999).

15. Regulation 6(7)(f)(ii) of the Miscellaneous Amendments Regulations 1999 (April 6, 1999).

16. Article 21(a)(i) of the Commencement No. 7 Order 1999 (June 1, 1999).

17. Article 21(a)(ii) of the Commencement No. 7 Order 1999 (June 1, 1999).

18. Article 21(b) of the Commencement No. 7 Order 1999 (June 1, 1999).

GENERAL NOTE

**4.281**     This Schedule makes provision for clean break settlements under court orders or written agreements made before the coming into force of the child support scheme. It provides for an allowance to be made in the absent parent's exempt income calculation based on a sliding scale which is fixed as follows. In the case of settlements expressly made solely in substitution for maintenance payments for a relevant child, the whole of the capital value is taken into account. In other cases, only half the capital value is used. Where the asset is an interest in land or a business asset which is mortgaged or charged, only the difference between the value of the asset and the outstanding principal secured is taken into account. Transfers from a parent with care to the absent parent are offset. The relevant value is that at the date of the order or agreement.

*Paragraph 1*
"*property*" The scope of the definition of property is limited. It does not include, for example, shares. Nor does it include cases where one party has conferred a benefit on the other by assuming responsibility for debts, such as mortgage debts.

*Paragraph 1*
"*qualifying transfer*" A qualifying transfer is one made between the absent parent and either the parent with care or a child. Accordingly, if the person with care is not a parent of the child (for example, a grandparent or a subsequent partner of one of the parents), the provisions of this Schedule can only apply if the settlement was between the absent parent and the child.

"*court order*" and "*written maintenance agreement*" See the general note to s.18 of the 1995 Act. It is arguable that in this context "written maintenance agreement" is not limited to agreements which fall within s.9(1) of the Act, as this would introduce an irrelevant and unnecessary limitation on the agreements that are covered by this Schedule.

In construing an order or agreement it is permissible to have regard to evidence contained in another document, such as a side letter, which is intended to contain terms of the arrangement (*CCS 16518/96*, para.7). In the case of a consent order, it is appropriate to interpret the undertakings and the orders of the court as a single whole, because the settlement was negotiated as a package *(CCS 316/98*, para.19).

*"executed"* This word is ambiguous. It is used in relation to agreements to mean either made or performed. It is suggested that the more natural meaning of the word is the former *(Terrapin International Ltd v Inland Revenue Commissioners* [1976] 2 All E.R. 461). Moreover, interpreting "executed" to mean the performance rather than the making of a written agreement would produce the anomaly that the relevant date for a transfer under a court order would be the date that order was made, whereas if the transfer were pursuant to a written agreement, the relevant date would be the date of the transfer.

*"asset"* It is important to identify clearly the asset being transferred.

*"expressly for the purpose only of compensating"* In deciding whether or not the specified purpose is expressed, the order or agreement is to be read as a whole *(CCS 16518/96*, para.12(3) and *CCS 316/98*, para.19).

The following are irrelevant: (i) subjective evidence of intention or motive; (ii) speculation or inference; (iii) calculations of who may have derived some direct or indirect benefit; (iv) any incidental benefit to a child, such as going on living at the family home after the transfer; (v) any mere statement of intention not affecting the actual interest taken or the terms on which the property is held, such as the standard certificate to postpone a legal aid charge, that the house is to be used by the parent with care as a home for herself or her dependants. See *CCS 1997/97*, para.15. The preservation of even a right to a nominal sum by way of maintenance for the other party prevents the transfer being a qualifying one *(CCS 16518/96*, paras 9 and 15).

*"loss"* This includes the partial loss of a right *(CCS 1554/97*, para.6 and *CCS 1997/97*, para.22).

*"any right to apply"* There are conflicting decisions by Commissioners on whether the reference to the loss of any right to apply for periodical payments or a capital sum means the loss of all right to apply *(CCS 16518/96*, para.12(1)) or the loss of a right to apply *(CCS 1997/97*, para.19). The question was left open in *CCS 1554/97*, para.6.

An Edinburgh-based Commissioner has decided that para.1(1)(e) can never be satisfied when the transfer is made in implementation of a Court decree *(CSCS 1/98* and *CSCS 2/98*). The Commissioner left open the position in the case of a written agreement *(ibid.*, para.13).

*Paragraph 5*

It is suggested that "money . . . derived from . . . capital" includes interest which has accrued to that money by the relevant date, namely, the date of the court order or the execution of the written maintenance agreement. This will catch, for example, interest earned on money which is raised from the sale, during the parties' divorce, of the former matrimonial home, but held on deposit in a bank account pending final resolution of the financial settlement.

[¹SCHEDULE 3B

AMOUNT TO BE ALLOWED IN RESPECT OF
TRAVELLING COSTS

**Interpretation**

**1.** In this Schedule—    4.282
    "day" means, in relation to a person who attends at a work place for one
        period of work which commences before midnight of one day and
        concludes the following day, the first of those days;

"journey" means a single journey, and "pair of journeys" means two journeys in opposing directions, between the same two places;

"relevant employment" means an employed earner's employment in which the relevant person is employed and in the course of which he is required to attend at a work place, and

"relevant employer" means the employer of the relevant person in that employment;

"relevant person" means—

(a) in the application of the provisions of this Schedule to regulation 9, the absent parent or the parent with care; and

(b) in the application of the provisions of this Schedule to regulation 11, the absent parent;

[[5]"straight-line distance" means the straight-line distance measured in kilometres and calculated to 2 decimal places, and, where that distance is not a whole number of kilometres, rounded to the nearest whole number of kilometres, a distance which exceeds a whole number of kilometres by 0.50 of a kilometre being rounded up;]

"travelling costs" means the costs of—

(a) purchasing either fuel or a ticket for the purpose of travel;

(b) contributing to the costs borne by a person other than a relevant employer in providing transport; or

(c) paying another to provide transport,

which are incurred by the relevant person in travelling between the relevant person's home and his work place, and where he has more than one relevant employment between any of his work places in those employments;

"work place" means the relevant person's normal place of employment in a relevant employment, and "deemed work place" means a place which has been selected by the [[4]Secretary of State] pursuant either to paragraph 8(2) or 15(2) for the purpose of calculating the amount to be allowed in respect of the relevant person's travelling costs.

### Computation of amount allowable in respect of travelling costs

4.283    **2.** For the purpose of regulation 9 and regulation 11 an amount in respect of the travelling costs of the relevant person shall be determined in accordance with the following provisions of this Schedule if the relevant person—

(a) has travelling costs; and

(b) provides the information required to enable the amount of the allowance to be determined.

### Computation in cases where there is one relevant employment and one work place in that employment

4.284    **3.** Subject to paragraphs 21 to 23, where the relevant person has one relevant employment and is normally required to attend at only one work place in the course of that employment the amount to be allowed in respect of travelling costs shall be determined in accordance with paragraphs 4 to 7 below.

4.285    **4.** There shall be calculated or, if that is impracticable, estimated—

(a) the straight-line distance between the relevant person's home and his work place;

(b) the number of journeys between the relevant person's home and his work place which he makes during a period comprising a whole number of weeks which appears to the [⁴Secretary of State] to be representative of his normal pattern of work, there being disregarded any pair of journeys between his work place and his home and where the first journey is from his work place to his home and where the time which elapses between the start of the first journey and the conclusion of the second is not more than two hours.

**5.** The results of the calculation or estimate produced by subparagraph (a) of paragraph 4 shall be multiplied by the result of the calculation or estimate required by sub-paragraph (b) of that paragraph.

4.286

**6.** The product of the multiplication required by paragraph 5 shall be divided by the number of weeks in the period.

4.287

**7.** Where the result of the division required by paragraph 6 is less than or equal to [⁶240], the amount to be allowed in respect of the relevant person's travelling costs shall be nil, and where it is greater than [⁶240] the weekly allowance to be made in respect of \the relevant person's travelling costs shall be [⁷6 pence] multiplied by the number by which that number exceeds [⁶240].

4.288

### Computation in cases where there is more than one work place but only one relevant employment

**8.**—(1) Subject to subparagraph (2) and paragraphs 21 to 23 below, where the relevant person has one relevant employment but attends at more than one work place the amount to be allowed in respect of travelling costs for the purposes of regulations 9 and 11 shall be determined in accordance with paragraphs 9 to [⁸14].

4.289

(2) Where it appears that the relevant person works at more than one work place but his pattern of work is not sufficiently regular to enable the calculation of the amount to be allowed in respect of his travelling costs to be made readily, the [⁴Secretary of State] may—

(a) select a place which is either one of the relevant person's work places or some other place which is connected with the relevant employment; and

(b) apply the provisions of paragraphs 4 to 7 above to calculate the amount of the allowance to be made in respect of travelling costs upon the basis that the relevant person makes one journey from his home to the deemed work place and one journey from the deemed work place to his home on each day on which he attends at a work place in connection with relevant employment, and the provisions of paragraphs 9 to [⁸14] shall not apply.

(3) For the purposes of sub-paragraph (2)(b) there shall be disregarded any day upon which the relevant person attends at a work place and in order to travel to or from that work place he undertakes a journey in respect of which—

(a) the travelling costs are borne wholly or in part by the relevant employer; or

(b) the relevant employer provides transport for any part of the journey for the use of the relevant person,

and where he attends at more than one work place on the same day that day shall be disregarded only if the condition specified in this sub-paragraph is satisfied in respect of all the work places at which he attends on that day.

4.290      **9.** There shall be calculated, or if that is impracticable, estimated—

    (a) the straight-line distances between the relevant person's home and each work place; and

    (b) the straight-line distances between each of the relevant person's work places, other than those between which he does not ordinarily travel.

4.291      **10.** Subject to paragraph 11, there shall be calculated for each pair of places referred to in paragraph 9 the number of journeys which the relevant person makes between them during a period comprising a whole number of weeks which appears to the [⁴Secretary of State] to be representative of the normal working pattern of the relevant person.

4.292      **11.** For the purposes of the calculation required by paragraph 10 there shall be disregarded—

    (a) any pair of journeys between the same work place and the relevant person's home where the first journey is from his work place to his home and the time which elapses between the start of the first journey and the conclusion of the second is not more than two hours; and

    (b) any journey in respect of which—

      (i) the travelling costs are borne wholly or in part by the relevant employer; or

      (ii) the relevant employer provides transport for any part of the journey for the use of the relevant person.

4.293      **12.** The result of the calculation of the number of journeys made between each pair of places required by paragraph 10 shall be multiplied by the result of the calculation or estimate of the straight-line distance between them required by paragraph 9.

4.294      **13.** All the products of the multiplications required by paragraph 12 shall be added together and the resulting sum divided by the number of weeks in the period.

4.295      **14.** Where the result of the division required by paragraph 13 is less than or equal to [⁹240], the amount to be allowed in respect of travelling costs shall be nil, and where it is greater than [⁹240], the weekly allowance to be made in respect of the relevant person's travelling costs shall be [¹⁰6 pence] multiplied by the number by which that number exceeds [⁹240].

### Computation in cases where there is more than one relevant employment

4.296      **15.**—(1) Subject to subparagraph (2) and paragraphs 21 to 23, where the relevant person has more than one relevant employment the amount to be allowed in respect of travelling costs for the purposes of regulations 9 and 11 shall be determined in accordance with paragraphs 16 to 20.

    (2) Where it appears that in respect of any of his relevant employments, whilst the relevant person works at more than one work place, his pattern

or work is not sufficiently regular to enable the calculation of the amount to be allowed in respect of his travelling costs to be made readily, the [4Secretary of State]—

(a) may select a place which is either one of the relevant person's work places in that relevant employment or some other place which is connected with that relevant employment;

(b) may calculate the weekly average distance travelled in the course of his journeys made in connection with the relevant employment upon the basis that—

(i) the relevant person makes one journey from his home, or from another work place or deemed work place in another relevant employment, to the deemed work place and one journey from the deemed work place to his home, or to another work place or deemed work place in another relevant employment, on each day on which he attends at a work place in connection with the relevant employment in relation to which the deemed work place has been selected; and

(ii) the distance he travels between those places is the straight-line distance between them; and

(c) shall disregard any journeys made between work places in the relevant employment in respect of which a deemed work place has been selected.

(3) For the purposes of subparagraph (2)(b) there shall be disregarded any day upon which the relevant person attends at a work place and in order to travel to or from that work place he undertakes a journey in respect of which—

(a) the travelling costs are borne wholly or in part by the relevant employer; or

(b) the relevant employer provides transport for any part of the journey for the use of the relevant person,

and where in the course of the particular relevant employment he attends at more than one work place on the same day, that day shall be disregarded only if the condition specified in this paragraph is satisfied in respect of all the work places at which he attends on that day in the course of that employment.

**16.** There shall be calculated, or if that is impracticable, estimated—    4.297

(a) the straight-line distances between the relevant person's home and each work place; and

(b) the straight-line distances between each of the relevant person's work places, except—

(i) those between which he does not ordinarily travel; and

(ii) those for which a calculation of the distance from the relevant person's home is not required by virtue of paragraph 15(c).

[²**17.** Subject to paragraph 17A, there shall be calculated, or if that is impracticable estimated, for each pair of places referred to in paragraph 16 between which the straight-line distances are required to be calculated or estimated, the number of journeys which the relevant person makes between them during a period comprising a whole number of weeks which appears to the [4Secretary of State] to be representative of the normal working pattern of the relevant person.]

4.298     [³**17A.** For the purpose of the calculation required by paragraph 17, there shall be disregarded—
    (a) any pair of journeys between the same work place and his home where the first journey is from his work place to his home and the time which elapses between the start of the first journey and the conclusion of the second is not more than two hours; and
    (b) any journey in respect of which—
      (i) the travelling costs are borne wholly or in part by the relevant employer; or
      (ii) the relevant employer provides transport for any part of the journey for the use of the relevant person.]

## Relevant employments in respect of which no amount is to be allowed

4.299     **18.** The result of the calculation or estimate of the number of journeys made between each pair of places required by paragraph 17 shall be multiplied by the result of the calculation or estimate of the straight-line distance between them required by paragraph 16.

4.300     **19.** All the products of the multiplications required by paragraph 18, shall be added together and the resulting sum divided by the number of weeks in the period.

4.301     **20.** Where the result of the division required by paragraph 19, plus where appropriate the result of the calculation required by paragraph 15 in respect of a relevant employment in which a deemed work place has been selected, is less than or equal to [¹¹240] the amount to be allowed in respect of travelling costs shall be nil, and where it is greater than [¹¹240], the weekly allowance to be made in respect of the relevant person's travelling costs shall be [¹²6 pence] multiplied by the number by which that number exceeds [¹¹240].

4.302     **21.**—(1) No allowance shall be made in respect of travelling costs in respect of journeys between the relevant person's home and his work place or between his work place and his home in a particular relevant employment if the condition set out in paragraph 22 or 23 is satisfied in respect of that employment.

    (2) The condition mentioned in paragraph 22, or as the case may be 23, is satisfied in relation to a case where the relevant person has more than one work place in a relevant employment only where the employer provides assistance of the kind mentioned in that paragraph in respect of all of the work places to or from which the relevant person travels in the course of that employment, but those journeys in respect of which that assistance is provided shall be disregarded in computing the total distance travelled by the relevant person in the course of the relevant employment.

4.303     **22.** The condition is that relevant employer provides transport of any description in connection with the employment which is available to the relevant person for any part of the journey between his home and his work place or between his work place and his home.

4.304     **23.** The condition is that the relevant employer bears any part of the travelling costs arising from the relevant person travelling between his home and his work place or between his work place and his home in connection with that employment, and for the purposes of this paragraph he does not bear any part of that cost where he does no more than—

(a) make a payment to the relevant person which would fall to be taken into account in determining the amount of the relevant person's net income;

(b) make a loan to the relevant person;

(c) pay to the relevant person an increased amount of remuneration,

to enable the relevant person to meet those costs himself.]

AMENDMENTS

1. Regulation 57 of and Sched.2 to the Amendment Regulations 1995 (April 18, 1995).    **4.305**

2. Regulation 49 of the Miscellaneous (No. 2) Regulations 1995 (January 22, 1996).

3. Regulation 49 of the Miscellaneous (No. 2) Regulations 1995 (January 22, 1996).

4. Article 22 of the Commencement No. 7 Order 1999 (June 1, 1999).

5. Regulation 5(4)(a) of the Miscellaneous Amendments Regulations 2004 (September 16, 2004).

6. Regulation 5(4)(b)(i) of the Miscellaneous Amendments Regulations 2004 (September 16, 2004).

7. Regulation 5(4)(b)(ii) of the Miscellaneous Amendments Regulations 2004 (September 16, 2004).

8. Regulation 5(4)(c) of the Miscellaneous Amendments Regulations 2004 (September 16, 2004).

9. Regulation 5(4)(b)(i) of the Miscellaneous Amendments Regulations 2004 (September 16, 2004).

10. Regulation 5(4)(b)(ii) of the Miscellaneous Amendments Regulations 2004 (September 16, 2004).

11. Regulation 5(4)(b)(i) of the Miscellaneous Amendments Regulations 2004 (September 16, 2004).

12. Regulation 5(4)(b)(ii) of the Miscellaneous Amendments Regulations 2004 (September 16, 2004).

GENERAL NOTE    **4.306**

This Schedule provides for allowance to be made in a parent's exempt income and in an absent parent's protected income in respect of costs of travelling between home and work. To qualify the parent must actually incur travelling costs. No sum is allowed, for example, if the parent walks or cycles to work or is taken by a relative or friend free of charge. If a parent does have travelling costs, an allowance is made. It is calculated or estimated by reference to the straight-line distance between home and work place and is based on the travel in a normal week. Straight-line measurement is the method which, by virtue of s.8 of the Interpretation Act 1978, would be applied unless the contrary intention appears. The express reference to this method of measurement avoids any argument that there was a contrary intention. Return journeys from work to home and back to work, for example for a meal or between shifts, are ignored if the return home lasts for two hours or less. The existence of physical obstructions, such as mountain ranges and river estuaries, is ignored as is the actual distance by road or rail. Where a parent has more than one employer or more than one work place, the decision-maker may deem one of them or some other connected place to be the place of work for the purpose of the calculation or estimate. No travelling costs are allowed if the employer provides transport for all or part of the journey or contributes toward the travelling costs, but no contribution is deemed to occur if the employer's sole contribution towards the costs of travel comprises a payment which would be taken into account in calculating net income, a loan or increased pay.

The calculation of distances by the Agency is made by a computer program based on post codes. If this issue arises on appeal, the tribunal will need to be satisfied on appropriate evidence of the following matters:

(i) The decision-maker will have to prove the accuracy of the Agency's computer program,

(ii) The post codes of the parent's home and place of work will need to be established,

(iii) It will have to be shown that the correct codes were put into the program, and the output from the program on the basis of that input will have to be shown. The tribunal will also need to bear in mind the following factors which may affect the relevance of the outcome of the program to the case under appeal.

(iv) The post code may, especially in a rural location, cover a fairly large area,

(v) A post code is only provided for buildings to which mail is delivered. Some employers will have mail delivered to a central location or to a Post Office Box number with the result that a person's particular place of work may not have a post code and may be some distance away from the building to which the post code applies. Finally, the tribunal will need to bear in mind two further factors.

(vi) There is no basis in the legislation for the calculation of distance by reference to post codes, so the tribunal may calculate the relevant distance by any means that will produce a sufficiently accurate result.

(vii) The tribunal will only need to concern itself with arguments over the accuracy of the Agency's calculation if the degree of error is likely to affect the ultimate decision.

## SCHEDULE 4

## CASES WHERE CHILD SUPPORT MAINTENANCE IS NOT TO BE PAYABLE

4.307    The payments and awards specified for the purposes of regulation 26(1)(b)(i) are—

(a) the following payments under the Contribution and Benefits Act—

[²(i) incapacity benefit under section 30A;

(ii) long-term incapacity benefit for widows under section 40;

(iii) long-term incapacity benefit for widowers under section 41;]

(iv) maternity allowance under section 35;

(v) [³. . .]

(vi) attendance allowance under section 64;

(vii) severe disablement allowance under section 68;

(viii) [⁴carer's allowance] under section 70;

(ix) disability living allowance under section 71;

(x) disablement benefit under section 103;

[⁵. . .]

(xii) statutory sick pay within the meaning of section 151;

(xiii) statutory maternity pay within the meaning of section 164;

(b) awards in respect of disablement made under (or under provisions analogous to)—

    (i) the War Pensions (Coastguards) Scheme 1944 (S.I. 1944 No. 500);

    (ii) the War Pensions (Naval Auxiliary Personnel) Scheme 1964 (S.I. 1964 No. 1985);

    (iii) the Pensions (Polish Forces) Scheme 1964 (S.I. 1964 No. 2007);

    (iv) the War Pensions (Mercantile Marine) Scheme 1964 (S.I. 1964 No. 2058);

    (v) the Royal Warrant of 21st December 1964 (service in the Home Guard before 1945) (Cmnd. 2563);

    (vi) the Order by Her Majesty of 22nd December 1964 concerning pensions and other grants in respect of disablement or death due to service in the Home Guard after 27th April 1952 (Cmnd. 2564);

    (vii) the Order by Her Majesty (Ulster Defence Regiment) of 4th January 1971 (Cmnd. 4567);

    (viii) the Personal Injuries (Civilians) Scheme 1983 (S.I. 1983 No. 686);

    (ix) the Naval, Military and Air Forces Etc. (Disablement and Death) Service Pensions Order 1983 (S.I. 1983 No. 883); [6. . .]

    [7(x) the Armed Forces (Pensions and Compensation) Act 2004; and]

(c) payments from [1the Independent Living (1993) Fund or the Independent Living (Extension) Fund].

AMENDMENTS

1. Regulation 34 of the Amendment Regulations (April 5, 1993).

2. Regulation 58(a) of the Amendment Regulations 1995 (April 13, 1995).

3. Regulation 58(b) of the Amendment Regulations 1995 (April 13, 1995)

4. Regulation 6(8)(a) of the Miscellaneous Amendments Regulations 2003 (April 1, 2003).

5. Regulation 6(8)(b) of the Miscellaneous Amendments Regulations 2003 (April 6, 2003).

6. Regulation 4(4)(a) of the Miscellaneous Amendments Regulations 2005 (March 16, 2005).

7. Regulation 4(4)(b) of the Miscellaneous Amendments Regulations 2005 (March 16, 2005).

DEFINITIONS

"Contributions and Benefits Act": see reg.1(2).    **4.308**
"Independent Living (1993) Fund": see reg.1(2).
"Independent Living (Extension) Fund": see reg.1(2)

[¹SCHEDULE 5

# PROVISIONS APPLYING TO CASES TO WHICH SECTION 43 OF THE ACT AND REGULATION 28 APPLY

[². . .]

4.309    [¹**9.** The provisions of paragraphs (1) and (2) of regulation 5 of the Child Support (Collection and Enforcement) Regulations 1992 shall apply to the transmission of payments in place of child support maintenance under section 43 of the Act and regulation 28 as they apply to the transmission of payments of child support maintenance.]

AMENDMENTS

1. Regulation 26(3) of, and the Schedule to, the Amendment Regulations (April 5, 1993).
2. Article 23 of the Commencement No.7 Order 1999 (June 1, 1999).

DEFINITION

4.310    "the Act": see reg.1(2).

## The Child Support Departure Direction and Consequential Amendments Regulations 1996

### (SI 1996/2907)

*Made by the Secretary of State for Social Security under sections 14(3), 21, 28A(3), 28B(2)(b), 28C, 28E(5), 28F, 28G, 28I(4)(c), 42, 51, 52(4) and 54 of, and paragraph 5 of Schedule 1, paragraphs 2, 4, 6, 7 and 9 of Schedule 4A, and Schedule 4B to, the Child Support Act 1991 and all other powers enabling him in that behalf and after consultation with the Council on Tribunals in accordance with section 8 of the Tribunals and Inquiries Act 1992.*

ARRANGEMENT OF REGULATIONS

PART I

*General*

4.311    1.   Citation, commencement and interpretation.
         2.   Documents.
         3.   Determination of amounts.

## Part II

*Procedure on an application for a departure direction and preliminary consideration*

## Part III

*Special expenses*

## Part IV

*Property or capital transfers*

## Part V

*Additional cases*

## PART X

### *Miscellaneous*

## PART XI

### *Transitional provisions*

## PART XII

### *Revocation*

[Regulations 52–68 make consequential amendments which are incorporated into the text of the relevant regulations.]

### SCHEDULE

#### EQUIVALENT WEEKLY VALUE OF A TRANSFER OF PROPERTY

### PART I

#### *General*

## Citation, commencement and interpretation

1.—(1) These Regulations may be cited as the Child Support Departure Direction and Consequential Amendments Regulations 1996 and shall come into force on 2nd December 1996.

4.312

961

(2) In these Regulations, unless the context otherwise requires—
"the Act" means the Child Support Act 1991;
. . .
"applicant" has the same meaning as in Schedule 4B to the Act;
"application" means [¹except in regulations 32A to 32G,] an application
for a departure direction;
. . .
"Contributions and Benefits Act" means the Social Security
Contributions and Benefits Act 1992;
"Departure Direction Anticipatory Application Regulations" means the
Child Support Departure Direction (Anticipatory Application)
Regulations 1996;
"departure direction application form" means the form provided by the
Secretary of State in accordance with regulation 4(1);
[²"designated authority" has the meaning it has in regulation 2(1) of the
Social Security (Work-focused Interviews) Regulations 2000;]
"effective date" in relation to a departure direction means the date on
which that direction takes effect;
. . .
"Maintenance Assessment Procedure Regulations" means the Child
Support (Maintenance Assessment Procedure) Regulations 1992;
"Maintenance Assessments and Special Cases Regulations" means the
Child Support (Maintenance Assessments and Special Cases)
Regulations 1992;
"maintenance period" has the same meaning as in regulation 33 of the
Maintenance Assessment Procedure Regulations;
"non-applicant" means—
(a) where the application has been made by a person with care, the
absent parent;
(b) where the application has been made by an absent parent, the person
with care;
[³"official error" means an error made by—
(a) an officer of the Department of Social Security acting as such which
no person outside that Department caused or to which no person
outside that Department materially contributed;]
[⁴(b) a person employed by a designated authority acting on behalf of
the authority, which no person outside that authority caused or to
which no person outside that authority materially contributed, but
excludes any error of law which is only shown to have been an error
by virtue of a subsequent decision of a Child Support Commissioner
or the court;]
"partner" has the same meaning as in paragraph (2) of regulation 1 of
the Maintenance Assessments and Special Cases Regulations;
"relevant person" means—
(a) an absent parent, or a person who is treated as an absent parent
under regulation 20 of the Maintenance Assessments and Special
Cases Regulations (persons treated as absent parents), whose
liability under a maintenance assessment may be affected by any
departure direction given following an application;
(b) a person with care, or a child to whom section 7 of the Act applies,
where the amount of child support maintenance payable under a

maintenance assessment relevant to that person with care or that child may be affected by any departure direction given following an application.

(3) In these Regulations, unless the context otherwise requires, a reference—

(a) to the Schedule, is to the Schedule to these Regulations;
(b) to a numbered regulation is to the regulation in these Regulations bearing that number;
(c) in a regulation or the Schedule to a numbered paragraph is to the graph in that regulation or the Schedule bearing that number;
(d) in a paragraph to a lettered or numbered subparagraph is to the subparagraph in that paragraph bearing that letter or number.

AMENDMENTS

1. Regulation 34(a) of the Miscellaneous Amendments (No. 2) Regulations 1999 (June 1, 1999).
2. Regulation 16(5) of, and para.9(a) of Sched.6 to, the Social Security (Work-focused Interviews) Regulations 2000 (April, 3, 2000).
3. Regulation 16(5) of, and para.9(b) of Sched.6 to, the Social Security (Work-focused Interviews) Regulations 2000 (April, 3, 2000).
4. Regulation 10 of the Miscellaneous Amendments Regulations 2000 (June 19, 2000).

GENERAL NOTE

*Paragraph (2)*                                                                                          **4.313**
The omitted definitions apply only to the consequential amendments made by regs 52–68.

## Documents

**2.**—(1) Except where express provision is made to the contrary, where,     **4.314**
under any provision of these Regulations—

(a) any document is given or sent to the Secretary of State, that document shall, subject to paragraph (2), be treated as having been so given or sent on the date it is received by the Secretary of State; and
(b) any document is given or sent to any other person, that document shall, if sent by post to that person's last known or notified address, and subject to paragraph (3), be treated as having been given or sent on the second day after the day of posting, excluding any Sunday or any day which is a Bank Holiday in England, Wales, Scotland or Northern Ireland under the Banking and Financial Dealings Act 1971.

(2) The Secretary of State may treat any document given or sent to him as given or sent on such day, earlier than the day it was received by him, as he may determine, if he is satisfied that there was unavoidable delay in his receiving the document in question.

(3) Where, by any provision of these Regulations, and in relation to a particular application, notice or notification—

(a) more than one document is required to be given or sent to a person, and more than one such document is sent by post to that person but not all the documents are posted on the same day; or

    (b)  documents are required to be given or sent to more than one person,
         and not all such documents are posted on the same day,

all those documents shall be treated as having been posted on the later or,
as the case may be, the latest day of posting.

## Determination of amounts

4.315      **3.**—(1) Where any amount is required to be determined for the purposes of these Regulations, it shall be determined as a weekly amount and, except where the context otherwise requires, any reference to such an amount shall be construed accordingly.

(2) Where any calculation made under these Regulations results in a fraction of a penny that fraction shall be treated as a penny if it is either one half or exceeds one half and shall be otherwise disregarded.

## PART II

## PROCEDURE ON AN APPLICATION FOR A DEPARTURE DIRECTION AND PRELIMINARY CONSIDERATION

### Application for a departure direction

4.316      **4.**—(1) Every application shall be made in writing on a form (a "departure direction application form") provided by the Secretary of State, or in such other manner, being in writing, as the Secretary of State may accept as sufficient in me circumstances of any particular case.

(2) Departure direction application forms shall be supplied without charge by such persons as the Secretary of State authorises for that purpose.

(3) Every application shall be given or sent to the Secretary of State or to such persons as he may authorise for that purpose.

(4) Where an application is defective at the date when it is received, or has been made in writing but not on the departure direction application form provided by the Secretary of State, the Secretary of State may refer that application to the person who made it or, as the case may be, supply him with a departure direction application form.

(5) In a case to which paragraph (4) applies, if the departure direction application form is received by the Secretary of State properly completed—

    (a)  within the specified period, he shall treat the application as if it had been duly made in the first instance;

    (b)  outside the specified period, unless he is satisfied that the delay has been unavoidable, he shall treat the application as a fresh application made on the date upon which the properly completed departure direction application form was received.

(6) An application which is made on a departure direction application form is, for the purposes of paragraph (5), properly completed if completed in accordance with the instructions on the form and defective if not so completed.

(7) In a case to which paragraph (4) applies, the specified period for the purposes of paragraph (5) shall be the period of 14 days commencing with

the date upon which, in accordance with paragraph (4), the application is referred to the person who made the defective application or a departure direction application form is given or sent to the person who made a written application but not on a departure direction application form.

(8) For the purposes of paragraph (7), the provisions of regulation 2 shall apply to an application referred to in paragraph (4).

(9) A person applying for a departure direction may authorise a representative, whether or not legally qualified, to receive notices and other documents on his behalf, and to act on his behalf in relation to an application.

(10) Where a person has, under paragraph (9), authorised a representative who is not legally qualified, he shall confirm that authorisation in writing, or as otherwise required, to the Secretary of State, unless such authorisation has already been approved by the Secretary of State under regulation 53 of the Maintenance Assessment Procedure Regulations (authorisation of representative).

[$^1$. . .]

AMENDMENT

1. Regulation 35 of the Miscellaneous Amendments (No. 2) Regulations 1999 (June 1, 1999).

DEFINITIONS

"application": see reg.1(2).                                                    4.317
"departure direction application form": see reg.1(2).
"Maintenance Assessment Procedure Regulations": see reg.1(2).

## Amendment or withdrawal of application

**5.** A person who has made an application may amend or withdraw his      4.318
application by notice in writing to the Secretary of State at any time prior
to a determination being made in relation to that application.

DEFINITION,

"application": see reg.1(2).                                                    4.319

## Provision of information

**6.**—(1) Where an application has been made, the Secretary of State may     4.320
request further information or evidence from the applicant to enable that
application to be determined.

(2) Any information or evidence requested by the Secretary of State in accordance with paragraph (1) shall be given within [$^1$one month, or such longer period as the Secretary of State is satisfied is reasonable in the circumstances of the case,] of the request for such information or evidence having been given or sent.

(3) Where the time limit specified in paragraph (2) is not complied with, the Secretary of State may determine that application, in the absence of that information or evidence.

AMENDMENT

1. Regulation 36 of the Miscellaneous Amendments (No. 2) Regulations 1999 (June 1, 1999).

DEFINITION

4.321    "application": see reg.1(2).

## Rejection of application on completion of a preliminary consideration

4.322    **7.**—(1) The Secretary of State may, on completing a preliminary consideration of an application, reject that application on the ground set out in section 28B(2)(b) of the Act if it appears to him that the difference between the current amount and the revised amount is less than £1.00.

(2) Where an application has been rejected in accordance with paragraph (1), the secretary of State shall, as soon as reasonably practicable, give notice of that rejection to the relevant persons.

DEFINITIONS

4.323    "the Act": see reg.1(2).
"application": see reg.1(2).
"relevant person": see reg.1(2).

## Procedure in relation to the determination of an application

4.324    **8.**—(1) Subject to paragraph 4, where an application has not failed within the meaning of section 28D of the Act, the Secretary of State shall[[1], unless he is satisfied on the information or evidence available to him that a departure direction is unlikely to be given]—

(a) give notice of that application to the relevant persons other than the applicant;

(b) send to them details of the grounds on which the application has been made and any relevant information or evidence the applicant has given, except details, information or evidence falling within paragraph (2);

(c) invite representations in writing from the relevant persons other than the applicant on any matter relating to that application; and

(d) set out the provisions of paragraphs (2), (5) and (6) in relation to such representations.

(2) The details, information or evidence referred to in paragraphs (l)(b), (6) and (7) are—

(a) medical evidence or medical advice that has not been disclosed to the applicant or a relevant person and which the Secretary of State considers would be harmful to the health of the applicant or that relevant person if disclosed to him;

(b) the address of a relevant person, or of any child in relation to whom the assessment was made in respect of which the application has been made, or any other information which could reasonably be expected to lead to that person or that child being located, where

that person has not agreed to disclosure of that address or that information, it is not known to the other party to that assessment and—
  (i) the Secretary of State is satisfied that that address or that information is not necessary for the determination of that application; or
  (ii) the Secretary of State is satisfied that that address or that information is necessary for the determination of that application and that there would be a risk of harm or undue distress to that person or that child if disclosure were made.

(3) Subject to paragraph (4), the notice referred to in paragraph (l)(a) shall be given as soon as reasonably practicable after—
  (a) completion of the preliminary consideration of that application under section 28B of the Act; or
  (b) where the Secretary of State has requested information or evidence under regulation 6, receipt of that information or evidence or the expiry of the period [³. . .] referred to in regulation 6(2).

(4) The provisions of paragraphs (1) and (3) shall not apply where information or evidence requested in accordance with regulation 6 has not been received by the Secretary of State within the period specified in paragraph (2) of that regulation and the Secretary of State is satisfied on the information or evidence available to him that a departure direction should not be given.

[²(4A) Where the provisions of paragraph (1) have not been complied with because the Secretary of State was satisfied on the information or evidence available to him that a departure direction was unlikely to be given, but on further consideration of the application he is minded to give a departure direction in that case, he shall, before doing so, comply with the provisions of this regulation.]

(5) Where the Secretary of State does not receive written representations from a relevant person within 14 days of the date on which representations were invited under paragraph (1), (6) or (7), he may, in the absence of written representations from that person, proceed to determine the application.

(6) The Secretary of State may, if he considers it reasonable to do so, send to the applicant a copy of any written representations made following an invitation under paragraph (l)(c), whether or not they were received within the time specified in paragraph (5), except to the extent that the representations contain information or evidence which falls within paragraph (2), and invite him to submit representations in writing on any matters contained in those representations.

(7) Where any information or evidence requested by the Secretary of State under regulation 6 is received after notification has been given under paragraph (1), the Secretary of State may, if he considers it reasonable to do so and except where that information or evidence falls within paragraph (2), send a copy of such information or evidence to the relevant persons and invite them to submit representations in writing on that information or evidence.

[⁸. . .]

(9) Where the Secretary of State has determined an application he shall, as soon as is reasonably practicable—

(a) notify the relevant persons of that determination;

(b) where a departure direction has been given, [⁶make a decision in accordance with regulation 17(2) or 20(2)(c) of the Maintenance Assessment Procedure Regulations].

(10) A notification under paragraph (9)(a) shall set out-

(a) the reasons for that determination;

(b) where a departure direction has been given, the basis on which the amount of child support maintenance is to be fixed by any assessment made in consequence of that direction.

[⁷. . .]

AMENDMENTS

1. Regulation 7(2) of the Miscellaneous Amendments Regulations 1998 (January 19, 1998).

2. Regulation 7(3) of the Miscellaneous Amendments Regulations 1998 (January 19, 1998).

3. Regulation 37(a) of the Miscellaneous Amendments (No. 2) Regulations 1999 (June 1, 1999).

6. Regulation 37(c) of the Miscellaneous Amendments (No. 2) Regulations 1999 (June 1, 1999)

7. Regulation 37(d) of the Miscellaneous Amendments (No. 2) Regulations 1999 (June 1, 1999)

8. Regulation 11 of the Miscellaneous Amendments Regulations 2000 (June 19, 2000).

DEFINITIONS

4.325

"the Act": see reg.1(2).

"applicant": see reg.1(2).

"application": see reg.1(2).

"relevant person": see reg.1(2).

## [¹Procedure in relation to determination of an application for a revision or a supersession of a decision with respect to a departure direction

4.326

**8A.**—(1) Subject to the modifications described in paragraph (2), regulation 8 shall apply to any application for a revision or a supersession of a decision with respect to a departure direction as it applies to an application for a departure direction.

(2) The modifications described in this paragraph are—

(a) for paragraph (1) there shall be substituted the following paragraphs-

"(1) Except where paragraph (1A) applies, the Secretary of State shall—

(a) give notice of an application for a revision or a supersession of a decision with respect to a departure direction to the relevant persons other than the applicant;

(b) inform them of the grounds on which the application has been made and any relevant information or evidence the applicant has given, except details, information or evidence falling within paragraph (2);

(c) invite representations from the relevant persons other than the applicant on any matter relating to that application; and

(d) explain the provisions of paragraphs (2), (5) and (6) in relation to such representations.

"(1A) This paragraph applies where an application for a revision or a supersession has been made and the Secretary of State is satisfied on the information or evidence available to him that either—

(a) a revision or supersession of a departure direction is unlikely to be made; or

(b) in a case where the applicant was the applicant for the decision which is to be revised or superseded, a ground on which the decision to be revised or superseded was made no longer applies.";

(b) paragraphs (3), (4) and (7) shall be omitted;

(c) in paragraph (4A) for the words from "that a departure direction" to the words "in that case" there shall be substituted the words "that a decision revising or superseding a direction with respect to a departure direction was unlikely to be made, but on further consideration of the application he is minded to make such a decision";

(d) in paragraph (5)—

    (i) for the words "(1), (6) or (7)" there shall be substituted the words "(1) or (6)";

    (ii) after the word "application" there shall be added the words "for a decision revising or superseding a decision";

(e) in paragraph (8)—

    (i) for the words "In deciding whether to give a departure direction" there shall be substituted the words "Before deciding whether or not to make a decision revising or, as the case may be, superseding a decision as to a departure direction in consequence of an application for such a decision"; and

    (ii) in sub-paragraph (a), for the words "by the applicant for that direction" there shall be substituted the words "in connection with the application";

(f) for paragraphs (9) and (10) there shall be substituted the following paragraph—

"(9) Where the Secretary of State has determined an application made for the purpose of revising or superseding a decision he shall, as soon as is reasonably practicable, notify the relevant persons of—

(a) that determination;

(b) the reasons for it; and

(c) where appropriate, the basis on which the amount of child support maintenance is to be fixed by any fresh assessment made in consequence of that determination.".]

AMENDMENT

1. Regulation 38 of the Miscellaneous Amendments (No. 2) Regulations 1999 (June 1, 1999).

## [¹Departure directions and persons in receipt of income support[³, state pension credit], income-based jobseeker's allowance [²or working tax credit]

4.327    **9.**—(1) The costs referred to in regulations 13 to 18 shall not constitute special expenses where they are or were incurred—

(a) by an absent parent to or in respect of whom income support[³, state pension credit] or income-based jobseeker's allowance is or was in payment at the date on which any departure direction given in response to that application would take effect;

(b) by a person with care to or in respect of whom income support[³, state pension credit], income-based jobseeker's allowance [²or working tax credit] is or was in payment at the date on which any departure direction given in response to that application would take effect; or

(c) by a person with care where, at the date on which any departure direction given in response to that application would take effect, income support[³, state pension credit] or income-based jobseeker's allowance is or was in payment to or in respect of the absent parent of the child or children in relation to whom the maintenance assessment in question is made.

(2) A transfer shall not constitute a transfer of property for the purposes of paragraph 3(1)(b) or 4(1)(b) of Schedule 4B to the Act, or of regulations 21 and 22, where the application is made—

(a) by an absent parent to or in respect of whom income support[³, state pension credit] or income-based jobseeker's allowance is or was in payment at the date on which any departure direction given in response to that application would take effect;

(b) by a person with care and, at the date on which any departure direction given in response to that application would take effect, income support[³, state pension credit] or income-based jobseeker's allowance is or was in payment to or in respect of the absent parent of the child or children in relation to whom the maintenance assessment in question is made.

(3) A case shall not constitute a case under regulations 23 to 29 where the application is made—

(a) by an absent parent to or in respect of whom income support[³, state pension credit] or income-based jobseeker's allowance is or was in payment at the date on which any departure direction given in response to that application would take effect;

(b) by an absent parent where, at the date on which any departure direction given in response to that application would take effect, income support[³, state pension credit], income-based jobseeker's allowance [²or working tax credit] is or was in payment to or in respect of the person with care of the child or children in relation to whom the maintenance assessment in question is made;

(c) by a person with care where, at the date on which any departure direction given in response to that application would take effect, income support[³, state pension credit] or income-based jobseeker's allowance is or was in payment to or in respect of the absent parent of the child or children in relation to whom the maintenance assessment is made.]

AMENDMENTS

1. Regulation 8 of the Miscellaneous Amendments Regulations 1998 (January 19, 1998).
2. Regulation 4(2) of the Miscellaneous Amendments Regulations 2003 (April 6, 2003).
3. Regulation 2(a) of the Miscellaneous Amendments (No. 2) Regulations 2003 (November 5, 2003).

DEFINITIONS

"the Act": see reg.1(2).    **4.328**
"application": see reg.1(2).

## Departure directions and interim maintenance assessments

**10.**—(1) For the purposes of section 28A(1) of the Act, the term   **4.329**
"maintenance assessment" does not include—
(a) a Category A or Category C interim maintenance assessment;
(b) a Category B interim maintenance assessment where the application is made under paragraph 2 of Schedule 4B to the Act in respect of expenses prescribed by regulation 18 and that Category B interim maintenance assessment was made because the applicant fell within paragraph (3)(b) of regulation 8 of the Maintenance Assessment Procedure Regulations;
(c) a Category D interim maintenance assessment, where the application is made under paragraph 3 or 4 of Schedule 4B to the Act or by an absent parent under paragraph 2 or 5 of that Schedule.
(2) For the purposes of this regulation, Category A, Category B, Category C and Category D interim maintenance assessments are defined in regulation 8(3) of the Maintenance Assessment Procedure Regulations (categories of interim maintenance assessment).

DEFINITIONS

"the Act": see reg.1(2).    **4.330**
"Maintenance Assessment Procedure Regulations": see reg.1(2).
[Regulation 11 was revoked by reg.39 of the Miscellaneous Amendments (No. 2) Regulations 1999 with effect from June 1, 1999.]

## [¹Meaning of "current assessment" for the purposes of the Act]

[²**11A.** Where—    **4.331**
(a) an application under section 28A of the Act has been made in respect of a current assessment; and
(b) after the making of that application, a fresh maintenance assessment has been made upon a revision of a decision as to a maintenance assessment under section 16 of the Act,
references to the current assessment in sections 28B(3), 28C(2)(a) and 28F(5) of, and in paragraph 8 of Schedule 4A and paragraphs 2, 3 and 4

of Schedule 4B to, the Act shall have effect as if they were references to the fresh maintenance assessment.]

AMENDMENTS

1. Regulation 10 of the Miscellaneous Amendments Regulations 1998 (January 19, 1998).
2. Regulation 40 of the Miscellaneous Amendments (No. 2) Regulations 1999 (June 1, 1999).

DEFINITIONS

**4.332**    "the Act": see reg.1(2).
"application": see reg.1(2).

## Meaning of "benefit" for the purposes of section 28E of the Act

**4.333**    **12.** For the purposes of section 28E of the Act, "benefit" means income support[², state pension credit], income-based jobseeker's allowance, [¹working tax credit], housing benefit, and council tax benefit.

AMENDMENT

1. Regulation 4 (3) of the Miscellaneous Amendments Regulations 2003 (April 6, 2003).
2. Regulation 2(b) of the Miscellaneous Amendments (No. 2) Regulations 2003 (November 5, 2003).

DEFINITION

**4.334**    "the Act": see reg.1(2).

PART III

SPECIAL EXPENSES

## Costs incurred in travelling to work

**4.335**    **13.**—(1) Subject to paragraphs (2) and (3), the following costs shall constitute expenses for the purposes of paragraph 2(2) of Schedule 4B to the Act where they are incurred by the applicant for the purposes of travel between his home and his normal place of work—
  (a) the cost of purchasing a ticket for such travel;
  (b) the cost of purchasing fuel, where such travel is by a vehicle which is not carrying fare-paying passengers; or
  (c) in exceptional circumstances, the taxi fare for a journey which must unavoidably be undertaken during hours when no other reasonable mode of travel is available,
and any minor incidental costs, such as tolls or fees for the use of a particular road or bridge, incurred in connection with such travel.

(2) Where the Secretary of State considers any costs referred to in paragraph (1) to be unreasonably high or to have been unreasonably incurred

he may substitute such lower amount as he considers reasonable, including a nil amount.

(3) Costs which can be set off against the income of the applicant under the Income and Corporation Taxes Act 1988 shall not constitute expenses for the purposes of paragraph (1).

DEFINITIONS

"the Act": see reg.1(2).                                                **4.336**
"applicant": see reg.1(2).

## Contact costs

**14.**—(1) Where at the time a departure direction is applied for a set pat-    **4.337**
tern has been established as to frequency of contact between the absent parent and a child in respect of whom the current assessment was made, the following costs, based upon that pattern and incurred by that absent parent for the purpose of maintaining contact with that child, shall, subject to paragraphs (2) to (6), constitute expenses for the purposes of paragraph 2(2) of Schedule 4B to the Act—

  (a) the cost of purchasing a ticket for travel for the purpose of maintaining that contact; or

  (b) the cost of purchasing fuel, where travel is for the purpose of maintaining that contact and is by a vehicle which is not carrying fare-paying passengers; or

  (c) the taxi fare for a journey or part of a journey to maintain that contact where the Secretary of State is satisfied that the disability of the absent parent makes it impracticable to use any other form of transport which might otherwise have been available to him,

and any minor incidental costs, such as tolls or fees for the use of a particular road or bridge, incurred in connection with such travel.

(2) Subject to paragraph (3), where the Secretary of State considers any costs referred to in paragraph (1) to be unreasonably high or to have been unreasonably incurred he may substitute such lower amount as he considers reasonable, including a nil amount.

(3) Any lower amount substituted by the Secretary of State under para- graph (2) shall not be so low as to make it impossible, in the Secretary of State's opinion, for contact to be maintained at the frequency specified in any court order made in respect of the absent parent and the child men- tioned in paragraph (1) where the absent parent is maintaining contact at that frequency.

(4) Paragraph (1) shall not apply where regulation 20 of the Maintenance Assessments and Special Cases Regulations (persons treated as absent parents) applies to the applicant.

(5) Where sub-paragraph (c) of paragraph (1) applies and the applicant has, at the date an application is made, received, or at that date is in receipt of, financial assistance from any source to meet, wholly or in part, costs of maintaining contact with the child who is referred to in paragraph (1), which arise wholly from his disability and which are in excess of the costs which would be incurred if that disability did not exist, only the net amount of the costs referred to in that sub-paragraph, after the deduction of that

financial assistance, shall constitute special expenses for the purposes of paragraph 2(2) of Schedule 4B to the Act.

(6) For the purposes of this regulation, a person is disabled if he is blind, deaf or dumb or is substantially or permanently handicapped by illness, injury, mental disorder or congenital deformity.

(7) Where, at the time a departure direction is applied for, no set pattern has been established as to frequency of contact between the absent parent and child in respect of whom the current assessment was made, but the Secretary of State is satisfied that that absent parent and the person with care of that child. have agreed upon a pattern of contact for the future, the costs mentioned in paragraph (1) and which are based upon that intended pattern of contact shall constitute expenses for the purposes of paragraph 2(2) of Schedule 4B to the Act, and paragraphs (2) to (6) shall apply to that application.

[[1](8) This regulation shall apply in relation to an application made for the purpose of superseding a decision with respect to a departure direction as though—

(a) for the words "at the time a departure direction is applied for" in paragraphs (1) and (7) there were substituted the words "at the time an application is made for a decision superseding a decision with respect to a departure direction";

(b) in paragraph (5), after the words "an application" there were inserted the words "for the supersession of a decision with respect to a departure direction."]

AMENDMENT

1. Regulation 41 of the Miscellaneous Amendments (No. 2) Regulations 1999 (June 1, 1999).

DEFINITIONS

4.338    "the Act": see reg.1(2).
"application": see reg.1(2).
"Maintenance Assessments and Special Cases Regulations": see reg.1(2).

## Illness or disability

4.339    **15.**—(1) Subject to paragraphs (2) to (4), the costs being met by the applicant in respect of the items listed in sub-paragraphs (a) to (m), which arise from long-term illness or disability of that applicant or a dependant of that applicant and which are in excess of the costs which would be incurred if that illness or disability did not exist, shall constitute special expenses for the purposes of paragraph 2(2) of Schedule 4B to the Act—

(a) personal care and attendance;
(b) personal communication needs;
(c) mobility;
(d) domestic help;
(e) medical aids where these cannot be provided under the health service;
(f) heating;

(g) clothing;

(h) laundry requirements;

(i) payments for food essential to comply with a diet recommended by a medical practitioner;

(j) adaptations required to the applicant's home; (k) day care;

(l) rehabilitation; or

(m) respite care.

(2) Where the Secretary of State considers any costs referred to in paragraph (1) to be unreasonably high or to have been unreasonably incurred he may substitute such lower amount as he considers reasonable, including a nil amount.

(3) [¹Subject to paragraph (4A),] where—

(a) an applicant or his dependant has, at the date an application is made, received, or at that date is in receipt of, financial assistance from any source in respect of his long-term illness or disability or that of his dependant; or

(b) that applicant or his dependant is adjudged eligible for either of the allowances referred to in paragraph (4),

only the net amount of the costs incurred in respect of the items listed in paragraph (1), after the deduction of the financial assistance referred to in sub-paragraph (a) and, where applicable, the allowance referred to in sub-paragraph (b) shall constitute special expenses for the purposes of paragraph 2(2) of Schedule 4B to the Act.

(4) [¹Subject to paragraph (4A),] where the Secretary of State considers that a person who has made an application in respect of special expenses falling with paragraph (1) or his dependant may be entitled to disability living allowance under section 71 of the Contributions and Benefits Act or attendance allowance under section 64 of that Act—

(a) if that applicant or his dependant has at the date of that application, or within a period of six weeks beginning with the giving or sending to him of notification of the possibility of entitlement to either of those allowances, applied for either of those allowances, the application made by that applicant shall not be determined until a decision has been made by the [³Secretary of State] on the eligibility for that allowance of that applicant or that dependant;

(b) if that applicant or his dependant has failed to apply for either of those allowances within the six week period specified in sub-paragraph (a), the Secretary of State shall determine the application for a departure direction made by that applicant on the basis that that applicant has income equivalent to the highest rate prescribed in respect of that allowance by or under those sections.

[²(4A) Paragraphs (3) and (4) shall not apply where the dependant of an applicant is adjudged eligible for either of the allowances referred to in paragraph (4) and in all the circumstances of the case the Secretary of State considers that the costs being met by the applicant in respect of the items listed in paragraph (1) shall constitute special expenses for the purposes of paragraph 2(2) of Schedule 4B to the Act without the deductions in paragraph (3) being made.]

(5) For the purposes of this regulation, a dependant of an applicant shall be

    (a)  where the applicant is an absent parent—
       (i)  the partner of that absent parent;
      (ii)  any child of whom that absent parent or his partner is a parent and who lives with them; or
    (b)  where the applicant is a parent with care—
       (i)  the partner of that parent with care;
      (ii)  any child of whom that parent with care or her partner is a parent and who lives with them, except any child in respect of whom the absent parent against whom the current assessment is made is the parent.
  (6)  For the purposes of this regulation—
    (a)  a person is disabled if he is blind, deaf or dumb or is substantially or permanently handicapped by illness, injury, mental disorder or congenital deformity;
    (b)  "long-term illness" means an illness from which the applicant or his dependant is suffering at the date of the application and which is likely to last for at least 52 weeks from that date or if likely to be shorter than 52 weeks, for the rest of the life of that applicant or his dependant;
    (c)  "the health service" has the same meaning as in section 128 of the National Health Service Act 1977 or in section 108(1) of the National Health Service (Scotland) Act 1978.

AMENDMENTS

1. Regulation 11(2) of the Miscellaneous Amendments Regulations 1998 (January 19, 1998).
2. Regulation 11(3) of the Miscellaneous Amendments Regulations 1998 (January 19, 1998).
3. Regulation 42 of the Miscellaneous Amendment (No. 2) Regulations 1999 (June 1, 1999).

DEFINITIONS

4.340      "the Act": see reg.1(2).
           "applicant": see reg.1(2).
           "application": see reg.1(2).
           "Contributions and Benefits Act": see reg.1(2).
           "partner": see reg.1(2).

### Debts incurred before the absent parent became an absent parent

4.341     **16.**—(1)  Subject to paragraphs (2) to (4), repayment of debts incurred—
    (a)  for the joint benefit of the applicant and the non-applicant parent;
    (b)  for the benefit of the non-applicant parent where the applicant remains legally liable to repay the whole or part of the debt;
    (c)  for the benefit of any person who at the time the debt was incurred—
       (i)  was a child;
      (ii)  lived with the applicant and non-applicant parent; and
      (iii)  of whom the applicant or the non-applicant parent is the parent both are the parents; or

(d) for the benefit of any child with respect to whom the current assessment was made,

shall constitute expenses for the purposes of paragraph 2(2) of Schedule 4B the Act where those debts were incurred before the absent parent became an absent parent in relation to a child with respect to whom the current assessment was made and at a time when the applicant and the non-applicant parent were a married or unmarried couple who were living together.

(2) Paragraph (1) shall not apply to repayment of—

(a) a debt which would otherwise fall within paragraph (1) where the applicant has retained for his own use and benefit the asset the purchase of which incurred the debt;

(b) a debt incurred for the purposes of any trade or business;

(c) a gambling debt;

(d) a fine imposed on the applicant;

(e) unpaid legal costs in respect of separation or divorce from the non-applicant parent;

(f) amounts due after use of a credit card;

(g) a debt incurred by the applicant to pay any of the items listed in sub-paragraphs (c) to (f) and (j);

(h) amounts payable by the applicant under a mortgage or loan taken out on the security of any property except where that mortgage or loan was taken out to facilitate the purchase of, or to pay for repairs or improvements to, any property which is the home of the parent with care and any child in respect of whom the current assessment was made;

(i) amounts payable by the applicant in respect of a policy of insurance of a kind referred to in paragraph 3(4) or (5) of Schedule 3 to the Maintenance Assessments and Special Cases Regulations (eligible housing costs) except where that policy of insurance was obtained or retained to discharge a mortgage or charge taken out to facilitate the purchase of, or to pay for repairs or improvements to, any property which is the home of the parent with care and any child in respect of whom the current assessment was made;

(j) bank overdraft except where the overdraft was, at the time it was taken out, agreed to be for a specified amount repayable over a specified period;

(k) a loan obtained by the applicant, other than a loan obtained from a qualifying lender or the applicant's current or former employer;

(l) a debt in respect of which a departure direction has already been given and which has not been repaid during the period for which that direction was in force except where the maintenance assessment in respect of which that direction was given was cancelled or ceased to have effect and, during the period for which that direction was in force, a further maintenance assessment was made in respect of the same applicant, non-applicant and qualifying child with respect to whom the earlier assessment was made; or

(m) any other debt which the Secretary of State is satisfied it is reasonable to exclude.

(3) Except where the repayment is of an amount which is payable under a mortgage or loan, or in respect of a policy of insurance, which falls within

the exception set out in sub-paragraph (h) or (i) of paragraph (2), repayment of a debt shall not constitute expenses for the purposes of paragraph (1) where the Secretary of State is satisfied that the applicant has taken responsibility for repayment of that debt, as, or as part of, a financial settlement with the non-applicant parent or by virtue of a court order.

(4) Where an applicant has incurred a debt partly to repay a debt or debts repayment of which would have fallen within paragraph (1), the repayment of that part of the debt incurred which is referable to the debts repayment of which would have fallen within that paragraph shall constitute expenses for the purposes of paragraph 2(2) of Schedule 4B to the Act.

(5) For the purposes of this regulation—

(a) "married or unmarried couple" has the meaning set out in regulation 1 of the Maintenance Assessments and Special Cases Regulations;

(b) "non-applicant parent" means—

   (i) where the applicant is the person with care, the absent parent;

   (ii) where the applicant is the absent parent, the partner of that absent parent at the time the debt in respect of which the application is made was entered into;

(c) "qualifying lender" has the meaning given to it in section 376(4) of the Income and Corporation Taxes Act 1988;

(d) "repairs and improvements" means major repairs necessary to maintain the fabric of the home and any of the measures set out in sub-paragraphs (a) to (j) of paragraph 2 of Schedule 3 to the Maintenance Assessments and Special Cases Regulations (eligible housing costs) and other improvements which the Secretary of State considers reasonable in the circumstances where those measures or other improvements are undertaken with a view to improving fitness for occupation of the home.

DEFINITIONS

4.342   "the Act": see reg.1(2).
   "applicant": see reg.1(2).
   "Maintenance Assessments and Special Cases Regulations": see reg.1(2).

## Pre-1993 financial commitments

4.343   17.—(1) A financial commitment entered into by an absent parent before 5th April 1993, except any commitment of a kind listed in paragraph (2)(b) to (g) and (j) of regulation 16 or which has been wholly or partly taken into account in the calculation of a maintenance assessment shall constitute expenses for the purposes of paragraph 2(2) of Schedule 4B to the Act where—

(a) there was in force on 5th April 1993 and at the date that commitment was entered into, [¹maintenance order or a written] maintenance agreement made before 5th April 1993 in respect of that absent parent and every child in respect of whom before that date, he was, or was found, or adjudged to be, the parent; [¹. . .]

[²(aa) at least one of the children referred to in sub-paragraph (a) is a child in respect of whom the current assessment was made; and]

978

(c)   the Secretary of State is satisfied that it is impossible for the absent
      parent to withdraw from that commitment or unreasonable to
      expect him to do so.

[³. . .]

AMENDMENTS

1. Regulation 12(2)(a) of the Miscellaneous Amendments Regulations 1998
(January 19, 1998).
2. Regulation 12(2)(b) of the Miscellaneous Amendments Regulations 1998
(January 19, 1998).
3. Regulation 12(3) of the Miscellaneous Amendments Regulations 1998
(January 19, 1998).

DEFINITIONS

"the Act": see reg.1 (2).                                                    4.344
"applicant": see reg.1(2).
"Maintenance Assessments and Special Cases Regulations": see reg.1(2).
"non-applicant": see reg.1(2).

## Costs incurred in supporting certain children

**18.**—(1) The costs incurred by a parent in supporting a child who is not   4.345
his child but who is part of his family [¹and who was, at the date on which
any departure direction given in response to an application under this regulation would take effect, living in the same household as that parent] (a
"relevant child") shall constitute special expenses for the purposes of paragraph 2(2) of Schedule 4B to the Act if the conditions set out in paragraph
(2) are satisfied and shall, if those conditions are satisfied, equal the amount
specified in paragraph (3).
  (2) The conditions referred to in paragraph (1) are—
  [²(a)  the child became a relevant child prior to 5th April 1993 and has
        remained a relevant child for the whole of the period from that date
        to the date on which any departure direction given in response to
        an application under this regulation would take effect;]
  [³(b)  subject to paragraph (7)—
        (i)   the liability of the absent parent of a relevant child to pay main-
              tenance to or for the benefit of that child under a maintenance
              order, a written maintenance agreement or a maintenance
              assessment; or
        (ii)  any deduction from benefit under section 43 of the Act in place
              of payment of child support maintenance to or for the benefit of
              that child, is less than the amount specified in paragraph (4), or
              there is no such liability or deduction; and]
  (c)    the net income of the parent's current partner where the relevant
        child is the child of that partner, calculated in accordance with
        paragraph (5), is less than the amount calculated in accordance
        with paragraph (6) ("the partner's outgoings").
  (3) [⁴Subject to paragraph (7A),] the amount referred to in paragraph
(1) constituting special expenses for a case falling within this regulation is
the difference between the amount specified in paragraph (4) and, subject

to paragraph (7), the liability of the absent parent of a relevant child to pay maintenance of a kind mentioned in paragraph (2)(b) [[5](i) or any deduction from benefit mentioned in paragraph (2)(b)(ii)], and if there is no such liability [[6]or deduction] is the amount specified in paragraph (4).

(4) [[7]Subject to paragraphs (4A) and (4B),] the amount referred to in paragraphs (2)(b) and (3) is the aggregate of—

(a) an amount in respect of each relevant child equal to the personal allowance for that child specified in column (2) of paragraph 2 of the relevant Schedule (income support personal allowance);

(b) if the conditions set out in paragraph 14(b) [[8]of] that Schedule (income support disabled child premium) are satisfied in respect of a relevant child, an amount equal to the amount specified in column (2) of paragraph 15(6) of that Schedule in respect of each such child; [[8]and]

[[9](c) except where the family includes other children of the parent, an amount equal to the income support family premium specified in paragraph 3(1)(b) of that Schedule that would be payable if the parent were a claimant.]

[[10]. . .]

[[11](4 A) Where day to day care of the relevant child is shared between the current partner of the person making an application under this regulation and the other parent of that child, the amounts referred to in paragraph (4) shall be reduced by the proportion of those amounts which is the same as the proportion of the week in respect of which the child is not living in the same household as the applicant.]

[[11](4B) Where an application under paragraph (1) is made in respect of more than one relevant child and the family does not include any other children of the parent, the amount applicable under sub-paragraph (c) of paragraph (4) in respect of each relevant child shall be calculated by dividing the amount referred to in that sub-paragraph by the number of relevant children in respect of whom that application is made.]

(5) For the purposes of paragraph (2)(c), the net income of the parent's partner shall be the aggregate of—

(a) the income of that partner, calculated in accordance with regulation 7(1) of the Maintenance Assessments and Special Cases Regulations (but excluding the amount mentioned in sub-paragraph (d) of that regulation) as if that partner were an absent parent to whom that regulation applied;

(b) the child benefit payable in respect of each relevant child; and

(c) any income, other than earnings, in excess of £10.00 per week in respect of each relevant child.

(6) For the purposes of paragraph (2)(c), a current partner's outgoings shall be the aggregate of—

(a) an amount equal to the amount specified in column (2) of paragraph 1(1)(e) of the relevant Schedule (income support personal allowance for a single claimant aged not less than 25);

(b) where a departure direction has already been given in a case falling within regulation 27 in respect of the housing costs attributable to the partner, the amount determined in accordance with regulation 40(7) as the housing costs the partner is able to contribute;

(c) the amount of any reduction in the parent's exempt income, calculated under paragraph (1) of regulation 9 of the Maintenance Assessments and Special Cases Regulations, in consequence of the application of paragraph (2) of that regulation; and

(d) the amount specified in paragraph (3) [¹²or the aggregate of those amounts where paragraph (7 A) applies to that partner.]

(7) The Secretary of State may, if he is satisfied that it is appropriate in the particular circumstances of the case, treat a liability of a kind mentioned in paragraph (2)(b) [¹³(i)] as not constituting a liability for the purposes of that paragraph and of paragraph (3).

[¹⁴(7A) Where an application is made in respect of relevant children of different parents, a separate calculation shall be made in accordance with paragraphs (3) and (4) in respect of each relevant child or group of relevant children who have the same parents and the amount constituting special expenses referred to in paragraph (1) shall be the aggregate of the amounts calculated in accordance with paragraph (3) in respect of each such relevant child or group of relevant children.

(8) For the purposes of this regulation—

[¹⁵(a) a child who is not the child of a particular person is a part of that person's family where—

(i) that child is the child of a current partner of that person; or

(ii) that child is the child of a former partner of that person and in the same household as the applicant for every night of week;]

(b) "relevant Schedule" means Schedule 2 to the Income Support (General) Regulations 1987.

AMENDMENTS

1. Regulation of 13(2) of the Miscellaneous Amendments Regulations 1998 (January 19, 1998).

2. Regulation of 13(3)(a) of the Miscellaneous Amendments Regulations 1998 (January 19, 1998)

3. Regulation of 13(3)(b) of the Miscellaneous Amendments Regulations 1998 (January 19, 1998)

4. Regulation of 13(4)(a) of the Miscellaneous Amendments Regulations 1998 (January 19, 1998).

5. Regulation of 13(4)(b) of the Miscellaneous Amendments Regulations 1998 (January 19, 1998).

6. Regulation of 13(4)(c) of the Miscellaneous Amendments Regulations 1998 (January 19, 1998).

7. Regulation of 13(5)(a) of the Miscellaneous Amendments Regulations 1998 (January 19, 1998).

8. Regulation of 13(5)(b) of the Miscellaneous Amendments Regulations 1998 (January 19, 1998).

9. Regulation of 14 of the Miscellaneous Amendments Regulations 1998 (April 6, 1998).

10. Regulation of 13(5)(d) of the Miscellaneous Amendments Regulations 1998 (January 19, 1998)

11. Regulation of 13(6) of the Miscellaneous Amendments Regulations 1998 (January 19, 1998).

12. Regulation of 13(7) of the Miscellaneous Amendments Regulations 1998 (January 19, 1998).

13. Regulation of 13(8) of the Miscellaneous Amendments Regulations 1998 (January 19, 1998).

14. Regulation of 13(9) of the Miscellaneous Amendments Regulations 1998 (January 19, 1998).

15. Regulation of 13(10) of the Miscellaneous Amendments Regulations 1998 (January 19, 1998).

DEFINITIONS

4.346    "the Act": see reg.1(2).
"Maintenance Assessments and Special Cases Regulations": see reg.1(2).
"partner": see reg.1(2).

## Special expenses for a case falling within regulation 13, 14, 16 or 17

4.347    **19.**—(1) This regulation applies where the expenses of an applicant fall within one or more of the descriptions of expenses falling within regulation 13 (travel to work costs), 14 (contact costs), 16 (debts incurred before the absent parent became an absent parent) or 17 (pre-1993 financial commitments).

(2) Special expenses for the purposes of paragraph 2(2) of Schedule 4B to the Act in respect of the expenses mentioned in paragraph (1) shall be—

(a) where the expenses fall within only one description of expenses, those expenses in excess of £15.00;

(b) where the expenses fall within more than one description of expenses, the aggregate of those expenses in excess of £15.00.

DEFINITIONS

4.348    "the Act": see reg.1(2).
"applicant": see reg.1(2).

## Application for a departure direction in respect of special expenses other than those with respect to which a direction has already been given

4.349    **20.** Where a departure direction with respect to special expenses falling within one or more of the descriptions of expenses falling within regulation 13, 14, 16 or 17 has already been given and an application with respect to special expenses falling within one or more of those descriptions of expenses is made where none of those expenses are ones with respect to which the earlier direction has been given, the special expenses with respect to which any later direction is given shall be the expenses, determined in accordance with regulation 13, 14, 16 or 17, as the case may be, with respect to which the later application is made, and the provisions of regulation 19 shall not apply.

PART IV

PROPERTY OR CAPITAL TRANSFERS

### Prescription of certain terms for the purposes of paragraphs 3 and 4 of Schedule 4B to the Act

**21.**—(1) For the purposes of paragraphs 3(l)(a) and 4(l)(a) of Schedule 4B to the Act—

  (a) a court order means an order made—

    (i) under one or more of the enactments listed in or prescribed under section 8(11) of the Act; and

    (ii) in connection with the transfer of property of a kind defined in paragraph (2);

  (b) an agreement means a written agreement made in connection with the transfer of property of a kind defined in paragraph (2).

(2) Subject to paragraphs (3) to (5), for the purposes of paragraph 3(l)(b) and 4(1)(b) of Schedule 4B to the Act, a transfer of property is a transfer by the absent parent of his beneficial interest in any asset to the person with care, to a child in respect of whom the current assessment was made, or to trustees where the object or one of the objects of the trust is the provision maintenance.

(3) Where a transfer of property would not originally have fallen within paragraph (2) but the Secretary of State is satisfied that some or all of the amount of that property transferred was subsequently transferred to the person currently with care of a child in respect of whom the current assessment was made, the transfer of that property to the person currently with care shall count as a transfer of property for the purposes of paragraph 3(l)(b) and 4(l)(b) of Schedule 4B to the Act.

(4) Where, if the Act had been in force at the time a transfer of property falling within paragraph (2) was made, the person who, at the time the application is made is the person with care would have been the absent parent and the person who, at the time the application is made is the absent parent would have been the person with care, that transfer shall not count as a transfer of property for the purposes of this regulation.

(5) For the purposes of paragraph 3(3) of Schedule 4B to the Act, the effect of a transfer of property is properly reflected in the current assessment if—

  (a) the amount of child support maintenance payable under any fresh maintenance assessment which would be made in consequence of a departure direction differs from the amount of child support maintenance payable under that current assessment by less than £1.00; or

  (b) the transfer referred to in paragraph (2) was for a specified period only and that period ended before the effective date of any departure direction which would otherwise have been given.

DEFINITIONS

"the Act": reg.1(2).

"maintenance": reg.22(4).

4.350

4.351

### Value of a transfer of property and its equivalent weekly value for a case falling within paragraph 3 of Schedule 4B to the Act

4.352    **22.**—(1) Where the conditions specified in paragraph 3(1) of Schedule 4B to the Act are satisfied, the value of a transfer of property for the purposes of that paragraph shall be that part of the transfer made by the absent parent (making allowance for any transfer by the person with care to the absent parent) which the Secretary of State is satisfied is in lieu of [¹periodical payments of] maintenance.

(2) The Secretary of State shall, in determining the value of a transfer of property in accordance with paragraph (1), assume that, unless evidence to the contrary is provided to him—

(a) the person with care and the absent parent had equal beneficial interests in the assets in relation to which the court order or agreement was made;

(b) where the person with care was married to the absent parent, one half of the value of the transfer was a transfer for the benefit of the person with care; and

(c) where the person with care has never been married to the absent parent, none of the value of the transfer was a transfer for the benefit of the person with care.

(3) The equivalent weekly value of a transfer of property shall be determined in accordance with the provisions of the Schedule.

(4) For the purposes of regulation 21 and this regulation, the term "maintenance" means the normal day-to-day living expenses of the child with respect to whom the current assessment was made.

AMENDMENT

1. Regulation 15 of the Miscellaneous Amendments Regulations 1998 (January 19, 1998).

DEFINITION

4.353    "the Act": see reg.1(2).

PART V

## ADDITIONAL CASES

### Assets capable of producing income or higher income

4.354    **23.**—(1) Subject to paragraphs (2) and (3), a case shall constitute a case for the purposes of paragraph 5(1) of Schedule 4B to the Act where—

(a) the Secretary of State is satisfied that any asset in which the non-applicant has a beneficial interest, or which he has the ability to control—

(i) is capable of being utilised to produce income but has not been so utilised;

(ii) has been invested in such a way that the income obtained from it is less than might reasonably be expected;

    (iii) is a chose in action which has not been enforced where the Secretary of State is satisfied that such enforcement would be reasonable;

    (iv) in Scotland, is monies due or an obligation owed, whether immediately payable or otherwise and whether the payment or obligation is secured or not and the Secretary of State is satisfied that requiring payment of the monies or implementation of the obligation would be reasonable;

    (v) has not been sold where the Secretary of State is satisfied that the sale of the asset would be reasonable;

(b) any asset has been transferred by the non-applicant to trustees and the non-applicant is a beneficiary of the trust so created; or

(c) any asset has become subject to a trust created by legal implication of which the non-applicant is a beneficiary.

(2) Paragraph (1) shall not apply where—

(a) the total value of the asset or assets referred to in that paragraph does not exceed £10,000.00 after deduction of the amount owing under any mortgage or charge on that asset; or

(b) the Secretary of State is satisfied that any asset referred to in that paragraph is being retained by the non-applicant to be used for a purpose which the Secretary of State considers reasonable in all the circumstances of the case[²; or

(c) if the non-applicant were a claimant, paragraph 64 of Schedule 10 to the Income Support (General) Regulations 1987 (treatment of relevant trust funds) would apply to the asset referred to in that paragraph.]

[¹. . .]

(4) For the purposes of this regulation the term "asset" means—

(a) money, whether in cash or on deposit;

(b) a beneficial interest in land and rights in or over land;

(c) shares as defined in section 744 of the Companies Act 1985, stock and unit trusts as defined in section 6 of the Charging Orders Act 1979, gilt edged securities as defined in paragraph 1 of Schedule 2 to the Capital Gains Tax Act 1979, and other similar financial instruments.

(5) For the purposes of paragraph (4) the term "asset" includes any ass falling within that paragraph which is located outside Great Britain.

AMENDMENTS

1. Regulation 16 of the Miscellaneous Amendments Regulations 1998 (January 19, 1998).

2. Regulation 3 of the Miscellaneous Amendments Regulations 2002 (April 30, 2002).

DEFINITIONS

"the Act": see reg.1(2).                          **4.355**
"non-applicant": see reg.1(2).

### Diversion of income

4.356    **24.** A case shall constitute a case for the purposes of paragraph 5(1) of Schedule 4B to the Act where—
  (a) the non-applicant has the ability to control the amount of income he receives, including earnings from employment or self-employment and dividends from shares, whether or not the whole of that income is derived from the company or business from which his earnings are derived; and
  (b) the Secretary of State is satisfied that the non-applicant has unreasonably reduced the amount of his income which would otherwise fall to be taken into account under regulation 7 or 8 of the Maintenance Assessments and Special Cases Regulations by diverting it to other persons or for purposes other than the provision of such income for himself

DEFINITIONS

4.357    "the Act": see reg.1(2).
  "Maintenance Assessments and Special Cases Regulations": see reg.1(2).
  "non-applicant": see reg.1(2).

### Life-style inconsistent with declared income

4.358    **25.**—(1) Subject to paragraph (2), a case shall constitute a case for the purposes of paragraph 5(1) of Schedule 4B to the Act where the Secretary of State is satisfied that the current [1. . .] assessment is based upon a level of income of the non-applicant which is substantially lower than the level of income required to support the overall life-style of that non-applicant.
  [2(2) Paragraph (1) shall not apply where the Secretary of State is satisfied that the life-style of the non-applicant is paid for—
  (a) out of capital belonging to him; or
  (b) by his partner, unless the non-applicant is able to influence or control the amount of income received by that partner.]
  (3) Where the Secretary of State is satisfied in a particular case that the provisions of paragraph (1) would apply but for the provisions of paragraph [3(2)(b)], he may, whether or not any application on that ground has been made, consider whether the case falls within regulation 27.

AMENDMENTS

  1. Regulation 17(2) of the Miscellaneous Amendments Regulations 1998 (January 19, 1998).
  2. Regulation 17(3) of the Miscellaneous Amendments Regulations 1998 (January 19, 1998).
  3. Regulation 17(4) of the Miscellaneous Amendments Regulations 1998 (January 19, 1998).

DEFINITIONS

4.359    "the Act": see reg.1(2).
  "non-applicant": see reg.1(2).
  "partner": see reg.1(2).

## Unreasonably high housing costs

**26.** A case shall constitute a case for the purposes of paragraph 5(1) of Schedule 4B to the Act where—

(a) the housing costs of the non-applicant exceed the limits set out in paragraph (1) of regulation 18 of the Maintenance Assessments and Special Cases Regulations (excessive housing costs);

(b) the non-applicant falls within paragraph (2) of that regulation or would fall within that paragraph if it applied to parents with care; and

(c) the Secretary of State is satisfied that the housing costs of the non-applicant are substantially higher than is necessary taking into account any special circumstances applicable to that non-applicant.

4.360

DEFINITIONS

"the Act": see reg.1(2).
"Maintenance Assessments and Special Cases Regulations": see reg.1(2).
"non-applicant": see reg.1(2).

4.361

## Partner's contribution to housing costs

**27.** A case shall constitute a case for the purposes of paragraph 5(1) of Schedule 4B to the Act where a partner of the non-applicant occupies the home with him and the Secretary of State considers that it is reasonable for that partner to contribute to the payment of the housing costs of the non-applicant.

4.362

DEFINITIONS

"the Act": see reg.1(2).
"non-applicant": see reg.1(2)
"partner": see reg.1(2).

4.363

## Unreasonably high travel costs

**28.** A case shall constitute a case for the purposes of paragraph 5(1) of Schedule 4B to the Act where an amount in respect of travel to work costs has been included in the calculation of exempt income of the non-applicant under regulation 9(1)(i) of the Maintenance Assessments and Special Cases Regulations (exempt income: calculation or estimation of E) or, as the case may be, under regulation 10 of those Regulations (exempt income: calculation or estimation of F) applying regulation 9(1)(i), and the Secretary of State is satisfied that, in all the circumstances of the case, that amount is unreasonably high.

4.364

DEFINITIONS

"the Act": see reg.1(2).
"Maintenance Assessments and Special Cases Regulations": see reg.1(2).
"non-applicant": see reg.1(2).

4.365

### Travel costs to be disregarded

4.366    **29.** A case shall constitute a case for the purposes of paragraph 5(1) of Schedule 4B to the Act where—

(a) an amount in respect of travel to work costs has, in the calculation of a maintenance assessment, been included in the calculation of the exempt income of the non-applicant under regulation 9(1)(i) of the Maintenance Assessments and Special Cases Regulations or, as the case may be, under regulation 10 of those Regulations applying regulation 9(l)(i); and

(b) the Secretary of State is satisfied that the non-applicant has sufficient income remaining after the deduction of the amount that would be payable under that assessment, had the amount referred to in sub-paragraph (a) not been included in its calculation, for it to be inappropriate for all or part of that amount to be included in the exempt income of the non-applicant.

DEFINITIONS

4.367    "the Act": see reg.1(2).
"Maintenance Assessments and Special Cases Regulations": see reg.1(2).
"non-applicant": see reg.1(2).

PART VI

## FACTORS TO BE TAKEN INTO ACCOUNT FOR THE PURPOSES OF SECTION 28F OF THE ACT

### Factors to be taken into account and not to be taken into account in determining whether it would be just and equitable to give a departure direction

4.368    **30.**—(1) The factors to be taken into account in determining whether it would be just and equitable to give a departure direction in any case shall include—

(a) where the application is made on any ground—

(i) whether, in the opinion of the Secretary of State, the giving of a departure direction would be likely to result in a relevant person ceasing paid employment;

(ii) if the applicant is the absent parent, the extent, if any, of his liability to pay child maintenance under a court order or other agreement in the period prior to the effective date of the maintenance assessment;

(b) where an application is made on the ground that the case falls within regulations 13 to 20 (special expenses), whether, in the opinion of the Secretary of State—

(i) the financial arrangements made by the applicant could have been such as to enable the whole or part of the expenses cited to be paid without a departure direction being given;

(ii) the applicant has at his disposal financial resources which are currently utilised for the payment of expenses other than those

arising from essential everyday requirements and which could
be used to pay the whole of part of the expenses cited.

(2) The following factors are not to be taken into account in determining whether it would be just and equitable to give a departure direction in any case—

(a) the fact that the conception of a child in respect of whom the current assessment was made was not planned by one or both of the parent;

(b) whether the parent with care or the absent parent was responsible for the breakdown of the relationship between them;

(c) the fact that the parent with care or the absent parent has formed a new relationship with a person who is not a parent of the child in respect of whom the current assessment was made;

(d) the existence of particular arrangements for contact with the child in respect of whom the current assessment was made, including whether any arrangements made are being adhered to by the parents;

(e) the failure by an absent parent to make payments under a maintenance order, a written maintenance agreement, or a maintenance assessment;

(f) representations made by persons other than the relevant persons.

DEFINITIONS

"applicant": see reg.1(2).　　　　　　　　　　　　　　　　　　　　　4.369
"application": see reg.1(2).
"relevant person": see reg.1(2).

PART VII

## EFFECTIVE DATE AND DURATION OF A DEPARTURE DIRECTION

**Refusal to give a departure direction under section 28F(4) of the Act**

**31.** The Secretary of State shall not give a departure direction in accordance with section 28F of the Act if he is satisfied that the difference between the current amount and the revised amount is less than £1.00.　　　4.370

DEFINITION

"the Act": see reg.1(2).　　　　　　　　　　　　　　　　　　　　　4.371

**Effective date of a departure direction**

**32.**—(1) Where an application is made on the grounds set out in section 28A(2)(a) of the Act (the effect of the current assessment) and that application is given or sent within [³one month] of the date of notification of the current assessment (whether or not that assessment has been made following an interim maintenance assessment), a departure direction given in response to that application shall take effect—　　4.372

989

(a) where it is given on grounds that relate to the whole of the period between the effective date of the current assessment and the date on which that assessment is made, on the effective date of that assessment;

(b) in a case not falling within sub-paragraph (a), on the first day of the maintenance period following the date upon which the circumstances giving rise to that application first arose.

(2) Where an application is made on the grounds set out in section 28A(2)(a) Act (the effect of the current assessment) and that application is given or sent later than [³one month] after the date of notification of the current assessment (whether or not that assessment has been made following an interim maintenance assessment)—

(a) subject to sub-paragraph (b), a departure direction given in response to that application shall take effect on the first day of the maintenance period during which that application is received;

(b) where the Secretary of State is satisfied that there was unavoidable delay, he may, for the purposes of determining the date on which a departure direction takes effect, treat the application as if it were given or sent within [³one month] of the date of notification of the current assessment.

(3) The provisions of paragraphs (1) and (2) are subject to the provisions of [¹paragraphs (3A) and (6)] and of regulations 47 to 50.

[²(3A) [⁴Subject to paragraph (3B), where] an application is determined in accordance with regulation 14 and is one to which paragraph (7) of that regulation applies, a departure direction given in response to that application shall take effect—

(a) from the first day of the maintenance period immediately following the date on which the absent parent and the parent with care have agreed the pattern of contact for the future is to commence; or

(b) where no such date has been so agreed, from the first day of the maintenance period immediately following the date upon which the departure direction is given.]

[⁵(3B) For the purposes of paragraph (3A), paragraph (8) of regulation 14 shall not apply.]

(4) Subject to paragraph (6), where an application for a departure direction is made on the grounds set out in section 28A(2)(b) of the Act (a material change in the circumstances of the case since the current assessment was made) any departure direction given shall take effect on the first day of the maintenance period during which the application was received.

(5) An application may be made on the grounds set out in section 28A(2)(b) of the Act only if the material change in the circumstances on which it is based has already occurred.

(6) Where—

(a) an application has been determined in accordance with regulation

(b) a subsequent application is made with respect to special expenses falling within regulation 15(1) each of which is an expense in respect of which the earlier application was made; and

(c) the Secretary of State is satisfied that there was good cause for the applicant or his dependant not applying for disability living allowance or, as the case may be, attendance allowance within the six week period specified in regulation 15(4)(a), any departure direction given in response to the later application shall take effect from the date that the earlier direction had effect, or would have had effect if an earlier direction had been given.

[6. . .]

AMENDMENTS

1. Regulation 18(2) of the Miscellaneous Amendments Regulations 1998 (January 19, 1998).
2. Regulation 18(3) of the Miscellaneous Amendments Regulations 1998 (January 19, 1998).
3. Regulation 43(a) of the Miscellaneous Amendments (No. 2) Regulations 1999 (June 1, 1999).
4. Regulation 43(b) of the Miscellaneous Amendments (No. 2) Regulations 1999 (June 1, 1999)—ambiguous as to the precise location.
5. Regulation 43(c) of the Miscellaneous Amendments (No. 2) Regulations 1999 (June 1, 1999).
6. Regulation 43(d) of the Miscellaneous Amendments (No. 2) Regulations 1999 (June 1, 1999).

DEFINITIONS

"the Act": see reg. 1(2).    4.373
"application": see reg.1(2).
"maintenance period": see reg.1(2).

## [¹Revision of decisions

**32A.**—(1) Subject to paragraphs (2) and (3), a decision of the Secretary    4.374
of State or any decision upon referral under section 28D(l)(b) of an appeal tribunal with respect to a departure direction may be revised by the Secretary of State under section 16 of the Act as extended by paragraph 1 of Schedule 4C to the Act—

(a) if the Secretary of State receives an application for the revision of a decision under section 16 of the Act as extended within one month of the date of notification of the decision or within such longer time as may be allowed by regulation 32B;

(b) if—

   (i) the Secretary of State notifies a person, who applied for a decision to be revised within the period specified in sub-paragraph (a), that the application is unsuccessful because the Secretary of State is not in possession of all of the information or evidence needed to make a decision; and

   (ii) that person reapplies for a decision to be revised within one month of the notification described in head (i) above or such longer period as the Secretary of State is satisfied is reasonable in the circumstances of the case, and provides in that application sufficient information or evidence to enable a decision to be made;

(c) if the decision arose from an official error;

(d) if the Secretary of State is satisfied that the original decision was erroneous due to a misrepresentation of, or failure to disclose, a

991

material fact and that the decision was more advantageous to the person who misrepresented or failed to disclose that fact than it would otherwise have been but for that error;

(e) where a departure direction takes effect in the circumstances described in regulation 35(3); or

(f) if the Secretary of State commences action leading to the revision of a decision within one month of the date of notification of the decision.

(2) Paragraph (1) shall apply neither—

(a) in respect of a material change of circumstances which—

   (i) occurred since [²the date on which the decision was made]; or

   (ii) is expected, according to information or evidence which the Secretary of State has, to occur; nor

(b) where—

   (i) an appeal against the original decision has been brought but not determined; and

   (ii) from the point of view of the appellant, a revision, if made, would be less to his advantage than the original decision.]

AMENDMENTS

1. Regulation 44 of the Miscellaneous Amendments (No. 2) Regulations 1999 (June 1, 1999).

2. Regulation 12 of the Miscellaneous Amendments Regulations 2000 (June 19, 2000).

DEFINITION

4.375     "the Act": see reg.1(2).

## [¹Late applications for a revision

4.376     **32B.**—(1) The period of one month specified in regulation 32A(1)(a) may be extended where the requirements specified in the following provisions of this regulation are met.

(2) An application for an extension of time shall be made by a relevant person or a person acting on his behalf.

(3) An application for an extension of time under this regulation shall—

(a) be made within 13 months of the date on which notification of the decision which it is sought to have revised was given or sent; and

(b) contain particulars of the grounds on which the extension of time is sought and shall contain sufficient details of the decision which it is sought to have revised to enable that decision to be identified.

(4) The application for an extension of time shall not be granted unless the person making the application, or any person acting for him, satisfies the Secretary of State that—

(a) it is reasonable to grant that application;

(b) the application for the decision to be revised has merit; and

(c) special circumstances are relevant to the application for an extension of time, and as a result of those special circumstances, it was not practicable for the application for a decision to be revised to be made within one month of the date of notification of the decision which it is sought to have revised.

(5) In determining whether it is reasonable to grant an application for an extension of time, the Secretary of State shall have regard to the principle that the greater the time that has elapsed between the expiration of the period of one month described in regulation 32A(l)(a) from the date of notification of the decision which it is sought to have revised and the making of the application for an extension of time, the more compelling should be the special circumstances on which the application is based.

(6) In determining whether it is reasonable to grant an application for an extension of time, no account shall be taken of the following—

(a) that the person making the application for an extension of time or any person acting for him was unaware of or misunderstood the law applicable to his case (including ignorance or misunderstanding of the time limits imposed by these Regulations);

(b) that a Child Support Commissioner or a court has taken a different view of the law from that previously understood and applied.

(7) An application under this regulation for an extension of time which has been refused may not be renewed.]

AMENDMENT

1. Regulation 44 of the Miscellaneous Amendments (No. 2) Regulations 1999 (June 1, 1999).

## [¹Date from which a revision of a decision takes effect

**32C.** Where the date from which a decision took effect is found to be erroneous on a revision, the revision shall take effect from the date on which the revised decision would have taken effect had the error not been made.]     4.377

AMENDMENT

1. Regulation 44 of the Miscellaneous Amendments (No. 2) Regulations 1999 (June 1, 1999).

## [¹Supersession of decisions

**32D.**—(1) For the purposes of section 17 of the Act as it applies in relation Ito decisions with respect to departure directions by virtue of paragraph 2 of Schedule 4C to the Act and subject to paragraphs (6), (9) and (10), the cases and circumstances in which a decision with respect to a departure direction may be made under that section are set out in paragraphs (2) to (5).     4.378

(2) A decision may be superseded by a decision made by the Secretary of |State acting on his own initiative where he is satisfied that—

(a) there has been a material change of circumstances since the decision was made; or

(b) the decision was made in ignorance of, or was based upon a mistake as to, some material fact.

(3) A decision may be superseded by a decision made by the Secretary of State where—

  (a) an application is made on the basis that—

    (i) there has been a change of circumstances since the decision was made; or

    (ii) it is expected that a change of circumstances will occur; and

  (b) the Secretary of State is satisfied that the change of circumstances is or would be material.

(4) A decision may be superseded by a decision made by the Secretary of State where—

  (a) an application is made on the basis that the decision was made in ignorance of, or was based upon a mistake as to, a fact; and

  (b) the Secretary of State is satisfied that the fact is or would be material.

(5) A decision, other than a decision given on appeal, may be superseded by a decision made by the Secretary of State—

  (a) where an application is made on the basis that the decision was erroneous in point of law; or

  (b) acting on his own initiative where he is satisfied that the decision was erroneous in point of law.

(6) Subject to paragraph (7), paragraphs (2)(a) and (3) shall not apply where, if a decision were to be superseded in accordance with section 17 of the Act, the difference between the current amount and the revised amount would be less than £1.00 per week.

(7) Paragraph (6) shall not apply where the Secretary of State is satisfied on the information or evidence available to him that a ground on which the decision to be superseded was made no longer applies.

(8) In paragraph (6) "revised amount" means the amount of child support maintenance which would be fixed if a decision with respect to a maintenance assessment were to be superseded by a decision made by the Secretary of State in accordance with paragraphs (2)(a) and (3) but for the operation of paragraph (6).

(9) The cases and circumstances in which a decision may be superseded by decision made by the Secretary of State shall not include any case or circumstances in which a decision may be revised.

(10) Subject to paragraph (11), paragraphs (2) and (5) shall apply in respect of neither—

  (a) a decision to reject or refuse an application for a departure direction; nor

  (b) a decision to cancel a departure direction.

(11) Paragraph (10) above shall not apply in a case to which either paragraph (2) or (3) of regulation 35 applies.]

AMENDMENT

1. Regulation 44 of the Miscellaneous Amendments (No. 2) Regulations 1999 (June 1, 1999).

DEFINITION

4.379    "the Act": see reg.1(2).

**[¹Date from which a superseding decision takes effect**

**32E.**—(1) This regulation contains exceptions to the provisions of sec-  4.380
tion 17(4) of the Act, as it applies in relation to decisions with respect to
departure directions by virtue of paragraph 2 of Schedule 4C to the Act, as
to the date from which decisions which supersede earlier decisions are to
take effect.

(2) Subject to paragraphs [²(3), (5) and (12)], where—

(a) a decision is made by the Secretary of State which supersedes an earlier decision in consequence of an application having been made
under section 17 of the Act as it applies in relation to decisions with
respect to departure directions by virtue of paragraph 2 of Schedule
4C to the Act; and

(b) the date on which the application is made is not the first day in a
maintenance period,

the decision shall take effect as from the first day of the maintenance period in which the application is made.

(3) [³Subject to paragraph (12), where a decision] is superseded by a
decision made by the Secretary of State in a case to which regulation
32D(2)(a) applies on the basis of evidence or information which was also
the basis of a decision made under section 9 or 10 of the Social Security
Act 1998 the superseding decision under section 17 of the Act as extended by paragraph 2 of Schedule 7 to the Act shall take effect as from the first
day of the maintenance period in which that evidence or information was
first brought to the attention of an officer exercising the functions of the
Secretary of State under the Act.

(4) Where a decision is superseded by a decision made by the Secretary
of State under regulation 32D(3) in consequence of an application made
on the basis that a material change of circumstances is expected to occur,
the superseding decision shall take effect as from the first day of the maintenance period which immediately succeeds the maintenance period in
which the material change of circumstances is expected to occur.

(5) Where the Secretary of State makes, on his own initiative, a decision
superseding a decision in consequence of evidence or information contained
in an unsuccessful application for a revision of that decision, the superseding decision shall take effect as from the first day of the maintenance period
in which that application was made.

(6) Where—

(a) a decision made by an appeal tribunal under section 20 of the Act as
extended by paragraph 3 of Schedule 4C to the Act is superseded on
the ground that it was erroneous due to a misrepresentation of, or
that there was a failure to disclose, a material fact; and

(b) the Secretary of State is satisfied that the decision was more advantageous to the person who misrepresented or failed to disclose that
fact than it would otherwise have been but for that error,

the superseding decision shall take effect as from the date the decision it
superseded took, or was to take, effect.

(7) Any decision given under section 17 of the Act as extended by
paragraph 2 of Schedule 4C to the Act in consequence of a decision which
is a relevant determination for the purposes of section 28ZC of the Act

(restrictions on liability in certain cases of error) shall take effect as from the date of the relevant determination.

(8) Where a decision with respect to a departure direction is superseded by a decision under section 17 of the Act as extended by paragraph 2 of Schedule 4C to the Act because the departure direction ceases to have effect in accordance with regulation 35(1), the superseding decision shall have effect as from the date on which the decision that the maintenance assessment is cancelled or ceases to have effect, takes or took effect.

(9) Where the superseding decision referred to in paragraph (8) above is itself superseded by a further decision made under section 17 of the Act as extended by paragraph 2 of Schedule 4C to the Act in the circumstances described in regulation 35(2), that further decision shall have effect as from the effective date of the fresh maintenance assessment.

(10) Where a decision with respect to a departure direction is superseded by a decision under section 17 of the Act as extended by paragraph 2 of Schedule 4C to the Act because the departure direction is suspended in accordance with regulation 35(4), the superseding decision shall have effect as from the effective date of the later interim maintenance assessment or, as the case may be, the interim maintenance assessment which replaces a maintenance assessment.

(11) Where the superseding decision referred to in paragraph (10) above is itself superseded by a further decision under section 17 as extended because the interim maintenance assessment referred to in regulation 35(4)(c) is followed by a maintenance assessment made in accordance with the provisions of Part I of Schedule 1 to the Act or by interim maintenance assessment to which regulation 10 does not apply, that further decision shall have effect as from the effective date of the fresh maintenance assessment or, as the case may be, interim maintenance assessment.]

[[4](12) Where a superseding decision is made in a case to which regulation 32D(2)(a) or (3) applies and the material circumstance is the death of a qualifying child or a qualifying child ceasing to be a qualifying child, the decision shall take effect from the first day of the maintenance period in which the change occurred.]

AMENDMENTS

1. Regulation 44 of the Miscellaneous Amendments (No. 2) Regulations 1999 (June 1, 1999).
2. Regulation 13(a) of the Miscellaneous Amendments Regulations 2000 (June 19, 2000).
3. Regulation 13(b) of the Miscellaneous Amendments Regulations 2000 (June 19, 2000).
4. Regulation 13(c) of the Miscellaneous Amendments Regulations 2000 (June 19, 2000).

DEFINITION

**4.381**     "the Act": see reg.1(2).

## [¹Cancellation of departure directions

**32F.** The Secretary of State may cancel a departure direction where—   4.382
   (a) regulation 32A(1) applies and he is satisfied that it was not
       appropriate to have given it; or
   (b) regulation 32D applies and he is satisfied that it is no longer
       appropriate for it to continue to have effect.]

AMENDMENT

1. Regulation 44 of the Miscellaneous Amendments (No. 2) Regulations 1999
(June 1, 1999).

## [¹Notification of right of appeal, decision and reason for decision

**32G.**—(1) The Secretary of State shall notify a person with a right of   4.383
appeal under the Act against the decision under section 16 or 17 of the Act
as those sections apply in relation to decisions with respect to departure
directions by virtue of paragraphs 1 and 2 of Schedule 4C to the Act with
respect to a departure direction—
   (a) that right;
   (b) that decision; and
   (c) the reasons for that decision.
   (2) A written notice provided under paragraph (1)—
   (a) shall also contain sufficient information to enable a relevant person
       to exercise a right of appeal; and
   (b) shall not contain any information which it is not necessary for a
       person to have in order to understand how the decision was
       reached.]

AMENDMENT

1. Regulation 44 of the Miscellaneous Amendments (No. 2) Regulations 1999
(June 1, 1999).
[Regulations 33 and 34 were revoked by reg.45 of the Miscellaneous
Amendments (No 2) Regulations 1999 with effect from June 1, 1999.]

## [¹Correction of accidental errors in departure directions

**34A.**—(1) Subject to paragraphs (3) and (4), accidental errors in any   4.384
departure direction made by the Secretary of State or record of such a
departure direction may, at any time, be corrected by the Secretary of State
and a correction made to, or to the record of, that departure direction shall
be deemed to be part of that direction or of that record.
   (2) Where the Secretary of State has made a correction under the provisions of paragraph (1), he shall immediately notify the persons who were
notified of the departure direction that has been corrected, so far as that is
reasonably practicable.
   (3) In determining whether the time limit specified in [²regulation 31(1)
(time within which an appeal is to be brought), or, as the case may be, regulation 32(1) (late appeals) of the Social Security and Child Support
(Decisions and Appeals) Regulations 1999] has been complied with, there

shall be disregarded any day falling before the day on which notification was given or sent under paragraph (2).

(4) The power to correct errors under this regulation shall not be taken to limit any other powers to correct errors that are exercisable apart from these Regulations.]

AMENDMENTS

1. Regulation 19 of the Miscellaneous Amendments Regulations 1998 (January 19, 1998).
2. Regulation 46 of the Miscellaneous Amendments (No. 2) Regulations 1999 (June 1, 1999).

## Termination and suspension of departure directions

4.385    35.—(1) Subject to paragraph (2), (3) and (4), where a departure direction has effect in relation to the amount of child support maintenance fixed by a maintenance assessment which is cancelled or ceases to have effect, that departure direction shall cease to have effect and shall subsequently take effect.

(2) Where [¹the Secretary of State] ceases to have jurisdiction to make a maintenance assessment and subsequently acquires jurisdiction to make a maintenance assessment in respect of the same absent parent, person with care and any child with respect to whom the earlier assessment was made, a departure direction for a case falling within paragraph 3 or 4 of Schedule 4B to the Act shall again take effect [². . .].

(3) Where a departure direction had effect in relation to the amount of child support maintenance fixed by a maintenance assessment which is, under regulation 8(2) of the Maintenance Arrangements and Jurisdiction Regulations (maintenance assessments and maintenance orders made in error), treated as not having been cancelled or not having ceased to have effect, that departure direction shall again take effect, [³. . .] except where there has, since that maintenance assessment was cancelled or ceased to have effect, been a material change of circumstances relevant to that departure direction.

(4) Where—
(a) a departure direction is in force in respect of an interim maintenance assessment or a maintenance assessment made in accordance with the provisions of Part I of Schedule 1 to the Act;
(b) that interim maintenance assessment is replaced by another ("the later interim maintenance assessment") or, as the case may be, that maintenance assessment is replaced by an interim maintenance assessment; and
(c) by virtue of regulation 10 a departure direction would not be given if that interim maintenance assessment or that later interim maintenance assessment had been in force at the time that departure direction was given,

that departure direction shall be suspended until that interim maintenance assessment or that later interim maintenance assessment has been cancelled or has ceased to have effect and shall again take effect [⁴where the interim maintenance assessment referred to in subparagraph (c) is followed by a maintenance assessment made in accordance with the provisions of Part I of Schedule 1 to the Act or by an interim maintenance assessment to which regulation 10 does not apply].

(5) For the purposes of paragraph (4), a departure direction which is in force shall include a departure direction which is suspended.

AMENDMENTS

1. Regulation 47(a)(i) of the Miscellaneous Amendments (No. 2) Regulations 1999 (June 1, 1999).
2. Regulation 47(a)(ii) of the Miscellaneous Amendments (No. 2) Regulations 1999 (June 1, 1999).
3. Regulation 47(b) of the Miscellaneous Amendments (No. 2) Regulations 1999 (June 1, 1999).
4. Regulation 47(c) of the Miscellaneous Amendments (No. 2) Regulations 1999 (June 1, 1999).

DEFINITIONS

"the Act": see reg.1(2).
"Maintenance Assessments and Jurisdiction Regulations": see reg.1(2).     4.386

PART VIII

## MAINTENANCE ASSESSMENT FOLLOWING A DEPARTURE DIRECTION

### Effect of a departure direction-general

**36.**—(1) Except where a case falls within regulation 22, 41, 42 or 43, a     4.387
departure direction shall specify, as the basis on which the amount of child support maintenance is to be fixed by any fresh assessment made in consequence of the direction, that the amount of net income or exempt income of the parent with care or absent parent or the amount of protected income of the absent parent be increased or, as the case may be, decreased in accordance with those provisions of regulations 37, 38 and 40 which are applicable to the particular case.

(2) Where the provisions of paragraph (1) apply to a departure direction, the amount of child support maintenance fixed by a fresh maintenance assessment shall be determined in accordance with the provisions of Part I of Schedule 1 to the Act, but with the substitution of the amounts changed in consequence of the direction for the amounts determined in accordance with those provisions.

DEFINITION

"the Act": see reg.1(2).     4.388

**Effect of a departure direction in respect of special expenses-exempt income**

4.389     **37.**—(1) Subject to paragraph (2), where a departure direction is given in respect of special expenses, the exempt income of the absent parent or, as the case may be, the parent with care shall be increased by [¹the amount specified in that departure direction being the whole or part of] the amount constituting the special expenses or the aggregate of the special expenses determined in accordance with regulations 13 to 20.

(2) Where a departure direction is given with respect to costs incurred in travelling to work or expenses which include such costs, and a component of exempt income has been determined in accordance with regulation 9(1)(i) of the Maintenance Assessments and Special Cases Regulations or regulation 10 of those Regulations applying regulation 9(1)(i), the increase in exempt income determined in accordance with paragraph (1) shall be reduced by that component of exempt income.

(3) A departure direction with respect to special expenses for a case falling within regulation 16 shall be given only for the repayment period remaining applicable to that debt at the date on which that direction takes effect except—

(a) where in consequence of the applicant's unemployment or incapacity for work, the repayment period of that debt has been extended by agreement with the creditor, a departure direction may be given to cover the additional weeks allowed for repayment; or

(b) where the Secretary of State is satisfied that, as a consequence of the income of the applicant having been substantially reduced the repayment period of that debt has been extended by agreement with the creditor, a departure direction may be given for such repayment period as the Secretary of State considers is reasonable.

(4) Where paragraph (4) of regulation 16 applies, a departure direction may be given in respect only of [²the whole or part of the amount required to repay] that part of the debt incurred which is referable to the debt, repayment of which would have fallen within paragraph (1) of that regulation, based upon the amount, rate of repayment and repayment period agreed in respect of that part at the time it was taken out.

AMENDMENTS

1. Regulation 20(2) of the Miscellaneous Amendments Regulations 1998 (January 19, 1998).
2. Regulation 20(3) of the Miscellaneous Amendments Regulations 1998 (January 19, 1998).

DEFINITIONS

4.390     "applicant": see reg.1(2).
"Maintenance Assessments and Special Cases Regulations": see reg.1(2).

### Effect of a departure direction in respect of special expenses-protected income

**38.**—(1) Subject to paragraphs (2) and (3), where a departure direction is given with respect to special expenses in response to an absent parent's application, his protected income shall be determined in accordance with paragraph (1) of regulation 11 of the Maintenance Assessments and Special Cases Regulations with the modification that the increase of exempt income as determined in accordance with regulation 37 shall be added to the aggregate of the amounts mentioned in sub-paragraphs (a) to (kk) of paragraph (1) of regulation 11 of the Maintenance Assessments and Special Cases Regulations.

(2) Protected income shall not be increased in accordance with paragraph (1) on account of special expenses constituted by costs falling within regulation 18 (costs incurred in supporting certain children).

(3) Where a departure direction is given with respect to costs which include costs incurred in travelling to work, the absent parent's protected income shall be determined in accordance with paragraph (1), but without inclusion of the amount determined in accordance with sub-paragraph (kk) of regulation 11(1) of the Maintenance Assessments and Special Cases Regulations within the aggregate of the amounts mentioned in that regulation.

4.391

DEFINITION

"Maintenance Assessments and Special Cases Regulations": see reg.1(2).

4.392

### Effect of a departure direction in respect of a transfer of property

**39.**—(1) Where a departure direction is given in respect of a transfer of property for a case falling within paragraph 3 of Schedule 4B to the Act—
   (a) where the exempt income of an absent parent includes a component exempt income determined in accordance with regulation 9(1)(bb) of the Maintenance Assessments and Special Cases Regulations, the exempt income of the absent parent shall be reduced by that component of exempt income;
[¹(b) subject to sub-paragraph (c) and paragraphs (2) and (3), the fresh maintenance assessment made in consequence of the direction shall be the lower of—
      (i) the amount, calculated in accordance with the provisions of paragraphs 1 to 5 and 7 to 10 of Part I of Schedule 1 to the Act, as modified in a case to which it applies by sub-paragraph (a) where that sub-paragraph is applicable to the case in question, reduced by the amount specified in that departure direction being the whole or part of the equivalent weekly value of the property transferred as determined in accordance with regulation 22; or
      (ii) where the provisions of paragraph 6 of Schedule 1 to the Act (protected income) apply, the amount, calculated in accordance with the provisions of Part I of Schedule 1 to the Act, as modified in a case to which it applies by sub-paragraph (a) where that sub-paragraph is applicable to the case in question;]

4.393

(c) where the equivalent weekly value is nil, the fresh maintenance assessment made in consequence of the direction shall be the maintenance assessment calculated in accordance with the provisions of Part I of Schedule 1 to the Act, as modified by sub-paragraph .(a), where that sub-paragraph is applicable to the case in question.

(2) The amount of child support maintenance fixed by an assessment made in consequence of a direction falling within paragraph (1) shall not be less than the amount prescribed by regulation 13 of the Maintenance Assessments and Special Cases Regulations.

(3) Where there has been a transfer by the applicant of property to trustees as set out in regulation 21(2) and the equivalent weekly value is greater than nil, any monies paid to the parent with care out of that trust fund for maintenance of a child with respect to whom the current assessment was made shall be disregarded in calculating the assessable income of that parent with care in accordance with the provisions of Part I of Schedule 1 to the Act.

(4) A departure direction falling within paragraph (1) shall cease to have effect at the end of the number of years of liability, as defined in paragraph 1 of the Schedule, for the case in question.

(5) Where a departure direction has ceased to have effect under the provisions of paragraph (4), the exempt income of an absent parent shall be determined as if regulation 9(l)(bb) of the Maintenance Assessments and Special Cases Regulations were omitted.

(6) Where a departure direction is given in respect of a transfer of property for a case falling within paragraph 4 of Schedule 4B to the Act, the exempt income of the absent parent shall be reduced by the component of exempt income determined in accordance with regulation 9(l)(bb) of the Maintenance Assessments and Special Cases Regulations.

(7) This regulation is subject to regulation 42.

AMENDMENT

1. Regulation 21 of the Miscellaneous Amendments Regulations 1998 (January 19, 1998).

DEFINITIONS

4.394    "the Act": see reg.1(2).
"applicant": see reg.1(2).
"Maintenance Assessments and Special Cases Regulations": see reg.1(2).

## Effect of a departure direction in respect of additional cases

4.395    **40.**—(1) This regulation applies where a departure direction is given for an additional case falling within paragraph 5 of Schedule 4B to the Act.

(2) In a case falling within paragraph (l)(a) of regulation 23 (assets capable of producing income or higher income), subject to paragraph (4), the net income of the non-applicant shall be increased by [¹the amount specified in that departure direction, being the whole or part of] an amount calculated by applying interest at the statutory rate prescribed for a judgment debt or, in Scotland, at the statutory rate in respect of interest included in

or payable under a decree in the Court of Session at the date on which the departure direction is given to—

(a) any moneys falling within that paragraph;

(b) the net value of any asset, other than monies, falling within that paragraph, after deduction of the amount owing on any mortgage or charge on that asset,

less any income received in respect of that asset which has been taken into account in the calculation of the current assessment.

(3) In a case falling within paragraph (1)(b) or (c) of regulation 23, subject to paragraph (4), the net income of the non-applicant shall be increased by [¹the amount specified in that departure direction, being the whole or part of] an amount calculated by applying interest at the statutory rate prescribed for a judgment debt or, in Scotland, at the statutory rate in respect of interest included in or payable under a decree in the Court of Session at the date of the application to the value of the asset subject to the trust less any income received from the trust which has been taken into account in the calculation of the current assessment.

(4) In a case to which regulation 24 (diversion of income) applies, the net income of the non-applicant who is a parent of a child in respect of whom the current assessment is made shall be increased by [¹the amount specified in that departure direction, being the whole or part of] the amount by which the Secretary of State is satisfied that that parent has reduced his income.

(5) In a case to which regulation 25 (life-style inconsistent with declared income) applies, the net income of the non-applicant who is a parent of a child in respect of whom the current assessment is made shall be increased by [¹the amount specified in that departure direction, being the whole or part of] the difference between the two levels of income referred to in paragraph (1) of that regulation.

(6) In a case to which regulation 26 applies (unreasonably high housing costs) »e amount of housing costs included in exempt income and the amount referred to in regulation 11(1)(b) of the Maintenance Assessments and Special Cases Regulations shall not exceed the amounts set out in regulation 18(1)(a) or (b), as case may be, of the Maintenance Assessments and Special Cases Regulations (excessive housing costs) and the provisions of regulation 18(2) of those Regulations shall not apply.

(7) In a case to which regulation 27 applies (partner's contribution to housing costs) that part of the exempt income constituted by the eligible housing determined in accordance with regulation 14 of the Maintenance Assessments and Special Cases Regulations (eligible housing costs) shall, subject to paragraphs (8) and (9), be reduced by the percentage of the housing costs which the Secretary of State considers appropriate, taking into account the income of that parent and the income or estimated income of that partner.

(8) Where paragraph (7) applies, the housing costs determined in accordance with regulation 11(1)(b) of the Maintenance Assessments and Special Cases Regulations (protected income) shall remain unchanged.

(9) Where a Category B interim maintenance assessment is in force in respect of a non-applicant, the whole of the eligible housing costs may be deducted from the exempt income of that non-applicant.

(10) In a case to which regulation 28 (unreasonably high travel costs) or regulation 29 (travel costs to be disregarded) applies, for the component of exempt income determined in accordance with regulation 9(1)(i) of the Maintenance Assessments and Special Cases Regulations or in accordance with that regulation as applied by regulation 10 of those Regulations and, in the case of an absent parent, for the amount determined in accordance with regulation 11(1)(kk) of those Regulations, there shall be substituted such amount, including a nil amount, as the Secretary of State considers to be appropriate in all the circumstances of the case.

AMENDMENT

1. Regulation 22 of the Miscellaneous Amendments Regulations 1998 (January 19, 1998).

DEFINITIONS

4.396    "the Act": see reg.1(2).
"Maintenance Assessments and Special Cases Regulations": see reg.1(2).
"non-applicant": see reg.1(2).

PART IX

MAINTENANCE ASSESSMENT FOLLOWING A DEPARTURE
DIRECTION: PARTICULAR CASES

**Child support maintenance payable where effect of a departure
direction would be to decrease an absent parent's assessable
income but case still fell within paragraph 2(3) of Schedule 1
to the Act**

4.397    **41.**—(1) Subject to regulation 42 and paragraph (8), where the effect of a departure direction would, but for the following provisions of this regulation, be to reduce an absent parent's assessable income and his assessable income following that direction would be such that the case fell within paragraph 2(3) of Schedule 1 to the Act (additional element of maintenance payable), the amount of child support maintenance payable shall be determined in accordance with paragraphs (2) to (5).

(2) There shall be calculated the amount equal to $A \times P$, where A is equal to the amount that would be the absent parent's assessable income if the departure direction referred to in paragraph (1) had been given and P has the value prescribed in regulation 5 of the Maintenance Assessments and Special Cases Regulations.

[1(3) There shall be determined the amount that would be payable under a maintenance assessment made in accordance with the provisions of Part I of Schedule 1 to the Act which would be in force at the date any departure direction referred to in paragraph (1) would take effect if it were to be given.]

[2(4) The revised amount for the purposes of regulation 7 (rejection of application on completion of a preliminary consideration) and regulation

1004

31 (refusal to give a departure direction under section 28F(4) of the Act) shall be the lowest of the following amounts —

   (a) the amount calculated in accordance with paragraph (2);

   (b) the amount determined in accordance with paragraph (3);

   (c) where the provisions of paragraph 6 of Schedule 1 to the Act (protected income) as modified in a case to which they apply by the provisions of regulation 38 (effect of a departure direction in respect of special expenses—protected income) would apply if a departure direction were given, the amount payable under those provisions,

and the Secretary of State may apply regulation 7 and shall apply regulation 31 in relation to the current amount and the revised amount as so construed.]

   (5) [³. . .] Where the application of the provisions of paragraph (4) results in a departure direction being given, the amount of child support maintenance payable following that direction shall be determined by [⁶the Secretary of State] as being the revised amount as defined in paragraph (4).

   (6) Where the assessable income of an absent parent changes following [⁷a decision under section 16 of the Act revising a decision as to a maintenance assessment or a decision under section 17 of the Act superseding a decision as to a maintenance assessment], the provisions of paragraphs (2) to (5) shall be applied to—

   (a) the amount calculated under paragraph (2) which takes account of the change in assessable income; and

   (b) the amount that would be payable under the maintenance assessment calculated in accordance with the provisions of Part I of Schedule 1 to the Act which takes account of that change in assessable income.

   [⁴. . .]

   (8) Where a departure direction given in accordance with the provisions of ['paragraphs (1) to (6)] has effect, those provisions shall apply, subject to the modifications set out in paragraph (9), where—

   (a) the effect of a later direction would, but for the provisions of paragraphs (2) to (5), be to change the absent parent's assessable income and his assessable income following the direction would be such that the case fell within paragraph 2(3) of Schedule 1 to the Act (additional element of maintenance payable); and

   (b) that assessable income following the later direction would be less than the assessable income would be if it were calculated in accordance with the provisions of Part I of Schedule 1 to the Act by reference to the circumstances at the time the application for the later direction is made.

   (9) The modifications referred to in paragraph (8) are—

   (a) in paragraph (2), A would be the absent parent's assessable income following the later direction but for the provisions of paragraphs (3) to (5);

   (b) the references to regulation 7 in paragraph (4) are omitted.

AMENDMENTS

1. Regulation 23(2) of the Miscellaneous Amendments Regulations 1998 (January 19, 1998).
2. Regulation 23(3) of the Miscellaneous Amendments Regulations 1998 (January 19, 1998).
3. Regulation 23(4) of the Miscellaneous Amendments Regulations 1998 (January 19, 1998).
4. Regulation 23(5) of the Miscellaneous Amendments Regulations 1998 (January 19, 1998).
5. Regulation 23(6) of the Miscellaneous Amendments Regulations 1998 (January 19, 1998).
6. Regulation 48(a) of the Miscellaneous Amendments (No. 2) Regulations 1999 (June 1 1999).
7. Regulation 48(b) of the Miscellaneous Amendments (No. 2) Regulations 1999 (June 1 1999).

DEFINITIONS

**4.398**    "the Act": see reg.1(2).
"Maintenance Assessments and Special Cases Regulations": see reg.1(2).

## Application of regulation 41 where there is a transfer of property falling within paragraph 3 of Schedule 4B to the Act

**42.**—[¹(1) Where an absent parent applies for a departure direction on the grounds that the case falls within both paragraph 2 of Schedule 4B to the Act (special expenses) and paragraph 3 of that Schedule (property or capital transfers), regulation 41 shall be applied subject to the modifications set out in paragraphs (1A) to (3).]

[¹(1A) In paragraph (1) of regulation 41, the reference to a departure direction shall be construed as a reference to any departure direction that would be given if the application had been made solely on the grounds that the case falls within paragraph 2 of Schedule 4B to the Act, and the reference to the absent parent's assessable income shall be construed as a reference to the assessable income calculated in consequence of such a direction.]

(2) Where the exempt income of an absent parent includes a component of exempt income determined in accordance with regulation 9(l)(bb) of the Maintenance Assessments and Special Cases Regulations, that amount shall be excluded—

(a) in calculating the amount A defined in paragraph (2) of regulation 41;

(b) in calculating the maintenance assessment specified in paragraph (3) of regulation 41.

[²(3) For the purposes of this regulation, the revised amount for the purposes of regulations 7 and 31 shall be—

(a) subject to sub-paragraph (b), the lower of the amounts specified in sub-paragraphs (a) and (b) of paragraph (4) of regulation 41, subject to paragraph (2) of this regulation, less the amount determined in accordance with regulation 22 (value of a transfer of property and its equivalent weekly value for a case falling within paragraph 3 of Schedule 4B to the Act);

(b) where the amount specified in sub-paragraph (c) of paragraph(4) of regulation 41 is lower than the amount determined in accordance with sub-paragraph (a), that amount.]

(4) Where the application of the provisions of paragraph (3) results in departure direction being given, the amount of child support maintenance payable [³determined by [⁴the Secretary of State] as being] the revised amount as defined in paragraph (3).

AMENDMENTS

1. Regulation 24(2) of the Miscellaneous Amendments Regulations 1998 (January 19, 1998).
2. Regulation 24(3) of the Miscellaneous Amendments Regulations 1998 (January 19, 1998).
3. Regulation 24(4) of the Miscellaneous Amendments Regulations 1998 (January 19, 1998).
4. Regulation 49 of the Miscellaneous Amendments (No. 2) Regulations 1999 (June 1, 1999).

DEFINITIONS

"the Act" see reg.1(2).
"Maintenance Assessments and Special Cases Regulations": see reg.1(2).     **4.399**

## [¹Application of regulation 41 where the case falls within paragraph 2 and paragraph 5 of Schedule 4B to the Act

**42A.**—(1) Where an absent parent applies for a departure direction on     **4.400** the grounds that the case falls within both paragraph 5 of Schedule 4B to the Act (additional cases) and paragraph 2 of that Schedule (special expenses), and the conditions set out in paragraph (1) of regulation 41 are satisfied, the amount of child support maintenance payable shall be determined in accordance with paragraphs (2) to (6).

(2) The application shall in the first instance be treated as an application (an "additional cases application") made solely on the grounds that the case falls within paragraph 5 of Schedule 4B to the Act, and a determination shall be made as to whether a departure direction would be given in response to that application.

(3) Following the determination mentioned in paragraph (2), the application shall be treated as an application (a "special expenses application") made solely on the grounds that the case falls within paragraph 2 of Schedule 4B to the Act, and the provisions of regulation 41 shall be applied to the special expenses application, subject to the provisions of paragraphs (4) to (6).

(4) Where no departure direction would be given in response to the additional cases application, the provisions of regulation 41 shall be applied to determine the amount of child support maintenance payable.

(5) Where a departure direction would be given in response to the additional cases application, the provisions of regulation 41 shall be applied to determine the amount of child support maintenance payable, subject to the modification set out in paragraph (6).

(6) For paragraph (3) of regulation 41 there shall be substituted the following paragraph—

"(3) There shall be determined the amount that would be payable under the maintenance assessment made in consequence of the direction that would be given in response to the additional cases application mentioned in paragraph (2) of regulation 42A which would be in force at the date any departure direction referred to in paragraph (1) would take effect if it were to be given."

(7) Where—

(a) a departure direction has been given in a case where regulation 41 has been applied and an application is then made on the grounds that the case falls within paragraph 5 of Schedule 4B to the Act; or

(b) a departure direction has been given on the grounds that the case falls within paragraph 5 of Schedule 4B to the Act, an application is then made on the grounds that the case falls within paragraph 2 of that Schedule, and the conditions set out in paragraph (1) of regulation 41 are satisfied,

the case shall be treated as a case which falls within paragraph (1), and the date of the later application treated as the date on which both applications were made.

(8) Where a departure direction is given in accordance with the provisions of paragraph (7), the earlier direction shall cease to have effect from the date we later direction has effect.]

AMENDMENT

1. Regulation 25 of the Miscellaneous Amendments Regulations 1998 (January 19. 1998).

DEFINITIONS

4.401    "the Act": see reg.1(2).
"application": see reg.1(2).

## Maintenance assessment following a departure direction for certain cases falling within regulation 22 of the Maintenance Assessments and Special Cases Regulations

4.402    **43.**—(1) Where the provisions of regulation 41 or 42 are applicable to a ca falling within regulation 22 of the Maintenance Assessments and Special Cases Regulations (multiple applications relating to an absent parent), those provision shall apply for the purposes of determining the total maintenance payable in consequence of a departure direction.

(2) In a case falling within paragraph (1), the amount of child support maintenance payable in respect of each application for child support maintenance following the direction shall be the [¹lowest] of—

(a) the amount as determined in accordance with paragraph (3) of regulation 41, subject to the modification that regulation 22 of the Maintenance Assessments and Special Cases Regulations is applied in determining the amount that would be payable ("Y");

(b) the amount calculated by the formula—

$$(A \times P) \times \frac{Y}{Q}$$

where A and P have the same meanings as in regulation 41(2) and Q is the sum of the amounts calculated in accordance with sub-paragraph (a) for each assessment;

[²(c) where the provisions of paragraph 6 of Schedule 1 to the Act (protected income) apply, as modified in a case to which they apply by the provisions of regulation 38 (effect of a departure direction in respect of special expenses—protected income) or, as the case may be, regulation 40(6), (8) or (10) (effect of a departure direction in respect of additional cases), the amount calculated as payable under those provisions.]

(3) Where, in a case falling within regulation 22 of the Maintenance Assessments and Special Cases Regulations, a departure direction has been given in respect of an absent parent in a case falling within paragraph 3 of Schedule 4B to the Act (property or capital transfers), the equivalent weekly value of the transfer of property as calculated in accordance with regulation 22 of these Regulations shall be deducted from the amount of the maintenance assessment in respect of the person with care or child to or in respect of whom the property transfer was made.

AMENDMENTS

1. Regulation 26(2) of the Miscellaneous Amendments Regulations 1998 (January 19, 1998).
2. Regulation 26(3) of the Miscellaneous Amendments Regulations 1998 (January 19, 1998).

DEFINITIONS

"the Act": see reg.1(2).
"Maintenance Assessments and Special Cases Regulations": see reg.1(2).      **4.403**

## Maintenance assessment following a departure direction where there is a phased maintenance assessment

**44.**—(1) Where a departure direction is given in a case falling within a relevant enactment, the assessment made in consequence of that direction shall be the assessment that fixes the amount of child support maintenance that would be payable but for the provisions of that enactment ("the unadjusted departure amount").

(2) Where a departure direction takes effect on the effective date of a maintenance assessment to which the provisions of a relevant enactment become applicable, those provisions shall remain applicable to that case following the departure direction.

(3) Where a departure direction takes effect on a date later than the date on which the provisions of a relevant enactment become applicable to a maintenance assessment, the amount of child support maintenance payable in consequence of that direction shall be—

(a) where the unadjusted departure amount is more than the formula amount, the phased amount plus the difference between the unadjusted departure amount and the formula amount;

(b) where the unadjusted departure amount is more than the phased amount but less than the formula amount, the phased amount;

(c) where the unadjusted departure amount is less than the phased amount, the unadjusted departure amount.

(4) Regulation 31 shall have effect for cases falling within paragraphs (1) to (3) as if "current amount" referred to the amount payable under the maintenance assessment that would be in force when the departure direction is given but for the provisions of the relevant enactment and "revised amount" referred to the unadjusted departure amount.

(5) [²Where the Secretary of State is satisfied that, were a decision as to a fresh maintenance assessment to be made under section 16 or, as the case may be, section 17 of the Act] in relation to a case to which the provisions of [¹paragraphs (1) to (3)] have been applied, and the amount payable under it ("[³the fresh unadjusted departure amount]") would be—

(a) more than the unadjusted departure amount, the amount of child support maintenance payable shall be the amount determined in accordance with paragraph (3), plus the difference between the unadjusted departure amount and [³the fresh unadjusted departure amount];

(b) less than the unadjusted departure amount but more than the phased amount, the amount of child support maintenance payable shall be the phased amount;

(c) less than the phased amount, the amount of child support maintenance payable shall be [³the fresh unadjusted departure amount].

(6) In this regulation—

"the 1992 enactment" means Part II of the Schedule to the Child Support Act 1991 (Commencement No. 3 and Transitional Provisions) Order 1992 (modification of maintenance assessment in certain cases);

"the 1994 enactment" means Part III of the Child Support (Miscellaneous Amendments and Transitional Provisions) Regulations 1994 (transitional provisions);

"formula amount" has the same meaning as in the relevant enactment;

"phased amount" means—

(a) where the 1992 enactment is applicable to the particular case, the modified amount as defined in paragraph 6 of that enactment;

(b) where the 1994 enactment is applicable to the particular case, the transitional amount as defined in regulation 6(1) of that enactment;

"relevant enactment" means—

(a) the 1992 enactment where that enactment is applicable to the particular case;

(b) the 1994 enactment where that enactment is applicable to the particular case.

AMENDMENTS

1. Regulation 27 of the Miscellaneous Amendments Regulations 1998 (January 19, 1998)
2. Regulation 50(a) of the Miscellaneous Amendments (No. 2) Regulations 1999 (June 1, 1999).
3. Regulation 50(b) of the Miscellaneous Amendments (No. 2) Regulations 1999 (June 1, 1999).

DEFINITION

"the Act": see reg.1(2).      **4.404**

PART X

MISCELLANEOUS

**Regular payments condition**

**45.**—(1) For the purposes of section 28C(2)(b) of the Act (regular pay-    **4.405**
ments condition-reduced payments), reduced payments shall, subject to
paragraph (3), be such payments as would be equal to the payments of
child support maintenance fixed by the fresh maintenance assessment that
would be made if the circumstances of the case were those set out in
paragraph (2).
  (2) The circumstances referred to in paragraph (1) are—
  (a) the Secretary of State is satisfied that the case is one which falls
     within paragraph 2 of Schedule 4B to the Act (special expenses);
  (b) the Secretary of State is satisfied that the expenses claimed by the
     absent parent are both being incurred and, for a case falling within
     regulation 13 (costs incurred in travelling to work), 14 (contact
     costs) or 15 (illness or disability), are neither unreasonably high nor
     being unreasonably incurred, and that it is just and equitable to
     give a departure direction in respect of the whole of those expenses;
     and
  (c) a departure direction is given in response to the application.
  (3) Where the Secretary of State considers it likely that the expenses
incurred by the absent parent are lower than those claimed by him or are
not reasonably incurred, he may fix such amount as he considers to be
reasonable in all the circumstances of the case.
  (4) Where the absent parent, following written notice under section
28C(8) of the Act, fails within 28 days of that notice to comply with the
regular payments condition that was imposed on him, the application shall
lapse.

DEFINITION

"the Act" see reg.1(2).      **4.406**

## Special case–departure direction having effect from date earlier than effective date of current assessment

4.407     **46.**—(1) A case shall be treated as a special case for the purposes of the Act if the conditions specified in paragraph (2) are satisfied.

(2) The conditions are—

(a) liability to pay child support maintenance commenced earlier than the effective date of the maintenance assessment in force ("the current assessment");

(b) an application is made or treated as made in relation to the current assessment which results in a departure direction being given in respect of that assessment [¹or, where regulation 11A (meaning of "current assessment" for the purposes of the Act) applies, in respect of the fresh maintenance assessment referred to in that regulation];

(c) the applicant was unable to make an application on a date falling within a period in respect of which an earlier assessment had effect because he had not been notified of that earlier assessment during that period; and

(d) if the applicant had been able to make such an application and had done so, the Secretary of State is satisfied that a departure direction would have been given in response to that application.

(3) Where a case falls within paragraph (2), references to ' 'the current assessment" and "the current amount" in these Regulations shall be construed as including references to an earlier assessment falling within paragraph (2)(c) and to the amount of child support maintenance fixed by it, and these Regulations shall be applied to such an earlier assessment accordingly.

AMENDMENT

1. Regulation 28 of the Miscellaneous Amendments Regulations 1998 (January 19, 1998).

DEFINITIONS

4.408     "the Act": see reg.1(2).
"applicant": see reg.1(2).
"application": see reg.1(2).

## [¹Cases to which regulation 11A applies

**46A.**—(1) A case where the conditions set out in paragraphs (a) [²and (b)] of regulation 11A (meaning of "current assessment" for the purposes of the Act) are satisfied shall be treated as a special case for the purposes of the Act.

(2) Where a case falls within paragraph (1), references to "the current assessment" and "the current amount" in these Regulations shall, subject to paragraph (3), be construed as including reference to the fresh maintenance assessment referred to in regulation 11 A.

(3) Paragraph (2) shall not apply to references to "the current assessment" in regulation 32, with the exception of the reference in paragraph (l)(a) of that regulation, and in regulations 46, 49 and 50.]

AMENDMENTS

1. Regulation 29 of the Miscellaneous Amendments Regulations 1998 (January 19, 1998).
2. Regulation 51 of the Miscellaneous Amendments (No. 2) Regulations 1999 (June 1, 1999).

DEFINITION

"the Act": reg.1(2).                                                      4.409

## PART XI

## TRANSITIONAL PROVISIONS

### Transitional provisions-application before 2nd December 1996

47.—(1) This paragraph applies in any case where an application for a     4.410
departure direction has been made before 2nd December 1996.

(2) Where paragraph (1) applies, the Secretary of State shall request the applicant to inform him in writing before 2nd December 1997–;

(a) whether he wishes the application to be treated as an application under these Regulations in respect of the maintenance assessment in force on 2nd December 1996; and

(b) whether there have been any changes in the circumstances which are relevant for the determination or, as the case may be, redetermination of the application which have occurred since his application and, if so, what those changes are.

(3) Where the applicant fully complies with the request set out in paragraph (2), and states that he wishes the application to be treated as described in paragraph (2)(a), the Secretary of State shall treat the application as an application under these Regulations which contains the statement mentioned in section 28A(2)(a) of the Act, and paragraphs (4) to (10) and regulation 48 shall apply.

(4) Where the applicant informs the Secretary of State that there have not been any changes of the kind mentioned in paragraph (2)(b), the Secretary of State shall nevertheless invite representations in writing from the relevant persons other than the applicant.

(5) Where the applicant informs the Secretary of State that there have been changes in the circumstances of the kind mentioned in paragraph (2)(b), the Secretary of State shall—

(a) give notice that he has been informed of such changes to the relevant persons other than the applicant;

(b) send to them the information as to such changes which the applicant has given except where the Secretary of State considers that information to be information of the kind falling within paragraph (2) of regulation 8;

(c) invite representations in writing from the relevant persons other than the applicant as to such changes; and

(d) set out the provisions of paragraph (6) in relation to such representations.

(6) The following provisions shall apply to information provided under paragraph (2)(b) or representations made following an invitation made in accordance with paragraph (4) or (5)(c)—

(a) paragraphs (2) [¹to (10)] of regulation 8, subject to the modification set out in paragraph (7);

(b) in relation to an applicant, regulations 6 and 7.

(7) The modification of regulation 8 mentioned in paragraph (6)(a) is that for the references to paragraph (1) or, as the case may be, paragraph (1)(c) of that regulation, there were substituted references to paragraph (5) or, as the case may be, paragraph (5)(c) of this regulation.

(8) Where the Secretary of State has not determined the application in accordance with the Departure Direction Anticipatory Application Regulations, a determination shall be made in accordance with these Regulations.

(9) Where the Secretary of State has determined the application in accordance with the Departure Direction Anticipatory Application Regulations, he shall determine whether there have been any changes in—

(a) the circumstances referred to in paragraph (2)(b);

(b) the relevant provisions of these Regulations compared with the corresponding provisions of the Departure Direction Anticipatory Application Regulations.

(10) Where the Secretary of State determines that there have been no changes ; of the kind referred to in paragraph (9)(a) or (b), and the relevant persons other than the applicant have not made any representations in accordance with paragraph (4), his determination of the application in accordance with the Departure Direction Anticipatory Application Regulations shall take effect.

(11) Where the Secretary of State determines that there have been changes of the kind referred to in paragraph (9)(a) or (b), or where the relevant persons other than the applicant have made representations, he shall make a determination of the application, taking those changes and representations into account, in accordance with these Regulations.

AMENDMENT

1. Regulation 52 of the Miscellaneous Amendments (No. 2) Regulations 1999 (June 1, 1999).

DEFINITIONS

4.411    "the Act": see reg.1(2).
"applicant": see reg.1(2).
"application": see reg.1(2).
"Departure Directions Anticipatory Application Regulations": see reg.1(2).
"relevant person": see reg.1(2).

### Effective date of departure direction for a case falling within regulation 47

4.412    **48.**—(1) Where the determination made by the Secretary of State by application of the provisions of paragraphs (1) to (10) of regulation 47 is to give a departure direction, that direction shall take effect on the first day of the first maintenance period commencing on or after 2nd December 1996.

(2) Where a case falls within paragraph (1) of regulation 47, and the applicant complies with the request for information mentioned in paragraph (2) of that regulation but not by the date mentioned in that paragraph, his response shall be treated as an application for a departure direction.

DEFINITIONS

"applicant": see reg.1(2).                                                       4.413
"application": see reg.1(2).
"maintenance period": see reg.1(2).

## Transitional provisions-no application before 2nd December 1996

**49.**—(1) Where—
(a) a maintenance assessment was in force on 2nd December 1996;             4.414
(b) no application has been made before that date by any of the persons with
(c) an application is made by one of those persons on the grounds set out in section 28A(2)(a) of the Act (the effect of the current assessment) on or after that date and before 2nd December 1997,
any departure direction given in response to that application shall take effect on the first day of the first maintenance period commencing on or after 2nd December 1996.

DEFINITIONS

"the Act": see reg.1(2).                                                         4.415
"application": see reg.1(2).
"maintenance period": see reg.1(2).

## Transitional provisions—new maintenance assessment made before 2nd December 1996 whose effective date is on or after 2nd December 1996

**50.** Where a new maintenance assessment is made before 2nd December   4.416
1996 but the effective date of that assessment is a date on or after 2nd December 1996—
(a) the provisions of paragraph (1) of regulation 32 shall apply as if for the reference to an application being given or sent within [¹one month] of the date of notification of the current assessment there were substituted a reference to an application being given or sent before 30th December 1996;
(b) the provisions of paragraph (2) of regulation 32 shall apply as if for the reference to an application being given or sent later than ['one month] after the date of notification of the current assessment there were substituted a reference to an application being given or sent after 29th December 1996.

AMENDMENT

1. Regulation 53 of the Miscellaneous Amendments (No. 2) Regulations 1999 (June 1, 1999).

DEFINITIONS

4.417    "application": see reg.1(2).
"effective date": see reg.1(2).


PART XII

REVOCATION

**Revocation of the Departure Direction Anticipatory Application Regulations**

4.418    **51.** The Departure Direction Anticipatory Application Regulations are hereby revoked.

DEFINITION

4.419    "Departure Direction Anticipatory Application Regulations": see reg.1(2).


SCHEDULE

EQUIVALENT WEEKLY VALUE OF A TRANSFER OF
A PROPERTY

4.420    **1.**—(1) Subject to paragraphs 3 and 4, the equivalent weekly value of a transfer of property shall be calculated by multiplying the value of a transfer of property determined in accordance with regulation 22(1) by the relevant factor specified in the Table set out in paragraph 2 ("the Table").

(2) For the purposes of sub-paragraph (1), the relevant factor is the number in the Table at the intersection of the column for the statutory rate and of the row for the number of years of liability.

(3) In sub-paragraph (2)—

(a) "the statutory rate" means interest at the statutory rate prescribed for a judgment debt or, in Scotland, the statutory rate in respect of interest included in or payable under a decree in the Court of Session, which in either case applies at the date of the court order or written agreement relating to the transfer of the property;

(b) "the number of years of liability" means the number of years, beginning on the date of the court order or written agreement relating to the transfer of property and ending on—

(i) the date specified in that order or agreement as the date on which maintenance for the youngest child in respect of whom that order or agreement was made shall cease; or

(ii) if no such date is specified, the date on which the youngest child specified in the order or agreement reaches the age of 18, and where that period includes a fraction of a year, that fraction shall be treated as a full year if it is either one-half or exceeds one-half of a year, and shall otherwise be disregarded.

**2.** The Table referred to in paragraph 1(1) is set out below—

**4.421**

THE TABLE

| Number of years of liability | Statutory Rate | | | | | | | |
|---|---|---|---|---|---|---|---|---|
| | 7.0% | 8.0% | 10.0% | 11.0% | 12.0% | 12.5% | 14.0% | 15.0% |
| 1 | 0.02058 | .02077 | .02115 | 0.02135 | .02154 | .02163 | .02192 | .02212 |
| 2 | 0.01064 | .01078 | .01108 | 0.02135 | .01138 | .01145 | .01168 | .01183 |
| 3 | 0.00733 | .00746 | .00773 | 0.00787 | .00801 | .00808 | .00828 | .00842 |
| 4 | 0.00568 | .00581 | .00607 | 0.00620 | .00633 | .00640 | .00660 | .00674 |
| 5 | 0.00469 | .00482 | .00507 | 0.00520 | .00533 | .00540 | .00560 | .00574 |
| 6 | 0.00403 | .00416 | .00442 | 0.00455 | .00468 | .00474 | .00495 | .00508 |
| 7 | 0.00357 | .00369 | .00395 | 0.00408 | .00421 | ʳ.00428 | .00448 | .00462 |
| 8 | 0.00322 | .00335 | .00360 | 0.00374 | .00387 | .00394 | .00415 | .00429 |
| 9 | 0.00295 | .00308 | .00334 | 0.00347 | .00361 | .00368 | .00389 | .00403 |
| 10 | 0.00274 | .00287 | .00313 | 0.00327 | .00340 | .00347 | .00369 | .00383 |
| 11 | 0.00256 | .00269 | .00296 | 0.00310 | .00324 | .00331 | .00353 | .00367 |
| 12 | 0.00242 | .00255 | .00282 | 0.00296 | .00310 | .00318 | .00340 | .00355 |
| 13 | 0.00230 | .00243 | .00271 | 0.00285 | .00299 | .00307 | .00329 | .00344 |
| 14 | 0.00220 | .00233 | .00261 | 0.00275 | .00290 | .00298 | .00320 | .00336 |
| 15 | 0.00211 | .00225 | .00253 | 0.00267 | .00282 | .00290 | .00313 | .00329 |
| 16 | 0.00204 | .00217 | .00246 | 0.00261 | .00276 | .00283 | .00307 | .00323 |
| 17 | 0.00197 | .00211 | .00240 | 0.00255 | .00270 | .00278 | .00302 | .00318 |
| 18 | 0.00191 | .00205 | .00234 | 0.00250 | .00265 | .00273 | .00297 | .00314 |

**3.** The equivalent weekly value of the property transferred shall be nil if the value of the transfer of the property is less than £5,000.

**4.421**

**4.** The Secretary of State may determine a lower equivalent weekly value than that determined in accordance with paragraphs 1 and 2 where the amount of child support maintenance that would be payable in consequence of a departure direction specifying that value is lower than the amount of [¹the periodical payments of maintenance which were] payable under the court order or written agreement referred to in regulation 21.

**4.422**

**4.423**

[². . .]

AMENDMENTS

1. Regulation 31(3) of the Miscellaneous Amendments Regulations 1998 (January 19, 1998).

2. Regulation 31(4) of the Miscellaneous Amendments Regulations 1998 (January 19, 1998).

# INDEX

# Index